FREE WITH NEW COPIES OF THIS TEXTBOOK*

brG8DqAX9z6ErRx4

Start using myBusinessCourse Today: www.mybusinesscourse.com

myBusinessCourse is a web-based learning and assessment program intended to complement your textbook and faculty instruction.

Student Benefits

- **eLectures**: These videos review the key concepts of each Learning Objective in each chapter.
- **Guided examples**: These videos provide step-by-step solutions for select problems in each chapter.
- **Auto-graded assignments**: Provide students with immediate feedback on select assignments. (**with Instructor-Led course ONLY**).
- **Quiz and Exam preparation**: myBusinessCourse provides students with additional practice and exam preparation materials to help students achieve better grades and content mastery.

You can access myBusinessCourse 24/7 from any web-enabled device, including iPads, smartphones, laptops, and tablets.

Interactive content that runs on any device.

Built for PCs, iPads, Laptops, Tablets, Smartphones

*Each access code is good for one use only. If the textbook is used for more than one course or term, students will have to purchase additional myBusinessCourse access codes. In addition, students who repeat a course for any reason will have to purchase a new access code. If you purchased a used book and the protective coating that covers the access code has been removed, your code may be invalid.

Access to myBusinessCourse is free ONLY with the purchase of a new textbook.

Financial Accounting for MBAs

Eighth Edition

Peter D. Easton

John J. Wild

Robert F. Halsey

Mary Lea McAnally

To my daughters, Joanne and Stacey
  —PDE

To my students and my loving family
  —JJW

To my wife Ellie and children, Grace and Christian
  —RFH

To my husband Brittan and children Loic, Cindy, Maclean, Lacey, Quinn, and Kay
  —MLM

Photo Credits
Module 1: iStock
Module 2: Shutterstock
Module 3: Shutterstock
Module 4: Shutterstock
Module 5: iStock
Module 6: Shutterstock
Module 7: Shutterstock
Module 8: Shutterstock
Module 9: Shutterstock
Module 10: Shutterstock
Module 11: Shutterstock
Module 12: iStock
Module 13: Shutterstock

Cambridge Business Publishers

FINANCIAL ACCOUNTING FOR MBAs, Eighth Edition, by Peter D. Easton, John J. Wild, Robert F. Halsey, and Mary Lea McAnally.

COPYRIGHT © 2021 by Cambridge Business Publishers, LLC. Published by Cambridge Business Publishers, LLC. Exclusive rights by Cambridge Business Publishers, LLC for manufacture and export.

ALL RIGHTS RESERVED. No part of this publication may be reproduced, distributed, or stored in a database or retrieval system in any form or by any means, without prior written consent of Cambridge Business Publishers, LLC, including, but not limited to, in any network or other electronic storage or transmission, or broadcast for distance learning.

Student Edition ISBN 978-1-61853-358-6

Bookstores & Faculty: to order this book, call **800-619-6473** or email customerservice@cambridgepub.com.

Students: to order this book, please visit the book's website and order directly online.

Printed in the United States of America.
10 9 8 7 6 5 4 3 2

About the Authors

The combined skills and expertise of Easton, Wild, Halsey, and McAnally create the ideal team to author the first new financial accounting textbook for MBAs in more than a generation. Their collective experience in award-winning teaching, consulting, and research in the area of financial accounting and analysis provides a powerful foundation for this innovative textbook.

PETER D. EASTON is an expert in accounting and valuation and holds the Notre Dame Alumni Chair in Accountancy in the Mendoza College of Business. Professor Easton's expertise is widely recognized by the academic research community and by the legal community. Professor Easton frequently serves as a consultant on accounting and valuation issues in federal and state courts.

Professor Easton holds undergraduate degrees from the University of Adelaide and the University of South Australia. He holds a graduate degree from the University of New England and a PhD in Business Administration (majoring in accounting and finance) from the University of California, Berkeley.

Professor Easton's research on corporate valuation has been published in the *Journal of Accounting and Economics, Journal of Accounting Research, The Accounting Review, Contemporary Accounting Research, Review of Accounting Studies,* and *Journal of Business Finance and Accounting.* Professor Easton has served as an associate editor for 11 leading accounting journals and he is currently an associate editor for the *Journal of Accounting Research, Journal of Business Finance and Accounting,* and *Journal of Accounting, Auditing, and Finance.* He is an editor of the *Review of Accounting Studies.*

Professor Easton has held appointments at the University of Chicago, the University of California at Berkeley, Ohio State University, Macquarie University, the Australian Graduate School of Management, the University of Melbourne, Tilburg University, National University of Singapore, Seoul National University, and Nyenrode University. He is the recipient of numerous awards for excellence in teaching and in research. Professor Easton regularly teaches accounting analysis and security valuation to MBAs. In addition, Professor Easton has taught managerial accounting at the graduate level.

JOHN J. WILD is a distinguished professor of accounting and business at the University of Wisconsin—Madison. He previously held appointments at Michigan State University and the University of Manchester in England. He received his BBA, MS, and PhD from the University of Wisconsin.

Professor Wild teaches courses in accounting and analysis at both the undergraduate and graduate levels. He has received the Mabel W. Chipman Excellence-in-Teaching Award, the departmental Excellence-in-Teaching Award, and the MBA Teaching Excellence Award (twice) from the EMBA graduation classes at the University of Wisconsin. He also received the Beta Alpha Psi and Salmonson Excellence-in-Teaching Award from Michigan State University. Professor Wild is a past KPMG Peat Marwick National Fellow and is a prior recipient of fellowships from the American Accounting Association and the Ernst & Young Foundation.

Professor Wild is an active member of the American Accounting Association and its sections. He has served on several committees of these organizations, including the Outstanding Accounting Educator Award, Wildman Award, National Program Advisory, Publications, and Research Committees. Professor Wild is author of several best-selling books. His research articles on financial accounting and analysis appear in *The Accounting Review, Journal of Accounting Research, Journal of Accounting and Economics, Contemporary Accounting Research, Journal of Accounting, Auditing & Finance, Journal of Accounting and Public Policy, Journal of Business Finance and Accounting, Auditing: A Journal of Theory and Practice,* and other accounting and business journals. He is past associate editor of *Contemporary Accounting Research* and has served on editorial boards of several respected journals, including *The Accounting Review* and the *Journal of Accounting and Public Policy.*

About the Authors

ROBERT F. HALSEY is Professor of Accounting at Babson College. He received his MBA and PhD from the University of Wisconsin. Prior to obtaining his PhD he worked as the chief financial officer (CFO) of a privately held retailing and manufacturing company and as the vice president and manager of the commercial lending division of a large bank.

Professor Halsey teaches courses in financial and managerial accounting at both the graduate and undergraduate levels, including a popular course in financial statement analysis for second-year MBA students. He has also taught numerous executive education courses for large multinational companies through Babson's school of Executive Education as well as for a number of stock brokerage firms in the Boston area. He is regarded as an innovative teacher and has been recognized for outstanding teaching at both the University of Wisconsin and Babson College.

Professor Halsey co-authors *Advanced Accounting* published by Cambridge Business Publishers. Professor Halsey's research interests are in the area of financial reporting, including firm valuation, financial statement analysis, and disclosure issues. He has publications in *Advances in Quantitative Analysis of Finance and Accounting, The Journal of the American Taxation Association, Issues in Accounting Education, The Portable MBA in Finance and Accounting,* the *CPA Journal, AICPA Professor/Practitioner Case Development Program,* and in other accounting and analysis journals.

Professor Halsey is an active member of the American Accounting Association and other accounting, analysis, and business organizations. He is widely recognized as an expert in the areas of financial reporting, financial analysis, and business valuation.

MARY LEA MCANALLY is the PwC Professor of Accounting at Mays Business School at Texas A&M University. She obtained her PhD from Stanford University and B. Comm. from the University of Alberta. She worked as a Chartered Accountant (in Canada) and is a Certified Internal Auditor. Prior to arriving at Texas A&M in 2002, Professor McAnally held positions at University of Texas at Austin, Canadian National Railways, and Dunwoody and Company.

Professor McAnally teaches financial reporting, analysis, and valuation in the full-time, Professional, and Executive MBA programs. Through the Mays Center for Executive Development, she works with a wide range of corporate clients. As a Certified Appreciative Inquiry Facilitator, Professor McAnally helps academic units (departments, colleges, and institutes) develop and implement strategic plans. She has also taught at the University of Alberta, University of Calgary, IMADEC (in Austria), and at the Indian School of Business at the Hyderabad and Mohali campuses. She has received numerous faculty-determined and student-initiated teaching awards at the MBA and executive levels.

Professor McAnally's research interests include accounting and disclosure in regulated environments, executive compensation, and accounting for risk. She has published articles in the leading academic journals including *Journal of Accounting and Economics, Journal of Accounting Research, The Accounting Review, Review of Accounting Studies,* and *Contemporary Accounting Research*. She was Associate Editor at *Accounting Horizons,* served on the editorial board of *Contemporary Accounting Research,* and was Guest Editor for the MBA-teaching volume of *Issues in Accounting Education.*

Preface

Welcome to the Eighth Edition of *Financial Accounting for MBAs*. Our main goal in writing this book was to satisfy the needs of today's business manager by providing the most contemporary, relevant, engaging, and user-oriented book available. This book is the product of extensive market research including focus groups, market surveys, class tests, manuscript reviews, and interviews with faculty from across the country. We are grateful to students and faculty who used the previous editions and whose feedback greatly benefited this new edition.

Target Audience

Financial Accounting for MBAs is intended for use in full-time, part-time, executive, and working professional MBA programs that include a financial accounting course as part of the curriculum, and one in which managerial decision making and analysis are emphasized. This book easily accommodates mini-courses lasting several days as well as extended courses lasting a full semester. The book and its resources are well suited for any instructional mode: face-to-face, online, flipped classroom, or any combination of delivery modes.

Innovative Approach

Financial Accounting for MBAs is managerially oriented and focuses on the most salient aspects of accounting. It helps MBA students learn how to read, analyze, and interpret financial accounting data to make informed business decisions. This text makes financial accounting **engaging, relevant,** and **contemporary.** To that end, it consistently incorporates **real company data,** both in the body of each module and throughout assignment material.

> "If you are looking for a book that students will actually read and learn from, look no further."
> **Andreas Simon**
> Pepperdine University

Flexible Structure

The MBA curricula, instructor preferences, and course lengths vary across colleges. Accordingly and to the extent possible, the 13 modules that make up *Financial Accounting for MBAs* were designed independently of one another. This modular presentation enables each college and instructor to "customize" the book to best fit the needs of their students. Our introduction and discussion of financial statements constitute Modules 1, 2, and 3. Module 4 presents the analysis of financial statements with an emphasis on analysis of operating profitability. Modules 5 through 10 highlight major financial accounting topics including assets, liabilities, equity, and off-balance-sheet financing. Module 11 details the process for preparing and analyzing the statement of cash flow. Module 12 explains forecasting financial statements and Module 13 introduces basic valuation models. At the end of each module, we present an ongoing analysis project that can be used as a guide for an independent project. Like the rest of the book, the project is independent across modules. At the end of the book, we include several useful resources. Appendix A contains compound interest tables and formulas. Appendix B is a chart of accounts used in the book along with abbreviations. Appendix C is an illustrative case that applies the techniques described in Modules 1 through 13 to an actual company, Harley-Davidson. Appendix C can be used as a guide, in conjunction with the module-end project questions, for students required to prepare a company analysis.

Transaction Analysis and Statement Preparation

Instructors differ in their coverage of accounting mechanics. Some focus on the effects of transactions on financial statements using the balance sheet equation format. Others include coverage of journal entries and T-accounts. We accommodate both teaching styles. Specifically, Module 2 provides an expanded discussion of the effects of transactions using our innovative financial statement effects template. Emphasis is on the analysis of Apple's summary transactions, which concludes with the preparation of its financial statements. Module 3, which is entirely optional, allows an instructor to drill down and focus on accounting mechanics: journal entries and T-accounts. It illustrates accounting for numerous transactions, including those involving accounting adjustments. It concludes with the preparation of financial statements. This detailed transaction analysis uses the same financial statement effects template, with journal entries and T-accounts highlighted in the margin. These two modules accommodate the spectrum of teaching styles—instructors can elect to use either or both modules to suit their preferences, and their students are not deprived of any information as a result of that selection.

> "The text does a balanced job of presenting real financial reporting situations without going too far into the debit/credit weeds."
> **Joshua Neil**
> University of Colorado—Boulder

> "The text allows me to easily tailor to topics I want to cover."
> **Joshua Neil**
> University of Colorado—Boulder

Flexibility for Courses of Varying Lengths

Many instructors have approached us to ask about suggested class structures based on courses of varying length. To that end, we provide the following table of common course designs.

	15 Week Semester-Course	10 Week Quarter-Course	6 Week, Mini-Course	1 Week Intensive-Course
Module 1: Financial Accounting for MBAs	Week 1	Week 1	Week 1	Day 1 (Module 1 and either Module 2 or Module 3)
Module 2: Introducing Financial Statements	Week 2	Week 2	Week 2	
Module 3: Transactions, Adjustments, and Financial Statements	Week 2 (optional)	Week 2 (optional)	Week 2 (optional)	
Module 4: Analyzing and Interpreting Financial Statements	Weeks 3 and 4	Week 3	Week 3	Day 2
Module 5: Revenues, Receivables, and Operating Expenses	Week 5	Week 4	Skim	Skim
Module 6: Inventories, Accounts Payable, and Long-Term Assets	Week 6	Week 5	Week 4	Day 3
Module 7: Current and Long-Term Liabilities	Week 7	Week 6	Week 5	Day 4
Module 8: Stock Transactions, Dividends, and EPS	Week 8	Week 7	Week 6	Day 5
Module 9: Intercorporate Investments	Week 9	Optional	Optional	Optional
Module 10: Leases, Pensions, and Income Taxes	Weeks 10 and 11	Week 8	Optional	Optional
Module 11: Cash Flows	Week 12	Week 9 (or Optional)	Optional	Optional
Module 12: Financial Statement Forecasting	Week 13	Week 10	Optional	Optional
Module 13: Using Financial Statements for Valuation	Week 14			

Managerial Emphasis

> "An excellent book if you are looking for great and extensive real world examples and application, as well as an analysis approach that distinguishes between operating and non-operating components of the IS and BS."
> **Galen Sevcik**
> Georgia State University

Tomorrow's MBA graduates must be skilled in using financial statements to make business decisions. These skills often require application of ratio analyses, benchmarking, forecasting, valuation, and other aspects of financial statement analysis for decision making. Tomorrow's MBA graduates must have the skills to go beyond basic financial statements and to interpret and apply nonfinancial statement disclosures, such as footnotes and supplementary reports. This book, therefore, emphasizes real company data, including detailed footnote and other management disclosures, and shows how to use this information to make managerial inferences and decisions. This approach makes financial accounting interesting and relevant for all MBA students.

As MBA instructors, we recognize that the core MBA financial accounting course is not directed toward accounting majors. *Financial Accounting for MBAs* embraces this reality. This book highlights **financial reporting, analysis, interpretation,** and **decision making.** We incorporate the following **financial statement effects template** to train MBA students in understanding the economic ramifications of transactions and their impact on financial statements. This analytical tool is a great resource for MBA students in learning accounting and applying it to their future courses and careers. Each transaction is identified in the "Transaction" column. Then, the dollar amounts (positive or negative) of the financial statement effects are recorded in the appropriate balance sheet or income statement columns. The template also reflects the statement of cash flow effects (via the cash column) and the statement of stockholders' equity effects (via the contributed capital and earned capital

> "It is an excellent Financial Accounting MBA textbook. It speaks the right language; does a great job relating accounting to business decisions."
> **Xiaofei Song**
> Saint Mary's University

columns). The earned capital account is immediately updated to reflect any income or loss arising from each transaction (denoted by the arrow line from net income to earned capital). This template is instructive as it reveals the financial impacts of transactions, and it provides insights into the effects of accounting choices.

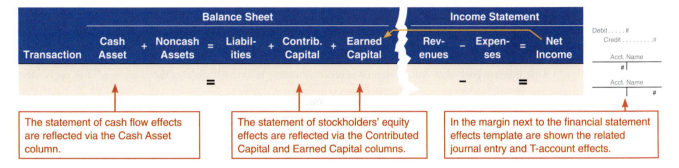

Innovative Pedagogy

Financial Accounting for MBAs includes special features specifically designed for the MBA student.

> "Excellent MBA-level text."
> **Nate Franke**
> University of California—Irvine

Focus Companies for Each Module

Each module's content is explained through the accounting and reporting activities of real companies. Each module incorporates a "focus company" for special emphasis and demonstration. The enhanced instructional value of focus companies comes from the way they engage MBA students in real analysis and interpretation. Focus companies were selected based on the industries that MBA students typically enter upon graduation.

MODULE 1	Apple	MODULE 8	Johnson & Johnson
MODULE 2	Apple	MODULE 9	Google
MODULE 3	Apple	MODULE 10	Microsoft, Deere, HP
MODULE 4	Boston Scientific	MODULE 11	Starbucks
MODULE 5	Pfizer	MODULE 12	Procter & Gamble
MODULE 6	Home Depot	MODULE 13	Procter & Gamble
MODULE 7	Verizon	APPENDIX C	Harley-Davidson

Real Company Data Throughout

Market research and reviewer feedback tell us that one of instructors' greatest frustrations with other MBA books is their lack of real company data. We have gone to great lengths to incorporate real company data throughout each module to reinforce important concepts and engage MBA students. We engage nonaccounting MBA students specializing in finance, taxation, marketing, management, real estate, operations, and so forth, with companies and scenarios that are relevant to them. For representative examples, **SEE PAGES 2-6, 4-16, 6-23, 7-3, 8-4, 9-10, 10-4, 11-6, and 12-17.**

Footnotes and Other Management Disclosures

Analyzed on their own, financial statements reveal only part of a corporation's economic story. Information essential for a complete analysis of a company's performance and financial position must be gleaned from the footnotes and other disclosures provided by the company. Consequently, we incorporate footnotes and other disclosures generously throughout the text and assignments. For representative examples, **SEE PAGES 2-24, 4-28, 5-3, 6-9, 7-6, 8-15, 9-7, and 12-5.**

> "Practical. Makes use of real-world examples and analyses."
> **Peter Wilson**
> Babson College

Dual Approach to ROE and Financial Statement Analysis

We continue to stress profitability and return analysis as a "hook" for student interest. The analysis framework includes disaggregation of ROE and application of several other key metrics.

- Module 4 opens with the traditional DuPont model as a simple, yet powerful, analysis framework.
- Later in Module 4, we disaggregate ROE into operating and nonoperating components as a natural extension of the traditional DuPont model.
- Later modules revisit the DuPont model, and text boxes throughout include deeper discussion of operating versus nonoperating activities.
- Later modules also discuss factors that affect operating performance and consider actions that managers can take to improve that performance.

Industry-Level Data

We repeatedly emphasize that financial analysis cannot be performed in a vacuum—appropriate benchmarks are critical to a complete understanding of a company's financial performance and position. To this point, we provide graphics that capture industry-level data including many of the ratios we discuss and compute in the modules. For representative examples, **SEE PAGES 4-1, 5-4, 6-26, 7-17, 8-29, and 10-14.**

Decision Making Orientation

One primary goal of an MBA financial accounting course is to teach students the skills needed to apply their accounting knowledge to solving real business problems and making informed business decisions. With that goal in mind, Managerial Decision boxes in each module encourage students to apply the material presented to solving actual business scenarios. For representative examples, **SEE PAGES 4-26, 5-4, 8-11, 10-8, and 11-15.** Each module also includes Analysis Insight boxes that provide insight into data analysis techniques and models that financial analysts typically use. For representative examples, **SEE PAGES 2-11, 6-13, 7-15, 9-17, 10-9, 11-28, and 12-24.**

Reviews for Each Learning Objective

Financial accounting can be challenging—especially for MBA students lacking business experience or previous exposure to business courses. To reinforce concepts presented in each module and to ensure student comprehension, we include reviews that require students to recall and apply the financial accounting techniques and concepts described in each section. Review questions usually include real financial statement data from a company in the same industry as the module's focus company.

Experiential Learning

Students retain information longer if they can apply the lessons learned from the module content. To meet this need for experiential learning, we conclude each module with a hands-on analysis project. A series of questions guides students' inquiry and helps students synthesize the material in the module and integrate material across modules.

Excellent, Class-Tested Assignment Materials

Excellent assignment material is a must-have component of any successful book (and class). We went to great lengths to create the best assignments possible from contemporary financial statements. In keeping with the rest of the book, we used real company data extensively. We also ensured that assignments reflect our belief that MBA students should be trained in analyzing accounting information to make business decisions, as opposed to working on mechanical bookkeeping tasks. There are six categories of assignments: **Questions**, **Mini Exercises**, **Exercises**, **Problems**, **IFRS Applications**, and **Management Applications**.

New Edition Changes

Based on classroom use and reviewer feedback, a number of substantive changes have been made in the new edition to further enhance the MBA students' experiences.

- **Digital delivery enhanced** To serve the expanding delivery modes of MBA education, we updated our in-chapter Reviews and Guided Example videos for all chapters (each Learning Objective has a Review/Guided Example, as well as a corresponding eLecture).

- **Data visualization and analytics** Companies are increasingly using data visualization (charts, pictures, and graphs) to more effectively convey financial information. To support student learning, each module opens with a data dashboard and includes end-of-chapter assignments that present data graphically and require students to analyze and interpret the data visualizations. We provide students with online access (via MBC) to author-created PowerBI dashboards where they can interact with the data and learn how to create their own data visualizations.

- **Content reflects new standards** This edition covers new standards on Revenue Recognition, Leases, and Marketable Securities. It also includes in-depth discussion of the Tax Cuts and Jobs Act and how new tax law impacts financial analysis.

- **Revenue, Operating Expenses, and Receivables** We expanded the discussion of revenue recognition following the new standard and included an illustration and analysis of Microsoft's revenue recognition. We also discuss sales returns and allowances and the effects of foreign currency exchange rates. Our operating expenses discussion introduces the effects of the Tax Cuts and Jobs Act, with a deeper discussion in Module 10.

- **Inventories** Our discussion of cash conversion cycle includes an illustration of management actions undertaken by Home Depot to streamline its supply chain to reduce days inventory outstanding.
- **Bond rating** A new section in Module 7 discusses Credit Analysis, including how bond ratings are determined. We provide an example of S&P Global's ratings for Verizon, following its purchase of Vodafone's interest in Verizon Wireless. We also simplify our discussion of bond pricing.
- **Share-based compensation** Module 8 includes an expanded discussion of share-based compensation, and Tesla's use of convertible debt.
- **Investments** We include a deeper discussion of the determination of fair value, including an expanded discussion of Level 3 inputs to value securities with limited markets and the accounting for those securities. Module 6 includes a new, expanded discussion of the new goodwill impairment standard.
- **Derivatives** We markedly revised our discussion of derivatives to simplify the exposition while maintaining the analysis coverage.
- **Equity Carve-Outs** The discussion of equity carve-outs is simplified and we provide examples of the accounting for Sell-offs, IPOs, Spin-offs, and Split-offs. We also discuss the deconsolidation of a subsidiary.
- **Leasing** Module 10 reflects the new lease standard including the analysis of right-of-use assets and differences between operating and financial leases. We discuss retrospective and prospective adoption, using Microsoft and Delta Airlines.
- **Pension disclosures** We markedly revised our discussion of pension accounting with a detailed illustration of the pension footnote disclosures. We include a section on fair valuation of pension obligations and the accounting for plan settlements.
- **Taxes** We provide an in-depth, completely revised, discussion of income tax expense, including the effects of the Tax Cuts and Jobs Act and the analysis implications during the transition period.
- **Updated Assignments** We updated all data and financial statements throughout the book to reflect each company's latest available financial statement filings and disclosures. Assignments include current financial statement excerpts and reflect new standards for Revenue Recognition, Leases, and Marketable Securities and the Tax Cuts and Jobs Act.

Fundamentals of Financial Accounting Tutorial

This interactive tutorial is intended for use in programs that either require or would like to offer a pre-term tutorial that creates a baseline of accounting knowledge for students with little to no prior exposure to financial accounting. Initially developed as a pre-term tutorial for first-year MBA students, this product can be used as a warm-up for any introductory-level financial accounting course. It is designed as an asynchronous, interactive, self-paced experience for students.

Available Learning Modules (You Select)

1. Introducing Financial Accounting (approximate completion time 2 hours)
2. Constructing Financial Statements (approximate completion time 4 hours)
3. Adjusting Entries and Completing the Accounting Cycle (approximate completion time 4 hours)
4. Reporting and Analyzing Cash Flows (approximate completion time 3.5 hours)
5. Analyzing and Interpreting Financial Statements (approximate completion time 3.5 hours)
6. Excel and Time-Value of Money Basics (approximate completion time 2 hours)

This is a separate, saleable item. Contact your sales representative to receive more information or email customerservice@cambridgepub.com.

Companion Casebook

Cases in Financial Reporting, 8th edition by Michael Drake (Brigham Young University), Ellen Engel (University of Illinois—Chicago), D. Eric Hirst (University of Texas—Austin), and Mary Lea McAnally (Texas A&M University). This book comprises 27 cases and is a perfect companion book for faculty interested in exposing students to a wide range of real financial statements. The cases cover companies from Japan, Sweden, Austria, the Netherlands, the UK, India, as well as from the U.S. Many of the U.S. companies are major multinationals. Each case deals with a specific financial accounting topic within the context of one (or more) company's financial statements. Each case contains financial statement information and a set of directed questions pertaining to one or two specific financial accounting issues. This is a separate, saleable casebook (**ISBN 978-1-61853-122-3**). Contact your sales representative to receive a desk copy or email customerservice@cambridgepub.com.

Supplement Package

For Instructors

myBusinessCourse: A web-based learning and assessment program intended to complement your book and classroom instruction. This easy-to-use course management system grades homework automatically and provides students with additional help when you are not available. In addition, detailed diagnostic tools assess class and individual performance. myBusinessCourse is ideal for online courses or traditional face-to-face courses for which the instructor wants to offer students more resources to succeed. Assignments with the MBC in the margin are available in myBusinessCourse. eLecture videos are available for the chapter Learning Objectives, and Guided Examples for the in-chapter Reviews are available to assign to students. MBC integrates with many learning management systems, including **Canvas**, **Blackboard**, **Moodle**, **D2L**, **Schoology**, and **Sakai**. The integration process is quick and easy, so you and your students are ready to go on day one.

Solutions Manual: Created by the authors, the *Solutions Manual* contains complete solutions to all assignments.

PowerPoint: Created by the authors, the PowerPoint slides outline key elements of each module.

Test Bank: Written by the authors, the test bank includes multiple-choice items, matching questions, short essay questions, and problems.

Website: All instructor materials are accessible via the book's website (password protected) along with other useful links and information. www.cambridgepub.com

For Students

eLectures: Created by the authors, each chapter's Learning Objective includes an eLecture video available in our online learning management system, myBusinessCourse (see below for more information).

Guided Examples: Created by the authors, Guided Example videos are available for each in-chapter Review, also in myBusinessCourse (see below for more information).

myBusinessCourse is a web-based learning and assessment program intended to complement your book and faculty instruction. This easy-to-use program provides additional help when the instructor is not available. Guided Example videos are available for all in-chapter Reviews, and eLecture videos are available for each Learning Objective. With Instructor-Led MBC courses, assignments with the MBC in the margin are also available and are automatically graded. Access is free with new copies of this book (look for page containing the access code towards the front of the book). If you buy a used copy of the book, you can purchase access at www.mybusinesscourse.com.

Student Solutions Manual: Created by the authors, the student solutions manual contains all solutions to the even-numbered assignment materials in the book. This is a **restricted** item that is only available to students after their instructor has authorized its purchase. ISBN 978-1-61853-373-9.

Website: Useful links are available to students free of charge on the book's website.

Acknowledgments

All editions of this book benefited greatly from the valuable feedback of focus group attendees, reviewers, students, and colleagues. We are extremely grateful to them for their help in making this project a success.

Beverley Alleyne, *Belmont University*
Ashiq Ali, *University of Texas—Dallas*
Dan Amiram, *Tel Aviv University*
Walter Austin, *Mercer University*
Steve Baginski, *University of Georgia*
Eli Bartov, *New York University*
Dan Bens, *INSEAD*
Richard Bernstein, *The University of Toledo*
James Biagi, *Marywood University*
Mark Bradshaw, *Boston College*
Dennis Bline, *Bryant University*
John Briginshaw, *Pepperdine University*
Thomas Buchman, *University of Colorado—Boulder*
Angela Busila, *Old Dominion University*
Edgar Carter, *University of Massachusetts—Lowell*
Mary Ellen Carter, *Boston College*
Sandra Cereola, *James Madison University*
Sumantra Chakravarty, *California State University—Fullerton*

Betty Chavis, *California State University—Fullerton*
Agnes Cheng, *Louisiana State University*
Ellen Cook, *University of Louisiana—Lafayette*
Erin Cornelsen, *University of South Dakota*
Michael Coyne, *Fairfield University*
Araya Debessay, *University of Delaware*
Roger Debreceny, *University of Hawaii—Manoa*
Carol Dee, *University of Colorado—Denver*
Rosemond Desir, *Colorado State University*
Vicki Dickinson, *University of Mississippi*
Jeffrey Doyle, *University of Utah*
Donald Drake, *Georgia State University*
Phil Drake, *Arizona State University*
Joanne Duke, *San Francisco State University*
Cindy Durtschi, *DePaul University*
Craig Emby, *Simon Fraser University*
Gerard Engeholm, *Pace University*
Kathryn Epps, *Kennesaw State University*

Lucile Faurel, *Arizona State University*
Bud Fennema, *Florida State University*
Mark Finn, *Northwestern University*
Carol Fischer, *St. Bonaventure University*
Tim Fogarty, *Case Western Reserve University*
Nate Franke, *University of California—Irvine*
Richard Frankel, *Washington University*
Waqar Ghani, *Saint Joseph's University*
Andy Garcia, *Bowling Green State University*
Maclean Gaulin, *Rice University*
Giorgio Gotti, *University of Texas—El Paso*
Julia Grant, *Case Western Reserve University*
Kris Gulick, *University of Iowa*
Karl Hackenbrack, *Vanderbilt University*
Bob Hartman, *University of Iowa*
Carla Hayn, *University of California— Los Angeles*
Frank Heflin, *University of Georgia*
Michele Henney, *University of Oregon*
Elaine Henry, *University of Miami*
Judith Hora, *University of San Diego*
Herbert Hunt, *California State University—Long Beach*
Ross Jennings, *University of Texas—Austin*
Greg Jonas, *Case Western Reserve University*
Greg Kane, *University of Delaware*
Victoria Kaskey, *Ashland University*
Zafar Khan, *Eastern Michigan University*
Saleha Khumawala, *University of Houston*
Marinilka Kimbro, *University of Washington—Tacoma*
Ron King, *Washington University*
Michael Kirschenheiter, *University of Illinois—Chicago*
Phillip J. Korb, *University of Baltimore*
Susan Kulp, *George Washington University*
Krishna Kumar, *George Washington University*
Lisa Kutcher, *University of Oregon*
Deborah Leitsch, *Goldey-Beacom College*
Brian Leventhal, *University of Illinois—Chicago*
Pierre Liang, *Carnegie Mellon University*
Joshua Livnat, *New York University*
Frank Longo, *Centenary University*
Benjamin Lonner, *New York University*
Barbara Lougee, *University of San Diego*
Yvonne Lu, *Lehigh University*
Jason MacGregor, *Baylor University*
Lois Mahoney, *Eastern Michigan University*
Michael Maier, *University of Alberta*
Ron Mano, *Westminster College*
Ronald Marcusson, *DePaul University*
Ariel Markelevich, *Suffolk University*
Jason Matthews, *University of Georgia*
Brian McAllister, *University of Colorado at Colorado Springs*
Bruce McClain, *Cleveland State University*
Karen McDougal, *St. Joseph's University*
Marc McIntosh, *Augsburg University*
James McKinney, *University of Maryland*
Gregory Merrill, *Saint Mary's University*
Jose Miranda-Lopez, *California State University—Fullerton*
Melanie Mogg, *University of Minnesota*
Steve Monahan, *INSEAD*
John Morris, *Kansas State University*
Philip Morris, *Sam Houston State University*
Dennis Murray, *University of Colorado—Denver*
Sandeep Nabar, *Oklahoma State University*
Suresh Nallareddy, *Columbia University*
Ramesh Narasimhan, *Montclair State University*
Siva Nathan, *Georgia State University*
Joshua Neil, *University of Colorado—Boulder*
Doron Nissim, *Columbia University*
Gary Olsen, *Carroll University*

Shail Pandit, *University of Illinois—Chicago*
Susan Parker, *Santa Clara University*
William Pasewark, *Texas Tech*
Stephen Penman, *Columbia University*
Mark Penno, *University of Iowa*
Gary Peters, *University of Arkansas*
Kathy Petroni, *Michigan State University*
Christine Petrovits, *New York University*
Kirk Philipich, *University of Michigan—Dearborn*
Morton Pincus, *University of California—Irvine*
Lincoln Pinto, *Concordia University*
Kay Poston, *University of Indianapolis*
Grace Pownall, *Emory University*
David Randolph, *Xavier University*
Laura Rickett, *Kent State University*
Susan Riffe, *Southern Methodist University*
Bruce Samuelson, *Pepperdine University*
Diane Satin, *California State University—East Bay*
Shahrokh Saudagaran, *University of Washington—Tacoma*
Andrew Schmidt, *North Carolina State University*
Chandra Seethamraju, *Washington University*
Stephen Sefcik, *University of Washington*
Galen Sevcik, *Georgia State University*
Lewis Shaw, *Suffolk University*
Kenneth Shaw, *University of Missouri*
Todd Shawver, *Bloomsburg University*
Evan Shough, *University of North Carolina—Greensboro*
Robin Shuler, *Seattle Pacific University*
Carl Shultz, *Rider University*
Paul Simko, *University of Virginia—Darden*
Andreas Simon, *Pepperdine University*
Kevin Smith, *University of Kansas*
Rod Smith, *California State University—Long Beach*
Hakjoon Song, *The University of Akron*
Xiaofei Song, *Saint Mary's University*
Jens Stephan, *Eastern Michigan University*
Jerry Strawser, *Texas A&M University*
Sherre Strickland, *University of Massachusetts—Lowell*
Chandra Subramaniam, *University of Texas—Austin*
K.R. Subramanyam, *University of Southern California*
Ziad Syed, *Texas A&M University*
Gregory Tanzola, *Saint Joseph's University*
Gary Taylor, *University of Alabama*
Mark Taylor, *Case Western Reserve University*
Suzanne Traylor, *State University of New York—Albany*
Sam Tiras, *Louisiana State University*
Brett Trueman, *University of California—Los Angeles*
Jerry Van Os, *Westminster College*
Lisa Victoravich, *University of Denver*
Marcia Vorholt, *Xavier University*
James Wallace, *Claremont Graduate School*
Charles Wasley, *University of Rochester*
Greg Waymire, *Emory University*
Andrea Weickgenannt, *Xavier University*
Daniel Weimer, *Wayne State University*
Edward Werner, *Drexel University*
Lourdes White, *University of Baltimore*
Jonathan M. Wild, *Oklahoma State University*
Jeffrey Williams, *University of Michigan*
Peter Wilson, *Babson College*
David Wright, *University of Michigan*
Michelle Yetman, *University of California—Davis*
Susan Young, *Fordham University*
Tzachi Zack, *Ohio State University*
Xiao-Jun Zhang, *University of California—Berkeley*
Yuan Zhang, *Columbia University*
Yuping Zhao, *University of Houston*

Very special thanks are extended to Susan Hamlen and Paul Hutchison for their thorough accuracy checking of the text and solutions manual. In addition, we are extremely grateful to George Werthman, Lorraine Gleeson, Jocelyn Mousel, Dana Vinyard, Debbie McQuade, Terry McQuade, and the entire team at Cambridge Business Publishers for their encouragement, enthusiasm, and guidance. Their market research, editorial development, and promotional efforts have made this book the best-selling MBA text in the market.

Peter   *John*   *Bob*   *Mary Lea*

February 2020

Brief Contents

About the Authors   iii

Preface   v

MODULE 1
Financial Accounting for MBAs 1-1

MODULE 2
Introducing Financial Statements 2-1

MODULE 3
Transactions, Adjustments, and Financial Statements 3-1

MODULE 4
Analyzing and Interpreting Financial Statements 4-1

MODULE 5
Revenues, Receivables, and Operating Expenses 5-1

MODULE 6
Inventories, Accounts Payable, and Long-Term Assets 6-1

MODULE 7
Current and Long-Term Liabilities 7-1

MODULE 8
Stock Transactions, Dividends, and EPS 8-1

MODULE 9
Intercorporate Investments 9-1

MODULE 10
Leases, Pensions, and Income Taxes 10-1

MODULE 11
Cash Flows 11-1

MODULE 12
Financial Statement Forecasting 12-1

MODULE 13
Using Financial Statements for Valuation 13-1

APPENDIX A
Compound Interest Tables A-1

APPENDIX B
Chart of Accounts with Acronyms B-1

APPENDIX C
Comprehensive Case (online only) C-1

Glossary   G-1

Index   I-1

Contents

About the Authors **iii**
Preface **v**

MODULE 1
Financial Accounting for MBAs 1-1

Preview 1-1
Reporting on Business Activities 1-3
Review 1-1 1-4
Financial Statements: Demand and Supply 1-4
    Demand for Information **1-4**
    Supply of Information **1-7**
    International Accounting Standards **1-8**
Review 1-2 1-9
Structure of Financial Statements 1-9
    Balance Sheet **1-10**
    Income Statement **1-13**
    Statement of Stockholders' Equity **1-14**
    Statement of Cash Flows **1-15**
    Information Beyond Financial Statements **1-16**
    Managerial Choices in Financial Accounting **1-17**
Review 1-3 1-18
Analysis of Financial Statements 1-18
    Return on Assets **1-18**
    Components of Return on Assets **1-18**
    Return on Equity **1-20**
    Are Financial Statements Relevant? **1-20**
Review 1-4 1-21
Financial Statements and Business Analysis 1-22
    Analyzing the Competitive Environment **1-22**
    SWOT Analysis of the Business Environment **1-23**
    Analyzing Competitive Advantage **1-24**
Review 1-5 1-25
Book Road Map 1-25
Global Accounting 1-26
Appendix 1A: Financial Statement Data and Analytics 1-26
    Data Analytics **1-29**
Appendix 1B: Accounting Principles and Governance 1-30
    Financial Accounting Environment **1-30**
    Audit Report **1-31**
Guidance Answers 1-34
Questions 1-34
Mini Exercises 1-35
Exercises 1-38
Problems 1-40
IFRS Applications 1-46
Management Applications 1-47
Ongoing Project 1-48
Solutions to Review Problems 1-48

MODULE 2
Introducing Financial Statements 2-1

Preview 2-1
Balance Sheet 2-3
    Balance Sheet and the Flow of Costs **2-3**
    Assets **2-4**
    Liabilities and Equity **2-6**
Review 2-1 2-13
Income Statement 2-13
    Recognizing Revenues and Expenses **2-14**
    Reporting of Transitory Items **2-15**
    Analyzing the Income Statement **2-16**
Review 2-2 2-17
Statement of Stockholders' Equity 2-17
Review 2-3 2-18
Statement of Cash Flows 2-18
    Statement Format and Data Sources **2-18**
Review 2-4 2-20
Articulation of Financial Statements 2-20
    Retained Earnings Reconciliation **2-20**
    Financial Statement Linkages **2-20**
Review 2-5 2-22
Additional Information Sources 2-22
    Form 10-K **2-22**
    Form 20-F and Form 40-F **2-24**
    Form 8-K **2-25**
    Analyst Reports **2-25**
    Credit Services **2-26**
    Data Services **2-26**
Review 2-6 2-26
Global Accounting 2-26
Guidance Answers 2-27
Questions 2-27
Mini Exercises 2-28
Exercises 2-29
Problems 2-34
IFRS Applications 2-38
Management Applications 2-38
Ongoing Project 2-39
Solutions to Review Problems 2-40

MODULE 3
Transactions, Adjustments, and Financial Statements 3-1

Preview 3-1
Basics of Accounting 3-3
    Four-Step Accounting Cycle **3-3**
    Financial Statement Effects Template **3-3**
Review 3-1 3-5
Accounting Cycle Step 1—Analyze Transactions and Prepare Entries 3-6
    Apple's Transactions **3-6**
    Applying the Financial Statement Effects Template **3-6**
    Applying the Journal Entry and T-Account **3-6**
Review 3-2 3-8
Accounting Cycle Step 2—Prepare Accounting Adjustments 3-9
    Prepaid Expenses **3-10**
    Unearned Revenues **3-10**
    Accrued Expenses **3-11**
    Accrued Revenues **3-12**
    Accounting Adjustments for Apple **3-12**
Review 3-3 3-13
Accounting Cycle Step 3—Prepare Financial Statements 3-13
    Income Statement **3-13**
    Balance Sheet **3-14**
    Statement of Stockholders' Equity **3-15**
Review 3-4 3-16
Accounting Cycle Step 4—Close the Books 3-16
Review 3-5 3-18
Global Accounting 3-18
Appendix 3A: FASB's Financial Statement Presentation Project 3-19
Guidance Answers 3-19
Questions 3-20
Mini Exercises 3-20
Exercises 3-23
Problems 3-27
IFRS Applications 3-32
Management Applications 3-33

xiii

MODULE 4
Analyzing and Interpreting Financial Statements 4-1

Preview... 4-1
Return on Equity (ROE)... 4-3
Review 4-1... 4-3
ROE Disaggregation: DuPont Analysis... 4-4
Review 4-2... 4-5
Return on Assets and Its Disaggregation... 4-6
    Analysis of Profitability and Productivity **4-7**
    Analysis of Profitability **4-8**
    Analysis of Productivity **4-9**
    Analysis of Financial Leverage **4-12**
Review 4-3... 4-14
Balance Sheet Analysis with an Operating Focus... 4-14
    Net Operating Assets (NOA) **4-15**
    Net Nonoperating Obligations (NNO) **4-17**
Review 4-4... 4-18
Income Statement Analysis with an Operating Focus... 4-19
Review 4-5... 4-22
Return on Net Operating Assets (RNOA)... 4-23
Review 4-6... 4-25
RNOA Disaggregation into Margin and Turnover... 4-25
    Net Operating Profit Margin **4-25**
    Net Operating Asset Turnover **4-26**
    Trade-Off between Margin and Turnover **4-27**
Review 4-7... 4-29
Global Accounting... 4-29
Appendix 4A: Operating versus Nonoperating Classification... 4-30
Appendix 4B: Nonoperating Return Component of ROE... 4-31
    Nonoperating Return **4-31**
    Nonoperating Return—With Substantial Net Nonoperating Assets: Amazon **4-33**
    Nonoperating Return—With Noncontrolling Interest: AT&T **4-34**
Review 4-8... 4-35
Appendix 4C: Liquidity and Solvency Analysis... 4-35
    Liquidity Analysis **4-36**
    Current Ratio **4-36**
    Quick Ratio **4-36**
    Solvency Analysis **4-37**
    Liabilities-to-Equity **4-37**
    Times Interest Earned **4-38**
    Vertical and Horizontal Analysis **4-38**
    Limitations of Ratio Analysis **4-40**
Review 4-9... 4-41
Guidance Answers... 4-41
Questions... 4-42
Mini Exercises... 4-42
Exercises... 4-46
Problems... 4-50
IFRS Applications... 4-57
Management Applications... 4-57
Ongoing Project... 4-58
Solutions to Review Problems... 4-59

MODULE 5
Revenues, Receivables, and Operating Expenses 5-1

Preview... 5-1
Revenue... 5-3
    Revenue Recognition Rules **5-4**
    Complications of Revenue Recognition **5-5**
    Performance Obligations Satisfied Over Time **5-7**
Review 5-1... 5-11
Sales Allowances... 5-11
    Accounting for Sales Allowances **5-11**
    Reporting Sales Allowances **5-12**
    Analysis of Sales Allowances **5-13**
Review 5-2... 5-13
Unearned (Deferred) Revenue... 5-14
Review 5-3... 5-15
Foreign Currency Effects on Revenue, Expenses, and Cash Flow... 5-15
    Foreign Currency and Cash Flows **5-16**
    Foreign Currency and Income **5-17**
    Foreign Currency and Future Results **5-17**
Review 5-4... 5-18
Accounts Receivable... 5-19
    Aging Analysis of Receivables **5-19**
    Accounting for Accounts Receivable **5-20**
    Analysis of Accounts Receivable—Magnitude **5-21**
    Analysis of Accounts Receivable—Quality **5-22**
Review 5-5... 5-24
Expenses and Losses... 5-25
    Deductions from Income **5-25**
    Research and Development Expense **5-26**
    Provision (Benefit) for Taxes on Income **5-28**
    Discontinued Operations **5-28**
Review 5-6... 5-30
Pro Forma Income Reporting... 5-31
    Regulation G Reconciliation **5-31**
    SEC Warnings about Pro Forma Numbers **5-32**
    Disclosures and Market Assessments **5-32**
Review 5-7... 5-34
Global Accounting... 5-35
Guidance Answers... 5-35
Questions... 5-35
Mini Exercises... 5-36
Exercises... 5-40
Problems... 5-47
IFRS Applications... 5-53
Management Applications... 5-54
Ongoing Project... 5-54
Solutions to Review Problems... 5-55

MODULE 6
Inventories, Accounts Payable, and Long-Term Assets 6-1

Preview... 6-1
Inventory—Costing Methods... 6-3
    First-In, First-Out (FIFO) **6-4**
    Last-In, First-Out (LIFO) **6-5**
    Average Cost (AC) **6-5**
    Financial Statement Effects of Inventory Costing **6-7**
Review 6-1... 6-8
Inventory—Reporting... 6-8
    Lower of Cost or Market (LCM) **6-8**
    LIFO Reserve Adjustments to Financial Statements **6-9**
    LIFO Liquidations **6-11**
Review 6-2... 6-11
Inventory—Analysis Tools... 6-12
    Gross Profit Analysis **6-12**
    Days Inventory Outstanding and Inventory Turnover **6-13**
    Days Payable Outstanding **6-15**
    Cash Conversion Cycle **6-16**
Review 6-3... 6-17
PPE Assets—Capitalization and Depreciation... 6-17
    Plant and Equipment **6-18**
    Research and Development Facilities and Equipment **6-19**
Review 6-4... 6-20
PPE Assets—Sales, Impairments, and Restructuring... 6-20
    Asset Sales **6-20**
    Asset Impairments **6-21**

Solutions to Review Problems... 3-35

Restructuring Costs **6-22**
Review 6-5 . . . . **6-24**
PPE Assets—Analysis Tools **6-25**
    PPE Turnover **6-25**
    PPE Useful Life **6-26**
    PPE Percent Used Up **6-27**
Review 6-6 . . . . **6-27**
Global Accounting **6-27**
Guidance Answers **6-28**
Questions **6-29**
Mini Exercises **6-30**
Exercises **6-32**
Problems **6-38**
IFRS Applications **6-40**
Management Applications **6-42**
Ongoing Project **6-42**
Solutions to Review Problems **6-43**

MODULE 7
Current and Long-Term Liabilities 7-1

Preview. **7-1**
Accrued Liabilities. **7-3**
    Accrued Liabilities Defined **7-3**
    Accruals for Contractual Liabilities—Wages Payable
      Example **7-4**
    Accruals for Contractual Liabilities—Deferred
      Revenue Example **7-4**
    Accruals for Contingent Liabilities **7-5**
    Accruals for Contingent Liabilities—Warranties Example **7-5**
Review 7-1 . . . . **7-7**
Short-Term Debt. **7-7**
    Accounting for Short-Term Debt **7-7**
    Current Maturities of Long-Term Debt **7-8**
Review 7-2 . . . . **7-9**
Long-Term Debt—Pricing. **7-9**
    Pricing of Bonds Issued at Par **7-10**
    Pricing of Bonds Issued at a Discount **7-10**
    Pricing of Bonds Issued at a Premium **7-11**
    Effective Cost of Debt **7-11**
Review 7-3 . . . . **7-13**
Long-Term Debt—Reporting. **7-13**
    Balance Sheet Reporting **7-13**
    Income Statement Reporting **7-14**
    Financial Statement Effects of Bond Repurchase **7-14**
    Fair Value Disclosures **7-15**
Review 7-4 . . . . **7-16**
Quality of Debt **7-16**
    Credit Analysis **7-16**
    What Are Credit Ratings? **7-18**
    What Determines Credit Ratings? **7-18**
    Verizon Credit Rating Example **7-21**
    Why Credit Ratings Matter **7-23**
Review 7-5 . . . . **7-24**
Global Accounting **7-24**
Appendix 7A: Time Value of Money **7-25**
    Present Value Concepts **7-25**
    Present Value of a Single Amount **7-25**
    Time Value of Money Tables **7-25**
    Present Value of an Annuity **7-26**
    Bond Valuation **7-27**
    Time Value of Money Computations Using a Calculator **7-28**
    Time Value of Money Computations Using Excel **7-28**
    Future Value Concepts **7-30**
    Future Value of a Single Amount **7-30**
    Future Value of an Annuity **7-30**
Review 7-6 . . . . **7-30**
Appendix 7B: Amortization of Debt **7-31**
    Amortization of Discount **7-31**
    Amortization of Premium **7-32**
Guidance Answers **7-32**
Questions **7-32**
Mini Exercises **7-33**
Exercises **7-36**
Problems **7-41**
IFRS Applications **7-46**
Management Applications **7-47**
Ongoing Project **7-47**
Solutions to Review Problems **7-48**

MODULE 8
Stock Transactions, Dividends, and EPS 8-1

Preview. **8-1**
Stockholders' Equity and Classes of Stock **8-3**
    Stockholders' Equity Accounts **8-3**
    Statement of Stockholders' Equity **8-5**
    Preferred Stock **8-6**
    Common Stock **8-7**
Review 8-1 . . . . **8-8**
Stock Transactions **8-9**
    Stock Issuance **8-9**
    Stock Repurchase (Treasury Stock) **8-10**
Review 8-2 . . . . **8-12**
Stock-Based Compensation. **8-13**
    Accounting for Stock-Based Compensation **8-14**
    Footnote Disclosures for Stock-Based Compensation **8-15**
Review 8-3 . . . . **8-16**
Dividends and Stock Splits. **8-16**
    Cash Dividend Disclosures **8-17**
    Dividend Payout and Yield **8-17**
    Cash Dividends Financial Effects **8-17**
    Stock Split **8-18**
Review 8-4 . . . . **8-19**
Accumulated Other Comprehensive Income **8-19**
    AOCI Components **8-19**
    AOCI Disclosures and Interpretation **8-20**
Review 8-5 . . . . **8-21**
Convertible Securities. **8-22**
Review 8-6 . . . . **8-23**
Earnings per Share (EPS) **8-23**
Review 8-7 . . . . **8-25**
Global Accounting **8-25**
Appendix 8A: Stock-Based Compensation: Reporting and
                  Analyzing. **8-26**
    Employee Stock Purchase Plans (ESPP) **8-26**
    Stock Awards **8-27**
    Stock Options **8-27**
    Stock Appreciation Rights (SAR) **8-28**
    Summary of Share-Based Compensation **8-28**
    Analysis Implications **8-28**
Guidance Answers **8-29**
Questions **8-30**
Mini Exercises **8-31**
Exercises **8-34**
Problems **8-39**
IFRS Applications **8-48**
Ongoing Project **8-50**
Solutions to Review Problems **8-51**

MODULE 9
Intercorporate Investments 9-1

Preview. **9-1**
Intercorporate Investments **9-3**
    Passive Investments in Equity Securities **9-4**
    Investments in Debt Securities **9-8**
Review 9-1 . . . . **9-11**
Equity Investments with Significant Influence. **9-12**

Accounting for Investments with Significant Influence **9-12**
Equity Method Accounting and ROE Effects **9-14**
Review 9-2 9-17
Equity Investments with Control 9-17
Accounting for Investments with Control **9-18**
Review 9-3 9-27
Global Accounting 9-28
Appendix 9A: Accounting for Derivatives 9-29
Analysis of Derivatives **9-30**
Review 9-4 9-31
Appendix 9B: Equity Carve-Outs 9-32
Analysis of Equity Carve-Outs **9-36**
Guidance Answers 9-36
Questions 9-36
Mini Exercises 9-37
Exercises 9-41
Problems 9-50
IFRS Applications 9-52
Management Applications 9-53
Ongoing Project 9-54
Solutions to Review Problems 9-55

MODULE 10
Leases, Pensions, and Income Taxes 10-1

Preview.. 10-1
Leases 10-3
New Lease Reporting Standard **10-3**
Lessee Reporting Example—Microsoft Corporation **10-4**
Lease Accounting **10-5**
Summary of Lease Accounting and Reporting **10-9**
Analysis Issues Relating to Leases **10-10**
Review 10-1 10-11
Pensions.. 10-11
Defined Benefit Pension Plans on the Balance Sheet **10-12**
Analysis Issue—Sufficiency of Plan Assets to Pay Pension Obligations **10-13**
Defined Benefit Pension Plans on the Income Statement **10-15**
Pension Expense Smoothing **10-16**
Fair Value Accounting for Pensions **10-19**
Footnote Disclosure—Key Assumptions **10-21**
Analysis Implications **10-22**
Other Post-Employment Benefits (OPEB) **10-23**
Review 10-2 10-23
Income Taxes 10-24
Timing Differences Create Deferred Tax Assets and Liabilities **10-24**
Disclosures for Income Taxes **10-29**
Analysis of Income Tax Disclosures **10-30**
Expanded Explanation of Deferred Taxes **10-31**
Review 10-3 10-33
Global Accounting 10-35
Appendix 10A: Lease Accounting Example—
Finance and Operating Leases 10-35
Questions 10-36
Mini Exercises 10-37
Exercises 10-42
Problems 10-50
IFRS Applications 10-59
Ongoing Project 10-61
Solutions to Review Problems 10-61

MODULE 11
Cash Flows 11-1

Preview.. 11-1
Framework for Statement of Cash Flows 11-3
Relation Among Financial Statements **11-3**
Statement of Cash Flows Structure **11-4**
Operating Activities Preview **11-5**
Investing Activities Preview **11-8**
Financing Activities Preview **11-8**
Review 11-1 11-8
Cash Flow from Operating Activities................. 11-9
Steps to Compute Net Cash Flow from Operating Activities **11-10**
Java House Case Illustration **11-11**
Review 11-2 11-15
Computing Cash Flows from Investing Activities ... 11-16
Analyze Remaining Noncash Assets **11-16**
Java House Case Illustration **11-16**
Review 11-3 11-18
Cash Flows from Financing Activities............... 11-18
Analyze Remaining Liabilities and Equity **11-18**
Java House Case Illustration **11-18**
Review 11-4A 11-19
Computing Cash Flows from Balance Sheet Accounts **11-19**
Supplemental Disclosures for the Indirect Method **11-20**
Review 11-4B 11-21
Analysis of Cash Flow Information.................. 11-21
Cash Flow Components **11-21**
Cash Flow Patterns **11-23**
Usefulness of the Statement of Cash Flows **11-25**
Review 11-5 11-27
Ratio Analyses of Cash Flows **11-27**
Free Cash Flow **11-28**
Review 11-6 11-29
Appendix 11A: Direct Method Reporting for Statement of Cash Flows 11-29
Cash Flows from Operating Activities **11-29**
Converting Revenues and Expenses to Cash Flows **11-29**
Java House Case Illustration **11-29**
Convert Sales to Cash Received from Customers **11-30**
Convert Cost of Goods Sold to Cash Paid for Merchandise Purchased **11-30**
Convert Wages Expense to Cash Paid to Employees **11-31**
Convert Insurance Expense to Cash Paid for Insurance **11-31**
Eliminate Depreciation Expense and Other Noncash Operating Expenses **11-31**
Convert Income Tax Expense to Cash Paid for Income Taxes **11-31**
Omit Gains and Losses Related to Investing and Financing Activities **11-31**
Cash Flows from Investing and Financing **11-32**
Supplemental Disclosures **11-32**
Review 11-7 11-32
Guidance Answers 11-32
Questions 11-33
Mini Exercises 11-34
Exercises 11-36
Problems 11-42
IFRS Applications 11-55
Solutions to Review Problems 11-56

MODULE 12
Financial Statement Forecasting 12-1

Preview.. 12-1
Forecasting Process.................................. 12-3
Company Guidance **12-5**
Review 12-1 12-6
Forecasting the Income Statement................... 12-8
Review 12-2 12-11
Forecasting the Balance Sheet 12-12
Review 12-3 12-16
Building Forecasts from the Bottom Up 12-16
Segment Data **12-16**
Review 12-4 12-18
Appendix 12A: Forecasting the Statement of Cash Flows... 12-19
Review 12-5 12-20

Appendix 12B: Multiyear Forecasting with Target Cash and New Debt Financing **12-20**
Review 12-6 .... **12-22**
Appendix 12C: Parsimonious Method for Forecasting NOPAT and NOA **12-22**
  Multiyear Forecasting with Parsimonious Method **12-22**
Review 12-7 .... **12-23**
Appendix 12D: Morgan Stanley's Forecast Report on Procter & Gamble **12-23**
Questions **12-31**
Mini Exercises **12-31**
Exercises **12-37**
Problems **12-45**
Ongoing Project **12-51**
Solutions to Review Problems **12-51**

MODULE 13
Using Financial Statements for Valuation 13-1
Preview **13-1**
Equity Valuation Models **13-3**
  Dividend Discount Model **13-3**
  Discounted Cash Flow Model **13-3**
  Residual Operating Income Model **13-3**
  Valuation Model Inputs **13-4**
Review 13-1 .... **13-5**
Discounted Cash Flow (DCF) Model **13-5**
  DCF Model Structure **13-5**
  Steps in Applying the DCF Model **13-6**
  Illustrating the DCF Model **13-6**
Review 13-2 .... **13-8**
Residual Operating Income (ROPI) Model **13-9**
  ROPI Model Structure **13-9**
  Steps in Applying the ROPI Model **13-9**
  Illustrating the ROPI Model **13-10**
Review 13-3 .... **13-11**
Further Considerations Involving Valuation Models **13-11**
  Managerial Insights from the ROPI Model **13-11**
  Assessment of Valuation Models **13-12**
Review 13-4 .... **13-13**
Global Accounting **13-14**
Appendix 13A: Derivation of Free Cash Flow Formula **13-14**
Appendix 13B: Deutsche Bank Valuation of Procter & Gamble **13-14**
  Qualitative and Quantitative Summary **13-14**

  Concluding Observations of Analyst Report **13-25**
Guidance Answers **13-25**
Questions **13-25**
Mini Exercises **13-26**
Exercises **13-27**
Problems **13-31**
Management Applications **13-36**
Ongoing Project **13-37**
Solutions to Review Problems **13-38**

APPENDIX A
Compound Interest Tables A-1

APPENDIX B
Chart of Accounts with Acronyms B-1
Assets B-1
Liabilities B-1
Equity B-1
Revenues and Expenses B-1

APPENDIX C (Online)
Comprehensive Case C-1
Preview **C-1**
Reviewing Financial Statements **C-3**
  Business Environment for Financial Reporting **C-3**
  Income Statement Reporting and Analysis **C-3**
  Balance Sheet Reporting and Analysis **C-9**
  Statement of Cash Flows Reporting and Analysis **C-21**
  Independent Audit Opinion **C-22**
Assessing Profitability and Creditworthiness ... **C-23**
  ROE Disaggregation—DuPont Analysis **C-23**
  ROE Disaggregation—Operating Focus **C-24**
  Disaggregation of RNOA—Margin and Turnover **C-25**
  Credit Analysis **C-26**
  Summarizing Profitability and Creditworthiness **C-26**
Forecasting Financial Statements **C-27**
Valuing Equity Securities **C-30**
  Discounted Cash Flow Valuation **C-31**
  Residual Operating Income Valuation **C-32**
  Assessment of the Valuation Estimate **C-32**
  Summary Observations **C-33**

Glossary G-1
Index I-1

Module 1
Financial Accounting for MBAs

Module Organization visually depicts key topics and their sequence.

Financial Accounting for MBAs

Information Environment	Financial Statements	Profitability Analysis	Business Environment	Regulatory and Legal Environment
■ Reporting on Business Activities ■ Demand for Information ■ Supply of Information	■ Balance Sheet ■ Income Statement ■ Statement of Stockholders' Equity ■ Statement of Cash Flows	■ Measuring Return on Assets ■ Disaggregating Return on Assets ■ Measuring Return on Equity ■ Relevance of Accounting	■ Competitive Analysis ■ Business Analysis ■ Analyzing Competitive Advantage	■ Financial Accounting Environment ■ Audits and Governance ■ SEC and the Courts
Review 1-1	Review 1-2	Review 1-3	Review 1-4	Review 1-5

A Preview introduces each module.

PREVIEW — AAPL

We introduce four financial statements
- ■ Balance sheet ■ Income statement ■ Statement of stockholders' equity ■ Statement of cash flows

We provide a simple, powerful set of metrics to analyze financial statements
- ■ Return on assets (ROA) ■ Net profit margin ■ Total asset turnover ■ Return on equity (ROE)

We discuss the broad context for analyzing a company's business
- ■ Porter's five forces ■ SWOT analysis ■ Analysis of competitive advantage

Each module lays out Learning Objectives and maps them to the module's eLectures, guided examples, and end-of-chapter problem assignments. Use the roadmap in each module to track your learning. Consider looping back to the Learning Objectives as we work through each module and ask whether we have learned that content.

A focus company in each module provides a real-world application.

Apple Inc. is the Module 1 focus company and we refer to its financial statements to illustrate key financial accounting issues. The dashboard here conveys information about Apple's balance sheet, income statement, and statement of cash flows over the past nine years.

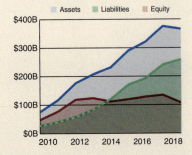
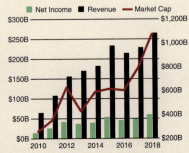
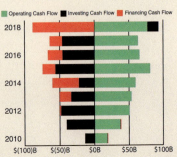

Road Map

Road Maps *visually organize the topics, eLecture videos, Guided Example videos, and assignments by Learning Objective.*

LO	Learning Objective | Topics	Page	eLecture	Guided Example	Assignments
1–1	**Explain and assess the four main business activities.** Planning :: Operating :: Investing :: Financing	1-3	e1–1	Review 1-1	1, 21, 58
1–2	**Identify and discuss the users and suppliers of financial statement information.** Information Demand :: Information Supply :: Global Setting	1-4	e1–2	Review 1-2	8, 9, 13, 17, 18, 22, 35, 39, 60
1–3	**Describe and examine the four financial statements, and define the accounting equation.** Balance Sheet :: Income Statement of Stockholders' Equity :: Statement of Cash Flows	1-9	e1–3	Review 1-3	2, 3, 4, 5, 6, 7, 21, 23, 24, 25, 26, 27, 28, 33, 34, 36, 42, 43, 44, 45, 46, 52, 56, 58, 59
1–4	**Explain and apply basic profitability analysis.** Return on Assets :: Return on Equity :: Relevance of Financial Statements	1-18	e1–4	Review 1-4	19, 20, 31, 37, 38, 40, 41, 42, 43, 44, 47, 48, 49, 50, 51, 57, 59
1–5	**Assess business operations within the context of a competitive environment.** Competitive Environment :: Business Environment :: Competitive Advantage	1-22	e1–5	Review 1-5	10, 11, 30
1–6	**Access and analyze financial datasets.** Datasets :: www.SEC.gov :: Data Analytics :: Excel :: Data Visualization	1-26	e1–6		12, 26, 27, 31
1–7	**Describe the accounting principles and regulations that frame financial statements (Appendix 1B).** Accounting Environment :: Auditing :: Regulatory and Legal	1-30	e1–7		14, 15, 16, 29, 32, 53, 54, 55, 61, 62

Reporting on Business Activities

LO1 Explain and assess the four main business activities.

*eLecture icons identify topics for which there are instructional videos in **myBusinessCourse** (MBC). See the Preface for more information on MBC.*

The main objective of financial reporting is to provide users with information that supports investment and management decisions. Although there are many users of financial statements provided by companies, there are three main user groups:

- *Investors and equity analysts* who use financial statement information to judge the company's profitability and financial strength and to make reasonable estimates of the value of the company's equity securities.
- *Lenders and credit analysts* who use financial statement information to assess the company's ability to repay its debts and to determine how to manage credit risk associated with the company's debt securities.
- *Company managers* who use financial statements to inform decisions such as where to invest scarce resources, how to finance those investments, how to maximize the company's profitability, and how much cash to maintain.

Business Activities To effectively analyze and use accounting information, we must consider the larger business context—see Exhibit 1.1. The yellow circle at the center of the exhibit captures the three types of ongoing business activities at every firm.

1. **Operating activities:** companies hire and train employees, manufacture products, deliver services, market and sell their products and services, and manage after-sale customer support.
2. **Investing activities:** companies acquire land, buildings and equipment, grow the business with new products and services, or acquire other companies to expand into new markets.
3. **Financing activities:** companies raise cash to fund the operating and investing activities. This includes selling stock to equity investors and borrowing from banks and other lenders.

Business activities occur within a particular business environment characterized by a number of **business forces**, including market conditions, competitive pressures, and regulations. These forces affect the way the company does business and shapes the company's overarching goals and objectives along with the company's strategy and its strategic planning process. Exhibit 1.1 depicts these forces and strategic plans in the outer (purplish) ring.

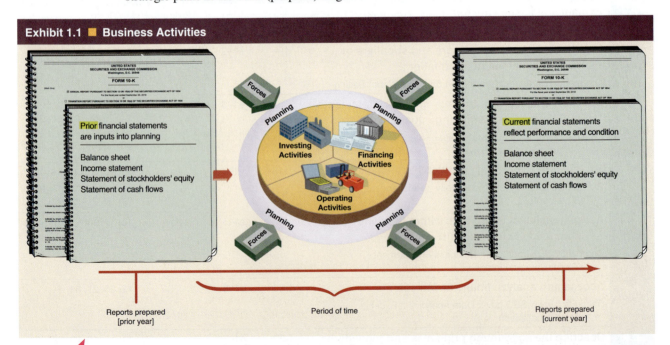

Exhibit 1.1 ■ Business Activities

Infographics are used to convey concepts and procedures.

Business Strategy A company's *strategic* (or *business*) *plan* reflects how it plans to achieve its goals and objectives. A plan's success depends on an effective analysis of market demand and supply.

Specifically, a company must assess demand for its products and services and assess the supply of its inputs (both labor and capital). The plan must also include competitive analyses, opportunity assessments, and consideration of business threats. We discuss competitive forces later in the module.

Past financial statements (depicted on the left of Exhibit 1.1) are an important input into the planning process. They provide information about the relative success of past strategic plans. Managers use that information to take corrective action and make new operating, investing, and financing decisions. These new actions yield the current financial statements (on the right hand side of Exhibit 1.1) and the process starts anew. Understanding a company's strategic plan helps focus our analysis of financial statements by placing them in proper context.

LO1 Review 1-1

Complete the statements by filling in the blanks.
1. Companies engage in the following three types of ongoing business activities: _____ activities, _____ activities, and _____ activities.
2. A company's _____ reflects how it plans to achieve its goals and objectives.
3. Investors use financial statement information to make reasonable estimates of the value of _____.
4. Lenders use financial statement information to assess the company's ability to _____.
5. Company managers use financial statements to decide where to invest _____ resources.
6. Indicate whether the following business activities are operating, investing, or financing activities.

- Manufacturing products
- Issuing stock to investors
- Repaying a mortgage
- Selling services to a client
- Acquiring land
- Engaging in after-sales support
- Constructing new manufacturing facilities
- Hiring and training employees
- Gaining control of the voting stock of a supplier to secure the supply chain
- Entering into a bank loan

Solution on p. 1-48.

Financial Statements: Demand and Supply

Demand for financial statements has existed for centuries as a means to facilitate efficient contracting and risk-sharing. Decision makers and other stakeholders demand information on a company's past and prospective returns and risks. Supply of financial statements is driven by companies' wish to lower financing costs and other costs such as political, contracting, and labor. Managers decide how much financial information to supply by weighing the costs of disclosure against the benefits of disclosure. Regulatory agencies intervene in this process with various disclosure requirements that establish a minimum supply of information.

LO2 Identify and discuss the users and suppliers of financial statement information.

Learning Objectives are highlighted at the start of the section covering that topic.

Demand for Information

The following broad classes of users demand financial accounting information.

- Managers and employees
- Investment analysts and information intermediaries
- Creditors and suppliers
- Stockholders and directors
- Customers and strategic partners
- Regulators and tax agencies
- Voters and their representatives

Managers and Employees

Managers and employees are interested in the company's current and future financial health. This leads to a demand for accounting information on the financial condition, profitability, and prospects of their companies as well as comparative financial information on competing companies and business opportunities. This permits them to benchmark their company's performance and condition. Managers and employees also demand financial accounting information for use in compensation and bonus contracts that are tied to such numbers. The popularity of employee profit sharing and stock ownership plans has further increased demand for financial information. Other sources of demand include union contracts that link wage negotiations to accounting numbers and monitor pension and benefit plans whose solvency depends on company performance. Financial statements provide useful information to company managers to address the following types of questions.

- What product lines, geographic areas, or other segments are performing well compared with our peer companies and our own benchmarks?
- Should we consider expanding or contracting our business?
- How will current profit levels impact incentive and share-based compensation?

Investment Analysts and Information Intermediaries

Investment analysts and other information intermediaries, such as financial press writers and business commentators, are interested in predicting companies' future performance. Expectations about future profitability and the ability to generate cash impact stock price and a company's ability to borrow money at favorable terms. Financial reports reflect information about past performance and current resources available to companies. These reports also provide information about claims on those resources, including claims by suppliers, creditors, lenders, and stockholders. This information allows analysts to make informed assessments about future financial performance and condition so they can provide stock recommendations or write commentaries. Financial statements provide useful information to investment analysts to address the following types of questions.

- What are expected future profits, cash flows, and dividends for input into stock-price models?
- Is the company financially solvent and able to meet its financial obligations?
- How do expectations about the economy, interest rates, and the competitive environment affect the company?

Analysts use financial information to prepare research reports similar to the one issued in 2019 by **Credit Suisse** on **Apple Inc.** (below). Analysts use balance sheet numbers, including debt and equity along with income statement numbers, including revenue, earnings per share (EPS), and earnings before interest, tax, depreciation, and amortization (EBITDA) to compute ratios that inform their price target ($209) and their stock rating (Neutral). We will discuss analysts and their activities in more depth later. For now, know that accounting information is a bedrock for equity analysis.

Excerpts *of reports from agencies such as Credit Suisse, Moody's, and Deutsche Bank illustrate how accounting information is used by financial services.*

Creditors and Suppliers

Banks and other lenders demand financial accounting information to help determine loan terms, loan amounts, interest rates, and required collateral. Loan agreements often include contractual requirements, called **covenants**, that restrict the borrower's behavior in some fashion. For example, loan covenants might require the loan recipient to maintain minimum levels of working capital, retained earnings, and interest coverage to safeguard lenders. If covenants are violated, the lender can demand early payment or other compensation. Suppliers demand financial information to establish credit terms and to determine their long-term commitment to supply-chain relations. Both creditors and suppliers use financial information to monitor and adjust their contracts and commitments with a company. Financial statements provide useful information to creditors and suppliers to address the following types of questions.

- Should we extend credit in the form of a loan or line of credit for inventory purchases?
- What interest rate is reasonable given the company's current debt load and overall risk profile?
- Is the company in compliance with the existing loan covenants (loan conditions that restrict the borrower's behavior in some fashion, such as minimum levels of working capital, retained earnings, and cash flow, which safeguard lenders)?

Following is Apple, Inc's disclosure of loan covenants on its credit facility (a line of credit) from a recent annual report.

> **Credit Facility** We are party to a credit agreement that provides revolving commitments for up to $1.25 billion of borrowings, as well as term loan commitments, in each case maturing in January 2021.... The credit agreement contains negative covenants that, subject to significant exceptions, limit our ability to, among other things, incur additional indebtedness, make restricted payments, pledge our assets as security, make investments, loans, advances, guarantees and acquisitions, undergo fundamental changes and enter into transactions with affiliates. We are also required to maintain a ratio of consolidated EBITDA, as defined in the credit agreement, to consolidated interest expense of not less than 3.50 to 1.00 and are not permitted to allow the ratio of consolidated total indebtedness to consolidated EBITDA to be greater than 3.25 to 1.00.... As of December 31, 2018, we were in compliance with these ratios.

Excerpts from recent financial statements are used to illustrate and reinforce concepts.

Stockholders and Directors

Stockholders and directors and others (such as investment analysts, brokers, and potential investors) demand financial accounting information to assess the profitability and risks of companies and other information useful in their investment decisions. **Fundamental analysis** uses financial information to estimate company value and to form buy-sell stock strategies. Both directors and stockholders use accounting information to evaluate managerial performance. Outside directors are crucial to determining who runs the company, and these directors use accounting information to help make leadership decisions. Financial statements provide useful information to stockholders and directors to address the following questions.

- Is company management demonstrating good stewardship of the resources that have been entrusted to it?
- Do we have the information we need to critically evaluate strategic initiatives that management proposes?

Customers and Strategic Partners

Customers (both current and potential) demand accounting information to assess a company's ability to provide products or services and to assess the company's staying power and reliability. Strategic partners wish to estimate the company's profitability to assess the fairness of returns on mutual transactions and strategic alliances. Financial statements provide useful information to customers and strategic partners to address the following questions.

- Will the company be a reliable supplier?
- Is the strategic partnership providing reasonable returns to both parties?

Regulators and Tax Agencies

Regulators (such as the Securities and Exchange Commission [SEC], the Federal Trade Commission, and the Federal Reserve Bank) and tax agencies demand accounting information for antitrust assessments, public protection, setting prices, import-export analyses, and setting tax policies. Timely and reliable information is crucial to effective regulatory policy, and accounting information is often central to social and economic policies. For example, governments often grant monopoly rights to electric and gas companies serving specific areas in exchange for regulation over prices charged to consumers. These prices are mainly determined from accounting measures.

Voters and Their Representatives

Voters and their representatives to national, state, and local governments demand accounting information for policy decisions. The decisions can involve economic, social, taxation, and other initiatives. Voters and their representatives also use accounting information to monitor government spending. Contributors to nonprofit organizations also demand accounting information to assess the impact of their donations.

Supply of Information

In general, the quantity and quality of accounting information that companies supply are determined by managers' assessment of the benefits and costs of disclosure. Managers release information provided the benefits of disclosing that information outweigh the costs of doing so. Both *regulation* and *bargaining power* affect disclosure costs and benefits and thus play roles in determining the supply of accounting information. Most areas of the world regulate the minimum levels of accounting disclosures. In the United States, publicly traded firms must file financial accounting information with the SEC. There are two main compulsory SEC filings.

- Form **10-K**: the audited annual report that includes the four financial statements, discussed below, with explanatory notes and the management's discussion and analysis (MD&A) of financial results.
- Form **10-Q**: the unaudited quarterly report that includes summary versions of the four financial statements and limited additional disclosures.

Forms 10-K (which must be filed within 60 [90] days of the year-end for larger [smaller] companies) and 10-Q (which must be filed within 40 [45] days of the quarter-end for larger [smaller] companies, except for the fourth quarter, when it is part of the 10-K) are available electronically from the SEC website (see Appendix 1A). The minimum, regulated level of information is prescribed by SEC regulations, but both the quantity and quality of information differ across companies and over time. We need only look at several annual reports to see considerable variance in the amount and type of accounting information supplied. For example, differences abound on disclosures for segment operations, product performance reports, and financing activities. Further, some stakeholders possess ample bargaining power to obtain accounting information for themselves. These typically include private lenders and major suppliers and customers.

There are a number of datasets that aggregate financial statement data (including SEC data), to aid access to financial statement information for a single firm or for large sets of firms. Most university libraries have subscriptions to one or more of the following datasets that we can access without charge.

- Compustat
- Mergent Online
- EMIS (for emerging-market companies)

Datasets consist of data that are "scrubbed" and formatted. Yet, we can use computer languages such as Python, R, or Java to gather data directly from the SEC website. This makes it possible to perform more-sophisticated textual analyses. For analyses in this text we use existing datasets and simpler programs such as Excel and Power BI, which are widely available Microsoft tools. We discuss this in more detail in Appendix 1A.

Benefits of Disclosure

The benefits of supplying accounting information extend to a company's capital, labor, input, and output markets. Companies must compete in these markets. For example, capital markets provide debt and equity financing; the better a company's prospects, the lower is its cost of capital (as reflected in lower interest rates or higher stock prices). The same holds for a company's recruiting efforts in labor markets and its ability to establish superior supplier-customer relations in the input and output markets.

A company's performance in these markets depends on success with its business activities *and* the market's awareness of that success. Companies reap the benefits of disclosure with good news about their products, processes, management, and so forth. That is, there are real economic incentives for companies to disclose reliable (audited) accounting information, enabling them to better compete in capital, labor, input, and output markets.

What inhibits companies from providing false or misleading good news? There are several constraints. An important constraint imposed by stakeholders is that of audit requirements and legal repercussions associated with inaccurate accounting information. Another relates to reputation effects from disclosures as subsequent events either support or refute earlier news.

Costs of Disclosure

Costs of supplying financial information include the following.

- **Preparation and dissemination costs**. Even though companies might already have gathered information for internal use, the cost of auditing the information and complying with the SEC's rules can be time consuming and costly.

- **Competitive disadvantages**. Disclosing product or segment successes, strategic alliances or pursuits, technological or system innovations, and product or process quality improvements could reduce or eliminate a company's competitive advantage.

- **Litigation**. Risk of litigation increases if companies disclose information that creates expectations that are not met. The cost of defending against customer or investor lawsuits in not inconsequential even for cases that are dismissed.

- **Political costs**. Highly visible companies can face political and public pressure. For example, government defense contractors, large software conglomerates, and oil companies are favorite targets of public scrutiny. Extra disclosure can increase this scrutiny.

The SEC adopted Regulation Fair Disclosure (FD), or Reg FD for short, to curb the practice of selective disclosure by public companies (called *issuers* by the SEC) to certain stockholders and financial analysts. In the past, many companies disclosed important information in meetings and conference calls that excluded individual stockholders. The goal of this rule is to level the playing field for all investors. Reg FD reads as follows: "Whenever an issuer discloses any material nonpublic information regarding that issuer, the issuer shall make public disclosure of that information . . . simultaneously, in the case of an intentional disclosure; and . . . promptly, in the case of a non-intentional disclosure." Reg FD increased the cost of voluntary financial disclosure and led some companies to curtail the supply of financial information to all users.

International Accounting Standards

Companies in more than 120 countries, including the European Union, the United Kingdom, Canada, and Japan use International Financial Reporting Standards (IFRS) for their financial reports. Headquartered in London, the International Accounting Standards Board (IASB) oversees the development of IFRS. While the IASB and the Financial Accounting Standards Board (FASB) operate as independent standard-setting bodies, the two boards work together cooperatively, often undertaking joint projects. Consequently, IFRS and U.S. GAAP (generally accepted accounting principles) are generally more alike than different for most transactions.

Currently, there is no formal plan for the U.S. to transition to IFRS or for the IASB and FASB to converge; however, both boards believe comparable global accounting standards are desirable because comparability would

- Improve the quality of financial reports.
- Benefit investors, companies, and other market participants who make global investment decisions.
- Reduce costs for both users and preparers of financial statements.
- Make worldwide capital markets more efficient.

Evidence of increasing "comparability" of U.S. GAAP and IFRS includes the following.

- Since 2007, the SEC has permitted foreign companies to file IFRS financial statements without requiring reconciliation to U.S. GAAP. Currently, more than 500 companies with a cumulative market capitalization of trillions of dollars report to the SEC using IFRS.
- The FASB participates actively in the development of IFRS, providing input on IASB projects through the IASB's Accounting Standards Advisory Forum (ASAF).
- Recent joint projects between the two boards relate to leases, financial instruments, revenue recognition, and insurance contracts.

We might ask: are financial statements prepared under IFRS substantially different from those prepared under U.S. GAAP? At a broad level, the answer is no. Both are prepared using accrual accounting and utilize somewhat similar conceptual frameworks. Both require the same set of financial statements: a balance sheet, an income statement, a statement of cash flows, a statement of stockholders' equity, and a set of explanatory footnotes. That does not mean that no differences exist. However, the differences are typically technical in nature, and do not differ on broad principles discussed in this book.

At the end of each module, we summarize key differences between U.S. GAAP and IFRS. Also, there are a variety of sources that provide more detailed and technical analysis of similarities and differences between U.S. GAAP and IFRS. The FASB, the IASB, and each of the "Big 4" accounting firms also maintain websites devoted to this issue. Search under IFRS and PwC, KPMG, EY, and Deloitte. The two standard-setting bodies also provide useful information. See: FASB (**www.fasb.org/intl/**) and IASB (**www.ifrs.org**).

Review Problems are self-study tools that require the application of accounting topics covered in each section. To aid learning, solutions are provided at the end of the module.

Review 1-2 LO2

Required
Match the users of financial statement information with the types of questions they would typically ask and answer using accounting data.

_____ I. Managers and employees
_____ II. Investment analysts and information intermediaries
_____ III. Creditors and suppliers
_____ IV. Stockholders and directors
_____ V. Customers and strategic partners
_____ VI. Regulators and tax agencies

a. Is company management demonstrating good stewardship of the resources that have been entrusted to it?
b. What product lines have performed well compared with competitors?
c. What regulated price is appropriate given the company's financial condition?
d. Is the strategic partnership providing reasonable returns to both parties?
e. What expectations about the company's future profit and cash flow should we use as input into the pricing of its stock?
f. Is the company in compliance with the contractual terms of its existing loan covenants?

Solution on p. 1-49.

Structure of Financial Statements

LO3 Describe and examine the four financial statements, and define the accounting equation.

Companies use four financial statements to periodically report on business activities. These statements are the balance sheet, income statement, statement of stockholders' equity, and statement of cash flows. Exhibit 1.2 shows how these statements are linked across time. A balance sheet reports on a company's financial position at a *point in time*. The income statement, statement of stockholders' equity, and the statement of cash flows report on performance over a *period of time*. The three statements in the middle of Exhibit 1.2 (period-of-time statements) link the balance sheet from the beginning to the end of a period.

A one-year, or annual, reporting period is common and is called the *accounting (fiscal) year*. Of course, firms prepare financial statements more frequently; semiannual, quarterly, and monthly financial statements are common. *Calendar-year* companies have reporting periods beginning on January 1 and ending on December 31. Some companies choose a fiscal year ending on a date other than December 31. Sometimes the fiscal year end coincides with a time when inventory is at a low point or at the end of a natural business cycle. Other times, the fiscal year is an industry standard. Most companies end their fiscal year on the same date each year (such as May 31). Other companies select a fiscal year that ends on the same week day each year. For example, many U.S. retailers have a fiscal year ending on the Saturday closest to February 1—some years that will be in late January, other years in early February. **Apple, Inc.** ends its fiscal year on the last Saturday in September.

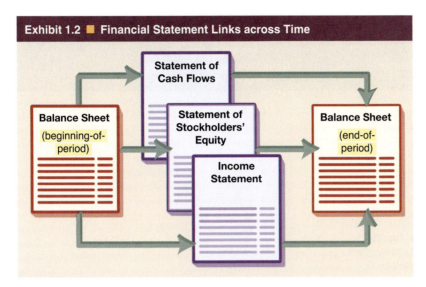

Exhibit 1.2 ■ Financial Statement Links across Time

Balance Sheet

A balance sheet reports a company's financial position at a point in time. The balance sheet reports the company's *resources* (*assets*), namely, what the company owns. The balance sheet also reports the *sources* of asset financing. There are two ways a company can finance its assets. It can raise money from stockholders; this is *owner financing*. It can also raise money from banks or other creditors and suppliers; this is *nonowner financing*. This means both owners and nonowners hold claims on company assets. Owner claims on assets are referred to as *equity,* and nonowner claims are referred to as *liabilities* (or debt). Since all financing must be invested in something, we obtain the following basic relation: *investing equals financing*. This equality is called the **accounting equation**, which follows.

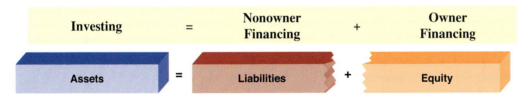

The accounting equation works for all companies at all points in time.

Apple's balance sheet (condensed) is in Exhibit 1.3. Its accounting equation follows ($ millions).

Real Companies and institutions are highlighted in bold, blue font.

Assets	=	Liabilities	+	Equity
$365,725	=	$258,578	+	$107,147

Investing Activities

Balance sheets are prepared at a point in time and are organized like the accounting equation. Investing activities are represented by the company's assets. These assets are financed by a combination of nonowner financing (liabilities) and owner financing (equity).

Apple's condensed balance sheet in Exhibit 1.3 categorizes assets into short-term and long-term assets (Module 2 explains the composition of assets in more detail). Assets are listed on the balance sheet in order of their nearness to cash, with short-term assets (also called current assets) expected to generate cash within one year from the balance sheet date. For example, the first short-term asset listed is cash, then accounts receivable (amounts owed to Apple by its customers that will be collected in cash in the near future), and then inventories (goods available for sale that must first be sold before cash can be collected). Land, buildings, and equipment (often referred to as property, plant, and equipment or just PPE) will generate cash over a long period of time and are, therefore, classified as long-term assets.

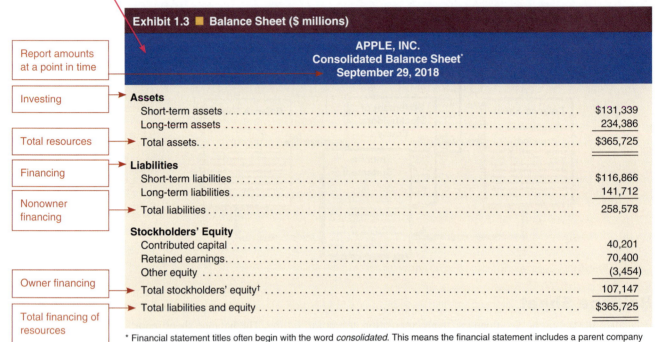

Exhibit 1.3 Balance Sheet ($ millions)

APPLE, INC.
Consolidated Balance Sheet*
September 29, 2018

Assets	
Short-term assets	$131,339
Long-term assets	234,386
Total assets	$365,725
Liabilities	
Short-term liabilities	$116,866
Long-term liabilities	141,712
Total liabilities	258,578
Stockholders' Equity	
Contributed capital	40,201
Retained earnings	70,400
Other equity	(3,454)
Total stockholders' equity†	107,147
Total liabilities and equity	$365,725

* Financial statement titles often begin with the word *consolidated*. This means the financial statement includes a parent company and one or more subsidiaries, which are companies the parent company controls.
† Components of equity are explained as part of Exhibit 1.5.

Labels: Report amounts at a point in time; Investing; Total resources; Financing; Nonowner financing; Owner financing; Total financing of resources.

Real financial data for focus companies illustrate key concepts of each module.

The relative proportion of short- and long-term assets is largely determined by a company's industry and business model. This is evident in the graph to the side that depicts the relative proportion of short- and long-term assets for a number of well-known companies.

■ Larger investments in short-term assets occur at companies such as **Best Buy**, **Starbucks**, and **Nordstrom's** that carry relatively high levels of inventories. High current assets also occur for technology companies like **Alphabet** (formerly Google) and **Cisco** that have high cash balances and large investments in marketable securities that are classified as short-term because they can be sold quickly in financial markets.

■ Manufacturers such as **3M**, **Johnson & Johnson**, and **Colgate-Palmolive** require more investment in property, plant, and equipment in addition to large investments in inventories and accounts receivable from customers.

■ At the other end of the spectrum are transportation companies like **Southwest Airlines** and communications companies like **Comcast** whose business models require significant investment in long-term equipment, such as planes and telecom infrastructure.

Although managers can influence the relative amounts and proportion of assets, their flexibility is somewhat limited by the nature of their industries.

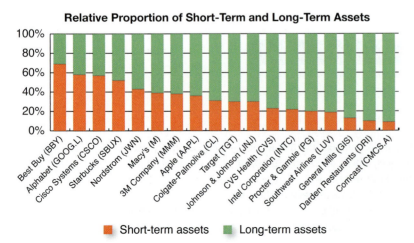

Financing Activities

To pay for assets, companies use a combination of owner (or equity) and nonowner financing (liabilities or debt). Owner financing has two components: resources (mostly cash, but sometimes noncash assets) contributed to the company by its owners, and profits retained by the company. Nonowner financing is borrowed money. We distinguish between these two financing sources for a reason: borrowed money must be repaid, and failure to do so can result in severe consequences for the borrower. Equity financing entails no such obligation for repayment.

The relative proportion of nonowner and owner financing is largely determined by a company's industry and business model. This is evident in the graph to the side.

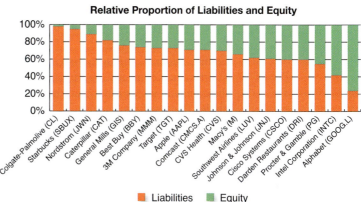

- Companies with relatively stable cash flows can operate more comfortably with a higher level of debt. **Caterpillar**, for example, sells much of its equipment on lease and the predictability of lease payments allows CAT to carry more debt. **General Mills** operates in the relatively stable consumer staples industry.

- **Colgate-Palmolive**, **Starbucks**, and **Best Buy** have used their stable cash flow to repurchase significant amounts of their common stock in order to boost returns for their shareholders. This has the effect of increasing debt relative to equity.

- At the other end of the spectrum are companies like **Alphabet**, and **Intel** that, like most technology companies, have higher levels of business risk. To offset the higher business risk, these companies reduce the level of financial risk by substituting equity capital for borrowed funds.

Most public companies tend to use slightly more debt than equity in their capital structures.

Manager Insights ▪ Balance sheet considerations

We have provided a sneak preview into the interplay among financial statements, managerial decisions, economic conditions, and the competitive landscape. We have used terms and concepts that might be unfamiliar to you. We might start thinking about the following sorts of questions from a manager's perspective.

- Alphabet reports $109.1 billion of cash on its 2018 balance sheet, nearly half of its total assets. Many high-tech companies do likewise. Why is that? Is it costly to carry too much cash?
- A company's business model largely dictates the relative proportion of short- and long-term assets. Why is this the case? Why is the composition of assets similar for companies in the same industry?
- What are the trade-offs in financing a company by owner versus nonowner financing? If nonowner financing is less costly, why don't companies finance themselves entirely with borrowed money?
- How might stockholders influence the strategic direction of a company? What about bankers and other lenders—can they influence strategic direction?
- Most assets and liabilities are reported on the balance sheet at the price the company paid to acquire them (called historical cost). Would reporting assets and liabilities at fair values be more informative? What problems might that cause?

Manager Insights challenge us to think like a manager and consider the company's accounting choices and their consequences.

IFRS Insights examine issues related to similarities and differences in accounting practices of U.S. and other countries.

IFRS Insight ▪ Balance Sheet Presentation and IFRS

Balance sheets prepared under IFRS often classify accounts in reverse order of liquidity (lack of nearness to cash), which is the opposite of what U.S. companies do. For example, intangible assets are typically listed first, and cash is listed last among assets. Also, equity is often listed before liabilities, where liabilities are again listed in order of decreasing liquidity. These choices reflect convention and *not* IFRS requirements.

Income Statement

An **income statement** reports on a company's performance over a period of time and lists amounts for its *top line* revenues (also called sales) and its expenses. Revenues less expenses equals the *bottom-line* net income amount (also called *profit* or *earnings*). Apple, as is typical of companies that sell products, reports two basic kinds of operating expenses.

- **Cost of goods sold** (COGS, also called cost of sales). While revenues represent the retail selling price of the goods sold to customers, cost of goods sold is the amount Apple paid to purchase or manufacture the goods (inventories) that it sold. Manufacturing and merchandising companies typically include a subtotal called *gross profit*, which is revenues less cost of goods sold. For example, if it costs a company $7 to purchase or manufacture an item of inventory and the item sells for $10, the income statement reports revenues of $10, cost of goods sold of $7, and a gross profit of $3. We use the term *gross* to mean the profit available to cover all other expenses.

- **Selling, general, and administrative expenses (SG&A).** This is Apple's overhead and includes salaries, marketing costs, occupancy costs, HR and IT costs, and all the other operating expenses the company incurs other than the cost of purchasing or manufacturing inventory (which is included in cost of goods sold).

Apple's income statement is in Exhibit 1.4. Refer to the income statement to verify the following: revenues of $265,595 million, cost of goods sold of $163,756 million, and operating expenses of $30,941 million. After interest income, net and income taxes, the company reports net income of $59,531 million. Net income reflects the profit (or earnings) to the company's shareholders for the period.

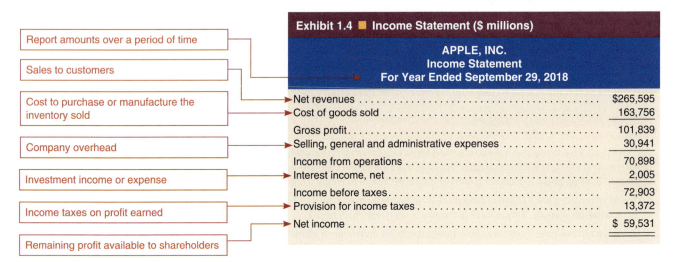

To generate net income, companies engage in operating activities that use company resources to produce, promote, and sell products and services. These activities extend from input markets involving suppliers of materials and labor to a company's output markets, involving customers of products and services. Input markets generate most *expenses* (or *costs*) such as inventory, salaries, materials, and logistics. Output markets generate *revenues* (or *sales*) to customers. Output markets also generate some expenses such as marketing and distributing products and services to customers. Net income arises when revenues exceed expenses. A net loss occurs when expenses exceed revenues.

Relative profitability (net income as a percent of sales) differs widely across industries and even among companies in the same industry. Although effective managers can increase their company's profitability, business models play a large part in determining profit levels. These differences are illustrated in the graph (below) of net income as a percent of sales for several companies.

- Retailers such as **Best Buy**, **CVS**, **Target**, **Nordstrom** and **Macy's** operate in a mature industry and have difficulty differentiating their products. Hence, their net income as a percent of sales is low.

- At the other end of the spectrum are companies like **Intel**, **Apple**, **Johnson & Johnson**, **Cisco**, and **Alphabet** that enjoy higher levels of operating profit resulting from patent protection for their intellectual property and companies like **Colgate-Palmolive**, **Procter & Gamble**, and **3M** whose brands are well-established and command higher market prices and yield higher levels of profitability.

Companies' ability to create barriers to competitive pressure, either by patent protection, effective marketing, or otherwise, is a key factor in determining their level of profitability. Those that compete in highly competitive markets with little product differentiation must concentrate on controlling operating expenses to offset lower gross profits.

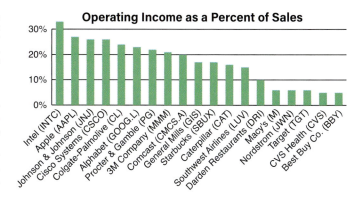

Manager Insights — Income statement considerations

Put yourself in the position of a senior company manager and think about the following situations.

- You sell to customers who promise to pay in 30 days. When should you (the seller) recognize the sale—when it is made or when cash is collected?
- Your company purchases a new building and reports the cost on the balance sheet as a long-term asset. What do you think of recording the entire cost of the building as an expense on the income statement in the year it is acquired?
- As a manufacturer, your company reports the cost of a product as an expense when the product is sold. How might you measure that cost? What sorts of items might be included in the calculation?
- If a piece of land increases in value, that increase is not reported as income until the land is sold. What consequences can you imagine if land appreciation *was* reported as income each year?
- Most of your employees are paid with a two-week lag. When should your company (the employer) record wages expense—in the period the employees worked or when you eventually pay the wages?
- Companies are not allowed to report profit when they sell their own shares of stock. Nor do they report an expense when dividends are paid to stockholders. Why do you suppose this is the case?

Statement of Stockholders' Equity

The **statement of stockholders' equity** reports on year-over-year changes in the equity accounts that are reported on the balance sheet. For each type of equity, the statement reports the beginning balance, a summary of the activity in the account during the year, and the ending balance. **Apple**'s statement of stockholders' equity is in Exhibit 1.5. During the recent period, its equity changed because Apple issued shares and retained a profit. The company classifies these changes into three categories.

- *Contributed capital*, the stockholders' net contributions to the company.
- *Retained earnings*, net income over the life of the company minus all dividends ever paid.
- *Other equity*, consists of amounts we explain later in the book.

Exhibit 1.5 reconciles the activity in each of the equity accounts from the balance sheet in Exhibit 1.3. We briefly discuss the two larger accounts here and explain the accounts in depth in Module 8.

- **Contributed capital** represents assets the company received from issuing stock to stockholders (also called shareholders). The balance of this account at the beginning of the year was $35,867 million. During the year, Apple sold additional shares for $4,334 million to yield a year-end balance of $40,201 million.
- **Retained earnings** (also called *earned capital* or *reinvested capital*) represent the cumulative total amount of income the company has earned and that has been retained in the business; that is, not distributed to stockholders in the form of dividends. The change in retained earnings links consecutive balance sheets via the income statement:

Beginning retained earnings
+ Net income for the period
− Dividends for the period
Ending retained earnings

Apple's retained earnings increased by the $59,531 million of net income reported in its income statement and decreased by the $13,735 million of dividends paid to shareholders. These dividends are *a distribution* of the shareholders' investment in the company and are not treated as an *expense* in the income statement. That is why they are included as a separate row in the computation of ending retained earnings. The table also reveals a decrease of ($73,056 + $670) million in retained earnings. This represents another distribution to the shareholders: the amount Apple paid to repurchase common stock from shareholders (Apple retired those shares, which we explain in Module 8).

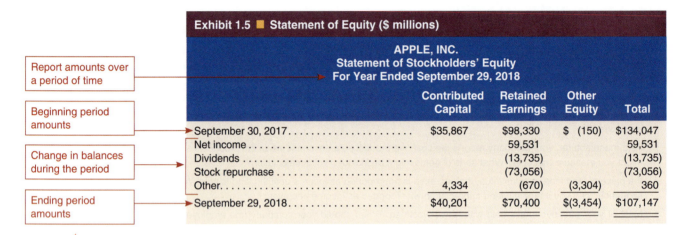

Exhibit 1.5 — Statement of Equity ($ millions)

Statement of Cash Flows

The **statement of cash flows** reports the change (either an increase or a decrease) in a company's cash balance over a period of time. The statement reports cash inflows and outflows from operating, investing, and financing activities over a period of time. Apple's statement of cash flows is shown in Exhibit 1.6.

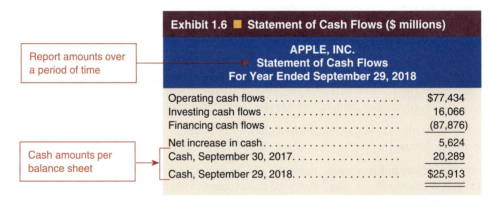

Exhibit 1.6 — Statement of Cash Flows ($ millions)

Apple's cash balance increased by $5,624 million in fiscal 2018 owing to the following three activities:

- **Operating activities.** The increase of $77,434 million from operating activities represents the net cash that Apple generated from its core business activities of making and selling products and services to its customers.

- **Investing activities.** Investing cash flows include cash outflows for the purchase of property, plant and equipment (PPE assets) and inflows and outflows of cash for sales and purchases of marketable securities. In 2018, Apple reduced its investments in marketable securities, which generated cash.

- **Financing activities.** Financing cash flows relate to borrowing and repayment of debt, sales and repurchases of stock, and the payment of dividends. During 2018, Apple's most significant items included a cash outflow of $13,712 million for dividends paid to shareholders and a cash outflow of $72,738 million to repurchase common stock from Apple shareholders.

It is important to reinforce one point that we cite above: Apple's cash flow from operating activities of $77,434 million does not equal its net income of $59,531 million. This is typical and is due to timing differences between when revenue and expense items are recognized on the income statement and when cash is received and paid. (We discuss this concept further in subsequent modules.)

Both cash flow and net income numbers are important for business decisions. Each is used in security valuation models, and both help users of accounting reports understand and assess a company's past, present, and future business activities.

Manager Insights — Statement of cash flows considerations

Put yourself in the position of a senior company manager and consider the following issues.

- Your accounting department prepares the statement of cash flows. Aren't the balance sheet and income statement sufficient?
- What types of information, disclosed in the statement of cash flows, can help you make important decisions?
- Is it critical for your company to report positive operating cash flow? What are the implications if operating cash flows are negative for an extended period of time?
- Why is it important for your company to report its investing cash flows? Which is more favorable, positive or negative investing cash flows?
- Is it useful to know the cash implications of your company's financing activities? What questions might that information help you answer?
- How might the composition of operating, investing, and financing cash flows change over your company's life cycle?

Review the Apple statement of cash flows summarized in Exhibit 1.6, and think about these questions. We provide answers for each of these questions as we progress through the book.

Information Beyond Financial Statements

Important financial information about a company is communicated to various decision makers through means other than the four financial statements. These include the following.

- Management Discussion and Analysis (MD&A)
- Independent auditor report
- Financial statement footnotes
- Regulatory filings, including proxy statements and other SEC filings

We describe and explain the usefulness of these additional information sources throughout the book.

Managerial Decisions require us to assume various roles within a business and use our accounting knowledge to address an issue. Solutions are provided at the end of the module.

Managerial Decision — You Are the Product Manager

There is often friction between investors' need for information and a company's desire to safeguard competitive advantages. Assume you are a key-product manager at your company. Your department has test-marketed a potentially lucrative new product, which it plans to further finance. You are asked for advice on the extent of information to disclose about the new product in the MD&A section of the company's upcoming annual report. What advice do you provide and why? [Answer, p. 1-34]

Managerial Choices in Financial Accounting

Some people mistakenly assume financial accounting is an exact discipline—that is, companies select the one proper accounting method to account for a transaction and then follow the rules. The reality is that GAAP allows companies choices in preparing financial statements. The choice of methods can yield financial statements that are markedly different from one another in terms of reported income, assets, liabilities, and equity amounts.

People often are surprised that financial statements comprise numerous estimates. For example, companies must estimate the amounts that will eventually be collected from customers, the length of time that buildings and equipment will be productive, the value impairments of assets, the future costs of warranty claims, the eventual payouts on pension plans, and numerous other estimates.

Historically, the FASB has promulgated standards that were quite complicated and replete with guidelines. In recent years, the pendulum has begun to swing away from such rigidity. Now, once financial statements are prepared, company management is required to step back from the details and make a judgment on whether the statements taken as a whole "fairly present" the financial condition of the company as is asserted in the company's audit report (see below).

Moreover, since the enactment of the *Sarbanes-Oxley Act* (SOX) in 2002, the SEC requires the chief executive officer (CEO) of the company and its chief financial officer (CFO) to personally sign a statement attesting to the accuracy and completeness of the financial statements. This requirement is an important step in maintaining confidence in the integrity of financial accounting. The statements signed by both the CEO and CFO contain the following declarations.

- Both the CEO and CFO have personally reviewed the annual report.
- There are no untrue statements of a material fact that would make the statements misleading.
- Financial statements fairly present in all material respects the financial condition of the company.
- All material facts are disclosed to the company's auditors and board of directors.
- No changes to its system of internal controls are made unless properly communicated.

SOX also imposed fines and potential jail time for executives for untrue statements or omissions of important facts. Presumably, the prospect of personal losses is designed to make these executives more vigilant in monitoring the financial accounting system. More recently, Congress passed the *Wall Street Reform and Consumer Protection Act* of 2010 (or the Dodd-Frank Act). Among the provisions of the act are rules that strengthened SOX by augmenting "claw-back" provisions for executives' ill-gotten gains.

Research Insight — Quality of Earnings

A recent study conducted a survey of nearly 400 CFOs on the definition and drivers of earnings quality, with an emphasis on the prevalence and detection of earnings misrepresentation. The CFOs cited the hallmarks of earnings quality as sustainability, absence of one-time items, and backing by actual cash flows. However, they also believe that, in any given period, a remarkable 20% of companies intentionally distort earnings, even while adhering to GAAP. The magnitude of the average misrepresentation is large: 10% of reported earnings.

What are the lessons for us? We can become informed and critical readers of financial reports by first understanding how reports are constructed and the types of assumptions and estimates that are used in their preparation. Much of this information is contained in the footnotes to the financial statements. This textbook will help you acquire the knowledge needed to become an informed and critical reader of financial reports.

Source: Ilia Dichev, John Graham, Campbell R. Harvey, and Shiva Rajgopal. 2016. "The Misrepresentation of Earnings" by *Financial Analyst Journal*, vol. 72, no. 1, pages 22–35.

Research Insights introduce relevant research findings on the topics presented.

LO3 Review 1-3

The following financial information is from Samsung Electronics, a competitor of Apple, for December 31, 2018 (in billions Korean won).

Short-term liabilities	₩ 69,082	Cost of goods sold	₩132,394
Cash flows from financing	(14,996)	Cash, beginning-year	30,545
Revenues	243,771	Income tax expense	16,815
Stockholders' equity	247,752	Short-term assets	174,697
Cash flows from operations	67,032	Long-term liabilities	22,523
SG&A expenses	52,490	Cash, end of year	30,341
Long-term assets	164,660	Cash flows from investing	(52,240)
Interest income, net	2,273		

Required
1. Prepare an income statement and statement of cash flows for Samsung Electronics for the year ended December 31, 2018. Prepare Samsung Electronics's balance sheet as of December 31, 2018.
2. Compare the balance sheet and income statement of Samsung Electronics with those of Apple, Inc. in Exhibits 1.3 and 1.4. What differences do we observe?

Guided Examples icons denote the availability of a demonstration video in **myBusinessCourse** (MBC) for each Review Problem— see the Preface for more on MBC.

Solution on p. 1-49.

Analysis of Financial Statements

This section previews the analysis framework of this book. This framework is used extensively by market professionals who analyze financial reports to evaluate company management and value the company's debt and equity securities. Analysis of financial performance is crucial in assessing prior strategic decisions and evaluating strategic alternatives.

LO4 Explain and apply basic profitability analysis.

Return on Assets

Suppose we learn that a company reports a profit of $10 million. Does the $10 million profit indicate the company is performing well? Knowing a company reports a profit is certainly positive as it indicates customers value its goods or services, and its revenues exceed expenses. However, we cannot assess how well it is performing without considering the context. To explain, suppose we learn this company has $500 million in assets. We now assess the $10 million profit as low because, relative to the size of its asset investment, the company earned a paltry 2% return ($10 million/$500 million). A 2% return on assets is what a lower-risk investment in government-backed bonds might yield. The important point is that a company's profitability must be assessed with respect to the size of its investment. This is done with a common metric: the *return on assets* (ROA)—defined as net income for that period divided by the average total assets during that period.

Components of Return on Assets

To further isolate components that are driving return on assets, we can separate ROA into two components: profitability and productivity.

- **Profitability relates profit to sales.** This ratio is called the *profit margin* (PM), and it reflects the net income (profit after tax) earned on each sales dollar. Management wants to earn as much profit as possible from sales.

- **Productivity relates sales to assets.** This component, called *asset turnover* (AT), reflects sales generated by each dollar of assets. Management wants to maximize asset productivity to achieve the highest possible sales level for a given level of assets (or to achieve a given level of sales with the smallest level of assets).

Exhibit 1.7 depicts the disaggregation of ROA into these two components. Profitability (PM) and productivity (AT) are multiplied to yield the ROA. Average assets are commonly defined as (beginning-year assets + ending-year assets)/2.

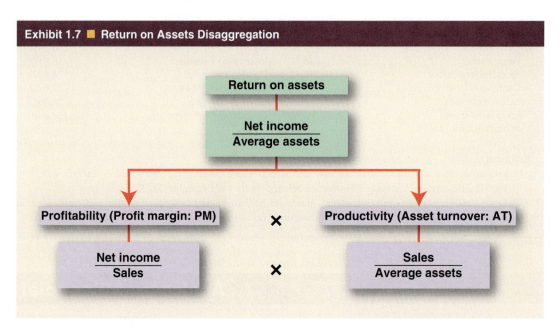

There are an infinite number of combinations of profit margin (PM) and asset turnover (AT) that yield the same ROA. To illustrate, Exhibit 1.8 graphs actual combinations of these two components for companies we highlight in this book (each is identified by its ticker symbol). The graph's green line represents possible combinations of margin and turnover to yield the 7.7% median ROA for the companies graphed here. The 7.7% ROA is higher than the 5.7% median ROA for all of the Standard & Poor's 500 companies for this same year. (Exhibit 1.8 focuses on core operating profit where we use earnings before unusual items and apply standardized tax rates to reduce variations from unusual activities.) Following are some general observations on Exhibit 1.8.

- **High margin and Low turnover.** Technology companies like Intel (INTC), Cisco (CSCO), Johnson & Johnson (JNJ), and Apple (AAPL) are characterized by high net profit margins resulting from patent protection that increase barriers to entry and reduce competition. These companies also report substantial assets, typically in the form of marketable securities and intangible assets that arise when these companies acquire other companies (a typical method of expansion in the high-tech industry). Because these securities and intangible assets do not generate "sales," the productivity ratio (AT) is decreased by the inflated assets in the denominator.

- **Low margin and High turnover.** At the other end of the spectrum, retailers like Nordstrom (JWN) and Target (TGT), Macy's (M), CVS (CVS), and Darden Restaurants (DRI) find it difficult to differentiate their products. This open competition keeps prices down, which yields lower profit margins. These retailing companies must focus on increasing AT to maintain an acceptable ROA. To do this, they watch inventory and PPE assets carefully and rarely have accounts receivable because most of their trade is cash-and-carry.

- **High performance.** The return on assets (ROA) is the product of profit margin and asset turnover and is higher as we move further away from the origin. Companies like Intel (INTC), Apple (AAPL), Colgate Palmolive (CL), Starbucks (SBUX), and Home Depot (HD) have higher ROAs than other companies. As we see, to achieve a high level of ROA, companies need to manage *both* profit margin and asset turnover. This is an important point—companies must manage both the income statement and the balance sheet to achieve high levels of financial performance. Managing one, but not the other, is generally not sufficient.

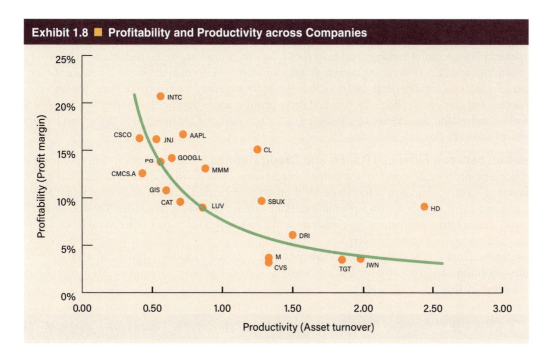

Return on Equity

Another important analysis measure is return on equity (ROE), which is defined as net income divided by average stockholders' equity, where average equity is commonly defined as (beginning-year equity + ending-year equity)/2. In this case, company earnings are compared to the level of stockholder investment. ROE reflects the return to stockholders, which is different from the return for the entire company (ROA). We return to ROE in more detail in Module 4.

Are Financial Statements Relevant?

Accounting, finance, and economic researchers have long investigated the role of financial statement data in capital markets.

Relation between Earnings and Stock Prices Early research focused on whether and how reported earnings are related to stock prices. There is a natural positive relation between expected earnings and stock prices, because stockholders expect dividends, which are paid out of earnings. Early research by Ball and Brown confirmed this expected relation, and the study produced the seminal graph shown here. (Source: Ball, R., and P. Brown. 1968. "An Empirical Evaluation of Accounting Income Numbers." *Journal of Accounting Research* (Autumn): 159–178.) It shows stock returns trending up during the year for companies that subsequently reported higher earnings (as compared with the prior year) and trending down for companies that subsequently reported lower earnings.

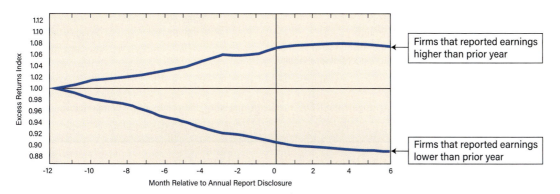

Subsequent research would show that persistent core earnings have the highest predictive ability for future earnings and cash flows. Rigorous financial statement analysis seeks to uncover a company's persistent core operating earnings and cash flows. In a later module, we consider how to forecast future earnings and cash flows using current financial statement information. We also consider financial statement analysis in more depth and conclude that rigorous analysis seeks to uncover the underlying economic and company-specific factors that drive profit margins and productivity ratios we observe. Once we understand the underlying dynamics of the business, we are better able to forecast its future earnings and cash flows.

Relation between Financial Ratios and Credit Ratings Financial markets also use forecasts to price a company's debt and to determine interest rates. As we will discuss in the module on debt financing, credit ratings are determined by a number of financial ratios based on balance sheet, income statement, and cash flow information. For example, Moody's Investors Service, one of the primary credit rating companies for corporate and municipal bonds, uses ratios such as that shown in the table below to evaluate a borrower's ability to repay its debt. Ratings are progressively riskier as we move from left to right in the following table. (Source: 'Moody's Financial Metrics™ Key Ratios by Rating and Industry for Global NonFinancial Corporates: December 2017' report dated 25 October 2018.)

Moody's Financial Ratios	Aaa	Aa	A	Baa	Ba	B	Caa
Debt/EBITDA	1.9	1.7	2.2	2.7	3.6	5.2	7.2
FCF/Debt	40.4%	45.9%	35.7%	28.2%	21.5%	13.2%	5.7%
EBITDA/Interest expense	12.0	20.7	11.4	6.4	3.7	2.0	0.7

These ratios use debt, EBITDA (earnings before interest, taxes, and amortization expense), and FCF (free cash flow, which is defined as operating cash flow less purchases of PPE). The table indicates that as the company credit ratings decline (Aaa, Aa, A, Baa, etc.), each ratio becomes progressively "weaker." So, to answer the question: Are financial statements relevant? Yes. They provide critical input into the pricing of equity and debt securities and, therefore, the creation of shareholder wealth. For that reason, they are also essential in the development and monitoring of corporate strategy.

> **Managerial Decision ■ You Are the Chief Financial Officer**
>
> You are reviewing your company's financial performance for the first six months of the year and are unsatisfied with the results. How can you disaggregate ROA to identify areas for improvement? [Answer, p. 1-34]

Review 1-4 LO4

Following are selected data from Apple's 2018 10-K.

$ millions	2018
Net sales	$265,595
Net income	59,531
Average assets	370,522
Average stockholders' equity	120,597

Required

Solution on p. 1-50.

a. Compute Apple's ROA. Disaggregate the ROA into its profitability and productivity components.
b. Compute Apple's ROE.

Financial Statements and Business Analysis

Analysis and interpretation of financial statements must consider the broader business context in which a company operates. This section describes how to systematically consider those broader business forces to enhance our analysis and interpretation. This business analysis can sharpen our insights and help us better estimate future performance and company value.

LO5 Assess business operations within the context of a competitive environment.

Analyzing the Competitive Environment

Financial statements are influenced by five important forces that determine competitive intensity: (A) industry competition, (B) buyer power, (C) supplier power, (D) product substitutes, and (E) threat of entry (for further discussion, see Porter, *Competitive Strategy: Techniques for Analyzing Industries and Competitors,* 1980 and 1998).

These five forces are depicted graphically in Exhibit 1.9 and are key determinants of profitability.

- **(A) Industry competition** Competition and rivalry raise the cost of doing business as companies must hire and train competitive workers, advertise products, research and develop products, and engage in other related activities.
- **(B) Bargaining power of buyers** Buyers with strong bargaining power can extract price concessions and demand a higher level of service and delayed payment terms; this force reduces both profits from sales and the operating cash flows to sellers.
- **(C) Bargaining power of suppliers** Suppliers with strong bargaining power can demand higher prices and earlier payments, yielding adverse effects on profits and cash flows to buyers.
- **(D) Threat of substitution** As the number of product substitutes increases, sellers have less power to raise prices and/or pass on costs to buyers; accordingly, threat of substitution places downward pressure on profits of sellers.
- **(E) Threat of entry** New market entrants increase competition; to mitigate that threat, companies expend monies on activities such as new technologies, promotion, and human development to erect *barriers to entry* and to create *economies of scale*.

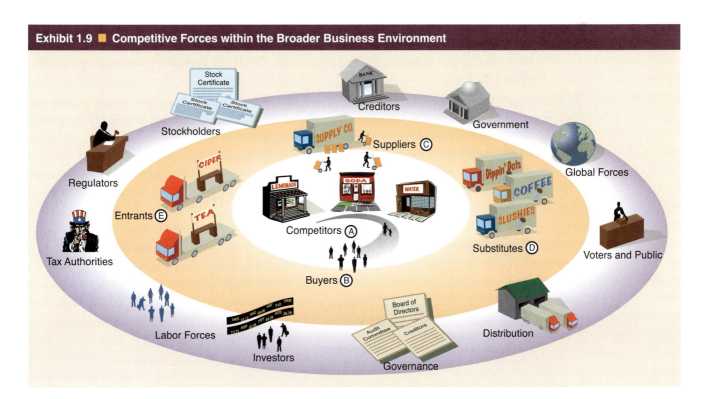

Exhibit 1.9 ■ Competitive Forces within the Broader Business Environment

The relative strength of companies within their industries, and vis-à-vis suppliers and customers, is an important determinant of both their profitability and the structure of their balance sheets. As competition intensifies, profitability likely declines, and the amount of assets companies need to carry on their balance sheet likely increases in an effort to generate more profit. Such changes are revealed in the income statement and the balance sheet.

SWOT Analysis of the Business Environment

As an alternative to Porter-based competitive analysis, some prefer a SWOT analysis of a company. SWOT is an acronym that stands for strengths, weaknesses, opportunities and threats. This analysis can be applied to almost any organization. This approach is universally applicable and easy to apply, and it can be graphically portrayed as follows:

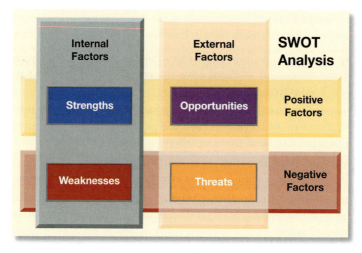

SWOT analysis has two parts.

- Looking internally, we review a company's strengths and weaknesses, while for external purposes, we review the opportunities of and threats to the company. SWOT analysis tries to understand particular strengths and weaknesses that give rise to specific opportunities (to exploit the strengths) and threats (caused by the weaknesses).

- When used as part of an overall strategic analysis, SWOT can provide a good review of strategic options.

However, SWOT is sometimes criticized as too subjective. Two individuals can identify entirely different factors from a SWOT analysis of the same company. This is partly because SWOT is intuitive and allows varying opinions on the relevant factors.

Following is an example of a SWOT analysis on Apple.

Competitive Analysis »

Apple, Inc. (AAPL) – Financial and Strategic SWOT Analysis

Strengths	Weaknesses
Strong brand image	Limited distribution network
High profit margins	High selling prices
Effective rapid innovation processes	Dependence of sales on high-end market segments

Opportunities	Threats
Expansion of distribution network	Aggressive competition
Higher sales volumes based on rising demand	Imitation
Development of new product lines	Rising labor cost in various countries

Analyzing Competitive Advantage

The goal of our analysis is to identify sustainable operating income and cash flow. This is true whether our analysis is focused on valuation of equity securities as a current or prospective investor or on a company's ability to repay its debt as a current or prospective creditor or on trying to grow company value as part of management. This analysis is much deeper than merely eliminating transitory (nonrecurring) items from financial statements. It is an exploration of the following two lines of thought.

1. Does the company have a competitive advantage, and, if so, what factors explain it? Further, is the competitive advantage sustainable?
2. If the company has no competitive advantage, does its management have a plan to develop a sustainable competitive advantage that can be implemented in an acceptable period of time and with a reasonable amount of investment?

Answers to these questions impact forecasts of the company's future performance.

Barriers to Entry Patents and other protections of intellectual property create **barriers to entry** that allow a company to achieve a competitive advantage and charge higher prices for their products or services and thereby earn excess returns. These legal barriers typically have a finite life, however, and a company must maintain a pipeline of innovations to replace intellectual property that loses patent protection.

Product Differentiation **Product differentiation** also allows companies to earn excess returns. Typically, differentiation is achieved from technological innovation that produces products and services with attributes valued by customers and not easily replicated by competitors. Differentiation along the dimensions of product design, marketing, distribution, and after-sale customer support are examples. Such differentiation has costs such as research and development, advertising, and other marketing expenses.

Cost Leader Another approach to achieve excess returns is to become a **cost leader**. Cost leadership can result from a number of factors, including access to low-cost raw materials or labor (while maintaining quality), manufacturing or service efficiency in the form of cost-efficient processes and manufacturing scale efficiencies, greater bargaining power with suppliers, sophisticated IT systems that permit timely collection of key information, and other avenues.

Other Factors In the absence of a competitive advantage, our analysis focuses on the likelihood that a company develops such an advantage. Management often discusses strategy with stockholders and equity analysts, which are recorded in conference calls that are readily available or reported in the financial press. In the case of a turnaround situation, our focus is on viability of the plan; that is, can it be achieved at an acceptable cost given the current state of the industry? Moreover, our focus is long term. Companies can often achieve short-term gains at long-term cost, such as by selling profitable segments. Such actions do not create long-term value.

Creating a sustainable competitive advantage that yields excess returns is difficult, and we are wary of forecasted excess returns for an extended period. Through a critical and thorough investigation of financial statements, and the footnotes, the MD&A, and all publicly available information, we can identify drivers of a company's competitive advantage. We then test the sustainability and validity of those drivers. This is an important step in assessing competitive advantage.

Review 1-5 LO5

Required

1. Match each of the following statements *a* through *f* with the category to which it relates.

   I. Analyzing the competitive environment
   II. SWOT analysis of the business environment
   III. Analyzing competitive advantage

   ___ *a.* Internal factors include a company's strengths and weaknesses.
   ___ *b.* Buyers with strong bargaining power can extract price concessions and demand a higher level of service and delayed payment terms; this force reduces both profits and operating cash flows to sellers.
   ___ *c.* The goal of our analysis is to identify sustainable operating income and cash flow.
   ___ *d.* New market entrants increase competition; to mitigate that threat, companies expend monies on activities such as new technologies, promotion, and human development to erect barriers to entry and to create economies of scale.
   ___ *e.* External factors include opportunities and threats.
   ___ *f.* If the company has no competitive advantage, does its management have a plan to develop a sustainable competitive advantage that can be implemented in an acceptable period of time and with a reasonable amount of investment?

2. Following are selected balance sheet and income statement accounts for Apple Inc. and Samsung Electronics. For both companies, compute ROA and its two components, PM and AT. Which company is performing better on these three measures?

	Apple ($ millions)	Samsung Electronics (Korean won billions)
Average assets...............	$370,522	₩320,555
Revenue.....................	265,595	243,771
Net income...................	59,531	44,345

Solution on p. 1-50.

Book Road Map

The book can be broken into four parts—see figure below.

- **Part 1** consists of Modules 1, 2, and 3 and offers an introduction of accounting fundamentals and the business environment.
- **Part 2** consists of Module 4, which introduces analysis of financial statements. Analysis of financial statements is aided by an understanding of how those statements are prepared.

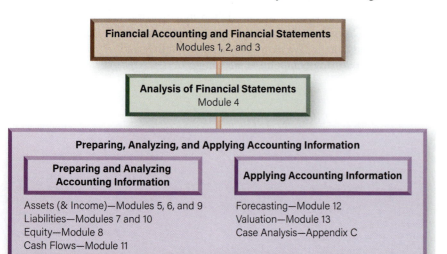

- **Part 3**, which consists of Modules 5 through 11, describes the accounting for assets, liabilities, and equity; this includes accounting for cash flows.
- **Part 4** consists of Modules 12 and 13, which explain the forecasting of financial statements and the valuation of equity. Appendix C is a comprehensive case, which applies many of the analysis tools introduced in this book.

Global Accounting

As we discussed, the United States is among only a few economically developed countries that do not use IFRS. While laws and enforcement mechanisms vary across countries, the demand and supply of accounting information are governed by global economic forces. Thus, it is not surprising that IFRS and U.S. GAAP both prescribe the same set of financial statements. While account titles and note details differ, the underlying principles are the same. That is, U.S. GAAP and IFRS both capture, aggregate, summarize, and report economic activities on an accrual basis.

Given the global economy and liquid transnational capital markets, along with the fact that many non-U.S. companies file IFRS financial statements with the SEC, it is useful for us to be conversant with both U.S. GAAP and IFRS. For this purpose, the final section of each module includes a summary of notable differences between these two systems of accounting for topics covered in that module. Also, each module has assignments that examine IFRS companies and their financial statements.

Global Accounting *sections summarize notable differences between IFRS and U.S. GAAP for topics covered in the module.*

Appendix 1A: Financial Statement Data and Analytics

SEC Filings

LO6 Access and analyze financial statement data.

As noted in the chapter, all publicly traded companies are required to file various reports with the SEC, two of which are the 10-Q (quarterly financial statements) and the 10-K (annual financial statements). Following is a brief tutorial to access these electronic filings. The SEC's website is **https://www.sec.gov/edgar/searchedgar/companysearch.html**.

1. In the **Company name** box, type in the name of the company we are looking for. In this case, we are searching for Apple, Inc. (AAPL). Then click Search.

2. Enter the form number under "filing type" we want to access. Click the Search button. In this case, we are looking for the 10-K.

3. Click on the document link for the year we want to access. The filing date listed (2018-11-05 for Apple) is about 5 weeks after the fiscal year end.

4. Exhibits relating to Apple's 10-K filing appear; click on the 10-K document.

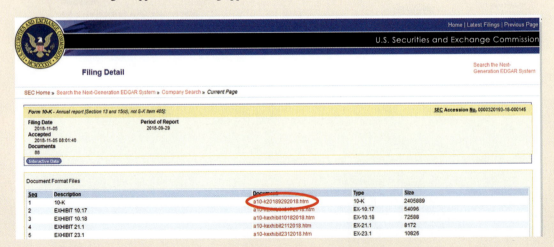

5. The Apple 10-K will open; the file is searchable.

6. An alternative is to download an Excel file of the financial statement data. From the Search Results page, click on "Interactive Data."

7. Click on "View Excel Document" to view or download as a spreadsheet. Or, to quickly view the financial statements or notes, use the links in the yellow box on the left.

Data Analytics

Data analytics is an umbrella term for diverse activities that gather, organize, and analyze raw data. Fueled by advances in computing power, mass storage, and machine learning, we have seen data analytics applications skyrocket in the past decade. Business has benefited greatly—consider the following:

- Data analytics can be applied to any type of information including structured data (such as spreadsheets and databases) and unstructured data (such as 10-K footnotes and transcripts of earnings calls). In the business realm, leaders use data analytics techniques to better understand and manage data related to customers, input costs, production, employees, operations, risks, prices, and other aspects.

- Data analytics provide the business intelligence that informs critical firm-level decisions such as lending at banks, production optimization at manufacturing plants, new product development at biotech firms, and commodity sales by agriculture cooperatives, and many additional applications.

- Financial information intermediaries have developed sophisticated data analytics techniques. Debt and equity analysts rely on data analytics, using large datasets (structured and unstructured) and writing algorithms to create industry benchmarks, assess firms' performance, forecast earnings, predict bankruptcy, and assign credit scores.

- Auditors—both internal and external—increasingly rely on data analytics to identify irregular accounts or activities that warrant closer inspection.

- Regulators including tax authorities and securities exchanges analyze disparate datasets to deter and detect fraud.

Types of Data Analytics

There are at least four types of data analytics.

1. **Descriptive analytics** summarize data and describe observable patterns. These analyses focus on understanding what has happened over a period of time. Did sales go up this month? Which product lines account for the biggest change in revenues? What proportion of sales of a new service line came from a particular sales region? Descriptive analytic techniques include statistics (such as totals, averages, and variances) and cross-tabulating the data (such as using pivot tables).
2. **Diagnostic analytics** seek to understand what happened and why. This involves more diverse data inputs and a deeper dive into the data. A hunch or hypothesis often guides the direction for a diagnostic analysis. Diagnostic analytic techniques involve correlations, regressions, and often culminate in dashboards that capture meaningful outcomes. Google Analytics is a prime example of diagnostic analytics.
3. **Predictive analytics** enable an understanding of what is likely going to happen or what will happen "if" something else happens. Sales forecasts depend on predictive analytics as do equity valuation models that financial analysts use. To be able to predict what will happen, we first need to understand how and why it happened in the past: predictive analytics builds on descriptive and diagnostic analytics. Predictive analytic techniques involve building models using past data and statistical techniques including regression and a deep understanding of cause and effect.
4. **Prescriptive analytics** address the question of what "should" be done and suggests next steps or complete courses of action. A classic example is the Waze navigation app that analyzes traffic and road data and recommends the best driving route. In the business domain, prescriptive analytics can be tremendously valuable for a company, but requires a deep knowledge of the company's objectives and values.

Importance of Data Analytics

Data analytics can provide fodder for well-informed, data-driven decisions. Understanding relevant data at a deeper level can give a firm a competitive advantage and help business leaders better meet their goals. At the firm level, consider for example the vast quantities of data generated by enterprise resource planning (ERP) systems, customer relationship management (CRM) systems, and point-of-sale (POS) systems.

Data analytics is especially relevant to financial statement analysis because there exist many large structured datasets of financial statement data including the SEC's XBRL data.

Data Visualization

Data visualization, the graphical display of numbers with charts, figures, and bars, is often a very effective way to convey meaning and trends vis-à-vis tabular data arrays. This is especially true for big data sets that can be so complex that visualization is a necessary first step for analyzing raw data. Companies and analysts used data visualization for descriptive and diagnostic data analytics, and to prepare reports that inform business decisions. A wide range of data visualization software packages is available, including Sisense, Microsoft PowerBI, Tableau, and IBM Watson Analytics, among others. These packages can accommodate structured and unstructured data and are user friendly; and most have a drag-and-drop user interface. A powerful feature of these data visualization tools is the "dashboard" that simultaneously displays a number of charts and graphics to capture key insights in one view.

In each module, we will encounter data visualization of competitor metrics, industry benchmarks, or time trends for critical accounting numbers. End-of-chapter exercises also present data graphically to create experiential learning opportunities. The text's MyBusinessCourse website provides online access to author-created PowerBI dashboards where we can interact with the data and learn how to create data visualizations of our own.

Appendix 1B: Accounting Principles and Governance

Financial Accounting Environment

LO7 Describe the accounting principles and regulations that frame financial statements.

Information in financial statements is crucial to valuing a company's debt and equity securities. Financial statement information can affect the price the market is willing to pay for the company's equity securities and interest rates attached to its debt securities.

The importance of financial statements means their reliability is paramount. This includes the crucial role of ethics. To the extent that financial performance and condition are accurately communicated to business decision makers, debt and equity securities are more accurately priced. When securities are mispriced, resources can be inefficiently allocated both within and across economies. Accurate, reliable financial statements are also important for the effective functioning of many other markets, such as labor, input, and output markets.

To illustrate, recall the consequences of a breakdown in the integrity of the financial accounting system at Enron. Once it became clear Enron had not faithfully and accurately reported its financial condition and performance, the market became unwilling to purchase Enron's securities. The value of its debt and equity securities dropped precipitously, and the company was unable to obtain cash needed for operating activities. Within months of the disclosure of its financial accounting irregularities, Enron, with revenues of more than $100 billion and total company value of more than $60 billion, the fifth largest U.S. company, was bankrupt!

Further historical evidence of the importance of financial accounting is provided by the Great Depression of the twentieth century. This depression was caused, in part, by the failure of companies to faithfully report their financial condition and performance.

Oversight of Financial Accounting

The stock market crash of 1929 and the ensuing Great Depression led Congress to pass the 1933 Securities Act. This act had two main objectives: (1) to require disclosure of financial and other information about securities being offered for public sale; and (2) to prohibit deceit, misrepresentations, and other fraud in the sale of securities. This act also required that companies register all securities proposed for public sale and disclose information about the securities being offered, including information about company financial condition and performance. This act became and remains a foundation for contemporary financial reporting.

Congress also passed the 1934 Securities Exchange Act, which created the **Securities and Exchange Commission** (SEC) and gave it broad powers to regulate the issuance and trading of securities. The act also provides that companies with more than $10 million in assets and whose securities are held by more than 500 owners must file annual and other periodic reports, including financial statements that are available for download from the SEC's database (**www.sec.gov**).

The SEC has ultimate authority over U.S. financial reporting, including setting accounting standards for preparing financial statements. Since 1939, however, the SEC has looked primarily to the private sector to set accounting standards. One such private sector organization is the American Institute of Certified Public Accountants (AICPA), whose two committees, the Committee on Accounting Procedure (1939–59) and the Accounting Principles Board (1959–73), authored the initial body of accounting standards.

The **Financial Accounting Standards Board (FASB)** sets U.S. financial accounting standards. The FASB is an independent body overseen by a foundation whose members include public accounting firms, investment managers, academics, and corporate managers. The FASB has published about 200 accounting standards governing the preparation of financial reports. This is in addition to more than 40 standards that were written by predecessor organizations to the FASB, numerous bulletins and interpretations, Emerging Issues Task Force (EITF) statements, AICPA statements of position (SOP), and direct SEC guidance, along with speeches made by high-ranking SEC personnel, all of which form the body of accounting standards governing financial statements. Collectively, these pronouncements, rules, and guidance create what is called **Generally Accepted Accounting Principles (GAAP)**. In 2009, the FASB rolled out the Accounting Standards Codification, to simplify user access to all authoritative U.S. GAAP. The Codification changed the structure of how GAAP are organized, from a standards-based model (with thousands of individual standards) to a topically based model (with roughly 90 topics). The Codification streamlined GAAP research for auditors, analysts, company managers, and students alike.

The standard-setting process is arduous, often lasting a decade and involving extensive comment by the public, public officials, accountants, academics, investors, analysts, and corporate preparers of financial reports. The reason for this involved process is that amendments to existing standards or the creation of new standards affect the reported financial performance and condition of companies. Consequently, given the widespread impact of financial accounting, there are considerable economic consequences as a result of accounting changes. To influence the standard-setting process, special interest groups often lobby members of Congress to pressure the SEC and, ultimately, the FASB, on issues about which constituents feel strongly.

Audits and Corporate Governance

Even though key executives must personally attest to the completeness and accuracy of company financial statements, markets demand further assurances from outside parties to achieve the level of confidence necessary to warrant investment, credit, and other business decisions. To that end, companies engage external auditors to provide an opinion about financial statements. Further, companies implement a system of checks and balances that monitor managers' actions, which is called *corporate governance*.

Audit Report

Financial statements for each publicly traded company must be audited by an independent audit firm. There are a number of large auditing firms that are authorized by the SEC to provide auditing services for companies that issue securities to the public: PwC, EY, KPMG, Deloitte, BDO, and RSM, to name a few. These firms provide opinions about financial statements for the large majority of publicly traded U.S. companies. A company's board of directors hires the auditors to review and express an opinion on its financial statements. The audit opinion expressed by Ernst & Young, LLP, on the financial statements of Apple Inc. is reproduced in Exhibit 1.10.

Exhibit 1.10 ■ Audit Report for Apple Inc.

Report of Independent Registered Public Accounting Firm

To the Shareholders and Board of Directors of Apple Inc.

Opinion on the Financial Statements

We have audited the accompanying consolidated balance sheets of Apple, Inc. as of September 29, 2018 and September 30, 2017, and the related statements of operations, comprehensive income, Shareholders' equity and cash flows for each of the three years in the period ended September 29, 2018, and the related notes (collectively referred to as the "financial statements"). In our opinion, the financial statements present fairly, in all material respects, the financial position of Apple, Inc. at September 29, 2018 and September 30, 2017, and the results of its operations and its cash flows for each of the three years in the period ended September 29, 2018, in conformity with U.S. generally accepted accounting principles.

We also have audited, in accordance with the standards of the Public Company Accounting Oversight Board (United States) (the "PCAOB"), Apple, Inc.'s internal control over financial reporting as of September 29, 2018, based on criteria established in *Internal Control—Integrated Framework* issued by the Comittee of Sponsoring Organizations of the Treadway Commission (2013 framework) and our report dated November 2, 2018 expressed an unqualified opinion thereon.

Basis for Opinion

These financial statements are the responsibility of Apple, Inc.'s management. Our responsibility is to express an opinion on Apple, Inc.'s financial statements based on our audits. We are a public accounting firm registered with the PCAOB and are required to be independent with respect to Apple, Inc. in accordance with the U.S. federal securities laws and the applicable rules and regulations of the U.S. Securities and Exchange Commission and the PCAOB.

We conducted our audits in accordance with the standards of the PCAOB. Those standards require that we plan and perform the audit to obtain reasonable assurance about whether the financial statements are free of material misstatement, whether due to error or fraud. Our audits included performing procedures to assess the risks of material misstatement of the financial statements, whether due to error or fraud, and performing procedures that respond to those risks. Such procedures included examining, on a test basis, evidence regarding the amounts and disclosures in the financial statements. Our audits also included evaluating the accounting principles used and significant estimates made by management, as well as evaluating the overall presentation of the financial statements. We believe that our audits provide a reasonable basis for our opinion.

/s/ Ernst & Young LLP

We have served as Apple, Inc.'s auditor since 2009.

San Jose, California
November 5, 2018

The basic "clean" audit report is consistent across companies and includes these assertions.

- Financial statements are management's responsibility. Auditor responsibility is to express an *opinion* on those statements.
- Auditing involves a sampling of transactions, not investigation of each transaction.
- Audit opinion provides *reasonable assurance* the statements are free of *material* misstatements, not a guarantee.
- Auditors review accounting policies used by management and the estimates used in preparing the statements.
- Financial statements *present fairly*, *in all material respects* a company's financial condition, in conformity with GAAP.

If the auditor cannot make all of these assertions, the auditor cannot issue a clean opinion. Instead, the auditor issues a "qualified" opinion and states the reasons a clean opinion cannot be issued. Financial report readers should scrutinize with care both the qualified audit opinion and the financial statements themselves.

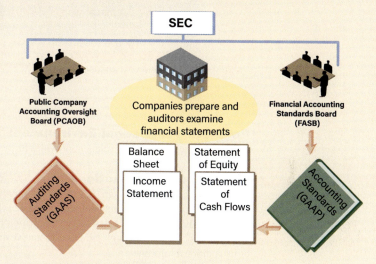

The audit opinion is not based on a test of each transaction. Instead, auditors usually develop statistical samples to make inferences about the larger set of transactions. The audit report is not a guarantee that no misstatements exist. Auditors only provide reasonable assurance that the statements are free of material misstatements. Their use of the word *reasonable* is deliberate, as they do not want to be held to an absolute standard should problems be subsequently uncovered. The word *material* is used in the sense that an item must be of sufficient magnitude to change the perceptions or decisions of the financial statement user (such as a decision to purchase stock or extend credit).

The requirement of auditor independence is the cornerstone of effective auditing and is subject to debate because the company pays the auditor's fees. Regulators have questioned the perceived lack of independence of auditing firms and the degree to which declining independence compromises the ability of auditing firms to challenge a client's dubious accounting.

SOX contains several provisions designed to encourage auditor independence.

1. It established the **Public Company Accounting Oversight Board** (PCAOB) to oversee the development of audit standards and to monitor the effectiveness of auditors.
2. It prohibits auditors from offering certain types of consulting services, and requires audit partners to rotate clients every five years.
3. It requires audit committees to consist of independent members.

Audit Committee

Law requires each publicly traded company to have a board of directors where stockholders elect each director. This board represents the company owners and oversees management. The board also hires the company's executive management and regularly reviews company operations.

The board of directors usually establishes several subcommittees to focus on particular governance tasks, such as compensation, strategic plans, and financial management. Governance committees are commonplace. One of these, the audit committee, oversees the financial accounting system. Exhibit 1.11 illustrates a typical organization of a company's governance structure.

The audit committee must consist solely of outside directors, and cannot include the CEO. As part of its oversight of the financial accounting system, the audit committee focuses on **internal controls**, which are the policies and procedures used to protect assets, ensure reliable accounting, promote efficient operations, and urge adherence to company policies.

Exhibit 1.11 ■ Corporate Governance Structure

Regulatory and Legal Environment
The regulatory and legal environment provides further assurance financial statements are complete and accurate.

SEC Enforcement Actions
Companies whose securities are issued to the public must file reports with the SEC (see **www.sec.gov**). One of these reports is the 10-K, which includes the annual financial statements (quarterly statements are filed on report 10-Q). The 10-K report provides more information than the company's glossy annual report, which is partly a marketing document (although the basic financial statements are identical). We prefer to use the 10-K because of its additional information.

The SEC critically reviews all the financial reports companies submit. If irregularities are found, the SEC has the authority to bring enforcement actions against companies it believes are misrepresenting their financial condition (remember the phrase in the audit opinion that requires companies to "present fairly, in all material respects, the financial position of . . ."). One such action was brought against **Celadon Group Inc.** and its executives. Following are excerpts from the SEC's press release 2019-60.

> **SEC Charges Truckload Freight Company with Accounting Fraud**
>
> *Washington D.C., April 25, 2019*—The Securities and Exchange Commission today charged Indianapolis-based Celadon Group Inc. with an accounting fraud that allowed the truckload freight company to avoid disclosing substantial losses and misrepresent its financial condition.
>
> In a complaint filed in federal court in Indianapolis, the SEC charged that between mid-2016 and April 2017, Celadon avoided recognizing at least $20 million in impairment charges and losses—almost two-thirds of its 2016 pre-tax income—by selling and buying used trucks at inflated prices from third parties. According to the complaint, as a result of the alleged scheme, Celadon overstated its pre-tax and net income and earnings per share in its annual report for the period ending June 30, 2016, and in its subsequent public filings for the first two fiscal quarters of 2017.
>
> "We allege that Celadon knowingly engaged in a multi-faceted scheme to hide at least $20 million in losses from its investors, and lied to its auditors to conceal the scheme," said Joel R. Levin, Director of the SEC's Chicago Regional Office. "We will continue to hold issuers accountable for such serious breaches of trust to the investing public."
>
> The SEC's complaint charges Celadon with fraud and with reporting, books and records, and internal control violations. Celadon admitted to those violations and agreed to a permanent injunction and to remediate the material weaknesses in its internal control over financial reporting. Celadon has also agreed to pay $7 million in disgorgement, which will be deemed satisfied by Celadon's payment of restitution in an action announced today by the Department of Justice. The settlement is subject to court approval.

Courts

Courts provide remedies to individuals and companies that suffer damages as a result of material misstatements in financial statements. Typical court actions involve stockholders who sue the company and its auditors, alleging the company disclosed, and the auditors attested to, false and misleading financial statements. Stockholder lawsuits are chronically in the news, although the number of such suits has declined in recent years. Stanford Law School's Securities Class Action Clearinghouse commented, "Two factors are likely responsible for the decline. First, lawsuits arising from the dramatic boom and bust of U.S. equities in the late 1990s and early 2000s are now largely behind us. Second, improved corporate governance in the wake of the Enron and WorldCom frauds likely reduced the actual incidence of fraud." Nevertheless, courts continue to wield considerable power.

> **Business Insight — Warren Buffett on Audit Committees**
>
> "Audit committees can't audit. Only a company's outside auditor can determine whether the earnings that a management purports to have made are suspect. Reforms that ignore this reality and that instead focus on the structure and charter of the audit committee will accomplish little. As we've discussed, far too many managers have fudged their company's numbers in recent years, using both accounting and operational techniques that are typically legal but that nevertheless materially mislead investors. Frequently, auditors knew about these deceptions. Too often, however, they remained silent. The key job of the audit committee is simply to get the auditors to divulge what they know. To do this job, the committee must make sure that the auditors worry more about misleading its members than about offending management. In recent years auditors have not felt that way. They have instead generally viewed the CEO, rather than the shareholders or directors, as their client. That has been a natural result of day-to-day working relationships and also of the auditors' understanding that, no matter what the book says, the CEO and CFO pay their fees and determine whether they are retained for both auditing and other work. The rules that have been recently instituted won't materially change this reality. What will break this cozy relationship is audit committees unequivocally putting auditors on the spot, making them understand they will become liable for major monetary penalties if they don't come forth with what they know or suspect."
>
> —Warren Buffett, Berkshire Hathaway Annual Report

Business Insights offer examples from the business news and popular press.

Guidance Answers

You Are the Product Manager

Pg. 1-16 As a manager, you must balance two conflicting objectives—namely, mandatory disclosure requirements and your company's need to protect its competitive advantages. You must comply with all minimum required disclosure rules. The extent to which you offer additional disclosures depends on the sensitivity of the information; that is, how beneficial it is to your existing and potential competitors. Another consideration is how the information disclosed will impact your existing and potential investors. Disclosures such as these can be beneficial in that they inform investors and others about your company's successful investments. Still, there are many stakeholders impacted by your disclosure decision, and each must be given due consideration.

You Are the Chief Financial Officer

Pg. 1-21 Financial performance is often measured by ROA, which can be disaggregated into the profit margin (profit after tax/sales) and AT (sales/average assets). This disaggregation might lead you to review factors affecting profitability (gross margins and expense control) and to assess how effectively your company is utilizing its assets (the turnover rates). Finding ways to increase profitability for a given level of investment or to reduce the amount of invested capital while not adversely impacting profitability contributes to improved financial performance.

Superscript $^{A(B)}$ denotes assignments based on Appendix 1A (1B).

Questions

Q1-1. Firms engage in four basic types of activities. List the activities. Describe how financial statements can provide useful information for each activity. How can subsequent financial statements be used to evaluate the success of each of the activities?

Q1-2. The accounting equation (Assets = Liabilities + Equity) is a fundamental business concept. Explain what this equation reveals about a company's sources and uses of funds and the claims on company resources.

Q1-3. Companies prepare four primary financial statements. What are those financial statements, and what information is typically conveyed by each?

Q1-4. Does a balance sheet report on a period of time or at a point in time? Explain the information conveyed in the balance sheet.

Q1-5. Does an income statement report on a period of time or at a point in time? Explain the information conveyed in the income statement.

Q1-6. Does a statement of cash flows report on a period of time or at a point in time? Explain the information and activities conveyed in the statement of cash flows.

Q1-7. Explain how a company's four primary financial statements are linked.

Q1-8. Financial statements are used by several interested stakeholders. List three or more potential external users of financial statements. Explain how each constituent on your list might use financial statement information in their decision-making process.

Q1-9. What ethical issues might managers face in dealing with confidential information?

Q1-10. What are the five important forces that confront the company and determine its competitive intensity?

Q1-11. What are the components of a SWOT analysis? For each component, indicate whether it is an internal or external environmental factor.

Seagate Technology (STX)

Q1-12.[A] Access the 2018 10-K for Seagate Technology plc at the SEC's database of financial reports (www.sec.gov). Who is the company's auditor? What specific language does the auditor use in expressing its opinion, and what responsibilities does it assume?

Q1-13. Business decision makers external to the company increasingly demand more financial information from the company. Discuss the reasons why companies have traditionally opposed the efforts of regulatory agencies like the SEC to require more disclosure.

Q1-14.[B] What are generally accepted accounting principles, and what organizations presently establish them?

Enron

Q1-15.[B] Corporate governance has received considerable attention since the collapse of Enron and other accounting-related scandals. What is meant by corporate governance? What are the primary means by which sound corporate governance is achieved?

Q1-16.[B] What is the primary function of the auditor? In your own words, describe what an audit opinion says.

Q1-17. Describe a decision that requires financial statement information, other than a stock investment decision. How is financial statement information useful in making this decision?

Q1-18. Users of financial statement information are vitally concerned with the company's strategic direction. Despite their understanding of this need for information, companies are reluctant to supply it. Why? In particular, what costs are companies concerned about?

Q1-19. One of Warren Buffett's acquisition criteria is to invest in businesses "earning good return on equity." The ROE formula uses both net income and stockholders' equity. Why is it important to relate net income to stockholders' equity? Why isn't it sufficient to merely concentrate on companies with the highest net income?

Q1-20. One of Warren Buffett's acquisition criteria is to invest in businesses "earning good return on equity while employing little or no debt." Why is Buffett concerned about debt?

Assignments with the MBC logo in the margin are available in myBusinessCourse. See the Preface of the book for details.

Mini Exercises

AT&T (T)

LO1 M1-21. **Understanding How the Four Business Activities Are Related**
In its November 2018 press release, AT&T revealed that CAPEX for fiscal 2019 (capital expenditures for additional property, plant and equipment) was expected to be in the $23 billion range. How will this planned expenditure affect operating, investing, and financing activities in 2019?

M1-22. Understanding What Information Financial Statement Users Demand LO2
Match each of the financial statement users listed to the question they are most likely to ask.

Financial Statement User	Questions
____ A. Current shareholders	1. What is the expected net income for next quarter?
____ B. Company CEO	2. Will the company have enough cash to pay dividends?
____ C. Banker	3. Has the company paid for inventory purchases promptly in the past?
____ D. Equity analyst	4. Will there be sufficient profits and cash flow to pay bonuses?
____ E. Supplier	5. Will the company have enough cash to repay its loans?

Homework icons indicate which assignments are available in **myBusinessCourse** (MBC). This feature is only available when the instructor incorporates MBC in the course.

M1-23. Balance Sheet Equation and Financing Sources LO3 Microsoft (MSFT)

In a recent year, the total assets of **Microsoft Corporation** equal $258,848 million, and its equity is $82,718 million.

Required
a. What is the amount of its liabilities?
b. Does Microsoft receive more financing from its owners or nonowners?
c. What percentage of financing is provided by Microsoft's owners?

M1-24. Balance Sheet Equation and Financing Sources LO3 Best Buy (BBY)

Best Buy's financial statements, dated February 2, 2019, report total assets of $12,901 million and total liabilities of $9,595 million.

Required
a. Why might Best Buy have chosen February 2 as a year-end date? Select all that apply.
   1. February is after the holiday season when sales are high. Best Buy wants to include those holiday sales in its results.
   2. A non-December year end will help reduce federal income taxes.
   3. In early February, inventory will be lower because of the holiday season sales and Best Buy can more easily (and inexpensively) count its inventory.
   4. Other retailers pick late January or early February, and so there is an industry standard that Best Buy wants to use.
b. What is the amount of Best Buy's equity at February 2, 2019?
c. Does Best Buy receive more financing from its owners or nonowners?
d. What percentage of financing is provided by Best Buy's nonowners?

M1-25. Applying the Accounting Equation and Computing Financing Proportions LO3

Use the accounting equation to compute the missing financial amounts (a), (b), and (c). Which of these companies is more owner-financed? Which of these companies is more nonowner-financed?

$ millions	Assets	=	Liabilities	+	Equity
Hewlett-Packard	$106,882	=	$78,731	+	$ (a)
General Mills	$ 21,712	=	$ (b)	+	$ 5,307
Target	$ (c)	=	$27,305	+	$12,957

Hewlett-Packard (HPQ)
General Mills (GIS)
Target (TGT)

M1-26.^A Identifying Key Numbers from Financial Statements LO3, 6 Starbucks (SBUX)

Access the September 30, 2018, 10-K for **Starbucks Corporation** at the SEC's database for financial reports (**www.sec.gov**).

Required
a. Fill in the amounts for Starbucks for fiscal year ended September 30, 2018.
   Total assets $_____   Total liabilities $_____   Total equity $_____
b. Confirm that the balance sheet equation holds.
c. What percent of Starbucks' assets is financed by owners?

M1-27.^A Analyzing Retained Earnings LO3, 6 Symantec Corp (SYMC)

Access the 2018 10-K for **Symantec Corp.** at the SEC's database of financial reports (www.sec.gov). Use the March 30, 2018, consolidated statement of stockholders' equity to fill in the blanks below to prepare a statement of retained earnings for the year ($ millions).

Symantec Corp.
Statement of Retained Earnings
For Year Ended March 30, 2018

Balance, beginning of year.........	$
Net income (loss)	
Cash dividends..................	
Balance, end of year.............	$

LO3 **M1-28. Identifying Financial Statement Line Items and Accounts**

Several line items and account titles are listed below. For each, indicate in which of the following financial statement(s) we would likely find the item or account: income statement (IS), balance sheet (BS), statement of stockholders' equity (SE), or statement of cash flows (SCF).

a.	Cash asset	d.	Contributed capital	g.	Cash inflow for stock issued
b.	Expenses	e.	Cash outflow for capital expenditures	h.	Cash outflow for dividends
c.	Noncash assets	f.	Retained earnings	i.	Revenue

LO7 **M1-29. Identifying Ethical Issues and Accounting Choices**

Assume you are a technology services provider and you must decide on whether to record revenue from the installation of computer software for one of your clients. Your contract calls for acceptance of the software by the client within six months of installation. According to the contract, you will be paid only when the client "accepts" the installation. Although you have not yet received your client's formal acceptance, you are confident it is forthcoming. Failure to record these revenues will cause your company to miss Wall Street's earnings estimates. What stakeholders will be affected by your decision, and how might they be affected?

LO5 **M1-30. Assessing the Competitive Environment**

For each of the following companies, briefly explain what type of competitive advantage(s) they have, if any. Select from: barriers to entry, product differentiation, cost leader, or buyer power.

a.	Apple	c.	Pfizer	e.	American Airlines	g.	McDonald's
b.	Walmart	d.	Uber	f.	UPS		

LO4, 6
Medtronic (MDT)
Boston Scientific (BSX)

M1-31.ᴬ Accessing SEC reports and Calculating Ratios

Access the financial reports for the fiscal year ending in 2018 at the SEC website for **Medtronic** and **Boston Scientific**, two competitors in the medical device industry.

a. Use data from the companies' balance sheets and income statements to complete the following table.

$ millions	Medtronic	Boston Scientific
Total assets, beginning of fiscal year	_____	_____
Total assets, end of fiscal year	_____	_____
Average total assets..................	_____	_____
Net income (consolidated)	_____	_____
Revenue...........................	_____	_____

b. Calculate the following ratios for each company.

$ millions	Medtronic	Boston Scientific
Return on assets (ROA)................	_____	_____
Profit margin (PM)	_____	_____
Asset turnover (AT)..................	_____	_____

c. Which company has the better ROA?
d. Which of the following is true?
    1. As compared to Boston Scientific, Medtronic has a better profit margin and a weaker asset turnover.
    2. As compared to Boston Scientific, Medtronic has a weaker profit margin and a weaker asset turnover.

3. As compared to Boston Scientific, Medtronic has a better profit margin and a better asset turnover.
4. As compared to Boston Scientific, Medtronic has a weaker profit margin and a better asset turnover.

M1-32. Understanding Internal Controls and Their Importance   **LO7**
SOX legislation requires companies to report on the effectiveness of their internal controls. The SEC administers SOX, and defines internal controls as follows.

Why would Congress believe internal controls are such an important area to monitor and report on?

> A process designed by, or under the supervision of, the registrant's principal executive and principal financial officers . . . to provide reasonable assurance regarding the reliability of financial reporting and the preparation of financial statements for external purposes in accordance with generally accepted accounting principles.

Exercises

E1-33. Composition of Accounts on the Balance Sheet   **LO3**
Answer the following questions about Target.

Target (TGT)

a. Briefly describe the types of assets Target is likely to include in its inventory.
b. What kinds of assets would Target likely include in its property and equipment?
c. Target's balance sheet reports about two-thirds of its total assets as long term. Given Target's business model, why do we see it report a relatively high proportion of long-term assets?

Ticker symbols are provided for companies so one can easily obtain additional information online.

E1-34. Applying the Accounting Equation and Assessing Financial Statement Linkages   **LO3**
The following information is available for Advanced Micro Devices (AMD) and Intel for the current year.
- AMD's assets increased by $1,004 million and its liabilities increased by $334 million.
- Intel's assets increased by $4,714 million and its liabilities decreased by $830 million.

Advanced Micro Devices (AMD)
Intel (INTC)

a. Complete the following table.

$ millions	Assets, beginning of year	Assets, end of year	Liabilities, beginning of year	Liabilities, end of year	Stockholders' Equity, end of year
Advanced Micro Devices	_____	$4,556	$2,956	_____	_____
Intel	$123,249	_____	_____	$53,400	_____

b. Calculate average assets for each company.

$ millions	Average Assets
Advanced Micro Devices	_____
Intel	_____

c. Which company has the larger proportion of its assets financed by the company's owners at year-end?

E1-35. Specifying Financial Information Users and Uses   **LO2**
Financial statements have a wide audience of interested stakeholders. Identify two or more financial statement users who are external to the company. For each user on your list, specify two questions that could be addressed with financial statement information.

E1-36. Applying Financial Statement Relations to Compute Dividends

a. Fill in the amounts for the Norfolk Southern statement of changes in retained earnings.

Norfolk Southern Inc. Consolidated Statements of Changes in Retained Income	
Beginning Balance at Dec. 31, 2015	$10,191
Net income	
Dividends on Common Stock	(695)
Share repurchases	(731)
Other	(8)
Ending Balance at Dec. 31, 2016	10,425
Net income	5,404
Dividends on Common Stock	
Share repurchases	(945)
Other	(5)
Ending Balance at Dec. 31, 2017	14,176
Net income	2,666
Dividends on Common Stock	(844)
Share repurchases	
Other	81
Ending Balance at Dec. 31, 2018	$13,440

b. Is it true (or false) that Norfolk Southern purchased its own shares back during each year from 2016 to 2018?

E1-37. Computing and Interpreting Financial Statement Ratios

Following are selected ratios of Norfolk Southern for 2018 and 2017.

Return on Assets (ROA) Component	2018	2017
Profitability (Net income/Sales)	23.3%	51.2%
Productivity (Sales/Average assets)	0.318	0.299

a. Was the company profitable in 2018?
b. Was the company more profitable in 2018 or 2017?
c. Is the change in productivity a **positive** or **negative** development?
d. Compute the company's ROA for 2018 and for 2017.
e. From the information provided, which of the following best explains the change in ROA during 2018?
  1. The company's profitability weakened considerably.
  2. The company's profitability weakened considerably and its productivity fell.
  3. The company had markedly more assets in 2018.
  4. The company had a marked drop in revenue in 2018.

E1-38. Computing Return on Assets and Applying the Accounting Equation

Nordstrom Inc. reports net income of $564 million for its fiscal year ended February 2019. At the beginning of that fiscal year, Nordstrom had $8,115 million in total assets. By fiscal year ended February 2019, total assets had decreased to $7,886 million. What is Nordstrom's ROA?

E1-39. Assessing the Role of Financial Statements in Society

Financial statement information plays an important role in modern society and business.

a. Identify two or more external stakeholders who are interested in a company's financial statements and what their particular interests are.
b. What are *generally accepted accounting principles*? What organizations have primary responsibility for the formulation of GAAP?
c. What role does financial statement information play in the allocation of society's financial resources?
d. What are three aspects of the accounting environment that can create ethical pressure on management?

E1-40. Computing Return on Equity

Starbucks reports net income for 2018 of $4,518.3 million. Its stockholders' equity is $5,450.1 million and $1,169.5 million for 2017 and 2018, respectively.

a. Compute its return on equity for 2018.
b. Starbucks repurchased over $7,208.7 million of its common stock in 2018. Did this repurchase increase or decrease Starbucks' ROE?
c. If Starbucks had not repurchased common stock in 2018, what would ROE have been?

LO4
Starbucks (SBUX)

Problems

P1-41. Computing Return on Equity and Return on Assets

The following table contains financial statement information for Walmart Inc.

$ millions	Total Assets	Net Income	Sales	Equity
2018	$219,295	$ 6,670	$510,329	$72,496
2017	204,522	9,862	495,761	77,869
2016	198,825	13,643	481,317	77,798

LO4
Walmart Inc. (WMT)

Required

a. Compute return on equity (ROE) for the two recent years.
b. Compute return on assets (ROA) for the two recent years.
c. Compute profit margin (PM) for the two recent years.
d. Compute asset turnover (AT) for the two recent years.
e. Which of the following best explains the change in ROA during 2018?
  1. The company's profitability weakened considerably.
  2. The company's asset productivity weakened considerably.
  3. The company had higher sales in 2018.
  4. The company had higher assets 2018.

P1-42. Formulating Financial Statements from Raw Data and Calculating Ratios

Following is selected financial information from General Mills Inc. for its fiscal year ended May 27, 2018 ($ millions).

LO3, 4
General Mills Inc. (GIS)

Cost of goods sold (COGS)	$10,312.9	Cash from operating activities	$ 2,841.0
Cash from investing activities	(8,685.4)	Noncash assets, end of year	30,225.0
Cash, end of year	399.0	Cash from financing activities*	5,477.3
Income tax expense	57.3	Total assets, beginning of year	21,812.6
Revenue	15,740.4	Total liabilities, end of year**	24,131.6
Total expenses, other than COGS and income tax	3,207.2	Stockholders' equity, end of year	6,492.4

* Cash from financing activities includes the effects of foreign exchange rate fluctuations.
** Total liabilities includes redeemable interest.

Required

a. Prepare the income statement for the year ended May 27, 2018.
b. Prepare the balance sheet as of May 27, 2018.
c. Prepare the statement of cash flows for the year ended May 27, 2018.
d. Compute ROA.
e. Compute profit margin (PM).
f. Compute asset turnover (AT).

LO3, 4   P1-43. Formulating Financial Statements from Raw Data and Calculating Ratios

Five Below, Inc. (FIVE)

Following is selected financial information from **Five Below** for its fiscal year ended February 2, 2019 ($ thousands).

Noncash assets, end of year	$ 700,516	Stockholders' equity, end of year	$615,094	
Cash from investing activities	(39,472)	Cash from financing activities	(5,582)	
Cash, end of year	251,748	Total assets, beginning of year	695,708	
Total liabilities, end of year	337,170	Cost of goods sold (COGS)	994,478	
Revenue	1,559,563	Cash, beginning of year	112,669	
Stockholders' equity, beginning of year	458,558	Total expenses, other than COGS and income tax	373,278	
Cash from operating activities	184,133	Income tax expense	42,162	

Required

a. Prepare the income statement for the year ended February 2, 2019.
b. Prepare the balance sheet as of February 2, 2019.
c. Prepare the statement of cash flows for the year ended February 2, 2019.
d. Compute ROA.
e. Compute profit margin (PM).
f. Compute asset turnover (AT).
g. Compute ROE.

LO3, 4   P1-44. Formulating Financial Statements from Raw Data and Calculating Ratios

JM Smucker Co. (SJM)

Following is selected financial information from **JM Smucker Co.** for the year ended April 30, 2018 ($ millions).

Current assets, end of year	$1,555.0	Long-term liabilities, end of year	$ 6,376.3	
Cash, end of year	192.6	Stockholders' equity, end of year	7,891.1	
Cash from investing activities	(277.6)	Cash from operating activities	1,218.0	
Cost of product sold	4,521.0	Total assets, beginning of year	15,639.7	
Total liabilities, end of year	7,410.1	Revenue	7,357.1	
Cash from financing activities*	(914.6)	Total expenses, other than cost of product sold	1,497.5	
Stockholders' equity, beginning of year	6,850.2	Dividends paid	350.3	

* Cash from financing activities includes the effects of foreign exchange rate fluctuations.

Required

a. Prepare the income statement for the year ended April 30, 2018.
b. Prepare the balance sheet as of April 30, 2018.
c. Prepare the statement of cash flows for the year ended April 30, 2018.
d. Compute ROA.
e. Compute profit margin (PM).
f. Compute asset turnover (AT).
g. Compute ROE.

LO3   P1-45. Formulating a Statement of Stockholders' Equity from Raw Data

Crocker Corporation began calendar-year 2019 with stockholders' equity of $150,000, consisting of contributed capital of $120,000 and retained earnings of $30,000. During 2019, it issued additional stock for total cash proceeds of $30,000. It also reported $50,000 of net income and paid $25,000 as a cash dividend to stockholders.

Required

Prepare the 2019 statement of stockholders' equity for Crocker Corporation.

P1-46. Formulating a Statement of Stockholders' Equity from Raw Data
Winnebago Industries Inc. reports the following selected information for its fiscal year ended August 25, 2018 ($ thousands).

Contributed capital, August 26, 2017	$ 106,289
Treasury stock, August 26, 2017	(342,730)
Retained earnings, August 26, 2017	679,138
Accumulated other comprehensive (loss) income, August 26, 2017	(1,023)

LO3
Winnebago Industries Inc. (WGO)

During fiscal year 2018, Winnebago reported the following.

Issuance of stock	$ 5,822	Cash dividends	$12,738
Repurchase of stock for resale	4,644	Other comprehensive income (loss)	1,915
Net income	102,416		

Required
Use this information to prepare the statement of stockholders' equity for Winnebago's fiscal year ended August 25, 2018.

P1-47. Computing, Analyzing, and Interpreting Return on Equity and Return on Assets
Following are summary financial statement data for Logitech International for 2016 through 2018.

$ thousands	2018	2017	2016
Sales	$2,566,863	$2,221,427	$2,018,100
Net income	208,542	205,876	119,317
Total assets	1,743,157	1,498,677	1,324,147
Equity	1,050,557	856,111	759,948

LO4
Logitech International (LGI)

Required
a. Compute the return on assets (ROA) for 2018 and 2017.
b. Compute the profit margin (PM) for 2018 and 2017.
c. Compute the asset turnover (AT) for 2018 and 2017.
d. Which component of ROA (profit margin or asset turnover or both) drives the change in ROA in 2018?
e. Compute the return on equity (ROE) for 2018 and 2017.
f. Logitech repurchased common shares in 2018 at a cost of $30 million. Did this repurchase increase or decrease the company's ROE?

P1-48. Computing, Analyzing, and Interpreting Return on Equity and Return on Assets
Following are summary financial statement data for Nordstrom Inc. for fiscal years ended 2017 through 2019.

$ millions	2019	2018	2017
Sales	$15,860	$15,478	$14,757
Net income	564	437	354
Total assets	7,886	8,115	7,858
Equity	873	977	870

LO4
Nordstrom Inc. (JWN)

Required
a. Compute the return on assets (ROA) for fiscal years ended 2019 and 2018.
b. Compute the profit margin (PM) or fiscal years ended 2019 and 2018.
c. Compute the asset turnover (AT) or fiscal years ended 2019 and 2018.
d. Which component of ROA (profit margin or asset turnover or both) drives the change in ROA in 2018?
e. Compute the return on equity (ROE) for fiscal years ended 2019 and 2018.
f. Nordstrom has a large negative balance in retained earnings (a retained deficit). How does this affect the company's ROE: does it increase it or decrease it?

LO4 **P1-49. Comparing Ratios for Luxury and Budget Retailers**

Capri Holdings (CPRI)
Five Below (FIVE)

Following are selected financial statement data from **Capri Holdings** (a retailer that owns upscale brands Michael Kors, Jimmy Choo, and Versace) and **Five Below** (a value-priced toy and novelty retailer).

	Capri Holdings ($ millions)		Five Below ($ thousands)	
	2018	2017	2018	2017
Sales...............	$4,718.6	$4,493.7	$1,559,563	$1,278,208
Cost of sales.........	1,859.3	1,832.3	994,478	814,795
Net income...........	592.1	551.5	149,645	102,451
Average equity........	1,805	1,794	536,826	394,982

Required
a. Calculate the gross profit for each company for both years. Gross profit is equal to sales minus the cost of sales.
b. Calculate gross profit as a percentage of sales for each company for both years.
c. Compute the return on equity for each company for both years.
d. Which of the following best explains why the ratios for Five Below and Capri Holdings differ.
   1. Capri Holdings is much larger than Five Below and so its ratios are naturally larger.
   2. Five Below is a younger company and so its ratios are naturally lower.
   3. Capri Holdings' brand recognition creates a competitive advantage, which allows the company to add a bigger markup to the products it sells.
   4. Five Below imports its products from Southeast Asia, which allows the company to keep product costs down.

LO4 **P1-50. Computing and Interpreting Return on Assets and Its Components**

McDonald's (MCD)

McDonald's Corporation (MCD) reported the following balance sheet and income statement data for 2016 through 2018.

$ millions	Total Assets	Net Income	Sales
2018.......................	$32,811.2	$5,924.3	$21,025.2
2017.......................	33,803.7	5,192.3	22,820.4
2016.......................	31,023.9	—	—

Required
a. What is McDonald's return on assets for 2018 and 2017?
b. Determine the profit margin for 2018 and 2017.
c. Calculate the asset turnover for 2018 and 2017.
d. What factor is mainly responsible for the change in McDonald's ROA over this period? Is it profit margin or asset turnover or both?

LO4 **P1-51. Disaggregating Return on Assets over Multiple Periods**

3M Company (MMM)

Following are selected financial statement data from **3M Company** for 2015 through 2018.

$ millions	Total Assets	Net Income	Sales
2015.......................	$32,883	$4,841	$30,274
2016.......................	32,906	5,058	30,109
2017.......................	37,987	4,869	31,657
2018.......................	36,500	5,363	32,765

Required
a. What was 3M Company's return on assets (ROA) for 2016, 2017, and 2018?
b. Determine profit margin (PM) for each of the three years 2016–2018.
c. Determine asset turnover (AT) for each of the three years 2016–2018.
d. What factor is mainly responsible for the change in 3M's ROA from 2016 to 2017? Is it profit margin or asset turnover or both?
e. What factor is mainly responsible for the change in 3M's ROA from 2017 to 2018? Is it profit margin or asset turnover or both?

P1-52. Data Visualization for Insights into Financial Statements

The following graphics relate to **Thermo Fisher Scientific** for 2009 through 2018. Access the dashboard at the text MyBusinessCourse website to answer the requirements.

LO3
Thermo Fisher Scientific (TMO)

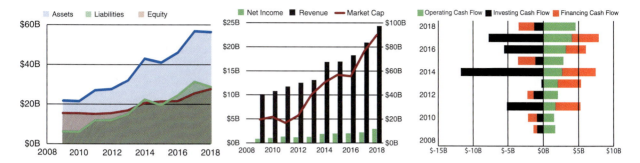

Required

a. The graphic on the left shows balance sheet data.
   i. Which year has the largest assets?
   ii. What general trend do we observe for Thermo Fisher's assets?
   iii. Which tracks more closely with total assets: liabilities or equity?
   iv. Over the 10-year period, how often did liabilities exceed equity?
b. The middle graphic shows income statement data and Thermo Fisher's market capitalization (the value of all the company's stock) each year.
   i. From 2009 to 2017, revenue roughly doubled from $10,110 million to $20,918 million. What was the growth in net income over that period?
   ii. What general pattern do we observe for revenue?
   iii. Which year had the biggest percentage increase in revenue?
   iv. Which year has a better profit margin (PM), 2017 or 2018?
   v. What is the company's market cap in 2018?
c. The graphic on the right shows cash flow data.
   i. Which year has the smallest operating cash flow?
   ii. In how many years were financing cash flows negative?
   iii. In all years but one, cumulative positive cash flows were about equal to cumulative negative cash flows. What year was the exception? Explain what the graphic shows for that year.
d. Use data from the left and middle graphics to calculate return on assets (ROA) and return on equity (ROE) for 2018.
e. Compare the data in all three graphics for 2014. What might explain the relation between the investing cash flow and the increase in revenue and assets for that year?

P1-53.[A] **Reading and Interpreting Audit Opinions**

Twitter Inc. financial statements include the following audit report from **Pricewaterhouse Coopers LLP**.

LO7
Twitter Inc. (TWTR)

> **Report of Independent Registered Public Accounting Firm**
>
> To the Board of Directors and Stockholders of Twitter, Inc.
>
> **Opinions on the Financial Statements and Internal Control over Financial Reporting**
>
> We have audited the accompanying consolidated balance sheets of Twitter, Inc. and its subsidiaries (the "Company") as of December 31, 2018 and 2017, and cash flows for each of the three years in the period ended December 31, 2018, including the related notes and financial statement schedule listed in the index appearing under Item 15.2 (collectively referred to as the "consolidated financial statements"). We also have audited the Company's internal control over financial reporting as of December 31, 2018, based on criteria established in Internal Control—Integrated Framework (2013) issued by the Committee of Sponsoring Organizations of the Treadway Commission (COSO).

continued

> In our opinion, the consolidated financial statements referred to above present fairly, in all material respects, the financial position of the Company as of December 31, 2018 and 2017, and the results of its operations and its cash flows for each of the three years in the period ended December 31, 2018, in conformity with accounting principles generally accepted in the United States of America. Also in our opinion, the Company maintained, in all material respects, effective internal control over financial reporting as of December 31, 2018, based on criteria established in Internal Control—Integrated Framework (2013) issued by the COSO.
>
> /s/ Pricewaterhouse Coopers LLP
> San Francisco, California
> February 20, 2019
> We have served as the Company's auditor since 2009.

Required

a. To whom is the audit report addressed?
b. Which of the following accurately describes the audit process or audit report? Select as many as apply.
   1. Auditors express an opinion as to whether Twitter's financial statements present a fair picture and are free from material misstatement.
   2. Auditors express an opinion that there was not fraudulent activity at Twitter.
   3. Auditors' opinion is that there are no misstatements in the related notes to Twitter's financial statements.
   4. Auditors separately audited Twitter's internal controls over the financial reporting process.
   5. Auditors examined most of Twitter's financial transactions to ensure they were accurate and not misstated.
c. What sort of opinion, *qualified* or *unqualified*, did PricewaterhouseCoopers provide?
d. PricewaterhouseCoopers provides two types of opinions in their report above. Which of the following accurately describes the scope of the two opinions?
   1. Financial statements and related footnotes.
   2. Material and nonmaterial respects.
   3. Financial statements and internal controls over financial reporting.
   4. Financial and nonfinancial information.
   5. Generally Accepted Accounting Principles (GAAP) and Committee of Sponsoring Organizations of the Treadway Commission (COSO).

LO7
Twitter, Inc. (TWTR)

P1-54. Reading and Interpreting CEO Certifications

Following is the CEO certification required by the Sarbanes-Oxley Act and signed by Twitter CEO Jack Dorsey. Twitter's Chief Financial Officer signed a similar form.

> **CERTIFICATIONS**
>
> I, Jack Dorsey, certify that:
>
> 1. I have reviewed this Annual Report on Form 10-K of Twitter, Inc.
> 2. Based on my knowledge, this report does not contain any untrue statement of a material fact or omit to state a material fact necessary to make the statements made, in light of the circumstances under which such statements were made, not misleading with respect to the period covered by this report;
> 3. Based on my knowledge, the financial statements, and other financial information included in this report, fairly present in all material respects the financial condition, results of operations and cash flows of the registrant as of, and for, the periods presented in this report;
> 4. The registrant's other certifying officer and I are responsible for establishing and maintaining disclosure controls and procedures (as defined in Exchange Act Rules 13–15(e) and 15d–15(e)) and internal control over financial reporting (as defined in Exchange Act Rules 13a–15(f) and 15d–15(f)) for the registrant and have:
>   (a) Designed such disclosure controls and procedures, or caused such disclosure controls and procedures to be designed under our supervision, to ensure that material information relating to the registrant, including its consolidated subsidiaries, is made known to us by others within those entities, particularly during the period in which this report is being prepared;

continued

(b) Designed such internal control over financial reporting, or caused such internal control over financial reporting to be designed under our supervision, to provide reasonable assurance regarding the reliability of financial reporting and the preparation of financial statements for external purposes in accordance with generally accepted accounting principles;

(c) Evaluated the effectiveness of the registrant's disclosure controls and procedures and presented in this report our conclusions about the effectiveness of the disclosure controls and procedures, as of the end of the period covered by this report based on such evaluation; and

(d) Disclosed in this report any change in the registrant's internal control over financial reporting that occurred during the registrant's most recent fiscal quarter (the registrant's fourth fiscal quarter in the case of an annual report) that has materially affected, or is reasonably likely to materially affect, the registrant's internal control over financial reporting; and;

5. The registrant's other certifying officer and I have disclosed, based on our most recent evaluation of internal control over financial reporting, to the registrant's auditors and the audit committee of the registrant's board of directors (or persons performing the equivalent functions):

(a) All significant deficiencies and material weaknesses in the design or operation of internal control over financial reporting which are reasonably likely to adversely affect the registrant's ability to record, process, summarize and report financial information; and

(b) Any fraud, whether or not material, that involves management or other employees who have a significant role in the registrant's internal control over financial reporting.

Date: February 20, 2019

/s/ Jack Dorsey

Jack Dorsey
Chief Executive Officer

Required
a. Summarize the assertions that Jack Dorsey made in this certification.
b. Why did Congress feel it important that CEOs and CFOs sign such certifications?
c. What potential liability do you believe the CEO and CFO are assuming by signing such certifications?

P1-55. Assessing Corporate Governance and Its Effects   **LO7**   General Electric (GE)

Review the corporate governance section of **General Electric**'s website (**http://www.ge.com**). Find and click on "investor relations"; then, find and click on "governance," and open the "Governance Principles" PDF.

Required
a. Briefly describe General Electric's governance structure.
b. What is the main purpose of its governance structure?

IFRS Applications

I1-56. Applying the Accounting Equation and Computing Financing Proportions   **LO3**   OMV Group, Ericsson, BAE Systems

Following is fiscal 2018 information for three companies that report under IFRS.

Required
a. Apply the accounting equation to compute the missing financial amounts (a), (b), and (c).
b. Which of the companies has the highest proportion of financing from owners?
c. Which of the companies has the highest proportion of financing from nonowners?

In millions	Assets	=	Liabilities	+	Equity
OMV Group (Austria)	€ 36,961		€21,619		(a)
Ericsson (Sweden)	SEK 268,761		(b)		SEK 87,770
BAE Systems (UK)	(c)		£24,746		£5,618

L04 I1-57. Computing Return on Equity and Return on Assets

The following table contains financial statement information for **OMV Group**, which is a petrochemical company headquartered in Vienna.

euros millions	2018	2017	2016	2015
Sales.............	€22,930	€20,222	€19,260	—
Net profit (Loss).....	3,298	1,486	(230)	—
Assets............	36,961	31,576	32,112	€32,664
Equity............	15,342	14,334	13,925	14,298

Required
a. What was OMV Group's return on assets (ROA) for 2016, 2017, and 2018?
b. Determine its profit margin (PM) for each of the three years 2016–2018.
c. Determine its asset turnover (AT) for each of the three years 2016–2018.
d. What factor is mainly responsible for the change in OMV's ROA from 2016 to 2017? Is it profit margin or asset turnover or both?
e. What factor is mainly responsible for the change in OMV's ROA from 2017 to 2018? Is it profit margin or asset turnover or both?
f. Determine OMV Group's return on equity (ROE) for each of the three years 2016–2018.

Management Applications

LO1, 3 MA1-58. Strategic Financing
You and your management team are working to develop the strategic direction of your company for the next three years. One issue you are discussing is how to finance the projected increases in operating assets. Your options are to rely more heavily on operating creditors, borrow the funds, or to sell additional stock in your company. Discuss the pros and cons of each source of financing.

LO3, 4 MA1-59. Statement Analysis
You are evaluating your company's recent operating performance and are trying to decide on the relative weights you should put on the income statement, the balance sheet, and the statement of cash flows. Discuss the information each of these statements provides and its role in evaluating operating performance.

LO2 MA1-60. Analyst Relations
Your investor relations department reports to you that stockholders and financial analysts evaluate the quality of a company's financial reports based on their "transparency," namely, the clarity and completeness of the company's financial disclosures. Discuss the trade-offs of providing more or less transparent financial reports.

LO7 MA1-61. Ethics and Governance: Management Communications
Many companies publicly describe their performance using terms such as *EBITDA* or *earnings purged of various expenses* because they believe these terms more effectively reflect their companies' performance than GAAP-defined terms such as *net income*. What ethical issues might arise from the use of such terms, and what challenges does their use present for the governance of a company by stockholders and directors?

LO7 MA1-62. Ethics and Governance: Auditor Independence
The SEC has been concerned with the "independence" of external auditing firms. It is especially concerned about how large nonaudit (such as consulting) fees might impact how aggressively auditing firms pursue accounting issues they uncover in their audits. Congress passed legislation that prohibits accounting firms from providing both consulting and auditing services to the same client. How might consulting fees affect auditor independence? What other conflicts of interest might exist for auditors? How do these conflicts impact the governance process?

Ongoing Project

An important part of learning is application. To learn accounting, we must practice the skills taught and apply those skills to real-world problems. To that end, we have designed a project to reinforce the lessons in each module and apply them to real companies. The goal of this project is to complete a comprehensive analysis of two (or more) companies in the same industry. We will then create a set of forecasted financial statements and a valuation of the companies' equity. This is essentially what financial analysts and many creditors do. We might not aspire to be an analyst or creditor, but by completing a project of this magnitude, we will have mastered financial reporting at a sufficient level to be able to step into any role in an organization. The goal of Module 1's assignment is to obtain and begin to explore the financial reports for two publicly traded companies that compete with each other.

- Select two publicly traded companies that compete with each other. They must be publicly traded, as private company financial statements will not be publicly available. While the two companies do not need to be head-to-head competitors, their main lines of business should broadly overlap.
- Download the annual reports for each company and peruse them. At this stage, choose companies that are profitable (net income is positive) and that have positive retained earnings and stockholders' equity. Select companies whose financial statements are not overly complicated. (Probably avoid the automotive, banking, insurance, and financial services industries. Automotive companies have large financial services subsidiaries that act like banks for customers, which complicates the analysis. Banking, insurance, and financial services have operations that differ drastically from the usual industrial companies common in practice. While these companies can be analyzed, they present challenges for the beginning analyst.)
- Use the SEC EDGAR website to locate the recent Form 10-K (or other annual report such as 20-F or 40-F) (**www.sec.gov**). Download a spreadsheet version of financial statements. Use Appendix 1A as a guide.
- Use the annual report and the financial statements, along with any websites, to assess the companies' business environment. Use Porter's five forces or a SWOT analysis to briefly analyze the competitive landscape for the two companies. The aim is to understand the competitive position of each company so we can assess their financial statements in a broader business context.
- Explore the financial statements, and familiarize yourself with the company basics. The following give an indication of some questions that guide us as we look for answers.
  - What accounting standards are used, U.S. GAAP, IFRS, or other?
  - What is the date of the most recent fiscal year-end?
  - Determine the relative proportion of short- and long-term assets.
  - Determine the relative proportion of liabilities and equity.
  - Calculate the return on assets (ROA) for the most recent year.
  - Disaggregate ROA into the two component parts as shown in Exhibit 1.7. Compare the numbers/ratios for each company.
  - Find the companies' audit reports. Who are the auditors? Are any concerns raised in the reports?
  - Do the audit reports differ significantly from the one for Under Armour in this module?

Solutions to Review Problems

Review 1-1—Solution

1. Companies engage in the following three types of ongoing business activities: <u>operating</u> activities, <u>investing</u> activities, and <u>financing</u> activities.
2. A company's <u>strategic plan</u> reflects how it plans to achieve its goals and objectives.
3. Investors use financial statement information to make reasonable estimates of the value of the <u>company's stock</u>.
4. Lenders use financial statement information to assess the company's ability to <u>repay its debt</u>.
5. Company managers use financial statements to decide where to invest <u>scarce</u> resources.
6.
• Manufacturing products	OPERATING		• Constructing new manufacturing facilities	INVESTING
• Issuing stock to investors	FINANCING		• Hiring and training employees	OPERATING
• Repaying a mortgage	FINANCING		• Gaining control of the voting stock of a supplier to secure the supply chain	INVESTING
• Selling services to a client	OPERATING			
• Acquiring land	INVESTING		• Entering into a bank loan	FINANCING
• Engaging in after-sales support	OPERATING			

Review 1-2—Solution

I. b
II. e
III. f
IV. a
V. d
VI. c

Review 1-3—Solution

1.

SAMSUNG ELECTRONICS
Balance Sheet (billions Korean won)
December 31, 2018

Short-term assets	₩174,697	Short-term liabilities	₩ 69,082
Long-term assets	164,660	Long-term liabilities	22,523
		Stockholders' equity	247,752
Total assets	₩339,357	Total liabilities and equity	₩339,357

SAMSUNG ELECTRONICS
Income Statement (billions Korean won)
For the Year Ended December 31, 2018

Revenues	₩243,771
Cost of goods sold	132,394
Gross profit	111,377
SG&A expenses	52,490
Income from operations	58,887
Interest income, net	2,273
Income before taxes	61,160
Provision for income taxes	16,815
Net income	₩ 44,345

SAMSUNG ELECTRONICS
Statement of Cash Flows (billions Korean won)
For the Year Ended December 31, 2018

Cash flows from operations	₩67,032
Cash flows from investing	(52,240)
Cash flows from financing	(14,996)
Net increase (decrease) in cash	(204)
Cash, beginning year	30,545
Cash, ending year	₩30,341

2. Both companies are very profitable. Samsung reports net income that is 18% of revenue while Apple's is 22%. Samsung's balance sheet reports about half of its assets as current, while Apple's balance shows a smaller proportion (about one-third). Samsung relies less on borrowed money; its stockholders' equity comprises 73% of total assets for Samsung compared to 29% for Apple. These are both financially strong companies and formidable competitors.

Review 1-4—Solution

a.

$ millions	
Net sales.	$265,595
Net income	59,531
Average assets.	370,522
ROA = Net income / Average assets = $59,531 / $370,522	16.1%
Asset turnover (AT) = Net sales / Average assets = $265,595 / $370,522	0.72
Profit margin (PM) = Net income / Net sales = $59,531 / $265,595	22.4%

b. ROE = Net income/Average stockholders' equity = $59,531/$120,597 = 49.4%.

Review 1-5—Solution

1. a. II
   b. I
   c. III
   d. I
   e. II
   f. III

2. Both of these companies are strong, but Apple's ROA is higher than Samsung's. While asset turnover rates are comparable, Apple's profitability is higher.

$ millions	Apple	Samsung
Average assets.	$370,522	₩320,555
Revenue.	265,595	243,771
Net income	59,531	44,345
ROA = Net income / Average assets	16.1%	13.8%
Asset turnover (AT) = Revenue / Average assets.	0.72	0.76
Profit margin (PM) = Net income / Revenue.	22.4%	18.2%

Module 2
Introducing Financial Statements

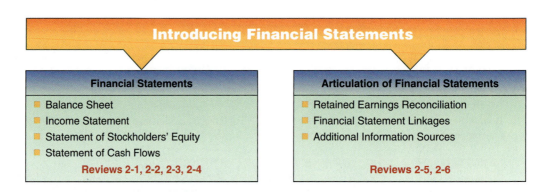

Introducing Financial Statements

Financial Statements
- Balance Sheet
- Income Statement
- Statement of Stockholders' Equity
- Statement of Cash Flows

Reviews 2-1, 2-2, 2-3, 2-4

Articulation of Financial Statements
- Retained Earnings Reconciliation
- Financial Statement Linkages
- Additional Information Sources

Reviews 2-5, 2-6

PREVIEW

AAPL

We examine, in detail, the
- balance sheet
- income statement
- statement of stockholders' equity
- statement of cash flows

We explain how financial statements are linked over time.

We use **Apple Inc.** as the focus company for this module. The following dashboard conveys key information from its balance sheet, income statement, and statement of cash flows.

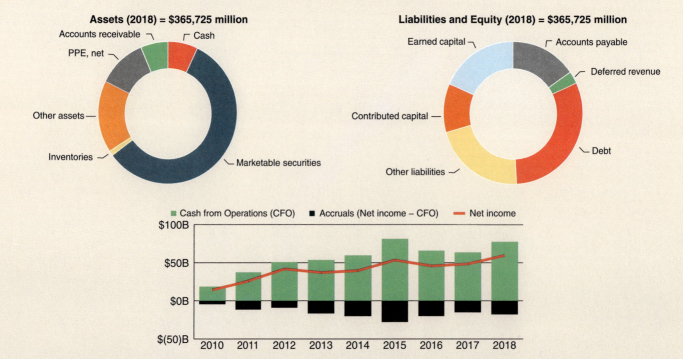

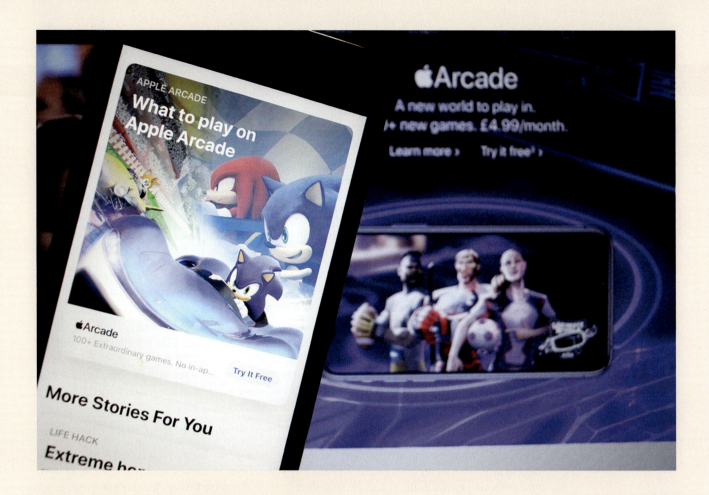

Road Map

LO	Learning Objective | Topics	Page	eLecture	Guided Example	Assignments
2-1	**Examine and interpret a balance sheet.** Cost Flows :: Assets :: Liabilities :: Equity	2-3	e2–1	Review 2-1	1, 2, 8, 9, 10, 11, 12, 13, 14, 15, 16, 17, 19, 20, 22, 26, 27, 28, 29, 30, 31, 32, 33, 34, 35, 36, 37, 38, 39, 41, 44, 45
2-2	**Examine and interpret an income statement.** Statement Format :: Revenue and Expense Recognition :: Analysis	2-13	e2–2	Review 2-2	3, 4, 8, 19, 20, 27, 28, 29, 30, 31, 32, 33, 34, 35, 36, 37, 39, 41, 42, 44, 46
2-3	**Examine and interpret a statement of stockholders' equity.** Statement Format :: Interpretation	2-17	e2–3	Review 2-3	5, 23, 24, 29, 30, 37
2-4	**Describe a statement of cash flows.** Statement Format :: Operating :: Investing :: Financing	2-18	e2–4	Review 2-4	6, 29, 30, 37, 42, 45
2-5	**Construct and apply linkages among the four financial statements.** Retained Earnings :: Linkages :: Articulation	2-20	e2–5	Review 2-5	7, 18, 29, 30, 37, 39
2-6	**Locate and use additional financial information from public sources.** Forms 10-K, 20-F, 40-F and 8-K :: Analyst Reports :: Credit and Data Services	2-22	e2–6	Review 2-6	21, 25, 26, 39, 40, 43

Balance Sheet

LO1 Examine and interpret a balance sheet.

The balance sheet is divided into three sections: assets, liabilities, and stockholders' equity. It provides information about the resources available to management and the claims against those resources by creditors and stockholders. The balance sheet reports the assets, liabilities, and equity at a *point* in time. Balance sheet accounts are called "permanent accounts" in that they carry over from period to period; that is, the ending balance from one period becomes the beginning balance for the next.

Balance Sheet and the Flow of Costs

Companies incur costs to acquire resources that will be used in operations. Every cost creates either an immediate or a future economic benefit. Determining when the company will realize the benefit from a cost is important.

- When a cost creates an *immediate* benefit, such as gasoline used in delivery vehicles, the company records the cost in the income statement as an expense.

- When a cost creates a *future* economic benefit, such as inventory to be resold or equipment to be later used for manufacturing, the company capitalizes the cost (i.e., adds it to the balance sheet as an asset). An asset remains on the company's balance sheet until it is used up. When an asset is used up, the company realizes the economic benefit from the asset; that is, there is no future economic benefit left, so there is no asset left. Then, the asset's cost is transferred from the balance sheet to the income statement, where it is recognized as an expense.

Two examples illustrate how asset costs are transferred from the balance sheet to the income statement.

- Inventory—when a company purchases or manufactures goods for resale, the cost is recorded on the balance sheet as an asset called *inventories*. When inventories are sold, they no longer have an economic benefit to the company, and their cost is transferred to the income statement in an expense called *cost of goods sold*.

- Equipment—when a company acquires equipment, the cost is recorded on the balance sheet in an asset called *equipment* (often included in the general category of property, plant, and equipment, or PPE). As the equipment is used in operations, a portion of the acquisition cost is transferred to the income statement as an expense. To illustrate, if an asset costs $100,000, and 10% is used up during the period in operating activities, then 10% of the asset's cost ($10,000) is transferred from the balance sheet to the income statement. This systematic allocation process is called *depreciation*.

Sometimes, however, companies immediately expense costs that are expected to provide future benefits because their future economic benefits cannot be reliably measured. Advertising and salary costs are examples. We expect, for example, that advertising will produce future benefits in the form of increased sales, but we cannot reliably measure those uncertain benefits. For that reason, we do not recognize an advertising asset; we expense that cost immediately. We immediately expense salaries for the same reason.

The point is that all costs are eventually recognized in the income statement as an expense. Those that create an immediate benefit are recognized as an expense immediately, and those that create a future benefit are added to the balance sheet as an asset (capitalized) and recognized as an expense in the future as the benefit is realized.

Exhibit 2.1 illustrates how costs flow from the balance sheet to the income statement.

Exhibit 2.1 ■ Flow of Costs

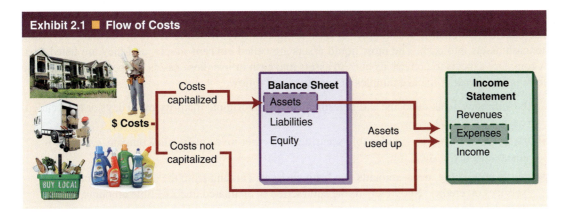

Assets

Companies acquire assets to yield a return for their shareholders. Assets are expected to produce economic benefits in the form of revenues, either directly, such as with inventory, or indirectly, such as with a manufacturing plant that produces inventories for sale. To create stockholder value, assets must yield income that is in excess of the cost of the funds used to acquire the assets.

The asset section of the **Apple** balance sheet is shown in Exhibit 2.2. Apple reports $365,725 million in total assets as of September 29, 2018, its year-end. Amounts reported on the balance sheet are at a *point in time*—that is, the close of business on the day of the report. An asset must possess two characteristics to be reported on the balance sheet.

1. It must be owned (or controlled) by the company.
2. It must confer expected future economic benefits that result from a past transaction or event.

The first requirement, owning or controlling an asset, implies that a company has legal title to the asset, such as the title to property, or has the unrestricted right to use the asset, such as a lease on the property. The second requirement implies that a company expects to realize a benefit from the asset. Benefits can be cash inflows from the sale of an asset or from sales of products produced by the asset. Benefits also can refer to the receipt of other assets, such as an account receivable from a credit sale; or benefits can arise from future services the company will receive, such as prepaying for a year-long insurance policy.

Exhibit 2.2 ■ Asset Section of Apple's Balance Sheet ($ millions)

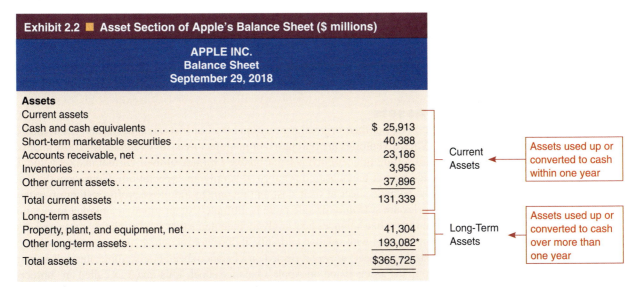

*Includes $170,799 million of long-term marketable securities

Current Assets

The balance sheet lists assets in order of decreasing **liquidity**, which refers to the ease of converting noncash assets into cash. The most liquid assets are called **current assets**, and they are listed first. A company expects to convert its current assets into cash or use those assets in operations within the coming fiscal year. Typical examples of current assets follow.

Cash—currency, bank deposits, and investments with an original maturity of 90 days or less (called *cash equivalents*).

Short-term investments—marketable securities and other investments the company expects to dispose of in the short run.

Accounts receivable, net—amounts due from customers arising from the sale of products and services on credit. "Net" refers to the subtraction of estimated uncollectible amounts. Also called Trade receivables.

Inventories—goods purchased or produced for sale to customers.

Prepaid expenses—costs paid in advance for rent, insurance, advertising, and other services.

Apple reports current assets of $131,339 million in 2018, which is 36% of its total assets. The amount of current assets is an important measure of liquidity, which relates to a company's ability to make short-term payments. Companies require a degree of liquidity to operate effectively, as they must be able to respond to changing market conditions and take advantage of opportunities. However, current assets such as receivables and inventories are expensive to hold (they must be stored, insured, monitored, financed, and so forth)—and they typically generate relatively low returns. As a result, companies seek to maintain only just enough current assets to cover liquidity needs, but not so much to unnecessarily reduce income.

Long-Term Assets

The second section of the balance sheet reports long-term (noncurrent) assets. Long-term assets include the following.

Property, plant, and equipment (PPE), net—land, factory buildings, warehouses, office buildings, machinery, motor vehicles, office equipment, and other items used in operating activities ("net" refers to the subtraction of accumulated depreciation, the portion of the assets' cost that has been expensed).

Long-term investments—investments the company does not intend to sell in the next fiscal year.

Intangible and other assets—assets without physical substance, including patents, trademarks, franchise rights, goodwill, and other costs the company incurred that provide future benefits.

Long-term assets are expected to generate economic benefits over a longer period of time and are, therefore, listed after current assets.

Measuring Assets

Most assets are reported at their original acquisition costs, or **historical costs**, and not at their current market values. When inventories are purchased or manufactured, for example, we know their cost and the expected retail selling price, which is a reasonable estimate of their current market value. But the actual selling price cannot be measured reliably (it is only an expectation). Consequently, we report inventories on the balance sheet at their cost and recognize the gross profit (selling price less cost) when the inventories are sold and the sale price is ultimately determined in a market transaction.[1]

It is important to realize balance sheets only include items that can be reliably measured. If a company cannot value an asset with relative certainty, it does not recognize an asset on the balance sheet. This means that sizable "assets" are *not* reflected on a balance sheet. For example, the well-known apple image is not among the assets listed on Apple's balance sheet. This image is called an "unrecognized

---

[1] However, one class of assets, marketable securities, is reported on the balance sheet at fair (market) value if the securities are frequently traded in organized markets with sufficient liquidity. Under those conditions, the fair value can be reliably measured. We discuss accounting for marketable securities in a later module.

intangible asset." While Apple owns the image and expects to realize future benefits from it, its value is not reliably measured. Other intangible assets missing from companies' balance sheets include the Coke bottle silhouette, the iPhone brand name, and the Nike swoosh. Companies only report intangible assets on the balance sheet when the assets are *purchased*. Any *internally created* intangible assets are not reported on a balance sheet.

Excluded intangible assets often relate to *knowledge-based* (intellectual) assets, such as a strong management team, a well-designed supply chain, or superior technology. Although these intangible assets confer a competitive advantage to the company and yield above-normal income (and clear economic benefits to those companies), they cannot be reliably measured. This is one reason why companies in knowledge-based industries are so difficult to analyze and value.

Presumably, however, companies' market values reflect these excluded intangible assets. This can yield a large difference between the market value of a company and the reported amount (book value) of stockholders' equity. This is illustrated in the following graph of Apple's market value per share (stock price) to book value per share from 2006 through 2019. Each year, market value is greater than book value but the difference between the two measures has widened over time. To put this into context, the ratio of Apple's market value to book value at fiscal 2019 year-end is 10.0 (computed as $225.74/$22.53) compared to a ratio of 3.3 for Target (computed as $71.17/$21.82 million).

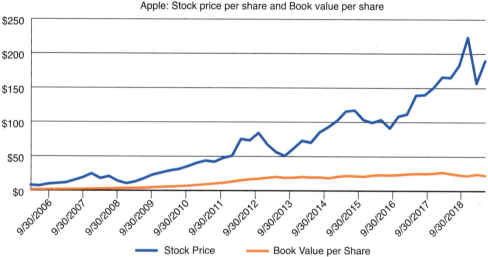

These market-to-book values (ratios) are greater for companies with large knowledge-based assets that are not reported on the balance sheet but are reflected in company market value (such as with Apple). Companies such as Target have fewer of these assets. Hence, their balance sheets usually reflect a greater portion of company value.

Liabilities and Equity

Liabilities and stockholders' equity (also called shareholders' equity) represent the sources of capital the company uses to finance the acquisition of assets.

- Liabilities represent a company's future economic sacrifices. Liabilities are borrowed funds, such as accounts payable and obligations to lenders. They can be interest-bearing or non-interest-bearing.
- Stockholders' equity represents capital that has been invested by the stockholders, either directly via the purchase of stock, or indirectly in the form of *retained earnings* that reflect profits that are reinvested in the business and not paid out as dividends.

The liabilities and stockholders' equity sections of the Apple balance sheet are reproduced in Exhibit 2.3. Apple reports $258,578 million of total liabilities and $107,147 million of stockholders' equity as of its 2018 year-end.

Why would Apple obtain capital from both borrowed funds and stockholders? Why not just one or the other? The answer lies in their relative costs and the contractual agreements Apple has with each.

Creditors have the first claim on the assets of the company. As a result, their position is not as risky and, accordingly, their expected return on investment is less than that required by stockholders. Also, interest is tax deductible, whereas dividends are not. This makes debt a less expensive source of capital than equity. So, then, why should a company not finance itself entirely with borrowed funds? The reason is that companies must repay the principal and interest on the debt. If a company cannot make these payments when they come due, creditors can force the company into bankruptcy and potentially put the company out of business. Stockholders, in contrast, cannot require a company to repurchase its stock or even to pay dividends. Thus, companies take on a level of debt they can comfortably repay at reasonable interest costs. The remaining balance required to fund business activities is financed with more costly equity capital.

Exhibit 2.3 ■ Liabilities and Equity Sections of Apple's Balance Sheet ($ millions)*

APPLE INC.
Balance Sheet
September 29, 2018

Liabilities and Shareholders' Equity

Liabilities:
Current liabilities
Accounts payable	$ 55,888
Accrued expenses (liabilities)	40,230
Other current liabilities	20,748
Total current liabilities	116,866

← Liabilities requiring payment within one year

Long-term debt	93,735
Other long-term liabilities	47,977
Long-term liabilities	141,712
Total liabilities	258,578

← Liabilities not requiring payment within one year

Equity:
Shareholders' equity
Common stock and additional paid-in capital, $0.00001 par value: 12,600,000 shares authorized; 4,754,986 shares issued and outstanding	40,201
Retained earnings	70,400
Other shareholders' equity	(3,454)
Total shareholders' equity	107,147
Total liabilities and shareholders' equity	$365,725

* In millions, except number of shares in thousands and par value.

Current Liabilities

The balance sheet lists liabilities in order of maturity. Obligations that must be settled within one year are called **current liabilities**. Examples of common current liabilities follow.

Accounts payable—amounts owed to suppliers for goods and services purchased on credit; also called trade payables or trade credit.

Accrued liabilities—obligations for expenses that have been incurred but not yet paid; also called accrued expenses.

Unearned revenues—cash the seller receives in advance from customers for goods or services it will deliver in the future; also called advances from customers, customer deposits, or deferred revenues.

Short-term debt—loans from banks or other creditors; includes short-term notes and commercial paper.

Current maturities of long-term debt—principal portion of long-term debt that is due to be paid within one year.

Apple reports current liabilities of $116,866 million on its 2018 balance sheet.

Accounts payable arise when one company purchases goods or services from another company. Typically, sellers offer credit terms when selling to other companies rather than expecting cash on delivery. The seller records an account receivable, and the buyer records an account payable. Apple reports accounts payable of $55,888 million as of the balance sheet date. Accounts payable are relatively uncomplicated liabilities. A transaction (say, an inventory purchase) occurs, a bill is sent by the seller, and the amount owed is reported on the buyer's balance sheet as a liability.

Accrued liabilities refer to incomplete transactions. For example, employees work and earn wages but usually are not paid until later, such as several days after the period-end. Wages must be reported as expense in the period employees earn them because those wages payable are obligations of the company, and a liability (wages payable) must be set up on the balance sheet. This is an *accrual*. Other common accruals include the recording of liabilities such as rent and utilities payable, taxes payable, and interest payable on borrowings. All of these accruals involve recognition of expense in the income statement and a liability on the balance sheet.

Apple has substantial unearned revenue because the company promises to provide after-sales support for each device or computer sold. These promises create obligations for the company that extend over the product's expected life. In its 2018 balance sheet, Apple reports current deferred revenue of $7,543 million and long-term deferred revenue of $2,797 million, which is cash Apple has received from its customers for future services, and therefore, represents revenue that has not yet been earned. Unearned revenue also arises for companies that sell gift cards, or offer subscription services, or take advance deposits from customers.

Net working capital, or simply working capital, reflects the difference between current assets and current liabilities and is defined as follows.

$$\text{Net working capital} = \text{Current assets} - \text{Current liabilities}$$

We usually prefer to see more current assets than current liabilities to ensure that companies are liquid. That is, companies should have sufficient funds to pay their short-term obligations as they come due. The net working capital required to conduct business depends on the company's **operating (or cash) cycle**, which is the time between paying cash for goods and receiving cash from customers—see Exhibit 2.4.

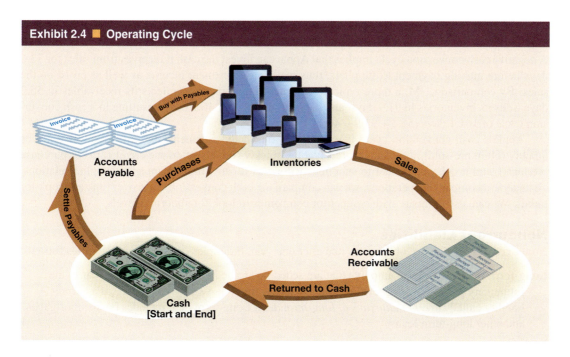

Exhibit 2.4 ■ Operating Cycle

Companies, for example, use cash to purchase or manufacture inventories. Inventories are usually purchased on credit from suppliers (accounts payable). This financing is called **trade credit**. Inventories are sold either for cash or on credit (accounts receivable). When accounts receivable are ultimately collected, a portion of the cash received is used to repay accounts payable, and the remainder goes to the cash account for the next operating cycle.

When cash is invested in inventory, the inventory can remain with the company for 30 to 90 days or more. Once inventory is sold, the resulting accounts receivable can remain with the company for another 30 to 90 days. Assets such as inventories and accounts receivable are costly to hold because they tie up cash. As companies complete one operating cycle, sales and gross profit are reported in the income statement, and cash is generated (equal to the sales proceeds less the purchase cost of the inventory sold). A prime objective is to shorten the operating cycle in order to complete as many cycles as possible during the year. Doing so maximizes profit and cash flow. To shorten the operating cycle, managers can undertake any or all of the following actions.

- Decrease accounts receivable with tighter credit-granting policies and more assertive collection procedures.
- Reduce inventory levels by improved production systems and management of the depth and breadth of inventory.
- Increase accounts payable (supplier credit) to minimize the cash invested in inventories.

Cash Conversion Cycle Analysts often use the "cash conversion cycle" to evaluate company liquidity. The cash conversion cycle is the number of days the company has its cash tied up in receivables and inventories less the number of days of trade credit provided by company suppliers.

Following are the cash conversion cycles for **Apple Inc.** and **3M Company** (a manufacturing company).

	Numbers in Days	Apple Inc.	3M Company
	Average Days Sales Outstanding.............................	28.2 days	55.3 days
+	Average Days Inventory Outstanding........................	9.8 days	91.9 days
−	Average Days Payable Outstanding.........................	111.6 days	46.1 days
=	Average Cash Conversion Cycle.............................	(73.6) days	101.1 days

On average, Apple collects its receivables in 28.2 days, sells its inventories in 9.8 days, and pays its accounts payable in 111.6 days, resulting in a cash conversion cycle of (73.6) days (28.2 + 9.8 − 111.6). A negative cash conversion cycle implies that Apple can invest the cash it receives from sales for 73.6 days before making payment to suppliers, thus realizing investment income as well as profit on the sales. By comparison, 3M, a more typical manufacturing company, collects its receivables in 55.3 days, sells its inventories in 91.9 days, and pays its suppliers in 46.1 days, resulting in a cash conversion cycle of 101.1 days (55.3 + 91.9 − 46.1).

Apple's cash conversion cycle is exceptional on all three dimensions: it sells its inventories quickly (often pre-sold), it collects its receivables quickly (buyers often use credit cards to purchase products), and it delays payment to suppliers as long as it can without damaging supplier relations. To analyze a company's operations, we can compare the cash conversion cycle over time and look for trends. We can also compare with competitor companies to look for abnormal levels.

Noncurrent Liabilities

Noncurrent liabilities are obligations due after one year. Examples of noncurrent liabilities follow.

Long-term debt—borrowed amounts that are scheduled to be repaid more than one year in the future; any portion of long-term debt that is due within one year is reclassified as a current liability called *current maturities of long-term debt*. Long-term debt includes bonds, mortgages, and other long-term loans.

Other long-term liabilities—various obligations, such as pension liabilities and long-term tax liabilities, that will be settled a year or more into the future.

Apple reports $141,712 million of noncurrent liabilities. Apple's noncurrent liabilities include long-term debt, deferred revenue, and deferred tax liability for income taxes the company will pay in the future. Deferred (unearned) revenue arises when a company receives cash in advance of providing a good or service.

Apple reports total assets of $365,725 million and liabilities of $258,578 million. This means that Apple finances 71% of its assets with borrowed funds ($258,578 million/$365,725 million), which is somewhat higher than average. For example, in 2018, the S&P 500 companies financed about 64% of assets with borrowed funds. Given Apple's level of profitability and the amount of cash it generates, this level of liabilities is less concerning than it would be for another company with lower and more volatile levels of cash flow. Companies must monitor their financing sources and amounts. Too much borrowing is risky in that borrowed money must be repaid with interest. The level of debt a company can effectively manage is directly related to the stability and reliability of its operating cash flows.

Stockholders' Equity

Stockholders' equity reflects financing provided from company owners. Equity is often referred to as *residual interest*. That is, stockholders have a claim on any assets in excess of what is needed to meet company obligations to creditors. The following are examples of items typically included in equity.

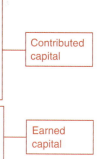

Common stock—par value received from the original sale of common stock to investors.

Additional paid-in capital—amounts received from the original sale of stock to investors in excess of the par value of stock.

Preferred stock—value received from the original sale of preferred stock to investors; preferred stock has fewer ownership rights than common stock.

Treasury stock—amount the company paid to reacquire its common stock from shareholders.

Retained earnings—accumulated net income (profit) that has not been distributed to stockholders as dividends or as stock repurchases.

Accumulated other comprehensive income or loss—accumulated changes in asset and liability fair values that are not reported in the income statement.

The equity section of a balance sheet consists of two basic components: contributed capital and earned capital.

Contributed Capital Contributed capital is the net funding a company received from issuing and reacquiring its shares; that is, the funds received from issuing shares less any funds paid to repurchase such. Apple reports $107,147 million in total stockholders' equity. Its contributed capital is $40,201 million. Apple's common stock has a par value of $0.00001 per share (see Exhibit 2.3). This means that, when Apple sells shares of stock, its Common stock account increases by the number of shares sold multiplied by $0.00001, and its Additional paid-in capital account increases by the remainder of the proceeds from the sale (Apple's balance sheet aggregates the common stock and additional paid-in capital accounts, which is acceptable under GAAP). Apple's stockholders (via its board of directors) have authorized the company to issue up to 12.6 billion shares of common stock. As of September 29, 2018, Apple has sold (issued) 4,754,986,000 shares for total proceeds of $40,201 million, or $8.45 per share, on average.

Earned Capital Earned capital primarily includes Retained earnings, which is the cumulative net income (loss) that the company has earned but not paid out to stockholders as dividends. Retained earnings also includes the cost of repurchased stock that the company has retired. Apple's Retained earnings totals $70,400 million as of its 2018 year-end. Its other earned capital accounts total $(3,454) million.

Analysis Insight ■ Common-Size Balance Sheet

One tool for analyzing a company's balance sheet is the *common-size balance sheet*. This is a balance sheet where each item is recast as a percent of total assets. It is called *common size* because each item is scaled by a common denominator. *Vertical analysis* and *"right-sized" balance sheet* are other phrases for common-size balance sheets. Common sizing the balance sheet enables us to perform the following types of analyses:

- Compare a company's balance sheets across two or more years. Companies provide side-by-side balance sheets for two years, and the 10-K often includes an 11-year history of key balance sheet accounts. If the company has grown or shrunk in size over time, comparing dollars (or other currency) masks shifts in relative size of balance sheet items. Percentages reveal a more accurate picture.

- Compare two or more companies' balance sheets. The common sizing eliminates size differences among companies—we can compare a small firm with a large firm because each asset, liability, and equity account is expressed in percentage terms. The other benefit is that common sizing is unit free, so we can compare companies that report in different currencies.

- Compare balance sheets with an industry average or some other benchmark. The percentages create a common basis for comparison, and this can help assess a particular company's financial position relative to others in the same industry.

Retained Earnings

There is an important relation for retained earnings that reconciles its beginning balance and its ending balance as follows. (Some might view stock repurchases and cancellations as a form of dividend.)

```
   Beginning retained earnings
+  Net income (or – Net loss)
–  Dividends
–  Stock repurchased and retired
=  Ending retained earnings
```

This is a useful relation to remember. Apple's retained earnings increases (or decreases) each year by the amount of its reported net income (loss) minus its dividends, and the cost of any shares the company repurchases and then retires. (There are other items that can impact retained earnings that we discuss in later modules.) After we explain the income statement, we will revisit this relation and show how retained earnings link the balance sheet and income statement.

Business Insight ■ Market Value vs. Book Value

Apple's market value has historically exceeded its book value of equity (see graph). Much of Apple's market value derives from intangible assets, such as brand equity, that are not fully reflected on its balance sheet and from favorable expectations of future financial performance (particularly in recent years). Apple has incurred many costs, such as research and development (R&D), advertising, and promotion, that will yield future economic benefits. However, Apple expensed these costs (did not capitalize them as assets) because their future benefits were uncertain and, therefore, could not be reliably measured. Companies capitalize intangible assets only when those assets are purchased, and not when they are internally developed. Consequently, Apple's balance sheet and the balance sheets of many knowledge-based companies are, arguably, less informative about company value.

Market Value vs. Book Value Stockholders' equity is the "value" of the company determined by generally accepted accounting principles (GAAP) and is commonly referred to as the company's **book value**. This book value is different from a company's **market value** (market capitalization or *market cap*), which is computed by multiplying the number of outstanding common shares by the company's stock price. To compute Apple's market cap, we multiply the number of outstanding shares at September 29, 2018 (4,754,986,000 shares), by stock price on that date ($225.74). This equals $1,073,391 million, which is considerably larger than Apple's book value of equity of $107,147 million on that date. Book value and market value can differ for several reasons, mostly related to the following.

- GAAP generally reports assets and liabilities at historical costs, whereas the market attempts to estimate fair market values.
- GAAP excludes resources that cannot be reliably measured (due to the absence of a past transaction or event), such as talented management, employee morale, recent innovations, and successful marketing, whereas the market attempts to value these.
- GAAP does not consider the business environment in which companies operate, such as competitive conditions and expected changes, whereas the market attempts to factor in these differences in determining value.
- GAAP does not usually capture expected future performance, whereas the market attempts to predict and value future performance.

As of the end of 2018, the median market-to-book ratio for U.S. companies included in the Russell 3000 Index is 1.8. (The Russell 3000 Index consists of the 3,000 largest public companies incorporated in the U.S. as measured by total market capitalization, and represents approximately 98% of the U.S. public equity market.) The 1.8 ratio value exceeds 1.0, which implies the market has drawn on information in addition to that provided in the balance sheet and income statement in valuing companies' stock. Some of this additional value-relevant information is in financial statement notes, but not all. It is important to understand that, eventually, factors determining company market value are reflected in financial statements and book value. Assets are eventually sold, and liabilities are settled. Moreover, talented management, employee morale, technological innovations, and successful marketing are eventually recognized in reported profit. The difference between book value and market value is one of timing.

Research Insight ◼ Market-to-Book Ratio

The market-to-book ratio is computed as a company's market value divided by the book value to total equity. It can also be computed as stock price per share divided by book value or equity per share. The market-to-book ratio varies considerably over time, reflecting the variability in the global economy. Specifically, over the past ten years, the median market-to-book ratio for the S&P 500 companies has ranged from a low of 2.05 to a high of 3.23.

Median Market-to-Book Ratios for S&P 500 Companies, 2009–2018

Review 2-1 LO1

Following are account balances ($ millions) for **Microsoft Corporation** as of the fiscal year ended June 30, 2018. Prepare Microsoft's balance sheet as of June 30, 2018.

Total revenue	$110,360	Cash flows for financing activities	$ (33,540)	
Accounts payable	8,617	Other current assets	6,751	
Cash and short-term investments	133,768	Accrued expenses	6,103	
Cash flows from operating activities	43,884	Other stockholders' equity	(2,187)	
Other current liabilities	43,768	Accounts receivable	26,481	
Inventories	2,662	Long-term liabilities	117,642	
Cost of goods sold	38,353	Cash at beginning of year	7,663	
Cash flows for investing activities	(6,061)	Other long-term assets	59,726	
Retained earnings	13,682	Other income	1,416	
Income tax expense	19,903	Property, plant, and equipment, net	29,460	
Operating expenses (other than COGS)	36,949	Common stock and paid-in capital	71,223	

Solution on p. 2-40.

Income Statement

LO2 Examine and interpret an income statement.

The income statement reports revenues earned from products sold and services provided during a period, the expenses incurred to produce those revenues, and the resulting net income or loss. The general structure of the income statement follows.

```
    Revenues
 –  Cost of goods sold
    ─────────────────────────────────────────
    Gross profit
 –  Operating expenses
    ─────────────────────────────────────────
    Operating profit
 –  Nonoperating expenses (+ Nonoperating revenues)
 –  Income tax expense
    ─────────────────────────────────────────
    Income from continuing operations
+/– Discontinued operations, net of tax
    ─────────────────────────────────────────
 =  Net income
```

On some income statements we see two lines after the net income line. These lines apportion "consolidated" net income between *net income attributable to noncontrolling interests* and *net income attributable to the parent company shareholders* (also called the controlling interest). Noncontrolling interests arise when a subsidiary company is partially owned by shareholders other than the parent company. We discuss noncontrolling interests in later modules.

See Exhibit 2.5 for **Apple**'s 2018 income statement (titled *statement of operations* by Apple). Apple reports net income of $59,531 million on sales of $265,595 million. This means about $0.22 of each dollar of sales is brought down to the bottom line ($59,531 million/$265,595 million). Apple's net income margin is higher than that of the average publicly-traded company (Russell 3000 companies) that reports about $0.065 in profit for each sales dollar. For Apple, the remaining $0.78 ($1.00 – $0.22) is consumed by expenses incurred to generate sales, including costs to manufacture Apple products (cost of sales), as well as wages, advertising, R&D, equipment costs (such as depreciation), and taxes.

Operating expenses are the usual and customary costs a company incurs to support its operating activities. Those include cost of goods sold, selling expenses, depreciation expense, and research and development expense. Not all of these expenses require a cash outlay; for example, depreciation expense is a noncash expense, as are many accrued expenses, such as wages payable, that recognize the expense in advance of cash payment.

Nonoperating income and expenses relate to the company's financing and investing activities and include interest expense, interest or dividend income, and gains and losses from the sale of securities. We see, for example, that Apple reports $2,005 million of other income. This is nonoperating income. It's important to understand that it is a company's operating activities that create value for shareholders. Granted, investments do earn additional returns, but only at the going market rate, and shareholders could invest at that rate themselves. Apple holding the investments does not create additional shareholder value. It is for this reason our analysis seeks to isolate the core (or sustainable) operating profit and cash flows. We discuss operating profit more thoroughly in a later module.

Alert The FASB has released a preliminary draft of a proposal to restructure financial statements to, among other things, better distinguish operating and nonoperating activities.

Exhibit 2.5 ■ Apple's Income Statement ($ millions)

APPLE INC.
Income Statement
For Year Ended September 29, 2018

Income statement	
Net sales.	$265,595
Cost of sales.	163,756
Gross margin	101,839
Operating expenses	
Research and development	14,236
Selling, general, and administrative	16,705
Total operating expenses	30,941
Operating income.	70,898
Other income, net.	2,005
Income before provision for income taxes	72,903
Provision for income taxes	13,372
Net income	$ 59,531

Managerial Decision ■ **You Are the Securities Analyst**

You are analyzing the performance of a company that hired a new chief executive officer (CEO) during the current year. The current year's income statement includes an expense labeled "asset write-offs." Write-offs represent the accelerated transfer of costs from the balance sheet to the income statement. Are you concerned about the legitimacy of these expenses? Why or why not? [Answer, p. 2-27]

Recognizing Revenues and Expenses

An important consideration in preparing the income statement is *when* to recognize revenues and expenses. For many revenues and expenses, the decision is easy. When a customer purchases an item, pays with cash, and walks out of the store with the item, we know the sale is made and revenue should be recognized. Or when companies receive and pay an electric bill, they have clearly incurred an expense that should be recognized.

However, should Apple recognize revenue when it sells products to a retailer that does not have to pay Apple for 60 days? Should Apple recognize an expense for employees who work this week but will not be paid until the first of next month? The answer to both of these questions is yes.

Two fundamental principles guide recognition of revenues and expenses.

Revenue recognition principle—recognize revenue when a performance obligation is satisfied by transferring to a customer a promised good or service.[2]

Expense recognition (matching) principle—recognize expenses when *incurred*.

---

[2] Revenue recognition follows the standard "Revenue from Contracts with Customers (Topic 606)," *Accounting Standards Update No. 2014-09*. The precise language follows: *An entity should recognize revenue when (or as) it satisfies a performance obligation by transferring a promised good or service to a customer. A good or service is transferred when (or as) the customer obtains control of that good or service. For each performance obligation, an entity should determine whether the entity satisfies the performance obligation over time by transferring control of a good or service over time. If an entity does not satisfy a performance obligation over time, the performance obligation is satisfied at a point in time.* We discuss revenue recognition more fully in Module 5.

These two principles are the foundation of **accrual accounting**, which is the accounting system used to prepare all GAAP-based financial statements. The general approach is this: first, recognize revenues in the time period when the company satisfies the performance obligations of the sales contract at the amount expected to be received; then, record all expenses *incurred* to generate those revenues during that same time period (this is called matching expenses to revenues). Net income is then correctly reported for that period.

Recognizing revenues does not necessarily imply the receipt of cash. Revenue is *recognized* when the company has done what it is obligated to do under the sales contract, such as when goods have been transferred or services performed for the customer. This means a sale of goods on credit would qualify for recognition as long as the goods have been transferred to the customer as laid out in the sales contract. The company records revenue but receives no cash; instead, it records an accounts receivable. Likewise, companies recognize an expense when it is *incurred*, even if no cash is paid. For example, companies recognize as expenses the wages earned by employees, even though they will not be paid until the next pay period. The company records an expense but pays no cash; instead, it records an accrued liability for the wages payable.

Accrual accounting requires estimates and assumptions. Examples include estimating how much revenue has been earned on a long-term contract, the amount of accounts receivable that will not be collected, the degree to which equipment has been "used up," and numerous other estimates. All of these estimates and assumptions affect both reported net income and the balance sheet. Judgments affect all financial statements. This is an important by-product of accrual accounting. We discuss these estimates and assumptions, and their effects on financial statements, throughout the book.

Managerial Decision ■ You Are the Operations Manager

You are the operations manager on a new consumer product that was launched this period with very successful sales. The chief financial officer (CFO) asks you to prepare an estimate of warranty costs to charge against those sales. Why does the CFO desire a warranty cost estimate? What issues must you address in arriving at such an estimate? [Answer, p. 2-27]

Reporting of Transitory Items

From time to time, companies will divest a segment of their business as their strategy changes. When they do, we see an additional component of net income located at the bottom of the statement called **discontinued operations**—see Exhibit 2.6. Discontinued operations has two components.

1. Net income (loss) from the discontinued segment's business activities prior to sale.
2. Any gain or loss on the actual sale of the discontinued segment.

The income statement separately reports the per share effects with two EPS numbers.

- Earnings per share from continuing operations.
- Earnings per share from discontinued operations.

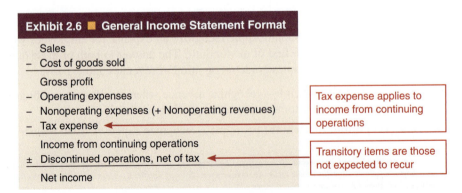

Exhibit 2.6 ■ General Income Statement Format

To be classified as a discontinued operation, the disposal of the business unit must represent a strategic shift that has, or will have, a major effect on the company's financial results. Because these divestitures represent strategic shifts with material financial effects, the reporting of discontinued operations is relatively infrequent.

Discontinued operations are segregated from "Income from continuing operations" because the discontinued operations affect the current and prior periods but will not recur. Many financial statement users analyze current-year financial statements to help predict future performance. One good example is a company's stock price, which is heavily influenced by expected future profits and cash flows. Although transitory items help us understand past performance, they are largely irrelevant to predicting future performance. Consequently, investors and other financial statement users focus on income from continuing operations because it represents the profitability that is likely to persist (continue) into the future. Likewise, the financial press tends to focus on income from continuing operations when it discloses corporate earnings (often described as earnings before one-time charges, or street earnings).

In addition to segregating the results of operations of the discontinued operation in the current and previous two years' income statements reported, companies are also required to segregate the discontinued operation's assets and liabilities that remain at year-end, on its current year's and prior year's balance sheets.

Analyzing the Income Statement

In the prior module, we described an analytical framework to disaggregate return on assets (ROA) into two important components: (1) profit margin, computed as Net income/Sales, and (2) asset turnover, computed as Sales/Average total assets. To augment the ROA analysis, we look at two additional profitability measures.

- Gross profit margin (Gross profit/Sales).
- Operating expense margins (Operating expense/Sales).

The **gross profit margin** is influenced by both the selling price of the company's products and the cost to make or buy those products. For example, if we purchase a product for $6 and sell it for $10, our gross profit margin is 40% ([$10 − $6]/$10). We analyze the gross profit margin by comparing the ratio over time and with peer companies' ratios. Typically, a high and/or increasing gross profit margin is a positive sign. A low or declining margin signals more intense competition or a lessening of the desirability of the company's product line or increasing inventory costs.

Analysis of **operating expenses** focuses on each expense category reported by the company as a percentage of sales over time and compared with peer companies. Any deviations from historical trends or significantly higher or lower levels from peer companies should be investigated to uncover causes. A particularly worrisome sign is when margins for operating expenses are declining in the face of falling profits. The concern is that the company has tried to address declining profits by reducing critical expenses such as R&D, marketing, or compensation costs. This generally leads to a short-term improvement at a long-term cost as market share declines and employee morale suffers. We discuss the analysis of the income statement in much more detail in Module 4.

Analysis Insight ■ Common-Size Income Statement

Analysts typically prepare common-size income statements as a starting point for their analysis; each income statement item is expressed as a percent of net sales. As with the common-size balance sheet, a common-size income statement facilitates the same three types of comparisons: one company across years (called time-series analysis), many companies across one year (called cross-sectional analysis), and to a benchmark such as an industry average. Common-size analysis is also referred to as "vertical analysis" because the percentages in the column on the income statement add up vertically to 100% of total sales (the top-line number on the income statement). A common-size balance sheet adds up vertically to 100% of total assets, and for that reason, is also called a vertical analysis.

Review 2-2 LO2

Refer to the data in Review 2-1 to answer the following requirement.

Required
Prepare Microsoft's income statement for the fiscal year ended June 30, 2018. *Hint:* Refer to Exhibits 2.5 and 2.6 for presentation guidance.

Solution on p. 2-40.

Statement of Stockholders' Equity

LO3 Examine and interpret a statement of stockholders' equity.

The statement of stockholders' equity reconciles the beginning and ending balances of stockholders' equity accounts. The statement of stockholders' equity for Apple is shown in Exhibit 2.7.

Exhibit 2.7 ■ Apple's Statement of Stockholders' Equity ($ millions)

APPLE INC.
Statement of Shareholders' Equity
For Year Ended September 29, 2018

	Common Stock and Additional Paid-in Capital	Retained Earnings	Accumulated Other Comprehensive Income (Loss)	Total Equity
September 30, 2017	$35,867	$98,330	$ (150)	$134,047
Stock issuance, net	4,334			3,386
Net income		59,531		59,531
Dividends and dividend equivalents declared		(13,735)		(13,735)
Repurchase of common stock		(73,056)		(73,056)
Other		278	(3,304)	(3,026)
September 29, 2018	$40,201	$70,400	$(3,454)	$107,147

Common stock and additional paid-in capital increase by the proceeds from the sale of stock. Retained earnings increase by the net income (or decrease by the net loss) reported in the income statement and decrease by the dividends to shareholders. Retained earnings also decrease if a company repurchases shares from stockholders and then retires the repurchased shares. These "buybacks" are another form of distribution to shareholders similar to the payment of dividends (which also decreases retained earnings).[3] Accumulated other comprehensive income (loss) increases and decreases by changes in asset and liability fair values that are not reported in the income statement (we discuss accumulated other comprehensive income in Module 8).

In sum, Apple's stockholders' equity begins the year at $134,047 million and ends fiscal 2018 with a balance of $107,147 million for a net decrease of $26,900 million. Stock issuances and net income increase total equity, whereas dividends, common stock repurchased and retired, and other adjustments decrease total equity.

---

[3] During the year, Apple paid $73,056 million to repurchase common stock from its shareholders and then retired those shares, which decreased retained earnings. Had Apple not retired the shares, they would have been reported in an account called *Treasury stock*, a stockholders' equity account that has a negative balance. Whether Apple retires repurchased shares or not, total stockholders' equity decreases by the buyback amount. Treasury shares that are not retired can be resold. Module 8 discusses treasury stock in more detail.

IFRS Insight ■ Balance Sheet and Income Statement under IFRS

U.S. GAAP and IFRS require a similar set of financial statements with similar formats. Both standards require current and long-term classifications for assets and liabilities, and both recognize revenues when earned (meaning when performance obligations are satisfied) and expenses when incurred. Although differences between U.S. GAAP and IFRS do exist at the "detailed level," there are two broader differences worth mention.

- SEC requires three years of comparative income statements, whereas IFRS requires only two.
- GAAP income statements categorize expenses by their function (e.g., cost of sales, selling, or administrative). For IFRS, expenses can be shown either by function or by nature (e.g., materials, labor, or overhead), whichever provides more reliable and relevant information.

LO3 Review 2-3

Use the data below to prepare **Microsoft**'s statement of stockholders' equity for the fiscal year ended June 30, 2018.

$ millions	Common Stock and Additional Paid-In Capital	Retained Earnings	Accumulated Other Comprehensive Income
Beginning balance	$69,315	$17,769	$627

Additional information for fiscal year 2018:
- Stock issuances, net increased common stock and additional paid-in capital by $1,908 million and decreased retained earnings by $(7,699) million.
- Accumulated other comprehensive income decreased by $2,814 million.
- Net income was $16,571 million.
- Dividends were $12,917 million.
- Other decreases in retained earnings total $42 million.

Solution on p. 2-40.

Statement of Cash Flows

The balance sheet and income statement are prepared using accrual accounting, in which revenues are recognized when earned and expenses when incurred. This means companies can report income even though no cash is received. Cash shortages—due to unexpected cash outlays or when customers refuse to or cannot pay—can create economic hardships for companies and even cause their demise.

To evaluate company performance, we must assess a company's cash management in addition to its profitability. Obligations to employees, creditors, and others are usually settled with cash. Illiquid companies (those lacking cash) are at risk for failure. Given the importance of cash management, companies must report a statement of cash flows in addition to the balance sheet, income statement, and statement of equity.

The income statement provides information about the economic viability of the company's products and services. It tells us whether the company can sell its products and services at prices that cover its costs and provide a reasonable return to lenders and stockholders. On the other hand, the statement of cash flows provides information about the company's ability to generate cash from those same transactions. It tells us from what sources the company has generated its cash (so we can evaluate whether those sources are persistent or transitory) and what it has done with the cash it generated.

Statement Format and Data Sources

The statement of cash flows is formatted to report cash inflows and cash outflows by the three primary business activities. To distinguish positive from negative cash flow, the statement of cash flows uses brackets to indicate cash *outflows*.

- **Cash flows from operating activities** Cash flows from the company's transactions and events that relate to its operations.
- **Cash flows from investing activities** Cash flows from acquisitions and divestitures of investments and long-term assets.
- **Cash flows from financing activities** Cash flows from issuances of and payments toward borrowings and equity.

The combined cash flows from these three sections yield the net change in cash for the period as illustrated by the following condensed cash flow statement for **Apple**.

Exhibit 2.8 ■ Apple's Statement of Cash Flows ($ millions)

APPLE INC.
Statement of Cash Flows
For Year Ended September 29, 2018

Cash generated by operating activities	$77,434
Cash from investing activities	16,066
Cash used in financing activities	(87,876)
Net change in cash	5,624
Cash balance, September 30, 2017	20,289
Cash balance, September 29, 2018	$25,913

Apple generated $77,434 million of cash from its operating activities. It generated $16,066 million of cash from investing activities, such as the purchase of PPE assets or marketable securities (Apple reported a net investing cash inflow because proceeds from the sale of marketable securities were greater than the outflow for the purchase of PPE). Apple used $(87,876) million of cash for financing activities, such as paying dividends, repurchasing common stock from the market, or reducing debt. The three types of cash flow together generated $5,624 million of cash during the year, thereby increasing the cash account from $20,289 million at the beginning of fiscal 2018 to $25,913 million at fiscal-year-end. Apple's cash flow picture is healthy: the company generated substantial cash from operating activities and from the sale of investments, and used that cash to invest in PPE infrastructure, reduce debt, and return cash to stockholders in the form of dividends and stock repurchases.

Our analysis of cash flows focuses on the sources and uses of cash.

- Is the company generating cash from operating activities?
- Is the operating cash flow sustainable?
- Is the company investing its cash to grow its infrastructure (PPE) or to enter new markets by acquiring other companies?
- Is the company using its excess cash to build liquidity (purchase of marketable securities)?
- Is the company paying down debt or paying dividends?
- Is the company repurchasing stock?

Ultimately, a company's ending cash balance must be positive. So, if operating cash flow is negative, the company must raise cash from investing activities (the sale of PPE assets or marketable securities) or financing activities (borrowing money, selling stock, or cutting dividends and share repurchases). In the long run, the amount of cash that can be raised from investing and financing activities is finite. Although companies can usually sustain a short-term negative operating cash flow, long-term operating cash outflows are a serious concern. We discuss the statement of cash flows in detail in a later module.

LO4 Review 2-4

Refer to the data in Review 2-1 to answer the following requirement.

Required
Prepare **Microsoft**'s statement of cash flows for the fiscal year ended June 30, 2018.

Solution on p. 2-41.

Articulation of Financial Statements

The four financial statements are linked with each other and linked across time. This section demonstrates the linkages (articulation) of financial statements using **Apple**.

LO5 Construct and apply linkages among the four financial statements.

Retained Earnings Reconciliation

One of the most important articulations between financial statements involves the balance sheet and income statement. The two statements are linked via retained earnings. Recall that retained earnings is updated each period as follows.

Beginning retained earnings
± Net income (loss)
− Dividends
− Shares repurchased and retired
= Ending retained earnings

Retained earnings reflect cumulative income that has not yet been distributed to shareholders. Exhibit 2.9 shows Apple's retained earnings reconciliation for 2018.

Exhibit 2.9 ■ Apple's Retained Earnings Reconciliation ($ millions)

APPLE INC.
Retained Earnings Reconciliation
For Year Ended September 29, 2018

Retained earnings, September 30, 2017	$98,330
Net income	59,531
Dividends declared	(13,735)
Repurchase and retirement of common stock	(73,056)
Other adjustments	(670)
Retained earnings, September 29, 2018	$70,400

This reconciliation of retained earnings links the balance sheet and the income statement.

In the absence of transactions with stockholders—such as stock issuances and repurchases, dividend payments, and other adjustments—the change in stockholders' equity equals income or loss for the period. The income statement, thus, measures the change in company value as measured by *GAAP*. This is not necessarily company value as measured by the *market*. Of course, all value-relevant items eventually find their way into the income statement. So, from a long-term perspective, the income statement does measure change in company value. This is why stock prices react to reported income and to analysts' expectations about future income.

Financial Statement Linkages

Exhibit 2.10 lays out the linkages among the four financial statements. Apple begins fiscal 2018 with assets of $375,319 million, consisting of cash of $20,289 million and noncash assets of $355,030 million. These investments are financed with $241,272 million from nonowners and $134,047 million

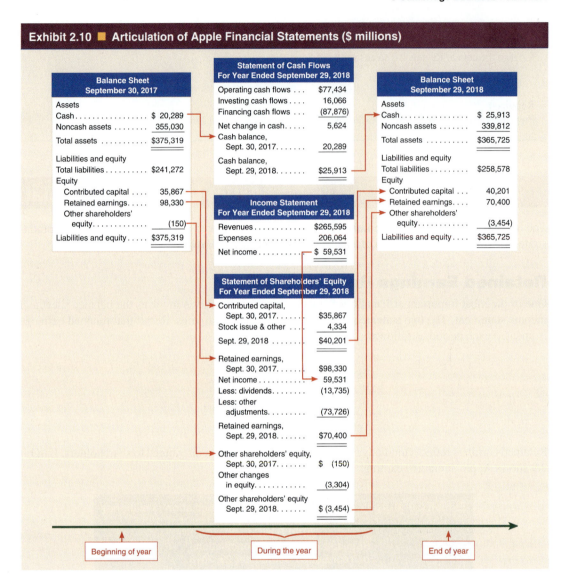

Exhibit 2.10 Articulation of Apple Financial Statements ($ millions)

from stockholders. Owner financing consists of contributed capital of $35,867 million, retained earnings of $98,330 million, and other shareholders' equity of $(150) million.

Exhibit 2.10 shows balance sheets at the beginning and end of Apple's fiscal year on the left and right columns, respectively. The middle column reflects annual operating activities. The statement of cash flows explains how operating, investing, and financing activities increase the cash balance by $5,624 million from $20,289 million at the beginning of the year to $25,913 million at year-end. The ending balance in cash is reported in the year-end balance sheet on the right.

Apple's $59,531 million net income reported on the income statement is linked to the statement of shareholders' equity. Apple's retained earnings increases by net income of $59,531 million and decreases by dividend payments of $(13,735) million, by the repurchase of stock of $(73,056) million, and by other items of $(670) million.

Understanding these linkages gives managers as well as external financial statement users a keener ability to assess the impact transactions have on the financial statements. Every transaction has at least two effects on the financial statements. For example, purchasing new PPE increases noncash assets and decreases cash on the balance sheet, which in turn affects the statement of cash flows. Many other transactions have more than two effects. For example, consider the cash sale of inventory. This transaction has the following income statement effects: (1) revenue increases, (2) expenses increase, and (3) net income increases (assuming the sales price exceeded the cost of the inventory). The balance sheet is affected as follows: (1) cash increases, (2) inventory decreases, and (3) retained earnings increases. Cash from operations increases on the statement of cash flows, and the statement of stockholders' equity is affected via retained earnings. With such an understanding, we can more accurately answer questions such as the following.

- What are the financial statement effects of purchasing new PPE versus renting it?
- How is ROA affected when the company discontinues certain operations?
- What are the income statement and balance sheet effects of outsourcing production?
- How will a proposed merger affect profit margin and asset turnover?

LO5 Review 2-5

Assume **Microsoft Corporation** reports the following balances for the prior-year balance sheet and current-year income statement ($ millions). Prepare the articulation of Microsoft's financial statements for fiscal years 2017 and 2018 following the format of Exhibit 2.10.

Balance Sheet, June 30, 2017	
Assets	
Cash	$ 7,663
Noncash assets	242,649
Total assets	$250,312
Liabilities and equity	
Total liabilities	$162,601
Equity	
Contributed capital	69,315
Retained earnings	17,769
Other stockholders' equity . . .	627
Liabilities and equity	$250,312

Income Statement, For Year Ended June 30, 2018	
Revenues	$110,360
Expenses	93,789
Net income	$ 16,571

Statement of Cash Flows, For Year Ended June 30, 2018	
Operating cash flows	$43,884
Investing cash flows	(6,061)
Financing cash flows	(33,540)
Net change in cash.	4,283
Cash balance, June 30, 2017.	7,663
Cash balance, June 30, 2018.	$11,946

Notes: 1. Stock issuances for the year are $1,098.
2. Dividends for the year are $12,917.
3. Other decreases in retained earnings are $7,741.
4. Change in other stockholders' equity for the year is $(2,814).
5. Total assets at June 30, 2018 are $258,848.

Solution on p. 2-41.

Additional Information Sources

The four financial statements are only a part of the information available to financial statement users. Additional information from a variety of sources provides useful insight into company operating activities and future prospects. This section highlights additional information sources.

LO6 Locate and use additional financial information from public sources.

Form 10-K

Companies with publicly traded securities must file with the SEC a detailed annual report and discussion of their business activities in their Form 10-K (quarterly reports are filed on Form 10-Q). Many of the disclosures in the 10-K are mandated by law and include the following general categories:

- **Item 1**, Business
- **Item 1A**, Risk Factors
- **Item 2**, Properties
- **Item 3**, Legal Proceedings
- **Item 4**, Submission of Matters to a Vote of Security Holders
- **Item 5**, Market for Registrant's Common Equity and Related Stockholder Matters

- **Item 6**, Selected Financial Data
- **Item 7**, Management's Discussion and Analysis of Financial Condition and Results of Operations
- **Item 7A**, Quantitative and Qualitative Disclosures About Market Risk
- **Item 8**, Financial Statements and Supplementary Data
- **Item 9**, Changes in and Disagreements with Accountants on Accounting and Financial Disclosure
- **Item 9A**, Controls and Procedures
- **Item 10**, Directors, Executive Officers, and Corporate Governance
- **Item 11**, Executive Compensation
- **Item 12**, Security Ownership of Certain Beneficial Owners and Management and Related Stockholder Matters
- **Item 13**, Certain Relationships and Related Transactions, and Director Independence
- **Item 14**, Principal Accountant Fees and Services

Description of Business (Item 1)

Companies must provide a general description of their business, including their principal products and services, the source and availability of required raw materials; all patents, trademarks, licenses, and important related agreements; seasonality of the business; any dependence upon a single customer; and competitive conditions, including particular markets in which the company competes, the product offerings in those markets, and the status of its competitive environment. Companies must also provide a description of their overall strategy. Apple's partial disclosure follows.

> **Business Strategy** The Company is committed to bringing the best user experience to its customers through its innovative hardware, software and services. The Company's business strategy leverages its unique ability to design and develop its own operating systems, hardware, application software and services to provide its customers products and solutions with innovative design, superior ease-of-use and seamless integration. As part of its strategy, the Company continues to expand its platform for the discovery and delivery of digital content and applications through its Digital Content and Services, which allows customers to discover and download or stream digital content, iOS, Mac, Apple Watch and Apple TV applications, and books through either a Mac or Windows personal computer or through iPhone, iPad and iPod touch® devices ("iOS devices"), Apple TV, Apple Watch and HomePod. The Company also supports a community for the development of third-party software and hardware products and digital content that complement the Company's offerings. The Company believes a high-quality buying experience with knowledgeable salespersons who can convey the value of the Company's products and services greatly enhances its ability to attract and retain customers. Therefore, the Company's strategy also includes building and expanding its own retail and online stores and its third-party distribution network to effectively reach more customers and provide them with a high-quality sales and post-sales support experience. The Company believes ongoing investment in research and development ("R&D"), marketing and advertising is critical to the development and sale of innovative products, services and technologies.

Management's Discussion and Analysis (Item 7)

The management discussion and analysis (MD&A) section of the 10-K contains valuable insight into the company's results of operations. In addition to an executive overview of company status and its recent operating results, the MD&A section includes information relating to critical accounting policies and estimates used in preparing the financial statements, a detailed discussion of sales activity; year-over-year comparisons of operating activities; analysis of gross margin, operating expenses, taxes, and off-balance-sheet and contractual obligations; assessment of factors that affect future results; and financial condition.

Item 7A reports quantitative and qualitative disclosures about market risk. For example, Apple makes the following disclosure relating to its Mac operating system and its iPods, iPhones, iPads, and other products.

Competition The markets for the Company's products and services are highly competitive and the Company is confronted by aggressive competition in all areas of its business. These markets are characterized by frequent product introductions and rapid technological advances that have substantially increased the capabilities and use of mobile communication and media devices, personal computers and other digital electronic devices. Many of the Company's competitors that sell mobile devices and personal computers based on other operating systems seek to compete primarily through aggressive pricing and very low cost structures. The Company's financial condition and operating results can be adversely affected by these and other industry-wide downward pressures on gross margins. Principal competitive factors important to the Company include price, product and service features (including security features), relative price and performance, product and service quality and reliability, design innovation, a strong third-party software and accessories ecosystem, marketing and distribution capability, service and support and corporate reputation.

Schedule II—Valuation and Qualifying Accounts

In addition to the 10-K sections described above, the SEC requires companies to report additional information about certain balance sheet accounts. That information explains reserves and allowances the company establishes to reflect expected losses or uncollectible amounts. (We explain these accounts in later modules.) Many companies comply with this requirement by including the required information in notes to financial statements or as additional information at the end of the 10-K. Exhibit 2.11 shows a typical disclosure from Cisco Inc. from its 2018 10-K.

Exhibit 2.11 ■ Cisco's Schedule II from 2018 10-K

SCHEDULE II
VALUATION AND QUALIFYING ACCOUNTS

	Allowances for	
Year Ended July 28, 2018 ($ millions)	Financing Receivables	Accounts Receivable
Balance at beginning of fiscal year..................................	$295	$211
Provisions (benefits)..	(89)	(45)
Write-offs net of recoveries...	(6)	(37)
Foreign exchange and other..	5	—
Balance at end of fiscal year	$205	$129

Cisco provides information relating to its reserves for anticipated losses on its financing receivables (leases and loans), and on its accounts receivable. Companies often provide similar analysis on estimated sales returns and deferred tax accounts. Our objective in reviewing these accounts is to determine if they are reasonable in amount and, if not, the extent to which our estimate of core operating income differs from that reported in the company's income statement. We discuss this analysis in later modules.

Form 20-F and Form 40-F

Non-U.S. companies that are publicly traded in the United States also file annual reports with the SEC. These foreign companies must furnish, within four months after the fiscal year-end, the same audited financial statements required on Form 10-K. The filing, labeled Form 20-F, requires that firms provide financial statements prepared according to U.S. GAAP or IFRS. If the company uses accounting standards other than GAAP or IFRS, Form 20-F must discuss major differences between the accounting principles used and GAAP and provide a table that reconciles net income as reported to U.S. GAAP net income. In addition, substantive balance sheet and cash flow items that differ from U.S. GAAP must be reconciled. Canadian companies file their annual reports, prepared under IFRS, using Form 40-F.

Form 8-K

Another useful report that is required by the SEC and is publicly available is the Form 8-K. This form must be filed within four business days of any of the following events.

- Quarterly earnings press release
- Entry into or termination of a material definitive agreement (including petition for bankruptcy)
- Exit from a line of business or impairment of assets
- Change in the company's certified public accounting firm
- Change in control of the company
- Departure of the company's executive officers
- Changes in the company's articles of incorporation or bylaws

Outsiders typically use Form 8-K to monitor for material adverse changes in the company.

Analyst Reports

Sell-side analysts provide their clients with objective analyses of company operating activities. Frequently, these reports include a discussion of the competitive environment for each of the company's principal product lines, strengths and weaknesses of the company, and an investment recommendation, including financial analysis and a stock price target. For example, **RBC Capital Markets** provides the following in its October 8, 2018, report to clients on Apple.

RBC Capital Markets

ROC Capital Markets, LLC
Amit Daryanani, CFA (Analyst)
(415) 633-8659
amit.daryanani@rbccm.com
Amitesh Bajad (Senior Associate)
(415) 633-8795
amitesh.bajod@rbccm.com

Irvin Liu (AVP)
(415) 633-8539
irvin.liu@rbccm.com

October 8, 2018

Apple Inc.

Data Download—Upside Ahead

Our view: We think AAPL should post strong Sep-qtr results helped by multiple factors including new products, ASP uplift, benign memory costs, Services tailwind, and continued buybacks.

Key points:

All You Need to Know: Heading into Sep-qtr earnings, we think investor sentiment is largely neutral to even slightly negative toward new iPhones and ability to maintain flat to up units in FY19. We expect AAPL to post Sep-qtr results slightly above Street expectations driven by revenues, modest upside to GMs, and continued buyback tailwinds. We think new iPhone launch will boost ASPs as well as units and note that last year iPhone X's delay should imply somewhat easier comps in Sep-qtr. Carrier promotions, which are more attractive this year, could be a driver of units upside. In addition, we think that the Others product segment could surprise positively given the new Apple Watch and rising AirPods attach rate. Overall, we see Sep-qtr revenues up mid/high teens vs. Sep-2017. While FX could be a slight headwind, AAPL's hedging program should largely offset that. On the GM side, in addition to ASP dynamic, we should start seeing impact of lower memory prices flowing through, particularly with the launch of new iPhones. Finally, services momentum should remain strong and we think AAPL's stock repurchase momentum remains strong. **Net/Net:** Maintaining Outperform rating and $250 price target.

Data Download: 1) On 9/12, AAPL announced its new lineup of phones: iPhone XS Max (6.5" OLED), iPhone XS (5.8" OLED), and iPhone XR (6.1" LCD). 2) For August, the contract price for 64Gb TLC wafer was flat m/m, for 128Gb TLC wafer declined −5.5% m/m, and for 256Gb TLC declined −12.8% m/m. 3) Aug DRAM contract prices were largely flat but spot was beginning to show some signs of softness. 4) On 9/25, JBL reported an Aug-qtr beat with revenue/EPS of $5.77B/$0.70 vs. Street at $5.41B/$0.68. 5) On 9/6, AVGO reported Jul-qtr revs/EPS of $5.07B/$4.98 vs. Street at $5.06B/$4.83.

Outperform
NASDAQ : AAPL; USD 224.29
Price Target USD 250.00

WHAT'S INSIDE	
☐ Rating/Risk Change	☐ Price Target Change
☐ In-Depth Report	☐ Est. Change
☐ Preview	☒ News Analysis

Scenario Analysis*

	Downside Scenario	Current Price	Price Target	Upside Scenario
	190.00 ↓14%	224.29	250.00 ↑12%	280.00 ↑26%

*Implied Total Returns

Key Statistics

Shares O/S (MM):	4,926.6	Market Cap (MM):		1,104,987
Dividend:	2.28	Yield:		1.0%
BVPS:	23.78	P/BVPS:		9.43x
		Avg. Daily Volume:		32,936,934

RBC Estimates

FY Sep	2016A	2017A	2018E	2019E
EPS, Ops Diluted	8.28	9.19	11.75	13.77
P/E	27.1x	24.4x	19.1x	16.3x
Revenue	215.6	229.2	264.9	286.4

EPS, Ops Diluted	Q1	Q2	Q3	Q4
2017	3.36A	2.10A	1.67A	2.07A
2018	3.89A	2.73A	2.34A	2.80E
2019	4.94E	3.16E	2.56E	3.11E
Revenue				
2017	78.4A	52.9A	45.4A	52.6A
2018	88.3A	61.1A	53.3A	62.2E
2019	95.2E	66.2E	57.9E	67.2E

All values in USD unless otherwise noted.

Credit Services

Several firms, including **S&P Global Ratings** (**StandardAndPoors.com**), **Moody's Investors Service** (**Moodys.com**), and **Fitch Ratings** (**FitchRatings.com**), provide credit analysis that assists potential lenders, investors, employees, and other users in evaluating a company's creditworthiness and future financial viability. Credit analysis is a specialized field of analysis, quite different from the equity analysis illustrated here. These firms issue credit ratings on publicly issued bonds as well as on firms' commercial paper.

Data Services

A number of companies supply financial statement data in easy-to-download spreadsheet formats. **Thomson Reuters Corporation** (**ThomsonReuters.com**) provides a wealth of information to its database subscribers, including the widely quoted *First Call* summary of analysts' earnings forecasts. S&P Global Ratings provides financial data for all publicly traded companies in its *Compustat* database. This database reports a plethora of individual data items for all publicly traded companies or for any specified subset of companies. These data are useful for performing statistical analysis and making comparisons across companies or within industries. Finally, **Capital IQ** (**CapitalIQ.com**), a division of Standard & Poor's, provides "as presented" financial data that conform to published financial statements, as well as additional statistical data and analysis.

LO6 Review 2-6

Use the SEC website (www.sec.gov/edgar/searchedgar/companysearch.html) to download **Microsoft**'s 2018 10-K, and answer the requirements.

Required
1. On what date did Microsoft file its 2018 10-K with the SEC? Compare this date with the company's fiscal year-end. Why do the two dates differ?
2. Item 1 of the 10-K lists the company's executive officers. What are the names of the CEO and CFO?
3. As of June 30, 2018, how many people worked for Microsoft, and where were they located?
4. Review the fiscal year highlights reported in the Overview (Part II, item 7). What specific products and services drive the company's 2018 revenue growth?
5. Who are the company's auditors?

Solution on p. 2-42.

Global Accounting

Both GAAP and IFRS use accrual accounting to prepare financial statements. Although there are vastly more similarities than differences, we highlight below a few of the more notable differences for financial statements.

Balance Sheet The most visible difference is that many IFRS-based balance sheets are presented in reverse order of liquidity. The least liquid asset, usually goodwill, is listed first, and the most liquid asset, cash, is last. The same inverse liquidity order applies to liabilities. There are also several detailed presentation and measurement differences that we explain in other modules. As one example, for GAAP-based balance sheets, bank overdrafts are often netted against cash balances. IFRS does not permit this netting on the balance sheet. However, the IFRS statement of cash flows *does* net the cash balance with any bank overdrafts and, thus, the cash balance on the statement of cash flows might not match the cash amount on the balance sheet.

Income Statement The most visible difference is that GAAP requires three years' of data on the income statement whereas IFRS requires only two. Another difference is that GAAP income statements classify expenses by *function* and must separately report cost of goods sold, whereas IFRS permits expense classification by *function* (cost of sales, selling and administrative, etc.) or by *type* (raw materials, labor, depreciation, etc.). This means, for example, there is no requirement to report a cost of sales figure under IFRS.

Guidance Answers

You Are the Securities Analyst
Pg. 2-14 Of special concern is the possibility that the new CEO is shifting costs to the current period in lieu of recording them in future periods. Evidence suggests such behavior occurs when a new management team takes control. The reasoning is that the new management can blame poor current period performance on prior management and, at the same time, rid the balance sheet (and the new management team) of costs that would normally be expensed in future periods.

You Are the Operations Manager
Pg. 2-15 The CFO desires a warranty cost estimate that corresponds to the sales generated from the new product. To arrive at such an estimate, you must estimate the expected number and types of deficiencies in your product and the costs to repair each deficiency per the warranty provisions. This is often a difficult task for product engineers because it forces them to focus on product failures and associated costs.

Questions

Q2-1. The balance sheet consists of assets, liabilities, and equity. Define each category, and provide two examples of accounts reported within each category.

Q2-2. Explain how we account for a cost that creates an immediate benefit versus a cost that creates a future benefit.

Q2-3. GAAP is based on the concept of accrual accounting. Define and describe accrual accounting.

Q2-4. Analysts attempt to identify transitory items in an income statement. Define transitory items. What is the purpose of identifying transitory items?

Q2-5. What is the statement of stockholders' equity? What useful information does it contain?

Q2-6. What is the statement of cash flows? What useful information does it contain?

Q2-7. Define and explain the concept of financial statement articulation. What insight comes from understanding articulation?

Q2-8. Describe the flow of costs for the purchase of a machine. At what point do such costs become expenses? Why is it necessary to record the expenses related to the machine in the same period as the revenues it produces?

Q2-9. What are the two essential characteristics of an asset?

Q2-10. What does the concept of liquidity refer to? Explain.

Q2-11. What does the term *current* denote when referring to assets?

Q2-12. Assets are recorded at historical costs even though current market values might, arguably, be more relevant to financial statement readers. Describe the reasoning behind historical cost usage.

Q2-13. Identify three intangible assets that are likely to be *excluded* from the balance sheet because they cannot be reliably measured.

Q2-14. Identify three intangible assets that are recorded on the balance sheet.

Q2-15. What are accrued liabilities? Provide an example.

Q2-16. Define net working capital. Explain how increasing the amount of trade credit can reduce the net working capital for a company.

Q2-17. What is the difference between company *book value* and *market value*? Explain why these two amounts differ.

Q2-18. Describe the linkage between the income statement and the equity section of the balance sheet. Describe the linkage between the statement of cash flows and the equity section of the balance sheet when a company pays dividends.

Mini Exercises

M2-19. Identify and Classify Financial Statement Items   LO1, 2

For each of the following items, indicate whether they would be reported in the balance sheet (B) or income statement (I).

___ a. Net income   ___ d. Accumulated depreciation   ___ g. Interest expense
___ b. Retained earnings   ___ e. Wages expense   ___ h. Interest payable
___ c. Depreciation expense   ___ f. Wages payable   ___ i. Sales

M2-20. Identify and Classify Financial Statement Items   LO1, 2

For each of the following items, indicate whether they would be reported in the balance sheet (B) or income statement (I).

___ a. Machinery   ___ e. Common stock   ___ i. Taxes expense
___ b. Supplies expense   ___ f. Factory buildings   ___ j. Cost of goods sold
___ c. Inventories   ___ g. Receivables   ___ k. Long-term debt
___ d. Sales   ___ h. Taxes payable   ___ l. Treasury stock

M2-21. Collect and Use Information from Form 8-K   LO6   Kraft Heinz (KHC)

On February 28, 2019, **Kraft Heinz** filed a Form 8-K Current Report with the SEC. What important announcement did Kraft make that day? *Hint:* Use the SEC website (www.sec.gov/edgar/searchedgar/companysearch.html) to find the Form 8-K.

M2-22. Assign Accounts to Sections of the Balance Sheet   LO1

Identify each of the following accounts as a component of assets (A), liabilities (L), or equity (E).

___ a. Cash and cash equivalents   ___ e. Long-term debt
___ b. Wages payable   ___ f. Retained earnings
___ c. Common stock   ___ g. Additional paid-in capital
___ d. Equipment   ___ h. Taxes payable

M2-23. Determine Missing Information Using the Accounting Equation   LO3

Use knowledge of accounting relations to complete the following table for Boatsman Company.

	2020	2019
Beginning retained earnings	$189,089	$?
Net income (loss)	?	48,192
Dividends	0	15,060
Ending retained earnings	169,634	?

M2-24. Reconcile Retained Earnings   LO3   Johnson & Johnson (JNJ)

Following is financial information from **Johnson & Johnson** for the year ended December 30, 2018. Prepare the retained earnings reconciliation for Johnson & Johnson for the year ended December 30, 2018 ($ millions).

Retained earnings, Dec. 31, 2017	$101,793	Dividends	$9,494
Net earnings	15,297	Retained earnings, Dec. 30, 2018	?
Other retained earnings changes	(1,380)		

Exercises

LO6
Credit Suisse Group (CS)

E2-25. Use Information from Form 20-F

Stock of **Credit Suisse Group** trades on the New York Stock Exchange as well as in various European stock markets. The company's Form 20-F reported the following.

> The accompanying consolidated financial statements of Credit Suisse Group AG (the Group) are prepared in accordance with accounting principles generally accepted in the US (US GAAP) and are stated in Swiss francs (CHF). The financial year for the Group ends on December 31.
>
> A major focus of US policy and regulation relating to financial institutions has been to combat money laundering and terrorist financing. These laws and regulations impose obligations to maintain appropriate policies, procedures and controls to detect, prevent and report money laundering and terrorist financing, verify the identity of customers and comply with economic sanctions. Any failure to maintain and implement adequate programs to combat money laundering and terrorist financing, and violations of such economic sanctions, laws and regulations, could have serious legal and reputational consequences. We take our obligations to prevent money laundering and terrorist financing in the US and globally very seriously, while appropriately respecting and protecting the confidentiality of clients. We have policies, procedures and training intended to ensure that our employees comply with "know your customer" regulations and understand when a client relationship or business should be evaluated as higher risk for us.

Required

a. Why would Credit Suisse prepare its financial statements in accordance with U.S. GAAP?
b. Credit Suisse discusses various criminal activities and explains its anti-corruption policies. Why might this be the case?

LO1, 6
H&R Block (HRB)

E2-26. Use Information from Form 20-F

H&R Block reports the following information in Schedule II of its 2018 Form 10-K. Accounts receivable represents the amount customers owe the company at year-end. The balance in the allowance for doubtful accounts is the company's best estimate of the amount customers will not repay.

VALUATION AND QUALIFYING ACCOUNTS				
For Year Ended April 30 ($ millions)	Balance at Beginning of Period	Additions Charged to Costs and Expenses	Deductions	Balance at End of Period
Allowance for doubtful accounts, April 30, 2016...	$54,527	$73,682	$(71,198)	$57,011
Allowance for doubtful accounts, April 30, 2017...	57,011	52,776	(54,491)	55,296
Allowance for doubtful accounts, April 30, 2018...	55,296	74,489	(47,972)	81,813

Required

The balance in the allowance account increased during 2018 (from $55,296 million to $81,813 million) after decreasing during 2017 (from $57,011 million to $55,296 million). What additional information would an analyst want to use to determine if this variability is of concern?

LO1, 2

E2-27. Construct Financial Statements from Account Data

Barth Company reports the following year-end account balances at December 31, 2019. Prepare the 2019 income statement and the balance sheet as of December 31, 2019.

Accounts payable	$ 16,000	Inventory	$ 36,000
Accounts receivable	30,000	Land	80,000
Bonds payable, long-term	200,000	Goodwill	8,000
Buildings	151,000	Retained earnings	160,000
Cash	148,000	Sales revenue	500,000
Common stock	150,000	Supplies inventory	3,000
Cost of goods sold	180,000	Supplies expense	6,000
Equipment	70,000	Wages expense	40,000

E2-28. Construct Financial Statements from Transaction Data   **LO1, 2**

Baiman Corporation commences operations at the beginning of January. It provides its services on credit and bills its customers $40,000 for January sales, which are unpaid at month-end. Its employees also earn January wages of $12,000 that are not paid until the first of February. Complete the following statements for the month-end of January.

Income Statement	
Sales	$
Wages expense	
Net income (loss)	$

Balance Sheet	
Cash	$
Accounts receivable	
Total assets	$
Wages payable	$
Retained earnings	
Total liabilities and equity	$

E2-29. Apply Financial Statement Linkages to Understand Transactions   **LO1, 2, 3, 4, 5**

Consider the effects of the independent transactions, *a* through *g*, on a company's balance sheet, income statement, and statement of cash flows. Complete the table below to explain the effects and financial statement linkages. Use "+" to indicate the account increases and "−" to indicate the account decreases. Refer to Exhibit 2.10 as a guide for the linkages.

	a.	b.	c.	d.	e.	f.	g.
Balance Sheet							
Cash							
Noncash assets							
Total liabilities							
Contributed capital							
Retained earnings							
Other equity							
Statement of Cash Flows							
Operating cash flow							
Investing cash flow							
Financing cash flow							
Income Statement							
Revenues							
Expenses							
Net income							
Statement of Stockholders' Equity							
Contributed capital							
Retained earnings							

    a. The company issued common stock in exchange for cash and property and equipment.
    b. The company paid cash for rent of office furnishings and facilities.
    c. The company performed services for clients and immediately received cash earned.
    d. The company performed services for clients and sent a bill with payment due within 60 days.

e. The company compensated an office employee with cash as salary.
f. The company received cash as partial payment on the amount owed from clients in transaction *d*.
g. The company paid cash in dividends.

LO1, 2, 3, 4, 5 **E2-30. Apply Financial Statement Linkages to Understand Transactions**

Consider the effects of the independent transactions, *a* through *g*, on a company's balance sheet, income statement, and statement of cash flow. Complete the table below to explain the effects and financial statement linkages. Use "+" to indicate the account increases and "−" to indicate the account decreases. Refer to Exhibit 2-10 as a guide for the linkages.

	a.	b.	c.	d.	e.	f.	g.
Balance Sheet							
Cash....................	___	___	___	___	___	___	___
Noncash assets	___	___	___	___	___	___	___
Total liabilities	___	___	___	___	___	___	___
Contributed capital	___	___	___	___	___	___	___
Retained earnings	___	___	___	___	___	___	___
Other equity	___	___	___	___	___	___	___
Statement of Cash Flows							
Operating cash flow	___	___	___	___	___	___	___
Investing cash flow.....	___	___	___	___	___	___	___
Financing cash flow	___	___	___	___	___	___	___
Income Statement							
Revenues.............	___	___	___	___	___	___	___
Expenses.............	___	___	___	___	___	___	___
Net income...........	___	___	___	___	___	___	___
Statement of Stockholders' Equity							
Contributed capital	___	___	___	___	___	___	___
Retained earnings	___	___	___	___	___	___	___

a. Owners invested cash in the company in exchange for shares of common stock.
b. The company received cash from the bank for a loan.
c. The company purchased equipment to manufacture goods for sale and paid with cash.
d. The company manufactured a custom piece of inventory and paid cash for materials and labor. The company sold the inventory for more than cost, and the customer promised to pay for the inventory in 30 days.
e. The company paid monthly rent for a manufacturing space.
f. The company paid cash dividends to the owners.
g. The company received cash from the customer in transaction *d*.

LO1, 2 **E2-31. Identify and Classify Balance Sheet and Income Statement Accounts**

Best Buy, Inc. (BBY)

Following are selected accounts for **Best Buy Inc.** for the fiscal year ended February 2, 2019.

a. Indicate whether each account appears on the balance sheet (B) or income statement (I).
b. Using the following data, compute total assets and total expenses.

$ millions	Amount	Classification
Sales....................................	$42,879	___
Accumulated depreciation	6,690	___
Depreciation expense.....................	770	___
Retained earnings	2,985	___
Net income..............................	1,464	___
Property, plant, and equipment, net	2,510	___
Selling, general, and administrative expense...	8,015	___
Accounts receivable......................	1,015	___
Total liabilities	9,595	___
Total stockholders' equity	3,306	___

E2-32. Identify and Classify Balance Sheet and Income Statement Accounts

Following are selected accounts for **Terex Corp** for the fiscal year ended December 31, 2018.

a. Indicate whether each account appears on the balance sheet (B) or income statement (I).
b. Using the following data, compute total assets and total expenses.

$ millions	Amount	Classification
Total revenues	$5,125.0	____
Accrued compensation and benefits	152.2	____
Depreciation and amortization expense	59.7	____
Retained earnings	749.0	____
Net income	113.7	____
Property, plant, and equipment, net	345.6	____
Selling, general, and administrative expense	673.5	____
Inventory	1,212.0	____
Total liabilities	2,624.9	____
Total stockholders' equity	861.0	____

LO1, 2
Terex Corp (TEX)

E2-33. Compare Income Statements and Balance Sheets of Competitors

Following are selected income statement and balance sheet data from two retailers, **Abercrombie & Fitch** (clothing retailer in the high-end market) and **TJX Companies** (clothing retailer in the value-priced market), for the fiscal year ended February 2, 2019.

Income Statement ($ thousands)	ANF	TJX
Sales	$3,590,109	$38,972,934
Cost of goods sold	1,430,193	27,831,177
Gross profit	2,159,916	11,141,757
Total expenses	2,081,108	8,081,959
Net income	$ 78,808	$ 3,059,798

Balance Sheet ($ thousands)	ANF	TJX
Current assets	$1,335,950	$ 8,469,222
Long-term assets	1,049,643	5,856,807
Total assets	$2,385,593	$14,326,029
Current liabilities	$ 558,917	$ 5,531,374
Long-term liabilities	608,055	3,746,049
Total liabilities	1,166,972	9,277,423
Stockholders' equity	1,218,621	5,048,606
Total liabilities and equity	$2,385,593	$14,326,029

LO1, 2
Abercrombie & Fitch (ANF)
TJX Companies (TJX)

a. Express each income statement amount as a percentage of sales. Comment on any differences observed between these two companies, especially as they relate to their respective business models.
b. Express each balance sheet amount as a percentage of total assets. Comment on any differences observed between these two companies, especially as they relate to their respective business models.
c. Which company has a lower proportion of debt? What do the ratios tell us about the relative riskiness of the two companies?

E2-34. Compare Income Statements and Balance Sheets of Competitors

Following are selected income statement and balance sheet data from two pharmaceutical companies, **Pfizer** and **Dr. Reddy's**, for their respective 2018 fiscal years.

LO1, 2
Pfizer, Inc (PFE)
Dr. Reddy's Laboratories (RDY)

Income Statement ($ millions)	Pfizer	Dr. Reddy's
Sales	$53,647	$2,181
Cost of goods sold	11,248	1,009
Gross profit	42,399	1,172
Total expenses	31,211	1,021
Net income	$11,188	$ 151

Balance Sheet ($ millions)	Pfizer	Dr. Reddy's
Current assets	$ 49,926	$1,684
Long-term assets	109,496	1,781
Total assets	$159,422	3,465
Current liabilities	$ 31,858	$1,070
Long-term liabilities	63,806	453
Total liabilities	95,664	1,523
Stockholders' equity	63,758	1,942
Total liabilities and equity	$159,422	$3,465

a. Express each income statement amount as a percentage of sales. Comment on any differences observed between the two companies, especially as they relate to their respective business models. (*Hint:* Pfizer's gross profit as a percentage of sales is considerably higher than Dr. Reddy's. What aspect of Pfizer's business do we believe is driving its profitability?)

b. Express each balance sheet amount as a percentage of total assets. Comment on any differences observed between the two companies. Pfizer has chosen to structure itself with a lower proportion of equity (and a higher proportion of debt) than Dr. Reddy's. How does this capital structure decision affect our evaluation of the relative riskiness of these two companies?

LO1, 2
Comcast (CMCSA)
Verizon (VZ)

E2-35. Compare Income Statements and Balance Sheets of Competitors

Following are selected income statement and balance sheet data for two communications companies, **Comcast** and **Verizon**, for the year ended December 31, 2018.

Income Statement ($ millions)	Comcast	Verizon
Sales	$94,507	$130,863
Operating costs	75,498	108,585
Operating profit	19,009	22,278
Nonoperating expenses	7,147	6,239
Net income	$11,862	$ 16,039

Balance Sheet ($ millions)	Comcast	Verizon
Current assets	$ 21,848	$ 34,636
Long-term assets	229,836	230,193
Total assets	$251,684	$264,829
Current liabilities	$ 27,603	$ 37,930
Long-term liabilities	151,579	172,189
Total liabilities	$179,182	210,119
Stockholders' equity*	72,502	54,710
Total liabilities and equity	$251,684	$264,829

*Includes noncontrolling interest

a. Express each income statement amount as a percentage of sales. Comment on any differences observed between the two companies.

b. Express each balance sheet amount as a percentage of total assets. Comment on any differences observed between the two companies, especially as they relate to their respective business models.

c. Both Verizon and Comcast have chosen a capital structure with a higher proportion of liabilities than equity. How does this capital structure decision affect our evaluation of the riskiness of these two companies? Take into consideration the large level of capital expenditures that each must make to remain competitive.

E2-36. Compare Financial Information Across Industries
Use the data and computations required in parts *a* and *b* of exercises E2-33 and E2-34 to compare TJX Companies and Pfizer, Inc.

LO1, 2
TJX Companies (TJX)
Pfizer, Inc. (PFE)

a. Compare gross profit and net income as a percentage of sales for these two companies. How might differences in their respective business models explain the differences observed?
b. Compare sales versus total assets. What do observed differences indicate about the relative capital intensity of these two industries?
c. Which company has the higher percentage of total liabilities to stockholders' equity? What do these ratios imply about the relative riskiness of these two companies?

E2-37. Apply Financial Statement Linkages to Understand Transactions
Consider the effects of the independent transactions, *a* through *h*, on a company's balance sheet, income statement, and statement of cash flow. Complete the table below to explain the effects and financial statement linkages. Use "+" to indicate the account increases and "−" to indicate the account decreases. Refer to Exhibit 2-10 as a guide for the linkages.

LO1, 2, 3, 4, 5

	a.	b.	c.	d.	e.	f.	g.	h.
Balance Sheet								
Cash								
Noncash assets								
Total liabilities								
Contributed capital								
Retained earnings								
Other equity								
Statement of Cash Flows								
Operating cash flow								
Investing cash flow								
Financing cash flow								
Income Statement								
Revenues								
Expenses								
Net income								
Statement of Stockholders' Equity								
Contributed capital								
Retained earnings								

a. Wages are earned by employees but not yet paid.
b. Inventory is purchased on credit.
c. Inventory purchased in transaction *b* is sold on credit (and for more than its cost).
d. Collected cash from transaction *c*.
e. Equipment is acquired for cash.
f. Paid cash for inventory purchased in transaction *b*.
g. Paid cash toward a note payable that came due.
h. Paid cash for interest on borrowings.

Problems

P2-38. Construct and Analyze Balance Sheet Amounts from Incomplete Data
Selected balance sheet amounts for 3M Company, a manufacturer of consumer and business products, for three recent years follow.

LO1
3M Company (MMM)

$ millions	Current Assets	Long-Term Assets	Total Assets	Current Liabilities	Long-Term Liabilities	Total Liabilities	Stockholders' Equity*
2018	$13,709	$?	$36,500	$?	$19,408	$26,652	$ 9,848
2017	14,277	23,710	?	7,687	18,678	?	11,622
2016	?	21,180	32,906	6,219	16,344	22,563	?

* Includes noncontrolling interest

Required

a. Compute the missing balance sheet amounts for each of the three years shown.
b. Which of the following would not be included among 3M's current assets? Select all that apply.

    1. Cash and cash equivalents   4. Accounts payable   7. Accrued expenses
    2. Property plant & equipment   5. Marketable securities   8. Prepaid expenses
    3. Inventory   6. Goodwill

c. Which of the following would be included among 3M's long-term assets? Select all that apply.

    1. Property plant & equipment   4. Work in process   7. Prepaid expenses
    2. Accounts payable   5. Goodwill   8. Long-term notes payable
    3. Intangible assets   6. Accrued expenses

LO1, 2, 5, 6
Community Health Systems (CYH)

P2-39. Use Additional Information from 10-K to Explain Linkages Among Financial Statements
Community Health Systems operates general acute care hospitals in communities across the United States. The company reports the following information in Schedule II of its 2017 10-K.

SCHEDULE II—VALUATION AND QUALIFYING ACCOUNTS

$ millions	Balance at Beginning of Year	Acquisitions and Dispositions	Bad Debt Expense	Write-Offs	Balance at End of Year
December 31, 2017, allowance for doubtful accounts	$3,773	$ (21)	$3,054	$(2,936)	$3,870
December 31, 2016, allowance for doubtful accounts	4,110	(365)	2,849	(2,821)	3,773
December 31, 2015, allowance for doubtful accounts	3,504	(17)	3,168	(2,545)	4,110

Accounts receivable represents the amount customers owe Community Health Systems for services rendered. The balance in the allowance for doubtful accounts is the company's best estimate of the amount that customers will not repay.

Community Health Systems' balance sheet and income statements reported the following.

$ millions	2017	2016	2015
Revenue	$18,398	$21,275	$22,564
Operating income (loss) before tax	(1,878)	(860)	1,337
Total assets	17,450	21,944	26,861

Required

a. Compute the common-size allowance for doubtful accounts for each year. Compare 2017 to the prior years; what do we observe? What is one conclusion analysts might draw from this analysis?
b. On average, the firms in the S&P 500 report common-size allowance for doubtful accounts between 3% and 5%. Why might Community Health Systems' ratio be so much higher? How could an analyst verify this inference?
c. Compute the common-size bad debt expense for each year. Interpret the ratio for 2017. What trend do we observe?
d. If the company had recorded bad debt expense of $2,554 in 2017 (which is $500 less than actually recorded), which of the following would be true? (Ignore taxes for this question.)
    1. The company would have reported operating loss of $1,378 and cash flow would have been $500 higher.
    2. The company would have reported operating loss of $2,378 and cash flow would have been $500 higher.
    3. The company would have reported operating loss of $1,378 and cash flow would have been unchanged.

4. The company would have reported operating loss of $1,878 and cash flow would have been unchanged.

P2-40. Collect and Use Additional Information from 10-K
Use the SEC website (www.sec.gov/edgar/searchedgar/companysearch.html) to download the 2018 10-K for **Facebook Inc.** and answer the following questions.

LO6
Facebook (FB)

a. On what date did Facebook file its 2018 10-K with the SEC? Compare this date to the company's fiscal year-end. Why do the two dates differ?
b. Item 1 of the 10-K reports the company's mission. What is its mission?
c. Who does Facebook see as its main competition? See Item 1 of the 10-K.
d. As of December 31, 2018, how many people worked for Facebook?
e. How many daily active users did Facebook have in December 2018? How does this compare with December 2017?
f. Many companies file Schedule II with the 10-K. One of the components of Schedule II is an estimate of the amount owing from customers that will not be collected (allowance for doubtful accounts). What does Facebook report concerning this schedule? Explain.
g. Who are the company's auditors?

P2-41. Compare Operating Characteristics Across Industries
Following are selected income statement and balance sheet data for companies in different industries.

LO1, 2

$ millions	Sales	Cost of Goods Sold	Net Income	Assets	Liabilities	Stockholders' Equity
Target Corp.	$75,356	$53,299	$ 2,937	$ 41,290	$29,993	$11,297
Nike Inc.	36,397	20,441	1,933	22,536	12,724	9,812
Harley-Davidson	5,717	3,352	531	10,666	8,892	1,774
Pfizer	53,647	11,248	11,188	159,422	95,664	63,758

Target Corp. (TGT)
Nike (NKE)
Harley-Davidson (HOG)
Pfizer (PFE)

Required
a. Compute the following ratios for each company.
   1. Gross profit/Sales
   2. Net income/Sales
   3. Net income/Stockholders' equity
   4. Liabilities/Stockholders' equity
b. Comment on any differences among the companies' gross profit-to-sales ratios and net income as a percentage of sales. Do differences in the companies' business models explain the differences observed?
c. Which company reports the highest ratio of net income to equity? Suggest one or more reasons for this result.
d. Which company has financed itself with the highest percentage of liabilities to equity? Suggest one or more reasons why this company can take on such debt levels.

P2-42. Compare Cash Flows Across Retailers
Following are selected accounts from the income statement and the statement of cash flows for several retailers, for their fiscal years ended in 2018.

LO2, 4

$ millions	Sales	Net Income	Cash Flows from Operating	Investing	Financing
Macy's	$ 25,739	$ 1,108	$ 1,735	$ (456)	$ (1,544)
Home Depot Inc.	108,203	11,121	13,038	(2,416)	(12,420)
Best Buy	42,879	1,464	2,408	508	(2,018)
Target Corp.	75,356	2,937	5,973	(3,416)	(3,644)
Walmart Stores	511,729	6,670	27,753	(24,036)	(2,537)

Macy's (M)
Home Depot (HD)
Best Buy (BBY)
Target (TGT)
Walmart (WMT)

Required
a. Compute the ratio of net income to sales for each company. Rank the companies on the basis of this ratio. Do their respective business models give insight into these differences?

b. Compute net cash flows from operating activities as a percentage of sales. Rank the companies on the basis of this ratio. Does this ranking coincide with the ratio rankings from part *a*? Suggest one or more reasons for any differences observed.

c. Compute net cash flows from investing activities as a percentage of sales. Rank the companies on the basis of this ratio. Does this ranking coincide with the ratio rankings from part *a*? Suggest one or more reasons for any differences observed.

LO6 P2-43 Interpret Data Visualization to Interpret Balance Sheet Data

Access the Power BI dashboard on **MyBusinessCourse** to use the data visualization for Apple's balance sheet and cash flow data.

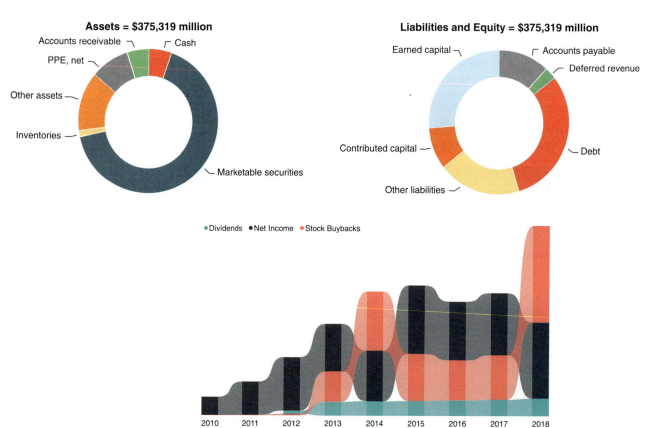

Required

a. Using this visualization, what is the largest asset? The smallest? What is the largest liability? Of the two equity components, which is smaller?

b. Compare this visualization of Apple's balance sheet (for 2017) with the Apple graphics on page 2-1 (for 2018).
   1. What do we observe about the relative size of Apple's balance sheet? How did the asset composition change across these years?
   2. Compare the liability and equity side of the balance sheet. How did the composition change during the year?

c. Consider the ribbon graph that depicts net income, dividends, and stock buybacks. In which year did Apple initiate dividends? What pattern do we observe with respect to dividends?

d. Compare net income and stock buybacks in the ribbon graph. What do we observe? What distinguishes 2014 and 2018 compared to all other years in this graphic?

e. From the ribbon graph, what can we conclude about the change in retained earnings between 2017 and 2018?

IFRS Applications

I2-44. Compare Income Statements and Balance Sheets of Competitors — **LO1, 2**

Following are selected income statement and balance sheet data from two European grocery chain companies: **Tesco PLC** (UK) and **Ahold** (the Netherlands).

Income Statements For Fiscal Year Ended	Tesco February 24, 2019 (£ millions)	Carrefour Group December 31, 2018 (€ millions)
Sales	£63,911	€77,917
Cost of goods sold	59,767	60,850
Gross profit	4,144	17,067
Total expenses	2,824	17,411
Net income	£ 1,320	€ (344)

Balance Sheet	Tesco February 24, 2019 (£ millions)	Carrefour Group December 31, 2018 (€ millions)
Current assets	£12,668	€18,670
Long-term assets	36,379	28,708
Total assets	£49,047	€47,378
Current liabilities	£20,680	€23,162
Long-term liabilities	13,533	12,930
Total liabilities	34,213	36,092
Stockholders' equity	14,834	11,286
Total liabilities and equity	£49,047	€47,378

Required

a. Prepare a common-size income statement. To do this, express each income statement amount as a percent of sales. Comment on any differences observed between the two companies.
b. Prepare a common-size balance sheet. To do this, express each balance sheet amount as a percent of total assets. Comment on any differences observed between the two companies.
c. Which company has chosen to structure itself with a higher proportion of equity (and a lower proportion of debt)? How does this capital structure decision affect our assessment of the relative riskiness of these two companies?

Management Applications

MA2-45. Explain the Company Operating Cycle and Management Strategy — **LO1, 4**

Consider the operating cycle as depicted in Exhibit 2.4 to answer the following questions.

a. Why might a company want to reduce its cash conversion cycle? (*Hint*: Consider the financial statement implications of reducing the cash conversion cycle.)
b. How might a company reduce its cash conversion cycle?
c. Examine and discuss the potential impacts on *customers* and *suppliers* of taking the actions identified in part *b*.

MA2-46. Ethics and Governance: Understand Revenue Recognition and Expense Recording — **LO2**

Revenue should be recognized when the performance obligation is satisfied and expense when incurred. Given some lack of specificity in these terms, companies have some latitude when applying GAAP to determine the timing and amount of revenues and expenses. A few companies use this latitude to manage reported earnings. Some have argued that it is not necessarily bad for companies to manage earnings in that, by doing so, management (1) can better provide investors and creditors with reported earnings that are closer to "core" earnings (i.e., management purges earnings of components deemed irrelevant or distracting so that share prices better reflect company performance) and (2) can present the company in the best light, which benefits both shareholders and employees—a Machiavellian argument that "the end justifies the means."

a. Is it good that GAAP is written as broadly as it is? Explain. What are the pros and cons of defining accounting terms more strictly?

b. Assess (both pro and con) the Machiavellian argument above that defends managing earnings.

Ongoing Project

(This ongoing project began in Module 1 and continues through most of the book; even if previous segments were not completed, the requirements are still applicable to any business analysis.) The goal of this module's project is to perform vertical analysis of the balance sheet and income statement, assess cash flows, and determine market capitalization.

1. *Balance Sheet Analysis.* Prepare a common-size balance sheet. To facilitate this, obtain the balance sheet in spreadsheet form from the SEC website at the the "Interactive Data" link on the search results page. Look for major differences over time. Some questions to consider:
   - What are the company's largest assets? Largest liabilities?
   - What proportion of total assets is financed by owners? (*Hint:* Compare with total equity.)
   - What proportion of total assets is financed by nonowners?

2. *Income Statement Analysis.* Prepare a common-size income statement. Express each item on the income statement as a percent of total sales or revenue. Do this for all years on the income statement. Look for major differences over time and between the companies. Do any patterns emerge? Some questions to consider:
   - What are the major expenses?
   - Are there any unusual or discontinued items? Are they large in magnitude?
   - Was the company more or less profitable when compared with the prior year?

3. *Statement of Cash Flows Analysis.* Determine the size and direction (cash source or use) of cash flows from operations, investing, and financing. One goal is to understand the company's pattern of cash flows and to form an opinion about the general strength of its cash flows. Some questions to consider:
   - What were the cash flows from operations? Were they positive?
   - Were operating cash flows smaller or larger than net income?
   - Did the company generate or use cash from investing activities?
   - Did the company generate or use cash from financing activities?

4. *Market Capitalization.* Determine the market capitalization at the most recent year-end. Determine the number of shares outstanding from the balance sheet. Recall that shares outstanding is total shares issued less any treasury shares. Obtain the year-end stock price from an investment website such as Seeking Alpha or Yahoo Finance. Compare market cap with the book value (total equity) of the company.

Solutions to Review Problems

Review 2-1—Solution ($ millions)

MICROSOFT CORPORATION
Balance Sheet
June 30, 2018

Cash and short-term investments	$133,768	Accounts payable	$ 8,617
Accounts receivable	26,481	Accrued expenses	6,103
Inventories	2,662	Other current liabilities	43,768
Other current assets	6,751	Total current liabilities	58,488
Total current assets	169,662	Long-term liabilities	117,642
Property, plant, and equipment, net	29,460	Total liabilities	176,130
Other long-term assets	59,726		
		Common stock and paid-in capital	71,223
		Retained earnings	13,682
		Other stockholders' equity	(2,187)
		Total stockholders' equity	82,718
Total assets	$258,848	Total liabilities and equity	$258,848

Review 2-2—Solution ($ millions)

MICROSOFT CORPORATION
Income Statement
For Year Ended June 30, 2018

Total revenue	$110,360
Cost of goods sold	38,353
Gross profit	72,007
Operating expenses	36,949
Operating income	35,058
Other income	1,416
Income before income tax	36,474
Income tax expense	19,903
Net income	$ 16,571

Review 2-3—Solution ($ millions)

MICROSOFT CORPORATION
Statement of Stockholders' Equity
For Year Ended June 30, 2018

	Common Stock and Paid-in Capital	Retained Earnings	Accumulated Other Comprehensive Income (Loss)	Total Equity
Beginning bal., June 30, 2017	$69,315	$17,769	$ 627	$87,711
Stock issuance, net	1,908	(7,699)		(5,791)
Net income		16,571		16,571
Dividends		(12,917)		(12,917)
Other		(42)	(2,814)	(2,856)
Ending bal., June 30, 2018	$71,223	$13,682	$(2,187)	$82,718

Review 2-4—Solution ($ millions)

MICROSOFT CORPORATION
Statement of Cash Flows
For Year Ended June 30, 2018

Cash flows from operating activities	$43,884
Cash flows used for investing activities	(6,061)
Cash flows used for financing activities	(33,540)
Net change in cash	4,283
Cash balance, beginning of year	7,663
Cash balance, end of year	$11,946

Review 2-5—Solution

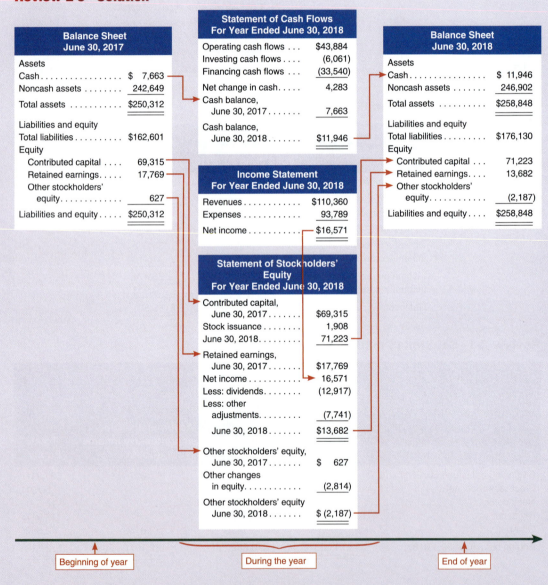

Review 2-6—Solution

1. The 10-K was filed on August 3, 2018, and the company's fiscal year-end was June 30, 2018. The SEC filing is a month after year-end because the auditors took a month to complete the audit.
2. The company's CEO is Satya Nadella, and the CFO is Amy E. Hood.
3. As of June 30, 2018, Microsoft employed approximately 131,000 people on a full-time basis, roughly 78,000 in the United States and 53,000 internationally.
4. The MD&A reports the growth in revenues is due to growth in "Productivity and Business Processes" and "Intelligent Cloud" segments and not from Personal Computing as we might have expected.
5. The company is audited by Deloitte and Touche out of the Seattle office.

Module 3
Transactions, Adjustments, and Financial Statements

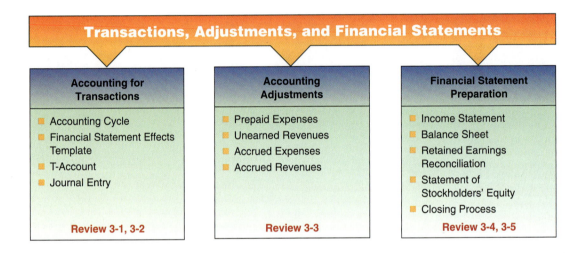

Transactions, Adjustments, and Financial Statements

Accounting for Transactions	Accounting Adjustments	Financial Statement Preparation
■ Accounting Cycle ■ Financial Statement Effects Template ■ T-Account ■ Journal Entry	■ Prepaid Expenses ■ Unearned Revenues ■ Accrued Expenses ■ Accrued Revenues	■ Income Statement ■ Balance Sheet ■ Retained Earnings Reconciliation ■ Statement of Stockholders' Equity ■ Closing Process
Review 3-1, 3-2	*Review 3-3*	*Review 3-4, 3-5*

PREVIEW — AAPL

- We describe how companies enter transactions into their financial records.
- We explain the adjustments companies make to their financial records after all transactions have been recorded and before the company issues financial statements.
- We show how financial statements are prepared from transactions and adjustments data.
- We describe how the books are closed at the end of each period to get ready for the next period.
- We use **Apple Inc.** as the focus company and the dashboard below conveys its revenue and expense information for 2018.

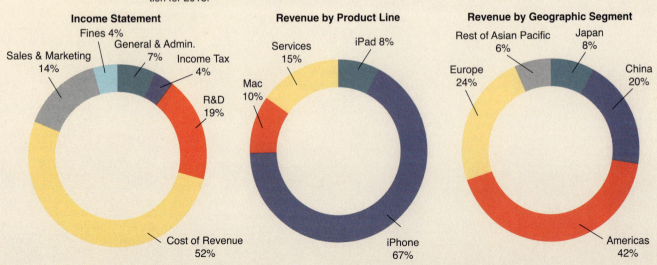

Income Statement: Sales & Marketing 14%, Fines 4%, General & Admin. 7%, Income Tax 4%, R&D 19%, Cost of Revenue 52%

Revenue by Product Line: Services 15%, iPad 8%, Mac 10%, iPhone 67%

Revenue by Geographic Segment: Rest of Asian Pacific 6%, Japan 8%, Europe 24%, China 20%, Americas 42%

Road Map

LO	Learning Objective | Topics	Page	eLecture	Guided Example	Assignments
3–1	**Explain the accounting cycle, and construct the financial statement effects template.** Accounting Cycle :: Template :: T-Account :: Journal Entry	3-3	e3–1	Review 3-1	1, 2, 3
3–2	**Apply the financial statement effects template to analyze accounting transactions.** Transactions :: Applying the Template :: Applying the T-Account and Journal Entry	3-6	e3–2	Review 3-2	7, 8, 12, 13, 14, 15, 16, 17, 20, 21, 24, 28, 36, 37, 39, 40, 42, 44, 47, 48, 49, 50, 56, 57, 58, 59, 60, 62, 63
3–3	**Prepare and explain accounting adjustments and their financial statement effects.** Prepaid Expenses :: Unearned Revenues :: Accrued Expenses :: Accrued Revenues	3-9	e3–3	Review 3-3	4, 5, 6, 7, 8, 9, 10, 16, 17, 18, 19, 26, 27, 29, 30, 31, 32, 33, 34, 35, 44, 45, 46, 47, 48, 49, 50, 51, 52, 53, 54, 55, 57, 58, 60, 62, 63, 64, 65
3–4	**Construct financial statements from accounting records.** Income Statement :: Retained Earnings Reconciliation :: Balance Sheet :: Statement of Equity	3-13	e3–4	Review 3-4	22, 26, 27, 41, 43, 55, 56, 58, 59, 60, 63
3–5	**Explain and apply the closing process.** Revenue Accounts :: Expense Accounts :: Dividend Account	3-16	e3–5	Review 3-5	11, 23, 25, 32, 38, 41, 55, 61

Basics of Accounting

LO1 Explain the accounting cycle, and construct the financial statement effects template.

Financial statements report on the financial performance and condition of a business. Those statements are tied to a period or point in time. The period of time is referred to as the accounting cycle, and each cycle consists of four activities.

Four-Step Accounting Cycle

The *accounting cycle* is illustrated in Exhibit 3.1.

- **Step 1** Record transactions in the accounting records. Each transaction is the result of an external or internal transaction or event, such as a sale to a customer or the payment of wages to employees.
- **Step 2** Prepare accounting adjustments, which recognize a number of events that have occurred but that have not yet been recorded. These might include the recognition of wage expense and the related wages payable for those employees who have earned wages but have not yet been paid or of depreciation expense for buildings and equipment.
- **Step 3** Prepare financial statements.
- **Step 4** Close the books in anticipation of the start of a new accounting cycle.

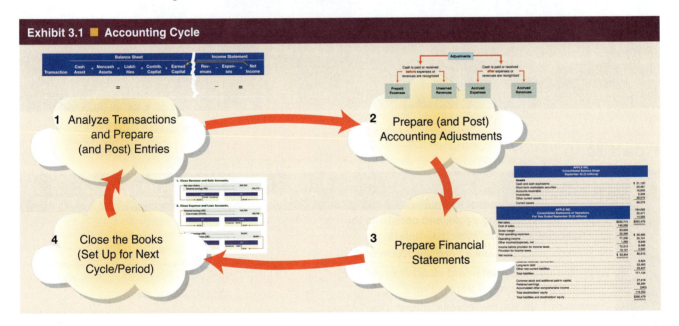

Exhibit 3.1 ■ Accounting Cycle

The purpose of this module is to explain the accounting cycle. We use Apple's financials to illustrate the four steps in the accounting cycle. Understanding the financial statement preparation process requires an understanding of the language used to record business transactions in accounting records. The recording and statement preparation processes are readily understood once we learn that language (of financial statement effects) and its mechanics (entries and posting). Even if we never post a transaction or prepare a financial statement, understanding the accounting process aids us in analyzing and interpreting accounting reports. Understanding the accounting language also facilitates our communication with business professionals within a company and with members of the business community outside of a company.

Financial Statement Effects Template

As of its 2018 year-end, Apple reports total assets of $365,725 million, total liabilities of $258,578 million, and equity of $107,147 million. The accounting equation for Apple follows ($ millions).

As financial statement users, we often draw on this relation to assess the effects of transactions and events, different accounting methods, and choices that managers make in preparing financial statements. For example, we are interested in knowing the effects of an asset acquisition or sale on the balance sheet, income statement, and statement of cash flows. Or, we might want to understand how the failure to recognize a liability would understate liabilities and overstate profits and equity. A useful tool to perform these sorts of analysis is the following **financial statement effects template**.

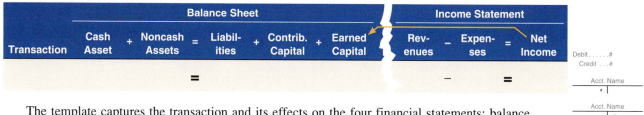

The template captures the transaction and its effects on the four financial statements: balance sheet, income statement, statement of stockholders' equity, and statement of cash flows. For the balance sheet, we differentiate between cash and noncash assets so as to identify the cash effects of transactions. Likewise, equity is separated into the contributed and earned capital components. Finally, income statement effects are separated into revenues, expenses, and net income (the updating of retained earnings is denoted with an arrow line running from net income to earned capital). This template provides a convenient means to represent relatively complex financial accounting transactions and events in a simple, concise manner for both analysis and interpretation.

In addition to using the template to show the dollar effects of a transaction on the four financial statements, we also include each transaction's *journal entry* and *T-account* representation in the margin. We explain journal entries and T-accounts in the next section; these are part of the bookkeeping aspects of accounting. The margin entries can be ignored without any loss of insight gained from the template.

T-accounts

The **T-account**, named for its likeness to a "T," is used to reflect increases and decreases to individual accounts. When a transaction occurs, it is recorded (*journalized*); once recorded, the specific accounts affected are updated in the accounting books (*general ledger*) of the company, and the affected accounts are increased or decreased. This process of continuously updating individual account balances is referred to as *posting* transactions to accounts. A T-account provides a simple illustration of the financial effects of each transaction.

Specifically, one side of the T-account is used for increases and the other for decreases. A convenient way to remember which side records increases is to recall the accounting equation: **Assets = Liabilities + Equity**. Assets are on the left side of the equation. So, the left side of an asset T-account records increases in the asset (referred to as the *normal balance* side), and the right side records decreases. Liabilities and equity are on the right side of the accounting equation. So, the right side of a liability and an equity T-account records increases (the *normal balance* side), and the left side records decreases. This relation is represented graphically as follows.

Journal Entries

Journal entries also capture the effects of transactions. Journal entries reflect increases and decreases to accounts using the language of debits and credits. Debits and credits simply refer to the left or right side of a T-account, respectively.

	Account Title	
Debit (Left side)	Credit (Right side)

The left side of the T-account is the debit side, and the right side is the credit side. This holds for all T-accounts. Thus, to record an increase in an asset, we enter an amount on the left, or debit, side of the T-account—that is, we *debit* the account. Decreases in assets are recorded with an entry on the opposite (credit) side. To record an increase in a liability or equity account, we enter an amount on the right, or credit, side of the T-account—we *credit* the account. Decreases in liability or equity accounts are recorded on the left (debit) side.

In the margin of our financial statement effects template, we show the journal entry first, followed by the related T-accounts. In accounting jargon, this sequence relates to *journalizing* the entry and *posting* it to the affected accounts. The T-accounts represent the financial impact of each transaction on the respective asset, liability, or equity accounts.

Review 3-1 LO1

The table below shows account names (in alphabetical order) from the balance sheet and income statement for **Apple Inc.**

Required
Indicate the column where each item best fits. The seven columns correspond to the seven account categories in the financial statement effects template.

Solution on p. 3-35.

	Cash Asset	Noncash Asset	Liabilities	Contributed Capital	Earned Capital	Revenues	Expenses
Accounts payable..................	___	___	___	___	___	___	___
Accounts receivable, less allowances.....	___	___	___	___	___	___	___
Accrued expenses................	___	___	___	___	___	___	___
Acquired intangible assets, net........	___	___	___	___	___	___	___
Cash and cash equivalents..........	___	___	___	___	___	___	___
Common stock and additional paid-in capital............	___	___	___	___	___	___	___
Cost of sales.....................	___	___	___	___	___	___	___
Current portion of long-term debt........	___	___	___	___	___	___	___
Deferred revenue..................	___	___	___	___	___	___	___
Deferred tax assets................	___	___	___	___	___	___	___
Goodwill.........................	___	___	___	___	___	___	___
Inventories.......................	___	___	___	___	___	___	___
Long-term debt....................	___	___	___	___	___	___	___
Long-term marketable securities........	___	___	___	___	___	___	___
Net sales........................	___	___	___	___	___	___	___
Other current assets................	___	___	___	___	___	___	___
Other noncurrent liabilities............	___	___	___	___	___	___	___
Property, plant, and equipment, net......	___	___	___	___	___	___	___
Provision for income taxes............	___	___	___	___	___	___	___
Research and development...........	___	___	___	___	___	___	___
Retained earnings.................	___	___	___	___	___	___	___
Selling, general, and administrative......	___	___	___	___	___	___	___

Accounting Cycle Step 1—Analyze Transactions and Prepare Entries

This section uses **Apple Inc.** to illustrate the accounting for selected business transactions. The assumed time frame is one fiscal year. We will begin with the account balances for Apple at the start of the 2018 fiscal year and illustrate the four steps in the accounting cycle. We construct its 2018 financial statements and close its books.

LO2 Apply the financial statement effects template to analyze accounting transactions.

Apple's Transactions

This section provides a comprehensive two-part illustration using the financial statement effects template with a number of transactions underlying Apple's 2018 financial statements.

- These summary transactions are described in the far left column of Exhibit 3.2, with their financial statement effects shown to the right-hand-side.
- Detailed explanations for each of the 16 fiscal year transactions are provided in Exhibit 3.3.

Applying the Financial Statement Effects Template

To illustrate Step 1 of the accounting cycle, we consider 16 transactions for Apple. Once details of each transaction are known to Apple's accounting department, entries are made in the company's accounting system. For our learning purposes, we use the financial statement effects template to record these transactions. (Adjusting entries 12 through 16 are described in the next section.)

In the first two rows of Exhibit 3.2, we present each of Apple's balance sheet accounts and related balances as of September 30, 2017. (The end of its 2017 fiscal year is the beginning of its 2018 fiscal year.) We have aggregated some accounts from the Apple balance sheet to keep the size of the financial statement effects template presentable.

Applying the Journal Entry and T-Account

Although we will not repeatedly refer to journal entries and T-accounts, we will describe them for the first transaction in Exhibit 3.2. Specifically, the $4,334 debit equals the $4,334 credit in the journal entry: assets ($4,334 cash) = liabilities ($0) + equity ($4,334 common stock). This balance in transactions is the basis of *double-entry accounting*. For simplicity, we use acronyms (such as CS for common stock) in journal entries and T-accounts. (A listing of accounts and acronyms is located in Appendix B near the end of the book.) The journal entry for this transaction is

Cash..................................	$4,334	
CS (common stock)		$4,334

Convention dictates that debits are listed first, followed by credits—the latter are indented.[1] The total debit(s) must always equal the total credit(s) for each transaction. The T-account representation for this transaction follows.

Cash is an asset; thus, a cash increase is recorded on the left or debit side of the T-account. Common stock (CS) is an equity account; thus, a common stock increase is recorded on the right or credit side.

---

[1] There can be more than one debit and one credit for a transaction. To illustrate, assume that Apple raises $300 cash, with $200 from investors and $100 borrowed from a bank. The resulting journal entry is

Cash............................	300	
CS (common stock)...........		200
NP (note payable)..........		100

Exhibit 3.2 ■ Financial Statement Effects Template for Apple ($ millions)

Transaction	Cash Asset	+	Noncash Assets	=	Liabilities	+	Contrib. Capital	+	Earned Capital*	Revenues	−	Expenses	=	Net Income
Balance, September 30, 2017	$20,289		$355,030		$241,272		$35,867		$98,180					
Step 1—Analyze Transactions, and Prepare Entries														
1. Issue common stock for $4,334 million cash	4,334						4,334 Common stock							
2. Purchase $162,857 million of inventories on account			162,857 Inventory		162,857 Accounts payable									
3. Sell inventories that cost $163,756 million for $265,551 million, on account			(163,756) Inventory 265,551 Accounts receivable						101,795 Retained earnings	$265,551 Sales		$163,756 Cost of sales		$101,795
4. Receive $260,239 million cash on account	260,239		(260,239) Accounts receivable											
5. Pay $151,211 million cash toward accounts payable	(151,211)				(151,211) Accounts payable									
6. Pay $13,137 million cash for operating expenses and $13,372 million cash for income taxes	(26,509)								(26,509) Retained earnings			13,137 Operating expenses 13,372 Income tax expenses		(26,509)
7. Pay cash to purchase current assets of $6,161 million, PPE of $16,821 million, and other long-term assets of $9,683 million	(32,665)		6,161 Current assets 16,821 PPE 9,683 Other long-term assets											
8. Sell for cash, $13,504 million short-term and $23,915 million long-term marketable securities at the amount reported on the balance sheet	37,419		(13,504) Short-term Marketable Securities (23,915) Long-term Marketable Securities											
9. Repay with cash, short-term debt of $13 million and long-term debt of $1,184 million	(1,197)				(13) Short-term debt (1,184) Long-term debt									
10. Pay $86,791 million cash for dividends and stock buybacks (Apple retired the shares)	(86,791)								(86,791) Retained earnings					
11. Receive $2,005 million cash for net investment income	2,005								2,005 Retained earnings			(2,005) Other income		2,005
Step 2—Prepare Accounting Adjustments														
12. Accrue operating expenses of $2,136 million (current liabilities) and $4,765 million (long-term liabilities)					2,136 Current accrued expenses 4,765 Long-term accrued expenses				(6,901) Retained earnings			6,901 Operating expenses		(6,901)
13. Record depreciation expense of $9,300 million			(9,300) PPE						(9,300) Retained earnings			9,300 Depreciation expense		(9,300)
14. Record amortization expense of $1,603 million on intangible assets			(1,603) Intangible assets						(1,603) Retained earnings			1,603 Amortization expense		(1,603)
15. Apple earns previously deferred revenue of $44 million					(44) Unearned Revenue				44 Retained earnings	44 Sales				44
16. Miscellaneous transactions			(3,974) Other long-term assets						(3,974) Other comprehensive loss					
Balance, September 29, 2018	$25,913		$339,812		$258,578		$40,201		$66,946	$265,595		$206,064		$59,531

* Earned capital includes retained earnings and accumulated other comprehensive loss, another earned capital account.

Exhibit 3.3 ■ Details of Transactions for Apple ($ millions)

Transaction	Description
1. Issue common stock for $4,334 million cash.	Cash, common stock, and additional paid-in capital all increase by the proceeds from issuance. (Apple combines common stock and additional paid-in capital on its balance sheet.) The sale of stock is not revenue. It is a financing transaction between the company and its owners (stockholders). Neither the sale or repurchase of stock, nor the payment of dividends to shareholders, affects revenue or expense. Transactions with stockholders never affect net income.
2. Purchase $162,857 million of inventories on account.	Inventories are often purchased *on account* (also called *on credit*), meaning that suppliers give the company a period of time in which to pay for the purchase. Inventory increases by the purchase price. Because the company has not yet paid for the purchase, accounts payable (a liability) also increases by the purchase price. Note that inventories are not recorded at their expected retail selling price.
3. Sell inventories that cost $163,756 million for $265,551 million on account.	The sale of inventory has two distinct parts: a) **Recognize revenue.** Revenue (net sales) can be recognized because ownership of inventory has transferred to the customer. Because the customer has not yet paid for the inventory, the amount owed to Apple is reported as an account receivable. To recognize revenue, Apple has to have performed its part of the sales contract (given possession of the inventory to the customer). The receipt of cash is not required to recognize revenue; an agreement to pay later is sufficient. b) **Record expense.** The cost of inventory is recognized as an expense at the time of sale. An asset remains on the balance sheet until it is used, at which time its cost is transferred to the income statement as an expense. Because Apple has now sold (used) the inventory, its cost is moved from the inventory account on the balance sheet to the income statement as an expense called cost of goods sold.
4. Receive $260,239 million cash on account.	Cash increases when customers settle their accounts and the accounts receivable balance decreases. Collection of a receivable is not revenue. Instead, revenue is recognized when earned, as in transaction 3.
5. Pay $151,211 million cash toward accounts payable.	Cash and accounts payable both decrease by the amount paid to suppliers to settle the account. Note that payment of a payable is not an expense. The expense was recognized when it was incurred, as in transaction 3.
6. Pay $13,137 million cash for operating expenses and $13,372 million cash for income taxes.	Operating expenses are costs incurred to earn revenue and do business. An example is salaries expense. Cash decreases when employees are paid and salaries expense is recorded in the income statement. Provision for income taxes (or tax expense) is also recognized in the income statement.
7. Pay cash to purchase current assets of $6,161 million, PPE of $16,821 million, and other long-term assets of $9,683 million.	Cash decreases and the company adds the purchase price to the balance sheet as assets. Purchasing assets does not generate an immediate expense because assets generate future economic benefits. But as the assets are consumed and the company realizes the intended benefits, the asset cost is transferred to the income statement as an expense. For example, the cost of PPE is transferred to the income statement as depreciation expense over the assets' useful lives.
8. Sell for cash, $13,504 million short-term and $23,915 million long-term marketable securities.	Apple invests its excess cash in marketable securities. This means cash decreases, and marketable securities accounts increase. The company plans to hold some of the investments for a year or less (short-term) and some for longer (long-term), depending on anticipated future cash needs. In the interim, the investments allow the company to earn interest, dividends, and any appreciation in value.
9. Repay with cash, short-term debt of $13 million and long-term debt of $1,184 million.	Cash decreases as Apple repays its short-term and long-term debt. As with the sale of stock, neither borrowing of money, nor its repayment, is recognized as revenue or expense. Only the interest related to the debt is an expense.
10. Pay $86,791 million cash for stock buybacks (Apple retired the shares) and dividends to stockholders.	Dividends reduce both cash and retained earnings. The payment of dividends is not an expense. It is a transaction with the company's owners (the stockholders), not with its customers, and no expense is recognized in the income statement. When Apple cancels the repurchased shares, it reduces retained earnings by the cost of the shares.
11. Receive $2,005 million cash for net investment income.	Cash increases, as does other income on the income statement. This income includes dividends, interest, and capital gains Apple earns on its short-term and long-term marketable securities. This is not classified as revenue because it is not earned from customers. We recorded other income as a negative expense, which lets us know it is an income item and not an expense.

LO2 Review 3-2

Prestige Inc. experienced the following 12 transactions during the month of January 2020.

1. Issue common stock for $3,000 cash.
2. Purchase inventory for $8,000 on credit.
3. Sell inventory costing $8,000 for $15,000 on credit.
4. Issue long-term debt for $10,000 cash.
5. Pay $15,000 cash for property, plant, and equipment (PPE).
6. Pay $500 cash for salaries.
7. Receive $300 cash in advance from client for future consulting services.

continued

continued from previous page

8. Pay $50 cash for interest on long-term debt.
9. Receive $3,000 cash from accounts receivable.
10. Pay $2,500 cash toward accounts payable.
11. Perform consulting services for client who previously paid in transaction 7.
12. Pay $100 cash for dividends.

Required

Record each transaction in the financial statement effects template. The beginning balances for each account are entered into the template. *Note:* The template includes rows for transactions 13 through 16, which are covered in Review 3-3, later in the module.

Solution on p. 3-36.

	Balance Sheet					Income Statement		
	Cash Assets +	Noncash Assets =	Liabil- ities +	Contrib. Capital +	Earned Capital	Rev- enues −	Expen- ses =	Net Income
Balance January 1, 2020	10,000	41,000	26,000	10,000	15,000	0	0	0
Transactions								
1. Issue common stock for $3,000 cash								
2. Purchase inventory for $8,000 on credit								
3. Sell inventory costing $8,000 for $15,000 on credit								
4. Issue long-term debt for $10,000 cash								
5. Pay $15,000 cash for PPE								
6. Pay $500 cash for salaries								
7. Receive $300 cash in advance for future consulting services								
8. Pay $50 cash for interest on long-term debt								
9. Receive $3,000 cash from accounts receivable								
10. Pay $2,500 cash toward accounts payable								
11. Perform consulting services for client who previously paid in 7								
12. Pay $100 cash for dividends								
Accounting Adjustments								
13. Record depreciation of $600								
14. Accrue salaries of $1,000								
15. Advertising costing $1,300 is aired								
16. Accrue income taxes of $1,200								
Balance January 31, 2020								

Accounting Cycle Step 2—Prepare Accounting Adjustments

LO3 Prepare and explain accounting adjustments and their financial statement effects.

Recognizing revenue when products and services are delivered at an amount expected to be received (even if not received in cash) *and* recording expenses when incurred (even if not paid in cash) are cornerstones of **accrual accounting**, which is required under GAAP. In addition, understanding accounting adjustments, commonly called *accruals*, is crucial to effectively analyzing and interpreting financial statements.

In this module's Apple illustration, we recorded inventory as a purchase even though no cash was paid, and we recognized the sale as revenue even though no cash was received. Both of these transactions reflect accrual accounting. Some accounting transactions affect the balance sheet alone (as with purchasing inventory on account in Exhibit 3.2, transaction 2). Other transactions affect the balance sheet *and* the income statement (as with selling inventory on account in Exhibit 3.2, transaction 3). Accounting transactions can affect asset, liability, or equity accounts and can either increase or decrease net income.

Companies record *adjustments* to more accurately report their financial performance and condition. For example, employees might not have been paid for wages earned at the end of an accounting period. Failure to recognize this labor cost would understate the company's total liabilities (because wages payable would be too low) and would overstate net income for the period (because wages expense would be too low). Thus, neither the balance sheet nor the income statement would be accurate without accounting adjustments.

Four Types of Accounting Adjustments Exhibit 3.4 identifies four general types of accounting adjustments, which are briefly described here.

- **Prepaid expenses** Prepaid expenses reflect advance cash payments that will ultimately become expenses. An example is the payment for radio advertising that will not be aired until sometime in the future.
- **Unearned revenues** Unearned revenues reflect cash received from customers before any services or goods are provided. An example is cash received from patrons for tickets to an upcoming concert.
- **Accrued expenses** Accrued expenses are expenses incurred and recognized on the income statement even though they are not yet paid in cash. An example is wages owed to employees who performed work but who have not yet been paid.
- **Accrued revenues** Accrued revenues are revenues earned and recognized on the income statement even though cash is not yet received. Examples include sales on credit and revenue earned under a long-term contract.

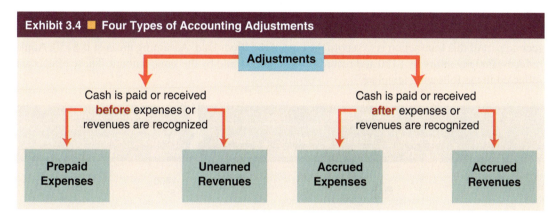

Exhibit 3.4 ■ Four Types of Accounting Adjustments

The remainder of this section illustrates how Apple's financial statements would reflect each of these four types of adjustments.

Prepaid Expenses

Assume Apple pays $200 to purchase time on MTV for iPod ads. Apple's cash account decreases by $200. Should the $200 advertising cost be recorded as an expense when Apple pays MTV, when MTV airs the ads, or at some other point? Under accrual accounting, Apple must record an expense when it is incurred. That means Apple should expense the cost of the ads when MTV airs them. When Apple pays for the advertisement, it records an asset; Apple "owns" air time that will presumably provide future benefits when the ads air. In the interim, the cost of the ads is an asset on the balance sheet. Apple's financial statement effects template follows for this transaction. There is a decrease in cash and an increase in the advertising asset, called prepaid advertising, when the ad time is paid for. At period-end, $50 of advertisements had aired. At that point, Apple must record an accounting adjustment to reduce the prepaid advertising account by $50 and transfer the cost to the income statement as advertising expense.

Transaction	Balance Sheet					Income Statement		
	Cash Asset	+ Noncash Assets	= Liabilities	+ Contrib. Capital	+ Earned Capital	Revenues	− Expenses	= Net Income
Pay $200 cash in advance for ad time	−200 Cash	+200 Prepaid Advertising	=				−	=
Record $50 cost of ad air time		−50 Prepaid Advertising	=		−50 Retained Earnings		− +50 Advertising Expense	= −50

PPDA . . . 200
Cash 200

PPDA
200 |
    | Cash
    | 200

AE 50
PPDA 50

AE
50 |

PPDA
    | 50

Unearned Revenues

Assume Apple receives $400 cash from a customer as advance payment on a multi-unit iPod sale to be delivered next month. Apple must record cash received on its balance sheet but cannot recognize revenue from the order until earned, which is generally when iPods are delivered to the customer. Until then, Apple must recognize a liability called unearned, or deferred, revenue that represents Apple's obligation to fulfill the order at some future point. The financial statement effects template for this transaction follows.

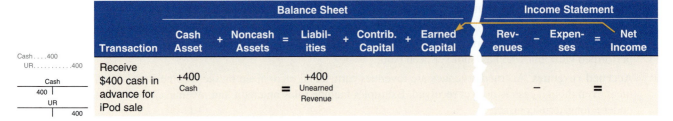

	Balance Sheet					Income Statement		
Transaction	Cash Asset	+ Noncash Assets	= Liabilities	+ Contrib. Capital	+ Earned Capital	Revenues	– Expenses	= Net Income
Receive $400 cash in advance for iPod sale	+400 Cash		= +400 Unearned Revenue				–	=

Assume Apple delivers the iPods a month later (but still within the fiscal quarter). Apple must recognize the $400 as revenue at delivery because it is now earned. Thus, net income increases by $400. The second part of this transaction is to record the cost of the iPods sold. Assuming the cost is $150, Apple reduces iPod inventory by $150 and records cost of goods sold by the same amount. These effects are reflected in the following template.

	Balance Sheet					Income Statement		
Transaction	Cash Asset	+ Noncash Assets	= Liabilities	+ Contrib. Capital	+ Earned Capital	Revenues	– Expenses	= Net Income
Deliver $400 of iPods paid in advance			= –400 Unearned Revenues		+400 Retained Earnings	+400 Sales	–	= +400
Record $150 cost of $400 iPod sale		–150 Inventory	=		–150 Retained Earnings		– +150 Cost of Goods Sold	= –150

Accrued Expenses

Assume Apple's sales staff earns $100 of sales commissions this period that will not be paid until next period. The sales staff earned the wages as they made the sales. However, because Apple pays its employees twice a month, the related cash payment will not occur until the next pay period. Should Apple record the wages earned by its employees as an expense even though payment has not yet been made? The answer is yes. The expense recognition principle requires Apple to recognize wages expense when it is *incurred*, even if not paid in cash. It must record wages expense incurred as a liability (wages payable). In the next period, when Apple pays the wages, it reduces both cash and wages payable. Net income is not affected by the cash payment; instead, net income decreased in the previous period when Apple accrued the wage expense.

	Balance Sheet					Income Statement		
Transaction	Cash Asset	+ Noncash Assets	= Liabilities	+ Contrib. Capital	+ Earned Capital	Revenues	– Expenses	= Net Income
Current period: Incur $100 of wages not yet paid			= +100 Wages Payable		–100 Retained Earnings		– +100 Wages Expense	= –100
Next period: Pay $100 cash for accrued wages	–100 Cash		= –100 Wages Payable				–	=

As another example of accrued expenses, assume Apple rents office space and that it owes $25 in rent at period-end. Apple has incurred rent expense in the current period, and that expense must be recorded this period. Failing to make this adjustment would mean Apple's liabilities (rent payable) would be understated and its income would be overstated. The entry to record the accrual of rent expense for office space follows.

Transaction	Balance Sheet					Income Statement			
	Cash Asset	+ Noncash Assets	= Liabilities	+ Contrib. Capital	+ Earned Capital	Revenues	− Expenses	= Net Income	
Incur $25 of rent not yet paid		=	+25 Rent Payable		−25 Retained Earnings		− +25 Rent Expense	= −25	

RNTE....25
    RNTP.........25

RNTE
| 25

RNTP
    | 25

Accrued Revenues

Assume Apple delivers iPods to a customer in Boston, Massachusetts, who will pay next quarter. The sales price for those units is $500, and the cost is $400. Apple has completed its revenue earning process with this sale and must accrue revenue from the Boston customer even though Apple received no cash. Like all sales transactions, Apple must record two parts, the sales revenue and the cost of sales. The financial effects template for this two-part transaction follows.

Transaction	Balance Sheet					Income Statement			
	Cash Asset	+ Noncash Assets	= Liabilities	+ Contrib. Capital	+ Earned Capital	Revenues	− Expenses	= Net Income	
Sell $500 of iPods on credit		+500 Accounts Receivable =			+500 Retained Earnings	+500 Sales	−	= +500	
Record $400 cost of $500 iPod sale		−400 Inventory =			−400 Retained Earnings		− +400 Cost of Goods Sold	= −400	

AR......500
    Sales.........500

AR
500 |

Sales
    | 500

COGS...400
    INV..........400

COGS
400 |

INV
    | 400

Accounting Adjustments for Apple

Entries 12 through 16 in Exhibit 3.2, which are explained in Exhibit 3.5, reflect the accounting adjustments Apple makes during its fiscal year. These accounting adjustments occur at the end of the accounting period, prior to the preparation of the financial statements. The purpose of accounting adjustments is to adjust balance sheet assets and liabilities so that the financial statements fairly present the company's financial performance and position.

Exhibit 3.5 ■ Details of Accounting Adjustments for Apple ($ millions)

Adjustment	Description
12. Accrue operating expenses of $2,136 million (current liabilities) and $4,765 million (long-term liabilities)	Accrued expenses represent liabilities that have been incurred before the end of the accounting period but have not been recorded. The accrual simultaneously increases liabilities on the balance sheet and expenses in the income statement. Failure to properly accrue expenses would understate liabilities and overstate profit (and retained earnings).
13. Record depreciation expense of $9,300 million	Each period that PPE is used, a portion of the cost of the PPE is transferred to the income statement as *depreciation expense* to reflect the fact that the PPE assets have been used during the period. Failure to record depreciation expense would overstate assets and net income (and retained earnings) for the period.
14. Record amortization expense of $1,603 million	Similar to PPE, certain intangible assets (those that have a limited useful life) are used up over time and amortized. This concept is the same as depreciation, but the word *amortization* is used instead. The accounting adjustment to amortize the intangible assets reduces the balance sheet value of the intangible assets and records an expense. Note that goodwill is not amortized because we assume it has an unlimited useful life. (We discuss intangible assets, including the goodwill asset, in Module 9.)
15. Apple earns previously deferred revenue of $44 million	When customers pay in advance, Apple records the cash pre-payment as a liability. Once Apple transfers the products or delivers the services to its customers, it can recognize revenue from the sale, typically with an accounting adjustment. The adjustment reduces the unearned revenue liability on the balance sheet and increases revenue in the income statement.
16. Miscellaneous transactions	Apple recognizes other comprehensive loss of $3,974 million, which reduces both earned capital and other long-term assets. We discuss other comprehensive income and loss in Modules 8 and 9.

Research Insight ■ Accruals: Good or Bad?

Researchers examine accounting accruals to study the effects of earnings management on financial accounting. Earnings management is broadly defined as the use of accounting discretion to distort reported earnings. Managers have incentives to manage earnings in many situations. For example, managers have tendencies to accelerate revenue recognition to increase stock prices prior to equity offerings. In contrast, other research shows that managers decelerate revenue recognition to depress stock prices prior to a management buyout (where management repurchases common stock and takes the company "private"). Research also shows that managers use discretion when reporting special items to either meet or beat analysts' forecasts of earnings and/ or to avoid reporting a loss. Not all earnings management occurs for opportunistic reasons. Research shows managers use accruals to communicate private information to outsiders about future profitability. For example, management might signal future profitability through use of income-decreasing accruals to show investors the company can afford to apply conservative accounting. This "signaling" through accruals is found to precede stock splits and dividend increases. In sum, we must look at reported earnings in conjunction with other earnings' quality signals (such as levels of disclosure, degree of corporate governance, and industry performance) to interpret information in accruals.

Review 3-3 LO3

Refer to the information in Review 3-2 for Prestige Inc., which is preparing to record its accounting adjustments for month-end January 2020.

Required
Enter the following accounting adjustments in the financial statement effects template, included in Review 3-2.

13. Record depreciation expense of $600.
14. Accrue salaries of $1,000.
15. Advertising costing $1,300 is aired. Prestige had previously paid cash for the advertising and recorded an asset labeled "Prepaid expense."
16. Accrue income taxes of $1,200.

Solution on p. 3-36.

Accounting Cycle Step 3—Prepare Financial Statements

LO4 Construct financial statements from the accounting records.

Once we enter all of the transactions and adjustments into the financial statement effects template, we sum each column to obtain ending balances for the accounts. This is shown on the bottom row of Exhibit 3.2, and reflects ending balances of accounts after all of the transactions have been recorded during the accounting period in Step 1 and all of the period-end adjustments have been entered into the accounting records in Step 2. With the accounts totaled, we can prepare the financial statements (Step 3).

There is an order to financial statement preparation.

- First, a company prepares its income statement using the income statement accounts. It then uses the net income number and dividend information to update the retained earnings account.
- Second, it prepares the balance sheet using the updated retained earnings account along with the remaining balance sheet accounts.
- Third, it prepares the statement of stockholders' equity.
- Fourth, it prepares the statement of cash flows using information from the cash account (and other sources).

Income Statement

Our financial statement effects spreadsheet in Exhibit 3.2 summarizes Apple's income statement accounts in the last three columns. We use the data from those columns to prepare the income statement in proper form. Apple aggregates its many operating expenses on a line labeled "Total operating expenses." Apple also combines interest expense with other nonoperating income and reports a line labeled "Other income/(expense), net." Apple's income statement for 2018 follows.

APPLE INC. Consolidated Statements of Operations For Year Ended September 29, 2018 ($ millions)	
Net sales.	$265,595
Cost of sales.	163,756
Gross margin	101,839
Total operating expenses	30,941
Operating income	70,898
Other income/(expense), net	2,005
Income before provision for income taxes	72,903
Provision for income taxes	13,372
Net income	$ 59,531

Apple's income statement includes a subtotal for gross margin, which is a common reporting practice that helps us evaluate company performance and profitability. Apple also reports a subtotal for operating profit. As we will discuss in Module 4, operating profit isolates those activities that create shareholder value and, for that reason, companies frequently report a subtotal for operating profit.

Retained Earnings Reconciliation

Once the income statement is prepared, companies update the retained earnings balance by adding net income and subtracting dividends. We can do likewise using the net income and dividend information from the financial statement effects spreadsheet in Exhibit 3.2. Apple's retained earnings reconciliation for 2018 follows.

APPLE INC. Retained Earnings Reconciliation For Year Ended September 29, 2018 ($ millions)	
Retained earnings, September 30, 2017	$98,330
Add: Net income	59,531
Deduct: Dividends	(13,735)
Deduct: Repurchase and retirement of common stock	(73,056)
Miscellaneous adjustments[1]	(670)
Retained earnings, September 29, 2018	$70,400

[1] This retained earnings reconciliation, also called *retained earnings statement*, is consistent with Apple's statement of shareholders' equity. The reconciliation here differs from Exhibit 3.2 where we combined retained earnings and AOCI into one account called Earned capital.

Balance Sheet

Once Apple computes the ending balance in retained earnings, it can prepare its balance sheet. Balance sheet accounts are called **permanent accounts** because their respective balances carry over from one period to the next. For example, the cash balance at the end of the current accounting period (ended September 29, 2018) is $25,913 million, which will be the balance at the beginning of the next accounting period (beginning September 30, 2018).

To prepare the balance sheet, we use the ending balances from the last row in the financial statement effects spreadsheet in Exhibit 3.2, along with specific details for accounts within several of the columns. We then apply proper balance sheet format that has subtotals for current assets, current liabilities, total liabilities, and equity to produce Apple's consolidated balance sheet for 2018 as follows.

APPLE INC.
Consolidated Balance Sheet
September 29, 2018 ($ millions)

Assets

Cash and cash equivalents	$ 25,913
Short-term marketable securities	40,388
Accounts receivable	23,186
Inventories	3,956
Other current assets	37,896
Current assets	131,339
Long-term marketable securities	170,799
Property, plant, and equipment, net	41,304
Other assets	22,283
Total assets	$365,725

Liabilities and equity

Accounts payable	$ 55,888
Accrued expenses	32,687
Deferred revenue	7,543
Commercial paper	11,964
Current portion of long-term debt	8,784
Current liabilities	116,866
Deferred revenue, noncurrent	2,797
Long-term debt	93,735
Other noncurrent liabilities	45,180
Total liabilities	258,578
Common stock and additional paid-in capital	40,201
Retained earnings	70,400
Accumulated other comprehensive income	(3,454)
Total shareholders' equity	107,147
Total liabilities and shareholders' equity	$365,725

Statement of Stockholders' Equity

We use the information from the financial statement effects template pertaining to contributed capital and earned capital to prepare the statement of stockholders' equity, as follows. (The final financial statement is the statement of cash flows, which we cover in detail in a later module.)

APPLE INC.
Statement of Shareholders' Equity
For Year Ended September 29, 2018

$ millions	Common Stock and Additional Paid-In Capital	Retained Earnings	Accumulated Other Comprehensive Income	Total Shareholders' Equity
Balance, September 30, 2017	$35,867	$98,330	$ (150)	$134,047
Stock issuance	4,334			4,334
Net income (loss)		59,531		59,531
Dividends		(13,735)		(13,735)
Common stock repurchased and retired		(73,056)		(73,056)
Other		(670)	(3,304)	(3,974)
Balance, September 29, 2018	$40,201	$70,400	$(3,454)	$107,147

LO4 Review 3-4

Refer to the information in Reviews 3-2 and 3-3 for Prestige Inc., which is preparing its financial statements for month-end January 2020. In addition, the financial statement effects template included the following (beginning) account balances at January 1, 2020.

Accounts receivable	$12,000	Accounts payable	$ 3,800
Inventory	7,200	Unearned revenue	200
Prepaid advertising	1,800	Long-term debt	22,000
PPE	20,000	Salaries payable	0
		Taxes payable	0

Required
1. List the 14 accounts, and determine the ending balance for each.
2. Prepare the income statement, retained earnings reconciliation, and balance sheet at the end of the period.

Solution on p. 3-37.

Accounting Cycle Step 4—Close the Books

The **closing process** (or *closing the books*) refers to "zeroing out" the temporary accounts by transferring their ending balances to retained earnings. Income statement accounts—revenues and expenses—and the dividend account are **temporary accounts** because their balances are zero at the start of each accounting period so that only the current period's activities are included. Balance sheet accounts carry over from period to period and are called permanent accounts. The closing process is typically carried out via a series of journal entries that successively zero out each revenue and expense account and the dividend account, transferring those balances to retained earnings. The result is that all income statement accounts and the dividend account begin the next period with zero balances. The balance sheet accounts do not need to be similarly adjusted because their balances carry over from period to period.

LO5 Explain and apply the closing process.

Closing with the Template It is important to distinguish our financial statement effects template from companies' accounting systems. The financial statement effects template and T-accounts are pedagogical tools that represent transactions' effects on financial statements. The template is highly stylized, but its simplicity is instructive.

Closing with Journal Entries In practice, managers use journal entries to record transactions and adjustments. The template captures these in summarized fashion. However, in practice, income statement transactions are not automatically transferred to retained earnings, and retained earnings is not continuously updated. Instead, companies have a formal "closing process" at the end of each reporting period—someone or some program must transfer the temporary account balances to retained earnings. Thus, it is important to understand the closing process and why companies "close" the books each period. We describe the mechanical details of the closing process.

Following are the journal entries, along with the T-account entries, Apple would make to close out its income statement accounts and dividend account to retained earnings (in millions).

1. Close Revenue and Gain Accounts.

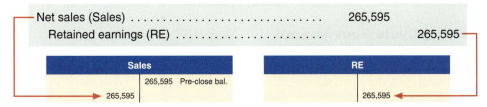

2. Close Expense and Loss Accounts.

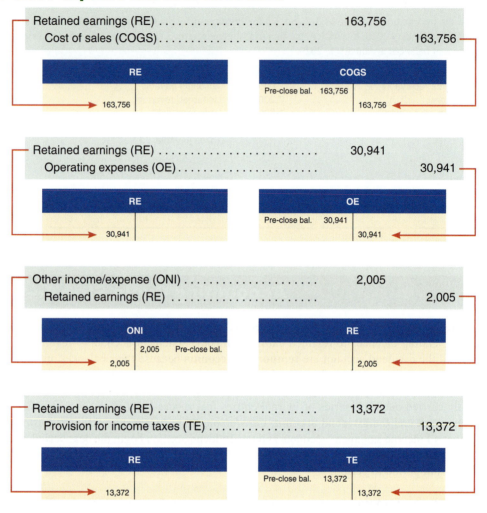

3. Close Dividend Account.

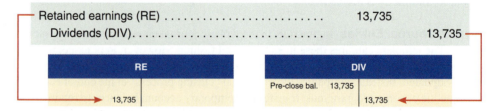

The closing process reduces all of the income statement accounts and the dividend account to zero to begin the next accounting period with a zero balance. This means revenues, expenses, and dividends are accumulated during a period so that the income statement only reflects activities for the period. In contrast, balance sheet accounts carry over from period to period. We can see this from our financial statement effects template for Apple where the bottom row balances as of September 29, 2018, become the top row in the template for the next fiscal year, which begins on September 30, 2018.

Accounting Cycle Summarized

The entire accounting process, from analysis of basic transactions to financial statement preparation to the closing process, is called the **accounting cycle**. As we discuss at the outset of this module and portray graphically in Exhibit 3.1, there are four basic processes in the accounting cycle.

❶ Analyze transactions and prepare (and post) entries.
❷ Prepare (and post) accounting adjustments.
❸ Prepare financial statements.
❹ Perform the closing process.

The analysis and posting of transactions are done regularly during each accounting period. However, the preparation of accounting adjustments and financial statements is only done at the end of an accounting period. At this point, we have explained and illustrated all aspects of the accounting cycle.

Managerial Decision ■ You Are the Chief Financial Officer

Assume that you learn of the leakage of hazardous waste from your company's factory. It is estimated that cleanup could cost $10 million. Part 1: What effect will recording this cost have on your company's balance sheet and its income statement? Part 2: Accounting rules require you to record this cost if it is both probable and can be reliably estimated. Although the cleanup is relatively certain, the cost is a guess at this point. Consequently, you have some discretion whether to record it. Discuss the parties that are likely affected by your decision on whether or not to record the liability and related expense and the ethical issues involved. (Answer, p. 3-19)

LO5 Review 3-5

Refer to the information in Reviews 3-2, 3-3, and 3-4 for Prestige Inc. It has prepared its financial statements and is ready to close its books for month-end January 2020.

Required

Prepare the entries required to close the temporary accounts for Prestige Inc. at the end of January 2020.

Solution on p. 3-37.

Global Accounting

The manner in which accounting data are gathered and recorded does not differ across accounting standards. Thus, the accounting cycle in Exhibit 3.1 applies in countries using IFRS in the same manner as in the United States. The difference is that companies create information systems that conform to the specific accounting rules in that country. For example, the rules for recording research and development (R&D) costs are different in the United States vis-à-vis Germany. Thus, the U.S. company and the German company would each tailor their accounting systems to properly record R&D costs so that each company's financial statements comply with their respective countries' accounting standards. The accounting cycle of each company still involves transactions and adjustments and a closing process. The result is that identical R&D expenditures are classified differently and the resulting financial statements diverge.

Large multinational companies often have subsidiaries in different countries. If a U.S. company has a foreign subsidiary, the foreign laws require a domestic set of financial statements for tax, regulatory, banking, or other purposes. For example, **Apple**'s Form 10-K reports it has three subsidiaries incorporated in Ireland. The Irish subsidiaries must prepare IFRS financial statements to file with the Irish Revenue Commission (the Irish equivalent of the IRS). During the closing process of the accounting cycle, Apple Inc. (the U.S. parent) must consolidate the subsidiaries, which means all assets and liabilities of the subsidiaries are included on Apple Inc.'s balance sheet. Similarly, all of the revenues and expenses of the subsidiaries are included on Apple Inc.'s income statement. It would not be appropriate for a simple summing of accounts because of differences between IFRS and U.S. GAAP. Instead, Apple Inc. must convert IFRS financial statements to U.S. GAAP equivalent (as well as convert euros to U.S. dollars). To accomplish this, Apple Inc. keeps two sets of accounting records for subsidiaries, one set in GAAP and the other in IFRS. This is not as complicated as it might seem. Companies like Apple use sophisticated computer accounting systems and enterprise resource planning (ERP) systems that are capable of supporting multiple sets of accounting standards.

Appendix 3A: FASB's Financial Statement Presentation Project

Preparers and users of financial statements have long expressed concern that existing accounting standards provide too little guidance on financial statement presentation. Popular opinion is that U.S. GAAP permits too many presentation formats and is silent on specific line items and on the level of detail required in financial statements. This lack of uniformity impairs comparability across companies. For example, some companies disaggregate product costs (such as materials and labor) as well as general and administrative costs (such as rent and utilities) in their income statements, and other entities present highly aggregated product costs and general and administrative expenses. Due to these concerns, there is broad support for a FASB project on financial statement presentation.

Under current accounting standards, the statement of cash flows categorizes a company's cash flows into three categories: operating, investing, and financing. The proposal under consideration at the FASB would require similar classification on the balance sheet and the income statement. The following table illustrates the proposed sections, categories, and subcategories in each financial statement. (Summarized from "Staff Draft of an Exposure Draft JULY 2010" © IFRS Foundation and made available by the FASB [FASB.org/cs/BlobServer?blobkey=id&blobnocache=true&blobwhere=1175820952961&blobheader=application%2Fpdf&blobheadername2=Content-Length&blobheadername1=Content-Disposition&blobheadervalue2=60259&blobheadervalue1=filename%3DIntroduction_Summary_Staff_draft_1_July.pdf&blobcol=urldata&blobtable=MungoBlobs].)

Statement of Financial Position (Balance Sheet)	Statement of Comprehensive Income	Statement of Cash Flows
Business section	**Business section**	**Business section**
Operating category	Operating category	Operating category
Operating finance subcategory	Operating finance subcategory	
Investing category	Investing category	Investing category
Financing section	**Financing section**	**Financing section**
Debt category	Debt category	
Equity category		
	Multi-category transaction section	**Multi-category transaction section**
Income tax section	**Income tax section**	**Income tax section**
Discontinued operation section	**Discontinued operation section,** net of tax	**Discontinued operation section**
	Other comprehensive income, net of tax	

The proposed presentation format is consistent with the approach we describe in Module 4—the separation of operating and nonoperating items on the income statement and balance sheet. The Module 4 approach extends the traditional DuPont analysis of return on equity (ROE) by isolating the operating activities of the business in order to evaluate what truly creates shareholder value. While the Module 4 approach sharpens our analysis of ROE, it requires additional effort at present because we must first parse operating from nonoperating components on the financial statements. Under the FASB proposal, financial statements would be formatted along these operating and nonoperating dimensions and standardized across companies. If adopted, the new format will make analysis less effortful.

Guidance Answers

You Are the Chief Financial Officer
Pg. 3-18 Part 1: Liabilities will increase by $10 million for the estimated amount of the cleanup, and an expense in that amount will be recognized in the income statement, thus reducing both income and retained earnings (equity) by $10 million. Part 2: Stakeholders affected by recognition decisions of this type are often much broader than first realized. Management is directly involved in the decision. Recording this cost can affect the market value of the company, its relations with lenders and suppliers, its auditors, and many other stakeholders. Further, if recording this cost is the right accounting decision, failure to do so can foster unethical behavior throughout the company, thus affecting additional company employees.

Questions

Q3-1. List the four steps in the accounting cycle.

Q3-2. What is the purpose of a general ledger?

Q3-3. Explain the process of posting.

Q3-4. What four different types of adjustments are frequently necessary before financial statements are prepared at the end of an accounting period? Give at least one example of each type.

Q3-5. On January 1, prepaid insurance was increased for $1,896 related to the cost of a two-year premium, with coverage beginning immediately. How should this account be adjusted on January 31 before financial statements are prepared for the current month?

Q3-6. At the beginning of January, the first month of the accounting year, the supplies account (asset) had a normal balance of $875. During January, purchases of $260 worth of supplies were added to the account. At the end of January, $630 of supplies were still available. How should this account be adjusted? If no adjustment is made, describe the impact on (a) the income statement for January and (b) the balance sheet prepared at January 31.

Q3-7. The publisher of *Accounting View*, a monthly magazine, received $9,768 cash on January 1 for new subscriptions covering the next 24 months, with service beginning immediately: (*a*) Use the financial statement effects template to record the receipt of the $9,768; and (*b*) use the template to show how the accounts should be adjusted at the end of January before financial statements are prepared for the current month.

Q3-8. Refer to Q3-7. Prepare journal entries for the receipt of cash and the delivery of the magazines.

Q3-9. Trombley Travel Agency pays an employee $950 in wages each Friday for the five-day work week ending on Friday. The last Friday of January falls on January 27. How should Trombley Travel Agency adjust wages expense on January 31, its fiscal year-end?

Q3-10. The Basu Company earns interest amounting to $720 per month on its investments. The company receives the interest revenue every six months, on December 31 and June 30. Monthly financial statements are prepared. Which accounts should Basu adjust on January 31?

Q3-11. What types of accounts are closed at the end of the accounting year? What are the three major steps in the closing process?

Assignments with the logo in the margin are available in *myBusinessCourse*.
See the Preface of the book for details.

Mini Exercises

M3-12. Assessing Financial Statement Effects of Transactions   **LO2**

K. Daniels started Daniels Services, a firm providing art services for advertisers, on June 1. The following accounts are needed to record the transactions for June: Cash, Accounts Receivable, Supplies, Office Equipment, Accounts Payable, Common Stock, Dividends, Service Fees Earned, Rent Expense, Utilities Expense, and Wages Expense. Record the following transactions for June using the financial statement effects template.

June 1 K. Daniels invested $12,000 cash to begin the business in exchange for common stock.
     2 Paid $950 cash for June rent. *Hint:* Record rent expense on June 2.
     3 Purchased $6,400 of office equipment on credit.
     6 Purchased $3,800 of art materials and other supplies; the company paid $1,800 cash with the remainder due within 30 days.
    11 Billed clients $4,700 for services rendered.
    17 Collected $3,250 cash from clients on their accounts billed on June 11.
    19 Paid $5,000 cash toward the account for office equipment (see June 3).
    25 Paid $900 cash for dividends.
    30 Paid $350 cash for June utilities.
    30 Paid $2,500 cash for June wages.

LO2 M3-13. Preparing Journal Entries and Posting

Refer to the information in M3-12. Prepare a journal entry for each transaction. Create a T-account for each account, and then post the journal entries to the T-accounts (use dates to reference each entry).

LO2 M3-14. Assessing Financial Statement Effects of Transactions

B. Fischer started Fischer Company, a cleaning services firm, on April 1. The company created the following accounts to record the transactions for April: Cash; Accounts Receivable; Supplies; Prepaid Van Lease; Equipment; Notes Payable; Accounts Payable; Common Stock; Dividends; Cleaning Fees Earned; Wages Expense; Advertising Expense; and Van Fuel Expense. Record the following transactions for April using the financial statement effects template.

April 1 B. Fischer invested $9,000 cash to begin the business in exchange for common stock.
  2 Paid $2,850 cash for six months' lease on a van for the business.
  3 Borrowed $10,000 cash from a bank and signed a note payable, agreeing to repay it in one year plus 10% interest.
  4 Purchased $5,500 in cleaning equipment; the company paid $2,500 cash with the remainder due within 30 days.
  5 Paid $4,300 cash for cleaning supplies.
  7 Paid $350 cash for advertisements to run in the area newspaper during April.
  21 Billed customers $3,500 for services performed.
  23 Paid $3,000 cash toward the account for cleaning equipment (see April 4).
  28 Collected $2,300 cash from customers on their accounts billed on April 21.
  29 Paid $1,000 cash for dividends.
  30 Paid $2,750 cash for April wages.
  30 Paid $995 cash for gasoline used during April.

LO2 M3-15. Preparing Journal Entries and Posting

Refer to the information in M3-14. Prepare a journal entry for each transaction. Create a T-account for each account, and then post the journal entries to the T-accounts (use dates to reference each entry).

LO2, 3 M3-16. Assessing Financial Statement Effects of Transactions and Adjustments

Schrand Services offers janitorial services on both a contract basis and an hourly basis. On January 1, Schrand collected $26,100 cash in advance on a six-month contract for work to be performed evenly during the next six months.

a. Prepare the entry on January 1 to reflect the receipt of $26,100 cash for contract work; use the financial statement effects template.
b. Adjust the appropriate accounts on January 31 for the contract work done during January; use the financial statement effects template.
c. At January 31, a total of 30 hours of hourly rate janitor work was performed but unbilled. The billing rate is $19 per hour. Prepare the accounting adjustment needed on January 31 using the financial statement effects template. (The firm uses the fees receivable account to reflect revenue earned but not yet billed.)

LO2, 3 M3-17. Preparing Accounting Adjustments

Refer to the information in M3-16. Prepare a journal entry for each of parts *a*, *b*, and *c*.

LO3 M3-18. Assessing Financial Statement Effects of Adjustments

Selected accounts of Portage Properties, a real estate management firm, are shown below as of January 31, before any accounts have been adjusted. All accounts have normal balances.

Prepaid insurance.............	$ 3,240		Unearned rent revenue..........	$ 5,550
Supplies	1,540		Salaries expense	2,325
Office equipment	6,240		Rent revenue	13,250

Portage Properties prepares monthly financial statements. Using the following information, adjust the accounts as necessary on January 31 using the financial statement effects template.

a. Prepaid insurance represents a two-year premium paid on January 1.
b. Supplies of $710 were still available on January 31.
c. Office equipment is expected to last eight years (or 96 months).
d. On January 1, Portage collected $5,550 for six months' rent in advance from a tenant renting space for $925 per month.
e. Salaries of $490 have been earned by employees but not yet recorded as of January 31.

M3-19. Preparing Accounting Adjustments   LO3

Refer to the information in M3-18. Prepare journal entries for each of parts *a* through *e*.

M3-20. Inferring Transactions from Financial Statements   LO2

Fitbit Inc. is a technology company that designs, manufactures, and sells wearable devices with software and services to help customers reach their health and fitness goals. During fiscal 2018, Fitbit purchased inventory costing $909,380 thousand. Assume Fitbit makes all purchases on credit and its accounts payable is only used for inventory purchases. The following T-accounts reflect information contained in the company's fiscal 2017 and 2018 balance sheets ($ thousands).

Fitbit Inc (FIT)

Inventories			Accounts Payable	
2017 Bal. 123,895				212,731 2017 Bal.
2018 Bal. 124,871				251,657 2018 Bal.

a. Use the financial statement effects template to record Fitbit's 2018 purchases.
b. What amount did it pay in cash to its suppliers during fiscal year 2018? Explain.
c. Use the financial statement effects template to record cost of goods sold for its fiscal year 2018.

M3-21. Preparing Journal Entries   LO2

Refer to the information in M3-20. Prepare journal entries for each of parts *a*, *b*, and *c*.

M3-22. Preparing a Statement of Stockholders' Equity   LO4

On December 31, 2019, the accounts of Leuz Architect Services showed credit balances in its common stock and retained earnings accounts of $30,000 and $18,000, respectively. The company's stock issuances for 2020 totaled $6,000, and it paid $9,700 in cash dividends. During 2020, the company had net income of $27,900. Prepare a 2020 statement of stockholders' equity for Leuz Architect Services.

M3-23. Preparing Closing Journal Entries   LO5

KLA-Tencor provides process control and yield management solutions for the semiconductor industry. Selected financial information for the year ended June 30, 2018, follows.

KLA-Tencor (KLAC)

$ millions	Debit	Credit
Net sales.		$4,036,701
Cost of sales.	$1,447,369	
Selling, general, and administrative expense and other.	1,019,025	
Interest expense, net	114,376	
Income tax expense	653,666	
Retained earnings at June 30, 2017.		848,457

Assume the company has not yet closed any accounts to retained earnings. Prepare journal entries to close the temporary accounts above. Set up the needed T-accounts, and post the closing entries. After these entries are posted, what is the balance of the retained earnings account?

M3-24. Inferring Transactions from Financial Statements   LO2

Lowe's is the second-largest home improvement retailer in the world, with 2,002 stores. During its fiscal year ended in February 2019, Lowe's purchased merchandise inventory at a cost of $49,569 ($ millions). Assume all purchases were made on account and accounts payable is only used for inventory purchases. The following T-accounts reflect information contained in the company's February 2018 and 2019 balance sheets.

Lowe's Companies (LOW)

Merchandise Inventories			Accounts Payable	
Feb. 2018 Bal. 8,911				5,124 Feb. 2018 Bal.
Feb. 2019 Bal. 9,458				5,633 Feb. 2019 Bal.

a. Use the financial statement effects template to record Lowe's purchases during the fiscal year ended February 2019.
b. What amount did Lowe's pay in cash to its suppliers during the fiscal year ended February 2019? Explain.
c. Use the financial statement effects template to record cost of sales for the fiscal year ended February 2019.

LO5 M3-25. Closing Process

At December 31, Hanlon Consulting's financial records show the following selected account information.

	Debit	Credit
Service fees earned		$80,300
Rent expense	$20,800	
Salaries expense	48,700	
Supplies expense	5,600	
Depreciation expense	10,200	
Retained earnings		67,000

Prepare entries to close these accounts in journal entry form. Set up T-accounts for each account and post the closing entries to the T-accounts. After these entries are posted, what is the balance of the retained earnings account?

LO3, 4 M3-26. Computing and Comparing Income and Cash Flow Measures

Penno Corporation recorded service revenues of $200,000 in 2020, of which $170,000 were on credit and $30,000 were for cash. Moreover, of the $170,000 credit sales for 2020, Penno collected $20,000 cash on those receivables before year-end 2020. The company also paid $25,000 cash for 2020 wages. Its employees also earned another $15,000 in wages for 2020, which were not yet paid at year-end 2020. (*a*) Compute the company's net income for 2020; and (*b*) how much net cash inflow or outflow did the company generate in 2020? Explain why Penno's net income and net cash flow differ.

LO3, 4 M3-27. Analyzing Transactions to Compute Net Income

Wasley Corp., a start-up company, provided services that were acceptable to its customers and billed those customers for $350,000 in 2019. However, Wasley collected only $280,000 cash in 2019, and the remaining $70,000 was collected in 2020. Wasley employees earned $225,000 in 2019 wages that were not paid until the first week of 2020. How much net income does Wasley report for 2019? For 2020 (assuming no additional transactions)?

LO2 M3-28. Analyzing Transactions Using the Financial Statement Effects Template

Report the effects for each of the following transactions using the financial statement effects template.

a. Issue stock for $1,000 cash.
b. Purchase inventory for $500 cash.
c. Sell inventory in transaction *b* for $3,000 on credit.
d. Receive $2,000 cash toward the transaction *c* receivable.

Exercises

LO3 E3-29. Assessing Financial Statement Effects of Adjustments

For each of the following separate situations, prepare the necessary accounting adjustments using the financial statement effects template.

a. Unrecorded depreciation on equipment is $720.
b. The supplies account has a balance of $3,870. Supplies still available at the end of the period total $1,100.
c. On the date for preparing financial statements, an estimated utilities expense of $430 has been incurred, but no utility bill has yet been received or paid.
d. On the first day of the current period, rent for four periods was paid and recorded as a $3,200 increase to prepaid rent and a $3,200 decrease to cash.
e. Nine months ago, a one-year service policy was sold to a customer, and the seller recorded the cash received by crediting unearned revenue for $1,872. No accounting adjustments have been prepared during the nine-month period. The seller is now preparing annual financial statements.
f. At the end of the period, employee wages of $965 have been incurred but not paid or recorded.
g. At the end of the period, $300 of interest has been earned but not yet received or recorded.

E3-30. Preparing Accounting Adjustments
Refer to the information in E3-29. Prepare journal entries for each accounting adjustment.

E3-31. Assessing Financial Statement Effects of Adjustments Across Two Periods
Oakmont Company closes its accounts on December 31 each year. The company works a five-day work week and pays its employees every two weeks. On December 31, Oakmont accrued $4,700 of salaries payable. On January 9 of the following year, the company paid salaries of $15,000 cash to employees. Prepare entries using the financial statement effects template to (*a*) accrue the salaries payable on December 31, and (*b*) record the salary payment nine days later on January 9.

E3-32. Preparing Accounting Adjustments
Refer to the information in E3-31. Prepare journal entries to accrue the salaries in December, close salaries expense for the year, and pay the salaries in January of the following year. Assume there is no change in the pay rate during the year and no change in the company's workforce.

E3-33. Financial Analysis Using Adjusted Account Data
Selected T-account balances for Bloomfield Company are shown below as of January 31, which reflect its accounting adjustments. The firm uses a calendar-year accounting period but prepares *monthly* accounting adjustments.

Supplies		Supplies Expense	
Jan. 31 Bal. 900		Jan. 31 Bal. 960	

Prepaid Insurance		Insurance Expense	
Jan. 31 Bal. 574		Jan. 31 Bal. 82	

Wages Payable		Wages Expense	
	700 Jan. 31 Bal.	Jan. 31 Bal. 3,200	

Truck		Accumulated Depreciation—Truck	
Jan. 31 Bal. 8,700			2,610 Jan. 31 Bal.

a. If the amount in supplies expense represents the January 31 adjustment for the supplies used in January, and $620 worth of supplies were purchased during January, what was the January 1 beginning balance of supplies?

b. The amount in the insurance expense account represents the adjustment made at January 31 for January insurance expense. If the original insurance premium was for one year, what was the amount of the premium, and on what date did the insurance policy start?

c. If we assume that no beginning balance existed in either wages payable or wages expense on January 1, how much cash was paid as wages during January?

d. If the truck has a useful life of five years (or 60 months), what is the monthly amount of depreciation expense, and how many months has Bloomfield owned the truck?

E3-34. Assessing Financial Statement Effects of Adjustments
L. Burnett began Burnett Refinishing Service on July 1. Selected accounts are shown below as of July 31, before any accounting adjustments have been made.

Prepaid rent	$6,900	Unearned refinishing fees.	$ 600
Prepaid advertising.	630	Refinishing fees revenue	2,500
Supplies	3,000		

Using the following information, prepare the accounting adjustments necessary on July 31 using the financial statement effects template.

a. On July 1, the firm paid one year's rent of $6,900 in cash.
b. On July 1, $630 cash was paid to the local newspaper for an advertisement to run daily for the months of July, August, and September.
c. Supplies still available at July 31 total $1,100.

d. At July 31, refinishing services of $800 have been performed but not yet recorded or billed to customers. The firm uses the fees receivable account to reflect amounts due but not yet billed.

e. In early July, a customer paid $600 in advance for a refinishing project. At July 31, the project is one-half complete.

LO3 E3-35. Preparing Accounting Adjustments and Posting

Refer to the information in E3-34. Prepare adjusting journal entries for each transaction. Set up T-accounts for each of the ledger accounts, and post the journal entries to them.

LO2 E3-36. Inferring Transactions from Financial Statements

The GAP is a global clothing retailer for men, women, children, and babies. The following information is taken from The Gap's annual report for the fiscal year ended February 2, 2019.

Selected Balance Sheet Data ($ millions)	February 2019	February 2018
Merchandise inventory	$2,131	$1,997
Accounts Payable	1,126	1,181

a. The Gap purchased inventories totaling $10,392 for the fiscal year ended February 2, 2019. Use the financial statement effects template to record cost of goods sold for The Gap's fiscal year ended February 2, 2019. (Assume accounts payable is used only for recording purchases of inventories and all inventories are purchased on credit.)

b. What amount did the company pay to suppliers during the year? Record this with the financial statement effects template.

LO2 E3-37. Inferring Transactions and Preparing Journal Entries

Refer to the information in E3-36. Prepare journal entries for each transaction.

LO5 E3-38. Preparing Closing Journal Entries

The following selected accounts appear in The GAP Inc.'s financial statements for the fiscal year ended February 2, 2019.

$ millions	Debit	Credit
Net sales		$16,580
Cost of goods sold	$10,258	
Operating expenses (other than COGS)	4,960	
Interest expense, net	40	
Income tax expense	319	
Retained earnings (beginning of year)		3,081

Prepare entries to close these accounts in journal entry form. Set up T-accounts for each of the accounts, and post the entries to them. After these entries are posted, what is the balance of the retained earnings account?

LO2 E3-39. Inferring Transactions from Financial Statements

Costco Wholesale Corporation operates membership warehouses selling food, appliances, consumer electronics, apparel, and other household goods at 762 U.S. and international locations. As of its fiscal year-end 2018, Costco had approximately 94.3 million members. Selected fiscal-year information from the company's balance sheets follows.

Selected Balance Sheet Data ($ millions)	2018	2017
Merchandise inventories	$11,040	$9,834
Deferred membership income (liability)	1,624	1,498

a. During fiscal 2018, Costco collected $3,268 million cash for membership fees. Use the financial statement effects template to record the cash collected for membership fees.

b. Costco recorded merchandise costs (cost of goods sold) of $123,152 million in fiscal 2018. Record this transaction in the financial statement effects template.

c. Determine the value of merchandise Costco purchased during fiscal 2018. Use the financial statement effects template to record these merchandise purchases. Assume all of Costco's purchases are on account, and recorded in accounts payable.

E3-40. Inferring Transactions and Preparing Journal Entries
Refer to the information in E3-39. Prepare journal entries for transactions in parts *a* through *c*.

E3-41. Preparing Financial Statements and Closing Process
Beneish Company has the following account balances at December 31, the end of its fiscal year.

	Debit	Credit
Cash	$ 8,000	
Accounts receivable	6,500	
Equipment	78,000	
Accumulated depreciation		$ 14,000
Notes payable		10,000
Common stock		43,000
Retained earnings		20,600
Dividends	8,000	
Service fees earned		75,000
Rent expense	18,000	
Salaries expense	37,100	
Depreciation expense	7,000	
Totals	$162,600	$162,600

a. Prepare Beneish Corporation's income statement and statement of stockholders' equity for year-end December 31 and its balance sheet as of December 31. There were no stock issuances or repurchases during the year.
b. Prepare journal entries to close Beneish's temporary accounts.
c. Set up T-accounts for each account and post the closing entries.

E3-42. Analyzing and Reporting Financial Statement Effects of Transactions
M. E. Carter launched Carter Company, a professional services firm on March 1. The firm will prepare financial statements at each month-end. In March (its first month), Carter executed the following transactions. Enter the transactions, *a* through *g*, into the financial statement effects template shown in the module.

a. Carter (owner) invested in the company $100,000 cash and $20,000 in property and equipment. The company issued common stock to Carter.
b. The company paid $3,200 cash for rent of office furnishings and facilities for March.
c. The company performed services for clients and immediately received $4,000 cash for these services.
d. The company performed services for clients and sent a bill for $24,000 with payment due within 60 days.
e. The company compensated an office employee with $4,800 cash as salary for March.
f. The company received $10,000 cash as partial payment on the amount owed from clients in transaction *d*.
g. The company paid $935 cash in dividends to Carter (owner).

E3-43. Analyzing Transactions Using the Financial Statement Effects Template
Refer to transactions *a* through *g* from E3-42. Prepare an income statement for Carter Company for the month of March.

E3-44. Analyzing Transactions and Adjustments Using the Financial Statement Effects Template
Record the effect of each of the following transactions for Hora Company using the financial statement effects template.

a. Wages of $500 are earned by employees but not yet paid.
b. $2,000 of inventory is purchased on credit.
c. Inventory purchased in transaction *b* is sold for $4,000 on credit.
d. Collected $3,000 cash from transaction *c*.
e. Equipment is acquired for $5,000 cash.
f. Recorded $1,000 depreciation expense on equipment from transaction *e*.
g. Paid $10,000 cash toward a note payable that came due.
h. Paid $2,000 cash for interest on borrowings.

Problems

LO3 P3-45. Assessing Financial Statement Effects of Adjustments

The following information relates to December 31 accounting adjustments for Fulton Fast Print Company. The firm's fiscal year ends on December 31.

1. Weekly salaries for a five-day week total $3,600, payable on Fridays. December 31 of the current year is a Tuesday.
2. Fulton Fast Print has $20,000 of notes payable outstanding at December 31. Interest of $200 has accrued on these notes by December 31 but will not be paid until the notes mature next year.
3. During December, Fulton Fast Print provided $900 of printing services to clients who will be billed on January 2. The firm uses the fees receivable account to reflect amounts earned but not yet billed.
4. Starting December 1, all maintenance work on Fulton Fast Print's equipment is handled by Richardson Repair Company under an agreement whereby Fulton Fast Print pays a fixed monthly charge of $400. Fulton Fast Print paid six months' service charge of $2,400 cash in advance on December 1 and increased its Prepaid maintenance account by $2,400.
5. The firm paid $900 cash on December 15 for a series of radio commercials to run during December and January. One-third of the commercials aired by December 31. The $900 payment was recorded in its prepaid advertising account.
6. Starting December 16, Fulton Fast Print rented 800 square feet of storage space from a neighboring business. The monthly rent of $0.80 per square foot is due in advance on the first of each month. Nothing was paid in December, however, because the neighboring business agreed to add the rent for one-half of December to the January 1 payment.
7. Fulton Fast Print invested $5,000 cash in securities on December 1 and earned interest of $38 on these securities by December 31. No interest will be received until January.
8. Annual depreciation on the firm's equipment is $2,175. No depreciation has been recorded during the year.

Required

Prepare Fulton Fast Print Company's accounting adjustments required at December 31 using the financial statement effects template.

LO3 P3-46. Preparing Accounting Adjustments

Refer to the information in P3-45. Prepare accounting adjustments required at December 31 using journal entries.

LO2, 3 P3-47. Assessing Financial Statement Effects of Transactions and Adjustments Across Two Periods

Sloan Company has the following account balances at December 31, the end of its fiscal year (all accounts have normal balances).

Prepaid advertising.............	$ 1,200	Unearned service fees..........	$ 5,400
Wages expense	43,800	Service fees earned	87,000
Prepaid insurance..............	3,420	Rental income.................	4,900

Required

a. Prepare Sloan Company's accounting adjustments at December 31 using the financial statement effects template and the following additional information.
   1. Prepaid advertising at December 31 is $800.
   2. Unpaid wages earned by employees in December are $2,600.
   3. Prepaid insurance at December 31 is $2,280.
   4. Unearned service fees at December 31 are $3,000.
   5. Rent revenue of $1,000 owed by a tenant is not recorded at December 31.

b. Use the financial statement effects template to record the following transactions on January 4 of the following year:
   1. Payment of $4,800 cash in wages.
   2. Cash receipt from the tenant of the $1,000 rent revenue.

P3-48. Preparing Accounting Transactions and Adjustments
Refer to the information in P3-47. Prepare journal entries for parts *a* and *b*.

LO2, 3

P3-49. Journalizing and Posting Transactions and Adjustments
D. Roulstone opened Roulstone Roofing Service on April 1. Transactions for April follow.

LO2, 3

Apr. 1 Roulstone contributed $11,500 cash to the business in exchange for common stock.
2 Paid $6,100 cash for the purchase of a used truck.
2 Purchased $6,200 of ladders and other equipment; the company paid $1,000 cash, with the balance due in 30 days.
3 Paid $2,880 cash for a two-year (or 24-month) premium toward liability insurance.
5 Purchased $1,200 of supplies on credit.
5 Received an advance of $1,800 cash from a customer for roof repairs to be done during April and May.
12 Billed customers $5,500 for roofing services performed.
18 Collected $4,900 cash from customers toward their accounts billed on April 12.
29 Paid $675 cash for truck fuel used in April.
30 Paid $100 cash for April newspaper advertising.
30 Paid $4,500 cash for assistants' wages earned.
30 Billed customers $4,000 for roofing services performed.

Required
a. Set up T-accounts for the following accounts: cash, accounts receivable, supplies, prepaid insurance, trucks, accumulated depreciation—trucks, equipment, accumulated depreciation—equipment, accounts payable, unearned roofing fees, common stock, roofing fees earned, fuel expense, advertising expense, wages expense, insurance expense, supplies expense, depreciation expense—trucks, and depreciation expense—equipment.
b. Record these transactions for April using journal entries.
c. Post the journal entries from part *b*. to their T-accounts (reference transactions in T-accounts by date).
d. Prepare journal entries to adjust the following accounts: insurance expense, supplies expense, depreciation expense—trucks, depreciation expense—equipment, and roofing fees earned. Supplies still available on April 30 amount to $200. Depreciation for April was $125 on the truck and $35 on equipment. One-fourth of the roofing fee received on April 5 was earned by April 30.
e. Post the adjusting journal entries from part *d*. to their T-accounts.

P3-50. Assessing Financial Statement Effects of Transactions and Adjustments
Refer to the information in P3-49.

LO2, 3

Required
a. Use the financial statement effects template to record the transactions for April.
b. Use the financial statement effects template to record the adjustments at the end of April (described in part *d* of P3-49).

P3-51. Preparing Accounting Adjustments
Pownall Photomake Company, a commercial photography studio, completed its first year of operations on December 31. Account balances before year-end adjustments follow; no adjustments have been made to the accounts at any time during the year. Assume that all balances are normal.

LO3

Cash	$ 4,300	Accounts payable	$ 4,060
Accounts receivable	3,800	Unearned photography fees	2,600
Prepaid rent	12,600	Common stock	24,000
Prepaid insurance	2,970	Photography fees earned	34,480
Supplies	4,250	Wages expense	11,000
Equipment	22,800	Utilities expense	3,420

An analysis of the firm's records discloses the following (business began on January 1).

1. Photography services of $1,850 have been rendered, but customers have not yet paid or been billed. The company uses the fees receivable account to reflect amounts due but not yet billed.
2. Equipment, purchased January 1, has an estimated life of 10 years.
3. Utilities expense for December is estimated to be $400, but the bill will not arrive or be paid until January of next year. (All prior months' utilities bills have been received and paid.)

4. The balance in prepaid rent represents the amount paid on January 1 for a two-year lease on the studio it operates from.
5. In November, customers paid $2,600 cash in advance for photos to be taken for the holiday season. When received, these fees were credited to unearned photography fees. By December 31, all of these fees are earned.
6. A three-year insurance premium paid on January 1 was debited to prepaid insurance.
7. Supplies still available at December 31 are $1,020.
8. At December 31, wages expense of $375 had been incurred but not yet paid or recorded.

Required
Prepare the required adjusting entries using the financial statement effects template.

LO3 P3-52. Recording Adjustments with Journal Entries and T-accounts
Refer to the information in P3-51.

Required
a. Prepare journal entries to record the accounting adjustments.
b. Set up T-accounts for each account, and post the journal entries to them.

LO3 P3-53. Preparing Accounting Adjustments
BensEx, a mailing service, has just completed its first year of operations on December 31. Its account balances before year-end adjustments follow; no adjusting entries have been made to the accounts at any time during the year. Assume all balances are normal.

Cash..........................	$ 1,700	Accounts payable...............	$ 2,700
Accounts receivable	5,120	Common stock	9,530
Prepaid advertising............	1,680	Mailing fees earned	86,000
Supplies	6,270	Wages expense	38,800
Equipment	42,240	Rent expense	6,900
Notes payable.................	7,500	Utilities expense	3,020

An analysis of the firm's records reveals the following (business began on January 1).

1. The balance in prepaid advertising represents the amount paid for newspaper advertising for one year. The agreement, which calls for the same amount of space each month, covers the period from February 1 of this first year to January 31 of the following year. BensEx did not advertise during its first month of operations.
2. Equipment, purchased January 1, has an estimated life of eight years.
3. Utilities expense does not include expense for December, estimated at $325. The bill will not arrive until January of the following year.
4. At year-end, employees have earned $2,400 in wages that will not be paid until January.
5. Supplies available at year-end amount to $1,520.
6. At year-end, unpaid interest of $450 has accrued on the notes payable.
7. The firm's lease calls for rent of $575 per month payable on the first of each month, plus an amount equal to 0.75% of annual mailing fees earned. The rental percentage is payable within 15 days after the end of the year.

Required
Prepare the required adjusting entries using the financial statement effects template.

LO3 P3-54. Recording Accounting Adjustments with Journal Entries and T-accounts
Refer to information in P3-53.

Required
a. Prepare journal entries to record the accounting adjustments.
b. Set up T-accounts for each account, and post the journal entries to them.

LO3, 4, 5 P3-55. Preparing Accounting Adjustments
Wysocki Wheels began operations on March 1 to provide automotive wheel alignment and balancing services. On March 31, accounting records revealed the following account balances.

	Debit	Credit
Cash	$ 2,900	
Accounts receivable	3,820	
Prepaid rent	4,770	
Supplies	3,700	
Equipment	36,180	
Accounts payable		$ 3,510
Unearned service revenue		1,000
Common stock		38,400
Service revenue		12,360
Wages expense	3,900	
Totals	$55,270	$55,270

The following information is also available.

1. The balance in prepaid rent was the amount paid on March 1 to cover the first six months' rent.
2. Supplies available on March 31 amounted to $1,360.
3. Equipment has an estimated life of nine years (or 108 months).
4. Unpaid and unrecorded wages at March 31 were $1,560.
5. Utility services used during March were estimated at $390; a bill is expected early in April.
6. The balance in unearned service revenue was the amount received on March 1 from a car dealer to cover alignment and balancing services on cars sold by the dealer in March and April. Wysocki Wheels agreed to provide the services at a fixed fee of $500 each month.

Required

a. Prepare the accounting adjustments at March 31 in journal entry form.
b. Set up T-accounts, and post the accounting adjustments to them.
c. Prepare the income statement for March and its balance sheet at March 31.
d. Prepare entries to close the temporary accounts in journal entry form. Post the closing entries to the T-accounts.

P3-56. Analyzing Transactions Using the Financial Statement Effects Template LO2, 4

Sefcik Company began operations on the first of October. Following are the transactions for its first month of business.

1. S. Sefcik launched Sefcik Company and invested $50,000 into the business in exchange for common stock. The company also borrowed $100,000 from a local bank.
2. Sefcik Company purchased equipment for $95,000 cash and inventory of $40,000 on credit (the company still owes its suppliers for the inventory at month-end).
3. Sefcik Company sold inventory costing $30,000 for $50,000 cash.
4. Sefcik Company paid $12,000 cash for wages owed employees for October work.
5. Sefcik Company paid interest on the bank loan of $1,000 cash.
6. Sefcik Company recorded $500 of depreciation expense related to its equipment.
7. Sefcik Company paid a dividend of $2,000 cash.

Required

a. Record the effects of each transaction using the financial statement effects template.
b. Prepare the income statement and balance sheet at the end of October.

P3-57. Analyzing Transactions and Adjustments Using the Financial Statement Effects Template LO2, 3

Following are selected transactions of Mogg Company. Record the effects of each using the financial statement effects template.

1. Shareholders contribute $10,000 cash to the business in exchange for common stock.
2. Employees earn $500 in wages that have not been paid at period-end.
3. Inventory of $3,000 is purchased on credit.
4. The inventory purchased in transaction 3 is sold for $4,500 on credit.
5. The company collected the $4,500 owed to it per transaction 4.
6. Equipment is purchased for $5,000 cash.

7. Depreciation of $1,000 is recorded on the equipment from transaction 6.
8. The supplies account had a $3,800 balance at the beginning of this period; a physical count at period-end shows that $800 of supplies are still available. No supplies were purchased during this period.
9. The company paid $12,000 cash toward the principal on a note payable; also, $500 cash is paid to cover this note's interest expense for the period.
10. The company received $8,000 cash in advance for services to be delivered next period.

LO2, 3, 4 **P3-58. Analyzing Transactions and Adjustments Using the Financial Statement Effects Template**
On March 1, S. Penman launched AniFoods Inc., an organic foods retailing company. Following are the transactions for its first month of business.

1. S. Penman contributed $100,000 cash to the company in return for common stock. Penman also lent the company $55,000. This $55,000 note is due one year hence.
2. The company purchased equipment in the amount of $50,000, paying $10,000 cash and signing a note payable to the equipment manufacturer for the remaining balance.
3. The company purchased inventory for $80,000 cash in March.
4. The company had March sales of $100,000, of which $60,000 was for cash and $40,000 on credit. Total cost of goods sold for its March sales was $70,000.
5. The company purchased future advertising time from a local radio station for $10,000 cash.
6. During March, $7,500 worth of radio spots purchased in transaction 5 are aired. The remaining spots will be aired in April.
7. Employee wages earned and paid during March total $17,000 cash.
8. Prior to disclosing the financial statements, the company recognized that employees had earned an additional $1,000 in wages that will be paid in the next period.
9. The company recorded $2,000 of depreciation for March relating to its equipment.

Required
a. Record the effect of each transaction using the financial statement effects template.
b. Prepare a March income statement and a balance sheet as of the end of March for AniFoods Inc.

LO2, 4 **P3-59. Analyzing Transactions Using the Financial Statement Effects Template**
Hanlon Advertising Company began the current month with the following balance sheet.

Cash	$ 80,000	Liabilities	$ 70,000
Noncash assets	135,000	Contributed capital	110,000
		Earned capital	35,000
Total assets	$215,000	Total liabilities and equity	$215,000

Following are summary transactions that occurred during the current month.

1. The company purchased supplies for $5,000 cash; none were used this month.
2. Services of $2,500 were performed this month on credit.
3. Services were performed for $10,000 cash this month.
4. The company purchased advertising for $8,000 cash; the ads will run next month.
5. The company received $1,200 cash as partial payment on accounts receivable from transaction 2.
6. The company paid $3,400 cash toward the accounts payable balance reported at the beginning of the month.
7. The company paid $3,500 cash toward this month's wages expense.
8. The company declared and paid dividends of $500 cash.

Required
a. Record the effects of each transaction using the financial statement effects template.
b. Prepare the income statement for this month and the balance sheet as of month-end.

LO2, 3, 4 **P3-60. Analyzing Transactions and Adjustments Using the Financial Statement Effects Template**
Werner Realty Company began the month with the following balance sheet.

Cash	$ 30,000	Liabilities	$ 90,000
Noncash assets	225,000	Contributed capital	45,000
		Earned capital	120,000
Total assets	$255,000	Total liabilities and equity	$255,000

Following are summary transactions that occurred during the current month.

1. The company purchased $6,000 of supplies on credit.
2. The company received $8,000 cash from a new customer for services to be performed next month.
3. The company paid $6,000 cash to cover office rent for two months (the current month and the next).
4. The company billed clients for $25,000 of work performed.
5. The company paid employees $6,000 cash for work performed.
6. The company collected $25,000 cash from accounts receivable in transaction 4.
7. The company recorded $4,000 depreciation on its equipment.
8. At month-end, $2,000 of supplies purchased in transaction 1 are still available; no supplies were available when the month began.

Required

a. Record the effects of each transaction using the financial statement effects template.
b. Prepare the income statement for this month and the balance sheet as of month-end.

IFRS Applications

I3-61. Preparing Closing Journal Entries
On June 30, 2018, Qantas Airlines reports the following balances.

LO5
Qantas Airlines

In AUD millions	Debit	Credit
Total passenger and freight revenue		A$17,060
Manpower and staff related	A$4,300	
Fuel	3,232	
Aircraft operating variable	3,596	
Depreciation and amortization	1,528	
Other expenses	2,831	
Finance costs, net	182	
Income tax expense	411	
Retained earnings, beginning of year		1,084

Assume the company has not yet closed any accounts to retained earnings. Prepare journal entries to close the temporary accounts above. Set up the needed T-accounts, and post the closing entries. After these entries are posted, what is the balance of the retained earnings account?

I3-62. Inferring Transactions and Adjustments from Financial Statements
Rio Tinto is a British-Australian multinational metals and mining corporation with headquarters in London, England, and a management office in Melbourne, Australia. Assume the following amounts have not been recorded for fiscal 2018 ($ millions).

LO2, 3
Rio Tinto

Sales revenue	$18,485
Depreciation and amortization expense	4,015
Income taxes paid	4,242

Use the financial statement effects template to record the following transactions for Rio Tinto for fiscal 2018.

a. Sales revenue. Assume 100% of the company's revenue is credit sales (meaning its sales are on accounts receivable).
b. Depreciation expense.
c. Income taxes paid. Assume this represents the portion of income tax expense paid in cash.

Management Applications

LO2, 3, 4   **MA3-63.**   **Preparing Accounting Transactions and Adjustments and Financial Statements**

Stocken Surf Shop began operations on July 1 with an initial investment of $50,000. During the first three months of operations, the following cash transactions were recorded in the firm's checking account.

Deposits	
Initial investment by owner	$ 50,000
Collected from customers	81,000
Borrowings from bank	10,000
	$141,000

Checks Drawn	
Rent	$ 24,000
Fixtures and equipment	25,000
Merchandise inventory	62,000
Salaries	8,000
Other expenses	13,000
	$132,000

Additional information:

1. Most sales were for cash; however, the store accepted a limited amount of credit sales; at September 30, customers owed the store $9,000.
2. Rent was paid on July 1 for six months. (The company recorded prepaid expense, an asset, on July 1.)
3. Salaries of $4,000 per month were paid on the first of each month for salaries earned in the month prior.
4. Inventories were purchased for cash; at September 30, inventory of $28,000 was still available.
5. Fixtures and equipment were expected to last five years (or 60 months), with zero salvage value.
6. The bank charges 12% annual interest (1% per month) on the $10,000 bank loan. Stocken took out the loan on July 1.

Required

a. Record all of Stocken's cash transactions, and prepare any necessary adjusting entries at September 30. You may either use the financial statement effects template or journal entries combined with T-accounts.
b. Prepare the income statement for the three months ended September 30 and the balance sheet at September 30.
c. Analyze the statements from part b, and assess the company's performance over its initial three months.

LO3   **MA3-64.**   **Analyzing Adjustments, Impacts on Financial Ratios, and Loan Covenants**

Kadous Consulting, a firm started three years ago by K. Kadous, offers consulting services for material handling and plant layout. Its balance sheet at the close of the current year follows.

KADOUS CONSULTING
Balance Sheet
December 31

Assets		Liabilities	
Cash	$ 3,400	Notes payable	$30,000
Accounts receivable	20,875	Accounts payable	4,200
Supplies	13,200	Unearned consulting fees	11,300
Prepaid insurance	6,500	Wages payable	400
Equipment, gross	68,500	Total liabilities	45,900
Less: Accumulated depreciation	23,975	**Equity**	
		Common stock	8,000
Equipment, net	44,525	Retained earnings	34,600
Total assets	$88,500	Total liabilities and equity	$88,500

Earlier in the year, Kadous obtained a bank loan of $30,000 cash for the firm. A provision of the loan is that the year-end debt-to-equity ratio (total liabilities to total equity) cannot exceed 1.0. Based on the above balance sheet, the ratio at December 31 of this year is 1.08. Kadous is concerned about being in violation of the loan agreement and requests assistance in reviewing the situation. Kadous believes she might have overlooked some items at year-end. Discussions with Kadous reveal the following.

1. On January 1 of this year, the firm paid a $6,500 insurance premium for two years of coverage; the amount in prepaid insurance has not yet been adjusted.
2. Depreciation on equipment should be 10% of cost per year; the company inadvertently recorded 15% for this year.
3. Interest on the bank loan has been paid through the end of this year.
4. The firm concluded a major consulting engagement in December, doing a plant layout analysis for a new factory. The $8,000 fee has not been billed or recorded in the accounts.
5. On December 1 of this year, the firm received an $11,300 cash advance payment from Dichev Corp. for consulting services to be rendered over a two-month period. This payment was credited to the unearned consulting fees account. One-half of this fee was earned but unrecorded by December 31 of this year.
6. Supplies costing $4,800 were available on December 31; the company has made no adjustment of its Supplies account.

Required
a. What is the correct debt-to-equity ratio at December 31?
b. Is the firm in violation of its loan agreement? Prepare computations to support the correct total liabilities and total equity figures at December 31.

MA3-65. Ethics, Accounting Adjustments, and Auditors   **LO3**

It is the end of the accounting year for Anne Beatty, controller of a medium-sized, publicly held corporation specializing in toxic waste cleanup. Within the corporation, only Beatty and the president know the firm has been negotiating for several months to land a large contract for waste cleanup in Western Europe. The president has hired another firm with excellent contacts in Western Europe to help with negotiations. The outside firm will charge an hourly fee plus expenses but has agreed not to submit a bill until the negotiations are in their final stages (expected to occur in another three to four months). Even if the contract falls through, the outside firm is entitled to receive payment for its services. Based on her discussion with a member of the outside firm, Beatty knows its charge for services provided to date will be $150,000. This is a material amount for the company.

Beatty knows the president wants negotiations to remain as secret as possible so competitors will not learn of the contract the company is pursuing in Europe. In fact, the president recently stated to her, "This is not the time to reveal our actions in Western Europe to other staff members, our auditors, or the readers of our financial statements; securing this contract is crucial to our future growth." No entry has been made in the accounting records for the cost of contract negotiations. Beatty now faces an uncomfortable situation. The company's outside auditor has just asked her if she knows of any year-end adjustments that have not yet been recorded.

Required
a. What are the ethical considerations Beatty faces in answering the auditor's question?
b. How should Beatty respond to the auditor's question?

Solutions to Review Problems

Review 3-1—Solution

	Cash Asset	Noncash Asset	Liabilities	Contributed Capital	Earned Capital	Revenues	Expenses
Accounts payable． ．			X				
Accounts receivable, less allowances ． ． ． ． ． ． ． ． .		X					
Accrued expenses ．			X				
Acquired intangible assets, net． ． ． ． ． ． ． ． ． ． ． ． ． .		X					
Cash and cash equivalents ． ． ． ． ． ． ． ． ． ． ． ． ． ． ． ．	X						
Common stock and additional paid-in capital． ． . .				X			
Cost of sales． ．							X
Current portion of long-term debt ． ． ． ． ． ． ． ． ． ． ． ． ．			X				
Deferred revenue ．			X				
Deferred tax assets ．		X					
Goodwill ．		X					
Inventories ．		X					
Long-term debt． ．			X				
Long-term marketable securities ． ． ． ． ． ． ． ． ． ． ． ．		X					
Net sales． ．						X	
Other current assets． ．		X					
Other noncurrent liabilities ． ． ． ． ． ． ． ． ． ． ． ． ． ． ． ． ．			X				
Property, plant, and equipment, net ． ． ． ． ． ． ． ． ． ．		X					
Provision for income taxes ． ． ． ． ． ． ． ． ． ． ． ． ． ． ． ． .							X
Research and development ． ． ． ． ． ． ． ． ． ． ． ． ． ． ． ．							X
Retained earnings ．					X		
Selling, general and administrative． ． ． ． ． ． ． ． ． ．							X

Review 3-2—Solution

	Balance Sheet					Income Statement		
	Cash Assets +	Noncash Assets =	Liabilities	+ Contrib. Capital	+ Earned Capital	Revenues −	Expenses =	Net Income
Balance January 1, 2020	10,000	41,000	26,000	10,000	15,000	0	0	0
Transactions								
1. Issue common stock for $3,000 cash	3,000			3,000				
2. Purchase inventory for $8,000 on credit		8,000 Inventory	8,000 Accounts payable					
3. Sell inventory costing $8,000 for $15,000 on credit		(8,000) Inventory 15,000 Accounts receivable			7,000 Retained earnings	15,000 Revenue	8,000 Cost of goods sold	7,000
4. Issue long-term debt for $10,000 cash	10,000		10,000 Long-term debt					
5. Pay $15,000 cash for PPE	(15,000)	15,000 PPE						
6. Pay $500 cash for salaries	(500)				(500) Retained earnings		500 Salaries expense	(500)
7. Receive $300 cash in advance for future consulting services	300		300 Unearned revenue					
8. Pay $50 cash for interest on long-term debt	(50)				(50) Retained earnings		50 Interest expense	(50)
9. Receive $3,000 cash from accounts receivable	3,000	(3,000) Accounts receivable						
10. Pay $2,500 cash toward accounts payable	(2,500)		(2,500) Accounts payable					
11. Perform consulting services for client who previously paid in 7			(300) Unearned revenue		300 Retained earnings	300 Revenue		300
12. Pay $100 cash for dividends	(100)				(100) Retained earnings			

Review 3-3—Solution

	Balance Sheet					Income Statement		
	Cash Assets +	Noncash Assets =	Liabilities	+ Contrib. Capital	+ Earned Capital	Revenues −	Expenses =	Net Income
Accounting Adjustments								
13. Record depreciation of $600		(600) PPE			(600) Retained earnings		600 Depreciation expense	(600)
14. Accrue salaries of $1,000			1,000 Salaries payable		(1,000) Retained earnings		1,000 Salaries expense	(1,000)
15. Advertising costing $1,300 is aired		(1,300) Prepaid expense			(1,300) Retained earnings		1,300 Advertising expense	(1,300)
16. Accrue income taxes of $1,200			1,200 Taxes payable		(1,200) Retained earnings		1,200 Tax expense	(1,200)
Balance January 31, 2020	8,150	66,100	43,700	13,000	17,550	15,300	12,650	2,650

Review 3-4—Solution

1.

Cash	$ 8,150	Taxes payable	$ 1,200
Accounts receivable	24,000	Unearned revenue	200
Inventory	7,200	Long-term debt	32,000
Prepaid advertising	500	Common stock	13,000
PPE	34,400	Retained earnings	17,550
Accounts payable	9,300	Revenues	15,300
Salaries payable	1,000	Expenses	12,650

2.

PRESTIGE INC.
Income Statement
For Month Ended January 31, 2020

Revenues	$15,300
Cost of goods sold	8,000
Gross profit	7,300
Salaries expense	1,500
Depreciation expense	600
Advertising expense	1,300
Operating profit	3,900
Interest expense	50
Profit before tax	3,850
Tax expense	1,200
Net income	$ 2,650

PRESTIGE INC.
Retained Earnings Reconciliation
For Month Ended January 31, 2020

Beginning retained earnings	$15,000
Net income	2,650
Dividends	(100)
Ending retained earnings	$17,550

PRESTIGE INC.
Balance Sheet
January 31, 2020

Cash	$ 8,150	Accounts payable	$ 9,300
Accounts receivable	24,000	Wages payable	1,000
Inventories	7,200	Taxes payable	1,200
Prepaid advertising	500	Unearned revenue	200
Current assets	39,850	Current liabilities	11,700
		Long-term debt	32,000
Property, plant, and equipment	34,400	Total liabilities	43,700
		Common stock	13,000
		Retained earnings	17,550
		Total stockholders' equity	30,550
Total assets	$74,250	Total liabilities and stockholders' equity	$74,250

Review 3-5—Solution

1. Close revenue account.

Revenues (REV)	15,300	
Retained earnings (RE)		15,300

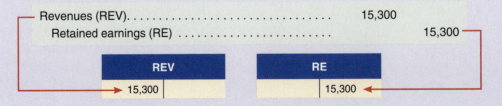

2. Close expense accounts.

| Retained earnings (RE) .... | 8,000 | |
| Cost of goods sold (COGS) .... | | 8,000 |

RE	COGS
8,000	8,000

| Retained earnings (RE) .... | 1,500 | |
| Salaries expense (SE) .... | | 1,500 |

RE	SE
1,500	1,500

| Retained earnings (RE) .... | 600 | |
| Depreciation expense (DE) .... | | 600 |

RE	DE
600	600

| Retained earnings (RE) .... | 1,300 | |
| Advertising expense (AE) .... | | 1,300 |

RE	AE
1,300	1,300

| Retained earnings (RE) .... | 50 | |
| Interest expense (IE) .... | | 50 |

RE	IE
50	50

| Retained earnings (RE) .... | 1,200 | |
| Tax expense (TE) .... | | 1,200 |

RE	TE
1,200	1,200

3. Close dividend account.

| Retained earnings (RE) .... | 100 | |
| Dividends (DIV) .... | | 100 |

RE	DIV
100	100

Module 4
Analyzing and Interpreting Financial Statements

Analyzing and Interpreting Financial Statements

Return on Equity (ROE)	Return on Assets (ROA)	Operating Focus	Nonoperating Return	Liquidity and Solvency
■ Measuring ROE ■ Disaggregating ROE with DuPont Analysis ■ Components: Return on Assets and Financial Leverage	■ Measuring ROA ■ Profitability (Profit Margin) ■ Productivity (Asset Turnover) ■ Financial Leverage: Link to ROE	■ Operating Revenues and Expenses ■ Tax on Operating Profit ■ Operating Assets and Liabilities ■ Disaggregating RNOA into Margin and Turnover	■ Measuring Nonoperating Return ■ Leveraging Debt to Increase ROE ■ Risks of Debt Financing ■ Debt Covenants	■ Liquidity: Current Ratio and Quick Ratio ■ Solvency: Liabilities-to-Equity and Times Interest Earned Ratios ■ Limitations of Ratio Analysis
Review 4-1, 4-2	Review 4-3	Review 4-4, 5, 6, 7	Review 4-8	Review 4-9

PREVIEW   BSX

- We explain several measures of performance that relate the income statement to the balance sheet:
  - Return on assets (ROA)
  - Return on equity (ROE)
  - Return on net operating assets (RNOA)
- We identify factors that drive these performance measures and how to interpret them.
- Boston Scientific is the focus company of this module.

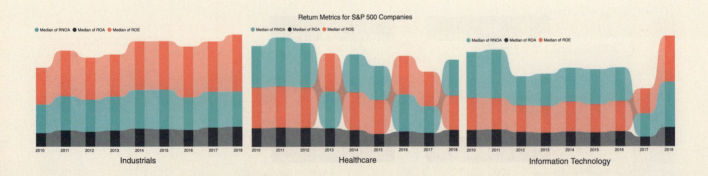

Return Metrics for S&P 500 Companies — Industrials, Healthcare, Information Technology

Road Map

LO	Learning Objective | Topics	Page	eLecture	Guided Example	Assignments
4-1	**Compute and interpret return on equity (ROE).** ROE Definition :: ROE Computation :: ROE Interpretation	4-3	e4-1	Review 4-1	1, 18, 26, 32, 34, 35, 36, 42, 48, 49, 51, 54
4-2	**Apply DuPont disaggregation of ROE into return on assets (ROA) and financial leverage.** ROE Disaggregation :: Return on Assets :: Financial Leverage	4-4	e4-2	Review 4-2	2, 19, 26, 32, 34, 36, 42, 51
4-3	**Disaggregate ROA into profitability and productivity and analyze both.** ROA Disaggregation :: Profitability :: Productivity :: Financial Leverage	4-6	e4-3	Review 4-3	3, 4, 5, 16, 19, 26, 31, 32, 34, 42, 51, 53, 56, 57, 58
4-4	**Identify balance sheet operating items and compute net operating assets.** Operating Focus on Balance Sheet :: RNOA Motivation :: NOA Computation	4-14	e4-4	Review 4-4	9, 14, 20, 24, 41, 45, 48, 50
4-5	**Identify income statement operating items and compute net operating profit after tax.** Operating Focus on Income Statement :: Operating vs Nonoperating :: NOPAT Computation :: Income Tax Expense	4-19	e4-5	Review 4-5	3, 7, 8, 14, 21, 25, 29, 40, 41, 45, 48, 50
4-6	**Compute and interpret return on net operating assets (RNOA).** RNOA Computation :: ROA vs RNOA :: ROA components :: Key Definitions	4-23	e4-6	Review 4-6	6, 22, 23, 27, 29, 33, 35, 36, 41, 45, 48, 50, 54
4-7	**Disaggregate RNOA into net operating profitability and net operating asset turnover.** RNOA Disaggregation :: Net Operating Profit Margin :: Net Operating Asset Turnover :: Trade-Off of Margin and Turnover	4-25	e4-7	Review 4-7	3, 4, 10, 11, 15, 22, 23, 27, 29, 33, 35, 41, 45, 48, 50, 52, 54
4-8	**Compute and interpret nonoperating return (Appendix 4B).** Nonoperating Return Components :: FLEV and Spread	4-31	e4-8	Review 4-8	37, 38, 41, 44, 47, 49
4-9	**Compute and interpret measures of liquidity and solvency (Appendix 4C).** Liquidity Analysis :: Solvency Analysis :: Vertical and Horizontal Analysis :: Limitations of Ratios	4-35	e4-9	Review 4-9	12, 13, 17, 28, 30, 39, 43, 46, 55

Return on Equity (ROE)

LO1 Compute and interpret return on equity (ROE).

The most common analysis metric used by managers and investors alike is **return on equity (ROE)**, a powerful summary measure of company performance defined as:

$$\text{ROE} = \frac{\text{Net income}}{\text{Average stockholders' equity}}$$

ROE relates net income to the average total stockholders' equity from the balance sheet. ROE measures return from the perspective of the company's stockholders. ROE uses net income, in the numerator, that represents profit earned *during* the year. The denominator would ideally reflect equity that the company had *throughout* the year. As an approximation, we use a simple average of the balance sheet values for equity at the start and end of the year. ROE is an important metric and, in the five years from 2014 to 2018, return on equity of the S&P 500 firms has ranged from 13.5% to 15.6%. The **Standard & Poor's (S&P) 500** consists of roughly 500 of the largest U.S. publicly traded companies and accounts for about 75% of the U.S. stock market capitalization. U.S.-based companies are selected for inclusion (by committee) based on market cap, industry, long-term profitability, and trading volume, and other factors. In 2019, Boston Scientific was #97 on the S&P 500. The **S&P 500 Index** is a market-capitalization-weighted index of the S&P 500 firms. Exhibit 4.1 includes the income statement and balance sheet data for **Boston Scientific Corporation**, our focus company for this module. We use these data to compute the ROE for 2018 of 21.24%.

Exhibit 4.1 ■ Financial Statement Data for Boston Scientific Corporation

$ millions	Dec. 29, 2018	Dec. 30, 2017
Sales.	$ 9,823	
Net income.	1,671	
Total assets	20,999	19,042
Total stockholders' equity.	8,726	7,012

$$\text{ROE} = \frac{\$1,671}{(\$8,726 + \$7,012)/2} = 21.24\%$$

ROE is a summary return metric that measures the return the company has earned on the book (reported) value of the shareholders' investment. It is one measure of how effective management has been in its role as stewards of the capital invested by shareholders. In our analysis of company performance, we seek to uncover the *drivers* of ROE and how those drivers have trended over time so that we are better able to predict future performance.

Review 4-1 LO1

Following are selected income statement and balance sheet data for **Stryker Corporation**.

$ millions	2018	2017
Sales.	$13,601	
Net income	3,553	
Total assets	27,229	22,197
Stockholders' equity	11,730	9,980

Required

Solution on p. 4-59.   Compute return on equity (ROE) for Stryker Corp. for 2018.

ROE Disaggregation: DuPont Analysis

There are two methods for disaggregating ROE into its components; each provides a different perspective that can inform our analysis.

LO2 Apply DuPont disaggregation of ROE into return on assets (ROA) and financial leverage.

- The first method is the traditional **DuPont analysis** that disaggregates return on equity into components of profitability, productivity, and leverage.
- The second method extends the traditional DuPont analysis by taking an **ROE analysis with an operating focus** that separates operating and nonoperating activities. Operating activities are the drivers of shareholder value. This method, which focuses on operating or core activities, provides insight into the factors that drive value creation.

Disaggregation of return on equity (ROE) was initially introduced by the **E.I. DuPont de Nemours and Company** to aid its managers in performance evaluation. DuPont realized that management's focus on profit alone was insufficient because profit can be increased simply by the purchase of additional investment in low-yielding, but safe, assets. DuPont wanted managers to think like investors and to manage their portfolio of activities using investment principles that allocate scarce investment capital to competing projects in descending order of return on investment (the capital budgeting approach). The DuPont model incorporates this investment perspective into performance measurement by disaggregating ROE into two components.

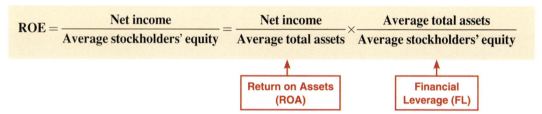

$$\text{ROE} = \frac{\text{Net income}}{\text{Average stockholders' equity}} = \underbrace{\frac{\text{Net income}}{\text{Average total assets}}}_{\text{Return on Assets (ROA)}} \times \underbrace{\frac{\text{Average total assets}}{\text{Average stockholders' equity}}}_{\text{Financial Leverage (FL)}}$$

Return on equity takes the perspective of a company's shareholders and measures rate of return on shareholders' investment—how much net income is earned relative to the equity invested by shareholders. It reflects *both* company performance (as measured by return on assets) *and* how assets are financed (relative use of liabilities and equity). ROE is higher when there is more debt and less equity for a given level of assets (this is because the denominator in ROE, equity, is smaller). There is, however, a trade-off: while using more debt and less equity results in higher ROE, the greater debt means higher risk for the company.

Return on Assets

Return on assets (ROA) measures return from the perspective of the entire company. This return includes both profitability (numerator) and total company assets (denominator). To earn a high return on assets, the company must be profitable *and* manage assets to minimize the assets invested to the level necessary to achieve its profit.

Most operating managers understand the income statement and the focus on profit. However, many of the same managers fail to manage the balance sheet (the denominator in ROA). ROA analysis encourages managers to focus on the profit achieved from the invested capital under their control. This means that managers seek to increase profits with the same level of assets *and* to decrease assets without decreasing the level of profit. It is this dual focus that makes return on assets a powerful performance measure—focusing managers' attention on *both* the income statement and balance sheet.

Boston Scientific's net income is $1,671 million, and its total assets are $20,999 million in 2018 and $19,042 million in 2017 (data from Exhibit 4.1). The company's 2018 return on assets is 8.35%, computed as follows ($ millions).

$$\text{ROA} = \frac{\$1,671}{(\$20,999 + \$19,042)/2} = 8.35\%$$

By comparison, the median return on assets of the S&P 500 companies for 2018 was 6.1% and ranged from 5.2% to 6.1% for the 2014–2018 period.

Financial Leverage

Financial leverage, the second component of ROE, measures the degree to which the company finances its assets with debt versus equity. There are many ways to measure financial leverage. In the DuPont analysis, we measure financial leverage (labeled FL) as the ratio of average total assets to average stockholders' equity. (In a later section of this module we show a different definition of financial leverage that excludes operating liabilities; we label that ratio FLEV.) An increase in this ratio implies an increase in the relative level of debt. This is evident from the accounting equation: assets = liabilities + equity. For example, if assets are financed equally with debt and equity, the accounting equation, expressed in percentage terms is: 100% = 50% + 50%, and financial leverage is 2.0 (100%/50%). If debt increases to 75%, the accounting equation is: 100% = 75% + 25%, and financial leverage is 4.0 (100%/25%).

Measuring financial leverage is important because debt is a contractual obligation and a company's failure to repay principal or interest can result in legal repercussions or even bankruptcy. As financial leverage increases so does the level of debt payments, which all else equal, increases the probability of default and possible bankruptcy. For 2018, Boston Scientific's financial leverage is 2.54, computed as ($ millions):

$$\text{Financial leverage (FL)} = \frac{(\$20{,}999 + \$19{,}042)/2}{(\$8{,}726 + \$7{,}012)/2} = 2.54$$

By comparison, the median financial leverage (FL) of the S&P 500 companies for 2018 was 2.66 and ranged from 2.46 to 2.74 for the 2014–2018 period.

Business Insight ■ Which Accounts Are Used to Compute ROE?

Return on equity has net income in the numerator and stockholders' equity in the denominator. The complexity of company financial statements, however, presents some complications: which net income and stockholders' equity accounts should we use?

- **Preferred Stock.** The ROE formula takes the perspective of the *common* stockholder in that it relates the income available to pay common dividends to the average common stockholder. The presence of preferred stock on the balance sheet requires two adjustments to ROE.

    1. Preferred dividends are subtracted from net income in the numerator.
    2. Preferred stock is subtracted from stockholders' equity in the denominator.

    This modified return on equity is labeled *return on common equity* (ROCE).

    $$\text{ROCE} = \frac{\text{Net income} - \text{Preferred dividends}}{\text{Average stockholders' equity} - \text{Average preferred equity}}$$

- **Noncontrolling interests.** Many companies have two sets of stockholders: those that own the common stock of the parent company whose financial statements are under analysis (called *controlling interest*) and those that own shares in one or more of the parent company's subsidiaries (called *noncontrolling interest*). Balance sheets separately identify the stockholders' equity relating to each group and, likewise, income statements separately identify net income attributable to each. ROE is computed from the perspective of the controlling (parent company) stockholders and, thus, the ratio is defined as:

    $$\text{ROE} = \frac{\text{Net income attributable to company shareholders}}{\text{Average equity attributable to company shareholders}}$$

    We explain controlling and noncontrolling interest in a later module and ROE computations with noncontrolling interests in Appendix 4B.

Review 4-2 LO2

Refer to the financial information for **Stryker Corp.** reported in Review 4-1.

continued

continued from previous page

> **Required**
> Compute return on assets (ROA) and financial leverage following the DuPont disaggregation of ROE for 2018. Confirm that ROA × Financial leverage (FL) = ROE.
>
> Solution on p. 4-59.

Return on Assets and Its Disaggregation

Return on assets (ROA) includes both profitability (in the numerator) and total assets (in the denominator). Managers can increase ROA by increasing profitability for a given level of asset investment or by reducing assets invested to generate a given level of profitability, or both. We gain insight into these two drivers by disaggregating return on assets into two components to isolate its profitability and asset investment levels as:

LO3 Disaggregate ROA into profitability and productivity and analyze both.

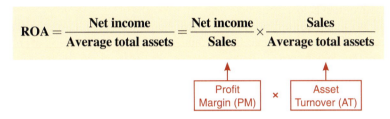

Return on assets is the product of profit margin and utilization of assets in generating sales (asset turnover). This is the insight that DuPont analysis offers as it focuses managers' attention on both profitability *and* management of the balance sheet. The two drivers of return on assets are:

- **Profit margin (PM).** PM is what the company earns on each sales dollar; a company increases profit margin by increasing its gross profit margin (Gross profit/Sales) and/or reducing its operating expenses as a percent of sales.

- **Asset turnover (AT).** AT is the sales level generated from each dollar invested in assets; a company increases asset turnover (*productivity*) by increasing sales volume with no increase in assets and/or by reducing assets invested without reducing sales.

Business Insight ■ Adjusted ROA

Return on assets is typically under the control of operating managers while the capital structure decision (the relative proportion of debt and equity) is not. Accordingly, a common adjustment is made to the numerator of ROA by adding back the after-tax net interest expense (net of any interest revenue or other nonoperating expense or revenue reported after operating income). The adjusted ROA for **Boston Scientific** is as follows ($ in millions).

$$\text{Adjusted ROA} = \frac{\text{Net income} + [\text{Net interest expense} \times (1 - \text{Statutory tax rate})]}{\text{Average total assets}}$$

$$\frac{\$1{,}671 + [(\$241 - \$156) \times (1 - 0.22)]}{(\$20{,}999 + \$19{,}042)/2} = 8.68\%$$

Net interest expense for Boston Scientific is interest expense less "other" nonoperating income (see Exhibit 4.6) "Statutory tax rate" in the adjusted ROA formula is the federal statutory tax rate *plus* the state tax rate net of any federal tax benefits; we use the assumed 22% federal and state tax rates as explained in the NOPAT computation later in this module. This adjusted numerator better reflects the company's operating profit as it measures return on assets exclusive of net nonoperating expense (or income) as we describe later in this module.

The goal is to increase the productivity of the company's assets in generating sales and then to bring as much of each sales dollar to the bottom line (net income). Managers usually understand product pricing, management of production costs, and control of overhead costs. Fewer managers understand the role of the balance sheet. The ROA approach to performance measurement encourages managers to focus on returns achieved from assets under their control, and ROA is maximized with a joint focus on both profitability and productivity.

Analysis of Profitability and Productivity

The complete DuPont return on equity disaggregation follows.

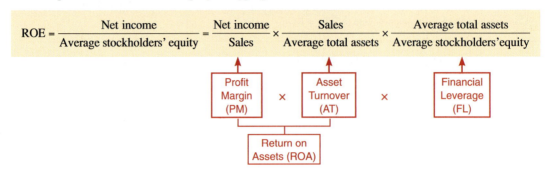

Return on equity increases with each of the three components (provided the company is profitable and reports a positive stockholders' equity).

In Exhibit 4.2, we compute the disaggregation of Boston Scientific's return into profit margin, asset turnover, and financial leverage. The analysis in Exhibit 4.2 represents a *first level* of analysis where we examine ROE over time and in comparison with peers to identify trends and differences from the norm.

Exhibit 4.2 ■ Disaggregation of Boston Scientific's ROE ($ millions)

Profit margin (PM)	Net income / Sales	$1,671 / $9,823	= 17.01%
×			×
Asset turnover (AT)	Sales / Average total assets	$9,823 / ($20,999 + $19,042)/2	= 0.49
=			=
Return on assets (ROA)	Net income / Average total assets	$1,671 / ($20,999 + $19,042)/2	= 8.35%
×			×
Financial leverage (FL)	Average total assets / Average stockholders' equity	($20,999 + $19,042)/2 / ($8,726 + $7,012)/2	= 2.54
=			=
Return on equity (ROE)	Net income / Average stockholders' equity	$1,671 / ($8,726 + $7,012)/2	= 21.24%

The *second level* analysis of the components of return on equity seeks to identify factors driving profitability (profit margin) and productivity (asset turnover) and to assess whether financial leverage increases the risk of default and bankruptcy beyond acceptable levels. The framework for second-level analysis is in Exhibit 4.3 and we explain each component in this module.

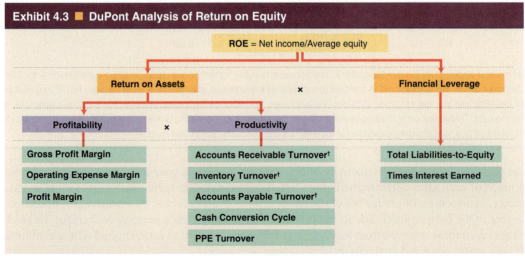

† This metric is also commonly measured "in days"—see discussion below.

Analysis of Profitability

Profit margin (Net income/Sales) reflects the profit in each dollar of sales. For 2018, the median profit margin for the S&P 500 companies was 11.2%. During 2009–2018, profit margin ranged from 7.1% in 2009 to 11.2% in 2018.

Profit margin, while an important measure of profitability, is influenced by *both* gross profit on sales and SG&A expenses. Consequently, we gain insight into profitability by separately examining gross profit margin and the SG&A expense margin.

Gross Profit Margin

Gross profit margin (Gross profit/Sales) is influenced by *both* the selling price of a company's products and the cost to make or buy those products. For 2018, the median gross profit margin for S&P 500 companies was 43.4% and it has trended upward over the past 10 years from a low of 40.4% in 2009. Gross profit margins differ greatly by industry and depend on a company's specific business model. Consequently, we must be careful in identifying peers for benchmarking to make sure their business models are similar.

We generally prefer gross profit margin to be high and increasing as the opposite usually signals more competition or less appeal for the company's product line. When analyzing gross profit margin, it is often helpful to view it on a unit basis, that is, as gross profit for one product unit. If, for example, we purchase a product for $6 and sell it for $10, the gross profit margin is 40% ([$10 − $6]/$10). A decline in gross profit margin, then, signals that the spread between the cost to make or buy the product and its selling price has narrowed. This narrowing could be due to several factors, all of which warrant investigation.

- Perhaps competitive intensity increased and selling prices have dropped to remain competitive.
- Perhaps the company's product line has lost appeal or its technology is not cutting edge.
- Perhaps the cost to make or buy products has increased due to increases in material or labor costs and the company cannot pass on that cost increase to customers.
- Perhaps there is a change in product mix away from high margin products to lower margin products (remember that sales and gross profit include *all* of the company's products, including both high margin and low margin products).
- Perhaps the volume of products sold has declined, resulting in an increase in manufacturing cost as factory overhead is spread out over a smaller number of units produced.

Business Insight **Business Model Affects Gross Margin**

The past few years have seen a sharp increase in the number of firms that use a subscription model—customers sign up for a monthly or annual payment plan. A wide variety of goods and services are now available by subscription, including apparel (such as Stitch Fix and Le Tote), healthcare and grooming (such as Bulu Box and Dollar Shave Club), entertainment (such as Netflix and PlayStation Vue), food and beverages (such as Blue Apron and WSJWine), and fitness (ClassPass and Fitocracy). More reliable revenue streams from subscribed customers and attractive margins drive this evolution. The largest shift, however, has been in the software sector with many vendors migrating to the "SaaS" (Software as a Service) business model, abandoning the traditional licensing model. The effects of this shift impact both revenues and cost of goods or services. In comparing margins over time, we need to keep in mind this dynamic business environment.

It is not enough for our analysis to reveal that a company's gross profit margin has increased or decreased. Instead, we must uncover the *reasons* for the change. It is only with analysis of the underlying cost and pricing structure of a company's products that we are able to predict future levels of gross profit. Many believe that a serious analysis should focus on the *individual product* level and the costs to make or buy those products along with the pricing strategy for the different markets served. That level of granularity is important for effective analysis of gross profit margin.

Operating Expense Margin

The operating expense margin, also referred to as SG&A expense margin (SG&A expense/Sales), measures general operating costs for each sales dollar. These costs include all costs other than those to make or buy the company's products. For 2018, the median SG&A expense margin for S&P 500 companies was 16.3% and that margin has declined steadily from a high of 19% since the economy emerged from recession in 2009.

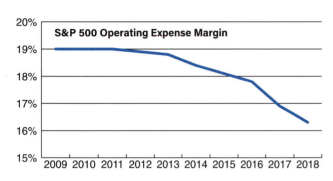

Analysis of operating expense margin focuses on each expense in whatever detail the company provides in its income statement. We compare the operating expense margin, and the margins for each of its components, over time and against peers (making sure that peers have similar business models). We investigate deviations from historical trends or benchmarks to uncover the cause. We are inclined to judge lower expense levels as favorable, but caution is advised. Perhaps a lower expense level happens because the company has tried to mitigate declining profits by reducing R&D, marketing, or compensation costs. Such activities tend to result in short-term improvements at long-term costs such as reduced market share and damaged employee morale.

Analysis of Productivity

Productivity is reflected in return on assets via turnover of total assets (Sales/Total assets). While a useful measure to gauge overall trend, a more rigorous analysis examines the productivity of each major asset category.

Analysis of Working Capital Components

All turnover ratios compare the activity on the income statement to the related balance sheet amount. The three most widely used turnover ratios follow.

Ratio	Computation
Accounts receivable turnover	Sales/Average accounts receivable
Inventory turnover	Cost of goods sold/Average inventories
Accounts payable turnover	Cost of goods sold/Average accounts payable

We discuss these turnover ratios in more detail in later modules; for now, know that they measure productivity, or efficiency, or throughput.

Turnover, while widely reported, has limited usefulness. For example, it is not easy to see how much cash is generated if accounts receivable turnover improves. It is more intuitive to think of the average number of days to collect accounts receivable, the average number of days to sell inventory, or the average number of days to pay accounts payable. Accordingly, a good analysis computes the "days" measures for working capital accounts. We compute annual measures as follows. When using quarterly financial statement data, use 90 or 91 days instead of 365.

Ratio	Computation
Days sales outstanding (DSO)	365/Accounts receivable turnover
+ Days inventory outstanding (DIO)	365/Inventory turnover
− Days payables outstanding (DPO)	365/Accounts payable turnover
= Cash conversion cycle	DSO + DIO − DPO

Cash Conversion Cycle

The three measures from the table above can be combined to yield the **cash conversion cycle** (Days sales outstanding + Days inventory outstanding – Days payables outstanding). The cash conversion cycle measures the average time (in days) to sell inventories, collect the receivables from the sale, pay the payables incurred for the inventory purchase, and return to cash. This is the same cash conversion cycle we describe in Module 2 (we use the term "operating cycle" in Exhibit 2.4 to describe the same concept). Each time a company completes one cash conversion cycle, it generates profit and cash flow. Managers aim to shorten the cash conversion cycle. The median cash conversion cycle for S&P 500 companies was 35 days in 2018 and has declined from a high of 39 days since the economy emerged from recession in 2009.

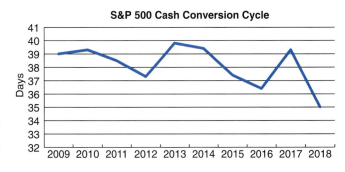

Cash conversion cycle depends on the business model of the company, which dictates:

- Credit terms offered to customers.
- Types of inventory carried and depth and breadth of product lines (which influence the time inventories remain unsold).
- Time period in which suppliers are paid for goods and services.

Diversity across business models is evident in the following graphic for medians of the cash conversion cycle for selected industries in 2018.

The variability in the cash conversion cycle across industries reflects fundamental differences in business models. Cash conversion cycle for the healthcare industry, for example, is much longer as a result of the extended period of time to collect receivables from third-party payers such as insurance companies and the government. In contrast, the utilities industry's quick cash conversion results from lower levels of inventory, and rapid collection of receivables from customers who typically pay their utility bill within a month.

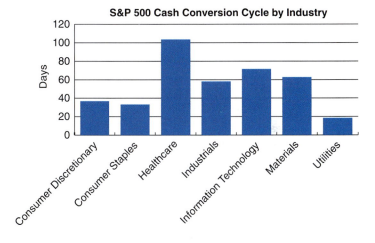

Generally companies prefer a lower cash conversion cycle. This means that the operating cycle is generating profit and cash flow quickly. Our analysis of this measure focuses on trends over time and comparisons to peers (with similar business models).

Sometimes, companies have a *negative* cash conversion cycle. **Apple**'s 2018 cash conversion cycle is one example.

Days sales outstanding (DSO).......	28.2
+ Days inventory outstanding (DIO)	9.8
– Days payables outstanding (DPO)....	(111.6)
= Cash conversion cycle (CCC)	(73.6)

Apple carries little inventory as its products are pre-sold and shipped when manufactured. Consequently, its quick sale of inventory and relatively longer time to pay suppliers result in a negative cash conversion cycle of (73.6) days. The negative number means that Apple is able to invest the cash it receives from the sale of its products for 73.6 days on average before that cash is needed to pay suppliers. This allows Apple to generate both profit from the sale *and* profit from investing cash. A negative cash conversion cycle is generally viewed positively.

A good analysis includes a review of cash conversion cycle over time. **Merck & Co.**, for example, reports improvement in its cash conversion cycle over the 2016–2018 period.

Amounts in Days	2018	2017	2016
Days sales outstanding (DSO)	61.0	63.4	62.1
+ Days inventory outstanding (DIO)	142.6	143.8	129.3
− Days payables outstanding (DPO)	(86.9)	(85.3)	(72.2)
= Cash conversion cycle (CCC)	116.7	121.9	119.2

The improvement in Merck's cash conversion cycle from 2017 to 2018 reflects improvement in all three working capital accounts.

- It is collecting receivables more quickly (an improvement).
- It is selling inventories faster (an improvement).
- It is delaying payment on payables (an improvement).

Each improvement generated additional cash during the period. To compute the amount of cash generated (or used) by changes in each of the measures, multiply the change in the the number of days by the related income statement account measured per day: Sales/365 for DSO, and COGS/365 for DIO and DPO. The table here illustrates these measures.

$ millions	Amounts in Days 2018	Amounts in Days 2017	Change		Sales (or COGS) per day		Cash savings
Days sales outstanding (DSO)	61.0	63.4	2.4	×	$115.9	=	$278.2
+ Days inventory outstanding (DIO)	142.6	143.8	1.2	×	37.0	=	44.4
− Days payables outstanding (DPO)	(86.9)	(85.3)	1.6	×	37.0	=	59.2
= Cash conversion cycle (CCC)	116.7	121.9					$381.8

In 2018, Merck's sales per day were $115.9 million such that collecting receivables 2.4 days sooner than in 2017 increased Merck's cash balance by $278.2 million ($115.9 × 2.4). In 2018, Merck recorded an average COGS of $37 million and sold inventory more quickly and paid suppliers more slowly as compared with 2017. These actions generated $44.4 million and $59.2 million, respectively. In total, by employing working capital more efficiently, Merck generated an additional $381.8 million of cash that could be invested in operating activities or in marketable securities or used to reduce interest-bearing debt, all of which increased profitability.

Although these trends for Merck are favorable, we must investigate whether they are *too* favorable. Companies can generate cash by restricting credit policies, by reducing the depth and breadth of their product offerings, and by delaying payment to suppliers ("leaning on the trade"). All of these actions can generate a short-term inflow of cash at a longer-term cost of market position and supplier relations if not managed properly. These questions must be answered by a review of nonfinancial information in the MD&A section of the 10-K, listening to conference calls with manaagement (on the Investor Relations portion of a company's website), reading the financial press, and reviewing analysts' reports.

Analysis of Plant, Property and Equipment (PPE)

The asset class for which analysis of turnover is most useful is PPE assets (Sales/Average PPE, gross). Lower levels of PPE turnover indicate a higher level of capital intensity. PPE asset turnover differs by industry as revealed in the graph for 2018 shown below for S&P 500 companies. The utilities industry requires high levels of capital investment and, consequently, reports low PPE turnover.

Because investment in PPE assets is often a large part of the balance sheet, improvement in plant asset turnover can greatly impact the company's return on assets and cash flow. Improvements in PPE turnover are not easy to achieve, however, often requiring:

- Divestiture of unproductive assets or entire business segments.
- Joint ventures with other companies to jointly use PPE assets such as distribution networks, information technology, production facilities, and warehouses.

- Divestiture of production facilities with agreements to purchase finished goods from the facilities' new owners.
- Sale and leaseback of administrative buildings.

Each of these activities is a strategic and financial event, often requiring integration within the supply chain, new financing, and relationship building. As such, improvements in PPE turnover can be difficult to achieve. If properly structured, however, they can markedly increase asset returns and cash flow.

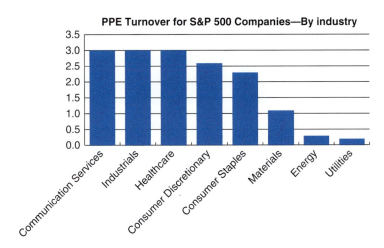

Analysis of Financial Leverage

As companies utilize a larger proportion of borrowed money in their capital structures, they incur obligations for interest payments and the repayment of the amount borrowed (the principal). Those obligations are typically evidenced by a loan agreement (or bond indenture) that contains some or all of the following.

- Restrictions on certain activities, such as mergers or acquisitions of other companies without approval of lenders.
- Prohibitions against dividend payments or the repurchase of common stock without approval of lenders.
- Covenants to maintain required levels of financial ratios, such as a maximum level of financial leverage, minimum levels of the current and quick ratios, minimum level of equity, and minimum level of working capital.
- Prohibitions against the pledging of assets to secure new borrowings.
- Remedies to lenders in event of default (failure to make required interest and principal payments when due). These remedies can include seizing company assets or, possibly, forcing the company into bankruptcy and requiring liquidation.

Judicial use of financial leverage is beneficial to stockholders (it is a relatively inexpensive source of capital), but the use of borrowed money adds risk as debt payments are contractual obligations. Analysis typically involves ratios that investigate the *level* of borrowed money relative to equity capital and the level of profitability and *cash flow* relative to required debt payments. Although there are dozens of financial leverage-related ratios in commercial databases, the following two ratios capture the spirit of such analysis.

- Total liabilities-to-equity ratio (Total liabilities/Stockholders' equity).
- Times interest earned ratio (Earnings before interest and taxes/Interest expense, gross).

As for all ratios, analysis of financial leverage ratios must consider ratios over time and comparisons with peers. Appropriate financial leverage varies across industries because different business models generate cash flow streams that differ in amount and variability over time. Generally, business models that generate high and stable levels of cash flow can support a higher level of debt.

The median liabilities-to-equity ratio for S&P 500 companies in 2018 was 1.69, indicating that companies typically report about 1.69 times more borrowed money than equity in their capital structures. The median financial leverage ratio for these companies has ranged from 1.56 to 1.76 from 2014 to 2018. Times interest earned ratios for S&P 500 companies was 7.7 in 2018, down markedly from a high of 9.3 in 2014. Again, we stress the importance of remembering that these (and all) ratios differ across industry and company size.

Exhibit 4.4 shows a summary of ratios used in the DuPont disaggregation of return on equity.

Exhibit 4.4 ■ Summary of Ratios in DuPont Disaggregation of Return on Equity

Ratio	Computation	What the Ratio Measures	Positive Indicators Include
Return on equity	Net income ÷ Avg. stockholders' equity, or Return on assets × Financial leverage	ROE measures accounting return to shareholders using net income and the book value of stockholders' equity.	• Improvement over time and favorable comparison to peers. • Greater proportion of ROE from ROA (operations) than financial leverage (risk).
Return on assets	Net income/Avg. total assets or Profit margin × Asset turnover	ROA measures the accounting return on total assets using net income and total assets.	• Improvement over time in both profit margin and asset turnover. • Improvement in gross margins and not solely from expense reduction.
PROFITABILITY			
Gross profit margin	Gross profit / Sales	Gross profit measures the difference between selling price and the cost to make or buy the products sold for the year.	• Improvement over time due to increases in selling prices and/or reductions in cost to make or buy without compromising product quality. • Favorable comparison to peers.
Operating expense margin (or SG&A expense margin)	SG&A expense / Sales	Operating expense margin measures total overhead expense (SG&A) as a percent of sales.	• Improvement over time. • Favorable comparison to peers. • No short-term gains at long-term cost (such as unusual reductions in marketing and R&D expenses).
Profit margin (or net profit margin)	Net income / Sales	Profit margin includes effects of both gross profit margin, the operating expense margin, and net nonoperating expenses.	• Improvement over time. • Favorable comparison to peers.
PRODUCTIVITY			
Accounts receivable turnover	Sales / Avg. accounts receivable	AR turnover reflects how effective a company manages the credit issued to customers.	• Improvement over time. • Favorable comparison to peers.
Days sales outstanding (DSO)	365/Accounts receivable turnover	DSO reflects how well a company's accounts receivables are managed.	• Maintain sales while reducing days to collect receivables.
Inventory turnover	COGS/Avg. inventory	Inventory turnover reflects the number of times inventory is sold or used during the period.	• Improvement over time. • Favorable comparison to peers.
Days inventory outstanding (DIO)	365/Inventory turnover	DIO reflects how many days it takes for a company to sell its inventory.	• Maintain sales while reducing days to sell inventory.
Accounts payable turnover	COGS/Avg. accounts payable	AP turnover reflects how many times a company pays off its suppliers during the period.	• Improvement over time. • Favorable comparison to peers.
Days payables outstanding (DPO)	365/Accounts payable turnover	DPO reflects how long it takes a company to pay its invoices from suppliers.	• Maintain supplier relations while delaying payment to suppliers.
Cash conversion cycle	DSO + DIO − DPO	Cash conversion (operating) cycle measures the days to convert cash to inventories, receivables to cash, cash to payables.	• Improvement over time. • Favorable comparison to peers.
PPE turnover	Sales/Avg. PPE assets	Plant asset turnover is a productivity measure, comparing the volume of sales generated by plant assets.	• Improvement over time. • Favorable comparison to peers.

continued

Exhibit 4.4 ■ Summary of Ratios in DuPont Disaggregation of Return on Equity (cont.)

Ratio	Computation	What the Ratio Measures	Positive Indicators Include
FINANCIAL LEVERAGE			
Total liabilities-to-equity	Total liabilities/Stockholders' equity	Proportion of liabilities vs. equity in the capital structure.	• Improvement over time. • Favorable comparison to peers. • Relatively lower levels are preferable.
Times interest earned	Earnings before interest and taxes/Interest expense, gross	Pool of operating profit before tax that a company earns relative to its interest expense, gross.	• Improvement over time. • Favorable comparison to peers. • Higher levels are preferable to lower levels.

LO3 Review 4-3

Refer to the income statement and balance sheet data for **Stryker Corp.** from Review 4-1 along with the following additional information.

$ millions	2018	2017
Cost of sales.	$ 4,663	$ 4,264
Accounts receivable	2,332	2,198
Inventories	2,955	2,465
Accounts payable	646	487
Liabilities.	15,499	12,217

Required

a. Disaggregate 2018 ROA into components of profitability margin (PM) and asset turnover (AT). Then, prove that their product (multiplication) results in ROA.
b. Compute the gross profit margin.
c. Compute the cash conversion cycle.
d. Compute the total liabilities-to-equity ratio for 2018.

Solution on p. 4-59.

Balance Sheet Analysis with an Operating Focus

ROE analysis with an operating focus recognizes that companies create value mainly through core operations of the business. Operating activities involve the manufacturing and selling of company products and services to customers. Nonoperating activities involve nonstrategic investments of cash into marketable securities and debt financing activities. The balance sheet and income statement include both operating and nonoperating items. Because operating activities affect company value much more than do nonoperating activities, our analysis of a company can, arguably, be improved if we separately identify these two components of the business and analyze them separately.

Operating and Nonoperating Returns Return on equity, computed using net income and total equity, reflects a blend of the return on the company's operating activities and the return that arises from the nonoperating activities. Specifically:

$$\text{ROE} = \text{Operating return} + \text{Nonoperating return}$$

This shows that ROE consists of two returns: (1) return from the company's operating activities, linked to revenues and expenses from the company's sale of products or services, and (2) return from financing and investing (nonoperating) activities. Companies can use debt to increase their return on equity, but this increases risk because the failure to make required debt payments can yield many legal consequences, including bankruptcy. This is one reason why many top investors such as Warren Buffett focus on acquiring companies whose return on equity is derived primarily from operating activities.

Operating and Nonoperating Liabilities A second, more subtle, issue arises in computing return on equity. In the traditional DuPont analysis, ROE is the product of the return on assets and financial leverage. Financial leverage is the ratio of total assets to stockholders' equity, which increases as the proportion of liabilities increases relative to equity. The problem is that the "liabilities" used in this computation includes *all* of the company's liabilities. However, there is a difference between borrowed money and operating liabilities such as accounts payable and accrued liabilities. Accounts payable and accruals are interest free and are *self-liquidating*, meaning that they are paid when receivables are collected as part of the cash conversion cycle. On the other hand, borrowed money is interest-bearing and often contains severe legal repercussions in the event of nonpayment, possibly risking bankruptcy. The operating focus treats these two types of liabilities differently for ROE analysis, treating borrowed money (debt) as a nonoperating item.

> The FASB released a draft of a proposed new format for financial statements to, among other things, distinguish operating and nonoperating activities.

Return on Net Operating Assets (RNOA)

Operating returns can be measured by the **return on net operating assets (RNOA)**.

$$\text{RNOA} = \frac{\text{Net operating profit after tax (NOPAT)}}{\text{Average net operating assets (NOA)}}$$

To implement this formula, we must first classify the balance sheet and income statement into operating and nonoperating components so that we can assess each separately. We first consider operating activities on the balance sheet and explain how to compute NOA. Second, we consider operating activities on the income statement and explain how to compute NOPAT. We summarize the classification method in Appendix 4A.

Net Operating Assets (NOA)

The balance sheet includes both operating and nonoperating assets and liabilites. NOA includes only operating items and we define NOA as follows.

$$\text{Net operating assets} = \text{Operating assets} - \text{Operating liabilities}$$

To compute NOA, we must partition the balance sheet into operating and nonoperating items.

Operating Assets

Operating assets are those assets directly linked to the company's ongoing (continuing) business operations of bringing its products or services to the market. The company needs these assets to operate normally and they typically include the following:

- Accounts receivable
- Inventories
- Prepaid expenses and supplies
- Property, plant, and equipment (PPE) including both assets that are owned outright and those that are leased[1]
- Intangible assets and Goodwill
- Deferred income tax assets
- "Equity method" investments, which are strategic investments with partners, associated companies, and joint ventures

Operating Liabilities

Operating liabilities are liabilities that arise from operating revenues and expenses, that is, relating to the core business activities of the company. Examples include:

---

[1] Leasing is a way to acquire an asset for use without the upfront cash outlay. If the leased asset is used for operations, then it is an operating asset and we categorize it as such regardless of how it is financed.

- Accounts payable
- Accrued expenses (for unpaid wages and other operating expenses)
- Unearned or deferred revenue (because it relates to operating revenue)
- Income taxes payable (both short-term and long-term)
- Deferred income tax liabilities
- Pension and other post-employment obligations (that relate to employee retirement and healthcare, which are operating activities)

"Other" Assets and Liabilities

Companies typically report "Other" assets and liabilities, both as current and long-term items. We *assume* that these are operating items *unless* information suggests otherwise. For example, details in footnotes might reveal that "other" consists of nonoperating items. In that case, we would classify the "other" as nonoperating. Or if the footnote revealed that "other" includes both operating and nonoperating items, we could consider partitioning the "other" line item into separate operating and nonoperating items.

Exhibit 4.5 shows Boston Scientific's balance sheet with operating assets and operating liabilities highlighted.

Exhibit 4.5 ■ Operating and Nonoperating Items in Boston Scientific's Balance Sheet

December 31, $ millions	2018	2017
Current assets		
Cash and cash equivalents	$ 146	$ 188
Trade accounts receivable, net	**1,608**	**1,548**
Inventories	**1,166**	**1,078**
Prepaid income taxes	**161**	**66**
Other current assets	**921**	**942**
Total current assets	4,002	3,822
Property, plant and equipment, net	**1,782**	**1,697**
Goodwill	**7,911**	**6,998**
Other intangible assets, net	**6,372**	**5,837**
Other long-term assets	**932**	**688**
Total assets	$20,999	$19,042
Current liabilities		
Current debt obligations	$ 2,253	$ 1,801
Accounts payable	**349**	**530**
Accrued expenses	**2,246**	**2,456**
Other current liabilities	**412**	**867**
Total current liabilities	5,260	5,654
Long-term debt	4,803	3,815
Deferred income taxes	**328**	**191**
Other long-term liabilities	**1,882**	**2,370**
Stockholders' equity		
Preferred stock	—	—
Common stock	16	16
Treasury stock, at cost	(1,717)	(1,717)
Additional paid-in capital	17,346	17,161
Accumulated deficit	(6,953)	(8,390)
Accumulated other comprehensive income (loss), net of tax:		
Foreign currency translation adjustment	(53)	(32)
Unrealized gain (loss) on derivative financial instruments	111	1
Unrealized gain (loss) on available-for-sale securities	0	(1)
Unrealized costs associated with defined benefit pensions and other items	(25)	(27)
Total stockholders' equity	8,726	7,012
Total liabilities and stockholders' equity	$20,999	$19,042

Operating assets
2018 = $20,853
2017 = $18,854

Operating liabilities
2018 = $5,217
2017 = $6,414

Net Operating Assets (NOA)

Using the classifications in Exhibit 4.5, Boston Scientific's net operating assets follow.

$ millions	2018	2017
Operating assets	$20,853	$18,854
Less operating liabilities	5,217	6,414
Net operating assets (NOA)	$15,636	$12,440

Net Nonoperating Obligations (NNO)

All balance sheets include nonoperating liabilities and/or nonoperating assets, although they are typically less numerous than the operating items. Generally, nonoperating refers to assets and liabilities that are not used as part of the core business activities of the company. As a rule of thumb, if the liability requires the payment of interest expense or if the asset earns interest or dividend income, it is classified as nonoperating. We compute net nonoperating obligations (NNO) as follows.

> Net nonoperating obligations (NNO) = Nonoperating liabilities – Nonoperating assets

See that NNO is net "obligations" whereas NOA is net "assets." We subtract any nonoperating assets from nonoperating liabilities to arrive at NNO. For most companies, NNO is a positive amount, meaning that nonoperating obligations are greater than nonoperating assets. We discuss situations where this is not the case in Appendix 4B.

Nonoperating Liabilities

Common nonoperating liabilities include:

- Short-term and long-term debt, regardless of the purpose of the borrowing
- Lease obligations, which are de facto debt liabilities, tied to major capital equipment or other long-term assets
- Interest payable
- Dividends payable
- Discontinued or held-for-sale liabilities[2]
- Derivative liabilities[3]

Nonoperating Assets

Common nonoperating assets are:

- Cash and cash equivalents
- Marketable securities (both current and noncurrent)
- Discontinued or held-for-sale assets
- Derivative assets

It might seem odd that we classify cash and cash equivalents as a nonoperating asset, but this account frequently consists almost totally of "cash equivalents," which are short-term investments with a

---

[2] **Discontinued operations** on the balance sheet represent assets and liabilities that the company no longer operates or has sold off. Companies separately disclose discontinued assets and liabilities on the balance sheet or in footnotes, to distinguish them from continuing items. Similarly, assets and liabilities "held for sale" are categorized as nonoperating because the company has formally decided to sell them to another party but has not yet concluded the sale. Thus, we categorize as nonoperating, all assets and liabilities that are labeled as discontinued or held-for-sale. We discuss discontinued operations in Modules 2 and 9.

[3] Companies use **derivatives** (including futures, forward contracts, options, swaps, and other derivative securities) to hedge (mitigate) risk or to speculate. Balance sheets report derivatives that are in loss positions as liabilities and those in gain positions as assets. For analysis purposes, we treat all derivatives as nonoperating items. Admittedly, some derivatives are operating assets or liabilities; for example, a forward contract on a company's manufacturing raw materials. Some derivatives are clearly nonoperating; for example, interest rate swaps. However, distinguishing between the two is complicated and often impossible for an external analyst. Accordingly, we treat all derivatives as nonoperating, both assets and liabilities. We discuss derivatives in Module 9.

scheduled maturity of 90 days or fewer. Technically, the cash needed to support routine business transactions is an operating asset. However, companies do not separately report that information and it is probably a small portion of the cash and cash equivalents line item. Therefore, we consider the entire cash and cash equivalents account as a nonoperating asset. This is consistent with current practice among external financial analysts.

Using the classified balance sheet for Boston Scientific in Exhibit 4.5, we can calculate net nonoperating obligations as follows.

$ millions	2018	2017
Nonoperating liabilities	$7,056	$5,616
Less nonoperating assets	146	188
Net nonoperating obligations (NNO)	$6,910	$5,428

LO4 Review 4-4

Refer to the following balance sheet for **Stryker Corporation**.

$ millions	Dec. 31, 2018	Dec. 31, 2017
Current assets		
Cash and cash equivalents	$ 3,616	$ 2,542
Marketable securities	83	251
Accounts receivable	2,332	2,198
Inventories	2,955	2,465
Prepaid expenses and other current assets	747	537
Total current assets	9,733	7,993
Property, plant and equipment, net	2,291	1,975
Goodwill	8,563	7,168
Other intangibles, net	4,163	3,477
Noncurrent deferred income tax assets	1,678	283
Other noncurrent assets	801	1,301
Total assets	$27,229	$22,197
Current liabilities		
Accounts payable	$ 646	$ 487
Accrued compensation	917	838
Income taxes	158	143
Dividend payable	192	178
Accrued expenses and other liabilities	1,521	1,207
Current maturities of debt	1,373	632
Total current liabilities	4,807	3,485
Long-term debt, excluding current maturities	8,486	6,590
Income taxes	1,228	1,261
Other noncurrent liabilities	978	881
Total liabilities	15,499	12,217
Shareholders' equity		
Common stock, $0.10 par value	37	37
Additional paid-in capital	1,559	1,496
Retained earnings	10,765	8,986
Other equity	(631)	(539)
Total shareholders' equity	11,730	9,980
Total liabilities and shareholders' equity	$27,229	$22,197

Required

a. Determine operating assets and operating liabilities for fiscal year-end 2017 and 2018.

b. Compute net operating assets (NOA) for fiscal year-end 2017 and 2018.

Solution on p. 4-60.

Income Statement Analysis with an Operating Focus

LO5 Identify income statement operating items and compute net operating profit after tax.

The income statement reports on both operating and nonoperating activities. Operating activities are those that relate to bringing a company's products or services to market and any after-sales support. The income statement captures operating revenues and expenses, yielding operating profit. Operating profit less income tax on operating profit results in net operating profit after tax (NOPAT). This measure of a company's operating performance warrants special attention because it is the lifeblood of a company's value creation and growth.

Net income (an after-tax measure) is not equivalent to net operating profit after tax because the income statement often includes nonoperating activities. These activities relate to such items as borrowed money that creates interest expense and nonstrategic investments in marketable securities that yield interest or dividend revenue. To more precisely analyze a company's operating activities, we separate the income statement into operating and nonoperating activities, as we did with the balance sheet.

To compute NOPAT, we start with net operating profit before tax from the income statement and use the following formula:

> Net operating profit after tax = Net operating profit before tax − Tax on operating profit

To measure net operating profit before tax (NOPBT), we classify the line items on the income statement as either operating or nonoperating.

Operating Line Items on the Income Statement

Operating activities relate to bringing a company's products or services to market and providing after-sales support. These include:

- Revenues
- Costs of goods sold (COGS)
- Selling, general, and administrative expense (SG&A) including wages, advertising, occupancy, insurance, depreciation and amortization, litigation, and restructuring expenses
- Research and development—often reported as part of SG&A
- Impairments of operating assets such as goodwill
- Income from strategic investments (*not* marketable securities)—including joint ventures, partnerships, associated companies, and equity-method investments
- Gains and losses on disposals of operating assets such as PPE and strategic investments
- "Other" operating expenses or income—unless footnote disclosures indicate that the items are nonoperating or they are included in the nonoperating portion of the income statement

Exhibit 4.6 presents Boston Scientific's income statement with operating revenues and expenses highlighted. We use this classified income statement to calculate the 2018 net operating profit before tax (NOPBT) as follows.

$$\text{NOPBT} = \text{Net sales} - \text{Cost of products sold} - \text{Operating expenses}$$
$$\text{NOPBT} = \$9{,}823 - \$2{,}813 - \$5{,}504 = \$1{,}506.$$

Boston Scientific reports NOPBT as a separate line item labeled "Operating income," but this is not required disclosure, and sometimes, a company's reported operating income is not equivalent to the NOPBT we calculate. The lesson here is that line-item classification and careful analysis are required.

Nonoperating Line Items on the Income Statement

Nonoperating income and expense items relate to nonoperating assets and liabilities. These items include:

- Interest expense on debt and lease obligations
- Loss or income relating to discontinued operations

- Debt issuance and retirement costs
- Interest and dividend income on nonstrategic investments (marketable securities)
- Gains or losses on the sale of nonstrategic investments
- "Other" income or expense *if reported separately* from operating income (usually following the operating section of the income statement)

Exhibit 4.6 ■ Operating and Nonoperating Items in Boston Scientific's Income Statement

For Year Ended December 31, $ millions	2018	2017	2016
Net sales	$9,823	$9,048	$8,386
Cost of products sold	2,813	2,593	2,424
Gross profit	7,010	6,455	5,962
Operating expenses			
Selling, general and administrative expenses	3,569	3,294	3,099
Research and development expenses	1,113	997	920
Royalty expense	70	68	79
Amortization expense	599	565	545
Intangible asset impairment charges	35	4	11
Contingent consideration expense (benefit)	(21)	(80)	29
Restructuring charges	36	37	28
Litigation-related charges	103	285	804
Operating expenses	5,504	5,170	5,515
Operating income	1,506	1,285	447
Other expense (income)			
Interest expense	241	229	233
Other expense (income), net	(156)	124	37
Income before income taxes	1,422	932	177
Income tax expense (benefit)	(249)	828	(170)
Net income	$1,671	$ 104	$ 347

For most companies, nonoperating activities create a pretax net nonoperating "expense" (meaning that interest expense exceeds interest and other nonoperating income). When the reverse is true (interest and other nonoperating income is greater than interest expense), then the net nonoperating item is "income" as depicted in the following examples.

	Pretax Nonoperating Expense	Pretax Nonoperating Income	Pretax Nonoperating Net
Company A	$100	$ 10	Expense = $ 90
Company B	50	300	Income = $250

Using Boston Scientific's classified income statement, we calculate 2018 pretax net nonoperating **expense** as $85 million (Interest expense of $241 million less Other income of $156 million).

Tax on Operating Profit The tax expense that companies report on their income statements pertains to both operating *and* nonoperating activities. To compute NOPAT, we need to compute the tax expense relating solely to operating profit as follows.

Tax on operating profit = Tax expense + (Pretax net nonoperating expense × Statutory tax rate)

Tax Shield

The amount in parentheses is called the tax shield, which are the taxes that a company saves by having tax-deductible nonoperating expenses (see Tax Shield box below for details). By definition, the taxes saved (by the tax shield) do not relate to operating profits; thus, we must add back the tax shield to total tax expense to compute the tax on operating profit.

For companies with nonoperating revenue and gains greater than nonoperating expenses, so-called nonoperating income, the "pretax net nonoperating expense" is a negative number which yields a negative tax shield. A negative tax shield implies that the company is paying more tax than it would have paid if not for the additional nonoperating income. Tax on operating profit is computed in the same manner as in the equation above: we add the negative tax shield to tax expense.

The Tax Cuts and Jobs Act (TCJA) of 2017 reduced the federal income tax rate for corporations from 35% to 21%. Most states and some local jurisdictions also impose an income tax on corporate income. On average, this adds 1% to the tax bill such that the combined statutory tax rate on operating profits is about 22%. Prior to the TCJA, the combined statutory rate was about 37%.

Applying the equations above to Boston Scientific for 2018, we calculate tax on operating profit and obtain NOPAT as follows ($ millions).

Net operating profit before tax (NOPBT)		$1,506
Less tax on operating profit		
Tax expense (benefit) per income statement	$(249)	
Plus tax shield $85 x 22%	19	(230)
Net operating profit after tax (NOPAT)		$1,736

Caveat In addition to lowering tax rates, the TCJA made sweeping changes to many aspects of tax law. Some companies benefitted greatly from the new tax rules while other companies came out behind. Many companies (including Boston Scientific) witnessed large swings in their overall tax bills in 2017 and 2018. This potential effect of the TCJA on the income statement necessitates caution when we compare after-tax profits over years that include 2017 and 2018. Module 10 further discusses the TCJA.

Boston Scientific	2018	2017
Income (loss) before income taxes	$1,422	$932
Income tax (benefit) expense	$ (249)	$828
Average tax rate (effective rate)	(17.5)%	88.8%

Business Insight ■ Tax Rates for Computing NOPAT

In our examples and assignments, we *assume* the statutory tax rate is 22% as this is the approximate average combined federal and state tax rate for public companies. We can, as an alternative, compute a company specific tax rate using the income tax footnote from the 10-K. For example, **Colgate-Palmolive** provides the following table in its 10-K for the year ended December 28, 2018. The federal statutory rate is 21.0%, and Colgate pays additional state taxes, net of 1% for a total of 22%.

Percentage of Income Before Income Taxes (For Fiscal Years Ended)	Dec. 28, 2018	Dec. 27, 2017	Dec. 26, 2016
Tax at United States statutory rate	21.0%	35.0%	35.0%
State income taxes, net of federal benefit	1.0	0.5	0.5
Earnings taxed at other than United States statutory rate	4.5	(3.4)	(2.7)
Charge for U.S. tax reform	2.3	7.9	—
Excess tax benefits from stock-based compensation	(0.3)	(1.4)	—
Foreign tax credit carryback	(1.7)	—	—
(Benefit) charge for foreign tax matters	(0.4)	—	(0.8)
(Benefit) from Venezuela remeasurement	—	—	(5.6)
Tax charge on incremental repatriation of foreign earnings	—	—	5.6
Other, net	(0.2)	(0.9)	(1.2)
Effective tax rate	26.2%	37.7%	30.8%

For forecasting purposes later in the text we look for a persistent effective tax rate. In 2018, Colgate paid additional taxes amounting to 4.2% of profit before tax, yielding an effective tax rate of 26.2%. When we forecast Colgate's future profitability (see Module 12), we must consider whether these additional taxes are likely to persist. In this case, the charge for U.S. tax reform (2.3%), foreign tax credit carryback (−1.7%), and the (benefit) charge for foreign tax matters (−0.4%) might be considered transitory items, and largely offsetting, leaving an effective tax rate of 26% for use in forecasting, computed as 21.0% + 1.0% + 4.5% − 0.3% − 0.2%.

Business Insight ■ Tax Shield

Persons with home mortgages understand well the beneficial effects of the "interest tax shield." To see how the interest tax shield works, consider two individuals, each with income of $50,000 and each with only one expense: a home. Assume that one person pays $10,000 per year in rent; the other pays $10,000 in interest on a home mortgage. Rent is not deductible for tax purposes, whereas mortgage interest (but not principal) is deductible. Assume that each person pays taxes at 25%, the personal tax rate for this income level. Their tax payments are as follows.

	Renter	Homeowner
Income before interest and taxes	$50,000	$50,000
Less interest deduction	0	(10,000)
Taxable income	$50,000	$40,000
Taxes paid (25% rate)	$12,500	$10,000

The renter reports $50,000 in taxable income and pays $12,500 in taxes. The homeowner deducts $10,000 in interest, which lowers taxable income to $40,000 and reduces taxes to $10,000. By deducting mortgage interest, the homeowner's tax bill is $2,500 lower. The $2,500 is the *interest tax shield*, and we can compute it directly as the $10,000 interest deduction multiplied by the 25% tax rate.

Net Nonoperating Expense (NNE)

Pretax nonoperating expense creates a tax shield. We can calculate net nonoperating expense, **after tax**, which we label, NNE.

NNE = Pretax net nonoperating expense − Tax shield
   = Pretax net nonoperating expense − (Pretax net nonoperating expense × Tax%)
   = Pretax net nonoperating expense × (1 − Tax%).

For Boston Scientific this yields NNE of $66 million, calculated as $85 × (1 − 22%).

Recall that net income includes both operating and nonoperating items, all measured after-tax. This means that Net income is equal to Net operating profit after tax (NOPAT) less Net nonoperating expense after tax (NNE). This is another way to calculate NOPAT.

$$\text{NOPAT} = \text{Net income} + \text{NNE}$$

Applying this to Boston Scientific, we compute NOPAT as $1,671 + $66 = $1,737. We see that this is off by $1 as compared to the NOPAT of $1,736 previously calculated ($ in millions). But recall, Boston Scientific's income statement suffers from a rounding discrepancy of $1 and this causes the two NOPAT calculations to deviate. Ordinarily, the two methods yield identical NOPAT numbers.

LO5 Review 4-5

Refer to the following income statement for **Stryker Corporation** to answer the requirements.

Stryker Corporation, $ millions	2018
Net sales	$13,601
Cost of sales	4,663
Gross profit	8,938
Research, development and engineering expenses	862
Selling, general and administrative expenses	5,099
Recall charges, net of insurance proceeds	23
Amortization of intangible assets	417
Total operating expenses	6,401
Operating income	2,537
Nonoperating expense, net	181
Earnings before income taxes	2,356
Income tax expense (benefit)	(1,197)
Net earnings	$ 3,553

continued

continued from previous page

Required
a. Determine net operating profit before tax (NOPBT) for fiscal 2018.
b. Compute tax on operating profit for fiscal 2018, assuming a 22% statutory tax rate.
c. Compute NOPAT using the formula: NOPBT − Tax on operating profit.
d. Compute after-tax net nonoperating expense, NNE.
e. Calculate NOPAT using the formula: Net income + NNE

Solution on p. 4-60.

Return on Net Operating Assets (RNOA)

LO6 Compute and interpret return on net operating assets (RNOA).

To determine average NOA, we take a simple average of two consecutive years' numbers. Return on net operating assets (RNOA) for Boston Scientific for 2018 is computed as follows ($ millions).

$$\text{RNOA} = \frac{\text{Net operating profit after tax}}{\text{Average net operating assets}} = \frac{\$1{,}737}{(\$15{,}636 + \$12{,}440)/2} = 12.37\%$$

Boston Scientific's 2018 RNOA is 12.37%. By comparison, the average RNOA for S&P 500 companies is 11.3% in 2018 and has ranged from 9.3% to 12.5% over the 2010-2018 period (see the Research Insight titled "Ratio Behavior over Time").

RNOA vs ROA A comparison of Boston Scientific's RNOA of 12.37% with the ROA of 8.35%, computed earlier, yields insight into the benefits of an operating focus.

DuPont vs Operating Focus, $ millions	DuPont	Operating	Computation
Net income	$ 1,671		
Net operating profit after tax (NOPAT)		$ 1,737	
Average assets	$20,021		($20,999 + $19,042)/2
Average net operating assets (NOA)		$14,038	($15,636 + $12,440)/2
ROA	8.35%		$1,671/$20,021
RNOA		12.37%	$1,737/$14,038
ROE	21.24%	21.24%	$1,671/[($8,726 + $7,012)/2]
ROE / ROA (or RNOA):			
DuPont (ROE/ROA)	2.54		21.24%/8.35%
Operating (ROE/ RNOA)		1.72	21.24%/12.37%

Boston Scientific's RNOA of 12.37% is larger than its ROA of 8.35% derived from the DuPont analysis. The reason for the difference is twofold.

1. **Numerator effect** RNOA focuses on NOPAT, which is $66 million higher than net income used in the DuPont ROA. The larger numerator in RNOA vis-a-vis the numerator in ROA pushes RNOA higher.
2. **Denominator effect** The operating approach focuses on net operating assets (NOA) while the DuPont analysis uses total assets. NOA is lower than total assets because operating liabilities have been subtracted to arrive at NOA. This creates a smaller denominator in the RNOA calculation ($14,038) as compared to ROA ($20,021), which makes the RNOA ratio higher.

We can disaggregate ROE into operating and nonoperating components.

$$\text{ROE} = \text{Operating return (via RNOA)} + \text{Nonoperating return}$$

Boston Scientific's ROE of 21.24% consists of an operating return of 12.37% (via RNOA) and nonoperating return of 8.87% (ROE − RNOA).

Financial leverage. As we discussed earlier in the module, financial leverage relates to the degree to which the company uses borrowed money, rather than shareholder equity investment, to fund operations and the acquisition of assets. The accounting equation (Assets = Liabilities + Equity) highlights the concept well. Holding total assets constant, as the amount of liabilities increases, means that stockholders' equity decreases, and consequently, financial leverage increases.

We are interested in financial leverage because it is an important measure of the risk a company is incurring with its reliance on debt. As debt increases so does the risk that the company is unable to pay the interest and principal payments on the debt. Financial leverage quantifies this risk.

While financial leverage increases risk, it also increases the return to shareholders *but only if the borrowing rate on the debt is less than the yield on the assets*. Thinking again about the accounting equation, if assets are yielding 12% and liabilities (debt) cost 10%, leverage is a positive force. If the spread between the asset returns and the debt cost is high, then, stockholders benefit even more from the borrowed money (debt). There is a trade-off, however, between the added return and the added risk created by debt. At some level of debt, the risk of default is too high and lenders will demand a higher rate and stockholders will no longer benefit from financial leverage. Continuing with the example, if the assets continue to yield 12% and additional debt costs 13%, leverage is a negative force.

While both the DuPont and Operating approaches consider the impact of financial leverage on ROE, they measure that impact in markedly different ways:

- **DuPont** approach measures the impact of financial leverage on ROE using only balance sheet numbers:

$$FL = \frac{\text{Average total assets}}{\text{Average stockholders' equity}} \quad (\text{and ROE} = \text{ROA} \times \text{FL})$$

- **Operating** approach measures the impact of financial leverage on ROE using **nonoperating returns**, which captures effects from both the balance sheet and the income statement. Recall, ROE– RNOA = Nonoperating returns. Nonoperating returns, therefore, provide a way to measure the impact of financial leverage on ROE. (In Appendix 4B we discuss financial leverage with an operating focus; that definition of financial leverage is labeled FLEV.)

In the table above, the DuPont approach measures the ratio of ROA/ROE as 39.3% and the Operating approach measures the ratio of RNOA/ROE as 58.2%. The DuPont approach ascribes a much smaller proportion of ROE to operating activities (as the effect of financial leverage is greater) than does the Operating approach. The Operating approach shows that much more of Boston Scientific's ROE is due to operating activities that make up its core business.

Divergent conclusions about the drivers of ROE are a key difference between the two approaches. While the difference between the DuPont approach and the Operating approach is moderate for Boston Scientific, for other companies the difference can be large. This is especially true for companies with large investments in marketable securities (such as big technology and pharmaceutical companies) where we come to opposite conclusions about ROE drivers when we use the Operating versus the DuPont approach. We discuss this concept further using Amazon as an example in Appendix 4B.

Exhibit 4.7 ■ Key Ratio and Acronym Definitions

Ratio		Definition
ROE:	Return on equity	Net income attributable to controlling interest/Average equity attributable to controlling interest
NOA:	Net operating assets	Operating assets less operating liabilities
NOPBT:	Net operating profit before tax	Revenue – Operating expenses including COGS
NNE:	Net nonoperating expense after tax	Pretax net nonoperating expense × (1 – Tax%)
NOPAT:	Net operating profit after tax	NOPBT – Tax on operating profit Or: Net income + NNE
RNOA:	Return on net operating assets	NOPAT / Average NOA

> ### Research Insight ■ Ratio Behavior over Time
>
> How do RNOA and ROE behave over time? Following is a graph of average RNOA and ROE for the S&P 500 companies from 2010 to 2018. The spread between ROE and RNOA has increased in recent years as many companies have utilized excess cash to invest in marketable securities and for stock buy-backs. Yet, in all periods for the S&P 500 companies, ROE exceeds RNOA. This is evidence of the positive effect of leverage on ROE. However, this relation varies by industry; the graphics at the start of this module show some industries where ROE is less than RNOA.
>
>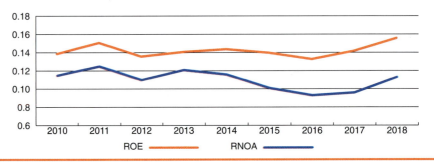

Review 4-6 LO6

Refer to Review 4-4 (for NOA) and 4-5 (for NOPAT) for **Stryker Corporation** to complete the following requirements.

Required
a. Compute and interpret return on net operating assets (RNOA) for fiscal year 2018.
b. Compare RNOA to the company's ROE of 32.73%. What proportion of the total return to shareholders comes from operations versus the effects of financial leverage?

Solution on p. 4-60.

RNOA Disaggregation into Margin and Turnover

LO7 Disaggregate RNOA into net operating profitability and net operating asset turnover.

Similar to the components of ROA, we can disaggregate RNOA into net operating profit margin and net operating asset turnover to gain further insights into a company's performance.

$$\text{RNOA} = \frac{\text{NOPAT}}{\text{Average NOA}} = \frac{\text{NOPAT}}{\text{Sales}} \times \frac{\text{Sales}}{\text{Average NOA}}$$

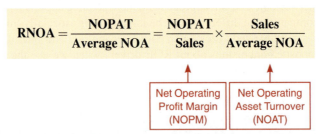

Net Operating Profit Margin (NOPM) — Net Operating Asset Turnover (NOAT)

Net Operating Profit Margin

Net operating profit margin (NOPM) reveals how much operating profit the company earns from each sales dollar. All things equal, a higher net operating profit margin is preferable. Net operating profit margin is affected by

- **Gross profit** (revenues − cost of goods sold) that the company earns on its products, which depends on product prices, manufacturing or purchase costs, and level of competition (that affects product pricing)
- Other operating expenses and all overhead costs that the company incurs to support its operating activities

Boston Scientific's net operating profit margin for 2018 follows ($ millions).

$$\text{Net operating profit margin (NOPM)} = \frac{\text{Net operating profit after tax}}{\text{Sales}} = \frac{\$1,737}{\$9,823} = 17.68\%$$

This result means that for each dollar of sales, the company earns almost 18¢ profit after all operating expenses and taxes. As a reference, the median NOPM for the S&P 500 companies in 2018 is about 12¢.

Analysis of net operating profit margin examines the ratio over time and in comparison with peers. As with net profit margin in the DuPont analysis, the net operating profit margin includes effects from the gross profit margin (Gross profit/Sales) and the operating expense margin (Operating expenses/Sales). A second-level analysis of net operating profit margin examines these components to uncover underlying trends that drive this ratio.

Net Operating Asset Turnover

Net operating asset turnover (NOAT) measures the productivity of the company's net operating assets. This metric reveals the level of sales the company realizes from each dollar invested in net operating assets. All things equal, a higher NOAT is preferable. Boston Scientific's net operating asset turnover ratio follows ($ millions).

$$\text{Net operating asset turnover} = \frac{\text{Sales}}{\text{Average net operating assets}} = \frac{\$9,823}{(\$15,636 + \$12,440)/2} = 0.70$$

This result means that for each dollar of net operating assets, Boston Scientific realizes $0.70 in sales. As a reference, the median NOAT for S&P 500 companies in 2018 is $0.96.

Companies can increase net operating asset turnover by either increasing sales for a given level of investment in operating assets, or by reducing the amount of operating assets necessary to generate a dollar of sales, or both. Reducing operating working capital (current operating assets less current operating liabilities) is usually easier than reducing long-term net operating assets. For example, companies can implement strategies to collect their receivables more quickly, reduce their inventories, and delay payments to their suppliers. All of these actions reduce operating working capital and, thereby, increase NOAT. These strategies must be managed, however, so as not to negatively impact sales or supplier relations. Working capital management is an important part of managing the company effectively.

It is usually more difficult to reduce the level of long-term net operating assets. The level of PPE required by the company is determined more by the nature of the company's business model than by management action. For example, telecommunications companies require more capital investment than do retail stores. Still, there are several actions that managers can take to reduce capital investment. Some companies pursue novel approaches, such as corporate alliances, outsourcing, and use of special-purpose entities; we discuss some of these approaches in later modules.

Analysis of net operating asset turnover examines the ratio over time and in comparison with peers. As with asset turnover in the DuPont analysis, the net operating asset turnover includes effects from the turnovers (and corresponding days) of each of the working capital accounts (accounts receivable, inventory, accounts payable) and effects from the long-term operating assets turnover. A second-level analysis of net operating profit margin examines these components to uncover underlying trends that drive this ratio.

Managerial Decision ■ You Are the CEO

You are analyzing the performance of your company. Your analysis of RNOA reveals the following (industry benchmarks in parentheses): RNOA is 16% (10%), NOPM is 18% (17%), and NOAT is 0.89 (0.59). What interpretations do you draw that are useful for managing your company? [Answer, p. 4-41]

Trade-Off between Margin and Turnover

Net operating profit margin and turnover of net operating assets are largely affected by a company's business model. This is an important concept. Specifically, an infinite number of combinations of net operating profit margin and net operating asset turnover will yield a given RNOA. This relation is depicted in Exhibit 4.8 (where the curved line reflects the median RNOA of 13.7% in 2018 for the S&P 500 companies included in this graphic).

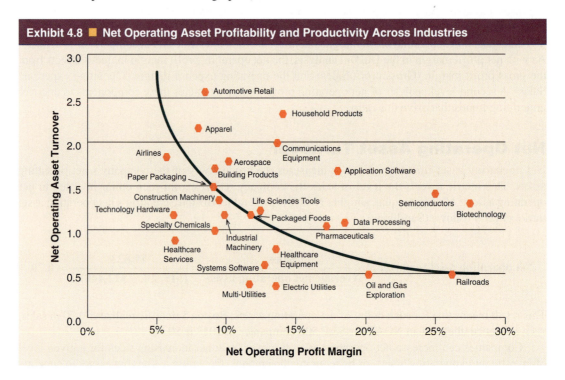

This exhibit reveals that some industries, such as railroads, oil and gas exploration, and utilities, are capital intensive with relatively low net operating asset turnover. For such industries to achieve an adequate RNOA (to be competitive in the overall market), they must obtain a higher profit margin. On the other hand, companies such as automotive retailing, apparel, and household products companies hold fewer assets and, therefore, can operate on lower net operating profit margins to achieve an adequate RNOA. This is because net operating asset turnover is greater.

This exhibit also warns of blindly comparing the performance of companies across different industries. For instance, a higher profit margin (NOPM) in the semiconductor and biotechnology industries compared with apparel and household products is not necessarily the result of better management. Instead, the semiconductor and biotechnology companies have higher operating assets (typically intangibles related to intellectual property) and thus, to achieve an equivalent RNOA, these companies must earn a higher profit margin (NOPM) to offset their lower asset turnover (NOAT). Economics suggests that all industries must earn an adequate return on investment (ROE and RNOA) if they are to continue to attract investors and survive.

The trade-off between margin and turnover is relatively straightforward when comparing companies that operate in one industry (*pure-play* firms). Analyzing conglomerates that operate in several industries is more challenging. The margins and turnover rates for companies that operate in more than one industry are a weighted average of the margins and turnover rates for the various industries in which they operate. For example, **Caterpillar Inc.** is a blend of a manufacturing company and a financial institution (**Caterpillar Financial Services Corp.**); thus, the margin and turnover benchmarks for Caterpillar on a consolidated basis are a weighted average of those two industries.

> **Research Insight ▪ NOPM and NOAT Explain Stock Prices**
>
> Research shows that stock returns are positively associated with earnings—when companies report higher than expected earnings, stock returns rise. Research also reports that the RNOA components (NOPM and NOAT) are more strongly associated with stock returns and future profitability than earnings (or return on assets) alone. This applies to the short-term market response to earnings announcements and long-term stock price changes. Thus, disaggregating earnings and the balance sheet into operating and nonoperating components is a useful analysis tool.
>
> Source: Soliman, Mark T., "Use of DuPont Analysis by Market Participants," *The Accounting Review*, May 2008, 83(3): 823–853.

Business Insight ▪ Return on Invested Capital (ROIC)

Many companies report alternative return metrics in their SEC filings (via their proxy statement or their MD&A in the 10-K). One common metric is the Return on Invested Capital (ROIC). Home Depot provides an example in the following excerpt from its 2019 10-K.

> **Return on Invested Capital** We believe ROIC is meaningful for investors and management because it measures how effectively we deploy our capital base. We define ROIC as NOPAT, a non-GAAP financial measure, for the most recent twelve-month period, divided by average debt and equity. We define average debt and equity as the average of beginning and ending long-term debt (including current installments) and equity for the most recent twelve-month period. The calculation of ROIC, together with a reconciliation of NOPAT to net earnings (the most comparable GAAP measure), follows.
>
> | Dollars in millions | Fiscal 2018 | Fiscal 2017 | Fiscal 2016 |
> |---|---|---|---|
> | Net earnings | $11,121 | $ 8,630 | $ 7,957 |
> | Interest and other, net | 974 | 983 | 936 |
> | Provision for income taxes | 3,435 | 5,068 | 4,534 |
> | Operating income | 15,530 | 14,681 | 13,427 |
> | Income tax adjustment | (3,665) | (5,432) | (4,874) |
> | NOPAT | $11,865 | $ 9,249 | $ 8,553 |
> | Average debt and equity | $26,492 | $27,074 | $27,203 |
> | ROIC | 44.8% | 34.2% | 31.4% |

At first glance, it might not be apparent but this definition of ROIC is nearly identical to the RNOA we use. Note that NOPAT can be computed as Net income + After-tax nonoperating expenses; if interest is the only nonoperating expense, then the ROIC and RNOA numerators are identical. As for the denominator, Home Depot sums average debt and average stockholder equity. Consider the accounting equation: Assets = Liabilities + Stockholders' equity, which can be rewritten as:

$$\text{Operating assets} + \text{Nonoperating assets} = \text{Operating liabilities} + \text{Nonoperating liabilities} + \text{Stockholders' equity}$$

By rearranging terms we see:

$$\text{Operating assets} - \text{Operating liabilities} = \text{Nonoperating liabilities} - \text{Nonoperating assets} + \text{Stockholders' equity}$$

On the left is net operating assets (the denominator in RNOA). The right has debt and stockholders' equity (the denominator in ROIC) less any nonoperating assets. Thus, RNOA and ROIC are nearly identical. Because companies generally report metrics that they adapt for their industry, it is important that we understand the exact definition of the metric before comparing metrics across different companies and industries.

Review 4-7 LO7

Use the income statement provided in Review 4-5 for **Stryker Corporation** and the RNOA computed in Review 4-6 to complete the following requirement.

Required
Disaggregate RNOA into components of net operating profit margin and net operating asset turnover for 2018.

Solution on p. 4-60.

Global Accounting

An important aim of this module is to distinguish between operating and nonoperating items for the balance sheet and income statement. U.S. GAAP and IFRS generally account for items similarly, but there are certain disclosure differences worth noting.

The IFRS balance sheet is similar to its U.S. GAAP counterpart, with the visible exception for the frequent, but not mandatory, reverse ordering of assets and liabilities. However, one notable difference is that IFRS companies routinely report "financial assets" or "financial liabilities" on the balance sheet. We must assess these items. IFRS defines financial assets to include receivables (operating item), loans to affiliates or associates (can be operating or nonoperating depending on the nature of the transactions), securities held as investments (nonoperating), and derivatives (nonoperating). IFRS notes to financial statements, which tend to be more detailed than U.S. GAAP notes, usually detail what financial assets and liabilities consist of. This helps us accurately determine NOA and net nonoperating obligations (NNO).

The IFRS income statement usually reports fewer line items than U.S. GAAP income statements and, further, there is no definition of "operating activities" under IFRS. This means we must devote attention to classify operating versus nonoperating income components. Following is a table that shows common U.S. GAAP income statement items and their classification as operating (O) or nonoperating (N). This table also indicates which items are required for IFRS income statements.

Income Statement Line Items	Operating (O) or Nonoperating (N)	Required on IFRS Income Statement
Net sales.	O	YES
Cost of sales.	O	—
Selling, general and administrative (SG&A) expense.	O	—
Provisions for doubtful accounts.	O	—
Nonoperating income.	N	—
Interest revenue and interest expense.	N	YES
Nonoperating expenses.	N	—
Income before income taxes.	O and N	—
Income tax expense.	O and N	YES
Earnings on equity investments (associates and joint ventures).	O	YES
Income from continuing operations.	O	—
Discontinued operations.	N	YES
Net income.	O and N	YES
Net income attributable to noncontrolling interest.	N	YES
Net income attributable to controlling interest.	O and N	YES
Earnings per share (Basic EPS and Diluted EPS).	O and N	YES

There is no requirement to report income from operations, yet many IFRS companies do so. However, items that are considered operating such as gains and losses on disposals of operating assets, or income from equity method investments, are often reported below the operating income line. We must examine IFRS income statements and their notes to make an independent assessment of what is operating. IFRS income statements usually report separately the other nonoperating revenues and expenses even though this is not required. We can better assess the nature of these items by reading the accompanying notes.

Appendix 4A: Operating versus Nonoperating Classification

Typical Balance Sheet Operating Items Highlighted in Green

Assets

Current Assets
Cash and cash equivalents
Short-term investments
Accounts receivable
Credit card and other financing receivables†
Unbilled revenues
Inventories
Prepaid expenses
Deferred income tax assets
Other current assets
Current assets of discontinued operations
Current assets held for sale
Loans receivable

Long-Term Assets
Long-term investments in securities
Property, plant and equipment, net
Capitalized lease assets‡
Natural resources
Equity method investments (including joint ventures, associated companies, and partnerships)
Goodwill and intangible assets
Deferred income tax assets
Other long-term assets
Long-term assets of discontinued operations
Long-term assets held for sale
Derivative assets

Liabilities and Equity

Current Liabilities
Short-term notes and interest payable
Current maturities of long-term debt
Interest payable
Dividends payable
Accounts payable
Accrued liabilities (Accrued expenses)
Unearned (deferred) revenue
Deferred income tax liabilities
Current liabilities of discontinued operations
Current liabilities related to assets held for sale

Long-Term Liabilities
Bonds and notes payable
Capitalized lease obligations
Pension and other post-employment liabilities
Deferred income tax liabilities
Long-term liabilities of discontinued operations
Long-term liabilities related to assets held for sale
Derivative liabilities

Stockholders' Equity
All equity accounts
Noncontrolling interest

† Some companies have their own financing arm (like Ford and Caterpillar) and many retailers have credit cards (including Kohls). Because these are integral to the company's operations, we consider these to be operating assets.

‡ Capitalized leases are recorded as assets (the term capitalized means added to the balance sheet) and are often called "right of use" assets because the lease allows the company to use or control some asset. For example, a long-term land lease would create a right of use asset.

Typical Income Statement Operating Items Highlighted in Green

Revenues
Cost of sales
Gross profit
Operating expenses
    Selling, general and administrative
    Depreciation and amortization expense
    Restructuring expense
    Research and development
    Asset impairment expense
    Gains and losses on PPE and other operating asset disposal
    Total operating expenses
Operating income
Interest expense

continued

continued from previous page

Typical Income Statement Operating Items Highlighted in Green
Gains and losses on debt retirement
Interest and dividend revenue
Investment gains and losses
Income from equity method investments (including joint ventures, associated companies, and partnerships)
Total nonoperating expenses (income), net
Income from continuing operations before taxes
Tax expense (**Tax on operating profit** ± Tax shield from net nonoperating expense)
Income from continuing operations
Income (loss) from discontinued operations, net of tax
Consolidated net income
Less: Consolidated net income attributable to noncontrolling interest
Consolidated net income attributable to controlling interest (parent company stockholders)

Appendix 4B: Nonoperating Return Component of ROE

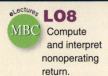

LO8 Compute and interpret nonoperating return.

Nonoperating Return

Recall that ROE can be written as:

$$\text{ROE} = \text{Operating return (RNOA)} + \text{Nonoperating return}$$

In simple form, return on nonoperating activities measures the extent to which a company is using debt to increase its return on equity.

We can infer the nonoperating return indirectly as the difference between ROE and RNOA. We can also compute the nonoperating return directly as follows.

$$\text{Nonoperating return} = \text{Financial Leverage (FLEV)} \times \text{Spread}$$

Conceptually Financial leverage and Spread can be understood as follows.

Financial leverage (FLEV): level of net debt (debt net of cash and investments) relative to the shareholders' investment

Spread: difference between what operating assets earn and what the net debt costs.

This means return on equity can be disaggregated as:

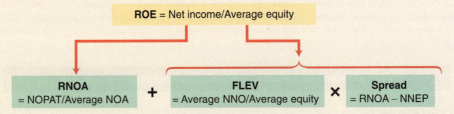

We see that the ratio definition of financial leverage here (labeled FLEV) differs from the definition in the ROA disaggregation (labeled FL). The main distinction is that FLEV uses NNO in the numerator instead of total assets. There are many ways to measure the concept of financial leverage; FL and FLEV are two distinct ways. Exhibit 4B.1 provides definitions for each of the terms required in this computation.

Exhibit 4B.1 ■ Nonoperating Return Definitions

NNO:	Net nonoperating obligations	Nonoperating liabilities less nonoperating assets
FLEV:	Financial leverage	Average NNO/Average total stockholders' equity
NNE:	Net nonoperating expense	NOPAT − Consolidated net income; or Nonoperating expenses × (1 − Statutory tax rate)
NNEP:	Net nonoperating expense percent	NNE/Average NNO
Spread:		RNOA − NNEP

This disaggregation of ROE explicitly recognizes that ROE can be increased by judicious use of debt (the nonoperating component of ROE). The idea is for a given level of RNOA, there are two ways a company could increase ROE.

1. **Increase FLEV**—the company would need to borrow more (proportionately), which would increase NNO relative to equity and increase FLEV
2. **Increase Spread**—the company (with RNOA held constant) would need to borrow at a lower cost, which would decrease NNEP and increase Spread

The upshot is that if the company can borrow more funds at the same rate of interest or borrow at a lower rate of interest, then stockholders will enjoy a higher ROE.

There is a limit: nonoperating return can only be increased as long as the company does not take on too much debt. Credit risk (the risk of default or bankruptcy) increases with the level of debt. As the company takes on more debt, lenders will mitigate the increased credit risk by charging higher interest rates. Further, as borrowing costs increase, there will be fewer investment opportunities (assets that the company can acquire) that earn an adequate return to justify the increased borrowing. At some point, further borrowing will not be cost-effective. This explains why we do not often see companies with excessive levels of financial leverage, or at least not over the long term.

BUSINESS INSIGHT ■ Financial Leverage and Spread Create Nonoperating return

$$\text{Nonoperating return} = \underbrace{\frac{\text{Average net nonoperating obligations (NNO)}}{\text{Average stockholders' equity (EQ)}}}_{\text{FLEV}} \times \underbrace{(\text{RNOA} - \text{NNEP})}_{\text{Spread}}$$

Financial Leverage (FLEV) Boston Scientific reports net nonoperating obligations as follows (see Exhibit 4.5 for balance sheet details).

$ millions	2018	2017	Average
Current debt obligations.......	$2,253	$1,801	
Long-term debt..............	4,803	3,815	
Cash and cash equivalents	(146)	(188)	
Net nonoperating obligations ...	$6,910	$5,428	$6,169

Boston Scientific's average stockholders' equity in 2018 is $7,869 million, calculated as ([$8,726 million + $7,012 million]/2), and its financial leverage is 0.784, computed as follows.

$$\text{Financial leverage (FLEV)} = \frac{\text{Average net nonoperating obligations}}{\text{Average stockholders' equity}} = \frac{\$6,169}{\$7,869} = 0.784$$

That the denominator in FLEV includes all equity and not just the equity to the parent company; that is, the denominator includes the equity of any noncontrolling interests.

Spread We first calculate net nonoperating expense in percentage terms (NNEP) as follows (see Exhibit 4.6 for income statement details). Recall that the company's operating return RNOA for 2018 is 12.37%.

Interest expense.....................................	$241
Other expense (income), net	(156)
Pretax net nonoperating expense.....................	85
Less: Tax shield (at 22%)............................	(19)
Net nonoperating expense (NNE)	$ 66

Then: NNEP = NNE/Average NNO   and   Spread = RNOA − NNEP
         = $66/$6,169 = 1.07%   = 12.37% − 1.07% = 11.3%

Nonoperating Return The benefit of financial leverage creates a nonoperating return of 8.86%.

Benefit (in %) of financial leverage = FLEV × Spread
= 0.784 × 11.3%
= 8.86%

Nonoperating Return—With Substantial Net Nonoperating Assets: Amazon

In 2018, nonoperating assets (cash and investments in marketable securities) comprised 10% of total assets for the average S&P 500 firm with over a third of firms reporting nonoperating asset balances exceeding 20% of total assets. About 35% of the S&P 500 have a negative NNO because nonoperating assets exceed nonoperating liabilities, which creates negative financial leverage (FLEV).

Two factors explain this. First, operating cash flows as a percentage of total revenues has increased steadily from 17% to 20% over the past decade, which has created large cash balances. The second factor relates to U.S. income tax law (before 2018) that compels firms to pay taxes only when they bring foreign earnings back to the U.S. in the form of dividends. To avoid these **repatriation taxes** over the past decade, firms left more and more international profits abroad and cash balances ballooned. For example, because of the way it structured its operations, Apple's earnings are generated primarily by it Irish subsidiaries. Worldwide profits have accumulated on the Irish subsidiaries' balance sheets such that in 2018, Apple reported $237,100 million in cash and investments, or 65% of its total assets. For all companies, this "trapped cash" was freed up somewhat when Congress passed the TCJA in 2017, reducing the tax rate from 35% to 21% and creating other incentives for firms to repatriate foreign profits.

How does negative FLEV affect the relation between ROE and RNOA? The short answer is that ROE is reduced as a consequence of the firm holding relatively low-earning financial assets that are financed by higher-cost debt. Negative FLEV companies typically report an acceptable level of ROE, but have foregone the opportunity to increase ROE even further. Amazon provides an example and its data follow.

Amazon (AMZN)	2018	2017	Average	Computation
Nonoperating assets: Cash and marketable securities	$ 41,250	$ 30,986		
Total assets	$162,648	$131,310		Reported on 2018 balance sheet
Current operating liabilities	$ (68,391)	$ (57,883)		
Long-term operating liabilities	$ (27,213)	$ (24,743)		
NOA	$ 25,794	$ 21,466	$ 23,630	
NNO	$ (17,755)	$ (6,243)	$(11,999)	Equity − NOA
Equity	$ 43,549	$ 27,709	$ 35,629	Reported on 2018 balance sheet
Pretax NNE	$ 1,160			Reported on 2018 income statement
Tax rate	22%			Assumed rate
NNE	$ 905			Pretax NNE × (1 − 0.22)
Net income	$ 10,073	—	—	Reported on 2018 income statement
NOPAT	$ 10,978	—	—	Net income + NNE
FLEV	(0.337)	—	—	$(11,999)/$35,629
RNOA	46.46%	—	—	$10,978/$23,630
NNEP	(7.54)%	—	—	$905/$(11,999)
Spread	54.00%	—	—	46.46% − (7.54%)
ROE	28.26%	—	—	$10,073/$35,629

We can disaggregate Amazon's ROE for 2018 as follows.

$$\begin{aligned}ROE &= RNOA + [\,FLEV \times Spread\,] \\ &= 46.46\% + [-0.337 \times 54.0\%] \\ &= 46.46\% + [-18.20\%] \\ &= 28.26\%\end{aligned}$$

Amazon's ROE is lower than its RNOA because of its large investment in marketable securities. That is, its excessive liquidity is reducing shareholder returns. Amazon's operating assets are providing an outstanding return (46.46%), much higher than the cost of its debt net of the return on its marketable securities (7.54%). Holding liquid assets that are less productive means that Amazon's stockholders are funding a mountain of cash and sacrificing returns in the process. (The graphic on the first page of this module shows that the median ROE for information technology companies exceeds the median RNOA in eight of the last 10 years.)

Why does Amazon hold so much cash? Many companies feel the need to maintain excessive liquidity to gain flexibility—the flexibility to take advantage of opportunities and to react quickly to competitor maneuvers. Amazon's management, evidently, feels that the investment of costly equity capital will reap future rewards for its stockholders. Its robust ROE of 28.26% provides some evidence that this strategy is not necessarily misguided.

While the Operating approach to ROE provides insight into the effects of financial leverage, it also offers deeper insight into the firm's operating performance than what we learn from the traditional Dupont approach.

The table below compares Amazon's ROA (from the DuPont approach) to its RNOA (from the Operating approach). The ROA for 2018 is 6.85% whereas RNOA is 46.46%, about seven times larger.

Analysis Approach, $ millions	DuPont	Operating	Computation
Net income	$ 10,073		
Net operating profit after tax (NOPAT)		$10,978	
Average assets	$146,979		($162,648 + $131,310)/2
Average net operating assets (NOA)		$23,630	($25,794 + $21,466)/2
ROA	6.85%		($10,073/$146,979)
RNOA		46.46%	($10,978/$23,630)

While both the numerator and denominator in the RNOA calculation reveal why ROA is so much smaller, the main reason for the drastic difference is in the denominator: ROA includes all of Amazon's assets whereas RNOA includes net operating assets (NOA). Specifically:

1. NOA excludes Amazon's sizable investment in cash marketable securities
2. NOA reveals the power of non-debt (interest-free) liabilities such as supplier credit and operating accruals such as payables for utilities, wages, and so forth

For all companies, NOA ≤ Total assets. However, for Amazon, this difference is dramatic as Amazon holds such sizeable investments in marketable securities. RNOA arguably measures Amazon's operating performance more accurately than does ROA. This is important because it is operating activities that drive shareholder value, not investment in marketable securities. In this case, the operating approach is a critical (and superior) measure of Amazon's company's financial performance.

Nonoperating Return—With Noncontrolling Interest: AT&T

When a company acquires controlling interest of the outstanding voting stock of another company, the parent company must consolidate the new subsidiary in its balance sheet and income statement. This means that the parent company must include 100% of the subsidiary's assets, liabilities, revenues, and expenses. If the parent acquires less than 100% of the subsidiary's voting stock, the remaining claim of noncontrolling stockholders is reported on the balance sheet as a component of stockholders' equity called noncontrolling interest, and net income is separated into income attributable to company stockholders and that attributable to noncontrolling interests. We need to amend the ROE calculation to measure the return to the parent company shareholders only, as follows.

$$\text{Return on equity (ROE)} = \frac{\text{Income attributable to parent company}}{\text{Average equity attributable to parent company}}$$

We compute RNOA as usual because NOPAT is operating income before any noncontrolling interest on the income statement, and NOA is unaffected by noncontrolling interest on the balance sheet. Similarly, we compute Spread and FLEV as usual.

However, we must modify the ROE = RNOA + [FLEV × Spread] formula slightly. Recall that a company's operating and nonoperating activities generate returns to both the controlling interest (labeled CI, which is the parent company's stockholders' equity) and the noncontrolling stockholders (labeled NCI). To account for this, we must multiply the ROE equation, RNOA + [FLEV × Spread], by a ratio that captures the relative income statement and balance sheet effects of the noncontrolling interest. This ratio is called the *noncontrolling interest ratio*, and is computed as follows.

$$\text{Noncontrolling interest ratio} = \left[\frac{\left(\frac{\text{Net income attributable to controlling interest (NI}_{CI})}{\text{Net income (NI)}} \right)}{\left(\frac{\text{Average equity attributable to controlling interest (CI)}}{\text{Average total equity (EQ)}} \right)} \right]$$

Hence, for companies with a noncontrolling interest (NCI), the disaggregated return on equity is expressed as:

$$\text{ROE} = [\text{RNOA} + (\text{FLEV} \times \text{Spread})] \times \text{NCI ratio}$$

To illustrate the calculation of ROE, FLEV, and Spread in the presence of noncontrolling interest, we consider the balance sheet and income statement items from **AT&T** ($ millions).

AT&T	2018	2017	Average
Balance sheet items			
Net operating assets (NOA)	$369,039	$258,925	$313,982
Net nonoperating obligations (NNO)	$175,155	$116,918	$146,037
Noncontrolling interest (NCI)	9,795	1,146	5,471
AT&T stockholders' equity (CI)	184,089	140,861	162,475
Total equity (EQ = NCI + CI)	193,884	142,007	167,946
Total net nonoperating obligations and Total equity (NNO + EQ)	$369,039	$258,925	$313,982
Income statement items			
Net operating profit after tax (NOPAT)	$ 19,037		
Net nonoperating expense (NNE)	(917)		
Net income (NOPAT + NNE)	19,953		
Net income attributable to noncontrolling interest (NI_{NCI})	583		
Net income attributable to AT&T stockholders (NI_{CI})	$ 19,370		

We compute AT&T's ROE for 2018 using the formula above (computations are in right column).

RNOA = NOPAT/Average NOA	6.06%	$19,037/$313,982
ROE = NI_{CI}/Average CI	11.92%	$19,370/$162,475
FLEV = Average NNO/Average EQ	0.8695	$146,037/$167,946
NNEP = NNE/Average NNO	(0.63)%	$(917)/$146,037
Spread = RNOA − NNEP	6.69%	6.06% − (0.63)%
Noncontrolling interest (NCI) ratio	1.0035	$\dfrac{\$19,370 \,/\, \$162,475}{\$19,953 \,/\, \$167,946}$
ROE = [RNOA + (FLEV × Spread)] × NCI ratio	11.92%	[6.06% + (0.8695 × 6.69%)] × 1.0035

Review 4-8 LO8

Refer to **Stryker Corporation**'s balance sheet from Review 4-4 and its income statement from Review 4-5, along with its ROE and RNOA computations from Reviews 4-1 and 4-6, respectively, to complete the requirements.

Required
a. Use ROE and RNOA ratios to determine the nonoperating return for 2018.
b. Compute net nonoperating obligations (NNO) for 2017 and 2018 and FLEV for 2018.
c. Compute net nonoperating expense (NNE) and net nonoperating expense as a percentage of NNO (NNEP).
d. Determine Spread using the formula: RNOA − NNEP.
e. Demonstrate that ROE = RNOA + (FLEV × Spread).

Solution on p. 4-60.

Appendix 4C: Liquidity and Solvency Analysis

LO9 Compute and interpret measures of liquidity and solvency.

Companies can effectively use debt to increase return on equity via nonoperating return. We might further ask: if a higher ROE is desirable, why don't companies use the maximum debt possible? The short answer is that lenders, such as banks and bondholders, charge successively higher interest rates for increasing levels of debt relative to the amount of equity investment. At some point, the cost of the additional debt exceeds the return on the additional assets acquired from the debt financing. Thereafter, further debt financing does not make economic sense. The market, in essence, places a limit on the level of debt that a company can effectively acquire. In sum, stockholders benefit from increased use of debt provided that the assets financed with the debt earn a return that exceeds the cost of the debt.

Creditors usually require a company to execute a loan agreement that places varying restrictions on the company's operating activities. These restrictions, called *covenants*, help safeguard debtholders in the face of increased risk. Covenants exist because debtholders do not have a voice on the board of directors like stockholders do. These debt covenants impose a "cost" on the company beyond that of the interest rate, and these covenants are more stringent as a company increases its reliance on debt financing.

In this appendix, we explore how much debt a company can reasonably manage. We examine a number of liquidity and solvency metrics that lenders use to assess the default risk and set interest rates. Credit analysts typically use the same ratios to develop credit ratings, which are key determinants of bond prices and cost of debt financing for public companies.

Liquidity Analysis

Liquidity refers to cash availability: how much cash a company has, and how much it can raise on short notice. Two of the most common ratios used to assess the degree of liquidity are the current ratio and the quick ratio. Both of these ratios link required near-term payments to cash available in the near-term.

Current Ratio

Current assets are assets that a company expects to convert into cash within the next operating cycle, which is typically a year. *Current liabilities* are liabilities that come due within the next year. An excess of current assets over current liabilities (Current assets − Current liabilities) is known as *net working capital* or simply *working capital*.[4] Positive working capital implies that cash generated by "liquidating" current assets would be sufficient to pay current liabilities. The current ratio expresses working capital as a ratio and is computed as follows.

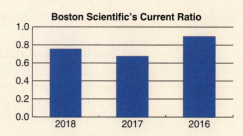

Boston Scientific's Current Ratio

$$\text{Current ratio} = \frac{\text{Current assets}}{\text{Current liabilities}}$$

A current ratio greater than 1.0 implies positive working capital. Both working capital and the current ratio consider existing balance sheet data only and ignore cash inflows from future sales or other sources. The current ratio is more commonly used than working capital because ratios allow comparisons across companies of different size. Generally, companies prefer a higher current ratio; however, an excessively high current ratio indicates inefficient asset use. Furthermore, a current ratio less than 1.0 is not always bad for at least two reasons:

1. A cash-and-carry company with comparatively fewer accounts receivable (like **Walmart** for example) can have potentially few current assets (and a low current ratio), but consistently large operating cash inflows ensure the company will be sufficiently liquid.
2. A company can efficiently manage its working capital by minimizing receivables and inventories and maximizing payables. **Walmart**, for example, uses its buying power to exact extended credit terms from suppliers. Consequently, because it is essentially a cash-and-carry company, its current ratio is less than 1.0 and is sufficiently liquid.

Boston Scientific's current ratio has declined over the recent past, mainly because it has initiated a program to reduce the level of accounts receivable and is paying its suppliers more quickly. In addition, the company's products are relatively slow-moving as they are technical and relatively high-priced in nature. The company reports that 40% of its finished goods inventory was at customer locations pursuant to consignment arrangements or held by sales representatives. Further, the company does not maintain large investments in marketable securities. All of these factors combine to reduce the level of current assets and the current ratio. Although its current ratio is not particularly high, Boston Scientific generates large cash inflows from operating activities that are more than sufficient to cover its operations, its investment in infrastructure, and its contractual obligations. We would not be concerned with the current ratio or its recent decline.

Quick Ratio

The quick ratio is a variant of the current ratio. It focuses on quick assets, which are assets likely to be converted to cash within a relatively short period of time. Specifically, quick assets include cash, marketable

---

[4] Both operating assets and operating liabilities can be either current or long-term. "Current" means that the asset is expected to be used, or the liability paid, within the next operating cycle or one year, whichever is longer, which for most companies means a year. Using the current versus long-term nature of operating assets and liabilities, we derive two types of net operating assets: net operating working capital (NOWC), and net long-term operating assets. Net operating working capital is defined as:

Net operating working capital (NOWC) = Current operating assets − Current operating liabilities

For Boston Scientific, NOWC is $849 million for 2018 ($1,608 million + $1,166 million + $161 million + $921 million − $349 million − $2,246 million − $412 million).

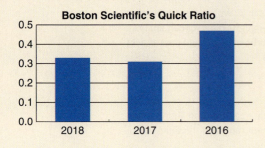

Boston Scientific's Quick Ratio

securities, and accounts receivable; they exclude inventories, prepaid assets, and other current assets. The quick ratio is defined as follows.

$$\text{Quick ratio} = \frac{\text{Cash} + \text{Marketable securities} + \text{Accounts receivable}}{\text{Current liabilities}}$$

The quick ratio reflects on a company's ability to meet its current liabilities without liquidating inventories. It is a more stringent test of liquidity than the current ratio.

Boston Scientific's 2018 quick ratio is 0.33 ($146 million + $1,608 million)/$5,260 million. Like the current ratio, Boston Scientific's quick ratio has declined slightly over the past three years mainly because the company is collecting accounts receivable and paying suppliers more quickly. It is not uncommon for a company's quick ratio to be less than 1.0. Again, Boston Scientific generates large cash inflows from operating activities that are more than sufficient to keep the company liquid.

Solvency Analysis

Solvency refers to a company's ability to meet its debt obligations, including both periodic interest payments and the repayment of the principal amount borrowed. Solvency is crucial because an insolvent company is a failed company. There are two general approaches to measuring solvency. The first approach uses balance sheet data and assesses the proportion of capital raised from creditors. The second approach uses income statement data and assesses the profit generated relative to interest payment obligations. We discuss each approach in turn.

Liabilities-to-Equity

The liabilities-to-equity ratio is a useful tool for the first type of solvency analysis. It is defined as follows.

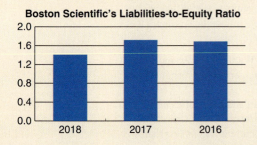

Boston Scientific's Liabilities-to-Equity Ratio

$$\text{Liabilities-to-equity ratio} = \frac{\text{Total liabilities}}{\text{Stockholders' equity}}$$

This ratio conveys how reliant a company is on creditor financing compared with equity financing. A higher ratio indicates less solvency, and more risk. Boston Scientific's 2018 liabilities-to-equity ratio is 1.41 ($5,260 million + $4,803 million + $328 million + $1,882 million)/$8,726 million). This ratio has steadily declined from 1.69 to 1.41 over the past three years, and is similar to the 1.67 average for S&P 500 firms in 2018.

As we would expect, the relative use of debt varies considerably across industries as illustrated in Exhibit 4C.1.

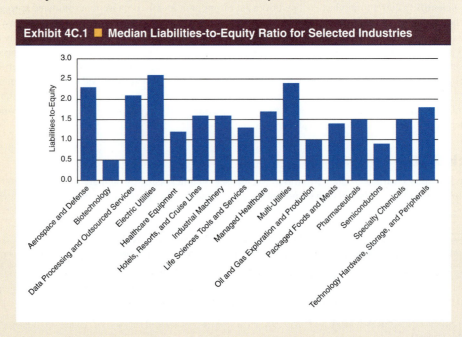

Exhibit 4C.1 ■ Median Liabilities-to-Equity Ratio for Selected Industries

Two factors explain why industries such as Aerospace, Data processing ("Cloud") companies, and Utilities have a larger proportion of debt. First, these industries are capital intensive, and second, they have relatively stable cash flows to cover higher interest costs and principal repayment.

A variant of the liabilities-to-equity ratio considers a company's long-term debt divided by equity. This ratio assumes that current liabilities are repaid from current assets (so-called self-liquidating). It assumes that creditors and stockholders need only focus on the relative proportion of long-term capital. In 2018, Boston Scientific's long-term debt divided by equity is 0.55, somewhat lower than the average of 0.62 for S&P 500 companies.

Times Interest Earned

The second type of solvency analysis compares profits to liabilities. This approach assesses how much operating profit is available to cover debt obligations. A common measure for this type of solvency analysis is the times interest earned ratio, defined as follows.

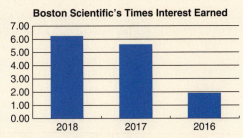

$$\text{Times interest earned} = \frac{\text{Earnings before interest and taxes}}{\text{Interest expense, gross}}$$

The times interest earned ratio reflects the operating income available to pay interest expense. The underlying assumption is that only interest needs to be paid because the principal will be refinanced. This ratio is sometimes abbreviated as EBIT/I. The numerator is similar to net operating profits after tax (NOPAT), but it is *pretax* instead of after tax. We use earnings before net interest expense, that is, net of any other nonoperating income or expenses. We use gross interest, which does not include interest income or other investment income or expenses. If the income statement reports Interest, net, the line item likely includes interest income. Footnotes or the MD&A section of Form 10-K typically report interest expense, gross.

The higher this ratio, the lower the risk of default. Boston Scientific's 2018 times interest earned is 6.25 ($1,506 million/$241 million), a large increase from the 1.92 reported two years prior. The level of this ratio implies that Boston Scientific could suffer a fairly large decline in profitability and still be able to service its interest payments when due. Notice that the times interest earned ratio uses interest expense in the denominator and analysts typically do not include "other" nonoperating income in this statistic. The ratio is also called a "coverage" ratio.

There are many variations of solvency and liquidity analysis and ratios. The basic idea is to construct measures that reflect a company's credit risk exposure. There is not one "best" financial leverage ratio. Instead, as financial statement users, we want to use measures that capture the risk we are most concerned with. It is also important to compute the ratios ourselves to ensure we know what is included and excluded from each ratio.

Vertical and Horizontal Analysis

Companies come in all sizes, which presents difficulties when making comparisons among firms, or between a firm and an industry benchmark, or over time. There are several methods that attempt to overcome this obstacle.

Vertical analysis expresses financial statements in ratio form. Specifically, we express income statement items as a percent of net sales, and balance sheet items as a percent of total assets. Such *common-size, or right-size, financial statements* facilitate comparisons *across companies* of different sizes and comparisons of accounts within a set of financial statements.

Horizontal analysis is the scrutiny of financial data *across time*. Comparing data across two or more consecutive periods assists in analyzing trends in company performance and in predicting future performance. There are two ways to perform a horizontal analysis.

- Compare the vertical analysis over time. Once the balance sheet or income statement is expressed in percentage terms, we can look for trends or changes year over year. This level of analysis points out areas that warrant additional research. We use footnotes, the MD&A section of the Form 10-K, and external sources to explain unusual changes or concerning trends.

- Compute the percentage change, for each line item, as follows.

$$(\text{Current balance} - \text{Previous balance})/\text{Previous balance}$$

Special attention is required when the previous balance is a negative number. Consider the example of a company that reports a net loss of $100 in 2017 and net income of $150 in 2018. Using the definition above, percentage change is *negative* 250%, calculated as $250/$(100), and we might erroneously conclude that the company's performance worsened in 2018. One fix is to adjust the denominator, as follows.

$$(\text{Current balance} - \text{Previous balance})/\text{Absolute value of previous balance}$$

Using this approach, we calculate a change of positive 250% and conclude that the company is improving.

Exhibits 4C.2 and 4C.3 report Boston Scientific's common-size balance sheets and income statements for the past three years. This presentation allows us to compare companies of different sizes by focusing on the relative proportions of balance sheet and income statement accounts. The vertical analysis also helps us more easily identify trends and changes. For example, looking at the balance sheet in dollars, we might conclude that trade accounts receivables increased during 2018 from $1,548 million to $1,608 million. But the vertical analysis reveals that trade receivables decreased in relative size from 8.1% to 7.7%.

Boston Scientific's asset composition has remained largely unchanged from 2016 to 2018. The most substantial assets are intangibles (Goodwill and other intangible assets), which comprise 68% of total assets in 2018 and are a testament to the company's long-standing strategy of growth by acquisition.

The composition of liability and equity has changed somewhat over the past three years. Boston Scientific has reduced the percentage of accounts payable and accrued expenses from 15.3% to 12.4% of total assets. On the other hand, its debt (current plus long-term) has increased. While it appears that treasury stock is stable, there was no balance in this account in 2016. The company repurchased sizeable amounts of its common stock in 2017 (nearly 10% of total assets).

While liquidity (as measured by the current ratio) has declined, Boston Scientific financed its 58.4% of its total assets with liabilities, down from 62.8% two years prior. This improvement in solvency (along with an improved times interest earned ratio) has improved the company's risk profile and its debt is rated as "investment grade" by all of the credit ratings companies (see Module 7 for a discussion of the credit rating analysis process).

From the vertical income statement, we see that Boston Scientific's cost of sales has decreased slightly from 28.9% in 2016 to 28.6% in 2018, for marginal increases to an already healthy gross profit margin. This margin reveals that Boston Scientific's product costs comprise relatively small amounts of materials and labor. Instead the company incurs sizeable research and development costs (11.3% of sales in 2018), which are not capitalized into inventory and, therefore, do not flow to the income statement as cost of products sold.

Over this three-year period, Boston Scientific's operating profit margin has increased from 5.3% to 15.3%, but much of this improvement is due to the steep drop in litigation expense.

Net income is 17% of sales in 2018, which seems to be a marked improvement from the 1.1% of sales reported in the prior year. However, the 2017 tax legislation and the consequent wild swings in tax expense make this line item nearly uninterpretable (see Modules 5 and 10 for a discussion of income tax expense). Better to consider pretax income where we observe steady improvement over the three-year period.

Bottom line, Boston Scientific is a profitable and well-capitalized company. It continues to invest in the future with research and development expenses and large corporate acquisitions to enhance its technology portfolio.

Exhibit 4C.2 ■ Boston Scientific Common-Size Balance Sheets

	2018	2017	2016
Current assets			
Cash and cash equivalents	0.7%	1.0%	1.1%
Trade accounts receivable, net	7.7%	8.1%	8.1%
Inventories	5.6%	5.7%	5.3%
Prepaid income taxes	0.8%	0.3%	0.4%
Other current assets	4.4%	4.9%	3.0%
Total current assets	19.1%	20.1%	17.9%
Property, plant and equipment, net	8.5%	8.9%	9.0%
Goodwill	37.7%	36.8%	36.9%
Other intangible assets, net	30.3%	30.7%	32.5%
Other long-term assets	4.4%	3.6%	3.7%
Total assets	100.0%	100.0%	100.0%
Current liabilities			
Current debt obligations	10.7%	9.5%	0.4%
Accounts payable	1.7%	2.8%	2.5%
Accrued expenses	10.7%	12.9%	12.8%
Other current liabilities	2.0%	4.6%	4.2%
Total current liabilities	25.0%	29.7%	19.8%
Long-term debt	22.9%	20.0%	30.0%
Deferred income taxes	1.6%	1.0%	0.1%
Other long-term liabilities	9.0%	12.4%	12.9%
Total liabilities	58.5%	63.1%	62.8%

continued

continued from previous page

Exhibit 4C.2 ■ Boston Scientific Common-Size Balance Sheets (cont.)

	2018	2017	2016
Stockholders' equity			
Preferred stock	—	—	—
Common stock	0.1%	0.1%	0.0%
Treasury stock	(8.2)%	(9.0)%	0.0%
Additional paid-in capital	82.6%	90.1%	0.0%
Accumulated deficit	(33.1)%	(44.1)%	(47.4)%
Accumulated other comprehensive income (loss), net of tax	0.0%	0.0%	0.0%
Foreign currency translation adjustment	(0.3)%	(0.2)%	(0.4)%
Unrealized gain (loss) on derivative financial instruments	0.5%	0.0%	0.6%
Unrealized gain (loss) on available-for-sale securities	0.0%	0.0%	0.0%
Unrealized costs associated with defined benefit pensions and other items	(0.1)%	(0.1)%	(0.1)%
Total stockholders' equity	41.6%	36.8%	37.2%
Total liabilities and stockholders' equity	100.0%	100.0%	100.0%

Exhibit 4C.3 ■ Boston Scientific Common-Size Income Statements

	2018	2017	2016
Net sales	100.0%	100.0%	100.0%
Cost of products sold	28.6%	28.7%	28.9%
Gross profit	71.4%	71.3%	71.1%
Operating expenses			
Selling, general and administrative expenses	36.3%	36.4%	37.0%
Research and development expenses	11.3%	11.0%	11.0%
Royalty expense	0.7%	0.8%	0.9%
Amortization expense	6.1%	6.2%	6.5%
Intangible asset impairment charges	0.4%	0.0%	0.1%
Contingent consideration expense (benefit)	(0.2)%	(0.9)%	0.3%
Restructuring charges (credits)	0.4%	0.4%	0.3%
Litigation-related charges (credits)	1.0%	3.1%	9.6%
Operating expenses	56.0%	57.1%	65.8%
Operating income (loss)	15.3%	14.2%	5.3%
Other income (expense)			
Interest expense	(2.5)%	(2.5)%	(2.8)%
Other, net	1.6%	(1.4)%	(0.4)%
Income (loss) before income taxes	14.5%	10.3%	2.1%
Income tax (benefit) expense	(2.5)%	9.2%	(2.0)%
Net income (loss)	17.0%	1.1%	4.1%

Limitations of Ratio Analysis

The quality of financial statement analysis depends on the quality of financial information. We ought not blindly analyze numbers; doing so can lead to faulty conclusions and suboptimal decisions. Instead, we need to acknowledge that current accounting rules (GAAP) have limitations, and be fully aware of the company's environment, its competitive pressures, and any structural and strategic changes. This section discusses some of the factors that limit the usefulness of financial accounting information for ratio analysis.

GAAP Limitations Several limitations in GAAP can distort financial ratios. Limitations include:

1. **Measurability**. Financial statements reflect what can be reliably measured. This results in nonrecognition of certain assets, often internally developed assets, the very assets that are most likely to confer a competitive advantage and create value. Examples are brand name, a superior management team, employee skills, and a reliable supply chain.

2. **Noncapitalized costs.** Related to the concept of measurability is the expensing of costs relating to "assets" that cannot be identified with enough precision to warrant capitalization. Examples are brand equity costs from advertising and other promotional activities, and research and development costs relating to future products.
3. **Historical costs.** Assets and liabilities are usually recorded at original acquisition or issuance costs. Subsequent increases in value are not recorded until realized, and declines in value are only recognized if deemed permanent.

Thus, GAAP balance sheets omit important and valuable assets. Our analysis of ROE and our assessment of liquidity and solvency must consider that assets can be underreported and that ratios can be distorted. We discuss many of these limitations in more detail in later modules.

Company Changes Many companies regularly undertake mergers, acquire new companies, and divest subsidiaries. Such major operational changes can impair the comparability of company ratios across time. Companies also change strategies, such as product pricing, R&D, and financing. We must understand the effects of such changes on ratios and exercise caution when we compare ratios from one period to the next. Companies also behave differently at different points in their life cycles. For instance, growth companies possess a different profile than do mature companies. Seasonal effects also markedly impact analysis of financial statements at different times of the year. Thus, we must consider life cycle and seasonality when we compare ratios across companies and over time.

Conglomerate Effects Few companies are a pure-play; instead, most companies operate in several businesses or industries. Most publicly traded companies consist of a parent company and multiple subsidiaries, often pursuing different lines of business. Most heavy equipment manufacturers, for example, have finance subsidiaries (**Ford Credit Corporation** and **Caterpillar Financial Services Corporation** are subsidiaries of **Ford** and **Caterpillar**, respectively). Financial statements of such conglomerates are consolidated and include the financial statements of the parent and its subsidiaries. Consequently, such consolidated statements are challenging to analyze. Typically, analysts break the financials apart into their component businesses and separately analyze each component. Fortunately, companies must report financial information (albeit limited) for major business segments in their 10-Ks.

Fuzzy View Ratios reduce, to a single number, the myriad complexities of a company's operations. No scalar can accurately capture all qualitative aspects of a company. Ratios cannot meaningfully convey a company's marketing and management philosophies, its human resource activities, its financing activities, its strategic initiatives, and its product management. In our analysis we must learn to look through the numbers and ratios to better understand the operational factors that drive financial results. Successful analysis seeks to gain insight into what a company is really about and what the future portends. Our overriding purpose in analysis is to understand the past and present to better predict the future. Calculating and analyzing ratios are crucial first steps in that process.

Review 4-9 LO9

Use the income statement and balance sheet for **Stryker Corporation** from Reviews 4-4 and 4-5.

Required

Solution on p. 4-61.
a. Compute measures of liquidity for 2018.
b. Compute liabilities-to-equity ratio and the times interest earned for 2018.

Guidance Answers

You Are the CEO
Pg. 4-26 Your company is performing substantially better than its competitors. Namely, your RNOA of 16% is markedly superior to competitors' RNOA of 10%. However, RNOA disaggregation shows that this is mainly attributed to your NOAT of 0.89 versus competitors' NOAT of 0.59. Your NOPM of 18% is essentially identical to competitors' NOPM of 17%. Accordingly, you will want to maintain your NOAT as further improvements are probably difficult to achieve. Importantly, you are likely to achieve the greatest benefit with efforts at improving your NOPM of 18%, which is only marginally better than the industry norm of 17%.

Superscript ᴮ⁽ᶜ⁾ denotes assignments based on Appendix 4B (4C).

Questions

Q4-1. Explain in general terms the concept of return on investment. Why is this concept important in the analysis of financial performance?

Q4-2.ᴮ (a) Explain how an increase in financial leverage can increase a company's ROE. (b) Given the potentially positive relation between financial leverage and ROE, why don't we see companies with 100% financial leverage (entirely nonowner financed)?

Q4-3. Gross profit margin (Gross profit/Sales) is an important determinant of NOPAT. Identify two factors that can cause gross profit margin to decline. Is a reduction in the gross profit margin always bad news? Explain.

Q4-4. When might a reduction in operating expenses as a percentage of sales denote a short-term gain at the cost of long-term performance?

Q4-5. Describe the concept of asset turnover. What does the concept mean and why is it so important to understanding and interpreting financial performance?

Q4-6. Explain what it means when a company's ROE exceeds its RNOA. What about when the reverse occurs?

Q4-7. Discontinued operations are typically viewed as a nonoperating activity in the analysis of the balance sheet and the income statement. What is the rationale for this treatment?

Q4-8. Describe what is meant by the "tax shield."

Q4-9. What is meant by the term "net" in net operating assets (NOA)?

Q4-10. Why is it important to disaggregate RNOA into net operating profit margin (NOPM) and net operating assets turnover (NOAT)?

Q4-11. What insights do we gain from the graphical relation between profit margin and asset turnover?

Q4-12. Explain the concept of liquidity and why it is crucial to company survival.

Q4-13. Identify at least two factors that limit the usefulness of ratio analysis.

Q4-14. Define (1) net nonoperating obligations and (2) net nonoperating expense.

Q4-15. What is the chief difference between the traditional DuPont disaggregation of ROE and the disaggregation based on RNOA?

Q4-16. What is meant by the term "cash conversion cycle"?

Q4-17. What insights can be gained from a common-size income statement or balance sheet?

Assignments with the ⓜⓑⓒ logo in the margin are available in myBusinessCourse.
See the Preface of the book for details.

Mini Exercises

M4-18. Compute ROE — LO1 — Facebook Inc. (FB)

Selected balance sheet and income statement information for Facebook Inc. follows. Compute the return on equity for the year ended December 31, 2018.

$ millions	Dec. 31, 2018	Dec. 31, 2017
Total assets	$97,334	$84,524
Total liabilities	13,207	10,177
Revenue	55,838	
Net income	22,112	

LO2, 3
Facebook Inc. (FB)

M4-19. Apply DuPont Disaggregation of ROE
Refer to the balance sheet and income statement information for Facebook Inc. from M4-18.

a. Compute ROE and disaggregate the ratio into its DuPont components of ROA and financial leverage.
b. Disaggregate ROA into profitability and productivity components.

LO4
Home Depot (HD)

M4-20. Compute Net Operating Assets (NOA)
Refer to the balance sheet information below for Home Depot. Compute net operating assets for the years ended February 3, 2019, and January 28, 2018.

$ millions	Feb. 3, 2019	Jan. 28, 2018
Operating assets	$ 42,225	$40,934
Nonoperating assets	1,778	3,595
Total assets	$ 44,003	$44,529
Operating liabilities	$ 16,679	$16,047
Nonoperating liabilities	29,202	27,028
Total liabilities	$ 45,881	$43,075
Net sales	$108,203	
Operating expense before tax	92,673	
Net operating profit before tax (NOPBT)	15,530	
Other expense	974	
Income before tax	14,556	
Tax expense	3,435	
Net earnings	$ 11,121	

LO5
Home Depot (HD)

M4-21. Compute Net Operating Profit after Tax
Refer to the income statement information for Home Depot from M4-20.
Assume a statutory tax rate of 22%.

a. Compute NOPAT using the formula: NOPAT = Net income + NNE
b. Compute NOPAT using the formula: NOPAT = NOPBT − Tax on operating profit

LO6, 7
Home Depot (HD)

M4-22. Compute RNOA with Disaggregation
Refer to the balance sheet and income statement information for Home Depot from M4-20.
a. Compute return on net operating assets (RNOA).
b. Disaggregate RNOA into components of profitability and productivity and show that the product of the two components equals RNOA.

LO6, 7
Netflix, Inc. (NFLX)

M4-23. Compute RNOA, Net Operating Profit Margin, and NOA Turnover
Selected balance sheet and income statement information for Netflix Inc. the world's leading Internet entertainment service, follows.

Company ($ thousands)	Ticker	2018 Revenue	2018 NOPAT	2018 Net Operating Assets	2017 Net Operating Assets
Netflix, Inc.	NFLX	$15,794,341	$1,506,681	$11,804,340	$7,258,593

a. Compute return on net operating assets (RNOA).
b. Disaggregate RNOA into net operating profit margin (NOPM) and net operating asset turnover (NOAT). Confirm that RNOA = NOPM × NOAT.

LO4
Lowe's Companies Inc. (LOW)

M4-24. Identify and Compute Net Operating Assets
Following is the balance sheet for Lowe's Companies Inc. Identify and compute net operating assets (NOA) as of February 1, 2019. Assume that long-term investments are nonoperating.

LOWE'S COMPANIES INC.
Consolidated Balance Sheet

$ millions, except par value	Feb. 1, 2019
Current assets	
Cash and cash equivalents	$ 511
Short-term investments	218
Merchandise inventory—net	12,561
Other current assets	938
Total current assets	14,228
Property, less accumulated depreciation	18,432
Long-term investments	256
Deferred income taxes—net	294
Goodwill	303
Other assets	995
Total assets	$34,508
Current liabilities	
Short-term borrowings	$ 722
Current maturities of long-term debt	1,110
Accounts payable	8,279
Accrued compensation and employee benefits	662
Deferred revenue	1,299
Other current liabilities	2,425
Total current liabilities	14,497
Long-term debt, excluding current maturities	14,391
Deferred revenue—extended protection plans	827
Other liabilities	1,149
Total liabilities	30,864
Shareholders' equity	
Preferred stock—$5 par value, none issued	0
Common stock—$0.50 par value	401
Capital in excess of par value	0
Retained earnings	3,452
Accumulated other comprehensive loss	(209)
Total shareholders' equity	3,644
Total liabilities and shareholders' equity	$34,508

M4-25. Identify and Compute NOPAT

Following is the income statement for **Lowe's Companies Inc.** Compute its net operating profit after tax (NOPAT) for the 12 months ended ended February 1, 2019, assuming a 22% total statutory tax rate.

LOWE'S COMPANIES INC.
Consolidated Statement of Earnings

Twelve Months Ended (In millions)	Feb. 1, 2019
Net sales	$71,309
Cost of sales	48,401
Gross margin	22,908
Expenses	
Selling, general and administrative	17,413
Depreciation and amortization	1,477
Operating income	4,018
Interest expense, net	624
Pretax earnings	3,394
Income tax provision	1,080
Net earnings	$ 2,314

M4-26. Compute DuPont Analysis Ratios

Selected balance sheet and income statement information for **Humana Inc.**, a health and well-being company, follows.

Company ($ millions)	Ticker	2018 Revenue	2018 Net income	2018 Assets	2017 Assets	2018 Stockholders' Equity	2017 Stockholders' Equity
Humana Inc	HUM	$56,912	$1,683	$25,413	$27,178	$10,161	$9,842

Compute the following 2018 ratios for Humana.
a. Return on equity (ROE)
b. Profit margin (PM)
c. Financial leverage (FL)

LO6, 7
Abercrombie & Fitch Co. (ANF)
TJX Companies Inc. (TJX)

M4-27. Compute RNOA, Net Operating Profit Margin, and NOA Turnover for Competitors
Selected balance sheet and income statement information for the fiscal year ended February 2, 2019, for **Abercrombie & Fitch Co.** and **TJX Companies Inc.**, clothing retailers in the high-end and value-priced segments, respectively, follows.

Company ($ millions)	Ticker	Sales	NOPAT	Current Year Net Operating Assets	Prior Year Net Operating Assets
Abercrombie & Fitch	ANF	$ 3,590.1	$ 87.4	$ 792.3	$ 877.3
TJX Companies	TJX	38,972.9	3,066.7	4,252.0	4,114.3

Compute the following ratios for both companies for the fiscal year ended February 2, 2019.
a. Return on net operating assets (RNOA)
b. Net operating profit margin (NOPM)
c. Net operating asset turnover (NOAT)

LO9
Verizon Communications Inc. (VZ)

M4-28. Compute Liquidity and Solvency Ratios
Selected balance sheet and income statement information from **Verizon Communications Inc.** follows.

$ millions	2018	2017
Current assets	$ 34,636	$ 29,913
Current liabilities	37,930	33,037
Total liabilities	382,308	391,875
Equity	54,710	44,687
Earnings before interest and taxes	22,278	27,425
Interest expense, gross	4,833	4,733
Net cash flow from operating activities	34,339	24,318

Compute the following ratios for Verizon for both 2018 and 2017.
a. Current ratio
b. Times interest earned
c. Liabilities-to-equity

LO5, 6, 7
Home Depot Inc. (HD)
Lowe's Companies Inc. (LOW)

M4-29. Compute NOPAT
Selected income statement information for 2018 is presented below for **Home Depot Inc.** and **Lowe's Companies Inc.** Assume the statutory tax rate is 22%.

Company ($ millions)	Ticker	Sales	NOPBT	Pretax Net Nonoperating Expense	Tax Expense	Average Net Operating Assets
Home Depot	HD	$108,203	$15,530	$974	$3,435	$25,217
Lowe's	LOW	71,309	4,018	624	1,080	20,326

a. Compute the following measures for both companies.

	Home Depot	Lowe's
1. Net operating profit (NOPAT)	_____	_____
2. Return on net operating assets (RNOA)	_____	_____
3. Net operating profit margin (NOPM)	_____	_____
4. Net operating asset turnover (NOAT)	_____	_____

b. Indicate which of these two companies:

	Home Depot	Lowe's
1. Is more profitable (in $s).	_____	_____
2. Produces the higher profit margin (in %).	_____	_____
3. Uses its NOA more efficiently.	_____	_____
4. Produces the higher return on NOA.	_____	_____

Exercises

E4-30. Compute Liquidity and Solvency Ratios for Competing Firms

Halliburton and **Schlumberger** compete in the oil field services sector. Refer to the following 2018 financial data for the two companies to answer the requirements.

LO9
Halliburton (HAL)
Schlumberger (SLB)

$ millions	HAL	SLB
Cash and equivalents.	$ 2,008	$ 1,433
Short-term investments	0	1,344
Accounts receivable.	5,234	7,881
Current assets	11,151	15,731
Current liabilities.	4,802	13,486
Total liabilities.	16,438	33,921
Total equity.	9,544	36,586
Earnings before interest and tax (EBIT).	2,467	3,050
Interest expense, gross	554	537

a. Compute the following measures for both companies.

	HAL	SLB
1. Current ratio	_____	_____
2. Quick ratio	_____	_____
3. Times interest earned	_____	_____
4. Liabilities-to-equity	_____	_____

	HAL	SLB
b. Which company appears more liquid?	_____	_____
c. Which company appears more solvent?	_____	_____

E4-31. Compute Cash Conversion Cycle for Competing Firms

Halliburton and **Schlumberger** compete in the oil field services sector. Refer to the following 2018 financial data for the two companies to answer the requirements.

LO3
Halliburton (HAL)
Schlumberger (SLB)

$ millions	HAL	SLB
Total revenue	$23,995	$32,815
Cost of sales and services	21,009	28,478
Average accounts receivable	5,135	7,983
Average inventory.	2,712	4,028
Average accounts payable.	2,786	10,130

a. Compute the following measures for both companies.

	HAL	SLB
1. Days sales outstanding (DSO)	_____	_____
2. Days inventory outstanding (DIO)	_____	_____
3. Days payables outstanding (DPO)	_____	_____
4. Cash conversion cycle (CCC)	_____	_____

	HAL	SLB
b. Which company better manages its accounts receivable?	_____	_____
c. Which company uses inventory more efficiently?	_____	_____
d. Which company better manages its accounts payable?	_____	_____

LO1, 2, 3

3M Company (MMM)

E4-32. Compute and Interpret Measures for DuPont Disaggregation Analysis

Use the information below for 2018 for **3M Company** to answer the requirements (perform these computations from the perspective of a 3M shareholder).

$ millions	2018	2017
Sales.	$32,765	
Net income, consolidated.	5,363	
Net income attributable to 3M shareholders.	5,349	
Pretax interest expense, net.	207	
Assets.	36,500	$37,987
Total equity.	9,848	11,622
Equity attributable to 3M shareholders.	9,796	11,563

a. Compute return on equity (ROE).
b. Compute the DuPont model components for profit margin (PM), asset turnover (AT), and financial leverage (FL).
c. Compute ROA.
d. Compute adjusted ROA. Assume a statutory tax rate of 22%.

LO6, 7

Halliburton (HAL)
Schlumberger (SLB)

E4-33. Compute, Disaggregate, and Interpret RNOA of Competitors

Halliburton and **Schlumberger** compete in the oil field services sector. Refer to the following 2018 financial data for the two companies to answer the requirements.

$ millions	HAL	SLB
Total revenue	$23,995	$32,815
Pretax net nonoperating expense.	653	426
Net income.	1,657	2,177
Average operating assets.	23,361	67,836
Average operating liabilities	5,888	16,499
Marginal tax rate.	22%	19%
Return on equity.	18.56%	5.86%

a. Compute return on net operating assets (RNOA) for each company.
b. Disaggregate RNOA into net operating profit margin (NOPM) and net operating asset turnover (NOAT) for each company.
c. Discuss any differences in these ratios for each company. Identify the factor(s) that drives the differences in RNOA observed from your analyses in parts a and b.

LO1, 2, 3

KLA-Tencor Corporation (KLAC)

E4-34. Disaggregate Traditional DuPont ROE

Graphical representations of the **KLA-Tencor** 2018 income statement and average balance sheet numbers (2017–2018) follow ($ thousands).

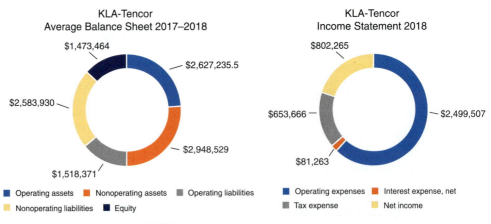

a. Compute return on equity (ROE).
b. Apply the DuPont disaggregation into return on assets (ROA) and financial leverage.
c. Calculate the profitability and productivity components of ROA.
d. Confirm the ROE from part a. above with the full DuPont disaggregation: ROE = PM × AT × FL.

E4-35. **Compute, Disaggregate, and Interpret ROE and RNOA**
Graphical representations of the **Ingersoll Rand** 2018 income statement and average balance sheets (2017–2018) follow.

LO1, 6, 7
Ingersoll Rand (IR)

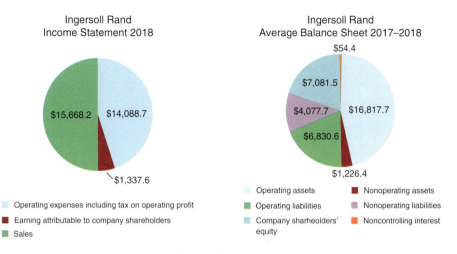

a. Compute the 2018 return on equity (ROE) and 2018 return on net operating assets (RNOA).
b. Disaggregate RNOA into net operating profit margin (NOPM) and net operating asset turnover (NOAT). What observations can we make about NOPM and NOAT?
c. Compute nonoperating return for 2018.

E4-36. **Compute and Compare ROE, ROA, and RNOA**
Refer to the balance sheet and income statement information for **KLA-Tencor Corporation** in E4-34.

LO1, 2, 6
KLA-Tencor (KLAC)

a. Compute return on equity (ROE).
b. Compute return on assets (ROA).
c. Compute return on net operating assets (RNOA).
d. Compare the three return metrics and explain what each one measures.

E4-37. **Directly Compute Nonoperating Return with Noncontrolling Interest**
Selected balance sheet and income statement information from **Abbott Laboratories** for 2018 follows ($ millions).

LO8
Abbott Laboratories (ABT)

Net income...	$ 2,368
Net income attributable to Company shareholders...................	2,368
Net operating profit after tax (NOPAT)...........................	2,940
Net nonoperating expense (NNE)...............................	572
Average net operating assets (NOA).............................	48,222
Average net nonoperating obligations (NNO)......................	17,312
Average total equity..	30,910
Average equity attributable to Company shareholders...............	30,711

Compute the following measures *a* through *h*.

a. Return on equity = (Net income attributable to Company shareholders/Average equity attributable to Company shareholders)
b. RNOA = NOPAT/Average NOA
c. Nonoperating return = ROE − RNOA
d. NNEP = NNE/Average NNO
e. Spread = RNOA − NNEP
f. FLEV = Average NNO/Average total equity
g. NCI ratio = (Net income attributable to Company shareholders/Net income)/(Average equity attributable to Company shareholders/Average total equity)
h. ROE = (RNOA + (Spread × FLEV)) × NCI ratio

LO8 E4-38. Directly Compute Nonoperating Return with Negative NNO

Amgen Inc. (AMGN)

Selected balance sheet and income statement information from **Amgen Inc.** for 2018 follows ($ millions).

Net income	$ 8,394
Net operating profit after tax (NOPAT)	8,954
Net nonoperating expense (NNE)	560
Average net operating assets (NOA)	18,015
Average net nonoperating obligations (NNO)	(856)
Average total equity	18,871

Compute the following measures.

a. Return on equity = Net income/Average total equity
b. RNOA = NOPAT/Average NOA
c. Nonoperating return = ROE − RNOA
d. NNEP = NNE/Average NNO
e. Spread = RNOA − NNEP
f. FLEV = Average NNO/Average total equity
g. ROE = RNOA + (Spread × FLEV)

LO9 E4-39. Compute and Interpret Solvency Ratios

TWDC Enterprises (DIS)

Selected balance sheet and income statement information from **TWDC Enterprises** from its 2018 Form 10-K follows.

$ millions	2018	2017
Cash and equivalents	$ 4,150	$ 4,017
Short-term investments	—	—
Accounts receivable	9,334	8,633
Current assets	16,825	15,889
Current liabilities	17,860	19,595
Total liabilities*	45,766	50,785
Total equity	52,832	45,004
Earnings before interest and tax (EBIT)	14,804	13,775
Interest expense, gross	682	507

*Includes redeemable noncontrolling interests

a. Compute the following measures for both years.

Measure	2018	2017
1. Current ratio	___	___
2. Quick ratio	___	___
3. Times interest earned	___	___
4. Liabilities-to-equity	___	___

	2018	2017
b. In which year does the company appear more liquid?	___	___
c. In which year does the company appear more solvent?	___	___

LO5 E4-40. Compute NOPAT

TJX Companies (TJX)

The income statement for **TJX Companies** follows.

TJX COMPANIES
Consolidated Statement of Income

Fiscal Year Ended ($ thousands)	February 2, 2019
Net sales	$38,972,934
Cost of sales, including buying and occupancy costs	27,831,177
Selling, general and administrative expenses	6,923,564
Pension settlement charge	36,122
Interest expense, net	8,860
Income before provision for income taxes	4,173,211
Provision for income taxes	1,113,413
Net income	$ 3,059,798

a. Compute NOPAT using the formula: NOPAT = Net income + NNE.
b. Compute NOPAT using the formula: NOPAT = NOPBT − Tax on operating profit.

Problems

P4-41. Analysis and Interpretation of Profitability LO4, 5, 6, 7, 8
Balance sheets and income statements for **3M Company** follow.

3M Company (MMM)

3M COMPANY
Consolidated Statements of Income

For Years Ended December 31 ($ millions)	2018	2017
Net sales	$32,765	$31,657
Operating expenses		
Cost of sales	16,682	16,055
Selling, general and administrative expenses	7,602	6,626
Research, development and related expenses	1,821	1,870
Gain on sale of businesses	(547)	(586)
Total operating expenses	25,558	23,965
Operating income	7,207	7,692
Other expense, net*	207	144
Income before income taxes	7,000	7,548
Provision for income taxes	1,637	2,679
Net income including noncontrolling interest	5,363	4,869
Less: Net income attributable to noncontrolling interest	14	11
Net income attributable to 3M	$ 5,349	$ 4,858

* Interest expense, gross is $350 million in 2018 and $322 million in 2017.

3M COMPANY
Consolidated Balance Sheets

At December 31 ($ millions)	2018	2017
Current assets		
Cash and cash equivalents	$ 2,853	$ 3,053
Marketable securities	380	1,076
Accounts receivable	5,020	4,911
Total inventories	4,366	4,034
Prepaids	741	937
Other current assets	349	266
Total current assets	13,709	14,277
Property, plant and equipment, net	8,738	8,866
Goodwill	10,051	10,513
Intangible assets—net	2,657	2,936
Other assets	1,345	1,395
Total assets	$36,500	$37,987
Current liabilities		
Short-term borrowings and current portion of long-term debt	$ 1,211	$ 1,853
Accounts payable	2,266	1,945
Accrued payroll	749	870
Accrued income taxes	243	310
Other current liabilities	2,775	2,709
Total current liabilities	7,244	7,687
Long-term debt	13,411	12,096
Pension and postretirement benefits	2,987	3,620
Other liabilities	3,010	2,962
Total liabilities	26,652	26,365

continued

continued from previous page

3M COMPANY Consolidated Balance Sheets		
At December 31 ($ millions)	2018	2017
3M Company shareholders' equity		
Common stock par value	9	9
Additional paid-in capital	5,643	5,352
Retained earnings	40,636	39,115
Treasury stock	(29,626)	(25,887)
Accumulated other comprehensive income (loss)	(6,866)	(7,026)
Total 3M Company shareholders' equity	9,796	11,563
Noncontrolling interest	52	59
Total equity	9,848	11,622
Total liabilities and equity	$36,500	$37,987

Required

a. Compute net operating profit after tax (NOPAT) for 2018. Assume that the combined federal and state statutory tax rate is 22%.
b. Compute net operating assets (NOA) for 2018 and 2017.
c. Compute and disaggregate 3M's RNOA into net operating profit margin (NOPM) and net operating asset turnover (NOAT) for 2018. Demonstrate that RNOA = NOPM × NOAT.
d. Compute net nonoperating obligations (NNO) for 2018 and 2017. Confirm the relation: NOA = NNO + Total equity.
e. Compute return on equity (ROE) for 2018.
f. What is the nonoperating return component of ROE for 2018?
g. Comment on the difference between ROE and RNOA. What inference can we draw from this comparison?

LO1, 2, 3
Facebook Inc. (FB)

P4-42. Compute the DuPont Disaggregation of ROE
Refer to the balance sheets and income statement below for **Facebook Inc.**

FACEBOOK INC. Consolidated Statement of Income	
For Year Ended December 31, $ millions	2018
Revenue	$55,838
Costs and expenses	
Cost of revenue	9,355
Research and development	10,273
Marketing and sales	7,846
General and administrative	3,451
Total costs and expenses	30,925
Income from operations	24,913
Interest and other income (expense), net	448
Income before provision for income taxes	25,361
Provision for income taxes	3,249
Net income	$22,112

FACEBOOK INC. Consolidated Balance Sheet		
At December 31, $ millions	2018	2017
Current assets		
Cash and cash equivalents..........................	$10,019	$ 8,079
Marketable securities	31,095	33,632
Accounts receivable, net..........................	7,587	5,832
Prepaid expenses and other current assets	1,779	1,020
Total current assets.............................	50,480	48,563
Property and equipment, net	24,683	13,721
Intangible assets, net	1,294	1,884
Goodwill	18,301	18,221
Other assets......................................	2,576	2,135
Total assets	$97,334	$84,524
Current liabilities		
Accounts payable	$ 820	$ 380
Partners payable................................	541	390
Accrued expenses and other current liabilities	5,509	2,892
Deferred revenue and deposits.....................	147	98
Total current liabilities	7,017	3,760
Other liabilities	6,190	6,417
Total liabilities	13,207	10,177
Stockholders' equity		
Common stock and additional paid-in capital..............	42,906	40,584
Accumulated other comprehensive loss..................	(760)	(227)
Retained earnings	41,981	33,990
Total stockholders' equity	84,127	74,347
Total liabilities and stockholders' equity	$97,334	$84,524

Required

a. Compute return on equity (ROE).
b. Apply the DuPont disaggregation into return on assets (ROA) and financial leverage.
c. Calculate the profitability and productivity components of ROA.
d. Confirm the full DuPont disaggregation: ROE = PM × AT × FL.

P4-43. Analysis and Interpretation of Liquidity and Solvency

Refer to the financial information of **3M Company** in P4-41 to answer the following requirements.

Required

a. Compute the current ratio and quick ratio for 2018 and 2017. Comment on any observed trends.
b. Compute times interest earned and liabilities-to-equity ratios for 2018 and 2017. Comment on any noticeable changes.
c. Summarize your findings about the company's liquidity and solvency. Do you have any concerns about its ability to meet its debt obligations?

P4-44. Direct Computation of Nonoperating Return

Refer to the financial information of **3M Company** in P4-41 to answer the following requirements. In 2018, 3M's return on equity (ROE) is 50.09% and its return on net operating assets (RNOA) is 25.89%.

Required

a. Compute net nonoperating expense (NNE) and net operating profit after tax (NOPAT).
b. Compute net nonoperating obligations (NNO).
c. Compute financial leverage (FLEV).
d. Compute NNEP and Spread.
e. Compute the noncontrolling interest ratio (NCI ratio).
f. Confirm the relation: ROE = [RNOA + (FLEV × Spread)] × NCI ratio.
g. What does the breakdown of nonoperating return imply about the company's use of borrowed funds?

LO4, 5, 6, 7 **P4-45. Analysis and Interpretation of Profitability**
Balance sheets and income statements for **Costco Wholesale Corporation** follow.

Costco Wholesale Corporation (COST)

COSTCO WHOLESALE CORPORATION
Consolidated Statement of Income

For Fiscal Years Ended ($ millions)	September 2, 2018
Total revenue	$141,576
Operating expenses	
Merchandise costs	123,152
Selling, general and administrative	13,876
Preopening expenses	68
Operating income	4,480
Other (income) expense	
Interest expense	159
Interest income and other, net	(121)
Income before income taxes	4,442
Provision for income taxes	1,263
Net income including noncontrolling interests	3,179
Net income attributable to noncontrolling interests	(45)
Net income attributable to Costco	$ 3,134

COSTCO WHOLESALE CORPORATION
Consolidated Balance Sheets

$ millions, except par value and share data	September 2, 2018	September 3, 2017
Current assets		
Cash and cash equivalents	$ 6,055	$ 4,546
Short-term investments	1,204	1,233
Receivables, net	1,669	1,432
Merchandise inventories	11,040	9,834
Other current assets	321	272
Total current assets	20,289	17,317
Net property and equipment	19,681	18,161
Other assets	860	869
Total assets	$40,830	$36,347
Current liabilities		
Accounts payable	$11,237	$ 9,608
Accrued salaries and benefits	2,994	2,703
Accrued member rewards	1,057	961
Deferred membership fees	1,624	1,498
Other current liabilities	3,014	2,725
Total current liabilities	19,926	17,495
Long-term debt	6,487	6,573
Other liabilities	1,314	1,200
Total liabilities	27,727	25,268
Equity		
Preferred stock $.01 par value	0	0
Common stock $0.01 par value	4	4
Additional paid-in capital	6,107	5,800
Accumulated other comprehensive loss	(1,199)	(1,014)
Retained earnings	7,887	5,988
Total Costco stockholders' equity	12,799	10,778
Noncontrolling interests	304	301
Total equity	13,103	11,079
Total liabilities and equity	$40,830	$36,347

Required

a. Compute net operating profit after tax (NOPAT) for 2018. Assume that the combined federal and state statutory tax rate is 22%.
b. Compute net operating assets (NOA) for 2018 and 2017.
c. Compute and disaggregate Costco's RNOA into net operating profit margin (NOPM) and net operating asset turnover (NOAT) for 2018; confirm that RNOA = NOPM × NOAT.
d. Compute net nonoperating obligations (NNO) for 2018 and 2017. Confirm the relation: NOA = NNO + Total equity.
e. Compute return on equity (ROE) for 2018.
f. Infer the nonoperating return component of ROE for 2018.
g. Comment on the difference between ROE and RNOA. What does this relation suggest about Costco's use of equity capital?

P4-46. Analysis and Interpretation of Liquidity and Solvency

Refer to the financial information of Costco Wholesale Corporation in P4-45 to answer the following requirements.

LO9

Costco Wholesale Corporation (COST)

Required

a. Compute Costco's current ratio and quick ratio for 2018 and 2017.
b. Compute Costco's times interest earned and its liabilities-to-equity ratios for 2018 and 2017. In 2017, Costco reported earnings before interest and tax (EBIT) of $4,111 million and interest expense of $134 million.
c. Summarize your findings about the company's liquidity and solvency. Do you have any concerns about Costco's ability to meet its debt obligations?

P4-47. Direct Computation of Nonoperating Return with Noncontrolling Interest

Refer to the financial information of Costco Wholesale Corporation in P4-45 to answer the following requirements. In 2018, Costco's return on equity (ROE) is 26.59% and its return on net operating assets (RNOA) is 26.52%.

LO8

Costco Wholesale Corporation (COST)

Required

a. Compute net nonoperating expense (NNE) and net operating profit after tax (NOPAT).
b. Compute net nonoperating obligations (NNO) for 2018 and 2017.
c. Compute financial leverage (FLEV).
d. Compute NNEP and Spread.
e. Compute the noncontrolling interest ratio (NCI ratio).
f. Confirm the relation: ROE = [RNOA + (FLEV × Spread)] × NCI ratio.
g. What does the breakdown of nonoperating return imply about the company's use of borrowed funds?

P4-48. Analysis and Interpretation of Ratios When RNOA Exceeds ROE

The balance sheets and income statement for Facebook Inc. are found in P4-42. Use these financial statements to answer the requirements.

LO1, 4, 5, 6, 7

Facebook Inc. (FB)

Required

a. Compute net operating profit after tax (NOPAT) for 2018. Assume that the combined federal and state statutory tax rate is 22%.
b. Compute net operating assets (NOA) for 2018 and 2017.
c. Compute RNOA and disaggregate it into net operating profit margin (NOPM) and net operating asset turnover (NOAT) for 2018.
d. Compute return on equity (ROE) for 2018.
e. Comment on the difference between ROE and RNOA. What is causing this difference?

P4-49. Compute ROE and Nonoperating Return with Negative NNO and No Noncontrolling Interest

Refer to the balance sheets and income statement for Facebook Inc. in P4-42. Use these financials to answer the requirements. For the 2018 fiscal year, Facebook had a return on net operating assets (RNOA) of 57.54%.

LO1, 8

Facebook Inc. (FB)

a. Compute ROE.
b. Compute net nonoperating obligations (NNO) for 2018 and 2017, net nonoperating expense (NNE), and the NNE as a percentage of NNO (NNEP), assuming a 22% statutory tax rate.
c. Compute FLEV and Spread.
d. Show that ROE = RNOA + (FLEV × Spread).
e. What is the nonoperating return for the year? Why is it negative? Is Facebook returning as much value to shareholders as possible? Explain.

LO4, 5, 6, 7

Netflix Inc. (NFLX)

P4-50. Analysis and Interpretation of ROE and RNOA with No Noncontrolling Interest

The 2018 balance sheets and income statement for **Netflix Inc.** follow. Refer to these financial statements to answer the requirements.

NETFLIX INC.
Consolidated Statement of Earnings

For Year Ended December 31, $ thousands	2018
Revenues	$15,794,341
Cost of revenues	9,967,538
Marketing	2,369,469
Technology and development	1,221,814
General and administrative	630,294
Operating income	1,605,226
Other income (expense)	
Interest expense	(420,493)
Interest and other income	41,725
Income before income taxes	1,226,458
Provision for income taxes	15,216
Net income	$ 1,211,242

NETFLIX INC.
Consolidated Balance Sheets

in thousands, except par value	2018	2017
Current assets		
Cash and cash equivalents	$3,794,483	$2,822,795
Current content assets, net	5,151,186	4,310,934
Other current assets	748,466	536,245
Total current assets	9,694,135	7,669,974
Noncurrent content assets, net	14,960,954	10,371,055
Property and equipment, net	418,281	319,404
Other noncurrent assets	901,030	652,309
Total assets	$25,974,400	$19,012,742
Current liabilities		
Current content liabilities	$ 4,686,019	$ 4,173,041
Accounts payable	562,985	359,555
Accrued expenses	477,417	315,094
Deferred revenue	760,899	618,622
Total current liabilities	6,487,320	5,466,312
Noncurrent content liabilities	3,759,026	3,329,796
Long-term debt	10,360,058	6,499,432
Other noncurrent liabilities	129,231	135,246
Total liabilities	20,735,635	15,430,786
Stockholders' equity		
Preferred stock, $0.001 par value	0	0
Common stock, $0.001 par value	2,315,988	1,871,396
Accumulated other comprehensive loss	(19,582)	(20,557)
Retained earnings	2,942,359	1,731,117
Total stockholders' equity	5,238,765	3,581,956
Total liabilities and stockholders' equity	$25,974,400	$19,012,742

Required

a. Compute net operating profit after tax (NOPAT) for 2018. Assume that the combined federal and state statutory tax rate is 22%.

b. Compute net operating assets (NOA) for 2018 and 2017.

c. Compute RNOA and disaggregate it into net operating profit margin (NOPM) and net operating asset turnover (NOAT) for 2018; confirm that RNOA = NOPM × NOAT.
d. Compute net nonoperating obligations (NNO) for 2018 and 2017. Confirm the relation: NOA = NNO + Shareholders' equity.
e. Compute return on equity (ROE) for 2018.
f. Infer the nonoperating return component of ROE for 2018.
g. Comment on the difference between ROE and RNOA. What does this relation suggest about Netflix's use of equity capital?

P4-51. Compute and Analyze Measures for DuPont Disaggregation Analysis

Refer to the 2018 financial data of **Netflix Inc.** in P4-50 to answer the following requirements.

LO1, 2, 3
Netflix Inc. (NFLX)

Required
a. Compute ROE and ROA for 2018.
b. Confirm that ROE equals ROE computed using the component measures for profit margin, assets turnover, and financial leverage: ROE = PM × AT × FL.
c. Compute adjusted ROA (assume a statutory tax rate of 22%).

P4-52. Analysis and Interpretation of Profit Margin, Asset Turnover, and RNOA

Net operating profit margin (NOPM) and net operating asset turnover (NOAT) for several selected companies for the most recent year follow.

LO7
Abbott Laboratories (ABT)
Costco (CSCO)
Netflix (NFLX)
Pfizer (PFE)
3M (MMM)
Halliburton (HAL)
Logitech (LOGI)
TJX (TJX)
Home Depot (HD)

	NOPM	NOAT		NOPM	NOAT
Abbott Laboratories...	9.61%	0.63	Halliburton...........	9.03%	1.37
Costco...............	2.27%	11.70	Logitech.............	8.05%	7.16
Netflix..............	9.54%	1.66	TJX..................	7.87%	9.32
Pfizer	23.93%	0.60	Home Depot	10.98%	4.29
3M.................	16.86%	1.54			

Required
a. Use Excel or some other visualization software to graphically represent NOPM and NOAT for each of these companies. Do you see a pattern that is similar to that shown in this module? Explain. (The graph in the module is based on medians for selected industries; the graph for this problem uses fewer companies than in the module and, thus, will not be as smooth.)
b. Consider the trade-off between profit margin and asset turnover. How can we evaluate companies on the profit margin and asset turnover trade-off? Explain.

P4-53. Compute Cash Conversion Cycle for Competing Firms

Kellogg's Company and **General Mills** compete in the consumer packaged goods (CPG) sector. Refer to the following 2018 financial data for the two companies to answer the requirements.

LO9
Kellogg's Company (K)
General Mills (GIS)

$ millions	K	GIS
Total revenue	$13,547.0	$15,740.4
Cost of sales and services	8,821.0	10,312.9
Average accounts receivable	1,382.0	1,557.2
Average inventory.............................	1,273.5	1,562.9
Average accounts payable	2,348.0	2,433.0

a. Compute the following measures for both companies.

	K	GIS
1. Days sales outstanding (DSO)	____	____
2. Days inventory outstanding (DIO)	____	____
3. Days payables outstanding (DPO)	____	____
4. Cash conversion cycle (CCC)	____	____

	K	GIS
b. Which company better manages its accounts receivable?	____	____
c. Which company uses inventory more efficiently?	____	____
d. Which company better manages its accounts payable?	____	____

IFRS Applications

LO1, 6, 7
Husky Energy Inc. (HUSKF)

I4-54. Compute, Disaggregate, and Interpret ROE and RNOA

Headquartered in Calgary, Alberta, Husky Energy Inc. is a publicly traded, integrated energy company. Selected fiscal year balance sheet and income statement information for Husky Energy follow (Canadian $ millions).

C$ millions	2018	2017
Revenues, net	$22,252	
Net income attributable to Husky	1,457	
Pretax NNE	236	
Operating assets	32,231	$30,222
Operating liabilities	9,864	9,520
Equity attributable to Husky shareholders	19,602	17,956
Tax rate	27.20%	

a. Compute the 2018 return on equity (ROE) and the 2018 return on net operating assets (RNOA).
b. Disaggregate RNOA into net operating profit margin (NOPM) and net operating asset turnover (NOAT).
c. Compute the percentage of RNOA to ROE, and compute Husky's nonoperating return for 2018.

LO9
Husky Energy Inc. (HUSKF)

I4-55. Analysis and Interpretation of Liquidity and Solvency

Headquartered in Calgary, Alberta, Husky Energy Inc. is a publicly traded, integrated energy company. Selected fiscal year balance sheet and income statement information for Husky Energy follow (Canadian $ millions).

C$ millions	2018	2017
Cash and equivalents	$2,866	$2,513
Short-term investments	0	0
Accounts receivable	1,355	1,355
Current assets	5,688	5,616
Current liabilities	4,994	3,507
Total liabilities	15,611	14,960
Total equity	19,614	17,967
Earnings before interest and tax (EBIT)	2,095	724
Interest expense, gross	314	392

Required
a. Compute the current ratio and quick ratio for 2018 and 2017. Comment on any observed trends.
b. Compute times interest earned and liabilities-to-equity ratios for 2018 and 2017. Comment on any noticeable changes.
c. Summarize the findings about the company's liquidity and solvency. Do we have any concerns about Husky Energy's ability to meet its debt obligations?

Management Applications

LO3 MA4-56. Gross Profit and Strategic Management

One way to increase overall profitability is to increase gross profit. This can be accomplished by raising prices and/or by reducing manufacturing costs.

Required
a. Will raising prices and/or reducing manufacturing costs unambiguously increase gross profit? Explain.
b. What strategy might you develop as a manager to (i) increase product prices, or (ii) reduce product manufacturing cost?

MA4-57. Asset Turnover and Strategic Management

Increasing net operating asset turnover requires some combination of increasing sales and/or decreasing net operating assets. For the latter, many companies consider ways to reduce their investment in working capital (current assets less current liabilities). This can be accomplished by reducing the level of accounts receivable and inventories, or by increasing the level of accounts payable.

Required

a. Develop a list of suggested actions that you, as a manager, could undertake to achieve these three objectives.
b. Describe the marketing implications of reducing receivables and inventories, and the supplier implications of delaying payment. How can a company reduce working capital without negatively impacting its performance?

MA4-58. Ethics and Governance: Earnings Management

Companies are aware that analysts focus on profitability in evaluating financial performance. Managers have historically utilized a number of methods to improve reported profitability that are cosmetic in nature and do not affect "real" operating performance. These methods are subsumed under the general heading of "earnings management." Justification for such actions typically includes the following arguments:

- Increasing stock price by managing earnings benefits stockholders; thus, no one is hurt by these actions.
- Earnings management is a temporary fix; such actions will be curtailed once "real" profitability improves, as managers expect.

Required

a. Identify the affected parties in any scheme to manage profits to prop up stock price.
b. Do the ends (of earnings management) justify the means? Explain.
c. To what extent are the objectives of managers different from those of stockholders?
d. What governance structure can you envision that might inhibit earnings management?

Ongoing Project

(This ongoing project began in Module 1 and continues through most of the book; even if previous segments were not completed, the requirements are still applicable to any business analysis.)

Analysis of financial statements commonly includes ROE disaggregation and scrutiny of its components as explained in this module.

1. Compute ROE for all three years reported on the income statement. (*Hint:* Do your companies report noncontrolling interest on the income statement and balance sheet? If so, make certain to use income available to the controlling interest (NICI) in the numerator and equity of the controlling interest (CI) in the denominator. To compute ROE for three years, we must determine average stockholders' equity for three years, which means we need four balance sheet amounts. Because the balance sheets of each company will report only two years, we must collect prior years' financial statements.)
2. Compute RNOA and its two components (NOPM and NOAT) for all three years reported on the income statement. We must use balance sheet numbers for four years to obtain three averages of net operating assets. Examine the income statements and balance sheets to determine the operating and nonoperating items. (*Hint:* Use an online source to understand any line items not described in the textbook. Use cell references in the spreadsheet to compute NOPAT and NOA and the various ratios.)

Compare ROE and RNOA and identify differences over time and between the companies. Evaluate the companies' returns and answer questions such as the following:

- Which company is more profitable?
- How do the operating and nonoperating portions of ROE compare?
- Compare the ROE and RNOA with the graph on page 4-25. If the ratios for the companies under analysis differ from the graph, is there an explanation?
- Is the net operating profit margin similar for the two companies? Given that they are roughly in the same industry, major differences should prompt further exploration.
- Are the companies' net operating asset turnover ratios similar or markedly different? Calculate and compare the cash conversion cycle for each year.

3. Determine FLEV and Spread and the noncontrolling interest ratio (if applicable). Show that:

$$\text{ROE} = [\text{RNOA} + (\text{FLEV} \times \text{Spread})] \times \text{Noncontrolling interest ratio}$$

Compare the components of the equation for each company over time and follow up on any differences.

4. Compute the four ratios from Appendix 4C for the recent three years for each company: current ratio, quick ratio, liabilities-to-equity, and times interest earned. Compare the ratios for the companies under analysis and identify differences over time and between companies. Evaluate each company's ability to pay its debts in the short term (liquidity) and the long term (solvency), and in the process address the following:

- Which company is more liquid? More solvent?
- Look at the bar chart in Exhibit 4C.1. If the ratios differ from the industry norm, is there an explanation(s)?
- Do the ratios change over time? If yes, does the change make sense given the economic and competitive factors that affect the industry and the companies?

Solutions to Review Problems

Review 4-1—Solution ($ millions)

$$\text{ROE} = \frac{\$3,553}{(\$11,730 + \$9,980)/2} = 32.73\%$$

Review 4-2—Solution ($ millions)

ROE = Return on assets (ROA) × Financial leverage

$$\text{ROA} = \frac{\$3,553}{(\$27,229 + \$22,197)/2} = 14.38\% \qquad \text{Financial leverage (FL)} = \frac{(\$27,229 + \$22,197)/2}{(\$11,730 + \$9,980)/2} = 2.28$$

ROE = 14.38% × 2.28 = 32.79% (.0006 rounding difference)

Review 4-3—Solution ($ millions)

a. $$\text{ROA} = \frac{\$3,553}{(\$27,229 + \$22,197)/2} = 14.38\%$$

$$\text{PM} = \frac{\$3,553}{\$13,601} = 26.12\%$$

$$\text{AT} = \frac{\$13,601}{(\$27,229 + \$22,197)/2} = 0.55$$

ROA = Profit Margin (PM) × Asset Turnover (AT)
ROA = 26.1% × 0.55 = 14.35% (0.0002 rounding difference)

b. Gross profit margin = ($13,601 − $4,663)/$13,601 = 65.72%

c. Days sales outstanding = 365 × [($2,332 + $2,198)/2]/$13,601 = 60.8
Days inventory outstanding = 365 × [($2,955 + $2,465)/2]/$4,663 = 212.1
Days accounts payable outstanding = 365 × [($646 + $487)/2]/$4,663 = 44.3
Cash conversion cycle = 60.8 + 212.1 − 44.3 = 228.6

d. $15,499/$11,730 = 1.32

Review 4-4—Solution ($ millions)

a.

$ millions	2018	2017
Accounts receivable	$ 2,332	$ 2,198
Inventories	2,955	2,465
Prepaid expenses and other current assets	747	537
Property, plant and equipment, net	2,291	1,975
Goodwill	8,563	7,168
Other intangibles, net	4,163	3,477
Noncurrent deferred income tax assets	1,678	283
Other noncurrent assets	801	1,301
Total operating assets	$23,530	$19,404
Accounts payable	$ 646	$ 487
Accrued compensation	917	838
Income taxes	158	143
Accrued expenses and other liabilities	1,521	1,207
Income taxes	1,228	1,261
Other noncurrent liabilities	978	881
Total operating liabilities	$ 5,448	$ 4,817

b.

$ millions
2018 NOA = $23,530 − $5,448 = $18,082
2017 NOA = $19,404 − $4,817 = $14,587

Review 4-5—Solution ($ millions)

a. NOPBT = Sales − Cost of Sales − Operating expenses = $13,601 − $4,663 − $6,401 = $2,537

b. Tax on operating profit = Tax expense or benefit + [Pretax net nonoperating expense × Statutory tax rate]
   = $(1,197) + [181 × 22%] = $(1,197) + $40 = $(1,157).

   Because of the new tax act changes, the company has a tax benefit (which is why it's a negative number).

c. NOPAT = NOPBT − Tax on operating profit = $2,537 − $(1,157) = $3,694

d. NNE = Pretax net nonoperating expense × (1 − Tax rate) = $181 × (1 − 22%) = $141

e. NOPAT = Net income + NNE = $3,553 + $141 = $3,694

Review 4-6—Solution ($ millions)

a. $\text{RNOA} = \dfrac{\$3,694}{(\$18,082 + \$14,587)/2} = 22.62\%$

b. RNOA/ROE = 22.62%/32.73% = 69.11%.

   Nearly 70% of the return to shareholders comes from the company's operating activities. Thus, about 30% is the effect of financial leverage.

Review 4-7—Solution ($ millions)

$\text{NOPM} = \dfrac{\$3,694}{\$13,601} = 27.16\%$

$\text{NOAT} = \dfrac{\$13,601}{(\$18,082 + \$14,587)/2} = 0.833$

RNOA = Net Operating Profit Margin (NOPM) × Net Operating Asset Turnover (NOAT)

= 27.16% × 0.833 = 22.62%

Review 4-8—Solution ($ millions)

a. ROE = Operating return (RNOA) + Nonoperating return
   32.73% = 22.62% + 10.11%

b.

	2018	2017
Dividend payable	$ 192	$ 178
Current maturities of debt	1,373	632
Long-term debt, excluding current maturities	8,486	6,590
Nonoperating liabilities	$10,051	$7,400
Cash and cash equivalents	$ 3,616	$2,542
Marketable securities	83	251
Nonoperating assets	$ 3,699	$2,793
NNO = Nonoperating liabilities − Nonoperating assets	$ 6,352	$4,607
Equity	$11,730	$9,980

FLEV = Average NNO/Average Total Equity

$$= \frac{[\$6{,}352 + \$(4{,}607)]/2}{(\$11{,}730 + \$9{,}980)/2} = 0.505$$

c.

Pretax net nonoperating expense	$181
Less Tax shield @ 22%	40
NNE	$141

$$\text{NNEP} = \frac{\$141}{(\$6{,}352 + \$4{,}607)/2} = 2.57\%$$

d. Spread = RNOA − NNEP

= 22.62% − 2.57%

= 20.05%

e. ROE = RNOA + (FLEV × Spread)

= 22.62% + (0.505 × 20.05%)

= 32.74% (0.001 rounding difference)

Review 4-9—Solution ($ millions)

a. Current ratio 2018: $9,733/$4,807 = 2.02

Quick ratio 2018: ($3,616 + $83 + $2,332)/$4,807 = 1.25

b. Liabilities-to-equity ratio 2018: $15,499/$11,730 = 1.32

Times interest earned ratio 2018: $2,537/$181 = 14.02

Module 5
Revenues, Receivables, and Operating Expenses

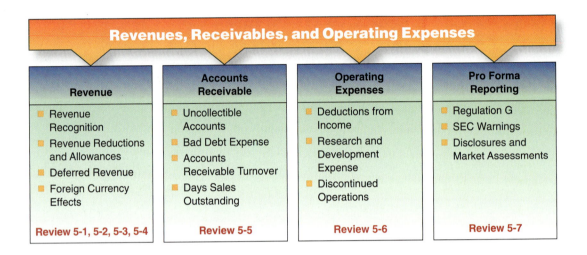

PREVIEW

- We examine how companies recognize revenue and account for sales returns and allowances, revenue paid in advance, and the effects of foreign currency exchange rates.
- We describe the accounting for and analysis of accounts receivable, the account most closely related to revenue.
- We discuss the typical expenses in income statements, including:
  - Cost of sales
  - Selling, general and administrative (SG&A) expense
  - Research and development (R&D) expense
  - Amortization of intangible assets
  - Restructuring expenses
  - Income tax expense
- We explain discontinued operations and the reporting of them.
- We examine income attributable to noncontrolling interests.
- We review pro forma income reporting.
- We use **Pfizer Inc.** as the focus company and the dashboard below conveys some key financial results.

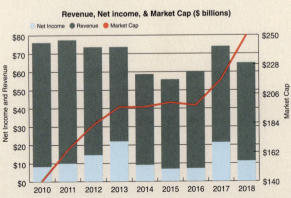

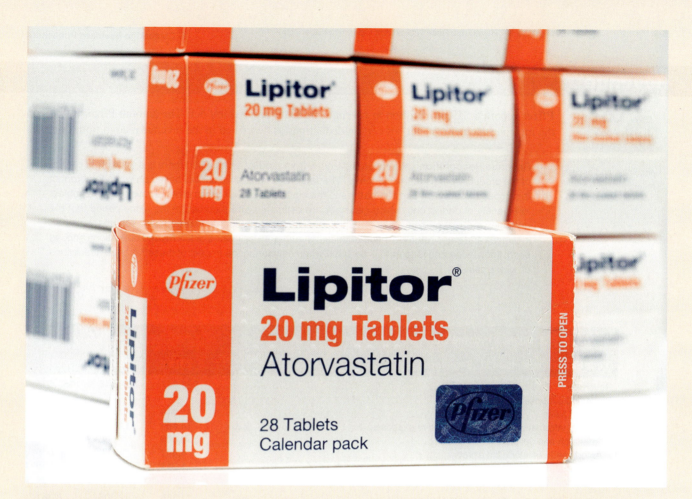

Road Map

LO	Learning Objective / Topics	Page	eLecture	Guided Example	Assignments
5-1	**Apply revenue recognition principles and assess results.** Recognition Rules :: Complications :: Long-Term Contracts :: Reporting	5-3	e5–1	Review 5-1	1, 8, 12, 13, 14, 15, 17, 29, 31, 32, 33, 34, 35, 40, 49, 51, 53, 54, 55, 56, 59, 61
5-2	**Examine and evaluate sales allowances.** Accounting :: Reporting & Disclosure :: Analysis	5-11	e5–2	Review 5-2	3, 17, 25, 51
5-3	**Analyze deferred revenue.** Accounting :: Illustrations :: Disclosure and Interpretation	5-14	e5–3	Review 5-3	10, 23, 24, 26, 29, 47, 55
5-4	**Evaluate how foreign currency exchange rates affect revenue.** Economics :: Cash Flows :: Income :: Forecasting	5-15	e5–4	Review 5-4	5, 6, 22, 27, 36, 39, 60
5-5	**Analyze accounts receivable and uncollectible amounts.** Aging :: Accounting :: Magnitude Analysis :: Quality Analysis	5-19	e5–5	Review 5-5	2, 7, 18, 19, 20, 21, 42, 43, 44, 45, 46, 49, 56, 58
5-6	**Evaluate operating expenses and discontinued operations.** Cost of Sales :: SG&A :: R&D :: Discontinued Operations	5-25	e5–6	Review 5-6	4, 11, 28, 30, 37, 38, 41, 48, 52, 57, 59
5-7	**Interpret pro forma and non-GAAP disclosures.** Regulation G :: SEC Warnings :: Market Assessments	5-31	e5–7	Review 5-7	9, 16, 39, 50

Revenue

LO1 Apply revenue recognition principles and assess results.

Pfizer reported $53,647 million in revenues in 2018; see Exhibit 5.1. The amount Pfizer reports on the income statement is "net" of certain deductions as described in the revenue recognition footnote.

> **Revenue Recognition** We record revenues from product sales when there is a transfer of control of the product from us to the customer. We determine transfer of control based on when the product is shipped or delivered and title passes to the customer... Our gross product revenues are subject to a variety of deductions, which generally are estimated and recorded in the same period that the revenues are recognized. Such variable consideration represents chargebacks, rebates, sales allowances and sales returns. These deductions represent estimates of the related obligations and, as such, knowledge and judgment is required when estimating the impact of these revenue deductions on gross sales.

Exhibit 5.1 ■ Pfizer's Income Statement

Year Ended December 31 ($ millions)	2018	2017	2016
Revenues	$53,647	$52,546	$52,824
Costs and expenses			
Cost of sales	11,248	11,228	12,322
Selling, informational, and administrative expenses	14,455	14,804	14,844
Research and development expenses	8,006	7,683	7,892
Amortization of intangible assets	4,893	4,758	4,056
Restructuring charges and certain acquisition-related costs	1,044	351	1,565
Other deductions—net	2,116	1,416	3,794
Income from continuing operations before provision (benefit) for taxes on income	11,885	12,305	8,351
Provision (benefit) for taxes on income	706	(9,049)	1,123
Income from continuing operations	11,179	21,353	7,229
Discontinued operations			
Income from discontinued operations—net of tax	10	(1)	16
Gain/(loss) on disposal of discontinued operations—net of tax	0	3	0
Discontinued operations—net of tax	10	2	17
Net income before allocation to noncontrolling interests	11,189	21,355	7,246
Less: Net income attributable to noncontrolling interests	36	47	31
Net income attributable to Pfizer Inc.	$11,153	$21,308	$ 7,215

The revenue recognition footnote shown above raises a number of issues related to revenue.

- **Revenue recognition.** Should revenue be recognized when an order is received? When products are shipped? When they are paid for? How should we recognize revenue for long-term contracts spanning more than one year?

- **Sales and related allowances.** How should we treat the various revenue deductions Pfizer references in its revenue footnote?

- **Deferred revenue.** How should we treat advance payments made by customers? Should we only recognize revenue when we receive cash?

- **Foreign currency exchange rates.** How do we account for revenues that are denominated in foreign currencies? In what way do fluctuations in exchange rates affect Pfizer's income statement?

Revenue (or sales) is the "top line" on the income statement and it includes transactions between the company and its customers during the past year (or, in the case of quarterly reports, during the prior three months). Revenue does not include gains or losses on the sale of assets such as property, plant and equipment (PPE) or investments (or the divestiture of a subsidiary company), nor does it include interest and dividend income on investments or gains or losses on their sale. Those items appear in different sections of the income statement.

Revenue Recognition Rules

New revenue recognition rules from the Financial Accounting Standards Board (FASB) went into effect for financial reporting periods beginning after December 15, 2017. The new rules modify the way in which companies recognize revenue (see the details in the text box below) but the core revenue recognition principles remain the same.

- Recognize revenue when the company transfers a good or service to a customer; that is, when the customer obtains control of that good or service.
- It is not necessary to receive cash to recognize revenue.

Every sale involves a contract (express or implied) between the customer and the company whereby the company agrees to transfer a good or service to the customer and the customer agrees to pay for it. All that is necessary for the company to recognize revenue is for the good to be transferred or the service performed. It is at that point the company's *performance obligation* under the contract is satisfied and revenue can be recognized.

Many sales are *on credit* (with accounts receivable), meaning the customer has agreed to pay the company in the future. The company still recognizes revenue when the good or service is transferred to the customer, and it records an account receivable that it will collect at a later date. The recognition of revenue is unaffected by the delayed receipt of cash if the company has fulfilled its performance obligation. (We discuss accounting for accounts receivable later in this module.)

When is the good or service transferred to the customer and the performance obligation satisfied? GAAP provides examples of evidence; a transfer is likely when:

- The customer has legal title to the goods or services purchased.
- The company has physically transferred the goods sold or has performed the service.
- The risks and rewards of ownership of the goods or service purchased transfer to the customer.
- The customer has accepted the goods or service and has agreed to pay the seller.

Manager Insights ■ Revenue Recognition in Practice

Revenue recognition can get complicated in practice, especially if the company sells a bundle of goods for a single price or delivers the goods over a period of time. **Microsoft** provides an example from its 2018 10-K.

> Revenue is recognized upon transfer of control of promised products or services to customers in an amount that reflects the consideration we expect to receive in exchange for those products or services. . . Our contracts with customers often include promises to transfer multiple products and services to a customer.

To recognize revenue, Microsoft first identifies each product and service that it sells and, then, sets a market price for that product or service. Although this may seem simple, Microsoft's contracts with customers often include the sale of multiple products and services for one contract price. This raises a number of product and service identification issues.

- When a cloud-based service includes both on-premises software licenses and cloud services, judgment is required to determine whether the software licenses are considered distinct (and accounted for separately) or not distinct and accounted for together with the cloud service and recognized over time.
- Certain cloud services depend on a significant level of integration, interdependency, and interrelation with the desktop applications. Consequently, the cloud services and desktop apps are accounted for together as one performance obligation even if the products or services can be separately identified.
- Some revenues are not recognized all at once. Revenues from the Office 365 software, for example, are recognized ratably over the period in which the cloud services are provided.

continued

There are also issues with determining the selling price, where judgment is required to determine the stand-alone selling price for each distinct performance obligation. If the products are sold separately, the price is usually determinable. But, in instances where stand-alone selling price is not directly observable, such as when Microsoft does not sell the product or service separately, the company must estimate the value of each product sold. Following is Microsoft's discussion of how it determines selling prices.

> Judgment is required to determine the stand-alone selling price ("SSP") for each distinct performance obligation. We use a single amount to estimate SSP for items that are not sold separately. . . We use a range of amounts to estimate SSP when we sell each of the products and services separately and need to determine whether there is a discount to be allocated based on the relative SSP of the various products and services.
>
> In instances where SSP is not directly observable, such as when we do not sell the product or service separately, we determine the SSP using information that may include market conditions and other observable inputs. We typically have more than one SSP for individual products and services due to the stratification of those products and services by customers and circumstances. In these instances, we may use information such as the size of the customer and geographic region in determining the SSP.

The FASB issued *Accounting Standards Update 2014-09 Revenue from Contracts with Customers (Topic 606)* that changed the way revenue is recognized starting in 2018 for most firms. The core principle of the new standard is that companies should recognize revenue relating to the transfer of promised goods or services to customers in an amount that reflects *the consideration to which the company expects to be entitled* in exchange for those goods or services. To achieve that core principle, companies need to apply the following steps.

1. **Identify the contract(s) with a customer.** The parties to the contract should be identifiable and the terms of the sale should be specified (including the items sold, the delivery terms, and the payments required).
2. **Identify the performance obligation(s) in the contract.** A performance obligation is the company's contractual promise to transfer a good or service to the customer. If the contract involves the transfer of more than one good or service to the customer, the company needs to account for each promised good or service as a separate performance obligation and recognize revenue separately for each.
3. **Determine the transaction price.** If the purchase price is variable, say dependent upon contingencies, the company should estimate revenue using the *expected* purchase price.
4. **Allocate the transaction price to the performance obligation(s).** For contracts with more than one performance obligation, the company must allocate the transaction price to *each* performance obligation at its *fair value*, that is, the standalone selling price of the distinct goods or services underlying each performance obligation. If published, standalone prices are not available, the company must use a reasonable estimate of the selling price.
5. **Recognize revenue when the performance obligation is satisfied.** Companies should recognize revenue when they satisfy the performance obligation—that is, when the customer obtains control of the goods or services. This will generally be when the company transfers the goods or services to the customer. Performance obligations that are satisfied over a period of time should be recognized as revenue over time.

Complications of Revenue Recognition

In retail settings, revenue recognition is straightforward: revenue is recognized at the point of sale. The customer takes physical possession of the purchased goods and the store immediately satisfies its performance obligation. In other settings, it can be more challenging. Following are some common types of transactions with complicated revenue recognition. Even though each of these situations is a bit more involved than a retail sale, the basic requirement for revenue recognition is the same: recognize revenue when the good or service is transferred to the customer.

- **Nonrefundable up-front fees.** In some industries, companies charge a fee at or near inception of the contract. These fees could be for setup, access, activation, initiation, or membership. In many cases, even though a nonrefundable up-front fee compels the company to undertake an activity at or near contract inception, that activity does not result in the transfer of the goods or service. Instead, the fee is an advance payment for future goods or services and, therefore, would be recognized as revenue when those future goods or services are provided.
- **Bill-and-hold arrangements.** Bill-and-hold arrangements arise when a customer is billed for goods that are ready for delivery, but the company "holds" the goods for shipment later. Revenue is recognized at the later date, when control of the goods transfers to the customer.
- **Consignment sales.** If the seller acts as an *agent* for another company, such as to sell another company's product on its website, it does not recognize the gross amount of the sale as revenue. Instead, it only recognizes its *commission* from the sale. Indicators that the seller is an agent include when the seller:
  - Is not responsible for fulfilling the contract.
  - Does not bear any risk associated with the inventory being sold.
  - Does not have full control over the selling price.
  - Does not bear the risk of loss for uncollectible accounts receivable.
  - Receives commission or another fee from the sale.
- **Licenses.** Software sales can take the form of licensing arrangements of intellectual property (IP). Revenue recognition depends on whether the arrangement confers a right to *use* the IP (arguing for recognition of revenue when the customer can first use the IP) or whether the contract promises to provide *access* to the company's IP (arguing for revenue recognition over a period of time).
- **Franchises.** Franchisors often sell both goods and consulting and other administrative services. The franchisor must separate the sale into separate components for goods and services and recognize the appropriate revenue for each component. The goods component is recognized when the goods are transferred to the buyer. The services component might involve use of a trade name or a license or other services that are provided over time. In such cases, revenue should be recognized as the services are delivered.
- **Variable consideration.** Portions of the selling price may depend upon future events, such as incentive payments, royalties, and volume discounts. If the good or service has been transferred to the customer and the payment is likely and can be reasonably estimated, the seller should estimate the expected amount to be received and recognize that amount in current revenue.
- **Multiple-element-contracts.** Many companies bundle multiple products and services together for one price. The added complication is that the seller might deliver some products and services at the point of sale and others in the future. In such cases, the seller must first separate the sale into distinct goods or services (components) that can each be valued on a stand-alone basis. Then, revenue is recognized separately on each distinct component (see the Manager Insight box for a discussion of how Microsoft deals with its multi-element contracts). Components are generally viewed as distinct if the:
  - Customer can use the good or service on its own.
  - Good or service is not highly interrelated with other goods or services sold per the contract.
- **Right of return.** Retailers typically offer a right of return if the customer is not satisfied with the product. Companies estimate the dollar amount of goods that are likely to be returned and deduct that amount from gross sales to arrive as the net sales reported in the income statement. We discuss rights of return and other sales allowances later in this module.
- **Gift cards.** When cash is received from the customer, the company records the receipt of cash and a deferred revenue liability. Then, revenue is recognized when the gift card is used by the customer to purchase goods or services. We discuss deferred revenue later in this module.

Performance Obligations Satisfied Over Time

Many companies enter into long-term contracts that obligate them to future performance. For example:

- **Spitz Inc.** enters into a construction contract with Disney World to design, manufacture, and install massive projection domes in the new Guardians of the Galaxy roller coaster experience.
- **Boeing** enters into a contract with domestic and international airlines and the U.S. military to construct planes.
- **Tata Consultancy Services** enters into long-term contracts with companies to design IT services, implement systems, and provide cloud-based services.

For these types of contracts, companies must determine the point at which their performance obligations have been satisfied so that revenue can be recognized. For a multiple-year contract, waiting to recognize revenue until the good is delivered would be problematic because the expense of constructing the product would be recognized as incurred whereas the revenue recorded only at the end of the contract. Although total revenue, expense, and profit would be accurate over the life of the contract, financial statements issued during the interim would report losses with a substantial profit at the end, making evaluation of the company's financial performance difficult during the interim.

Cost-to-Cost Method An accepted practice for many years has been to recognize revenue over the life of a long-term contract in amounts that track the percentage of completion of the contract. Companies typically use the percentage of projected contract costs that have been incurred to estimate the contract's percentage of completion. This method is called the *cost-to-cost method*. (There are other ways to determine percentage of completion, but cost-to-cost is the most common.) For example, if a company incurred 15% of the total expected cost to create the product in the current period, it would recognize revenues equal to 15% of the contract amount. **Raytheon**, a U.S. conglomerate ranked 114 among the Fortune 500, specializes in aerospace, defense, civil government, and cybersecurity. The company describes its revenue recognition practice as follows.

> Because of control transferring over time, revenue is recognized based on the extent of progress towards completion of the performance obligation. . . We generally use the cost-to-cost measure of progress for our contracts because it best depicts the transfer of control to the customer which occurs as we incur costs on our contracts. Under the cost-to-cost measure of progress, the extent of progress towards completion is measured based on the ratio of costs incurred to date, to the total estimated costs at completion of the performance obligation. Revenues, including estimated fees or profits, are recorded proportionally as costs are incurred.

To illustrate accounting for long-term contracts using the *cost-to-cost* approach, assume Raytheon signs a $10 million contract to develop a prototype for a defense system. Bayer estimates construction will take two years and will cost $7,500,000. This means the contract yields an expected gross profit of $2,500,000 over two years. The following table summarizes costs incurred each year and the revenue Raytheon recognizes.

	Costs Incurred	Percentage Complete	Revenue Recognized
Year 1	$4,500,000	$\frac{\$4,500,000}{\$7,500,000} = 60\%$	$10,000,000 × 60% = $6,000,000
Year 2	$3,000,000	$\frac{\$3,000,000}{\$7,500,000} = 40\%$	$10,000,000 × 40% = $4,000,000

This table reveals Raytheon would report $6 million in revenue and $1.5 million ($6 million − $4.5 million) in gross profit on the project in the first year; it would report $4 million in revenue and $1 million ($4 million − $3 million) in gross profit in the second year.

The following template captures the recognition of revenue and expense over this two-year period (M indicates millions).

Transaction	Balance Sheet					Income Statement		
	Cash Asset	+ Noncash Assets	= Liabilities	+ Contrib. Capital	+ Earned Capital	Revenues	− Expenses	= Net Income
Year 1: Record $4.5M costs	−4.5M Cash		=		−4.5M Retained Earnings		+4.5M Cost of Sales	= −4.5M
Year 1: Recognize $6M revenue on partly completed contract		+6M Accounts Receivable	=		+6M Retained Earnings	+6M Revenue		= +6M
Year 2: Record $3M costs	−3M Cash		=		−3M Retained Earnings		+3M Cost of Sales	= −3M
Year 2: Recognize $4M revenue for completed contract		+4M Accounts Receivable	=		+4M Retained Earnings	+4M Revenue		= +4M

```
COGS.... 4.5M
   Cash ........ 4.5M
          COGS
        4.5M |
             |  Cash
             |     4.5M

AR...... 6M
   REV .......... 6M
           AR
         6M |
             |  REV
             |     6M

COGS... 3M
   Cash ........ 3M
          COGS
        3M |
             |  Cash
             |     3M

AR...... 4M
   Rev .......... 4M
           AR
         4M |
             |  Rev
             |     4M
```

Cost-to-Cost Reporting Raytheon's reported revenues and expenses for years 1 and year 2 follow.

At December 31	Year 1	Year 2
Revenues	$6,000,000	$4,000,000
Expenses	4,500,000	3,000,000
Gross profit	$1,500,000	$1,000,000

Over the two-year period, Raytheon recognizes total revenues of $10 million, contract expenses of $7.5 million, and a contract gross profit of $2.5 million.

How Raytheon recognizes profit on long-term contracts affects its income statements. In addition, there are often timing differences between when contract costs are paid and when the customer is billed for work performed. These timing differences affect the balance sheet. Raytheon describes the accounting for these timing differences in the following footnote.

> Under the typical payment terms of our U.S. government fixed-price contracts, the customer pays us either performance based payments (PBPs) or progress payments . . . Because the customer retains a portion of the contract price until completion of the contract, our U.S. government fixed-price contracts generally result in revenue recognized in excess of billings which we present as contract assets on the balance sheet. Amounts billed and due from our customers are classified as receivables on the balance sheet. . . For non-U.S. government contracts, we typically receive interim payments as work progresses, although for some contracts, we may be entitled to receive an advance payment. We recognize a liability for these advance payments in excess of revenue recognized and present it as contract liabilities on the balance sheet.

When Raytheon receives cash in advance of incurring costs under the contract, it records a liability that represents the obligation to deliver the product for which it has been paid. When Raytheon incurs costs to construct the product in excess of the amount it bills the customer, it recognizes that excess as a current asset, contracts in process, as illustrated in the "current assets" section of Raytheon's 2018 balance sheet.

At December 31 ($ millions)	2018	2017
Current assets		
Cash and cash equivalents.	$ 3,608	$ 3,103
Short-term investments.	—	297
Receivables, net.	1,648	1,324
Contract assets.	**5,594**	**5,247**
Inventories	758	594
Prepaid expenses and other current assets	528	761
Total current assets.	$12,136	$11,326

The cost-to-cost method of revenue recognition requires an estimate of total costs. This estimate is made at the beginning of the contract and is typically the one used to bid the contract. However, estimates are inherently inaccurate. If the estimate changes during the construction period, the percentage of completion is computed as the total costs incurred to date divided by the *current* estimate of total anticipated costs (costs incurred to date plus total estimated costs to complete).

If total construction costs are underestimated, the percentage of completion is overestimated (the denominator is too low) and revenue and gross profit to date are overstated. The estimation process inherent in this method has the potential for inaccurate or even improper revenue recognition. In addition, estimates of remaining costs to complete projects are difficult for the auditors to verify. This uncertainty adds additional risk to financial statement analysis.

Business Insight ■ Disney's Revenue Recognition

The Walt Disney Company uses a percentage of completion method similar to the cost-to-cost method to determine the amount of production cost to match against film and television revenues. Following is an excerpt from its 10-K.

> **Film and Television Revenues and Costs** We expense film and television production, participation and residual costs over the applicable product life cycle based upon the ratio of the current period's revenues to the estimated remaining total revenues (Ultimate Revenues) for each production... For film productions, Ultimate Revenues include revenues from all sources that will be earned within ten years from the date of the initial theatrical release. For television series, Ultimate Revenues include revenues that will be earned within ten years from delivery of the first episode, or if still in production, five years from delivery of the most recent episode, if later.

As Disney pays production costs, it records those costs on the balance sheet as inventory. Then, as film and television revenues are recognized, the company matches a portion of production costs (from inventory) against revenues in computing income. Each period, the costs recognized are equal to the proportion of total revenues recognized in the period to the total revenues expected over the "product life cycle" of the film or television show. Thus, estimates of both costs and income depend on the quality of Disney's revenue estimates, which are, likely, imprecise.

Business Insight ■ Impacts of New Revenue Recognition Standard

There was widespread concern that the new revenue recognition standard could significantly impact a company's reported financial performance. To address this, **PwC** surveyed more than 700 finance executives to learn details about the impact, asking this question: Do you expect the new revenue recognition standard to have a material impact on your company's income statement and/or balance sheet?

continued

continued from previous page

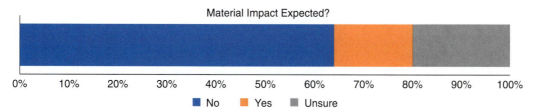

While the new standard's impact varies by industry, and is high for companies with licensing or complex revenue arrangements, the overall impact is not expected to be material. However, the impact extends beyond accounting. Consider the responses to the following PwC survey questions (for those responding "Somewhat difficult" to "Very difficult"):

How difficult will it be to implement the new standard in the following areas?	
Reviewing customer contracts	78%
Documenting the conversion process	76%
Quantifying the revenue adjustments	72%
Managing projects	71%
Revising processes and information systems	68%

An important characteristic of financial statements is comparability. By adopting the new standard, companies changed how they measure revenue beginning in 2018, thereby impairing the comparability of the 2016 and 2017 numbers reported on the 2018 income statement. To avoid this, companies can choose to restate all comparative numbers shown on the 2018 income statement but are not required to do so. For example, consider the following disclosure by **Amazon.com**.

> We adopted (the standard) on January 1, 2018 for all revenue contracts . . . The adjustment primarily relates to the unredeemed portion of our gift cards, which are now recognized over the expected customer usage period rather than waiting until gift cards expire or when the likelihood of redemption becomes remote. We changed the recognition and classification of Amazon Prime memberships, which are now accounted for as a single performance obligation and recognized ratably over the membership period as service sales. Previously, Prime memberships were considered to be arrangements with multiple deliverables and were allocated among product sales and service sales. Other changes relate primarily to the presentation of revenue. Certain advertising services are now classified as revenue rather than a reduction in cost of sales, and sales of apps, in-app content, and certain digital media content are presented on a net basis. Prior year amounts have not been adjusted and continue to be reported in accordance with our historic accounting policy.

While a more detailed discussion of the transition for accounting is beyond the scope of this text, three important things to remember are:

1. Footnotes will describe the impact of the new standard on 2018 revenue and we can use those disclosures to determine the size and direction of the effect.
2. Comparative years presented in the income statement (2017 and prior) may or may not reflect the new revenue recognition standard. We must use caution when we calculate growth and any ratios that include balance sheet numbers from prior years.
3. We will observe "cumulative adjustments" to firms' retained earnings balances in the statement of equity to reflect the catch-up effect of the new standard on prior years' numbers. As an example, Amazon.com reported a significant cumulative effect related to several new accounting standards (including revenue recognition adjustment of $650 million) in its 2018 Form 10-K.

Retained Earnings Balance as of December 31, 2017	$ 8,636
Cumulative effect of changes in accounting principles related to revenue recognition, income taxes, and financial instruments	916
Net income	10,073
Retained Earnings Balance as of December 31, 2018	$19,625

Review 5-1 LO1

Part I Indicate how revenue should be recognized for each of the following independent situations.

1. A clothing store sells goods to customers who use the store's proprietary (captive) credit card. The store estimates that 2% of the clothes will be returned.
2. A customer purchases a copy machine whose purchase price includes an agreement under which the seller will provide monthly service of the machine for two years at no additional cost.
3. A health club charges an up-front fee to join. Customers are entitled to use the club for one year.
4. A company lists products of other companies on its website and receives a commission equal to a percentage of the selling price when the goods are sold.
5. A franchisor sells franchisees product for sale and provides accounting services on a monthly basis.

Part II A construction company expends $500,000 for work performed under a contract with a total contract price of $3,000,000 and estimated costs of $2,500,000. It sends a bill to the customer for $400,000 under the terms of the contract.

1. How much revenue and gross profit should the company recognize in the income statement?
2. How is the $400,000 billing reported on the balance sheet?

Solution on p. 5-55.

Sales Allowances

LO2 Examine and evaluate sales allowances.

Many companies offer customers a variety of sales allowances, including rights of return, sales discounts for volume purchases, and retailer promotions (point-of-sale price markdowns and other promotions). Sales allowances are especially prevalent in industries with undifferentiated, commoditized products. For example, **Levi Strauss** discusses allowances in its 2018 10-K.

> The apparel industry is characterized by low barriers to entry for both suppliers and marketers, global sourcing through suppliers located throughout the world, trade liberalization, continuing movement of product sourcing to lower cost countries, regular promotional activity, and the ongoing emergence of new competitors with widely varying strategies and resources. These factors have contributed, and may continue to contribute in the future, to intense pricing pressure and uncertainty throughout the supply chain. Pricing pressure has been exacerbated by the variability of raw materials in recent years. This pressure could have adverse effects on our business and financial condition, including:
> - reduced gross margins across our product lines and distribution channels;
> - increased retailer demands for allowances, incentives and other forms of economic support; and
> - increased pressure on us to reduce our production costs and operating expenses.

Levi Strauss is actively growing its direct-to-consumer (DTC) sales channel because e-commerce sites typically yield higher gross margins than retail-outlet sales. In 2018, Levi Strauss generated 35% of its total revenues through the DTC channel, which increased overall gross margin by 1.5 percentage points to 53.8%.

Accounting for Sales Allowances

GAAP requires companies to report sales revenue at the net amount the company expects to receive. This means companies are to deduct from gross sales the expected sales returns and other allowances. For example, Levi Strauss reports the following in its revenue recognition footnote.

> We recognize allowances for estimated returns in the period in which the related sale is recorded. We recognize allowances for estimated discounts, retailer promotions and other similar incentives at the later of the period in which the related sale is recorded or the period in which the sales incentive is offered to the customer.

When Levi Strauss recognizes revenue, it increases both sales and cash or accounts receivable, by the gross amount of the sale and then reduces the gross sales amount by two specific types of sales allowance: returns and discounts/incentives. To illustrate the allowance for sales returns, assume Levi Strauss sells jeans costing $80 to a customer for $130 on account. Levi Strauss recognizes $130 as revenue and $80 as cost of goods sold (COGS). Because Levi Strauss has offered its customers a right of return, and because prior experience leads the company to expect that returns will occur, Levi Strauss must also set up a reserve for estimated returns. Let's assume Levi Strauss expects returns to amount to 3% of sales. In the same period in which Levi Strauss records the revenue, it also records the estimated returns as follows.

Transaction	Balance Sheet					Income Statement		
	Cash Asset	+ Noncash Assets	= Liabilities	+ Contrib. Capital	+ Earned Capital	Revenues	− Expenses	= Net Income
Establish allowance for sales returns (3% × $130)		−3.90 Allowance for Sales Returns			−3.90 Retained Earnings	−3.90 Sales Returns and Allowances		−3.90
Adjust COGS ([$80/$130] × $3.90)		2.40 Inventory Adj. for Estimated Returns			2.40 Retained Earnings		−2.40 COGS Adj. for Estimated Returns	2.40

In the first entry, Levi Strauss reduces sales by $3.90 to reflect expected merchandise returns with a corresponding reduction of accounts receivable (similar to the allowance for uncollectible accounts). The second entry reduces COGS by the COGS percentage ($80/$130) and increases inventory for the expected returns. Levi Strauss income statement (through gross profit) follows for the illustration above.

Sales, net ($130 − $3.90)	$126.10
Cost of goods sold ($80 − $2.40)	77.60
Gross profit	$ 48.50

Levi Strauss will also report accounts receivable of $126.10, and the estimated product returns of $2.40 will be reported in its inventory account.

Reporting Sales Allowances

Levi Strauss provides a reconciliation of the beginning and ending balances for the past three years for its allowance for sales returns and for its sales discounts and incentives in its 2018 10-K. This is a typical disclosure for companies with sales returns, discounts, and other sales allowances.

Sales Returns ($ thousands)	Balance at Beginning of Period	Additions During the Year	Deductions	Balance at End of Period
November 25, 2018	$47,401	$245,665	$239,382	$53,684
November 26, 2017	36,457	211,741	200,797	47,401
November 27, 2016	34,021	195,718	193,282	36,457

Sales Discounts ($ thousands)	Balance at Beginning of Period	Additions During the Year	Deductions	Balance at End of Period
November 25, 2018	$135,139	$357,929	$372,364	$120,704
November 26, 2017	105,477	342,169	312,507	135,139
November 27, 2016	86,274	325,843	306,640	105,477

Analysis of Sales Allowances

We use data in the table below to calculate three metrics to analyze sales allowances.

1. **"Additions charged during the year" as compared with gross sales for both sales returns and sales discounts.** This ratio reveals any effects of the pricing pressure on net sales and we would expect the percentage of sales allowances to gross sales to increase (thus reducing net sales) as pricing pressure increases. Over the three-year period, Levi Strauss has reduced the sales returns and discounts given to customers, from 10.3% to 9.8% of gross sales. The company attributes this favorable trend to an increase in its direct-to-consumer (DTC) channel: "Sales directly to consumers generally have higher gross margins than sales through third parties, although these sales typically have higher selling expenses." Although it may not seem like much of an impact, an increase in net sales by 50 basis points (½ percentage point change from 10.3% to 9.8%), for a company with a net profit margin of 5.1% in 2018, is substantial. This explains why analysts focus on the sales allowances, monitoring and following up on any material changes.

2. **Allowances as a percentage of gross sales.** The allowance balance has fluctuated over the three-year period, increasing fairly significantly in 2017 (up from 2.8% to 3.3%) but returning to prior levels in 2018.

$ thousands	2018	2017	2016
Net sales..................................	$5,575,440	$4,904,030	$4,552,739
Additions charged during the year			
Sales returns	245,665	211,741	195,718
Sales discounts	357,929	342,169	325,843
Total additions charged during the year	603,594	553,910	521,561
Gross sales...............................	$6,179,034	$5,457,940	$5,074,300
Additions charged during the year/Gross sales ...	9.8%	10.1%	10.3%
Allowance balance at year-end			
Sales returns	$ 53,684	$ 47,401	$ 36,457
Sales discounts	120,704	135,139	105,477
Total allowances.........................	$ 174,388	$ 182,540	$ 141,934
Allowances/Gross sales	2.8%	3.3%	2.8%

3. **Adequacy of the allowance account.** This analysis compares the dollar amount Levi Strauss estimates for future sales returns with the amount actually realized during the year. If the company's estimates are 100% accurate, the two amounts will be roughly the same (with some variance due to sales and returns that cross a fiscal year-end). If the amount charged to sales is greater than the cost incurred, the company has reduced sales more than is needed and has reduced its profit accordingly. If the amount charged to sales is less than the cost incurred, the company has under-reserved the allowance account, thus increasing profit. There is not much concern for the adequacy of Levi Strauss's allowance account—the ratio is near 1.0 each year with a moderate amount of variation. We would conclude that Levi Strauss is accurately estimating its sales returns and discounts.

$ thousands	2018	2017	2016
Estimated (total additions charged in the year) ...	$603,594 ($245,655 + $357,929)	$553,910 ($211,741 + $342,169)	$521,561 ($195,718 + $325,843)
Actual (total deductions in the year)............	611,746 ($239,382 + $372,364)	513,304 ($200,797 + $312,507)	499,922 ($193,282 + $306,640)
Adequacy (Estimated/Actual).................	98.7%	107.9%	104.3%

Review 5-2 LO2

Tiffany & Co. reports the following in its 2019 annual report.

Years Ended January 31 (in millions)	2019	2018	2017
Net sales.......................................	$4,442.1	$4,169.8	$4,001.8

continued

> **Revenue Recognition.** The Company's performance obligations consist primarily of transferring control of merchandise to customers. Sales are recognized upon transfer of control, which occurs when merchandise is taken in an "over-the-counter" transaction or upon receipt by a customer in a shipped transaction, such as through the Internet and catalog channels. Sales are reported net of returns, sales tax and other similar taxes. . . The Company maintains a reserve for potential product returns and records (as a reduction to sales and cost of sales) its provision for estimated product returns, which is determined based on historical experience.

The company reports the following data related to Tiffany's sales return allowance ($ millions).

Year ended January 31	Balance at Beginning of Period	Charged to Costs and Expenses	Deductions	Balance at End of Period
2019	$15.0	$12.6	$10.1	$17.5
2018	9.6	7.5	2.1	15.0
2017	8.3	2.5	1.2	9.6

Required
1. The reconciliation includes "Charged to costs and expenses" of $12.6 million for the year ended January 31, 2019. What does this item refer to?
2. The reconciliation includes "Deductions" of $10.1 million. What does this item refer to?
3. Compute the following metrics for the past three years and comment on the results.
    a. Sales returns allowance/Gross sales.
    b. Charged to costs and expenses/Gross sales.
    c. Adequacy of the allowance account.

Solution on p. 5-55.

Unearned (Deferred) Revenue

LO3 Analyze deferred revenue.

In some industries, it is common to receive cash before recording revenue. Customers might pay in advance for special orders, make deposits for future services, or buy concert tickets, subscriptions, or gift cards. In those cases, companies must record unearned revenues, and only record revenue when those products and services are provided. Specifically, deposits or advance payments are not recorded as revenue until the company performs the services owed or delivers the goods. Until then, the company's balance sheet shows the advance payment as a liability (called unearned revenue or deferred revenue) because the company is obligated to deliver those products and services.

Unearned revenue is particularly common among retailers that:

- Receive advance payments from customers for products that are not yet delivered.
- Offer gift cards.
- Sell extended-protection plan contracts.

Lowe's Companies, the home improvement company, provides several examples of transactions that require revenue to be deferred, as illustrated in the following excerpts from the revenue recognition footnote in its 10-K for the 2018 fiscal year ended February 1, 2019.

> **In-store and on-line sales.** Revenues from in-store and online merchandise purchases are recognized at the point in time when the customer obtains control of the merchandise, which is at the time of in-store purchase or delivery of the product to the customer. A provision for anticipated merchandise returns is provided through a reduction of sales and cost of sales in the period that the related sales are recorded.

continued

> **Service revenue.** Revenues from services primarily relate to professional installation services the Company provides through subcontractors related to merchandise purchased by a customer. The Company recognizes revenue associated with services as they are rendered, and the majority of services are completed less than one week from initiation.
>
> **Stored-value cards.** The Company defers revenues from stored-value cards, which include gift cards and returned merchandise credits, and recognizes revenue into sales when the cards are redeemed.
>
> **Extended protection plans.** The Company also defers revenues for its separately-priced extended protection plan contracts. The Company recognizes revenue from extended protection plan sales on a straight-line basis over the respective contract term.

As we evaluate profitability for companies that report substantial amounts of deferred revenue, we must be aware of changes in deferred revenue liabilities on the balance sheet. Should deferred revenue liabilities decrease, we infer the company's *current* reported revenue was collected from customers in a *prior* accounting period and there have been fewer new prepayments for which revenue will be recognized in future periods. Such a trend could predict future declines in revenue and profit.

The following schedule allows us to track the deferred revenue liability related to Lowe's extended protection plan contracts.

$ millions	FY2018	FY2017	FY2016
Deferred revenue—extended protection plans, beginning of year	$803	$763	$729
Additions to deferred revenue	414	398	387
Deferred revenue recognized	(390)	(358)	(353)
Deferred revenue—extended protection plans, end of year	$827	$803	$763

During the 2018 fiscal year ended February 1, 2019, Lowe's received cash from customers of $414 million for new extended protection plan contracts and recognized revenue of $390 million that related to cash received in prior years. As a result, the balance in the deferred revenue liability account increased from $803 million to $827 million at the end of fiscal year 2018.

From this reconciliation, we would have no reason to predict future revenue declines.

Review 5-3 LO3

Microsoft reports a significant amount of unearned revenue mainly from cloud-services subscriptions. During 2018, Microsoft included the following information in a footnote ($ millions).

Deferred revenue balance, beginning of period	$26,656
Deferred revenue balance, end of period	32,720
Previously unearned revenue, recognized in 2018	(55,078)

Required
Determine the amount of cash Microsoft collected from customers in advance of recognizing revenue during 2018.

Solution on p. 5-56.

Foreign Currency Effects on Revenue, Expenses, and Cash Flow

 **LO4** Evaluate how foreign currency exchange rates affect revenue.

Exhibit 5.1 shows **Pfizer**'s income statement that reports an increase in revenues of $1.1 billion from 2017 to 2018. Pfizer explains that changes in foreign exchange rates during 2018 accounted for $310 million of the $1.1 billion total. A footnote describes Pfizer's foreign currency exposure.

> Significant portions of our revenues, costs and expenses, as well as our substantial international net assets, are exposed to changes in foreign exchange rates. 53% of our total 2018 revenues were derived from international operations, including 21% from Europe and 22% from China, Japan and the rest of Asia. As we operate in multiple foreign currencies, including the euro, the Japanese yen, the Chinese Renminbi, the U.K. pound, the Canadian dollar and approximately 100 other currencies, changes in those currencies relative to the U.S. dollar will impact our revenues and expenses. If the U.S. dollar were to weaken against another currency, assuming all other variables remained constant, our revenues would increase, having a positive impact on earnings, and our overall expenses would increase, having a negative impact on earnings. Conversely, if the U.S. dollar were to strengthen against another currency, assuming all other variables remained constant, our revenues would decrease, having a negative impact on earnings, and our overall expenses would decrease, having a positive impact on earnings. Therefore, significant changes in foreign exchange rates can impact our results and our financial guidance. . . Revenues in 2018 increased by $1.1 billion, or 2%, compared to 2017, which reflects operational growth of $791 million, or 2%, and the favorable impact of foreign exchange of $310 million.

Increased revenue was not the only foreign exchange impact. The weakening U.S. dollar ($US) also increased Pfizer's COGS and other operating expenses. Because Pfizer is profitable (revenues > expenses), the foreign currency fluctuations had the net effect of increasing Pfizer's net income for 2018.

Companies routinely conduct business in foreign currencies. Although Pfizer's U.S.-based companies may write purchase and sales contracts that are denominated in foreign currencies, Pfizer's foreign subsidiaries likely transact business almost entirely in foreign currencies. These foreign subsidiaries not only conduct business in foreign currencies, they also maintain their accounting records in currencies other than the $US. Before the financial statements of those subsidiaries can be consolidated with the U.S. parent company, they must first be translated into $US.

As the $US weakens vis-à-vis other world currencies in which Pfizer conducts its business, each foreign currency buys more $US. When Pfizer translates a subsidiary's foreign-currency denominated income statement into $US, the income statement grows: reported revenues, expenses, and profit are all larger than before the dollar weakened. In the consolidation process, Pfizer must also translate the foreign subsidiary's balance sheet and, with a weaker $US, the foreign currency-denominated balance sheet grows as well, reporting higher assets, liabilities, and equity. We examine the income statement and cash flow effects of foreign currency here, and we defer our discussion of the balance sheet effects to Module 9, when we discuss the consolidation process.

Foreign Currency and Cash Flows

Following are three examples of the ways in which foreign currency gains and losses may affect *cash flow*.

1. **When the $US company transacts business denominated in foreign currencies.** A U.S. company might denominate a sales contract in Euros, for example. If the $US weakens between the date of the sale and the ultimate collection of the Euro-denominated account receivable, the U.S. company realizes a foreign currency transaction gain. Conversely, if the U.S. company purchases goods, the foreign currency denominated account payable would grow and more $US would be required to settle the obligation, resulting in a foreign currency transaction loss.

2. **When the U.S. parent company borrows money that is denominated in a foreign currency.** If the U.S. parent company borrows in foreign currencies and the $US weakens, it will require more in $US to repay the foreign currency-denominated liability. If the company planned to repay the loan with $US, the company will realize a loss as it repays the foreign currency-denominated loan.

3. **When the foreign subsidiary's cash is repatriated to the United States.** Most foreign subsidiaries maintain cash in foreign bank accounts (local to the subsidiary) for use in ongoing operations. If the U.S. parent repatriates that cash, however, say, by a cash dividend from the subsidiary to the U.S. parent company, a foreign currency transaction gain may arise if the dollar weakens before the foreign currency is converted into $US to pay the dividend.

The difference between these three situations and the translation adjustment that arises solely from the consolidation of Pfizer's foreign subsidiaries' profits is that these three transactions describe *realized* losses, whereas the translation losses that Pfizer reports above are *unrealized*.

Regarding contracts denominated in foreign currencies (#1 above) and borrowing in foreign currencies (#2 above), companies frequently hedge their exposures to these potential realized losses by using financial derivative securities. These derivative securities act like an insurance policy to offset the income statement effects of realized gains and losses by transferring some of the risk for foreign currency fluctuations to other parties who are willing to accept that risk for a fee. An effective hedging process reduces the effects of realized gains and losses and greatly reduces the impact on net income. We discuss hedging in more detail in Appendix 9A.

Accordingly, the *realized* foreign currency translation effects of #1 and #2 above are likely small, and the foreign currency translation gains (the increase in revenues, expenses, and profit Pfizer discusses above) are, therefore, likely to be primarily *unrealized* noncash losses.

Regarding the repatriation of foreign earnings (#3 above), until recently, firms infrequently repatriated foreign earnings (or repatriated only small proportions). Recent estimates are that U.S. companies hold $1 trillion of overseas earnings, mostly invested in U.S. marketable securities. However, the Tax Cuts and Jobs Act (TCJA) removed a major tax barrier to repatriation. From 2017 onward, companies must pay a one-time tax of 15.5% (down from 35%) on repatriated earnings. Since the new tax law was passed, many companies have started to bring foreign profits back to the U.S. One study finds that companies repatriated more earnings in the first sixth months of 2018 than in 2015, 2016, and 2017 combined.

Foreign Currency and Income

So, how should we treat the foreign currency translation effects on the income statement given that the currency fluctuations reduced Pfizer's revenues, expenses, and profit? When we use the income statement numbers, as reported, to calculate metrics such as NOPAT and ratios such as ROE and RNOA, we implicitly include the effects of foreign currency translation. One approach would be to back out the revenue and expense effects to yield income statements that are not affected by these foreign currency fluctuations. Pfizer identifies numerous effects on its 2018 income statement in the management discussion and analysis (MD&A) section of its 10-K, including the following.

1. Revenues were increased by $310 million.
2. COGS was increased by $153 million.

Backing out these foreign currency translation effects on the 2018 income statement (with similar adjustments to prior year financial statements) would allow us to better isolate Pfizer's operating profit without the distortion of foreign currency exchange rate effects. The impact on Pfizer's gross profit for 2018 is $157 million ($310 million − $153 million). This amounts to 1.4% of net income ($157 million/$11,153 million). A thorough analysis computes ratios and numbers with and without the effect of foreign currency.

Foreign Currency and Future Results

Companies frequently provide guidance for analysts to forecast future income statements. Pfizer's 2018 10-K includes the following guidance to analysts for 2019.

Our Financial Guidance for 2019 The following table provides our financial guidance for full-year 2019:

Revenues	$52.0 to $54.0 billion
Adjusted cost of sales as a percentage of revenues	20.8% to 21.8%
Adjusted selling, informational and administrative expenses	$13.5 to $14.5 billion
Adjusted research and development expenses	$7.8 to $8.3 billion
Adjusted other (income) deductions	Approximately $100 million of income
Effective tax rate on adjusted income	Approximately 16.0%
Adjusted diluted EPS	$2.82 to $2.92

Pfizer also includes a footnote to its guidance relating to foreign currency effects (on revenue only).

> Exchange rates assumed are as of mid-January 2019. Reflects the anticipated unfavorable impact of approximately $0.9 billion on revenues and approximately $0.06 on adjusted diluted EPS as a result of changes in foreign exchange rates relative to the U.S. dollar compared to foreign exchange rates from 2018.

Because foreign currency effects are unpredictable and out of the company's direct control, we exclude these effects to better forecast operating cash flow.

LO4 Review 5-4

Alphabet Inc. (Google) reports the following in the notes to its 2018 10-K. EMEA is the acronym for Alphabet's operations in Europe, the Middle East, and Africa.

> The effect of currency exchange rates on our business is an important factor in understanding period-to-period comparisons. Our international revenues are favorably affected as the U.S. dollar weakens relative to other foreign currencies, and unfavorably affected as the U.S. dollar strengthens relative to other foreign currencies. Our international revenues are also favorably affected by net hedging gains and unfavorably affected by net hedging losses. We use non-GAAP constant currency revenues and constant currency revenue growth for financial and operational decision-making and as a means to evaluate period-to-period comparisons. We believe the presentation of results on a constant currency basis in addition to GAAP results helps improve the ability to understand our performance because they exclude the effects of foreign currency volatility that are not indicative of our core operating results. Our revenues and revenue growth from 2017 to 2018 were favorably affected by changes in foreign currency exchange rates, primarily due to the U.S. dollar weakening relative to the Euro and British pound.

Year Ended December 31 ($ millions)	2016	2017	2018
EMEA revenues	$30,304	$36,046	$44,567
Exclude foreign exchange effect on current period revenues using prior year rates	1,291	(5)	(1,325)
Exclude hedging effect recognized in current period	(479)	190	172
EMEA constant currency revenues	$31,116	$36,231	$43,414
EMEA revenue growth		19%	24%
EMEA constant currency revenue growth		21%	20%

Required
1. Explain how fluctuations in foreign currency exchange rates affected Google's EMEA revenues in 2018 and 2017. Why do these fluctuations occur?
2. What other portions of the income statement are likely affected by these exchange rate fluctuations?
3. How do these fluctuations in foreign exchange rates affect Google's cash flow?

Solution on p. 5-56.

Accounts Receivable

LO5 Analyze accounts receivable and uncollectible amounts.

Pfizer reports $8,025 million of net trade accounts receivable in the current asset section of its balance sheet.

As of December 31 ($ millions)	2018	2017
Cash and cash equivalents	$ 1,139	$ 1,342
Short-term investments	17,694	18,650
Trade accounts receivable, less allowance for doubtful accounts: 2018—$541; 2017—$584	8,025	8,221

Selling goods on account carries the risk that some customers encounter financial difficulty and are unable to pay the amount due. GAAP recognizes this possibility and requires companies to estimate the dollar amount of receivables that are likely to be uncollectible and to report only the net collectible amount on the balance sheet. Pfizer reports net receivables of $8,025 million and estimates that $541 million of its total accounts receivable are uncollectible. From this, we can determine that the gross accounts receivable (the total amount customers owe to Pfizer) is $8,566 million ($8,025 million + $541 million). Pfizer estimates, therefore, that 6.3% ($541 million/$8,566 million) of the total amount of receivables owed is likely uncollectible.

Aging Analysis of Receivables

Companies frequently employ an **aging analysis** of their accounts receivable to estimate the uncollectible amounts. An aging analysis groups accounts receivable by number of days past due (days after the scheduled due date). A common grouping method uses 30-day or 60-day intervals, as shown in the following.

Age of Accounts	Receivable Balance	Estimated Percent Uncollectible	Estimated Uncollectible Accounts
Current	$ 50,000	2%	$1,000
1–60 days past due	30,000	3%	900
61–90 days past due	15,000	4%	600
Over 90 days past due	5,000	8%	400
Total	$100,000		$2,900

In this example, we assume the seller's credit terms are a typical "2/10, net 30" (customers receive a 2% discount from the amount owed if they make payment within 10 days of the invoice date; or the full amount owed is due 30 days from the invoice date). Accounts listed as 1–60 days past due are those 1 to 60 days past their due date. This would include an account that is 45 days outstanding for a net 30-day invoice. Given this aging schedule, the company draws upon its previous experience of uncollectible accounts of that age. The company has experience that if an account is 1–60 days past due, about 3% of the balance is not collected. Based on that past experience, the company estimates a potential loss of $900 for the $30,000 in the 1–60 days past due group. As expected, the percent uncollectible increases with the age of the account.

The company estimates that $2,900, or 2.9% of its $100,000 of gross accounts receivable, is likely uncollectible. The net amount, $97,100, represents the company's best estimate of what it expects to ultimately collect from its customers.

Accounting for Accounts Receivable

To account for uncollectible amounts, companies use an allowance account similar to the ones discussed above for sales returns and other allowances. The *allowance for uncollectible accounts* (also called the allowance for doubtful accounts) reduces the gross amount of receivables that are reported on the balance sheet.

To illustrate, assume the company sells goods on account for $100,000 and, at the end of the accounting period, performs an aging analysis and establishes the allowance for uncollectible accounts in the amount of $2,900. Our financial statement effects for the sale and the estimate of uncollectible accounts receivable are as follows.

Transaction	Balance Sheet					Income Statement		
	Cash Asset	+ Noncash Assets	= Liabilities	+ Contrib. Capital	+ Earned Capital	Revenues	− Expenses	= Net Income
Sale on account		100,000 Accounts Receivable			100,000 Retained Earnings	100,000 Sales	−	= 100,000
Establish allowance and record bad debts expense		−2,900 Allowance for Uncollectible Accounts			−2,900 Retained Earnings		+2,900 Bad Debts Expense	= −2,900

```
AR......100,000
  Rev......100,000

     AR
100,000 |
           Rev
           | 100,000

BDE ....2,900
  AU..........2,900

    BDE
  2,900 |
           AU
           | 2,900
```

The allowance for uncollectible accounts is subtracted from the gross accounts receivable, and the net amount collectible is reported on the balance sheet.

Accounts receivable (gross amount owed)............................	$100,000
Less: Allowance for uncollectible accounts	(2,900)
Accounts receivable, net (reported on balance sheet).....................	$ 97,100

Companies typically report the allowance for uncollectible accounts along with accounts receivable as follows.

Accounts receivable, less allowance for uncollectible accounts of $2,900........	$97,100

By setting up the allowance, the company has established a reserve, or a cushion, that it can use to absorb credit losses as they occur. To see how this works, assume a customer who owes $500 files for bankruptcy. If the company determines the receivable is now uncollectible, it must write off the receivable. This is absorbed by the allowance for uncollectible accounts as follows.

Transaction	Balance Sheet					Income Statement		
	Cash Asset	+ Noncash Assets	= Liabilities	+ Contrib. Capital	+ Earned Capital	Revenues	− Expenses	= Net Income
Write off $500 of uncollectible accounts receivable		500 Allowance for Uncollectible Accounts = −500 Accounts Receivable					−	=

```
AU......500
  AR..........500

    AU
   500 |
           AR
           | 500
```

The write-off of the uncollectible account receivable results in the following balances at the end of the period.

Accounts receivable (gross amount owed)	$99,500	($100,000 − $500)
Less: Allowance for uncollectible accounts	(2,400)	($2,900 − $500)
Accounts receivable, net (reported on balance sheet)	$97,100	

We see that the net amount of accounts receivable the company will report at the end of the period is the same $97,100 balance it reported *before* the write-off of the uncollectible account (i.e., because the write-off was completely absorbed by the allowance account established in the previous period). This leaves the reported amount of net accounts receivable on the balance sheet unchanged. The write-off used up some of the reserve as the allowance decreased from $2,900 to $2,400. Future write-offs will reduce the allowance further. Each period, the company replenishes the allowance account and then draws it down for write-offs.

Analysis of Accounts Receivable–Magnitude

An important analysis tool for accounts receivable is to determine the magnitude and quality of the receivables. The relative magnitude of accounts receivable is usually measured with respect to sales volume using either of the following ratios. (Average accounts receivable is a simple average: (Current year balance + Prior year balance)/2.

- **Accounts receivable turnover**

$$\text{Accounts receivable turnover} = \frac{\text{Sales}}{\text{Average accounts receivable}}$$

- **Days sales outstanding (DSO)**

$$\text{Days sales outstanding} = \frac{365 \text{ days}}{\text{Accounts receivable turnover}} = \frac{365 \times \text{Average accounts receivable}}{\text{Sales}}$$

DSO is, arguably, the most intuitive of the ratios, and it reveals the number of days, on average, that accounts receivable are outstanding before they are paid. The DSO statistic can be:

- Compared with the company's established credit terms to investigate if the company's customers are conforming to those credit terms.
- Computed over several years for the same company to investigate trends.
- Compared with peer companies.

A lower accounts receivable turnover, a higher percentage of accounts receivable to sales, and a lengthening of the DSO all provide a signal that accounts receivable have grown more quickly than sales. Generally, such a trend is not favorable for two possible reasons.

- **The company is becoming more lenient in granting credit to its customers.** Perhaps this is in response to greater competition, or perhaps the company is finding it difficult to maintain sales volume and is reaching for additional volume by selling to new customers with weaker credit scores.
- **Credit quality is deteriorating.** If existing customers are not paying on time, the level of accounts receivable relative to the level of sales will increase. This will be highlighted in the DSO statistic, which will increase as the percentage of receivables to sales grows. (A third explanation is that the mix of products sold has changed toward markets with longer payment terms.)

What further steps can analysts take to assess an adverse trend in DSO? A first step is to review the MD&A section of the 10-K to learn management's interpretation of the adverse trend. A second step is to review the financial press, analyst reports, and other external reports about the company to glean additional insight.

The ratios we highlight above are often reported in commercial databases that are regularly used by analysts. For example, **Standard & Poors' Capital IQ** reports the following data for Pfizer.

Pfizer Inc. (NYSE:PFE) Financial Ratios					
Ratios for Fiscal Period Ending	2018	2017	2016	2015	2014
Asset turnover					
Total asset turnover	0.3	0.3	0.3	0.3	0.3
Fixed asset turnover	3.9	3.9	3.9	3.8	4.1
Accounts receivable turnover	6.6	6.4	6.4	5.9	5.6
Inventory turnover	1.5	1.5	1.7	1.4	1.5
Short-term liquidity					
Current ratio	1.6	1.4	1.3	1.5	2.6
Quick ratio	1.0	1.0	0.9	1.2	2.2
Cash from operations to current liabilities	0.5	0.6	0.5	0.5	0.8
Average days sales outstanding	55.3	57.1	56.8	61.9	65.3
Average days inventory outstanding	247.4	247.8	219.5	256.9	239.0
Average days payable outstanding	154.0	147.5	133.4	111.2	137.9
Average cash conversion cycle	148.7	157.4	142.9	207.6	166.5

We have highlighted the accounts receivable turnover and days sales outstanding (DSO). To compute these ratios for 2018, Capital IQ uses Pfizer's 2018 sales of $53,647 million and its accounts receivable, net of $8,025 million and $8,221 million for 2018 and 2017, respectively:

$$2018 \text{ accounts receivable turnover} = \frac{\$53,647}{(\$8,025 + \$8,221)/2} = 6.6 \text{ times}$$

$$2018 \text{ days sales outstanding} = \frac{365 \text{ days}}{6.6 \text{ times per year}} = 55.3 \text{ days}$$

A review of the Capital IQ data reveals that Pfizer's accounts receivable turnover has increased over the past five years—a good sign. The downward trend for DSO is another way to measure the positive trend. The metric has declined by 10 days from 65.3 days in 2014 to 55.3 days in 2018. Generally, the analysis of accounts receivable focuses on the levels of the turnover and DSO ratios compared with peer companies (shedding evidence on the company's ability to collect its receivables relative to competitors) and trends in these ratios (providing a bigger picture and insight into the company's cash-collection patterns). To assess the 10-day decrease, we would compare to a set of Pfizer's peers.

Collecting receivables more quickly increases operating cash flow. At the current sales volume of $53,647 million, the average sales per day is $147 million ($53,647 million/365), and collecting receivables 10 days more quickly generated an additional (one-time) $1.47 billion of cash in 2018 ($147 million per day × 10 days).

Data Analytics Insight ▪ Reducing Days to Collect Accounts Receivable

A company can generate cash by reducing the days to collect receivables from its customer. On the other side of the transaction, customers that pay earlier will see their cash position reduced. Consequently, efforts to collect receivables more quickly must be done with care so as not to damage customer relationships. One approach is to become smarter about credit decisions. Companies maintain extensive data on their customers and can use data analytics to identify customer profiles and behaviors. Armed with these insights, companies can make more-informed credit decisions, for example, to extend credit on a more selective basis, to offer more generous terms to faster-paying customers, and to reduce credit to slow payers. Thanks to this sort of data analytics, we have FICO credit scores that banks and credit card companies use to determine consumer lines of credit and loan amounts and terms.

Analysis of Accounts Receivable—Quality

To analyze the quality of accounts receivable, we focus on the allowance for uncollectible accounts. Companies are required to report on their balance sheet the amount of accounts receivable they expect to collect (the gross amount of accounts receivable less the estimated uncollectible accounts). Levi Strauss reports its accounts receivable as follows in its 2018 balance sheet.

$ thousands	Nov. 25, 2018	Nov. 26, 2017
Current assets		
Cash and cash equivalents.	$713,120	$633,622
Trade receivables, net of allowance for doubtful accounts of $10,037 and $11,726	**534,164**	**485,485**

The company also includes Schedule II in its 10-K, where it reports a "roll forward" of the allowance for uncollectible accounts that shows movements in the account.

Allowance for Doubtful Accounts ($ thousands)	Balance at Beginning of Period		Additions Charged to Expenses		Deductions		Balance at End of Period
November 25, 2018	$11,726	+	$2,284	–	$3,973	=	$10,037
November 26, 2017	$11,974	+	$1,645	–	$1,893	=	$11,726
November 27, 2016	$11,025	+	$2,195	–	$1,246	=	$11,974

Reconciling the allowance account from the beginning to the end of the year yields useful insights (in $000s). The allowance account began 2018 with a balance of $11,726. Levi Strauss increased the allowance by $2,284 and recognized bad debt expense (included in selling, general and administrative expense) equal to that amount. The allowance was reduced by $3,973 to absorb the write-off of uncollectible accounts receivable during 2018 and ended the year with a balance of $10,037. The decrease in the account during the year means that Levi Strauss wrote off more than it added to its allowance account. We observe the same pattern in 2017, when the company added $1,645 and wrote off $1,893. However, in 2016, the opposite holds true, additions to the allowance were greater than the write-offs. Over the three-year period, the company wrote off $7,112 ($3,973 + $1,893 + $1,246) while only increasing the allowance account by $6,124 ($2,284 + $1,645 + $2,195).

Because Levi Strauss has not replenished the allowance account for the amount of the write-offs for three years, the balance of the allowance account has declined from $11,025 at the beginning of 2016 to $10,037 at the end of 2018. This would not be an issue if gross receivables had declined proportionately, but this is not the case. Instead, the allowance account as a percentage of gross accounts receivable has declined.

$ thousands	2018	2017
Accounts receivable (net).	$534,164	$485,485
Allowance account	10,037	11,726
Accounts receivable (gross)	$544,201	$497,211
Allowance account / Accounts receivable (gross)	1.84%	2.36%

There are two possible interpretations for this change.

1. **Credit quality has improved.** If Levi Strauss believes the collectability of its remaining receivables has improved, it can feel confident in allowing the allowance for uncollectible accounts to decline. An improvement in credit quality might be plausible given that the recession ended during this period and customers are in better financial condition.

2. **Levi Strauss is underestimating the allowance account.** This is the more troubling of the two possibilities. Remember, Levi Strauss reports bad debt expense in its income statement when it *increases* its allowance account. Write-offs have no effect on profit; only the estimation of the loss affects income. So, Levi Strauss might be attempting to increase its profitability by not *adding* to the allowance account, and, thus, avoiding more bad debt expense.

How can we determine which of these two possibilities is more likely? We might compare Levi Strauss with its peer companies to determine if its ratio of allowance account to gross accounts receivable is higher or lower. If Levi Strauss's ratio exceeds industry or peer benchmarks, then the decrease might be reasonable. If Levi Strauss's ratio is lower than industry or peer benchmarks, Levi Strauss may be attempting to inflate its earnings by avoiding the additional drag on profits from bad debt expense (maybe to meet analyst forecasts or to avoid a default in loan covenants). All we know for certain is the allowance account has declined, both in absolute dollar amount and as a percentage of gross accounts receivable. It is difficult to know the reasons unless the company discusses those reasons in its MD&A section of the 10-K or in conference calls with analysts.

Managerial Decision ■ You Are the Receivables Manager

You are analyzing your receivables for the period and you are concerned that the average collection period is lengthening. What specific actions can you take to reduce the average collection period? [Answer, p. 5-35]

LO5 Review 5-5

Coca-Cola reports the following in its 2018 10-K about its credit policy for accounts receivable.

> We record trade accounts receivable at net realizable value. This value includes an appropriate allowance for estimated uncollectible accounts to reflect any loss anticipated on the trade accounts receivable balances and charged to the provision for doubtful accounts. We calculate this allowance based on our history of write-offs, the level of past-due accounts based on the contractual terms of the receivables, and our relationships with, and the economic status of, our bottling partners and customers.

Assume that Coca-Cola's customers owe the company $3,885 million as of December 31, 2018, and that an aging analysis of accounts receivable reveals the following.

$ millions	Accounts Receivable	% Uncollectible
Current	$1,554	1.5%
1–30 days past due	971	5.0%
31–60 days past due	544	14.0%
61–90 days past due	427	25.0%
91–120 days past due	272	54.0%
Over 120 days past due	117	75.0%
Total	$3,885	

Required
1. Compute the dollar amount that Coca-Cola should report in its December 31, 2018, balance sheet for the allowance for doubtful accounts and the net balance of accounts receivable it will report on its balance sheet as of that date.
2. Assume that Coca-Cola's estimated uncollectible accounts on December 31, 2017, were $477 million and that the company wrote off $17 million of accounts receivable during 2018. What dollar amount of expense will Coca-Cola report in its 2018 income statement?
3. Coca-Cola's 2017 balance sheet reported accounts receivable, net of $3,667 million. Are Coca-Cola's accounts receivable of higher or lower quality in 2018 as compared with 2017?

Solution on p. 5-57.

Expenses and Losses

LO6 Evaluate operating expenses and discontinued operations.

Pfizer's income statement in Exhibit 5.1 reports a number of expense and loss items.

Deductions from Income

The following expense and loss items reported by **Pfizer** are typical of many companies.

- **Cost of sales.** This is the cost Pfizer incurred to make or buy the products it sold during the year. As goods are manufactured or purchased, the cost is recognized as inventory on the balance sheet. The inventory remains there until the product is sold, at which time the cost is transferred from the balance sheet into the income statement as cost of goods sold. Given that the product is sold, revenue from the sale of the product is also added to the income statement. The difference between revenue and cost of sales is the gross profit on the sale. We discuss this cost together with inventories in Module 6 and the analysis of the gross profit margin (Gross profit / Sales) in Module 4.

- **Selling, informational and administrative expense.** Usually, this expense category is labeled Selling, general and administrative (SG&A) expense, and it includes a number of general overhead expense categories, such as:
  - Salaries and benefits for administrative personnel and executives.
  - Rent and utilities for office facilities.
  - Marketing and selling expenses.
  - IT, legal, and accounting expenses.
  - Depreciation for Pfizer's depreciable assets that are used for administrative purposes (we discuss this expense together with property, plant, and equipment in Module 6).

- **Research and development expense.** This is the amount Pfizer incurs to conduct research for new products. We discuss this cost in a separate section below.

- **Amortization of intangible assets.** When Pfizer acquires an intangible asset, such as a patent, it amortizes that cost over the useful life of the patent (the period of time Pfizer expects the patent to produce cash flow). Amortization expense is a noncash expense, similar to depreciation expense. Often, it is included with the SG&A expense.

- **Restructuring charges.** This represents the cost Pfizer has incurred and expects to incur to restructure its operations, say, by the elimination of lines of business, consolidation of operations, reduction of the number of employees, and the like. We discuss restructuring charges in Module 6.

- **Provision for taxes on income.** The tax provision shown on the income statement relates to Pfizer's profit. These are taxes that will be paid to federal and state taxing authorities as well as income taxes levied by foreign governments and municipalities. We discuss income tax expense in a separate section below and, in greater depth, in Module 10. Other types of taxes, such as sales tax or employment taxes, are included in SG&A and not with the income tax expense.

- **Discontinued operations.** This represents the operating profit (or loss) plus the gain (or loss) on the sale of businesses Pfizer has decided to divest. We discuss discontinued operations in a separate section below.

- **Income attributable to noncontrolling interest.** Noncontrolling interest arises because Pfizer has one or more subsidiaries where Pfizer does not own 100% of the voting stock. So, while Pfizer owns the controlling interest, other shareholders own the balance of the stock (the noncontrolling interest). The income attributable to the noncontrolling interest is their portion of the subsidiary's income (and is added to the noncontrolling interest equity account on Pfizer's balance sheet). The remainder of the subsidiary's net income is credited to Pfizer's shareholders and is added to retained earnings on Pfizer's balance sheet. We discuss noncontrolling interest in greater depth in Module 9.

Research and Development Expense

Companies in many industries depend heavily on research and development (R&D) for new and improved products and services. For these companies, R&D is critical because failure to offer "cutting edge" technology can lead to loss of market share and even bankruptcy. R&D costs broadly consist of the following.

- Salaries and benefits for researchers and developers.
- Supplies needed to conduct the research.
- Licensing fees for intellectual property or software used in the R&D process.
- Third-party payments to collaborators at other firms and universities.
- Laboratory and other equipment.
- Property and buildings to be used as research facilities. As we discuss in a later module, research facilities are included in PPE and the depreciation on research facilities is included in R&D expense each year.

Accounting for R&D is straightforward: R&D costs are expensed as incurred.

R&D Spending

Exhibit 5.2 shows the median level of R&D spending in 2018 for the S&P 500 firms that report R&D expense on the income statement.

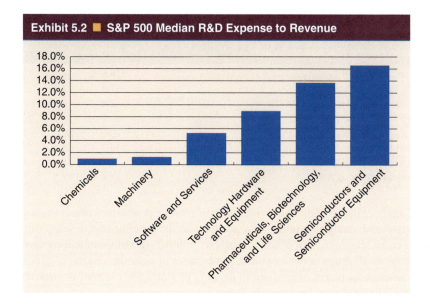

Analysis of R&D

Our analysis of R&D starts with measuring R&D expense in dollars and as a percentage of total revenues. It is important to compare a company's R&D spending to its peers.

R&D is a significant expense for Pfizer as it seeks new compounds and drugs to bring to market. In 2018, Pfizer's R&D expense is $8,006 million or 14.9% of total revenues. As Exhibit 5.3 shows, Pfizer's R&D expense has ranged between 13% and 16% of total revenues over the past six years, in line with the 13.7% median for the pharmaceutical and biotech sector.

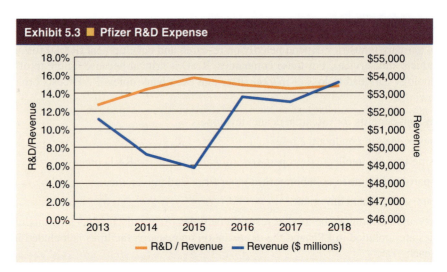

Among Pfizer's peers there are significant differences in the percentage of revenues devoted to R&D expenditures (see Exhibit 5.4). Pfizer's R&D is about average among its peers. Our analysis focuses on trends over time and whether other firms are experiencing the same trends. As we saw in Exhibit 5.3, R&D spending might vary in percentage terms due to changes in revenue; our analysis needs to consider both dollar levels and percentages.

Exhibit 5.4 R&D Expenditures to Revenue

Company Name (Exchange:Ticker)	2016	2017	2018
Pfizer Inc. (NYSE:PFE)	14.9%	14.5%	14.8%
AbbVie Inc. (NYSE:ABBV)	17.1	17.7	16.1
Bayer Aktiengesellschaft (DB:BAYN)	12.4	12.8	12.3
GlaxoSmithKline plc (LSE:GSK)	12.7	13.0	12.3
Eli Lilly and Company (NYSE:LLY)	25.0	23.4	21.6
Johnson & Johnson (NYSE:JNJ)	12.7	13.9	13.2
Merck & Co. Inc. (NYSE:MRK)	17.4	24.5	22.8
Novartis AG (SWX:NOVN)	17.4	17.3	17.1

Financial analysts usually aim to develop *forward-looking* predictions of a company's income and cash flow. To that end, analysts monitor new products in the pipeline and develop estimates of their ultimate commercial feasibility. For example, analysts following pharmaceutical companies frequently prepare schedules of all drugs in development and monitor closely the success of experimental trials. Analysts also monitor the patent expirations of existing products and estimate the impact on sales after a patent expires. The challenge for analysts is two-fold; not only must we estimate the magnitude of future revenues, but we must estimate revenue timing as well. There is often a considerable lag between when R&D expenditures occur and when the resulting revenue is earned. But while the income statement might suffer from such lags, the company's market cap reflects at least some of the future revenue related to current period R&D expenditure. This is one reason why we observe market-to-book ratios much greater than 1.0 for R&D intensive firms.

Manager Insights R&D Projects

Company managers aim to maximize return on R&D investments by selecting projects to fund. Managers have a considerable amount of proprietary information about each R&D project, which they can use to make investment decisions. The goal is to maximize the return on the R&D investment by focusing on the following areas:

R&D Costs. Companies can reduce R&D costs by strategically managing the procurement of raw materials and equipment as they do for other business units, by monitoring closely the investment at each stage of the research process (reducing investment cost in high-risk areas and increasing that investment if and when the risk level

continued

continued from previous page

falls), by outsourcing portions of the research process as they do for other production and business processes, by identifying failed research ventures early and cutting their losses, by partnering with other companies interested in the research to share the investment cost and the risk, and a variety of other measures.

Speed of research effort. Companies can reduce the period of time over which the research is conducted (and thus the cost of the research) with careful planning and control. Some of the same production and scheduling techniques that companies have applied to their manufacturing processes can be applied to the research units. These include project management techniques, parallel processing, and a number of other techniques discussed in operations courses.

Quality of decisions. Each R&D project requires constant monitoring and numerous decisions relating to a succession of investments and go versus no-go decisions. Failed projects need to be identified early and culled from the research portfolio and managers need to continually analyze the extent to which the research is creating knowledge that will lead to commercially feasible products.

It is important for managers to adopt the mindset that each R&D project is a separate investment decision similar to other capital-budgeting decisions and one which typically involves a series of related investment decisions. It is only with this degree of discipline that the R&D process will achieve maximum returns on investment. Ultimately, firms invest in R&D to earn future revenues. There is an argument to be made that R&D investments create an asset that should be added to the balance sheet and then depreciated over the expected life of the new product.

Provision (Benefit) for Taxes on Income

The tax expense reported on the income statement (also called *tax provision*) relates to taxes the company expects to pay to federal, state and municipal taxing authorities as well as income taxes levied by foreign governments. In 2016, Pfizer reported an income tax provision of $1,123 million, or 13.4% of the $8,351 million reported pretax income. This "effective" tax rate of 13.4% is lower than the 20%–30% rate the company reported in years before 2016.

Oddly, in 2017, Pfizer reported a tax *benefit* of $9,049 million that actually *increased* its net income. This unusual tax activity arose as a result of the U.S. Tax Cuts and Jobs Act (TCJA) of 2017. The TCJA made sweeping changes that significantly impacted companies' income statements. In particular, the new tax law:

- Reduced the corporate tax rate from 35% to 21%.
- Imposed tax on all *future* income earned outside of the U.S. even if the cash profits remain abroad.
- Reduced the repatriation tax on *prior* foreign earnings to 15.5% (from 35%).

In the two years after the TJCA passed, the tax provision line on U.S. companies' income statements gyrated wildly. Some companies reported significant spikes in tax expense in 2017 while others reported dramatic decreases. More than a few, including Pfizer, experienced tax benefits (a *negative* tax expense), which served to increase reported profits in 2017. The effects of the TJCA continued into 2018 as companies responded to the new rules by realigning operations and repatriating past foreign earnings. For example, Pfizer's effective tax rate in 2018 dipped to 5.9% (tax expense of only $706 million on pretax income of $11,885).

Neither the income tax benefit of $9,049 million in 2017 nor the relatively low tax expense of $706 million in 2018 accurately represent the income tax expense that Pfizer will report in future years. Pfizer's guidance for 2019 to analysts (presented earlier in this module) projects a 16% tax rate. We discuss income taxes more fully in Module 10. For now, we should recognize that the forecast of future tax rates is critical to an effective forecast of profit and cash flow. To forecast as accurately as possible, we must carefully read the information the company provides about its current and future income tax expense.

Discontinued Operations

From time to time, as strategy changes, companies will divest a segment of their business. When this occurs (or when there is a definitive agreement to sell the segment), the company reports the event at the bottom of the income statement by segregating income from continuing versus **discontinued operations**. The line item for discontinued operations has two distinct components.

- Net income (or loss) from the segment's business activities prior to the divestiture or sale.
- Any gain (or loss) on the sale of the business.

Following is the portion of Pfizer's income statement that reports on its discontinued operations.

Year Ended December 31 ($ millions)	2018	2017	2016
Income from continuing operations	$11,179	$21,353	$7,229
Discontinued operations			
Income from discontinued operations—net of tax	10	(1)	16
Gain on disposal of discontinued operations—net of tax	—	3	—
Discontinued operations—net of tax	10	2	17
Net income before allocation to noncontrolling interests	$11,189	$21,355	$7,246

In addition to segregating the results of operations of the discontinued operation in the current and previous two years' income statements reported, companies are also required to segregate the discontinued operation's assets and liabilities on the current and prior year's balance sheets.

Although the financial effects of Pfizer's discontinued operations were not significant in the most recent years, they have been in the past. In 2013 for example, Pfizer sold its animal health business to a newly formed company, Zoetis. Prior to the sale, the animal health business reported a net income of $308 million. Pfizer reported these operating results as "Income from discontinued operations—net of tax" in the 2013 income statement excerpt below. The sale of the animal health business created a gain on sale of $10,354 million, net of tax. That gain represents the difference between the sales proceeds Pfizer received from Zoetis and the amount at which the animal health business was reported on Pfizer's balance sheet on the date of the sale, that is, its net book value or carrying value.

Footnotes to Pfizer's 2013 10-K provide data relating to both the income earned by the animal health business through the date of sale along with the gain realized when the business was sold.

Year Ended ($ millions)	December 31, 2013
Revenues	$51,584
⋮	
Pretax income from discontinued operations	408
Provision for taxes on income	100
Income from discontinued operations—net of tax	308
Pretax gain on disposal of discontinued operations	10,446
Provision for taxes on income	92
Gain on disposal of discontinued operations—net of tax	10,354
Discontinued operations—net of tax	$10,662

Discontinued operations are segregated in the income statement because they represent a *transitory* item; that is, transactions or events that affect the current period (and in prior periods while the operation was owned by the company) but will not recur. Many readers of financial statements analyze current-year financial statements to gain clues to better predict *future* performance (stock prices, for example, are based on a company's expected profits and cash flows). Although the segregation of transitory items can help us analyze past performance to uncover core operating profit, they are largely irrelevant to predicting future performance. This means investors and other users tend to focus on income from continuing operations because that is the level of profitability that is likely to *persist* (continue) into the future. Likewise, the financial press tends to focus on income from continuing operations when it discloses corporate earnings (often described as "earnings before one-time charges").

Accounting standards relating to discontinued operations have recently changed and have restricted the types of disposals that will be accounted for as discontinued operations. Under the new accounting standard, in order to be classified as a discontinued operation, the disposal of the business unit must represent a *strategic shift* for the company that has or will have a *major effect* on a company's financial results. This represents a substantial hurdle because the company will have to demonstrate that a divestiture represents a strategic shift *and* creates large financial effects. Consequently, the reporting of discontinued operations is likely to be less frequent in the future.

LO6 Review 5-6

Hewlett-Packard Enterprise Co. (HPE) reports the following income statement for 2018 and 2017.

HEWLETT-PACKARD ENTERPRISE COMPANY AND SUBSIDIARIES
Consolidated Statements of Earnings

For fiscal years ended October 31 (in millions)	2018	2017
Net revenue		
Products	$19,504	$17,597
Services	10,901	10,878
Financing income	447	396
Total net revenue	30,852	28,871
Costs and expenses		
Cost of products	14,079	12,715
Cost of services	7,203	7,197
Financing interest	278	265
Research and development	1,663	1,486
Selling, general and administrative	4,851	5,006
Amortization of intangible assets	294	321
Impairment of goodwill	88	—
Restructuring charges	19	417
Transformation costs	425	359
Disaster charges	—	93
Acquisition and other related charges	82	203
Separation costs	12	248
Defined benefit plan settlement charges and remeasurement (benefit)	—	(64)
Gain on H3C and MphasiS divestitures	—	—
Total costs and expenses	28,994	28,246
Earnings from continuing operations	1,858	625
Interest and other, net	(274)	(327)
Tax indemnification adjustments	(1,354)	(3)
Earnings (loss) from equity interests	38	(23)
Earnings from continuing operations before taxes	268	272
Benefit (provision) for taxes	1,744	164
Net earnings from continuing operations	2,012	436
Net loss from discontinued operations	(104)	(92)
Net earnings	$ 1,908	$ 344

Required

1. Which of the following expenses would **not** be included in selling, general, and administrative expense on the income statement?
   - Salary for the chief executive officer
   - Office supplies
   - Utilities for the research laboratories
   - Depreciation on the company jet
   - Wages for manufacturing employees
   - Shipping costs for products delivered to customers
   - License fees for software used to develop new products
   - Depreciation on machines that package and label finished goods

2. Compare R&D expense for 2017 and 2018. (*Hint:* First determine the common-size expense.) List three types of activities that are included in total R&D expense for HPE.

3. Explain the item on the income statement labeled "Earnings from discontinued operations."

Solution on p. 5-57.

Pro Forma Income Reporting

L07 Interpret pro forma and non-GAAP disclosures.

In its fourth quarter earnings release for 2018, Pfizer described its financial performance as follows.

PFIZER REPORTS FOURTH-QUARTER AND FULL-YEAR 2018 RESULTS PROVIDES 2019 FINANCIAL GUIDANCE

- Full-Year 2018 Revenues of $53.6 Billion, Reflecting 2% Operational Growth; Fourth-Quarter 2018 Revenues of $14.0 Billion, Reflecting 5% Operational Growth
- Full-Year 2018 Reported Diluted EPS of $1.87, **Adjusted Diluted EPS** of $3.00; Fourth-Quarter 2018 Reported Loss Per Share of $0.07, Adjusted Diluted EPS of $0.64
- Returned $20.2 Billion Directly to Shareholders in 2018 Through Share Repurchases and Dividends; Anticipates Repurchasing Approximately $9 Billion of Shares in 2019

The company reports revenue growth and specifically highlights "adjusted diluted EPS" (boldface emphasis added). What is this metric, and why does Pfizer report it? To arrive at the adjusted EPS number, Pfizer made a number of deductions and additions to its published GAAP financials because company management believes doing so provides a better measure of Pfizer's financial performance. These adjusted income statements (sometimes referred to as *pro forma* income statements or non-GAAP numbers) are increasingly common.

Regulation G Reconciliation

The Securities and Exchange Commission (SEC), which oversees all publicly traded companies in the United States, requires that companies reconcile such non-GAAP information to GAAP numbers so financial statement readers can have a basis for comparison and can evaluate the excluded items (Regulation G). To comply with the regulation, Pfizer provides the following adjusted income statement in the management discussion and analysis (MD&A).

Twelve Months Ended December 31, 2018 (In millions, except per common share data)	GAAP Reported	Purchase Accounting Adjustments	Acquisition-Related Costs	Discontinued Operations	Certain Significant Items	Non-GAAP Adjusted
Revenues	$53,647	$ —	$ —	$ —	$ —	$53,647
Cost of sales	11,248	3	(10)	—	(110)	11,130
Selling, informational and administrative expenses	14,455	2	(2)	—	(222)	14,232
Research and development expenses	8,006	3	—	—	(47)	7,962
Amortization of intangible assets	4,893	(4,612)	—	—	—	281
Restructuring charges and certain acquisition-related costs	1,044	—	(299)	—	(745)	—
Other (income) deductions—net	2,116	(182)	(7)	—	(3,181)	(1,253)
Income from continuing operations before provision (benefit) for taxes on income	11,885	4,786	318	—	4,305	21,294
Provision (benefit) for taxes on income	706	915	54	—	1,625	3,301
Income from continuing operations	11,179	3,871	264	—	2,680	17,994
Discontinued operations—net of tax	10	—	—	(10)	—	—
Net income attributable to noncontrolling interests	36	—	—	—	—	36
Net income attributable to Pfizer Inc.	11,153	3,871	264	(10)	2,680	17,958
Earnings per common share attributable to Pfizer Inc.—diluted	1.87	0.65	0.04	—	0.45	3.00

Adjusted income is an alternative view of performance used by management . . . Because Adjusted income is an important internal measurement for Pfizer, we believe that investors' understanding of our performance is enhanced by disclosing this performance measure . . . We have defined Adjusted income as Net income attributable to Pfizer Inc. before the impact of purchase accounting for acquisitions, acquisition-related costs, discontinued operations and certain significant items.

Pfizer's "adjusted" net income is $17,958 million (as compared with GAAP net income of $11,153 million), and excludes costs primarily relating to transitory items, such as costs relating to acquisitions completed during the year, discontinued operations, and other one-time nonrecurring items.

Pfizer's management appears to be thorough in its reporting of "adjusted" income statement items, but other companies may not be. It is important to remember that a company's purpose for making a non-GAAP disclosure is to portray its financial performance the way that management would like us to analyze it. Unscrupulous companies can attempt to lower the bar for analysis by presenting financial results in the best possible light.

SEC Warnings about Pro Forma Numbers

The SEC is very mindful of the potential for abuse in pro forma income statements and cautions investors as follows. (Excerpted from Securities and Exchange Commission (Release Nos. 33-8039, 34-45124, FR-59) "Cautionary Advice Regarding the Use of 'Pro Forma' Financial Information in Earnings Releases," https://www.sec.gov/rules/other/33-8039.htm.)

> We believe it is appropriate to sound a warning to public companies and other registrants who present to the public their earnings and results of operations on the basis of methodologies other than Generally Accepted Accounting Principles ("GAAP"). This presentation in an earnings release is often referred to as "pro forma" financial information. In this context, that term has no defined meaning and no uniform characteristics. We wish to caution public companies on their use of this "pro forma" financial information and to alert investors to the potential dangers of such information.
>
> "Pro forma" financial information can serve useful purposes. Public companies may quite appropriately wish to focus investors' attention on critical components of quarterly or annual financial results in order to provide a meaningful comparison to results for the same period of prior years or to emphasize the results of core operations. To a large extent, this has been the intended function of disclosures in a company's Management's Discussion and Analysis section of its reports. There is no prohibition preventing public companies from publishing interpretations of their results, or publishing summaries of GAAP financial statements. . .
>
> Nonetheless, we are concerned that "pro forma" financial information, under certain circumstances, can mislead investors if it obscures GAAP results. Because this "pro forma" financial information by its very nature departs from traditional accounting conventions, its use can make it hard for investors to compare an issuer's financial information with other reporting periods and with other companies.
>
> For these reasons . . . we encourage investors to compare any summary or "pro forma" financial presentation with the results reported on GAAP-based financials by the same company. Read before you invest; understand before you commit.

When we read adjusted (pro forma) income statements, it is important to remember they represent management's interpretation of the company's financial performance. We must view those representations as such, not as statements of fact.[1]

Disclosures and Market Assessments

Pro forma income statements must be read and analyzed within the context of the GAAP statements. It is only by a thorough analysis of the GAAP financial statements that we can understand the reasons for, and the implications of, the adjustments management is making with the pro forma statements. We recommend the following steps for a thorough reading of the GAAP financials.

- Read the reports from the external auditor, and take special note of any deviation from boilerplate language.

- Peruse the footnote on accounting policies (typically footnote 1), and compare the company's policies with its industry peers. Deviations from the norm can signal opportunism.

- Examine changes in accounting policies. What would the company have reported absent the change? Did the new policy help it avoid reporting a loss or violating a debt covenant?

- Compare key ratios over time. Follow up on marked increases or decreases in ratios, read footnotes and the MD&A to see how management explains such changes. Follow up on ratios that do not change when a change is expected. For example, during the tech bubble, Worldcom Inc. reported an

---

[1] For a good discussion of the issue of accounting *quality*, see Dechow, P., and C. Schrand. "Earnings Quality," The Research Foundation of CFA Institute. Charlottesville, VA 2004.

expense-to-revenue ratio (ER ratio) of 42% quarter after quarter, despite worsening economic conditions. Later, it was discovered that managers had deliberately underreported expenses to maintain the ER ratio. The lesson is that sometimes no change signals managerial intervention.

- Review ratios of competitors, and consider macroeconomic conditions and how they have shifted over time. Are the ratios reasonable in light of current conditions? Are changes in the income statement aligning with changes on the balance sheet?
- Identify nonrecurring items, and separately assess their impact on company performance and position.
- Recast financial statements as necessary to reflect an accounting policy(ies) that is more in line with competitors or one that better reflects economically relevant numbers. We illustrate recasting at several points in future modules.

Business Insight — Creative Accounting

Pfizer calls its non-GAAP earnings "Adjusted earnings." Other companies use more creative labels. Consider the following examples of pro forma metrics and their effects reported during 2018 and 2019.

UBER *Core-platform contribution margin*, which changed a $3 billion loss to a non-GAAP profit of $940 million.

WeWork *Community-adjusted EBITDA*, which allowed the company to report non-GAAP profit of $467 million instead of a *loss* of $1.9 billion.

Lyft *Adjusted contribution margin*, which was $384.9 million versus a GAAP loss of $1,138.5 million.

Other recent creative non-GAAP measures include:

- Annual recurring revenue
- Bookings
- Cumulative billings
- Adjusted consolidated segment operating income (ACSOI)
- Profit including back-log sales

These pro forma reporting practices are reminiscent of the dot-com bubble of the early 2000s and, like then, are most prevalent among tech and start-up companies. It remains to be seen if investors are any savvier this time around, or whether the rosier non-GAAP profits hold sway.

The purported motive for reporting pro forma income is to eliminate transitory (one-time) items to enhance year-to-year comparability. Although this might be justified on the basis that pro forma income has greater predictive ability, important information could be lost in the process. One role for accounting is to report how effective management has been in its stewardship of invested capital. Asset write-downs, liability accruals, and other charges that are eliminated in calculating pro forma income often reflect outcomes of poor management decisions. Our analysis must not blindly eliminate information contained in nonrecurring items by focusing solely on pro forma income. Critics of pro forma income also argue that the items excluded by managers from GAAP income are inconsistent across companies and time. They contend that a major motive for pro forma income is to mislead stakeholders. Legendary investor Warren Buffett puts pro forma in context: "When companies or investment professionals use terms such as 'EBITDA' and 'pro forma,' they want you to unthinkingly accept concepts that are dangerously flawed." (Berkshire Hathaway, Annual Report)

Research Insight — Assessing Earnings Quality

It is no secret that corporate executives can and do make choices to deliberately influence reported earnings. GAAP permits choices so that each company can make its financial reports as relevant as possible. But the latitude granted by GAAP opens the door for potential abuse that reduces the quality of financial reports in general and of net earnings in particular. But how prevalent is such deliberate intervention? Can it be detected?

Recently, a team of accounting researchers surveyed and interviewed chief financial officers (CFOs) and other finance executives at 400 firms (169 public and 231 private). The research aimed to uncover CFOs' thinking about earnings quality and reasons for deliberate intervention in the reporting process. According to the CFOs, nearly 20% of public companies and 25% of private companies use allowable discretion in GAAP to misrepresent earnings with average misrepresentations of 12 cents on the dollar. Interestingly, 33% of the misrepresentations *decreased* earnings.

When asked about potential motivations for deliberately misrepresenting earnings, CFOs almost unanimously agreed it was "to influence stock price," "to hit earnings benchmarks," and "to influence executive compensation." The researchers compiled a list of 20 red flags that suggest earnings misrepresentation according to the CFOs.

continued

1. GAAP earnings and cash flow from operations move in different direction for 6–8 quarters.
2. Deviations from industry norms on critical metrics, including cash cycle, average profitability, revenue growth, asset impairment, level of disclosure.
3. Consistently meeting or beating earnings targets.
4. Large or frequent one-time items, such as restructuring charges, write-downs, or gains and losses on asset sales.
5. Large changes in accruals or capitalized costs and insufficient explanation of such changes.
6. Too smooth of an earnings progression (relative to economy, market).
7. Frequent changes in significant accounting policies.
8. Using non-GAAP metrics.
9. High executive and employee turnover, sudden change in top management.
10. Inventory buildup and mismatch between inventory and COGS.
11. Wide swings in earnings, especially without real change in business.
12. Buildups of receivables, deterioration of days sales outstanding.
13. Aggressive use of long-term estimates and lack of explanatory detail on estimates.
14. SEC filings becoming less transparent, uninformative MD&A, complex footnotes.
15. Major jumps or turnarounds or breaks with historical performance.
16. Large incentive compensation payment and management turnover after bonus payments.
17. Repeated restatement of earnings and prior period adjustments.
18. Accruals, assets, and working capital growing faster or slower than revenue.
19. Increased debt and high liabilities.
20. Weak sales growth or declining performance versus the industry.

Source: Dichev, I. D., Graham, J. R., Harvey, C. R., and Rajgopal, S., "Earnings Quality: Evidence from the Field" (2013). Available at SSRN: http://ssrn.com/abstract=2103384 or http://dx.doi.org/10.2139/ssrn.2103384.

LO7 Review 5-7

In its SEC 10-K filing for 2018, **Merck & Co. Inc.** provided the proforma disclosures below. Use this information to answer the requirements.

A reconciliation between GAAP financial measures and non-GAAP financial measures is as follows: ($ in millions)	2018	2017	2016
Income before taxes as reported under GAAP.	$ 8,701	$ 6,521	$ 4,659
Increase (decrease) for excluded items:			
Acquisition and divestiture-related costs.	3,066	3,760	7,312
Restructuring costs	658	927	1,069
Other items:			
Charge related to the formation of an oncology collaboration with Eisai.	1,400	—	—
Charge related to the termination of a collaboration with Samsung	423	—	—
Charge for the acquisition of Viralytics	344	—	—
Charge related to the formation of an oncology collaboration with AstraZeneca	—	2,350	—
Charge related to the settlement of worldwide Keytruda patent litigation	—	—	625
Other	(57)	(16)	(67)
Non-GAAP income before taxes	14,535	13,542	13,598
Taxes on income as reported under GAAP	2,508	4,103	718
Estimated tax benefit on excluded items	535	785	2,321
Net tax charge related to the enactment of the TCJA.	(160)	(2,625)	—
Net tax benefit from the settlement of certain federal income tax issues	—	234	—
Tax benefit related to the settlement of a state income tax issue	—	88	—
Non-GAAP taxes on income.	2,883	2,585	3,039
Non-GAAP net income	$11,652	$10,957	$10,559

Required
1. Why do firms, including Merck, publicly report non-GAAP information?
2. What are the significant items and the effect of the proposed adjustments on non-GAAP net income?

Solution on p. 5-58.

Global Accounting

Revenue Recognition
The new revenue recognition standard, as discussed in this module, eliminates many prior differences between U.S. GAAP and IFRS. That is, the accounting for revenue is now nearly identical between the two systems.

Accounts Receivable
Accounts receivable are accounted for identically with one notable exception. Under IFRS, all receivables are treated as financial assets. This means future cash flows from accounts receivable must be discounted and reported at net present value. This measurement applies to both short- and long-term receivables, assuming the effect of discounting is material. For analysis purposes, we review the notes to determine the discount rate used by the company using IFRS and assess the significance of any discounting. Ratios using accounts receivable (such as turnover ratios and current ratios) can be affected.

Research and Development
Accounting for R&D represents an ongoing difference between U.S. GAAP and IFRS. International standards required that all research expenditures be expensed in the period in which they are incurred. This is consistent with U.S. GAAP. The two standards diverge when it comes to development costs. Under IFRS standard 38, companies *shall capitalize and recognize* as intangible assets, all development costs related to products and services when the company can demonstrate the following:

- Intangible asset's technical feasibility;
- Intention to complete the development of the intangible asset;
- Ability to use or sell the intangible asset;
- How the intangible asset will generate probable future economic benefits (for example, the existence of a market for the output of the intangible asset or for the intangible asset itself);
- Availability of resources to complete the development; and
- Ability to reliably measure the related expenditures (costs pertaining to the intangible asset).

These *internally generated intangible assets* are amortized over their useful lives and periodically assessed for impairment. As such, we observe larger intangible assets on the balance sheets of IFRS companies.

Guidance Answers

You Are the Receivables Manager
Pg. 5-24 First, we must realize that extending credit is an important tool in the marketing of your products, often as important as advertising and promotion. Given that receivables are necessary, there are certain ways to speed their collection. (1) We can better screen the customers to whom we extend credit. (2) We can negotiate advance or progress payments from customers. (3) We can use bank letters of credit or other automatic drafting procedures that obviate billing. (4) We can make sure products are sent as ordered, to reduce disputes. (5) We can improve administration of past-due accounts to provide for more timely notices of delinquencies and better collection procedures.

Questions

Q5-1. What is a performance obligation and how is it related to revenue recognition?

Q5-2. Explain how management can shift income from one period into another by using the allowance for uncollectibles account.

Q5-3. Why do companies allow sales returns, and how does this business practice affect reported revenue?

Q5-4. The income statement line item "Discontinued operations" typically comprises two distinct components. What are they?

Q5-5. What effect, if any, does a weakening $US have on reported sales and net income for subsidiaries of U.S. companies?

Q5-6. Explain why analysts might remove foreign exchange gains or losses when analyzing revenue and expenses for the year.

Q5-7. What is meant by "aging" of accounts receivable?

Q5-8. Under what circumstances is it appropriate to use the cost-to-cost method to measure revenue?

Q5-9. What is the concept of pro forma income and why has this income measure been criticized?

Q5-10. What is unearned revenue? Provide three examples of unearned revenue.

Q5-11. What is the current U.S. GAAP accounting treatment for research and development costs?

Q5-12. How would a company recognize revenue on a sale that includes equipment and a multi-year service contract all for one price?

Assignments with the MBC logo in the margin are available in *myBusinessCourse*.
See the Preface of the book for details.

Mini Exercises

M5-13. Computing Revenues under Long-Term Contracts   **LO1**
Camden Corporation agreed to build a warehouse for a client at an agreed contract price of $900,000. Expected (and actual) costs for the warehouse follow: 2016, $202,500; 2017, $337,500; and 2018, $135,000. The company completed the warehouse in 2018. Compute revenues, expenses, and income for each year 2016 through 2018, and for all three years combined, using the cost-to-cost method.

M5-14. Applying the Financial Statement Effects Template   **LO1**
Refer to the information for Camden Corporation in M5-13.
  a. Use the financial statement effects template to record contract revenues and expenses for each year 2016 through 2018 using the cost-to-cost method.
  b. Prepare journal entries and T-accounts to record contract revenues and expenses for each year 2016 through 2018 using the cost-to-cost method. Assume Camden does not receive payment until the contract is completed. All costs are paid in cash.

M5-15. Assessing Revenue Recognition of Companies   **LO1**
Match each of the following companies, to the appropriate revenue recognition policy, listed below.
  a. **The GAP**: The GAP is a retailer of clothing items for all ages.
  b. **GlaxoSmithKline**: GSK develops, manufactures, and markets pharmaceutical products. It sells its drugs (many of which have regulated expiry dates) to retailers such as CVS and Walgreens.
  c. **Deere & Company**: Deere manufactures heavy equipment. It sells equipment to a network of independent distributors, who in turn sell the equipment to customers. Deere provides financing and insurance services both to distributors and customers.
  d. **Bank of America**: Bank of America is a banking institution. It lends money to individuals and corporations and invests excess funds in marketable securities.
  e. **Johnson Controls**: Johnson Controls manufactures products for the government under long-term contracts.

The GAP (GPS)
GlaxoSmithKline (GSK)
Deere & Company (DE)
Bank of America (BAC)
Johnson Controls (JCI)

  1. The performance obligation is to build and complete projects for specific customers. Revenue is recognized for long-term construction contracts under the percentage-of-completion method, typically using cost-to-cost method to identify the percentage of the project that is complete.
  2. The performance obligation is fulfilled when the customer takes delivery of the merchandise and the right of return period for regulated products has expired or costs of returns can be reasonably estimated. The company will also establish an allowance for uncollectible accounts receivable when revenue is recognized.
  3. The performance obligation is recorded when the customer takes the merchandise (for in-store sales) or when the goods are delivered (for online sales). The company estimates product returns and records an allowance at the time of sale.
  4. The performance obligation is fulfilled when the customer takes the merchandise. The company will also establish allowances for product returns, uncollectible accounts, and a reserve for anticipated warranty costs. Revenues for financial or insurance services are recognized when the services are provided.
  5. The performance obligation is fulfilled with the passage of time. Interest is earned by the passage of time. Each period income is accrued on loans even if customers have not yet paid the interest.

LO7
OptimizeRx (OPRX)

M5-16. Non-GAAP Disclosure

OptimizeRx provides digital health messaging via electronic health records to provide a direct channel for pharmaceutical companies to communicate with healthcare providers and patients. The company reported the following in its 2018 earnings release.

Reconciliation of Non-GAAP to GAAP Financial Measures	For the Three Months Ended Dec. 31, 2018	For the Twelve Months Ended Dec. 31, 2018
Net income (loss)	$(109,914)	$ 226,344
Depreciation and amortization	153,085	316,502
Stock-based compensation	798,866	2,520,852
Non GAAP net income	$ 842,037	$3,063,698

a. Explain in plain language the two adjustments that OptimizeRx makes to arrive at non-GAAP net income.
b. How did the adjustments affect non-GAAP net income for the fiscal quarter ended December 31, 2018? For the 2018 fiscal year? Are these effects significant?

LO1, 2
ModCloth Inc.

M5-17. Estimating Revenue Recognition with Right of Return

ModCloth Inc. offers an unconditional return policy. It normally expects 2% of sales at retail selling prices to be returned before the return period expires. Assuming ModCloth records total sales of $10 million for the current period, what amount of *net* sales should it record for this period?

LO5

M5-18. Estimating Uncollectible Accounts and Reporting Accounts Receivable

Mohan Company estimates its uncollectible accounts by aging its accounts receivable and applying percentages to various aged categories of accounts. Mohan computes a total of $2,100 in estimated uncollectible accounts as of its current year-end. Its accounts receivable has a balance of $86,000, and its allowance for uncollectible accounts has an unused balance of $700 before any year-end adjustments.

a. What amount of bad debt expense will Mohan report in its income statement for the current year?
b. Determine the net amount of accounts receivable reported in current assets at year-end.

LO5 **M5-19. Interpreting the Allowance Method for Accounts Receivable**

At a recent board of directors meeting of Bismark Corp., one of the directors expressed concern over the allowance for uncollectible accounts appearing in the company's balance sheet. "I don't understand this account," he said. "Why don't we just show accounts receivable at the amount owed to us and get rid of that allowance?" Respond to the director's question; include in your response (a) an explanation of why the company has an allowance account, (b) what the balance sheet presentation of accounts receivable is intended to show, and (c) how accrual accounting (as opposed to the cash-basis accounting) affects the presentation of accounts receivable.

LO5
Mondelēz International (MDLZ)

M5-20. Analyzing the Allowance for Uncollectible Accounts

Following is the current asset section from the Mondelēz balance sheet.

$ millions	Dec. 31, 2018	Dec. 31, 2017
Cash and cash equivalents	$ 1,100	$ 761
Trade receivables (net of allowances of $40 at 2018 and $50 at 2017). . . .	2,262	2,691
Other receivables (net of allowances of $47 at 2018 and $98 at 2017). . . .	744	835
Inventories, net.	2,592	2,557
Other current assets.	906	676
Total current assets	$ 7,604	$ 7,520
Total assets	$62,729	$62,957

a. What is the common-size trade receivables, net, at year-end 2018?
  i. 29.75%
  ii. 3.94%
  iii. 3.61%
  iv. 4.79%
b. What do Mondelez's customers owe the company at December 31, 2018 ($ millions)?
  i. $2,262
  ii. $2,302
  iii. $2,222
  iv. $3,006

c. What does Mondelez expect to collect from its customers as of December 31, 2017 ($ millions)?
  i. $2,691
  ii. $2,741
  iii. $2,641
  iv. $3,526
d. What is the GROSS Receivables at year-end 2018 ($ millions)?
  i. $2,302
  ii. $3,093
  iii. $3,006
  iv. $2,919
e. What percentage of trade receivables does the company deem uncollectible as of year-end 2018?
  i. 1.77%
  ii. 3.85%
  iii. 1.80%
  iv. 1.74%
f. Based on the analysis above, in which year does the company have higher quality trade receivables?
  i. 2018
  ii. 2017

M5-21. Evaluating Accounts Receivable Turnover for Competitors

The Procter & Gamble Company and Colgate-Palmolive Company report the following sales and accounts receivable balances.

$ millions	Procter & Gamble	Colgate-Palmolive
2018 Net sales	$66,832	$15,544
2018 Accounts receivable	4,686	1,400
2017 Accounts receivable	4,594	1,480

LO5
The Procter & Gamble Company (PG)
Colgate-Palmolive Company (CL)

a. Compute the accounts receivable turnover and DSO for both companies for 2018.
b. Identify and discuss a potential explanation for the difference between these competitors' accounts receivable ratios.

M5-22. Interpreting Foreign Currency Translation Disclosure

Procter & Gamble reports the following table in its 10-K report relating to the change in sales from 2017 to 2018.

LO4
Procter & Gamble Company (PNG)

Net Sales Change Drivers 2018 vs. 2017	Volume	Foreign Exchange	Price	Mix	Net Sales Growth
Beauty	2%	2%	—	5%	9%
Grooming	—	3%	(3)%	(1)%	(1)%
Health care	3%	3%	(1)%	—	5%
Fabric & home care	3%	1%	(1)%	—	3%
Baby, feminine & family care	(1)%	1%	(1)%	—	(1)%
Total company	1%	2%	(1)%	1%	3%

a. Did total company net sales increase or decrease during the year? By what percentage? How much of this change is attributable to volume versus price changes?
b. What was the effect of foreign exchange rates on sales during the year? From this result, what can we infer about the relative strength of the $US during the period?
c. The Grooming and the Baby, Feminine & Family Care segment sales both decreased by 1%. From this result, can we conclude that the dollar decrease in sales was the same for both segments? Explain.

M5-23. Assessing Revenue Recognition for Advance Payments

Hamilton Company operates a performing arts center. The company sells tickets for its upcoming season of six Broadway musicals and receives $630,000 cash. The performances occur monthly over the next six months.

LO3

a. When should Hamilton record revenue for the Broadway musical series?
b. Use the financial statement effects template to show the $630,000 cash receipt and recognition of the first month's revenue.

M5-24. Reporting Unearned Revenue

Target sells gift cards that can be used at any of the company's Target stores or on Target.com. Target encodes information on the card's magnetic strip about the card's value and the store where it was purchased. Target gift cards do not have expiration dates.
a. When does Target record revenue from the gift card?
  i. Two years after the date of the sale, which is when the gift card expires.
  ii. When the gift card is sold.

LO3
Target Corporation (TGT)

iii. When the customer uses the gift card, at which point, Target also records an allowance for estimated product returns.

iv. 90 days after the date the customer uses the gift card, which is when the product return period expires.

b. How will Target's balance sheet reflect the gift card when it is initially sold?

i. As an asset: cash and cash equivalents.
ii. As an asset: allowance for product sales.
iii. As sales revenue.
iv. As a liability: unearned revenue.

LO2 M5-25. Sales Returns

Which of the following statements is true relating to the allowance for sales returns?

a. Sales returns are treated as an expense in the income statement and, therefore, reduce profit for the period.

b. An excess of the amount by which the allowance for sales returns is increased compared with the actual returns for the period indicates the company may have inflated profit for the period.

c. The amount by which the allowance for sales returns is reduced during the period is recognized as a reduction of sales for the period, thus reducing profit.

d. Increasing the allowance for sales returns by an amount that is less than the actual returns recognized for the period may indicate either the company is attempting to increase profit for the period or it estimates that less of its products will be returned in the future.

LO3 M5-26. Deferred Revenue

True or false: A reduction of the deferred revenue account can be interpreted as a leading indicator of lower future revenues. Explain.

LO4 M5-27. Foreign Exchange Effects on Sales

True or false: A multinational company reports that a large amount of its sales is generated in foreign currencies that have strengthened vis-à-vis the $US. Consolidated revenues are likely lower than would have been reported in the absence of such a shift in exchange rates.

LO6 M5-28. Operating Expenses

Indicate whether each of the following is true or false.

a. Amortization expense is a noncash expense similar to depreciation, except it applies to intangible assets.
b. Income attributable to noncontrolling interests is an expense item that reduces net income.
c. Discontinued operations relate to any segment of the business a company is selling.
d. The income (loss) of Discontinued operations and gain (loss) on their sale are reported in the income statement like other revenue and expense items.

LO1, 3 M5-29. Revenue Disclosure and Unearned Revenue

American Airlines (AMR)

American Airlines disclosed the following in its Form 10-Q for the first quarter ended March 31, 2019.

> On March 13, 2019, the Federal Aviation Administration (FAA) grounded all U.S.-registered Boeing 737 MAX aircraft. Our fleet currently includes 24 Boeing 737 MAX aircraft with an additional 76 aircraft on order. As a result, we canceled approximately 1,200 flights in the first quarter of 2019.
>
> In aggregate, we estimate that these grounded aircraft and associated flight cancellations decreased our first quarter 2019 pre-tax income by approximately $80 million.
>
> We have removed all Boeing 737 MAX flying from our flight schedule through August 19, 2019, which is approximately 115 flights per day. These flights represent approximately 2% of our total capacity each day this summer. Although these aircraft represent a small portion of our total fleet, its financial impact is disproportionate as most of the revenue from the cancellations is lost while the vast majority of the costs remain in place. In total, we currently estimate the Boeing 737 MAX cancellations, which are assumed to extend through August 19, 2019, to decrease our 2019 pre-tax income by approximately $350 million.

a. Why does American Airlines disclose this information?
b. What would be the effect on deferred revenue on the March 31, 2019, balance sheet (relative to the prior year-end December 31, 2018) because of these flight cancellations?

LO6 M5-30. Discontinued Operations

Campbell Soup (CPB)

Campbell Soup reported discontinued operations in its Form 10-Q for the third quarter ended April 28, 2019. The company reported that, during the third quarter, it sold its Garden Fresh Gourmet business for approximately $55 million and also signed a definitive agreement for the sale of Bolthouse Farms for $510 million and expects to close the deal before July 2019. The company disclosed the following related to these discontinued operations ($ millions).

For the Nine Months Ended	April 28, 2019
Net sales.	$ 666
Earnings (loss) from operations, after-tax	$(279)
Loss on sale of businesses, net of tax	(52)
Loss from discontinued operations.	$(331)

a. Which of the following best describes how Campbell Soup reported the Bolthouse transaction?
   i. Campbell Soup will report the Bolthouse unit as discontinued operations in the quarter in which the unit is formally sold.
   ii. Campbell Soup reported the Bolthouse unit as discontinued operations in the April 28, 2019, income statement even though the unit had not been formally sold by then.
   iii. Campbell Soup will retroactively report the Bolthouse unit as discontinued operations in the year in which the unit is formally sold.
   iv. Campbell Soup will pro-rate the effects of the Bolthouse unit sale (as discontinued operations) event among the fiscal quarters in year in which the unit is formally sold.

b. What amount of sales revenue did Campbell Soup earn from Garden Fresh Gourmet and Bolthouse for the first three quarters of fiscal 2019?

c. What amount of earnings did Campbell Soup report from Garden Fresh Gourmet and Bolthouse for the first three quarters of fiscal 2019?

d. What was the combined selling price for Garden Fresh Gourmet and Bolthouse Farms?

e. Ignoring tax effects, what is the approximate combined net book value of Garden Fresh Gourmet and Bolthouse Farms at the date of their respective disposals?

Exercises

E5-31. Assessing Revenue Recognition Timing LO1
Explain when each of the following businesses fulfills the performance obligations implicit in the sales contract.

a. A clothing retailer like **American Eagle Outfitters Inc.**
b. A contractor like **Raytheon Company** that performs work under long-term government contracts.
c. A grocery store like **Supervalu Inc.**
d. A producer of television shows like **MTV** that syndicates its content to television stations.
e. A residential real estate developer that constructs only speculative houses and later sells these houses to buyers.
f. A banking institution like **Bank of America Corp.** that lends money for home mortgages.
g. A manufacturer like **Harley-Davidson Inc.**
h. A publisher of magazines such as **Time-Warner Inc.**

American Eagle Outfitters Inc. (AEO)
Raytheon Company (RTN)
Supervalu Inc. (SVU)
MTV
Bank of America Corp. (BAC)
Harley-Davidson Inc. (HOG)
Time-Warner Inc. (TWX)

E5-32. Assessing Revenue Recognition Timing and Income Measurement LO1
Explain when each of the following businesses fulfills the performance obligations implicit in the sales contract and recognizes revenue. Identify any revenue measurement issues that could arise.

a. RealMoney.Com, a division of **TheStreet Inc.**, provides investment advice to customers for an up-front fee. It provides these customers with password-protected access to its website, where they can download investment reports. RealMoney has an obligation to provide updates on its website.

b. **Oracle Corp.** develops general ledger and other business application software that it sells to its customers. The customer pays an up-front fee for the right to use the software and a monthly fee for support services.

c. **Intuit Inc.** develops tax preparation software that it sells to its customers for a flat fee. No further payment is required, and the software cannot be returned, only exchanged if defective.

d. **Electronic Arts** develops and sells computer games. The company will provide a full refund within 24 hours after the game is first launched or within 14 days from the date of sale, if the game has not been launched. After that, there is no refund.

TheStreet Inc. (TST)

Oracle Corp. (ORCL)

Intuit Inc. (INTU)

Electronic Arts (EA)

LO1
GE Hitachi Nuclear Energy (GEH)

E5-33. Constructing and Assessing Income Statements Using Cost-to-Cost Method

Assume **GE Hitachi Nuclear Energy** agreed in May 2019 to construct a nuclear generator for NSTAR, a utility company serving the Boston area. GE Hitachi estimated that its construction costs would be $600 million. The contract price of $750 million is to be paid as follows: $250 million at the time of signing; $250 million on December 31, 2019; and $250 million at completion in May 2020. GE Hitachi Nuclear Energy incurred the following costs in constructing the generator: $240 million in 2019 and $360 million in 2020.

a. Compute the revenue, expense, and income for both 2019 and 2020, and for both years combined, under the company's cost-to-cost revenue recognition method.

b. Discuss whether or not we believe the cost-to-cost method provides a good measure of the company's performance under the contract.

LO1

E5-34. Constructing and Assessing Income Statements Using Cost-to-Cost Method

On March 15, 2019, Gilbert Construction contracted to build a shopping center at a contract price of $220 million. The schedule of expected (which equals actual) cash collections and contract costs follows.

Year	Cash Collections	Cost Incurred
2019	$ 55 million	$ 36 million
2020	88 million	81 million
2021	77 million	63 million
Total	$220 million	$180 million

a. Calculate the amount of revenue, expense, and net income for each of the three years 2019 through 2021, and for all three years combined, using the cost-to-cost revenue recognition method.

b. Discuss whether or not the cost-to-cost method provides a good measure of this construction company's performance under the contract.

LO1
Beyond Meat, Inc. (BYND)

E5-35. Analyzing Segment Revenue Disclosures from Quarterly Data

Beyond Meat disclosed the following in its Form 10-Q for the first quarter ended March 30, 2019. The company had its initial public offering (IPO) in May 2019.

The Company's net revenues by platform and channel are included in the tables below:

For Three Months Ended (in thousands)	March 30, 2019	March 31, 2018
Net revenues		
Fresh platform.	$38,806	$ 9,596
Frozen platform.	4,512	4,748
Less: discounts	(3,112)	(1,568)
Net revenues	$40,206	$12,776

For Three Months Ended (in thousands)	March 30, 2019	March 31, 2018
Net revenues		
Retail.	$19,579	$ 9,288
Restaurant and foodservice	20,627	3,488
Net revenues	$40,206	$12,776

Two distributors each accounted for approximately 21% of the Company's gross revenues in the three months ended March 30, 2019; and three distributors accounted for approximately 34%, 14% and 11%, respectively, of the Company's gross revenues in the three months ended March 31, 2018.

a. Calculate the average discount given to customers for the two quarters presented. Why might a company like Beyond Meat grant such generous discounts? What do we observe about the level of the discounts across the two quarters?

b. Beyond Meat's revenue grew tremendously between March 2018 and March 2019. Determine growth rates for each of the platforms and channels disclosed (Fresh, Frozen, Retail, and Restaurant). Use these ratios to explain overall revenue growth.

c. Explain why the company disclosed the proportion of sales to its major distributors. Why would investors care to know this information?

E5-36. Foreign Currency Impact
Kellogg included the following note in its fiscal 2018 10-K report ($ millions).

Adjusted net income attributable to Kellogg	$1,510
Foreign currency impact	4
Currency-neutral adjusted net income attributable to Kellogg	$1,506

LO4
Kellogg Company (K)

a. Assume the foreign currency impact related entirely to foreign sales. Determine whether the $US strengthened or weakened vis-à-vis the currencies in which Kellogg conducts business.
b. Assume the foreign currency impact related entirely to purchases of goods from foreign vendors. Determine whether the $US strengthened or weakened vis-à-vis the currencies in which Kellogg conducts business.
c. As an analyst, how would we treat this foreign currency impact in our analysis of Kellogg?

E5-37. Identifying Operating Income Components
Following is the income statement information from Apollo Medical Devices. Identify the components that we would consider operating.

LO6

$ thousands	2020
Net sales	$4,163,770
Cost of sales before special charges	1,382,235
Special inventory obsolescence charge	27,876
Total cost of sales	1,410,111
Gross profit	2,753,659
Selling, general and administrative expense	1,570,667
Research and development expense	531,086
Merger and acquisition costs	46,914
In-process research and development charges	12,244
Litigation settlement	16,500
Operating profit	576,248
Interest expense	(57,372)
Interest income	2,076
Gain on disposal of fixed assets	4,929
Impairment of marketable securities	(5,222)
Other income (expense), net	(2,857)
Earnings before income taxes	517,802
Income tax expense	191,587
Net earnings	$ 326,215

E5-38. Identifying Operating Income Components
Following is the Deere & Company income statement for 2018.

LO6

Deere & Company (DE)

$ millions	2018
Net sales and revenues	
Net sales	$33,350.7
Finance and interest income	3,106.6
Other income	900.4
Total	$37,357.7
Costs and expenses	
Cost of sales	$25,571.2
Research and development expenses	1,399.1
Selling, administrative and general expenses	1,657.6
Interest expense	3,455.5
Other operating expenses	1,203.6
Total	33,287.0

continued

continued from previous page

$ millions	2018
Income of consolidated group before income taxes.	4,070.7
Provision for income taxes	1,726.9
Income of consolidated group	2,343.8
Equity in income of unconsolidated affiliates	26.8
Net income	2,370.6
Less: Net income attributable to noncontrolling interests	2.2
Net income attributable to Deere & Company	$ 2,368.4

Notes:
- The income statement includes John Deere commercial and consumer tractor segment, a finance subsidiary that provides loan and lease financing relating to the sales of those tractors, and a healthcare segment that provides managed healthcare services for the company and certain outside customers.
- Equity in income of unconsolidated affiliates refers to income John Deere has earned on investments made for strategic purposes.

  a. Identify the components in its income statement that we would consider operating.
  b. Discuss our treatment of the company's finance and interest income and the income from the unconsolidated affiliates. Would these items be treated as operating or nonoperating?

LO4, 7
Kellogg Co. (K)

E5-39. Analyzing and Interpreting Foreign Currency Translation Effects and Non-GAAP Disclosures
Kellogg Co. reports the following table and discussion in its 2018 10-K for its reportable segments.

The following table provides an analysis of operating profit for the year ended December 29, 2018.

$ millions	U.S Morning Foods	U.S. Snacks	U.S. Specialty	North America Other	Europe	Latin America	Asia Pacific	Corporate	Kellogg Consolidated
2018 Reported operating profit	$446	$478	$251	$222	$297	$102	$128	$(218)	$1,706
Mark-to-market	—	—	—	—	—	—	—	7	7
Project K and cost-reduction activities . . .	(28)	(50)	(4)	(25)	(33)	(15)	(11)	(7)	(173)
Brexit impacts	—	—	—	—	(3)	—	—	—	(3)
Business and portfolio realignment	(3)	—	—	—	—	—	—	(2)	(5)
Adjusted operating profit	477	528	255	247	333	117	139	(216)	1,880
Foreign currency impact	—	—	—	(2)	6	(3)	(7)	3	(3)
2018 Currency-neutral adjusted operating profit	$477	$528	$255	$249	$327	$120	$146	$(219)	$1,883
2017 Reported operating profit	$138	$567	$312	$229	$276	$108	$84	$(327)	$1,387
2017 Currency-neutral adjusted operating profit	$447	$585	$314	$245	$316	$116	$95	$(239)	$1,879
Operating Profit 2018 vs. 2017									
Reported growth	224.4%	(15.7)%	(19.8)%	(3.0)%	7.8%	(5.2)%	50.7%	33.1%	22.9%
Mark-to-market	—	—	—	—	—	—	—	25.2%	7.3%
Project K and cost-reduction activities . . .	218.3%	(6.0)%	(0.7)%	(3.9)%	3.1%	(5.6)%	6.1%	(0.5)%	16.1%
Brexit impacts	—	—	—	—	(0.9)%	—	—	—	(0.2)%
Business and portfolio realignment	(0.8)%	—	—	—	—	—	—	(0.8)%	(0.3)%
Adjusted growth	6.9%	(9.7)%	(19.1)%	0.9%	5.6%	0.4%	44.6%	9.2%	—
Foreign currency impact	—	—	—	(0.4)%	1.9%	(2.8)%	(7.2)%	0.6%	(0.1)%
Currency-neutral adjusted growth	6.9%	(9.7)%	(19.1)%	1.3%	3.7%	3.2%	51.8%	8.6%	0.1%

Brexit: We recognize that there are still significant uncertainties surrounding the ultimate resolution of Brexit negotiations, and we will continue to monitor any changes that may arise and assess their potential impact on our business.

Project K restructuring: Since inception, Project K has reduced the Company's cost structure, and is expected to provide enduring benefits, including an optimized supply chain infrastructure, an efficient global business services model, a global focus on categories, increased agility from a more efficient organization design, and improved effectiveness in go-to-market models. These benefits are intended to strengthen existing businesses in core markets, increase growth in developing and emerging markets, and drive an increased level of value-added innovation.

continued

continued from previous page

> **Foreign currency risk:** Our company is exposed to fluctuations in foreign currency cash flows related primarily to third-party purchases, intercompany transactions, and when applicable, non-functional currency denominated third-party debt. Our company is also exposed to fluctuations in the value of foreign currency investments in subsidiaries and cash flows related to repatriation of these investments. Additionally, our company is exposed to volatility in the translation of foreign currency denominated earnings to U.S. dollars. Primary exposures include the U.S. dollar versus the euro, British pound, Australian dollar, Canadian dollar, Mexican peso, Brazilian real, Nigerian naira, Russian ruble and Egyptian pound.

a. Complete the following table that summarizes the information that Kellogg reports in the excerpt above. Confirm the % change that Kellogg reports.

Kellogg Consolidated	2018	2017	% change (2017 to 2018)
Reported operating profit			
Currency-neutral adjusted operating profit			

b. Kellogg reports "Adjusted growth" that shows various adjustments to reported growth numbers. Explain why Kellogg provides this information in its financial statements. Briefly explain how Project K and Brexit impacted operating profits in 2018.
c. How did foreign currency exchange rates affect operating profit at each of the geographic segments? What can we infer about the strength of the $US vis-à-vis the currencies in Kellogg's segments?
d. Describe how the accounting for foreign exchange translation affects reported operating profit.
e. What are the three sources of Kellogg's foreign exchange exposure?

E5-40. Interpreting Revenue Recognition Disclosure for Multi-channel Retailer

LO1
Amazon.com (AMZN)

Amazon.com reports the following in footnotes to its 2018 financial statements.

> We serve consumers through our online and physical stores and focus on selection, price, and convenience. We design our stores to enable hundreds of millions of unique products to be sold by us and by third parties across dozens of product categories. Customers access our offerings through our websites, mobile apps, Alexa, and physically visiting our stores. We also manufacture and sell electronic devices, including Kindle e-readers, Fire tablets, Fire TVs, and Echo devices, and we develop and produce media content. In addition, we offer Amazon Prime, a membership program that includes unlimited free shipping on over 100 million items, access to unlimited streaming of thousands of movies and TV episodes, and other benefits.

For each of the following revenue streams, list the nature of the performance obligation and when Amazon would recognize revenue for that performance obligation.

a. Online sale of merchandise owned by Amazon
b. Online sale of merchandise owned by third parties
c. Sale of a Kindle e-reader
d. Collecting cash for an Amazon Prime membership
e. Sale of media content such as a movie available for download

E5-41. Operating Expenses

LO6
Target Corp. (TGT)

Target Corporation's footnote from a recent annual report table illustrates the primary items classified in each major expense category: cost of sales (COS), or selling, general and administrative (SG&A). For each expense, indicate whether the item would be included in COS or SG&A.

a. Advertising expenses .... _____
b. Compensation and benefits costs for headquarters employees. .... _____
c. Compensation and benefits costs for store employees .... _____
d. Compensation and benefits costs for distribution center employees .... _____
e. Distribution center costs .... _____
f. Freight expenses associated with moving merchandise from our vendors to our distribution centers and our retail stores.. _____
g. Freight expenses associated with moving merchandise among our distribution and retail stores .... _____

continued

continued from previous page

- h. Import costs . . . . _____
- i. Inventory shrink and theft . . . . _____
- j. Litigation and defense costs and related insurance recovery . . . . _____
- k. Markdowns on slow moving inventory . . . . _____
- l. Occupancy and operating costs for headquarters facilities . . . . _____
- m. Occupancy and operating costs of retail locations . . . . _____
- n. Outbound shipping and handling expenses associated with sales to our guests . . . . _____
- o. Payment term cash discounts to our vendors . . . . _____
- p. Pre-opening costs of stores and other facilities . . . . _____
- q. U.S. credit cards servicing expenses . . . . _____
- r. Vendor reimbursement of specific, incremental, and identifiable advertising costs . . . . _____

L05 E5-42. Estimating Uncollectible Accounts and Reporting Accounts Receivable

Collins Company analyzes its accounts receivable at December 31 and arrives at the age categories below along with the percentages that are estimated as uncollectible. The balance of the allowance for uncollectible accounts is $1,100 on December 31, before any adjustments.

Age Group	Accounts Receivable	Estimated Loss %
0–30 days past due	$110,000	1%
31–60 days past due	40,000	2
61–120 days past due	27,000	5
121–180 days past due	14,000	10
Over 180 days past due	9,000	25
Total accounts receivable	$200,000	

a. What amount of bad debts expense will Collins report in its income statement for the year?
b. Use the financial statement effects template to record Collins's bad debts expense for the year.
c. What is the balance of accounts receivable on its December 31 balance sheet?

L05 E5-43. Analyzing and Reporting Receivable Transactions and Uncollectible Accounts Using Percentage-of-Sales Method to Estimate Bad Debt Expense

At the beginning of the year, Penman Company had the following account balances.

Accounts receivable	$356,000
Allowance for uncollectible accounts	21,400

During the year, Penman's credit sales were $2,008,000, and collections on accounts receivable were $1,963,000. The following additional transactions occurred during the year.

Feb. 17 Wrote off Bava's account, $8,200.
May 28 Wrote off Reed's account, $4,800.
Dec. 15 Wrote off Fischer's account, $2,300.
Dec. 31 Recorded the bad debts expense assuming Penman's policy is to record bad debts expense as 0.9% of credit sales. (*Hint*: The allowance account is increased by 0.9% of credit sales regardless of write-offs.)

Compute the ending balances in accounts receivable and the allowance for uncollectible accounts. Show how Penman's December 31 balance sheet reports the two accounts.

L05 E5-44. Interpreting the Accounts Receivable Footnote

HP Inc. (HPQ)

HP Inc. reports the following in its 2018 10-K report.

October 31 ($ millions)	2018	2017
Accounts receivable	$5,113	$4,414

Footnotes to the company's 10-K provide the following additional information relating to its allowance for doubtful accounts.

For Fiscal Years Ended October 31 ($ millions)	2018	2017	2016
Allowance for doubtful accounts—accounts receivable			
Balance, beginning of period	$101	$107	$ 80
Provision for doubtful accounts	57	30	65
Deductions, net of recoveries	(29)	(36)	(38)
Balance, end of period	$129	$101	$107

a. What is the gross amount of accounts receivables for HP in fiscal 2018 and 2017?
b. What is the percentage of the allowance for doubtful accounts to gross accounts receivable for 2018 and 2017?
c. What amount of bad debts expense did HP report each year 2016 through 2018? How does bad debts expense compare with the amounts of its accounts receivable actually written off? (Identify the amounts and explain.)
d. Explain the changes in the allowance for doubtful accounts from 2016 through 2018. Does it appear that HP increased or decreased its allowance for doubtful accounts in any particular year beyond what seems reasonable?

E5-45. Estimating Bad Debts Expense and Reporting Receivables

At December 31, Barber Company had a balance of $420,000 in its accounts receivable and an unused balance of $2,600 in its allowance for uncollectible accounts. The company then aged its accounts as follows.

Current	$346,000
1–60 days past due	48,000
61–180 days past due	17,000
Over 180 days past due	9,000
Total accounts receivable	$420,000

The company has experienced losses as follows: 1% of current balances, 5% of balances 1–60 days past due, 15% of balances 61–180 days past due, and 40% of balances over 180 days past due. The company continues to base its allowance for uncollectible accounts on this aging analysis and percentages.

a. What amount of bad debts expense does Barber report on its income statement for the year?
b. Show how Barber's December 31 balance sheet will report the accounts receivable and the allowance for uncollectible accounts.

E5-46. Estimating Uncollectible Accounts and Reporting Receivables over Multiple Periods

Weiss Company, which has been in business for three years, makes all of its sales on credit and does not offer cash discounts. Its credit sales, customer collections, and write-offs of uncollectible accounts for its first three years follow.

Year	Sales	Collections	Accounts Written Off
2018	$733,000	$716,000	$5,300
2019	857,000	842,000	5,800
2020	945,000	928,000	6,500

a. Weiss recognizes bad debts expense as 1% of sales. (*Hint:* This means the allowance account is increased by 1% of credit sales regardless of any write-offs and unused balances.) What does Weiss's 2020 balance sheet report for accounts receivable and the allowance for uncollectible accounts? What total amount of bad debts expense appears on Weiss's income statement for each of the three years?
b. Comment on the appropriateness of the 1% rate used to provide for bad debts based on our analysis in part *a*.

E5-47. Interpreting Graphical Data to Analyze Deferred Revenue

Use the graphic below that depicts common size deferred revenue for several industries from 2010 to 2018 to answer the requirements.

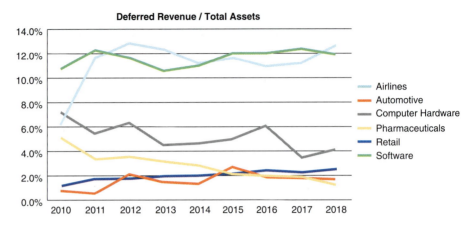

a. Explain how deferred revenue arises for firms in each industry.
b. What might explain the relative size of the deferred revenue of Airlines and Software compared to Pharmaceuticals?

LO6 E5-48. Interpreting Graphical Data to Analyze R&D and Market Capitalization

Consider the graphic below that depicts common-size R&D expense and the market-to-book ratio for several industries in 2018.

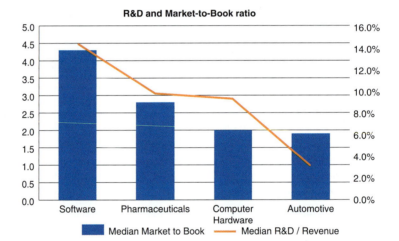

a. What explains the common-size R&D expense across the four industries?
b. What relation do we observe between common-size R&D expense and the market-to-book ratio? Explain.

Problems

LO1, 5 P5-49. Analyzing Segment Disclosures
Raytheon Company (RTN)

Raytheon Company disclosed the following data related to segment sales and operating profits for fiscal 2018.

	Total Net Sales			Operating Income		
$ millions	2018	2017	2016	2018	2017	2016
Integrated defense systems	$ 6,180	$ 5,804	$ 5,529	$1,023	$ 935	$971
Intelligence, information and services	6,722	6,177	6,169	538	455	467
Missile systems	8,298	7,787	7,096	973	1,010	921
Space and airborne systems	6,748	6,430	6,182	884	862	808
Forcepoint	634	608	586	5	33	90
Eliminations	(1,514)	(1,423)	(1,361)			
Total net sales	$27,068	$25,383	$24,201			

The company also reported the following on its balance sheet.

$ millions	2018	2017
Receivables, net of allowance for doubtful accounts of $12 and $8.	$1,648	$1,324

Required

a. Which segment is largest in 2018? Has this ranking changed over the three-year period?
b. Calculate the operating profit margin for each segment and determine which segment is most profitable in 2018 by this measure.
c. Which segment's sales grew the most in 2018? How does this compare to 2017 sales growth?
d. Calculate the company's accounts receivable turnover and its days sales outstanding (DSO) for 2018. Does this seem reasonable? What might explain the DSO?
e. Assess the size of the receivables allowance. Does it seem reasonable?

P5-50. Non-GAAP Disclosures

General Electric (GE) disclosed the following non-GAAP reconciliation for its Industrial segment from its 2018 Form 10-K.

$ millions	2018	2017	2016
GE Industrial earnings (loss)	$(20,587)	$(1,841)	$ 9,048
Less: Nonoperating pension benefit costs (net of tax)	(2,184)	(1,550)	(1,527)
Less: Gains and impairments for disposed or held for sale businesses (net of tax)	974	864	2,374
Less: Restructuring and other (net of tax)	(2,948)	(2,778)	(2,483)
Less: Goodwill impairments (net of tax)	(22,371)	(1,156)	—
Less: GE Industrial U.S. tax reform enactment adjustment	(38)	(4,905)	—
Adjusted GE Industrial earnings (loss) (Non-GAAP)	$ 5,980	$ 7,685	$10,684

Required

a. Explain how the non-GAAP items (in total) affected adjusted earnings each year. Are the adjustments significant?
b. GE makes five specific adjustments. Are any of the adjustments likely beyond the company's control?
c. Calculate the year-over-year change (in % terms) in reported net income for 2017 and 2018. Calculate the year-over-year change (in % terms) in the non-GAAP net income. Which trend do we believe more accurately depicts GE's performance over this period?

P5-51. Revenue Recognition and Sales Allowances

Target Corporation reported the following on its income statement.

For 12 Months Ended ($ millions)	Feb. 2, 2019	Feb. 3, 2018	Jan. 28, 2017
Total revenue	$75,356	$72,714	$70,271
Cost of sales	53,299	51,125	49,145

The revenue recognition footnote from the 10-K for the year ended February 2, 2019, includes the following.

> - We record almost all retail store revenues at the point of sale.
> - Digital channel sales include shipping revenue and are recorded upon delivery to the guest or upon guest pickup at the store.
> - Total revenues do not include sales tax because we are a pass-through conduit for collecting and remitting sales taxes.
> - Generally, guests may return national brand merchandise within 90 days of purchase and owned and exclusive brands within one year of purchase. Revenues are recognized net of expected returns, which we estimate using historical return patterns as a percentage of sales and our expectations of future returns.
> - Revenue from gift card sales is recognized upon gift card redemption. Our gift cards do not expire. Based on historical redemption rates, a small and relatively stable percentage of gift cards will

continued

> continued from previous page
>
> - never be redeemed, referred to as "breakage." Estimated breakage revenue is recognized over time in proportion to actual gift card redemptions.
> - Guests receive a 5 percent discount on virtually all purchases and receive free shipping at Target.com when they use their REDcard. This discount is included as a sales reduction in our Consolidated Statements of Operations and was $953 million, $933 million, and $899 million in the fiscal years ended February 2019, 2018, and 2017 respectively.

Required

a. Use the financial statement effects template to record retail cash sales of $1,000 in a state with a sales-tax rate of 8%. For this question, assume 10% of all merchandise sold is returned within 90 days.

b. Use the financial statement effects template to record the following transaction: On March 4, an internet customer places an order for $2,000 and pays online with a credit card (which is equivalent to cash for accounting purposes). The goods are shipped from the warehouse on March 6, and FedEx confirms delivery on March 7. Ignore shipping costs, sales tax, and returns.

c. Use the financial statement effects template to record the gift card activity during the fiscal year ended February 2, 2019. Ignore sales tax and returns. Details are as follows.

$ millions	
Gift card liability, February 3, 2018	$727
Gift cards issued during current period but not redeemed	645
Revenue recognized from beginning liability	(532)
Gift card liability, February 2, 2019	$840

d. Determine the amount of revenue Target collected from customers who used their loyalty card (REDcard™) for each of the fiscal years reported above. What proportion of total revenues come from REDcard™ customers each year? Does the loyalty program seem to be working? Explain.

LO6 **P5-52. Research and Development Expense**

International Business Machines Corporation (IBM)

International Business Machines Corporation (IBM) reported the following on its 2018 form 10-K.

$ millions	2018	2017	2016
Total revenue	$79,591	$79,139	$79,919
Research, development and engineering expense	5,379	5,590	5,726
Number of new patents awarded	9,100	9,043	8,088

Required

a. Calculate IBM's common-size research, development and engineering expense for each year. What pattern do we observe? Is this of potential concern to investors?

b. Compute the research, development and engineering expense per new patent for each year. What pattern do we observe? What flaw is there in this metric?

c. What other data might analysts and investors collect to form an opinion about the level and effectiveness of IBM's R&D endeavors?

LO1 **P5-53. Analyzing and Interpreting Revenue Recognition Policies and Adoption of the New Standard**

Barnes & Noble (BKS)

Barnes & Noble provides the following explanation of its gift card liabilities.

> **Gift Cards** The Company sells gift cards, which can be used in its stores, on www.barnesandnoble.com, on NOOK® devices and at Barnes & Noble Education, Inc. (B&N Education) stores. Upon the purchase of a gift card, a liability is established for its cash value. Revenue associated with gift cards is deferred until redemption of the gift card. Over time, a portion of the gift cards issued is typically not redeemed. This is referred to as gift card breakage. Effective April 29, 2018, the Company adopted Topic 606. The adoption of Topic 606 resulted in changes in the timing of revenue recognition for gift card breakage. The Company estimates the portion of the gift card liability for which the likelihood of redemption is remote based upon the Company's historical redemption patterns. Prior to adoption of Topic 606, the Company recorded this amount in revenue on a straight-line basis over a 12-month period beginning in the 13th month after the month the gift card was originally sold. Upon adoption, the Company now recognizes estimated gift card

continued

continued from previous page

> breakage as revenue proportionately as redemption occurs. Below is a summary of the changes to the company's gift card liability during fiscal 2019 (in thousands):
>
> | | |
> |---|---:|
> | Gift card liabilities balance as of April 28, 2018 | $323,465 |
> | Adoption of Topic 606 Revenue Recognition | (90,147) |
> | Gift card breakage | (42,282) |
> | Gift card redemptions | (247,231) |
> | Gift card issuances | 271,654 |
> | Gift card liabilities balance as of April 27, 2019 | $215,459 |

Required
a. Explain in plain language "breakage" of gift cards.
b. The company adopted the new revenue recognition standard effective April 29, 2018. Explain how the company accounted for breakage (i) before adopting the new standard and (ii) after adoption.
c. Did the new revenue recognition standard slow down or speed up revenue recognition?
d. What effect did the new revenue recognition standard have on Barnes & Noble's unearned revenue account? Explain.

P5-54. **Analyzing and Interpreting Income Disclosures**   **LO1**
Sales information for Tesla Inc. follows.

Tesla Inc. (TSLA)

> | Year Ended December 31 ($ thousands) | 2018 | 2017 | 2016 |
> |---|---:|---:|---:|
> | Automotive sales | $17,631,522 | $8,534,752 | $5,589,007 |
> | Automotive leasing | 883,461 | 1,106,548 | 761,759 |
> | Total automotive revenues | 18,514,983 | 9,641,300 | 6,350,766 |
> | Services and other | 1,391,041 | 1,001,185 | 467,972 |
> | Total automotive & services and other segment revenue | 19,906,024 | 10,642,485 | 6,818,738 |
> | Energy generation and storage segment revenue | 1,555,244 | 1,116,266 | 181,394 |
> | Total revenues | $21,461,268 | $11,758,751 | $7,000,132 |
>
> Automotive sales revenue includes revenues related to sale of new Model S, Model X and Model 3 vehicles, including access to our Supercharger network, internet connectivity, Autopilot, full self-driving and over-the-air software updates.
>
> Automotive leasing revenue includes the amortization of revenue for Model S and Model X vehicles under direct lease agreements as well as those sold with resale value guarantees accounted for as operating leases under lease accounting. We do not yet offer leasing for Model 3 vehicles.
>
> Services and other revenue consists of non-warranty after-sales vehicle services, sales of used vehicles, sales of electric vehicle components and systems to other manufacturers, retail merchandise, and sales by our acquired subsidiaries to third party customers.
>
> Energy generation and storage revenues consists of the sale of solar energy systems and energy storage systems to residential, small commercial, and large commercial and utility grade customers.

Required
a. Tesla reports several sources of revenue. How should revenue be recognized for each of these business activities? Explain.
b. Compute the relative size of sales revenue from the four types of revenue Tesla discloses. (*Hint:* Scale each type of revenue by total revenue.) What observations can be made about the different sources of revenue?
c. Compute the growth in sales revenue for both years from each of the four types of revenue. What do we observe?

LO1, 3 **P5-55. Analyzing Unearned Revenue Disclosures**

The following disclosures (excerpted) are from the September 2, 2018, annual report of **Costco Wholesale Corporation**.

Costco Wholesale (COST)

> The Company generally recognizes sales, net of returns, at the time the member takes possession of merchandise or receives services.
>
> When the Company collects payments from members prior to the transfer of ownership of merchandise or the performance of services, the amounts received are generally recorded as deferred sales, included in other current liabilities in the consolidated balance sheets, until the sale or service is completed.
>
> The Company reserves for estimated sales returns based on historical trends in merchandise returns and reduces sales and merchandise costs accordingly.
>
> The Company accounts for membership fee revenue, net of refunds, on a deferred basis, ratably over the one-year membership.
>
> The Company's Executive members qualify for a 2% reward on qualified purchases (up to a maximum reward of approximately $1,000 per year), which can be redeemed only at Costco warehouses. The Company accounts for this reward as a reduction in sales. The sales reduction and corresponding liability (classified as accrued member rewards in the consolidated balance sheets) are computed after giving effect to the estimated impact of non-redemptions, based on historical data. The net reduction in sales was $1,394, $1,281, and $1,172 in 2018, 2017, and 2016, respectively.

Revenue ($ millions)	Sept. 2, 2018	Sept. 3, 2017	Aug. 28, 2016
Net sales.	$138,434	$126,172	$116,073
Membership fees	3,142	2,853	2,646
Total revenue	$141,576	$129,025	$118,719

Current Liabilities ($ millions)	Sept. 2, 2018	Sept. 3, 2017
Accounts payable	$11,237	$9,608
Accrued salaries and benefits	2,994	2,703
Accrued member rewards	1,057	961
Deferred membership fees.	1,624	1,498
Other current liabilities	3,014	2,725
Total current liabilities.	$19,926	$17,495

Required

a. Explain in layman's terms how Costco accounts for the cash received for membership fees.
b. Use the balance sheet information on Costco's deferred membership fees liability account and its income statement revenues related to membership fees earned during fiscal 2018 to compute the cash Costco received during fiscal 2018 for membership fees.
c. Use the financial statement effects template to show the effect of the cash Costco received during fiscal 2018 for membership fees and the recognition of membership fees revenue for fiscal 2018.
d. Explain in plain language the "accrued member rewards" liability.
e. Complete the following sentence. Costco recorded sales of at least $_____ from the Company's Executive members, during fiscal 2018.

LO1, 5 **P5-56. Interpreting Accounts Receivable and Related Footnote Disclosure**

Following is information from the **Fitbit Inc.** financial statements.

Fitbit Inc. (FIT)

$ thousands	Dec. 31, 2018	Dec. 31, 2017	Dec. 31, 2016
Revenue.	$1,511,983	$1,615,519	$2,169,461
Accounts receivable, net	414,209	406,019	477,825

continued

continued from previous page

Allowance for Doubtful Accounts ($ thousands)	2018	2017	2016
Beginning balance	$9,229	$ 282	$1,825
Increases	56	30,551	339
Write-offs	(5,543)	(21,604)	(1,882)
Ending balance	$3,742	$ 9,229	$ 282

Customer Bankruptcy In September 2017, Wynit Distribution filed for bankruptcy protection under Chapter 11 of the United States Bankruptcy Code. Wynit was the Company's largest customer, historically representing 11% of total revenue during the six months ended July 1, 2017 and 19% of total accounts receivables as of July 1, 2017. In connection with Wynit's bankruptcy filing, the Company believed that the collectability of the product shipments to Wynit during the third quarter of 2017 was not reasonably assured. However, as of July 1, 2017, collectability of accounts receivables from Wynit was reasonably assured. The Company ceased to recognize revenue from Wynit, which totaled $8.1 million during the third quarter of 2017. Additionally, the Company recorded a charge of $35.8 million during the third quarter ended September 30, 2017 comprised of cost of revenue of $5.5 million associated with shipments to Wynit in the third quarter of 2017 and bad debt expense of $30.3 million associated with all of Wynit's outstanding accounts receivables.

Required

a. What amount do customers owe Fitbit at each of the year-ends 2016 through 2018?
b. What percentage of its total accounts receivable does Fitbit deem uncollectible? (*Hint:* Percentage of uncollectible accounts = Allowance for uncollectible accounts/Gross accounts receivable.)
c. What amount of bad debts expense did Fitbit report in its income statement for each of the years 2016 through 2018? Is this a significant expense? (*Hint:* Calculate the common-size expense.)
d. Consider the information about Wynit Distribution. How might we adjust our analyses in parts *a* through *c* to reflect this information?
e. Calculate the average number of days that it took Fitbit to collect its receivables during 2018 and 2017.
f. Overall, what is our assessment of the quality of Fitbit's accounts receivable?

P5-57. Analyzing and Interpreting Operating Expenses for an Early Stage Company **LO6**
The graphic below depicts revenue, cost of goods sold, and R&D expense for **Tesla Inc.** for 2010 through 2018 ($ in millions).   **Tesla Inc. (TSLA)**

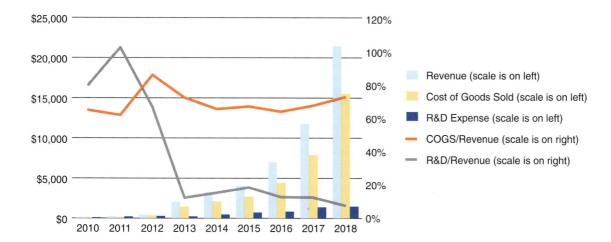

a. What pattern do we observe for revenue over the eight years?
b. What pattern do we observe for COGS and R&D expense over the eight years?
c. What explains the volatile pattern of cost of goods sold and R&D expense relative to revenue in the earlier years? How would analysts interpret the declining R&D as a % of revenue over time?

IFRS Applications

LO5

Lupin Pharmaceuticals (LUPIN)

I5-58. Analyzing Accounts Receivable

Lupin Pharmaceuticals, an Indian transnational pharmaceutical company, develops and markets a wide portfolio of branded and generic products. The company reported the following in its 2018 annual report.

INR millions	2018	2017	2016
Trade receivables.............................	52,229.0	43,391.8	45,946.3
Less provision for doubtful receivables	306.9	318.4	448.2
Trade receivables, net	51,922.1	43,073.4	45,498.1
Total assets	140,958	146,544	127,375
Revenue from operations.....................	158,042	174,943	142,555

Required

a. Calculate days sale outstanding (DSO) for 2018 and 2017.
b. Determine the total amount that customers owe Lupin each year.
c. What proportion of trade receivables is doubtful each year? From this ratio, what do we conclude about the quality of its trade receivables over time?

LO1, 6

Repsol S.A. (REPYY)

I5-59. Identifying Operating Income Components

Repsol S.A. is a Spanish energy company based in Madrid. It carries out upstream and downstream activities throughout the entire world.

Repsol, S.A. and investees comprising the Repsol Group Consolidated income statement for years ending December 31, 2018 (€ Million)	
Sales...	€49,701
Income from services rendered and other income.................................	172
Changes in inventories of finished goods and work in progress	130
Reversal of impairment provisions and gains on disposal of assets	277
Other operating income	1,073
Operating income..	51,353
Supplies	(38,056)
Amortization of noncurrent assets	(2,140)
Personnel expenses..	(1,874)
Transport and freights..	(1,114)
Supplies	(739)
Impairment loss provisions recognized and losses on disposal of assets	(1,281)
Other operating expenses	(3,696)
Operating costs	(48,900)
Operating income..	2,453
Net interest...	(230)
Change in fair value of financial instruments	200
Exchange gains (losses)	467
Impairment of financial instruments	(370)
Other finance income and expenses	(240)
Financial result..	(173)
Income investments accounted for using the equity method	1,053
Net income before tax	3,333
Income tax	(1,386)
Profit from continuing operations	1,947
Income from continuing operations attributed to noncurrent interests	(18)
Income from continuing operations attributed to the parent........................	€ 1,929

Required

a. Identify the components considered operating for each year.
b. Identify the nonrecurring operating items for 2018 and explain how financial analysts would treat these items.

Management Applications

MA5-60. Managing Foreign Currency Risk **LO4**

Fluctuations in foreign currency exchange rates can result in increased volatility of revenues, expenses, and profits. Companies generally attempt to reduce this volatility.

a. Identify two possible solutions to reduce the volatility effect of foreign exchange rate fluctuations.
b. What costs would arise if you implemented each of your solutions?

MA5-61. Ethics and Governance: Revenue Recognition **LO1**

GAAP revenue recognition standards are based on broad principles rather than bright-line rules. This creates a certain amount of latitude in determining when revenue is earned. Assume a company that normally requires acceptance by its customers prior to recording revenue as earned delivers a product to a customer near the end of the quarter. The company believes customer acceptance is assured but cannot obtain it prior to quarter-end. Recording the revenue would assure "making its numbers" for the quarter. Although formal acceptance is not obtained, the salesperson records the sale, fully intending to obtain written acceptance as soon as possible.

a. What are the revenue recognition requirements in this case?
b. What are the ethical issues relating to this sale?
c. Assume you are on the board of directors of this company. What safeguards can you put in place to ensure the company's revenue recognition policy is followed?

Ongoing Project

(This ongoing project began in Module 1 and continues through most of the book; even if previous segments were not completed, the requirements are still applicable to any business analysis.) Analysis of financial statements commonly includes operating income and its components as explained in this module.

1. *Revenue Recognition* Revenue is the largest item on the income statement, and we must assess it on a quantitative and qualitative basis.
   - Use horizontal analysis to identify any time trends.
   - Compare the horizontal analyses of the two companies.
   - Consider the current economic environment and the companies' competitive landscape. Given they operate in the same industry, you might expect similar revenue trends.
   - Read the management's discussion and analysis (MD&A) section of the 10-K to learn how the companies' senior managers explain revenue levels and changes.

   Our goal is to determine whether each company's revenue levels and changes seem appropriate and in line with external factors. *Additional analysis*: (a) If the company distinguishes among types of revenue on the income statement, use horizontal and vertical analyses to identify any changes in the product line mix or where sales are growing most quickly. Find the footnote on segment revenues and profits, and identify trends or significant changes. (b) Assess each company's revenue recognition policy by comparing it with the other and with those of some other close competitors. (c) Consider unearned revenue on the balance sheet. How big is it (common size), and is it fluctuating over time? (d) For companies that operate globally, determine the effect of foreign currency fluctuations on revenue. If these are substantial year after year, it might indicate that managers are not effectively hedging, and this would warrant additional investigation.

2. *Accounts Receivable* The following provides some guidance for analyzing a company's accounts receivable.
   - Are sales primarily on credit, or is a typical sale transacted in cash? Consider the industry and the companies' business model.
   - What is the relative size of accounts receivable? How has this changed over the recent three-year period?
   - Determine the accounts receivable balance relative to gross accounts receivable.
   - What did the company record for bad debt expense? Compute the common size amount.

- Compute accounts receivable turnover and days sales outstanding for all three years reported on the income statement. One will need to obtain additional balance sheet information to be able to compute average balances for the denominator. Consider the current economic environment and the company's competitive landscape. Would one expect collection to have slowed down or sped up during the year?
- Does the company have any large customers that increase its credit risk?

For each point of analysis, compare across companies and over time. The goal is to determine whether each company's accounts receivable (levels and changes) seems appropriate and to gauge the quality of the receivables.

3. *Operating Expenses* Review and analyze the income statement items.
   - Prepare a common-sized income statement by dividing each item on the income statement by total revenues, net.
   - Compare the common-sized values for the three years presented in the income statement. What changes are there, if any? Are material changes explained in the MD&A? Do the explanations seem reasonable given the current economic environment?
   - Does the company engage in research and development activities? Quantify the amount in dollar terms and common size. Do you observe any patterns? Is the level of R&D expense consistent with peers and industry?
   - Does the company have discontinued operations? If so, how will this impact future operations?

4. *Accounting Quality* Evaluating accounting quality is more of an art than a science. The point is to form an overall opinion about the reliability of the numbers in the financial statements.
   - Does the company report non-GAAP earnings? What items do they exclude or include? Do the two companies report similar one-time items? Do the items seem reasonable, or do we detect some self-serving disclosures?
   - Consider the list in the Research Insight Box in the module, and use it to assess the quality of the two companies' reported numbers.
   - Use an online investment website to find key ratios for close competitors. Compare to our companies.
   - Find the consensus analysts' EPS forecast for the recent year-end. How did our companies fare? Were there any one-time items or unusual changes in any expenses that might have caused the company to just meet or beat the forecast? This could indicate earnings management.

Solutions to Review Problems

Review 5-1—Solution

Part I

1. Revenue is recognized for the amount the company expects to receive, which is sales price less anticipated returns.

2. The purchase price is apportioned between two components (performance obligations): the value of the copier and the value of the two-year service agreement. Revenue is immediately recognized on the first component. For the second component, revenue is deferred and recognized ratably over two years.

3. Revenue is recognized ratably over the year despite the fact that customers pay up front.

4. Revenue is recognized for the commission only, not the full sales price, because the company is acting as an agent for the other companies.

5. Product sales are recognized as revenue when the product is delivered to the franchisee. Accounting services are recognized as revenue on a monthly basis as the service is provided.

Part II

1. Revenue = $3,000,000 × ($500,000/$2,500,000) = $600,000.

   Gross profit = $600,000 − $500,000 = $100,000.

2. The cost of $500,000 exceeds the billing of $400,000, and the excess of $100,000 is reported as a current asset (such as construction in progress).

Review 5-2—Solution

1. "Charged to costs and expenses" represents the amount of returns allowances recorded during fiscal 2018 for sales during that year. This amount is included in Tiffany's income statement for the fiscal year.

2. "Deductions" is the dollar value of actual returns offset by the value of the merchandise returned (that reduces COGS by the same amount). The actual returns number is $10.1 million, which is close to the estimated amount charged to costs and expenses of $12.6 million. This indicates that Tiffany & Co is fairly accurate in its estimation process.

3. *a.*

$ millions	2019	2018	2017
Net sales	$4,442.1	$4,169.8	$4,001.8
Charged to costs and expenses	12.6	7.5	2.5
Gross sales	$4,454.7	$4,177.3	$4,004.3
Allowance at year end	$17.5	$15	$9.6
Allowance/Gross sales	0.39%	0.36%	0.24%

The sales return allowance is small at year end, compared to gross sales, likely because sales returns are made quickly after the purchase so the balance outstanding at any time is small. In fact, the amount outstanding is roughly equal to one day's sales ($4,442.1/365 days = $12.2).The amount has been increasing over time but is not of concern given its magnitude.

b.

$ millions	2019	2018	2017
Charged to costs and expenses	$ 12.6	$ 7.5	$ 2.5
Gross sales	$4,454.7	$4,177.3	$4,004.3
% returned merchandise	0.28%	0.18%	0.06%

The % of merchandise that Tiffany estimates will be returned has steadily increased over the three years, but the amount is so low as to be immaterial. There is no cause for concern here.

c. Tiffany's sales returns allowance seems a bit high considering the following ratio of actual to estimate.

$ millions	2019	2018	2017
Estimated returns for the year	$12.6	$7.5	$2.5
Actual returns during the year	$10.1	$2.1	$1.2
Adequacy	125%	357%	208%

Review 5-3—Solution

The amount of cash received from the customers is the amount added to the liability.

Advanced Billings and Customer Deposits ($ millions)	
Balance at 1/1/2018	$26,656
+ Cash prepayments by customers during the year	??
− Revenue recognized during the year	(55,078)
= Balance at 12/31/2018	$32,720

Cash prepayments by customers during the year = $32,720 + $55,078 − $26,656 = $61,142

Review 5-4—Solution

1. In 2018, Google's EMEA revenues were 4 percentage points higher (24% versus 20% growth) as a result of the weakening $US vis-à-vis the other currencies in that region. As the $US weakened, foreign currency denominated income statements grew when translated into in $US. In 2017, the opposite was true, EMEA revenue growth would have been 2 percentage points higher (19% versus 21%) if not for the negative effect of the stronger $US.

2. All accounts in the income statement grow when the $US weakens: revenues, expenses, and profit. Because Alphabet is profitable (revenues are greater than expenses), the company will appear more profitable as a result of the weakening U.S. dollar.

3. Translation of the income statement does not affect cash flow. However, to the extent that Google transacts business in these foreign currencies, the amount of cash collected will likely be higher as the $US weakens.

Review 5-5—Solution

1. The estimate of total uncollectible accounts receivable as of December 31, 2018, for Coca-Cola is $490 million, calculated as follows. Coca-Cola will report Accounts receivable net of $3,395 million ($3,885 million − $490 million).

$ millions	Accounts Receivable	% Uncollectible	Estimated Allowance for Uncollectible Accounts (Receivable × % Uncollectible)
Current	$1,554	1.5%	$ 23
1–30 days past due	971	5.0%	49
31–60 days past due	544	14.0%	76
61–90 days past due	427	25.0%	107
91–120 days past due	272	54.0%	147
Over 120 days past due	117	75.0%	88
Total	$3,885		$490

2. Coca-Cola must increase the allowance for uncollectible accounts balance by $30 million. The increase of $30 million in the allowance account is bad debt expense. Coca-Cola will record this amount in the 2018 income statement.

Allowance for Uncollectible Accounts	
Balance as of beginning of the year	$477
Plus: addition to the allowance for uncollectible accounts recognized as expense	30
Less: write-offs of uncollectible accounts	(17)
Balance at end of year	$490

3. Coca-Cola's accounts receivable are of higher quality in 2017 because the allowance was proportionately smaller than in 2018.

	2018	2017
Accounts receivable, net	$3,395	$3,667
Allowance for doubtful accounts	490	477
Accounts receivable, gross	$3,885	$4,144
Allowance/AR gross	12.6%	11.5%

Review 5-6—Solution

1. The following would **not** be included in selling, general and administrative expense.
   - Utilities for the research laboratories—this would be included in the research and development expense because it relates to those activities.
   - Wages for manufacturing employees—these are costs to manufacture goods and would be included in cost of products sold.
   - License fees for software used to develop new products is part of the research and development process, so these costs would be included on that income statement line item.
   - Depreciation on machines that package and label finished goods—this is part of the cost to get the inventory ready for sale and would be included in cost of products sold.

2. Following is a summary of HPE's R&D expense for 2017 and 2018.

	2018	2017
R&D expense in $ millions	$1,663	$1,486
R&D expense as % of revenue	5.39%	5.15%

HPE has held R&D spending relatively constant over the two-year period. R&D costs include salaries and overhead for R&D employees including scientists, lab workers directly involved with R&D, as well as for personnel who indirectly assist and support R&D activities.

3. HPE discontinued (that is, sold off or closed) some operations during the 2018 fiscal year. The "Loss from discontinued operations" of $104 million included any profit or loss from those discontinued operations during the year. The loss also includes any gain or loss that HPE realized when it disposed of any assets of the discontinued operations.

Review 5-7—Solution

1. Companies, including Merck, publicly report non-GAAP information to communicate their view of the companies' ongoing, persistent earnings. Skeptics of such pro forma numbers suggest companies are simply trying to present their financial results in the best possible light.

2. First, Merck adjusts for one-time charges relating to acquisitions/divestitures and restructurings. In 2018, these include costs of $3,066 million and $658 million, respectively. Then, Merck adds back the cost of new joint ventures and collaborations including charges relating to the formation of oncology collaborations in 2018 (Eisai, $1,400 million) and 2017 (AstraZeneca, $2,350 million). Lastly, Merck adjusts for the tax effects of the adjustments and for the effects of the recent tax law changes. This latter charge was particularly large in 2017.

Module 6

Inventories, Accounts Payable, and Long-Term Assets

Inventories, Accounts Payable, and Long-Term Assets

Inventories and Accounts Payable
- Inventory Costing Methods
- Footnote Disclosures
- Effects of Inventory Costing
- Inventory Disclosures
- Inventory Analysis
- Cash Conversion Cycle

Review 6-1, 6-2, 6-3

Property, Plant & Equipment
- Depreciation and Book Value
- Disposals, Impairments and Restructuring
- Footnote Disclosures
- Analysis Tools—Turnover, Useful Life, and Percent Used Up

Review 6-4, 6-5, 6-6

PREVIEW

HD

We examine three balance sheet elements
- Inventories
- Accounts payable
- Long-term assets (PPE assets and intangible assets)

We review the accounting mechanics followed by an analysis of these elements. **Home Depot** is the focus company and the dashboard below conveys income statement and balance sheet information for 2000 through 2018.

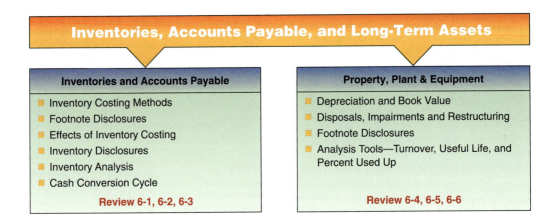

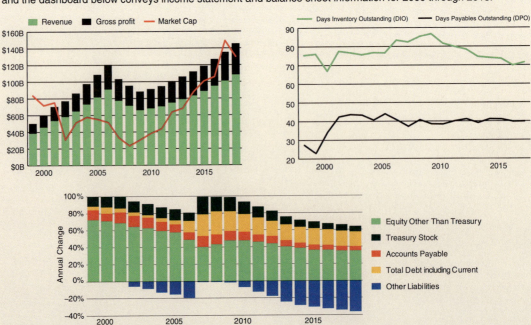

Road Map

LO	Learning Objective | Topics	Page	eLecture	Guided Example	Assignments
6-1	**Apply inventory costing methods.** Cost Flows :: FIFO :: LIFO :: Average Cost :: Financial Effects	6-3	e6–1	Review 6-1	1, 2, 3, 4, 13, 14, 23
6-2	**Examine inventory disclosures in financial statements.** LCM :: LIFO Liquidation :: LIFO Reserve and Adjustments	6-8	e6–2	Review 6-2	5, 11, 22, 24, 25, 26, 37
6-3	**Analyze inventories and the related accounts payable.** Gross Profit Margin :: Days Inventory Outstanding :: Inventory Turnover :: Days Payable Outstanding :: Cash Conversion Cycle	6-12	e6–3	Review 6-3	6, 10, 15, 19, 20, 22, 25, 27, 29, 32, 35, 36, 37, 41, 43
6-4	**Apply capitalization and depreciation of tangible assets.** Property :: Plant & Equipment :: Depreciation Methods :: R&D Facilities & Equipment	6-17	e6–4	Review 6-4	7, 8, 16, 17, 28, 33
6-5	**Evaluate asset sales, impairments, and restructuring activities.** Asset Sales :: Gains and Losses :: Asset Impairments	6-20	e6–5	Review 6-5	9, 12, 21, 28, 30, 33, 40, 42
6-6	**Analyze tangible assets and related activities.** PPE Turnover :: PPE Useful Life :: PPE Percent Used Up	6-25	e6–6	Review 6-6	18, 31, 32, 34, 38, 39, 42, 43

Inventory—Costing Methods

LO1 Apply inventory costing methods.

For many companies, inventory is among the four largest assets on the balance sheet (along with receivables, property, plant & equipment (PPE), and intangible assets such as goodwill). On the income statement, cost of goods sold (which is directly related to inventory) is the largest expense for many companies and certainly for those in retailing and manufacturing. Companies can choose from among several methods to account for inventory costs and these accounting choices can greatly impact the balance sheet and income statement. Although rare, companies can and do change inventory costing methods if doing so enhances the quality of their financial reports and the company can justify the change. A company must disclose the change in financial statements.

In Module 2 we describe the following flow of costs.

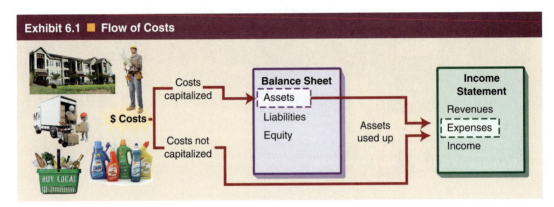

Exhibit 6.1 ■ Flow of Costs

Inventory expenditures follow the "Costs capitalized" line at the top of the graphic.

- Cost of **inventory** is added to the balance sheet as an asset (capitalized) when it is purchased or manufactured.[1]

- Inventory cost is transferred from the balance sheet to the income statement as **cost of goods sold** (COGS) when sold.[2] This COGS is deducted from sales to yield **gross profit**.

A typical income statement reports cost of goods sold as follows.

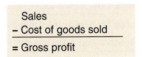

Sales
− Cost of goods sold
= Gross profit

As companies purchase or manufacture inventories, those costs are added to the balance sheet. Likewise, as companies sell inventories, they transfer the cost of those inventories to the income statement.

Measuring and analyzing the flow of inventory costs are important. If all inventory purchased or manufactured during the period is sold, then COGS is equal to the cost of the goods purchased or manufactured. However, when inventory remains at the end of a period (the usual case), companies must distinguish the cost of the inventories that are sold (reported as cost of goods sold in the income statement) from the cost of the inventories that remain as an asset on the balance sheet. The remaining inventory is available for sale in the next period. Exhibit 6.2 shows this cost flow graphically.

---

[1] **Manufacturing costs** consist of three components: cost of **direct (raw) materials** used in the product, cost of **direct labor** to manufacture the product, and **manufacturing overhead**. Direct materials cost is relatively easy to compute. Design specifications list the components of each product, and their purchase costs are readily determined. The direct labor cost per unit of inventory depends on how long each unit takes to construct and the wages and salaries paid for employees who work on that product. Overhead costs are also capitalized into inventory. These include all manufacturing costs other than direct materials and direct labor, such as utilities, supervisory personnel, repairs and depreciation on manufacturing PPE, and other related costs.

[2] Before issuing financial statements, companies compare the amount at which inventories are reported on the balance sheet with the current "market" value of the inventories. If the market value is less than the reported cost of the inventory, the company "writes down" the inventory to its market value. This process is called reporting inventories at the **lower of cost or market**, which we discuss later in the module.

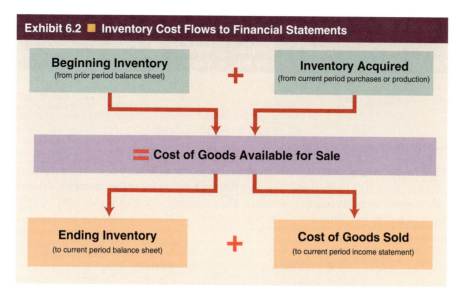

Companies have a choice when it comes to determining the cost of goods sold and the cost of the inventory remaining on the balance sheet. To understand this, consider the example in Exhibit 6.3.

Exhibit 6.3 ■ Summary Inventory Records

Inventory available on January 1	500 units	@ $100 per unit	$ 50,000
Inventory purchased during the period	200 units	@ $150 per unit	30,000
Total cost of goods available for sale	700 units		$ 80,000
Inventory sold during the period	450 units	@ $250 per unit	$112,500

This company began the period with 500 units of inventory that were purchased or manufactured for $50,000 ($100 each). During the period the company purchased and/or manufactured an additional 200 units costing $30,000. The total cost of goods available for sale for this period equals $80,000.

The company sold 450 units during the period for $250 per unit for total sales of $112,500. Accordingly, the company must remove the cost of the 450 units sold from the inventory account on the balance sheet and match this cost against the revenues generated from the sale. An important question is which costs should management remove from the balance sheet and report as cost of goods sold in the income statement? Three inventory costing methods (FIFO, LIFO, and average cost) are common and all are acceptable for U.S. GAAP.

First-In, First-Out (FIFO)

The FIFO inventory costing method transfers costs from inventory in the order that they were initially recorded. That is, FIFO assumes that the first costs recorded in inventory (first-in) are the first costs transferred from inventory (first-out). Applying FIFO to the data in Exhibit 6.3 means that the costs of the 450 units sold comes from *beginning* inventory, which consists of 500 units costing $100 each. The company's cost of goods sold and gross profit, using FIFO, is computed as follows.

Sales.	$112,500
COGS (450 @ $100 each).	45,000
Gross profit.	$ 67,500

The cost remaining in inventory and reported on the year-end balance sheet is $35,000 ($80,000 goods available for sale less $45,000 COGS). The following financial statement effects template captures the transaction.

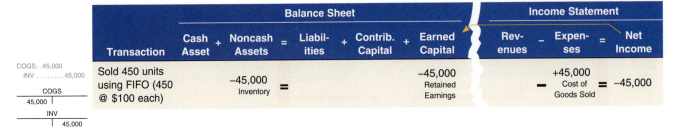

Last-In, First-Out (LIFO)

The LIFO inventory costing method transfers the most recent inventory costs from the balance sheet to COGS. That is, the LIFO method assumes that the most recent inventory purchases (last-in) are the first costs transferred from inventory (first-out). The company's cost of goods sold and gross profit, using LIFO, is computed as follows.

Sales.		$112,500
COGS: 200 @ $150 per unit	$30,000	
250 @ $100 per unit	25,000	55,000
Gross profit.		$ 57,500

The cost remaining in inventory and reported on the year-end balance sheet is $25,000 (computed as $80,000 − $55,000). This is reflected in our financial statements effects template as follows.

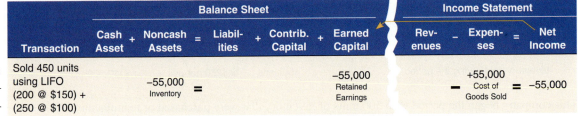

Average Cost (AC)

The average cost method computes the cost of goods sold as an average of the cost to purchase or manufacture all of the inventories that were available for sale during the period. To calculate the average cost of $114.286 per unit, the company divides the total cost of goods available for sale by the number of units available for sale ($80,000/700 units). The company's sales, cost of sales, and gross profit follow.

Sales.	$112,500
COGS (450 @ $114.286 per unit)	51,429
Gross profit.	$ 61,071

The cost remaining in inventory and reported on the year-end balance sheet is $28,571 ($80,000 − $51,429). This is reflected in our financial statements effects template as follows.

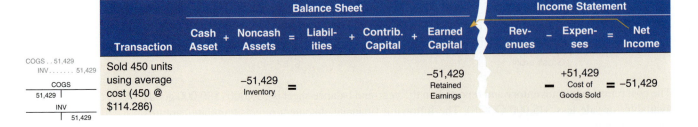

The average cost method is commonly adopted when inventory purchases and sales are continuous during the year. This method is especially common for retail companies that stock (and constantly restock) nonseasonal items and for manufacturing companies that use commodities (or commoditized items) as raw materials. Technological advances such as bar codes, scanners, and RFIDs have enabled continuous inventory tracking, tracing, and counting. Enterprise resource planning (ERP) systems interface with these inventory management systems, and, together, these advances reduce the costs associated with inventory costing prompting more firms to adopt the average cost method. In its fiscal 2019 financial statements, **CVS Health Corporation** reports the following.

> Inventories are valued at the lower of cost or net realizable value using the weighted average cost method. Physical inventory counts are taken on a regular basis in each retail store and LTC pharmacy and a continuous cycle count process is the primary procedure used to validate the inventory balances on hand in each distribution center and mail facility to ensure that the amounts reflected in the accompanying consolidated financial statements are properly stated. During the interim period between physical inventory counts, CVS Health accrues for anticipated physical inventory losses on a location-by-location basis based on historical results and current trends.

It is important to understand that the inventory costing method a company chooses to prepare its income statement is independent of the actual flow of inventory. For example, the **Kroger** grocery store chain uses LIFO inventory but certainly does not sell the freshest products first.

Business Insight ▪ Retail Method for Inventory Costing

Retailers such as Home Depot and Lowe's commonly estimate the cost of ending inventories using the *retail inventory method* (RIM). Retailers know the **cost** of the inventories purchased as well as their **retail** selling price. From this, the retailer computes the **cost-to-retail percentage** and applies that percentage to estimate the cost of the inventory still available at year-end (the ending inventory) as follows.

	Purchase Cost	Retail Selling Price
Beginning inventories	$100,000	$160,000
+ Purchases during the period	300,000	500,000
= Cost of goods available for sale	400,000	660,000
(Cost-to-retail percentage: $400,000/$660,000 = 60.6%)		
Sales		(420,000)
Estimated ending inventory at retail selling prices		$240,000
Estimated ending inventory at cost (60.6% × $240,000 retail)	(145,440)	
= Cost of goods sold	$254,560	

This retailer reports inventory of $145,440 on its balance sheet at year-end. The income statement reports sales of $420,000, cost of goods sold of $254,560, and gross profit of $165,440.

This method allows retailers to readily compute ending inventories at retail selling prices (Quantities available × Selling price). The company's inventory system tracks both the purchase cost and the retail selling price of inventories. These are inputs in the cost-to-retail percentage calculation. The cost-to-retail percentage is important and managers review the ratio regularly for reliability. **Home Depot** describes its inventory costing method as follows.

> The majority of the Company's Merchandise Inventories are stated at the lower of cost (first-in, first-out) or market, as determined by the *retail inventory method* . . . Independent physical inventory counts . . . are taken on a regular basis in each store and distribution center to ensure that amounts reflected in the accompanying Consolidated Financial Statements for Merchandise Inventories are properly stated.

Financial Statement Effects of Inventory Costing

This section describes the financial statement effects of different inventory costing methods.

Income Statement Effects

The three inventory costing methods yield differing levels of gross profit as Exhibit 6.4 shows.

Exhibit 6.4 ■ Income Effects from Inventory Costing Methods			
	Sales	Cost of Goods Sold	Gross Profit
FIFO..................	$112,500	$45,000	$67,500
LIFO..................	112,500	55,000	57,500
Average cost...........	112,500	51,429	61,071

Recall that inventory costs *rose* during this period from $100 per unit to $150 per unit. The higher gross profit reported under FIFO arises because FIFO matches older, lower-cost inventory against current selling prices. To generalize: in an inflationary environment, FIFO yields higher gross profit than do LIFO or average cost methods.

In recent years, the gross profit impact from using the FIFO method has been minimal for companies due to lower rates of inflation and increased management focus on reducing inventory quantities through improved manufacturing processes and better inventory controls. The FIFO gross profit effect can still arise, however, with companies subject to high inflation and slow inventory turnover.

Balance Sheet Effects

In our illustration above, the ending inventory using LIFO is less than that reported using FIFO. In periods of rising costs, LIFO inventories are markedly lower than under FIFO. As a result, balance sheets using LIFO do not accurately represent the cost that a company would incur to replace its current investment in inventories. A second issue is that financial statement users cannot compare LIFO and FIFO inventory numbers across firms as the balance sheet and income statement numbers are not equivalent. Thus, U.S. GAAP requires that firms choosing LIFO also report (in their footnotes) the equivalent FIFO inventory amounts. The difference between FIFO and LIFO inventories is called the **LIFO reserve**. We discuss, below, how to use the LIFO reserve to better analyze inventories.

Caterpillar Inc. (CAT), for example, uses LIFO and reports inventories of $11,529 million on its 2018 balance sheet. CAT's inventory footnote (below) reports that under FIFO costing, inventories would have been $2,009 million greater, a 17% difference. This suggests that CAT's balance sheet omits over $2 billion in inventories.

> Inventories are stated at the lower of cost or net realizable value. Cost is principally determined using the last-in, first-out (LIFO) method. The value of inventories on the LIFO basis represented about 65 percent of total inventories at December 31, 2018 and 2017. If the FIFO (first-in, first-out) method had been in use, inventories would have been $2,009 million and $1,934 million higher than reported at December 31, 2018 and 2017, respectively.

Cash Flow Effects

When inventory costs rise, the LIFO method yields lower net income. Assuming that companies and investors prefer higher net income, one wonders why any company would use LIFO. The answer is taxes. Unlike most other accounting method choices, inventory costing methods affect taxable income. (U.S. IRS is the only taxing authority in the world to allow LIFO; LIFO is not permitted under IFRS. For background, see: https://www.researchgate.net/publication/268365773.) Using LIFO increases COGS, which reduces taxable income and taxes paid. The net result is a real cash savings. Companies weigh the cash flow effect against the financial reporting effect when selecting among LIFO, FIFO, and average cost.

Could companies strategically use FIFO for financial reporting (and present high net income to investors) and LIFO for tax purposes (and pay as little tax as possible)? The answer is NO. A "LIFO conformity rule" in the IRS tax code stipulates that if a company uses LIFO for its tax filing, it must also adopt LIFO for financial reporting. This rule limits companies' ability to cherry-pick among accounting methods. Further, the LIFO reserve quantifies the difference that LIFO creates.

Caterpillar's use of LIFO has created significant tax savings over the years. We compute this tax savings using CAT's footnote data.

	LIFO Reserve	Tax Rate	Tax Saving
LIFO reserve (cumulative through 2017)	$1,934 million	35%	$677 million
Change to the LIFO reserve in 2018	75 million	21%	16 million
LIFO reserve (cumulative through 2018)	$2,009 million		$693 million

Through 2017, CAT's cumulative taxable income was reduced by $1,934 million. (Cumulative here means the aggregate amount over the company's entire history.) With the 35% tax rate in effect during that period, the company saved $677 million in taxes ($1,934 × 35%), which increased after-tax cash flow by the same amount. In 2018, the LIFO reserve increased by another $75 million for a cumulative total of $2,009 million. In 2018, the tax laws changed and reduced the corporate tax rate to 21% (see discussions of the new tax act, in Modules 5 and 10). At 21%, the 2018 tax saving was $16 million. Through 2018, CAT's cumulative tax savings is $693 million. The upshot is that CAT's cumulative cash flows were higher by that amount because the company used LIFO for inventory costing.

While tax savings have traditionally motivated companies to choose LIFO, the drop in the corporate tax rate in 2017 has reduced potential tax savings. With smaller benefits associated with LIFO, we might see a decline in the number of companies using LIFO.

LO1 Review 6-1

At the beginning of the current period, assume that one of **Home Depot**'s subsidiary companies holds 1,000 units of a certain product with a unit cost of $18. A summary of purchases during the current period follows. During the current period, the HD subsidiary sells 2,800 units.

		Units	Unit Cost	Cost
Beginning Inventory		1,000	$18.00	$18,000
Purchases:	#1	1,800	18.25	32,850
	#2	800	18.50	14,800
	#3	1,200	19.00	22,800
Cost of goods available for sale		4,800		$88,450

Required

1. Assume that the HD subsidiary uses the first-in, first-out (FIFO) method for this product. Compute the product's cost of goods sold for the current period and the ending inventory balance.
2. Assume that the HD subsidiary uses the last-in, first-out (LIFO) method for this product. Compute the product's cost of goods sold for the current period and the ending inventory balance.
3. Assume that the HD subsidiary uses the average cost (AC) method for this product. Compute the product's cost of goods sold for the current period and the ending inventory balance.
4. As manager, which of these three inventory costing methods would you choose:
   a. To reflect what is probably the physical flow of goods? Explain.
   b. To minimize income taxes for the period? Explain.

Solution on p. 6-43.

Inventory—Reporting

Lower of Cost or Market (LCM)

Footnotes to financial statements describe the inventory accounting method a company uses. To illustrate, **Home Depot** reports $13,925 million in inventory on its balance sheet as a current asset for the year ended February 3, 2019. Following is an excerpt from Home Depot's footnote.

> The majority of our merchandise inventories are stated at the lower of cost (first-in, first-out) or market, as determined by the retail inventory method. As the inventory retail value is adjusted regularly to reflect market conditions, the inventory valued using the retail method approximates the lower of cost or market. We evaluate the inventory valued using a cost method at the end of each quarter to ensure that it is carried at the lower of cost or net realizable value.

Like many retailers, Home Depot uses FIFO to cost its inventory along with the retail inventory method that we explained above. Then, at the end of each accounting period, Home Depot compares the ending FIFO inventory balance with the market value of the inventory (its replacement cost). If the market value is less than the FIFO amount, Home Depot "writes down" the inventory to its market value. The result is that the inventory is carried on the balance sheet at whichever amount is lower: the cost of the inventory *or* its market value. This process is called reporting inventories at the **lower of cost or market** and creates the following financial statement effects.

- Inventory book value is written down to current market value (replacement cost), reducing inventory and total assets.
- Inventory write-down is reflected as an expense (part of cost of goods sold) on the income statement, reducing current period gross profit, income, and equity.

To illustrate, assume that a company has inventory on its balance sheet at a cost of $27,000. Management learns that the inventory's replacement cost is $23,000 and writes inventories down to a balance of $23,000. The following financial statement effects template shows the adjustment.

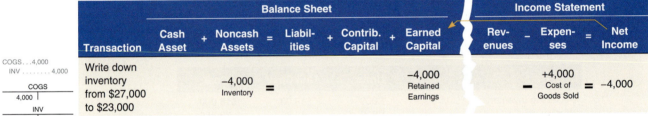

The inventory write-down (a noncash expense) is reflected in cost of goods sold and reduces gross profit by $4,000. Inventory write-downs are included in cost of goods sold. They are *not* reported in selling, general, and administrative expenses, which is common for other asset write-downs. A common occurrence of inventory write-downs is in connection with restructuring activities.

LIFO Reserve Adjustments to Financial Statements

CAT uses LIFO for most of its inventories. (Neither the IRS nor GAAP requires use of a single inventory costing method. That is, companies are allowed to, and frequently do, use different inventory costing methods for different types of inventory (such as spare parts versus finished goods) or inventory in different geographical locations.) We can use a LIFO reserve to adjust LIFO inventories on the balance sheet to their FIFO value using the following equation.

> **FIFO Inventory = LIFO Inventory + LIFO Reserve**

We adjust CAT's inventory balances for 2017 and 2018 using balance sheet and footnote data as follows ($ in millions).

2018 FIFO inventory = $11,529 LIFO inventory + $2,009 LIFO reserve = $13,538

2017 FIFO inventory = $10,018 LIFO inventory + $1,934 LIFO reserve = $11,952

Comparing LIFO inventory balances across years for the same company can conceal any changes or trends, and thus, analysts typically adjust to FIFO numbers before calculating inventory ratios.

Disclosures for a LIFO Reserve Because companies can choose among the various inventory costing methods, their financial statements are often not comparable. The problem is most serious when companies hold large amounts of inventory and when prices markedly rise or fall. For example, consider comparing CAT to **Kubota**, a close competitor that uses the FIFO method to cost its inventory. The table below reports certain financial information for both companies for fiscal 2018.

Monetary amounts in millions	CAT LIFO as Reported	CAT FIFO as Adjusted	Kubota as Reported
Inventory	$11,529	$13,538	¥ 370,698
LIFO reserve, 2018	$ 2,009	—	—
LIFO reserve, 2017	$ 1,934	—	—
Total assets	$78,509	$80,518	¥2,895,655
Inventory as a % of total assets	**15%**	**17%**	**13%**
Cost of goods sold	$36,997	$36,922	¥1,332,930
Revenue (equipment sales)	$51,822	$51,822	¥1,850,316
Cost of goods sold as a % of revenue	71.39%	71.25%	72.04%

If we compare the information reported on each company's financial statements ('CAT LIFO as Reported' vs. 'Kubota as Reported') we would conclude that Caterpillar holds slightly more inventory than Kubota—15% of total assets for CAT vs. 13% for Kubota. But this is not an apples-to-apples comparison and such a conclusion is erroneous. Fortunately, companies that use LIFO must report their LIFO reserve, and we can use these disclosures to adjust the LIFO numbers to their FIFO equivalents. Once we convert CAT's inventory and its total assets to FIFO (by adding the LIFO reserve, as explained above), we find that the company holds 17% of total assets as inventory, a greater difference than first noted.

Balance Sheet Adjustments for a LIFO Reserve In general, to adjust for LIFO on the balance sheet, we must make three modifications and then recompute balance sheet totals and subtotals (current assets, total assets, and total equity).

- Increase inventories by the LIFO reserve.
- Increase tax liabilities by the tax rate applied to the LIFO reserve.
- Increase retained earnings for the difference.

As an example, to adjust CAT's 2018 balance sheet, we would:

- Increase inventories by $2,009 million.
- Increase tax liabilities by $693 million (see our computation on page 6-8).
- Increase retained earnings by the difference of $1,316 million (computed as $2,009 million − $693 million).

Income Statement Adjustments for a LIFO Reserve To compare the income statements of companies that use LIFO, we must adjust cost of goods sold from LIFO to FIFO. Recall that: Cost of Goods Sold = Beginning Inventories + Purchases − Ending Inventories. To determine FIFO COGS, we must use the *change* in the LIFO reserve as follows.

> **FIFO COGS = LIFO COGS − Increase in LIFO Reserve (or + Decrease)**

During 2018, the change in CAT's LIFO reserve was $75 million ($2,009 million − $1,934 million). Had CAT *always used* FIFO, its 2018 COGS would have been $75 million lower (meaning gross profit and pretax income would be $75 million higher), and the company would have paid $16 million ($75 million × 21%) more in taxes. This does not make much difference either in dollar or percentage terms for CAT in 2018 because the LIFO reserve increased only slightly during the year. But in other years, and for other companies, the impact can be great.

LIFO Liquidations

When LIFO companies acquire inventory at different costs, they are required to account for each cost level as a separate inventory pool or layer (for example, there are the $100 and $150 units in our Exhibit 6.3 illustration). When companies reduce inventory levels, older inventory costs flow to the income statement. These older LIFO costs are often markedly lower than current inventory costs, assuming an inflationary environment. The net effect is that the LIFO cost of sales is lower than the equivalent FIFO cost of sales (the reverse of the typical situation). The liquidation boosts gross profit as older, lower costs are matched against current selling prices on the income statement.

The increase in gross profit resulting from a reduction of inventory quantities in the presence of rising costs is called **LIFO liquidation**. The effect of LIFO liquidation is evident in the following footnote from **Rite Aid**'s 10-K for the fiscal year ended March 2, 2019 (which Rite Aid labels fiscal 2019).

> **Inventory** (in $000s) At March 2, 2019 and March 3, 2018, inventories were $604,444 and $581,090, respectively, lower than the amounts that would have been reported using the first-in, first-out ("FIFO") cost flow assumption. . . During fiscal 2019, 2018 and 2017, a reduction in non-pharmacy inventories resulted in the liquidation of applicable LIFO inventory quantities carried at lower costs in prior years. This LIFO liquidation resulted in a $5,884, $2,707 and $2,375 cost of revenues decrease, with a corresponding reduction to the adjustment to LIFO for fiscal 2019, fiscal 2018 and fiscal 2017, respectively.

Rite Aid reports that reductions in inventory quantities in 2018 led to the sale (at current selling prices) of inventory that had a low balance sheet value—the inventory was valued using costs from prior years when those costs were much lower. As a result of these inventory reductions, COGS was lower, which increased income by $5,884 thousand in fiscal 2019. Fiscal years 2018 and 2017 were similarly affected.

IFRS Insight ■ Inventory Measurement under IFRS

Like GAAP, IFRS measures inventories at the lower of cost or market. The cost of inventory generally is determined using the FIFO (first-in, first-out) or average cost method; use of the LIFO (last-in, first-out) method is prohibited under IFRS.

Review 6-2 L02

Refer to the information in Review 6-1. Consider each of the following as separate situations.

Required
1. Assume HD reports its inventories using the FIFO cost flow assumption as in #1 in Review 6-1 and that the market value (replacement cost) of the inventories on the financial statement date is $30,000. At what amount is inventories reported on the balance sheet?
2. Assume that the HD subsidiary utilizes the LIFO method and delays purchasing lot #3 until the next period. Compute cost of goods sold under this scenario and discuss how the LIFO liquidation affects profit.
3. Assume that the subsidiary uses LIFO for this product. In that case, the company would compute and report a LIFO reserve. What is the amount of LIFO reserve? How would that reserve affect the subsidiary's tax expense for the current period (as compared to FIFO) assuming a marginal tax rate of 21%?

Solution on p. 6-43.

Inventory—Analysis Tools

This section describes several useful tools for analysis of inventory and related accounts.

LO3
Analyze inventories and the related accounts payable.

Gross Profit Analysis

The **gross profit margin (GPM)** is gross profit divided by sales. This important ratio is closely monitored by management, analysts, and other external financial statement users. Exhibit 6.5 shows the gross profit margin on **Home Depot**'s sales for the past three years.

Exhibit 6.5 ■ Gross Profit Margin and Related Data for Home Depot

$ millions	Feb. 3, 2019 Fiscal 2018	Jan. 28, 2018 Fiscal 2017	Jan. 29, 2017 Fiscal 2016
Net sales................	$108,203	$100,904	$94,595
Cost of sales.............	71,043	66,548	62,282
Gross profit...............	$ 37,160	$ 34,356	$32,313
Gross profit margin.........	34.3%	34.0%	34.2%
Inventories...............	$ 13,925	$ 12,748	
Accounts payable..........	7,755	7,244	

The gross profit margin is commonly used instead of the dollar amount of gross profit as the GPM allows for comparisons across companies and over time. A decline in GPM is usually cause for concern since it indicates that the company has less ability to pass on increased product cost to customers or that the company is not effectively managing product costs. Home Depot's gross profit margin on product sales increased by 0.3 percentage points (from 34.0% to 34.3%) during the fiscal year ended February 3, 2019 (HD refers to this as fiscal 2018). Following is Home Depot's discussion of its gross profit from its Form 10-K.

> Gross profit increased $2.8 billion, or 8.2%, to $37.2 billion in fiscal 2018. Gross profit as a percent of net sales, or gross profit margin, was 34.3% in fiscal 2018 compared to 34.0% in fiscal 2017. The increase in gross profit margin for fiscal 2018 was primarily driven by a $598 million benefit from the adoption of ASU No. 2014-09 and a benefit from mix of products sold, partially offset by higher transportation and fuel costs in our supply chain and shrink. The additional week in fiscal 2018 contributed $615 million to gross profit.

The increase in Home Depot's gross profit margin in fiscal 2018 was partly due to factors outside Home Depot's control.

- It adopted the new revenue recognition standard (ASU No. 2014-09, see Module 5), which impacted the timing of revenue recognition. Footnote disclosures reveal that, due to the new standard: sales increased by $216 million, COGS decreased by $382 million, and gross profit increased by $598 million.

- The fiscal year that ended in February 2019 included a 53rd week. Home Depot, like most retailers, operates on a 52- or 53-week year. The company closes its fiscal year on the Sunday nearest to January 31st each year. That date was January 28 in 2018 (fiscal 2017) and February 3 in 2019 (fiscal 2018). This created a 53rd week for fiscal 2018. Home Depot 10-K revealed that the additional week contributed $615 million to gross profit. While this additional week adds to gross profit, it will have a negligible effect on gross profit margin because both cost of sales and sales will include the 53rd week.

It also reported that a portion of the change in gross profit resulted from operating factors within the company's control.

- It changed the mix of products sold and its gross margin increased. From this we can conclude that it sold higher-margin products, on average. However, it incurred higher transportation and fuel costs in the supply chain. Home Depot's use of the word *shrink* relates to the loss of inventory due to obsolescence, damage, theft, and a variety of other causes. The amount of this shrink is included in cost of goods sold.

It is important to distinguish between factors that Home Depot can control and those it cannot. These factors cause cash flow changes and, consequently, impact shareholder value.

Following is a brief list of factors that can adversely affect gross profit margins.

- Changes in product mix toward lower-margin products.
- New products introduced at low prices to gain market share.
- Increases in production costs.
- Decrease in production volume (lower production volume spreads out manufacturing overhead over a smaller number of units produced, thus increasing the cost per unit produced).
- Increases in supply-chain costs (such as procurement, transportation, technology, and insurance).
- More generous sales discounts or sales returns policies.
- Inventory obsolescence and/or overstocking.
- Warranty costs.
- General decline in economic activity.
- New competitors in the market.
- Regulation that inhibits sales or adds fees or taxes to products sold.

Competitive pressures mean that companies rarely have the opportunity to completely control gross profit with price increases. Improvements in gross profit on existing product lines typically arise from better management of supply chains, production processes, or distribution networks. Companies that succeed do so because of better performance on basic business processes.

Data Analytics Insight — Inventory Optimization

Companies have long used information technology including bar codes and RFIDs to manage inventory levels. The explosion of big data and powerful data analytics tools allow companies to better manage inventory quantity and quality and it enhances management of the supply chain. It is common to track inventory as it moves from manufacturer to distributor and to the final customer using scanning and GSP tracking technology. Expensive IT investments pay off when they help companies avoid upset customers, inventory carrying costs, and obsolescence write-downs. Predictive data analytics are especially common for retailers. AI-based tools can integrate internal sales and pricing data with macro-economic indicators, consumer demographics, social-media data, and weather forecasts, to fine-tune inventory items store by store and anticipate the timing of sales. Further, online shopping apps make "helpful suggestions" for additional purchases based on prior purchases and other data.

Days Inventory Outstanding and Inventory Turnover

A useful way to analyze inventory is to compare the income statement activity related to inventory (COGS) to inventory levels on the balance sheet. This helps us assess inventory management and provides insight into the company's efficiency in generating sales. We commonly calculate two inventory ratios.

Inventory turnover (IT) measures the number of times during the period that the company sells its inventory and is computed as follows.

$$\text{Inventory Turnover} = \text{Cost of Goods Sold} / \text{Average Inventory}$$

Average days inventory outstanding (DIO), also called *days inventory outstanding*, measures the days required to sell the average inventory available for sale and it is computed as follows.

$$\text{Average Days Inventory Outstanding} = 365/\text{Inventory Turnover} = \frac{365 \times \text{Average Inventory}}{\text{COGS}}$$

We use cost of goods sold in these ratios (instead of sales) because inventory is reported at cost whereas sales includes any gross profit on the inventory. We calculate average inventory as a simple average of the balance at the beginning and the balance at the end of the period.[3]

Recall that Home Depot's fiscal year that ends February 3, 2019, includes a 53rd week. We want to compare inventory turnover and DIO across years for Home Depot as well as to competitors. To do this, we begin with the data from Exhibit 6.3 and adjust the cost of goods sold for the 53rd week. The common approach is to multiply COGS by 52/53 under that assumption that Home Depot sold inventory evenly over all weeks in the fiscal year. (The inventory reported on the balance sheet is the amount at February 3, 2019, and does not require any adjustment.)

For Year Ended, $ millions	As Reported, February 3, 2019 (53 weeks)	As Adjusted, February 3, 2019 (52 weeks)
COGS.	$71,043	$69,703 $71,043 × 52/53

Using the adjusted COGS, we calculate the two ratios for the year ended February 2019 ($ millions).

$$\text{Inventory Turnover} = \frac{\$69,703}{(\$13,925 + \$12,748)/2} = 5.23 \text{ times}$$

$$\text{Average Days Inventory Outstanding} = \frac{365}{5.23} = 69.8 \text{ days}$$

The results imply that Home Depot turned over (sold) its entire inventory 5.23 times during the year and that it took the company about 70 days, on average, to sell its average inventory. (Had we not adjusted for the 53rd week, the DIO would have been 68.5 days.)

The number of days required to turn over inventory varies widely by industry. At the high end, pharmaceutical and biotechnology companies have raw materials and finished goods inventory that include rare ingredients or patented molecules. At the low end are transportation and utility companies whose inventory line item on the balance sheet likely reflects fuel and other consumables primarily for internal use.

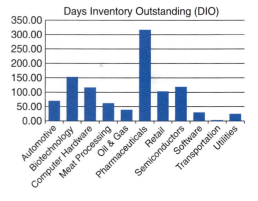

Overall, analysis of days inventory outstanding is important for at least two reasons.

1. *Inventory quality.* The ratios can be compared over time and across competitors. Fewer days is viewed favorably, because it implies that products are salable, preferably without undue discounting (we would compare profit margins to assess discounting). Conversely, more days implies that inventory is on the shelves for a longer period of time, perhaps from excessive purchases or production, missed fashion trends or technological advances, increased competition, and so forth. Our conclusions about higher or lower days inventory outstanding must consider alternative explanations including the following.

    - Product mix can include more (or less) higher margin inventories that sell more slowly. This can occur from business acquisitions that consolidate different types of inventory.
    - A company can change its promotion policies. Increased, effective advertising is likely to decrease days inventory outstanding. Advertising expense is in SG&A, not COGS. This means the additional advertising cost is in operating expenses, but the benefit is in gross profit and

---

[3] This formula uses average inventories. A variant of the ratio considers the number of days to sell the *ending* inventories (365 × Ending inventories/ COGS). For the year ended February 3, 2019, this ratio is as follows: Days Inventory Outstanding = $\frac{365}{(\$69,703/\$13,925)}$ = 72.9. These two approaches address different issues: the "average days" tells us the number of days it took Home Depot to sell the inventory available for sale during the year. The second approach tells us the number of days it would take Home Depot to sell the current *ending* inventories. It is important that we first identify the issue under investigation and then choose the formula that best addresses that issue.

fewer days. If the promotion campaign is successful, the positive effects in margin and days should more than offset the promotion cost in SG&A.
- A company can realize improvements in manufacturing efficiency and lower investments in direct materials and work-in-process inventories. Such improvements reduce inventory and, consequently, decrease days inventory outstanding. Although a good sign, it does not yield any information about the desirability of a company's product line.

2. *Asset utilization.* Companies strive to optimize their inventory investment. Carrying too much inventory is expensive, and too little inventory risks stock-outs and lost sales (current and future). Companies can make the following operational changes to optimize inventory.
    - Improved manufacturing processes can eliminate bottlenecks and the consequent buildup of work-in-process inventories.
    - Just-in-time (JIT) deliveries from suppliers, which provide raw materials to the production line when needed, can reduce the level of raw materials and associated holding costs.
    - Demand-pull production, in which raw materials are released into the production process when final goods are demanded by customers instead of producing for estimated demand, can reduce inventory levels. **Harley-Davidson**, for example, does not manufacture a motorcycle until it receives the customer's order; thus, Harley produces for actual, rather than estimated, demand.

Reducing inventories reduces inventory carrying costs, thus improving profitability and increasing cash flows. The reduction in inventory is reflected as an operating cash inflow in the statement of cash flows.

There is normal tension between the sales side of a company that argues for depth and breadth of inventory, and the finance side that monitors inventory carrying costs and seeks to maximize cash flow. Companies, therefore, seek to *optimize* inventory investment, not minimize it.

Days Payable Outstanding

Most companies purchase inventories on credit, meaning that suppliers allow companies to pay later. The supplier sets credit terms that specify when the invoice must be paid. Sometimes the supplier will offer a discount if the company pays more quickly. A typical invoice might include payment terms of 2/10, net 30, which means that the seller offers a 2% discount if the invoice is paid within 10 days and, if not, requires payment in full to be made in 30 days. Business-to-business (B2B) payables are usually non-interest bearing. This means accounts payable represent a low-cost financing source and companies should defer payment as long as allowed by the vendor.

Consistent with the ratios we calculated to analyze inventory, we can calculate **accounts payable turnover (APT)** that measures the number of payment cycles in the year.

$$\text{Accounts Payable Turnover} = \frac{\text{COGS}}{\text{Average Accounts Payable}}$$

The average length of time a company takes to pay its suppliers is reflected in the **days payable outstanding (DPO)** ratio.

$$\text{Days Payable Outstanding} = \frac{365}{\text{Accounts Payable Turnover}} = \frac{365 \times \text{Average Accounts Payable}}{\text{COGS}}$$

Similar to the inventory metrics above, we use COGS in the accounts payable ratios because payables relate to the purchase of inventories, which are reported at cost.[4] Again, we use the COGS adjusted for the 53rd week for Home Depot for the year ended February 2019; the two ratios are:

---

[4] Alternate versions of APT and DPO use inventory purchases instead of COGS (which are inventory sales). The rationale for this alternate definition is that the activity in accounts payable is directly related to purchases from and payments to suppliers. The link from COGS to payables is indirect, via the inventory account, which increases with inventory purchases and decreases with COGS. Nonetheless, it is more common to use COGS because they typically are a close approximation of purchases (and it's simpler).

$$\text{Accounts payable turnover} = \frac{\$69{,}703}{(\$7{,}755 + \$7{,}244)/2} = 9.29 \text{ times}$$

$$\text{Days payable outstanding} = \frac{365}{9.29} = 39.3 \text{ days}$$

This means Home Depot pays its suppliers in 39.3 days, on average. This is slightly longer than the typical supplier payment terms of 30 days. (Had we not adjusted for the 53rd week, the DPO would have been 38.5 days.)

Delaying payment to suppliers allows the purchasing company to increase its available cash (in other words, reduce its necessary level of cash). However, excessive delays (called "leaning on the trade") can damage supplier relationships. Remember, the purchaser's days payable outstanding is the seller's days sales outstanding in accounts receivable—this means as the purchaser gains cash from delaying payment, the seller loses an equal amount. As such, if delays become excessive, sellers might increase product cost or even choose to not sell to the purchaser. In managing the days accounts payable outstanding, companies must take care to maximize available cash while minimizing supply-chain disruption.

Cash Conversion Cycle

The cash conversion cycle is defined as:

```
  Days sales outstanding (accounts receivable)
+ Days inventory outstanding
− Days payable outstanding
= Cash conversion cycle
```

Each time a company completes one cash conversion cycle, it has purchased and sold inventory (realizing sales and gross profit), and paid accounts payable and collected accounts receivable. The cycle increases cash flow (unless the sales are unprofitable). The aim is to minimize the time to complete a cycle.

Home Depot's cash conversion cycle for the three-year period ending February 3, 2019, follows.

Amounts in Days	Feb. 3, 2019 (52 weeks adjusted)	Jan. 28, 2018	Jan. 29, 2017
Days sales outstanding (DSO)*	6.7	7.2	7.8
+ Days inventory outstanding (DIO)	69.8	69.4	73.5
− Days payable outstanding (DPO)	(39.3)	(39.1)	(41.0)
= Cash conversion cycle	37.2	37.5	40.3

* We discuss DSO in Module 5.

Over the past three years, Home Depot has improved its cash conversion cycle from 40.3 days to 37.2 days. The biggest improvement was for inventory days, which dropped 3.7 days over the three-year period (73.5 days − 69.8 days = 3.7 days). Inventory management has been a strategic focus for Home Depot as explained in its February 2019 MD&A.

> We centrally forecast and replenish over 98% of our store products through sophisticated inventory management systems and utilize a network of over 200 distribution centers to serve both our stores' and customers' needs. This network includes multiple distribution center platforms in the U.S., Canada, and Mexico tailored to meet the needs of our stores and customers based on the types of products, location, transportation, and delivery requirements. These platforms primarily include rapid deployment centers, stocking distribution centers, bulk distribution centers, and direct fulfillment centers. As part of our investment in One Home Depot Supply Chain, we will add a number of different fulfillment facilities designed to help us meet our goal of reaching 90% of the U.S. population with same or next day delivery for an extended home improvement product offering, including big and bulky goods. These facilities include more direct fulfillment centers and market delivery operations, or MDOs, which function as local hubs to consolidate freight for dispatch to customers for the final mile of delivery. In fiscal 2018, we began piloting these facilities.

Supply chain optimization is often cited as a key for effective inventory management. Inventories are recognized on the balance sheet when received at the distribution center and the days inventories outstanding clock starts ticking at that moment. Home Depot's challenge, then, is to minimize the time it takes to get the right amount of product from the distribution center to the store shelves. This involves accurate estimates of customer demand for products and an efficient logistics network.

As inventories decrease (all else equal), cash increases, and that increase can be large. For example, from 2017 to 2018, Home Depot reduced its DIO by 4.1 days from 73.5 to 69.4, which increased the company's cash balance by $747.5 million, computed as (Δ refers to 'change in'):

$$\Delta \text{ Cash} = \Delta \text{ Days Inventory Outstanding} \times (\text{COGS}/365)$$
$$= 4.1 \text{ days} \times (\$66{,}548 \text{ million}/365 \text{ days}) = \$747.5 \text{ million}$$

Managerial Decision ■ You Are the Operations Manager

You are analyzing your inventory turnover report for the month and are concerned that the average days inventory outstanding is lengthening. What actions can you take to reduce average days inventory outstanding? [Answer, p. 6-28]

Review 6-3 LO3

Lowe's Companies Inc. is a competitor of Home Depot. It reports the following financial statement data for 2017, 2018 and 2019. Use these data to answer the requirements below.

$ millions	2017	2018	2019
Revenue....................	$65,017	$68,619	$71,309
Cost of goods sold...............	43,343	46,185	48,394
Gross profit....................	21,674	22,434	22,915
Accounts receivable.............	0	0	0
Inventory.....................	10,458	11,393	12,561
Accounts payable...............	6,651	6,590	8,279

Required
1. Compute the gross profit margin for 2017, 2018, and 2019.
2. Compute the days inventory outstanding for 2018 and 2019.
3. Compute the days payable outstanding for 2018 and 2019.
4. Compute the cash conversion cycle for 2018 and 2019. By how many days did the cash conversion cycle improve during 2019?
5. Compute the cash effect in 2019 due to the 2019 change in the cash conversion cycle.

Solution on p. 6-44.

PPE Assets—Capitalization and Depreciation

LO4 Apply capitalization and depreciation of tangible assets.

Property, plant and equipment (PPE or PP&E, also called tangible or fixed assets) is the largest asset for most companies, and depreciation is often second in expenses to cost of goods sold on the income statement. Companies choose the method to compute depreciation, which can markedly impact the income statement and balance sheet. When companies dispose of PPE, a gain or loss often results. Understanding gains and losses on asset sales is important as we assess performance. Also, asset write-downs (and impairments) impact companies' current financial performance *and* future profitability. We must understand these accounting effects when we read and analyze and forecast financial statements.

When PPE is acquired, it is recorded at cost on the balance sheet. This is called *capitalization*, which explains why *expenditures* for PPE are called CAPEX. The amount capitalized on the balance sheet includes all costs to put the assets into service. This includes the cost of the PPE as well as transportation, duties, tax, and necessary costs to install and test the assets.

Instead of purchasing PPE outright, companies often enter into long-term equipment leases to increase operational flexibility or to take advantage of attractive financing terms. If the lease terms convey the "risks and rewards" of ownership, the equipment is capitalized just like other tangible assets. These lease assets are included in the company's PPE even though the company does not legally own the assets. The rationale is that the company operates the assets as if it did own them. (We discuss capital leases in detail in Module 10.)

Plant and Equipment

Once capitalized, the cost of plant and equipment is recognized as expense over the period of time that the assets produce revenues (directly or indirectly) in a process called depreciation. Depreciation recognizes *using up* of the asset over its useful life. Only assets that have a useful life are depreciated—**land, for example, does not have a determinable useful life and is therefore *not* depreciated**.

To determine depreciation expense, a company makes three estimates.

1. **Useful life**—period of time over which the asset is expected to generate measurable benefits.
2. **Salvage value**—amount expected for the asset when disposed of at the end of its useful life.
3. **Depreciation method**—estimate of how the asset is used up over its useful life.

With these three estimates, the company can determine a depreciation rate that approximates how the asset is used up over its life. The company uses that rate to systematically decrease the asset's balance sheet value (called the carrying value) such that, at the end of its useful life, the asset's carrying value equals its salvage value. When the asset is sold, the difference between the sales proceeds and its book value is recorded as a gain or loss on sale in the income statement.

Companies can use any reasonable method to depreciate assets. Straight-line depreciation is the most common method in the U.S. and around the world. Other methods include accelerated methods and the units of production method. Because these methods are infrequently used or are common to only certain industries, we discuss them only briefly.

Straight-Line Method

To illustrate, consider a machine with the following details: $100,000 cost, $10,000 salvage value, and a five-year useful life. Depreciation expense is recognized evenly over the estimated useful life of the asset as follows.

Depreciation Base	Depreciation Rate
Cost − Salvage value = $100,000 − $10,000 = $90,000	1/Estimated useful life = 1/5 years = 20%

Depreciation expense per year for this asset is $18,000, computed as $90,000 × 20%. For the asset's first full year of usage, $18,000 of depreciation expense is reported in the income statement. (If an asset is purchased midyear, it is typically depreciated only for the portion of the year it is used. For example, had the asset in this illustration been purchased on May 31, the company would report $10,500 of depreciation in the first year, computed as 7/12 × $18,000, assuming the company has a December 31 year-end.) This depreciation is reflected in the company's financial statements as follows.

The accumulated depreciation (contra asset) account increases by $18,000, thus reducing net PPE by the same amount. Also, $18,000 of the asset cost is transferred from the balance sheet to the income statement as depreciation expense. At the end of the first year the asset is reported on the balance sheet as follows.

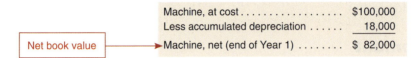

Accumulated depreciation is the sum of all depreciation expense that has been recorded to date. The asset **net book value (NBV)**, or *carrying value*, is cost less accumulated depreciation. Although the word *value* is used here, it does not refer to market value. Depreciation is a cost allocation concept (transfer of costs from the balance sheet to the income statement), not a valuation concept.

In the second year of usage, another $18,000 of depreciation expense is recorded in the income statement and the net book value of the asset on the balance sheet follows.

```
                      Machine, at cost...............  $100,000
                      Less accumulated depreciation......  36,000
Net book value  ───►  Machine, net (end of Year 2) ........  $ 64,000
```

Accumulated depreciation of $36,000 now includes the sum of the first and second years' depreciation, and the net book value of the asset is now reduced to $64,000. After the fifth year, a total of $90,000 of accumulated depreciation will be recorded ($18,000 per year × 5 years), yielding a net book value for the machine of $10,000. The net book value at the end of the machine's useful life is exactly equal to the salvage value that management estimated when the asset was acquired.

Other Depreciation Methods

Accelerated depreciation methods record more depreciation in the early years of an asset's useful life (hence the term *accelerated*) and less depreciation in later years. At the end of the asset's useful life, the balance sheet will still report a net book value equal to the asset's salvage value. The difference between straight-line and accelerated depreciation methods is not in the total amount of depreciation, but in the rate at which costs are transferred from the balance sheet to the income statement.

Units-of-production method records depreciation according to asset use. Specifically, the depreciation base is cost less salvage value, and the depreciation rate is the units produced and sold during the year compared with the total expected units to be produced and sold. For example, if a truck is driven 10,000 miles out of a total expected 100,000 miles, 10% of its depreciable cost is reflected as depreciation expense. This method is common for extractive industries including oil and gas, timber, and coal.

Modified Accelerated Cost Recovery System (MACRS), an accelerated method, is required by the U.S. IRS to calculate taxable income. We discuss this in Module 10. It is important to note that regardless of the depreciation method a company chooses *for its published financial statements*, it has no impact on taxes paid.

Research and Development Facilities and Equipment

In a prior module, we introduce R&D expense and explain that it includes costs associated with property and buildings to be used as research facilities. Importantly, **R&D facilities and equipment** are not immediately expensed. If they are *general-use* in nature (such as a general research laboratory that can be used for many types of activities), the costs are capitalized on the balance sheet and depreciated over its useful life like other depreciable assets. Only those R&D facilities and equipment that are purchased specifically for a single R&D project, and have *no alternative use*, are expensed immediately in the income statement (an unusual situation).

Companies expect R&D efforts ultimately to yield new tangible products and services. This might suggest that *all* R&D costs be capitalized (recognized as assets) on the balance sheet. After all, R&D can create future revenues like other assets including PPE.

However, with the exception of facilities and equipment that have alternative uses, R&D costs are *not* capitalized. Instead, R&D costs are expensed in the income statement as they are incurred. The rationale for this accounting treatment is threefold.

- Whether any tangible projects or services will be developed is often uncertain while the R&D is ongoing. Indeed, many R&D efforts fail to produce any benefits whatsoever.
- Even for R&D programs that look promising, the timing of future products and services is uncertain.
- Salaries for R&D personnel are no different than for other personnel whose salaries and wages are expensed when incurred.

It is generally acknowledged that R&D costs, especially development costs associated with clearly defined products for which a workable prototype has been proven, do create future benefits and have the characteristics of assets. However, the measurement uncertainty argument prevails and R&D costs are not capitalized under GAAP and, with the exception of general-use R&D PPE assets, they are expensed when incurred.

LO4 Review 6-4

On January 2, assume that one of **Home Depot**'s subsidiary companies purchases equipment that fabricates a key product part. The equipment costs $95,000, and its estimated useful life is five years, after which it is expected to be sold for $10,000.

Required
1. Compute depreciation expense for each year of the equipment's useful life using the straight-line method of depreciation.
2. Show how the HD subsidiary reports the equipment on its balance sheet at the end of the third year assuming straight-line depreciation.

Solution on p. 6-44.

PPE Assets—Sales, Impairments, and Restructuring

This section discusses gains and losses from asset sales, restructurings, and the computation and disclosure of asset impairments.

LO5 Evaluate asset sales, impairments, and restructuring activities.

Asset Sales

The gain or loss on the sale (disposition) of a tangible asset is computed as follows.

> **Gain or Loss on Asset Sale = Proceeds from Sale – Net Book Value of Asset Sold**

An asset's net book value is its acquisition cost less accumulated depreciation. When an asset is sold, its acquisition cost and related accumulated depreciation are both removed from the balance sheet, and any gain or loss is reported in income from continuing operations.

Gains and losses on asset sales can be large, and analysts must be aware that these gains and losses are usually *transitory operating* income components. Financial statements do not typically report gains and losses from tangible asset sales because, if the gain or loss is small (immaterial), companies include the item in selling, general and administrative expenses. Footnotes can sometimes be informative. To illustrate, **Macy's Inc.** provides the following footnote disclosure relating to certain real estate sales.

> **Gains on Sale of Real Estate** The Company recognized gains of $389 million in 2018 associated with sales of real estate, as compared to $544 million in 2017. 2018 included gains of $178 million related to the I. Magnin building in Union Square San Francisco. 2017 included gains of $234 million related to the Macy's Union Square location, $71 million related to the Macy's Brooklyn transaction, $47 million related to the downtown Minneapolis properties and $40 million related to the downtown Seattle Macy's location.

The various gains on sale that Macy's recognized reflect the difference between the sale proceeds and the amount at which the properties were reported on Macy's balance sheet on the date of sale, that is, their net book value (also called carrying value).

Asset Impairments

Tangible assets are reported at their net book values (original cost less accumulated depreciation). This is the case even if the market values of these assets increase subsequent to acquisition. As a result, there can be unrecognized gains hidden within the balance sheet.

On the other hand, if market values of PPE assets subsequently decrease—and the asset value is deemed to be permanently impaired—then, companies must write off the impaired cost and recognize losses on those assets. **Impairment** of PPE assets is determined by comparing the asset's net book value to the sum of the asset's *expected* future (undiscounted) cash flows. If the sum of expected cash flow is greater than net book value, there is no impairment. However, if the sum of the expected cash flow is less than net book value, the asset is deemed impaired and it is written down to its current fair value (generally, the present value of those expected cash flows). Exhibit 6.6 depicts this impairment analysis.

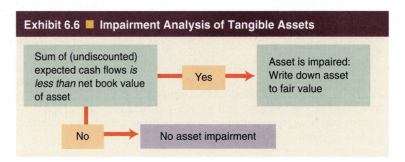

To record an impairment charge, the company reduces assets by the amount of the write-down and recognizes a loss in the income statement. To illustrate, a footnote to the 2018 Form 10-K of **Dean Foods Company** reports the following about asset impairments.

> **Asset Impairment Charges** We evaluate our finite-lived intangible and long-lived assets for impairment when circumstances indicate that the carrying value may not be recoverable. Indicators of impairment could include, among other factors, significant changes in the business environment, the planned closure of a facility, or deteriorations in operating cash flows. . . The results of our 2018 impairment analysis indicated an impairment of our property, plant, and equipment at five of our production facilities, totaling $13.7 million. The impairments were the result of declines in operating cash flows at these production facilities on both a historical and forecasted basis. These impairment charges were recorded during the year ended December 31, 2018.

As operating cash flows declined in five of their production facilities, the management of Dean Foods concluded that it was unlikely that these locations would generate enough cash flow to absorb the cost of the PPE assets. Consequently, the facilities were deemed to be impaired and the assets were written down to their fair values, resulting in an impairment expense for 2018 of $13.7 million.

IFRS Insight ■ PPE Valuation under IFRS

Like GAAP, companies reporting under IFRS must periodically assess long-lived assets for possible impairment. Unlike the two-step GAAP approach, IFRS uses a one-step approach: firms compare an asset's net book value to its current fair value (estimated as discounted expected future cash flows) to test for impairment and then reduce net book value to that fair value. Under IFRS, impairment losses can be reversed if the PPE subsequently regains its value. The PPE account is increased to the newly estimated recoverable amount, not to exceed the assets' initial cost adjusted for depreciation. GAAP prohibits such reversals.

Restructuring Costs

It is not uncommon for a company to face corporate challenges that are so great that the only way forward is to alter its organizational, operational, and financial structures. Such corporate "restructurings" are designed to turn a company around and are frequently initiated in response to poor performance, mounting debt, and shareholder pressure. A restructuring can involve eliminating business segments, selling major assets, downsizing the workforce, and reconfiguring debt. Ultimately, the goal of a restructuring is to positively impact a company's long-term financial performance. But in the short term, restructurings usually have large negative impacts on the company's income statement.

Disclosure of Restructuring Costs

Because of their magnitude, restructurings require enhanced disclosure either as a separate line item in the income statement or as a footnote. Restructuring costs typically include three components:

1. Employee severance or relocation costs.
2. Asset write-downs.
3. Other restructuring costs.

Reporting of employee severance or relocation costs. The first part, **employee severance or relocation costs**, represents accrued (estimated) costs to terminate or relocate employees as part of a restructuring program. To accrue those expenses, the company must:

- Estimate total costs of terminating or relocating selected employees; these costs might include severance pay (typically a number of weeks of pay based on the employee's tenure with the company), outplacement costs, and relocation or retraining costs for remaining employees.

- Report *total* estimated costs as an expense (and a liability) in the period the restructuring program is announced. Subsequent payments to employees reduce the restructuring accrual (the liability).

Reporting of asset write-downs. The second part of restructuring costs is **asset write-downs**, also called *write-offs* or *charge-offs*. Restructuring activities usually involve closure or relocation of manufacturing or administrative facilities. This can require the write-down of assets whose fair value is less than book value. For example, restructurings can necessitate the write-down of long-term assets (such as plant assets or goodwill) and of inventories. To determine the amount of the write-down, the company follows the approach in Exhibit 6.6. Remember that write-downs have no cash flow effects unless the write-down has tax consequences.

Reporting of other restructuring costs. The third part of restructuring costs is typically labeled "Other" and includes costs of vacating duplicative facilities, fees to terminate contracts (such as lease agreements and service contracts), and other exit costs (such as legal and asset-appraisal fees). Companies estimate and accrue these costs and reduce the restructuring liability as those costs are paid in cash.

For a company to use the term *restructuring* in the income statement and to accrue restructuring liabilities, the company is required to have a formal restructuring plan that is approved by its board of directors. Also, a company must identify the relevant employees and notify them of its plan. In each subsequent year, the company must disclose in its footnotes the original amount of the Restructuring liability (accrual), how much of that liability is settled in the current period (such as employee payments), how much of the original liability has been reversed because of original cost overestimation, any new accruals for unforeseen costs, and the current balance of the liability. This creates more transparent financial statements, which allow readers to see, in hindsight, if the initial restructuring accrual was overstated (requiring subsequent reversal) or understated (requiring subsequent additions to the restructuring accrual).

> **Business Insight | Pfizer's Restructuring**
>
> **Pfizer** explains its restructuring efforts as follows in its 2018 10-K.
>
> > We incur significant costs in connection with acquiring, integrating and restructuring businesses and in connection with our global cost-reduction/productivity initiatives. For example:
> >
> > - In connection with acquisition activity, we typically incur costs associated with executing the transactions, integrating the acquired operations (which may include expenditures for consulting and the integration of systems and processes), and restructuring the combined company (which may include charges related to employees, assets and activities that will not continue in the combined company); and
> >
> > - In connection with our cost-reduction/productivity initiatives, we typically incur costs and charges associated with site closings and other facility rationalization actions, workforce reductions and the expansion of shared services, including the development of global systems.
> >
> > All of our businesses and functions may be impacted by these actions, including sales and marketing, manufacturing and R&D, as well as groups such as information technology, shared services and corporate operations. The following table provides the components of costs associated with acquisitions and cost-reduction/productivity initiatives:
>
> | $ millions | Employee Termination Costs | Asset Impairment Charges | Exit Costs | Accrual |
> |---|---|---|---|---|
> | Balance, January 1, 2017........ | $1,547 | $ — | $ 36 | $1,583 |
> | Provision (Credit) .... | (181) | 190 | 21 | 30 |
> | Utilization and other .... | (326) | (190) | 9 | (508) |
> | Balance, December 31, 2017.... | 1,039 | — | 66 | 1,105 |
> | Provision.................... | 459 | 290 | 33 | 782 |
> | Utilization and other .... | (295) | (290) | (51) | (636) |
> | Balance, December 31, 2018.... | $1,203 | $ — | $ 49 | $1,252 |

The table reflects Pfizer's restructuring transactions for 2017 and 2018. Companies are required to disclose the beginning-year balance of the restructuring liability. Pfizer reports this in the right-most "Accrual" column ($1,105 million for fiscal 2018). Companies must also report the changes in the restructuring liability for the year, which Pfizer reports separately for the three types of restructuring costs.

During 2018, Pfizer added a total of $782 million to the liability and recorded that amount as restructuring expense in its 2018 income statement. (On the income statement, Pfizer aggregated the $782 million with additional costs relating to other acquisitions, for a total of $1,044 million). During the year, the company reduced the liability by $636 million for the payment of employee termination costs ($295 million), asset impairment charges ($290 million), and exit costs ($51 million). The ending balance of $1,252 million is reported on Pfizer's 2018 balance sheet as a liability.

Analysis of Restructuring Costs

Restructuring costs are typically large and, as such, greatly affect reported profits. Our analysis must consider whether these costs are associated with the accounting period in which they are recognized. Following are some guidelines relating to the components of restructuring costs.

Analyzing employee severance or relocation costs and other costs. Companies are allowed to record costs relating to employee separation or relocation that are *incremental* and that do not benefit future periods. Similarly, other accrued costs must be related to the restructuring and not to expenses that would otherwise have been incurred in the future. Thus, accrual of these costs is treated like other liability accruals. We must, however, be aware of over- or understated costs and their effect on current and future profitability. Disclosure rules require a reconciliation of this restructuring accrual in future years (see the preceding Business Insight on Pfizer's restructuring). A reconciliation reveals either overstatements or understatements: overstatements are followed by a reversal of the restructuring liability, and understatements are followed by further accruals. Should a company develop a reputation for recurring reversals or understatements, its management loses credibility.

Research Insight — Restructuring Costs and Managerial Incentives

Research has investigated the circumstances and effects of restructuring costs. Some research finds that stock prices increase when a company announces a restructuring as if the market appreciates the company's candor. Research also finds that many companies that reduce income through restructuring costs later reverse a portion of those costs, resulting in a substantial income boost for the period of reversal. These reversals often occur when the company would have otherwise reported an earnings decline. Whether or not the market responds favorably to trimming the fat or simply disregards restructuring costs as transitory and, thus, as uninformative, managers have incentives to characterize such income-decreasing items as "one-time" on the income statement and routinely exclude such charges in non-GAAP, pro forma disclosures. These incentives often derive from contracts such as debt covenants and managerial bonus plans.

Analyzing asset write-downs. Asset write-downs accelerate (or catch up) the depreciation process to reflect asset impairment. Impairment implies the loss of cash-generating capability and, likely, occurs over several years. Thus, prior periods' profits were arguably not as high as reported, and the current period's profit is not as low. This measurement error is difficult to estimate and, thus, many analysts do not adjust balance sheets and income statements for write-downs. At a minimum, however, we must recognize the qualitative implications of restructuring costs for the profitability of recent prior periods and the current period.

Managerial Decision — You Are the Financial Analyst

You are analyzing the 10-K of a company that reports a large restructuring expense, involving employee severance and asset write-downs. How do you interpret and treat this cost in your analysis of the company's current and future profitability? [Answer, p. 6-29]

LO5 Review 6-5

Part 1. Refer to information in Review 6-4 and to its solution to answer the following requirements.

Required

a. Assume that the HD subsidiary uses the straight-line method of depreciation and estimates that, at the end of the third year, the equipment will generate $40,000 in cash flow over its remaining life and that it has a current fair value of $36,000. Is the equipment impaired? If so, what is the effect on the HD subsidiary financial statements?
b. Instead of the facts in part *a*, assume that, at the end of the third year, the HD subsidiary sells the equipment for $50,000 cash. What amount of gain or loss does the HD subsidiary report from this sale?

Part 2. The Coca-Cola Company reports the following reconciliation of its restructuring liability for 2018.

$ millions	Severance Pay and Benefits	Outside Services	Other Direct Costs	Total
Accrued balance as of December 31, 2017...	$190	$ 1	$ 15	$206
2018				
Costs incurred	$164	$92	$252	$508
Payments	(209)	(83)	(211)	(503)
Noncash and exchange	(69)	—	(52)	(121)
Accrued balance as of December 31, 2018...	$ 76	$10	$ 4	$ 90

Required

a. What amount of expense did Coca-Cola report in its income statement as restructuring expense in 2018?
b. What amount of restructuring liability did Coca-Cola report on its balance sheet for 2018?

Solution on p. 6-44.

PPE Assets—Analysis Tools

LO6 Analyze tangible assets and related activities.

Home Depot reports $22,375 million of property and equipment, net of accumulated depreciation, on its balance sheet at February 3, 2019. Footnote disclosures reveal the following.

Net Property and Equipment The components of net property and equipment follow.

in millions	February 3, 2019	January 28, 2018
Land.	$ 8,363	$ 8,352
Buildings.	18,199	18,073
Furniture, fixtures, and equipment	12,460	11,506
Leasehold improvements	1,705	1,637
Construction in process	820	538
Capital leases.	1,392	1,308
Property and equipment, at cost.	42,939	41,414
Less accumulated depreciation and capital lease amortization	20,564	19,339
Net property and equipment.	$22,375	$22,075

Depreciation and capital lease amortization expense, including depreciation expense included in cost of sales, follows.

For Fiscal Year Ended, in millions	Feb. 3, 2019 (Fiscal 2018)	Jan. 28, 2018 (Fiscal 2017)	Jan. 29, 2017 (Fiscal 2016)
Depreciation and capital lease amortization expense	$2,076	$1,983	$1,899

Property and Equipment, including Capitalized Lease Assets Building, furniture, fixtures, and equipment are recorded at cost and depreciated using the straight-line method over their estimated useful lives. Leaseholder improvements are amortized using the straight-line method over the original term of the lease or the useful life of the improvement, whichever is shorter. The estimated useful lives of our property and equipment follow.

	Life
Buildings.	5–45 years
Furniture, fixtures and equipment.	2–20 years
Leasehold improvements	5–45 years

We can use these data to compute key ratios to assess the productivity of Home Depot's PPE and its assets' relative age.

PPE Turnover

A crucial issue in analyzing PPE is determining their productivity (utilization). For example, what level of plant assets is necessary to generate a dollar of revenues? How capital intensive are the company and its competitors? To address these and similar questions, we use **PPE turnover**, defined as follows.

$$\text{PPE Turnover (PPET)} = \text{Sales/Average PPE, net}$$

To calculate PPE turnover for Home Depot, we must adjust Sales for the 53rd week for the fiscal year ended February 3, 2019, as discussed earlier in the module: $108,203 × 52/53 = $106,161. Home Depot's PPE turnover is 4.8 ($106,161 million/[($22,375 million + $22,075 million)/2]).

Higher PPE turnover is preferable to lower. A higher PPE turnover implies a lower capital investment for a given level of sales. Higher turnover, therefore, increases profitability because the company avoids asset carrying costs and because the freed-up assets can generate operating cash flow.

PPE turnover is lower for capital-intensive manufacturing companies than it is for companies in service or knowledge-based industries. To this point, consider the following chart of PPE turnover for selected industries. (The term *turnover* is a bit of a misnomer for PPE. Intuitively we can understand how accounts receivable, inventory, and accounts payable "turn over" as customers pay, and the company sells inventory and pays suppliers. But for PPE, there is no equivalent concept and perhaps the ratio would be better named PPE productivity. Nonetheless, the label PPE turnover is widely used.)

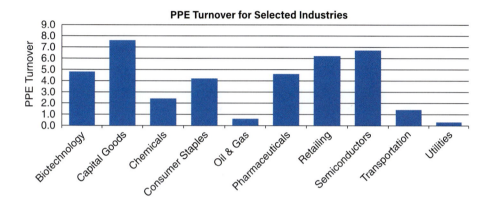

There is wide variability in PPE turnover rate across industries. Capital intensive industries such as utilities, transportation, and oil & gas report relatively low turnover rates, reflecting large levels of capital investment required to compete in those areas.

PPE Useful Life

Home Depot reports that the useful lives of its depreciable assets range from two years for furniture, fixtures and equipment to 45 years for buildings and leasehold improvements. The longer an asset's useful life, the lower the annual depreciation expense reported in the income statement and the higher the income each year. It might be of interest, therefore, to know whether a company's useful life estimates are more conservative or more aggressive than its competitors.

If we assume straight-line (SL) depreciation (which is consistent with the company's policy) and zero salvage value, we can estimate the average useful life for depreciable assets as follows.

> **Average useful life = Average depreciable asset cost / Depreciation expense**

We compute depreciable assets for 2018, by excluding two items from gross PPE of $42,939.

- Land of $8,363 million, which is never depreciated.
- Construction-in-progress of $820 million, which is not depreciated until the assets under construction are completed and placed into service, which is when the company begins to use the assets.

Depreciable assets for 2018 are, therefore, $33,756 million ($42,939 million − $8,363 million − $820 million), and for 2017 are $32,524 million. The footnote disclosures reveal that the reported amount of $2,076 million of depreciation and amortization expense includes depreciation of the owned PPE assets and amortization of the leased PPE assets (capital lease assets), which are treated like purchased PPE assets for accounting purposes.

This means the average useful life for 2018 is

$$\text{Average useful life for 2018} = \frac{(\$33{,}756 + \$32{,}524)/2}{\$2{,}076} = 16 \text{ years}$$

PPE Percent Used Up

We can also estimate the proportion of a company's depreciable assets that have already been transferred to the income statement. This ratio reflects the percent of depreciable assets that are no longer productive and is computed as follows.

> **Percent used up = Accumulated depreciation / Average depreciable asset cost**

Home Depot's assets are 62% used up, computed as $20,564 million/([$33,756 million + $32,524 million]/2]). If a company replaced all of its assets evenly each year, the percent used up ratio would be 50%. Home Depot's depreciable assets are slightly older than this benchmark. Knowing the degree to which a company's assets are used up is of interest in forecasting future cash flows. If, for example, depreciable assets are 80% used up, we might anticipate a higher level of capital expenditures to replace aging assets in the near future. We also expect that older assets are less efficient and will incur higher maintenance costs.

Managerial Decision ■ You Are the Division Manager

You are the manager for a main operating division of your company. You are concerned that a declining PPE turnover is adversely affecting your division's return on net operating assets. What specific actions can you take to increase PPE turnover? [Answer, p. 6-29]

Review 6-6 LO6

Lowe's Companies Inc. reports the following selected financial data for 2019, 2018, and 2017.

$ millions	2019	2018	2017
Revenue.................................	$71,309	$68,619	$65,017
Depreciation and amortization	1,454	1,540	1,590
Gross property, plant, and equipment	35,863	36,940	36,918
Accumulated depreciation	(17,431)	(17,219)	(16,969)
Net property, plant and equipment	18,432	19,721	19,949
Footnote data			
Land.....................................	7,196	7,414	7,329
Buildings.................................	18,052	18,521	18,147
Machinery...............................	10,090	10,475	10,978
Construction in progress..................	525	530	464

Required

Compute the following measures for 2019 and 2018. (For simplicity, assume that the entire amortization expense relates to property, plant and equipment assets.)
1. PPE turnover.
2. Average useful life.
3. Percent used up.

Solution on p. 6-44.

Global Accounting

Both GAAP and IFRS account similarly for operating assets. Although similarities in accounting dwarf any differences, we highlight some of the more notable differences.

Inventory There are two notable differences in accounting for inventory.
1. IFRS does not permit use of the LIFO method.
2. IFRS permits companies to reverse inventory write-downs; GAAP does not. This means that if markets recover and inventory previously "impaired" regains some or all of its value, it can be

revalued upwards. IFRS notes disclose this revaluation, if material, which permits us to recompute inventory and cost of sales amounts that are comparable to GAAP.

Property, plant, and equipment In accounting for tangible assets, four notable differences deserve mention.

1. GAAP requires the total cost of a tangible asset to be capitalized and depreciated over its useful life. Under IFRS, tangible assets are disaggregated into individual components and then each component is separately depreciated over its useful life. Thus, assets with components with vastly different useful lives can yield IFRS depreciation expense that is markedly different from that computed using GAAP.
2. Property, plant and equipment can be revalued upward to fair market value under IFRS. The latter will cause IFRS book values of PPE to be higher. Few companies have opted to revalue assets upwards but in some industries, such as real estate, the practice is common.
3. U.S. GAAP applies a two-step approach for determining impairments. Step 1: compare book value to *undiscounted* expected future cash flows; and Step 2: if book value is higher, measure impairment using *discounted* expected future cash flows. IFRS uses *discounted* expected future cash flows for both steps, which means IFRS uses one step. This results in more asset impairments under IFRS.
4. IFRS fair-value impairments for tangible assets can be reversed; that is, written back up after being written down. The notes to PPE articulate such reversals.

Research and Development All R&D costs are expensed under GAAP whereas IFRS allows development costs (but not research costs) to be capitalized as an intangible asset if all of the following six criteria are met.

- It is technically feasible to complete the asset.
- The company intends to complete the asset and use or sell it.
- The company is able to use or sell the asset.
- The company can use the asset to create economic benefits or there is a profitable market for the asset.
- The company has adequate resources to complete the asset.
- Costs related to the asset can be reliably measured.

For some companies and some industries these intangible assets are significant and the IFRS financial statements can be markedly different.

Restructuring There are two differences worth noting.

1. Under IFRS, restructuring expense is recognized when there is a plan for the restructuring and if the affected employees expect the plan to be implemented. Under GAAP, restructuring expense can be recognized earlier because the trigger is board approval of a plan.
2. Consistent with other IFRS accruals, a restructuring provision is recorded at its best estimate. This is usually the expected value or, in the case of a range of possible outcomes that are equally likely, the provision is recorded at the *midpoint* of the range. The GAAP estimate is at the most-likely outcome; and if there is a range of possible outcomes, the provision is recorded as the *minimum* amount of the range.

Guidance Answers

You Are the Operations Manager

Pg. 6-17 Companies need inventories to avoid lost sales opportunities; however, there are several ways to minimize inventory needs. (1) We can reduce product costs by improving product design to eliminate costly features that customers don't value. (2) We can use more cost-efficient suppliers; possibly producing in lower wage-rate parts of the world. (3) We can reduce raw material inventories with just-in-time delivery from suppliers. (4) We can eliminate production bottlenecks that increase work-in-process inventories. (5) We can manufacture for orders rather than for estimated demand to reduce finished goods inventories. (6) We can improve warehousing and distribution to reduce duplicate inventories. (7) We can monitor product sales and adjust product mix as demand changes to reduce finished goods inventories.

You Are the Financial Analyst

Pg. 6-24 Typically, restructuring charges have three components: severance costs, other restructuring-related expenses, and asset write-downs (including inventories, PPE, intangible assets, and goodwill). Write-downs occur when an asset's ability to generate cash flow declines and this decline reduces the asset's fair value below its book value (as reported on the balance sheet). Arguably, this decline in cash flow generating ability did not occur solely in the current year. Most likely the decline developed over several periods. It is not uncommon for companies to delay loss recognition, such as write-downs of assets. Thus, prior period income is, arguably, overstated and the current period income is understated. Turning to severance and other costs, GAAP permits restructuring expense to include only those costs that are *incremental* and will *not* benefit future periods. Like other accruals, restructuring might be over- or understated. In future periods, the company reports actual restructuring costs incurred, which will provide insight into the adequacy of the accrual in the earlier period.

You Are the Division Manager

Pg. 6-27 PPE is a difficult asset to reduce. Because companies need long-term operating assets, managers usually try to maximize throughput to reduce unit costs. Also, many companies form alliances to share administrative, production, logistics, customer service, IT, and other functions. These alliances take many forms (such as joint ventures) and are designed to spread ownership of assets among many users. The goal is to identify underutilized assets and to increase capacity utilization. Another solution might be to reconfigure the value chain from raw material to end user. Examples include the sharing of IT, or manufacturing facilities, outsourcing of production or administration such as customer service centers, and the use of special-purpose entities for asset securitization.

Questions

Q6-1. Why do relatively stable inventory costs across periods reduce the importance of management's choice of an inventory costing method?

Q6-2. Explain why using the FIFO inventory costing method will increase gross profit during periods of rising inventory costs.

Q6-3. If inventory costs are rising, which inventory costing method—first-in, first-out; last-in, first-out; or average cost—yields the (a) lowest ending inventory? (b) lowest net income? (c) largest ending inventory? (d) largest net income? (e) greatest cash flow, assuming the same method is used for tax purposes?

Q6-4. Even though it may not reflect their physical flow of goods, why might companies adopt last-in, first-out inventory costing in periods when costs are consistently rising?

Q6-5. In a recent annual report, Kaiser Aluminum Corporation made the following statement in reference to its inventories: "The Company recorded pretax charges of approximately $19.4 million because of a reduction in the carrying values of its inventories caused principally by prevailing lower prices for alumina, primary aluminum, and fabricated products." What basic accounting principle caused Kaiser Aluminum to record this $19.4 million pretax charge? Briefly describe the rationale for this principle.

Kaiser Aluminum Corporation (KALU)

Q6-6. What does the cash conversion cycle measure?

Q6-7. How might a company affect its depreciation expense computation by selecting useful life and salvage value?

Q6-8. What is the benefit of accelerated depreciation for income tax purposes when the total depreciation taken over the asset's life is identical under any method of depreciation?

Q6-9. What factors determine the gain or loss on the sale of a PPE asset?

Q6-10 What three metrics comprise the cash conversion cycle? How could companies manage each of the three components to improve CCC?

Q6-11 Explain the concept of lower of cost or market. What benefit does the LCM rule create for financial statement users?

Q6-12. Identify the three typical categories of restructuring costs and their effects on the balance sheet and the income statement.

Mini Exercises

M6-13. Computing Cost of Goods Sold and Ending Inventory Under FIFO, LIFO, and Average Cost **LO1**
Assume that Madden Company reports the following initial balance and subsequent purchase of inventory.

Inventory balance at beginning of year.	1,300 units @ $150 each	$195,000
Inventory purchased during the year	1,700 units @ $180 each	306,000
Cost of goods available for sale during the year . . .	3,000 units	$501,000

Assume that 2,000 units are sold during the year. Compute the cost of goods sold for the year and the inventory on the year-end balance sheet under the following inventory costing methods.

a. FIFO
b. LIFO
c. Average Cost

M6-14. Computing Cost of Goods Sold and Ending Inventory Under FIFO, LIFO, and Average Cost **LO1**
Wong Corporation reports the following beginning inventory and inventory purchases.

Inventory balance at beginning of year.	400 units @ $12 each	$ 4,800
Inventory purchased during the year	700 units @ $14 each	9,800
Cost of goods available for sale during the year . . .	1,100 units	$14,600

Wong sells 600 of its inventory units during the year. Compute the cost of goods sold for the year and the inventory on the year-end balance sheet under the following inventory costing methods.

a. FIFO
b. LIFO
c. Average Cost

M6-15. Computing and Evaluating Inventory Turnover for Two Companies **LO3**
PriceSmart and **Nordstrom** report the following information in their respective 10-K reports relating to their two most recent fiscal years.

PriceSmart (PSMT)
JW Nordstrom (JWN)

	PriceSmart ($ thousands)			Nordstrom ($ millions)		
	Sales	Cost of Goods Sold	Inventories	Sales	Cost of Goods Sold	Inventories
2018	$3,053,754	$2,610,111	$321,025	$15,480	$10,155	$1,978
2017	2,910,062	2,487,146	310,946	15,137	9,890	2,027

a. Compute the 2018 inventory turnover for each of these two retailers.
b. Discuss any difference we observe in inventory turnover between these two companies. Does the difference confirm our expectations given their respective business models? Explain. (*Hint*: Nordstrom is a higher-end retailer and PriceSmart operates no-frills, warehouse stores.)
c. Describe ways that a retailer can improve its inventory turnover.

M6-16. Computing Depreciation **LO4**
A delivery van costing $37,000 is expected to have a $2,900 salvage value at the end of its useful life of five years. Assume that the truck was purchased on January 1. Compute the depreciation expense for the first two calendar years under the straight-line depreciation method.

LO4 M6-17. Computing Depreciation for Partial Years

A company with a calendar year-end purchases a machine costing $129,000 on July 1, 2020. The machine is expected to be obsolete after five years (60 months) and, thereafter, no longer useful to the company. The estimated salvage value is $6,000. The company's depreciation policy is to record depreciation for the portion of the year that the asset is in service. Compute depreciation expense for both 2020 and 2021 under the straight-line depreciation method.

LO6 M6-18. Computing and Comparing PPE Turnover for Two Companies

Texas Instruments Inc. and Intel Corporation report the following information.

$ millions	Intel Corporation		Texas Instruments	
	Sales	Plant, Property and Equipment, net	Sales	Plant, Property and Equipment, net
2018	$70,848	$48,976	$15,784	$3,183
2017	62,761	41,109	14,961	2,664

a. Compute the 2018 PPE turnover for both companies. Comment on any difference observed.
b. Discuss ways in which high-tech manufacturing companies like these can increase their PPE turnover.

LO3 M6-19. Computing Cash Conversion Cycle for Two Years

Winnebago Industries has the following metrics for 2018 and 2017.

Amounts in days	2018	2017
Days sales outstanding	26.2	22.5
Days inventory outstanding	35.9	36.5
Days payable outstanding	17.0	17.0

Compute the cash conversion cycle for both years. What accounts for the change between the years?

LO3 M6-20. Using Inventory Analysis Tools

AutoZone and O'Reilly are two competitors in the retail automotive parts industry.

$ thousands	AutoZone	O'Reilly
Average 2018 Inventory	$ 3,912,878	$3,101,572
2018 Sales	11,221,077	9,536,428
2018 Cost of goods sold	5,247,331	4,496,462
Average 2017 Inventory	$ 3,757,001	$2,894,388
2017 Sales	10,888,676	8,977,726
2017 Cost of goods sold	5,149,056	4,257,043

a. Use the information above to compute the companies' gross profit margin and days inventory outstanding for both years.
b. Based on these two ratios, which company is more profitable selling its inventory? How has that changed from 2017 to 2018?
c. Based on these two ratios, which company is more efficient with its inventory? How has that changed from 2017 to 2018?

LO5 M6-21. Asset Impairment

Winnebago Industries recorded an impairment loss of $462,000 on its corporate plane during a recent year. Assume that the plane originally cost the company $2,350,000 and had accumulated depreciation of $1,598,000 at the time of the impairment charge.

a. Why did the company record an impairment loss on the plane?
b. Explain how the company determined the amount of the impairment loss.
c. What was the plane's fair value at the end of the year?

Exercises

E6-22. Analyzing Inventory Levels and Write-downs

Quarterly data for **Nvidia Inc.** for the most recent 10 quarters follows ($ millions).

LO2, 3
Nvidia (NVDA)

Fiscal Year	Fiscal Quarter	Total Assets	Cost of Goods Sold	Inventories	Revenue
2016.......	4	$ 9,841	$ 824	$ 794	$2,173
2017.......	1	9,410	740	821	1,937
2017.......	2	9,402	879	855	2,230
2017.......	3	9,830	1,018	857	2,636
2017.......	4	11,241	1,056	796	2,911
2018.......	1	11,460	1,082	797	3,207
2018.......	2	12,882	1,089	1,090	3,123
2018.......	3	13,657	1,178	1,417	3,181
2018.......	4	13,292	899	1,575	2,205
2019.......	1	14,021	833	1,426	2,220

On November 16, 2018, after Nvidia's third quarter (Q3) 2018 earnings release, ExtremeTech reported:

> - Nvidia stocks plummeted on Friday after the company released its earnings report. The company has, as of this writing, lost about 16 percent of its previous valuation. But what happens to a company after it reports earnings doesn't always make sense from a technical perspective.
> - Nvidia's stock has taken a hammering today for basically having a weak Q3. Revenue in Nvidia's fiscal year Q3 2019 (Nvidia's calendar runs a year ahead of the actual physical date) was up significantly compared with the same time last year, but flat in Q3 compared with Q2. Nvidia's margin slipped a tiny bit but it's the company's inventory build that has analysts worried. Nvidia is currently holding $1.417B in product, up from $796M in January 2018 and $1.09B in Q2 2018. Nvidia blames this problem entirely on the decline of the cryptography market and has stated it will ship no new midrange cards to market through Q4 to give the channel time to work through the excess inventory build-up. Source: https://www.extremetech.com/gaming/280800-nvidia-stock-plummets-on-high-inventory-fears

a. Calculate the inventory as a percent of total assets. Is the "inventory build" referred to by ExtremeTech significant in common-size terms?
b. Determine the gross profit margin for each quarter. Did the margin slip a "tiny bit" in Q3 2018?
c. Have margins and inventory levels improved in the quarters subsequent to the ExtremeTech report?

E6-23. Applying and Analyzing Inventory Costing Methods

At the beginning of the current period, Chen carried 1,000 units of its product with a unit cost of $32. A summary of purchases during the current period follows. Also, during the current period, Chen sold 2,800 units.

LO1

	Units	Unit Cost	Cost
Beginning Inventory.........	1,000	$32	$32,000
Purchases: #1..............	1,800	34	61,200
#2	800	38	30,400
#3	1,200	41	49,200

a. Assume that Chen uses the first-in, first-out method. Compute both cost of goods sold for the current period and the ending inventory balance. Use the financial statement effects template to record cost of goods sold for the period.
b. Assume that Chen uses the last-in, first-out method. Compute both cost of goods sold for the current period and the ending inventory balance.
c. Assume that Chen uses the average cost method. Compute both cost of goods sold for the current period and the ending inventory balance.

d. Which of these three inventory costing methods would we choose to:
1. Reflect what is probably the physical flow of goods? Explain.
2. Minimize income taxes for the period? Explain.
3. Report the largest amount of income for the period? Explain.

LO2

Illinois Tool Works (ITW)

E6-24. Analyzing an Inventory Footnote Disclosure

Illinois Tool Works reports the following footnote in its 10-K report. The company reports its inventories using the LIFO inventory costing method.

December 31 ($ millions)	2018	2017
Raw material..........................	$ 523	$ 465
Work-in-process.....................	161	141
Finished goods.......................	731	703
LIFO reserve..........................	(97)	(89)
Total inventories.....................	$1,318	$1,220

a. What is the balance in inventories reported on the 2018 balance sheet?
b. What would the 2018 balance sheet have reported for inventories had the company used FIFO inventory costing?
c. What cumulative effect has the company's choice of LIFO over FIFO had on its pretax income as of year-end 2018? Explain.
d. Assume the company has a 35% income tax rate for years prior to 2017 and a 21% rate thereafter. ITW's LIFO reserve was $86 million at December 31, 2016. As of the 2018 year-end, how much has the company saved in taxes by choosing the LIFO over FIFO method for costing inventory? Has the use of LIFO increased or decreased the company's cumulative taxes paid?
e. What effect has the use of LIFO inventory costing had on the company's pretax income and tax expense for 2018 only (assume a 21% income tax rate)?

LO2, 3

Under Armour, Inc (UAA)

E6-25. Quantifying the Effect of Inventory Write-offs on Ratios

Under Armour reported the following in its 2018 Form 10-K. Under Armour's income statement reported 2018 cost of goods sold of $2,852,714 thousand. Its balance sheet reported inventories of $1,019,496 thousand in 2018 and $1,158,548 thousand in 2017.

Restructuring Plans As previously announced, our Board of Directors approved restructuring plans designed to more closely align our financial resources with the critical priorities of our business and optimize operations. We recognized approximately $203.9 million of pre-tax charges in connection with our restructuring plan. The costs incurred during the year ended December 31, 2018, include the following:

Costs recorded in cost of goods sold ($ thousands)	2018
Inventory write-offs...	$20,801
Total cost recorded in cost of goods sold............	$20,801

a. Explain why Under Armour recorded an inventory write-off.
b. What effect did the 2018 inventory write-off have on pretax income during 2018?
c. Calculate inventory turnover and days inventory outstanding for 2018.
d. If Under Armour had not written off inventory in 2018, what would it have reported for cost of goods sold in 2018? What would have been the inventory balances in 2018 and 2017?
e. Use the adjusted cost of goods sold and inventory balances to recalculate inventory turnover and days inventory outstanding. Did the inventory write-off make a significant difference?

LO2

Deere & Co. (DE)

E6-26. Analyzing an Inventory Footnote Disclosure

The inventory footnote from **Deere & Company**'s 2018 10-K follows.

Inventories A majority of inventory owned by Deere & Company and its U.S. equipment subsidiaries are valued at cost, on the "last-in, first-out" (LIFO) basis. Remaining inventories are

continued

continued from previous page

generally valued at the lower of cost, on the "first-in, first-out" (FIFO) basis, or net realizable value. The value of gross inventories on the LIFO basis at October 28, 2018, and October 29, 2017, represented 54 percent and 61 percent, respectively, of worldwide gross inventories at FIFO value. If all inventories had been valued on a FIFO basis, estimated inventories by major classification at October 28, 2018, and October 29, 2017, in millions of dollars would have been as follows:

$ millions	2018	2017
Raw materials and supplies	$2,233	$1,688
Work-in-process	776	495
Finished goods and parts	4,777	3,182
Total FIFO value	7,786	5,365
Less adjustment to LIFO value	1,637	1,461
Inventories	$6,149	$3,904

This footnote reveals that not all of Deere's inventories are reported using the same inventory costing method (companies can use different inventory costing methods for different inventory pools).

a. What amount does Deere report for inventories on its 2018 balance sheet?
b. What would Deere have reported as inventories on its 2018 balance sheet had the company used FIFO inventory costing for all of its inventories?
c. What cumulative effect has the use of LIFO inventory costing had, as of year-end 2018, on Deere's pretax income compared with the pretax income it would have reported had it used FIFO inventory costing for all of its inventories? Explain.
d. Assuming an average (cumulative) income tax rate of 30%, by what cumulative dollar amount has Deere's tax expense been affected by use of LIFO inventory costing as of year-end 2018? Has the use of LIFO inventory costing increased or decreased Deere's cumulative tax expense?
e. What effect has the use of LIFO inventory costing had on Deere's pretax income and tax expense for 2018 only (assume a 21% income tax rate)?

E6-27. Analyzing Inventory from Data Visualization

LO3
Amazon Inc. (AMZN)

The following data visualization depicts quarterly revenue, cost of goods sold, and gross profit margin for Amazon from Q2 2010 through Q1 2019.

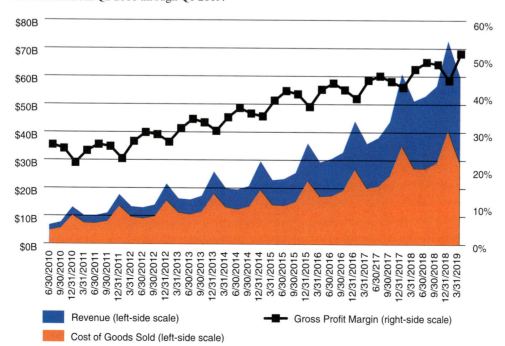

a. What trend do we observe in all three metrics from 2010 to 2019?
b. When does revenue spike each year? Why?
c. What pattern do we observe between revenue and gross margin? Explain.

LO4, 5

E6-28. Computing Depreciation, Net Book Value, and Gain or Loss on Asset Sale
Zimmer Company owns an executive plane that originally cost $1,280,000. It has recorded straight-line depreciation on the plane for seven full years, calculated assuming a $160,000 expected salvage value at the end of its estimated 10-year useful life. Zimmer disposes of the plane at the end of the seventh year.

a. At the disposal date, what is the (1) cumulative depreciation expense and (2) net book value of the plane?
b. How much gain or loss is reported at disposal if the sales price is:
   1. A cash amount equal to the plane's net book value.
   2. $285,000 cash.
   3. $700,000 cash.

LO3

E6-29. Analyzing Inventory with Data Visualization
Consider the following inventory graphics for **Walmart** and **Target**, two large US retailers who compete head to head. The graphs depict quarterly revenue, cost of goods sold, and gross profit margin from 2010 through 2019.

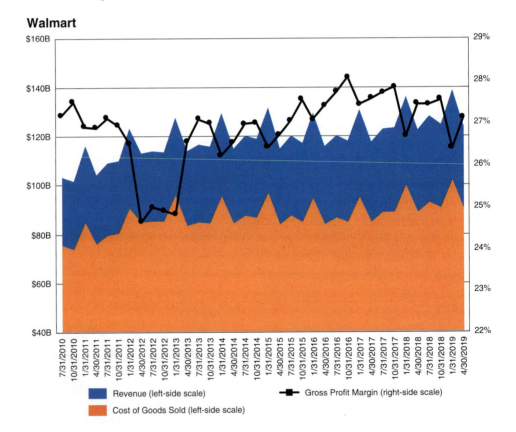

Target

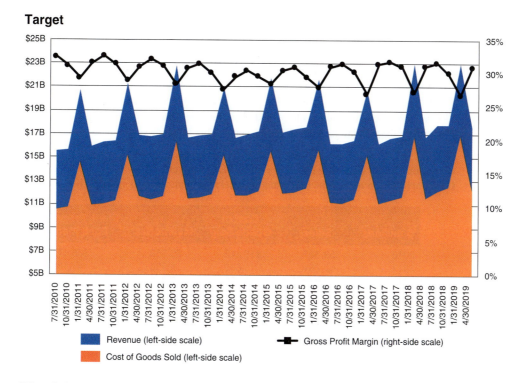

What similarities and differences do we see as compared to the Amazon graphic in E6-27?

E6-30. Computing Depreciation, Net Book Value, and Gain or Loss on Asset Sale **LO5**
Lynch Company owns and operates a delivery van that originally cost $46,400. Lynch has recorded straight-line depreciation on the van for four years, calculated assuming a $5,000 expected salvage value at the end of its estimated six-year useful life. Depreciation was last recorded at the end of the fourth year, at which time Lynch disposed of this van.

a. Compute the net book value of the van on the disposal date.
b. Compute the gain or loss on sale of the van if the disposal proceeds are:
   1. A cash amount equal to the van's net book value.
   2. $21,000 cash.
   3. $17,000 cash.

E6-31. Estimating Useful Life and Percent Used Up **LO6**
The property and equipment footnote from Tesla follows. Assume that 25% of the amount classified as "Land and buildings" pertains to the cost of the Land.

Tesla Inc. (TSLA)

Property, Plant and Equipment Our property, plant and equipment, net, consists of the following (in thousands):

December 31	2018	2017
Machinery, equipment, vehicles and office furniture	$ 6,328,966	$ 4,251,711
Tooling	1,397,514	1,255,952
Leaseholder improvements	960,971	789,751
Land and buildings	4,047,006	2,517,247
Computer equipment, hardware and software	487,421	395,067
Construction in progress	807,297	2,541,588
	14,029,175	11,751,316
Less: Accumulated depreciation	(2,699,098)	(1,723,794)
Total	$11,330,077	$10,027,522

continued

continued from previous page

> Depreciation expense during the years ended December 31, 2018, 2017, and 2016 was $1.11 billion, $769.3 million, and $477.3 million, respectively.

a. Compute the average useful life of Tesla's depreciable assets at year-end 2018.
b. Estimate the percent used up of Tesla's depreciable assets at year-end 2018. How do we interpret this figure?

LO3, 6
Intel Corp. (INTC)

E6-32. Computing and Evaluating Inventory and PPE Turnovers
Intel Corporation reports the following financial statement amounts in its 10-K reports.

$ millions	Sales	Cost of Goods Sold	Inventories	Plant, Property and Equipment, Net
2016	$59,387	$15,313	$5,553	$36,171
2017	62,761	15,685	6,983	41,109
2018	70,848	18,226	7,253	48,976

a. Compute the inventory and PPE turnover ratios for both 2017 and 2018.
b. What changes are evident in the turnover rates of Intel for these years? Discuss ways in which a company such as Intel can improve inventory and PPE turnover ratios.

LO4, 5

E6-33. Computing and Assessing Plant Asset Impairment
On July 1, Arcola Company purchases equipment for $330,000. The equipment has an estimated useful life of 10 years and expected salvage value of $40,000. The company uses straight-line depreciation. Four years later, economic factors cause the fair value of the equipment to decline to $160,000. On this date, Arcola examines the equipment for impairment and estimates $185,000 in undiscounted expected cash inflows from this equipment.

a. Compute the annual depreciation expense relating to this equipment.
b. Compute the equipment's net book value at the end of the fourth year.
c. Apply the test of impairment to this equipment as of the end of the fourth year. Is the equipment impaired? Show supporting computations.
d. If the equipment is impaired at the end of the fourth year, compute the impairment loss.

LO6
J.M. Smucker Co. (SJM)

E6-34. Computing Asset Related Ratios
J.M. Smucker included the following information in its April 2019 10-K.

$ millions	Apr. 30, 2019	Apr. 30, 2018
Sales	$7,838.0	
Depreciation expense	206.0	
Land	$ 122.1	$ 120.1
Buildings and fixtures	903.2	812.6
Machinery and equipment	2,185.0	2,111.5
Construction in progress	321.8	212.1
Gross property, plant, and equipment	3,532.1	3,256.3
Accumulated depreciation	(1,619.7)	(1,527.2)
Total property, plant, and equipment	$1,912.4	$1,729.1

Required
a. Compute PPE turnover for fiscal year ended April 30, 2019.
b. Compute the average useful life of depreciable assets at April 30, 2019.
c. Compute the percentage used up of the PPE at April 30, 2019.

E6-35. Evaluating Grocery Stores Using Efficiency Ratios

Below are data for three publicly traded grocery stores that range in size from local (**Village Super Markets**) to regional (**Publix**) to national (**Kroger**). Use the ratios below to answer the requirements. Assume that the companies sell roughly the same mix of products and face about the same inventory costs.

LO3
Publix Super Markets Inc. (PUSH)
Kroger Co. (KR)
Village Super Market (VLGEA)

Fiscal 2018	Publix	Kroger	Village Super Market
Gross profit margin %.............	29.6%	21.7%	27.2%
Number of stores at year-end...........	1,211	2,764	30
Sales ($ per square foot)............	$639	$677	$1,165
Sales per store ($ millions)...........	$ 30	$ 44	$ 54
Average store size (thousand square feet)...	47	65	46
COGS (per square foot).............	$450	$530	$ 848
Days inventory outstanding	26.5	25.7	12.6

Required
a. On average, which company has the freshest food?
b. Which company is least efficient with its space?
c. Which company has the lowest prices?
d. Which company is busiest?
e. Which company has the smallest stores?

Problems

P6-36. Evaluating Turnover and Nontraditional Efficiency Ratios Across Industries

The following information is taken from publicly traded retailers. The data come from the balance sheet, income statement, and Item 2 on the companies' Form 10-K filings. Use the information to answer the requirements.

LO3

Autozone (AZO)
Costco (COST)
Home Depot (HD)
Lowe's (LOW)
O'Reilly (ORLY)
Walmart (WMT)

$ millions	Revenue	COGS	Average Inventory	Retail SQ Footage (000s)	# of Stores
Autozone......	$ 11,221	$ 4,902	$ 3,913	41,066	6,202
Costco........	141,576	121,715	10,437	110,700	762
Home Depot ...	108,203	71,043	13,337	237,700	2,287
Lowe's........	71,309	48,396	11,977	209,000	2,015
O'Reilly	9,536	4,237	3,102	38,455	5,219
Walmart.......	511,729	374,623	44,026	1,129,000	11,361

Required
a. Compute the days inventory outstanding (DIO) for each company.
b. Compute the gross profit margin for each company.
c. Compare the DIO and gross profit margin for each of the three combinations of competitors. What do we observe? How are the two ratios related?
d. Compute the following two nontraditional efficiency metrics: Revenue per square foot and Revenue per store. What do we observe?

P6-37. Analyzing Inventories with Quarterly Data and LIFO Liquidation

The inventory footnote from **The Dow Chemical Company**'s first quarter 2019 SEC report follows. The company also reports cost of goods sold for Q1 of 2019 of $10,707 million.

LO2, 3
Dow Chemical Co. (DOW)

Inventories, in millions	Mar. 31, 2019	Dec. 31, 2018
Finished goods........................	$5,703	$5,640
Work in process	2,239	2,214
Raw materials........................	940	941
Supplies	891	880
Total	$9,773	$9,675
Adjustment of inventories to a LIFO basis ...	(265)	(415)
Total inventories	$9,508	$9,260

Required

a. What inventory costing method does Dow Chemical use? As of Q1 of 2019, what is the effect on cumulative pretax income and cash flow of using this inventory costing method? (Assume a 30% average cumulative tax rate.) What is the effect on Q1 of 2019 pretax income and cash flow of using this inventory costing method, assuming a 21% tax rate?

b. Compute inventory turnover and average inventory days outstanding for Q1 of 2019. (*Hint:* How do we adjust the ratio for the number of days in a quarter instead of a year?) Comment on the level of these two ratios. Is the level what we expected?

c. Determine the FIFO values for inventories and cost of goods sold for Q1 of 2019. Recompute inventory turnover and DIO. Compare the ratios to those from part *b*. Which set of ratios would provide more useful analysis?

d. Explain why a reduction in the LIFO reserve increased income in Q1 of 2019.

LO6 **P6-38. Estimating Useful Life and Percent Used Up**

lululemon athletica (LULU)

The property and equipment section of the **lululemon athletica** 2018 balance sheet follows.

Property and Equipment (in thousands)	Feb. 3, 2019	Jan. 28, 2018
Land	$ 78,636	$ 83,048
Buildings	38,030	39,278
Leasehold improvements	362,571	301,449
Furniture and fixtures	103,733	91,778
Computer hardware	69,542	61,734
Computer software	230,689	173,997
Equipment and vehicles	15,009	14,806
Work in progress	74,271	51,260
Property and equipment, gross	972,481	817,350
Accumulated depreciation	(405,244)	(343,708)
Property and equipment, net	$567,237	$473,642

Depreciation expense related to property and equipment was $122.4 million and $108.0 million for the years ended February 3, 2019, and January 28, 2018, respectively.

Required

a. Consider the level of the various PPE components. Does it seem likely that the company manufactures its own inventory? Why or why not?

b. What is meant by "work in progress"? Explain how this item will be accounted for in the coming months at lululemon.

c. Compute the estimated useful life of lululemon's depreciable assets.

d. Compute the estimated percent used up of lululemon's depreciable assets. How do we interpret this figure?

LO6 **P6-39. Interpreting and Applying Disclosures on Property and Equipment**

Facebook Inc. (FB)

Following are selected disclosures from the 10-K report of **Facebook Inc.** Facebook reported 2018 sales of $55,838 million.

Property and Equipment, Net

December 31, $ millions	2018	2017
Land	$ 899	$ 798
Buildings	7,401	4,909
Leasehold improvements	1,841	959
Network equipment	13,017	7,998
Computer software, office equipment and other	1,187	681
Construction in progress	7,228	2,992
Total	31,573	18,337
Less: Accumulated depreciation	(6,890)	(4,616)
Property and equipment, net	$24,683	$13,721

continued

> Depreciation expense on property and equipment was $3.68 billion and $2.33 billion during 2018 and 2017, respectively.

Required

a. Compute the PPE turnover for 2018.
b. Estimate the useful life, on average, for its depreciable PPE assets.
c. By what percentage are Facebook's assets "used up" in 2018? What implication does the assets used up computation have for forecasting cash flows?
d. Consider the ratios in parts *a*, *b*, and *c*. Interpret them in light of the company's age and business model.
e. The list of PPE assets includes an asset labeled "Construction in progress." What is this asset and what types of costs are included on the balance sheet?

P6-40. Analyzing and Interpreting Restructuring Costs and Effects

General Electric (GE) reports the following footnote disclosure (excerpted) in its 2018 10-K relating to its restructuring program.

LO5
General Electric (GE)

> **RESTRUCTURING** Restructuring actions are an essential component of our cost improvement efforts to both existing operations and those recently acquired. Restructuring and other charges relate primarily to workforce reductions, facility exit costs associated with the consolidation of sales, service and manufacturing facilities, the integration of recent acquisitions, and other asset write-downs. We continue to closely monitor the economic environment and may undertake further restructuring actions to more closely align our cost structure with earnings and cost reduction goals.
>
> | Restructuring and Other Charges (In billions) | 2018 | 2017 | 2016 |
> |---|---|---|---|
> | Workforce reductions | $0.9 | $1.2 | $1.3 |
> | Plant closures & associated costs and other asset write-downs | 1.8 | 1.9 | 1.3 |
> | Acquisition/disposition net charges | 0.8 | 0.8 | 0.6 |
> | Other | 0.1 | 0.2 | 0.3 |
> | Total | $3.6 | $4.1 | $3.5 |
>
> For 2018, restructuring and other charges were $3.6 billion of which approximately $1.4 billion was reported in cost of products/services and $2.1 billion was reported in selling, general and administrative expenses (SG&A). These activities were primarily at Power, Corporate and Oil & Gas. Cash expenditures for restructuring and other charges were approximately $2.0 billion for the twelve months ended December 31, 2018.

Required

a. Briefly describe the company's 2018 restructuring program. Provide two examples of common noncash charges associated with corporate restructuring activities.
b. Using the financial statement effects template, show the effects on financial statements of the (1) 2018 restructuring charge of $3.6 billion, and (2) 2018 cash payment of $2.0 billion.
c. Assume that instead of accurately estimating the anticipated restructuring charge in 2018, the company overestimated them by $30 million. How would this overestimation affect financial statements in (1) 2018, and (2) 2019 when severance costs are paid in cash?

IFRS Applications

I6-41. Analyzing Inventory for Two Retail Grocery Companies

Carrefour Group (headquartered in Boulogne-Billancourt, France) and Tesco PLC (headquartered in Welwyn Garden City, UK) compete head-to-head in the grocery space in the UK, Ireland, Central Europe, and North Africa. The following information comes from their 2018 annual reports.

LO3
Carrefour Group
Tesco PLC

	Carrefour Group in € millions		Tesco PLC in £ millions	
	2018	2017	2018	2017
Sales.	€76,000	€78,315	£57,491	€55,917
Cost of sales.	60,850	62,311	54,141	53,015
Gross profit.	15,150	16,004	3,350	2,902
Inventory.	6,135	6,690	2,263	2,301
Total assets	47,378	47,813	44,862	45,853

Required

a. Calculate gross profit margin for each year for both companies.
b. Determine the common-size inventory for each year for both companies.
c. Compute inventory turnover and days average inventory outstanding for 2018.
d. Based on the metrics in parts *a*, *b*, and *c*, how do we assess the two companies' inventory management?

LO5, 6
Husky Energy (HSE)

I6-42. Estimating Useful Life, Percent Used Up, and Gain or Loss on Disposal

Husky Energy is one of Canada's largest integrated energy companies. Based in Calgary, Alberta, Husky is publicly traded on the Toronto Stock Exchange. The Company operates in Western and Atlantic Canada, the United States and the Asia Pacific Region with upstream and downstream business segments. The company uses IFRS to prepare its financial statements. During 2018, the company reported depreciation expense of $2,591 million. The property and equipment footnote follows.

Property, Plant and Equipment (in C$ millions)	Oil and Gas Properties	Processing, Transportation and Storage	Upgrading	Refining	Retail and Other	Total
Cost						
December 31, 2017	$ 41,815	$ 86	$ 2,599	$ 9,191	$ 2,930	$ 56,621
Additions.	2,465	12	62	744	151	3,434
Acquisitions.	64	—	—	3	—	67
Transfers from exploration and evaluation.	79	—	—	—	—	79
Intersegment transfers	—	—	—	(5)	5	—
Changes in asset retirement obligations.	43	2	(2)	(5)	7	45
Disposals and derecognition.	(632)	—	—	(10)	(1)	(643)
Exchange adjustments	362	1	—	773	3	1,139
December 31, 2018	$ 44,196	$101	$ 2,659	$10,691	$ 3,095	$ 60,742
Accumulated depletion, depreciation, amortization, and impairment						
December 31, 2017	$(26,016)	$ (47)	$(1,462)	$ (3,176)	$(1,842)	$(32,543)
Depletion, depreciation, amortization, and impairment.	(1,811)	(2)	(123)	(503)	(152)	(2,591)
Disposals and derecognition.	586	—	—	10	—	596
Exchange adjustments	(138)	(1)	—	(264)	(1)	(404)
December 31, 2018	$(27,379)	$ (50)	$(1,585)	$ (3,933)	$(1,995)	$(34,942)
Net book value						
December 31, 2017	$15,799	$ 39	$ 1,137	$ 6,015	$ 1,088	$ 24,078
December 31, 2018	16,817	51	1,074	6,758	1,100	25,800

Required

a. Compute the average useful life of Husky Energy's depreciable assets in 2018. Assume that land is 10% of "Refining."
b. Estimate the percent used up of Husky Energy's depreciable assets in 2018. How do we interpret this figure?
c. Consider the disposals and derecognition during the year. This refers to assets that were sold and removed from the balance sheet during 2018. Calculate the net book value of the total PPE disposed during the year. Assume that Husky Energy received $4 million cash proceeds for the year. Determine the gain or loss on the disposal.

Management Applications

MA6-43. Managing Operating Asset Reduction   **LO3, 6**

Return on net operating assets (RNOA = NOPAT/Average NOA, see Module 4) is commonly used to evaluate financial performance. If managers cannot increase NOPAT, they can still increase this return by reducing the amount of net operating assets (NOA). List specific ways that managers could manage the following operating items.

    a. Inventories   *b.* Plant, property and equipment   *c.* Accounts payable

Ongoing Project

(This ongoing project began in Module 1 and continues through most of the book; even if previous segments were not completed, the requirements are still applicable to any business analysis.)

1. *Inventory* The following provides some guidance for analysis of a company's inventory.
   - What is inventory for the company? Does the company manufacture inventory? What proportion of total inventory is raw materials? Work in process? Finished goods?
   - Compare the two companies' inventory costing methods. Adjust LIFO inventory and cost of goods sold if the company uses LIFO. Is the LIFO reserve significant? Estimate the tax savings associated with LIFO costing method. (Use the adjusted COGS and inventory figures for all calculations and ratios.)
   - What is the relative size of inventory? How has this changed over the recent three-year period?
   - Compute inventory turnover and days inventory outstanding and the cash conversion cycle for all three years reported on the income statement.
   - Compute gross profit margin in percentage terms. Consider the current economic environment and the companies' competitive landscape. Can we explain any changes in gross profit levels? Have costs for raw materials and labor increased during the year? Have sales volumes softened? What has happened to unit prices? Read the MD&A to determine senior management's take.
   - Does the company face any inventory-related risk? What has been done to mitigate this risk? Read the MD&A.

   For each point of analysis, compare across companies and over time.

2. *Tangible Assets* The following provides some guidance to the companies' long-term (tangible) assets.
   - Are tangible assets significant for the companies? What proportion of total assets is held as tangible assets (PPE)? What exactly are the companies' tangible assets? That is, what is their nature?
   - Compare the two companies' depreciation policies. Do they differ markedly?
   - What is the relative size of tangible assets? How has this changed over the three-year period?
   - Did the company increase tangible assets during the year? Was the increase for outright asset purchases or did the company acquire assets via a merger or acquisition?
   - Compute PPE turnover.
   - Compute the average age of assets and percentage used up.
   - Are any assets impaired? Is the impairment charge significant? Is the impairment specific to the company or is the industry experiencing a downturn?

   For each point of analysis, compare across companies and over time.

3. *Restructuring Activities* Have the companies restructured operations in the past three years?
   - Determine the amount of the expense on the income statement—look in the footnotes or the MD&A for additional information.
   - Are other close competitors also restructuring during this time period?
   - Read the footnotes and assess the company's restructuring plans. How many years will it take to fully execute the plan? What additional expenditures are required?
   - Find the restructuring liability on the balance sheet (again the notes will help). Does the liability seem reasonable over time? Compare it to total assets and total liabilities each year and look for any patterns.

Solutions to Review Problems

Review 6-1—Solution

Preliminary computation: Units in ending inventory = 4,800 available − 2,800 sold = 2,000 units

1. First-in, first-out (FIFO)

Cost of goods sold computation:	Units		Cost		Total
	1,000	@	$18.00	=	$18,000
	1,800	@	$18.25	=	32,850
	2,800				$50,850

   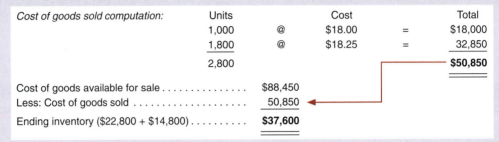

Cost of goods available for sale	$88,450
Less: Cost of goods sold	50,850
Ending inventory ($22,800 + $14,800)	**$37,600**

2. Last-in, first-out (LIFO)

Cost of goods sold computation:	Units		Cost		Total
	1,200	@	$19.00	=	$22,800
	800	@	$18.50	=	14,800
	800	@	$18.25	=	14,600
	2,800				$52,200

   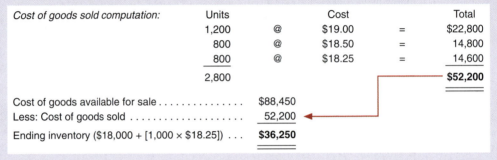

Cost of goods available for sale	$88,450
Less: Cost of goods sold	52,200
Ending inventory ($18,000 + [1,000 × $18.25]) . . .	**$36,250**

3. Average cost (AC)

Average unit cost	= $88,450/4,800 units	= $18.427
Cost of goods sold	= 2,800 × $18.427	= $51,596
Ending inventory	= 2,000 × $18.427	= $36,854

4. a. FIFO is normally the method that most closely reflects physical flow. For example, FIFO would apply to the physical flow of perishable units and to situations where the earlier units acquired are moved out first because of risk of deterioration or obsolescence.
   b. LIFO results in the highest cost of goods sold during periods of rising costs (as in the HD subsidiary case); and, accordingly, LIFO yields the lowest net income and the lowest income taxes.

Review 6-2—Solution

1. Because the $30,000 market value of the inventories is less than the carrying value of the inventories under FIFO inventory costing, the inventories must be written down to their market value with the write-down reported in the income statement as an increase in COGS. The balance sheet will report the inventory at $30,000.
2. Last-in, first-out with LIFO liquidation

Cost of goods sold computation:	Units		Cost		Total
	800	@	$18.50	=	$14,800
	1,800	@	$18.25	=	32,850
	200	@	$18.00	=	3,600
	2,800				$51,250

   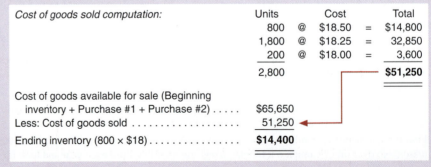

Cost of goods available for sale (Beginning inventory + Purchase #1 + Purchase #2)	$65,650
Less: Cost of goods sold	51,250
Ending inventory (800 × $18)	**$14,400**

The company's LIFO gross profit has increased by $950 ($52,200 − $51,250) because of the LIFO liquidation. The reduction of inventory quantities matched older (lower) cost layers against current selling prices. The company has, in effect, dipped into lower-cost layers to boost current-period profit—all from a simple delay of inventory purchases.

3. The LIFO reserve is computed as the difference between the inventory cost at LIFO and FIFO. This is $37,600 − $36,250 = $1,350. Using LIFO for inventory costing for the subsidiary resulted in $284 of taxes being deferred in the current period, computed as $1,350 × 21%.

Review 6-3—Solution

$ millions	2019	2018	2017
1. Gross profit margin	$\dfrac{\$22,915}{\$71,309} = 32.1\%$	$\dfrac{\$22,434}{\$68,619} = 32.7\%$	$\dfrac{\$21,674}{\$65,017} = 33.3\%$
2. Days inventory outstanding	$\dfrac{365}{\left[\dfrac{\$48,394}{\dfrac{\$12,561+\$11,393}{2}}\right]} = 90.3$	$\dfrac{365}{\left[\dfrac{\$46,185}{\dfrac{\$11,393+\$10,458}{2}}\right]} = 86.3$	
3. Days payable outstanding	$\dfrac{365}{\left[\dfrac{\$48,394}{\dfrac{\$8,279+\$6,590}{2}}\right]} = 56.1$	$\dfrac{365}{\left[\dfrac{\$46,185}{\dfrac{\$6,590+\$6,651}{2}}\right]} = 52.3$	

4. Cash conversion cycle .... 0 + 90.3 − 56.1 = 34.2   0 + 86.3 − 52.3 = 34.0
   Analysis: Cash conversion cycle did not improve; the cycle got longer (worsened), going from 34.0 days to 34.2 days.
5. Δ Cash = Δ Cash Conversion Cycle Days × (COGS/365) = −0.2 days × ($48,394/365 days) = $(26.5) million

Review 6-4—Solution

1. Straight-line depreciation expense = ($95,000 − $10,000)/5 years = $17,000 per year
2. The HD subsidiary reports equipment on its balance sheet at its net book value of $44,000.

Equipment, cost	$95,000
Less accumulated depreciation ($17,000 × 3)	51,000
Equipment, net (end of Year 3)	$44,000

Review 6-5—Solution

Part 1.
a. The equipment is impaired since the undiscounted expected cash flows of $40,000 are less than the $44,000 net book value of the equipment. The HD subsidiary must write down the equipment to its fair value of $36,000. The effect of this write-down is to reduce the net book value of the equipment by $8,000 ($44,000 − $36,000) and recognize a loss in the income statement.
b. The HD subsidiary must report a gain on this sale of $6,000, computed as proceeds of $50,000 less the net book value of the equipment of $44,000 (see Review 6-4, part 2).

Part 2.
a. Coca-Cola's restructuring expense for 2018 is the increase in the restructuring liability of $508 million.
b. Coca-Cola reports a restructuring liability of $90 million on its 2018 balance sheet.

Review 6-6—Solution

$ millions	2019	2018
PPE turnover	$\dfrac{\$71,309}{\left(\dfrac{\$18,432+\$19,721}{2}\right)} = 3.7$	$\dfrac{\$68,619}{\left(\dfrac{\$19,721+\$19,949}{2}\right)} = 3.5$
Average useful life	$\dfrac{(\$18,052+\$10,090+\$18,521+\$10,475)/2}{\$1,454} = 19.6$	$\dfrac{(\$18,521+\$10,475+\$18,147+\$10,978)/2}{\$1,540} = 18.9$
Percent used up	$\dfrac{\$17,431}{(\$18,052+\$10,090+\$18,521+\$10,475)/2} = 61\%$	$\dfrac{\$17,219}{(\$18,521+\$10,475+\$18,147+\$10,978)/2} = 59\%$

Module 7
Current and Long-Term Liabilities

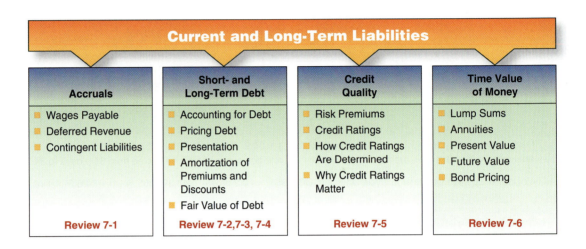

Accruals	Short- and Long-Term Debt	Credit Quality	Time Value of Money
■ Wages Payable ■ Deferred Revenue ■ Contingent Liabilities	■ Accounting for Debt ■ Pricing Debt ■ Presentation ■ Amortization of Premiums and Discounts ■ Fair Value of Debt	■ Risk Premiums ■ Credit Ratings ■ How Credit Ratings Are Determined ■ Why Credit Ratings Matter	■ Lump Sums ■ Annuities ■ Present Value ■ Future Value ■ Bond Pricing
Review 7-1	Review 7-2, 7-3, 7-4	Review 7-5	Review 7-6

PREVIEW — VZ

We examine current and long-term liabilities
- Current liabilities
  ○ Accrued liabilities, deferred revenue, and contingent liabilities (such as warranties)
  ○ Short-term debt and current maturities of long-term debt
- Long-term liabilities
  ○ Bond pricing and the effective cost of debt
  ○ Footnote disclosures of long-term debt
  ○ Financial statement effects of bond repurchases
  ○ Fair-value disclosures
- Bond credit ratings
  ○ Determinants of credit ratings
  ○ How credit ratings influence the effective cost of debt
  ○ Investment grade versus noninvestment grade credit ratings
  ○ Example of credit rating analysis for Verizon
  ○ Predictive ability of credit ratings for future rates
- **Verizon Communications** is the focus company and the dashboard below conveys key financial information

Equity, Operating Liabilities, and Debt

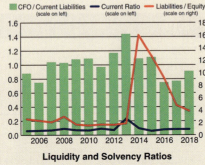
Liquidity and Solvency Ratios

Revenue, Assets, and Market Capitalization

Road Map

LO	Learning Objective | Topics	Page	eLecture	Guided Example	Assignments
7–1	**Explain accounting for accrued liabilities.** Defined :: Contractual Liabilities :: Contingent Liabilities	7-3	e7–1	Review 7-1	1, 2, 7, 9, 13, 21, 27, 28, 29, 30, 50
7–2	**Analyze reporting for short-term debt.** Accounting for ST Debt :: Interest :: Maturities of LT Debt	7-7	e7–2	Review 7-2	8, 17, 46
7–3	**Determine the pricing of long-term debt.** Bond Details :: Par Bonds :: Discount Bonds :: Premium Bonds :: Cost of Debt	7-9	e7–3	Review 7-3	3, 10, 19, 20, 22, 31, 34, 35, 36, 37, 39, 45, 46, 47, 49, 51
7–4	**Analyze reporting for long-term debt.** Debt Disclosures :: Amortization :: Bond Repurchase :: Bond Fair Value	7-13	e7–4	Review 7-4	4, 6, 11, 12, 13, 14, 15, 16, 22, 26, 31, 32, 34, 35, 36, 37, 39, 46, 47, 48, 49
7–5	**Explain how quality of debt is determined.** Credit Ratings Defined :: Determinants of Ratings :: Importance of Ratings	7-16	e7–5	Review 7-5	5, 10, 18, 23, 33, 40, 41, 42, 46, 48, 52
7–6	**Apply time value of money concepts (Appendix 7A).** Present & Future Values :: Single Amounts and Annuities :: Using Excel or Calculator	7-25	e7–6	Review 7-6	19, 20, 22, 24, 25, 38, 43, 44

Accrued Liabilities

The current liabilities section of the balance sheet reports liabilities that will normally mature within one year from the balance sheet date. Following is the information that **Verizon Communications Inc.** provides in its 2018 annual report and footnotes.

Verizon Current Liabilities ($ millions)			
Reported on balance sheet		**Reported in footnotes**	
Current liabilities		Accounts payable and accrued liabilities	
Debt maturing within one year	$ 7,190	Accounts payable	$ 7,232
Accounts payable and accrued liabilities	22,501	Accrued expenses	5,948
Other current liabilities	8,239	Accrued vacation, salaries and wages	6,268
Total current liabilities	$37,930	Interest payable	1,570
		Taxes payable	1,483
			$22,501
		Other current liabilities	
		Dividends payable	$ 2,512
		Contract liability	4,207
		Other	1,520
			$ 8,239

Verizon's current liabilities of $37,930 million includes the following usual categories.

- **Debt maturing within one year and short-term debt.** This category typically includes loans from banks, commercial paper borrowings, and scheduled maturities of long-term bonds and notes. These are nonoperating liabilities.
- **Accounts payable.** These are amounts owed to suppliers for the purchase of goods and services on account and are, therefore, operating liabilities. We discuss accounts payable with inventory in a prior module because accounts payable are typically related to inventory purchases.
- **Accrued liabilities.** This category typically includes many different accruals. For Verizon, accrued liabilities includes unpaid salaries and wages, interest and taxes, customer deposits, and dividends payable to shareholders.

Accrued Liabilities Defined

LO1 Explain accounting for accrued liabilities.

Accrued liabilities (or accruals) are adjustments that accountants make to the balance sheet after all transactions have been entered into the accounting records, and prior to the issuance of the financial statements, so that those statements fairly present the financial condition of the company. These adjustments recognize liabilities on the balance sheet (and the related expense on the income statement) that are not the result of external transactions (such as the purchase of goods or services on account that are recognized as accounts payable). Accrued liabilities are incurred in the current period and, therefore, must be recognized in the current period. Accrued liabilities fall into two broad categories.

1. **Accruals for routine contractual liabilities.** These accruals include items such as:
   - Wages that the company is contractually obligated to pay to employees for work performed, but not yet paid for in the current period.
   - Interest that is due in the current period on borrowed money, but has not yet been paid.
   - Income taxes that are owed, but not yet paid, as a result of profit earned during the period.
   - Other operating liabilities that have been incurred but not yet paid for in the current period (like rent, utilities, etc.).
2. **Accruals for contingent liabilities.** Contingent liabilities depend on the occurrence of a future uncertain event in order to determine whether a liability exists and, if so, in what amount. An example is litigation that has been brought against the company whose outcome and amount depends

upon adjudication. Another is warranty liabilities for products sold which depend upon the occurrence of product defects to require the company to repair or replace the product purchased.

Accruals for Contractual Liabilities—Wages Payable Example

Many companies pay employees bi-monthly. In the last two weeks of the month, then, employees have worked for the company, have earned wages, but have not yet been paid. If the liability for unpaid wages is not reflected on the month-end balance sheet, liabilities will be understated and wage expense will not be reflected in the income statement, thus overstating profit for the period. To correct for this, accountants make an entry to reflect the unpaid wage liability on the balance sheet and recognize wage expense in the income statement. When the wages are subsequently paid in the following month, cash decreases as does the wage liability.

The accrual entry and subsequent payment are reflected in our financial statement effects template.

Transaction	Balance Sheet					Income Statement		
	Cash Asset	+ Noncash Assets	= Liabilities	+ Contrib. Capital	+ Earned Capital	Revenues	− Expenses	= Net Income
Period 1: Accrued $75 for employee wages earned at period-end		=	+75 Wages Payable		−75 Retained Earnings		+75 Wages Expense	= −75
Period 2: Paid $75 for wages earned in prior period	−75 Cash	=	−75 Wages Payable				−	=

WE 75
  WP 75

WE
75 |
WP
    | 75

WP 75
  Cash 75

WP
75 |
Cash
    | 75

The following financial statement effects result from this accrual and subsequent payment of employee wages.

- The effect of the accrual in period 1 is to increase wages payable on the balance sheet and to recognize wages expense on the income statement. Failure to recognize this liability and associated expense would understate liabilities on the balance sheet and overstate income in the current period.

- When the company pays employees in the following period, cash and wages payable both decrease. This payment does not result in expense because the expense was recognized in the prior period when the wages were earned by employees and the liability to pay those wages was incurred.

For example, Verizon reports accrued vacation, salaries, and wages of $6,268 million at the 2018 year-end. This represents the anticipated salaries and benefits earned by employees in 2018 that will be paid in 2019.

Other contractual accruals of this type are common and they relate to events that are certain. For example, companies can estimate fairly precisely unpaid rent and utilities, the amount of interest that is due in the current period on borrowed money, and income taxes that are owed as a result of profit earned during the period. All of these are included in accrued liabilities.

Accruals for Contractual Liabilities—Deferred Revenue Example

Deferred (or unearned) revenue represents deposits or other prepayments from customers that the company has not yet earned. Verizon collects cash in advance from customers who opt for prepaid phone plans, which are plans that enable customers to obtain wireless services without credit verification by paying for all services in advance. In some cases, Verizon collects deposits from commercial customers in advance of a major installation of communication equipment. Both of these types of prepayments are accrued liabilities until Verizon provides the related services; that is, until the prepaid plan is used or the installation is completed. At the end of fiscal 2018, Verizon's Other current liabilities account includes $4,207 million for Contract liabilities, which is deferred revenue that the company will earn in 2019. (We discuss deferred revenue more fully in a prior module.)

Accruals for Contingent Liabilities

Some accrued liabilities are less certain than others because the ultimate settlement of the liability is contingent on the outcome of some future event(s). Companies must record an accrual (a contingent liability) on the balance sheet, when two conditions are met.

1. It is "probable" that one or more future events will confirm that a liability existed at the financial statement date.
2. The amount required to settle the liability in the future can be reasonably determined at the financial statement date. The amount recorded should be the best estimate of the future expenditure required to settle the obligation. (If the best estimate of the expenditure is a range, and no amount in the range is a better estimate than any other, the company records the minimum amount in the range.)

Common examples of contingent liabilities include:

- Guarantees on the debt of another entity.
- Lawsuits (only for losses, never for lawsuits where the company stands to win).
- Product warranties and recalls.
- Environmental disasters and remediation.

Accruals for Contingent Liabilities—Warranties Example

Warranty liabilities are commitments that manufacturers make to their customers to repair or replace defective products within a specified period of time. If the obligation is *probable* and the amount *estimable* with reasonable certainty, GAAP requires manufacturers to record the expected cost of warranties as a liability and to record the related expected warranty expense in the income statement in the same period that the sales revenue is reported. And, for warranty liabilities, both the probability and the likely amount can be reasonably estimated based on past experience.

To illustrate, assume that a company estimates from past experience that defective units amount to 2% of sales and that each unit will cost $5 to replace. If sales during the period are $10,000, the estimated warranty expense is $1,000 ($10,000 × 2% × $5), and the entries to accrue this liability and to reflect its ultimate payment are shown in the template that follows.

Accruing warranty liabilities has the same effect on financial statements as accruing wages expense. That is, a liability is recorded on the balance sheet and an expense is reported in the income statement. When the defective product is later replaced (or repaired), the liability is reduced together with the cost of the inventory, cash paid for labor to repair the product, parts used in the repair, and any other costs that were necessary to satisfy the claim. (Only a portion of the products estimated to fail does so in the current period; we expect other product failures in future periods. Management monitors this estimate and adjusts it if failure is higher or lower than expected.) As in the accrual of wages, the expense and the liability are reported when incurred and not when paid.

		Balance Sheet					Income Statement		
Transaction	Cash Asset	+ Noncash Assets	= Liabil- ities	+ Contrib. Capital	+ Earned Capital		Rev- enues	− Expen- ses	= Net Income
Accrued $1,000 of expected warranty costs on units sold during the period			= +1,000 Warranty Payable		−1,000 Retained Earnings			− +1,000 Warranty Expense	= −1,000
Delivered $1,000 in replacement products to settle warranty claims		−1,000 Inventory	= −1,000 Warranty Payable					−	=

WRE.. 1,000
  WRP 1,000

WRE
1,000 |
    WRP
    | 1,000

WRP.. 1,000
  INV 1,000

WRP
1,000 |
    INV
    | 1,000

Because the warranty liability and related expense are typically important items for manufacturing companies, information relating to this liability for the current and prior two periods is disclosed in the footnotes to the financial statements. **Harley-Davidson's** warranty footnote in its 2018 annual report is an example.

> **Product Warranty and Recall** The Company currently provides a standard two-year limited warranty on all new motorcycles sold worldwide, except for Japan, where the Company provides a standard three-year limited warranty on all new motorcycles sold. In addition, the Company offers a one-year warranty for Parts & Accessories (P&A). The warranty coverage for the retail customer generally begins when the product is sold to a retail customer. The Company accrues for future warranty claims using an estimated cost based primarily on historical Company claim information. Additionally, the Company has from time-to-time initiated certain voluntary recall campaigns. The Company accrues for the estimated cost associated with voluntary recalls in the period that management approves and commits to the recall. Changes in the Company's warranty and recall liability were as follows (in thousands):
>
> | | 2018 | 2017 | 2016 |
> |---|---|---|---|
> | Balance, beginning of period | $ 94,200 | $79,482 | $74,217 |
> | Warranties issued during the period | 53,367 | 57,834 | 60,215 |
> | Settlements made during the period | (79,300) | (82,554) | (99,298) |
> | Recalls and changes to pre-existing warranty liabilities | 63,473 | 39,438 | 44,348 |
> | Balance, end of period | $131,740 | $94,200 | $79,482 |
>
> The liability associated with recalls was $73.3 million, $35.3 million, and $13.6 million at December 31, 2018, 2017, and 2016, respectively.

At the beginning of 2018, Harley-Davidson reported a reserve of $94,200 for estimated product warranty and safety recall costs (all $ in thousands for this discussion). During 2018, the company added $53,367 to the reserve relating to warranties on products sold in 2018. Then, the company added another $63,473 to update the estimates it made in prior periods—the actual costs to replace and repair recalled equipment came in significantly higher than anticipated and the company needed a catch-up accrual. As a result of these two accruals, Harley-Davidson recognized an expense of $116,840 ($53,367 + $63,473) in its 2018 income statement.

During 2018, the company paid out $79,300 to settle warranty claims. The settlements include cash paid to customers for refunds, wages paid to employees who repair the motorcycles, and the cost of parts used in repairs.

It is important to understand that only the increase in the liability impacts the income statement—the accrual ($116,840 in 2018) is recorded as warranty expense, which reduces pre-tax income. Payments made to settle warranty claims do not affect current-period income; they merely reduce the pre-existing liability.

GAAP requires that the warranty liability should reflect the estimated cost that the company expects to incur as a result of warranty claims. This is often a difficult estimate to make and is prone to error. Each period, the company examines the liability and updates the amount to reflect new, more accurate information, as we saw above, for Harley-Davidson. There is also the possibility that a company might intentionally underestimate its warranty liability to report higher current income, or overestimate it so as to depress current income and create an additional liability on the balance sheet (*cookie jar reserve*) that can be used to absorb future warranty costs and, thus, to reduce *future* expenses. The overestimation would shift income from the current period to one or more future periods. Warranty liabilities must, therefore, be examined closely and compared with sales levels. Any deviations from the historical relation of the warranty liability to sales, or from levels reported by competitors, should be scrutinized.

> **IFRS Insight** ■ **Provisions and Contingencies under IFRS**
>
> IFRS requires that a "provision" be recognized as a liability if a present obligation exists, if it is probable that an outflow of resources is required, and if the obligation can be reasonably estimated. These provisions are roughly equivalent to GAAP contingent liabilities that meet the bar for recognition on the balance sheet such as warranties and lawsuits that are probable and can be reasonably estimated. IFRS defines contingent liabilities as "possible but not probable" future obligations and, like under GAAP, are disclosed in footnotes, but not accrued.

Review 7-1 LO1

Consider the balance in the warranty and recall liability at Harley-Davidson for 2018 from the information above. Assume that in the next fiscal year, Harley-Davidson estimates a warranty liability of $70,000 on product sold and incurs a cost of $85,000 during the year to repair or replace defective products. (All $ in thousands for this review.)

Required
a. What amount of warranty expense will Harley-Davidson report in its income statement in 2019?
b. What will be the amount of warranty liability that Harley-Davidson reports on its 2019 balance sheet?
c. Assume that Harley-Davidson mistakenly accrues $90,000 for warranty liability in 2019 (instead of $70,000). What effect will this accrual mistake have on future income statements and balance sheets?

Solution on p. 7-48.

Short-Term Debt

LO2 Analyze reporting for short-term debt.

Companies generally seek to match the maturity of borrowings with the assets they are financing. While PPE assets are appropriately financed with long-term debt and/or equity, seasonal swings in working capital are often financed with a bank line of credit (short-term debt). In this case the bank commits to lend up to a maximum amount with the understanding that the amounts borrowed will be repaid in full sometime during the year. An interest-bearing note evidences any such borrowing.

When the company borrows these short-term funds, it reports the cash received on the balance sheet together with an increase in liabilities (notes payable). The note is reported as a current liability because the company expects to repay it within a year. Although this borrowing has no effect on income or equity, the borrower incurs (and the lender earns) *interest* on the note as time passes. GAAP requires the borrower to accrue the interest liability and the related interest expense each time financial statements are issued.

Accounting for Short-Term Debt

To illustrate, assume that Verizon borrows $1,000 cash on January 1. The note bears interest at a 12% annual rate, and the interest (3% per quarter) is payable on the first day of each subsequent quarter (April 1, July 1, October 1, January 1). Assuming that Verizon issues calendar-quarter financial statements, this borrowing results in the following financial statement effects for January 1 through April 1.

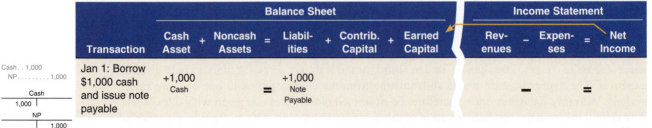

continued

Transaction	Balance Sheet						Income Statement			
	Cash Asset	+	Noncash Assets	=	Liabil- ities	+ Contrib. Capital + Earned Capital	Rev- enues	−	Expen- ses	= Net Income
Mar 31: Accrue quarterly interest on 12%, $1,000 note payable				=	+30 Interest Payable	−30 Retained Earnings		−	+30 Interest Expense	= −30
Apr 1: Pay $30 cash for interest due	−30 Cash			=	−30 Interest Payable			−		=

```
IE . . . . . . .30
   IP. . . . . . . . . . . .30
           IE
        30 |
              IP
               |   30

IP . . . . . . .30
   Cash . . . . . . . . . .30
           IP
        30 |
              Cash
               |   30
```

The January 1 borrowing increases both cash and notes payable. On March 31, Verizon issues its quarterly financial statements. Although interest is not paid until April 1, the company has incurred three months' interest obligation as of March 31. Failure to recognize this liability and the expense incurred would not fairly present the financial condition of the company. Accordingly, the quarterly accrued interest payable is computed as follows.

$$\text{Interest Expense} = \text{Principal} \times \text{Annual Rate} \times \text{Portion of Year Outstanding}$$
$$\$30 = \$1,000 \times 12\% \times 3/12$$

The subsequent interest payment on April 1 reduces both cash and the interest payable that Verizon accrued on March 31. There is no expense reported on April 1, as it was recorded the previous day (March 31) when Verizon prepared its financial statements. (For fixed-maturity borrowings specified in days, such as a 90-day note, we assume a 365-day year for interest accrual computations; see Review 7-2.)

Current Maturities of Long-Term Debt

Principal payments that must be made during the upcoming 12 months on long-term debt (such as for a mortgage or a maturing bond) are reported as current liabilities called *current maturities of long-term debt*. The current liabilities section of the Verizon 2018 balance sheet includes $7,190 million of "Debt maturing within one year." Some long-term debt, including mortgages, requires a periodic payment that is part principal and part interest. Note that the current maturity is the principal portion only of the payments that will be made in the upcoming year. Consider a five-year, 4% mortgage of $1 million that requires annual payments of $224,627. We can use a loan-amortization schedule such as the one below, to determine the principal amount outstanding at each reporting period.

Year	Interest at 4% on Principal Balance	Annual Payment	Principal Reduction (Ann Pymt− Int)	Principal Balance (Prior Bal.−Prin. Red.)
0				$1,000,000
1	$40,000	$224,627	$184,627	815,373
2	32,615	224,627	192,012	623,361
3	24,934	224,627	199,693	423,668
4	16,947	224,627	207,680	215,988
5	8,640	224,627	215,988	0

In the first year, the amount of interest accrued on the loan is $40,000 ($1 million × 4%). The remainder of the annual payment of $224,627 is a reduction of the principal amount of the loan. On the day the mortgage was taken out, the balance sheet would show a current maturity of $184,627 with the remainder, $815,373, included in long-term debt. As the balance owed on the mortgage decreases, so too does the interest; the current portion increases each year.

Review 7-2 LO2

Assume that on January 15, Comcast borrowed $10,000 million on a 90-day, 6% note payable. The bank accrues interest daily based on a 365-day year. Comcast has a December 31 fiscal year-end.

Required
Use the financial statement effects template to show the following:
1. The interest accrual Comcast would make on March 31 when it prepares its first-quarter financial statements.
2. Comcast's payment of principal and interest when the note matures on April 14.

Solution on p. 7-49.

Long-Term Debt—Pricing

LO3 Determine the pricing of long-term debt.

Companies often include long-term nonoperating liabilities in their capital structure to fund long-term assets. Smaller amounts of long-term debt can be readily obtained from banks, private placements with insurance companies, and other credit sources. However, when a large amount of financing is required, the issuance of bonds (and notes) in capital markets is a cost-efficient way to raise funds. The following discussion uses bonds for illustration, but the concepts also apply to long-term notes.

Bonds are structured like any other borrowing. The borrower receives cash and agrees to pay it back with interest. Generally, the entire **face amount** (principal) of the bond is repaid at maturity (at the end of the bond's life) and interest payments are made in the interim (usually semiannually).

Companies that raise funds in the bond market normally work with an underwriter (like Goldman Sachs) to set the terms of the bond issue. The underwriter then sells individual bonds (usually in $1,000 denominations) from this general bond issue to its retail clients and professional portfolio managers (like The Vanguard Group), and receives a fee for underwriting the bond issue. These bonds are investments for individual investors, other companies, retirement plans and insurance companies.

After they are issued, the bonds can trade in the secondary market just like stocks. Market prices of bonds fluctuate daily despite the fact that the company's obligation for payment of principal and interest normally remains fixed throughout the life of the bond. Then, why do bond prices change? The answer is that the bond's fixed rate of interest can be higher or lower than the interest rates offered on other securities of similar risk. Because bonds compete with other possible investments, bond prices are set relative to the prices of other investments. In a competitive investment market, a particular bond will become more or less desirable depending on the general level of interest rates offered by competing securities. Just as for any item, competitive pressures will cause bond prices to rise and fall.

Before we discuss the mechanics of long-term debt pricing, we need to define two types of interest rates that we will use to price bonds.

- **Coupon (contract** or **stated) rate** The coupon rate of interest is stated in the bond contract; it is used to compute the dollar amount of interest payments that are paid (in cash) to bondholders during the life of the bond issue.

- **Market (yield** or **effective) rate** This is the interest rate that investors expect to earn on the investment in this debt security; this rate is used to price the bond.

The coupon (contract) rate is used to compute interest payments and the market (yield) rate is used to price the bond. The coupon rate and the market rate are nearly always different. This is because the coupon rate is fixed prior to issuance of the bond and normally remains fixed throughout its life. Market rates of interest, on the other hand, fluctuate continually with the supply and demand for bonds in the marketplace, general macroeconomic conditions, and the borrower's financial condition.

The bond price, both its initial sales price and the price it trades at in the secondary market subsequent to issuance, equals the present value of the expected cash flows to the bondholder. Specifically, bondholders normally expect to receive two different types of cash flows.

1. **Periodic interest payments** (usually semiannual) during the bond's life; these payments are called an *annuity* because they are equal in amount and made at regular intervals.
2. **Single payment** of the face (principal) amount of the bond at maturity; this is called a *lump-sum* because it occurs only once.

The bond price equals the present value of the periodic interest payments plus the present value of the single payment. If the present value of the two cash flows is equal to the bond's face value, the bond is sold at par. If the present value is less than or greater than the bond's face value, the bond sells at a discount or premium, respectively. We next illustrate the issuance of bonds at three different prices: at par, at a discount, and at a premium.

Pricing of Bonds Issued at Par

To illustrate a bond issued (sold) at par, assume that a bond with a face amount of $10 million has a 6% annual coupon rate payable semiannually (3% semiannual rate) and a maturity of 10 years. Semiannual interest payments are typical for bonds. This means that the issuer pays bondholders two interest payments per year. Each semiannual interest payment is equal to the bond's face value times the annual rate divided by two. Investors purchasing these bonds receive the following cash flows.

Cash Flows	Number of Payments	Dollars per Payment	Total Cash Flows
Semiannual interest payments......	10 years × 2 = 20	$10,000,000 × 3% = $300,000	$ 6,000,000
Principal payment at maturity.......	1	$10,000,000	10,000,000
			$16,000,000

Specifically, the bond agreement dictates that the borrower must make 20 semiannual payments of $300,000 each, computed as $10,000,000 × (6%/2). At maturity, the borrower must repay the $10,000,000 face amount. To price bonds, investors identify the *number* of interest payments and use that number when computing the present value of *both* the interest payments and the principal (face) payment at maturity.

The bond price is the present value of the periodic interest payments (the annuity) plus the present value of the principal payment (the lump sum). In our example, assuming that investors desire a 3% semiannual market rate (yield), the bond sells for $10,000,000, which is computed as follows.

	Payment	Present Value Factor[a]	Present Value
Interest.................	$ 300,000	14.87747[b]	$ 4,463,200[d]
Principal	$10,000,000	0.55368[c]	5,536,800
			$10,000,000

[a] Mechanics of using tables to compute present values are explained in Appendix 7A; present value factors come from Appendix A near the end of the book.
[b] Present value of an ordinary annuity for 20 periods discounted at 3% per period.
[c] Present value of a single payment in 20 periods discounted at 3% per period.
[d] Rounded.

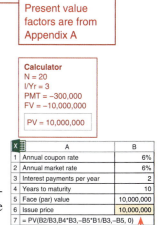

Because the bond contract pays investors a 3% semiannual rate when investors demand a 3% semiannual market rate, given the borrower's credit rating and the time to maturity, the investors purchase those bonds at the **par (face) value** of $10 million.

Pricing of Bonds Issued at a Discount

As a second illustration, assume investors demand a 4% semiannual return for the 3% semiannual coupon bond, while all other details remain the same. The bond now sells for $8,640,999, computed as follows.

Calculator
N = 20
I/Yr = 4
PMT = −300,000
FV = −10,000,000

PV = 8,640,967*

*rounding difference

	A	B
1	Annual coupon rate	6%
2	Annual market rate	8%
3	Interest payments per year	2
4	Years to maturity	10
5	Face (par) value	10,000,000
6	Issue price	8,640,967
7	= PV(B2/B3,B4*B3,−B5*B1/B3,−B5, 0)	
8	= 8,640,967	

	Payment	Present Value Factor	Present Value
Interest	$ 300,000	13.59033[a]	$4,077,099
Principal	$10,000,000	0.45639[b]	4,563,900
			$8,640,999

[a] Present value of an ordinary annuity for 20 periods discounted at 4% per period.
[b] Present value of a single payment in 20 periods discounted at 4% per period.

Because the bond carries a coupon rate *lower* than what investors demand, the bond is less desirable and sells at a **discount**. More generally, bonds sell at a discount whenever the coupon rate is less than the market rate.

Pricing of Bonds Issued at a Premium

As a third illustration, assume that investors demand a 2% semiannual return for the 3% semiannual coupon bonds, while all other details remain the same. The bond now sells for $11,635,129, computed as follows.

Calculator
N = 20
I/Yr = 2
PMT = −300,000
FV = −10,000,000

PV = 11,635,143*

*rounding difference

	A	B
1	Annual coupon rate	6%
2	Annual market rate	4%
3	Interest payments per year	2
4	Years to maturity	10
5	Face (par) value	10,000,000
6	Issue price	11,635,143
7	= PV(B2/B3,B4*B3,−B5*B1/B3,−B5, 0)	
8	= 11,635,143	

	Payment	Present Value Factor	Present Value
Interest	$ 300,000	16.35143[a]	$ 4,905,429
Principal	$10,000,000	0.67297[b]	6,729,700
			$11,635,129

[a] Present value of an ordinary annuity for 20 periods discounted at 2% per period.
[b] Present value of a single payment in 20 periods discounted at 2% per period.

Because the bond carries a coupon rate *higher* than what investors demand, the bond is more desirable and sells at a **premium**. More generally, bonds sell at a premium whenever the coupon rate is greater than the market rate.[1] Exhibit 7.1 summarizes this relation for bond pricing.

Exhibit 7.1 ■ Coupon Rate, Market Rate, and Bond Pricing

Coupon rate > market rate	→	Bond sells at a **premium** (above face amount)
Coupon rate = market rate	→	Bond sells at **par** (at face amount)
Coupon rate < market rate	→	Bond sells at a **discount** (below face amount)

Effective Cost of Debt

When a bond sells for par, the cost to the issuing company is the cash interest paid. In our first illustration above, the *effective cost* of the bond is the 6% interest paid by the issuer.

When a bond sells at a discount, the issuer must repay more (the face value when the bond matures) than the cash received at issuance (the discounted bond proceeds). This means that the effective cost of a discount bond is greater than if the bond had sold at par. A discount is a cost and, like any other cost, must eventually be transferred from the balance sheet to the income statement as an expense.

When a bond sells at a premium, the borrower received more cash at issuance than it must repay. The difference, the premium, is a benefit that must eventually find its way into the income statement as a *reduction* of interest expense. As a result of the premium, the effective cost of a premium bond is less than if the bond had sold at par.

Bonds are priced to yield the return (market rate) demanded by investors. Consequently, the effective rate of a bond *always* equals the yield (market) rate demanded by investors,

---

[1] Bond prices are often stated in percent form. For example, a bond sold at par is said to be sold at 100 (that is, 100% of par). The bond sold at $8,640,999 is said to be sold at 86.41 (86.41% of par, computed as $8,640,999/$10,000,000). The bond sold for a premium is said to be sold at 116.35 (116.35% of the bond's face value).

regardless of the coupon rate of the bond. This means that companies cannot influence the effective cost of debt by raising or lowering the coupon rate. Doing so will only result in a bond premium or discount. We discuss the factors affecting the yield demanded by investors later in the module.

The effective cost of debt is reflected in the amount of interest expense reported in the issuer's income statement. Because of bond discounts and premiums, interest expense is usually different from the cash interest paid.

Exhibit 7.2 demonstrates the difference between coupon rates and effective rates of interest. On April 2, 2019, **Verizon** issued €2,500 million and £500 million of debt including 0.875% notes with a face value of €1,250 million due April 8, 2027. The exhibit shows that the issue price of these notes was 99.631 (this is the percent of par value and indicates that the bonds were sold at a discount). Verizon's underwriters charged 0.3% in underwriting fees (€3,750,000) for underwriting and selling this debt issue, and thus, Verizon received proceeds of 99.331% of the face value, or €1,241,637,500. These notes paid interest annually on April 8. If we assume the notes were sold on April 8, 2019 (to simplify the calculations), we can determine that the effective rate on these notes was 0.9623%.

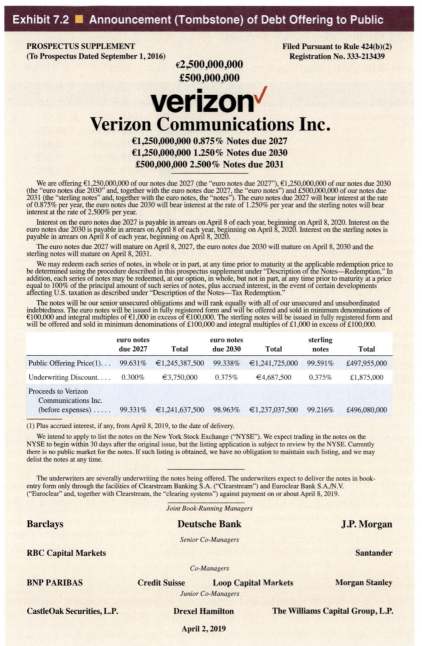

Source: Thomson Reuters WESTLAW

Review 7-3 LO3

On January 1, assume that **Comcast** issues $300,000 of 15-year, 10% bonds payable, yielding an effective semiannual interest rate of 4%. Interest is payable semiannually on June 30 and December 31.

Required

1. Calculate the issue price of this bond.
2. What would the bond issue price be if the semiannual effective interest rate is 6% instead of 4%?

Solution on p. 7-49.

Long-Term Debt—Reporting

Balance Sheet Reporting

LO4 Analyze reporting for long-term debt.

Companies typically have many debt issues outstanding and disclose the total amount owed as a long-term liability on the balance sheet. Footnotes provide details about each of the company's outstanding bonds and notes like the following for **Verizon**.

Long-Term Debt Outstanding long-term debt obligations as of December 31, 2018, are as follows.

At December 31,	Rates%	Maturities	2018	2017
Verizon Communications	1.38–4.00	2018–2042	$ 29,651	$ 31,370
	4.05–5.51	2020–2055	66,230	67,906
	5.82–6.90	2026–2054	5,658	5,835
	7.35–8.95	2029–2039	1,076	1,106
	Floating	2018–2025	4,657	6,684
VerizonWireless	6.80–7.88	2029–2032	234	234
Telephone subsidiaries—debentures	5.13–6.50	2028–2033	226	226
	7.38–7.88	2022–2032	341	341
	8.00–8.75	2022–2031	229	229
Other subsidiaries—notes payable, debentures and other	6.70–8.75	2018–2028	444	748
VerizonWireless and other subsidiaries—asset-backed debt	1.42–3.55	2021–2023	7,962	6,293
	Floating	2021–2023	2,139	2,620
Capital lease obligations (average rate of 4.1% and 3.6% in 2018 and 2017, respectively).			905	1,020
Unamortized discount, net of premium.			(6,298)	(7,133)
Unamortized debt issuance costs.			(541)	(534)
Total long-term debt, including current maturities.			112,913	116,945
Less long-term debt maturing within one year			7,040	3,303
Total long-term debt			$105,873	$113,642

In general, companies report debt net of any discount (or including any premium) and also net of any debt issuance costs. Verizon subtracts Unamortized discount, net of premium, of $6,298 million and Unamortized debt issuance costs of $541 million to arrive at Total long-term debt, including current maturities, of $112,913 million in 2018. Then, Verizon subtracts $7,040 million, the amount of the debt that matures in the next year to arrive at the $105,873 million that is reported in the noncurrent liability section of the 2018 balance sheet.

Companies must provide a schedule of the maturities of their long-term debt in the footnotes to the financial statements. Following is the footnote disclosure of debt maturities in Verizon's 2018 annual report.

> Maturities of long-term debt (secured and unsecured) outstanding, including current maturities, excluding unamortized debt issuance costs, at December 31, 2018.

continued

continued from previous page

Years	(dollars in millions)
2019	$ 7,058
2020	7,380
2021	6,999
2022	7,674
2023	5,903
Thereafter	78,439

The $7,058 million of long-term debt scheduled to mature in 2019 includes debt issuance costs of $18 million. The net amount $7,040 is reported as a current liability in the 2018 balance sheet (as reported in the debt footnote above). The remaining amounts through 2023 are scheduled maturities of long-term debt included in long-term debt on the balance sheet. In general, we look for significant amounts maturing in any one year as this raises the question whether the company will have the cash flow to make the required payment. We prefer to see a relatively level debt repayment schedule, like the one above, which allows for an orderly payment or refinancing. To assess whether these amounts are large, consider that Verizon's operating cash flow for 2018 is $34,339 million. So, while the amounts of maturing debt are not insignificant, they should be manageable for Verizon. The size of Verizon's total debt, however, is one reason why the company's credit rating is not high (we discuss credit ratings later in this module).

Income Statement Reporting

As discussed above, companies report long-term debt on the balance sheet net of the discount and debt issuance costs. When its bonds mature, however, the company must pay the face amount (the amount borrowed). This means that between the bond issuance and its maturity, the discount and debt issuance must decline to zero. This reduction of the discount and debt issuance over the life of the bond is called **amortization**, and the discount amortization results in additional interest expense in the income statement. This amortization causes the total interest expense to be greater than the cash interest payments. The opposite holds true for bonds and notes issued at a premium—the total interest expense is less than the cash interest paid. Consequently, the interest expense reported on the income statement each year represents the *effective cost* of debt, including both the cash interest paid plus a portion of the additional borrowing costs (or less a portion of the benefit of the premium). We discuss the amortization process in Appendix 7B.

Financial Statement Effects of Bond Repurchase

Companies report bonds payable at *historical (adjusted) cost*. Specifically, net bonds payable amounts follow from the amortization table, as do the related cash flows and income statement numbers. All financial statement relations are set when the bond is issued; they do not subsequently change.

Once issued, however, bonds trade in secondary markets. The yield rate used to compute bond prices for these subsequent transactions is the market interest rate prevailing at the time. These rates change daily based on the level of interest rates in the economy and the perceived creditworthiness of the bond issuer.

Companies can and sometimes do repurchase (or redeem or *retire*) their bonds prior to maturity. The bond indenture (contract agreement) can include provisions giving the company the right to repurchase its bonds directly from the bond holders. Or, the company can repurchase bonds in the open market. **Verizon** reports a "loss on the early extinguishment of debt" of $700 million in 2018 as described in the financial statement footnotes as follows.

> During 2018 and 2017, we recorded losses on early debt redemptions of $0.7 billion and $2.0 billion, respectively. We recognize losses on early debt redemptions in Other income (expense), net, in our consolidated statements of income and within our Net cash used in financing activities in our consolidated statements of cash flows.

When a bond repurchase occurs, a gain or loss usually results, and is computed as follows.

> **Gain or Loss on Bond Repurchase = Net Bonds Payable − Repurchase Payment**

The net bonds payable, also referred to as the *book value,* is the net amount reported on the balance sheet. If the issuer pays more to retire the bonds than the amount carried on its balance sheet, it reports a loss on its income statement, usually called *loss on bond retirement.* The issuer reports a *gain on bond retirement* if the repurchase price is less than the net bonds payable.

How should we treat these gains and losses for analysis purposes? That is, do they carry economic effects? The answer is no—the gain or loss on repurchase is exactly offset by the present value of the future cash flow implications of the repurchase. (The Accounting Insight box that follows demonstrates this.) Further, the gain or loss on early retirement is a transitory item and, consequently, will not be repeated in future income statements.

Accounting Insight ■ Economics of Gains and Losses on Bond Repurchases

CVS repurchased its 6.25% Notes in 2014 and recorded a loss on the early extinguishment of debt. At the same time, CVS issued $850 million of 2.25% Notes. CVS used part of the proceeds to fund the repurchase of the 6.25% Notes. Because interest rates had dropped since the 6.25% Notes were issued, the market value of the 6.25% Notes had increased to $521 million in excess of their carrying amount. To repurchase the Notes, CVS had to pay the market price (and not the face value), which created a large "loss on the early extinguishment of debt."

Although CVS reported the $521 million loss in its income statement, there was no *economic* loss. We use a simple example to explain. Please refer to Exhibit 7B.1 relating to a $600,000 bond with a 3% coupon rate that was sold at a discount to yield 4%. At the end of period 2, the bond has a carrying amount on the balance sheet of $588,576.81.

Assume that at the end of period 2, the market rate of interest declines from 4% when the bond was issued, to 2% (1% semiannually). The drop in market rates will affect the market value of the bond. At the end of period 2, there are four interest payments of $9,000 remaining plus the $600,000 face amount of the bond at maturity. The present value of that stream of payments, discounted at the current market rate of 1% semiannual rate, is equal to $611,705.90 (the Excel formula is = PV(1%, 4, −9,000, −600,000)). To repurchase the bond, CVS would have to issue a new bond in the amount of $611,705.90 carrying a 1% coupon rate. Either way, CVS would report a loss on the early extinguishment of debt of $23,129.09 ($611,705.90 − $588,576.81).

Despite reporting an accounting loss on the early extinguishment of debt of $23,129.09, there is no economic loss. Why? Because the present value of the new debt is equal to $611,705.90 (the Excel formula is = PV(1%, 4, −6,117.06, −611,705.90), where 6,117.06 = $611,705.90 × 1%). The present value of the new debt is, therefore, equal to the present value of the remaining payments on the old debt, discounted at the new semiannual market rate of 1%. They are, therefore, equivalent and no economic loss has been sustained.

Fair Value Disclosures

An important analysis issue involves assessing the fair value of bonds and other long-term liabilities. This information is relevant for investors and creditors because it reveals unrealized gains and losses (similar to that reported for marketable securities). GAAP requires companies to provide information about current fair values of their long-term liabilities in footnotes as Verizon does in its 2018 10-K.

> **Fair Value of Short-Term and Long-Term Debt** The fair value of our debt is determined using various methods, including quoted prices for identical terms and maturities, which is a Level 1 measurement, as well as quoted prices for similar terms and maturities in inactive markets and future cash flows discounted at current rates, which are Level 2 measurements. The fair value of our short-term and long-term debt, excluding capital leases, was as follows:
>
> | | 2018 | | 2017 | |
> |---|---|---|---|---|
> | At December 31 (dollars in millions) | Carrying Amount | Fair Value | Carrying Amount | Fair Value |
> | Short- and long-term debt, excluding capital leases . . . . | $112,159 | $118,535 | $116,075 | $128,658 |

The increase in fair value is due to a decline in market rates of interest since the debt was initially issued (or to an increase in the credit rating of the company). These fair values are *not* reported on the balance sheet and changes in these fair values are not reflected in net income. The chief justification for not recognizing fair-value gain and losses is that such amounts can reverse with subsequent fluctuations in market rates of interest and the bonds are repaid at par at maturity.

LO4 Review 7-4

Assume that on January 1 **Comcast** issues $300,000 of 15-year, 10% bonds payable for $351,876, yielding an effective semiannual interest rate of 4%. Interest is payable semiannually on June 30 and December 31.

1. Show computations to confirm the issue price of $351,876.
2. Complete Comcast's financial statement effects template for
   a. bond issuance,
   b. semiannual interest payment and premium amortization on June 30 of the first year, and
   c. semiannual interest payment and premium amortization on December 31 of the first year.
3. Prepare an amortization table for the bonds for the first five years (See Exhibit 7B.2 for guidance).
4. Assume that at the end of year 5, Comcast repurchases the bonds on the open market. The effective semiannual interest rate has fallen to 2%. What will Comcast have to pay to repurchase these bonds? Determine any gain or loss on the repurchase transaction.

Solution on p. 7-49.

Quality of Debt

Credit Analysis

Credit analysis differs from the analysis of equity securities. While equity investors are focused on upside potential, lenders are primarily concerned with recouping the amount loaned (the "principal"), together with the interest earned on their loan. (We use the term "**lenders**" broadly to include traditional bank loans or bonds and notes that trade on the open market.) Their focus is on the company's ability to repay, which is largely determined by two factors.

1. **Level of indebtedness**—amount of principal and interest that must be repaid.
2. **Excess cash that the company is able to generate**—this provides the cash needed to repay the debt. The term "excess cash" means the cash the company is able to generate over and above what is needed for ongoing operating and investing activities, including bringing its products and/or services to market and maintaining and growing PPE infrastructure via capital expenditures (CAPEX).

The first factor is a *levels-based* focus and the second is a *flow-based* approach, and both are essential to a thorough investigation of a company's creditworthiness.

We discuss the credit analysis performed by Standard & Poor's in more detail below.[2] While each credit rating agency develops its own proprietary models, in general, the rating agencies take a *two-step approach* to evaluate the riskiness of a company's debt. The *first step* is to assess the likelihood of default (the nonpayment of amounts owed), relative to the likelihood of default for other companies. The relative likelihood of default can be gauged by an analysis of historical and forecasted levels of debt and the excess cash flow available to pay the indebtedness. The *second step* is to assess the potential loss that the lender will suffer in the event of default. The potential loss given default is generally a function of the structure of the debt. The following factors help to assess the collectibility of debt in the event of default.

- How does the debt rank (senior or junior in order of payment) relative to other issuances by the same borrower?

---

[2] S&P Global Ratings (S&P) closest competitors are Moody's Investors Service and Fitch Ratings. Together, they are referred to as the Big Three credit rating agencies and they play a key role in global capital markets where they provide credit analysis for financial institutions, individual investors, and regulators.

- What collateral, if any, has been pledged to secure the debt in the event of nonpayment?
- What controls and restrictions have the lenders placed on the company to limit risk exposure?

Generally, lenders will require a higher interest rate as the creditworthiness of the borrower declines. This increase in interest rate is referred to as a *risk premium*. Earlier in the module we explained that the effective cost of debt to the issuing company is the market (yield) rate of interest used to price the bond, regardless of the bond coupon rate. The market rate of interest is usually defined as the yield on U.S. Government borrowings such as treasury bills, notes, and bonds, called the *risk-free rate*, plus a *risk premium* (also called a *spread*).

$$\text{Yield Rate} = \text{Risk-Free Rate} + \text{Risk Premium}$$

Both the treasury yield (the so-called risk-free rate) and the corporate yield vary over time as illustrated in the following graphic.

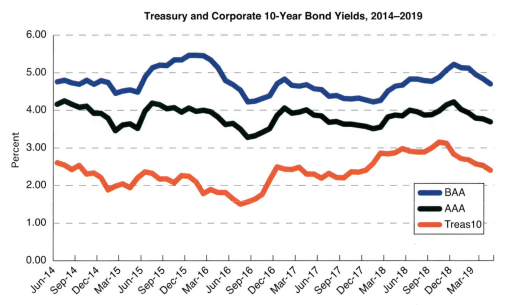

Source: Federal Reserve Bank of St. Louis.

The rate of interest that investors expect for a particular bond is a function of the risk-free rate and the risk premium, where the latter depends on the creditworthiness of the issuing entity.

The yield increases (shifts upward) as debt quality moves from Treasury securities (generally considered to be risk free), which is the highest-quality debt reflected in the lowest line in the graph, to the Aaa (highest) rated corporates and, finally, to the Baa (lower-rated) corporates shown in this graph. That is, higher credit-rated issuers warrant a lower rate than lower credit-rated issuers. This difference is substantial. For example, in May 2019, the average 10-year treasury bond yield was 2.40%, while the Aaa corporate bond yield was 3.69% and the average Baa (the lowest investment grade corporate bond) yield was 4.70%.

Research Insight — Accounting Conservatism and Cost of Debt

Research indicates that companies that use more conservative accounting policies incur a lower cost of debt. Research also suggests that while accounting conservatism can lead to lower-quality accounting income (because such income does not fully reflect economic reality), creditors are more confident in the numbers and view them as more credible. Evidence also implies that companies can lower the required return demanded by creditors (the risk premium) by issuing high-quality financial reports that include enhanced footnote disclosures and detailed supplemental reports.

What Are Credit Ratings?

A company's credit rating, also referred to as debt rating, credit quality, or creditworthiness, is related to default risk. **Default** refers to the nonpayment of interest and principal and/or the failure to adhere to the various terms and conditions (covenants) of the bond indenture. Companies that want to obtain bond financing from the capital markets normally first seek a rating on their proposed debt issuance from one of several rating agencies such as S&P Global Ratings, Moody's Investors Service, or Fitch Ratings. The aim of rating agencies is to rate debt so that its default risk is more accurately conveyed to, and priced by, the market. Each rating agency uses its own rating system, as Exhibit 7.3 shows. This exhibit includes the general description for each rating class—for example, AAA is assigned to debt of prime maximum safety (highest in creditworthiness). The dotted green line separates investment grade bonds from noninvestment grade or speculative bonds. Many investment managers are precluded from purchasing noninvestment grade bonds for their client portfolios, thus lessening the liquidity of the bonds.

Exhibit 7.3 ■ Corporate Debt Ratings and Descriptions

S&P	Moody's	Fitch	Description
AAA	Aaa	AAA	Prime Maximum Safety
AA+ AA AA−	Aa1 Aa2 Aa3	AA+ AA AA−	High Grade, High Quality
A+ A A−	A1 A2 A3	A+ A A−	Upper-Medium Grade
BBB+ BBB BBB2	Baa1 Baa2 Baa3	BBB+ BBB BBB2	Lower-Medium Grade
BB+ BB BB−	Ba1 Ba2 Ba3	BB+ BB BB−	Noninvestment Grade Speculative
B+ B B−	B1 B2 B3	B+ B B−	Highly Speculative
CCC+ CCC CCC−	Caa1 Caa2 Caa3	CCC	Substantial Risk In Poor Standing
CC	Ca		Extremely Speculative
C	C		May be in Default
D		DDD DD D	Default

What Determines Credit Ratings?

Verizon bonds are rated BBB+, Baa1, and A− by S&P Global Ratings, Moody's, and Fitch, respectively, as of 2018. In the text box, we provide excerpts from the S&P Global Ratings Credit Report for Verizon in 2019.

S&P Global Ratings determines its "anchor" credit rating from an analysis of the borrower's business risk and financial risk. It then adjusts the anchor credit rating by applying several modifiers: diversification of the borrower's revenue stream, capital structure, financial policy, liquidity and management/governance, and comparable ratings. This process is depicted in the following graphic.

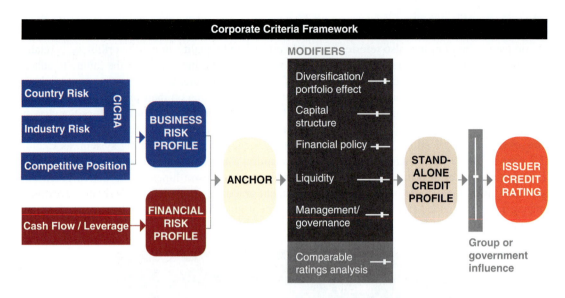

The objective of credit analysis is to assess the probability that the company will be able to make all required principal and interest payments when they come due. Large companies that are conservatively financed, dominant in their markets, and with large and predictable cash flows are more likely to meet debt obligations. Conversely, smaller companies facing intense competition in volatile markets carry more risk for lenders and will receive lower credit ratings.

Credit Ratings and Financial Ratios

Credit rating agencies use a variety of financial ratios to assess the level of debt relative to other balance sheet accounts and the required principal and interest payments relative to profitability and cash flow. Exhibit 7.4 provides a sample of these ratios. This table includes median values for each ratio across a range of credit ratings. As we move from the highest quality (Aaa) to speculative grade (Caaa-C) debt, the ratios weaken. For example, EBITA/Average assets is a variant of the Return on assets (ROA) metric that we discuss in Module 4. For the highest-rated companies, the median for this statistic in 2017 is 12.3%. The lowest-rated companies are one-third of that level. For operating margins (Operating profit / Sales) the range is even more striking with the highest-rated companies reporting a median operating margin of 24.8% and the lowest a median of 3.8%.

Similarly, the (Funds from operations (FFO) + Interest expense)/Interest expense is a variant of the times interest earned ratio that we discuss in the solvency section of Module 4. The highest-rated companies report a median value of 18.0 while the lowest report a level of 1.7, which means available funds barely cover interest payments. The FFO/Debt ratio, measuring the company's operating cash flow relative to the level of its debt, ranges from 40.4% to 5.7%.

Business Insight — Credit Rating Factors for Verizon Debt

S&P's credit analysis of Verizon's debt anchors on its **Business** risk and its **Financial** risk as of December 2018 year-end.

Business Risk: Strong

The business risk assessment reflects Verizon's strong position as the largest wireless provider in the U.S., with a leading brand and reputation for network quality. It also reflects the strength of its wireless EBITDA margins with substantial scale advantages and growth from Fios broadband services. Partial mitigating factors include a mature wireless market with limited near-term growth potential, as well as secular industry pressures and weak margins in its wireline business.

Financial Risk: Intermediate

We expect modest improvement in adjusted net leverage to around 2.6x to 2.7x in 2019 from 2.8x in 2018. We believe Verizon has good prospects to reduce leverage to the 2.5x area (our threshold for a higher rating) by 2020, although this depends on the amount and timing of spectrum license acquisitions. Additionally, the company's recently stated target for net unsecured debt to EBITDA of 1.75x–2.0x provides greater clarity on financial policy. We estimate that the upper end of this range translates into our adjusted leverage of 2.5x. We also expect FFO to total debt will be in the high-20% area, which is somewhat weak for our financial risk assessment.

Liquidity: Adequate

Our liquidity assessment is adequate and the short-term commercial paper (CP) rating is 'A-2'. We expect sources of liquidity to cover uses by about 1.3x for the next 12 months and for net sources to be positive even with a 15% decline in forecasted EBITDA. In addition, we believe Verizon has a high standing in the credit markets, evidenced by its track record of accessing both domestic and international debt markets, demonstrates prudent risk management, and has flexibility around the timing and amount of capital expenditures.

Verizon Communications Inc.

Ratings Score Snapshot

Issuer Credit Rating

BBB+/Positive/A-2

Business risk: Strong
- Country risk: Very low
- Industry risk: Intermediate
- Competitive position: Strong

Financial risk: Intermediate
- Cash flow/Leverage: Intermediate

Anchor: a–

Modifiers
- Diversification/Portfolio effect: Neutral (no impact)
- Capital structure: Neutral (no impact)
- Financial policy: Neutral (no impact)
- Liquidity: Adequate (no impact)
- Management and governance: Strong (no impact)
- Comparable rating analysis: Negative (–1 notch)

Stand-alone credit profile: bbb+
- Group credit profile: bbb+

The Business and Financial risk assessments combine to yield an overall rating of a–/bbb+ as shown in this matrix.

Business and Financial Risk Matrix

Business Risk Profile	Financial Risk Profile					
	Minimal	Modest	Intermediate	Significant	Aggressive	Highly Leveraged
Excellent	aaa/a+	aa	a+/a	a–	bbb	bbb–/bb+
Strong	aa/aa–	a+/a	a–/bbb+	bbb	bb+	bb
Satisfactory	a/a–	bbb+	bbb/bbb–	bbb–/bb+	bb	b+
Fair	bbb/bbb–	bbb–	bb+	bb	bb–	b
Weak	bb+	bb+	bb	bb–	b+	b/b–
Vulnerable	bb–	bb–	bb–/b+	b+	b	b–

The **Liquidity** assessment as "adequate" reduces the anchor rating to the lower end of the range for bbb+.

Exhibit 7.4 ■ Ratio Values for Different Credit Ratings*

	EBITA/ Avg AT	EBITA/ Int Exp	EBITA Margin	Oper Margin	(FFO + Int Exp)/Int Exp	FFO/ Debt	RCF/Net Debt	Debt/ EBITDA	Debt/ Book Cap	CAPEX/ Dep Exp	Rev Vol
Aaa	12.3%	12.0	30.6%	24.8%	18.0	40.4%	32.3%	1.9	42.8%	1.1	6.8
Aa	14.7%	20.7	24.9%	24.2%	20.0	45.9%	35.5%	1.7	41.5%	1.3	11.1
A	13.5%	11.4	19.0%	16.9%	11.9	35.7%	27.7%	2.2	46.7%	1.2	6.8
Baa	10.4%	6.4	16.3%	15.0%	8.1	28.2%	27.5%	2.7	48.4%	1.2	10.7
Ba	8.8%	3.7	13.3%	11.2%	5.4	21.5%	22.1%	3.6	55.9%	1.1	14.4
B	6.6%	2.0	9.4%	7.6%	3.3	13.2%	13.5%	5.2	68.1%	1.0	18.7
Caa-C	4.9%	0.7	6.5%	3.8%	1.7	5.7%	6.6%	7.2	94.4%	0.8	24.8

* Table reports 2017 median values by credit rating; from Moody's Financial Metrics™, Key Ratios by Rating and Industry for North American Non-Financial Corporates: December 2017 (reproduced with permission).

Ratio	Definition
EBITA/Average Assets	EBITA/Average of Current and Previous Year Assets
EBITA/Interest Expense	EBITA/Interest Expense
EBITA Margin	EBITA/Net Revenue
Operating Margin	Operating Profit/Net Revenue
(FFO + Interest Exp)/Interest Exp	(Funds From Operations + Interest Expense)/Interest Expense
FFO/Debt	Funds From Operations/(Short-Term Debt + Long-Term Debt)
RCF/Net Debt	(FFO – Preferred Dividends – Common Dividends – Minority Dividends)/(Short-Term Debt + Long-Term Debt – Cash & Cash Equivalents)
Debt/EBITDA	(Short-Term Debt + Long-Term Debt)/EBITDA
Debt/Book Capitalization	(Short-Term Debt + Long-Term Debt)/(Short-Term Debt + Long-Term Debt + Deferred Taxes + Minority Interest + Book Equity)
CAPEX/Depreciation Exp	Capital Expenditures/Depreciation Expense
Revenue Volatility	Standard Deviation of Trailing Five Years of Net Revenue Growth

where: EBITA = Earnings from continuing operations before interest, taxes, and amortization
EBITDA = Earnings from continuing operations before interest, taxes, depreciation, and amortization
FFO = Funds from Operations = Net income from continuing operations plus depreciation, amortization, deferred income taxes, and other noncash items

A review of these ratios indicates that Moody's considers the following factors, grouped by area of emphasis, as relevant in evaluating a company's ability to meet its debt service requirements.

1. Profitability ratios (first four metrics in footnote to Exhibit 7.4)
2. Cash flow ratios (metrics five, six, and seven in footnote to Exhibit 7.4)
3. Solvency ratios (metrics eight, nine, ten, and eleven in footnote to Exhibit 7.4)

A company's profitability, cash flow, and solvency are important factors in assessing the likelihood that it will successfully meet its debt obligations. In addition, credit rating agencies consider various aspects of the structure of the debt, including the following:

- **Collateral** Companies can provide security for debt by pledging certain assets against the bond. This is like mortgages on assets. To the extent debt is secured, the debt holder is in a preferred position vis-à-vis other creditors.

- **Covenants** Debt agreements (indentures) can restrict the behavior of the issuing company so as to protect debt holders. For example, covenants commonly prohibit excessive dividend payments, mergers and acquisitions, further borrowing, and commonly prescribe minimum levels for key liquidity and solvency ratios. These covenants provide debt holders an element of control over the issuer's operations because, unlike equity investors, debt holders have no voting rights.

- **Options** Options are sometimes written into debt contracts. Examples are options to convert debt into stock and options allowing the issuing company to repurchase its debt before maturity (usually at a premium).

Verizon Credit Rating Example

In September 2013, Verizon entered into an agreement with Vodafone Group Plc to acquire Vodafone's 45% interest in Verizon Wireless, giving it sole ownership of the wireless carrier. The deal closed in 2014 with a purchase price of $130 billion, paid in a combination of cash and stock. During 2013 and 2014, Verizon's long-term debt increased from $48 billion to $116 billion. The increase in financial leverage resulted in a downgrade in Verizon's credit rating. As Moody's reported "the deal will cause leverage to spike and remain elevated for an extended time frame as higher interest expense and increased dividend payments offset the distributions that Verizon will retain as a result of acquiring 100% ownership of [Verizon Wireless], reducing the amount of cash available for debt reduction."

In the years following the acquisition, Verizon's creditworthiness has become important as bond buyers look to ascertain the company's ability to manage its debt load in addition to meeting significant competitive challenges from **AT&T** for wireless and **Comcast** on the cable side of its business. In this section, we discuss in depth the credit analysis on Verizon performed by S&P Global Ratings in 2019.

S&P Global Ratings provides the following summary of its credit analysis of Verizon.

Verizon Communications Inc.

Business Risk: STRONG
Vulnerable — Excellent

Financial Risk: INTERMEDIATE
Highly leveraged — Minimal

Anchor: a- to bbb+ to bbb+
Modifiers | Group/Gov't

Issuer Credit Rating

BBB+ / Positive / A-2

Credit Highlights

Overview

Key Strengths	Key Risks
Strong market position as the largest wireless carrier in the U.S., with a leading brand reputation for network quality.	Modest wireless revenue growth due to mature industry conditions and significant competition.
Industry leader in wireless EBITDA margins with substantial scale advantages.	Secular industry declines for linear video and landline phone services.
Growth from Fios broadband services.	Weak wireline margins.
Consistent financial policy and commitment to leverage improvement.	Fifth generation (5G) wireless services will require substantial financial resources for spectrum license acquisitions and network deployment, with material revenue opportunities five to 10 years away.

Outlook: Positive

The positive outlook reflects our expectation for low-single-digit percent EBITDA growth, leverage approaching 2.5x, and funds from operations (FFO) to total debt in the high-20% area over the next couple of years. That said, potential debt-financed acquisitions, spectrum purchases, and higher levels of capital spending on network upgrades to support growth in data and video consumption could constrain near-term leverage improvement.

Downside scenario
We could revise the outlook to stable if the company allocates excess cash flow to share repurchases or makes a debt-financed acquisition. Given that 5G revenue opportunities are still uncertain and do not ramp until 2020–2021, at the earliest, we could revise the outlook back to stable if spectrum purchases are materially higher than our base case. While less likely, we could also revise the outlook to stable if wireless operations deteriorate, resulting in service revenue declines because of more aggressive competition.

Upside scenario
We could raise the rating if the company reaches and maintains S&P adjusted leverage of less than 2.5x. Given our expectation for very modest EBITDA growth over the next couple of years, we believe this could occur if Verizon commits to using excess cash flow for debt reduction. An upgrade would also need to be accompanied by growth in wireless revenue and a commitment to maintaining leverage below 2.5x longer term.

S&P Global Ratings cites Verizon's size, strong market position, greater profitability than its peers, and its consistent and transparent financial policy as contributory factors in its credit rating. Constraining the credit rating are the maturity of the industry (which limits growth potential), possible increases in competition, and uncertain costs of future licenses. S&P Global Ratings concludes with its expectation that Verizon will continue in its stated objective to reduce debt.

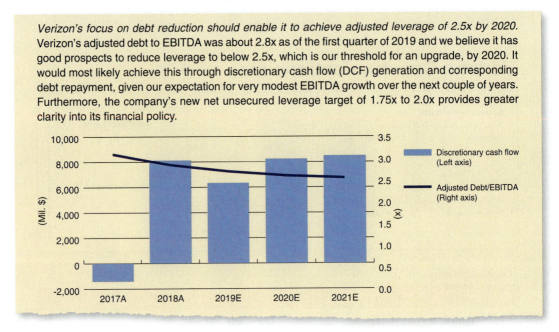

Why Credit Ratings Matter

Credit raters seek to estimate the relative probability that the company will default on its debt obligations (compared with companies in other credit ratings categories). As its credit ratings deteriorate, a company is more likely to be unable to make its debt payments and, consequently, it must pay a higher rate of interest on its borrowings to compensate investors for the risk of default.

So, how good are credit ratings at predicting defaults? Moody's provides the following graphic that illustrates the default rates for each ratings category five years into the future.

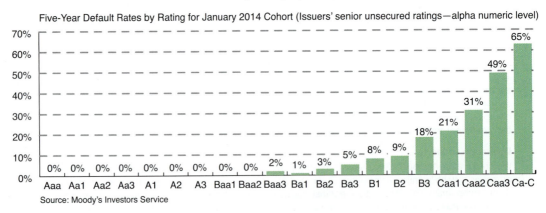

The forecast of default rates for 10 years after the initial rating is similar, and Moody's summarizes its findings as follows.

The five-year performance of Moody's January 2014 ratings was also strong. Five-year cumulative default rates through December 2018 by rating category increase moving down the rating scale, which shows that our ratings provided a strong rank-ordering of credit risk. Over the five-year period from January 2014 through December 2018, 291 issuers defaulted that had ratings outstanding at

continued

the beginning of the period. Of these defaulters, 262 (90%) had a rating of B3 or lower one year prior to default, indicating that the ratings provided strong advance warning of default. None of the 291 defaulters had investment-grade ratings one year before default and only five had ratings higher than B1.

In Exhibit 7.3, we identify Baa as the lowest investment grade security, and the graphic above provides corroborating evidence. Below Baa2, the probability of a default begins to increase. On balance, the ratings methodologies used by S&P Global Ratings, Moody's, and Fitch are quite thorough and have a good track record of predicting default rates far into the future.

Managerial Decision ■ You Are the Vice President of Finance

Your company is currently rated B1/B+ by the **Moody's** and **S&P Global Ratings** credit rating agencies, respectively. You are considering restructuring to increase your company's credit rating. What types of restructurings might you consider? What benefits will your company receive from those restructurings? What costs will your company incur to implement such restructurings? [Answer, p. 7-32]

LO5 Review 7-5

Assume that **Comcast's** financial statements for the current period yield the following ratios.

Operating margin	14.2%	FFO/Debt	32.9%
Debt/EBITDA	2.1	EBITA/Interest Expense	3.9

Required
Using the four measures above for Comcast, infer a reasonable credit rating for Comcast.

Solution on p. 7-51.

Global Accounting

The FASB and the IASB have worked on a number of joint projects and the differences in accounting for liabilities are limited. We list here some differences that we encounter in studying IFRS financial statements and the implications for comparing GAAP and IFRS companies.

- Under U.S. GAAP, if a contingent liability is probable *and* if it can be reasonably estimated, it must be accrued. Under IFRS, companies can limit disclosure of contingent liabilities if doing so would severely prejudice the entity's competitive or legal position; for example, disclosing the amount of a potential loss on a lawsuit could sway the legal outcome. Accordingly, IFRS likely yields less disclosure of contingencies.

- Accruals sometimes involve a range of estimates. If all amounts within the range are equally probable, U.S. GAAP requires the company to accrue the lowest number in the range whereas IFRS requires the company to accrue the expected amount. Also, contingencies are discounted under IFRS whereas U.S. GAAP records contingencies at their nominal value. For both of these reasons, contingent liabilities are likely smaller under U.S. GAAP.

- IFRS offers more disclosure of liabilities and accruals. For each IFRS provision (the term used for accrued liabilities and expenses), the company must reconcile the opening and closing carrying amounts, describe any additional provision for the period, and explain any reversals for the period. Reconciliation is less prevalent under U.S. GAAP (required for example for allowance for doubtful accounts, warranty accruals, restructuring accruals). Recall that an over-accrual in one period shifts income to a subsequent period when the accrual is reversed. This increased transparency under IFRS might make it easier to spot earnings management.

Appendix 7A: Time Value of Money

LO6 Apply time value of money concepts.

This appendix explains the time value of money, which includes the concepts of present and future value. Time value of money concepts are important for pricing long-term bonds and notes, understanding the accounting for debt and other analysis purposes.

Present Value Concepts

Would you rather receive a dollar now or a dollar one year from now? Most people would answer a dollar now. Intuition tells us that a dollar received now is more valuable than the same amount received sometime in the future. Sound reasons exist for choosing the dollar now, the most obvious of which concerns risk. Because the future is uncertain, any number of events can prevent us from receiving the dollar a year from now. To avoid this risk, we choose the earlier date. Another reason is that the dollar received now could be invested. That is, one year from now, we would have the dollar and the interest earned on that dollar.

Present Value of a Single Amount

Risk and interest factors yield the following generalizations: (1) the right to receive an amount of money now, its **present value**, is worth more than the right to receive the same amount later, its **future value**; (2) the longer we must wait to receive an amount, the less attractive the receipt is; (3) the greater the interest rate the greater the amount we will receive in the future. (Putting 2 and 3 together we see that the difference between the present value of an amount and its future value is a function of both interest rate and time, that is, Principal × Interest Rate × Time); and (4) the more risk associated with any situation, the higher the interest rate.

To illustrate, let's compute the amount we would need to receive today (the present value) that would be equivalent to receiving $100 one year from now if money can be invested at 10%. We recognize intuitively that, with a 10% interest rate, the present value (the equivalent amount today) will be less than $100. The $100 received in the future must include 10% interest earned for the year. Thus, the $100 received in one year (the future value) must be 1.10 times the amount received today (the present value). Dividing $100/1.10, we obtain a present value of $90.91 (rounded). This means that we would do as well to accept $90.91 today as to wait one year and receive $100. To confirm the equality of the $90.91 receipt now to a $100 receipt one year later, we calculate the future value of $90.91 at 10% for one year as follows.

$$\$90.91 \times 1.10 \times 1 \text{ year} = \$100 \text{ (rounded)}$$

To generalize, we compute the present value of a future receipt by *discounting* the future receipt back to the present at an appropriate interest rate (also called the *discount rate*). We present this schematically below.

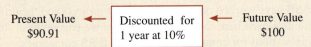

If either the time period or the interest rate were increased, the resulting present value would decrease. If more than one time period is involved, our future receipts include interest on interest. This is called *compounding*.

Time Value of Money Tables

Appendix A near the end of the book includes time value of money tables. Table 1 is a present value table that we can use to compute the present value of future amounts. A present value table provides present value factors (multipliers) for many combinations of time periods and interest rates that determine the present value of $1.

Present value tables are used as follows. First, determine the number of interest compounding periods involved (three years compounded annually are 3 periods, and three years compounded semiannually are 6 periods). The extreme left-hand column indicates the number of periods. It is important to distinguish between years and compounding periods. The table is for compounding periods (years × number of compounding periods per year).

Next, determine the interest rate per compounding period. Interest rates are usually quoted on a *per year* (annual) basis. The rate per compounding period is the annual rate divided by the number of compounding periods per year. For example, an interest rate of 10% *per year* would be 10% per period if compounded annually, and 5% *per period* if compounded semiannually.

Finally, locate the present value factor, which is at the intersection of the row of the appropriate number of compounding periods and the column of the appropriate interest rate per compounding period. Multiply this factor by the dollars that will be paid or received in the future.

All values in Table 1 are less than 1.0 because the present value of $1 received in the future is always smaller than $1. As the interest rate increases (moving from left to right in the table) or the number of periods increases (moving from top to bottom), the present value factors decline. This illustrates two important facts: (1) present values decline as interest rates increase, and (2) present values decline as the time lengthens. Consider the following three cases.

Case 1. Compute the present value of $100 to be received one year from today, discounted at 10% compounded semiannually.

Number of periods (one year, semiannually) = 2
Rate per period (10%/2) = 5%
Multiplier = 0.90703
Present value = $100.00 × 0.90703 = $90.70 (rounded)

Calculator
N = 2
I/Yr = 5
PMT = 0
FV = 100
PV = −90.70

	A	B
1	Discount Rate (rate)	5%
2	Number of Periods (nper)	2
3	Annuity (pmt)	0
4	Future value (fv)	100
5	Present value (pv)	(90.70)
6	= PV(B1,B2,B3,B4)	
7	= (90.70)	

Case 2. Compute the present value of $100 to be received two years from today, discounted at 10% compounded semiannually.

Number of periods (two years, semiannually) = 4
Rate per period (10%/2) = 5%
Multiplier = 0.82270
Present value = $100 × 0.82270 = $82.27 (rounded)

Calculator
N = 4
I/Yr = 5
PMT = 0
FV = 100
PV = −82.27

	A	B
1	Discount Rate (rate)	5%
2	Number of periods (nper)	4
3	Annuity (pmt)	0
4	Future value (fv)	100
5	Present value (pv)	(82.27)
6	= PV(B1,B2,B3,B4)	
7	= (82.27)	

Case 3. Compute the present value of $100 to be received two years from today, discounted at 12% compounded semiannually.

Number of periods (two years, semiannually) = 4
Rate per period (12%/2) = 6%
Multiplier = 0.79209
Present value = $100 = 0.79209 = $79.21 (rounded)

Calculator
N = 4
I/Yr = 6
PMT = 0
FV = 100
PV = −79.21

	A	B
1	Discount Rate (rate)	6%
2	Number of Periods (nper)	4
3	Annuity (pmt)	0
4	Future value (fv)	100
5	Present value (pv)	(79.21)
6	= PV(B1,B2,B3,B4)	
7	= (79.21)	

In Case 2, the present value of $82.27 is less than in Case 1 ($90.70) because the time increased from two to four compounding periods—the longer we must wait for money, the lower its value to us today. Then in Case 3, the present value of $79.21 was lower than in Case 2 because, while there were still four compounding periods, the interest rate per year was higher (12% annually instead of 10%)—the higher the interest rate the more interest that could have been earned on the money and therefore the lower the value today.

Present Value of an Annuity

In the examples above, we computed the present value of a single amount (also called a lump sum) made or received in the future. Often, future cash flows involve the same amount being paid or received each period. Examples include semiannual interest payments on bonds, quarterly dividend receipts, or monthly insurance premiums. If the payment or the receipt (the cash flow) is equally spaced over time and each cash flow is the same dollar amount, we have an *annuity*. One way to calculate the present value of the annuity would be to calculate the present value of each future cash flow separately. However, there is a more convenient method.

To illustrate, assume $100 is to be received at the end of each of the next three years as an annuity. When annuity amounts occur at the *end of each period*, the annuity is called an *ordinary annuity*. As shown below, the present value of this ordinary annuity can be computed from Table 1 by computing the present value of each of the three individual receipts and summing them (assume a 5% annual rate).

Future Receipts (ordinary annuity)			PV Multiplier (Table 1)		Present Value
Year 1	Year 2	Year 3			
$100			× 0.95238	=	$ 95.24
	$100		× 0.90703	=	90.70
		$100	× 0.86384	=	86.38
			2.72325		$272.32

Calculator
N = 3
I/Yr = 5
PMT = 100
FV = 0
PV = −272.32

	A	B
1	Discount Rate (rate)	5%
2	Number of Periods (nper)	3
3	Annuity (pmt)	100
4	Future value (fv)	0
5	Present value (pv)	(272.32)
6	= PV(B1,B2,B3,B4)	
7	= (272.32)	

Table 2 in Appendix A provides a single multiplier for computing the present value of an ordinary annuity. Referring to Table 2 in the row for three periods and the column for 5%, we see that the multiplier is 2.72325. When applied to the $100 annuity amount, the multiplier gives a present value of $272.33. As shown above, the same present value (with 1 cent rounding error) is derived by summing the three separate multipliers from Table 1. Considerable computations are avoided by using annuity tables.

Bond Valuation

Recall that a bond agreement specifies a pattern of future cash flows—usually a series of interest payments (cash outflow) and a single payment of the face amount at maturity (cash outflow), and bonds are priced using the prevailing market rate on the day the bond is sold (cash inflow). This is the case for the original bond issuance and for subsequent open-market sales. The market rate on the date of the sale is the rate we use to determine the bond's market value (its price). That rate is the bond's *yield*. The selling price of a bond is determined as follows.

1. Use Table 1 to compute the present value of the future principal payment at the prevailing market rate.
2. Use Table 2 to compute the present value of the future series of interest payments (the annuity) at the prevailing market rate.
3. Add the present values from steps 1 and 2.

We illustrate in Exhibit 7A.1 the price of $100,000, 8%, four-year bonds paying interest semiannually and sold when the prevailing market rate was (1) 8%, (2) 10%, or (3) 6%. Note that the price of 8% bonds sold to yield 8% is the face (or par) value of the bonds. A bond issue price of $93,537 (discount bond) yields 10%. A bond issue price of $107,020 (premium bond) yields 6%.

Calculator
N = 8
I/Yr = 4
PMT = −4,000
FV = −100,000
PV = 100,000

	A	B
1	Annual coupon rate	8%
2	Annual market rate	8%
3	Interest payments per year	2
4	Years to maturity	4
5	Face (par) value	100,000
6	Issue price	100,000
7	= PV(B2/B3,B4*B3,−B5*B1/B3,−B5, 0)	
8	= 100,000	

Calculator
N = 8
I/Yr = 5
PMT = −4,000
FV = −100,000
PV = 93,537

	A	B
1	Annual coupon rate	8%
2	Annual market rate	10%
3	Interest payments per year	2
4	Years to maturity	4
5	Face (par) value	100,000
6	Issue price	93,537
7	= PV(B2/B3,B4*B3,−B5*B1/B3,−B5, 0)	
8	= 93,537	

Calculator
N = 8
I/Yr = 3
PMT = −4,000
FV = −100,000
PV = 107,020

	A	B
1	Annual coupon rate	8%
2	Annual market rate	6%
3	Interest payments per year	2
4	Years to maturity	4
5	Face (par) value	100,000
6	Issue price	107,020
7	= PV(B2/B3,B4*B3,−B5*B1/B3,−B5, 0)	
8	= 107,020	

Exhibit 7A.1 ■ Calculation of Bond Price Using Present Value Tables

Future Cash Flows	Multiplier (Table 1)	Multiplier (Table 2)	Present Values at 4% Semiannually
(1) $100,000 of 8%, 4-year bonds with interest payable semiannually priced to yield 8%.			
Principal payment, $100,000 (a single amount received after 8 semiannual periods)	0.73069		$ 73,069
Interest payments, $4,000 at end of each of 8 semiannual periods		6.73274	26,931
Present value (issue price) of bonds			$100,000

Future Cash Flows	Multiplier (Table 1)	Multiplier (Table 2)	Present Values at 5% Semiannually
(2) $100,000 of 8%, 4-year bonds with interest payable semiannually priced to yield 10%.			
Principal payment, $100,000 (a single amount received after 8 semiannual periods)	0.67684		$ 67,684
Interest payments, $4,000 at end of each of 8 semiannual periods		6.46321	25,853
Present value (issue price) of bonds			$ 93,537

Future Cash Flows	Multiplier (Table 1)	Multiplier (Table 2)	Present Values at 3% Semiannually
(3) $100,000 of 8%, 4-year bonds with interest payable semiannually priced to yield 6%.			
Principal repayment, $100,000 (a single amount received after 8 semiannual periods)	0.78941		$ 78,941
Interest payments, $4,000 at end of each of 8 semiannual periods		7.01969	28,079
Present value (issue price) of bonds			$107,020

Time Value of Money Computations Using a Calculator

We can use a financial calculator for time value of money computations. There are five important function keys for these calculations. If we know values for four of those five, the calculator will compute the fifth. Those function keys are:

N	Number of compounding (or discounting) periods
I/Yr	Interest (yield) rate per period—entered in % terms, for example, 12% is entered as 12 and not as 0.12. This key is labeled "interest per year" but it can handle any rate per different compounding periods; for example, if we have semiannual interest payments, our compounding periods are semiannual and the interest rate is the semiannual rate.
FV	Future value of the cash flows; this is a lump sum
PMT	Annuity (coupon) per discount period
PV	Present value of the cash flows; this is a lump sum

Calculator inputs follow for the three examples in Exhibit 7A.1. In these examples, the unknown value is the bond price, which is the present value (PV) of the bond's cash flows. (For additional instruction on entering inputs into a specific calculator, or how to do more complicated computations, review the calculator's user manual or review online calculator tutorials.)

A note about positive and negative signs for variables. Financial calculators use a convention to capture the direction of cash flows. This can be understood by thinking about the direction of the cash flows from the company's perspective. Consider the examples in Exhibit 7A.1. The unknown value is the bond proceeds, the present value. From the perspective of the company, the interest payment is a cash outflow. We enter this in the calculator as a negative. Again, from the company's perspective, the cash paid to investors when the bond matures is a cash outflow (negative in the calculator). With both PMT and FV entered as negative numbers, the calculator returns a positive number—this can be understood as a cash inflow to the company. As long as we are consistent in the sign of our variables and we understand the calculator convention, we can interpret the result from the calculator. For example, if we enter PMT and FV as positive numbers, the PV returned is a negative number. (This would be considering cash flows from the investor's perspective.) Yet, be careful; if we enter PMT and FV with opposite signs, the result is nonsensical.

Example (1), Exhibit 7A.1: Bond priced to yield 8%.

N	=	8 (4 years × 2 periods per year = 8 semiannual periods)
I/Yr	=	4 (8% annual yield ÷ 2 periods per year = 4% semiannually)
FV	=	−100,000 (face value, which is the lump sum that must be repaid in the future, a cash outflow)
PMT	=	−4,000 ($100,000 × 4% semiannual coupon rate, a cash outflow)
PV	=	100,000 (output obtained from calculator)

Example (2), Exhibit 7A.1: Bond priced to yield 10%.

N = 8   I/Yr = 5   FV = −100,000   PMT = −4,000   PV = 93,537

Example (3), Exhibit 7A.1: Bond priced to yield 6%.

N = 8   I/Yr = 3   FV = −100,000   PMT = −4,000   PV = 107,020

Time Value of Money Computations Using Excel

We can use Excel or other spreadsheet software, to perform time value of money calculations. There are a number of functions for time value of money, but all of them involve the same six variables, which are:

rate	Interest (yield) rate per period, entered as either a percent (4%) or as a number 0.04. The variable is labeled rate and should be understood to mean per period; if we have semiannual interest payments, our compounding periods are semiannual and the interest rate is the semiannual rate

continued

continued from previous page

nper	Number of compounding or discounting periods
pmt	Annuity per discounting or compounding period; if there is no annuity, enter 0
pv	Present value of the cash flow; this is a lump sum
fv	Future value of the cash flow; this is a lump sum
type	Timing of the annuity payment, this is a 0 or 1 variable; if the annuity is paid at the end of each compounding period (as for interest payments), then type =0; if the annuity is paid at the beginning of each compounding period, then type =1 (type = 0 is the default value in Excel)

The Excel functions for present value and future value are as follows.

= pv(rate,nper,pmt,fv,type)
= fv(rate,nper,pmt,pv,type)

Unlike for a calculator, the variables must be entered in the correct order. Yet, once we open the bracket in the function, Excel prompts us for the variables in order. Similar to the calculator, Excel maintains the convention for positive and negative cash flows.

Example (1), Exhibit 7A.1: Bond priced to yield 8%.

rate	=	4% (8%/2 compounding periods = 4% semiannually)
nper	=	8 (4 years × 2 compounding periods = 8 semiannual periods)
pmt	=	−4,000 ($100,000 × 4% semiannual interest rate); this is a cash outflow so we enter a negative value
fv	=	−100,000 face value, which is the lump sum to be repaid in the future; this is a cash outflow so we enter a negative value
type	=	0 because interest is paid at the end of each semiannual period
	=	PV(rate,nper,pmt,fv,type)
	=	PV(4%, 8, −4000, −100000, 0) = 100,000

Example (2), Exhibit 7A.1: Bond priced to yield 10%.

= PV(5%, 8, −4000, −100000, 0) = 93,537

Example (3), Exhibit 7A.1: Bond priced to yield 6%.

= PV(3%, 8, −4000, −100000, 0) = 107,020

Excel is more powerful than a calculator because we can use cell addresses for the variables. For example, consider the three examples in Exhibit 7A.1 that could be defined as follows.

	A	B
1	Annual coupon rate	8%
2	Annual market rate	8%
3	Interest payments per year	2
4	Years to maturity	4
5	Face (par) value	100,000
6	Annuity type	0
7	Issue price	100,000
8	= PV(B2/B3,B4*B3,−B5*B1/B3,−B5, B6)	
9	= 100,000	

The value in cell B7 is 100,000. By changing cell B2 to 10%, the present value in B7 immediately changes to $93,537 and then when B2 is set to 6%, cell B7 displays $107,020.

Future Value Concepts
Future Value of a Single Amount

The **future value** of a single sum is the amount that a specific investment is worth at a future date if invested at a given rate of compound interest. To illustrate, suppose that we decide to invest $6,000 in a savings account that pays 6% annual interest and we intend to leave the principal and interest in the account for five years. We assume that interest is credited to the account at the end of each year. The balance in the account at the end of five years is determined using Table 3 in Appendix A, which gives the future value of a dollar, as follows.

$$\textbf{Principal} \times \textbf{Factor} = \textbf{Future Value}$$
$$\$6{,}000 \times 1.33823 = \$8{,}029$$

Calculator
N = 5
I/Yr = 6
PMT = 0
PV = −6,000
FV = 8,029.35

	A	B
1	Discount Rate (rate)	6%
2	Number of Periods (nper)	5
3	Annuity (pmt)	0
4	Present value (pv)	−6,000
5	Future value (fv)	8,029.35
6	= FV(B1,B2,B3,B4)	
7	= 8,029.35	

The factor 1.33823 is at the intersection of the row for five periods and the column for 6%.

Next, suppose that the interest is credited to the account semiannually rather than annually. In this situation, there are 10 compounding periods, and we use a 3% semiannual rate (one-half the annual rate because there are two compounding periods per year). The future value calculation follows.

$$\textbf{Principal} \times \textbf{Factor} = \textbf{Future Value}$$
$$\$6{,}000 \times 1.34392 = \$8{,}064$$

Calculator
N = 10
I/Yr = 3
PMT = 0
PV = −6,000
FV = 8,063.50

	A	B
1	Discount Rate (rate)	3%
2	Number of Periods (nper)	10
3	Annuity (pmt)	0
4	Present value (pv)	−6,000
5	Future value (fv)	8,063.50
6	= FV(B1,B2,B3,B4)	
7	= 8,063.50	

Future Value of an Annuity

If, instead of investing a single amount, we invest a specified amount *each period,* then we have an annuity. To illustrate, assume that we decide to invest $2,000 at the end of each year for five years at an 8% annual rate of return. To determine the accumulated amount of principal and interest at the end of five years, we refer to Table 4 in Appendix A, which furnishes the future value of a dollar invested at the end of each period. The factor 5.86660 is in the row for five periods and the column for 8%, and the calculation is as follows.

$$\textbf{Periodic Payment} \times \textbf{Factor} = \textbf{Future Value}$$
$$\$2{,}000 \times 5.86660 = \$11{,}733$$

Calculator
N = 5
I/Yr = 8
PMT = −2,000
PV = 0
FV = 11,733.20

	A	B
1	Discount Rate (rate)	8%
2	Number of Periods (nper)	5
3	Annuity (pmt)	−2,000
4	Present value (pv)	0
5	Future value (fv)	11,733.20
6	= FV(B1,B2,B3,B4)	
7	= 11,733.20	

If we decide to invest $1,000 at the end of each six months for five years at an 8% annual rate of return, we would use the factor for 10 periods at 4%, as follows.

$$\textbf{Periodic Payment} \times \textbf{Factor} = \textbf{Future Value}$$
$$\$1{,}000 \times 12.00611 = \$12{,}006$$

LO6 Review 7-6

For each of the separate cases *a*, *b*, and *c*, compute the sale price of a $5,000, five-year bond with a 6% coupon rate (annual rate with interest paid semiannually) sold to yield an annual rate of:

a. 4%
b. 6%
c. 8%

Solution on p. 7-51.

Appendix 7B: Amortization of Debt

As we saw in Exhibit 7.2, Verizon received €1,241,637,500 when it issued the €1,250,000,000 0.875% notes due in 2027. As detailed in the prospectus, the difference of €8,362,500 has two parts: the discount of €4,612,500 (€1,250,000,000 − €1,245,387,500) and the fees paid to bankers and underwriters to sell the notes of €3,750,000. The total difference of €8,462,500 is an additional borrowing cost for Verizon, a cost over and above the 0.875% interest the company will pay in cash each year. This additional borrowing cost is expensed on the income statement over the life of the notes (from 2019 to 2027) and reported with the 0.875% cash interest that Verizon pays to its lenders. Conversely, if Verizon had sold the notes at a premium, it would have received proceeds in excess of the €1,250 million face amount and that premium would subsequently be reported as a *reduction* of interest expense over the life of the notes. The process of recognizing the discount or premium as an adjustment to interest expense is called **amortization**.

Amortization of Discount

Calculator
N = 6
I/Yr = 2
PMT = −9,000
FV = −600,000

PV = 583,195.71

	A	B
1	Annual coupon rate	3%
2	Annual market rate	4%
3	Interest payments per year	2
4	Years to maturity	3
5	Face (par) value	600,000
6	Issue price	583,195.71
7	= PV(B2/B3,B4*B3,−B5*B1/B3,−B5, 0)	
8	= 583,195.71	

Companies amortize discounts and premiums using the effective interest method. To illustrate, assume that **Verizon** issues bonds with a face amount of $600,000, a 3% annual coupon rate payable semiannually (1.5% semiannual rate), a maturity of three years (six semiannual payment periods), and a market (yield) rate of 4% annual (2% semiannual). These facts yield a bond issue price of $583,195.71, which we round to $583,196 for the bond discount amortization table of Exhibit 7B.1.

The interest period is denoted in the left-most column. Period 0 is the point at which the bond is issued, and period 1 and following are successive six-month periods (recall, interest is paid semiannually). Column [A] is interest expense, which is reported in the income statement. Interest expense is computed as the bond's net balance sheet value (the carrying amount of the bond) at the beginning of the period (column [E]) multiplied by the 2% semiannual rate used to compute the bond issue price. Column [B] is cash interest paid, which is a constant $9,000 per the bond contract (face amount × coupon rate). Column [C] is discount amortization, which is the difference between interest expense and cash interest paid. Column [D] is the discount balance, which is the previous balance of the discount less the discount amortization in column [C]. Column [E] is the net bond payable, which is the $600,000 face amount less the unamortized discount from column [D].

Exhibit 7B.1 Bond Discount Amortization Table

Period	[A] ([E] × market%) Interest Expense	[B] (Face × coupon%) Cash Interest Paid	[C] ([A] − [B]) Discount Amortization	[D] (Prior bal − [C]) Discount Balance	[E] (Face − [D]) Bond Payable, Net
0				$16,804	$583,196
1	$11,664	$ 9,000	$ 2,664	14,140	585,860
2	11,717	9,000	2,717	11,423	588,577
3	11,772	9,000	2,772	8,651	591,349
4	11,827	9,000	2,827	5,824	594,176
5	11,884	9,000	2,884	2,940	597,060
6	11,940	9,000	2,940	0	600,000
	$70,804	$54,000	$16,804		

Cash paid *plus* discount amortization equals interest expense

During the bond life, carrying value is adjusted to par and the discount to zero

The table shows amounts for the six interest payment periods. The amortization process continues until period 6, at which time the discount balance is 0 and the net bond payable is $600,000 (the maturity value). Each semiannual period, interest expense is recorded at 2%, the market rate of interest at the bond's issuance. This rate does not change over the life of the bond, even if the prevailing market interest rates change. An amortization table reveals the financial statement effects of the bond for its duration. Specifically, we see the income statement effects in column [A], the cash effects in column [B], and the balance sheet effects in columns [D] and [E].

Amortization of Premium

To illustrate amortization of a premium bond, we assume that Verizon issues bonds with a $600,000 face value, a 3% annual coupon rate payable semiannually (1.5% semiannual rate), a maturity of three years (six semiannual interest payments), and a 2% annual (1% semiannual) market interest rate. These facts yield a bond issue price of $617,386.43, which we round to $617,386. Exhibit 7B.2 shows the premium amortization table for this bond.

Interest expense is computed using the same process that we used for discount bonds. The difference is that the yield rate is 1% semiannual in the premium case. Cash interest paid follows from the bond contract (face amount × coupon rate), and the other columns' computations reflect the premium amortization. After period 6, the premium is fully amortized (equals zero) and the net bond payable balance is $600,000, the amount owed at maturity. Again, an amortization table reveals the financial statement effects of the bond—the income statement effects in column [A], the cash effects in column [B], and the balance sheet effects in columns [D] and [E].

Calculator
N = 6
I/Yr = 1
PMT = −9,000
FV = −600,000
PV = 617,386.43

	A	B
1	Annual coupon rate	3%
2	Annual market rate	2%
3	Interest payments per year	2
4	Years to maturity	3
5	Face (par) value	600,000
6	Issue price	617,386.43
7	= PV(B2/B3,B4*B3,−B5*B1/B3,−B5, 0)	
8	= 617,386.43	

Exhibit 7B.2 ■ Bond Premium Amortization Table

Period	[A] ([E] × market%) Interest Expense	[B] (Face × coupon%) Cash Interest Paid	[C] ([B] − [A]) Premium Amortization	[D] (Prior bal − [C]) Premium Balance	[E] (Face + [D]) Bond Payable, Net
0				$17,386	$617,386
1	$ 6,174	$ 9,000	$ 2,826	14,560	614,560
2	6,146	9,000	2,854	11,706	611,706
3	6,117	9,000	2,883	8,823	608,823
4	6,088	9,000	2,912	5,911	605,911
5	6,059	9,000	2,941	2,970	602,970
6	6,030	9,000	2,970	0	600,000
	$36,614	$54,000	$17,386		

During the bond life, carrying value is adjusted to par and the premium to zero

Cash paid *less* premium amortization equals interest expense

Guidance Answers

You Are the Vice President of Finance
Pg. 7-24 You might consider the types of restructuring that would strengthen financial ratios typically used to assess liquidity and solvency by the rating agencies. Such restructuring includes generating cash by reducing inventory, reallocating cash outflows from investing activities (PPE) to debt reduction, and issuing stock for cash and using the proceeds to reduce debt (an equity for debt recapitalization). These actions increase liquidity or reduce financial leverage and, thus, should improve debt rating. An improved debt rating will attract more investors because your current debt rating is below investment grade and is not a suitable investment for many professionally managed portfolios. An improved debt rating will also lower the interest rate on your debt. Offsetting these benefits are costs such as the following: (1) potential loss of sales from inventory stock-outs; (2) potential future cash flow reductions and loss of market power from reduced PPE investments; and (3) costs of equity issuances (equity costs more than debt because investors demand a higher return to compensate for added risk and, unlike interest payments, dividends are not tax deductible for the company), which can yield a net increase in the total cost of capital. All cost and benefits must be assessed before you pursue any restructuring.

Questions

Q7-1. What does the term *current liabilities* mean? What assets are usually used to settle current liabilities?

Q7-2. What is an accrual? How do accruals impact the balance sheet and the income statement?

Q7-3. What is the difference between a bond's coupon rate and its market interest rate (yield)?

Q7-4. Why do companies report a gain or loss when they repurchase their bonds? Is this a real economic gain or loss?

Q7-5. How do credit (debt) ratings affect the cost of borrowing for a company?

Q7-6. How would you interpret a company's reported gain or loss on the repurchase of its bonds?

Assignments with the logo in the margin are available in *my* BusinessCourse.
See the Preface of the book for details.

Mini Exercises

LO1
NCI Building Systems (NCS)

M7-7. Interpreting a Contingent Liability Footnote

NCI Building Systems reports the following footnote to one of its recent 10-Ks related to its manufacturing of metal coil coatings and metal building components.

> We have discovered the existence of trichloroethylene in the ground water at our Southlake, Texas facility. Horizontal delineation concentrations in excess of applicable residential assessment levels have not been fully identified. We have filed an application with the Texas Commission of Environmental Quality ("TCEQ") for entry into the voluntary cleanup program. The cost of required remediation, if any, will vary depending on the nature and extent of the contamination. As of October 28, we have accrued $0.1 million to complete site analysis and testing. At this time, we cannot estimate a loss for any potential remediation costs, but we do not believe there will be a material adverse effect on our Consolidated Financial Statements.

a. How has NCI reported this potential liability on its balance sheet?
b. Does the $0.1 million accrual "to complete site analysis and testing" relate to a contingent liability? Explain.

LO2

M7-8. Analyzing and Computing Financial Statement Effects of Interest

Leahy Inc. signed a 90-day, 8% note payable for $13,800 on December 16. Use the financial statement effects template to illustrate the year-end December 31 accounting adjustment Leahy must make.

LO1

M7-9. Analyzing and Determining Liability Amounts

For each of the following situations, indicate the liability amount, if any, that is reported on the balance sheet of Bloomington Inc. at December 31, 2019.

a. Bloomington owes $220,000 at year-end 2019 for inventory purchases.
b. Bloomington agreed to purchase a $28,000 drill press in January 2020.
c. During November and December of 2019, Bloomington sold products to a customer and warranted them against product failure for 90 days. Estimated costs of honoring this 90-day warranty during 2020 are $3,100.
d. Bloomington provides a profit-sharing bonus for its executives equal to 5% of reported pretax annual income. The estimated pretax income for 2019 is $800,000. Bonuses are not paid until January of the following year.

LO3, 5
Citigroup Inc. (C)

M7-10. Interpreting Relations among Bond Price, Coupon, Yield, and Credit Rating

The following appeared in **Markets Insider** (https://markets.businessinsider.com/bonds) regarding outstanding bonds issued by **Citigroup Inc.**

Price	Coupon (%)	Maturity	Yield to Maturity (%)	Moody's Ratings
166.43	6.80	2038	2.40	A3
122.70	5.15	2026	1.59	A3

a. Discuss the relation among the coupon rate, price, and yield for the bond maturing in 2038.
b. Compare the yields on the two bonds. Why are the yields different when the credit ratings are the same?

M7-11. Determining Gain or Loss on Bond Redemption
On April 30, one year before maturity, Middleton Company retired $200,000 of its 9% bonds payable at the current market price of 101 (101% of the bond face amount, or $200,000 × 1.01 = $202,000). The bond book value on April 30 is $196,600, reflecting an unamortized discount of $3,400. Bond interest is currently fully paid and recorded up to the date of retirement. What is the gain or loss on retirement of these bonds? Is this gain or loss a real economic gain or loss? Explain.

M7-12. Interpreting Bond Footnote Disclosures
Marriott International reports the following long-term debt as part of its MD&A in its 2018 10-K.

	Obligations Expiring by Period ($ millions)						
Maturity Date	Total	2019	2020	2021	2022	2023	Later Years
Long-term debt	$9,347	$833	$912	$3,108	$1,114	$695	$2,685

a. What does this information indicate about Marriott's future payment obligations for 2019 through 2021?
b. What implications does this payment schedule have for our evaluation of Marriott's liquidity and solvency?

M7-13. Classifying Liability-Related Accounts as Balance Sheet or Income Statement Items
Indicate the proper financial statement classification (balance sheet or income statement) for each of the following liability-related accounts.

a. Gain on Bond Retirement
b. Discount on Bonds Payable
c. Mortgage Notes Payable
d. Bonds Payable
e. Bond Interest Expense
f. Bond Interest Payable (due next period)
g. Premium on Bonds Payable
h. Loss on Bond Retirement

M7-14. Interpreting Bond Footnote Disclosures
Netflix reports the following information from the Management Discussion and Analysis section of its 2018 10-K.

> The Notes include, among other terms and conditions, limitations on the Company's ability to create, incur or allow certain liens; enter into sale and lease-back transactions; create, assume, incur or guarantee additional indebtedness of certain of the Company's subsidiaries; and consolidate or merge with, or convey, transfer or lease all or substantially all of the Company's and its subsidiaries assets, to another person. As of December 31, 2018 and December 31, 2017, the Company was in compliance with all related covenants.

a. The operating and financing restrictions that Netflix reports are similar to those discussed in the section on credit ratings and the cost of debt. What effects might these covenants have on the degree of freedom that management has in running Netflix?
b. What pressures might management face if the company's ratios are near covenant limits?

M7-15. Analyzing Financial Statement Effects of Bond Redemption
Weiss Corporation issued $600,000 of 10%, 20-year bonds at 106 on January 1, 2015. Interest is payable semiannually on June 30 and December 31. Through January 1, 2020, Weiss amortized $10,000 of the bond premium. On January 1, 2020, Weiss retired the bonds at 103. Use the financial statement effects template to illustrate the bond retirement at January 1, 2020.

M7-16. Analyzing Financial Statement Effects of Bond Redemption
Camden Inc. issued $450,000 of 8%, 15-year bonds at 96 on July 1, 2015. Interest is payable semiannually on December 31 and June 30. Through June 30, 2020, Camden amortized $6,000 of the bond discount. On July 1, 2020, Camden retired the bonds at 101. Use the financial statement effects template to record the bond retirement.

LO2

M7-17. Analyzing and Computing Accrued Interest on Notes

During the current year, Penman Inc. issued three short-term notes payable with principal and interest due at the end of the term of the note. Compute interest accrued for each of the notes payable as of December 31 of the current year (assume a 365-day year).

Lender	Issuance Date	Principal	Interest Rate (%)	Term
Nissim......	11/21	$30,000	10%	120 days
Klein.......	12/13	22,000	8	90 days
Bildersee....	12/19	26,000	6	60 days

LO5
KLA-Tencor (KLAC)

M7-18. Interpreting Credit Ratings

KLA-Tencor reports the following information in the Management Discussion & Analysis section of its 2018 10-K report.

> Our credit ratings as of June 30, 2018 are summarized below:
>
> | Credit Rating Agency | Rating |
> |---|---|
> | Fitch..................................... | BBB+ |
> | Moody's................................. | Baa+ |
> | Standard & Poor's......................... | BBB |
>
> Factors that can affect our credit ratings include changes in our operating performance, the economic environment, conditions in the semiconductor and semiconductor equipment industries, business acquisitions, our financial position and changes in our business strategy.

a. Is KLA-Tencor above or below investment grade? *Hint:* See Exhibit 7.3.
b. KLA-Tencor has reduced the level of its financial leverage over the past several years. How does the reduction in financial leverage likely affect the company's credit ratings?
c. What effect will less financial leverage have on the company's borrowing costs? Explain.

LO3, 6

M7-19. Computing Bond Issue Price

Abbington Inc. issues $700,000 of 9% bonds that pay interest semiannually and mature in 10 years. Compute the bond issue price assuming that the prevailing market rate of interest is:

a. 8% per year compounded semiannually.
b. 10% per year compounded semiannually.

LO3, 6

M7-20. Computing Issue Price for Zero Coupon Bonds

Underwood Inc. issues $350,000 of zero coupon bonds that mature in 10 years. Compute the bond issue price assuming that the bonds' market rate is:

a. 8% per year compounded semiannually.
b. 10% per year compounded semiannually.

LO1

M7-21. Determining the Financial Statement Effects of Accounts Payable Transactions

Hobson Company had the following transactions relating to its accounts payable. Use the financial statement effects template to identify the effects (both amounts and accounts) for these transactions.

a. Purchases $1,260 of inventory on credit.
b. Sells inventory for $1,650 on credit.
c. Records $1,260 cost of sales for transaction b.
d. Receives $1,650 cash toward accounts receivable.
e. Pays $1,260 cash to settle accounts payable.

LO3, 4, 6

M7-22. Computing Bond Issue Price and Preparing an Amortization Table in Excel

On January 1, 2021, Springfield Inc. issues $400,000 of 8% bonds that pay interest semiannually and mature in 10 years (December 31, 2030).

a. Using the Excel PRICE function, compute the issue price assuming that the bonds' market rate is 7% per year compounded semiannually. (Use 100 for the redemption value to get a price as a percentage of the face amount, and use 1 for the basis.)
b. Prepare an amortization table in Excel to demonstrate the amortization of the book (carrying) value to the $400,000 maturity value at the end of the 20th semiannual period.

M7-23. Determining Credit Ratings

The chart below shows financial ratios for three companies. Use the data, along with Exhibit 7.4 to determine a bond rating for each of the three companies below.

	EBITA/ Average Assets	Operating Margin	EBITA Margin	EBITA/ Interest Expense	(FFO + Int Exp)/ Int Exp	Debt/ EBITDA	DEBT/ Book Capital-ization	FFO/ Debt	Retained Cash Flow/Net Debt	CAPEX/ Depre-ciation	Revenue Volatility
Company 1..	12.80%	16.30%	18.82%	15.0	13.4	1.6	38.12%	44.72%	37.64%	1.3	10.1
Company 2..	9.20%	11.40%	13.00%	2.8	5.1	3.3	48.60%	21.73%	21.92%	1.2	16.0
Company 3..	13.87%	18.62%	20.76%	22.2	20.5	1.3	39.87%	60.82%	32.79%	1.3	6.3

M7-24. Applying Time Value of Money Concepts

Complete the missing information in the table below. Assume that all bonds pay interest semiannually.

	Annual Yield	Years to Maturity	Coupon Rate	Face Value	Issue Proceeds
Firm 1...	8.00%	15	7.00%	$ 300,000	?
Firm 2...	3.00%	10	0.00%	?	$ 556,853
Firm 3...	6.50%	?	5.00%	$ 500,000	$ 468,416
Firm 4...	?	12	3.50%	$1,000,000	$1,147,822
Firm 5...	0.80%	20	2.00%	$ 500,000	?

M7-25. Applying Time Value of Money Concepts

Ozona Minerals issued bonds that mature in 10 years. As is typical for bonds, Ozona Minerals must pay interest only on the $250 million face value. As part of the bond indenture, Ozona Minerals must make annual payments to a sinking fund, which is a pool of money set aside to help repay the bond issue. The sinking fund must be equal to 50% of the face value of the bonds in 10 years (at maturity). If Ozona Minerals can invest at 5%, what amount must the company add to the sinking fund each year to comply with the sinking fund requirement?

M7-26. Calculating Gains and Losses on Early Retirement of Debt

The data below pertain to bonds outstanding at 2020 year-end. For each of the following outstanding bonds, determine whether the company would record a gain or a loss if it decided to retire the bonds at the end of fiscal 2020. Calculate the amount of gain or loss.

	Face Value	Premium (Discount)	Fair Value
Firm 1......	$ 450,000	$42,300	$502,189
Firm 2......	1,000,000	(69,034)	947,482
Firm 3......	250,000	—	244,893
Firm 4......	500,000	2,033	498,574

Exercises

E7-27. Analyzing and Computing Accrued Warranty Liability and Expense

Canton Company sells a motor that carries a 60-day unconditional warranty against product failure. From prior years' experience, Canton estimates that 3% of units sold each period will require repair at an average cost of $160 per unit. During the current period, Canton sold 100,000 units and repaired 2,400 of those units.

a. How much warranty expense must Canton report in its current-period income statement?
b. What warranty liability related to current-period sales will Canton report on its current period-end balance sheet? Assume that actual repair costs are as estimated. (*Hint:* Remember that some units were repaired in the current period.)
c. What analysis issues must we consider with respect to reported warranty liabilities?

LO1

E7-28. Analyzing Contingent and Other Liabilities
The following independent situations represent various types of liabilities. Analyze each situation and indicate which of the following is the proper accounting treatment for the company: (a) record a liability on the balance sheet, (b) disclose the liability in a financial statement footnote, or (c) neither record nor disclose any liability.

1. A stockholder has filed a lawsuit against Windsor Corporation. Windsor's attorneys have reviewed the facts of the case. Their review revealed that similar lawsuits have never resulted in a cash award and it is highly unlikely that this lawsuit will either.
2. Sterling Company signed a 60-day, 10% note when it purchased items from another company.
3. The Environmental Protection Agency notifies Stark Industries that a state where it has a plant is filing a lawsuit for groundwater pollution against Stark and another company that has a plant adjacent to Stark's plant. Test results have not identified the exact source of the pollution. Stark's manufacturing process often produces by-products that can pollute groundwater.
4. Franklin Company manufactured and sold products to a retailer that later sold the products to consumers. Franklin Company will replace the product if it is found to be defective within 90 days of the sale to the consumer. Historically, 1.2% of the products are returned for replacement.

LO1
Harley-Davidson Inc. (HOG)

E7-29. Recording and Analyzing Warranty Accrual and Payment
Refer to the discussion of and excerpt from the **Harley-Davidson Inc.** warranty reserve on page 7-6 to answer the following questions.

a. Using the financial statement effects template, record separately the 2018 warranty liability transactions relating to the (1) "Warranties issued during the period," (2) "Recalls and changes to preexisting warranty obligations," and (3) "Settlements made during the period."
b. Does the level of Harley-Davidson's warranty accrual appear to be reasonable?

LO1

E7-30. Analyzing and Computing Accrued Wages Liability and Expense
Demski Company pays its employees on the 1st and 15th of each month. It is March 31 and the company is preparing financial statements for this quarter. Its employees have earned $96,000 since the 15th of March and have not yet been paid. How will Demski's balance sheet and income statement reflect the accrual of wages on March 31? What balance sheet and income statement accounts would be incorrectly reported if Demski failed to make this accrual (for each account indicate whether it would be overstated or understated)?

LO3, 4

E7-31. Analyzing and Reporting Financial Statement Effects of Bond Transactions
On January 1, Remington Corp. issued $500,000 of 15-year, 10% bonds payable for $586,460 yielding an effective interest rate of 8%. Interest is payable semiannually on June 30 and December 31.

a. Show computations to confirm the issue price of $586,460.
b. Indicate the financial statement effects using the template for (1) bond issuance, (2) semiannual interest payment and premium amortization on June 30 of the first year, and (3) semiannual interest payment and premium amortization on December 31 of the first year.

LO4

E7-32. Analyzing and Reporting Financial Statement Effects of Mortgages
On January 1, Patterson Inc. borrowed $1,000,000 on a 10%, 15-year mortgage note payable. The note is to be repaid in equal semiannual installments of $65,051 (payable on June 30 and December 31). Each mortgage payment includes principal and interest. Interest is computed using the effective interest method. Indicate the financial statement effects using the template for (a) issuance of the mortgage note payable, (b) payment of the first installment on June 30, and (c) payment of the second installment on December 31.

LO5
Ford Motor Co. (F)

E7-33. Assessing the Effects of Bond Credit Rating Changes
Ford Motor Co. reports the following information from the Risk Factors and the Management Discussion and Analysis sections of its 2018 10-K report.

> **Credit Ratings** Our short-term and long-term debt is rated by four credit rating agencies designated as nationally recognized statistical rating organizations ("NRSROs") by the U.S. Securities and Exchange Commission: DBRS, Fitch, Moody's, and S&P Global Ratings.
> In several markets, locally-recognized rating agencies also rate us. A credit rating reflects an assessment by the rating agency of the credit risk associated with a corporate entity or

continued

continued from previous page

particular securities issued by that entity. Rating agencies' ratings of us are based on information provided by us and other sources. Credit ratings are not recommendations to buy, sell, or hold securities, and are subject to revision or withdrawal at any time by the assigning rating agency. Each rating agency may have different criteria for evaluating company risk and, therefore, ratings should be evaluated independently for each rating agency.

There have been no rating actions taken by these NRSROs since the filing of our Quarterly Report on Form 10-Q for the quarter ended September 30, 2018.

The following chart summarizes certain of the credit ratings and outlook presently assigned by these four NRSROs:

	NRSRO RATINGS						
	Ford			Ford Credit			NRSROs
	Issuer Default Corporate/ Issuer Rating"	Long-Term Senior Unsecured	Outlook / Trend	Long-Term Senior Unsecured	Short-Term Unsecured	Outlook/ Trend	Minimum Long-Term Investment Grade Rating
DBRS	BBB	BBB	Stable	BBB	R-2M	Stable	BBB (low)
Fitch	BBB	BBB	Stable	BBB	F2	Stable	BBB–
Moody's . . .	N/A	Baa3	Negative	Baa3	P-3	Negative	Baa3
S&P	BBB	BBB	Negative	BBB	A-2	Negative	BBB–

    a. What financial ratios do credit rating companies such as the four NRSROs listed above use to evaluate the relative riskiness of borrowers?
    b. What economic consequences would there be if any of the four NRSROs upgraded Ford's credit rating? How would this affect the fair value of the company's bonds?
    c. What type of actions can Ford take to improve its credit ratings?

E7-34. Analyzing and Reporting Financial Statement Effects of Bond Transactions **LO3, 4**
Winston Inc. reports financial statements each December 31. On May 1, of the current year, it issues $400,000 of 9%, 15-year bonds, with interest payable on October 31 and April 30. Assuming the bonds are sold at par on May 1, complete the financial statement effects template to reflect the following events: (a) bond issuance, (b) the first semiannual interest payment, and (c) retirement of $150,000 of the bonds at 102 on November 1 of the current year.

E7-35. Analyzing and Reporting Financial Statement Effects of Bond Transactions **LO3, 4**
On January 1 of the current year, Banek Inc. issued $350,000 of 8%, nine-year bonds for $309,086, which implies a market (yield) rate of 10%. Semiannual interest is payable on June 30 and December 31 of each year.

    a. Show computations to confirm the bond issue price.
    b. Indicate the financial statement effects using the template for (1) bond issuance, (2) semiannual interest payment and discount amortization on June 30 of the current year, and (3) semiannual interest payment and discount amortization on December 31 of the current year.

E7-36. Analyzing and Reporting Financial Statement Effects of Bond Transactions **LO3, 4**
On January 1 of the current year, Shields Inc. issued $1,000,000 of 9%, 20-year bonds for $1,098,964, yielding a market (yield) rate of 8%. Semiannual interest is payable on June 30 and December 31 of each year.

    a. Show computations to confirm the bond issue price.
    b. Indicate the financial statement effects using the template for (1) bond issuance, (2) semiannual interest payment and premium amortization on June 30 of the current year, and (3) semiannual interest payment and premium amortization on December 31 of the current year.

E7-37. Determining Bond Prices, Interest Rates, and Financial Statement Effects **LO3, 4**
Deere & Company's 2018 10-K reports the following footnote relating to long-term debt for its equipment operations subsidiary. Deere's borrowings include $300 million, 7.125% notes, due in 2031 (highlighted below).

Deere & Co (DE)

Long-term borrowings at October 28 consisted of the following in millions of dollars:

Notes and Debentures	2018	2017
4.375% notes due 2019		$ 750
8-1/2% debentures due 2022	$ 105	105
2.60% notes due 2022	1,000	1,000
6.55% debentures due 2028	200	200
5.375% notes due 2029	500	500
8.10% debentures due 2030	250	250
7.125% notes due 2031	**300**	**300**
3.90% notes due 2042	1,250	1,250
Other notes	1,109	1,136
Total	$4,714	$5,491

A recent price quote (from **Markets Insider**) on Deere's 7.125% notes follows.

Type	Issuer	Price	Coupon (%)	Maturity	Yield (%)	Moody's Rating	Callable
Corp	Deere & CO	131.03	7.125	2031	2.82%	A2	No

This price quote indicates that Deere's 7.125% notes have a market price of 131.03 (131.03% of face value), resulting in a yield of 2.82%.

a. Assuming that these notes were originally issued at par value, what does the market price reveal about interest rate changes since Deere issued its notes? (Assume that Deere's credit rating has remained the same.)
b. Does the change in interest rates since the issuance of these notes affect the amount of interest expense that Deere reports in its income statement? Explain.
c. How much cash would Deere have to pay to repurchase the 7.125% notes at the quoted market price of 131.03%? (Assume no interest is owed when Deere repurchases the notes.) How would the repurchase affect Deere's current income?
d. Assuming that the notes remain outstanding until their maturity, at what market price will the notes sell on their due date in 2031?

LO6 E7-38. Computing Present Values of Single Amounts and Annuities
Refer to Tables 1 and 2 in Appendix A near the end of the book to compute the present value for each of the following amounts.

a. $120,000 received 10 years hence if the annual interest rate is:
 1. 10% compounded annually.
 2. 10% compounded semiannually.
b. $2,000 received at the end of each year for the next eight years discounted at 8% compounded annually.
c. $800 received at the end of each six months for the next 15 years if the interest rate is 10% per year compounded semiannually.
d. $250,000 received 10 years hence discounted at 10% per year compounded annually.

LO3, 4 E7-39. Analyzing and Reporting Financial Statement Effects of Bond Transactions
On January 1 of the current year, Arbor Corporation issued $800,000 of 20-year, 11% bonds for $739,815, yielding a market (yield) rate of 12%. Interest is payable semiannually on June 30 and December 31.

a. Confirm the bond issue price.
b. Indicate the financial statement effects using the template for (1) bond issuance, (2) semiannual interest payment and discount amortization on June 30 of the current year, and (3) semiannual interest payment and discount amortization on December 31 of the current year.

E7-40. **Interpreting Credit Rating Action**
Moody's Investors Service issued the following press release (excerpts) on December 14, 2018, pertaining to a credit rating action for **Xerox Corporation**.

> New York, December 14, 2018—Moody's Investors Service downgraded Xerox Corporation's senior unsecured debt ratings to Ba1 from Baa3. The rating outlook is negative. As part of the rating actions, Moody's assigned Xerox a Ba1 Corporate Family Rating (CFR).
>
> **RATINGS RATIONALE** The downgrades reflect uncertainty about the company's ability to stabilize and grow its revenue base over the next few years given the secular decline in copier and printing demand as well as intense global competition. Xerox reported seven consecutive quarters of year over year revenue declines on a constant currency basis since the spin-off of the business process outsourcing segment despite major product launches in 2017.
>
> Moody's expects organic revenues to continue on a flat to declining trajectory over the next 12 to 18 months in the absence of an unlikely fundamental change in the company's revenue mix or market share.
>
> Xerox's Ba1 CFR is supported by the company's good market position in its core mid-range print and document outsourcing markets as well as solid leverage and free cash flow metrics. Roughly 78% of Xerox's revenue is derived from post-sale activities that include document outsourcing, managed print services, maintenance service, supplies (toner and paper), and finance income. These elements come with higher operating margins and provide some revenue predictability.
>
> The negative outlook reflects the persistent pressures on the company's core copier and printing business as well as execution challenges. The outlook could be changed to stable if the company demonstrates progress in stabilizing revenues and if Moody's expects the company will be able to maintain operating margins and free cash flow generation while keeping leverage in line with current levels.

a. What rating action did Moody's take on Xerox in December 2018?
b. Did the rating action change the investment grade of Moody's debt? (*Hint:* See Exhibit 7.3.) What is a likely economic outcome for Xerox?
c. What is the primary rationale for the downgrade?
d. Despite the downgrade, Moody's cites four reasons for the rating to be as high as it is. What are these four reasons?

E7-41. **Calculating Ratios and Estimating Credit Rating**
The following data are from **Amazon**'s 2018 10-K report ($ millions).

Revenue	$232,887	Net income	$ 10,073
Interest expense	1,417	Capital expenditures (CAPEX)	13,427
Tax expense	1,197	Total debt	23,495
Amortization expense	8,979	Average assets	146,979
Depreciation expense	6,362		

a. Use the data above to calculate the following ratios: EBITA/Average assets, EBITA Margin, EBITA/Interest expense, Debt/EBITDA, CAPEX/Depreciation Expense. Definitions for these ratios are in Exhibit 7.4.
b. Refer to Exhibit 7.4 and the ratios you calculated in part *a*. Estimate the credit rating that Moody's might assign to Amazon.

E7-42. **Calculating Ratios and Estimating Credit Rating**
The following data are from **Kellogg**'s 10-K report dated December 29, 2018 ($ millions).

Revenue	$13,547	Earnings from continuing operations	$ 1,344
Interest expense	287	Capital expenditures (CAPEX)	578
Tax expense	181	Total debt	8,893
Amortization expense	23	Average assets	17,066
Depreciation expense	493		

a. Use the data above to calculate the following ratios: EBITA/Average assets, EBITA Margin, EBITA/Interest expense, Debt/EBITDA, CAPEX/Depreciation Expense. Definitions for these ratios are in Exhibit 7.4.
b. Refer to Exhibit 7.4 and the ratios you calculated in part *a*. Estimate the credit rating that Moody's might assign to Kellogg.

LO6 **E7-43. Applying Time Value of Money Concepts**

Fulton Corporation purchases new manufacturing facilities and assumes a 10-year mortgage of $4 million. The annual interest rate on the mortgage is 5.5% and payments are due at the end of each year.

a. Determine the mortgage payment that Fulton Corporation must make each year.
b. Use Excel to prepare a mortgage amortization schedule for the 10 years.
c. At the end of the first year, what amount will Fulton include as "current maturities of long-term debt" on its balance sheet?

LO6 **E7-44. Applying Time Value of Money Concepts**

Manchester Corporation takes a 20-year mortgage of $15 million. The annual interest rate on the mortgage is 7% and payments are due at the end of each year.

a. Determine the annual mortgage payment.
b. Use the financial statement effects template to record the mortgage proceeds.
c. Use the financial statement effects template to record the first two mortgage payments.

LO3
Boston Scientific
(BSX)

E7-45. Interpreting Graphical Bond Prices

Consider the following price chart for Boston Scientific's 4.00% bond. The bond was issued at par in February 2018 and matures in March 2028. The following screen shot is from Markets Insider (August 9, 2019) and tracks the bond's daily price since issuance.

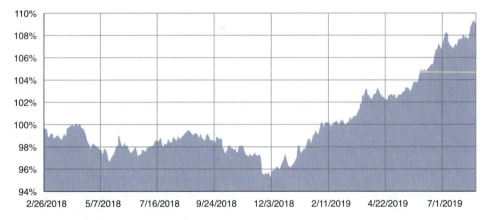

a. At what approximate price is the bond trading on August 9, 2019?
b. In late 2018, the bond was significantly below par. Explain how this could have happened.
c. Consider the price movement during 2019. What is the relation of the bond's price to its yield during this period?
d. Suggest three reasons for Boston Scientific's bond price to increase so significantly during the first half of 2019.

Problems

LO2, 3, 4, 5
PepsiCo Inc.
(PEP)

P7-46. Interpreting and Analyzing Debt Footnotes

PepsiCo Inc. reports $32,248 million of long-term debt outstanding as of December 2018 in the following schedule to its 10-K report.

The following table summarizes the Company's debt obligations:

Debt Obligations ($ millions)	2018	2017
Short-term debt obligations		
Current maturities of long-term debt	$ 3,953	$ 4,020
Commercial paper (1.3%)	—	1,385
Other borrowings (6.0% and 4.7%)	73	80
	$ 4,026	$ 5,485
Long-term debt obligations		
Notes due 2018 (2.4%)	$ —	$ 4,016
Notes due 2019 (3.1% and 2.1%)	3,948	3,933
Notes due 2020 (3.9% and 3.1%)	3,784	3,792
Notes due 2021 (3.1% and 2.4%)	3,257	3,300
Notes due 2022 (2.8% and 2.6%)	3,802	3,853
Notes due 2023 (2.9% and 2.4%)	1,270	1,257
Notes due 2024–2047 (3.7% and 3.8%)	16,161	17,634
Other, due 2018–2026 (1.3% and 1.3%)	26	31
	32,248	37,816
Less: current maturities of long-term debt obligations	(3,953)	(4,020)
Total	$28,295	$33,796

In 2018, we completed a cash tender offer for certain notes issued by PepsiCo and predecessors to a PepsiCo subsidiary for $1.6 billion in cash to redeem the following amounts:

Interest Rate	Maturity Date	Amount Tendered
7.290%	September 2026	$ 11
7.440%	September 2026	$ 4
7.000%	March 2029	$357
5.500%	May 2035	$138
4.875%	November 2040	$410
5.500%	January 2040	$408

Our borrowing costs and access to capital and credit markets may be adversely affected by a downgrade or potential downgrade of our credit ratings.

Rating agencies routinely evaluate us, and their ratings of our long-term and short-term debt are based on a number of factors, including our cash generating capability, levels of indebtedness, policies with respect to shareholder distributions and our financial strength generally, as well as factors beyond our control, such as the then-current state of the economy and our industry generally. Any downgrade of our credit ratings by a credit rating agency, especially any downgrade to below investment grade, whether as a result of our actions or factors which are beyond our control, could increase our future borrowing costs, impair our ability to access capital and credit markets on terms commercially acceptable to us or at all, and result in a reduction in our liquidity.

Moody's Investors Service (www.moodys.com) reported the following regarding PepsiCo.

Rating Action: Moody's rates PepsiCo's new notes at A1; outlook stable
New York, July 25, 2019—Moody's today assigned an A1 rating to PepsiCo, Inc.'s senior unsecured notes being issued in 10 and 30 year tranches. All other ratings for the company remain unchanged. The outlook is stable. The proceeds will be used for general corporate purposes.

On August 9, 2019, **Markets Insider** reported the following details for notes due in 2022.

Type	Issuer	Price	Coupon(%)	Maturity	YTM(%)	Moody's Ratings
Corp......	PEPSICO INC	102.27	2.75%	3/5/2022	1.87%	A1

Required

a. PepsiCo reports current maturities of long-term debt of $3,953 million as part of short-term debt. Why is this amount reported that way? Is this amount important to our analysis of PepsiCo? Explain.

b. The Markets Insider excerpt above reveals that the 2.75% notes due in 2022 are priced at 102.27, resulting in a yield to maturity of 1.87%. Assuming that the credit rating of PepsiCo has not changed, what does the pricing of this bond imply about interest rate changes since PepsiCo issued the bond?

c. During 2018, PepsiCo retired certain notes (early) with a cash tender offer. What was the total amount tendered? PepsiCo paid $1.6 billion cash for the tendered notes. Assume that the reported amounts tendered represent the net book value of the notes. What gain or loss did the company report on this early retirement of debt?

d. The Moody's rating action excerpt above reveals that the company issued new notes in 2019. From this ratings action, what can investors infer about PepsiCo's creditworthiness in 2019? How does this rating action affect the issue proceeds?

e. What type of actions can PepsiCo take to improve its credit ratings?

LO3, 4
Boston Scientific Corporation (BSX)

P7-47. Interpreting Debt Footnotes on Interest Rates and Interest Expense

Boston Scientific discloses the following as part of its long-term debt footnote in its December 31, 2018 10-K.

Borrowings and Credit Agreements

In millions, except interest rates	Issuance Date	Maturity Date	As of December 31, 2018	As of December 31, 2017	Semi-annual Coupon Rate
January 2020 Notes............	December 2009	January 2020	$ 850	$ 850	6.000%
May 2020 Notes...............	May 2015	May 2020	600	600	2.850%
May 2022 Notes...............	May 2015	May 2022	500	500	3.375%
October 2023 Notes............	August 2013	October 2023	450	450	4.125%
May 2025 Notes...............	May 2015	May 2025	750	750	3.850%
March 2028 Notes	February 2018	March 2028	1,000	—	4.000%
November 2035 Notes⁽¹⁾........	November 2005	November 2035	350	350	7.000%
January 2040 Notes............	December 2009	January 2040	300	300	7.375%
Unamortized debt insurance discount and deferred financing cost		2020–2040	(29)	(24)	
Unamortized gain on fair value hedge		2020—2025	26	38	
Capital lease obligation		Various	6	1	
Long-term debt................................			$4,803	$3,815	

⁽¹⁾ Corporate credit rating improvements may result in a decrease in the adjusted interest rate on our November 2035 Notes to the extent that our lowest credit rating is above BBB– or Baa3. The interest rates on our November 2035 notes will be permanently reinstated to the issuance rate if the lowest credit ratings assigned to these senior notes is either A– or A3 or higher.

Boston Scientific discloses its required principal debt repayments due during each of the next five years and thereafter.

In millions	
2019	$2,248
2020	1,540
2021	0
2022	500
2023	450
Thereafter	2,400

Boston Scientific also discloses the following information.

Interest Expense The following table provides a summary of our *Interest expense* and average borrowing rate :

Year Ended December 31 (in millions)	2018	2017	2016
Interest expense	$(241)	$(229)	$(233)
Weighted average borrowing rate	3.6%	3.8%	4.0%
Cash paid for interest	$(262)	$(235)	$(233)

The price of the Boston Scientific's bonds in February 2019 follows.

Maturity date	Coupon	Current Price	Current Yield	Moody's Rating (02/21/2019)
2028	4.00%	109.35	2.80%	Baa2
2023	4.125%	101.57	2.41%	Baa2

Required
a. What amount of Boston Scientific's long-term debt is due in 2019?
b. What is the total amount of Boston Scientific's long-term debt at December 31, 2018, including the current maturities?
c. The company's balance sheet reports short-term debt including current maturities of $2,253 million and $1,801 million in 2018 and 2017, respectively. Compute the average effective interest rate on the company's total debt for fiscal 2018. Compare this to the average interest rate the company reports.
d. Explain how the amount of cash paid for interest can differ from the amount of interest expense recorded in the income statement.
e. The $1,000 million 4.00% note due in 2028 is priced at 109.35 (109.35% of face value, or $1,093.50 million) as of early 2019, resulting in a current yield of 2.8%. Assuming that the company's credit rating has not changed since the bond was issued, what does the pricing of this 4.00% bond imply about interest rate changes since Boston Scientific issued the bond?
f. Compare the bonds that mature in 2023 and 2028. Explain why the bond with the higher coupon rate (4.125%) has the lower yield (2.41%).

LO4, 5
Oracle Corp. (ORCL)

P7-48. Analyzing Debt Terms, Yields, Prices, and Credit Ratings
Reproduced below is the debt footnote from the May 31, 2019, 10-K report of Oracle Corporation.

$ millions	May 31, 2019	May 31, 2018
Fixed-rate senior notes:		
$1,500, 2.375%, due January 2019	—	$ 1,500
$1,750, 5.00%, due July 2019	$ 1,750	1,750
$2,000, 2.25%, due October 2019	2,000	2,000
$1,000, 3.875%, due July 2020	1,000	1,000
€1,250, 2.25%, due January 2021	1,393	1,446
$1,500, 2.80%, due July 2021	1,500	1,500
$4,250, 1.90%, due September 2021	4,250	4,250
$2,500, 2.50%, due May 2022	2,500	2,500
$2,500, 2.50%, due October 2022	2,500	2,500
$1,250, 2.625%, due February 2023	1,250	1,250
$1,000, 3.625%, due July 2023	1,000	1,000
$2,500, 2.40%, due September 2023	2,500	2,500
$2,000, 3.40%, due July 2024	2,000	2,000
$2,000, 2.95%, due November 2024	2,000	2,000
$2,500, 2.95%, due May 2025	2,500	2,500
€750, 3.125%, due July 2025	836	868
$3,000, 2.65%, due July 2026	3,000	3,000
$2,750, 3.25%, due November 2027	2,750	2,750
$500, 3.25%, due May 2030	500	500
$1,750, 4.30%, due July 2034	1,750	1,750
$1,250, 3.90%, due May 2035	1,250	1,250
$1,250, 3.85%, due July 2036	1,250	1,250
$1,750, 3.80%, due November 2037	1,750	1,750
$1,250, 6.50%, due April 2038	1,250	1,250
$1,250, 6.125%, due July 2039	1,250	1,250
$2,250, 5.375%, due July 2040	2,250	2,250
$1,000, 4.50%, due July 2044	1,000	1,000
$2,000, 4.125%, due May 2045	2,000	2,000
$3,000, 4.00%, due July 2046	3,000	3,000
$2,250, 4.00%, due November 2047	2,250	2,250
$1,250, 4.375%, due May 2055	1,250	1,250
Floating-rate senior notes:		
$500, three-month LIBOR plus 0.58%, due January 2019	—	500
$750, three-month LIBOR plus 0.51%, due October 2019	750	750
Revolving credit agreements and other borrowings:		
$2,500, LIBOR plus 0.50%, due June 2018	—	2,500
Other borrowings due August 2025	113	113
Total senior notes and other borrowings	56,342	60,927
Unamortized discount/issuance costs	(202)	(282)
Hedge accounting fair value adjustments(1)(4)	27	(26)
Total notes payable and other borrowings	56,167	60,619
Notes payable and other borrowings, current	4,494	4,491
Notes payable and other borrowings, noncurrent	$51,673	$56,128

Future principal payments (adjusted for the effects of the cross-currency swap agreements associated with the January 2021 Notes and July 2025 Notes) for all of our borrowings at May 31, 2019, were as follows:

$ millions	
Fiscal 2020	$ 4,500
Fiscal 2021	2,631
Fiscal 2022	8,250
Fiscal 2023	3,750
Fiscal 2024	3,500
Thereafter	33,984
Total	$56,615

Reproduced below is a summary of the market values as of August 10, 2019, of select Oracle bonds. Source: **Markets Insider** (https://markets.businessinsider.com/bonds).

Maturity Date	Amount $	Price	Coupon %	Yield to Maturity %
July 2020	$1,000	109.47	3.875%	2.613%
April 2038	$1,250	136.78	6.5%	3.36%
July 2039	$1,250	120.47	6.125%	3.45%

Required

a. What is the amount of debt reported on Oracle's May 31, 2019, balance sheet? What are the scheduled maturities for this indebtedness? Why is information relating to a company's scheduled maturities of debt useful in an analysis of its financial condition?

b. Oracle reported $2,082 million in interest expense in the notes to its 2019 income statement. In the note to its statement of cash flows, Oracle indicates that the cash portion of this expense is $2,059 million. What could account for the difference between interest expense and interest paid? Explain.

c. Oracle's long-term debt is rated A1 by Moody's, A+ by S&P Global Ratings, and A+ by Fitch. What factors would be important to consider in attempting to quantify the relative riskiness of Oracle compared with other borrowers? Explain.

d. Oracle's $1,250 million 6.5% notes traded at 136.78 as of August 10, 2019. What is the market value of these notes on that date? How is the difference between this market value and the $1,250 million face value reflected in Oracle's financial statements? What effect would the repurchase of this entire note issue have on Oracle's financial statements? What does the 136.78 price tell us about the general trend in interest rates since Oracle sold this bond issue? Explain.

e. Examine the yields to maturity of the three bonds in the table above. What relation do we observe between these yields and the maturities of the bonds? Also, explain why this relation applies in general.

IFRS Applications

I7-49. **Interpreting Bond Footnote Disclosures and Computing Effective Interest Rate**
In 2019, French grocery retailer **Carrefour** issued bonds as follows.

Issue date	May 7, 2019
Issue amount (€M)	500
Annual coupon rate	1%
Maturity	May 17, 2027
Issue price	99.534

LO3, 4
Carrefour SA
(CRRFY)

a. Determine the annual interest payments.
b. Determine the effective interest rate.
c. What amount of interest expense does the company report related to these bonds for the fiscal year ended December 31, 2019?

LO1
Bombardier Inc.
(BDRBF)

I7-50. Analyzing Contingent Liabilities: Warranty Reserves

Headquartered in Montreal, Quebec, Canada, **Bombardier Inc.** is a multinational aerospace and transportation company, founded in 1941. The company manufactures regional aircraft, business jets, mass transportation equipment, and recreational equipment and is also a financial services provider. Bombardier is a Fortune Global 500 company and operates two segments: BA (Aerospace) and BT (Transportation). Bombardier's 2018 annual report is presented in U.S. dollars, and includes the following details about the company's provision for product warranties ($ millions).

Balance as at December 31 2017	$672
Additions	206
Utilization	(223)
Reversals	(106)
Accretion expense	2
Effect of changes in discount rates	(1)
Disposal of CSALP business	(15)
Effect of foreign currency exchange rate changes	(20)
Balance as at December 31, 2018	**$515**
Of which current	$403
Of which noncurrent	112
	$515

Required

a. In common language, explain what a provision for product warranties is. When do companies create such provisions?
b. What amount is included on the 2018 balance sheet for warranty provision?
c. What amount is included on the 2018 income statement related to warranties?
d. What is meant by "Utilization" in the table? What sort of costs does this entail?

Management Applications

LO3 MA7-51. Coupon Rate versus Effective Rate

Assume that you are the CFO of a company that intends to issue bonds to finance a new manufacturing facility. A subordinate suggests lowering the coupon rate on the bond to lower interest expense and to increase the profitability of your company. Is the rationale for this suggestion a good one? Explain.

LO5 MA7-52. Ethics and Governance: Bond Covenants

Because lenders do not have voting rights like shareholders do, they often reduce their risk by invoking various bond covenants that restrict the company's operating, financing, and investing activities. For example, debt covenants often restrict the amount of debt that the company can issue (in relation to its equity) and impose operating restrictions (such as the ability to acquire other companies or to pay dividends). Failure to abide by these restrictions can have serious consequences, including forcing the company into bankruptcy and potential liquidation. Assume that you are on the board of directors of a company that issues bonds with such restrictions. What safeguards can you identify to ensure compliance with those restrictions?

Ongoing Project

(This ongoing project began in Module 1 and continues through most of the book; even if previous segments were not completed, the requirements are still applicable to any business analysis.) Review liabilities that arise from operating and financing transactions, including the type and quantity of both categories. The goal is to consider how the companies are financed and whether they can repay their obligations as they come due in the short and longer term.

1. *Accrued liabilities.* Accrued liabilities arise from ordinary operations and provide interest-free financing.
   - Are operating liabilities large for the companies? Compare common-size amounts. What proportion of total liabilities are operating?
   - What are the companies' main operating liabilities?
   - Are there substantial contingencies? What gives rise to these? Read the footnote and determine whether the company has recorded a liability on its balance sheet for these contingencies.

2. *Short and Long-Term Debt.* Examine the debt footnote and consider the following questions.
   - What is the common-size debt and how does that compare to published industry averages?
   - What types of debt does the company have? Is it publicly traded? Are there bank loans? Other types of debt?
   - When does the debt mature? Determine if there is a large proportion due in the next year or two. If so, can the company refinance given its current level of debt?
   - What is the average interest rate on debt? Compare it to the coupon rates reported.
   - Read the footnote and the MD&A to see if there are any debt covenants and whether the company is in compliance.
   - If the company has publicly traded debt, determine its current price. Sharp drops in bond prices could indicate a deterioration in the company's credit quality.

3. *Credit Ratings.* Find the companies' credit ratings at two or three ratings agencies' websites.
   - What are the credit ratings and how do they compare across the agencies? Are the two companies similarly rated?
   - Have the ratings changed during the year? If so, why?
   - Are the companies on a credit watch or a downgrade list?
   - If possible, find a credit report online and read it to gain a better understanding of the companies' creditworthiness.
   - Calculate the ratios in Exhibit 7.4 for your firms. Compare the ratios to those for firms with similar credit ratings. Do the credit ratings for the firms seem reasonable?

Solutions to Review Problems

Review 7-1—Solution (in $000s)

a. $70,000, the amount of the additional warranty liability arising from current-year sales.

b. $131,740 (from the current year-end balance) + $70,000 − $85,000 = $116,740

c. The 2019 income statement understates profit by the additional mistaken accrual of $20,000. Thus, next year's balance sheet reports a warranty liability that is $20,000 too high. In a subsequent period, assuming that the actual warranty costs incurred are, indeed, $20,000 lower than originally estimated, the company will not need to accrue as much warranty liability. Consequently, future profit will be higher until the reported warranty liability is reduced (by recognition of costs incurred) to an accurate level. Profit has, therefore, been shifted from next year to a future period(s).

Review 7-2—Solution

($ millions)	Balance Sheet					Income Statement		
Transaction	Cash Asset	+ Noncash Assets	= Liabilities	+ Contrib. Capital	+ Earned Capital	Revenues	− Expenses	= Net Income
Mar. 31: Accrue $125 interest expense*			+125 Interest Payable		−125 Retained Earnings		+125 Interest Expense	−125
Apr 14: Pay principal and interest on note**	−10,148		−125 Interest Payable −10,000 Note Payable		−23 Retained Earnings		+23 Interest Expense	−23

*Accrued interest = $10,000 × 0.06 × 76/365 = $125
** Interest expense = $10,000 × 0.06 × 14/365 = $23

```
IE ...... 125
  IP .......... 125
        IE
       125 |
            IP
           125
NP ... 10,000
IP .....  125
IE ......   23
  Cash ...... 10,148
        NP
      10,000 |
            IP
           125 |
            IE
            23 |
          Cash
              | 10,148
```

Review 7-3—Solution

Calculator
N = 30
I/Yr = 4
PMT = −15,000
FV = −300,000
PV = 351,876

Issue price for $300,000, 15-year bonds that pay 10% interest discounted at 4% semiannually:

Present value of principal payment ($300,000 × 0.30832)........................	$ 92,496
Present value of semiannual interest payments ($15,000 × 17.29203)...........	259,380
Issue price of bonds	$351,876

	A	B
1	Annual coupon rate	10%
2	Annual market rate	8%
3	Interest payments per year	2
4	Years to maturity	15
5	Face (par) value	300,000
6	Issue price	351,876
7	= PV(B2/B3,B4*B3,−B5*B1/B3,−B5, 0)	
8	= 351,876	

Calculator
N = 30
I/Yr = 6
PMT = −15,000
FV = −300,000
PV = 258,706

Issue price for $300,000, 15-year bonds that pay 10% interest, discounted at 6% semiannually:

Present value of principal payment ($300,000 × 0.17411)........................	$ 52,233
Present value of semiannual interest payments ($15,000 × 13.76483)...........	206,472
Issue price of bonds	$258,705

	A	B
1	Annual coupon rate	10%
2	Annual market rate	12%
3	Interest payments per year	2
4	Years to maturity	15
5	Face (par) value	300,000
6	Issue price	258,706
7	= PV(B2/B3,B4*B3,−B5*B1/B3,−B5, 0)	
8	= 258,706	

Review 7-4—Solution

1.

Calculator
N = 30
I/Yr = 4
PMT = −15,000
FV = −300,000
PV = 351,876

Issue price for $300,000, 15-year bonds that pay 10% interest, discounted at 4% semiannually:

Present value of principal payment ($300,000 × 0.30832)........................	$ 92,496
Present value of semiannual interest payments ($15,000 × 17.29203)...........	259,380
Issue price of bonds	$351,876

	A	B
1	Annual coupon rate	10%
2	Annual market rate	8%
3	Interest payments per year	2
4	Years to maturity	15
5	Face (par) value	300,000
6	Issue price	351,876
7	= PV(B2/B3,B4*B3,−B5*B1/B3,−B5, 0)	
8	= 351,876	

2.

Transaction	Balance Sheet					Income Statement		
	Cash Asset	+ Noncash Assets	= Liabilities	+ Contrib. Capital	+ Earned Capital	Revenues	− Expenses	= Net Income
January 1: Issue 10% bonds	+351,876		+351,876 Long-Term Debt					
June 30: Pay interest and amortize bond premium[1]	−15,000		−925 Long-Term Debt		−14,075 Retained Earnings		+14,075 Interest Expense	−14,075
December 31: Pay interest and amortize bond premium[2]	−15,000		−962 Long-Term Debt		−14,038 Retained Earnings		+14,038 Interest Expense	−14,038

Cash 351,876
LTD 351,876

Cash
351,876 |
LTD
       | 351,876

IE ... 14,075
LTD .. 925
   Cash 15,000

IE
14,075 |
LTD
925 |
Cash
       | 15,000

IE ... 14,038
LTD .. 962
   Cash 15,000

IE
14,038 |
LTD
962 |
Cash
       | 15,000

[1] $300,000 × 0.10 × 6/12 = $15,000 cash payment; 0.04 × $351,876 = $14,075 interest expense; the difference of $925 is the bond premium amortization, which reduces the net bond carrying amount.

[2] 0.04 × ($351,876 − $925) = $14,038 interest expense. The difference between this amount and the $15,000 cash payment ($962) is the premium amortization, which reduces the net bond carrying amount.

3.

Period	Interest Expense	Cash Interest Paid	Premium Amortization	Premium Balance	Bond Payable, Net
0				$51,876	$351,876
1	$14,075	$15,000	$ 925	50,951	350,951
2	14,038	15,000	962	49,989	349,989
3	14,000	15,000	1,000	48,989	348,989
4	13,960	15,000	1,040	47,949	347,949
5	13,918	15,000	1,082	46,867	346,867
6	13,875	15,000	1,125	45,742	345,742
7	13,830	15,000	1,170	44,572	344,572
8	13,783	15,000	1,217	43,355	343,355
9	13,734	15,000	1,266	42,089	342,089
10	13,684	15,000	1,316	40,773	340,773

4. Comcast would have to pay $447,163 to repurchase the bonds. This would yield a loss on debt repurchase of $106,390 computed as $447,163 − $340,773.

Calculator
N = 20
I/Yr = 2
PMT = −15,000
FV = −300,000
PV = 447,163

	A	B
1	Annual coupon rate	10%
2	Annual market rate	4%
3	Interest payments per year	2
4	Years to maturity	10
5	Face (par) value	300,000
6	Issue price	447,163
7	= PV(B2/B3,B4*B3,−B5*B1/B3,−B5, 0)	
8	= 447,163	

Review 7-5—Solution

Ratio	Result	Rating
Operating margin	14.2%	Baa
Debt/EBITDA	2.1	A
FFO/Debt	32.9%	Baa
EBITA/Interest Expense	3.9	Ba
Overall composite		**Baa**

Review 7-6—Solution

Using the Excel formula PV(rate,nper, pmt,[fv],[type])

a. $5,449.13

b. $5,000.00

c. $4,594.46

Module 8

Stock Transactions, Dividends, and EPS

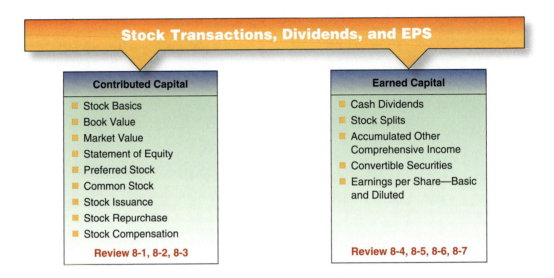

PREVIEW   JNJ

- We examine topics related to stockholders' equity, including:
  - Issuance and repurchase of common stock
  - Payment of dividends
  - Stock splits
  - Convertible securities
  - Stock-based compensation
  - Earnings per share and book value per share
  - Accumulated other comprehensive income

- **Johnson & Johnson** is the focus company and the dashboard below conveys key financial information.

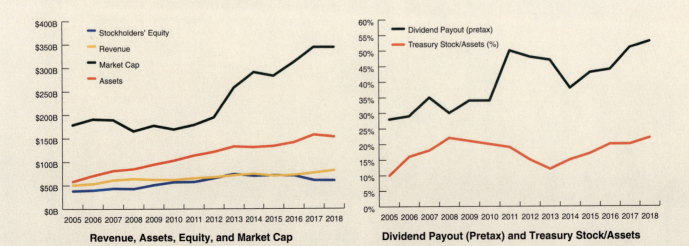

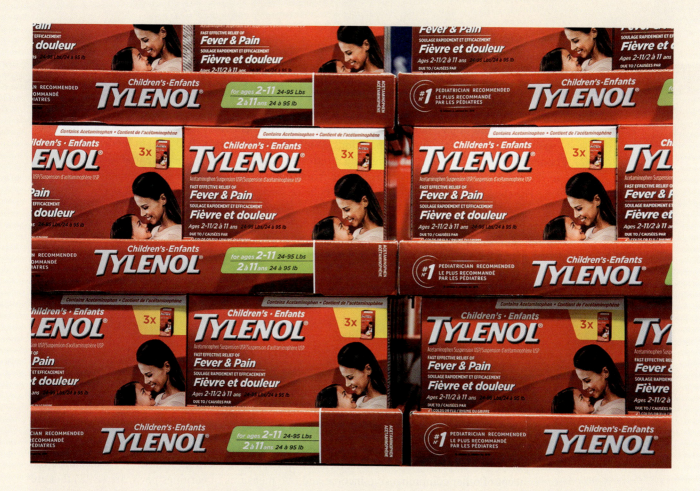

Road Map

LO	Learning Objective | Topics	Page	eLecture	Guided Example	Assignments
8–1	**Examine stock as a financing source and explain its various features.** Equity Terms :: Stockholders' Equity :: Preferred Stock :: Common Stock :: Market Capitalization	8-3	e8–1	Review 8-1	1, 2, 3, 6, 7, 11, 12, 13, 15, 21, 24, 37, 40, 45, 46, 48, 49, 52, 53, 54, 55, 62, 63
8–2	**Analyze stock issuances and repurchases.** Stock Issuance :: Stock Repurchase :: Retirement of Repurchases	8-9	e8–2	Review 8-2	5, 7, 9, 10, 19, 22, 35, 36, 37, 40, 42, 45, 46, 49, 50, 52, 53, 54, 55, 62, 63
8–3	**Interpret stock-based compensation, including restricted stock and options.** Compensation Types :: Compensation Accounting :: Disclosures	8-13	e8–3	Review 8-3	17, 26, 37, 38, 51, 54, 55, 58, 59, 61, 63
8–4	**Analyze cash dividends and stock splits.** Dividend Payout :: Dividend Yield :: Financial Effects :: Stock Splits	8-16	e8–4	Review 8-4	4, 8, 23, 25, 27, 28, 29, 31, 32, 39, 41, 42, 43, 44, 45, 53, 54, 62, 63
8–5	**Interpret accumulated other comprehensive income and its components.** AOCI Disclosure and Interpretation :: Other Comprehensive Income	8-19	e8–5	Review 8-5	16, 33, 50, 54, 55, 62, 63
8–6	**Analyze convertible securities and their financial effects.** Disclosures and Interpretation :: Financial Effects	8-22	e8–6	Review 8-6	18, 34, 47, 50, 56, 57
8–7	**Interpret earnings per share.** Basic EPS :: Diluted EPS	8-23	e8–7	Review 8-7	14, 20, 30, 47, 56, 60

Stockholders' Equity and Classes of Stock

LO1 Examine stock as a financing source and explain its various features.

Companies raise funds by selling shares of stock to investors in addition to borrowing. But, unlike debtholders and other lenders to the company, shareholders elect a Board of Directors that hires executives to oversee company operations. While interest and principal paid to lenders is fixed by contract, shareholders have no contractual return. There is, however, the potential for shareholders to receive dividends and derive large value from future price appreciation of company stock.

The stockholders' equity section of the balance sheet reports the book value of the stockholders' investment, as determined under accounting rules (GAAP). This measurement of book value differs from the market value of stockholders' investment, which is computed as share price multiplied by the number of shares outstanding. Market value is determined by supply and demand for the company's outstanding shares in the marketplace as shares are actively traded among investors.

There are two types of stockholders' equity accounts: contributed capital and earned capital. **Contributed capital** is the net funding a company receives from issuing and reacquiring its shares; that is, the funds received from issuing shares less any funds paid to repurchase such shares. **Earned capital** includes two accounts: retained earnings and accumulated other comprehensive income (AOCI). Retained earnings is the cumulative net income (loss) that the company has earned but not paid out to stockholders as dividends. (Retained earnings can include the effects of retiring common stock as we discuss in the Business Insight box later in the module.) AOCI is the cumulative net *unrealized* (holding) gains or losses related to key balance sheet accounts (primarily pensions, investment securities, derivatives, and foreign currencies). These holding gains and losses will flow to the income statement, and be included in retained earnings, when they are *realized*.

We explain the components of stockholders' equity section of the balance sheet, the different classes of stock, how we account for share issuances (sales) and repurchases (Treasury stock), and the reporting for dividends to shareholders, stock splits, and convertible securities. We also describe the concept of other comprehensive income and two measures of earnings per share (EPS) that are regularly discussed in the financial press.

Stockholders' Equity Accounts

When the company is incorporated, shareholders of the company authorize management to issue (sell) shares of stock. After that, the company's management is free to manage the company, consistent with its policies and under the watchful eye of the Board of Directors (representatives of the shareholders who are elected by them and look out for their interests). Over time, stockholders expect their equity to increase and the stockholders' equity section of the balance sheet represents a score card, in a sense, that records how well management has performed with the capital entrusted to them by the shareholders.

The stockholders' equity section of Johnson & Johnson's (JNJ) balance sheet, shown in Exhibit 8.1, includes the following accounts (see the Business Insight box for definitions).

Contributed Capital

- **Preferred stock.** Johnson & Johnson is authorized to issue up to 2,000,000 preferred shares, but to date has not issued any—the balance is $0.
- **Common stock.** The balance sheet reveals a number of details about the Johnson & Johnson common stock:
  - **Par value.** The par value of its common stock (as stated in its charter) is $1 per share.
  - **Authorized shares.** It can issue up to 4,320,000,000 shares without further approval from shareholders.
  - **Issued shares.** To date, it has sold (issued) 3,119,843,000 shares at the $1 par value and thus, the common stock account has a balance of $3,120 million. It does not report any additional

paid-in capital. We can infer that no shares were sold for more than the $1 par value. (See the Coca-Cola illustration on page 8-9 for an example of additional paid-in capital, which Coca-Cola labels "capital surplus.")

Earned Capital

- **Treasury stock.** The company routinely repurchases its own shares on the open market. As of the 2018 year-end, the company held 457,519,000 treasury shares for which it paid $34,362 million. Like all balance sheet accounts, the treasury stock balance is a cumulative amount that reflects open-market repurchases and subsequent resale of its shares. The account has increased during the year, which implies that Johnson & Johnson purchased additional shares during the current year, net of any shares sold back to the market or granted to employees.
- **Accumulated Other Comprehensive Income (AOCI).** This account reflects the cumulative total of changes to stockholders' equity other than from transactions with owners and transactions reflected in net income. This account can be a positive or negative amount.
- **Retained earnings.** Defined as the cumulative net income recorded since the company's inception less all of the dividends the company has ever paid out to shareholders, which nets to $106,216 million. Retained earnings increased in 2018 primarily because during that year net income exceeded the amount of dividends paid out.

Exhibit 8.1 ■ Stockholders' Equity Section from Johnson & Johnson's Balance Sheet

Shareholders' equity ($ millions, except par value per share)	2018	2017
Preferred stock — without par value (authorized and unissued 2,000,000 shares)...	$ —	$ —
Common stock — par value $1.00 per share		
(authorized 4,320,000,000 shares; issued 3,119,843,000 shares)...............	3,120	3,120
Accumulated other comprehensive income (loss)	(15,222)	(13,199)
Retained earnings	106,216	101,793
	94,114	91,714
Less: common stock held in treasury, at cost		
(457,519,000 shares and 437,318,000 shares)	34,362	31,554
Total shareholders' equity..	$ 59,752	$ 60,160

Book Value per Share A measure commonly used by analysts and the financial press is *book value per share*. This is the equity (net book value) of the company that is available to common shareholders and is defined as:

$$\text{Book value per share} = \left(\text{Stockholders' equity} - \text{Preferred stock}\right) \Big/ \text{Number of common shares outstanding}$$

Johnson & Johnson's book value per share at the end of 2018 follows:

$$\text{JNJ book value per share} = \$59,752 \text{ million} \Big/ \left(3,119,843 \text{ thousand shares} - 457,519 \text{ thousand shares}\right) = \$22.44 \text{ per share}$$

Market-to-Book In comparison, JNJ's market price per share was $129.05 on December 31, 2018 (the last trading day before JNJ's fiscal year-end). The ratio of market price per share to book value per share is the **market-to-book ratio**. For JNJ, at year-end 2018, market-to-book was 5.75. The median market-to-book for the S&P 500 companies at the end of 2018 was 2.91. So, the market values JNJ higher (relative to the book value of its equity) than the median S&P 500 company.

> ### Business Insight ■ Stockholders' Equity Terms and Phrases
>
> Following are common terms and phrases relating to stockholders' equity that we encounter in the financial press.
>
> - **Board of directors.** Shareholders' elected representatives who hire the CEO and oversee company operations.
> - **Preferred stock.** Generally non-voting shares that convey, 1) a dividend preference—preferred stockholders receive dividends on their shares before common stockholders, and 2) a liquidation preference—if a company fails and is liquidated, the assets are sold and liabilities paid; then any remaining cash is paid first to preferred shareholders before payment is made to common shareholders.
> - **Common stock.** Shares that allow the holder to elect the company's board of directors and vote on important company issues such as whether to adopt employee benefit plans, acquire other companies, divest current companies, and reorganize or liquidate the company. Common shares receive dividends after preferred shareholders have been paid their required dividends.
> - **Dividends.** Company profit that is distributed to shareholders. Profit not distributed as dividends is reinvested in the business and shown on the balance sheet as retained earnings.
> - **Declaration date.** The date the board of directors authorizes the payment of the dividend (declares the dividend).
> - **Date of record.** The date the company prepares the list of current stockholders to which the dividend will be paid.
> - **Date of payment.** The date the dividend is paid to stockholders (who held the stock on the date of record).
> - **Residual claim.** When a company voluntarily ceases operations or fails and is liquidated, all assets are sold and liabilities paid. Each shareholder is entitled to their proportional share of the residual cash, if any. Shareholders are called residual claimants.
> - **Authorized shares.** The maximum number of shares that a company can sell (issue) without approval from the shareholders.
> - **Issued shares.** The number of shares that have been sold (issued) to date. This is a cumulative number.
> - **Outstanding shares.** The number of shares that are outstanding in the market, determined as the number of issued shares less the number of shares that have been repurchased by the company.
> - **Treasury shares.** The number of shares that the company has repurchased and holds for resale or for employee compensation plans.
> - **Initial public offering (IPO).** An initial sale of stock to the public.
> - **Par value** and **Additional paid-in capital.** The per share amount (stated in a company's charter) that will be recorded in the common stock account when stock is sold (issued). Par value is unrelated to the stock's market value. The excess of the issue price over the par value is added to the Additional paid-in capital account (also called capital surplus, or capital in excess of par).
> - **Paid-in capital.** The *total* amount of cash and other assets paid in to the company by stockholders in exchange for capital stock.
> - **Market price.** The published price at which a share of stock can be purchased ("ask") or sold ("bid").
> - **Market capitalization.** The market value of all outstanding shares; also called *market cap*.
> - **Stock split.** Proportional issuance of shares to stockholders (and a consequent proportional reduction in par value) with no exchange of cash. A stock split does not affect the value of the company. Because the number of outstanding shares increases, while the value of the company remains unchanged, the share price declines proportionally. One goal of a stock split is to reduce the share price to make the stock more marketable.

Statement of Stockholders' Equity

The statement of stockholders' equity reconciles the beginning and ending balances of the contributed and earned stockholders' equity accounts. It highlights the following.

- How net income and dividends impact retained earnings.
- Cash raised from new shares issued.
- Cash used to repurchase shares in the open market.
- Changes in key balance sheet accounts not recorded in net income or not arising from transactions with shareholders. Each year, these changes are included in an account called **Other Comprehensive Income** (OCI), and the *cumulative* sum of that account is reflected in an equity account called **Accumulated Other Comprehensive Income** (AOCI).

Johnson & Johnson's statement of stockholders' equity, shown in Exhibit 8.2, reveals the following key activities from 2018.

❶ Net income is added to retained earnings, increasing it by $15,297 million.

❷ Cash dividends paid to stockholders reduce retained earnings by $9,494 million.

❸ JNJ's policy is to use treasury shares for employee stock-based compensation plans—see discussion of stock-based compensation later in the module. Treasury stock always has a negative balance because stock buybacks are the opposite of a stock sale. In the statement of stockholders' equity, the positive $3,060 indicates that treasury stock is *reduced* by $3,060 million, which is the *original cost* of the treasury shares used for compensation during the year. In exchange for the shares, employees paid cash of $1,949 million only because Johnson & Johnson awarded the stock-based compensation grants when the stock price was lower. The $1,111 million difference reduced retained earnings.

❹ JNJ purchased additional stock on the open market during the year at a cost of $5,868 million, which is shown as a negative number, increasing the treasury stock account. A portion of the stock repurchase was related to a general share buy-back program. Another portion was to forestall a potential drop in stock price from a dilution related to the stock-based compensation plans.

❺ JNJ reported other comprehensive loss of $1,791 million—we explain this in the accumulated other comprehensive income section of this module. Changes in AOCI can be positive or negative.

In 2018, certain accounting rules changed, including those for revenue recognition and income taxes (see Module 5 for a detailed discussion). In adopting the new rules, companies had to make retrospective "catch-up" adjustments to certain equity accounts. JNJ reported a total cumulative adjustment of $(486) million, split between retained earnings $(254 million) and AOCI $(232 million)—see the first row following the beginning balance in Exhibit 8.2.

Exhibit 8.2 ■ Johnson & Johnson's Statement of Stockholders' Equity

$ millions	Total	Retained Earnings	Accumulated Other Comprehensive Income	Common Stock Issued	Treasury Stock
Balance, December 31, 2017....	$60,160	$101,793	$(13,199)	$3,120	$(31,554)
Cumulative adjustment.........	(486)	(254)	(232)		
❶ Net earnings.................	15,297	15,297			
❷ Cash dividends paid...........	(9,494)	(9,494)			
❸ Employee compensation and stock option plans...........	1,949	(1,111)			3,060
❹ Repurchase of common stock ...	(5,868)				(5,868)
Other.......................	(15)	(15)			
❺ Other comprehensive income (loss), net of tax	(1,791)		(1,791)		
Balance, December 30, 2018....	$59,752	$106,216	$(15,222)	$3,120	$(34,362)

Preferred Stock

Preferred stock is a multi-use security with a number of desirable features. In addition to usual dividend and liquidation preferences, preferred stock has two other common features.

- **Yield.** Preferred stock can be structured to provide investors with a dividend yield that is similar to an interest rate on a bond. Dividends, unlike interest expense, are not deductible for tax purposes. Therefore, the after-tax cost to the company for preferred dividends is higher than the after-tax effective interest rate on a bond.
- **Conversion privileges.** Preferred stock can contain an option that allows investors to convert their preferred shares into common shares at a predetermined number of common shares per preferred share.

Both of these features are illustrated in the Corning Inc. convertible preferred stock as reported on its balance sheet and related footnote.

At December 31 (In millions, except share amounts)	2018	2017
Shareholders' Equity		
Convertible preferred stock, Series A—Par value 100 per share; shares authorized 3,100; shares issued: 2,300	$2,300	$2,300

> **Fixed Rate Cumulative Convertible Preferred Stock, Series A.** On January 15, 2014, Corning designated a new series of its preferred stock as Fixed Rate Cumulative Convertible Preferred Stock, Series A, par value $100 per share, and issued 1,900 shares of preferred stock at an issue price of $1 million per share, for an aggregate issue price of $1.9 billion, to Samsung Display with the acquisition of its equity interest in Samsung Corning Precision Materials. Corning also issued to Samsung Display an additional amount of preferred stock at closing, for an aggregate issue price of $400 million in cash.
>
> Dividends on the preferred stock are cumulative and accrue at the annual rate of 4.25% on the per share issue price of $1 million…The preferred stock is convertible at the option of the holder and the Company upon certain events, at a conversion rate of 50,000 shares of Corning's common stock per one share of preferred stock… The Company has the right, at its option, to cause some or all the shares of preferred stock to be converted into common stock, if, for 25 trading days (whether or not consecutive) within any period of 40 consecutive trading days, the closing price of common stock exceeds $35 per share.

Corning's convertible preferred stock pays a dividend of 4.25% of par value, meaning that the preferred shareholder, Samsung Display, receives an annual dividend of $97.75 million ($2,300 million × 4.25%). Interestingly, this yield is higher than the effective rate on the company's debt securities.

The conversion would have a number of effects creating some pros and cons to the conversion. The preferred shareholder would convert each preferred share into 50,000 common shares. Each preferred share was issued for $1 million, which would convert to $1.5105 million of common stock (2018 year-end stock price of $30.21 × 50,000 shares). And Samsung Display would benefit from any future price appreciation in Corning's common stock. This seems like a good trade. However, there is a downside—the preferred dividend per share is $42,500 whereas the dividends on 50,000 common shares in 2018 were only $9,000 ($0.18 per share). Thus, under the conversion the preferred shareholder would receive a much lower yield. They would also relinquish their liquidation preference—senior position in bankruptcy—although this is only an issue if Corning is in financial difficulty. The conversion decision depends upon a careful evaluation of Corning's future prospects and consequent stock-price increase.

Common Stock

Johnson & Johnson has one class of common stock that has the following attributes (see Exhibit 8.1).

- A par value of $1.00 per share. **Par value** is an arbitrary amount set when the company was formed and has no relation to, or impact on, the stock's market value. Generally, par value is irrelevant from an analysis perspective. It is only used to allocate proceeds from stock issuances between the two contributed capital accounts on the balance sheet: common stock and additional paid-in capital.

- 4,320,000,000 shares of stock have been **authorized** for issuance. The company cannot issue (sell) more shares than have been authorized. If more shares are needed, say for an acquisition, the stockholders must vote to authorize more shares.

- To date, JNJ has **issued** (sold) 3,119,843,000 shares of common stock. The number of issued shares is a cumulative amount. Year-over-year changes in the number of issued shares represent the number of shares of stock issued in the current year.

- To date, JNJ has repurchased 457,519,000 shares from its stockholders at a cumulative cost of $34,362 million. These shares are currently held in the company's treasury, hence the name **treasury stock**. These shares neither have voting rights nor do they receive dividends.
- Number of **outstanding shares** is equal to the issued shares less treasury shares. There were 2,662,324,000 (3,119,843,000 − 457,519,000) shares outstanding at the end of 2018.
- Number of outstanding common shares multiplied by the market price per share yields the **market capitalization** (or *market cap*) for the company. As of December 31, 2018, JNJ's market capitalization was $343.6 billion (2,662,324,000 shares outstanding × $129.05 per share).

Business Insight ■ Noncontrolling Interests

Many companies report an additional equity account called **noncontrolling interest**. This account arises when the company controls a subsidiary but does not own all of the subsidiary's stock. That is, the company has control of the subsidiary but does not own 100% of its stock. The noncontrolling interest is the portion of the subsidiary's stock NOT owned by the company. The noncontrolling interest account increases with any additional investment made by the noncontrolling shareholders and by their share of the subsidiary's net income whose common stock they own. The account decreases by any dividends paid to the noncontrolling shareholders and by their share of any net losses of the subsidiary. For most companies, the dollar amount of noncontrolling interest is small as illustrated in the following excerpt from the equity section of **PepsiCo**'s 2018 balance sheet.

In millions, except per share amounts	2018	2017
Preferred stock, no par value	$ —	$ 41
Repurchased preferred stock	—	(197)
PepsiCo Common Shareholders' Equity		
Common stock, par value 1 2/3¢ per share (authorized 3,600 shares; issued, net of repurchased common stock at par value: 1,409 and 1,420 shares, respectively)	$ 23	$ 24
Capital in excess of par value	3,953	3,996
Retained earnings	59,947	52,839
Accumulated other comprehensive loss	(15,119)	(13,057)
Repurchased common stock, in excess of par value (458 and 446 shares, respectively)	(34,286)	(32,757)
Total PepsiCo Common Shareholders' Equity	14,518	11,045
Noncontrolling interests	84	92
Total Equity	$14,602	$10,981

The relative magnitude of noncontrolling interest that PepsiCo reports ($84 million compared with $14,602 million of total equity) is typical. For comparison, the median noncontrolling interest as a percent of total liabilities and equity for the S&P 500 companies in 2018 was 0.04% (only 50 companies in the S&P 500 report noncontrolling interest as a percent of total liabilities and equity of greater than 10%). We further explain noncontrolling interest in a later module.

LO1 Review 8-1

Stockholders' equity reflects owner financing of an enterprise.

Required
For each of the following, (1) indicate whether the statement is true or false regarding stockholders' equity, and (2) for any identified false statement, indicate how to correct that statement.

___ a. Stockholders' equity represents the market value of the company.
___ b. Stockholders do not manage the company directly, but oversee its operations through its Board of Directors.
___ c. Issued shares represents the number of shares that have been sold to investors.
___ d. Outstanding shares represents the number of shares issued less the number of shares repurchased by the company.
___ e. Preferred stock is entitled to the same per share dividends as common stock.
___ f. Treasury stock represents the cumulative total cost of shares that the company has repurchased, net of any subsequent sales of the treasury shares. Assume no repurchased shares are retired.

Solution on p. 8-51.

Stock Transactions

LO2 Analyze stock issuances and repurchases.

Stock Issuance

Companies issue stock to obtain cash and other assets for use in their business. Stock issuances increase assets (cash) by the issue proceeds: the number of shares sold multiplied by the price of the stock on the issue date. Equity increases by the same amount, which is reflected in contributed capital accounts. If the stock has a par value, the common stock account increases by the number of shares sold multiplied by its par value. The additional paid-in capital account increases by the remainder. Stock can also be issued as "no-par" or as "no-par with a stated value." For no-par stock, the common stock account is increased by the entire proceeds of the sale and no amount is assigned to additional paid-in capital. For no-par stock with a stated value, the stated value is treated just like par value; that is, common stock is increased by the number of shares multiplied by the stated value, and the remainder is assigned to the additional paid-in capital account.

Stock Issuance Financial Effects To illustrate, assume that JNJ issues 1,000 shares with a $1.00 par value common stock at a market price of $100 cash per share. This stock issuance has the following financial statement effects.

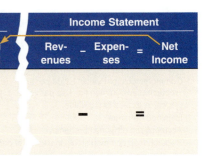

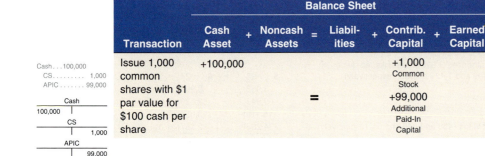

Specifically, the stock issuance affects the financial statements as follows.

1. Cash increases by $100,000 (1,000 shares × $100 per share).
2. Common stock increases by the par value of shares sold: 1,000 shares × $1 par value = $1,000.
3. Additional paid-in capital increases by the $99,000 difference between the issue proceeds and par value ($100,000 − $1,000).

Once shares are issued, they are traded in the open market among investors. The proceeds of those sales and their associated gains and losses, as well as fluctuations in the company's stock price subsequent to issuance, do not affect the issuing company and are not recorded in its accounting records.

Stock Disclosures and Interpretation Using our stock issuance illustration above, we can interpret the common stock and additional paid-in capital (capital surplus) disclosures on **Coca-Cola**'s balance sheet.

December 31 (In millions, except par value)	2018	2017
The Coca-Cola Company Shareowners' Equity		
Common stock, $0.25 par value; Authorized—11,200 shares;		
Issued—7,040 and 7,040 shares, respectively	$ 1,760	$ 1,760
Capital surplus	16,520	15,864
Reinvested earnings	63,234	60,430
Accumulated other comprehensive income (loss)	(12,814)	(10,305)
Treasury stock, at cost — 2,772 and 2,781 shares, respectively	(51,719)	(50,677)
Equity attributable to shareowners of the Coca-Cola Company	$16,981	$17,072

As of December 31, 2018, Coca-Cola has issued 7,040 million shares of common stock for total proceeds of $18,280 million ($1,760 million + $16,520 million). The $1,760 million in common stock is the total par value for the 7,040 million shares ($0.25 × 7,040 million). The $16,520 million capital surplus account (another title for additional paid-in capital) is the difference between the $18,280 million total issue proceeds and the $1,760 million par value. The average price at which Coke issued the 7,040 million shares is $2.60 ($18,280 million/7,040 million shares issued).

> **IFRS Alert**
> Stock terminology can differ between IFRS and GAAP. Under IFRS, common stock is called *share capital* and additional paid-in capital (APIC) is called *share premium*. Despite different terminology, the accounting is similar.

Research Insight ■ Stock Issuance and Stock Returns

Research shows that, historically, companies issuing equity securities experience unusually low stock returns for several years following those offerings. Evidence suggests that this poor performance is partly due to overly optimistic estimates of long-term growth by equity analysts. That optimism causes offering prices to be too high. This over-optimism is most pronounced when the analyst is employed by the brokerage firm that underwrites the stock issue. There is also evidence that companies manage earnings upward prior to an equity offering. This means the observed decrease in returns following an issuance likely reflects the market's negative reaction, on average, to lower earnings, especially if the company fails to meet analysts' forecasts.

Stock Repurchase (Treasury Stock)

JNJ has repurchased 457,519,000 shares of its common stock for a cumulative cost of $34,362 million as of December 31, 2018 (see Exhibit 8.1). One reason a company repurchases shares is because it believes that the market undervalues them. The logic is that the repurchase sends a favorable signal to the market about the company's financial condition, which positively impacts its share price and, thus, allows it to resell those shares for a "gain." Any such gain on resale, however, is *never* reflected in the income statement. Instead, any excess of the resale price over the repurchase price is added to additional paid-in capital. GAAP prohibits companies from reporting gains and losses from stock transactions with their own stockholders.

Another reason companies repurchase shares is to offset the dilutive effects of share-based compensation plans including an employee stock option program. When an employee exercises stock options, the number of shares outstanding increases. Because net income is unchanged, these additional shares reduce earnings per share and are, therefore, *dilutive*. In response, many companies repurchase an equivalent number of shares in the open market to keep outstanding shares constant.

A stock repurchase reduces the size of the company (cash declines and, thus, total assets decline). A repurchase has the opposite financial statement effects from a stock issuance. That is, cash decreases by the price of the shares repurchased (number of shares repurchased multiplied by the purchase price per share), and stockholders' equity decreases by the same amount. The decrease in equity is recorded in a contra equity account called treasury stock. Treasury stock (the contra equity account) has a negative balance, which reduces stockholders' equity. Thus, when the treasury stock contra equity account increases, total stockholders' equity decreases.

When the company subsequently resells treasury stock, there is no accounting gain or loss. Instead, the difference between the proceeds received and the original purchase price of the treasury stock is reflected as an increase or decrease to additional paid-in capital.

Stock Repurchase Financial Effects To illustrate, assume that 200 common shares of JNJ previously issued for $100 are repurchased for $90 cash per share. This repurchase has the following financial statement effects.

Transaction	Balance Sheet							Income Statement		
	Cash Asset	+ Noncash Assets	= Liabilities	+ Contrib. Capital	+ Earned Capital			Revenues	− Expenses	= Net Income
Repurchase 200 common shares for $90 cash per share	−18,000 Cash		=	−18,000 Treasury Stock					−	=

TS......18,000
   Cash.......18,000

```
       TS
 18,000 |
        |
       Cash
        | 18,000
```

Assets (cash) and stockholders' equity both decrease. Treasury stock (a contra equity account) increases by $18,000, which reduces stockholders' equity by that amount.

Reselling Treasury Stock Assume that these 200 shares of treasury stock are subsequently resold for $95 cash per share. This resale of treasury stock has the following financial statement effects.

```
Cash....19,000
 TS........ 18,000
 APIC....... 1,000

    Cash
 19,000 |
        |
    TS
        | 18,000
    APIC
        | 1,000
```

	Balance Sheet						Income Statement		
Transaction	Cash Asset	+ Noncash Assets	= Liabilities	+ Contrib. Capital	+ Earned Capital		Revenues	− Expenses	= Net Income
Resell 200 treasury (common) shares for $95 cash per share	+19,000 Cash		=	+18,000 Treasury Stock +1,000 Additional Paid-In Capital				−	=

Cash assets increase by $19,000 (200 shares × $95 per share), the treasury stock account is reduced by the $18,000 cost of the treasury shares issued (thus increasing contributed capital), and the $1,000 excess (200 shares × $5 per share) is reported as an increase in additional paid-in capital. (If the resale price is below the repurchase price, then additional paid-in capital is reduced until it reaches a zero balance, after which retained earnings is reduced.) Again, there is no effect on the income statement as companies are prohibited from reporting gains and losses from repurchases and reissuances of their own stock.

IFRS Alert
Accounting for stock repurchases under IFRS is similar to GAAP except that IFRS provides little guidance on how to allocate the treasury stock to equity accounts. Thus, repurchases can be recorded as an increase to treasury stock, or as a decrease to common stock and APIC (share capital and premium), retained earnings (reserves), or some combination.

Treasury Stock Disclosures and Interpretation The treasury stock section of JNJ's balance sheet is reproduced below.

In millions, except for share amounts	2018	2017
Common stock held in treasury, at cost (457,519,000 shares and 437,318,000 shares)	34,362	31,554

JNJ repurchased a cumulative total of 457,519,000 shares of common stock for $34,362 million, an average repurchase price of $75.10 per share. These shares, while legally owned by JNJ, have no voting rights and receive no dividends. Treasury shares can be resold should JNJ need to raise capital or acquire another entity. Treasury shares can also be used to compensate employees and executives. Sometimes, companies "retire" treasury stock. In that event, the treasury stock account is reduced by the cost of the treasury shares retired (thus increasing stockholders' equity) and the common stock and APIC accounts are likewise reduced (thus reducing stockholders' equity by the same amount). When treasury shares are retired, total stockholders' equity remains unchanged.

Managerial Decision ■ You Are the Chief Financial Officer

As CFO, you believe that your company's stock price is lower than its real value. You are considering various alternatives to increase that price, including the repurchase of company stock in the market. What are some factors you should consider before making your decision? [Answer, p. 8-29]

Business Insight ■ Companies Increasingly Choose Retirement for Treasury Stock

In recent years, a large number of companies have not applied the *Treasury Stock* method as described in this section, but instead applied the *Retirement* method. Under the retirement method, stock repurchases reduce both common stock and additional paid-in capital for the average original issue price. Then, retained earnings are adjusted for the difference between the amount paid and the common stock and APIC. (Some states, such as California and Massachusetts, now require this method.)

continued

continued from previous page

The following stockholders' equity statement from **Microsoft** demonstrates the retirement method. We see that the repurchase reduces common stock (and APIC) by $3,033 million and retained earnings by $7,699 million for a total cost of $10,732 million. Interestingly, this helps explain why Microsoft reports such a low balance for retained earnings.

Microsoft's Statement of Stockholders' Equity

Year Ended June 30 (In millions)	2018
Common stock and paid-in capital	
Balance, beginning of period	$69,315
Common stock issued	1,002
Common stock repurchased	(3,033)
Stock-based compensation expense	3,940
Other, net	(1)
Balance, end of period	71,223
Retained earnings	
Balance, beginning of period	17,769
Net income	16,571
Common stock cash dividends	(12,917)
Common stock repurchased	(7,699)
Cumulative effect of accounting change	(42)
Balance, end of period	13,682
Accumulated other comprehensive income	
Balance, beginning of period	627
Other comprehensive income (loss)	(2,856)
Cumulative effect of accounting change	42
Balance, end of period	(2,187)
Total stockholders' equity	$82,718

LO2 Review 8-2

Following is the equity section of **Coca-Cola Company** balance sheet for December 31, 2018 and 2017.

COCA-COLA COMPANY SHAREOWNERS' EQUITY (In millions, except par value)	Dec. 31, 2018	Dec. 31, 2017
Common stock, $0.25 par value; Authorized—11,200 shares; Issued—7,040 and 7,040 shares, respectively	$ 1,760	$ 1,760
Capital surplus	16,520	15,864
Reinvested earnings	63,234	60,430
Accumulated other comprehensive income (loss)	(12,814)	(10,305)
Treasury stock, at cost — 2,772 and 2,781 shares, respectively	(51,719)	(50,677)
Equity attributable to shareowners of the Coca-Cola Company	16,981	17,072
Equity attributable to noncontrolling interests	2,077	1,905
Total equity	$19,058	$18,977

Required

a. How much additional common stock did Coca-Cola issue during the first quarter of 2018? Explain.
b. Assume that Coca-Cola issued 400,000 shares during the first quarter at $45 per share. Use the financial statement effects template to record this transaction.
c. Assume that during the first quarter, Coca-Cola purchased approximately 22 million shares on the open market at an average price of $43.45 per share. Use the financial statement effects template to record this transaction. Round numbers to millions.
d. Assume the company sold 30 million shares of treasury stock for $964 million. The treasury shares had an original cost of $15.77 per share. Determine the effect of this transaction on the treasury stock and capital surplus accounts. Round numbers to millions.

Solution on p. 8-51.

Stock-Based Compensation

LO3 Interpret stock-based compensation, including restricted stock and options.

Common stock has been an important component of executive compensation for decades. The general idea follows: If the company executives own stock, they will have an incentive to increase its value. This aligns the executives' interests with those of other stockholders. Although the strength of this alignment is the subject of much debate, its logic compels boards of directors of most American companies to use stock-based compensation.

Characteristics of Stock-Based Compensation Plans

Companies use a range of stock-based compensation plans. The Business Insight box below provides details of the types of plans, but they share the following features.

- **Create incentives for employees to think and act like shareholders.** The amount of the stock award is often tied to corporate performance targets including sales, income, and stock price. Stock-based compensation plans motivate employees to work hard and make decisions that improve company performance.
- **Encourage employee retention and longevity.** With most plans, employees earn the right to own or purchase shares over time. The period of time over which ownership rights are earned is called the *vesting* period (usually a few years). During this vesting period, employees have greater incentive to stay with the company.

Johnson & Johnson's compensation plans include stock options, restricted stock units (RSUs), and performance share units (these are RSUs that will only be awarded if certain performance targets are met, which creates additional incentives for employees).

Business Insight — Types of Stock-Based Compensation Plans

The following stock-based compensation plans are widely in use today and we often see companies maintain more than one of these plans at the same time.

- **Restricted stock.** Shares are issued to the employee but the employee is *not* free to sell the shares during a restriction period. This creates an incentive for the employee to remain with the company. During the restriction period, the employee has the rights of a shareholder, other than the ability to sell the shares.
- **Restricted stock units (RSUs).** Employee is awarded the right to receive a specified number of shares (or cash equivalent) after a vesting period. Unlike restricted stock, shares are not issued to the employee until after the restriction period, at which time the employee has all of the rights of a shareholder (but not during the vesting period).
- **Employee stock options.** Employees are given the right to purchase shares at a fixed (strike) price for a specified period of time. Similar to restricted stock, there is a waiting period (called a vesting period) before the employee can purchase the shares.
- **Stock appreciation rights (SARs).** Employees are paid in cash or stock for the increase in share price, but do not purchase shares of stock. This is similar to a stock option but with no share purchase required.
- **Employee share purchase plans.** Employees are permitted to purchase shares directly from the company at a discounted price, typically a set percentage (such as 85%) of the prevailing market price.

Most stock-based compensation plans contain forfeiture provisions—if the employee is terminated for cause or leaves the company before the rights to receive shares are vested, the award is forfeited.

Analysis of Stock-Based Compensation Plans

There are two analysis issues relating to stock-based compensation plans: recognition of the *expense* and potential *dilution*.

Expense Recognition The expense side is straightforward. When shares or options are awarded to employees, companies estimate the fair value of the award and recognize the fair value as compensation expense in the income statement over the period in which the employee provides service.

Potential Dilution Dilution relates to the number of common shares outstanding that have a claim against the company's earnings or net assets. For example, if a company earns $1 million and there are 1,000,000 shares outstanding, the earnings per share (EPS) available to pay dividends is $1. But, if there are 2,000,000 shares outstanding, the EPS available to pay dividends is only $0.50. The drop in EPS due to the increase in the number of outstanding shares is called *dilution* and companies are required to report diluted EPS in their annual reports—we discuss EPS later in this module. In the same way, dilution affects the value of each share of stock. If a company is worth $10 million, the per share price of the company's stock will be half as much if there are 2,000,000 shares outstanding than if there are only 1,000,000.

Mindful of shareholder concerns about the potential dilution of their stock holdings, companies often repurchase shares in an effort to counter the dilutive effects of share issuances under stock-based compensation plans. Johnson & Johnson describes this in its footnotes.

> The Company settles employee benefit equity issuances with treasury shares. Treasury shares are replenished throughout the year for the number of shares used to settle employee benefit equity issuances.

To work through the analysis issues relating to employee stock compensation plans, it is important for us to understand:

- How stock-based compensation expense is measured and recorded in the income statement.
- Dilutive effects of stock-based compensation and the cash cost incurred to offset that dilution.
- Dilutive effects of stock-based compensation on earnings per share (EPS).

Accounting for Stock-Based Compensation

Regardless of the type of stock-based compensation plan, there are common accounting steps.

- When the award is granted to employees, the company estimates the fair value of the award.
- The fair value of the award is recorded as an expense in the income statement, ratably over the vesting period, and APIC is increased by the same amount.
- When the shares are issued, common stock and additional paid-in capital increase in the same manner as for cash-based stock issuances, as described above.

Stock-based compensation expense is included on the income statement but rarely reported as a separate line item. Like other forms of compensation, the expense is included in cost of goods sold (for employees in R&D and manufacturing) or selling general and administrative expense (for employees in selling and administration and executive roles). However, we can determine the amount of the expense from the statement of cash flows. Because stock-based compensation expense is a noncash expense, companies add back this expense in the statement of cash flow as in the following excerpt from the JNJ statement from 2018.

JOHNSON & JOHNSON AND SUBSIDIARIES Consolidated Statements of Cash Flows			
$ millions	2018	2017	2016
Cash flows from operating activities			
Net earnings	$15,297	$1,300	$16,540
Adjustments to reconcile net earnings to cash flows from operating activities:			
Depreciation and amortization of property and intangibles	6,929	5,642	3,754
Stock-based compensation	**978**	**962**	**878**

JNJ adds back the $978 million of stock-based compensation expense, which is included in net income on the income statement, to arrive at cash from operations. (This is similar to the $6,929 million add-back for depreciation expense.)

Interpretation of Stock-Based Compensation The stock-based compensation add-back might lead some to conclude that this form of compensation is cash free. But this is erroneous—a real cash cost occurs when the company buys new treasury shares in the open market to offset the dilution created by the share award to the employees. Consider also that the company used stock-based compensation instead of paying higher salaries or bonuses in cash. The employees bartered for stock. So while companies and analysts often add stock-based compensation expense back when computing and reporting non-GAAP measures such as EBIT and EBITDA, that treatment is not correct. *Stock-based compensation expense* is a real cash cost. To accurately evaluate and forecast operating cash flow, analysts must either include stock-based compensation expense or recognize the related treasury-stock purchase as an operating cash outflow.

In addition to the cash cost that JNJ will incur to offset the potential dilution relating to shares that will be issued to employees, JNJ's earnings per share will be affected. Fortunately, the effect of this potential dilution is a required disclosure in a statistic called diluted earnings per share that is reported on the income statement with details provided in a related footnote disclosure. We discuss diluted earnings per share later in this module.

Footnote Disclosures for Stock-Based Compensation

Footnotes to the 10-K contain extensive descriptions of stock-based compensation plans that describe two facets of a company's stock-based compensation: plan activity and fair value.

Plan Activity Disclosure for plan activity includes:

- Number of shares granted to employees during the year (to illustrate potential dilution to existing shareholders).
- Number of shares issued during the year to satisfy awards that vested.
- Any shares forfeited—when employees leave the company or fail to exercise options within the specified time period.

For example, Johnson & Johnson provides the following information related to activity for its three types of compensation plans.

Shares in thousands	Outstanding Stock Options	Outstanding Restricted Share Units	Outstanding Performance Share Units
Shares at December 31, 2017	111,306	20,161	2,625
Granted	17,115	6,074	1,142
Issued		(6,684)	(1,151)
Options exercised	(16,228)		
Canceled or forfeited or adjusted	(2,541)	(1,091)	(122)
Shares at December 30, 2018	109,652	18,460	2,494

Fair Value and Expense Disclosure for fair value and expense includes:

- Fair value of the stock-based compensation awards.
- How fair value is determined. Restricted stock awards are valued using the share price on the date of the award. Stock option plans are valued using option pricing models. The two most common models are the Black-Scholes model and the bilateral model (also called lattice method).
- The expense on the income statement.
- Value of the shares issued to employees over and above the price the employee paid for shares. This difference is called the intrinsic value.

For example, JNJ provides fair value details for its stock option plan in its 2018 10-K. Similar schedules are usually provided for each type of stock-based compensation plan.

	2018	2017	2016
Risk-free rate	2.77%	2.25%	1.51%
Expected volatility	15.77%	15.30%	15.76%
Expected life (in years)	7.0	7.0	7.0
Expected dividend yield	2.70%	2.90%	3.10%

JNJ disclosed the following per share fair values for stock-based awards during the year.

Stock options	$17.98
Restricted share units	119.67
Performance share units	120.64

Interpretation of Fair Values for Different Stock-Based Awards For JNJ, the fair value of RSUs is much higher than the fair value of the options because the two compensation arrangements differ greatly. If stock price drops between the grant date and the time the shares are issued, the employee with the RSU will still receive something of value (the share). The employee with an option could buy the stock at the predetermined (higher) price. Because it makes no economic sense to pay more for the stock than its market value, the option is worthless and the employee is left empty handed.

The appendix to this module discusses additional accounting and analysis issues for share-based compensation.

LO3 Review 8-3

Coca-Cola Company has a number of stock-based compensation plans including stock options, RSUs, and employee stock purchase plans. The company reports the following activity for its stock options.

In millions	Shares
Outstanding on January 1, 2018	173
Granted	8
Exercised	(47)
Forfeited/expired	(1)
Outstanding on December 31, 2018	133

The company also reports the following information in its footnotes.
- Total stock-based compensation expense of $225 million for 2018.
- Fair value of stock options granted during 2018 of $10.58 and the options' strike price averaged $36.74.
- Granted 2,183 thousand performance share units during 2018 with a fair value of $38.45 per share.

Required
a. How did Coca-Cola's stock-based compensation expense affect net income for the year?
b. How did the stock-based compensation expense affect cash from operations? Can we infer from this that the expense involves no cash outflow for Coca-Cola?
c. Consider the fair value of the stock options granted during the year. If these options vest over four years, determine the related compensation expense for 2018.
d. Consider the fair value of the performance share units granted during the year. If the average restriction period is two years, determine the related compensation expense for 2018.
e. Explain why the fair value per share of the performance share units is so much larger than the stock option fair value.

Solution on p. 8-52.

Dividends and Stock Splits

In this section, we discuss the following topics related to earned capital accounts.

LO4 Analyze cash dividends and stock splits.

- Dividends, which can be paid in cash, in land, in other property, or in additional shares of stock (stock dividends).
- Stock splits, where the company distributes additional shares of stock to existing shareholders.

Cash Dividend Disclosures

Johnson & Johnson reports retained earnings of $106,216 million, which is higher than the prior year. Many companies, but not all, pay dividends and reasons for dividend payments vary. JNJ reports that it "increased its dividend in 2018 for the 56th consecutive year," paying $3.54 per share in 2018. Companies typically pay dividends on a quarterly basis.

Investors and financial analysts closely monitor dividend payments. It is generally perceived that the level of dividend payments is related to the company's expected long-term recurring income. Accordingly, dividend increases are usually viewed as positive signals about future performance and are accompanied by stock price increases. By that logic, companies rarely reduce their dividends unless absolutely necessary because dividend reductions are often met with substantial stock price declines.

Dividend Payout and Yield

> **IFRS Alert**
> The dividend payout ratio is called "dividend cover" in some IFRS countries.

Two common metrics that analysts use to assess a company's dividends are dividend payout and dividend yield. These ratios are computed for common stock dividends and not for preferred stock because, as we explain below, most preferred stock has a stated dividend rate such that a "payout" ratio is not meaningful.

Dividend Payout The dividend payout ratio measures the proportion of the company's earnings that is paid out as dividend—it is defined as:

$$\text{Dividend payout} = \frac{\text{Common stock dividends per share}}{\text{Basic earnings per share (EPS)}}$$

During 2018, JNJ reported dividends per share of $3.54 and basic earnings per share of $5.70. The dividend payout ratio is 62% ($3.54/$5.70). By comparison, the median dividend payout ratio for S&P 500 companies in 2018 is 30%, with 17% of those companies not paying any dividends at all. More mature, profitable companies, such as JNJ, tend to have a higher payout ratio because they have fewer investment opportunities that require cash.

Dividend Yield Dividend yield is tied to the current market value of the company's stock and is defined as:

$$\text{Dividend yield} = \frac{\text{Common stock dividends per share}}{\text{Current share price}}$$

The ratio measures the cash return to stockholders given the cash investment. Of course, the other way to earn a return is via stock price appreciation, but dividend yield reflects only the one-year cash return. Given JNJ's dividends per share in 2018 of $3.54 and its closing share price on December 31, 2018, of $129.05, the dividend yield is 2.7% ($3.54/$129.05).

Cash Dividends Financial Effects

Cash dividends reduce both cash and retained earnings by the amount of the cash dividends paid. To illustrate, assume that JNJ declares and pays cash dividends in the amount of $10 million. The financial statement effects of this cash dividend payment are as follows.

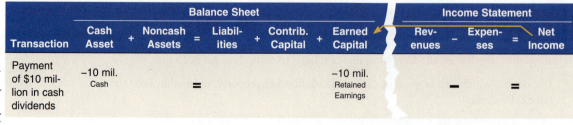

Dividend payments *do not* affect net income. They directly reduce retained earnings and bypass the income statement.

Cumulative Dividends in Arrears Dividends on preferred stock have priority over those on common stock, including unpaid prior years' preferred dividends (called *dividends in arrears*) when preferred stock is cumulative. To illustrate, assume that a company has 15,000 shares of $50 par value, 8% preferred stock outstanding; assume that the preferred stock is cumulative, which means that any unpaid dividends accumulate and must be paid before common dividends. The company also has 50,000 shares of $5 par value common stock outstanding. During its first three years in business, assume that the company declares $20,000 dividends in the first year, $260,000 of dividends in the second year, and $60,000 of dividends in the third year. Cash dividends paid to each class of stock in each of the three years follows.

	Preferred Stock	Common Stock
Year 1—$20,000 cash dividends paid		
Current-year dividend (15,000 shares × $50 par × 8%; but only $20,000 paid, leaving $40,000 in arrears)......	$20,000	
Balance to common		$ 0
Year 2—$260,000 cash dividends paid		
Dividends in arrears from Year 1 ([15,000 shares × $50 par × 8%] − $20,000)	40,000	
Current-year dividend (15,000 shares × $50 par × 8%)	60,000	
Balance to common		160,000
Year 3—$60,000 cash dividends paid		
Current-year dividend (15,000 shares × $50 par × 8%)	60,000	
Balance to common		0

Dividends need not be paid in cash. Many companies pay dividends in the form of additional shares of stock. Companies can also distribute additional shares to their shareholders via a stock split. We cover both of these distributions in this section.

Stock Split

A **stock split** happens when a company issues additional common shares to its existing stockholders. Stock splits are usually prompted by the company's desire to reduce its stock price in order to improve marketability of the shares. There seems to be a psychological hurdle for investors when the price of a share exceeds $100. A typical stock split is 2-for-1, which means that the company distributes one additional share for each share owned by shareholders. Because there is no cash flow effect from a stock split, the company's market cap is unaffected by the split. Following the distribution each investor owns twice as many shares that are each worth approximately half as much. So the total market value of their investment is unchanged. Although the split itself has little effect on shareholders, the price per share is reduced, thus increasing the marketability of the shares.

A stock split is not a monetary transaction and, as such, there are no financial statement effects. However, companies must disclose the number of shares outstanding for all periods presented in the financial statements. Additionally, companies must reduce the par value of the stock proportionally (to ½ of the previous par value for a 2:1 stock split) and historical financial statements presented in the current 10-K must be adjusted likewise.

Stock Split in Form of Dividend One common way to perform a stock split is to declare a dividend *payable in company stock*. The company adds the par value of the stock distributed to the common stock account and subtracts the same amount from retained earnings (similar to a cash dividend). Thus, there is no net effect on total stockholders' equity. For example, **TJX Companies Inc.** announced a two-for-one stock split in the form of a stock dividend, paid on November 6, 2018, to the shareholders of record at the close of business on October 30, 2018. After the split, outstanding common shares doubled to approximately 1.3 million shares.

Review 8-4 LO4

Wells Fargo (WFC) reports the following information in its 2018 financial statements.

For 12 Months Ended	2018	2017
Preferred stock: Cash dividends paid ($ millions)	$(1,622)	$(1,629)
Common stock: Cash dividends paid ($ millions).	$(7,692)	$(7,480)
Earnings per common share ($ per share).	$4.31	$4.14
Dividends declared per common share ($ per share)	$1.64	$1.54

Required
- a. Use the financial statement effects template to record the preferred and common stock dividends for 2018.
- b. If Wells Fargo had paid $100 million more in common stock dividends in 2018, what would have been the after-tax effect on net income for that year?
- c. Compute the dividend payout ratio for 2017 and 2018.
- d. Given Wells Fargo's closing stock price of $46.08 on December 31, 2018, compute the dividend yield ratio for 2018.

Solution on p. 8-52.

Accumulated Other Comprehensive Income

LO5 Interpret accumulated other comprehensive income and its components.

Unrealized gains and losses arise when the fair value of an asset or liability on the balance sheet differs from its cost. For most assets and liabilities (see below), unrealized gains and losses are not reflected in net income nor in retained earnings because the company has had no transaction to create a realized gain or loss.

There are selected items recorded on the balance sheet at fair value—see list below. For the accounts listed below, any unrealized gains or losses are captured in the asset or liability section of the balance sheet. However, because unrealized gains or losses are not reported in net income or retained earnings, the balance sheet does not balance. To solve this issue, unrealized gains and losses are added to **accumulated other comprehensive income (AOCI)**, a stockholders' equity account that captures unrealized gains and losses on certain assets and liabilities. Unrealized gains and losses are "held" in AOCI until the related asset is sold (or liability settled) and any gain or loss is realized.

AOCI Components

Following are common items in AOCI—we further describe these items in later modules.

- **Foreign currency translation adjustments.** Foreign subsidiaries often maintain their financial statements in foreign currencies and these statements are translated into $US before the subsidiaries' financial statements are included in the company's 10-K. The strengthening and weakening of the $US vis-à-vis foreign currencies results in decreases and increases in the $US-value of subsidiaries' assets and liabilities. Because subsidiaries normally have positive equity (assets exceed liabilities), a weaker $US creates an unrealized foreign currency gain. Conversely, a stronger $US creates an unrealized loss. These unrealized gains or losses in the $US value of foreign subsidiaries' assets and liabilities are included in AOCI.

- **Gains and losses on available-for-sale investments in debt securities.** Investments in certain types of marketable debt securities are reported at fair value on the asset side of a company's balance sheet. If the fair value differs from the securities' cost, there are unrealized gains and losses on these securities included in AOCI. Beginning in 2018, gains and losses on available-for-sale *equity* securities are no longer deferred in AOCI until the securities are sold. New standards require firms measure these equity securities at fair value with changes in the fair value flowing to the income statement.

- **Employee benefit plans.** Unrealized gains and losses on some pension investments and pension liabilities are reported in AOCI.
- **Gains and losses on derivatives and hedges.** Unrealized gains and losses on certain financial securities (derivatives) that companies purchase to hedge exposures to interest rate, foreign exchange rate, and commodity price risks are included in AOCI.

AOCI Disclosures and Interpretation

Following is the reconciliation of beginning and ending balances in AOCI for Johnson & Johnson.

$ millions	Foreign Currency Translation	Gain/(Loss) On Securities	Employee Benefit Plans	Gain/(Loss) On Derivatives and Hedges	Total Accumulated Other Comprehensive Income (Loss)
January 3, 2016	$(8,435)	$604	$(5,298)	$ (36)	$(13,165)
Net 2016 changes	(612)	(193)	(682)	(249)	(1,736)
January 1, 2017	(9,047)	411	(5,980)	(285)	(14,901)
Net 2017 changes	1,696	(179)	(170)	355	1,702
December 31, 2017	(7,351)	232	(6,150)	70	(13,199)
Cumulative adjustment to retained earnings		(232)			(232)
Net 2018 changes	(1,518)	—	(8)	(265)	(1,791)
December 30, 2018	$(8,869)	$ —	$(6,158)	$(195)	$(15,222)

As is typical of many companies, JNJ's accumulated other comprehensive income account has become more negative over the past few years for two main reasons.

1. **Foreign currency translation.** JNJ's foreign subsidiaries maintain financial statements in their domestic currencies. To consolidate (combine) those income statements and balance sheets, JNJ first translates all the foreign currency numbers into $US using the rates that prevail on the balance sheet date. As the $US weakens or strengthens vis-à-vis foreign currencies, JNJ's foreign subsidiaries' assets and liabilities are translated into higher or lower amounts, respectively. This creates foreign currency translation gains or losses, which are aggregated each period in AOCI. A stronger US dollar in 2018 created additional unrealized losses of $1,518 million and AOCI became more negative. We discuss the effects of foreign currency translation in Module 9.
2. **Employee benefit plans.** Certain gains and losses on pension and other post-retirement benefit plans are not included in net income but are instead deferred and held in AOCI until recognized on the income statement in future years. We discuss the accounting for pension and other post-retirement benefit plans in Module 10.

Gains and losses on securities and on derivatives are less significant for JNJ (and for most other companies) because these activities are much smaller than foreign subsidiaries and pension plans. Gains and losses on securities have a $0 balance for JNJ in 2018 owing to the new accounting rules for marketable securities. JNJ, like many other companies, made a cumulative adjustment to the opening balance of AOCI (and to retained earnings) in 2018 when the company adopted the new marketable-securities standard. We discuss the accounting for investments in marketable securities in Module 9 and investments in derivative securities in Module 10.

Comprehensive Income During the year, market values on the AOCI items inevitably change and so do the unrealized gains and losses in AOCI. Remember, changes in unrealized gains and losses do not flow to the income statement as they are not part of net income. Instead, those changes are aggregated and labeled **other comprehensive income (OCI)**. The following graphic depicts the relation between net income and retained earnings and between comprehensive income and AOCI.

Following is JNJ's statement of comprehensive income for the year.

Consolidated Statements of Comprehensive Income ($ millions)	12 Months Ended		
	2018	2107	2016
Net earnings..	$15,297	$1,300	$16,540
Other comprehensive income (loss), net of tax			
Foreign currency translation.........................	(1,518)	1,696	(612)
Securities:			
Unrealized holding gain (loss) arising during period...	(1)	159	(52)
Reclassifications to earnings......................	1	(338)	(141)
Net change......................................	—	(179)	(193)
Employee benefit plans:			
Prior service credit (cost), net of amortization........	(44)	2	21
Gain (loss), net of amortization....................	(56)	29	(862)
Effect of exchange rates..........................	92	(201)	159
Net change......................................	(8)	(170)	(682)
Derivatives & hedges:			
Unrealized gain (loss) arising during period.........	(73)	(4)	(359)
Reclassifications to earnings......................	(192)	359	110
Net change......................................	(265)	355	(249)
Other comprehensive income (loss)...................	(1,791)	1,702	(1,736)
Comprehensive income...............................	$13,506	$3,002	$14,804

During 2018, JNJ reported other comprehensive loss of $1,791 million. This represents the amount by which AOCI changed during the year, primarily due to the foreign currency translation loss of $1,518 million owing to a stronger US dollar. (See that the components of other comprehensive income are the same components as shown in the "Net 2018 changes" row of Johnson & Johnson's AOCI reconciliation. There is no cash effect from unrealized gains and losses or from any changes in unrealized gains and losses over time.)

For analysis purposes, recall that unrealized gains or losses do not affect net income until the assets are sold or the liabilities settled. If the company anticipates selling the assets or settling the liabilities in the short run (say, within the next quarter), those unrealized gains or losses would flow to net income and this could affect our assessment of company profitability and cash flow. But over the long run, unrealized gains and losses might change substantially (as market prices move) and thus, there is no reliable way to include unrealized gains and losses in our analysis.

Review 8-5 LO5

The annual report of **The Coca-Cola Company** discloses the following related to accumulated other comprehensive income (AOCI).

Year Ended December 31	2018	2017	2016
Net foreign currency translation adjustments....................	$(2,035)	$861	$ (626)
Net gains (losses) on derivatives...........................	(7)	(433)	(382)
Net unrealized gains (losses) on available-for-sale securities......	(34)	188	17
Net change in pension and other benefit liabilities...............	29	322	(53)
Accumulated other comprehensive income (loss)..............	$(2,047)	$938	$(1,044)

continued

continued from previous page

> **Required**
> a. On average, during 2018, did the $US strengthen or weaken vis-à-vis currencies of countries where Coca-Cola has subsidiaries? How do we know?
> b. Consider unrealized losses on the available-for-sale securities of $34 million at year-end. What would have been the effect on pretax income if Coca-Cola had sold all of these securities on December 31, 2018?
> c. Consider an unrealized loss on the derivatives of $7 million at year-end. Is it accurate to conclude that the market value of these derivatives decreased during the year? Explain.
>
> Solution on p. 8-52.

Convertible Securities

LO6 Analyze convertible securities and their financial effects.

When common stock is issued, the company receives proceeds equal to the market price of the stock multiplied by the number of shares sold. So, the higher the stock price, the greater the proceeds. Preferred stock and long-term bonds are sold in much the same way, and their market price on the date of sale determines the cash proceeds to the company.

Companies can increase the cash proceeds by including provisions in the preferred stock and bonds agreements that make the securities more desirable. One such provision is a **conversion option** that allows the holder of those securities to convert them into common stock at a preset price. While investors own the preferred stock or long-term bond, they receive dividend or interest payments and will have a senior position to common shareholders in the event that the company fails and is liquidated (meaning the preferred stock or bond investors are paid before the common shareholders).

On the other hand, if the company performs well and its prospects are good, the preferred stock or bond investors can exchange their securities for common stock at a pre-agreed exchange ratio. They have the option to become common shareholders. In that case, they can benefit from the company's upside potential and the value of their common shares will increase as the market value of the company increases. This conversion option is valuable to investors and they are willing to pay a higher price for convertible preferred stock or convertible bonds when they are issued. For the company, the issue proceeds are higher.

Convertible Securities Disclosures and Interpretation Earlier in this module we described a 4.25% convertible preferred stock at **Corning Inc.** that is convertible (at the shareholder's option) into 50,000 common shares for each preferred share. This is an attractive feature for investors and it allowed Corning to realize a higher market price for its preferred stock.

Bonds can have a similar conversion option. Until bonds are converted, bondholders enjoy interest income and a senior position in liquidation. But, if the company performs well, bondholders can convert their bonds into common stock and enjoy all of the benefits of a common shareholder.

For many years, **Tesla** has used convertible bonds to finance its growth. As of 2018, Tesla had outstanding convertible bonds amounting to $5.7 billion, over half of its total long-term debt of $11 billion. By way of example, consider the following disclosure in Tesla's 10-K.

> In March 2017, we issued $977.5 million in aggregate principal amount of 2.375% Convertible Senior Notes due in March 2022 in a public offering. The net proceeds from the issuance, after deducting transaction costs, were $965.9 million. Each $1,000 of principal of the 2022 Notes is initially convertible into 3.0534 shares of our common stock, which is equivalent to an initial conversion price of $327.50 per share. Holders of the 2022 Notes may convert, at their option, on or after December 15, 2021.

After December 15, 2021, bondholders can exchange each $1,000 bond for 3.0534 shares of Tesla common stock. Until then, the bondholders earn 2.375% interest. Conversion of these bonds is advantageous to the bondholder if Tesla's stock rises above the $327.50 conversion price (computed as $1,000/3.0534). On December 31, 2018, Tesla common stock was valued at $332.80, making conversion attractive, but that option was not available because the conversion feature kicks in on December 15, 2021.

Convertible Securities Financial Effects To see the effects that conversion would have on Tesla's financial statements, assume that on December 31, 2021, bondholders convert $600 million (of the total $977.5 million bond issue) into 1,832,040 common shares of common stock with a par value of $0.001 per share ([$600 million/$1,000] × 3.0534 shares). The financial statement effects of the conversion are as follows (Tesla reports its balance sheet in $000s).

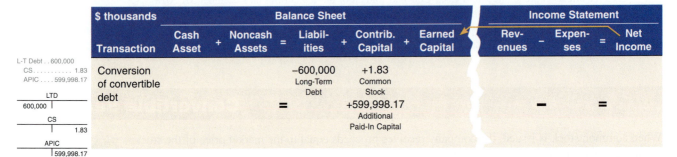

Upon conversion, the debt is removed from the balance sheet at its book value ($600 million assumed in this case) and the common stock is issued for that amount, resulting in an increase in the Common Stock account of $1,832 (1,832,040 shares at par value of $0.001 per share). Additional paid-in capital is increased for the remaining amount. No gain or loss (or cash inflow or outflow) is recognized as a result of the conversion.

IFRS Insight ■ Convertible Securities under IFRS

Unlike GAAP, convertible securities (called *compound financial instruments* under IFRS) are split into separate debt and equity components. The idea is that the conversion premium is akin to a call option on the company's stock. This embedded option has a value of its own even if it is not legally detachable. Thus, under IFRS, the proceeds from the issuance are allocated between the liability component (at fair value) and an equity component (the residual amount).

Review 8-6 LO6

Assume that **Express Scripts Inc.** has issued the following convertible debentures: each $1,000 bond is convertible into 200 shares of $1 par common. Assume that the bonds were sold at a discount, and that each bond has a current unamortized discount equal to $150.

Required
Solution on p. 8-53. Use the financial statements effect template to record the conversion of one of these convertible debentures.

Earnings per Share (EPS)

LO7 Interpret earnings per share.

A common metric reported in the financial press is earnings per share (EPS). EPS is the only ratio defined by GAAP, a testimony to this ratio's perceived importance for users. During the "earnings season"—the time each quarter when public companies release their quarterly earnings reports—EPS disclosures are followed obsessively by Wall Street analysts and investors.

We must be careful in using EPS when comparing companies' operating results, as the number of shares outstanding is not necessarily proportional to the income level—that is, a company with twice the level of net income does not necessarily have double the number of common shares outstanding. Management controls the number of common shares outstanding and there is no relation between firm size and number of shares outstanding. For example, consider that JNJ reports Basic EPS of $5.70 for 2018, while in the same year, **Berkshire Hathaway** reports Basic EPS of $2,446! This is because Berkshire Hathaway has so few common shares outstanding, not necessarily because it has stellar profits.

Potential ownership dilution is another concern. As we described earlier, stock options awarded to employees under stock-based compensation plans and convertible securities, such as Dow's convertible preferred stock and Xilinx's convertible notes, all have the potential to increase the number of common shares outstanding. Existing shareholders usually take a dim view of this because more common stock outstanding dilutes the ownership of existing shareholders. This is because there are more shareholders laying claim to the available dividends *and* the new shareholders will share equally in the proceeds of liquidation if the company fails. Current shareholders are, therefore, concerned about potential dilution.

To communicate the potential impact of dilution in earnings available for the payment of dividends to shareholders, accounting regulation requires companies to report two EPS statistics.

- **Basic EPS**. Basic EPS is computed as:

$$\text{Basic EPS} = \frac{\text{Net income} - \text{Dividends on preferred stock}}{\text{Weighted average number of common shares outstanding during the year}}$$

Subtracting preferred stock dividends, in the numerator, yields the income available for dividend payments to common shareholders. The denominator is the average number of common shares outstanding during the year.

- **Diluted EPS**. Diluted EPS reflects the impact of additional shares that would be issued if all stock options and convertible securities are converted into common shares at the beginning of the year. Diluted EPS never exceeds basic EPS.

Exhibit 8.3 highlights the difference between the two ratios.

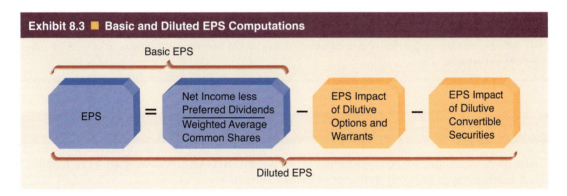

Exhibit 8.3 ■ Basic and Diluted EPS Computations

EPS Disclosures JNJ reports the following table of basic and diluted EPS for 2018.

In millions, except per share amounts†	2018	2017	2016
Basic net earnings per share	$5.70	$0.48	$6.04
Average shares outstanding—basic.	2,681.5	2,692.0	2,737.3
Potential shares exercisable under stock option plans.	139.0	139.7	142.4
Less: shares repurchased under treasury stock method	(92.5)	(87.3)	(92.1)
Convertible debt shares	0.7	0.9	1.3
Adjusted average shares outstanding—diluted	2,728.7	2,745.3	2,788.9
Diluted net earnings per share	$5.61	$0.47	$5.93

† The diluted net earnings per share calculation included the dilutive effect of convertible debt that is offset by the related reduction in interest expense of $1 million after-tax for 2018 and 2017, and $2 million for 2016. The diluted net earnings per share calculation for 2018, 2017, and 2016 included all shares related to stock options, as the exercise price of all options was less than the average market value of the Company's stock.

The denominator in diluted earnings per share calculation presumes the most-extreme case: at the beginning of the year, all employees exercise their right to purchase common shares and all convertible debt holders convert their notes to common shares.

JNJ uses the treasury-stock method to determine the dilutive effect of stock options. The method assumes that all options are exercised (139.0 million shares) and that the company uses the proceeds to repurchase shares on the open market at the current stock price (92.5 million shares). The 46.5 million share increase is the net of the shares issued to option holders less the new treasury shares (139.0 million − 92.5 million).

The combined effect is to increase the number of shares in the denominator from 2,681.5 million shares used for the basic EPS calculation to 2,728.7 shares used for the diluted EPS calculation.[1] The increase in the number of shares in the denominator reduces $5.70 for basic EPS to $5.61 for diluted EPS. Diluted EPS is never greater than basic EPS.

Review 8-7 LO7

Autozone reports the following reconciliation of basic net earnings per share to diluted net earnings per share for 2018.

In thousands	2018
Net income (basic and diluted).........................	$1,337,536
Weighted average shares outstanding—basic...........	26,970
Effect of dilutive stock equivalents.....................	454

Required
a. Compute basic EPS for 2018.
b. Compute diluted EPS 2018.
c. Autozone's footnotes contain the following statement: "There were 847,279 stock options excluded from the diluted earnings per share calculation because they would have been anti-dilutive as of 2018." Explain this statement.

Solution on p. 8-53.

Global Accounting

Under IFRS, accounting for equity is similar to that under U.S. GAAP. Following are a few terminology differences (seen primarily in European balance sheets).

U.S. GAAP	IFRS
Common stock	Share capital *or* Ordinary shares
Preferred shares	Preference shares
Additional paid-in capital	Share premium
Retained earnings	Reserves
Accumulated other comprehensive income	Other equity *or* Other components of equity
—	Revaluation surplus *or* Revaluation reserve*
Treasury stock	Own shares

* Certain assets including fixed assets and intangible assets may be revalued upwards (and later, revalued downwards) under IFRS. These revaluations do not affect net income or retained earnings but, instead, are reported in a separate equity account. For comparative purposes our analysis might exclude revaluations from both equity and the asset accounts to which they relate.

U.S. GAAP has a more narrow definition of liabilities than IFRS. Therefore, more items are classified as liabilities under IFRS. For example, some preferred shares are deemed liabilities under IFRS and equity under GAAP. (Both systems classify preferred shares that are mandatorily redeemable or

---

[1] JNJ notes that diluted EPS includes the dilutive effect of the exercise of all outstanding stock options. The effects of dilutive securities are only included if they actually reduce the EPS number. **Antidilutive** securities *increase* EPS, and are, thus, excluded from the computation. An example of an antidilutive security is employee stock options with an exercise price greater than the stock's current market price. The company could repurchase more shares than would be issued to option holders. This would decrease the number of shares outstanding. These underwater (or out-of-the-money) options are antidilutive and are, therefore, excluded from the EPS computation.

redeemable at the option of the shareholder, as liabilities.) For comparative purposes, we look at classification of preferred shares that are not mandatorily redeemable and make the numbers consistent. To do this we add preference shares classified as liabilities under IFRS to equity.

Treasury stock transactions are sometimes difficult to identify under IFRS because companies are not required to report a separate line item for treasury shares on the balance sheet. Instead treasury share transactions reduce share capital and share premium. We must review the statement of shareholders' equity to assess stock repurchases for IFRS companies.

For example, at March 31, 2018, BT Group plc reports the following in the equity section of its IFRS balance sheet (in £ millions).

Ordinary shares	£ 499
Share premium	1,051
Own shares	(186)
Merger reserve	6,647
Other reserves	534
Retained profit (loss)	1,759
Total equity	**£10,304**

Its balance sheet reports no treasury stock line item, but footnotes disclose that BT Group's "own shares" of £(186) million changed as follows over the prior year.

£ millions	Own Shares
At 1 April 2017	£ (96)
Net buyback of own shares	(90)
At 31 March 2018	£(186)

Appendix 8A: Stock-Based Compensation: Reporting and Analyzing

There are four broad types of share-based compensation plans.

1. Employee stock purchase plans
2. Stock awards (unrestricted and restricted)
3. Stock options
4. Stock appreciation rights

Whichever type of plan is used, the accounting objective is the same: *to record the fair value of compensation as expense over the periods in which employees perform services* (the vesting period).

This requires determining the fair value of the compensation and the vesting period. The fair value for each of the types is discussed below along with some important features of each.

Employee Stock Purchase Plans (ESPP)

Compensation expense is the amount of any discount the employee receives when stock is purchased. Common features are:

- Employees can purchase the company's stock at a discount, commonly ~15%.
- Employees can purchase stock up to a maximum that can be a flat amount (such as $25,000) or based on the employee's salary (such as 15% of gross salary).
- Payroll deductions are made monthly and employees can choose when to purchase the stock (such as purchasing when price is low).

Stock Awards

Compensation expense is market price of the stock at the grant date. Common feature is:

- Employee granted shares with no restrictions. Not a strong incentive because employee can sell stock or leave the company.

Stock Awards—Restricted Stock Awards

Compensation expense is the market price of the stock at the grant date. Common features are:

- Employee granted shares (and legally owns them) but is "restricted" from selling shares until the vesting date (to encourage employee retention).
- Shares are forfeited if employee quits before vesting date.
- Often shares are forfeited if performance targets are not met.
- Employee may or may not receive dividends between the grant date and the vesting date, depending on the plan details. But, restricted stock holds no vote.

Stock Awards—Restricted Stock Units (RSU)

Compensation expense is market price of the stock at the grant date. Common features are:

- Employee receives a stock "unit" but no actual stock, the employee does not legally own any stock. A stock unit is typically equivalent to one share.
- Employer delivers stock (or cash) to the employee based on a vesting schedule.
- Employee cannot receive dividends during restriction period as employee does not own any stock.
- Often RSUs are forfeited if performance targets are not met.
- Unlike restricted stock, RSUs do not dilute EPS because no shares are issued.

Stock Options

Compensation expense is the estimated fair value of the options at the grant date. Fair value is measured with a model that requires assumptions. Common features are:

- Employee has right to buy shares in the future, at a price specified at the grant date.
- The employee cannot buy shares before the vesting date.
- Options are forfeited if employee quits before vesting period.
- The employee cannot sell the options.

For stock options, understanding some of the vocabulary is helpful:

- *Employee stock option:* Security that gives employee the right, but not obligation, to purchase stock at a predetermined price.
- *Grant date:* Date the option is awarded to the employee.
- *Exercise:* Purchase of stock pursuant to an option.
- *Exercise price:* Predetermined price at which the stock can be purchased. This is also called the strike price or grant price. In most plans, the exercise price is the stock price on the grant date.
- *Option term:* Length of time employee can hold the option before it expires. Typically 7–10 years.
- *Vesting:* Requirement(s) that must be met for employee to have right to exercise the option. Usually options vest with continuation of employment for a specific period of time (such as 4 years) or the meeting of a performance goal (such as revenue growth).
- *Expiry date:* Date after which the option can no longer be exercised. Once vested, the employee can exercise the option at the grant price at any time over the option term up to the expiration date.
- *Intrinsic value:* Difference between the current stock price and the exercise price. As the stock price rises so does intrinsic value.

At-the-money option	Intrinsic value = 0	Current stock price = Exercise price
In-the-money option	Intrinsic value > 0	Current stock price > Exercise price
Out-of-the-money option	Intrinsic value < 0	Current stock price < Exercise price

- *Option fair value:* Value of the option that considers the intrinsic value and the time value of the option. Determined with a valuation model, most frequently Black-Scholes or lattice model.

Stock Appreciation Rights (SAR)

Compensation expense is the estimated fair value of the SARs at the grant date. Fair value is measured with a model that requires assumptions. Fair value is usually the same as an option with similar terms. Common features are:

- Employee benefits by the amount of any stock price increase but without having to buy shares.
- Settlement date is determined at the grant date (similar to vesting period).
- "Stock appreciation" is the increase in the market price since the grant date; SAR has no value if stock price falls.
- SARs can be settled in stock or cash, depending on plan details.
- Similar to stock option but with no exercise price.

Some plans allow for RSUs and SARs to settle in either stock or cash. If they settle in cash (or if the employee has a cash option), the RSU or SAR is considered a liability. The amount of compensation (and related liability) is estimated each period and adjusted quarterly to reflect changes in the fair value of the RSUs or SARs until the settlement date.

Summary of Share-Based Compensation

The following chart summarizes the accounting for various types of stock-based compensation plans.

	Cash	Liability	Common Stock	APIC	Deferred Comp	Treasury Stock	Retained Earnings	Comp Expense
Employee stock purchase plan								
At purchase: Compensation expense	+		+	+			−	+
Stock grants (awards)								
Grant: Fair value of stock			+	+			−	+
Restricted stock								
Grant: Fair value of restricted stock				+	−			
Vesting: Proportion of restricted stock that vests					+		−	+
Restricted stock units or Stock appreciation rights settled in cash								
Grant: Fair value of restricted stock unit		+					−	+
Settlement: Cash to employee	−	−						
Stock options								
Grant: Fair value of options				+			−	+
Exercise: New shares issued	+		+	+				
Exercise: Treasury shares issued	+					+		

The chart shows that some plans have cash effects while others do not. Some plans affect common stock and APIC when shares are issued; other plans have no such effect because stock is not issued at all.

Analysis Implications

There are several analysis implications for share-based compensation.

- **Magnitude of Awards**—We consider both the absolute and relative size of compensation expense each period. Large increases or decreases are examined to determine the cause. Footnotes and the MD&A section provide details. For JNJ, stock compensation is increasing in dollar terms, but fairly constant relative to total sales, over the past five years. The proportion of stock-based compensation to sales varies greatly by industry (see graphic), which highlights the need to evaluate any metric against competitors and industry benchmarks.

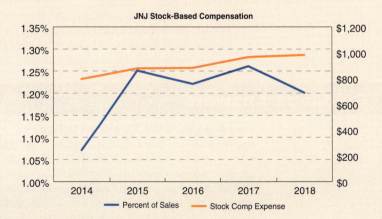

- **Dilution potential**—Large compensation plans can create large dilution that is not fully captured in diluted EPS. The dilution calculation for EPS includes all vested shares but none of the unvested shares.

For example, JNJ's diluted EPS included 38.2 million dilutive shares, net (2,795.4 million − 2,757.2 million). But the footnotes reveal that an additional 486 million shares are yet to be granted and, as such, are not included in diluted EPS. One way to quantify this missing dilution is to recompute EPS with a denominator that includes unvested shares. This will be a worst-case scenario because not all unvested shares are ultimately issued, but the adjusted EPS measure could be informative.

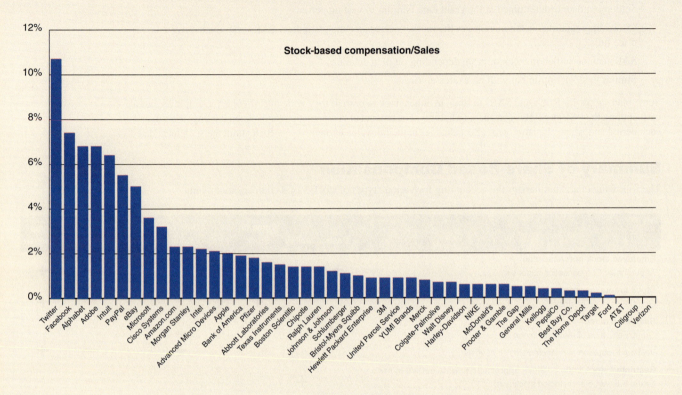

- **Tax benefit**—Companies cannot deduct GAAP share-based compensation expense for tax purposes. The tax laws do permit companies to deduct the *intrinsic* value of shares issued. This can be much larger than the GAAP expense and can create large tax savings. To assess this, analysts look at footnotes to determine the size of the tax benefit in the current period as well as the *intrinsic* value of outstanding shares and options. For example, JNJ reports the total intrinsic value of options exercised was $1,028 million, which gave rise to a tax benefit of $192 million. The intrinsic value of outstanding options is $3,214 million, a considerable amount of potential future cash flow. Footnotes to the financial statements include these details.

- **Model assumptions**—Companies select assumptions used in the models that they use to estimate fair value. Analysts examine the assumptions, compare them to prior years and to assumptions used by competitors.

- **Cash flow implications**—When plans allow employees the choice to settle the award in cash instead of in stock, the company must record a liability for the potential cash outflow. This liability must be adjusted each quarter to reflect current stock price. Analysts must consider that for "hot" stocks, this means the liability on the balance sheet might understate the eventual cash outflow.

Guidance Answers

You Are the Chief Financial Officer

Pg. 8-11 Several points must be considered. (1) Buying stock back reduces the number of shares outstanding, which can prop up earnings per share (EPS). However, foregone earnings from the cash used for repurchases can dampen earnings. The net effect is that EPS is likely to increase because of the reduced shares in the denominator. (2) Another motivation is that, if the shares are sufficiently undervalued (in management's opinion), the stock repurchase and subsequent resale can provide a better return than alternative investments. (3) Stock repurchases send a strong signal to the market that management feels its stock is undervalued. This is more credible than merely making that argument with analysts. On the other hand, company cash is diverted from other investments. This is bothersome if such investments are mutually exclusive either now or in the future.

Superscript ^A denotes assignments based on Appendix 8A.

Questions

Q8-1. Define *par value stock*. What is the significance of a stock's par value from an accounting and analysis perspective?

Q8-2. What are the basic differences between preferred stock and common stock? That is, what are the typical features of preferred stock?

Q8-3. What features make preferred stock similar to debt? Similar to common stock?

Q8-4. What is meant by preferred dividends in arrears? If dividends are two years in arrears on $500,000 of 6% preferred stock, and dividends are declared at the end of this year, what amount of total dividends must the company pay to preferred stockholders before paying any dividends to common stockholders?

Q8-5. Distinguish between authorized shares and issued shares. Why might the number of shares issued be more than the number of shares outstanding?

Q8-6. Describe the difference between contributed capital and earned capital. Specifically, how can earned capital be considered as an investment by the company's stockholders?

Q8-7. How does the account "additional paid-in capital" (APIC) arise? Does the amount of APIC reported on the balance sheet relative to the common stock amount provide any information about the financial condition of the company?

Q8-8. Define *stock split*. What are the major reasons for a stock split?

Q8-9. Define *treasury stock*. Why might a corporation acquire treasury stock? How is treasury stock reported in the balance sheet?

Q8-10. If a corporation purchases 10,000 shares of its own common stock at $10 per share and resells them at $14 per share, where would the $40,000 increase in capital be reported in the financial statements? Why is no gain reported?

Q8-11. A corporation has total stockholders' equity of $18,995,250 and one class of $2 par value common stock. The corporation has 500,000 shares authorized; 300,000 shares issued; and 15,000 shares as treasury stock. What is its book value per share?

Q8-12. What is meant by the *market cap* of a company and how is it determined?

Q8-13. When a company reports negative retained earnings on the balance sheet (a deficit), can we conclude that the company has reported significant net losses on the income statement?

Q8-14. Employee stock options potentially dilute earnings per share (EPS). What can companies do to offset these dilutive effects and how might this action affect the balance sheet?

Q8-15. What information is reported in a statement of stockholders' equity?

Q8-16. What items are typically reported under the stockholders' equity category of accumulated other comprehensive income (AOCI)?

Q8-17. What are three common forms of stock-based compensation and why do companies use such forms of compensation?

Q8-18. Describe the accounting for a convertible bond. Can the conversion ever result in the recognition of a gain in the income statement?

Mini Exercises

LO2 M8-19. Analyzing and Identifying Financial Statement Effects of Stock Issuances
During the current year, Austin Company, (*a*) issues 8,000 shares of $50 par value preferred stock at $84 cash per share and (*b*) issues 19,000 shares of $1 par value common stock at $10 cash per share. Indicate the financial statement effects of these two issuances using the financial statement effects template.

LO7 M8-20. Understanding EPS Calculations
On its Form 10-K for the year ended December 31, 2018, **Bank of America Corp.** reported information related to basic earnings per share. Fill in the missing information.

$ millions, except per share amounts	2018	2017	2016
Net income	$28,147	$18,232	d
Preferred stock dividends	1,451	b	$ 1,682
Net income applicable to common shareholders	26,696	c	$16,140
Average common shares outstanding	10,096.5	10,195.6	e
Basic earnings per share	a	$1.63	$1.57

LO1 M8-21. Distinguishing Between Common Stock and Additional Paid-in Capital
Following is the stockholders' equity section from the **Cisco Systems Inc.** balance sheet for the third quarter of fiscal 2019.

Shareholders' Equity (in millions, except par value)	April 27, 2019
Preferred stock, no par value: 5 shares authorized; none issued and outstanding	$ —
Common stock and additional paid-in capital, $0.001 par value: 20,000 shares authorized; 4,313 shares issued and outstanding	40,577
Retained earnings (Accumulated deficit)	(2,877)
Accumulated other comprehensive income (loss)	(896)
Total equity	$36,804

a. For the $40,577 million reported as "common stock and additional paid-in capital," what portion is common stock and what portion is additional paid-in capital?
b. Explain why Cisco does not report the two components described in part *a* separately.
c. Cisco's stock price was $55.88 on April 26, 2019 (the closest trading day to fiscal year-end). Determine Cisco's market capitalization that day.

LO2 M8-22. Identifying Financial Statement Effects of Stock Issuance and Repurchase
On January 1, Centaur Inc. issues 7,000 shares of $100 par value preferred stock at $300 cash per share. On March 1, the company repurchases 7,000 shares of previously issued $1 par value common stock at $156 cash per share. Use the financial statement effects template to record these two transactions.

LO4 M8-23. Assessing the Financial Statement Effects of a Stock Split
The following is taken from a Motley Fool article dated June 15, 2018, concerning **Aflac Inc.**

> **Quacking about a split.** Supplemental-insurance giant Aflac is best known for the white duck it has as its spokesperson, but the insurance products it provides to workers in the U.S. and Japan help millions get the coverage they need in areas that few insurance companies cover. That's been a successful model, and the insurer has seen its share price rise substantially over the years. In February, Aflac announced that it would do a 2-for-1 split effective March 16, putting it in the form of a 100% stock dividend. CEO Daniel Amos celebrated the announcement, noting that "this is the ninth split of the company's common stock since listing on the NYSE in 1974 and the first in 17 years." Aflac pointed to improving liquidity as a key reason for the move.

a. Aflac's common stock has a par value of $0.10. What adjustments will it make to its balance sheet as a result of the stock split?
b. Why is Aflac splitting its stock?

M8-24. Reconciling Common Stock and Treasury Stock Balances
Following is the stockholders' equity section from the **The Walt Disney Company** balance sheet.

The Walt Disney Company (TWDC)

Stockholders' equity, $ millions	Sep. 29, 2018	Sep. 30, 2017
Preferred stock...	$ 0	$ 0
Common stock, $0.01 par value, Authorized—4.6 billion shares, Issued—2.9 billion shares	36,779	36,248
Retained earnings	82,679	72,606
Accumulated other comprehensive loss...............	(3,097)	(3,528)
Stockholders' Equity subtotal before Treasury Stock, Total	116,361	105,326
Treasury stock, at cost, 1.4 billion shares................	(67,588)	(64,011)
Total Disney Shareholders' equity	48,773	41,315
Noncontrolling interests	4,059	3,689
Total equity..	$ 52,832	$ 45,004

a. How many shares are issued at September 29, 2018? The par value of these shares is $0.01 per share. Where is this information reported on the balance sheet?
b. How many shares are outstanding at 2018 fiscal year-end?
c. Determine the average price at which Disney issued its common stock.
d. Use the treasury stock account to determine the average price Disney paid when it repurchased its common shares.

M8-25. Identifying and Analyzing Financial Statement Effects of Cash Dividends
On March 15, 2018, **Bank of America** issued 94,000 shares of 5.875% Fixed-to-Floating Rate Non-Cumulative Preferred Stock, Series FF for $2.35 billion. Dividends are payable semiannually on or about March 15 and September 15.

Bank of America Corp. (BAC)

a. Assume the stock was issued at face value. What is the face value of each Series FF share?
b. What will be the total dividend for the year ended December 31, 2018, assuming that the number of shares remains unchanged?

M8-26.^A Estimating Stock-Based Compensation Expense
Pedernales Corp. has several types of stock-based compensation plans including a stock purchase plan that allows employees to buy shares at a 15% discount. During the current year, employees purchased 25,000 shares under this plan. Also, the company granted 20,000 stock options with estimated fair value of $10.10 per option. The options vest ratably over three years. Pedernales's average stock price during this year was $78.94. Determine Pedernales's stock-based compensation expense for the current year.

M8-27. Identifying, Analyzing, and Explaining the Effects of a Stock Split
On September 1, Apstein Company has 300,000 shares of $9 par value ($148 market value) common stock that are issued and outstanding. Its balance sheet on that date shows the following account balances relating to its common stock.

Common stock	$2,700,000
Paid-in capital in excess of par value	1,680,000

On September 2, Apstein splits its stock 3-for-2 and reduces the par value to $6 per share.

a. How many shares of common stock are issued and outstanding immediately after the stock split?
b. What is the dollar balance of the common stock account immediately after the stock split?
c. What is the likely reason that Apstein Company split its stock?

M8-28. Determining Cash Dividends to Preferred and Common Shareholders
Sinclair Company has outstanding 40,000 shares of $50 par value, 6% cumulative preferred stock and 100,000 shares of $10 par value common stock. The company declares and pays cash dividends amounting to $280,000.

a. If there are no preferred dividends in arrears, how much in total dividends, and in dividends per share, does Sinclair pay to each class of stock?
b. If there are one year's dividends in arrears on the preferred stock, how much in total dividends, and in dividends per share, does Sinclair pay to each class of stock?

LO4

M8-29. Reconciling Retained Earnings

Use the following data to reconcile the 2019 retained earnings for Springwerth Company (that is, explain the change in retained earnings during the year).

Total retained earnings, December 31, 2018	$537,000
Stock dividends declared and paid in 2019	46,000
Cash dividends declared and paid in 2019	55,000
Net income for 2019	203,000

LO7
Wells Fargo (WFC)

M8-30. Calculating and Interpreting EPS Information

Wells Fargo reports the following information in its Form 10-K.

In millions	2018	2017
Wells Fargo net income	$22,393	$22,183
Preferred stock dividends	$ 1,556	$ 1,629
Common stock dividends	$ 7,955	$ 7,708
Average common shares outstanding	4,799.7	4,964.6
Diluted average common shares outstanding	4,838.4	5,017.3

a. Determine Wells Fargo's basic EPS for fiscal 2018 and for fiscal 2017.
b. Compare the number of common shares outstanding used for the 2018 Basic and Diluted EPS ratios. Provide three examples that explain why the two numbers differ.

LO4
McDonald's (MCD)

M8-31. Calculating and Recording Cash Dividends

On May 23, 2019, **McDonald**'s Board of Directors declared a quarterly cash dividend of $1.16 per share of common stock payable on June 17, 2019, to shareholders of record at the close of business on June 3, 2019. Assume that there were 785.2 million shares outstanding during this time period.

Use the financial statement effects template to record the transactions for the following dates:

a. May 23, 2019
b. June 3, 2019
c. June 17, 2019

LO4
Apple Inc. (AAPL)

M8-32. Determining Effects of Stock Splits

Apple Inc. has had the following stock splits since its inception.

Effective Date	Split Amount
June 9, 2014	7 for 1
February 28, 2005	2 for 1
June 21, 2000	2 for 1
June 16, 1987	2 for 1

a. If the par value of Apple shares was originally $1, what would Apple report as par value per share on its 2018 balance sheet?
b. On August 23, 2019, Apple's stock traded for about $206.50. All things equal, if Apple had never had a stock split, what would a share of Apple have traded for that same day?

LO5

M8-33. Interpreting Comprehensive Income and AOCI

Indicate whether each of the following statements is true or false. If false, indicate how to correct the statement.

a. The amount reported for accumulated other comprehensive income (AOCI) on the balance sheet must be a positive amount consistent with all other stockholders' equity accounts.
b. Changes in AOCI are reflected in other comprehensive income, which is different from net income.
c. Other comprehensive income does not imply a change in cash.

M8-34. Analyzing Financial Statement Effects of Convertible Securities

CenterPoint Energy reports the following footnote to its 2018 10-K. *Note:* A **depositary share** is a U.S. dollar-denominated equity *share* of a foreign-based company available for purchase on an American stock exchange.

LO6
CenterPoint Energy (CNP)

> **Series B Preferred Stock** On October 1, 2018, CenterPoint Energy completed the issuance of 19,550,000 depositary shares, each representing a 1/20th interest in a share of its Series B Preferred Stock, at a price of $50 per depositary share. The Series B Preferred Stock has a per share value of $1,000. A holder of the Series B Preferred Stock may, at any time prior to September 1, 2021, elect to convert shares of the Series B Preferred Stock at the conversion rate of 30.5820 shares of Common Stock per share of the Series B Preferred Stock.

a. How many Series B Preferred share equivalents did CenterPoint issue on October 1, 2018?
b. Describe the effects on CenterPoint's balance sheet if the preferred stock are all converted prior to September 1, 2021.
c. Would the conversion affect earnings? Explain.

Exercises

E8-35. Identifying and Analyzing Financial Statement Effects of Stock Transactions

Melo Company reports the following transactions relating to its stock accounts in the current year. Use the financial statement effects template to indicate the effects from each of these transactions.

LO2

Mar. 2	Issued 10,000 shares of $1 par value common stock at $30 cash per share.
Apr. 14	Issued 15,000 shares of $100 par value, 8% preferred stock at $250 cash per share.
June 30	Purchased 3,000 shares of its own common stock at $22 cash per share.
Sep. 25	Sold 1,500 shares of its treasury stock at $26 cash per share.

E8-36. Identifying and Analyzing Financial Statement Effects of Stock Transactions

Pyle Corp. reports the following transactions relating to its stock accounts in the current year. Use the financial statement effects template to indicate the effects from each of these transactions.

LO2

Feb. 3	Issued 40,000 shares of $5 par value common stock at $27 cash per share.
Feb. 27	Issued 9,000 shares of $50 par value, 8% preferred stock at $88 cash per share.
Mar. 31	Purchased 5,000 shares of its own common stock at $30 cash per share.
June 25	Sold 3,000 shares of its treasury stock at $38 cash per share.
July 15	Sold the remaining 2,000 shares of treasury stock at $29 cash per share.

E8-37. Analyzing and Computing Average Issue Price and Treasury Stock Cost

Following is the stockholders' equity section from the **Campbell Soup Company** balance sheet. *Note:* Campbell's uses *shareowners' equity* in lieu of the more common title of stockholders' equity.

LO1, 2, 3
Campbell Soup Co. (CPB)

Shareowners' Equity (millions, except per share amounts)	July 29, 2018	July 30, 2017
Preferred stock: authorized 40 shares; none issued	$ —	$ —
Capital stock, $.0375 par value; authorized 560 shares; issued 323 shares	12	12
Additional paid-in capital	349	359
Earnings retained in the business	2,224	2,385
Capital stock in treasury, at cost	(1,103)	(1,066)
Accumulated other comprehensive loss	(118)	(53)
Total Campbell Soup Company shareowners' equity	1,364	1,637
Noncontrolling interests	9	8
Total equity	$1,373	$1,645

Campbell Soup Company also reports the following statement of stockholders' equity.

(millions, except per share amounts)	Capital Stock				Additional Paid-in Capital	Earnings Retained in the Business	Accumulated Other Comprehensive Income (Loss)	Noncontrolling Interests	Total Equity
	Issued		In Treasury						
	Shares	Amount	Shares	Amount					
Balance at July 30, 2017............	323	$12	(22)	$(1,066)	$359	$2,385	$(53)	$8	$1,645
Net earnings........................						261			261
Other comprehensive income (loss)......							(65)	1	(64)
Dividends ($1.40 per share)..............						(422)			(422)
Treasury stock purchased			(2)	(86)					(86)
Treasury stock issued under management incentive and stock option plans..........			2	49	(10)				39
Balance at July 29, 2018	323	$12	(22)	$(1,103)	$349	$2,224	$(118)	$9	$1,373

a. Show the computation, using par value and share numbers, to arrive at the $12 million in the capital (common) stock account.

b. At what average price were the Campbell Soup shares issued?

c. Reconcile the beginning and ending balances of retained earnings.

d. Campbell Soup reports an increase in shareowners' equity relating to the exercise of stock options (titled "Treasury stock issued under management incentive and stock option plans"). This transaction involves the purchase of common stock by employees at a preset price. Describe how this set of transactions affects stockholders' equity.

e. Describe the transaction relating to the "Treasury stock purchased" line in the statement of shareowners' equity.

f. Campbell Soup's stock price was $32.99 on July 29, 2018. Determine the company's market capitalization that day.

g. Calculate and interpret the company's market-to-book ratio at July 29, 2018.

LO3 E8-38.[A] **Analyzing Stock-Based Compensation**

Hearne Inc. began business on March 1, 2020. At that time, it granted 250,000 options, with a strike price of $5, to computer engineers in lieu of signing bonuses. The fair value of each option was estimated at $1 and the options vest over four years.

a. What benefits did Hearne create by granting options to the engineers instead of cash signing bonuses?

b. What is the total expense that the company will record associated with the options granted in 2020?

c. What will Hearne record in 2020 for stock-option compensation expense?

d. How will the exercise of the options impact the balance sheet, income statement, and statement of cash flows?

LO4 E8-39. Analyzing Cash Dividends on Preferred and Common Stock

Haas Enterprise Inc. has outstanding 30,000 shares of $50 par value, 6% preferred stock and 70,000 shares of $1 par value common stock. During its first three years in business, it declared and paid no cash dividends in the first year, $310,000 in the second year, and $90,000 in the third year.

a. If the preferred stock is cumulative, determine the total amount of cash dividends paid to each class of stock in each of the three years.

b. If the preferred stock is noncumulative, determine the total amount of cash dividends paid to each class of stock in each of the three years.

E8-40. Analyzing and Computing Issue Price and Shares Outstanding
Following is the stockholders' equity section from **Public Storage**'s 2018 balance sheet.

(in thousands, except share data)	December 31, 2018
Preferred Shares, $0.01 par value, 100,000,000 shares authorized, 161,000 shares issued and outstanding	$4,025,000
Common Shares, $0.10 par value, 650,000,000 shares authorized, 174,130,881 shares issued and outstanding	17,413
Paid-in capital	5,718,485
Accumulated deficit	(577,360)
Accumulated other comprehensive loss	(64,060)
Total Public Storage shareholders' equity	9,119,478
Noncontrolling interests	25,250
Total equity	$9,144,728

a. Show the computation to derive the $17,413 thousand for common stock.
b. At what average price has Public Storage issued its common stock?
c. At what average price has the company issued its preferred shares?
d. The company reports Accumulated deficit of $(577,360). What would this account be called if the balance was positive rather than negative?
e. Public Storage has reported more than $1 billion in net income in each of the past five years. Given this, what are two plausible reasons for the accumulated deficit?
f. What does the Noncontrolling interests account of $25,250 thousand represent?

E8-41. Analyzing Cash Dividends on Preferred and Common Stock
Torres Company began business on June 30, 2018. At that time, it issued 25,000 shares of $40 par value, 8% cumulative preferred stock and 100,000 shares of $5 par value common stock. Through the end of 2020, there has been no change in the number of preferred and common shares outstanding.

a. Assume the company declared and paid cash dividends of $103,000 in 2018, $0 in 2019, and $461,000 in 2020. Compute the total cash dividends and the dividends per share paid to each class of stock in 2018, 2019, and 2020.
b. Assume the company declared and paid cash dividends of $0 in 2018, $160,000 in 2019, and $278,000 in 2020. Compute the total cash dividends and the dividends per share paid to each class of stock in 2018, 2019, and 2020.

E8-42. Identifying and Analyzing Financial Statement Effects of Stock Repurchase and Dividends
Quinn Company has outstanding 25,000 shares of $10 par value common stock that was issued for an average of $24 per share. It also has $514,000 of retained earnings. The company repurchases and retires 2,000 shares at $32 per share. Near the current year-end, the company declares and pays a cash dividend of $1.80 per share. Use the financial statement effects template to record the share repurchase and dividend transactions.

E8-43. Identifying and Analyzing Financial Statement Effects of Dividends
The statement of shareholders' equity of **Public Storage Corporation** for the year ended December 31, 2018, reports the following dividends paid to shareholders ($ thousands).

Distributions to equity holders	
Preferred shares	$ 216,316
Common shares	$1,396,364

The 2018 balance sheet includes the following ($ thousands).

Preferred Shares, $0.01 par value, 100,000,000 shares authorized, 161,000 shares issued and outstanding	$4,025,000
Common Shares, $0.10 par value, 650,000,000 shares authorized, 174,130,881 shares issued and outstanding	$ 17,413

a. Use the financial statement effects template to indicate the effects of the dividend payments.
b. Determine the dividends per share for both classes of stock.

LO4 **E8-44. Analyzing Financial Statement Effects of Dividends**

The stockholders' equity of DiFrancesco Company at March 31, 2019, is shown below.

4% preferred stock, $1,000 par value, 25,000 shares authorized, 10,000 shares issued and outstanding..	$10,000,000
Common stock, $1 par value, 3,000,000 shares authorized, 700,000 shares issued ...	700,000
Additional paid-in capital—preferred stock..	60,000
Additional paid-in capital—common stock	17,150,000
Retained earnings	49,005,689
Total stockholders' equity..	$76,915,689

The following transactions, among others, occurred during the fiscal year ended March 31, 2020.

April 15, 2019	Declare and pay preferred dividends of $400,000
April 15, 2019	Declare and pay common dividends of $1.30 per share
October 1, 2019	Execute a 3-for-1 stock split of the common stock when the stock price was $140 per share
March 1, 2020	Declare and pay common dividends of $0.50 per share

a. Use the financial statement effects template to indicate the effects of these transactions.
b. At March 31, 2020, the company reported net income for the year of $8,900,610. Compute retained earnings as of March 31, 2020.

LO1, 2, 4 **E8-45. Analyzing Shareholders' Equity Transactions Using Graphical Data**

The following dashboard was developed using **PowerBI** with data collected from 10-K filings for the S&P 500 for fiscal 2010 through 2018. Access the dashboard at the myBusinessCourse website to answer the requirements.

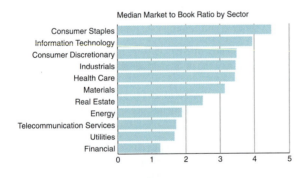
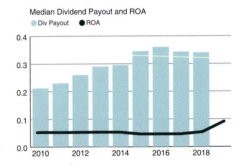
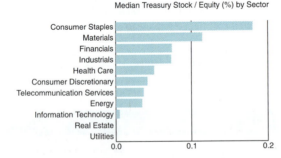
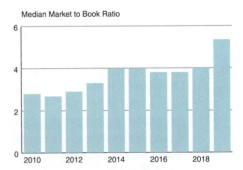

a. Which industry sector exhibits the highest market-to-book ratios, on average? Does the proportion of treasury shares held by firms in this sector explain the high market-to-book ratio?
b. What industry sectors exhibit the lowest market-to-book ratios? What might explain low ratios in these sectors?
c. What pattern do we observe in market-to-book ratios over time?
d. From the graphic of dividend payout ratio and return on assets, we might conclude that there is no relation between the two metrics. From the online dashboard, display the graphic for the Energy sector. What relation do we observe and what might explain this. *Hint:* Is this relation mechanical in any way?

E8-46. **Analyzing and Computing Issue Price, Treasury Stock Cost, and Shares Outstanding**
Following is the stockholders' equity section of the December 31, 2018, Caterpillar Inc. balance sheet.

LO1, 2
Caterpillar Inc.
(CAT)

Stockholders' Equity ($ millions)	2018
Common stock of $1.00 par; Authorized shares: 2,000,000,000; Issued 814,894,624 shares at paid-in amount	$ 5,827
Treasury stock 239,351,886 shares, at cost.	(20,531)
Profit employed in the business	30,427
Accumulated other comprehensive income (loss)	(1,684)
Noncontrolling interests	41
Total stockholders' equity	$14,080

a. How many shares of Caterpillar common stock are outstanding at year-end 2018?
b. What does the phrase "at paid-in amount" in the common stock account mean?
c. At what average cost has Caterpillar repurchased its stock as of year-end 2018?
d. Why would a company such as Caterpillar want to repurchase its common stock?
e. What is meant by "Profit employed in the business"? The account balance was $26,301 million at the start of the year and the company reported net income of $6,147 million for the year. What amount did the company record as dividends in 2018?

E8-47. **Analyzing Convertible Preferred Stock**
Xerox Corp. reports the following stockholders' equity information in its 10-K report.

LO6, 7
Xerox Corporation
(XRX)

Shareholders' Equity (in millions, except par value)	December 31 2018	2017
Series A convertible preferred stock.	$ 214	$ 214
Common stock, $1 par value	232	255
Additional paid-in capital.	3,321	3,893
Treasury stock, at cost	(55)	0
Retained earnings	5,072	4,856
Accumulated other comprehensive loss.	(3,565)	(3,748)
Xerox shareholders' equity.	$5,005	$5,256

Preferred Stock As of December 31, 2018, we had one class of preferred stock outstanding. We have issued 180,000 shares of Series B Convertible Perpetual Preferred Stock that have an aggregate liquidation value of $180 and a carrying value of $214. The Series B Convertible Preferred Stock pays quarterly cash dividends at a rate of 8% per year. Each share of Preferred Stock is convertible at any time, at the option of the holder, into 37.4532 shares of common stock for a total of 6,742 thousand shares (reflecting an initial conversion price of approximately $26.70 per share of common stock), subject to customary anti-dilution adjustments.

Required
a. At December 31, 2018, Xerox reports $214 million of 8% Series B Convertible Preferred stock. What is the dollar amount of dividends that Xerox must pay on this stock (assume a par value of $1,000 per share)?
b. Describe the effects that will occur to Xerox's balance sheet and its income statement when the Convertible Preferred stock is converted.
c. What is the benefit, if any, of issuing equity securities with a conversion feature? How are these securities treated in the computation of earnings per share (EPS)?

LO1 E8-48. Analyzing and Computing Issue Price, Treasury Stock Cost, and Shares Outstanding

Merck & Co. Inc. (MRK)

Following is the stockholders' equity section of the 2018 Merck & Co. Inc. balance sheet.

Stockholders' Equity ($ millions)	2018
Common stock, $0.50 par value; Authorized—6,500,000,000 shares; Issued—3,577,103,522 shares.................................	$ 1,788
Other paid-in capital	38,808
Retained earnings	42,579
Accumulated other comprehensive loss.....................	(5,545)
Stockholders' equity before deduction for treasury stock..........	77,630
Less treasury stock, at cost: 984,543,979 shares	50,929
Total Merck & Co. Inc. stockholders' equity	$26,701

a. Show the computation of the $1,788 million in the common stock account.
b. At what average price were the Merck common shares issued?
c. At what average cost was the Merck treasury stock purchased?
d. How many common shares are outstanding as of December 31, 2018?
e. Use an online investment site to determine Merck's closing stock price on December 31, 2018. Use that amount to calculate the company's market cap for that day.

Problems

LO1, 2 P8-49. Identifying and Analyzing Financial Statement Effects of Stock Transactions

The stockholders' equity section of XPress Media Company for the current year follows.

8% preferred stock, $25 par value, 50,000 shares authorized; 8,400 shares issued and outstanding.........................	$210,000
Common stock, $10 par value, 200,000 shares authorized; 50,000 shares issued and outstanding.........................	500,000
Paid-in capital in excess of par value—preferred stock	85,000
Paid-in capital in excess of par value—common stock	300,000
Retained earnings	370,000

During the year, the following transactions occurred.

Jan. 10	Issued 28,000 shares of common stock for $18 cash per share.
Jan. 23	Repurchased 8,000 shares of common stock at $20 cash per share.
Mar. 14	Sold one-half of the treasury shares acquired January 23 for $22 cash per share.
July 15	Issued 2,600 shares of preferred stock for $128,000 cash.
Nov. 15	Sold 1,000 of the treasury shares acquired January 23 for $26 cash per share.

Required

a. Use the financial statement effects template to indicate the effects from each of these transactions.
b. Prepare the stockholders' equity section of the balance sheet assuming the company reports net income of $121,000 for the current year.

LO2, 5, 6 P8-50. Analyzing Stockholders' Equity Including AOCI and Convertible Securities

Under Armour Inc. (UA)

Under Armour reported the following stockholders' equity section of the balance sheet for the fiscal year ended December 31, 2018.

Stockholders' Equity ($ 000s)	2018	2017
Class A Common Stock, $0.0003 1/3 par value; 400,000,000 shares authorized as of December 31, 2018 and 2017; 187,710,319 shares issued and outstanding as of December 31, 2018 and 185,257,423 shares issued and outstanding as of December 31, 2017..................	$ 62	$ 61
Class B Convertible Common Stock, $0.0003 1/3 par value; 34,450,000 shares authorized, issued and outstanding as of December 31, 2018 and 2017	11	11
Class C Common Stock, $0.0003 1/3 par value; 400,000,000 shares authorized as of December 31, 2018 and 2017; 226,421,963 shares issued and outstanding as of December 31, 2018, and 222,375,079 shares issued and outstanding as of December 31, 2017..................	75	74
Additional paid-in capital..	916,628	872,266
Retained earnings	1,139,082	1,184,441
Accumulated other comprehensive loss	(38,987)	(38,211)
Total stockholders' equity...	$2,016,871	$2,018,642

Under Armour reports additional information related to the three classes of stock in its 10-K.

> Under Armour's Class A Common Stock and Class C Common Stock are traded on the New York Stock Exchange under the symbols "UAA" and "UA", respectively. As of January 31, 2019, there were 1,628 record holders of our Class A Common Stock, 6 record holders of Class B Convertible Common Stock which are beneficially owned by our Chief Executive Officer and Chairman of the Board Kevin A. Plank, and 1,216 record holders of our Class C Common Stock. Our Class A common stock has one vote per share, our Class B common stock has 10 votes per share and our Class C common stock has no voting rights (except in limited circumstances).

Required

a. Complete the following table to determine the % ownership and voting power for each class of stock.

	Class A	Class B	Class C	Total
Shares authorized				
Shares issued and outstanding				
Proportion of ownership of Under Armour ...				100%
Shareholders of record..................				NA
Votes per share				NA
Total votes				
Proportion of voting rights................				100%

b. Class B Convertible Common Stock can be converted on a 1-for-1 basis into Class A stock. Explain the balance sheet effect if all outstanding shares were converted. What repercussions would this have for the CEO, Kevin Plank?

c. In June 2015, the company created nonvoting Class C common stock and issued Class C shares primarily for employee share-based compensation plans. Explain the incentives such compensation plans create. Why would Under Armour create another class of stock for this purpose?

d. During the year, foreign currency translation losses increased by $23,576 and unrealized losses on cash flow hedges (derivatives) decreased by $22,800. Use this information to reconcile the accumulated other comprehensive loss account. What can you conclude about changes in $US against currencies of countries where Under Armour has subsidiaries?

LO3 **P8-51. Identifying and Analyzing Financial Statement Effects of Stock-Based Compensation**

The stockholders' equity of Aspen Corporation at December 31, 2019, follows.

7% Preferred stock, $100 par value, 20,000 shares authorized; 4,000 shares issued and outstanding	$ 400,000
Common stock, $15 par value, 300,000 shares authorized; 30,000 shares issued and outstanding	450,000
Paid-in capital in excess of par value—preferred stock	36,000
Paid-in capital in excess of par value—common stock	360,000
Retained earnings	325,000
Total stockholders' equity	$1,571,000

The following transactions, among others, occurred during the following year.
- Employees exercised 12,000 stock options that were granted in 2015 and had a three-year vesting period. These options had an estimated fair value of $2 at the grant date, and an exercise price of $16. There were no other vested or unvested options after this exercise.
- Awarded 1,000 shares of stock to new executives, when the stock price was $36.
- Sold 10,000 shares to employees under the company-wide stock purchase plan. Under the plan, employees purchased the shares at a 10% discount when the stock price was $33 per share.
- Granted 40,000 new stock options, with a strike price of $34 and an estimated fair value of $6. The options vest over three years.

Required

Prepare the December 31, 2019, statement of stockholders' equity assuming that the company reports 2019 pretax income of $483,000 before the effects of stock-based compensation. Assume the company has a 35% tax rate.

LO1, 2 **P8-52. Identifying and Analyzing Financial Statement Effects of Stock Transactions**

The stockholders' equity of Gaulin Company at the start of the current year follows.

Common stock, $5 par value, 500,000 shares authorized; 350,000 shares issued and outstanding	$1,750,000
Paid-in capital in excess of par value	800,000
Retained earnings	634,000

During the current year, the following transactions occurred.

Jan.	5	Issued 10,000 shares of common stock for $13 cash per share.
Jan.	18	Repurchased 4,000 shares of common stock at $16 cash per share.
Mar.	12	Sold one-fourth of the treasury shares acquired January 18 for $19 cash per share.
July	17	Sold 500 shares of treasury stock for $14 cash per share.
Oct.	1	Issued 5,000 shares of 8%, $25 par value preferred stock for $36 cash per share. This is the first issuance of preferred shares from the 50,000 authorized preferred shares.

Required
a. Use the financial statement effects template to indicate the effects of each transaction.
b. Prepare the current year, stockholders' equity section of the balance sheet assuming that the company reports net income of $76,900 for the year.

LO1, 2, 4 **P8-53. Identifying and Analyzing Financial Statement Effects of Stock Transactions**

Following is the stockholders' equity of Sharp Corporation at the start of the current year.

8% preferred stock, $50 par value, 10,000 shares authorized; 8,000 shares issued and outstanding	$ 400,000
Common stock, $20 par value, 50,000 shares authorized; 25,000 shares issued and outstanding	500,000
Paid-in capital in excess of par value—preferred stock	70,000
Paid-in capital in excess of par value—common stock	385,000
Retained earnings	238,000
Total stockholders' equity	$1,593,000

The following transactions, among others, occurred during the current year.

Jan. 15 Issued 1,000 shares of preferred stock for $60 cash per share.
Jan. 20 Issued 4,000 shares of common stock at $34 cash per share.
May 18 Announced a 2-for-1 common stock split, reducing the par value of the common stock to $10 per share. The number of shares authorized was increased to 100,000 shares.
June 1 Issued 2,000 shares of common stock for $56,000 cash.
Sep. 1 Repurchased 2,500 shares of common stock at $16 cash per share.
Oct. 12 Sold 900 treasury shares at $19 cash per share.
Dec. 22 Issued 500 shares of preferred stock for $57 cash per share.

Required
Use the financial statement effects template to indicate the effects of each transaction.

P8-54. Analyzing and Interpreting Equity Accounts and Comprehensive Income   **LO1, 2, 3, 4, 5**

Following is the statement of shareholders' equity from the 2019 10-K for **Procter & Gamble Company**.

The Procter & Gamble Company (PG)

Consolidated Statement of Shareholders' Equity

Dollars in millions; Shares in thousands	Common Shares Outstanding	Common Stock	Preferred Stock	Additional Paid-in Capital	Reserve for ESOP Debt Retirement	Accumulated Other Comprehensive Income (Loss)	Treasury Stock	Retained Earnings	Non-controlling Interest	Total
Balance, June 30, 2018	2,498,093	$4,009	$967	$63,846	$(1,204)	$(14,749)	$(99,217)	$98,641	$590	$52,883
Impact of adoption of new accounting standards						(326)		(200)	(27)	(553)
Net earnings								3,897	69	3,966
Other comprehensive income (loss)						139			1	140
Dividends and dividend equivalents ($2.8975 per share)										
Common								(7,256)		(7,256)
Preferred, net of tax benefits								(263)		(263)
Treasury stock purchases	(53,714)						(5,003)			(5,003)
Employee stock plans	55,734			93			3,781			3,874
Preferred stock conversions	4,638		(39)	6			33			—
ESOP debt impacts					58			99		157
Noncontrolling interest, net				(118)					(248)	(366)
Balance, June 30, 2019	2,504,751	$4,009	$928	$63,827	$(1,146)	$(14,936)	$(100,406)	$94,918	$385	$47,579

Required

a. How many shares of common stock did Procter & Gamble issue when convertible Class A preferred stock was converted during fiscal year ended June 30, 2019? At what average price were the preferred shares converted? Did the company issue new (previously unissued) shares for the preferred share conversion?

b. How many shares did the company issue for employee stock plans during the year? At what average price were the common shares issued to employees? Did the company issue new shares for the employee stock plans awards?

c. The company reported basic EPS of $1.40 for the year. The company's stock price on June 28, 2019 (the closest day before the fiscal year-end) was $109.65. Calculate the dividend payout and dividend yield ratios.

d. How many shares of stock did PG repurchase during the year? At what average price per share? Why does PG repurchase its own stock?

e. Compute the company's market cap at June 28, 2019. What is the market-to-book ratio on that day?

LO1, 2, 3, 5
Alphabet Inc. (GOOG)

P8-55. Analyzing and Interpreting Equity Accounts and Accumulated Other Comprehensive Income
Following is the stockholders' equity section of **Alphabet Inc.** along with its components of AOCI and related footnote disclosures.

Alphabet Inc.
CONSOLIDATED STATEMENTS OF STOCKHOLDERS' EQUITY
(In millions, except share amounts which are reflected in thousands)

	Class A and Class B Common Stock, Class C Capital Stock and Additional Paid-In Capital		Accumulated Other Comprehensive Income (Loss)	Retained Earnings	Total Stockholders' Equity
	Shares	Amount			
Balance as of December 31, 2017	694,783	$40,247	$(992)	$113,247	$152,502
Cumulative effect of accounting change	0	0	(98)	(599)	(697)
Common and capital stock issued	8,975	148	0	0	148
Stock-based compensation expense	0	9,353	0	0	9,353
Tax withholding related to vesting of restricted stock units and other	0	(4,782)	0	0	(4,782)
Repurchases of capital stock	(8,202)	(576)	0	(8,499)	(9,075)
Sale of subsidiary shares	0	659	0	0	659
Net income	0	0	0	30,736	30,736
Other comprehensive loss	0	0	(1,216)	0	(1,216)
Balance as of December 31, 2018	695,556	$45,049	$(2,306)	$134,885	$177,628

The components of AOCI, net of tax, were as follows (in millions).

	Foreign Currency Translation Adjustments	Unrealized Gains (Losses) on Available-for-Sale Investments	Unrealized Gains (Losses) on Cash Flow Hedges	Total
Balance as of December 31, 2017	$(1,103)	$ 233	$(122)	$ (992)
Other comprehensive income (loss) before reclassifications	(781)	(10)	264	(527)
Amounts excluded from the assessment of hedge effectiveness recorded in AOCI	0	0	26	26
Amounts reclassified from AOCI	0	(911)	98	(813)
Other comprehensive income (loss)	(781)	(921)	388	(1,314)
Balance as of December 31, 2018	$(1,884)	$(688)	$ 266	$(2,306)

Class A and Class B Common Stock and Class C Capital Stock Our board of directors has authorized three classes of stock, Class A and Class B common stock, and Class C capital stock. The rights of the holders of each class of our common and capital stock are identical, except with respect to voting. Each share of Class A common stock is entitled to one vote per share. Each share of Class B common stock is entitled to 10 votes per share. Class C capital stock has no voting rights, except as required by applicable law. Shares of Class B common stock may be converted at any time at the option of the stockholder and automatically convert upon sale or transfer to Class A common stock.

Share Repurchases In October 2016, the board of directors of Alphabet authorized the company to repurchase up to $7.0 billion of its Class C capital stock, which was completed during 2018. In January 2018, the board of directors of Alphabet authorized the company to repurchase up to $8.6 billion of its Class C capital stock. The repurchases are being executed from time to time, subject to general business and market conditions and other investment opportunities. The repurchase program does not have an expiration date.

Required

a. What amount of dividends did Alphabet pay in 2018 for all three classes of common stock combined?
b. Alphabet uses stock-based compensation for broad classes of employees. What amount did the company record for this expense in 2018? What was the total cash effect of this expense in 2018?
c. During 2018, Alphabet issued common stock, primarily for share-based compensation awards. How many shares did the company issue? At what average price were these shares issued?
d. During 2018, the company repurchased Class C capital stock for cash. How many shares did the company repurchase and retire? What was the total amount of cash used for the transaction? What was the average price paid for the shares? At what average price were these shares originally issued? (*Hint:* See Additional paid-in capital account on the statement of shareholders' equity.)
e. What items affect Alphabet's accumulated other comprehensive income? Consider the foreign currency translation adjustment of $781 million. Explain how this loss arose during 2018.

P8-56. Interpreting Disclosure on Convertible Debentures   **LO6, 7**
On March 2, 2017, **Snapchat** undertook its initial public offering (IPO). Following is Snapchat's balance sheet for its first two fiscal years as a public company.

Snapchat (SNAP)

Consolidated Balance Sheets

December 31 (in thousands, except par value)	2017	2018
Assets		
Current assets		
Cash and cash equivalents	$ 334,063	$ 387,149
Marketable securities	1,708,976	891,914
Accounts receivable, net of allowance	279,473	354,965
Prepaid expenses and other current assets	44,282	41,900
Total current assets	2,366,794	1,675,928
Property and equipment, net	166,762	212,560
Intangible assets, net	166,473	126,054
Goodwill	639,882	632,370
Other assets	81,655	67,194
Total assets	$3,421,566	$2,714,106
Liabilities and Stockholders' Equity		
Current liabilities		
Accounts payable	$ 71,194	$ 30,876
Accrued expenses and other current liabilities	275,062	261,815
Total current liabilities	346,256	292,691
Other liabilities	82,983	110,416
Total liabilities	429,239	403,107
Commitments and contingencies		
Stockholders' equity		
Class A nonvoting common stock, $0,00001 par value. 3,000,000 shares authorized, 883,022 shares issued and outstanding at December 31, 2017, and 3,000,000 shares authorized, 999,304 shares issued and outstanding at December 31, 2018.	9	10
Class B voting common stock, $0.0000 par value. 700,000 shares authorized, 122,564 shares issued and outstanding at December 31, 2017, and 700,000 shares authorized, 93,845 shares issued and outstanding at December 31, 2018.	1	1
Class C voting common stock, $0.0000 1 par value. 260,888 shares authorized, 216,616 shares issued and outstanding at December 31, 2017, and 260,888 shares authorized, 224,611 shares issued and outstanding at December 31, 2018.	2	2
Additional paid-in capital	7,634,825	8,220,417
Accumulated other comprehensive income	14,157	3,147
Accumulated deficit	(4,656,667)	(5,912,578)
Total stockholders' equity	2,992,327	2,310,999
Total liabilities and stockholders' equity	$3,421,566	$2,714,106

Snapchat reported the following in a Form 8-K dated August 9, 2019.

> **Purchase Agreement** On August 6, 2019, we entered into a purchase agreement with Goldman Sachs, Morgan Stanley, and J.P. Morgan relating to the sale by us of an aggregate of $1.265 billion principal amount of our 0.75% Convertible Senior Notes due 2026 in a private offering. The Notes are convertible into cash, shares of our Class A common stock, or a combination thereof, at our election, at an initial conversion rate of 43.8481 shares of Class A common stock per $1,000 principal amount of the Notes, which is equivalent to an initial conversion price of approximately $22.81 per share of Class A common stock. Holders of the Notes may convert all or a portion of their Notes at their option prior to May 1, 2026, in multiples of $1,000 principal amount, only under the following circumstances:
> - during any calendar quarter commencing after December 31, 2019, if the last reported sale price of Class A common stock for at least 20 trading days (whether or not consecutive) during the period of 30 consecutive trading days . . . is greater than or equal to 130% of the applicable conversion price of the Notes on each such trading day;

Required:

a. Why did Snapchat wait two years to issue debt? Why did the company not do so during the time of the IPO?
b. What will be the balance sheet effect of the sale of the convertible senior notes? How will this affect the company's leverage?
c. Confirm the initial conversion price of $22.81 per share. At what price did SNAP stock close on August 9, 2019 (use on online investment site to determine the closing price that day)? Compare the two prices and explain why the three investment banks might enter into the purchase agreement described above.
d. After December 31, 2019, what minimum stock price is required to permit note holders to convert to Class A common stock?
e. What will Snapchat record as interest expense on the convertible senior notes in fiscal 2019?
f. How will the convertible senior notes impact the computation of basic and diluted earnings per share (EPS)?
g. Assume that on January 2020, SNAP has traded at around $30 for a month and that bondholders convert $400 million notes. Explain how the conversion will affect debt and equity. Which accounts and by how much?

LO6 **P8-57. Interpreting Disclosure on Convertible Preferred Securities**
Gladiator Investment Corporation (GAIN)

Gladiator Investment Corporation includes the following in its 10-K for the fiscal year ended March 31, 2019.

Mandatorily Redeemable Senior Securities ($ thousands)	
Class and Year	Amount Outstanding
7.125% Series A Cumulative Term Preferred Stock	
March 31, 2019	—
March 31, 2018	—
6.75% Series B Cumulative Term Preferred Stock	
March 31, 2019	—
March 31, 2018	41,400
6.50% Series C Cumulative Term Preferred Stock due 2022	
March 31, 2019	—
March 31, 2018	40,250
6.25% Series D Cumulative Term Preferred Stock due 2023	
March 31, 2019	57,500
March 31, 2018	57,500
6.375% Series E Cumulative Term Preferred Stock due 2025	
March 31, 2019	74,750
March 31, 2018	—

Required

a. Explain what is meant by "mandatorily redeemable preferred stock."
b. Assume that the company issued new stock on the first day of the fiscal year. What total amount of preferred stock dividends must Gladiator Investment pay during the year ended March 31, 2018?
c. What total amount of preferred stock dividends must Gladiator Investment pay during the year ended March 31, 2019?
d. During the fiscal year ended March 31, 2018, the company issued Series E preferred stock and used the proceeds to redeem all of the Series B and Series C stock at face value. Use the financial statement effects template to record these transactions.

P8-58. Identifying and Analyzing Financial Statement Effects of Share-Based Compensation

Weaver Industries implements a new share-based compensation plan in 2017. Under the plan, the company's CEO and CFO each will receive nonqualified stock options to purchase 100,000, no par shares. The options vest ratably (1/3 of the options each year) over three years, expire in 10 years, and have an exercise (strike) price of $27 per share. Weaver uses the Black-Scholes model to estimate a fair value per option of $18.

Required

a. Use the financial statement effects template to record the compensation expense related to these options for each year 2017 through 2019.
b. In 2020, the company's stock price is $24. If you were the Weaver Industries CEO, would you exercise your options? Explain.
c. In 2022, the company's stock price is $46 and the CEO exercises all of her options. Use the financial statement effects template to record the exercise.

P8-59. Interpreting Disclosure on Employee Stock Options

Intel Corporation reported the following in its 2018 10-K report.

> **Share-Based Compensation** Share-based compensation recognized in 2018 was $1.5 billion ($1.4 billion in 2017 and $1.4 billion in 2016). During 2018, the tax benefit that we realized for the tax deduction from share-based awards totaled $399 million ($520 million in 2017 and $616 million in 2016). We grant RSUs with a service condition, as well as RSUs with both a market condition and a service condition, which we call outperformance stock units (OSUs). We estimate the fair value of Restricted Stock Units (RSUs) with a service condition using the value of our common stock on the date of grant, reduced by the present value of dividends expected to be paid on our shares of common stock prior to vesting. We estimate the fair value of OSUs using a Monte Carlo simulation model on the date of grant. We base expected volatility for OSUs on historical volatility. We based the weighted average estimated value of RSU and OSU grants on the weighted average assumptions for each period as follows.
>
> | RSUs and OSUs | Dec 29, 2018 | Dec 30, 2017 | Dec 31, 2016 |
> | --- | --- | --- | --- |
> | Estimated values | $48.95 | $35.30 | $29.76 |
> | Risk-free interest rate | 2.4% | 1.4% | 0.9% |
> | Dividend yield | 2.4% | 2.9% | 3.3% |
> | Volatility | 22% | 23% | 23% |
>
> Additional information with respect to RSU activity is as follows.
>
> **Restricted Stock Unit Awards** RSU activity in 2018 was as follows.
>
> | | Number of RSUs (in millions) | Weighted Average Grant-Date Fair Value |
> | --- | --- | --- |
> | December 30, 2017 | 100.4 | $32.36 |
> | Granted | 36.4 | 48.95 |
> | Vested | (39.5) | 31.64 |
> | Forfeited | (7.4) | 36.23 |
> | December 29, 2018 | 89.9 | $39.07 |

Required
a. What is the main difference between Intel's RSUs and OSUs?
b. What amount did Intel record in 2018 for share-based compensation expense?
c. What is the total fair value of RSUs granted in 2018? Why is this amount not equal to the 2018 share-based compensation expense?
d. Imagine that during 2018, all employees immediately sold their shares when their RSUs vested. What profit would the employees have made (before tax)? *Hint:* Use the RSU average grant-date fair value to approximate Intel's average stock price in 2018.
e. Provide two reasons why an employee would forfeit their RSUs.

P8-60. Analyzing Stockholders' Equity and EPS
The following dashboard depicts equity related information for firms in four industries: Pharmaceuticals, Financial services, Retail, and Heavy equipment manufacturers. Access the dashboard at the myBusinessCourse website to answer the requirements.

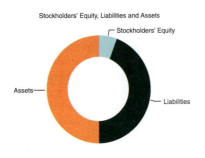
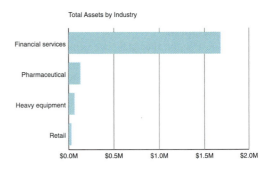
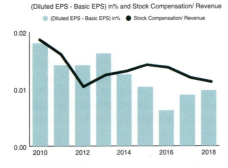
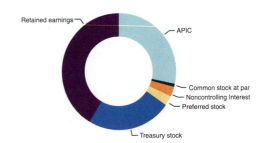

Required
a. Which industry has the smallest proportion of assets financed by owners? Why might that be?
b. Which industry has the largest proportion of treasury stock in their capital structure?
c. Across all four industries, what pattern do we observe in diluted versus basic EPS over time? Is this pattern different for any of the four industries?

P8-61. Interpreting Disclosure on Share-Based Compensation

lululemon athletica reported the following information for the fiscal year ended February 3, 2019.

A summary of the balances of the Company's stock-based compensation plans as of February 3, 2019, January 28, 2018, and January during the fiscal years then ended is presented below:

(In thousands, except per share amounts)	Stock Options Number	Stock Options Weighted-Average Exercise Price	Performance-Based Restricted Stock Units Number	Performance-Based Restricted Stock Units Weighted-Average Grant Date Fair Value	Restricted Shares Number	Restricted Shares Weighted-Average Grant Date Fair Value	Restricted Stock Units Number	Restricted Stock Units Weighted-Average Grant Date Fair Value
Balance at January 31, 2016	867	$49.54	395	$58.58	31	$57.67	333	$55.91
Granted	428	68.63	164	68.64	17	69.94	216	68.15
Exercised/vested	191	36.76	7	64.36	34	58.39	91	56.87
Forfeited/expired	186	58.87	162	62.54	—	—	98	55.95
Balance at January 29, 2017	918	$59.20	390	$61.05	14	$70.54	360	$62.99
Granted	619	52.34	192	52.38	24	52.38	336	52.83
Exercised/vested	109	51.62	—	—	14	70.29	135	60.64
Forfeited/expired	311	58.09	253	55.30	3	51.72	134	57.28
Balance at January 28, 2018	1,117	$56.44	329	$60.42	21	$52.45	427	$57.54
Granted	388	96.96	123	102.49	6	124.19	257	88.75
Exercised/vested	316	56.29	39	63.04	21	52.45	174	58.94
Forfeited/expired	319	59.76	133	61.71	—	—	70	66.90
Balance at February 3, 2019	870	$73.34	280	$78.01	6	$124.19	440	$73.73

Stock-based compensation expense charged to income for the plans was $29.6 million, $17.6 million, and $16.8 million for the years ended February 3, 2019, January 28, 2018, and January 29, 2017, respectively.

Required

a. How do stock options and restricted shares differ? In what respects are they the same?
b. Why do companies impose vesting periods on restricted stock grants?
c. Consider the stock option activity. Compare the weighted average exercise price of the granted stock options and exercised options each year. What explains the difference in the two amounts each year?
d. Use the financial statement effects template to record the restricted shares granted during 2018. The common stock has a $0.005 par value per share.
e. Use the financial statement effects template to record the total 2018 compensation expense related to Lululemon's share-based compensation activity. Include the tax effects of the compensation expense. Assume a tax rate of 21%.

IFRS Applications

I8-62. Analyzing and Interpreting Equity Accounts and Comprehensive Income

Henkel AG & Co. is an international, fast-moving consumer goods (FMCG) company headquartered in Düsseldorf, Germany. Following is its shareholders' equity statement, prepared using IFRS, from its 2018 annual report.

In millions euro	Issued Capital					Other Components of Equity					
	Ordinary Shares	Preferred Shares	Capital Reserve	Treasury Shares	Retained Earnings	Currency Translation	Hedge Reserve	Reserve for Equity & Debt Instruments	Shareholders of Henkel AG & Co. KGaA	Non-Controlling Interests	Total
At January 1, 2018 (adjusted)	€260	€178	€652	€(91)	€16,042	€(1,332)	€(198)	€3	€15,514	€ 74	€15,588
Net income	—	—	—	—	2,311	—	—	—	2,311	19	2,330
Other comprehensive income	—	—	—	—	(134)	146	(1)	—	11	—	11
Total comprehensive income for the period	—	—	—	—	2,177	146	(1)	—	2,322	19	2,341
Dividends	—	—	—	—	(772)	—	—	—	(772)	(16)	(788)
Sale of treasury shares	—	—	—	—	—	—	—	—	—	—	—
Changes in ownership interest with no change in control	—	—	—	—	—	—	—	—	—	—	—
Other changes in equity	—	—	—	—	(48)	—	—	—	(48)	—	(48)
At December 31, 2018	€260	€178	€652	€(91)	€17,399	€(1,186)	€(199)	€3	€17,016	€ 77	€17,093

Required

a. Did Henkel issue any additional ordinary or preferred shares during 2018?
b. How much did Henkel pay in dividends during 2018? To whom were these dividends paid?
c. Did the company repurchase any stock during 2018?
d. Did Henkel sell any treasury shares?
e. Consider the currency translation account. Explain how the change of €146 arose during the year.
f. Henkel reports noncontrolling interest of €77. Why did this account increase during the year?
g. Compute return on equity for 2018. (*Hint:* Use the net income attributable to controlling interest [shareholders of Henkel] and equity attributable to controlling interest.)

LO1, 2, 3, 4, 5
Nutrien Ltd. (NTR)

I8-63. Analyzing Stockholders' Equity Accounts and Transactions

Nutrien Ltd.—the world's largest potash producer—is a Canadian corporation based in Saskatoon, Saskatchewan. The following is information taken from its financial statements reported in $US but prepared in accordance with IFRS.

Accumulated Other Comprehensive (Loss) Income ("AOCI")									
(In millions of dollars)	Share Capital	Contributed Surplus	Net Fair Value Loss on Investments	Net Actuarial Gain on Defined Benefit Plans	Loss on Currency Translation of Foreign Operations	Other	Total Accumulated Other Comprehensive Income	Retained Earnings	Total Equity
Balance—December 31, 2017	$ 1,806	$230	$73	$—	$(2)	$(46)	$25	$6,242	$ 8,303
Merger impact (Notes 3 and 11)	15,898	7	—	—	—	—	—	(1)	15,904
Net earnings	—	—	—	—	—	—	—	3,573	3,573
Other comprehensive (loss) income	—	—	(99)	54	(249)	(8)	(302)	—	(302)
Share repurchased (Note 24)	(998)	(23)	—	—	—	—	—	(831)	(1,852)
Dividends declared	—	—	—	—	—	—	—	(1,273)	(1,273)
Effect of share-based compensation including issuance of common shares	34	17	—	—	—	—	—	—	51
Transfer of net actuarial gain on defined benefit plans	—	—	—	(54)	—	—	(54)	54	—
Transfer of net loss on sale of investment	—	—	19	—	—	—	19	(19)	—
Transfer of net loss on cash flow hedges	—	—	—	—	—	21	21	—	21
Balance—December 31, 2018	$16,740	$231	$(7)	$—	$(251)	$(33)	$(291)	$7,745	$24,425

continued

continued from previous page

Authorized The company is authorized to issue an unlimited number of common shares without par value and an unlimited number of preferred shares. The common shares are not redeemable or convertible. The preferred shares may be issued in one or more series with rights and conditions to be determined by the Board of Directors. No first preferred shares have been issued.

Issued	Number of Common Shares
Balance, December 31, 2017	644,197,473
Issued under option plans	670,201
Repurchased	(36,332,197)
Balance, December 31, 2018	608,535,477

a. How many shares are authorized at December 31, 2018?
b. How many shares are issued at December 31, 2018? At what average price were these shares issued as of December 31, 2018?
c. How many shares are issued under option plans at December 31, 2018? At what average price were these shares issued?
d. Does the company have any treasury stock? How do we know?
e. On December 14, 2018, the company's Board of Directors declared a quarterly dividend of $0.43 per share, payable to all shareholders of record on March 29, 2019. Assuming that the number of shares outstanding on March 29, 2019, is the same as on December 31, 2018, what dividends will the company pay?
f. Comprehensive income includes net income plus other comprehensive income. What was the company's comprehensive income for 2018? Why does it differ from net income for 2018?

Ongoing Project

(This ongoing project began in Module 1 and continues through most of the book; even if previous segments were not completed, the requirements are still applicable to any business analysis.) Company analysis should consider how the companies are financed and what transactions were executed with stockholders during the recent year.

1. *Contributed Capital.* Use the balance sheet and the statement of stockholders' equity to determine how the company has structured its equity.

   - What proportion of assets are financed with equity?
   - What classes of equity does the company have? What transactions occurred during the year?
   - Does the company have treasury stock? Read the MD&A and the footnotes to determine the main reason for holding treasury stock. Assess the treasury stock transactions during the year. How much was spent and/or received? What did the company do with the proceeds? Compare the average price paid for treasury shares to the current stock price.
   - Does the company use share-based compensation? What types of plans are used? What was the magnitude of the compensation? What is the magnitude of the outstanding (unvested) options and/or shares? Compare the level of treasury shares to outstanding (unvested) options and/or shares.
   - Compute the market capitalization of the firms and compare to the book value of equity. Find an online source for the average market-to-book ratio for the industry and see where the firms fit. Follow up on anything unusual.

2. *Earned Capital.* Recall that the least costly form of financing is internal—that is, plowing earned profits (and cash) into new investments is a low-cost means to grow the company and return even more to stockholders.

   - How profitable were the companies? Compare return on equity for the three-year period and determine causes for major differences over time and between companies.
   - Review accumulated other comprehensive income and determine the main components of that account. How did AOCI change during the year?

- Did the companies pay dividends? Compute the dividend payout and the dividend yield for all three years and compare them.
- Did the company have any stock splits?

3. *Convertible Securities.* Read the debt footnote to determine if the company has any convertible securities.
   - What types of convertible securities are outstanding?
   - Are these securities substantive? To assess this, consider their common size and their effect on diluted earnings per share.
   - Did the company have any convertible transactions during the year? If yes, determine the effect on the balance sheet and income statement.

Solutions to Review Problems

Review 8-1—Solution

a. **False.** Stockholders' equity is the book value (determined in accordance with GAAP) of the company. It represents the claim that shareholders have against the net assets (assets less liabilities) of the company.

b. **True.** The Board of Directors is the elected representatives of the shareholders who hire the company's CEO and oversee its operations.

c. **True.** Issued shares represents the cumulative number of shares that have been sold (issued) to date.

d. **True.** Outstanding shares is equal to the cumulative number of shares that have been issued less the cumulative number of shares that have been subsequently repurchased by the company.

e. **False.** The amount of annual dividends per share for preferred stock is usually fixed. Common stock receives any remaining dividends after preferred shareholders have been paid and there is no limit to the amount of dividends that common shareholders can receive.

f. **True.** Treasury stock represents the cumulative dollar amount of all share repurchases and subsequent resales on the open market.

Review 8-2—Solution

a. The common stock account did not change during this period, either in the number of shares issued (7,040 million) or in dollars ($1,760 million). Thus, we conclude that the company issued no new stock during the year.

b. (in millions)

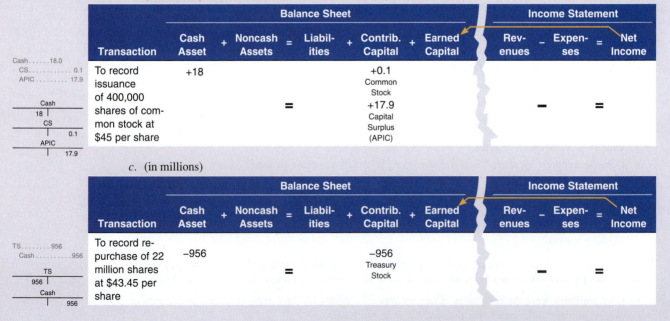

c. (in millions)

d. The company will decrease the treasury stock account by $473 million, the original cost of the shares (30 million shares × $15.77 per share). The difference between the market value of the treasury shares ($964 million) and the cost ($473 million) is added to the Capital Surplus account, increasing it by $491 million.

Review 8-3—Solution

a. Coca-Cola's income before tax was reduced by $225 million for the stock-based compensation expense. This was included in "other" line items on the income statement rather than disclosed separately.

b. Stock-based compensation does not affect cash flow; it is a noncash expense. There is a real cash outflow associated with the compensation—the company buys treasury shares to use for compensation instead of issuing new stock. The cost of the treasury shares is a real cash cost.

c. The fair value of the total stock option grant is $84.64 million computed as $10.58 fair value per share × 8 million shares. With a vesting period of four years, the amount of stock option compensation expense on the 2018 income statement is $21.16 million.

d. The fair value of the total performance share units grant is $83.9 million computed as $38.45 fair value per share × 2,183 thousand shares. With a restriction period of two years, the amount of stock option compensation expense on the 2018 income statement is $41.95 million.

e. There is a chance that the options will not be exercised. If the stock price falls below the option strike price of $36.74 by the time the options expire, the option will have no value to the employee. But even if the stock price falls, the performance share units will have value, albeit less than at the grant date. The other issue is that the restriction period for the performance share units is only two years, whereas the vesting period for the options is four years.

Review 8-4—Solution

a. (in millions)

b. If Wells Fargo had paid $100 million more in common stock dividends in 2018, net income would not have been affected. Dividends are not included when we determine net income; they are a return of the net income to shareholders.

c.

	2018	2017
Dividends declared per common share ($ per share)	$1.64	$1.54
Earnings per common share ($ per share)	$4.31	$4.14
Dividend payout ratio	38.1%	37.2%

d. The WFC closing stock price on December 31, 2018, was $46.08. The dividend yield ratio for 2018 is 3.56% ($1.64/$46.08).

Review 8-5—Solution

a. The unrealized loss increased during the year. On average, the U.S. dollar strengthened in 2018 vis-à-vis currencies of countries where Coca-Cola has subsidiaries. This means that the assets and liabilities of foreign subsidiaries, when translated to U.S. dollars, lost value. If the subsidiary is solvent (assets > liabilities), then equity declines and that is reflected in negative other comprehensive income.

b. If the securities had been sold, the unrealized loss of $34 million would be realized in the income statement as a reduction in "other income" before tax.

c. Yes, the unrealized "loss" of $7 million arises because the fair value of the derivative investments has declined during the year.

Review 8-6—Solution

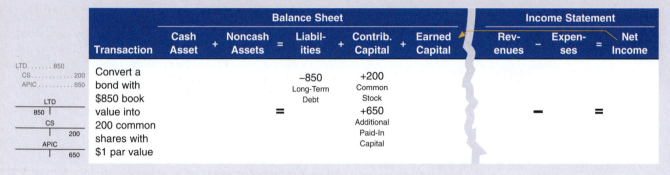

Review 8-7—Solution

a. $\text{Basic EPS} = \dfrac{\$1{,}337{,}536{,}000}{26{,}970{,}000} = \$49.59$

b. $\text{Diluted EPS} = \dfrac{\$1{,}337{,}536{,}000}{(26{,}970{,}000 + 454{,}000)} = \$48.77$

c. Anti-dilutive means that including the stock-option effects would increase EPS (as opposed to diluting the EPS) because the options' exercise price is greater than the stock's current market price. These underwater (or out-of-the-money) options are anti-dilutive and are, therefore, excluded from the diluted EPS computation.

Module 9
Intercorporate Investments

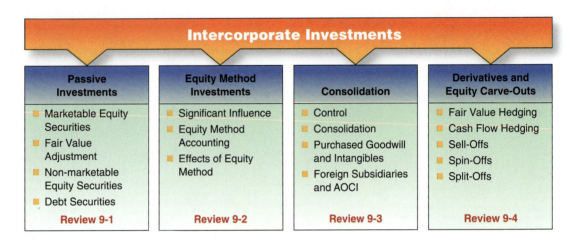

PREVIEW — GOOG

We examine topics related to investments, including the following.

- Investments of excess cash in marketable equity and debt securities.
- Strategic investments in equity securities in which the investor company has significant influence.
- Investments in equity securities of privately held companies prior to an initial public offering.
- Consolidation of subsidiaries that the investor company (the parent) controls.
- Recognition of intangibles, including goodwill.
- Hedging of risks using derivatives (Appendix A).
- Unlocking business value using equity carve outs (Appendix B).
- **Alphabet Inc.** is the focus company and the dashboard below conveys key financial information.

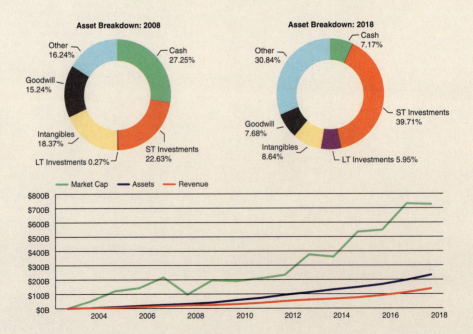

Road Map

LO	Learning Objective | Topics	Page	eLecture	Guided Example	Assignments
9–1	**Examine and interpret marketable securities reporting.** Passive Investments :: Marketable Equity Securities :: Fair Value Adjustment :: Non-Marketable Equity Securities :: Debt Securities	9-3	e9–1	Review 9-1	1, 2, 3, 13, 14, 19, 27, 28, 29, 30, 31, 34, 47, 52
9–2	**Analyze and interpret equity method investments.** Significant Influence :: Equity Method Accounting :: Effects of Equity Method	9-12	e9–2	Review 9-2	4, 5, 17, 18, 20, 32, 34, 35, 36, 37, 48, 51, 52
9–3	**Explain consolidation and interpret consolidated reports.** Control :: Consolidation for Investments with Control :: Purchased Goodwill and Intangibles :: Foreign Subsidiaries and AOCI :: Limitations of Consolidated Reporting	9-17	e9–3	Review 9-3	6, 7, 10, 11, 21, 22, 23, 30, 33, 38, 39, 41, 42, 43, 44, 49, 50, 52
9–4	**Describe and interpret derivative disclosures (Appendix 9A).** Fair Value Hedging :: Cash Flow Hedging :: Analysis of Derivatives	9-29	e9–4	Review 9-4	8, 9, 15, 16, 44, 45, 46
9–5	**Explain equity carve-outs and their financial statement impact (Appendix 9B).** Sell-offs :: Split-offs :: Spin-offs :: Analysis of Equity Carve-outs	9-32			12, 24, 25, 26, 40, 53

Intercorporate Investments

LO1 Examine and interpret marketable securities reporting.

It is common for one company to purchase the voting stock of another. These purchases, called *intercorporate equity investments*, typically have one or more of the following strategic aims.

- **Short-term investment of excess cash.** Companies might invest excess cash during slow times of the year (after receivables are collected and before seasonal production begins), or to maintain liquidity in order to counter strategic moves by competitors, or to quickly respond to acquisition opportunities.

- **Strategic alliances.** Companies use intercorporate investments to gain access to needed resources or expertise such as research and development activities, an established supply chain or distribution market, or production and marketing expertise.

- **Targeted projects.** Companies might invest in a partnership or joint venture (with equity ownership) to accomplish specific short- to medium-term outcomes such as construction projects or research endeavors. Partnerships and joint ventures can increase the return to the venture partners' investments and reduce risks associated with going it alone.

- **Market penetration or expansion.** Companies might acquire control of other companies to integrate vertically (by buying a supplier or a customer) or horizontally (by buying a competitor). These investments can help the company expand in existing product or geographic markets or penetrate new markets.

The level of ownership interest the investor (the purchaser) acquires directly affects the level of influence or control the investor has over the investee company (the company whose securities are purchased), as shown in Exhibit 9.1.

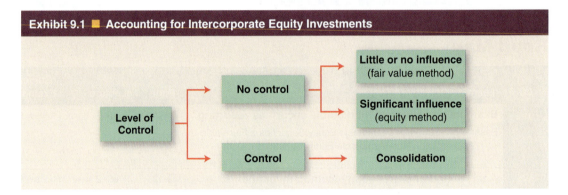

Exhibit 9.1 ■ Accounting for Intercorporate Equity Investments

There are three levels of influence or control.

- **Little or no influence (passive investments).** The investor has a relatively small investment and cannot exert influence over the investee. The investor's goal is to realize dividend income and capital gains. Generally, the investor is deemed to have little to no influence if it owns less than 20% of the investee's outstanding voting stock.

- **Significant influence.** The investor can exert "significant influence" over the investee by virtue of the percentage of the outstanding voting stock it owns or owing to legal agreements between the investor and investee, such as a license to use technology. Absent evidence to the contrary, significant influence is presumed when the investor owns between 20% and 50% of the outstanding voting shares.

- **Control.** When a company has control over an investee, it has the ability to elect a majority of the board of directors and, as a result, the ability to affect the investee's strategic direction and the hiring of executive management. Control is generally presumed if the investor company owns more than 50% of the outstanding voting stock of the investee company but can sometimes occur at less than 50% stock ownership by virtue of legal agreements, technology licensing, or other contractual means. The determining factor is the ability to control strategic decisions.

The level of influence/control determines the specific accounting method applied and its financial statement implications as outlined in Exhibit 9.2.

Exhibit 9.2 ■ Investment Type, Accounting Treatment, and Financial Statement Effects

	Accounting	Balance Sheet Effects	Income Statement Effects	Cash Flow Effects
Little or no influence (passive investment)	Fair value method	• Investment account is reported at fair value	• Dividends and capital gains and losses included in income • Interim changes in fair value affect income	• Dividends are operating cash inflows • Sale proceeds are investing cash inflows • Purchases are cash outflows from investing activities
Significant influence	Equity method	• Investment account equals percent owned of investee company's equity since acquired*	• Dividends reduce investment account • Investor reports income equal to percent owned of investee income • Sale of investment yields capital gain or loss	• Dividends are operating cash inflows • Sale proceeds are investing cash inflows • Purchases are cash outflows from investing activities
Control	Consolidation	• Balance sheets of investor and investee are combined	• Income statements of investor and investee are combined • Sale of investee yields capital gain or loss	• Cash flows of investor and investee are combined and retain original classification (operating, investing, or financing) • Sale and purchase of investee are investing cash flows

*Investments are often acquired at purchase prices in excess of book value (the median market price of S&P 500 companies was 2.7 times their book value as of August 2019). In this case, the investment account exceeds the proportionate ownership of the investee's equity.

As Exhibit 9.2 shows, there are three basic reporting issues to consider: (1) how investment income and capital gains are recognized in the income statement, (2) at what amount the investment is reported on the balance sheet, and (3) how the cash flow statement classifies cash received and used for the investment. Next we discuss these issues for the three investment types.

Passive Investments in Equity Securities

There are many types of equity securities and many reasons for investing in them. Most often, companies buy marketable equity securities as a passive investment because they provide a short-term return. Marketable equity securities are financial instruments that can be bought and sold on a public exchange whereas non-marketable equity securities are shares of stock of private companies. In this section we examine the accounting for both marketable and non-marketable equity securities. Accounting differs for equity versus debt and, in a later section, we discuss debt investments.

Acquisition and Sale

When a company makes a passive investment in marketable or non-marketable equity securities, it records the shares acquired on the balance sheet at fair value; that is, the purchase price. This is the same as accounting for the acquisition of other assets, such as inventories or PPE. Subsequent to acquisition, these investments are classified on the balance sheet as current or long-term assets, depending on management's expectations about their ultimate holding period.

When investments are sold, any recognized gain or loss on sale is equal to the difference between the proceeds received and the book (carrying) value of the investment on the balance sheet as follows.

Gain or Loss on Sale = Proceeds from Sale − Book Value of Investment Sold

To illustrate the acquisition and sale of a passive investment in equity securities, assume **Alphabet** purchases 1,000 shares of **Juniper Networks** for $20 cash per share (this includes transaction costs such as brokerage fees). Alphabet subsequently sells 400 of the 1,000 shares for $23 cash per share (assume no change in the investment book value). The following financial statement effects template shows how these transactions affect Alphabet.

Module 9 Intercorporate Investments

	Balance Sheet					Income Statement		
Transaction	Cash Asset	+ Noncash Assets	= Liabilities	+ Contrib. Capital	+ Earned Capital	Revenues	− Expenses	= Net Income
1. Purchase 1,000 shares of Juniper common stock for $20 cash per share	−20,000 Cash	+20,000 Marketable Securities	=			−		=
2. Sell 400 shares of Juniper common stock for $23 cash per share	+9,200 Cash	−8,000 Marketable Securities	=		+1,200 Retained Earnings	+1,200 Gain on Sale	−	= +1,200

```
MS .... 20,000
  Cash .... 20,000

      MS
 20,000 |
         |  Cash
         |  20,000

Cash .... 9,200
  MS ........ 8,000
  GN ........ 1,200

      Cash
  9,200 |
         |  MS
         |  8,000
         |  GN
         |  1,200
```

Income statements include the gain or loss on sale of marketable securities as a component of *other income*, which is typically reported separately from operating income and often aggregated with interest and dividend income.

Fair-Value Method for Investments in Equity Security

On the balance sheet, companies must report all passive investments in equity securities at fair value. Moreover, changes in the fair value of equity securities during the current period flow to current period net income. As the market value of equity securities fluctuates so do the balance sheet and the income statement. This is known as fair-value method of accounting.

What is fair value? Accounting rules lay out three specific ways to determine fair value and all three are acceptable (in order of preferred usage).

- **Level 1** Quoted market prices if the security is traded in active markets.
- **Level 2** Quoted market prices in active markets for similar securities and model-based valuation techniques if all significant inputs are observable in the market or can be derived from observable market data.
- **Level 3** Unobservable inputs that are supported by little or no market activities.

When we think of investments in equity securities, we generally think of investments in marketable securities that are traded on organized exchanges (such as NYSE and NASDAQ). These securities are reported at fair value at each reporting date using their quoted market prices (Level 1) or quoted market prices for similar securities (Level 2). For non-marketable securities, companies use Level 3 inputs to determine the fair value, as we explain below.

Fair Value Adjustments To illustrate the accounting for changes in fair value subsequent to purchase (and before sale), assume Alphabet's investment in Juniper Networks (600 remaining shares purchased for $20 per share) increases in value to $25 per share at year-end. The investment account must be adjusted to fair value to reflect the $3,000 unrealized gain ($5-per-share increase for 600 shares) as follows.

	Balance Sheet					Income Statement		
Transaction	Cash Asset	+ Noncash Assets	= Liabilities	+ Contrib. Capital	+ Earned Capital	Revenues	− Expenses	= Net Income
$5 increase in fair value of Juniper investment		+3,000 Marketable Securities	=		+3,000 Retained Earnings	+3,000 Unrealized Gain	−	= +3,000

```
MS ...... 3,000
  UG ........ 3,000

      MS
  3,000 |
         |  UG
         |  3,000
```

The investment account increases by $3,000 to reflect the increase in the stock's fair value, and the unrealized gain is recorded as income, thus increasing both reported income and retained earnings for the period. (Our illustration uses a portfolio with only one security for simplicity. Portfolios usually consist of multiple securities, and the unrealized gain or loss is computed based on the total cost and total market value of the entire portfolio.)

Marketable Equity Securities

Alphabet has investments in marketable equity securities of $1,222 million at December 31, 2018. In a footnote, the company reports the following ($ millions).

> From time to time, we may hold marketable equity securities obtained through acquisitions or strategic investments in private companies that subsequently go public.
>
> | As of December 31, 2018 | Cash and Cash Equivalents | Marketable Securities |
> |---|---|---|
> | **Level 1:** | | |
> | Money market funds. . . . . | $3,493 | $ 0 |
> | Marketable equity securities. . . . . | 0 | 994 |
> | | 3,493 | 994 |
> | **Level 2:** | | |
> | Mutual funds. . . . . | 0 | 228 |
> | Total. . . . . | $3,493 | $1,222 |

Some of Alphabet's marketable equity securities trade frequently and prices are easily observable, and for those securities, Alphabet reported Level 1 fair value of $994 million. The mutual funds are apparently infrequently traded and Alphabet reported Level 2 fair value of $228 million. The total of $1,222 million is not reported as a separate balance sheet line item, but instead, reported along with marketable debt securities.

Non-Marketable Equity Securities

In addition to its marketable equity securities, Alphabet invests in non-marketable equity securities—the stock of privately held companies with no publicly available stock price. These investments allow Alphabet early access to new technologies or the opportunity to invest prior to an initial public offering.

Because, by definition, investments in non-marketable securities lack readily determined market values, we might think that they would be exempt from fair-value adjustment. However, this is not so. Accounting rules require that such securities must also be reported at fair value on the balance sheet with fair-value changes recognized in current income.

Companies use Level 3 inputs to value these non-marketable securities and valuation techniques commonly include the use of market multiples, discounted cash flow approaches, and a variety of other methods that utilize forecasts and other inputs in a valuation model to estimate the fair value of the security.

At year-end 2018, Alphabet's non-marketable equity security portfolio had a fair value of $12.3 billion. Alphabet discusses the inherent difficulty of valuing these securities in this excerpt from its 2018 10-K.

> Our non-marketable equity securities not accounted for under the equity method are adjusted to fair value for observable transactions for identical or similar investments of the same issuer or impairment (referred to as the measurement alternative). . . These investments, especially those that are in the early stages, are inherently risky because the technologies or products these companies have under development are typically in the early phases and may never materialize and they may experience a decline in financial condition, which could result in a loss of a substantial part of our investment in these companies. The success of our investment in any private company is also typically dependent on the likelihood of our ability to realize value in our investments through liquidity events such as public offerings, acquisitions, private sales or other favorable market events reflecting appreciation to the cost of our initial investment. As of December 31, 2018, the carrying value of our non-marketable equity securities, which were accounted for under the measurement (i.e. fair-value) alternative, was $12.3 billion. Valuations of our equity investments in private companies are inherently more complex due to the lack of readily available market data. Volatility in the global economic climate and financial markets could result in a significant impairment charge on our non-marketable equity securities.

Initial Adoption of New Accounting Rules

Prior to January 1, 2018, companies accounted for non-marketable equity securities at cost (original purchase cost), recognizing as income any dividends received and any gains and losses realized on sale of securities. This meant unrealized gains and losses were omitted from both the balance sheet and the income statement. As an example, immediately prior to adopting the new accounting standard, Alphabet reported non-marketable securities on the balance sheet at a cost of $4.5 billion when those same securities had a fair value of $8.8 billion. This meant the previous accounting rules omitted $4.3 billion of unrealized gains for Alphabet. This was indicative of a larger issue among U.S. companies.

Many companies, including Alphabet, adopted the new accounting standard *prospectively*, meaning that the company did *not* go back and restate prior financial statements; instead, they recognized any gains or losses in the adoption year. Following is Alphabet's description of its adoption of the new accounting standard in 2018.

> Our non-marketable equity securities are investments in privately held companies without readily determinable market values. Because we adopted ASU 2016-01 prospectively, we recognize unrealized gains that occurred in prior periods in the first period after January 1, 2018 when there is an observable transaction for our securities. The following is a summary of unrealized gains and losses recorded in other income (expense), net, and included as adjustments to the carrying value of non-marketable equity securities held as of December 31, 2018 (in millions):
>
> | Twelve Months Ended | December 31, 2018 |
> |---|---|
> | Upward adjustments. . . . . | $4,285 |
> | Downward adjustments (including impairment) . . . . | (178) |
> | Total unrealized gain (loss) for non-marketable equity securities. . . . . | $4,107 |

The newly adopted fair-value method caused an upward adjustment of $4,107 million to Alphabet's investments account on the balance sheet. Alphabet also included that upward adjustment in its 2018 income statement on the "Other income" line (highlighted in following table). The following excerpt comes from Alphabet's 2018 income statement, where the total $8,592 million includes the $4,107 million of unrealized gains along with $4,487 million of interest income, realized gains on sales of securities, and other items).

Year Ended December 31, in millions	2016	2017	2018
Income from operations	$23,716	$26,146	$26,321
Other income (expense), net	434	1,047	8,592
Income before income taxes	24,150	27,193	34,913
Provision for income taxes	4,672	14,531	4,177
Net income	$19,478	$12,662	$30,736

This one-time (transitory) income item helps explain the significant increase in Alphabet's profitability in 2018 compared with the prior year. (Another factor is income tax expense that increased significantly in 2017 as a result of tax legislation passed that year; see our discussion of income taxes in Modules 5 and 10.)

Investments in Debt Securities

Companies often purchase debt securities, including bonds issued by other companies or by the U.S. government. For example, Alphabet reports investments in time deposits, corporate bonds, U.S. government agency bonds, and municipal securities. Companies can choose to classify investments in debt securities as either:

- **Held-to-maturity securities (HTM).** Debt securities that the investor has the intent and ability to hold to their maturity.
- **Available-for-sale securities (AFS).** Debt securities that may be sold prior to their scheduled maturities to meet liquidity needs or risk management objectives.
- **Trading securities.** Debt securities that are held for a short period of time and are intended to be actively traded. These securities are accounted for like equity securities (reported at fair value on the balance sheet with changes in fair value recognized in current income).

Held-to-Maturity (HTM) Debt Securities

Many debt securities have maturity dates—dates when the security must be repaid by the borrower. If a company buys debt securities, and *management intends to hold the securities to maturity* (as opposed to selling them early), the securities are classified as **held-to-maturity** (HTM). Exhibit 9.3 identifies the reporting of these securities.

Changes in fair value of held-to-maturity securities do not affect either the balance sheet or the income statement. The presumption is that these investments will indeed be held to maturity, at which time their market value will be exactly equal to their face value. Fluctuations in fair value, as a result, are less relevant. Any interest earned is recorded in current income. (GAAP gives companies an option to report held-to-maturity investments at fair value; if this fair value option is elected, the accounting for held-to-maturity securities is like that for marketable equity securities, discussed above.)

Exhibit 9.3 ■ Accounting Treatment for Held-to-Maturity Debt Investments

Investment Classification	Reporting of Fair Value Changes	Reporting Interest Received and the Gains and Losses on Sale
Held-to-Maturity (HTM)	Fair value changes are *not* reported in either the balance sheet or income statement (HTM is reported at *amortized cost*)	Interest reported as *other income* in income statement If sold before maturity (the exception), any gain or loss on sale is reported in income statement

Because the value of debt securities fluctuates with the prevailing rate of interest, the market value of the security will be greater than its face value if current market interest rates are lower than what the security pays for interest. In that case, the acquirer will pay a premium for the security. Conversely, if current market interest rates exceed what the security pays in interest, the acquirer will purchase the security at a discount. (We cover premiums and discounts on debt securities in more detail in more detail in Module 7.) Either way, the company records the investment at its acquisition cost (like any other asset) and amortizes any discount or premium over the remaining life of the held-to-maturity investment. At any point in time, the acquirer's balance sheet carries the investment at "amortized cost," which is never adjusted for subsequent market value changes.

Available-for-Sale Debt Securities

Like marketable equity securities, available-for-sale (AFS) debt securities are reported at fair value on the balance sheet. However, changes in fair value for AFS debt securities do ***not*** flow to the income statement. Instead, these unrealized gains and losses are transferred to the equity section of the balance sheet to an account called "accumulated other comprehensive income" (AOCI).

Fair Value and Unrealized Gains To illustrate, assume that the fair value of a company's AFS debt securities increased by $3,000 during the year they were acquired. The company increases the fair value on the balance sheet by $3,000 and the unrecognized gain is reported in accumulated other comprehensive income (AOCI). The financial statement effects template below shows this accounting.

Transaction	Balance Sheet					Income Statement		
	Cash Asset	+ Noncash Assets	= Liabilities	+ Contrib. Capital	+ Earned Capital	Revenues	− Expenses	= Net Income
Recognize $3,000 increase in market value of AFS debt securities		+3,000 Marketable Securities	=		+3,000 AOCI		−	=

MS 3,000
 AOCI 3,000

MS
3,000

AOCI
	3,000

Alphabet describes its investment in AFS debt securities (which totals over $91 billion) as follows.

> We have classified and accounted for our marketable debt securities as available-for-sale. After consideration of our risk versus reward objectives, as well as our liquidity requirements, we may sell these debt securities prior to their stated maturities. As we view these securities as available to support current operations, we classify highly liquid securities with maturities beyond 12 months as current assets under the caption marketable securities on the Consolidated Balance Sheets. We carry these securities at fair value, and report the unrealized gains and losses, net of taxes, as a component of stockholders' equity, except for unrealized losses determined to be other-than-temporary, which we record within other income (expense), net. We determine any realized gains or losses on the sale of marketable debt securities on a specific identification method, and we record such gains and losses as a component of other income (expense), net.

The following table provides details of Alphabet's debt securities portfolio ($ millions).

As of December 31, 2018	Adjusted Cost	Gross Unrealized Gains	Gross Unrealized Losses	Fair Value	Cash and Cash Equivalents	Marketable Securities	Non-Marketable Securities
Level 2:							
Time deposits	$ 2,202	$ 0	$ 0	$ 2,202	$2,202	$ 0	$ 0
Government bonds	53,634	71	(414)	53,291	3,717	49,574	0
Corporate debt securities	25,383	15	(316)	25,082	44	25,038	0
Mortgage-backed and asset-backed securities	16,918	11	(324)	16,605	0	16,605	0
	98,137	97	(1,054)	97,180	5,963	91,217	0
Level 3:							
Non-marketable debt securities	147	116	0	263	0	0	263
Total	$98,284	$213	$(1,054)	$97,443	$5,963	$91,217	$263

This footnote discloses adjusted cost of $98,284 million and fair value of $97,443 million. Alphabet reports the total fair value of these securities in three line items on the balance sheet: cash and cash equivalents of $5,963 million, marketable securities of $91,217 million, and non-marketable debt securities of $263 million. As the table reveals, the company values most of these debt securities using Level 2 inputs.

Realized Gains When the company ultimately sells the securities, it transfers any related gains or losses from AOCI into current-period income. That is, the previously unrealized gain or loss is now realized because of the sale and therefore recognized on the income statement. During 2018, Alphabet "reclassified" a previously deferred gain of $911 million relating to the sale of its AFS debt securities as reported in the following table.

Alphabet Inc.
CONSOLIDATED STATEMENTS OF COMPREHENSIVE INCOME

Year Ended December 31 (In millions)	2016	2017	2018
Net income	$19,478	$12,662	$30,736
Other comprehensive income (loss):			
Change in foreign currency translation adjustment	(599)	1,543	(781)
Available-for-sale investments:			
Change in net unrealized gains (losses)	(314)	307	88
Less: reclassification adjustment for net (gains) losses included in net income	221	105	(911)
Net change (net of tax effect of $0, $0, and $156)	(93)	412	(823)
Cash flow hedges:			
Change in net unrealized gains (losses)	515	(638)	290
Less: reclassification adjustment for net (gains) losses included in net income	(351)	93	98
Net change (net of tax effect of $64, $247, and $103)	164	(545)	388
Other comprehensive income (loss)	(528)	1,410	(1,216)
Comprehensive income	$18,950	$14,072	$29,520

Financial Statement Disclosures

Companies are required to disclose cost and fair values of their passive investment portfolios in footnotes to financial statements. **Alphabet** reports the accounting policies for its investments in the following footnote to its 2018 10-K report.

> **Cash, Cash Equivalents, and Marketable Securities** We invest all excess cash primarily in government bonds, corporate debt securities, mortgage-backed and asset-backed securities, time deposits, and money market funds. We classify all investments that are readily convertible to known amounts of cash and have stated maturities of three months or less from the date of purchase as cash equivalents and those with stated maturities of greater than three months as marketable securities.

Following is the asset section of Alphabet's 2018 balance sheet (in millions).

December 31	2017	2018
Assets		
Current assets		
Cash and cash equivalents	$ 10,715	$ 16,701
Marketable securities	91,156	92,439
Total cash, cash equivalents, and marketable securities	101,871	109,140
Accounts receivable, net of allowance of $674 and $729	18,336	20,838
Income taxes receivable, net	369	355
Inventory	749	1,107
Other current assets	2,983	4,236
Total current assets	124,308	135,676
Non-marketable investments	7,813	13,859
Deferred income taxes	680	737
Property and equipment, net	42,383	59,719
Intangible assets, net	2,692	2,220
Goodwill	16,747	17,888
Other noncurrent assets	2,672	2,693
Total assets	$197,295	$232,792

Alphabet's investments are reported in the three highlighted line items: cash and cash equivalents (marketable securities that mature within 90 days of the balance sheet date are essentially equivalent to cash and are therefore included in cash and cash equivalents), marketable securities, and non-marketable investments.

The following table reconciles these three balance sheet line items to the various investments discussed above.

December 31, 2018 ($ millions)	Cash and Cash Equivalents	Marketable Securities	Non-marketable Investments
Cash....................	$ 7,245		
Marketable equity securities.......	3,493	$ 1,222	
Non-marketable equity securities...			$12,275
Equity-method investments........			1,321
Debt securities	5,963	91,217	263
Balance sheet total..............	$16,701	$92,439	$13,859

Review 9-1 LO1

Assume **Microsoft** had the following four transactions involving investments in marketable securities. Use this information to answer requirement *a*.

1. Purchased 1,000 shares of **Juniper Networks** common stock for $22 cash per share.
2. Received cash dividend of $2.50 per share on Juniper Networks common stock.
3. Year-end market price of Juniper Networks common stock is $27 per share.
4. Sold all 1,000 shares of Juniper Networks common stock for $27,000 cash in the next period.

Microsoft reports the following table in the footnotes to its 2018 10-K. Use this information to answer requirements *b* through *d*.

In millions	Cost Basis	Unrealized Gains	Unrealized Losses	Recorded Basis	Cash and Cash Equivalents	Short-Term Investments	Equity and Other Investments
June 30, 2018							
Cash.....................	$ 3,942	$ 0	$ 0	$ 3,942	$ 3,942	$ 0	$ 0
Mutual funds...............	246	0	0	246	246	0	0
Commercial paper	2,513	0	0	2,513	2,215	298	0
Certificates of deposit.........	2,058	0	0	2,058	1,865	193	0
U.S. government and agency securities.................	109,862	62	(1,167)	108,757	3,678	105,079	0
Foreign government bonds.....	5,182	1	(10)	5,173	0	5,173	0
Mortgage- and asset-backed securities.................	3,868	4	(13)	3,859	0	3,859	0
Corporate notes and bonds	6,947	21	(56)	6,912	0	6,912	0
Municipal securities	271	37	(1)	307	0	307	0
Common and preferred stock...	1,220	95	(10)	1,305	0	0	1,305
Other investments	558	0	0	558	0	1	557
Total	$136,667	$220	$(1,257)	$135,630	$11,946	$121,822	$1,862

Required

a. Use the financial statement effects template to record the four transactions.
b. What amount does Microsoft report as investments on its balance sheet? What does this balance represent?
c. What proportion of the total portfolio is equity securities?
d. Compare the cost and fair value of the portfolio. What accounts for the difference in value?

Solution on p. 9-55.

Equity Investments with Significant Influence

Many companies make equity investments that yield them significant influence over the investee companies. These intercorporate investments are usually made for strategic reasons such as the following.

- **Prelude to acquisition.** Significant ownership can allow the investor company to gain a seat on the board of directors, from which it can learn much about the investee company, its products, and its industry.

- **Strategic alliance.** Strategic alliances permit the investor to gain trade secrets, technical know-how, or access to restricted markets. For example, a company might buy an equity interest in a company that provides inputs for the investor's production process. This relationship is closer than the usual supplier–buyer relationship and will convey benefits to the investor company.

- **Pursuit of research and development.** Many research activities in the pharmaceutical, software, and oil and gas industries are conducted jointly. The common motivation is to reduce the investor's risk or the amount of capital investment. The investment often carries an option to purchase additional shares, which the investor can exercise if the research activities are fruitful.

LO2 Analyze and interpret equity method investments.

The investment can take a number of forms, including marketable securities, as well as other ownership arrangements, such as partnerships, joint ventures, and limited liability companies. A crucial feature in each of these investments is that the investor company has a level of ownership that is sufficient for it to exert *significant influence* over the investee company. GAAP requires that such investments be accounted for using the *equity method*.

Significant influence is the ability of the investor to affect the financing, investing, and operating policies of the investee. Ownership levels of 20% to 50% of the outstanding common stock of the investee typically convey significant influence. Significant influence can also exist when ownership is less than 20%. Evidence of such influence can be that the investor company is able to gain a seat on the board of directors of the investee, or the investor controls technical know-how or patents that are used by the investee, or the investor is able to exert significant influence by virtue of legal contracts with the investee. (There is growing pressure from regulators for determining significant influence by the facts and circumstances of the investment instead of a strict ownership percentage rule.)

Accounting for Investments with Significant Influence

Companies must use the **equity method** when significant influence exists. The equity method reports the investment on the balance sheet at an amount equal to the percentage of the investee's equity owned by the investor; hence, the name equity method. (This assumes acquisition at book value; acquisition at an amount greater than book value is covered later in this section.) Unlike passive investments, whose carrying amounts increase or decrease with the *market value* of the investee's stock, equity method investments increase (decrease) with increases (decreases) in the investee's *stockholders' equity*.

Equity method accounting is summarized as follows.

- Investments are recorded at their purchase cost.

- Dividends received are treated as a recovery of the investment and, thus, reduce the investment balance (dividends are not reported as income).

- The investor reports income equal to its percentage share of the investee's reported net income; the investment account is increased by the percentage share of the investee's income or decreased by the percentage share of any loss.

- Changes in fair value do not affect the investment's carrying value. (GAAP gives companies an option to report equity method investments at fair value unless those investments relate to consolidated subsidiaries; we discuss consolidation later in the module.)

To illustrate the equity method, consider the following scenario: Assume Google (an Alphabet subsidiary) acquires a 30% interest in Mitel Networks, a company seeking to develop a new technology. This investment is a strategic alliance for Google. At the acquisition date, Mitel's balance sheet reports $1,000 of stockholders' equity, and Google purchases a 30% stake for $300, giving it the ability to exert significant influence over Mitel. At the first year-end, Mitel reports profits of $100 and pays $20 in cash dividends to its shareholders ($6 to Google). Following are the financial statement effects for Google from this investment using the equity method.

Transaction	Balance Sheet					Income Statement		
	Cash Asset	+ Noncash Assets	= Liabilities	+ Contrib. Capital	+ Earned Capital	Revenues	− Expenses	= Net Income
1. Purchase 30% investment in Mitel for $300 cash	−300 Cash	+300 Investment in Mitel	=				−	=
2. Mitel reports $100 income; Google's share is $30		+30 Investment in Mitel	=		+30 Retained Earnings	+30 Equity Income	−	= +30
3. Mitel pays $20 cash dividends; $6 to Google	+6 Cash	−6 Investment in Mitel	=				−	=
Ending balance of Google's investment account		324						

The investment is initially reported on Google's balance sheet at its purchase price of $300, representing a 30% interest in Mitel's total stockholders' equity of $1,000. During the year, Mitel's equity increases to $1,080 ($1,000 plus $100 income and less $20 dividends). Likewise, Google's investment increases by $30 to reflect its 30% share of Mitel's $100 income, and decreases by $6, relating to its share of Mitel's dividends. After these transactions, Google's investment in Mitel is reported on Google's balance sheet at 30% of $1,080, or $324.

Google's investment in Mitel is an asset just like any other asset. As such, it must be tested annually for impairment. If the investment is found to be permanently impaired, Google must reduce the investment amount on the balance sheet and report a loss on the write-down of the investment in its income statement (unlike investments accounted for using the market method, equity method investments are not written up if fair values increase). If and when Google sells Mitel, any gain or loss on the sale is reported in Google's income statement. The gain or loss is computed as the difference between the sales proceeds and the investment's carrying value on the balance sheet. For example, if Google sold Mitel for $500, Google would report a gain on sale of $176 ($500 proceeds − $324 balance sheet value).

Companies often pay more than book value when they make equity investments. For example, if Google paid $400 for its 30% stake in Mitel, Google would initially report its investment at its $400 purchase price. The $400 investment consists of two parts: the $300 equity investment described above and the $100 additional investment. Google is willing to pay the higher purchase price because it believes Mitel's reported equity is below its current market value. Perhaps some of Mitel's assets are reported at costs that are below market values or Mitel has intangible assets such as a patent or internally generated goodwill that are missing from its balance sheet. The $300 portion of the investment is accounted for as described above. Google's management must decide how to allocate the excess of the amount paid over the book value of the investee company's equity and account for the excess accordingly. For example, if management decides the $100 relates to unrecognized depreciable assets, the $100 is depreciated over the assets' estimated useful lives. Or, if it relates to identifiable intangible assets that have a determinable useful life (such as patents), it is amortized over the useful lives of the intangible assets (however, if it relates to goodwill, it is not amortized).

Two final points about equity method accounting: First, there can be a substantial difference between the book value of an equity method investment and its fair value. An increase in value is not recognized until the investment is sold. If the fair value of the investment has permanently declined, however, the investment is deemed impaired and written down to that lower fair value. Second, if the investee company reports income, the investor company reports its share. Recognition of equity income by the investor, however, does not mean it has received that income in cash. Cash is only received if the investee pays a dividend. To highlight this, the operating section of the investor's statement of cash flows (prepared using the indirect method) will include a reconciling item (a deduction from net income in computing operating cash flow) for its percentage share of the investee's net income in excess of cash dividends received.

Research Insight ■ Equity Income and Stock Prices

Under the equity method of accounting, the investor does not recognize as income any dividends received from the investee, nor any changes in the investee's fair value, until the investment is sold. However, research has found a positive relation between investors' and investees' stock prices at the time of investees' earnings and dividend announcements. This suggests the market includes information regarding investees' earnings and dividends when assessing the stock prices of investor companies and implies the market looks beyond the book value of the investment account in determining stock prices of investor companies.

Equity Method Accounting and ROE Effects

The investor company reports equity method investments on the balance sheet at an amount equal to the percentage owned of the investee company's equity when that investment is acquired at book value. To illustrate, consider the case of the **Altria Group Inc.**'s equity investment in **AB InBev/SABMiller**. Altria owns approximately 10.1% economic and voting interest of AB InBev and provides the following disclosure in its 2018 10-K.

> **Investment in AB InBev/SABMiller** At December 31, 2018, Altria had an approximate 10.1% ownership of AB InBev, consisting of approximately 185 million restricted shares of AB InBev (the "Restricted Shares") and approximately 12 million ordinary shares of AB InBev. Altria accounts for its investment in AB InBev under the equity method of accounting because Altria has the ability to exercise significant influence over the operating and financial policies of AB InBev, including having active representation on AB InBev's Board of Directors ("AB InBev Board") and certain AB InBev Board Committees. Through this representation, Altria participates in AB InBev policy making processes. Summary financial data of AB InBev is as follows:
>
> | For the Years Ended December 31 ($ millions) | 2018[1] | 2017[1] |
> |---|---|---|
> | Net revenues | $55,500 | $56,004 |
> | Gross profit | 34,986 | 34,376 |
> | Earnings from continuing operations | 9,020 | 6,769 |
> | Net earnings | 9,020 | 6,845 |
> | Net earnings attributable to AB InBev | 7,641 | 5,473 |
>
> | At December 31 ($ millions) | 2018[1] | 2017[1] |
> |---|---|---|
> | Current assets | $ 20,289 | $ 30,920 |
> | Long-term assets | 207,921 | 213,696 |
> | Current liabilities | 32,019 | 37,765 |
> | Long-term liabilities | 130,812 | 134,236 |
> | Noncontrolling interests | 7,251 | 10,639 |
>
> [1] Reflects one-quarter lag.
>
> At December 31, 2018, Altria's carrying amount of its equity investment in AB InBev exceeded its share of AB InBev's net assets attributable to equity holders of AB InBev by approximately $11.8 billion. Substantially all of this difference is comprised of goodwill and other indefinite-lived intangible assets (consisting primarily of trademarks). . . The fair value of Altria's equity investment in AB

continued

continued from previous page

> InBev at December 31, 2018 and 2017 was $13.1 billion and $22.1 billion, respectively, compared with its carrying value of $17.7 billion and $18.0 billion, respectively. Based on Altria's evaluation of the duration and magnitude of the fair value decline, AB InBev's financial condition and near-term prospects, and Altria's intent and ability to hold its investment in AB InBev until recovery, Altria concluded that the decline in fair value of its investment in AB InBev below its carrying value is temporary and, therefore, no impairment was recorded.

From the table above, we can derive AB InBev's 2018 balance sheet as follows.

$ millions	
Current assets	$ 20,289
Long-term assets	207,921
Total assets	$228,210
Current liabilities	$ 32,019
Long-term liabilities	130,812
Total liabilities	162,831
AB InBev equity	58,128
Noncontrolling interests	7,251
Total equity	65,379
Total liabilities and equity	$228,210

Altria's share of AB InBev's equity is $5.9 billion (calculated 10.1% × $58,128 million). But Altria's footnote discloses that the carrying value of the AB InBev investment is $17.7 billion. The excess of $11.8 billion ($17.7 billion − $5.9 billion) relates to "goodwill and other indefinite-lived intangible assets." Because these intangible assets are viewed as "indefinite-lived," Altria is not required to amortize them, thereby avoiding additional amortization expense in Altria's income statement.

Altria avoided another expense related to the AB InBev investment. As of 2018, the $17.7 billion carrying value exceeded the investment's $13.1 billion fair value. Had Altria deemed the decline to be "other than temporary," the company would have had to write down the investment to fair value. This would have created an impairment loss of $4.6 billion on Altria's 2018 income statement. Altria concluded, however, that the investment's decline in fair value is temporary, thereby avoiding a significant income-statement impact.

Underlying Financial Statement Components It is helpful to visualize the equity investment in relation to the underlying assets and liabilities. Following is a summary of the Altria 2018 balance sheet ($ millions).

Altria	
Cash	$ 1,333
Noncash assets	36,605
Investment in AB InBev	17,700
Total assets	$55,638

AB InBev	
Total assets	$228,210
Liabilities	$162,831
Stockholders' equity	65,379
Liabilities and equity	$228,210

The $17,700 million equity investment on Altria's balance sheet represents a 10.1% investment in a very large company with assets of over $228 billion and liabilities of nearly $163 billion. Although unreported liabilities are not a serious concern for beer manufacturers, we might want to know more about the investee company if the investment were in a pharmaceutical company with significant potential liabilities or in a venture with highly variable cash flows. The investor company may have no direct legal obligation for the investee's liabilities, but it might need to fund the investee company, via additional investment or advances to maintain the investee's viability, if the company is important to the investor's strategic plan. Further, companies that routinely fund research and development activities through equity investments in other companies, a common practice in the pharmaceutical and software industries, can find themselves supporting underperforming equity-method investments to ensure continued external funding. One cannot always assume, therefore, the investee's liabilities and business fortunes will not adversely affect the investor.

Unreported liabilities are of particular concern when the investee company reports losses that are substantial. In extreme cases, the investee company can become insolvent (when equity is negative) as the growing negative balance in retained earnings more than offsets contributed capital. Once the equity of the investee company reaches zero, the investor must discontinue accounting for the investment by the equity method. Instead, it accounts for the investment at cost with a zero balance and no further recognition of its proportionate share of investee company losses (until the investee company's equity becomes positive again). In this case, the investor's income statement no longer includes the losses of the investee company and its balance sheet no longer reports the troubled investee company. Unreported liabilities can be especially problematic in this case.

To summarize, under equity method accounting, only the investor's proportion of the investee's equity is reported on the balance sheet (not the underlying assets and liabilities), and only the investor's proportion of the investee's earnings is reported in the income statement (not the underlying sales and expenses). This is illustrated as follows using Google's 30% investment in Mitel. The investee's income statement and balance sheet at the end of the first year is as follows.

Analysis Implications From an analysis standpoint, because the assets and liabilities are left off the Google balance sheet, and because the sales and expenses are omitted from the Google income statement, the *components* of ROE are markedly affected as follows.

- **Net operating profit margin (NOPM = NOPAT/Sales).** Most analysts include equity income (sales less expenses) in NOPAT because it relates to operating investments. However, investee's sales are not included in the NOPM denominator. The reported NOPM is, thus, overstated.

- **Net operating asset turnover (NOAT = Sales/Average NOA).** Investee's sales are excluded from the NOAT numerator, and net operating assets in excess of the investment balance are excluded from the denominator. This means the impact on NOAT is *indeterminate*.

- **Financial leverage (FLEV = Net nonoperating obligations/Average equity).** Financial leverage is understated due to the absence of investee liabilities in the numerator.

Although ROE components are affected, ROE is unaffected by equity method accounting because the correct amount of investee net income and equity *is* included in the ROE numerator and denominator, respectively. Still, the evaluation of the quality of ROE is affected. Analysis using reported equity method accounting numbers would use an overstated NOPM and an understated FLEV because the numbers are based on net balance sheet and net income statement numbers. As we discuss in a later module, analysts should adjust reported financial statements for these types of items before conducting analysis. One such adjustment might be to consolidate (for analysis purposes) the equity method investee with the investor company.

> **Managerial Decision** ■ **You Are the Chief Financial Officer**
>
> You are receiving capital expenditure requests for long-term operating asset purchases from various managers. What potential courses of action can you consider? Explain. [Answer, p. 9-36]

Review 9-2 LO2

Consider the following items related to equity method investments at **Intel** for fiscal 2018.

a. Record the following five hypothetical transactions at Intel, using a financial statement effects template.
   1. Purchased 5,000 shares of **LookSmart** common stock at $10 cash per share; these shares reflect 30% ownership of LookSmart.
   2. Received a $2-per-share cash dividend on LookSmart common stock.
   3. Recorded an accounting adjustment to reflect $100,000 income reported by LookSmart.
   4. Year-end market price of LookSmart has increased to $12 per common share.
   5. Sold all 5,000 shares of LookSmart common stock for $90,000 cash in 2019.

b. Intel reports a 49% equity investment in **IM Flash Technologies LLC (IMFT)**, which is a joint venture with Micron Technology Inc. Assume that on its 2018 financial statements, IMFT reports net income of $750 million and stockholders' equity of $4,000 million. What will Intel report in 2018 as equity-method income related to IMFT? What will be the carrying value of the IMFT equity investment on Intel's 2018 balance sheet (assume the investment was purchased at book value)?

c. Intel reported the following in its 2018 10-K. Describe the reason for and the effect of the impairment charge.

> "In July 2018, Intel and Micron announced that they agreed to complete joint development for the second generation of 3D XPoint technology, which is expected to occur in the first half of 2019 and technology development beyond that generation will be pursued independently by the two companies to optimize the technology for their respective product and business needs. We recognized an impairment charge of $290 million during the third quarter of 2018. This reduced the carrying value of our equity method investment in IMFT to $1.6 billion in line with our expectation of future cash flows."

Solution on p. 9-55.

Equity Investments with Control

 **LO3** Explain consolidation, and interpret consolidated reports.

This section discusses accounting for investments where the investor company "controls" the investee company. For example, in its footnote describing its accounting policies, **Alphabet** reports the following.

> **Basis of Consolidation** The consolidated financial statements of Alphabet include the accounts of Alphabet and entities consolidated under the variable interest and voting models. Noncontrolling interests are not presented separately as the amounts are not material. All intercompany balances and transactions have been eliminated.

This means Alphabet financial statements are an aggregation (an adding up) of those of the parent company, Alphabet, and all its subsidiary companies less any intercompany activities such as intercompany sales or receivables.

Accounting for Investments with Control

Accounting for business combinations (acquiring a controlling interest) goes one step beyond equity method accounting. Under the equity method, the investor's investment balance represents the proportion of the investee's equity owned by the investor, and the investor company's income statement includes its proportionate share of the investee's income. Once control over the investee company is achieved, GAAP requires consolidation for financial statements issued to the public (but not for the internal financial records of the separate companies).

What is control? The big picture is that control is exercised through economic power. Determining economic power can be complicated, but the following items are consistent with economic power.

- The investor has the ability to influence the investee's decision-making.
- The investor can influence the investee's financial results through contractual rights and obligations.
- The investor is exposed to variable returns; that is, the investor will absorb any losses as well as benefit from any gains.
- The investor has the right to receive residual returns.

If these items are in play, the investment is a **variable interest entity (VIE)** where the investor is the primary beneficiary. All VIEs must be consolidated.

If the VIE test is *not* met, there is a second test: the voting interest test. This test is much more straightforward. If the investor holds more than 50% of the voting stock of the investee, then economic control is in evidence and the investment must be consolidated. We see from Alphabet's footnote above that it consolidates VIEs and all wholly-owned entities (as Alphabet owns 100% of the voting stock).

Consolidation accounting includes 100% of the investee's assets and liabilities on the investor's balance sheet and 100% of the investee's sales and expenses on the investor's income statement. Specifically, the consolidated balance sheet includes the gross assets and liabilities of the investee company, and the income statement includes the investee's gross sales and expenses rather than just the investor's share of the investee company's net assets or income. All intercompany sales and expenses, and receivables and payables, are eliminated in the consolidation process to avoid double-counting when, for example, goods are sold from the investee (called a subsidiary) to the investor (called the parent company) for resale to the parent's ultimate customers.

IFRS Alert Consolidation accounting is generally similar to IFRS; differences exist in technical details, but not with presentation of consolidated financial statements.

Investments Purchased at Book Value: Subsidiary Wholly-Owned To illustrate, consider the following scenario. Penman Company acquires 100% of the common stock of Nissim Company and issues its own stock to Nissim shareholders. The purchase price of $3,000 (in Penman stock) is equal to the book value of Nissim's stockholders' equity ($2,000 contributed capital plus $1,000 retained earnings). During the next year, Nissim earned $400, bringing its retained earnings to $1,400. On its balance sheet, Penman accounts for the investment in Nissim using the equity method. This is important. Even if the investor (the parent) owns 100% of the investee (the subsidiary), the investor may still record the investment on its (parent-company) balance sheet using the equity method described in the previous section. That is, Penman records an initial balance in the equity investment account in the amount of the purchase price, which is equal to Nissim's stockholders' equity. Thereafter, the equity investment account on Penman's balance sheet will increase and decrease with Nissim's stockholders' equity, reflecting profits earned, losses incurred, and dividends paid.

Because Penman Company owns 100% of the stock of its subsidiary (and, therefore, controls the activities of Nissim), GAAP requires consolidation. That process, shown in Exhibit 9.4, involves summing each balance sheet and income statement account for the two companies *after eliminating any intercompany transactions* (such as the investment Penman has in Nissim Company, together with any intercompany sales/purchases and receivables/payables).

Exhibit 9.4 shows the balance sheets of Penman and Nissim in the first two columns, the consolidating adjustments in the next column, and the consolidated balance sheet in the far right column. The consolidated balance sheet reports total assets of $21,400, total liabilities of $7,000, and equity of $14,400. Because Penman owns 100% of the stock of Nissim and the purchase was made at book value, the equity investment account on Penman's balance sheet equals Nissim's stockholders' equity to which it relates. Both amounts are removed in the consolidation process and each row in the balance sheet is then summed to arrive at the consolidated totals. The result of this process is to remove both the equity investment account and Nissim's stockholders' equity from the consolidated balance sheet and to replace the equity investment with the assets and liabilities of Nissim to which it relates. *The consolidated stockholders' equity equals the equity of the parent company—this is always the case when the subsidiary is wholly owned.*

The consolidated income statement is shown in Exhibit 9.4. Penman reports equity income in its income statement equal to the net income reported by Nissim Company. The effect of the consolidation process is to remove the equity income account in Penman's income statement and replace it with the sales and expenses of Nissim Company to which it relates. This is accomplished by summing the rows in the income statement and eliminating the equity income account to yield the consolidated income statement. *The consolidated net income equals the net income of the parent company—this is always the case* (because the equity income the parent reports equals the net income of the subsidiary when the subsidiary is wholly owned).

Exhibit 9.4 ■ Mechanics of Consolidation Accounting (Wholly-Owned Subsidiary, Purchased at Book Value)

	Penman Company	Nissim Company	Consolidating Adjustments	Consolidated
Balance Sheet				
Current assets	$ 6,000	$ 1,400		$ 7,400
Investment in Nissim	3,400	0	(3,400)	0
PPE, net	10,000	4,000		14,000
Total assets	$19,400	$ 5,400		$21,400
Liabilities	$ 5,000	$ 2,000		$ 7,000
Contributed capital	10,000	2,000	(2,000)	10,000
Retained earnings	4,400	1,400	(1,400)	4,400
Total liabilities and equity	$19,400	$ 5,400		$21,400
Income statement				
Sales	$25,000	$10,000		$35,000
Cost of goods sold	(20,000)	(7,000)		(27,000)
Gross profit	5,000	3,000		8,000
Operating expenses	(3,600)	(2,600)		(6,200)
Equity income from investment	400	—	(400)	0
Net income	$ 1,800	$ 400		$ 1,800

Investments Purchased at Book Value: Subsidiary Not Wholly-Owned When a subsidiary is not wholly-owned, we account for the equity interest of noncontrolling shareholders in addition to that of the parent's stockholders. This will affect both the balance sheet and the income statement. To illustrate, assume Penman acquires 80% of Nissim instead of 100%, as in our previous example. Now, the equity investment account on Penman's balance sheet will reflect only 80% of Nissim's equity, and the equity income it reports in its income statement will only reflect 80% of Nissim's net income. The remaining 20% of the net assets of the subsidiary and its net income are owned by noncontrolling shareholders. Their share in the net assets of Nissim is reflected on the consolidated balance sheet in a new account titled **noncontrolling interest**. In addition, we apportion Nissim's net income into the 80%, or $320, attributed to Penman's shareholders and the 20%, or $80, attributed to noncontrolling shareholders.

We demonstrate the accounting for noncontrolling interests in Exhibit 9.5. Again, the balance sheets of Penman and Nissim are shown in the first two columns. The consolidating adjustments are shown in the third column and the consolidated balance sheet and income statement in the last column. The claim of noncontrolling shareholders on Nissim's net assets is recognized in consolidated equity in an account called noncontrolling interest. The $680 noncontrolling interest on the consolidated balance sheet represents the 20% share of the net assets at acquisition ($3,000 × 20% = $600) plus the 20% share of Nissim's net income ($400 × 20% = $80). The $2,720 equity investment account on Penman's balance sheet reflects its 80% interest in Nissim's equity ([$2,000 + $1,400] × 80%). That equity investment account is eliminated in the consolidation process.

Business Insight ■ Accounting for Noncontrolling Interests

When a company acquires less than 100% of a subsidiary, it must account for the interests of the noncontrolling shareholders separately from those of its own shareholders. This has two implications for consolidated financial statements.

1. Consolidated net income is first computed for the company as a whole as revenues less expenses. Then, it is allocated to the portion attributable to the parent's shareholders and the noncontrolling shareholders in proportion to their respective ownership interests.
2. The cumulative balance of the noncontrolling interests is reported on the balance sheet in the stockholders' equity section. It is increased each year by the net income allocated to noncontrolling interests and is decreased by any dividends paid to those noncontrolling shareholders.

The consolidated income statement shows the consolidated revenues, consolidated expenses, and consolidated net income. The $320 equity income account in Penman's income statement reflects 80% of Nissim's net income that it owns ($400 × 80%). This equity income account is eliminated in the consolidation process just like the equity investment account on the balance sheet. When less than 100% of the subsidiary is owned by the parent, the consolidated income statement allocates net income into that portion *attributable to the parent (controlling) shareholders* (80% here) and that portion *attributable to the noncontrolling shareholders* (20% here).

Exhibit 9.5 ■ Mechanics of Consolidation Accounting (Subsidiary Not Wholly-Owned, Purchased at Book Value)

	Penman Company	Nissim Company	Consolidating Adjustments	Consolidated
Balance Sheet				
Current assets	$ 6,000	$1,400		$ 7,400
Investment in Nissim	2,720	0	2,720	0
PPE, net	10,000	4,000		14,000
Total assets	$18,720	$5,400		$21,400
Liabilities	$ 5,000	$2,000		$ 7,000
Contributed capital	9,400	2,000	(2,000)	9,400
Retained earnings	4,320	1,400	(1,400)	4,320
Noncontrolling interest			680	680
Total liabilities and equity	$18,720	$5,400		$21,400
Income statement				
Sales	$25,000	$10,000		$35,000
Cost of goods sold	(20,000)	(7,000)		(27,000)
Gross profit	5,000	3,000		8,000
Operating expenses	(3,600)	(2,600)		(6,200)
Equity income from investment	320	—	(320)	0
Net income	$ 1,720	$ 400		$ 1,800
Net income attributable to noncontrolling interest				80
Net income attributable to Penman shareholders				$ 1,720

Investments Purchased <u>above</u> Book Value The illustrations above assume the purchase price of the acquisition equals the book value of the investee company. It is more often the case, however, that the purchase price exceeds the book value. This might arise, for example, if an investor company believes it is acquiring something of value that is not reported on the investee's balance sheet—such as tangible assets whose market values have risen above book value or unrecorded intangible assets, such as patents or corporate synergies. When the acquisition price exceeds book value, all net assets acquired (both tangible and intangible) must be recognized on the consolidated balance sheet.

To illustrate, let's return to the example of Exhibit 9.4 in which Penman acquires 100% interest in Nissim. Let's now assume Penman paid a premium to Nissim of $1,000 more than the book value of Nissim's stockholders' equity on the acquisition date (see the increase in Penman's contributed capital to $11,000 reflecting the additional $1,000 of stock issued to Nissim's shareholders). Assume Penman paid the additional $1,000 because Penman expects to realize $1,000 in additional value from corporate synergies, such as increased market presence, ability to consolidate offices, and increased buying power. General synergies such as this are recognized on the balance sheet as an intangible asset with an indefinite useful life, called **goodwill**. The $4,000 investment account now reflects two components: the book value acquired of $3,000 (as before) and an additional $1,000 of newly acquired assets (goodwill asset). Exhibit 9.6 shows the balance sheets of the two companies along with the consolidating adjustments and the consolidated balance sheet, on the date of acquisition. (Note that this example is at the acquisition date and does not include the $400 earned by Nissim during the ensuing year.)

Exhibit 9.6 ■ Mechanics of Consolidation Accounting (Purchase Price above Book Value)

	Penman Company	Nissim Company	Consolidating Adjustments	Consolidated
Current assets	$ 6,000	$1,000		$ 7,000
Investment in Nissim	4,000	0	(4,000)	0
PPE, net	10,000	4,000		14,000
Goodwill			1,000	1,000
Total assets	$20,000	$5,000		$22,000
Liabilities	$ 5,000	$2,000		$ 7,000
Contributed capital	11,000	2,000	(2,000)	11,000
Retained earnings	4,000	1,000	(1,000)	4,000
Total liabilities and equity	$20,000	$5,000		$22,000

The consolidated current assets and liabilities are the sum of those accounts on each company's balance sheet. The investment account, however, includes $1,000 of the newly acquired goodwill asset that must now be reported on the consolidated balance sheet. The consolidation process in this case has two steps. First, the $3,000 equity of Nissim Company is eliminated against the equity investment account as before. Then, the remaining $1,000 of the investment account is eliminated and the newly acquired asset ($1,000 of goodwill, which is not reported on Nissim's balance sheet) is added to the consolidated balance sheet. The goodwill asset is now recognized on the consolidated balance sheet as a separate asset that has an indefinite life. This means goodwill is not routinely amortized. But, like all other assets, goodwill must be tested annually for impairment and written down (or written off entirely) if found to be impaired.

In our example here, we recognized just one intangible asset: goodwill. Often, the excess purchase price is assigned to several intangible assets that have a useful life (such as the value of brands, patents, licensing agreements, and customer relationships; see the text box below for more details). If recognized, the costs of such intangible assets (other than goodwill) are amortized over their useful lives in the same manner we depreciate a tangible asset. Consolidated net income is reduced by the amortization of those intangible assets. As with goodwill, the other intangible assets are tested periodically for impairment and adjusted as needed with any write-off reflected as a reduction of equity income.

Under current accounting standards, companies are required to assess the possible impairment of goodwill on an annual basis or more often if circumstances indicate that impairment is likely.

That assessment compares the fair value of the investment in the subsidiary with the amount at which the subsidiary is reported on the parent's balance sheet (the book value of the equity investment). If the fair value is less, the parent company must write down the equity investment to its fair value and record the impairment loss in its income statement.

The **Kraft Heinz Company** provides an example. In 2018, the company reported an impairment loss of $15.5 billion as described in its footnote disclosures.

> For the fourth quarter of 2018, in connection with the preparation of our year-end financial statements, we assessed the changes in circumstances that occurred during the quarter to determine if it was more likely than not that the fair values of any reporting units or brands were below their carrying amounts. Although our annual impairment test is performed during the second quarter, we perform this qualitative assessment each interim reporting period.
>
> While there was no single determinative event or factor, the consideration in totality of several factors that developed during the fourth quarter of 2018 led us to conclude that it was more likely than not that the fair values of certain reporting units and brands were below their carrying amounts. These factors included: (i) a sustained decrease in our share price in November and December of 2018 . . . (ii) the completion of our fourth quarter results, which were below management's expectations . . . (iii) the development and approval of our 2019 annual operating plan in December 2018, which provided additional insights into expectations and priorities for the coming years, such as lower growth and margin expectations; (iv) the announcement in November 2018 to sell certain assets in our natural cheese portfolio in Canada . . . (v) fluctuations in foreign exchange rates in certain countries; (vi) increased interest rates in certain locations, including an increase in the United States in December 2018; and (vii) increased and prolonged economic and regulatory uncertainty in the United States and global economies as of the end of December 2018.
>
> As we determined that it was more likely than not that the fair values of certain reporting units or brands were below their carrying amounts, we performed an interim impairment test as of December 29, 2018. As a result of our interim impairment test, we recognized goodwill impairment losses of $6.9 billion and indefinite-lived intangible asset impairment losses of $8.6 billion in the fourth quarter of 2018.

The combined impairment charges of $15.5 billion resulted in a net loss of $10.2 billion on Kraft Heinz's 2018 income statement. Although the write-off is a noncash charge, it sent investors a message about management's expectations for its brands. Shares of Kraft Heinz dropped 27% following the announcement.

Accounting Insight ■ Accounting for Acquired Intangible Assets

The market value of a company's equity can differ substantially from its book value because of unrecorded assets. These unrecorded assets typically relate to intangible assets such as market position, brand equity, managerial talent, and internally developed technology. When companies are acquired, however, such unrecorded assets are recognized on the acquirer's balance sheet. The purchase price is allocated to the assets acquired and the liabilities assumed. First tangible assets, such as PPE and inventory, are identified and valued. Then, intangible assets are identified and valued. All these assets are recorded on the acquirer's consolidated balance sheet at fair market value just like any other purchased asset. Finally, any excess purchase price is allocated to Goodwill. Common types of intangible assets recognized during acquisitions follow.

- Marketing-related assets such as trademarks and Internet domain names
- Customer-related assets such as customer lists and customer contracts
- Artistic-related assets such as plays, books, and videos
- Contract-based assets such as licensing, lease contracts, and franchise and royalty agreements
- Technology-based assets such as patents, in-process research and development, software, databases, and trade secrets

For example, in 2015, when **Heinz** acquired **Kraft** for $52,637 million, the purchase price was allocated to the acquired assets and liabilities as follows ($ millions).

continued

continued from previous page

Cash	$ 314
Other current assets	3,423
Property, plant and equipment	4,193
Identifiable intangible assets	49,749
Other noncurrent assets	214
Trade and other payables	(3,026)
Long-term debt	(9,286)
Net postemployment benefits and other noncurrent liabilities	(4,734)
Deferred income tax liabilities	(17,239)
Net assets acquired	23,608
Goodwill on acquisition	29,029
Total consideration	$52,637

Heinz allocated $49,749 million of the purchase price to identifiable intangible assets, which consisted of the following.

	Preliminary Fair Value ($ millions)	Weighted Average Life (in years)
Indefinite-lived trademarks	$45,082	—
Definite-lived trademarks	1,690	24
Customer relationships	2,977	29
Total identifiable intangible assets	$49,749	

Once recognized, intangible assets with definite useful lives are amortized over their remaining lives. For example, Heinz will amortize the customer relationships over 29 years. Other intangible assets that are considered to be indefinite-lived assets (such as the indefinite-lived trademarks) remain on the balance sheet at their initial value. Annually, Heinz tested the fair value of the acquired intangible assets, and as we saw above, deemed them impaired in 2018. The company recorded a $15.5 billion impairment charge, reducing the balance sheet value of the assets by 20% only three years after their acquisition.

Consolidation of Foreign Subsidiaries (Cumulative Translation Adjustment)

Foreign subsidiaries that are headquartered outside of the U.S. typically conduct business and maintain their accounting records in their own domestic currencies rather than in U.S. dollars. Before the U.S. parent company can consolidate the foreign subsidiary, the foreign currency denominated financial statements must be translated into $US. From day to day, the exchange rate between the $US and the foreign currency changes. So while the value of any of the subsidiary's transactions is known with certainty, its $US equivalent will change depending on the prevailing exchange rate the day the financials are translated.

Consider the example below where a European subsidiary has no changes in its balance sheet during the year (including no net income). Assume the $US strengthens during the year vis-à-vis the euro, such that each euro purchases fewer $US ($1.25 dropping to $1.10).

	December 31, 2017		December 31, 2018	
Balance Sheet	€	$	€	$
Assets	$2,000	$2,500	$2,000	$2,200
Liabilities	500	625	500	550
Net assets	1,500	**1,875**	1,500	**1,650**
Exchange Rates				
$US/Euro	1.25		1.100	

The euro-denominated balance sheet does not change year over year, but the translated and consolidated values vary greatly. The upshot is the foreign currency-denominated balance sheet shrinks when the $US strengthens.[1]

At consolidation, the foreign subsidiary's assets and liabilities are reported on the parent's balance sheet at their $US value translated at the rate prevailing on the balance sheet date. Recall that during consolidation, the subsidiary's equity is *not* added to the parent's balance sheet. From the example above, we see that adding the assets and liabilities causes the balance sheet to be out of balance in $US. To balance, we adjust stockholders' equity for the difference. We add the change in net assets arising from the change exchange rate to an account called the **cumulative translation adjustment**. In the example above, the net assets of €1,500 translates to **$1,875** at the start of the year (December 31, 2017) and **$1,650** at the end (December 31, 2018), a decrease of $225. To balance, we adjust equity downward by $225. Thus, the cumulative translation adjustment account has a negative balance. This balance is reported in AOCI. The parent's consolidated balance sheet will include the following amounts.

December 31, 2018	€	$
Assets.	$2,000	$2,200
Liabilities.	500	550
Cumulative translation adjustment		(225)

To sum up, when the $US strengthens, the cumulative translation adjustment is negative. Conversely, when the $US weakens, the foreign subsidiary's assets and liabilities increase, as does stockholders' equity, and that increase is evidenced by a positive cumulative translation adjustment on the parent's balance sheet. The cumulative translation adjustment account remains on the balance sheet as long as the company owns the foreign subsidiary. The account balance typically fluctuates between negative and positive values as the $US strengthens and weakens vis-à-vis foreign currencies over time. If the subsidiary is sold, however, the related cumulative translation adjustment amount is transferred from AOCI into current income. The following footnote disclosure from **The Hershey Company** in 2018 is illustrative (in $000s).

	Pre-Tax Amount	Tax (Expense) Benefit	After-Tax Amount
Net income including noncontrolling interest			$1,171,051
Foreign currency translation adjustments			
Foreign currency translation gains (losses) during period	$(31,143)	$—	(31,143)
Reclassification to earnings due to the sale of businesses	25,131	—	25,131
	⋮	⋮	⋮

During 2018, the $US strengthened and The Hershey Company recorded other comprehensive loss of $31,143 thousand. Also during 2018, the company sold a subsidiary and reclassified a related foreign currency translation gain of $25,131 thousand into current income. The sale of the subsidiary converted the previously unrealized currency translation gain to a realized gain and this increased the total gain on the sale of the subsidiary in 2018.

Most companies aggregate the cumulative translation adjustment with similar adjustments in AOCI.[2] **Alphabet** reports AOCI as part of its stockholders' equity accounts, as follows.

---

[1] We discuss this same effect on the income statement in Module 5. In short, when the foreign currency-denominated income statement is translated to $US, a stronger $US means lower sales, expenses, and profit.

[2] Other adjustments that are included in AOCI relate to available-for-sale debt securities and derivative securities, as discussed in this module, and pension adjustments, discussed in a later module. The common feature of all of these adjustments is that they represent unrealized gains and losses on various assets and liabilities. The unrealized gains and losses are recognized in income (realized) *only when* the asset or liability is removed from the balance sheet (sold, settled, or disposed of).

Stockholders' Equity as of December 31 ($ millions)	2017	2018
Convertible preferred stock, $0.001 par value per share, 100,000 shares authorized; no shares issued and outstanding	$ 0	$ 0
Class A and Class B common stock, and Class C capital stock and additional paid-in capital, $0.001 par value per share: 15,000,000 shares authorized (Class A 9,000,000, Class B 3,000,000, Class C 3,000,000); 694,783 (Class A 298,470, Class B 46,972, Class C 349,341) and 695,556 (Class A 299,242, Class B 46,636, Class C 349,678) shares issued and outstanding	40,247	45,049
Accumulated other comprehensive income (loss)	(992)	(2,306)
Retained earnings	113,247	134,885
Total stockholders' equity	$152,502	$177,628

For Alphabet, AOCI decreases by $1,314 million in 2018. The change includes other comprehensive loss of $1,216 million (as detailed below) and an adjustment of $(98) million to the AOCI beginning balance for catch-up charges related to various accounting rule changes during the year.

The year-over-year change in AOCI is formally called **other comprehensive income (or loss)**. The financial statements for all companies include a statement of comprehensive income that explains the changes in the AOCI account. The statement of comprehensive income is either presented at the bottom of the income statement or on its own immediately after the income statement. Alphabet, for example, chose the latter. (As explained in more detail in a prior module, Comprehensive income = Net income + Other comprehensive income. For Alphabet in 2018, Comprehensive income = $29,520 million, the sum of Net income ($30,736 million) and Other comprehensive loss ($1,216 million).)

ALPHABET INC.
Consolidated Statements of Comprehensive Income

Year Ended December 31 ($ millions)	2016	2017	2018
Net income	$19,478	$12,662	$30,736
Other comprehensive income (loss):			
Change in foreign currency translation adjustment	(599)	1,543	(781)
Available-for-sale investments:			
Change in net unrealized gains (losses)	(314)	307	88
Less: reclassification adjustment for net (gains) losses included in net income	221	105	(911)
Net change (net of tax effect of $0, $0, and $156)	(93)	412	(823)
Cash flow hedges:			
Change in net unrealized gains (losses)	515	(638)	290
Less: reclassification adjustment for net (gains) losses included in net income	(351)	93	98
Net change (net of tax effect of $64, $247, and $103)	164	(545)	388
Other comprehensive income (loss)	(528)	1,410	(1,216)
Comprehensive income	$18,950	$14,072	$29,520

To conclude, the strengthening or weakening of the $US that causes fluctuations in assets and liabilities, and the cumulative translation adjustment has no effect on cash flow. Changes in the cumulative translation adjustment account are not reflected in net income; the fluctuations are included in AOCI and remain in stockholders' equity as long as the parent owns the foreign subsidiary. If and when a foreign subsidiary is sold, any remaining amount in AOCI that relates to the foreign subsidiary is removed from stockholders' equity and reported in net income.

Consolidation Disclosures To illustrate consolidation mechanics, we consider **Caterpillar**. The company's Form 10-K reports consolidated financial statements: the parent company financial statements (Machinery and Power Systems) are combined with those of the subsidiary (Financial Products). Exhibit 9.7 (taken from Caterpillar's 10-K) reports the parent and the subsidiary balance sheets separately as well as the adjustments that yield the consolidated financial statements.

Exhibit 9.7 Caterpillar Consolidated Balance Sheet

December 31, 2018 ($ millions)	Machinery & Power Systems	Financial Products	Consolidating Adjustments	Consolidated
Balance sheet				
Current assets	$24,401	$15,862	❹ $(1,660)	$38,603
Noncurrent assets	20,402	20,206	❹ (702)	39,906
Investment in Financial Products subsidiaries	❶ 3,672		❸ (3,672)	—
Total assets	$48,475	$36,068	$(6,034)	$78,509
Current liabilities	$15,814	$14,065	❹ $(1,661)	$28,218
Long-term liabilities	18,581	18,331	❹ (701)	36,211
Stockholders' Equity:				
Common stock	5,827	919	(919)	5,827
Treasury stock	(20,531)	0		(20,531)
Retained earnings	30,427	3,543	(3,543)	30,427
Accumulated other comprehensive income	(1,684)	(943)	943	(1,684)
Noncontrolling interests	41	153	(153)	41
Total stockholders' equity	14,080	❷ 3,672	❸ (3,672)	14,080
Total liabilities and equity	$48,475	$36,068	$(6,034)	$78,509
Income statement				
Revenues	$51,822	$ 3,362	❹ $ (462)	$54,722
Operating costs	(43,667)	(2,840)	❹ 78	(46,429)
Operating profit	8,155	522	(384)	8,293
Other income (expense)	(815)	(16)	❹ 384	(447)
Profit before taxes	7,340	506	0	7,846
Provision for income taxes	(1,574)	(124)	—	(1,698)
Equity in profit of Financial Products subsidiaries	❺ 362		❺ (362)	—
Profit of consolidated companies	6,128	382	(362)	6,148
Less: profit (loss) attributable to noncontrolling interests	(19)	20		1
Profit attributable to Caterpillar shareholders	$ 6,147	$ 362	$ (362)	$ 6,147

Following are a few observations relating to Exhibit 9.7.

❶ The parent company (Machinery and Power Systems) reports an investment on its balance sheet called "Investment in Financial Products subsidiaries" with a balance of $3,672 million in 2018. This investment represents the parent's investment in its wholly-owned subsidiaries, and it is accounted for using the equity method. On the parent's books, this investment account represents net assets (total assets less total liabilities) of the Financial Products subsidiaries in the same way **Altria**'s balance sheet represents the percentage it owns of the net assets of AB InBev. The parent maintains its separate parent company financial records for taxation and other internal decision-making purposes. But for external reporting purposes, Caterpillar must present consolidated financial statements. (Caterpillar controls its Financial Products subsidiaries. Altria does not control AB InBev. That is why Caterpillar must consolidate its Financial Products subsidiaries while Altria reports AB InBev as an equity investment.)

❷ The subsidiary balance sheet reports total stockholders' equity in the amount of $3,672 million, the same amount as the equity investment on the parent's balance sheet. That is not a coincidence. As we discuss earlier in this module, if the investment is acquired at book value and the investee company is wholly-owned, the investment account on the parent's balance sheet will always be equal to the stockholders' equity of the subsidiary (investee) company. In this case, Caterpillar formed (not acquired) its financial products subsidiary, which is why the equity investment balance equals the equity of the financial products subsidiary and there are no recorded intangible assets.

❸ The consolidation process eliminates all intercompany investments, including intercompany sales and receivables, which we discuss below. Then, the rows are summed to yield the consolidated totals reported. This first group of eliminations removes the equity investment of $3,672 million from total assets and the subsidiary's stockholders' equity. Notice that the equity investment shows a zero balance (and is, therefore, not reported) on the consolidated balance sheet. Notice also that consolidated stockholders' equity is equal to parent company stockholders' equity (that will always be the case if the parent uses the equity method to account for its investment in the subsidiary).

❹ All intercompany transactions are eliminated in both the income statement and the balance sheet to avoid double counting. These include intercompany sales (and offsetting purchases) and intercompany receivables (and offsetting payables).

❺ Finally, because the subsidiaries are wholly-owned, the parent company reports equity income equal to the net income of its subsidiaries ($362 million). This income statement line is eliminated during the consolidation process and replaced by the revenues and expenses to which it relates. Net income remains unchanged, but the consolidated income statement reports the sales and expenses of its Financial Products subsidiaries rather than just the net income.

Following the eliminations of *all intercompany transactions*, the adjusted balance sheets and income statement line items are summed to yield the financial statements reported in Caterpillar's 10-K. In the case that a subsidiary is controlled but not wholly-owned, the consolidated financial statements will also reflect the *noncontrolling interest*, which we discuss above.

Limitations of Consolidation Reporting

Consolidation of financial statements is meant to present a financial picture of the entire set of companies under the control of the parent. Because investors typically purchase stock in the parent company and not in the subsidiaries, a consolidated view is more relevant than the parent company reporting subsidiaries as equity investments in its balance sheet. Still, we must be aware of certain limitations of consolidation.

1. Consolidated income does not imply the parent company has received any or all of the subsidiaries' net income as cash. The parent can only receive cash from subsidiaries via dividend payments. Conversely, the consolidated cash is not automatically available to the individual subsidiaries. It is quite possible, therefore, for an individual subsidiary to experience cash flow problems even though the consolidated group has strong cash flows. Likewise, unguaranteed debts of a subsidiary are not obligations of the consolidated group. Thus, even if the consolidated balance sheet is strong, creditors of a failing subsidiary are often unable to sue the parent or other subsidiaries to recoup losses.

2. Consolidated balance sheets and income statements are a mix of the various subsidiaries, often from different industries. Comparisons across companies, even if in similar industries, are often complicated by the different mix of subsidiary companies.

3. Consolidated disclosures are highly aggregated, which can preclude effective analysis. Consolidated numbers can mask poorly performing subsidiaries whose losses are offset by the positive performance of others.

Review 9-3 LO3

On January 1, assume Intel purchased all of the common shares of EarthLink for $600,000 cash—this is $200,000 more than the book value of EarthLink's stockholders' equity. Balance sheets of the two companies immediately after the acquisition follow.

continued

continued from previous page

	Intel (Parent)	EarthLink (Subsidiary)	Consolidating Adjustments	Consolidated
Current assets	$1,000,000	$100,000		
Investment in EarthLink	600,000	—		
PPE, net	3,000,000	400,000		
Total assets	$4,600,000	$500,000		
Liabilities	$1,000,000	$100,000		
Contributed capital	2,000,000	200,000		
Retained earnings	1,600,000	200,000		
Total liabilities and equity	$4,600,000	$500,000		

During purchase negotiations, EarthLink's PPE was appraised at $500,000, and Earthlink had unrecorded patents with a fair value of $25,000. All of EarthLink's remaining assets and liabilities were appraised at values approximating their book values. Also, Intel concluded that payment of an additional $75,000 was warranted because of anticipated corporate synergies. Prepare the consolidating adjustments and the consolidated balance sheet at acquisition.

Solution on p. 9-56.

Global Accounting

Both U.S. GAAP and IFRS account similarly for investments by companies in the debt and equity securities of other companies. However, differences exist, and we highlight the notable ones here.

Passive Investments

- Under IFRS, the definition of financial instrument is much broader, including, for example, accounts receivable and loans to customers or associates. For analysis, such instruments are disclosed in the notes, which will aid our reclassification for comparison purposes.

- Under IFRS, all equity instruments are measured at fair value through profit or loss (FVTPL). Companies can make an irrevocable choice to measure equity instruments at fair value through other comprehensive income (FVOCI) with no subsequent reclassification to profit or loss.

- Under IFRS, there are three classifications of investments in debt instruments: (1) amortized cost, (2) FVOCI (with subsequent reclassification to profit or loss), or (3) FVTPL, depending on the company's reasons for holding the instruments.

Equity Method Investment

- U.S. GAAP permits companies to elect to report equity method investments at fair value with changes in fair value to net income. IFRS only permits this option for mutual funds, insurance companies, and similar entities.

- IFRS distinguishes between joint ventures (where the parties have claims on the net assets of the venture) and joint operations (where parties have direct rights to the assets and obligations of the venture). IFRS companies account for joint ventures like GAAP companies, where they use equity method of accounting. However, for joint operations, companies include their share of assets, liabilities, income and expenses.

Consolidation
GAAP sets out two ways to determine whether or not consolidation is required—the VIE model and the voting interest model, as discussed above. Under IFRS, consolidation is required when the investor controls the investee; that is, when the investor has power over the investee, is exposed to variable returns from the investee, or can exercise power to affect the amount of return from the investee.

- Under IFRS, companies can measure noncontrolling interests either at fair value (full goodwill approach) or at the proportionate share of the identifiable net assets acquired (purchased goodwill approach). U.S. GAAP permits fair value only. This IFRS-GAAP difference affects ratios based on operating assets, such as return on net operating assets (RNOA). Because goodwill is not routinely amortized, the difference will have no income statement impact (recall that we exclude noncontrolling interest from our calculation of return on equity).

- Under U.S. GAAP, parent and subsidiary accounting policies do not need to conform. Under IFRS, parent and subsidiary accounting policies must conform.

- IFRS fair value impairments for intangible assets, excluding goodwill, can be later reversed (that is, written back up after being written down). Companies must have reliable evidence that the value of the intangible has been restored, and the reversal cannot exceed the original impairment.

Appendix 9A: Accounting for Derivatives

LO4 Describe and interpret derivative disclosures.

Companies routinely face many market-related risks in addition to the risks they face in the ordinary course of business. These risks derive from changes in:

- Interest rates
- Foreign exchange rates
- Commodity prices
- Marketable security prices

Generally, these risks are beyond the company's control and can cause earnings and cash flow volatility that is difficult to manage. Fortunately, companies can mitigate these types of risk exposures by purchasing a financial security whose value is negatively correlated with the specific risk the company faces or by entering into a contract that locks in a future value. This transfer of risk is called hedging and it works best when the hedging instrument (including futures and forward contracts, swap agreements, and options) generates earnings and cash flows that exactly offset the adverse effects of the hedged item (debt, commodities, foreign currency or marketable securities). Collectively, these contracts and securities are called **derivatives** because their value derives from the value of some underlying asset. Derivatives, therefore, act like an insurance policy. However, while the company may protect itself from loss by using a derivative, it also gives up the prospect of gains. That is, if the hedged item increases in value, the gain will be offset by a loss on the derivative. The core idea of hedging is to insulate against potential losses and not to speculate on potential gains.

The following excerpts from the 10-K footnotes provide good examples.

- **Tiffany & Co.** "The Company periodically hedges a portion of its forecasted purchases of precious metals for use in its internal manufacturing operations in order to manage the effect of volatility in precious metal prices."

- **Michael Kors Holdings LTD.** "The Company in its normal course of business enters into transactions with foreign suppliers and seeks to minimize risks related to certain forecasted inventory purchases."

- **Harley-Davidson Inc.** "The Company utilizes commodity contracts to hedge portions of the cost of certain commodities consumed in the Company's motorcycle production and distribution operations."

- **Southwest Airlines Inc.** "The Company purchases jet fuel at prevailing market prices, but seeks to manage market risk through execution of a documented hedging strategy. The Company utilizes financial derivative instruments, on both a short-term and a long-term basis, as a form of insurance against the potential for significant increases in fuel prices."

- **Cisco Systems Inc.** "Our equity portfolio consists of securities with characteristics that most closely match the Standard & Poor's 500 Index or Nasdaq Composite Index . . . To manage our exposure to changes in the fair value of certain equity securities, we may enter into equity derivatives designated as hedging instruments."

- **Verizon** "We enter into interest rate swaps to achieve a targeted mix of fixed and variable rate debt. We principally receive fixed rates and pay variable rates based on the LIBOR, resulting in a net increase or decrease to Interest expense."

Hedge accounting is complex and derivative footnotes are among the most difficult to interpret. In general, hedging transactions fall into two groups.

1. **Hedging the fair value of a recognized asset or liability.** **Cisco** reports marketable securities on its balance sheet that are subject to price fluctuations. To protect against price declines, Cisco can purchase put options to lock in the sale price of the securities. **Verizon** has fixed-rate debt, the fair value of which

changes inversely with interest rates. Verizon can use a fixed-to-floating interest rate swap to hedge the value of the debt. The hedging of reported assets and liabilities is called a **fair value hedge**.
2. **Hedging future cash flows from forecasted transactions.** **Tiffany**, **Michael Kors**, **Harley-Davidson** and **Southwest Airlines** all face risks that purchase costs may increase, thus lessening profit as higher costs are matched against sales. To protect against adverse price increases, these companies can execute forward contracts or other securities that lock in the future cost. The hedging of forecasted transactions is called a **cash flow hedge**.

Like other marketable securities that we discussed earlier, derivatives are subject to fair value accounting.

- **Fair value hedges.** Both the derivative and the recognized asset or liability (the hedged item) are reported at fair value on the balance sheet. Changes in fair value for both are recognized in current earnings. If the hedge is effective, changes in the fair value of the hedged asset or liability will be offset by opposite changes in the fair value of the derivative, leaving income relatively unaffected.
- **Cash flow hedges.** The derivative is reported at fair value on the balance sheet. Recall, there is no hedged item with a cash flow hedge. Because cash flow hedges relate to *forecasted* transactions, changes in the fair value of the derivative are deferred until the related transaction occurs. The unrealized gain or loss is included in other comprehensive income and recognized in stockholders' equity as accumulated other comprehensive income. Then, when the hedged transaction occurs, the deferred gain or loss is transferred ("reclassified") from AOCI into current earnings in the same income statement line item that includes the hedged transaction.

The bottom line is that all changes in the fair value of the derivative securities are recognized in income, just like for any other marketable security. The only difference between the two types of derivative transactions is one of timing, where fair value hedges are recognized immediately and cash flow hedges are deferred until the hedged transaction occurs.

Business Insight ■ Counterparty Risk

The purpose of derivatives is to transfer risk from one company to another. For example, a company might be concerned about the possible decline in the $US value of an account receivable denominated in euros. In order to hedge that risk, the company might execute a forward contract to sell euros and receive $US. That forward contract only has value, however, if the party on the other side of the transaction (the counterparty) ultimately buys euros from the company when the contract matures. If the counterparty fails to honor its part of the agreement, the forward contract is of no value. The risk that the other party might not live up to its part of the bargain is known as *counterparty risk*. Counterparty risk is very real. Many companies require counterparties to back up their agreement with cash collateral or other acceptable forms of guarantees (e.g., a bank letter of credit). As a result, there is a hidden risk in companies' use of derivatives that is difficult to quantify.

Analysis of Derivatives

The footnote disclosures relating to financial derivatives provide details about the amounts and types of derivatives used by the company and the purposes for which they are used. Tables report:

- Notional (contact) amounts of derivatives in force.
- Fair values.
- Balance sheet location of where these derivative assets and liabilities are reported.

Companies also typically disclose that they do not use derivatives for speculative purposes. The implication is that there is some asset or liability or anticipated transaction offsetting the effect of the derivative so that the gains or losses are not one-sided.

One of the key analysis questions relates to the impact of derivatives on profitability and cash flow.

- For **fair value hedges**, as the fair value of the hedged item (asset or liability) changes, so does the fair value of the hedge (derivative security). Both changes are included in current earnings and their offsetting effects leaving net income relatively unaffected. So, the effect of fair value hedges on reported profit is usually not significant.
- For **cash flow hedges**, it is different. Hedges are purchased in advance of an anticipated or forecasted transaction, sometimes with a long lead time. The forecasted amount and timing of the transaction might not perfectly coincide with the actual transaction. As a result, the gain or loss on the derivative may not match the amount of the loss or gain on the transaction, leaving net income exposed to volatility—albeit

by less volatility than if the forecasted transaction had not been hedged. The most significant disclosure relates to the dollar amount of deferred gain or loss that is transferred into current earnings from AOCI during the year. This is the amount by which current profit has been affected by the company's use of derivatives to hedge market risk.

Although footnote disclosures (which are extensive) provide information about the magnitude of the company's use of derivatives to mitigate risk and the impact on current earnings of the reclassification of deferred gains and losses on cash flow hedged, they do not provide us with a clear picture of the degree of risk the company faces or the extent to which that risk has been mitigated. That has been an ongoing objection to the derivative disclosures and, in 2013 the **CFA Institute**, a global association of investment professionals, published a report titled "User Perspectives on Financial Instrument Risk Disclosures Under International Financial Reporting Standards Derivatives and Hedging Activities Disclosures (Volume 2)" that compiled feedback from investment managers relating to the quality of derivatives disclosures. The study focused on disclosures mandated by IFRS, but the findings are relevant for U.S. GAAP as well in that the derivative accounting standards are similar under both standards.

The 2013 CFA Institute study reported low user satisfaction with the quality of derivative disclosures. The report summarized its finding as follows:

> Respondents indicated that hedge accounting and disclosure requirements are complex and confusing for users and they do not readily communicate key economic information (e.g. nature of hedging strategies, hedged versus unhedged exposures and hedge effectiveness). The highly complex and arcane nature of hedge accounting rules, along with the partial information regarding hedging activities addressed by hedge accounting disclosures, does not help users to discern the entirety of risk management practices of reporting companies. This explains the ratings of moderate importance of, and low satisfaction with, hedge accounting disclosures.

In sum, footnote disclosures relating to derivatives are very complex, often quite lengthy, and difficult to decipher. While we do obtain some important information about how changes in derivatives' fair values affect reported profit, on balance, the disclosures do not inform us about the company's overall risk exposure and the degree to which management has hedged the company's exposure.

Review 9-4 LO4

PepsiCo Inc. reports the following table in its footnote relating to derivatives.

Losses/(gains) on our hedging instruments are categorized as follows:

	Fair Value/Non-designated Hedges		Cash Flow and Net Investment Hedges			
	Losses/(Gains) Recognized in Income Statement[a]		Losses/(Gains) Recognized in Accumulated Other Comprehensive Loss		Losses/(Gains) Reclassified from Accumulated Other Comprehensive Loss into Income Statement[b]	
	2018	2017	2018	2017	2018	2017
Foreign exchange...	$ 9	$(15)	$(52)	$ 62	$ (8)	$ 10
Interest rate	53	101	110	(195)	119	(184)
Commodity	117	(48)	3	3	—	3
Net investment	—	—	(77)	157	—	—
Total	$179	$ 38	$(16)	$ 27	$111	$(171)

[a] Foreign exchange derivative losses/gains are primarily included in selling, general, and administrative expenses. Interest rate derivative losses/gains are primarily from fair value hedges and are included in interest expense. These losses/gains are substantially offset by decreases/increases in the value of the underlying debt, which are also included in interest expense. Commodity derivative losses/gains are included in either cost of sales or selling, general and administrative expenses, depending on the underlying commodity.

[b] Foreign exchange derivative losses/gains are primarily included in cost of sales. Interest rate derivative losses/gains are included in interest expense. Commodity derivative losses/gains are included in either cost of sales or selling, general and administrative expenses, depending on the underlying commodity.

Required
1. What types of risks did PepsiCo hedge with its derivatives in 2018?
2. Did PepsiCo classify these derivatives as fair or cash flow hedges? How do we know?
3. What types of commodities might PepsiCo hedge? What income statement account would include gains and losses on these commodity hedges?

Solution on p. 9-56.

Appendix 9B: Equity Carve-Outs

Companies divest their subsidiaries, in whole or in part, for a variety of reasons, including the following.

- As strategies evolve, some businesses in the consolidated entity might no longer be consistent with the current strategy and divestment allows management to focus on "core" operating activities.
- Divestiture can help capture some of the value created by high-performing subsidiaries whose performance is obscured by highly aggregated consolidated financial statements and related disclosures.
- Divestitures may present an effective means to raise cash for expansion, to bolster liquidity, or to reduce debt.
- Regulatory authorities might insist a company divest of certain business lines to increase competition as a precondition for approval of an acquisition.

LO5 Explain equity carve-outs and their financial statement impact.

These divestitures, or **equity carve-outs**, take many forms including the following.

① **Sell-offs.** The parent company sells its shares of the subsidiary company to an unrelated party.
② **IPOs.** The subsidiary company sells unissued shares to the public making the event an initial public offering. The parent company's ownership will be diluted but control can be retained (or not). If the parent retains control, the larger subsidiary company has new noncontrolling shareholders.
③ **Spin-offs.** The parent company declares a dividend, and instead of using cash, distributes all of the shares in the subsidiary company. The former subsidiary can have new leadership, free of the former parent company, and the subsidiary's shares can be publicly traded on an organized exchange.
④ **Split-offs.** The parent company repurchases its own shares. But rather than using cash for the buyback, the parent uses shares of the subsidiary company. As with a spin-off, the former subsidiary can be publicly traded. The chief difference between a spin-off and a split-off is the voluntary nature of a split-off; each shareholder decides whether or not to exchange their shares.

We illustrate the accounting for each of these transactions in Exhibit 9B.1.

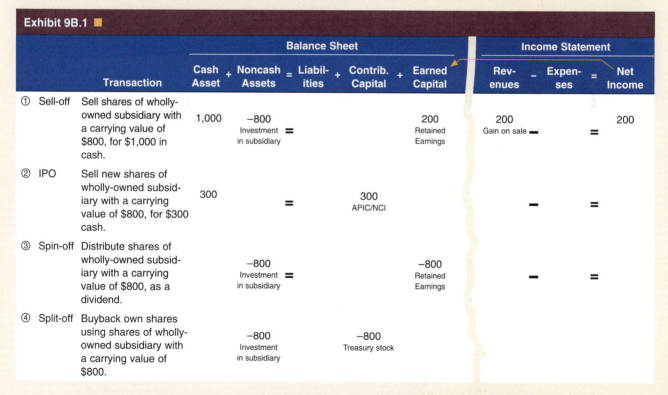

Exhibit 9B.1

① **Sell-offs.** The simplest form of divestiture is a sell-off, the outright sale of a business unit. In this case, the company sells its equity interest to an unrelated party. The sale is accounted for just like the sale of any other asset. Specifically, any excess (deficit) of cash received over the book value of the business unit sold is recorded as a gain (loss) on the sale. To illustrate, in 2018, **International Paper Company** sold its **North American Consumer Packaging** business as disclosed in the following 10-K excerpt ($ millions).

> On January 1, 2018, the Company completed the transfer of its North American Consumer Packaging business. . . to Graphic Packaging International Partners, LLC. International Paper is accounting for its ownership interest in the combined business under the equity method. The Company determined the fair value of its investment in the combined business to be $1.1 billion and recorded a pre-tax gain of $488 million ($364 million, net of tax) in 2018. The fair value was calculated using a market approach using inputs classified as Level 2 and Level 3 within the fair value hierarchy.

The financial statement effects of this transaction follow.
- International Paper received consideration of $1.1 billion.
- International Paper reported a gain on sale of $488 million, implying that the carrying value of the investment in the North American Consumer Packaging business was $612 million ($1.1 billion − $488 million).
- On the statement of cash flows, International Paper subtracts the $488 million noncash gain on sale to reconcile net income and cash from operating activities. The $1.1 billion cash proceeds are reported as a cash inflow in the investing section.

Because selling off the North American Consumer Packaging business represented a strategic business shift having a major effect on International Paper's operations and financial results, the company reported the North American Consumer Packaging business as a discontinued operation.

② **IPOs.** An initial public offering (IPO) by a subsidiary involves the sale of previously unissued shares to the public. To record the stock sale, the subsidiary increases both cash and paid-in capital as we discuss in Module 8 (see *Stock issuance*). The parent company reports the subsidiary as an equity-method investment on its balance sheet as we discuss earlier in this module. To reflect the change in percentage ownership of the subsidiary, the parent adjusts the carrying value of the equity-method investment and balances the transaction by adjusting its own additional paid-in capital. At consolidation, the parent reports a new noncontrolling interest to reflect the IPO shares. We illustrate these steps with the following example.
- Assume a wholly-owned subsidiary has a book value of stockholders' equity of $800,000, with 800,000 shares outstanding.
- The parent's balance sheet reports the subsidiary as an equity-method investment of $800,000 (that is, the parent acquired the subsidiary at book value).
- The subsidiary sells 200,000 no-par shares to unrelated parties for $300,000, bringing the outstanding shares increase to 1,000,000. The parent's ownership interest falls to 80%.
- The subsidiary's stockholders' equity increases to $1,100,000 ($800,000 before the stock issuance + $300,000 proceeds from the stock issuance). The parent now owns an 80% interest in a subsidiary that has stockholders' equity of $1,100,000.
- The parent makes the following accounting adjustments:
  - Increases the equity-method investment by $80,000 ($1,100,000 × 80% − $800,000) bringing the carrying value to $880,000.
  - Increases APIC by $80,000.
- In the consolidation process, the parent eliminates the equity-method investment together with the stockholders' equity of the subsidiary. The parent records noncontrolling interest of $220,000 ($1,100,000 × 20%).

Each of these steps is illustrated in the following table (in thousands).

	Transaction	Cash Asset	+	Noncash Assets	=	Liabilities	+	Contrib. Capital	+	Earned Capital	Revenues	−	Expenses	=	Net Income
② IPO	Step 1: subsidiary records the sale of stock	+300			=			+300 APIC				−		=	
	Step 2: parent increases equity investment to recognize the stock sale by the subsidiary			+80 Equity investment	=			+80 APIC				−		=	

continued

Transaction		Balance Sheet					Income Statement		
		Cash Asset +	Noncash Assets =	Liabil- ities +	Contrib. Capital +	Earned Capital	Rev- enues −	Expen- ses =	Net Income
② IPO	Step 3: consolidation elimination entries		−880 Equity investment =		−1,100 Subsidiary's equity +220 Noncontrolling interest			− 	=
	Net effect of steps 1–3	+300			+80 − APIC +220 Noncontrolling interest				

③ **Spin-offs.** In a spin-off, the parent company distributes to its stockholders the shares of the subsidiary company as a dividend, giving its stockholders direct ownership of the subsidiary rather than through the parent company. In recording this dividend, the parent company reduces retained earnings by the book value of the equity method investment, thereby removing the investment in the subsidiary from the parent's balance sheet. The accounting is similar to a cash dividend in that retained earnings is reduced by the dollar amount of the dividend. The difference is that the dividend is paid in shares of stock (a property dividend) rather than in cash.

Netgear Inc. combined an IPO of its subsidiary with a subsequent spin-off of that subsidiary.

On February 6, 2018, the Company announced that its Board of Directors had unanimously approved the pursuit of a separation of its smart camera business "Arlo" from NETGEAR (the "Separation") to be effected by way of initial public offering ("IPO") and spin-off. On August 2, 2018, Arlo and NETGEAR announced the pricing of Arlo's IPO and subsequently listed on the New York Stock Exchange on August 3, 2018 under the symbol "ARLO". On August 7, 2018, we completed the IPO of 11,747,250 shares of common stock . . . (and) the Company held 62,500,000 shares of Arlo common stock, representing approximately 84.2% of the outstanding shares. On December 31, 2018, the Company completed the distribution of these 62,500,000 shares to its stockholders (the "Distribution") and no longer owns any shares of Arlo common stock. Upon completion of the Distribution, the Company ceased to own a controlling financial interest in Arlo and Arlo's historical financial results for periods presented are reflected in our consolidated financial statements as discontinued operations.

NETGEAR, INC.
CONSOLIDATED STATEMENTS OF STOCKHOLDERS' EQUITY

(In thousands)	Common Stock		Additional Paid-In Capital	Accumulated Other Comprehensive Income (Loss)	Retained Earnings (Losses)	Non- controlling Interest	Total
	Shares	Amount					
Balance as of December 31, 2017..........	31,320	$31	$603,137	$(851)	$128,168	$ —	$730,485
Adoption of ASU 2014-09 (ASC 606 Rev Rec), ASU2016-16, and ASU 2018-02, net of tax ...	—	—	—	—	8,593	—	8,593
Change in unrealized gains and losses on available-for-sale securities, net of tax	—	—	—	78	—	—	78
Change in unrealized gains and losses on derivatives, net of tax..................	—	—	—	758	—	—	758
Net loss attributable to NETGEAR, Inc.........	—	—	—	—	(9,162)	—	(9,162)
Net loss attributable to noncontrolling interest	—	—	—	—	—	(9,167)	(9,167)
Stock-based compensation expense..........	—	—	31,966	—	—	—	31,966
Stock-based compensation expense for Arlo's shares.........................	—	—	—	—	—	942	942
A Sale of Arlo's common stock	—	—	146,088	—	—	24,158	170,246
Repurchases of common stock	(473)	—	—	—	(30,000)	—	(30,000)
Restricted stock unit withholdings	(138)	—	—	—	(8,065)	—	(8,065)
Issuance of common stock under stock- based compensation plans................	853	1	12,394	—	—	—	12,395
B Distribution of Arlo	—	—	—	—	(255,584)	(15,933)	(271,517)
December 31, 2018.....................	31,562	$32	$793,585	$ (15)	$(166,050)	$ —	$627,552

To recap the transactions: Netgear owned 62,500,000 shares (100% ownership) of Arlo Technologies. In August 2018, Arlo sold 11,747,250 shares of stock to the public (on the NYSE) bringing the total shares outstanding to 74,247,250 and dropping Netgear's ownership to 84.2%. This transaction (highlighted and marked A, in the table above) shows the IPO increased APIC by $146,088 thousand and noncontrolling interest by $24,128 thousand. Then, on December 31, 2018, Netgear distributed all of its 62,500,000 shares of Arlo to Netgear shareholders. This "dividend" (highlighted and marked B, in the table above) decreases retained earnings by $255,584 thousand and decreases noncontrolling interest by $15,933 thousand.

Accounting Insight ■ Deconsolidation of a Subsidiary

When a subsidiary issues stock in an IPO, the parent's percentage of ownership decreases. In the examples in this section, the parent retains control over the subsidiary. However, an IPO could conceivably reduce the parent's ownership to the point at which it no longer controls the subsidiary. In that case, the parent must deconsolidate the subsidiary— the equity-method investment is increased (or decreased) to its fair value and a gain (or loss) on the revaluation is recognized in current earnings. Subsequently, the former parent company will account for the investment using the methods appropriate given the level of ownership and the marketability of the former subsidiary's stock (equity method, fair value, or non-marketable securities). **Nextera Energy Inc.** (NEE) deconsolidated one of its subsidiary companies (NEP) in 2018 as disclosed in this excerpt from its 10-K filing.

> NextEra Energy Partners, LP - NEP owns or has an interest in a portfolio of wind and solar projects and a portfolio of seven long-term contracted natural gas pipeline assets located in Texas. NEP was deconsolidated from NEE for financial reporting purposes in January 2018 . . . Subsequent to deconsolidation, NEE owns a noncontrolling interest in NEP and began reflecting its ownership interest in NEP as an equity method investment with its earnings from NEP as equity in earnings of equity method investees . . . In connection with the deconsolidation, NEE recorded an initial investment in NEP of approximately $4.4 billion based on the fair value of NEP common units. The fair value was based on the market price of NEP common units as of January 1, 2018, which ==resulted in NEE recording a gain of approximately $3.9 billion ($3.0 billion after tax) for the year ended December 31, 2018==. Total assets of approximately $7.8 billion, primarily property, plant and equipment, total liabilities of approximately $4.8 billion, primarily long-term debt, and total noncontrolling interests of approximately $2.7 billion were removed from NEE's balance sheet as part of the deconsolidation. [emphasis added]

Once Nextera no longer controlled NEP, it deconsolidated the subsidiary. On its balance sheet, Nextera increased the fair value of NEE to $4.4 billion and recognized a gain of $3.9 billion, which represented more than half of Nextera's 2018 pre-tax profit of $7.4 billion.

---

④ **Split-offs.** The split-off is a fourth form of equity carve-out, where the parent company buys back its own stock using the shares of the subsidiary company instead of cash. After completing this transaction, the subsidiary is an independent, publicly traded company. The parent treats the split-off like any other purchase of treasury stock. As such, the parent increases its treasury stock account and decreases the equity method investment account, reflecting the distribution of that asset. **CBS Corporation** provides an example in this excerpt from its 2018 10-K.

> On November 16, 2017, the Company completed the split-off of CBS Radio through an exchange offer, in which the Company accepted 17.9 million shares of CBS Corp Class B Common Stock from its stockholders in exchange for the 101.4 million shares of CBS Radio common stock that it owned... CBS Radio has been presented as a discontinued operation in the consolidated financial statements for all periods presented.

CBS CORPORATION AND SUBSIDIARIES
CONSOLIDATED STATEMENTS OF STOCKHOLDERS' EQUITY

Year Ended December 31 (In millions)	2018 Shares	2018 Amount	2017 Shares	2017 Amount	2016 Shares	2016 Amount
Treasury Stock, at cost:						
Balance beginning of year	489	(22,258)	455	(20,201)	401	(17,205)
Class B Common Stock purchased	11	(600)	16	(1,050)	54	(2,997)
CBS Radio Split-Off	—	—	18	(1,007)	—	—
Shares paid for tax withholding for stock-based compensation . . .	1	(59)	1	(89)	1	(58)
Issuance of stock for deferred compensation.	—	—	—	—	—	1
Retirement of treasury stock.	(1)	59	(1)	89	(1)	58
Balance, end of year.	500	(22,858)	489	(22,258)	455	(20,201)

continued from previous page

As the highlighted transaction in the table above shows, CBS Corp recorded a treasury stock transaction where shares of stock were distributed rather than cash. The treasury stock account decreased by $1,007 million as did the carrying value of CBS Corp's equity method investment in CBS Radio.

Analysis of Equity Carve-Outs

We see that the only type of equity carve-out that affects the income statement is a sell-off, which is the outright sale of the subsidiary. After an equity carve-out, the consolidated entity will no longer report the profits and cash flow (positive or negative) of the divested business unit. As such, the divestiture should be treated like any other nonoperating transaction as the consolidated entity will no longer include the operations of the divested subsidiary. And, although many equity carve-out transactions relate to discontinued operations, they may not be reported as such because the rules for reporting discontinued operations require a strategic change for the company and a significant financial effect. Footnotes will reveal the details of the transaction and whether it is reported as a discontinued operation or comingled with other operating activities.

Business Insight ■ Bloomberg U.S. Spin-Off Index

Equity carve-outs can unlock significant value for shareholders. When no longer operated as a subsidiary of a large conglomerate, a company can often be more nimble and responsive to a fast-changing business environment. In short, the operations are worth more as a standalone than as a subsidiary. A number of studies show that equity carve-outs historically have generated far better returns than the overall stock market. The Bloomberg U.S. Spin-Off Index tracks the stock price performance of companies spun off from larger companies within the past three years. In 2018, the index included 35 equities each with a value over $1 billion and the index as a whole outperformed the broader market by nine percentage points.

Guidance Answers

You Are the Chief Financial Officer

Pg. 9-17 Capacity utilization is important. If long-term operating assets are used inefficiently, cost per unit produced is too high. Cost per unit does not relate solely to manufacturing products. It also applies to the cost of providing services and many other operating activities. However, if we purchase assets with little productive slack, our costs of production at peak levels can be excessive. Further, the company may be unable to service peak demand and risks losing customers. In response, the company might explore strategic alliances. These take many forms. Some require a simple contract to use another company's manufacturing, service, or administrative capability for a fee (*Note:* These executory contracts are not recorded under GAAP). Another type of alliance is a joint venture to share ownership of manufacturing or IT facilities. In this case, if demand can be coordinated with that of a partner, perhaps operating assets can be more effectively used. As chief financial officer, what thoughts do you have?

Superscript [A(B)] denotes assignments based on Appendix 9A(9B).

Questions

Q9-1. What is a passive investment? Why do companies have passive investments?

Q9-2. What is an unrealized gain (loss)? Explain.

Q9-3. Where are unrealized gains and losses related to marketable equity securities reported in the financial statements?

Q9-4. What does significant influence imply regarding intercorporate investments? Describe the accounting procedures used for such investments.

Q9-5. On January 1 of the current year, Tse Company purchases 30% of the common stock of Green Company for $1,300,000 cash. This ownership allows Tse to exert significant influence over Green. During the year, Green reports $220,000 of net income and pays $42,000 in cash dividends. At year-end, what amount should appear in Tse's balance sheet for its investment in Green?

Q9-6. What accounting method is used when a stock investment represents more than 50% of the investee company's voting stock and allows the investor company to "control" the investee company? Explain.

Q9-7. What is the underlying objective of consolidated financial statements?

Q9-8.ᴬ What is a derivative? How do companies use them to hedge risk?

Q9-9.ᴬ For accounting purposes, what are the two types of hedges? How are unrealized derivative gains and losses treated under each accounting method?

Q9-10. What are some limitations of consolidated financial statements?

Q9-11. How does a weakening $US affect the consolidated balance sheet of a company with foreign subsidiaries?

Q9-12.ᴮ What is the difference between a spin-off and a split-off?

Assignments with the logo in the margin are available in *BusinessCourse*.
See the Preface of the book for details.

Mini Exercises

LO1 M9-13. Accounting for Marketable Equity Securities

Assume that Bava Company purchases 23,000 common shares of Jones Company for $12 cash per share. During the year, Bava receives a cash dividend of $1.30 per common share from Jones, and the year-end market price of Jones common stock is $13 per share. How much income does Bava report relating to this investment for the year?

LO1 M9-14. Interpreting Disclosures of Investment Securities

Amgen Inc. (AMGN)

Amgen Inc. reports the following disclosure relating to its accumulated other comprehensive income.

$ millions	Foreign Currency Translation	Cash Flow Hedges	Available-for-Sale Securities	Other	AOCI
Balance as of December 31, 2017	$(529)	$(6)	$ (144)	$—	$(679)
Cumulative effect of change in accounting principle, net of tax	—	—	(9)	—	(9)
Foreign currency translation adjustments.	(141)	—	—	—	(141)
Unrealized (losses) gains	—	61	(556)	—	(495)
Reclassification adjustments to income	—	262	365	—	627
Other.	—	—	—	(2)	(2)
Income taxes	—	(76)	6	—	(70)
Balance as of December 31, 2018	$(670)	$241	$(338)	$ (2)	$(769)

a. Amgen reports unrealized gains and losses on available-for-sale securities as part of AOCI. Which of the following types of investments could be included in this account? Select all that apply.
   i. Bonds issued by US corporations.
   ii. Common stock traded on US stock exchange.
   iii. Common stock traded on foreign stock exchange.
   iv. Debt securities issued by a foreign government.
   v. Municipal bonds.
   vi. U.S. Treasury bills.

b. Consider the securities held in the available-for-sale portfolio at December 31, 2018. Which of the following is true?
   i. At December 31, 2018, the fair value of the securities was $338 million less than their amortized cost.
   ii. At December 31, 2018, the fair value of the securities was $338 million greater than their amortized cost.
   iii. At December 31, 2018, the fair value of the securities was $338 million lower than their value at December 31, 2017.

iv. At December 31, 2018, the fair value of the securities was $194 million lower than their value at December 31, 2017.

c. Consider the securities held in the available-for-sale portfolio at December 31, 2018. During the year, by how much did the market value of those securities increase or decrease?
   i. Decreased by $338 million.
   ii. Decreased by $556 million.
   iii. Increased by $556 million.
   iv. Decreased by $191 million.

d. Amgen increased AOCI by $365 million for reclassification adjustments to income. Which of the following best describes what this line item means.
   i. During 2018, Amgen sold available-for-sale securities and realized a loss of $365 million.
   ii. During 2018, Amgen sold available-for-sale securities and realized a gain of $365 million.
   iii. During 2018, Amgen sold available-for-sale securities that had unrealized gains of $365 million at December 31, 2017.
   iv. During 2018, Amgen sold available-for-sale securities that had unrealized losses of $365 million at December 31, 2017.

M9-15. Analyzing Derivatives and Hedging

Refer to the information for **Amgen** in M9-14. This information reports activity related to Amgen's cash flow hedges.

a. Explain how this type of hedging works. Provide an example of how Amgen might use this type of hedging strategy.
b. How did the hedges affect net income for 2018?
c. If these same hedges had instead been fair value hedges, what amount would have been added to AOCI for the year?

M9-16. Analyzing Derivatives and Hedging

For each of the following, indicate whether the hedge would be classified as a fair value hedge or a cash flow hedge.

a. **Morningstar** locks in a price on a forward contract to buy soybeans over the next 12 months.
b. **General Motors** enters into a foreign currency futures contract on Canadian dollars to hedge its C$200 million bond issuance.
c. **American Airlines** takes delivery of 10 new Airbus jets. The contract was denominated in euros instead of $US. American Airlines will settle the accounts payable in six months. To hedge its exposure, American Airlines buys € denominated futures contracts.
d. **Apple Inc.** has foreign currency options to buy Chinese Yuan to hedge payments to FoxConn, the Chinese company that manufactures Apple products.
e. **Poole Construction** signs a contract to build a soccer stadium in Mexico. The contract is denominated in Mexican pesos. Poole buys foreign currency options to sell Mexican pesos.

M9-17. Analyzing and Interpreting Equity Method Investments

Concord Company purchases an investment in Bloomingdale Company at a purchase price of $2 million cash, representing 30% of the book value of Bloomingdale. During the year, Bloomingdale reports net income of $300,000 and pays cash dividends of $90,000. At the end of the year, the fair value of Concord's investment is $2.4 million.

a. What amount does Concord report on its balance sheet for its investment in Bloomingdale at year-end?
b. What amount of income from investments does Concord report for the year? Explain.
c. The fair value of Bloomingdale increased during the year creating an unrealized gain for Concord. This unrealized gain in the fair value of the Bloomingdale investment (choose one and explain):
   (1) Is not reflected on either its income statement or balance sheet.
   (2) Is reported in its current income.
   (3) Is reported on its balance sheet only.
   (4) Is reported in its accumulated other comprehensive income.

M9-18. Computing Income for Equity Method Investments

Kross Company purchases an equity investment in Penno Company at a purchase price of $2.5 million, representing 40% of the book value of Penno. During the current year, Penno reports net income of $300,000 and pays cash dividends of $100,000. At the end of the year, the fair value of Kross's investment is $2.65 million. What amount of income does Kross report relating to this investment in Penno for the year? Explain.

LO1 **M9-19. Marketable Debt Securities**

Facebook Inc (FACE)

Facebook reports the following in its 2018 10-K.

The following table summarizes, for assets or liabilities measured at fair value, the respective fair value and the classification by level of input within the fair value hierarchy (in millions):

Description	December 31, 2018	Quoted Prices in Active Markets for Identical Assets (Level 1)	Significant Other Observable Inputs (Level 2)	Significant Unobservable Inputs (Level 3)
Cash equivalents:				
Money market funds	$ 6,792	$ 6,792	$ —	$—
U.S. government securities	90	90	—	—
U.S. government agency securities	54	54	—	—
Certificate of deposits and time deposits	369	—	369	—
Corporate debt securities	1	—	1	—
Marketable securities:				
U.S. government securities	13,836	13,836	—	—
U.S. government agency securities	8,333	8,333	—	—
Corporate debt securities	8,926	—	8,926	—
Total cash equivalents and marketable securities	$38,401	$29,105	$9,296	$—

The gross unrealized losses on our marketable securities were $357 million and $289 million as of December 31, 2018 and 2017, respectively. The gross unrealized gains for both periods were not significant.

a. What does Facebook report as Cash equivalents at December 31, 2018? As Marketable securities?
b. What is the chief difference between Cash equivalents and Marketable securities?
c. What is the cost of its marketable securities? *Hint:* Consider that its marketable securities are in a loss position.

LO2 **M9-20. Interpreting Disclosures on Investments in Affiliates**

Pfizer, Inc. (PFE)

Pfizer's 10-K report includes the following footnote disclosure.

On December 19, 2018, we announced that we entered into a definitive agreement with GSK under which we . . . will combine our respective consumer healthcare businesses into a new consumer healthcare joint venture that will operate globally under the GSK Consumer Healthcare name. In exchange for contributing our Consumer Healthcare business, we will receive a 32% equity stake in the company and GSK will own the remaining 68%.

a. How will Pfizer account for its 32% equity stake in GSK Consumer Healthcare?
b. If the joint venture distributes cash of $350 million in 2019 what will be the effect on Pfizer's 2019 balance sheet and income statement?
c. Assume that the joint venture generated profit of $1,400 million in 2019. How will this affect Pfizer's 2019 income statement?

LO3 **M9-21. Computing Consolidating Adjustments and Noncontrolling Interest**

Patterson Company purchases 80% of Kensington Company's common stock for $400,000 cash when Kensington Company has $200,000 of common stock and $300,000 of retained earnings. If a consolidated balance sheet is prepared immediately after the acquisition, what amounts are eliminated when preparing that statement? What amount of noncontrolling interest appears in the consolidated balance sheet?

LO3 **M9-22. Computing Consolidated Net Income**

Bedford Company purchased a 90% interest in Midway Company on January 1 of the current year, and the purchase price reflected 90% of Midway's book value of equity. Bedford Company had $400,000 net income for the current year *before* recognizing its share of Midway Company's net income. If Midway Company had net income of $90,000 for the year, what is the consolidated net income attributable to Bedford shareholders for the year?

M9-23. **Assigning Purchase Price in Acquisitions** **LO3**
Jasper Company acquired 80% of Fey Company at the beginning of the current year. Jasper paid $150,000 more than the book value of Fey's stockholders' equity and determined that this excess purchase price related to intangible assets. How does the $150,000 appear on the consolidated Jasper Company balance sheet if the intangible assets acquired related to (*a*) patents or, alternatively, (*b*) goodwill? How would each scenario affect the consolidated income statement?

M9-24. **Interpreting a Divestiture Disclosure** **LO5**
In early 2018, Jack in the Box completed its divestiture of wholly-owned subsidiary Qdoba, to private investors for $305 million. CNBC.com reported the following statement attributed to Lenny Comma, CEO and chairman of Jack in the Box.

Jack in the Box (JACK)

> For the past several months, we have worked closely with our financial advisors and evaluated various strategic alternatives with respect to Qdoba, including a sale or spin-off, as well as opportunities to refranchise company restaurants. Following the completion of this robust process, our Board of Directors has determined that the sale of Qdoba is the best alternative for enhancing shareholder value and is consistent with the Company's desire to transition to a less capital-intensive business model."

a. From the facts provided, what sort of equity carve-out does this seem to be?
b. Explain how the deal could "enhance value" for Jack in the Box shareholders.
c. What effects will the Qdoba carve-out have on Jack in the Box's balance sheet and income statement.

M9-25. **Interpreting a Proposed Split-Off Disclosure** **LO5**
On October 19, 2015, the following was reported in an article at StreetInsider.com.

General Electric (GE)

> General Electric commenced an offer to exchange GE common stock for common stock of Synchrony Financial presently owned by GE. This exchange offer is in connection with the previously announced separation of Synchrony, the largest provider of private label credit cards in the United States, from GE. The exchange offer is expected to conclude the week of November 16, 2015. The exchange offer is designed to provide GE shareholders an opportunity to exchange their shares of GE common stock for shares of Synchrony common stock at a 7% discount, subject to an upper limit of 1.1308 shares of Synchrony common stock per share of GE common stock.

a. This transaction is a split-off. How do we know?
b. How will the proposed split-off affect the number of GE shares outstanding?
c. Given the details revealed in the news article, does the split-off appear to be pro-rata or non pro-rata?

M9-26. **Interpreting Disclosure Related to IPO Carve-Out** **LO5**
The Gap reports the following in its Form 8-K dated February 28, 2019.

Gap Inc. (GPS)

> GAP Inc. today announced plans to create two independent publicly traded companies: Old Navy, a category-leader in family apparel, and a yet-to-be-named company ("NewCo"), which will consist of the iconic Gap brand, Athleta, Banana Republic, Intermix and Hill City. Gap Inc. expects to effect the separation through a spin-off that is intended to generally be tax-free to Gap Inc.'s shareholders for U.S. federal income tax purposes. Upon separation, Gap Inc. shareholders are expected to receive a pro-rata stock distribution and as a result own shares in both NewCo and Old Navy in equal proportion. The transaction is currently targeted to be completed in 2020.

a. Describe the accounting for the spin-off component of this transaction.
b. What effects did this transaction have on The Gap balance sheet and income statement?

Exercises

LO1 E9-27. Assessing Financial Statement Effects of Marketable Equity Securities
Use the financial statement effects template to record the following four transactions involving investments in marketable equity securities.

a. Purchased 18,000 common shares of Baez Inc. for $12 cash per share.
b. Received a cash dividend of $1.20 per common share from Baez.
c. Year-end market price of Baez common stock was $11.25 per share.
d. Sold all 18,000 common shares of Baez for $213,600.

LO1 E9-28. Assessing Financial Statement Effects of Marketable Equity Securities
Use the financial statement effects template to record the accounts and amounts for the following four transactions involving investments in marketable equity securities.

a. Purchased 20,000 common shares of Heller Co. at $16 cash per share.
b. Received a cash dividend of $1.25 per common share from Heller.
c. Year-end market price of Heller common stock is $17.50 per share.
d. Sold all 20,000 common shares of Heller for $315,600 cash.

LO1 E9-29. Marketable Debt Securities
Use the financial statement effects template to record the accounts and amounts for the following four transactions involving investments in marketable debt securities classified as available-for-sale securities.

a. Purchased 5,000 bonds with a face value of $1,000 per bond. The bonds are purchased at par for cash and pay interest at an annual rate of 4%.
b. Received semi-annual cash interest of $100,000.
c. Year-end fair value of the bonds is $978 per bond.
d. Shortly after year-end, Loudder sold all 5,000 bonds for $970 per bond.

LO1, 3 E9-30. Interpreting Footnotes on Security Investments
Snapchat Inc. (SNAP)
Snapchat reports the following information in its 2018 10-K report.

The table below presents the changes in accumulated other comprehensive income (loss) ("AOCI") by component and the reclassifications out of AOCI:

$ thousands	Marketable Securities	Foreign Currency Translation	Total
Balance at December 31, 2017	$(1,078)	$15,235	$14,157
OCI before reclassifications	710	(11,720)	(11,010)
Amounts reclassified from AOCI	—	—	—
Net current period OCI	710	(11,720)	(11,010)
Balance at December 31, 2018	$ (368)	$ 3,515	$ 3,147

Footnotes report the following information on Snapchat's marketable debt securities.

$ thousands	Cost or Amortized Cost	Gross Unrealized Gains	Gross Unrealized Losses	Total Estimated Fair Value
Cash	$ 279,950	$ —	$ —	$ 279,950
Level 1 securities:				
U.S. government securities	735,988	12	(175)	735,825
U.S. government agency securities	181,032	4	(36)	181,000
Level 2 securities:				
Corporate debt securities	35,819	1	(18)	35,802
Commercial paper	33,193	—	—	33,193
Certificates of deposit	13,293	—	—	13,293
Total	$1,279,275	$17	$(229)	$1,279,063

a. Snapchat's AOCI account includes unrealized gains and losses from two sources. What are those sources?
b. Snapchat reported net loss for the year of $1,255,911 thousand. Determine comprehensive income for the year.
c. During 2018, did the currencies in the countries where Snapchat's subsidiaries were headquartered weaken or strengthen?
d. Snapchat uses Level 1 and Level 2 inputs to determine fair value for its marketable debt investments. Explain the difference between these two inputs.
e. Consider the Level 1 securities, which relate to investments in U.S. government debt securities. On average, has the market rate of interest for these securities increased or decreased since Snapchat bought these securities?

E9-31. Interpreting Footnote Disclosures for Investments
CNA Financial Corporation provides the following footnote to its 2018 10-K report.

LO1

CNA Financial Corporation (CNA)

> **Investments** The company classifies its fixed maturity securities as either available-for-sale or trading, and as such, they are carried at fair value. Changes in fair value of trading securities are reported within Net investment income on the Consolidated Statements of Operations. Changes in fair value related to available-for-sale securities are reported as a component of Other comprehensive income.

The following table provides a summary of fixed maturity and equity securities.

December 31, 2018 ($ millions)	Cost or Amortized Cost	Gross Unrealized Gains	Gross Unrealized Losses	Estimated Fair Value
Fixed maturity securities available-for-sale				
Corporate and other bonds....................	$18,764	$791	$395	$19,160
States, municipalities and political subdivisions.......	9,681	1,076	9	10,748
Asset-backed:				
Residential mortgage-backed....................	4,815	68	57	4,826
Commercial mortgage-backed....................	2,200	28	32	2,196
Other asset-backed............................	1,975	11	24	1,962
Total asset-backed.............................	8,990	107	113	8,984
U.S. Treasury and obligations of government sponsored enterprises.....	156	3	—	159
Foreign government...........................	480	5	4	481
Redeemable preferred stock....................	10	—	—	10
Total fixed maturity securities available-for-sale.........	38,081	1,982	521	39,542
Total fixed maturity securities trading.................	4	—	—	4
Total fixed maturity securities.....................	**$38,085**	**$1,982**	**$521**	**$39,546**

a. At what amount does CNA report its investment in marketable debt securities on its balance sheet? In your answer, identify the portfolio's fair value, cost, and any unrealized gains and losses.
b. Compute the net unrealized gain or loss on CNA's investment portfolio. How do CNA's balance sheet and income statement reflect this net unrealized gain or loss?
c. How do CNA's balance sheet and income statement reflect gains and losses realized from the sale of available-for-sale securities?

E9-32. Assessing Financial Statement Effects of Equity Method Securities
Use the financial statement effects template (with amounts and accounts) to record the following transactions involving investments in marketable securities accounted for using the equity method.

a. Purchased 12,000 common shares of Bakersfield Co. at $9 per share; the shares represent 30% ownership in Bakersfield.
b. Received a cash dividend of $1.25 per common share from Bakersfield.
c. Bakersfield reported annual net income of $60,000.
d. Sold all 12,000 common shares of Bakersfield for $114,500.

LO2

E9-33. Assessing Acquisition Announcement

Salesforce Inc. included the following note with its 10-Q dated July 31, 2019.

> **Subsequent event** On August 1, 2019, pursuant to an Agreement and Plan of Merger dated June 9, 2019, the Company acquired all of the outstanding capital stock of Tableau, which provides a self-service analytics platform that enables users to easily access, prepare, analyze, and present findings in their data. The preliminary acquisition date fair value of the consideration transferred for Tableau is estimated to be approximately $14.9 billion comprised of $14.6 billion in common stock issued, or approximately 96 million shares, and $0.3 billion related to the fair value of stock options and restricted stock awards assumed. The Company will include the financial results of Tableau in the condensed consolidated financial statements from the date of the acquisition on August 1, 2019.

a. How will the investment in Tableau appear on the Salesforce parent-only balance sheet?
b. In its SEC filings, how will Salesforce Inc. account for the investment in Tableau?
c. In its June 30, 2019, 10-Q report, Tableau reported net assets of just over $1 billion. What is an approximation of the intangible assets and goodwill that Salesforce will report on its consolidated balance sheet?

E9-34. Assessing Financial Statement Effects Investments

On January 1, 2018, Ball Corporation purchased shares of Leftwich Company common stock.

a. Assume that the stock acquired by Ball represents 15% of Leftwich's voting stock and that Ball has no influence over Leftwich's business decisions. Use the financial statement effects template (with amounts and accounts) to record the following transactions.
  1. Ball purchased 5,000 common shares of Leftwich at $15 cash per share.
  2. Leftwich reported annual net income of $40,000.
  3. Ball received a cash dividend of $1.10 per common share from Leftwich.
  4. Year-end market price of Leftwich common stock is $19 per share.

b. Assume that the stock acquired by Ball represents 30% of Leftwich's voting stock and that Ball accounts for this investment using the equity method because it is able to exert significant influence. Use the financial statement effects template (with amounts and accounts) to record the following transactions.
  1. Ball purchased 5,000 common shares of Leftwich at $15 cash per share.
  2. Leftwich reported annual net income of $40,000.
  3. Ball received a cash dividend of $1.10 per common share from Leftwich.
  4. Year-end market price of Leftwich common stock is $19 per share.

E9-35. Interpreting Equity Method Investment Footnotes

Ford Motor Company includes the following table in its 2018 Form 10-K. The table reports the ownership percentages and carrying value of equity method investments (in millions, except percentages).

Automotive Sector	Investment Balance 2017	Investment Balance 2018	Ownership Percentage December 31, 2018
Changan Ford Automobile Corporation, Limited	$1,144	$ 950	50.0%
Jiangling Motors Corporation, Limited	675	543	32.0
AutoAlliance (Thailand) Co., Ltd.	439	431	50.0
Ford Otomotiv Sanayi Anonim Sirketi	329	247	41.0
Getrag Ford Transmissions GmbH	222	236	50.0
FFS Finance South Africa (Pty) Limited	71	81	50.0
Changan Ford Mazda Engine Company, Ltd.	84	71	25.0
Ionity Holding GmbH & Co. KG	12	42	25.0
DealerDirect LLC	33	33	97.7
RouteOne LLC	24	31	30.0
Thirdware Solutions Limited	12	12	20.0
Percepta, LLC	8	10	45.0
Chongqing ANTE Trading Co., Ltd.	5	6	10.0
U.S. Council for Automotive Research LLC	5	6	33.3
Crash Avoidance Metrics Partnership LLC	3	4	50.0
Blue Diamond Parts, LLC	3	3	25.0
CNF-Administradora de Consorcio Nacional Ltda	6	3	33.3
Automotive Fuel Cell Cooperation Corporation	10	—	49.9
Total Automotive sector	$3,085	$2,709	

a. What does Ford report on its balance sheet at December 31, 2018, for its investment in equity method affiliates? Does this reflect the adjusted cost or fair value of Ford's interest in these companies?
b. Approximate the total stockholders' equity of the Changan Ford Mazda Engine Company at the end of 2018. Explain.
c. Ford owns 97.7% of DealerDirect LLC yet this investment was not consolidated. Speculate on why this might be the case.
d. Assume Getrag Ford Transmission GmbH paid no dividends in 2018. Determine Getrag's net income for the year.
e. Explain why Ford has so many equity-method investments.
f. Ford's 2018 income statement included income from equity method investments of $1,780 million. Approximate the dividends and distributions that Ford received from the equity method affiliates during 2018.

E9-36. Analyzing and Interpreting Disclosures on Equity Method Investments

LO2

Cummins Inc. (CMI)

Cummins Inc. reports investments in affiliated companies, consisting mainly of investments in six manufacturing joint ventures. Cummins provides the following financial information on its investee companies in a footnote to its 10-K report.

Equity Investee Financial Summary, $ millions	For years ended December 31		
	2018	2017	2016
Net sales	$7,352	$7,050	$5,654
Gross margin	1,373	1,422	1,182
Net income	647	680	499
Cummins' share of net income	$ 336	$ 308	$ 260
Royalty and interest income	58	49	41
Total equity, royalty and interest from investees	$ 394	$ 357	$ 301
Current assets	$3,401	$3,416	
Noncurrent assets	1,449	1,379	
Current liabilities	(2,669)	(2,567)	
Noncurrent liabilities	(218)	(237)	
Net assets	$1,963	$1,991	
Cummins' share of net assets	$1,144	$1,116	

a. What assets and liabilities of unconsolidated affiliates are omitted from Cummins' balance sheet as a result of the equity method of accounting for those investments?
b. Do the liabilities of the unconsolidated affiliates affect Cummins directly? Explain.
c. How does the equity method impact Cummins' ROE and its RNOA components (net operating asset turnover and net operating profit margin)?

E9-37. Interpreting Equity Method Investment Footnotes

LO2

AT&T reports the following footnote to its 2018 10-K report.

> **Equity Method Investments** Investments in partnerships, joint ventures and less than majority-owned subsidiaries in which we have significant influence are accounted for under the equity method . . . The following table is a reconciliation of our investments in equity affiliates as presented on our consolidated balance sheets.
>
> | $ millions | 2018 | 2017 |
> |---|---|---|
> | Beginning of year | $1,560 | $1,674 |
> | Additional investments | 237 | 51 |
> | Time Warner investments acquired | 4,912 | — |
> | Acquisition of remaining interest in Otter Media | (166) | — |
> | Equity in net income of affiliates | (48) | (128) |
> | Dividends and distributions received | (243) | (46) |
> | Sale of América Móvil shares | (14) | 22 |
> | Other adjustments | 7 | (13) |
> | End of year | $6,245 | $1,560 |
>
> Undistributed earnings from equity affiliates were $292 and $174 at December 31, 2018 and 2017, respectively.

a. At what amount is the equity investment in affiliates reported on AT&T's balance sheet?
b. Did affiliates pay dividends in 2018? How do you know?
c. How much income did AT&T report in 2018 relating to this investment in affiliates?
d. Interpret the AT&T statement that "undistributed earnings from equity affiliates were $292 and $174 at December 31, 2018 and 2017, respectively."
e. How does use of the equity method impact AT&T's ROE and its RNOA components (net operating asset turnover and net operating profit margin)?
f. AT&T accounts for its investment in affiliates under the equity method. Why?

LO3 E9-38. Constructing the Consolidated Balance Sheet at Acquisition

On January 1 of the current year, Liu Company purchased all of the common shares of Reed Company for $380,000 cash. Balance sheets of the two firms immediately after the acquisition follow.

	Liu Company	Reed Company	Consolidating Adjustments	Consolidated
Current assets	$ 950,000	$ 70,000		
Investment in Reed	380,000	—		
PPE, net	1,600,000	305,000		
Goodwill	—	—		
Total assets	$2,930,000	$375,000		
Liabilities	$ 450,000	$ 55,000		
Contributed capital	1,850,000	280,000		
Retained earnings	630,000	40,000		
Total liabilities and equity	$2,930,000	$375,000		

During purchase negotiations, Reed's PPE was appraised at $332,000, and all of its remaining assets and liabilities were appraised at values approximating their book values. Liu also concluded that an additional $33,000 (for goodwill) demanded by Reed's shareholders was warranted because Reed's earning power was better than the industry average. Prepare the consolidating adjustments and the consolidated balance sheet at acquisition.

LO3 E9-39. Constructing the Consolidated Balance Sheet at Acquisition

Winston Company purchased all of Marcus Company's common stock for $600,000 cash on January 1, at which time the separate balance sheets of the two corporations appeared as follows.

	Winston Company	Marcus Company	Consolidating Adjustments	Consolidated
Investment in Marcus	$ 600,000	$ —		
Other assets	2,300,000	700,000		
Goodwill	—	—		
Total assets	$2,900,000	$700,000		
Liabilities	$ 900,000	$160,000		
Contributed capital	1,400,000	300,000		
Retained earnings	600,000	240,000		
Total liabilities and equity	$2,900,000	$700,000		

During purchase negotiations, Winston determined the appraised value of Marcus's Other Assets was $720,000, and all of its remaining assets and liabilities were appraised at values approximating their book values. The balance of the purchase price was ascribed to goodwill. Prepare the consolidating adjustments and the consolidated balance sheet at acquisition.

LO5 E9-40. Assessing Financial Statement Effects from a Subsidiary Stock Issuance

Sykora Company owns 80% of Walton Company. Information reported by Sykora and Walton as of the current year-end follows.

Sykora Company
Shares owned of Walton	80,000
Book value of investment in Walton	$720,000

Walton Company
Shares outstanding	100,000
Book value of equity	$900,000
Book value per share	$9

Assume Walton issues 60,000 additional shares of previously authorized but unissued common stock solely to outside investors (none to Sykora) for $14 cash per share. Indicate the financial statement effects of this stock issuance on Sykora using the financial statement effects template.

E9-41. Estimating Goodwill Impairment

On January 1 of the current year, Engel Company purchases 100% of Ball Company for $8.4 million. At the time of acquisition, the fair value of Ball's tangible net assets (excluding goodwill) is $8.1 million. Engel ascribes the excess of $300,000 to goodwill. Assume the fair value of Ball declines to $6.25 million and the fair value of Ball's tangible net assets is estimated at $6.15 million as of December 31.

a. Determine if the goodwill has become impaired and, if so, the amount of the impairment.
b. What impact does the impairment of goodwill have on Engel's financial statements?

E9-42. Allocating Purchase Price

Capri Holdings, the parent company of Michael Kors and Jimmy Choo, reports the following footnote to its 10-K report dated March 31, 2019.

Capri Holdings (CPRI)

On December 31, 2018, the Company completed the acquisition of Versace for a total enterprise value of approximately €1.753 billion (or approximately $2.005 billion). The following table summarizes the preliminary purchase price allocation of fair values of the assets acquired and liabilities assumed at the date of acquisition (in millions).

	December 31, 2018
Cash and cash equivalents	$ 41
Accounts receivable	82
Inventory	197
Other current assets	39
Current assets	359
Property and equipment	89
Goodwill	878
Brand	948
Customer relationships	203
Favorable lease	16
Deferred tax assets	24
Other assets	135
Total assets acquired	$2,652
Accounts payable	$ 144
Short-term debt	57
Other current liabilities	99
Current liabilities	300
Deferred tax liabilities	289
Other liabilities	54
Total liabilities assumed	$ 643
Less: Noncontrolling interest in joint ventures	$ 4
Fair value of net assets acquired	$2,005
Fair value of acquisition consideration	$2,005

a. Of the total assets acquired, what portion is allocated to net intangible assets? What amount was allocated to tangible assets such as inventory and PPE?
b. Are Versace's assets and liabilities reported on the Capri Holdings consolidated balance sheet at the book value or at the fair value on the date of the acquisition? Explain.
c. How are each of the intangible assets accounted for subsequent to the acquisition?
d. Describe the accounting for goodwill. Why is an impairment test difficult to apply?

E9-43. Constructing the Consolidated Balance Sheet at Acquisition

Easton Company acquires 100 percent of the outstanding voting shares of Harris Company. To obtain these shares, Easton pays $420,000 in cash and issues 5,000 of its $10 par value common stock. On this date, Easton's stock has a fair value of $72 per share, and Harris's book value of stockholders' equity is $560,000. Easton is willing to pay $780,000 for a company with a book value of $560,000 because it believes that (1) Harris's buildings are undervalued by $80,000 and (2) Harris has an unrecorded patent that Easton values at $60,000. Easton considers the remaining balance sheet items to be fairly valued (no book-to-market difference). The remaining $80,000 of the purchase price is ascribed to corporate synergies and other general unidentifiable intangible assets (goodwill). The balance sheets at the acquisition date follow.

	Easton Company	Harris Company	Consolidating Adjustments	Consolidated
Cash....................	$ 168,000	$ 80,000		
Receivables	320,000	180,000		
Inventory................	440,000	260,000		
Investment in Harris	780,000	—		
Land	200,000	120,000		
Buildings, net	800,000	220,000		
Equipment, net...........	240,000	100,000		
Total assets	$2,948,000	$960,000		
Accounts payable.........	$ 320,000	$ 60,000		
Long-term liabilities.......	760,000	340,000		
Common stock	1,000,000	80,000		
Additional paid-in capital...	148,000	—		
Retained earnings	720,000	480,000		
Total liabilities & equity....	$2,948,000	$960,000		

a. Show the breakdown of the investment into the book value acquired, the excess of fair value over book value, and the portion of the investment representing goodwill.
b. Prepare the consolidating adjustments and the consolidated balance sheet on the date of acquisition.
c. How will the excess of the purchase price over book value acquired be treated in years subsequent to the acquisition?

LO3, 4
General Mills Inc. (GIS)

E9-44. Foreign Currency Translation Adjustment and Derivatives
General Mills reported the following statement of comprehensive income in its fiscal 2019 Form 10-K.

For 12 Months Ended ($ millions)	May 26, 2019	May 27, 2018	May 28, 2017
Net earnings, including earnings attributable to redeemable and noncontrolling interests	$1,786.2	$2,163.0	$1,701.1
Other comprehensive income (loss), net of tax:			
Foreign currency translation.......................	(82.8)	(37.0)	6.3
Net actuarial (loss) income.......................	(253.4)	140.1	197.9
Other fair value changes:			
Securities.....................................	—	1.2	0.8
Hedge derivatives	12.1	(50.8)	53.3
Reclassification to earnings:			
Securities.....................................	(2.0)	(5.1)	—
Hedge derivatives	0.9	17.4	(25.7)
Amortization of losses and prior service costs.........	84.6	117.6	122.5
Other comprehensive (loss) income, net of tax	(240.6)	183.4	355.1
Total comprehensive income	1,545.6	2,346.4	2,056.2
Comprehensive(loss) income attributable to redeemable and noncontrolling interests	(10.7)	70.5	31.0
Comprehensive income attributable to General Mills....	$1,556.3	$2,275.9	$2,025.2

Required
a. Comprehensive income for fiscal year ended May 26, 2019, includes a loss of $82.8 million related to foreign currency translation. Explain what this loss means.
b. On average, did the $US weaken or strengthen vis-à-vis the currencies of the companies' foreign subsidiaries?

c. What was the cash portion of the foreign currency translation loss in fiscal year 2019?
d. Comprehensive income for fiscal year ended May 26, 2019, includes a gain of $12.1 million related to hedge derivatives. Is this a fair value or a cash flow hedge?
e. Provide four examples of hedging transactions General Mills might engage in.
f. How did the cash flow hedges affect net income during the fiscal year ended May 26, 2019?

E9-45. Hedging and Use of Derivatives
Intel reports the following in its Form 10-K for fiscal 2018.

> We are exposed to currency exchange risks of non-U.S.-dollar-denominated investments in debt instruments and loans receivable, and may economically hedge this risk with foreign currency contracts, such as currency forward contracts or currency interest rate swaps. Gains or losses on these non-U.S.-currency investments are generally offset by corresponding losses or gains on the related hedging instruments. We are exposed to currency exchange risks from our non-U.S.-dollar-denominated debt indebtedness and may use foreign currency contracts designated as cash flow hedges to manage this risk.
>
> Substantially all of our revenue is transacted in U.S. dollars. However, a significant portion of our operating expenditures and capital purchases are incurred in other currencies, primarily the euro, the Japanese yen, the Israeli shekel, and the Chinese yuan. We have established currency risk management programs to protect against currency exchange rate risks associated with non-U.S. dollar forecasted future cash flows and existing non-U.S. dollar monetary assets and liabilities. We may also hedge currency risk arising from funding of foreign currency-denominated future investments. We may utilize foreign currency contracts, such as currency forwards or option contracts in these hedging programs.

Required
a. Consider the first paragraph in Intel's footnote. Explain whether this describes fair value or cash flow hedges.
b. Suppose, at year-end, there was an unrealized loss on Intel's currency forward contracts described in the first paragraph. How would Intel report the derivative on the balance sheet? How would the income statement be affected?
c. Consider the second paragraph in Intel's footnote. Explain whether this describes fair value or cash flow hedges.
d. Suppose, at year-end, there was an unrealized loss on Intel's currency forward contracts that hedge forecasted future cash flows as described in the second paragraph. How would Intel report the derivative on the balance sheet? How would the income statement be affected?
e. What is hedge ineffectiveness and how does it affect Intel's income statement?

E9-46. Hedging and Use of Derivatives
Ford Motor Company reports the following in its Form 10-K for fiscal 2018.

> Commodity price risk is the possibility that our financial results could be worse than planned because of changes in the prices of commodities used in the production of motor vehicles, such as base metals (e.g., steel, copper, and aluminum), precious metals (e.g., palladium), energy (e.g., natural gas and electricity), and plastics/resins (e.g., polypropylene). Accordingly, our normal practice is to use derivative instruments, when available, to hedge the price risk with respect to forecasted purchases of certain commodities that we can economically hedge (primarily base metals and precious metals). In our hedging actions, we use derivative instruments commonly used by corporations to reduce commodity price risk (e.g., financially settled forward contracts).

Ford's statement of comprehensive income for 2018 follows.

$ millions	2016	2017	2018
Net income	$4,600	$7,757	$3,695
Other comprehensive income (loss), net of tax			
Foreign currency translation	(1,024)	314	(523)
Marketable securities	(8)	(34)	(11)
Derivative instruments	219	(265)	183
Pension and other postretirement benefits	56	37	(56)
Total other comprehensive income (loss), net of tax	(757)	52	(407)
Comprehensive income	3,843	7,809	3,288
Less: Comprehensive income (loss) attributable to noncontrolling interests	10	24	18
Comprehensive income attributable to Ford Motor Company	$3,833	$7,785	$3,270

Required

a. What sort of risks does Ford hedge?
b. Ford describes its hedging strategy. What sort of hedges are these, cash flow or fair value? Explain.
c. The statement of comprehensive income discloses a line item labeled "Derivative instruments." What does this line item represent?
d. The comprehensive income (loss) from derivatives instruments is $219 million for 2016, $(265) million for 2017, and $183 million for 2018. What can we conclude about the fair value of the derivatives for each of these years?

E9-47. Interpreting Graphical Data to Assess Investments
The graphics below include data for all S&P 500 information-technology companies with positive equity for 2008 to 2018. Access the dashboard at the **myBusinessCourse** website to answer the requirements.

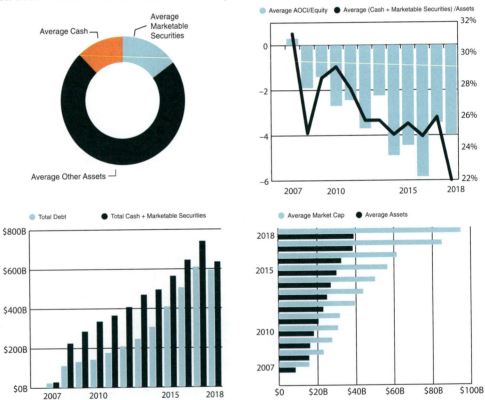

Required

a. Consider the pie chart. Explain what the graph depicts. What is included in the black portion of the graphic? In what year is the proportion of Cash the smallest? *Hint*: Interact with data in the dashboard to answer this question.
b. The bar-line graphic (top right panel) reports the average AOCI as a proportion of equity, by year. What do we observe about the magnitude of AOCI across the 11 years? Does the average firm have

unrealized gains or losses? What does the line in this graphic measure? Does it reveal any deeper understanding about the magnitude of AOCI?

c. Consider the vertical bar chart that depicts total debt and total liquid assets (the aggregate for all the companies in the data set) (bottom left panel). In what year was the total debt outstanding at its peak? What amount of debt was outstanding?

d. Consider the vertical bar chart (bottom left panel) and compare the aggregate total debt and total liquid assets. Interpret the trend. What two or three conclusions can we make from this graphic? Does the relation between the two measures hold true for all firms in the dataset?

e. The horizontal bar graph (bottom right panel) plots total assets and market cap over time. What trend do we observe over time? What is the relation between the two metrics over time? Provide two or three explanations for what we observe.

Problems

P9-48. Analyzing and Interpreting Disclosures on Equity Method Investments

LO2
General Mills Inc. (GIS)

General Mills Inc. invests in a number of joint ventures to manufacture and distribute its food products, as discussed in the following footnote to its 10-K report for the fiscal year ended May 26, 2019.

INVESTMENTS IN UNCONSOLIDATED JOINT VENTURES

We have a 50 percent equity interest in Cereal Partners Worldwide (CPW), which manufactures and markets ready-to-eat cereal products in more than 130 countries outside the United States and Canada. CPW also markets cereal bars in several European countries and manufactures private label cereals for customers in the United Kingdom. We have guaranteed a portion of CPW's debt and its pension obligation in the United Kingdom.

We also have a 50 percent equity interest in Häagen-Dazs Japan, Inc. (HDJ). This joint venture manufactures and markets Häagen-Dazs ice cream products and frozen novelties.

Results from our CPW and HDJ joint ventures are reported for the 12 months ended March 31. Joint venture related balance sheet activity follows:

$ millions	May 26, 2019	May 27, 2018
Cumulative investments	$452.9	$499.6
Goodwill and other intangibles	472.1	488.7
Aggregate advances included in cumulative investments	249.0	295.3

Joint venture earnings and cash flow activity follows:

Fiscal Year ($ millions)	2019	2018	2017
Sales to joint ventures	$ 4.2	$ 7.4	$ 7.0
Net advances (repayments)	(0.1)	17.3	(3.3)
Dividends received	86.7	113.2	75.6

Summary combined financial information for the joint ventures on a 100 percent basis follows:

Fiscal Year ($ millions)	2019	2018	2017
Net sales			
CPW	$1,674.7	$1,734.0	$1.648.4
HDJ	396.2	430.4	435.1
Total net sales	2,043.9	2,164.4	2,083.5
Gross margin	744.4	853.6	865.9
Earnings before income taxes	155.4	216.2	243.3
Earnings after income taxes	111.9	176.7	190.3

$ millions	May 26, 2019	May 27, 2018
Current assets	$ 895.6	$ 938.5
Noncurrent assets	839.2	902.5
Current liabilities	1,517.3	1,579.3
Noncurrent liabilities	77.1	72.6

Required

a. How does General Mills account for its investments in joint ventures? How are these investments reflected on General Mills' balance sheet, and how, generally, is income recognized on these investments? Estimate the amount of income that General Mills included in its 2019 income statement as Equity method income.

b. Does the $117.5 million investment reported on General Mills' balance sheet sufficiently reflect the assets and liabilities required to conduct these operations? Explain. *Note:* The $452.9 million disclosed includes cash advances to the joint venture partners of $335.4 million. The net $117.5 million represents the equity method investment.

c. Do you believe the liabilities of these joint venture entities represent actual obligations of General Mills? Explain.

d. What potential problem(s) does equity method accounting present for analysis purposes?

LO3

Snap-on Incorporated (SNA)

P9-49. Analyzing and Interpreting Disclosures on Consolidations

Snap-on Incorporated consists of two business units: the manufacturing company (parent corporation) and a wholly-owned finance subsidiary. These two units are consolidated in Snap-on's 10-K report. Following is a supplemental disclosure Snap-on includes in its 10-K report that shows the separate balance sheets of the parent and the subsidiary. This supplemental disclosure is not mandated under GAAP but is voluntarily reported by Snap-on as useful information for investors and creditors. Using this disclosure, answer the following questions.

Required

a. Do the parent and subsidiary companies each maintain their own financial statements? Explain. Why does GAAP require consolidation instead of separate financial statements of individual companies?

b. What is the balance of Investments in Financial Services as of December 31, 2018, on the parent's balance sheet? What is the equity balance of the financial services subsidiary to which this relates as of December 31, 2018? Do you see a relation? Will this relation always exist?

c. Refer to your answer for part *a*. How does the equity method of accounting for the investment in the subsidiary obscure the actual financial condition of the parent company as compared with the consolidated financial statements?

d. Recall that the parent company uses the equity method of accounting for its investment in the subsidiary and that this account is eliminated in the consolidation process. What is the relation between consolidated net income and the net income of the parent company? Explain.

e. What is the implication for the consolidated balance sheet if the fair value of the financial services subsidiary (subsequent to acquisition) is greater than the book value of its stockholders' equity?

$ millions	Operations* 2018	Operations* 2017	Financial Services 2018	Financial Services 2017
Assets				
Current assets				
Cash and cash equivalents..................	$ 140.5	$ 91.8	$ 0.4	$ 0.2
Intersegment receivables	15.1	17.1	—	—
Trade and other accounts receivable—net..............	692.1	674.9	0.5	0.7
Finance receivables—net...........................	—	—	518.5	505.4
Contract receivables—net..........................	6.6	9.4	91.7	87.4
Inventories—net	673.8	638.8	—	—
Prepaid expenses and other assets	100.2	117.6	0.5	0.7
Total current assets........................	1,628.3	1,549.6	611.6	594.4
Property and equipment—net......................	493.5	482.4	1.6	2.0
Investment in Financial Services	329.5	317.4	—	—
Deferred income tax assets	45.8	25.2	18.9	26.8
Intersegment long-term notes receivable	701.3	583.7	—	—
Long-term finance receivables—net.................	—	—	1,074.4	1,039.2
Long-term contract receivables—net	11.9	13.2	333.0	309.4
Goodwill	902.2	924.1	—	—
Other intangibles—net	232.9	253.7	—	—
Other assets.............................	51.9	63.1	0.1	—
Total assets	$4,397.3	$4,212.4	$2,039.6	$1,971.8

continued

continued from previous page

$ millions	Operations* 2018	Operations* 2017	Financial Services 2018	Financial Services 2017
Liabilities and Equity				
Current liabilities				
Notes payable and current maturities of long-term debt	$ 186.3	$ 183.2	$ —	$ 250.0
Accounts payable	199.6	177.1	1.5	1.1
Intersegment payables	—	—	15.1	17.1
Accrued benefits	52.0	55.8	—	—
Accrued compensation	66.8	67.8	4.7	3.7
Franchisee deposits	67.5	66.5	—	—
Other accrued liabilities	355.4	366.0	26.1	29.7
Total current liabilities	927.6	916.4	47.4	301.6
Long-term debt and intersegment long-term debt	—	—	1,647.3	1,337.3
Deferred income tax liabilities	41.4	28.4	—	—
Retiree health care benefits	31.8	36.0	—	—
Pension liabilities	171.3	158.9	—	—
Other long-term liabilities	106.6	100.4	15.4	15.5
Total liabilities	1,278.7	1,240.1	1,710.1	1,654.4
Total shareholders' equity attributable to Snap-on Inc.	3,098.8	2,953.9	329.5	317.4
Noncontrolling interests	19.8	18.4	—	—
Total equity	3,118.6	2,972.3	329.5	317.4
Total liabilities and equity	$4,397.3	$4,212.4	$2,039.6	$1,971.8

*Snap-on Operations include Financial Services using the equity method.

IFRS Applications

I9-50. Allocating Purchase Price Including Intangibles

LO3
Deutsche Telekom AG

Deutsche Telekom AG, headquartered in Bonn, Germany, is the largest telecommunications company in Europe. The company uses IFRS to prepare its financial statements. Assume that during 2019, Deutsche Telekom acquired a controlling interest in Hellenic Telecommunications Organization S.A. (Hellenic). The table below shows the pre- and post-acquisition values of Hellenic's assets.

€ millions	Fair Value at Acquisition Date	Carrying Amounts Immediately Prior to Acquisition
Cash and cash equivalents	€ 1,558	€ 1,558
Noncurrent assets	195	158
Other assets	1,716	1,716
Current assets	3,469	3,432
Intangible assets	5,348	4,734
Goodwill	2,500	3,835
Property, plant, and equipment	6,965	5,581
Other assets	823	782
Noncurrent assets	15,636	14,932
Assets	€19,105	€18,364

Required

a. At the acquisition, which measurement does the company use, fair value or carrying value, to record the acquired tangible and intangible assets on its consolidated balance sheet?
b. At the acquisition date, why is fair value of goodwill less than its carrying value?
c. What are some possible reasons why intangible assets increased in value at the acquisition date?
d. Describe accounting for goodwill. Why is an impairment test challenging?

LO2 I9-51. Interpreting Equity Method Investment Footnotes

BHP Billiton Limited discovers, acquires, develops, and markets natural resources worldwide. Headquartered in Melbourne Australia, the company explores for, develops, produces, and markets oil and gas in the Gulf of Mexico, Western Australia, and Trinidad and Tobago. It also explores for copper, silver, lead, zinc, molybdenum, uranium, gold, iron ore, and metallurgical and thermal coal. The company's 2018 annual report included the following disclosure related to its many equity-method investments.

The movement for the year in the Group's investments accounted for using the equity method is as follows:

Year ended 30 June 2018 (US$M)	Investment in Associates
At the beginning of the financial year.	$2,448
Share of operating profit of equity accounted investments. . . .	656
Investment in equity accounted investments	62
Dividends received from equity accounted investments.	(693)
At the end of the financial year.	$2,473

BHP reports additional information for its equity method investments including the following information pertaining to two specific equity method investments. During the year, these two associates, Cerrejon and Antamina, reported net profit of $576 million and $1,613 million, respectively.

Shareholdings in Associates	Country of Incorporation/ Principal Place of Business	Principal Activity	Reporting Date	Ownership Interest 2018%
Carbones del Cerrejón LLC (Cerrejón)	Anguilla/ Colombia	Coal mining in Colombia	31 December	33.33
Compañía Minera Antamina S.A. (Antamina)	Peru	Copper and zinc mining	31 December	33.75

Required

a. The company uses the equity method to account for its investment in associates and joint ventures. Why is this the appropriate method for the two investments disclosed in the footnotes?

b. What total amount of equity method income did BHP include in its 2018 income statement? What amount did BHP include from the two specific associates, Cerrejon and Antamina?

c. Explain why dividends received of $693 million are shown as a decrease to the equity method investment account.

d. How does the use of the equity method impact Billiton's ROE and its RNOA components (net operating asset turnover and net operating profit margin) as compared to the case of consolidation?

Management Applications

LO1, 2, 3 MA9-52. Determining the Reporting of an Investment

Assume your company acquires 20% of the outstanding common stock of APEX Software as an investment. You also have an option to purchase the remaining 80%. APEX is developing software (its only activity) it hopes to eventually package and sell to customers. You do not intend to exercise your option unless its software product reaches commercial feasibility. APEX has employed your software engineers to assist in the development efforts, and you are integrally involved in its software design. Your ownership interest is significant enough to give you influence over APEX's software design specifications.

Required

a. Describe the financial statement effects of the three possible methods to accounting for this investment (fair value, equity, and consolidation).

b. What method of accounting is appropriate for this investment (fair value, equity, or consolidation)? Explain.

Ongoing Project

(This ongoing project began in Module 1 and continues through most of the book; even if previous segments were not completed, the requirements are still applicable to any business analysis.) Company analysis should include an assessment of the companies' various investments, transactions during the year, the effect on net income, and the balance sheet results at year-end.

1. *Investments in Marketable Securities.* To analyze nonoperating investments in marketable debt and equity securities, consider the following questions that will help us understand both companies' level of excess cash and how they invest it:
    - What is the magnitude of the investments in common-size terms? Has this changed over time? What proportion is short-term versus long-term?
    - What types of investments does the company hold—debt, equity, private-company equity?
    - What explanation do the companies provide for their level of investments? Does the MD&A section of the Form 10-K discuss plans for expansion or other strategic initiatives that would require cash?

2. *Investments with Significant Influence.* Our goal is to assess how the companies structure their operations to better understand their strategies.
    - What types of investments does the company have: associates, joint ventures, or other?
    - Why does the company engage in equity-method investments; what is their intent? Read the MD&A section of the Form 10-K and the financial statement footnotes.
    - What are the main equity-method investments? (IFRS: Does the company have any proportionate consolidation?) How large are these in common-size terms?
    - Have there been changes during the year in terms of new investments or disposals? The MD&A and footnotes will be instructive.
    - Are the equity method investments profitable? Do they provide cash dividends?

3. *Investments with Control (Consolidations).* Most multinational corporations are consolidated entities that structure their operations to meet many goals, including legal requirements, tax planning, and foreign ownership restrictions. Financial statements will not report information to completely comprehend all these intricacies; the goal here is to understand the companies' structure at a very high level.
    - What types of companies does the company control? What are the main subsidiaries?
    - What strategic advantages do these subsidiaries afford? Foreign? Domestic? Supplier or distributors? Read the MD&A section of the Form 10-K and the financial statement footnotes to learn about strategic investment and plans for the future.
    - Have there been new investments during the year? How were these acquisitions financed (debt, equity)? Did these yield intangible assets including goodwill? What proportion of the acquisition price was allocated to intangibles?
    - Were there disposals during the year? Why were these made? Did the transaction cause a gain or loss?
    - Gauge the significance of previously acquired intangibles in common-size terms. Have any been impaired during the year?
    - If the company reports subsidiary-level profit, which are the most profitable? The least?

Solutions to Review Problems

Review 9-1—Solution

a.

Transaction	Balance Sheet						Income Statement		
	Cash Asset	+ Noncash Assets	= Liabilities	+ Contrib. Capital	+ Earned Capital		Revenues	− Expenses	= Net Income
1. Purchased 1,000 shares of Juniper common stock for $22 cash per share	−22,000 Cash	+22,000 Marketable Securities	=					−	=
2. Received cash dividend of $2.50 per share on Juniper common stock	+2,500 Cash		=		+2,500 Retained Earnings		+2,500 Dividend Income	−	= +2,500
3. Year-end market price of Juniper common stock is $27 per share		+5,000 Marketable Securities	=		+5,000 Retained Earnings		+5,000 Unrealized Gain	−	= +5,000
4. Sold 1,000 shares of Juniper common stock for $27,000 cash	+27,000 Cash	−27,000 Marketable Securities	=					−	=

MS.....22,000
  Cash.......22,000

MS	
22,000	
	Cash
	22,000

Cash.....2,500
  DI..........2,500

Cash	
2,500	
	DI
	2,500

MS......5,000
  UG..........5,000

MS	
5,000	
	UG
	5,000

Cash....27,000
  MS.........27,000

Cash	
27,000	
	MS
	27,000

b. Microsoft's investment portfolio includes both debt and equity securities. The balance sheet reports the investments at fair value totaling $135,630 million (which Microsoft calls "Recorded Basis" in the footnote).

c. Less than 1% of the total portfolio is equity securities ($1,305 million/$135,630 million).

d. Microsoft's investment portfolio has a cost of $136,667 million and a fair value of $135,630 million. Most of the unrealized loss related to U.S. government bonds whose market values have declined as interest rates have risen. These unrealized losses are unlikely to be realized, however, if the bonds are held to maturity as they will mature at par value.

Review 9-2—Solution

a.

Transaction	Balance Sheet						Income Statement		
	Cash Asset	+ Noncash Assets	= Liabilities	+ Contrib. Capital	+ Earned Capital		Revenues	− Expenses	= Net Income
1. Purchased 5,000 shares of LookSmart common stock at $10 cash per share; these shares reflect 30% ownership	−50,000 Cash	+50,000 Investment in LookSmart	=					−	=
2. Received a $2 per share cash dividend on LookSmart stock	+10,000 Cash	−10,000 Investment in LookSmart	=					−	=
3. Record 30% share of the $100,000 income reported by LookSmart		+30,000 Investment in LookSmart	=		+30,000 Retained Earnings		+30,000 Equity Income	−	= +30,000

EMI.....50,000
  Cash.......50,000

EMI	
50,000	
	Cash
	50,000

Cash....10,000
  EMI........10,000

Cash	
10,000	
	EMI
	10,000

EMI.....30,000
  EI..........30,000

EMI	
30,000	
	EI
	30,000

continued

continued from previous page

Transaction	Balance Sheet					Income Statement		
	Cash Asset +	Noncash Assets =	Liabil- ities +	Contrib. Capital +	Earned Capital	Rev- enues −	Expen- ses =	Net Income
4. Market value has increased to $12 per share	colspan NOTHING RECORDED							
5. Sold all 5,000 shares of LookSmart stock for $90,000	+90,000 Cash	−70,000 Investment in LookSmart			+20,000 Retained Earnings	+20,000 Gain on Sale		+20,000

b. Intel owns 49% of IMFT. It will, therefore, report $367.5 million of equity income and its equity investment will be carried at $1,960 million on its balance sheet (assuming the investment was purchased at book value).

c. The investment must be written down to fair value if the decline in value is deemed to be other than temporary. In this case, Intel determined that the expected cash flows for IMFT had declined and are expected to remain at lower levels indefinitely. Consequently, it reduced the carrying amount of its equity investment and recorded an impairment charge for the write-down, which affected net income for the year of the write-down.

Review 9-3—Solution

	Intel (Parent)	EarthLink (Subsidiary)	Consolidating Adjustments	Consolidated
Current assets	$1,000,000	$100,000		$1,100,000
Investment in EarthLink	600,000	—	(600,000)	
PPE, net	3,000,000	400,000	100,000	3,500,000
Intangible assets (patents)	—	—	25,000	25,000
Goodwill	—	—	75,000	75,000
Total assets	$4,600,000	$500,000		$4,700,000
Liabilities	$1,000,000	$100,000		$1,100,000
Contributed capital	2,000,000	200,000	(200,000)	2,000,000
Retained earnings	1,600,000	200,000	(200,000)	1,600,000
Total liabilities and equity	$4,600,000	$500,000		$4,700,000

Explanation: The $600,000 investment account is eliminated together with the $400,000 book value of EarthLink's equity to which Intel's investment relates. The remaining $200,000 consists of the additional $100,000 in PPE assets, $25,000 in unrecorded intangibles, and $75,000 in goodwill from expected corporate synergies. Following these adjustments, the balance sheet items are summed to yield the consolidated balance sheet.

Review 9-4—Solution

1. PepsiCo used derivatives to hedge foreign currency risk, interest rate risk, and price risk in the commodities it uses to produce its products.
2. PepsiCo employs both fair value and cash flow hedges. We see this by looking at the column headings in the table, both fair value and cash flow hedges are tabulated.
3. PepsiCo would likely hedge sugar (for sodas), corn and wheat (for snack products), and aluminum (for cans), among other types of commodities. Gains and losses on these derivatives would be included in cost of goods sold. The footnote corroborates that conclusion.

Module 10
Leases, Pensions, and Income Taxes

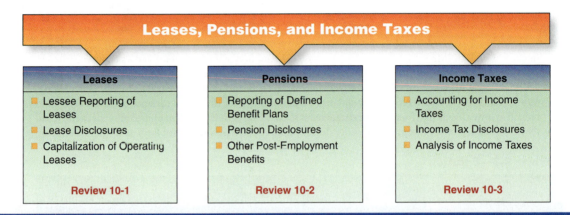

Leases, Pensions, and Income Taxes

Leases
- Lessee Reporting of Leases
- Lease Disclosures
- Capitalization of Operating Leases

Review 10-1

Pensions
- Reporting of Defined Benefit Plans
- Pension Disclosures
- Other Post-Employment Benefits

Review 10-2

Income Taxes
- Accounting for Income Taxes
- Income Tax Disclosures
- Analysis of Income Taxes

Review 10-3

PREVIEW   MSFT DE HPQ

We analyze three important items that affect financial statements.
- **Leases**
  - New lease accounting standard that requires firms to recognize on the balance sheet most leases.
  - Lease accounting disclosures.
- **Pensions and other post-employment benefit plans**
  - Recognition of pension assets and obligations on the balance sheet and income statement.
  - How companies use current pension accounting standards to smooth effects of pension expense.
  - Sufficiency of pension plan assets to cover promised pension payments to retirees.
  - Effects of changing estimates used to compute pension liability and expense.
  - Mark-to-market pension accounting and pension settlements.
- **Income taxes**
  - Balance sheet and income statement differences between U.S. GAAP and tax regulations.
  - Deferred tax assets and liabilities.
  - How changes in the valuation allowance for deferred tax assets affect net income.
  - Income tax footnote disclosures.
  - Financial reporting consequences of the U.S. Tax Cuts and Jobs Act of 2017.
- The dashboard below conveys financial information for Module 10 focus companies: **Microsoft**, **Deere** and **HP**.

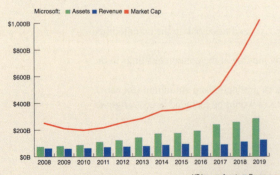

Road Map

LO	Learning Objective | Topics	Page	eLecture	Guided Example	Assignments
10–1	**Analyze and interpret lease disclosures.** Lessee Reporting :: New Lease Rules :: Footnote Disclosure :: Capitalization	10-3	e10–1	Review 10-1	1, 2, 3, 14, 15, 20, 28, 29, 30, 36, 38, 39, 40
10–2	**Analyze and interpret pension disclosures.** Reporting of Defined Benefit Pensions :: Balance Sheet :: Income Statement :: Fair Value Accounting :: Footnote Disclosure—Pension Plan Assets and PBO :: Future Cash Flows :: Profit and Analysis Implications :: Other Post-Employment Benefits	10-11	e10–2	Review 10-2	4, 5, 6, 7, 12, 16, 17, 18, 19, 21, 26, 27, 31, 32, 33, 37, 41, 42, 46
10–3	**Analyze and interpret income tax reporting.** Timing Differences :: Deferred Tax Assets and Liabilities :: Disclosures for Income Taxes :: Analysis of Income Taxes	10-24	e10–3	Review 10-3	8, 9, 10, 11, 13, 22, 23, 24, 25, 34, 35, 43, 44, 45, 47

Leases

LO1 Analyze and interpret lease disclosures.

A lease is a contract between the owner of an asset (the **lessor**) and the party desiring to use that asset (the **lessee**). Since this is a private arrangement between two willing parties, it is governed only by applicable commercial law and can include whatever provisions the parties negotiate. Leases generally include the following terms.

- Lessor grants the lessee the unrestricted right to use the asset during the lease term.
- Lessee agrees to maintain the asset and make periodic payments to the lessor. Lease payments are set at an amount that yields an acceptable return on the lessor's investment in the leased asset, commensurate with the lessee's credit rating.
- Title to the asset remains with the lessor, who usually takes physical possession of the asset at lease-end unless the lessee negotiates the right to purchase the asset at its market value or other predetermined price.

Leases serve as a financing vehicle similar to a secured bank loan. However, leasing has a few advantages compared to bank financing.

- Leases often require less equity investment by the lessee (borrower). Leases usually require the first lease payment be made at the inception of the lease. For a 60-month lease, this amounts to a 1/60 (1.7%) investment by the lessee, compared with a bank loan typically requiring 20%–30% equity investment by the borrower.
- Because leases are contracts between two parties, their terms can be structured to meet both parties' needs. For example, a lease can allow variable payments to match the lessee's seasonal cash inflows or have graduated payments for start-up companies.
- Leasing can be utilized to finance the acquisition of any asset, including vehicles, equipment, and real estate.

The ability to finance a greater proportion of the asset's cost, coupled with the flexibility that the leasing contract provides, has made this a popular form of financing, amounting to over $1 trillion in equipment financing alone (Source: Equipment Leasing & Finance Foundation, 2017).

New Lease Reporting Standard

The FASB issued a new lease accounting standard effective for all U.S. companies in 2019. Under the pre-2019 accounting standard, companies' balance sheets did not include the lease assets and lease liabilities if the company classified the lease as an "operating" lease (see the Practice Insight box "Delta Airlines Prospective Adoption of 2019 Lease Accounting Standard"). Under current GAAP, these operating lease assets and liabilities are now included on companies' balance sheets.

The new standard requires companies classify all leases as either a finance lease or an operating lease.

- **Finance leases** transfer **control of the lease asset** to the lessee. Finance leases are effectively like purchasing the asset and financing the purchase with a collateralized loan.
- **Operating leases** transfer **control of the use of the lease asset**, but not the asset itself. Any lease of 12 months or more not classified as a finance lease is classified as an operating lease.

As they adopt the new standard, companies must choose between two transition options.

1. **Retroactive adoption:** implement the new standard in the current year and restate all prior periods presented in the financial statements. This means that the current-year financial statements and the comparative financial statements (the prior year balance sheet and the two prior years' income statements) all conform to the new standard.
2. **Prospective adoption:** implement the new standard without restatement of the prior periods. This means that the company reports current-period leasing activities under the *new* accounting standard and leasing activities in the prior periods under the *old* standard.

Microsoft chose the first (retroactive) approach and restated its prior year's financial statements in the year of adoption. Consequently, Microsoft's current balance sheet reports both operating and finance leases under the current lease accounting standard for both years. Thus, we can directly compare the financial statements in the current 10-K, across the years presented.

Delta Airlines chose the second (prospective) approach. (See the Practice Insight box "Delta Airlines Prospective Adoption of the 2019 Lease Accounting Standard"). As a result of its prospective adoption of the new standard, Delta's fiscal 2019 financial statements include both the new lease-accounting standard (2019 numbers) and the old standard (2018 and 2017 numbers). Unlike for Microsoft, we cannot directly compare the financial statement in Delta's current 10-K, across the years.

Because companies were free to decide whether they would use the retroactive approach or the prospective approach, financial statements will reflect a mix of old and new standards for the next few years. Consequently, it's important for us to understand both lease standards and this module addresses both.

We begin with a general discussion of lease accounting and then use Microsoft Corporation to illustrate the accounting mechanics.

Lessee Reporting Example—Microsoft Corporation

Companies report all leases on the balance sheet as both lease assets and lease liabilities. As companies describe their leases in footnotes, they distinguish between operating and finance leases. Microsoft provides the following lease disclosure in its 2019 10-K.

> **Leases** We have operating and finance leases for datacenters, corporate offices, research and development facilities, retail stores, and certain equipment. Our leases have remaining lease terms of 1 year to 20 years, some of which include options to extend the leases for up to 5 years, and some of which include options to terminate the leases within 1 year... We determine if an arrangement is a lease at inception. Operating leases are included in operating lease right-of-use ("ROU") assets, other current liabilities, and operating lease liabilities in our consolidated balance sheets. Finance leases are included in property and equipment, other current liabilities, and other long-term liabilities in our consolidated balance sheets. ROU assets represent our right to use an underlying asset for the lease term and lease liabilities represent our obligation to make lease payments arising from the lease. Operating lease ROU assets and liabilities are recognized at commencement date based on the present value of lease payments over the lease term. As most of our leases do not provide an implicit rate, we generally use our incremental borrowing rate based on the estimated rate of interest for collateralized borrowing over a similar term of the lease payments at commencement date. The operating lease ROU asset also includes any lease payments made and excludes lease incentives. Our lease terms may include options to extend or terminate the lease when it is reasonably certain that we will exercise that option. Lease expense for lease payments is recognized on a straight-line basis over the lease term.

On its balance sheet, Microsoft reports assets relating to both operating and finance leases.

June 30 ($ in millions)	2019	2018
Assets		
Current assets		
Cash and cash equivalents	$ 11,356	$ 11,946
Short-term investments	122,463	121,822
Total cash, cash equivalents, and short-term investments	133,819	133,768
Accounts receivable, net of allowance for doubtful accounts of $411 and $377	29,524	26,481
Inventories	2,063	2,662
Other	10,146	6,751
Total current assets	175,552	169,662
Property and equipment, net of accumulated depreciation of $35,330 and $29,223	36,477	29,460 ← Finance leases
Operating lease right-of-use assets	7,379	6,686 ← Operating leases
Equity investments	2,649	1,862
Goodwill	42,026	35,683
Intangible assets, net	7,750	8,053
Other long-term assets	14,723	7,442
Total assets	$286,556	$258,848

Microsoft includes the finance lease assets in PPE and reports the operating lease right-of-use assets (highlighted) on a separate line item. Microsoft reports the lease liabilities on its 2019 balance sheet.

June 30 ($ in millions)	2019	2018
Liabilities and stockholders' equity		
Current liabilities		
Accounts payable..	$ 9,382	$ 8,617
Current portion of long-term debt........................... [Operating and Finance leases]	5,516	3,998
Accrued compensation	6,830	6,103
Short-term income taxes	5,665	2,121
Short-term unearned revenue	32,676	28,905
Other	9,351	8,744
Total current liabilities......................................	69,420	58,488
Long-term debt.. [Finance leases]	66,662	72,242
Long-term income taxes......................................	29,612	30,265
Long-term unearned revenue...............................	4,530	3,815
Deferred income taxes	233	541
Operating lease liabilities.................................... [Operating leases]	6,188	5,568
Other long-term liabilities	7,581	5,211
Total liabilities...	184,226	176,130
Stockholders' equity		
Common stock and paid-in capital – shares authorized 24,000; outstanding 7,643 and 7,677	78,520	71,223
Retained earnings	24,150	13,682
Accumulated other comprehensive loss	(340)	(2,187)
Total stockholders' equity................................	102,330	82,718
Total liabilities and stockholders' equity	$286,556	$258,848

Under the pre-2019 accounting standard, operating leases were *omitted* from the balance sheet. With over $7 billion in operating leases, Microsoft's balance sheet demonstrates that these omissions can be large. Under the old standard, assets and liabilities were both understated, which markedly affected profitability, asset use, and especially leverage ratios. The analyst community lobbied FASB for many years to correct this accounting issue, and it was finally resolved by the passage of the new standard.

We now turn to lease accounting: how operating and financing leases are reported on the balance sheet, the ways lease costs are reflected as expenses in the income statement, and how these lease costs affect the statement of cash flows.

Lease Accounting

The first step in lease accounting is to determine whether a lease is operating or financing. If the lease is economically similar to the purchase of an asset, the company must classify the lease as financing. In particular, finance leases meet one or more of the following criteria.

- **Transfer of ownership.** The lease transfers ownership of the underlying asset to the lessee by the end of the lease term.
- **Purchase option.** The lease grants the lessee an option to purchase the underlying asset that the lessee is reasonably certain to exercise.
- **Lease term.** The lease term is for a major part of the remaining economic life of the underlying asset.
- **Present value.** The present value of the sum of the lease payments and any residual value guaranteed by the lessee that is not already included in the lease payments equals or exceeds substantially all of the fair value of the underlying asset.
- **Specialized asset.** The underlying asset is of such a specialized nature that it is expected to have no alternative use to the lessor at the end of the lease term.

Any lease of 12 months or more not classified as a finance lease is classified as an operating lease.

Lease Accounting and the Balance Sheet

Both operating and finance leases are recognized on the balance sheet.

- A **lease liability** is recognized at the present value of the remaining lease payments (see below).
- A **right-of-use asset** is recognized at an amount calculated as follows.

	Amount of the lease obligation
+	Lease payments made to the lessor at or before the lease commencement date
−	Lease incentives received from the lessor
+	Initial direct costs of right-of-use asset incurred by the lessee.
=	Right-of-use asset

This means the right-of-use asset will often be greater than the related lease liability at inception of the lease. (The difference is the net cash paid for the upfront costs.) The year the company adopts the new accounting standard is considered to be the year of inception for preexisting operating leases.

The balance sheet presents lease liabilities and right-of-use assets separately (not the net amount). Finance lease assets are typically included in PPE, and lease liabilities are included with debt. Operating lease assets and liabilities are each reported in a separate line item if material.

The amount reported on the balance sheet for the lease obligation and right-of-use lease asset relates to the payments that the company will make under the lease terms. Footnotes also disclose a schedule of such lease payments for both operating and finance leases. For example, Microsoft discloses the following in its 2019 10-K.

Maturities of lease liabilities were as follows:

Year Ending June 30 (In millions)	Operating Leases	Finance Leases
2020	$1,678	$ 591
2021	1,438	616
2022	1,235	626
2023	1,036	631
2024	839	641
Thereafter	2,438	5,671
Total lease payments	8,664	8,776
Less imputed interest	(961)	(2,202)
Total	$7,703	$6,574

Total forecasted lease payments for operating leases are $8,664 million in FY2019. However, Microsoft's balance sheet includes liabilities of $7,703 million (current liability of $1,515 million relating to payments to be made in the upcoming year and long-term liability of $6,188 million), which is the present value of the forecasted lease payments discounted at 3.15%. Exhibit 10.1 illustrates the present value calculation. The Business Insight box below explains the discount rate. (The 3.15% discount rate used in this example is consistent with the assumed payment stream, an approach commonly used in practice. Microsoft's actual discount rate is 3%, as disclosed in its 2019 10-K.)

Exhibit 10.1 ■ Present Value of Operating Lease Payments ($ millions)

	A	B	C	D	E
1	Year	Operating Lease Payment	Discount Factor ($i = 0.0315$)	Present Value	Cell Formula
2	1	$1,678	0.96946	$1,627	=PV(B10,A2,0,−B2)
3	2	1,438	0.93986	1,352	=PV(B10,A3,0,−B3)
4	3	1,235	0.91116	1,125	=PV(B10,A4,0,−B4)
5	4	1,036	0.88333	915	=PV(B10,A5,0,−B5)
6	5	839	0.85636	718	=PV(B10,A6,0,−B6)
7	>5	$2,438 ($839 × 2.906 years)	2.73602 × 0.85636	1,966	=PV(B10,B9,−B6,0,0)*PV(B10,A6,0,−1)
8	Total payments	$8,664		$7,703	=SUM(D2:D7)
9	Remaining life	2.906			=B7/B6
10	Discount rate	3.15%			

The total *operating* lease liability of $7,703 million consists of a portion maturing in the next year, which is reported as a current liability and the remainder, reported as a long-term liability, as highlighted in Microsoft's balance sheet above. The table above shows a current portion of $1,627 million, slightly higher than the $1,515 million Microsoft reports in its footnotes. The difference arises because Microsoft uses a specific discount rate for each lease, whereas we use an average of 3.15% for all leases.

Microsoft uses the same approach to compute the present value of its forecasted *finance* lease payments and reports $6,574 million on the balance sheet. (See "Maturities of lease liabilities" table above.) Of the total finance lease liability, Microsoft includes $317 million in the Current portion of long-term debt and $6,257 million in Long-term debt (disclosed in footnotes). In subsequent years, these leases will be reported at the present value of the remaining lease payments, and are included with any new leases on the balance sheet.

Business Insight — Imputed Discount Rate Computation for Leases

Microsoft reports total undiscounted minimum operating lease payments of $8,664 million and a discounted value for those lease payments of $7,703 million. Using Excel, we can use the IRR function to estimate the *implicit* discount rate that Microsoft used for its lease computations. The following spreadsheet lays out the calculations.

Amounts in cells B2 through G2 are from Microsoft's lease footnote shown earlier in this section. Cells H2 through J2 sum to $2,438 million, the total lease payments due after 2023 (year 5). We assume that Microsoft continues to pay $839 million per year (the same as in 2023) with a final payment of $760 million, until the $2,438 million is used up. The IRR functions estimates that Microsoft used a discount rate of 3.15% to capitalize its operating leases in its FY2019 balance sheet.

In this method we make assumptions about the remaining useful life of the lease assets (total remaining payments divided by the payment in year 5). Many firms disclose the weighted average discount rate and the weighted average remaining lease term used to determine the present value of future lease payments. If provided, these assumptions are a more exact way to corroborate the disclosed present value or implicit interest rates.

	A	B	C	D	E	F	G	H	I	J
1	N	0	1	2	3	4	5	6	7	8
2	Amount	(7,703)	1,678	1,438	1,235	1,036	839	839	839	760
3	IRR*	3.15%								
4									=2,438	
5		*Formula for cell B3 is =IRR(B2:J2,0.1), as shown in the formula bar at the top of the sheet								

B3 formula: =IRR(B2:J2,0.1)

Lease Accounting and the Income Statement

Total expense over the lifetime of the lease is recognized in the income statement in an amount equal to the total remaining lease payments plus total amortization of any up-front costs. Assume, for example, a company executes a five-year lease requiring annual payments of $22,463 and pays $5,000 of initial direct costs prior to commencing the lease. The present value of the lease payments at 4% is $100,000 and the company recognizes a lease liability for that amount. The company also recognizes a right-of-use asset of $105,000 (the $100,000 present value of the lease payments plus the $5,000 up-front direct costs).

The total lease cost under both operating and finance leases over the five-year life of the lease is: $22,463 lease payments × 5 years + $5,000 upfront costs = $117,314. The income statement will reflect this amount differently, however, for operating and finance leases.

- **Operating lease.** Lease expense of $23,463 ($117,314/5 years) is recognized each period as rent expense in arriving at income from operating activities.
- **Finance lease.** Lease expense includes interest on the lease liability plus straight-line amortization of the right-of-use asset. For the first year, lease expense is equal to $100,000 × 4% + $105,000/5 = $25,000. Also:
  - Amortization of the right-of-use asset will be included in income from operations (similar to depreciation expense relating to PPE assets).
  - Interest expense will be reported after operating income.
  - Operating profit will be higher than by the amount of interest expense recognized as nonoperating.

Appendix 10A provides a detailed example of the accounting for operating and finance leases.

Statement of Cash Flows

The statement of cash flows will be impacted by the classification of leases in a similar manner to the income statement.

- **Operating lease.** Cash flow from operating activities includes the entire lease payment.
- **Finance lease.** The lease payments include payment of accrued interest and reduction of the principal balance of the lease liability. The interest portion is included in net income and, therefore, in net cash flows from operating activities. The portion representing the payment of the principal balance of the lease liability is considered a financing activity. Net cash flows from operating activities will therefore be higher for finance leases by the amount of the payment allocated to reduction of the lease liability.

Practice Insight ■ **Delta Airlines Prospective Adoption of 2019 Lease Accounting Standard**

Delta Airlines adopted the new lease accounting standard as disclosed in notes to its 2019 10-K.

> **Leases** During the December 2018 quarter, we adopted ASU No. 2016-02, "Leases (Topic 842)," which requires leases with durations greater than twelve months to be recognized on the balance sheet. We adopted the standard using the modified retrospective approach with an effective date as of the beginning of our fiscal year, January 1, 2018. Prior year financial statements were not recast under the new standard and, therefore, those amounts are not presented below.

Contrary to Microsoft's retroactive adoption of the standard, Delta did not restate its 2017 balance sheet. Consequently, operating leases are recognized on the balance sheet for 2018 (the year of adoption) and not for 2017 (under the previous accounting standard—see the following Accounting Insight box). Delta's noncurrent assets increased in 2018 by $5,994 million as seen in this excerpt from its balance sheet.

December 31 (in millions)	2018	2017
Noncurrent Assets		
Property and equipment, net of accumulated depreciation and amortization of $15,823 and $14,097 at December 31, 2018 and 2017, respectively	$28,335	$26,563
Operating lease right-of-use assets	5,994	0
Goodwill	9,781	9,794
Identifiable intangibles, net of accumulated amortization of $862 and $845 at December 31, 2018 and 2017, respectively	4,830	4,847
Cash restricted for airport construction	1,136	0
Deferred income taxes, net	242	1,354
Other noncurrent assets	3,608	3,309
Total noncurrent assets	$53,926	$45,867

Likewise, Delta's liabilities increased by $6,756 million; and $5,801 million of this is reported separately as a noncurrent liability (the remainder is included in current liabilities).

December 31 (in millions)	2018	2017
Noncurrent Liabilities		
Long-term debt and finance leases	$ 8,253	$ 6,592
Pension, postretirement and related benefits	9,163	9,810
Loyalty program deferred revenue	3,652	3,559
Noncurrent operating leases	5,801	—
Other noncurrent liabilities	1,132	2,221
Total noncurrent liabilities	$28,001	$22,182

Because it chose not to adopt the new leasing standard retrospectively, Delta's 2017 balance sheet is prepared under the former lease standard, impairing the comparability between the two years. Analysts must, therefore, adjust Delta's prior year balance sheet as we discuss in our "Analysis Issues" section of the text.

Accounting Insight ■ Pre-2019 Lease Accounting Standard

Under the pre-2019 lease accounting standard, GAAP identified two different approaches for the reporting of leases by the lessee. These are summarized in Exhibit 10.2.

Exhibit 10.2 ■ Financial Statement Effects of Lease Type for the Lessee

Lease Type	Assets	Liabilities	Expenses	Cash Flows
Capital......	Lease asset reported	Lease liability reported	Depreciation and interest expense	Payments per lease contract
Operating....	Lease asset **not** reported	Lease liability **not** reported	Rent expense	Payments per lease contract

Under the **operating lease method**, lease assets and lease liabilities were not recorded on the balance sheet. The company merely disclosed key details of the transaction in the lease footnote. The income statement reported the lease payment as rent expense. The cash outflows (payments to lessor) per the lease contract were included in the operating section of the statement of cash flows. (This is still the case with the post-2019 accounting standards.)

For **capital leases**, both the lease asset and lease liability were reported on the balance sheet. In the income statement, depreciation of the lease asset and interest expense on the lease liability were reported instead of rent expense. Further, although the cash payments to the lessor are identical whether or not the lease is capitalized on the balance sheet, the cash flows were classified differently for capital leases—that is, each payment was part interest (operating cash flow) and part principal (financing cash flow). Consequently, operating cash flows were greater when a lease was classified as a capital lease. (This is still the case with the post-2019 accounting standards.)

The benefits of applying the operating method for leases were obvious to managers (including healthier Du Pont ratios). Thus, some managers actively avoided capital lease treatment. Moreover, the pre-2019 rigid capitalization rules created an unintended negative consequence: managers seeking off-balance-sheet financing could, and routinely did, deliberately structure their leases around GAAP rules so as to avoid capital lease treatment. Analysts and other financial statement users objected to the pre-2019 rules that skewed ratios and created hidden leverage.

Summary of Lease Accounting and Reporting

A summary of the effects of the new standard on the balance sheet, the income statement, and the statement of cash flows follows.

	Operating Lease	Finance Lease
Balance Sheet (same for both operating and finance leases)	<ul><li>All leases are recognized on the balance sheet (except leases with a term of less than 12 months).</li><li>Lease asset is reported as either PPE or a "right-of-use" asset that is amortized over the lease life.</li><li>Lease liability is reduced by principal payments each period, like a mortgage.</li><li>Accounting treatment is similar to recording a PPE asset that is purchased and financed with borrowed money (both the asset and liability are reported on the balance sheet).</li></ul>	
Income Statement	<ul><li>Rent expense is recognized for the straight-line amortization of the total lease payments plus up-front costs.</li></ul>	<ul><li>Straight-line amortization expense of the right-of-use asset, *plus*</li><li>Interest expense is recognized on the lease liability.</li></ul>
Statement of Cash Flows	<ul><li>Lease payments are classified as operating cash flow.</li></ul>	<ul><li>Interest portion of lease payments is classified as operating cash flow.</li><li>Principal portion of lease payments is classified as financing cash flow.</li></ul>

For both operating and financing leases, the balance sheet treatment is identical. However, the income statement and statement of cash flows presentation depend on the lease classification (operating versus financing).

- ■ Income statement
    - Operating leases: Level rent expense recorded each period (an operating item).

- Finance leases: Amortization expense recorded each period (an operating item) and interest expense accrued on the lease liability (a nonoperating item). The expense decreases each year because the total expense includes a level asset amortization expense plus a decreasing interest expense (lower in later years because the interest accrual is calculated on a decreasing lease liability).
■ Statement of cash flows
- Operating leases: Rent expense is reported in net income and, thus, is included in net cash from operating activities. The amortization of direct costs (non-cash portion of rent expense) is added back as a reconciling item.
- Finance leases: Amortization expense is an add-back in net cash from operating activities. Interest expense is reported in net income and, thus, is included in net cash from operating activities. Repayment of the lease obligation is classified as a financing activity.

Analysis Issues Relating to Leases

There are two significant analysis issues relating to leases.

1. Treatment of operating leases prior to adoption of the 2019 accounting standard.
2. Different accounting treatments for operating and finance leases.

Delta Airlines provides an example of the first analysis issue (see the Practice Insight box above). In 2018, Delta adopted the new lease accounting standard prospectively and recognized right-of-use assets and lease liabilities for operating leases for 2018 only. Delta did not restate the prior year balance sheet and income statement, thereby impairing comparability. This is evident from Delta Airlines balance sheet that reports $5,994 million in right-of-use assets and $5,801 million in noncurrent operating lease liabilities for 2018, with $0 reported as a comparable number in 2017. Although comparability will increase over time as previous lease accounting standards are no longer reported alongside the new standard, the lack of comparability will continue to plague analysis of older financial statements. Thus, we need an approach to restore comparability of the financial statements across time.

The second issue relates to the differing accounting treatment for operating and finance leases. This clouds analysis for companies that have both types of leases. It also impairs cross-firm comparisons when companies have differing proportions of operating and finance leases.

Credit rating companies consider the following issues and they adjust for lease reporting issues.

1. **Postadoption reporting of leases—balance sheet.** Generally, credit raters accept the dollar amounts reported by companies for right-of-use assets and lease obligations.
2. **Postadoption reporting of leases—income statement.** Postadoption balance sheets reflect operating and finance leases equally and therefore credit raters simply compare balance sheets across firms. However, income statements and statements of cash flow are not comparable, as we discussed above. Therefore, credit rating companies must adjust for these differences before comparing one company to another.
3. **Prospective adoption of the lease standard.** For companies that adopt the new lease accounting standard on a prospective basis, current and prior years are not comparable (see our Practice Insight box "Delta Airlines Prospective Adoption of 2019 Lease Accounting Standard"). Credit raters' adjustment follows the same method discussed above to capitalize the operating leases using footnote disclosures of future operating lease payments.

The credit rating companies' objective is to recognize all lease assets and lease obligations on the balance sheet and to present lease expense uniformly.

IFRS Insight ■ Lease Accounting under IFRS

Post 2019, there are few differences between U.S. GAAP and IFRS lease accounting standards. One distinction is that IFRS has a single model of lease classification: all leases are accounted for similar to a finance lease under U.S. GAAP.

Review 10-1 LO1

Following is the leasing footnote disclosure from Delta Airlines's 2018 10-K report.

We lease property and equipment under finance and operating leases. For leases with terms greater than 12 months, we record the related asset and obligation at the present value of lease payments over the term.

The table below reconciles the undiscounted cash flows for each of the first five years and total of the remaining years to the finance lease liabilities and operating lease liabilities recorded on the balance sheet.

(in millions)	Operating Leases	Finance Leases
2019	$ 1,172	$ 127
2020	1,000	89
2021	819	75
2022	692	33
2023	654	27
Thereafter	4,200	111
Total minimum lease payments	8,537	462
Less: amount of lease payments representing interest	(1,781)	(59)
Present value of future minimum lease payments	6,756	403
Less: current obligations under leases	(955)	(109)
Long-term lease obligations	$ 5,801	$ 294

Required

1. Using Excel and a discount rate of 4.42%, confirm the present value of the future minimum lease payments for operating leases of $6,756 million.
2. Describe how the $6,756 million will appear on Delta Airlines's balance sheet for 2018.

Solution on p. 10-67.

Pensions

LO2 Analyze and interpret pension disclosures.

Companies frequently offer postretirement benefit plans for their employees. There are two general types of plans.

1. **Defined contribution plan.** This plan requires the company to make periodic contributions to an employee's account (usually with a third-party trustee like a bank), and many plans require an employee matching contribution. Following retirement, the employee makes periodic withdrawals from that account. A tax-advantaged 401(k) account is a typical example. Under a 401(k) plan, the employee makes contributions that are exempt from federal taxes until they are withdrawn by the employee after retirement.

2. **Defined benefit plan.** This plan also requires the company make periodic payments to a third party, which then makes payments to an employee after retirement. Payments are usually based on years of service and the employee's salary. The company may *or may not* set aside sufficient funds to cover these obligations (federal law does set minimum funding requirements). As a result, defined benefit plans can be overfunded or underfunded. All pension investments are retained by the third party until paid to the employee. In the event of bankruptcy, employees have the standing of a general creditor, but usually have additional protection in the form of government pension benefit insurance.

The financial statement implications and the accounting for defined contribution plans is similar to a simple accrual of wages payable. When the company becomes liable to make its contribution, it accrues the liability and related expense. Later, when the company makes the payment, its cash and the liability are reduced. The amount of the liability is certain and the company's obligation is fully satisfied once payment has been made.

A defined benefit plan is not so simple. For that type of plan, the company has made a promise to make annual payments to retirees based on a formula that typically includes the employee's final salary level and years of service, both of which are not determined for maybe 30–40 years in the future. Estimating the amount of the liability is difficult and prone to error. While companies typically set aside some cash to fund promised future payments, usually they make only the minimum contribution required by law. This makes it uncertain whether there will be sufficient funds available to make required payments to retirees.

The accounting for defined benefit plans is subjective, amounts are uncertain, and companies frequently revise their estimates. Footnote disclosures are often lengthy and difficult to decipher. Nonetheless, it is possible to use the disclosures to assess how a defined benefit plan impacts company performance and financial condition.

Defined Benefit Pension Plans on the Balance Sheet

The amount reported on the balance sheet for pension and other post-employment obligations is actually a net amount (Projected benefit obligation – Pension plan assets). This amount is called the *funded status* and is most often a net liability because companies' pension obligations are typically greater than the pension plan assets set aside to pay those liabilities. Funded status is reported on the balance sheet as follows.

Assets	Liabilities and Equity
Cash	Accounts payable
Accounts receivable	Accrued liabilities
⋮	⋮
	Long-term debt
PPE, net	Pension and Postretirement Benefit Obligations
Intangible assets	⋮
⋮	Stockholders' equity
Total Assets	Total Liabilities and Equity

Here we label the funded status as Pension and Postretirement Benefit Obligations, but companies use many other account titles. Funded status is the net balance of two accounts.

- **Pension plan assets.** Think of this account as an investment portfolio with a variety of marketable debt and equity securities. The portfolio provides a return that will fund future payments to retirees. Each period the investment account increases with investment income (interest, dividends, and gains) and as the company contributes additional cash to the portfolio. The investment account decreases with investment losses and as cash is paid to retirees.
- **Projected benefit obligation (PBO).** This liability represents the present value of the company's estimated future payments to retirees. It is similar in concept to the present value of the lease liability that we computed earlier. A company must estimate its future payments that will be required. The following factors make it difficult to project future payments (and companies typically hire actuarial advisors to do this job).
  - Payments often do not occur for many decades into the future.
  - Number of eligible employees is uncertain.
  - Employees' longevity with the company is unknown.
  - Payments depend on employees' final salary levels, which must be estimated.

  A company must then compute the present value of the future cash outflows to determine the projected benefit obligation. This liability decreases when the company pays benefits to its retirees.
- **Funded status.** The balance sheet reports the funded status, calculated as the difference between the projected benefit obligation and the market value of the plan assets. If the plan assets exceed the projected benefit obligation, the pension plan is said to be *overfunded* and a net asset is reported on the balance sheet. However, as is more often the case, the funded status is a net liability. In this case, the pension plan is said to be *underfunded* and a liability for the unfunded amount is reported on the balance sheet.

For S&P 500 firms from 2009–2018, pension assets have averaged about 80% of projected benefit obligations, indicating that underfunding is common. As the stock market increased in value during the 2016–2018 period, plan assets as a percentage of pension obligations increased to nearly 87%.

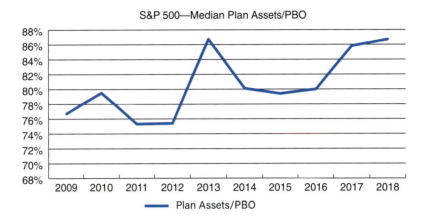

Analysis Issue—Sufficiency of Plan Assets to Pay Pension Obligations

An analysis issue arises when the plan assets are insufficient to cover the PBO. For example, **FedEx** reported the following fiscal year 2019 balances for its projected benefit obligations (PBO), pension plan assets, and funded status.

$ millions	U.S. Pension Plans		International Pension Plans		Postretirement Healthcare Plans	
	2019	2018	2019	2018	2019	2018
PBO/APBO at the end of year	$26,554	$22,653	$2,301	$2,167	$1,221	$955
Change in plan assets						
Fair value of plan assets at the beginning of year	$22,057	$24,933	$1,509	$1,379	$ —	$ —
Actual return on plan assets	984	1,609	94	49	—	—
Company contributions	1,034	2,547	91	84	73	42
Benefits paid	(755)	(854)	(38)	(46)	(123)	(80)
Settlements	—	(6,178)	(13)	(5)	—	—
Other	—	—	(65)	48	50	38
Fair value of plan assets at the end of year	$23,320	$22,057	$1,578	$1,509	$ —	$ —
Funded status of the plans	$ (3,234)	$ (596)	$ (723)	$ (658)	$(1,221)	$(955)

For 2019, FedEx reported domestic and international pension plans along with postretirement healthcare plans with a combined negative funded status of $5,178 million ($3,234 million + $723 million + $1,221 million). This represents significantly underfunded plans. Employees and analysts are keenly interested in the likelihood that the company will be able to pay its pension obligations to retirees. This negative funded status is, therefore, cause for some concern.

However, funded status is not the only measure we can use to assess the company's ability to pay its pension obligations. While comparing the pension assets and liabilities is important, it is more important to consider cash flow in the coming years. Companies are required to provide a schedule of the expected benefit payments to retirees for the next five years and for the five-year period thereafter (this is a similar schedule to the projected lease payments that we illustrated earlier in this module). FedEx provides the following schedule in its 2019 10-K.

> Benefit payments, which reflect expected future service, are expected to be paid as follows for the years ending May 31 (in millions):
>
> | | U.S. Pension Plans | International Pension Plans | Postretirement Healthcare Plans |
> | --- | --- | --- | --- |
> | 2020 | $1,027 | $ 45 | $ 87 |
> | 2021 | 971 | 46 | 98 |
> | 2022 | 1,051 | 47 | 109 |
> | 2023 | 1,138 | 55 | 117 |
> | 2024 | 1,230 | 61 | 121 |
> | 2025–2029 | 7,515 | 396 | 473 |

For fiscal 2020, FedEx forecasts payments of $1,159 million for its combined plans ($1,027 million + $45 million + $87 million) and expects payments to retirees to increase slightly over the ensuing years. The analysis question is whether the pension plan assets will generate investment returns sufficient to cover the required pension payments to retirees.

In 2019, FedEx generated Pension plan (domestic and international) asset returns of $1,078 million ($984 million + $94 million), exceeding the $793 million of benefit payments required that year ($755 million + $38 million). The graph below reports plan asset returns and benefit payments for the past 10 years for FedEx.

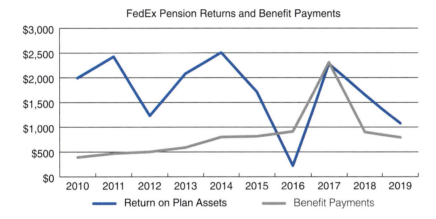

Over the past 10 years, FedEx has generated $17.2 billion of investment returns and paid $8.5 billion of benefits to retirees. Although the Pension and Healthcare plans report a negative funded status, the plans are generating sufficient returns to cover benefit payments. (Benefit payments were higher in 2017 because FedEx's U.S. Pension Plans were amended to permit former employees with a vested traditional pension benefit to make a one-time, irrevocable election to receive their benefits in a lump-sum distribution. Approximately 18,300 former employees elected to receive this lump-sum distribution and FedEx paid a total of $1.3 billion in May 2017.)

The bottom line is that the cash for benefit payments must come from the pension plan assets. Either the plan assets must generate sufficient returns to fund benefit payments (which they did for FedEx), or the company must make additional contributions to the pension plan assets. Severely underfunded plans might not have sufficient assets to cover the projected payments to retirees. In this case, the company might need to use operating cash flow, or worse, borrow to cover its pension benefit obligations. The decline in the financial condition and ultimate bankruptcy of **General Motors** was due in large part to its inability to pay its pension and healthcare obligations from pension assets. The company was forced to divert much needed operating cash flow and to borrow funds to meet its pension payment obligations.

To summarize, the PBO is the present value of the expected benefit payments, and the plan assets is the fair value of the investment portfolio on the statement date. Companies net these two amounts and report the funded status on the balance sheet. Computing the PBO presents a big challenge for the reasons listed above. Given these difficulties, we must remember that the PBO is an *informed* estimate full of uncertainty.

> **IFRS Insight** ■ Reporting of Pension Funded Status under IFRS
>
> Like U.S. GAAP, IFRS requires companies to report the funded status of their defined benefit pension plans on the balance sheet. The IFRS calculation of the unfunded status is slightly different than under GAAP. The IFRS unfunded status is calculated as projected benefit obligation minus the fair value of plan assets; but, unlike GAAP, any actuarial gains are added (losses are subtracted). There are other differences in detailed computations, which means that for pension assets and liabilities it is difficult to reliably compare GAAP and IFRS reports.

Defined Benefit Pension Plans on the Income Statement

A useful way to think about pensions and healthcare expense in the income statement is to recall the accounting equation and how it applies to the funded status liability.

$$\text{Assets} = \text{Liabilities} + \text{Equity}$$

As liabilities increase, holding assets constant, equity must decrease (an expense). And, as liabilities fall, equity must increase (income). Recall that companies report the funded status of their pension plan (PBO − Plan assets) and that the funded status is frequently a net liability. Looking at a funded status liability, then, we are talking about increases and decreases to the liability, other than from company cash contributions and cash payment of benefits to retirees (those cash payments are not expenses).

Apart from the cash contributions and payments, there are several items that cause the funded status liability to increase or decrease. These items create pension expense in the income statement.

Item	Effect on Funded Status Liability	Effect on Income Statement
Service cost	Increase	Expense
Interest cost	Increase	Expense
Returns on plan assets	Increase (Decrease)	Income (Expense)
Actuarial adjustments	Increase (Decrease)	(Expense) Income

- **Service cost.** Pension benefits are usually based on years of service and salary levels at retirement. As employees work another year for the company, their cumulative years of service increase as does their salary level. This increases the benefits due to them at retirement. The increase in the funded status liability results in pension expense, and this expense is called *service cost* since it relates to the service provided to the company by employees that year.
- **Interest cost.** The PBO is computed as the present value of the expected benefit payments. Each year, the liability increases by the interest accrued on the PBO liability, computed using the discount rate. This expense is called *interest cost*.
- **Investment returns.** If a pension investment portfolio generates a positive investment return, plan assets increase and the funded status liability decreases. This creates income (a reduction of pension expense). However, if the pension investment portfolio reports a loss, plan assets decrease and the funded status liability increases, resulting in additional pension expense.
- **Actuarial adjustments.** The computation of the PBO requires a number of estimates about future payments, pension investment portfolio returns, and discount rates. Companies can, and often do, change these estimates, which affects the amount of the PBO and the funded status liability.
  - *Wage inflation.* If a company increases its assumption about the level of wage inflation, estimated salary levels at retirement will be higher and the pension liability increases, resulting in expense in the income statement.
  - *Years of benefit payments.* If the company assumes a longer period of time for the payment of benefits to retirees, the pension liability increases, resulting in expense in the income statement.
  - *Discount rate.* While a higher discount rate reduces the present value of the PBO, the ensuing annual interest cost is at a higher rate but accrued on a lower PBO. The net effect on

the pension liability is, therefore, indeterminate. An increase in the discount rate may or may not create additional pension expense.

- *Investment returns.* Investment returns on plan assets offset pension expense. So as investment returns increase, pension expense decreases (we discuss below the different ways in which investment returns are recognized in the income statement).

As the company changes estimates, pension expense reported in the income statement changes as well. Fortunately, companies are required to report the levels of these estimates in footnote disclosures, and these disclosures help analysts to better understand the effects on reported profits. We will discuss the analysis of these footnote disclosures later. Before that, we need to better understand the different ways in which pension expense is recognized in the income statement.

Pension Expense Smoothing

Reporting the funded status net liability, rather than reporting pension assets and the pension benefit obligation (PBO) separately, was a concession by the FASB to gain support for passage of the pension accounting standard. During deliberation of the pension standard, companies expressed concern over recognizing the full PBO as a liability on the balance sheet and found the recognition of a net (smaller) liability more palatable.

The FASB also made another significant concession. Companies were concerned about the increase in volatility of reported earnings that would result if changes in plan assets and the PBO were reflected in current earnings. For example, as pension asset returns increased in bull markets and decreased in bear markets, so would reported earnings. And if, for example, companies lowered the estimated discount rate, the PBO would increase and that increase would hit current earnings as an expense.

To allay these concerns, the FASB agreed to a mechanism that would *smooth* pension expense: companies could hold certain gains and losses in accumulated other comprehensive income (AOCI) in the equity section of the balance sheet and transfer them to the income statement over time. In particular, the income effects relating to the following two items would be included in other comprehensive income (rather than in net income) and carried in AOCI (rather than in retained earnings):

1. Large investment gains and losses on pension assets.
2. Changes in the PBO that arise from changes in estimates in actuarial assumptions.

This AOCI mechanism essentially defers gains and losses arising from these two sources. These deferred amounts remain in AOCI unless they became very large, at which point, they are reclassified from AOCI into the current period income statement as either income or expense. (To avoid reclassification, the deferred amounts must be less than 10% of the PBO or pension plan asset investments, whichever is greater. The excess, if any, is amortized to the income statement until no further excess remains. When the excess is eliminated, for example, by investment returns or company contributions, the amortization ceases.) The bottom line is that as long as the total deferred gains or losses are not excessive, they remain on the balance sheet in AOCI and are, therefore, not included in the income statement.

Details of how the deferral mechanism works follow.

1. Instead of recognizing actual returns on pension assets in the income statement, companies recognize an **expected return** that represents the long-term rate of return that the company expects to earn on pension investments given the expected composition of the investment portfolio.
2. Only the amortization of *excess* deferred gains or losses is recognized in current income.

For most companies, pension expense is computed as follows.

	Net Pension Expense
	Service cost
+	Interest cost
−	*Expected* return on pension plan assets
±	Amortization of deferred amounts, if any
=	Net pension expense

With this background, we can now better understand how the pension plan assets and pension benefit obligation (PBO) are updated each year.

Pension Plan Assets
Pension plan assets, beginning balance
+ Actual returns on investments (interest, dividends, gains and losses)
+ Company contributions to pension plan
− Benefits paid to retirees
= Pension plan assets, ending balance

Projected Benefit Obligation
Projected benefit obligation, beginning balance
+ Service cost
+ Interest cost
+/− Actuarial losses (gains)
− Benefits paid to retirees
= Projected benefit obligation, ending balance

- **Pension plan assets** increase by actual investment returns or decrease by investment losses and by additional contributions by the company. The plan assets decrease by any benefits paid to retirees.
- **Projected benefit obligation (PBO)** increases to recognize additional service provided by employees (service cost) and by interest accrued on the PBO liability. It also increases (decreases) as deferred losses (gains) are recognized in income, and it decreases by any benefit payments paid to retirees.

We see that benefits are paid from the pension plan assets, and the payments reduce both the plan assets and the PBO liability when paid.

Pension footnotes disclose details about plan assets and the PBO as well as the components of pension expense. We use **Deere & Company** as an example and focus only on its U.S. Pension Benefit plan to simplify our exposition. The Deere footnotes provide a good illustration of how pension expense is smoothed for the vast majority of companies. The following disclosures come from Deere's 2018 10-K.

Pension Plan ($ millions)	2018	2017
Change in benefit obligations		
Beginning of year balance	$(13,166)	$(13,086)
❶ Service cost	(293)	(274)
❷ Interest cost	(390)	(361)
❹ Actuarial gain (loss)	1,012	(35)
❺ Benefits paid	711	704
Settlements/curtailments		2
Acquisition*	(29)	
Foreign exchange and other	47	(116)
End of year balance	(12,108)	(13,166)
Change in plan assets (fair value)		
Beginning of year balance	12,093	11,137
❸ Actual return on plan assets	316	1,517
❻ Employer contribution	938	62
❺ Benefits paid	(711)	(704)
Settlements		(2)
Foreign exchange and other	(34)	83
End of year balance	12,602	12,093
❼ Funded status	$ 494	$ (1,073)
Weighted-average assumptions		
Discount rates	4.1%	3.6%
Rate of compensation increase	3.8%	3.8%

Net Periodic Pension Cost ($ millions)	2018	2017
Pensions		
❶ Service cost	$293	$274
❷ Interest cost	390	361
❸ Expected return on plan assets	(775)	(790)
❹ Amortization of actuarial loss	226	247
Amortization of prior service cost	12	12
Settlements/curtailments	8	2
Net cost	$154	$106
Weighted-average assumptions		
Discount rates—service cost	3.5%	3.5%
Discount rates—interest cost	3.2%	3.0%
Rate of compensation increase	3.8%	3.8%
Expected long-term rates of return	6.9%	7.3%

Deere discloses the funded status (the net of the PBO liability and pension plan assets) on the left-hand side of the table. We see that the funded status is positive in 2018 (a net asset) and negative in 2017 (a net liability). Deere discloses the pension expense components on the right-hand side of the table. Items that increase (decrease) the funded status are recognized as expense (income). Remember that pension expense or income is only recognized from accruals, not from cash contributions by the company or cash payments to retirees.

Service and interest cost

❶ **Service cost.** Deere employees provided another year of service to the company, which increases future benefits and the PBO by $293 million (liabilities are reported as a negative amount in this table). We see that the service cost increase in PBO is also reflected as an increase in pension cost. Under current GAAP, only the service cost is reported in operating income. The other components of pension cost are reported as other income (expense) below income from operations.

❷ **Interest cost.** PBO is the present value of forecasted pension obligations and is initially recognized as its present value. Each year the company accrues interest on the PBO using the discount rate. In 2018, this increased the PBO by $390 million. The interest cost component of pension expense increased by the same amount.

Investment returns

❸ Actual returns on pension investments for 2018 were $316 million and these increased the plan assets. Returns include gains (losses) on sales of investments along with interest and dividend income. In both 2017 and 2018, investment returns were positive, but returns can also be negative (for example, in a bear market).

Actual returns are not a component of pension expense. Rather *expected* return is recognized as income, which reduces pension cost. In 2018, expected return was $775 million. Deere estimates the expected return using an expected long-term rate of return on plan assets, which was 6.9% in 2018. Comparing the expected returns in the pension expense table to actual returns in the plan assets table, we see that the latter are relatively more volatile over time. As a result, pension expense is smoother by the use of expected returns rather than actual returns. This was the intended stabilizing effect of the pension accounting standard.

Actuarial gains (losses)

❹ **Actuarial gain (loss).** Deere invokes a number of actuarial assumptions in estimating PBO. Deere can change these assumptions to reflect changing macroeconomic conditions. The increases (decreases) in PBO that result from changes in actuarial assumptions are called actuarial gains (losses). In 2018, Deere increased the discount rate from 3.6% to 4.1% (see the 'Weighted-average assumptions' at the bottom of the table). The increase in discount rate lowered the PBO liability, which was reflected as a $1,012 million *gain* in Deere's PBO table.

The vast majority of companies do not reflect current period actuarial gains and losses in pension expense. Instead, companies carry the gains and losses in AOCI and gradually amortize them to pension expense. Deere amortizes $226 million of deferred actuarial losses during 2018. We see that the amortization is of a deferred loss (because it increases pension expense in 2018), but Deere recognized an actuarial *gain* of $1,012 million in the PBO in 2018. These two amounts will often be quite different because the PBO reflects the current period actuarial gains or losses and the pension expense represents the amortization of the cumulative actuarial gains or losses. The bottom line is that only a small proportion of the gains (losses) recognized in the PBO will ever be reflected in pension expense. That is the smoothing effect of the pension accounting standard. (See the text box on Amortization of Deferred Amounts).

Cash transactions

❺ **Benefits paid.** During 2018, benefits of $711 million were paid to retirees and Deere decreased the PBO by that amount. The payments came from the investment portfolio (pension plan assets) and so Deere also decreased that account by $711 million. Remember that payments to retirees do not affect pension expense for the year.

❻ **Employer contributions.** Deere's 2018 cash contributions of $938 million are reflected as an increase in the pension plan assets (and not reflected in income).

Funded status

❼ **Funded status.** Deere ended the year with a PBO balance of $12,108 million, pension plan assets of $12,602 million, and a positive funded status of $494 million (a net asset). This means that the pension plan was over-funded at the end of the year. In the previous year, Deere reported a funded status liability of $(1,073) million, indicating an under-funded plan.

> ### Accounting Insight ■ Amortization of Deferred Amounts
>
> Pension expense includes amortization of previously deferred amounts that arise from two sources: unexpected return on pension assets and changes in actuarial assumptions.
>
> **Unexpected returns on pension plan assets.** Pension expense includes the *expected* rate of return on pension assets rather than the *actual* rate of return. Pension assets increase with positive returns and decrease with negative returns, and those increases and decreases result in increases and decreases in equity, just like the effects of changes in the PBO. Using *actual* returns on pension assets would make pension expense and net income more volatile. To win approval for the pension standard from corporations, the FASB offered the use of a more stable long-term *expected* rate of return in the computation of pension expense. Actual returns usually differ from expected returns, and that *unexpected* return is included in OCI (and carried in AOCI) just like the deferred actuarial gains and losses relating to the PBO.
>
> AOCI includes both deferred actuarial gains and losses on the PBO and deferred unexpected gains and losses on pension assets. The AOCI balance, therefore, fluctuates over time, becoming positive in some years and negative in others. As long as it doesn't become too large, these deferred gains and losses remain on the balance sheet, not in the income statement.
>
> **Changes in actuarial assumptions.** To estimate the projected benefit obligation (PBO), companies must make assumptions about the following:
>
> - Proportion of current workers that will ultimately retire from the company and will become eligible for pension payments.
> - Expected rate of wage inflation that will, together with length of service, determine employees' benefits.
> - Number of years that employees will live (will receive annual pension payments) after retirement.
> - Discount rate to use in computing the present value of the estimated payments upon retirement.
>
> Each of these estimates is called an actuarial assumption and companies frequently change these assumptions as inflation rates and interest rates change and as new information about the employee population becomes available.
>
> A change in any of these actuarial assumptions changes the PBO liability. From the accounting equation (Assets = Liabilities + Equity), we know that if liabilities increase, equity must decrease, and if liabilities decrease, equity must increase. The vast majority of companies treat the change in equity arising from a change in estimates as a deferred gain (if the PBO decreases) or a deferred loss (if the PBO increases), recognizing the deferred gain or loss in other comprehensive income in the current year and, ultimately, in accumulated other comprehensive income (AOCI), a component of equity on the balance sheet. Those deferred gains and losses continue to be recognized in AOCI until they become large, at which point, they are reclassified from AOCI into the current period income statement as either income or expense.[1] As long as the total deferred gains or losses are not excessive, they can remain on the balance sheet in AOCI for a very long time. The deferral of actuarial gains and losses was a concession by the FASB to pave the way for passage of the pension accounting standard.

Fair Value Accounting for Pensions

The use of expected returns and the deferral and future amortization of actuarial gains and losses serves to smooth reported pension expense and, thereby, dampens earnings volatility. While the majority of companies continue to defer unexpected returns and actuarial gains and losses, recognizing them only if they exceed certain size limits, a number of large public companies have started to recognize those gains and losses in current earnings. AT&T, for example, adopted fair-value accounting for pensions in 2010 and now recognizes in current income the actual returns on pension assets (rather than expected returns) and gains (losses) arising from changes in actuarial assumptions. Following is an excerpt from the AT&T 2018 Form 10-K ($ millions).

---

[1] To avoid amortization, the deferred amounts must be less than 10% of the PBO or pension investments, whichever is greater. The excess, if any, is amortized until no further excess remains. When the excess is eliminated (by investment returns or company contributions, for example), the amortization ceases.

> We recognize gains and losses on pension and postretirement plan assets and obligations immediately in our operating results... Our combined net pension and postretirement cost (credit) recognized in our consolidated statements of income was $(4,251), $155 and $303 for the years ended December 31, 2018, 2017 and 2016.

AT&T's actuarial gain arose from a higher discount rate used to compute the PBO, which reduced the PBO and created a gain. The gain was offset, in part, by the fact that the actual return on pension assets was less than the expected return. The net actuarial (non-cash) gain increased AT&T's earnings by $4,117 million in 2018, or 16.5% of pretax earnings. Had AT&T accounted for its pension and other postretirement plans (OPEB) using the conventional approach, the gains would have flowed through other comprehensive income and earnings would have been unaffected.

AT&T's fair-value approach greatly increases earnings volatility as illustrated in the following graph that shows AT&T's actuarial gains and losses over the past six years.

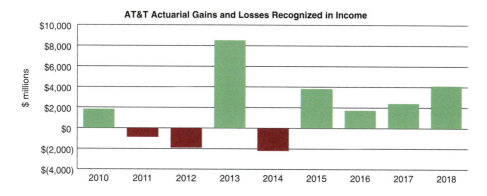

Other companies that have adopted fair value accounting for pensions and OPEB include **Verizon**, **IBM**, **Honeywell**, **FedEx** and **UPS**.

Although U.S. GAAP allows companies to recognize actuarial gains either immediately in current income or deferred in accumulated other comprehensive income (AOCI) and, subsequently amortized to income if they exceed certain limits, International Financial Reporting Standards (IFRS) does not allow an option to recognize actuarial gains and losses in income at all. Instead, IFRS requires actuarial gains and losses be deferred in accumulated other comprehensive income with no subsequent amortization. As a result, these gains are deferred indefinitely.

Research Insight ■ Valuation Implications of Pension Footnote Disclosures

The FASB requires footnote disclosure of the major components of pension cost presumably because it is useful for investors. Pension-related research has examined whether investors assign different valuation multiples to the components of pension cost when assessing company market value. Research finds that the market does, indeed, attach different interpretations to pension components, reflecting differences in information about perceived permanence in earnings.

Business Insight ■ Accounting for Pension Plan Settlements

Companies have long been moving away from traditional pensions and replacing them with Defined Contribution Plans (such as 401k plans), stock-based plans, and other forms of compensation. Under U.S. GAAP, pension obligations are deemed "settled" if the company makes an irrevocable action that relieves the company of its responsibility for pension benefit payments in the future.

Often companies settle their pension obligations by making lump-sum cash payments to plan participants. Another means to settle the obligation is to purchase nonparticipating annuity contracts from insurance companies

continued

continued from previous page

to cover vested benefits (buy-out contracts). The contracts off-load the responsibility for pension benefit payments to the insurance company. **FedEx** is an example of this sort of arrangement. In 2018, FedEx entered into an agreement with **Metropolitan Life Insurance Co.** to purchase a group annuity contract that transfers responsibility of pension benefits for 41,000 FedEx retirees and beneficiaries. FedEx described the transaction in a May 2018 press release.

> MEMPHIS, Tenn., May 8, 2018—FedEx Corp. (NYSE: FDX) announced today it has entered into an agreement with Metropolitan Life Insurance Company ("Metropolitan Life") to purchase a group annuity contract and transfer approximately $6 billion of the company's U.S. pension plan obligations. . . As a result of the transaction, FedEx expects to recognize a one-time non-cash pension settlement charge, which will be included in the fiscal 2018 year-end mark-to-market pension accounting adjustments that will be reported in the company's fiscal 2018 fourth quarter earnings release.

Settlement of the pension obligations triggers a settlement gain or loss that generally equals the net gain or loss remaining in AOCI, including any new actuarial gain or loss resulting from the measurement of the PBO and the plan assets on the settlement date. FedEx recognized a $210 million settlement loss in its 2018 income statement.

Footnote Disclosure—Key Assumptions

Recall the following earlier breakdown for pension expense.

	Net Pension Expense
	Service cost
+	Interest cost
−	*Expected* return on pension plan assets
±	Amortization of deferred amounts, if any
=	Net pension expense

Interest cost is the product of the PBO and the discount rate. This discount rate is set by the company. The expected dollar return on pension assets is the product of the pension plan asset balance and the expected long-run rate of return on the investment portfolio. This rate is also set by the company. Further, PBO is affected by the expected rate of wage inflation, termination and mortality rates, all of which are estimated by the company.

Under U.S. GAAP, companies must disclose the rates and assumptions used to estimate PBO and pension expense. (Pension plan assets do not rely on rate assumptions because the returns and asset fair values are directly measurable.) Deere reported the rates it used immediately beneath the tables in its pension footnote. Other companies report these assumptions separately in other footnotes. During 2018, Deere increased the discount rate used to compute the present value of its PBO, from 3.6% to 4.1%, while leaving unchanged its estimate of the rate of compensation increase. The increase in the discount rate reduced the PBO present value by $1,012 million, resulting in an actuarial gain of that amount. On the expense side, Deere increased the interest rate used to compute the interest component of pension expense from 3.0% to 3.2% and reduced the expected long-term rate of return on pension investments from 7.3% to 6.9%. Respectively, these changes resulted in increased interest cost and reduced investment returns, both of which increased pension expense for the year.

Changes in assumptions have the following general effects on pension expense and, thus, profitability. This table summarizes the effects of increases in the various rates. Decreases have the exact opposite effects.

Assumption Change	Probable Effect on Pension Expense	Reason for Effect
Discount (interest) rate ↑	↑ or ↓	While the higher discount rate reduces the PBO, the lower PBO is multiplied by a higher rate when the company computes the interest component of pension expense. The net effect is, therefore, indeterminate.
Investment return ↑	↓	The dollar amount of expected return on plan assets is the product of the plan assets balance and the expected long-term rate of return. Increasing the return increases the expected return on plan assets, thus reducing pension expense.
Wage inflation ↑	↑	The expected rate of wage inflation affects future wage levels that determine expected pension payments. An increase, thus, increases PBO, which increases both the service and interest cost components of pension expense.

Analysis Implications

There are three important analysis issues relating to pensions.

1. To what extent will the company's pension plans compete with investing and financing needs for the available cash flows?
2. In what ways has the company's choice of estimates affected its profitability?
3. Should pension costs and funded status be treated as operating or nonoperating?

Regarding the first issue, pension plan assets are the source of funds to pay benefits to retirees, and federal law (Employee Retirement Income Security Act) sets minimum standards for pension contributions. Consequently, if investment returns are insufficient, companies must make up the shortfall with additional contributions. Any such additional contributions compete for available operating cash flows with other investing and financing activities. This can be especially severe in a business downturn when operating cash flows are depressed. As pension payments are contractual, companies can be forced to postpone needed capital investment to make the contributions necessary to ensure funding of their pension plans as required by law or labor agreements. Analysts must be aware of funding requirements when projecting future cash flows.

Regarding the second issue, accounting for pensions requires several assumptions, including the expected return on pension investments, the expected rate of wage inflation, the discount rate used to compute the PBO, and other actuarial assumptions that are not reported in footnotes (mortality rates, for example). Each of these assumptions affects reported profit, and analysts must be aware of changes in these assumptions and their effects on profitability. An increase in reported profit that is due to an increase in the expected return on pension investments, for example, is not related to core operating activities and, further, might not be sustainable. Such changes in estimates must be considered in our evaluation of reported profitability.

The third analysis issue relates to the operating vs. nonoperating treatment of pension expense and funded status. Pension expense includes service cost, interest costs, and actuarial cost components (and gains and losses for companies that opt for fair-value accounting). Service cost is, arguably, more related to operating activities than the other components, because service cost arises from the increase in pension benefits earned by employees as they continue to work for the company. Consequently, many analysts argue for operating treatment of service costs. In 2017, the FASB issued new accounting standards relating to the recognition of pension cost. Under current GAAP, companies are required to report the service cost component of pension cost in the same line item or items as other compensation costs. The other components of pension expense are to be presented in the income statement separately from the service cost component and outside of income from operations.

The operating vs. nonoperating analysis of the funded status on the balance sheet is more difficult. The pension obligation represents a form of compensation and, in that sense, it is operating in nature. However, U.S. GAAP defines the PBO as the "actuarial *present value* . . . of all benefits attributed by the pension benefit formula to employee service rendered before that date" [emphasis ours]. It is the present-value requirement that results in the need to accrue interest expense as a component of pension expense, leading to the argument that a portion of the PBO might be considered as nonoperating. In our view, the GAAP requirement to discount future pension obligations does not change the character of the obligation and, for that reason, we treat the funded status liability as operating. (Very few companies report a net pension *asset*. But, if they do, we consider the PBO to be equal to zero and treat the excess pension assets as nonoperating as they comprise marketable securities, which we generally treat as nonoperating.)

Other Post-Employment Benefits (OPEB)

In addition to pension benefits, many companies provide healthcare and insurance benefits to retired employees. These benefits are referred to as **other post-employment benefits (OPEB)**. These benefits present reporting challenges similar to pension accounting. However, companies most often provide these benefits on a "pay-as-you-go" basis and it is rare for companies to make contributions in advance for OPEB. As a result, this liability, known as the **accumulated post-employment benefit obligation (APBO)**, is largely, if not totally, unfunded. GAAP requires that the unfunded APBO liability, net of any unrecognized amounts, be reported in the balance sheet and the annual service costs and interest costs be accrued as expenses each year. This requirement is controversial for two reasons. First, future healthcare costs are especially difficult to estimate, so the value of the resulting APBO (the present value of the future benefits) is fraught with error. Second, these benefits are provided at the discretion of the employer and can be altered or terminated at any time. Consequently, employers argue that without a legal obligation to pay these benefits, the liability should not be reported in the balance sheet. (For a more complete discussion of OPEB issues, see: https://www.pwc.com/us/en/corporate-governance/assets/pension-paper.pdf.)

These other post-employment benefits can produce large liabilities. For example, **Deere**'s footnotes report a funded status for the company's healthcare obligation of $(4,753) million in 2018, consisting of an APBO liability of $5,472 million and OPEB plan assets of $719 million. Our analysis of cash flows related to pension obligations can be extended to other post-employment benefit obligations. For example, in addition to its pension payments, Deere discloses that it is obligated to make healthcare payments to retirees totaling about $320 million to $345 million per year. Because healthcare obligations are rarely funded until payment is required (federal minimum funding standards do not apply to OPEB and there is no tax benefit to pre-funding), there are no investment returns to fund the payments. Our analysis of projected cash flows must consider this potential cash outflow in addition to that relating to pension obligations.

Research Insight ■ Valuation of Nonpension Post-Employment Benefits

The FASB requires employers to accrue the costs of all nonpension post-employment benefits, known as *accumulated post-employment benefit obligation* (APBO). These benefits consist primarily of healthcare and insurance. This requirement is controversial due to concerns about the reliability of the liability estimate. Research finds that the APBO (alone) is associated with company value. However, when other pension-related variables are included in the research, the APBO liability is no longer useful in explaining company value. Research concludes that the pension-related variables do a better job at conveying value-relevant information than the APBO number alone, which implies that the APBO number is less reliable.

Review 10-2 LO2

Following is the pension disclosure footnote from **American Airlines**' 10-K report (in millions).

Pension Benefits	2018	2017
Benefit obligation at beginning of period	$18,275	$17,238
Service cost	3	2
Interest cost	674	721
Actuarial (gain) loss	(1,910)	1,016
Settlements	(4)	(4)
Benefit payments	(662)	(726)
Other	2	28
Obligation at December 31	$16,378	$18,275

continued

continued from previous page

Pension Benefits	2018	2017
Fair value of plan assets at beginning of period	$11,395	$10,017
Actual return on plan assets	(1,151)	1,797
Employer contributions	475	286
Settlements	(4)	(4)
Benefit payments	(662)	(726)
Other	—	25
Fair value of plan assets at end of period	$10,053	$11,395
Funded status at end of period	$ (6,325)	$ (6,880)

Following is American Airlines' footnote for its pension cost as reported in its income statement (in millions).

Pension Benefits	2018	2017
Defined benefit plans:		
Service cost	$ 3	$ 2
Interest cost	674	721
Expected return on assets	(905)	(790)
Settlements	—	1
Amortization of:		
Prior service cost (benefit)	28	28
Unrecognized net loss (gain)	141	144
Net periodic benefit cost (income)	$ (59)	$106

Required

1. What factors impact American Airlines' pension benefit obligation during 2018?
2. What factors impact American Airlines' pension plan assets during 2018?
3. What amount is reported on the balance sheet relating to American Airlines defined benefit pension plan?
4. How does the expected return on plan assets affect pension expense?
5. How does American Airlines' expected return on plan assets compare with its actual return (in $ millions) for 2018?
6. How much net pension expense is reflected in American Airlines' 2018 income statement?
7. Assess American Airlines' ability to meet payment obligations to retirees.

Solution on p. 10-68.

Income Taxes

When preparing financial statements for stockholders and other external constituents, companies use GAAP. But when companies prepare their income tax returns, they prepare financial statements using the *Internal Revenue Code (IRC)*. These two sets of accounting rules recognize revenues and expenses differently in many cases and, as a result, can yield markedly different levels of income. In general, companies desire to report lower income to taxing authorities than they do to their stockholders so that they can reduce their tax liability and increase after-tax cash flow. This practice is acceptable so long as the financial statements are prepared in conformity with GAAP and tax returns are filed in accordance with the IRC.

LO3 Analyze and interpret income tax reporting.

Timing Differences Create Deferred Tax Assets and Liabilities

As an example, consider the depreciation of long-term assets. For financial reports, companies typically depreciate long-term assets using straight-line depreciation (meaning the same amount of depreciation expense is reported each year over the useful life of the asset). However, for tax returns, companies use an *accelerated* method of depreciation (meaning more depreciation is taken in the early years of the asset's life and less depreciation in later years). When a company depreciates assets at an accelerated rate for tax purposes, the depreciation deduction for tax purposes is higher and taxable income is lower in the early years of the assets' lives. As a result, taxable income and tax payments are reduced and after-tax cash flow is increased. That excess cash can then be reinvested in the business to increase its returns to stockholders.

To illustrate, assume that Southwest Airlines purchases an asset with a five-year life. It depreciates that asset using the straight-line method (equal expense per year) when reporting to stockholders and depreciates the asset at a faster rate (accelerated depreciation) for tax purposes. Annual (full year) depreciation expense under these two methods is depicted in Exhibit 10.3.

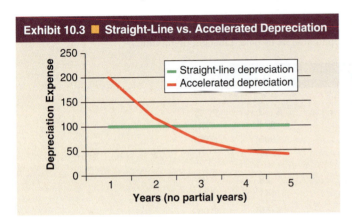

During the first 2.5 years in this example, depreciation is higher in the company's tax returns than it is in its GAAP financial statements. In the last 2.5 years, this is reversed, with lower depreciation expense for tax purposes. Taxable income and tax payments are, therefore, higher during the last 2.5 years. The same total amount of depreciation is recognized under both methods over the five-year life of the asset. Only the timing of the recognition of the expense differs.[2]

Illustration of Deferred Tax Liabilities We use this timing concept to illustrate the accounting for a **deferred tax liability**. Assume that a company purchases a depreciable asset with a cost of $100 and a two-year useful life. For financial reporting purposes (for GAAP-based reports), it depreciates the asset using the straight-line method, which yields depreciation expense of $50 per year. For tax reporting (when filing income tax returns), it depreciates the asset on an accelerated basis, which yields depreciation deduction of $75 in the first year and $25 in the second year (the same total amount of depreciation is reported under the two depreciation methods; only the amount of depreciation reported per year differs). Assume that this company reports income before depreciation and taxes of $200 and that its tax rate is 40%. Its income statements, for both financial reporting and tax reporting, for the asset's first year are in Exhibit 10.4A.

Exhibit 10.4A ■ Year 1 Income Statements: Financial Reporting vs. Tax Reporting		
Year 1	**Financial Reporting**	**Tax Reporting**
Income before depreciation	$200	$200
Depreciation	50	75
Income before tax.	150	125
Income tax (40%)	60 [expense]	50 [cash paid]
Net income	$ 90	$ 75

This company records income tax expense and a related deferred tax liability for the first year as reflected in the following financial statement effects template:

---

[2] The Modified Accelerated Cost Recovery System (MACRS) is the current method of accelerated asset depreciation required by the United States income tax code. Under MACRS, all assets are divided into classes that dictate the number of years over which an asset's cost is "recovered" and the percentage of the asset cost that can be depreciated per year is fixed by regulation. For a five-year asset, such as in our example, the MACRS depreciation percentages per year are 20%, 32%, 19.2%, 11.52%, 11.52%, and 5.76%. MACRS assumes that assets are acquired in the middle of the year, hence a half-year depreciation in Year 1 and a half-year depreciation in Year 6. The point after which straight-line depreciation exceeds MACRS depreciation is after about 2.5 years as assumed in the example.

Year 1 Transaction	Balance Sheet					Income Statement		
	Cash Asset	+ Noncash Assets	= Liabilities	+ Contrib. Capital	+ Earned Capital	Revenues	− Expenses	= Net Income
Record tax expense: expense exceeds cash because of deferral of tax	−50 Cash		= +10 Deferred Tax Liability		−60 Retained Earnings		+60 Tax Expense	−60

```
TE.........60
   DTL...........10
   Cash..........50

   TE
   60 |
       DTL
          | 10
       Cash
          | 50
```

The reduction in cash reflects the payment of taxes owed to the taxing authority. The increase in deferred tax liability represents an estimate of additional tax that will be payable in the second year (which is the tax liability deferred in the first year). This liability for a future tax payment arises because second-year depreciation expense for tax purposes will be only $25, resulting in taxes payable of $70, which is $10 more than the income tax expense the company reports in its income statement to shareholders in Year 2 as we illustrate in Exhibit 10.4B.

Exhibit 10.4B ■ Year 2 Income Statements: Financial Reporting vs. Tax Reporting

Year 2	Financial Reporting	Tax Reporting
Income before depreciation	$200	$200
Depreciation	50	25
Income before tax	150	175
Income tax (40%)	60 [expense]	70 [cash paid]
Net income	$ 90	$105

At the end of Year 1, the company knows that this additional tax must be paid in Year 2 because the financial reporting and tax reporting depreciation schedules are set when the asset is placed in service. Given these known amounts, the company accrues the deferred tax liability in Year 1 in the same manner as it would accrue any estimated future liability, say for wages payable, by recognizing a liability and the related expense.

At the end of Year 2, the additional income tax is paid and the company's deferred tax liability is now satisfied. Financial statement effects related to the tax payment and expense in Year 2 are reflected in the following template:

Year 2 Transaction	Balance Sheet					Income Statement		
	Cash Asset	+ Noncash Assets	= Liabilities	+ Contrib. Capital	+ Earned Capital	Revenues	− Expenses	= Net Income
Record tax expense: cash exceeds expense because deferred taxes are reversed	−70 Cash		= −10 Deferred Tax Liability		−60 Retained Earnings		+60 Tax Expense	−60

```
TE.........60
   DTL........10
       Cash..........70

   TE
   60 |
       DTL
       10 |
           Cash
              | 70
```

The income tax expense for financial reporting purposes is $60 each year. However, the cash payment for taxes is $70 in Year 2; the $10 excess reduces the deferred tax liability accrued in Year 1.

Illustration of Deferred Tax Assets Deferred tax assets arise when the tax payment is *greater* than the tax expense for financial reporting purposes (opposite of the illustration above).

For example, restructuring accruals give rise to deferred tax assets. In the year in which a company approves a reorganization plan, it will accrue a restructuring liability for estimated employee severance payments and other costs and it will write down assets to their market values (this reduces the net book value of those assets on the balance sheet). However, for tax purposes, restructuring costs are not deductible until paid in the future, and asset write-downs are not deductible until the loss is realized when the asset is sold. As a result, the restructuring accrual is not a liability for tax reporting until the company makes the payment, and the write-down of assets is not a deductible expense for tax purposes until the assets are sold. Both of these differences (the liability and the assets) give rise to a deferred tax asset. The deferred tax asset will be transferred to the income statement in the future as an expense when the company pays the restructuring costs and sells the impaired assets for a loss.

Another common deferred tax asset relates to **tax loss carryforwards**. Specifically, when a company reports a loss for tax purposes, it can carry the loss forward indefinitely to reduce future taxable income. (Prior to the 2017 tax law changes, losses could be carried back two years and forward for 20 years. See the Analysis Insight box on page 10-30.) This creates a benefit (an "asset") for tax reporting for which there is no corresponding financial reporting asset. Thus, the company records a deferred tax asset but only if the company is "more likely than not" to be able to use the loss to reduce future taxes. This depends on the company's assessment of whether it will have sufficient profits in the future. (We return to this issue later in the module.)

Reporting Deferred Tax Assets and Liabilities

In financial statement footnotes, companies must disclose the components of deferred tax liabilities and assets. **HP Inc.**'s deferred tax footnote (shown in Exhibit 10.5) reports net deferred tax assets of $2,624 million and total deferred tax liabilities of $293 million at the end of fiscal 2018. HP's deferred tax assets primarily relate to loss carryforwards. Its deferred tax liabilities relate to estimated tax on unremitted earnings for foreign subsidiaries (see the text box below). Other companies with significant investments in PPE assets report deferred tax liabilities relating to accelerated depreciation, as illustrated at the start of this section.

Exhibit 10.5 ■ Deferred Taxes Footnote for HP Inc.

As of October 31 (in millions)	2018	2017
Deferred Tax Assets		
Loss and credit carryforwards	$ 8,204	$ 9,914
Intercompany transactions—excluding inventory	994	1,901
Fixed assets	151	256
Warranty	194	219
Employee and retiree benefits	401	519
Deferred Revenue	164	231
Other	422	511
Gross Deferred Tax Assets	10,530	13,551
Valuation allowances	(7,906)	(8,807)
Net Deferred Tax Assets	2,624	4,744
Deferred Tax Liabilities		
Unremitted earnings of foreign subsidiaries	(31)	(5,554)
Intangible assets	(229)	(209)
Other	(33)	(49)
Total Deferred Tax Liabilities	(293)	(5,812)
Net Deferred Tax Assets (Liabilities)	$ 2,331	$ (1,068)

Under U.S. GAAP, companies compute deferred tax assets and liabilities as follows.

- **Deferred tax asset** Future estimated tax deductible expense or loss × Estimated tax rate
- **Deferred tax liability** Future estimated taxable income × Estimated tax rate

Deferred tax assets. HP reports tax loss carryforwards that can be applied to reduce future taxable income and decrease HP's income tax bill that year. The $8,204 million deferred tax asset represents the cash benefit HP will receive when loss carryforwards are applied to reduce future taxable income. This means that HP expects to save $8,204 million in future taxes. HP computes the reported amount as: Estimated tax deductible *loss* that will be applied to future tax returns × Estimated tax rate.

Deferred tax liabilities. The $31 million that HP reports for estimated future taxes on unremitted earnings of foreign subsidiaries represents the cash HP will pay in tax when the foreign subsidiary profits become taxable. The $31 million reported amount is computed as: Estimated future taxable *income* × Estimated tax rate.

Both deferred tax assets and deferred tax liabilities are computed using the tax rates in effect when the financial statements are prepared. If the tax rates change, so do the reported deferred tax assets and liabilities. The text box below discusses the effects of the U.S. Tax Cuts and Jobs Act of 2017 (TCJA).

Valuation Allowance for Deferred Tax Assets

Companies must establish a valuation allowance for deferred tax assets if the future realization of the tax benefits is uncertain. (HP provides an allowance of $7,906 million in Exhibit 10.5 above) The allowance reduces reported assets and increases tax expense, which reduces equity. (This allowance is similar to accounting for the write-down of any asset.) Once the deferred tax asset valuation allowance is established, it can be reduced (reversed) by one of two events.

- **The company writes off a deferred tax asset.** In this case, the asset is reduced to zero and the amount written off is subtracted from the deferred tax valuation allowance. There is no effect on income from this write-off. (This is similar to the accounting for a write-off of an uncollectible account receivable against the allowance for uncollectible accounts, which has no effect on income.) A typical example of a deferred tax asset write-off occurs when net operating loss carryforwards (NOLs) expire before they can be used to offset other profits.
- **The company determines that the deferred tax assets *will* be realized.** If the company decides that the realization of the deferred tax assets is more likely than not, it can reverse the deferred tax asset valuation allowance. In that case, the deferred tax asset valuation allowance is reduced and tax expense is reduced by the same amount, thus *increasing* net income.

We see that HP's deferred tax footnote in Exhibit 10.5, includes a valuation allowance in both 2017 and 2018 and that the allowance decreased in 2018. The footnote below explains that in 2018 the company adjusted the valuation allowance because certain foreign tax rules changed during the year, thereby increasing the value of the future benefit.

Taxes on Earnings

HP recognizes deferred tax assets and liabilities for the expected tax consequences of temporary differences between the tax bases of assets and liabilities and their reported amounts using enacted tax rates in effect for the year the differences are expected to reverse. HP records a valuation allowance to reduce the deferred tax assets to the amount that is more likely than not to be realized.

Deferred Tax Asset Valuation Allowance

The deferred tax asset valuation allowance and changes were as follows:

As of October 31 (in millions)	2018	2017	2016
Balance at beginning of year	$8,807	$8,520	$7,114
Income tax (benefit) expense	(897)	297	1,421
Other comprehensive income, currency translation and charges to other accounts	(4)	(10)	(15)
Balance at end of year	$7,906	$8,807	$8,520

Gross deferred tax assets as of October 31, 2018, 2017 and 2016, were reduced by valuation allowances of $7.9 billion, $8.8 billion and $8.5 billion, respectively. The total valuation allowance decreased by $901 million in fiscal year 2018, associated primarily with foreign net operating losses and U.S. deferred tax assets that are anticipated to be realized at a lower effective rate than the federal statutory tax rate due to certain future U.S. international tax reform implications.

The decrease in the valuation allowance had the following effects: HP's deferred tax assets and net income both increased by $901 million in 2018 ($897 million + $4 million).

Disclosures for Income Taxes

Following is an excerpt from HP's 2018 income statement (highlight ours).

For Fiscal Years Ended October 31 ($ millions)	2018	2017	2016
Earnings from continuing operations before taxes	$3,013	$3,276	$3,761
Benefit from (provision for) taxes	2,314	(750)	(1,095)
Net earnings from continuing operations	5,327	2,526	2,666
Net loss from discontinued operations	—	—	(170)
Net earnings	$5,327	$2,526	$2,496

The tax expense reported on the income statement relates to taxes that will be paid to federal, state, and municipal taxing authorities as well as income taxes levied by foreign governments. We see that HP reported a tax benefit in FY2018 that resulted from the U.S. Tax Cuts and Jobs Act of 2017 (TCJA) (see text box below). That tax benefit increased HP's net income by $2,314 million in 2018.

Companies are required to disclose in their footnotes the portion of income tax expense that is currently payable and the amount that relates to deferred taxes. HP's disclosure for fiscal 2018 follows.

For Fiscal Years Ended October 31 ($ millions)	2018	2017	2016
U.S. federal taxes:			
Current	$ 751	$189	$ 439
Deferred	(3,132)	197	470
Non-U.S. taxes:			
Current	528	302	288
Deferred	(563)	4	(123)
State taxes:			
Current	61	20	(35)
Deferred	41	38	56
	$(2,314)	$750	$1,095

- **Current tax expense.** Current tax expense is determined from the company's tax returns; it is the amount that must be paid (in cash) to tax authorities for current year operations. Some of these taxes are paid during the year as the company makes installments. The remaining balance is included as a current liability. For fiscal 2018, HP's current tax expense was $1,340 million (= $751 million + $528 million + $61 million).
- **Deferred tax expense.** Deferred tax expense is the effect on tax expense from changes in deferred tax liabilities and deferred tax assets. For fiscal 2018, this was a net tax benefit of $3,654 million, reducing tax expense and increasing deferred tax assets.

Companies are also required to reconcile the difference between the U.S. corporate tax rate and the company's **effective tax rate** (computed as Tax expense/Pretax income). HP's tax reconciliation table follows.

For Fiscal Years Ended October 31 ($ millions)	2018	2017	2016
U.S. federal statutory income tax rate from continuing operations	23.3%	35.0%	35.0%
State income taxes from continuing operations, net of federal tax benefit	0.5%	1.4%	1.1%
Lower rates in other jurisdictions, net	(10.9)%	(13.2)%	(9.3)%
U.S. tax reform impacts	(35.8)%	—%	—%
Research and development ("R&D") credit	(0.7)%	(0.5)%	(2.4)%
Valuation allowances	(9.3)%	(1.9)%	(1.2)%
Uncertain tax positions and audit settlements	(50.3)%	0.4%	11.7%
Indemnification related items	5.2%	(0.3)%	(4.1)%
Other, net	1.2%	2.0%	(1.7)%
	(76.8)%	22.9%	29.1%

The effective tax rate reconciliation table not only provides insight into the company's effective tax rate, it also provides valuable information about transitory items that have affected income taxes and, therefore, net income. In 2018, for example, HP reported reductions to the effective tax rate of 35.8% from U.S. Tax Reform impacts and 50.3% from "Uncertain tax positions and audit settlements." Tax reductions like these are not likely to recur in the foreseeable future. Accordingly, we would likely not want to use this negative 2018 tax rate to forecast future tax rates.

Analysis of Income Tax Disclosures

Analysis of deferred taxes can yield useful insights. Some revenue accruals (such as accounts receivable for longer-term contracts) increase deferred tax liabilities as GAAP income exceeds taxable income (similar to the effect of using straight-line depreciation for financial reporting purposes and accelerated depreciation for tax returns).

An increase in deferred tax liabilities indicates that a company is reporting higher GAAP income relative to taxable income and can indicate the company is managing earnings upwards. Although an increase in deferred tax liabilities can legitimately result, for example, from an increase in depreciable assets and the use of accelerated depreciation for tax purposes, we must be aware of the possibility that the company might be improperly reporting revenues.

The income tax footnote also reveals any changes in the deferred tax asset valuation account. A decrease in the valuation allowance is often triggered by the write-off of deferred tax assets, typically relating to net operating loss carryforwards (NOLs). These carryforwards allow companies to offset current losses against future income indefinitely, but they are capped to 80% of taxable income. NOL carryforwards cannot be used to offset profits across subsidiary companies. (Prior to the TCJA, firms could carry NOLs back two years and forward 20 years. The TCJA eliminated the carryback and extended carry forwards indefinitely. These new rules changed the likelihood that NOLs would be used for many firms, which increased the deferred tax asset, or reduced the related valuation allowances.)

As we illustrate with HP, Inc. above, companies can (and do) increase their estimate on the recoverability of deferred tax assets. When they do, the valuation allowance is reduced, thereby increasing deferred tax assets and increasing net income dollar-for-dollar by a reduction of income tax expense. The income tax footnote will reveal any such changes in the deferred tax valuation allowance and also the impact on net income.

The reconciliation of statutory and effective tax rates can reveal important transitory items that might impact our forecast of future tax rates. Income tax expense is a large expense item for most companies and the rate we use in our forecasts can greatly affect our expectations of future net income.

Analysis Insight ■ U.S. Tax Cuts and Jobs Act of 2017

HP reported a tax *benefit* of $2,314 million in 2018, compared with a tax *expense* of $750 million in the prior year on comparable levels of reported pretax profit. This unusual tax situation for HP and a myriad of other companies arose from the U.S. Tax Cuts and Jobs Act of 2017. This new tax law significantly changed the income tax structure for U.S. corporations in key ways.

- It reduced the corporate tax rate from 35% to 21%.
- It taxed income earned outside the U.S. even if the cash profit remained abroad.

As a result of this legislation, some companies reported significant tax expense increases in 2017 and 2018 and others, like HP, reported tax decreases that significantly increased reported profits. The effects of this tax legislation are great for many companies, and will confound any historical analysis of the income statement. HP discusses the significant effects of the TCJA in the following excerpt from its income tax footnote.

> In fiscal year 2018, HP recorded $2.8 billion of net income tax benefits related to discrete items in the provision for taxes which include impacts of the TCJA . . . [A]s of October 31, 2018, HP recorded a . . . $5.6 billion net benefit for the decrease in its deferred tax liability on unremitted foreign earnings, partially offset by $3.3 billion net expense for the deemed repatriation tax payable in installments over eight years, a $1.2 billion net expense for the remeasurement of its deferred assets and liabilities to the new U.S. statutory tax rate and a $317 million valuation allowance on net expense related to deferred tax assets that are expected to be realized at a lower rate.

continued

continued from previous page

There were two main tax effects of the TCJA on income tax expense for U.S. companies.

1. **Tax on unremitted profit on foreign subsidiaries.** Under prior tax laws, profits earned by foreign subsidiaries were not taxed in the U.S. until the cash was repatriated via a dividend to the U.S. parent company. U.S. GAAP allowed companies to postpone recording the related tax expense, provided that the company asserted the foreign profits were "indefinitely invested abroad." These incentives to keep foreign profits outside the U.S. led to nearly $3 trillion cumulative unrepatriated foreign earnings of U.S. companies in 2017. The TCJA moved the U.S. to a territorial system, meaning that companies could repatriate foreign profits earned after 2017, without triggering any U.S. tax. The TCJA also mandated that *previously earned* foreign profits would be taxed in 2018, whether foreign earnings were ever repatriated. While companies can elect to pay the "mandatory transition tax" over eight years, under U.S. GAAP, companies must recognize the entire transition tax liability and related income tax expense in 2018.
2. **Reduction of deferred tax assets (liabilities).** Under U.S. GAAP, deferred tax assets and liabilities are computed as the product of future taxable loss (income) and the estimated tax rate, which was 35% prior to the TCJA. With the passage of the TCJA, the corporate tax rate fell to 21%. This had the effect of reducing all deferred taxes, both assets and liabilities. A decrease to the deferred tax asset account resulted in additional tax expense and lower net income. A reduction in deferred tax liabilities had the opposite effect, a tax benefit (a negative tax expense) increased net income. The TCJA created winners and losers: companies with significant deferred tax assets reported lower net income while companies with significant deferred tax liabilities saw tax expenses plummet. Many companies reported large tax benefits and inflated net income in 2017 (or in 2018 for non-calendar-year companies like HP).

The "catch-up" tax on income previously earned by foreign subsidiaries and the revaluation of deferred tax assets and liabilities using the lower corporate tax rates *are both transitory items* that affected the income statements of U.S. companies in 2017 or 2018. These tax impacts were substantial for many companies, resulting in a lack of comparability with prior years and complicating the choice of the appropriate tax rate to use to analyze performance analysis and to forecast future income statements (see Module 12).

Expanded Explanation of Deferred Taxes

The earlier example showed that total depreciation over the life of the asset is the same under both tax and financial reporting, and that the only difference is the timing of the expense or tax deduction. Because depreciation differs each year, the amount at which the equipment is reported will differ as well for book and tax purposes (cost less accumulated depreciation is called *net book value* for financial reporting purposes and *tax basis* for tax purposes). These book vs. tax differences are eliminated at the end of the asset's useful life.

Expanded Example of a Deferred Tax Liability: PPE

To understand this concept more completely, we modify the example from the module to include a third year. Assume that the company purchases PPE assets at the start of Year 1 for $120. For financial reporting purposes, the company uses straight-line depreciation and records depreciation of $40 each year (with zero salvage). For tax purposes, assume that the company takes tax depreciation deductions of $60, $50, and $10. Exhibit 10.6 reports the annual depreciation along with the asset's net book value and its tax basis, for each year-end.

The third column in Exhibit 10.6 shows the "book-tax" difference, which is the difference between GAAP net book value and the tax basis at the end of each year. The fourth column shows the deferred tax liability at the end of each period, computed as the book-tax difference times the tax rate. We see from the fourth column that when the financial reporting net book value is greater than the tax basis, the company has a deferred tax liability on its balance sheet (as in Years 1 and 2). Companies' footnotes provide information about deferred taxes. For example, **Southwest Airlines'** footnote reports a deferred tax liability of $4,429 million for its accelerated depreciation on its property, plant and equipment, which indicates the tax basis for PPE is less than GAAP net book value, on average, for Southwest's PPE.

Accounting standards require a company to first compute the taxes it owes (per its tax return), then to compute any changes in deferred tax liabilities and assets, and finally to compute tax expense

Exhibit 10.6 — Book and Tax Depreciation and Carrying Value

	Financial Reporting (Net Book Value)	Tax Reporting (Tax Basis)	Book vs. Tax Difference	Deferred Tax Liability (Book vs. Tax Difference × Tax Rate)	Deferred Tax Expense (Increase or Decrease in Deferred Tax Liability)
At purchase: PPE carrying value	$120	$120	$ 0	$ 0	
Year 1: Depreciation	(40)	(60)			
End of Year 1: PPE carrying value	80	60	$20 ($80 − $60)	$ 8 ($20 × 40%)	$ 8 ($8 − $0)
Year 2: Depreciation	(40)	(50)			
End of Year 2: PPE carrying value	40	10	$30 ($40 − $10)	$12 ($30 × 40%)	$ 4 ($12 − $8)
Year 3: Depreciation	(40)	(10)			
End of Year 3: PPE carrying value	0	0	$ 0 ($0 − $0)	$ 0	$(12) ($0 − $12)

reported in the income statement (as a residual amount). Thus, tax expense is not computed as pretax income multiplied by the company's tax rate as we might initially expect. Instead, tax expense is computed as follows.

Tax Expense = Taxes Paid − Increase (or + Decrease) in Deferred Tax Assets + Increase (or − Decrease) in Deferred Tax Liabilities

The far-right column in Exhibit 10.6 shows the deferred tax expense per year, which is the amount added to, or subtracted from, taxes paid, to arrive at the tax expense. If we assume this company had $100 of pre-depreciation income, its taxable income and tax expense (assuming a 40% rate) follow.

	Taxes Paid	Deferred Tax Expense	Total Tax Expense
Year 1	$16 ($100 − $60) × 40%	$ 8	$24
Year 2	$20 ($100 − $50) × 40%	$ 4	$24
Year 3	$36 ($100 − $10) × 40%	$(12)	$24

In this example, the timing difference between the financial reporting and tax reporting derives from PPE and creates a deferred tax liability. Other differences between the two sets of books create other types of deferred tax accounts.

Rules for Deferred Tax Assets and Liabilities from Timing Differences Between GAAP and Tax

Exhibit 10.7 shows the relation between the financial reporting and tax reporting net book values, and the resulting deferred taxes (liability or asset) on the balance sheet.

Exhibit 10.7 — Sources of Deferred Tax Assets and Liabilities

For Assets...

| Financial reporting net book value | > | Tax reporting net book value | → | Deferred tax liability on balance sheet |
| Financial reporting net book value | < | Tax reporting net book value | → | Deferred tax asset on balance sheet |

For Liabilities...

| Financial reporting net book value | < | Tax reporting net book value | → | Deferred tax liability on balance sheet |
| Financial reporting net book value | > | Tax reporting net book value | → | Deferred tax asset on balance sheet |

Expanded Example of a Deferred Tax Asset: Restructuring Costs

A common deferred tax asset relates to accrued restructuring costs (a liability for financial reporting purposes). Restructuring costs are not deductible for tax purposes until paid in the future and, thus, there is no accrual restructuring liability for tax reporting, which means it has a tax basis of $0. To explain how this timing difference affects tax expense, assume that a company accrues $300 of restructuring costs in Year 1 and settles the liability in Year 2 as follows.

	Financial Reporting (Net Book Value)	Tax Reporting (Tax Basis)	Book vs. Tax Difference	Deferred Tax Asset (Book vs. Tax Difference × Tax Rate)	Deferred Tax Expense (Change in Deferred Tax Asset)
Year 1: Accrue restructuring costs...	$(300)	$ 0			
End of Year 1: Liability book value...	$ 300	$ 0	$300 ($300 − $0)	$120 ($300 × 40%)	$(120) ($120 − $0)
Year 2: Pay restructuring costs......		$(300)			
End of Year 2: Liability book value...	$ 0	0	$ 0 ($0 − $0)	$ 0 ($0 × 40%)	$120 ($120 − $0)

Timing differences created by the restructuring liability yield a deferred tax asset in Year 1. Timing differences disappear in Year 2 when the company pays cash for restructuring costs. To see how tax expense is determined, assume that this company has $500 of pre-restructuring income each year; computations follow.

	Taxes Paid	Deferred Tax Expense	Total Tax Expense
Year 1.........	$200 ($500 − $0) × 40%	$(120)	$ 80
Year 2.........	$ 80 ($500 − $300) × 40%	$ 120	$200

Deferred tax accounts derive from timing differences between GAAP expenses and tax deductions. This creates differences between the net book value and the tax basis for many assets and liabilities. **HP**'s deferred tax footnote (see Exhibit 10.5) reports several deferred tax assets and liabilities that explain its book-tax difference and the tax basis.

Review 10-3 LO3

Part 1

Refer to the following information from footnotes to **FedEx**'s 2018 Form 10-K.

The components of the provision for income taxes for the years ended May 31 were as follows ($ millions):

	2018	2017	2016
Current provision (benefit)			
Domestic			
Federal.............................	$(540)	$ 269	$513
State and local......................	43	88	72
Foreign.............................	461	285	200
	(36)	642	785
Deferred provision (benefit)			
Domestic			
Federal.............................	271	989	155
State and local......................	125	59	(18)
Foreign.............................	(579)	(108)	(2)
	(183)	940	135
Provision for income taxes...............	$(219)	$1,582	$920

continued

continued from previous page

A reconciliation of total income tax expense and the amount computed by applying the statutory federal income tax rate (29.2% in 2018 and 35% in 2017 and 2016) to income before taxes for the years ended May 31 is as follows (in millions):

	2018	2017	2016
Taxes computed at federal statutory rate	$ 1,271	$1,603	$959
Increases (decreases) in income tax from:			
Goodwill impairment charge	109	—	—
State and local income taxes, net of federal benefit	119	99	33
Foreign operations	43	(19)	(50)
Corporate structuring transactions	(255)	(68)	(76)
Tax Cuts and Jobs Act	(1,357)	—	—
Foreign tax credits from distributions	(225)	—	—
Uncertain tax positions	86	—	—
TNT Express integration and acquisition costs	20	25	40
Other, net	(30)	(58)	14
	$ (219)	$1,582	$920
Effective Tax Rate	(5.0)%	34.6%	33.6%

Required
1. What is the total income tax expense that FedEx reports in its 2018 income statement?
2. What amount of its total tax expense did (or will) FedEx pay in cash (that is, what amount is currently payable)?
3. Explain how FedEx calculates its income tax expense.
4. What was the effective tax rate for FedEx for 2018? Why is FedEx reporting a negative effective tax rate for 2018?

Part 2
Refer to the footnote disclosures from **FedEx** above along with the following additional disclosures.

	2018		2017	
$ millions	Deferred Tax Assets	Deferred Tax Liabilities	Deferred Tax Assets	Deferred Tax Liabilities
Property equipment, leases and intangibles	$ 752	$3,663	$ 124	$4,993
Employee benefits	595	31	1,951	—
Self-insurance accruals	494	—	745	—
Other	416	602	692	660
Net operating loss/credit carryforwards	1,146	—	1,069	—
Valuation allowances	(711)	—	(738)	—
	$2,692	$4,296	$3,843	$5,653

Our 2018 tax rate was favorably impacted by the enactment of the TCJA during the third quarter. In accordance with SAB 118, we have recorded a provisional benefit of $1.15 billion related to the remeasurement of our net U.S. deferred tax liability.

Required
1. To what does the property, equipment, leases and intangibles deferred tax liability of $3,663 million relate?
2. To what does the employee benefits deferred tax asset of $595 million relate?
3. Describe the way in which the property, equipment, leases and intangibles deferred tax liability is computed. Why did FedEx report a $1.15 billion income tax benefit as a result of the TCJA

Solution on p. 10-68.

Global Accounting

We discussed three major areas of reporting in this module: leases, pensions, and taxes. There are several differences between U.S. GAAP and IFRS on these items, which we highlight below.

Leases The new lease accounting rules narrowed the difference between U.S. GAAP and IFRS. Under both standards, companies must recognize a right-of-use (ROU) asset and a lease liability on the balance sheet. This means the balance sheets of U.S. and international companies will be comparable. However, the income statement treatment and cash flow presentation differ. IFRS does not allow for operating leases; all leases under IFRS must be classified as finance leases with interest expense and ROU amortization on the income statement. Investors can overcome analytical challenges with the adjustments laid out earlier in this module.

Pensions For pension accounting, there are several disclosure differences and one notable accounting difference. The accounting difference pertains to actuarial gains and losses. U.S. GAAP permits deferral of actuarial gains and losses and then amortizes them to net income over time. A notable difference is that IFRS companies can recognize all actuarial gains and losses in comprehensive income in the year they occur, and they are *never* reported on the IFRS income statement. Many IFRS companies select this option. Turning to disclosure, one difference is that pension expense is not reported as a single item under IFRS; various components can be aggregated with other expenses. For example, interest cost can be included with other interest expenses and reported as finance expense under IFRS. A second disclosure difference is that IFRS companies do not disclose the full funded status of their pension plan on the balance sheet as U.S. GAAP requires. However, they must do so in the footnotes.

Income Taxes The two accounting standards are largely the same when it comes to accounting for deferred taxes. One difference of note, pertains to the valuation allowance. Under GAAP, deferred tax assets are recognized in full, and then reduced by a valuation allowance if it is considered more likely than not that some portion of the deferred taxes will not be realized. With IFRS, deferred tax assets are recognized net, that is, if it is more likely than not that future taxable profits will be high enough for the company to use the deferred tax assets. The end result is the same but without the initial recognition of a valuation allowance and any subsequent reversal.

Appendix 10A: Lease Accounting Example—Finance and Operating Leases

We illustrate the accounting for finance leases and operating leases under the 2019 accounting standard. Assume a company leases equipment with the following lease terms.

- Term: 5 years.
- Annual Payments: $22,463 at year-end.
- Initial direct costs paid by lessee: $5,000.
- Present value of lease payments, discounted at 4%: $100,000.

The table below shows the accounting treatment for both a finance lease and an operating lease.

	Lease Liability				Finance Lease			Operating Lease		
Year	Payments	Interest Portion	Decrease in Lease Liability	Lease Liability Balance	ROU Asset Amortization Expense	ROU Asset Balance	Interest Expense + Amortization Expense	Rent Expense	ROU Asset Amortization	ROU Asset Balance
0				❶ $100,000		❺ $105,000				❼ $105,000
1	$ 22,463	❷ $ 4,000	❸ $18,463	❹ $ 81,537	❻ $ 21,000	84,000	$25,000	❽ $ 23,463	❾ $ 19,463	85,537
2	22,463	3,261	19,201	62,336	21,000	63,000	24,261	23,463	20,201	65,336
3	22,463	2,493	19,969	42,367	21,000	42,000	23,493	23,463	20,969	44,367
4	22,463	1,695	20,768	21,599	21,000	21,000	22,695	23,463	21,768	22,599
5	22,463	864	21,599	0	21,000	0	21,864	23,463	22,599	—
Total	$112,314	$12,314			$105,000		$117,314	$117,314	$105,000	

❶ The lease liability, for both the finance lease and operating lease, is recognized at $100,000, which is the present value of the remaining lease payments discounted at 4%.
❷ The interest portion is the beginning balance of the lease liability × discount rate: $4,000 = $100,000 × 4% for Year 1.
❸ The lease liability is reduced by the difference between the lease payment and the interest portion: $18,463 = $22,463 − $4,000 for Year 1.
❹ The lease liability ending balance is equal to the beginning balance less the liability reduction during the year: $81,537 = $100,000 − $18,463 for Year 1.
❺ Right-of-use (ROU) asset is recognized at the initial balance of the lease liability plus any lease payments made to the lessor at or before the commencement date (and less any lease incentives received) and plus any initial direct costs incurred by the lessee: $105,000 = $100,000 + $5,000.
❻ ROU amortization for the finance lease is straight-line over the lease term: $21,000 = $105,000 / 5 years.
❼ ROU recognized for the operating lease is the same as for the finance lease at the inception of the lease. Over time, the two amounts deviate because the asset is amortized straight-line for finance leases but not for operating leases. (See #9, below).
❽ Rent expense recognized in the income statement for an operating lease is equal to the lease payment plus the straight-line amortization of any initial direct costs incurred by the lessee: $23,463 = $22,463 + $5,000/5 years.
❾ ROU amortization for an operating lease is not straight-line. It is equal to the rent expense for the operating lease less the interest amount for the year: $19,463 = $22,463 − $4,000 for Year 1. Interest is *not* recorded as an expense for an operating lease, but the amount is relevant because it is used to compute ROU amortization.

We see that lease expense for a finance lease exceeds that for an operating lease in the early years and is less in later years.

For companies with leases at approximately their mid-point in duration, the expense will be about the same for the two different lease types. However, income statement classification of total lease expense differs across the two lease types as follows.

▪ Expense for a finance lease consists of interest (nonoperating) and amortization of the right-of-use asset (operating).
▪ Expense for an operating lease is rent expense (operating).

Questions

Q10-1. Under the lease standards effective for 2019, how are leases treated on the balance sheet?

Q10-2. What are the four criteria that distinguish a finance lease from an operating lease?

Q10-3. Is the expense of a lease over its entire life the same for operating and finance leases? Explain.

Q10-4. What are the economic and accounting differences between a defined contribution plan and a defined benefit plan?

Q10-5. Under what circumstances will a company report a net pension asset? A net pension liability?

Q10-6. What are the components of pension expense that are reported in the income statement?

Q10-7. What effect does the use of expected returns on pension investments and the deferral of unexpected gains and losses on those investments have on income?

Q10-8. What are the two components of income tax expense?

Q10-9. Why do deferred taxes arise?

Q10-10. What is a valuation allowance for deferred tax assets?

Q10-11. Describe the income statement effect if a company reduced a deferred tax asset valuation allowance by $10 million.

Q10-12. What is a tax loss carryforward and how does it create an economic benefit for a company?

Q10-13. How do companies compute income tax expense for financial reporting purposes?

Assignments with the MBC logo in the margin are available in myBusinessCourse. See the Preface of the book for details.

Mini Exercises

LO1
The GAP Inc. (GPS)

M10-14. Analyzing and Interpreting Lease Footnote Disclosures

The GAP Inc. discloses the following schedule to its fiscal 2018 (ended February 2, 2019) 10-K report relating to its operating leasing activities.

The aggregate minimum noncancelable annual lease payments under leases in effect on February 2, 2019, are as follows:

Fiscal Year ($ millions)	
2019	$1,156
2020	1,098
2021	892
2022	730
2023	539
Thereafter	1,520
Total minimum lease commitments	$5,935

a. Compute the present value of GAP's operating leases using a 6% discount rate and round the remaining lease term to the nearest whole year.

b. GAP disclosed in a footnote that it will adopt the new lease accounting standard in the next fiscal year. Had the company adopted the standard for the year ended February 2, 2019, and classified its leases as operating leases, what would have been the balance sheet impact from the leases disclosed above?

LO1
Costco Wholesale Corpation (COST)

M10-15. Analyzing and Capitalizing Operating Lease Payments Disclosed in Footnotes

Costco Wholesale Corporation discloses the following in footnotes to its 10-K report relating to its leasing activities.

At September 2, 2018, we operated 762 membership warehouses.

	Own Land and Building	Lease Land and/or Building	Total
United States and Puerto Rico	426	101	527
Canada	86	14	100
Mexico	38	1	39
United Kingdom	22	6	28
Japan	12	14	26
Korea	11	4	15
Taiwan	—	13	13
Australia	7	3	10
Spain	2	—	2
Iceland	—	1	1
France	1	—	1
Total	605	157	762

continued

continued from previous page

At September 2, 2018, our commitments to make future payments under contractual obligations were as follows:

Contractual obligations	Payments Due by Fiscal Year				
	2019	2020 to 2021	2022 to 2023	2024 and thereafter	Total
Operating leases	$227	$407	$358	$2,215	$3,207
Capital lease obligations	34	71	72	647	824

a. From these disclosures it appears that Costco has not yet adopted the new leasing standard. How do we know this?
b. How would Costco determine if each of the lease contracts listed under Lease Land and/or Building would be a finance lease or an operating lease?
c. From the disclosure details, do you think the Lease Land and/or Building leases are operating or finance leases?

M10-16. Analyzing and Interpreting Pension Disclosures—Expenses and Returns
Stanley Black & Decker Inc. discloses the following pension footnote for 2018 in its 10-K report.

$ millions	U.S. Plans	Non-U.S. Plans	Total
Service cost	$ 7.5	$15.2	$ 22.7
Interest cost	42.8	28.6	71.4
Expected return on plan assets	(68.7)	(46.5)	(115.2)
Amortization of prior service cost (credit)	1.1	(1.3)	(0.2)
Actuarial loss amortization	7.8	8.5	16.3
Settlement/curtailment loss	—	0.7	0.7
Net periodic pension (benefit) expense	$ (9.5)	$ 5.2	$ (4.3)

a. How much pension expense does Stanley Black & Decker report in its 2018 income statement?
b. Explain, in general, how expected return on plan assets affects reported pension expense. How did expected return affect Stanley Black & Decker's 2018 pension expense?
c. Explain use of the word "expected" as it relates to pension plan assets.

M10-17. Analyzing and Interpreting Pension Disclosures—PBO and Funded Status
YUM! Brands Inc. discloses the following pension footnote in its 10-K report.

Pension Benefit Obligation ($ millions)	2018
Change in benefit obligation	
Benefit obligation at beginning of year	$1,007
Service cost	8
Interest cost	38
Plan amendments	1
Special termination benefits	1
Benefits paid	(73)
Actuarial (gain) loss	(109)
Benefit obligation at end of year	$ 873

a. Explain the terms "service cost" and "interest cost."
b. How do actuarial losses arise?
c. The fair value of YUM!'s pension assets is $755 million as of 2018. What is the funded status of the plan, and how will this be reflected on YUM!'s balance sheet?

LO2
YUM! Brands Inc. (YUM)

M10-18. Analyzing and Interpreting Pension Disclosures—Plan Assets and Cash Flow

YUM! Brands Inc. discloses the following pension footnote in its 10-K report.

Pension Plan Assets ($ millions)	2018
Fair value of plan assets at beginning of year	$864
Actual return on plan assets	(49)
Employer contributions	13
Benefits paid	(73)
Fair value of plan assets at end of year	$755

a. How does the "actual return on plan assets" of $(49) million affect YUM!'s reported profits for 2018?
b. YUM! Brands contributed $13 million cash to the pension plan investment account (asset) during the year. Which of the following is true?
   i. YUM! recognized the $13 million cash payment as a pension expense in 2018.
   ii. YUM! did not recognize the $13 million cash payment as a pension expense in 2018 because it is not tax deductible.
   iii. YUM! did not recognize the 13 million cash payment as a pension expense in 2018 because it relates to employees' service in prior periods.
   iv. YUM! did not recognize the $13 million cash payment as a pension expense in 2018 because benefits of $73 million were paid to employees and that amount represents the pension expense.
   v. None of the above.
c. YUM!'s pension plan paid out $73 million in benefits during 2018. How is this payment reported?

LO2
lululemon athletica inc. (LULU)

M10-19. Analyzing and Interpreting Retirement Benefit Footnote

lululemon athletica discloses the following footnote relating to its retirement plans in its 10-K report for the year ended February 3, 2019.

> During fiscal 2016, the Company began offering pension plans to its eligible employees in Canada and the United States. Participating employees may elect to defer and contribute a portion of their eligible compensation to a plan up to limits stated in the plan documents, not to exceed the dollar amounts set by applicable laws. The Company matches 50% to 75% of the contribution depending on the participant's length of service, and the contribution is subject to a two year vesting period. The Company's net expense for the plans was $6.4 million, $5.2 million, and $3.2 million for the years ended February 3, 2019, January 28, 2018, and January 29, 2017, respectively.

a. Does lululemon athletica have a defined contribution or defined benefit pension plan? Explain.
b. How does lululemon athletica account for its contributions to its retirement plan?
c. How does lululemon athletica report its obligation for its retirement plan on the balance sheet?

LO1
AT&T Inc. (T)

M10-20. Analyzing Adoption of New Lease Standard

AT&T Inc. provided the following footnote in its 10-Q report for the first quarter of fiscal 2019.

> As of January 1, 2019, we adopted, with modified retrospective application, Accounting Standards Update (ASU) No. 2016-02, Leases (Topic 842) as modified (ASC 842), which replaces existing leasing rules with a comprehensive lease measurement and recognition standard and expanded disclosure requirements.
>
> Using the modified retrospective transition method of adoption, we did not adjust the balance sheet for comparative periods but recorded a cumulative effect adjustment to retained earnings on January 1, 2019. We elected the package of practical expedients permitted under the transition guidance within the new standard. Our accounting for finance leases did not change from our prior accounting for capital leases.
>
> The adoption of ASC 842 resulted in the recognition of an operating lease liability of $22,121 and an operating right-of-use asset of the same amount. Existing prepaid and deferred rent accruals were recorded as an offset to the right-of-use asset, resulting in a net asset of $20,960. The cumulative effect of the adoption to retained earnings was an increase of $316 reflecting the reclassification of deferred gains related to sale/leaseback transactions. The standard will have no impact on our debt-covenant compliance under our current agreements.

On January 1, 2019, after adopting the new standard, AT&T's balance sheet reported the following amounts ($ millions).

Total assets ..... $531,864   Total liabilities .... $445,290   Total equity $86,574

Required
a. When AT&T adopted the new standard, what were the dollar effects on total assets and on total liabilities?
b. AT&T used the modified retrospective transition method of adoption. Explain what this means and describe the dollar impact on retained earnings.
c. Quantify in percentage terms, the size of the dollar effect of the adoption of the new standard on AT&T's assets, liabilities, and equity.

M10-21. Analyzing and Interpreting Pension Plan Benefit Footnotes

Lockheed Martin Corporation discloses the following funded status for its defined benefit pension plans in its 10-K report.

Defined Benefit Pension Plans ($ millions)	2018
Unfunded status of the plans	$(11,303)

Lockheed contributed $5,000 million to its pension plan assets in 2018, up drastically from $46 million in the prior year. The company also reports that it is obligated for the following expected payments to retirees in the next five years.

$ millions	Qualified Pension Benefits
2019	$ 2,350
2020	2,390
2021	2,470
2022	2,550
2023	2,610
Years 2024–2028	13,670

a. How is this funded status reported in Lockheed's balance sheet under current GAAP?
b. How should we interpret this funded status in our analysis of the company?
c. What likely effect did the bull market from 2015 through 2019 have on Lockheed's contribution to its pension plans? Explain.

M10-22. Analyzing and Interpreting Income Tax Disclosures

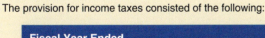 **Apple Inc.** reports the following footnote disclosure to its 2018 10-K report ($ millions).

The provision for income taxes consisted of the following:

Fiscal Year Ended	September 29, 2018
Federal	
Current	$41,425
Deferred	(33,819)
	7,606
State	
Current	551
Deferred	48
	599
Foreign	
Current	3,986
Deferred	1,181
	5,167
Total	$13,372

a. What amount of income tax expense does Apple report in its income statement for 2018?
b. How much of Apple's income tax expense is current (as opposed to deferred)?
c. Why do deferred tax assets and liabilities arise? How do they impact the tax expense that Apple reports in its 2018 income statement?

LO3
Walmart (WMT)

M10-23. Analyzing and Interpreting Income Tax Footnote
The following is an excerpt from **Walmart**'s Form 10-K for the fiscal year ended January 31, 2019.

A summary of the provision for income taxes is as follows ($ millions):

Current:	
U.S. federal.	$2,763
U.S. state and local.	493
International	1,495
Total current tax provision	4,751
Deferred:	
U.S. federal.	(361)
U.S. state and local.	(16)
International	(93)
Total deferred tax expense (benefit).	$ (470)

Required
a. What amount of income tax expense does Walmart report in its income statement for the fiscal year ended January 31, 2019?
b. How much of Walmart's income tax expense was determined from the company's tax returns?
c. How did deferred taxes affect Walmart's tax expense for the year?

LO3
Walmart (WMT)

M10-24. Analyzing Tax Expense
Refer to the excerpt from **Walmart**'s Form 10-K in M10-23. Consider the deferred portion of Walmart's tax provision. Which of the following is plausible? (*Hint*: Consider the tax expense equation.)
a. Walmart's deferred tax assets increased during the year.
b. Walmart's deferred tax liabilities decreased during the year.
c. Both *a* and *b* are plausible.
d. Neither *a* nor *b* is plausible.

LO3

M10-25. Analyzing Tax Expense
Crestview Holdings reported the following in its 2020 financial statements.

$ millions	2020	2019
Total deferred tax assets	$ 821	$ 764
Total deferred tax liabilities.	4,089	3,126
Current provision for income taxes.	1,372	134

Required
Compute the deferred tax expense for the company for 2020.

LO2
Bristol Myers Squibb (BMY)

M10-26. Analyzing Footnote Disclosure of Pension Buy-out
In a press release dated December 3, 2018, **Bristol Myers Squibb** disclosed the following with respect to its pension plans (excerpted).

> NEW YORK (BUSINESS WIRE) Bristol-Myers Squibb Company (NYSE: BMY) today announced it will transfer $3.8 billion of U.S. pension obligations through a full termination of its U.S. Retirement Income Plan. The obligations will be distributed through a combination of lump sums to Plan participants who elect such payments, and the purchase of a group annuity contract from Athene Annuity and Life Company, for all remaining liabilities.

continued

continued from previous page

> The Plan includes approximately 4,800 active employees, 1,400 retirees and their beneficiaries receiving benefits, and 18,000 prior Bristol-Myers Squibb employees who have not yet initiated their benefits. Current Plan provisions, benefit payment options and in-pay benefits will remain available for all participants.
>
> Upon closing of this transaction in the third quarter of 2019, the Company expects a non-cash pre-tax pension settlement charge of approximately $1.5 billion–$2 billion.

Required

a. In plain language, explain this transaction. Why would the company engage in such a transaction?
b. What are the two payout options available to the company's employees, retirees, and prior employees?
c. At December 31, 2018, Bristol Myers Squibb reported a funded status of $163 million on its balance sheet. What will be the net funded status at December 31, 2019? For this question, assume the $163 million relate solely to the U.S. Retirement Income Plan.

M10-27. Analyzing Footnote Disclosure of Pension Income

In its 2018 10-K, **Norfolk Southern Railroad** reported the following in a footnote labeled "Other income, net."

LO2
Norfolk Southern Railroad (NSC)

($ in millions)	2018	2017	2016
Net pension and other postretirement benefit cost	$61	$ 64	$ 65
Rental income	5	87	93
External advisor costs	—	—	(20)
Other	1	5	(2)
Total	$67	$156	$136

Required

a. Explain how Norfolk Southern could report "income" of $61 million related to its pension and other postretirement plans as opposed to an expense.
b. For purposes of analysis, would we classify this 'Other income, net' as operating or nonoperating?

Exercises

E10-28. Analyzing and Interpreting Leasing Footnote

Lowe's Companies reports the following footnote relating to its leased facilities in its first quarter report dated May 3, 2019

LO1
Lowe's Companies Inc. (LOW)

> During the first quarter of fiscal 2019, the Company adopted ASU 2016-02, Leases (Topic 842), which requires leases to be recognized on the balance sheet. The Company leases certain retail stores, warehouses, distribution centers, office space, land and equipment under finance and operating leases.
>
> The table below presents the Company's operating lease-related assets and liabilities recorded on the balance sheet.

(in millions)	Classification	May 3, 2019
Assets		
Operating lease assets	Operating lease right-of-use assets	$3,926
Liabilities		
Current	Current operating lease liabilities	500
Noncurrent	Noncurrent operating lease liabilities	4,064

continued

continued from prior page

Maturity of Lease Liabilities (In millions)	Operating Leases
2019	$ 463
2020	664
2021	636
2022	642
2023	554
After 2023	2,934
Total lease payments	5,893
Less: interest	(1,329)
Present value of lease liabilities	$4,564

a. Use Excel to confirm that Lowe's capitalized its operating leases using a rate of about 4%. *Note:* The company discloses the remaining maturity of its operating leases is 10.68 years (after 2023), which can be used to determine the annual payment in years after 2023.
b. What effect did the initial capitalization of the operating leases have on Lowe's assets and liabilities?
c. How will Lowe's treat the operating right-of-use asset on its balance sheet over the life of the lease?
d. How will Lowe's treat the operating lease liability on its balance sheet over the life of the lease?

E10-29. **Analyzing and Interpreting Footnote on Operating and Capital Leases**
Verizon Communications Inc. provides the following footnote relating to adoption of the new lease accounting standards (Topic 842) in its 10-Q report for the quarter ended March 31, 2019.

The cumulative after-tax effect of the changes made to our condensed consolidated balance sheet for the adoption of Topic 842 were as follows:

($ millions)	At December 31, 2018	Adjustments due to Topic 842	At January 1, 2019
Prepaid expenses and other	$ 5,453	$ (329)	$5,124
Operating lease right-of-use assets	—	23,241	23,241
Other assets	11,717	(2,048)	9,669
Accounts payable and accrued liabilities	22,501	(3)	22,498
Other current liabilities	8,239	(2)	8,237
Current operating lease liabilities	—	2,931	2,931
Deferred income taxes	33,795	139	33,934
Noncurrent operating lease liabilities	—	19,203	19,203
Other liabilities	13,922	(1,815)	12,107
Retained earnings	43,542	410	43,952
Noncontrolling interests	1,565	1	1,566

Rent expense for operating leases is recognized on a straight-line basis over the term of the lease and is included in either Cost of services or Selling, general and administrative expense in our condensed consolidated statements of income, based on the use of the facility on which rent is being paid.

a. What is the amount of the right-of-use asset the company added to its balance sheet upon adoption of the new standard?
b. How will Verizon treat the right-of-use asset on the balance sheet during the life of the lease?
c. Assume the right-of-use assets had a weighted average lease term of 12 years. Approximate the effect the operating leases had on Verizon's income statement in Q1 2019.
d. What is the amount of the total operating lease liabilities the company added to its balance sheet upon adoption of the new standard? Explain what this amount represents.
e. The company decided to adopt the standard with a modified retrospective method and did not adjust numbers on the comparative balance sheet. What analysis challenges does this create?

E10-30. Analyzing, Interpreting, and Capitalizing Operating Leases

TJX Companies Inc. reports the following balance sheet in its 2019 first-quarter report (10-Q).

LO1
TJX Companies Inc.
(TJX)

$ thousands	May 4, 2019	February 2, 2019
Assets		
Current assets		
Cash and cash equivalents	$ 2,235,056	$ 3,030,229
Accounts receivable, net	393,276	346,298
Merchandise inventories	5,057,202	4,579,033
Prepaid expenses and other current assets	381,678	513,662
Total current assets	8,067,212	8,469,222
Net property at cost	5,018,598	5,255,208
Noncurrent deferred income taxes, net	5,801	6,467
Operating lease right-of-use assets	8,810,367	—
Goodwill	96,685	97,552
Other assets	490,401	497,580
Total Assets	$22,489,064	$14,326,029
Liabilities		
Current liabilities		
Accounts payable	$ 2,578,370	$ 2,644,143
Accrued expenses and other current liabilities	2,468,588	2,733,076
Current portion of operating lease liabilities	1,343,243	—
Federal, state and foreign income taxes payable	190,818	154,155
Total current liabilities	6,581,019	5,531,374
Other long-term liabilities	752,968	1,354,242
Noncurrent deferred income taxes, net	167,283	158,191
Long-term operating lease liabilities	7,621,531	—
Long-term debt	2,234,368	2,233,616
Shareholders' Equity		
Preferred stock, authorized 5,000,000 shares, par value $1, no shares issued	—	—
Common stock, authorized 1,800,000,000 shares, par value $1, issued and outstanding 1,212,667,546; 1,217,182,508 and 1,250,405,376 respectively	1,212,668	1,217,183
Additional paid-in capital	—	—
Accumulated other comprehensive loss	(633,282)	(630,321)
Retained earnings	4,552,509	4,461,744
Total shareholders' equity	5,131,895	5,048,606
Total Liabilities and Shareholders' Equity	$22,489,064	$14,326,029

TJX reported the following in its 10-K report for the year ended February 2, 2019.

The following is a schedule of future minimum lease payments for continuing operations as of February 2, 2019:

In thousands	Operating Leases
Fiscal year 2020	$1,676,700
2021	1,603,378
2022	1,441,444
2023	1,253,420
2024	1,042,184
Later years	2,774,845
Total future minimum lease payments	$9,791,971

Required

a. The company adopted the new lease standard using the modified retrospective method which does not require restatement of comparative numbers on the balance sheet. What analysis challenge does this present if we want to analyze TJX at May 4, 2019?

b. Assume a discount rate of 3.75% to determine the present value of the operating lease payments at fiscal-year-end February 2, 2019. Use Excel and do not round any of your numbers or subtotals.

c. What adjustments might we make to the fiscal-year-end numbers to increase comparability of the TJX balance sheet numbers?

d. Did the new lease standard have a material effect on the TJX balance sheet? Explain.

LO2 **E10-31. Analyzing and Interpreting Pension Disclosures**

General Mills Inc. (GIS)

General Mills Inc. reports the following pension footnote in its 10-K report.

Defined Benefit Pension Plans ($ millions)	Fiscal Year 2019
Change in Plan Assets	
Fair value at beginning of year	$6,177.4
Actual return on assets	391.9
Employer contributions	30.4
Plan participant contributions	3.9
Benefits payments	(305.2)
Foreign currency	(6.8)
Fair value at end of year	$6,291.6
Change in Projected Benefit Obligation	
Benefit obligation at beginning of year	$6,416.0
Service cost	94.6
Interest cost	248.0
Curtailment/other	(0.7)
Plan participant contributions	3.9
Actuarial loss	301.8
Benefits payments	(305.8)
Foreign currency	(7.1)
Projected benefit obligation at end of year	$6,750.7

Estimated benefit payments . . . are expected to be paid from fiscal 2020–2029 as follows:

$ millions	Defined Benefit Pension Plans
2020	$ 319.0
2021	324.9
2022	331.8
2023	338.8
2024	346.3
2025–2029	1,856.4

a. Describe what is meant by *service cost* and *interest cost*.

b. What is the total amount paid to retirees during fiscal 2019? What is the source of funds to make these payments to retirees?

c. Compute the 2019 funded status for the company's pension plan.

d. What are actuarial gains and losses? What are the plan amendment adjustments, and how do they differ from the actuarial gains and losses?

e. General Mills projects payments to retirees of between $320 and $350 million per year. How is the company able to contribute only $30.4 million to its pension plan?

f. What effect would a substantial decline in the financial markets have on General Mills' contribution to its pension plans?

E10-32. Analyzing and Interpreting Pension and Healthcare Footnote

Norfolk Southern Railroad reports the following pension and other postretirement benefits footnote as part of its 10-K report.

Norfolk Southern Railroad Inc. (NSC)

December 31, 2018 ($ millions)	Pension Benefits	Other Post-Retirement Benefits
Change in Benefit Obligation		
Benefit obligation at beginning of year	$2,541	$510
Service cost	39	7
Interest cost	83	15
Actuarial losses (gains)	(149)	(24)
Benefits paid/settlements	(143)	(42)
Benefit obligation at end of year	$2,371	$466
Change in plan assets		
Fair value of plan assets at beginning of year	$2,373	$201
Actual return on plan assets	(143)	(19)
Employer contribution	18	18
Benefits paid	(143)	(42)
Fair value of plan assets at end of year	$2,105	$158
Net cost benefit		
Service cost	$ 39	$ 7
Interest cost	83	15
Expected return on plan assets	(177)	(15)
Amortization of net losses	57	—
Amortization of prior service cost (benefit)	—	(24)
Net cost (benefit)	$ 2	$ (17)

a. Describe what is meant by *service cost* and *interest cost* (the service and interest costs appear both in the reconciliation of the PBO and in the computation of pension expense).

b. What is the actual return on the pension and other postretirement benefits plan investments in 2018? Was Norfolk Southern's profitability impacted by this amount?

c. Provide an example under which an "actuarial gain," such as the 2018 gain of $149 million that Norfolk Southern reports, might arise.

d. What is the source of funds to make payments to retirees?

e. How much did Norfolk Southern contribute to its pension and other postretirement benefits plans in 2018?

f. How much cash did retirees receive from the pension plan and the other post-retirement benefits plans in 2018? How much cash did Norfolk Southern pay these retirees?

g. Show the computation of the funded status for the pension and other postretirement benefits plans in 2018.

E10-33. Analyzing and Interpreting Pension and Healthcare Disclosures

Verizon Communications Inc. reports the following pension footnote as part of its 10-K report.

Verizon Communications Inc. (VZ)

December 31, 2018 ($ millions)	Pension
Change in Benefit Obligations	
Beginning of year	$21,531
Service cost	284
Interest cost	690
Plan amendments	230
Actuarial (gain) loss, net	(1,418)
Benefits paid	(1,475)
Curtailment and termination benefits	181
Settlements paid	(456)
End of year	$19,567

continued

continued from prior page

December 31, 2018 ($ millions)	Pension
Change in Plan Assets	
Beginning of year	$19,175
Actual return on plan assets	(494)
Company contributions	1,066
Benefits paid	(1,475)
Settlements paid	(456)
End of year	$17,816

The following table summarizes the components of net periodic benefit cost related to our pension plans.

Years Ended December 31, 2018 ($ millions)	Pension
Service cost—cost of services	$ 230
Service cost—selling, general and administrative expense	54
Service cost	284
Amortization of prior service cost (credit)	48
Expected return on plan assets	(1,293)
Interest cost	690
Remeasurement loss (gain), net	369
Curtailment and termination benefits	181
Total	$ 279

Verizon discloses the following assumptions related to its pension plans.

At December 31	2018	2017
Discount rate used in determining benefit obligations	4.4%	3.7%
Expected return on plan assets	7.0%	7.7%

a. Describe what is meant by *service cost* and *interest cost*.
b. What payments did retirees receive during fiscal 2018 from the pension plans? What is the source of funds to make payments to retirees?
c. Show the computation of Verizon's 2018 funded status for the pension plans.
d. What expense does Verizon's income statement report for its pension plans?
e. Why does Verizon distinguish between the Service cost for Cost of services and for Selling, general and administrative expense?
f. Consider the two pension-related assumptions above. Indicate whether the 2018 assumptions will increase, decrease, or have no effect on each of the following three pension plan elements *relative to the assumption in 2017*: PBO; Pension Plan Assets; and 2018 Pension Expense.

LO3 **E10-34. Analyzing and Interpreting Income Tax Disclosures**

The Boeing Company (BA)

The income tax footnote to the 2018 financial statements for **Boeing** follows.

The components of income before tax were:

Years ended December 31 ($ millions)	2018	2017	2016
U.S.	$11,166	$9,660	$5,386
Non-U.S.	438	447	397
Total	$11,604	$10,107	$5,783

continued

Income tax expense/(benefit) consisted of the following:

Years ended December 31 ($ millions)	2018	2017	2016
Current tax expense			
U.S. federal	$1,873	$1,276	$1,193
Non-U.S.	169	149	133
U.S. state	97	23	15
Total current	$2,139	$1,448	$1,341
Deferred tax expense			
U.S. federal	$ (996)	$ 204	$ (544)
Non-U.S.	(4)	3	(4)
U.S. state	5	(6)	(44)
Total deferred	$ (995)	$ 201	$ (592)

a. What is the amount of income tax expense reported by Boeing each year?
b. What percentage of total tax expense is currently payable for each year?
c. What is Boeing's effective (average) tax rate for each year?
d. Use the pretax information to determine the effective tax rate for U.S. and Non-U.S. operations for each year. What do we observe?
e. Determine the cash tax rate for U.S. operations for each year. *Hint:* Current tax expense is paid in cash; compare the rates calculated to the U.S. statutory rates each year: 2017 and 2018: 21%, and 2016: 35%.

E10-35. Analyzing and Interpreting Income Tax Disclosures
Colgate-Palmolive reports the following income tax footnote disclosure in its 10-K report.

LO3
Colgate-Palmolive
(CL)

Deferred Tax Balances at December 31 ($ millions)	2018	2017
Deferred tax liabilities		
Goodwill and intangible assets	$(344)	$(311)
Property, plant and equipment	(311)	(306)
Deferred withholding tax	(181)	(119)
Other	(75)	(63)
Total deferred tax liabilities	(911)	(799)
Deferred tax assets		
Pension and other retiree benefits	354	375
Tax credits and tax loss carryforwards	89	48
Accrued liabilities	180	197
Stock-based compensation	95	90
Other	164	82
Total deferred tax assets	882	792
Valuation allowance	(54)	(9)
Net deferred tax assets	828	783
Net deferred income taxes	$ (83)	$ (16)
Deferred taxes included within		
Assets		
Deferred income taxes	152	188
Liabilities		
Deferred income taxes	(235)	(204)
Net deferred income taxes	$ (83)	$ (16)

a. Colgate reports $311 million of deferred tax liabilities in 2018 relating to "Property." Explain how such liabilities arise.
b. Describe how a deferred tax asset can arise from pension and other retiree benefits.
c. Colgate reports $89 million in deferred tax assets for 2018 relating to tax loss and tax credit carryforwards. Describe how tax loss carryforwards arise and under what conditions the resulting deferred tax assets will be realized.
d. Colgate's income statement reports income tax expense of $906 million in 2018. Assume that cash paid for income tax is $847 million and that taxes payable decreased by $8 million. Use the financial statement effects template to record tax expense for 2018. (*Hint:* Show the effects of changes in deferred taxes.)

LO1 E10-36. Using Graphical Data to Interpret Operating Lease Footnotes
The following graphics relate to operating leases for S&P 500 firms from 2010 through 2018. The data come from the period before the new lease standards because most firms adopted the standard in fiscal 2019 (the first mandated year). Present values are calculated with a 5% discount rate. Access the dashboard at myBusinessCourse to answer the requirements.

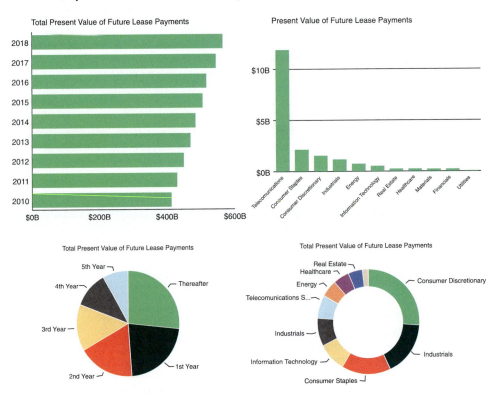

Required
a. Consider the top left panel. What pattern do we observe for the overall level of operating leases over time? How does this affect our analysis of a company's leverage?
b. Consider the bottom right panel. Which industrial sector has the most operating leases? What types of companies are in that sector? What sort of assets are typically leased in this sector?
c. Consider the top right panel. Which industrial sector has the largest average operating leases? What types of companies are in that sector? What sorts of assets are typically leased in this sector?
d. Consider the pie chart that shows lease payments by year (bottom left panel). How could we use this graphic to determine which sector has the longest lease terms?

LO2 E10-37. Using Graphical Data to Interpret Pension Footnotes
The following graphics relate to pensions for S&P 500 firms from 2010 through 2018. Access the dashboard at myBusinessCourse to answer the requirements.

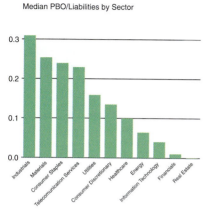
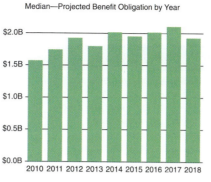
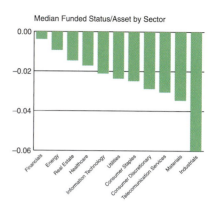
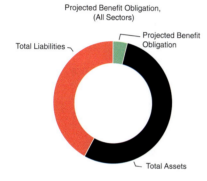

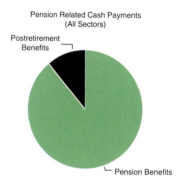

Required

a. Which sector has the largest PBO? What types of companies are in that sector?
b. Do we observe a pattern for PBO over time? Looking across all sectors, which year had the highest median PBO? Does that hold for all sectors?
c. Compare the size of the PBO by sector to the funded status by sector (top left graphic compared to top right graphic). What pattern do we observe?
d. Consider the graphic in the lower middle. This displays the actual return on pension assets minus the expected returns (in $ millions). Explain how actual returns could differ from expected returns. What does it mean for bars above versus below the $0 line in this graphic?
e. Consider the pie chart that displays the cash payments for pension and healthcare benefits. Looking across all sectors, what is the relative magnitude of the two cash outflows? In which sector are postretirement benefits the largest compared to pension benefits paid?

Problems

P10-38. Analyzing, Interpreting, and Capitalizing Operating Leases

Goldman Sachs' SEC filing for the quarter ended March 31, 2019, report contains the following lease footnote.

LO1

The Goldman Sachs Group Inc. (GS)

> **Leases (ASC 842).** In February 2016, the FASB issued ASU No. 2016-02, Leases (Topic 842). This ASU requires that, for leases longer than one year, a lessee recognize in the statements of financial condition a right-of-use asset and a lease liability. It also requires that for finance leases, a lessee recognize interest expense on the lease liability, separately from the amortization of the right-of-use asset in the statements of earnings, while for operating leases, such amounts should be recognized as a combined expense. The firm adopted this ASU in January 2019 under a modified retrospective approach.

continued

continued from previous page

The table below presents other assets by type.

$ in millions	March 2019	December 2018
Property, leasehold improvements and equipment	$19,277	$18,317
Held-to-maturity securities	5,841	1,288
Goodwill and identifiable intangible assets	4,092	4,082
Operating lease right-of-use assets	2,386	—
Income tax-related assets	1,729	1,529
Miscellaneous receivables and other	4,358	5,424
Total	$37,683	$30,640

The table below presents other liabilities by type.

$ in millions	March 2019	December 2018
Compensation and benefits	$ 3,110	$ 6,834
Income tax-related liabilities	3,080	2,864
Operating lease liabilities	2,413	—
Noncontrolling interests	1,565	1,568
Employee interests in consolidated funds	122	122
Accrued expenses and other	5,884	6,219
Total	$16,174	$17,607

The table below presents information about future operating lease payments.

$ in millions	March 2019
Remainder of 2019	$ 318
2020	341
2021	262
2022	235
2023	204
2024	193
2025–thereafter	2,494
Total undiscounted lease payments	4,047
Imputed interest	(1,634)
Total operating lease liabilities	$ 2,413
Weighted average remaining lease term	18 years
Weighted average discount rate	4.85%

Goldman Sachs's 10-K report for the year ended December 31, 2018, included the following table about future cash payments required under operating leases.

The table below presents future minimum rental payments, net of minimum sublease rentals.

$ in millions	December 2018
2019	$ 281
2020	271
2021	218
2022	177
2023	142
2024 – thereafter	1,310
Total	$2,399

Required

a. Explain in plain language what "right-to-use assets" are; that is, how do they convey an economic benefit to the company?
b. What operating lease liability did Goldman Sachs report for the quarter ended March 31, 2019?
c. How does Goldman Sachs determine the amount of operating lease liabilities to add to its balance sheet?
d. Use an Excel spreadsheet and the information on future operating lease payments to verify the total liabilities of $2,413 million on the 2019 Form 10-Q. *Hint*: The amount might not be exactly $2,413.
e. What right-of-use assets did Goldman Sachs report for the quarter ended March 31, 2019? Given Goldman Sachs' business, what does the company lease under its operating leases?
f. Why might the right-of-use asset amount that Goldman Sachs added to the January 2019 balance sheet differ from the related operating lease liabilities?
g. Use the information on rental payments from the December 2018 Form 10-K, to calculate the present value of future payments at year-end. Use the same average weighted lease term and discount rate Goldman Sachs discloses in the 2019 Form 10-Q.
h. How would we adjust the December 2018 balance sheet to enhance comparability?

P10-39. Applying New Lease Accounting Standards for Operating Leases

On January 1 of the current year, CCH Corporation entered into the following lease contract. Based on the facts, CCH Corporation classifies the lease as an operating lease. The company has a 5% cost of debt capital.

Leased asset: Office space.
Lease term: 5 years.
Annual lease payment: $115,487 due at each year-end.
Upfront fees: $10,000 paid in cash.

Required

a. Explain how the facts support the classification of the lease as an operating lease.
b. Determine the amount of the lease liability that CCH will add to its balance sheet at the inception of the lease.
c. What amount will be added to the balance sheet as an asset? What will CCH Corporation call the asset on the balance sheet?
d. Prepare a lease amortization schedule that shows the interest and principal portions of each lease payment.
e. Use the financial statement effects template to record the lease inception and lease payments for the first two years of the lease term. Also show the asset and lease amortization for those same two years.
f. At the end of the current year, what additional disclosure would CCH make in its footnotes pertaining to the four remaining lease payments?
g. CCH Corporation also has finance leases. To enhance comparability, what adjustments would we make to the CCH income statement in the current year?

P10-40. Analyzing, Interpreting, and Capitalizing Operating Leases

On January 1, 2020, Alexander Mack Adventures Inc. entered into land leases that grant unrestricted access to property in Texas where the company plans to build an RV resort. Lease details follow.

- Lease term: 15 years.
- Upfront fees: $450,000 paid in cash.
- Annual lease payment: $500,000 due at each year-end.
- Lessee responsible for property tax and insurance.

The company also leased computer equipment with the following details.

- Lease term: 4 years.
- Upfront fees: $5,000.
- Annual lease payments: $24,694.
- Lessee has option to purchase equipment for $1 at end of lease.

Required

a. Given the lease contract facts, determine the classification for each of the two leases (operating or finance).
b. Determine the amount of the lease liability that Alexander Mack will add to its balance sheet at the inception of each lease. The company has a 9% cost of debt capital.
c. What asset will the company add to its balance sheet for each lease?
d. For each lease, prepare an amortization schedule that shows the interest and principal portions of each lease payment.
e. What will be the income statement effect of the land lease in 2020?

f. What will be the income statement effect of the equipment lease in 2020?
g. For fiscal 2020, what additional disclosure would Alexander Mack make in its footnotes pertaining to the remaining land lease payments?
h. On December 31, 2021, what amount will be on the balance sheet (asset and liability) for each of the leases?
i. To enhance comparability, what adjustments would we make to the Alexander Mack income statement in 2020?

LO2 **P10-41. Analyzing and Interpreting Pension Disclosures**

DowDuPont Inc. (DD)

DowDuPont's 10-K report has the following disclosures related to its retirement plans ($ millions).

Obligations and Funded Status ($ millions)	December 31, 2018
Change in projected benefit obligations	
Benefit obligations at beginning of year	$ 57,401
Service cost	651
Interest cost	1,638
Plan participants' contributions	29
Actuarial changes in assumptions and experience	(2,832)
Benefits paid	(3,223)
Plan amendments	34
Acquisitions/divestitures/other	(57)
Effect of foreign exchange rates	(627)
Benefit obligation at end of year	$53,014
Change in plan assets	
Fair value of plan assets at beginning of year	$ 43,685
Actual return on plan assets	(1,524)
Employer contributions	2,964
Plan participants' contributions	29
Benefits paid	(3,223)
Acquisitions/divestitures/other	(7)
Effect of foreign exchange rates	(462)
Fair value of plan assets at end of year	$ 41,462
Funded status	
U.S. plan with plan assets	$ (6,956)
Non-U.S. plans with plan assets	(2,751)
All other plans	(1,845)
Funded status at end of year	$(11,552)

Components of Net Periodic Benefit Cost ($ millions)	December 31, 2018
Net periodic benefit cost	
Service cost	$ 651
Interest cost	1,638
Expected return on plan assets	(2,846)
Amortization of prior service credit	(24)
Amortization of unrecognized (gain) loss	649
Curtailment/settlement/other	(10)
Net periodic benefit costs—Total	$ 58

Weighted-Average Assumptions used to Determine Net Periodic Benefit Cost for Years Ended December 31	2018	2017
Discount rate	3.80%	3.26%
Expected return on plan assets	6.68%	6.94%
Rate of compensation increase	3.95%	3.88%

The following benefit payments, which reflect future service, as appropriate, are expected to be paid:

$ millions	Pension Benefits
2019	$ 3,197
2020	3,172
2021	3,182
2022	3,198
2023	3,219
2024–2028	16,078
Total	$32,046

Required

a. How much pension expense does DowDuPont report in its 2018 income statement? Would 2018 pension expense have been higher or lower if DowDuPont had not changed the "Rate of compensation increase" from 2017 to 2018?

b. DowDuPont reports a $2,846 million expected return on pension plan assets as an offset to 2018 pension expense. Estimate what the expected return would have been had DowDupont not changed the assumption on the expected return in 2018. What is DowDuPont's actual gain or loss realized on its 2018 pension plan assets? What is the purpose of using this expected return instead of the actual gain or loss (return)?

c. What main factors (and dollar amounts) affected DowDuPont's pension liability during 2018? What main factors (and dollar amounts) affected its pension plan assets during 2018?

d. What does the term *funded status* mean? What is the funded status of the 2018 DowDuPont pension plans?

e. DowDuPont increased its discount rate during 2018. What effect(s) does this have on its balance sheet and its income statement?

f. How did DowDuPont's pension plan affect the company's cash flow in 2018? (Identify any inflows and outflows, including amounts.)

g. Explain how the returns on pension assets affect the amount of cash that DowDuPont must contribute to fund the pension plan.

P10-42. Analyzing and Interpreting Pension Disclosures

LO2
Johnson & Johnson (JNJ)

Johnson & Johnson provides the following footnote disclosures in its 10-K report relating to its defined benefit pension plans and its other postretirement benefits.

December 31, 2018 ($ millions)	Retirement Plans	Other Benefit Plans
Change in Benefit Obligation		
Projected benefit obligation—beginning of year	$33,221	$4,582
Service cost	1,283	269
Interest cost	996	148
Plan participant contributions	66	—
Amendments	26	—
Actuarial (gains) losses	(2,326)	(119)
Divestitures & acquisitions	(29)	—
Curtailments & settlements & restructuring	(21)	—
Benefits paid from plan	(1,018)	(383)
Effect of exchange rates	(528)	(17)
Projected benefit obligation—end of year	$31,670	$ 4,480

continued

Module 10 | Leases, Pensions, and Income Taxes

continued from previous page

December 31, 2018 ($ millions)	Retirement Plans	Other Benefit Plans
Change in Plan Assets		
Plan assets at fair value—beginning of year	$28,404	$ 281
Actual return (loss) on plan assets	(1,269)	—
Company contributions	1,140	282
Plan participant contributions	66	—
Settlements	(13)	—
Divestitures & acquisitions	(17)	—
Benefits paid from plan assets	(1,018)	(383)
Effect of exchange rates	(475)	—
Plan assets at fair value—end of year	$26,818	$ 180
Funded status—end of year	$ (4,852)	$(4,300)

December 31, 2018 ($ millions)	Retirement Plans	Other Benefit Plans
Service cost	$1,283	$269
Interest cost	996	148
Expected return on plan assets	(2,212)	(7)
Amortization of prior service cost (credit)	3	(31)
Recognized actuarial losses	852	123
Curtailments and settlements	1	—
Net periodic benefit cost	$ 923	$502

Worldwide Benefit Plans	Retirement Plans		Other Benefit Plans	
	2018	2017	2018	2017
Discount rate	3.60%	3.98%	3.62%	3.94%
Expected long-term rate of return on plan assets	8.46	8.43	—	—
Rate of increase in compensation levels	3.98	4.01	4.29	4.31

Required

a. How much pension and other benefit expense does Johnson & Johnson report in its 2018 income statement?

b. The company reports a $2,212 million expected return on pension plan assets as an offset to 2018 pension expense. Approximately, how is this amount computed? What is the actual gain or loss realized on its 2018 pension plan assets? What is the purpose of using this expected return instead of the actual gain or loss?

c. What factors affected the company's pension liability during 2018? What factors affected the pension plan assets during 2018?

d. What does the term *funded status* mean? What is the funded status of the 2018 pension plans and postretirement benefit plans?

e. The company decreased its discount rate on retirement plans from 3.98% to 3.60%. What effect(s) does this decrease have on its balance sheet and its income statement?

f. How did Johnson & Johnson's pension plan affect the company's cash flow in 2018?

g. Why are the plan assets so small for Other benefit plans compared to the Pension plans?

h. The company reports an actuarial gain of $2,326, which is subtracted from the PBO. Explain what this is and how this item affected net income in 2018.

LO3 **P10-43. Analyzing and Interpreting Tax Footnote (Financial Statement Effects Template)**

Snapchat Inc. (SNAP)

Snapchat Inc. reports total tax expense of $2,547 thousand on its income statement for year ended December 31, 2018, and paid cash of $3,958 thousand for taxes and decreased taxes payable by $755 thousand. The tax footnote in the company's 10-K filing reports the following deferred tax assets and liabilities information.

The domestic and foreign components of pre-tax loss were as follows:

Year Ended December 31 (in thousands)	2017	2018
Domestic	$ (969,922)	$(3,027,580)
Foreign	(283,442)	(435,828)
Loss before income taxes	$(1,253,364)	$(3,463,408)

The significant components of net deferred tax balances were as follows:

December 31 (in thousands)	2017	2018
Deferred tax assets		
Accrued expenses	$ 10,534	$ 21,056
Deferred revenue	2,142	976
Intangible assets	140,771	140,494
Stock-based compensation	396,604	254,255
Net operating losses	473,110	849,224
Tax credit carryforwards	124,078	235,300
Property and equipment	—	203
Other	2,015	322
Total deferred tax assets	$1,149,254	$1,501,830
Deferred tax liability		
Property and equipment	$ (5,883)	$ —
Total deferred tax liabilities	(5,883)	—
Total net deferred tax assets before valuation allowance	1,143,371	1,501,830
Valuation allowance	(1,144,543)	(1,502,346)
Net deferred taxes	$ (1,172)	$ (516)

Required

a. Snapchat's gross deferred tax assets increased during 2018. What two items explain the majority of the increase?

b. In 2017, Snapchat reported deferred tax liabilities. Explain how this liability arose.

c. Why does the company record a valuation allowance? Given the size of the 2018 allowance, what is the company's expectation of future pretax income?

d. Explain how the valuation allowance affected 2018 net income.

e. Use the financial statement effects template to record income tax expense for fiscal year 2018 along with the changes in both deferred tax assets and liabilities and the valuation allowance.

P10-44. Analyzing and Interpreting Income Tax Footnote

Consider the following income tax footnote information for **Oracle** for the fiscal year ended May 31, 2019 (fiscal year 2019).

LO3
Oracle Corporation
(ORCL)

The following is a geographical breakdown of income before the provision for income taxes:

Year Ended May 31 (in millions)	2019	2018	2017
Domestic	$ 3,774	$ 3,366	$ 3,674
Foreign	8,494	9,058	8,006
Income before provision for income taxes	$12,268	$12,424	$11,680

continued

continued from previous page

The provision for income taxes consisted of the following:

Year Ended May 31 ($ in millions)	2019	2018	2017
Current provision:			
Federal	$ 979	$8,320	$ 936
State	300	264	257
Foreign	1,097	1,100	1,475
Total current provision	$2,376	$9,684	$2,668
Deferred benefit:			
Federal	$ 483	$ (827)	$ (158)
State	(28)	(26)	(29)
Foreign	(1,646)	6	(253)
Total deferred benefit	$(1,191)	$ (847)	$ (440)
Total provision for income taxes	$ 1,185	$8,837	$2,228

The provision for income taxes differed from the amount computed by applying the federal statutory rate to our income before provision for income taxes as follows:

Year Ended May 31 ($ in millions)	2019	2018	2017
U.S. federal statutory tax rate	21.0%	29.2%	35.0%
Tax provision at statutory rate	$2,576	$3,629	$4,088
Impact of the Tax Act of 2017:			
One-time transition tax	(529)	7,781	—
Deferred tax effects	140	(911)	—
Foreign earnings at other than United States rates	(789)	(995)	(1,312)
State tax expense, net of federal benefit	197	142	150
Settlements and releases from judicial decisions and statute expirations, net	(132)	(252)	(189)
Domestic production activity deduction	—	(87)	(119)
Federal research and development credit	(158)	(174)	(127)
Stock-based compensation	(201)	(302)	(149)
Other, net	81	6	(114)
Total provision for income taxes	$1,185	$8,837	$2,228

The components of our deferred tax assets and liabilities were as follows:

May 31 (in millions)	2019	2018
Deferred tax assets:		
Accruals and allowances	$ 541	$ 567
Employee compensation and benefits	646	664
Differences in timing of revenue recognition	322	338
Basis of property, plant and equipment and intangible assets	1,238	—
Tax credit and net operating loss carryforwards	3,717	2,614
Total deferred tax assets	6,464	4,183
Valuation allowance	(1,266)	(1,308)
Total deferred tax assets, net	5,198	2,875
Deferred tax liabilities:		
Unrealized gain on stock	(78)	(78)
Acquired intangible assets	(973)	(1,254)
GILTI deferred	(1,515)	—
Basis of property, plant and equipment and intangible assets	—	(158)
Other	(200)	(48)
Total deferred tax liabilities	(2,766)	(1,538)
Net deferred tax assets	$2,432	$1,337

Required

a. What is the total amount of income tax expense that Oracle reports in its fiscal 2019 income statement? What portion of this expense did Oracle pay during 2019 or expect to pay in 2020?
b. Explain how the deferred tax liability called "Acquired intangible assets" arises. Under what circumstances will the company settle this liability? Under what circumstances might this liability be deferred indefinitely?
c. Explain how the deferred tax asset called "Employee compensation and benefits" arises. Why is it recognized as an asset?
d. Explain how the deferred tax asset called "Tax credit and net operating loss carryforwards" arises. Under what circumstances will Oracle realize the benefits of this asset?
e. Oracle reports a 2019 valuation allowance of $1,266 million. How does this valuation allowance arise? How did the change in valuation allowance for 2019 affect net income? Valuation allowances typically relate to questions about the realizability of tax loss carryforwards. Under what circumstances might Oracle not realize the benefits of its tax loss carryforwards?
f. Calculate Oracle's effective (average) tax rate for each year.
g. Oracle reconciles the difference between its total provision for income tax and the statutory rate. What item explains most of the difference in fiscal 2017 compared to fiscal 2018?
h. If not for the effects of the Tax Cuts and Jobs Act of 2017, what would have been Oracle's effective tax rate each year?

P10-45. Analyzing and Interpreting Effects of TCJA Tax Law Changes

Pfizer Inc. reports the following footnote disclosure in its 2018 Form 10-K.

LO3
Pfizer Inc. (PFE)

The following table provides the components of *Income from continuing operations before provision (benefit) for taxes on income*:

Year Ended December 31, $ millions	2018	2017	2016
United States	$ (4,403)	$ (6,879)	$(8,534)
International	16,288	19,184	16,886
Income from continuing operations before provision for taxes	$11,885	$12,305	$ 8,351

The following table provides the components of *Provision (benefit) for taxes on income* based on the location of the taxing authorities:

$ millions	2018	2017	2016
United States			
Current income taxes:			
Federal	$ 668	$ 1,267	$ 342
State and local	9	45	(52)
Deferred income taxes:			
Federal	$(1,663)	$ (2,064)	$ (419)
State and local	16	(304)	(106)
Total U.S. tax provision	$ (970)	$ (1,055)	$ (235)
TCJA(a)			
Current income taxes	$(3,035)	$ 13,135	—
Deferred income taxes	2,439	(23,795)	—
Total TCJA tax provision	$ (596)	$(10,660)	—
International			
Current income taxes	$ 2,831	$ 2,709	$1,532
Deferred income taxes	(558)	(42)	(175)
Total international tax provision	$ 2,273	$ 2,667	$1,358

(a) In the fourth quarter of 2017, we recorded an estimate of certain tax effects of the TCJA, including (i) the impact on deferred tax assets and liabilities from the reduction in the U.S. Federal corporate tax rate from 35% to 21%, (ii) the impact on valuation allowances and other state income tax considerations, (iii) the $15.2 billion repatriation tax liability on accumulated post-1986 foreign earnings for which we plan to elect, with the filing of our 2018 U.S. Federal Consolidated Income Tax Return, payment over eight years through 2026 that is reported in Other taxes payable in our consolidated balance sheet as of December 31, 2017 and (iv) deferred taxes on basis differences expected to give rise to future taxes on global intangible low-taxed income. As a result of the TCJA, in the fourth quarter of 2017, we reversed an estimate of the deferred taxes that are no longer expected to be needed due to the change to the territorial tax system.

Required

a. What is the amount of income tax expense reported by Pfizer for each year? What amount is current versus deferred?
b. What is Pfizer's effective (average) tax rate for each year?
c. Use the pretax information to determine the effective tax rate for U.S. operations for each year.
d. The footnote includes amounts related to the TCJA of 2017. What was the effect on the company's tax expense in 2017 and 2018 due to the TCJA?
e. Pfizer lists four TCJA items that impacted their 2017 tax provision. Explain how each of the four items might have affected Pfizer's 2017 tax expense.

IFRS Applications

LO2
Nutrien Ltd. (NTR)

I10-46. Analyzing and Interpreting Pension Disclosures

Nutrien, the world's largest potash producer, is a multinational corporation based in Saskatoon, Saskatchewan. The company produces nitrogen and phosphate used to produce fertilizer. At the end of 2018, the company controlled 34% of the world's potash production capacity. Below is Nutrien's pension footnote for 2018.

$ millions	Obligation	Plan Assets	Net
Balance—December 31, 2017	$(1,831)	$1,380	$(451)
Merger impact[1]	(347)	205	(142)
Components of defined benefit expense recognized in earnings			
Current service cost for benefits earned during the year	(67)	—	(67)
Interest (expense) income	(77)	62	(15)
Past service cost, including curtailment gains and settlements	157	—	157
Foreign exchange rate changes and other	39	(27)	12
Subtotal of components of defined benefit expense recognized in earnings	52	35	87
Remeasurements of the net defined benefit liability recognized in OCI during the year			
Actuarial gain arising from:			
Changes in financial assumptions	210	—	210
Changes in demographic assumptions	11	—	11
Loss on plan assets (excluding amounts included in net interest)	—	(149)	(149)
Subtotal of remeasurements	221	(149)	72
Cash flows			
Contributions by plan participants	(6)	6	—
Employer contributions	—	53	53
Benefits paid	114	(114)	—
Subtotal of cash flows	108	(55)	53
Balance—December 31, 2018	$(1,797)	$1,416	$(381)

[1]The Company acquired Agrium's pension and other postretirement benefit obligations, representing the fair values at the acquisition date as described in Note 3.

Required

a. How much pension expense does the company report in its 2018 income statement?
b. What factors affected the company's pension liability during 2018? What factors affected the pension plan assets during 2018?
c. What does the term *funded status* mean? What is the funded status of the 2018 pension plans and postretirement benefit plans?
d. The company increased its discount rate on the pension obligation from 3.65% to 4.22% in 2018. What effect(s) does this increase have on the company's balance sheet and income statement?
e. How did Nutrien's pension plan affect the company's cash flow in 2018?

LO3
BMW Group (BMW)

I10-47. Analyzing and Interpreting Income Tax Footnote

Bayerische Motoren Werke AG, commonly referred to as **BMW**, is a German multinational company that produces automobiles and motorcycles. The company was founded in 1916 as a manufacturer of aircraft engines, which it produced from 1917 until 1918 and again from 1933 to 1945. BMW includes the following footnotes in its 2018 annual report.

Taxes on income of the BMW Group comprise the following:

in € million	2018	2017*
Current tax expense	€2,220	€2,558
Deferred tax expense (+)/deferred tax income (−)	355	−558
thereof relating to temporary differences	641	−502
thereof relating to tax loss carryforwards and tax credits	−286	−56
Income taxes	€2,575	€2,000

The difference between the expected tax expense based on the underlying tax rate for Germany and actual tax expense is explained in the following reconciliation:

in € million	2018	2017*
Profit before tax	€9,815	€10,675
Tax rate applicable in Germany	30.8%	30.7%
Expected tax expense	3,023	3,277
Variances due to different tax rates	−359	−1,026
Tax increases (+)/tax reductions (−) as a result of nondeductible expenses and tax-exempt income	141	58
Tax expense (+)/benefits (−) for prior years	−16	−104
Other variances	−214	−205
Actual tax expense	2,575	€ 2,000

The allocation of deferred tax assets and liabilities to balance sheet line items at 31 December is shown in the following table:

in € million	Deferred Tax Assets 2018	Deferred Tax Liabilities 2018
Intangible assets	€ 22	€ 3,077
Property, plant and equipment	171	359
Leased products	487	5,210
Other investments	3	20
Sundry other assets	1,185	3,254
Tax loss carryforwards and capital losses	891	—
Provisions	5,323	29
Liabilities	2,570	620
Eliminations	3,180	981
	13,832	13,550
Valuation allowances on tax loss carryforwards and capital losses	−498	—
Netting within tax jurisdictions	−11,744	−11,744
Deferred taxes	1,590	1,806
	€ —	€ 216

Required

a. What income tax expense does BMW report in its 2018 income statement? How much of this expense was paid during the year or is currently payable?
b. Determine the company's effective tax rate.
c. What is the company's marginal (statutory) tax rate?
d. Does BMW report a net deferred tax asset or liability on its balance sheet?
e. BMW reports a deferred tax asset and a deferred tax liability related to "Property, plant and equipment." Explain how both an asset and a liability can arise from this item.
f. BMW includes a valuation allowance of €498 million related to tax loss carryforwards. Explain how this valuation allowance arises.

Ongoing Project

(This ongoing project began in Module 1 and continues through most of the book; even if previous segments were not completed, the requirements are still applicable to any business analysis.) Your project should include a discussion of leases (capital and operating), defined benefit obligations, as well as deferred tax assets and liabilities. The objective is to gain a deeper understanding of all of the obligations the company faces and how they affect key performance and leverage ratios.

1. *Financing and Operating Leases.* Read the debt and lease footnotes to determine whether the company uses leases.
   - Does the company use leases? What types of assets are leased?
   - What proportion of leases are finance versus operating?
   - Are leases a substantial component of overall financing?
   - Determine the discount rate implicit in the company's leases.
   - Has the company adopted the new standard for leases? What was the balance sheet impact of the adoption?

2. *Pensions.* Read the pension footnote to determine whether the company has defined benefit obligations.
   - What is the funded status of the pension and other benefits plans? Is the underfunded or overfunded obligation substantial? Compare between the companies.
   - Are the plans substantial to the company?
   - How much pension expense does each company report in its income statement? Is this a substantial amount?
   - Compare the cash paid into the plan assets to the amounts paid to retirees. Assess the cash flow implications of the company's future payment obligations. The point is to determine whether the company will be able to meet its obligations as they come due.

3. *Income Tax Disclosures and Strategies.* Examine the income tax expense and deferred tax assets and liabilities.
   - Analyze the footnotes and assess the company's effective tax rate. Is it a consistent rate? If not, do the fluctuations seem reasonable?
   - What was the effect of the 2017 TCJA on the provision for income taxes? How did the new law change the company's effective tax rate?
   - Do the deferred tax assets and liabilities seem appropriate given the company's industry?
   - Is there a valuation allowance? If so, how big is it relative to total deferred tax assets? Has the valuation allowance changed markedly during the year? This might indicate income shifting.

Solutions to Review Problems

Review 10-1—Solution

1. Using Excel, the present value of $6,756 million for operating leases, discounted at 4.42%, is computed as follows ($2 rounding difference).

Year ($ millions)	Operating Lease Payment	Discount Factor 4.42%	Present Value
1	$1,172	0.95767	$1,122
2	1,000	0.91713	$917
3	819	0.87831	$719
4	692	0.84113	$582
5	654	0.80553	$527
>5	4,200	5.48688 × 0.80553	$2,891
Remaining life	6.422*		$6,758
Total payments	$8,537		

* $4,200/$654 = 6.422 years

2. Delta Airlines' balance sheet will recognize a lease liability of $6,758 million together with a lease asset (titled as "Operating lease right-of-use assets") of about the same amount.

Review 10-2—Solution

1. American Airlines' pension benefit obligation increases by service cost and interest cost, and decreases with actuarial gains (which are decreases in the pension liability as a result of changes in actuarial assumptions). It is decreased by the payment of benefits to retirees.
2. American Airlines' pension assets decrease by negative investment returns for the period and increase by cash contributions made by the company. Assets decrease by benefits paid to retirees.
3. American Airlines' funded status is $(6,325) million ($16,378 million PBO – $10,053 million pension assets) as of 2018. The negative amount indicates that the plan is underfunded. Consequently, this amount is reflected as a liability on American's balance sheet.
4. Expected return on plan assets acts as an offset to service cost and interest cost in computing net pension cost. As the expected return increases, net pension expense decreases.
5. American Airlines' expected loss of $905 million is less than its actual loss of $1,151 million in 2018.
6. American Airlines reports a net pension *income* of $59 million in its 2018 income statement.
7. American Airlines' funded status is negative, indicating an underfunded plan. In 2018, the company contributed $475 million to the pension plan, up from $286 million in the prior year. If returns on pension plan assets continue to decline, the company will be forced to increase its cash contribution.

Review 10-3—Solution

Part 1

1. Total income tax benefit was $219 million in 2018, compared with tax expense of $1,582 million in the prior year.
2. The current portion of FedEx's tax provision was $(36) million.
3. Income tax expense is the sum of current taxes (that is, currently payable as determined from the company's federal, state, and foreign tax returns) plus the change in deferred tax assets and liabilities. It is a calculated figure, not a percentage that is applied to pretax income. For 2018, FedEx tax expense was decreased by the deferred provision (an asset) of $183 million.
4. FedEx's effective tax rate for fiscal 2018 is (5.0)%. FedEx's tax reconciliation indicates that it received a tax benefit of $1,357 from the Tax Cuts and Jobs Act of 2017. Benefits such as these typically result from the reduction of deferred tax liabilities that are now computed using a lower tax rate than the one in effect when the liabilities were initially recognized.

Part 2

1. FedEx is depreciating its long-term PPE and lease assets more quickly for tax purposes than it does for financial reporting purposes. Consequently, FedEx' taxable income will be higher in future years as less depreciation expense is recognized, resulting in additional income tax liability that is recognized as a deferred tax lability on its balance sheet.
2. FedEx is recognizing accrued employee benefit expense in its income statement that will not be deductible for tax purposes until paid in the future. These future payments will reduce taxable income and the income tax liability, and that future reduction of tax liability is a future benefit that is recognized on the balance sheet as a deferred tax asset.
3. The total expected increase in taxable income (from lower expected tax depreciation expense) is multiplied by the expected tax rate to yield the dollar amount of deferred tax assets and liabilities that are reported on the balance sheet. Prior to the passage of the TCJA, this future taxable income was multiplied by the 35% corporate tax rate. After passage of the TCJA, this future income was multiplied by the new 21% corporate tax rate, resulting in lower deferred tax liability. The reduction of the deferred tax liability is recognized in the income statement as a reduction of income tax expense, thus increasing net income dollar-for-dollar.

Module 11
Cash Flows

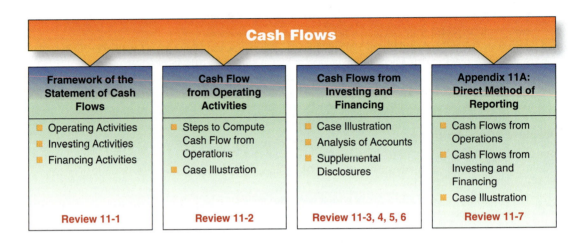

PREVIEW — SBUX

We examine the statement of cash flows, including

- Preparing the statement of cash flows, including how to determine net cash flows from
  - **Operating activities**
  - **Investing activities**
  - **Financing activities**
- Analyzing and interpreting the statement of cash flows.
- Drawing insights from cash flows that are not apparent from the income statement and balance sheet.
- Preparing a direct-method statement of cash flows.

Cash Flow by Type

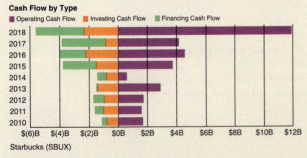

Starbucks (SBUX)

S&P 500

Net Income, Operating Cash Flow, and Market Cap

Starbucks (SBUX)

S&P 500

11-1

Road Map

LO	Learning Objective | Topics	Page	eLecture	Guided Example	Assignments
11–1	**Describe the framework for the statement of cash flows.** Relations Among Financial Statements :: Statement of Cash Flows Structure :: Operating Activities Preview :: Investing Activities Preview :: Financing Activities Preview	11-3	e11–1	Review 11-1	1, 2, 3, 4, 22, 23, 30, 49, 50, 51, 56, 57, 58
11–2	**Determine and analyze net cash flows from operating activities.** Steps to Compute Net Cash Flows from Operating Activities	11-9	e11–2	Review 11-2	9, 10, 11, 13, 24, 25, 31, 32, 33, 34, 43, 44, 45, 46, 47, 48, 49, 50, 51
11–3	**Determine and analyze net cash flows from investing activities.** Analyze Remaining Noncash Assets	11-16	e11–3	Review 11-3	5, 10, 12, 32, 36, 38, 43, 44, 45, 46, 47, 48, 49, 50, 52, 53, 54, 55
11–4	**Determine and analyze net cash flows from financing activities.** Analyze Liabilities and Equity :: Balance Sheet Accounts and Cash Flow Effects :: Supplemental Disclosures for Indirect Method	11-18	e11–4	Review 11-4	5, 6, 12, 32, 36, 38, 43, 44, 45, 46, 47, 48, 49, 50, 52, 53, 54, 55
11–5	**Examine and interpret cash flow information.** Cash Flow Components :: Cash Flow Patterns :: Usefulness of Statement of Cash Flows	11-21	e11–5	Review 11-5	7, 21, 28, 39, 40, 42, 49, 50, 51, 56, 57, 58
11–6	**Compute and interpret ratios based on operating cash flows.** Ratio Analyses of Cash Flows :: Free Cash Flow	11-27	e11–6	Review 11-6	19, 20, 29, 41, 42, 56, 57
11–7	**Explain and construct a direct method statement of cash flows (Appendix 11A).** Cash Flows from Operating Activities :: Cash Flows from Investing and Financing	11-29	e11–7	Review 11-7	8, 14, 15, 16, 17, 18, 26, 27, 35, 36, 37, 52, 53, 54, 55

Framework for Statement of Cash Flows

LO1 Describe the framework for the statement of cash flows.

The **statement of cash flows** is a financial statement that summarizes information about the flow of cash into and out of a company.[1] Information provided in a statement of cash flows helps managers, investors, and creditors assess the company's ability to generate positive future net cash flows and to meet its debt obligations, its need for external financing, and its ability to pay its dividends. The balance sheet reports the company's financial position at a point in time (the end of each period), whereas the statement of cash flows explains the change in one of its components—cash—from one balance sheet date to the next. The income statement reveals the results of the company's operating activities for the period, and these operating activities are a major contributor to the change in cash as reported in the statement of cash flows.

Relation Among Financial Statements

Each financial statement reveals a different view of the company, and a thorough financial analysis requires us to scrutinize the information contained in each.

Income Statement Insights The income statement informs us about the degree to which consumers value the products and/or services offered by the company. How much does it cost to produce them, and can the company set prices that pass on these production costs to its customers? Is the company able to control labor costs, both for salaries and wages and for benefits offered to employees? Can the company effectively manage its overhead costs? How well is it insulated against fluctuations in interest rates, commodity prices, or foreign exchange rates? How well can it control its income tax obligations? These are but a few of the important questions that can be answered by our analysis of the income statement.

Balance Sheet Insights The balance sheet informs us about the resources available to the company and the claims against those resources by creditors and owners. From the balance sheet, we learn about the magnitude of investment in net working capital and PPE assets required for the company to conduct business. This is impacted by the company's business model and the norms of the industries in which the company operates. We are able to estimate the extent to which the company relies upon borrowed funds, the structure of that indebtedness, and the degree to which the company has (or can generate) the liquidity required to meet its debt obligations. We also learn about the company's equity investors and the claims they have on the net assets and income of the company. Whereas the income statement provides us with insight into the economics of the company's operations, the balance sheet informs us about the resources the company uses in its operations and the claims against those resources.

Statement of Cash Flows Insights As we will learn in this module, the statement of cash flows is prepared from the company's income statement and comparative balance sheets. At first glance, it might appear that the information contained in the statement of cash flows is redundant. However, to treat the statement of cash flows as a secondary statement would ignore potential information that can assist us in our analysis of the company. In particular, the statement of cash flows offers information along the following four dimensions.

- **Activity type** The statement of cash flows is structured to highlight three primary activities of the company: **operating activities**, **investing activities**, and **financing activities**. Neither the income statement nor the balance sheet presents that perspective.

- **Liquidity** The statement of cash flows emphasizes the role cash plays in the company's day-to-day operations; it is cash that pays employees, cash that pays debt, and cash that provides a return to equity holders in the form of dividends. Finance professionals often focus on free cash flow, and for good reason. Companies that fail typically do so because they lack the cash flow necessary to conduct their business. A focus solely on GAAP profit can obscure a deterioration of liquidity that can lead to company failure.

---

[1] The statement of cash flows explains the change in a firm's cash *and* cash equivalents. **Cash equivalents** are short-term, highly liquid investments that are (1) easily convertible into a known cash amount and (2) close enough to maturity so that their market value is not sensitive to interest rate changes (generally, investments with initial maturities of three months or less). Treasury bills, commercial paper (short-term notes issued by corporations), and money market funds are typical examples of cash equivalents.

- **Additional detail** As an added benefit, the statement of cash flows highlights important operating items that are often not reported as separate line items in the income statement, such as depreciation on building and equipment assets, impairments of tangible and intangible assets, the cost of stock-based compensation, the excess of reported equity income over dividends received from investee companies, the cash portion of interest expense and income tax expense, and the gain or loss on the sales of assets. In addition, the statement of cash flows highlights items that are *not* reflected in the income statement, such as capital expenditures (CAPEX), dividend payments, and the repayment of the principal portion of company debt.

- **Earnings quality** The statement of cash flows provides insight into the "quality" of company earnings. All profit must eventually be received in cash. So, when profit and operating cash flow diverge, we must investigate the reasons for the divergence because cash flow ultimately drives company value. If net income grows at a faster pace than operating cash flows, our analysis attempts to understand whether cash flow will increase in the future or whether income has been improperly recognized, only to be reversed in the future. Our assessment of the quality of company earnings is a difficult challenge but one that is aided considerably by a thorough understanding of the statement of cash flows.

Statement of Cash Flows Structure

The statement of cash flows classifies cash receipts and cash payments into one of three categories.

- **Operating activities** Operating activities measure the net cash inflows and outflows as a result of the company's transactions with its customers. We generally prefer operating cash flows to be positive, although companies can report net cash outflows for operating activities in the short run during periods of growth (as the company builds up inventory and hires staff to grow operations in anticipation of future sales and cash inflows).

- **Investing activities** Investing activities relate to investments, joint ventures, and capital expenditures for PPE. Outflows occur when a company purchases these assets, and inflows occur when they are sold.

- **Financing activities** Financing activities relate to long-term debt and stockholders' equity. Cash inflows result from borrowing money and issuing stock to investors. Outflows occur when a company repays debt, repurchases stock, or pays dividends to shareholders.

The combined effects on cash of all three categories explain the net change in cash for that period:

```
    Beginning cash balance (the ending cash balance from prior year's balance sheet)
+   Change in cash during the period
=   Ending cash balance for current year (reported on current year's balance sheet)
```

Statement of Cash Flows Preparation Overview The statement of cash flows is prepared using data from the income statement and the balance sheet.

- **Income statement** For the *indirect* method of preparing the operating section, we begin with net income as a source of cash and adjust net income for noncash items that are included in the computation of net income.[2]

- **Balance sheet** We consider the change in each balance sheet account and determine the cash generated or used by the change in the account balance. The graphic below shows how balance sheet categories relate to the three sections of the statement of cash flows.

---

[2] Firms can choose to present operating cash flows either directly, by reporting operating cash receipts from customers and cash payments to suppliers and employees, or indirectly, by reconciling net income and cash flow from operating activities. While firms are encouraged to use the simpler direct method, most U.S. companies continue to use the indirect method. Our discussion here addresses the indirect method, and we return to the direct method at the end of the module.

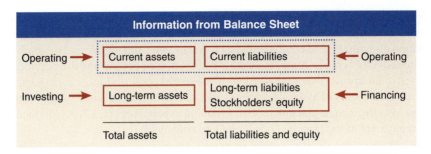

There are two exceptions to the balance sheet classification in the graphic above; both involve the current section of the balance sheet where items are not classified as operating activities.

- **Current (Nonoperating) assets** classified as investing activities such as marketable securities.
- **Current (Nonoperating) liabilities** classified as financing activities such as the principal balance of short-term debt and current maturities of long-term debt.

Statement of Cash Flows for Starbucks Exhibit 11.1 reproduces Starbucks' statement of cash flows. Starbucks reports $11,937.8 million in net cash inflows from operating activities in 2018. This is much greater than its net income of $4,518.0 million, which highlights that net income and operating cash flow are different measures. (Later in this module, we explain all the items included in the operating section of Starbucks' statement of cash flows). The company used $2,361.5 million of cash for investing activities, primarily for purchases of PPE (called capital expenditures or CAPEX), and also used $3,242.8 million of cash for financing activities to pay dividends and repurchase common stock. In sum, Starbucks increased its cash by $6,294 million (after considering foreign exchange effects), from $2,462.3 million at the beginning of fiscal 2018 to $8,756.3 million at the end of fiscal 2018.

Overall, Starbucks' cash flow picture is strong for three reasons.

- The company is generating positive cash from operating activities, its core business.
- The company is investing in the maintenance and growth of its infrastructure with capital expenditures (CAPEX).
- The company is returning cash to shareholders through dividends and share repurchases.

In analyzing the statement of cash flows, we should not necessarily conclude the company is better off if the ending balance of cash increases and worse off if cash decreases. It is not the *change* in cash that is most important but the reasons behind the change. For example, what are the sources of cash inflows? Are these sources of cash transitory, or can we expect the cash flows to continue? Are these sources mainly from operating activities, or did sales of investments or PPE generate cash flow? To what uses have cash inflows been put? Such questions and answers are key to properly using the statement of cash flows.

Operating Activities Preview

The focus of **operating activities** of companies is to generate cash from selling goods or services at a profit. Following are examples of cash inflows and outflows relating to operating activities.

Operating Activities	
Cash Inflows ↑	**Cash Outflows** ↓
■ Receipts from customers for sales made or services rendered.	■ Payments to employees or suppliers.
■ Receipts of interest and dividends.	■ Payments to purchase inventories.
■ Other receipts that are not related to investing or financing activities, such as lawsuit settlements and refunds received from suppliers.	■ Payments of interest to creditors.
	■ Payments of taxes to government.
	■ Other payments that are not related to investing or financing activities, such as contributions to charity.

Exhibit 11.1 ■ Statement of Cash Flows for Starbucks Corporation

Fiscal Year Ended ($ millions)	Sept. 30, 2018	Oct. 1, 2017	Oct. 2, 2016
Operating Activities			
Net earnings including noncontrolling interests	$4,518.0	$2,884.9	$2,818.9
Adjustments to reconcile net earnings to net cash provided by operating activities:			
Depreciation and amortization	1,305.9	1,067.1	1,030.1
Deferred income taxes, net	714.9	95.1	265.7
Income earned from equity method investees	(242.8)	(310.2)	(250.2)
Distributions received from equity method investees	226.8	186.6	223.3
Gain resulting from acquisition of joint venture	(1,376.4)	—	—
Net gain resulting from divestiture of certain retail operations	(499.2)	(93.5)	(6.1)
Stock-based compensation	250.3	176.0	218.1
Goodwill impairments	37.6	87.2	—
Other	89.0	68.9	45.1
Cash provided by changes in operating assets and liabilities:			
Accounts receivable	131.0	(96.8)	(55.6)
Inventories	(41.2)	14.0	(67.5)
Accounts payable	391.6	46.4	46.9
Deferred revenue	7,109.4	130.8	180.4
Other operating assets and liabilities	(677.1)	(4.7)	248.8
Net cash provided by operating activities	11,937.8	4,251.8	4,697.9
Investing Activities			
Purchase of investments	(191.9)	(674.4)	(1,585.7)
Sales of investments	459.0	1,054.5	680.7
Maturities and calls of investments	45.3	149.6	27.9
Acquisitions, net of cash acquired	(1,311.3)	—	—
Additions to property, plant and equipment	(1,976.4)	(1,519.4)	(1,440.3)
Net proceeds from the divestiture of certain operations	608.2	85.4	69.6
Other	5.6	54.3	24.9
Net cash used by investing activities	(2,361.5)	(850.0)	(2,222.9)
Financing Activities			
Proceeds from issuance of long-term debt	5,584.1	750.2	1,254.5
Repayments of long-term debt	—	(400.0)	—
Proceeds from issuance of common stock	153.9	150.8	160.7
Cash dividends paid	(1,743.4)	(1,450.4)	(1,178.0)
Repurchase of common stock	(7,133.5)	(2,042.5)	(1,995.6)
Minimum tax withholdings on share-based awards	(62.7)	(82.8)	(106.0)
Other	(41.2)	(4.4)	(8.4)
Net cash used by financing activities	(3,242.8)	(3,079.1)	(1,872.8)
Effect of exchange rate changes on cash and cash equivalents	(39.5)	10.8	(3.5)
Net increase in cash and cash equivalents	6,294.0	333.5	598.7
Cash and Cash Equivalents:			
Beginning of period	2,462.3	2,128.8	1,530.1
End of period	$8,756.3	$2,462.3	$2,128.8

These cash inflows and outflows affect net income. Accordingly, net income is the first line of the operating cash flow section of the statement of cash flows. This reflects the idea that the company generates cash from selling its goods or services to its customers.

Net income commonly includes items that do not involve the receipt or payment of cash. Depreciation expense is an example. Cash is spent when the depreciable asset (such as equipment or a building) is purchased. Depreciation expense is an accounting process that allocates the cash cost over the useful life of the asset. Although there is no cash outflow with annual depreciation expense, it is reported as an expense in computing net income. Because the focus of the statement of cash flows is on cash, we need to "undo" the effect of depreciation and other noncash expenses. We do that by *adding it back* to offset the expense (i.e., undo the negative effect) in the income statement.

Let's consider further adjustments to get operating cash flow. During the year, the company might decide whether to use cash to grow the firm. For example, the company might purchase additional inventories to have goods available for future sales. This use of cash increases inventory but has no effect on net income. As another example, the company can extend credit to its customers as a strategic move to generate additional sales. This action increases sales, but instead of receiving cash, the company's accounts receivable increases. The statement of cash flows shows an increase in inventories and an increase in accounts receivable as negative amounts to indicate the company has invested cash in the growth of assets (inventory and accounts receivable). Conversely, cash is freed up when the company reduces its receivables or inventory levels, and the statement of cash flows shows such decreases as positive amounts.

On the liability side, companies can conserve cash by borrowing from their suppliers or other operating creditors. An increase in liabilities signals an increase in borrowing, an inflow of cash, which is reported as a positive amount in the statement of cash flows. As the company uses cash to repay borrowed amounts, the statement of cash flows shows the reduction of the liability as a negative amount, indicating a cash outflow.

Companies prepare the statement of cash flows using their income statement and balance sheets (to calculate changes in accounts between the current and prior years). The preparation is mainly a mechanical process with limited discretion. A simple but common computation of operating cash flow follows.

	Net income (– if a net loss)
+	Depreciation expense
–	Increases in current assets
+	Decreases in current assets
+	Increases in current liabilities
–	Decreases in current liabilities
=	Cash from operating activities

Understanding how increases and decreases in assets and liabilities affect cash flow is key to understanding the information contained in the statement of cash flows. To help, keep the following decision rules in mind.

Balance Sheet Account	Increase in Account	Decrease in Account
Assets (noncash)	Cash Outflow	Cash Inflow
Liabilities and equity	Cash Inflow	Cash Outflow

This table applies to all sections of the statement of cash flows. (When we examine a statement of cash flows such as Starbucks', see Exhibit 11.1, the cash flow effect of an item does not always agree with the change in the balance sheet account. This can be due to several factors. One factor is when a company uses its own stock to acquire another entity. There is no cash effect from a stock acquisition and, hence, it is not reported in the statement of cash flows. Yet, the company does increase its assets and liabilities when it adds the acquired company's assets and liabilities to its balance sheet.)

Knowledge of how companies record cash inflows and outflows not only sheds light on the information contained in the statement of cash flows, it also helps managers with business decisions. For instance, managers can increase cash by decreasing the levels of receivables and inventories, perhaps by better managing the quantities and types of inventories to reduce slow-moving items or by being smarter about which customers to extend credit to, and in what amounts, to minimize slow-paying customers. Similarly, managers can increase cash by increasing the levels of accounts payable and accrued liabilities. (This must be done with care, however, as one company's payables are another company's receivables and slowing down payment could jeopardize future transactions with the vendor or supplier.) Managing cash balances by managing current asset and current liability accounts is called *working capital management*, an important activity for all companies.

Investing Activities Preview

A firm's transactions involving (1) the acquisition and disposal of PPE assets and intangible assets, (2) the purchase and sale of stocks, bonds, and other securities (that are not cash equivalents), and (3) the lending and subsequent collection of money constitute the basic components of its **investing activities**. The related cash receipts and payments appear in the investing activities section of the statement of cash flows. Examples of these cash flows follow.

Investing Activities

Cash Inflows
- Receipts from sales of PPE assets and intangible assets.
- Receipts from sales of investments in stocks, bonds, and other securities (other than cash equivalents).
- Receipts from repayments of loans by borrowers.

Cash Outflows
- Payments to purchase PPE assets and intangible assets.
- Payments to purchase stocks, bonds, and other securities (other than cash equivalents).
- Payments made to lend money to borrowers.

Financing Activities Preview

A firm engages in **financing activities** when it obtains resources from owners, returns resources to owners, borrows resources from creditors, and repays amounts borrowed. Cash flows related to these transactions are reported in the financing activities section of the statement of cash flows. Examples of these cash flows follow.

Financing Activities

Cash Inflows
- Receipts from issuances of common stock and preferred stock and from sales of treasury stock.
- Receipts from issuances of bonds payable, mortgage notes payable, and other notes payable.

Cash Outflows
- Payments to acquire treasury stock.
- Payments of dividends.
- Payments to settle outstanding bonds payable, mortgage notes payable, and other notes payable.

LO1 Review 11-1

Identify each transaction as one of the following activities: operating (O), investing (I), or financing (F).

Transaction	Classification
1. Payments of dividends	_____
2. Payments to purchase PPE assets and intangible assets	_____
3. Payments to employees or suppliers	_____
4. Payments to purchase inventories	_____
5. Receipts from issuances of bonds payable, mortgage notes payable, and other notes payable	_____
6. Receipts from sales of investments in stocks, bonds, and other securities (other than cash equivalents)	_____

continued

continued from previous page

Transaction	Classification
7. Payments of interest to creditors	_____
8. Receipts from issuances of common stock and preferred stock and from sales of treasury stock	_____
9. Receipts of interest and dividends	_____
10. Payments to purchase stocks, bonds, and other securities (other than cash equivalents)	_____
11. Receipts from customers for sales made or services rendered.	_____
12. Payments to acquire treasury stock	_____
13. Other receipts such as lawsuit settlements and refunds received from suppliers	_____
14. Payments of taxes to government	_____
15. Payments to settle outstanding bonds payable, mortgage notes payable, and other notes payable	_____
16. Receipts from sales of PPE assets and intangible assets	_____
17. Other payments such as contributions to charity	_____
18. Receipts from repayments of loans by borrowers	_____
19. Payments made to lend money to borrowers	_____

Solution on p. 11-56.

Cash Flow from Operating Activities

LO2 Determine and analyze net cash flows from operating activities.

The first section of a statement of cash flows presents a firm's net cash flow from operating activities. Two alternative formats are used to report the net cash flow from operating activities: the *indirect method* and the *direct method*. *Both methods report the same amount of net cash flow from operating activities.* (Net cash flows from investing and financing activities are prepared in the same manner under both the indirect and direct methods; only the format for cash flows from operating activities differs.)

The **indirect method** starts with net income and applies a series of adjustments to net income to convert it to net cash flow from operating activities. *More than 98% of companies preparing the statement of cash flows use the indirect method.* The indirect method is popular because it is easier and less expensive to prepare than the direct method and the direct method requires a supplemental disclosure showing the indirect method (thus, essentially reporting both methods).

The remainder of this module discusses the preparation of the statement of cash flows. The indirect method is presented in this section, and the direct method is presented in the Appendix. (These discussions are independent of each other; both provide complete coverage of the preparation of the statement of cash flows.)

To prepare a statement of cash flows, we need a firm's income statement, comparative balance sheets, and some additional data taken from the accounting records. Exhibit 11.2 presents this information for Java House. We use these data to prepare Java House's 2020 statement of cash flows using the indirect method. Java House's statement of cash flows explains the $25,000 increase in cash (from $10,000 to $35,000) that occurred during 2020 by classifying the firm's cash flows into operating, investing, and financing categories.

Exhibit 11.2 ■ Financial Data of Java House

JAVA HOUSE
Income Statement
For Year Ended December 31, 2020

Sales..................		$250,000
Cost of goods sold.......	$148,000	
Wages expense..........	52,000	
Insurance expense.......	5,000	
Depreciation expense.....	10,000	
Income tax expense......	11,000	
Gain on sale of land......	(8,000)	218,000
Net income.............		$ 32,000

Additional Data for 2020
1. Purchased all of the long-term investments for cash at year-end.
2. Sold land costing $20,000 for $28,000 cash.
3. Acquired a $60,000 patent at year-end by issuing common stock.
4. All accounts payable relate to merchandise purchases.
5. Issued common stock for $10,000 cash.
6. Declared and paid cash dividends of $13,000.

JAVA HOUSE
Balance Sheet

	Dec. 31, 2020	Dec. 31, 2019
Assets		
Cash.....................	$ 35,000	$ 10,000
Accounts receivable.........	39,000	34,000
Inventory.................	54,000	60,000
Prepaid insurance...........	17,000	4,000
Long-term investments.......	15,000	—
PPE	180,000	200,000
Accumulated depreciation ...	(50,000)	(40,000)
Patent...................	60,000	—
Total assets	$350,000	$268,000
Liabilities and Equity		
Accounts payable...........	$ 10,000	$ 19,000
Income tax payable	5,000	3,000
Common stock	260,000	190,000
Retained earnings	75,000	56,000
Total liabilities and equity	$350,000	$268,000

Steps to Compute Net Cash Flow from Operating Activities

The following four steps are applied to construct the operating activities section of the statement of cash flows.

① **Begin with net income** The first line of the operating activities section of the statement of cash flows is net income, which is the bottom line from the income statement. This amount is recorded as a positive amount for net income and as a negative amount for a net loss.

② **Adjust net income (loss) for *noncash* revenues, expenses, gains, and losses**
   a. **Noncash revenues and expenses** The income statement often includes noncash expenses, such as depreciation and amortization. These expenses are allocations of asset costs over their useful lives to match the revenues generated from those assets. The cash outflow normally occurs when the asset is acquired, which is reported in the *investing* section. Depreciation and amortization expenses do not entail cash outflows. Hence, we must eliminate them from the statement of cash flows by adding them back (to "zero them out" because they are negative amounts in the net income computation).
   b. **Gains and losses** Gains and losses on sales of assets are part of investing activities, not operating activities (unless the company is in the business of buying and selling assets). Thus, we must remove them from the operating section and record the net cash inflows or outflows in the investing section; namely, gains on sales are subtracted from income and losses on sales are added to income.

③ **Adjust net income (loss) for changes in current assets and current liabilities** Net income must be adjusted for changes in current assets and current liabilities (the operating section of the balance sheet). A decrease (from prior year to current year) in a noncash current asset is identified as a cash inflow, and an increase is identified as a cash outflow. Conversely, an increase in a current liability is identified as a cash inflow and a decrease as a cash outflow. To make this computation, we use the following guide.

Balance Sheet Account	Increase in Account	Decrease in Account
Current assets (excluding cash)	Cash Outflow	Cash Inflow
Current liabilities	Cash Inflow	Cash Outflow

④ **Sum the amounts from Steps 1, 2, and 3 to get net cash flows from operating activities**

Exhibit 11.3 summarizes the adjustments to net income in determining operating cash flows. These are adjustments applied under the indirect method of computing cash flow from operations.

Exhibit 11.3 ■ Converting Net Income to Net Cash Flow from Operating Activities

	Add (+) or Subtract (−) from Net Income
Net income	$ #
Adjustments for noncash revenues, expenses, gains, and losses:	
Add depreciation and amortization	+
Add (subtract) losses (gains) on asset and liability dispositions	+ or −
Adjustments for changes in noncash current assets and current liabilities:	
Adjust for changes in noncash current assets	
Subtract increases in noncash current assets	−
Add decreases in noncash current assets	+
Adjust for changes in current liabilities	
Add increases in current liabilities	+
Subtract decreases in current liabilities	−
Net cash flow from operating activities	$ #

To better understand the adjustments for current assets and current liabilities, the following table provides brief explanations of adjustments for receivables, inventories, and payables and other accruals.

	Change in Account Balance	Inference Drawn	Adjustment to Net Income to Operating Cash Flow
Receivables	Increase	Sales and net income increase, but cash is not yet received	Deduct increase in receivables from net income
	Decrease	More cash is received than is reported in sales and net income	Add decrease in receivables to net income
Inventories	Increase	Cash is paid for inventories that are not yet reflected in cost of goods sold	Deduct increase in inventories from net income
	Decrease	Cost of goods sold includes inventory costs that were paid for in a prior period	Add decrease in inventories to net income
Payables and Accruals	Increase	More goods and services are acquired on credit, delaying cash payment	Add increase in payables and accruals to net income
	Decrease	More cash is paid than that reflected in cost of goods sold or operating expenses	Deduct decrease in payables and accruals from net income

Java House Case Illustration

We next explain and illustrate these adjustments with Java House's data from Exhibit 11.2.

Revenues and Expenses with No Cash Flow Effects

Depreciation and amortization expenses represent write-offs of previously recorded assets, so-called noncash expenses. Because depreciation and amortization expenses are subtracted in computing net income, we add these expenses to net income as we convert it to a related net operating cash flow. Adding these expenses to net income eliminates them from the income statement and is a necessary adjustment to obtain cash income. Java House had $10,000 of 2020 depreciation expense, so this amount is added to Java House's net income of $32,000.

Net income	$32,000
Add depreciation	**10,000**

Gains and Losses with No Cash Flow Effects

The income statement can contain gains and losses that relate to investing or financing activities. Gains and losses from the sale of investments, PPE assets, or intangible assets illustrate gains and losses from investing (not operating) activities. A gain or loss from the retirement of bonds payable is an example of a financing gain or loss. The full cash flow effect from these types of events is reported in the investing or financing sections of the statement of cash flows. Therefore, the related gains or losses must be eliminated as we convert net income to net cash flow from operating activities. To eliminate their impact on net income, gains are subtracted and losses are added to net income. Java House had an $8,000 gain from the sale of land. This gain relates to an investing activity, so it is subtracted from Java House's net income.

Net income	$32,000
Add depreciation	10,000
Subtract gain on sale of land	**(8,000)**

Change in Current Operating Assets—Accounts Receivable

Credit sales increase accounts receivable; cash collections on account decrease accounts receivable. If, overall, accounts receivable decrease during a year, then cash collections from customers exceed credit sales revenue by the amount of the decrease. Because sales are added in computing net income, the decrease in accounts receivable is added to net income. In essence, this adjustment replaces the sales amount with the larger amount of cash collections from customers. If accounts receivable increase during a year, then sales revenue exceeds the cash collections from customers by the amount of the increase. Because sales are added in computing net income, the increase in accounts receivable is subtracted from net income as we convert it to a net cash flow from operating activities. In essence, this adjustment replaces the sales amount with the smaller amount of cash collections from customers. Java House's accounts receivable increased $5,000, so this increase is subtracted from net income under the indirect method.

Net income	$32,000
Add depreciation	10,000
Subtract gain on sale of land	(8,000)
Subtract accounts receivable increase	**(5,000)**

Change in Current Operating Assets—Inventory

The adjustment for an inventory change is one of two adjustments to net income that together cause the cost of goods sold expense to be replaced by an amount representing the cash paid during the period for merchandise purchased. The second adjustment, which we examine shortly, is for the change in accounts payable. The effect of the inventory adjustment alone is to adjust net income for the difference between the cost of goods sold and the cost of merchandise purchased during the period. The cost of merchandise purchased increases inventory; the cost of goods sold decreases inventory. An overall decrease in inventory during a period must mean, therefore, that the cost of merchandise purchased was less than the cost of goods sold, by the amount of the decrease. Because cost of goods sold was subtracted in computing net income, the inventory decrease is added to net income. After this adjustment, the effect of the cost of goods sold on net income has been replaced by the smaller cost of merchandise purchased. Similarly, if inventory increased during a period, the cost of merchandise purchased is larger than the cost of goods sold by the amount of the increase. To replace the cost of goods sold with the cost of merchandise purchased, the inventory increase is subtracted from net income. Java House's inventory decreased $6,000, so this decrease is added to net income.

Net income	$32,000
Add depreciation	10,000
Subtract gain on sale of land	(8,000)
Subtract accounts receivable increase	(5,000)
Add inventory decrease	**6,000**

Change in Current Operating Assets—Prepaid Expenses

Cash prepayments of various expenses increase a firm's prepaid expenses. When the related expenses for the period are subsequently recorded, the prepaid expenses decrease. An overall decrease in prepaid expenses for a period means the cash prepayments were less than the related expenses. Because the expenses were subtracted in determining net income, the indirect method adds the decrease in prepaid expenses to net income as it is converted to a cash flow amount. The effect of the addition is to replace the expense amount with the smaller cash payment amount. Similarly, an increase in prepaid expenses is subtracted from net income because an increase means the cash prepayments during the year were more than the related expenses. Java House's prepaid insurance increased $13,000, so this increase is deducted from net income.

Net income	$32,000
Add depreciation	10,000
Subtract gain on sale of land	(8,000)
Subtract accounts receivable increase	(5,000)
Add inventory decrease	6,000
Subtract prepaid insurance increase	**(13,000)**

Change in Current Operating Liabilities—Accounts Payable

When merchandise is purchased on account, accounts payable increase by the cost of the goods purchased. Accounts payable decrease when cash payments are made to settle the accounts. An overall decrease in accounts payable during a year means cash payments for purchases were more than the cost of the purchases. An accounts payable decrease, therefore, is subtracted from net income under the indirect method. The deduction, in effect, replaces the cost of merchandise purchased with the larger cash payments for merchandise purchased. (Recall that the earlier inventory adjustment replaced the cost of goods sold with the cost of merchandise purchased.) In contrast, an increase in accounts payable means cash payments for purchases were less than the cost of purchases for the period. Thus, an accounts payable increase is added to net income as it is converted to a cash flow amount. Java House shows a $9,000 decrease in accounts payable. This decrease is subtracted from net income.

Net income	$32,000
Add depreciation	10,000
Subtract gain on sale of land	(8,000)
Subtract accounts receivable increase	(5,000)
Add inventory decrease	6,000
Subtract prepaid insurance increase	(13,000)
Subtract accounts payable decrease	**(9,000)**

Change in Current Operating Liabilities—Accrued Liabilities

Changes in accrued liabilities are interpreted the same way as changes in accounts payable. A decrease means cash payments exceeded the related expense amounts; an increase means cash payments were less than the related expenses. Decreases are subtracted from net income; increases are added to net income. Java has one accrued liability, income tax payable, and it increased by $2,000. The $2,000 increase is added to net income.

Net income	$32,000
Add depreciation	10,000
Subtract gain on sale of land	(8,000)
Subtract accounts receivable increase	(5,000)
Add inventory decrease	6,000
Subtract prepaid insurance increase	(13,000)
Subtract accounts payable decrease	(9,000)
Add income tax payable increase	**2,000**

Net Cash from Operating Activities

We have identified all of the adjustments to convert Java House's net income to its net cash flow from operating activities. The operating activities section of the statement of cash flows appears as follows under the indirect method.

Net income	$32,000
Add (deduct) items to convert net income to cash basis:	
Depreciation	10,000
Gain on sale of land	(8,000)
Accounts receivable increase	(5,000)
Inventory decrease	6,000
Prepaid insurance increase	(13,000)
Accounts payable decrease	(9,000)
Income tax payable increase	2,000
Net cash provided by operating activities	**$15,000**

To summarize, net cash from operating activities begins with net income (loss) and eliminates noncash expenses (such as depreciation) and noncash revenues, and any noncash gains and losses that are properly reported in the investing and financing sections. Next, cash inflows (outflows) relating to changes in the level of current operating assets and liabilities are added (subtracted) to yield net cash flows from operating activities. During the period, Java House earned cash operating profits of $34,000 ($32,000 + $10,000 − $8,000) and used $19,000 of cash (−$5,000 + $6,000 − $13,000 − $9,000 + $2,000) to increase net working capital. Cash outflows relating to the increase in net working capital are a common occurrence for growing companies, and this net asset increase must be financed just like the increase in PPE assets.

> **Business Insight** ■ **Starbucks' Adjustments for Operating Cash Flow**
>
> **Starbucks** reports $4,518.0 million for 2018 net earnings, including noncontrolling interests, along with $11,937.8 million of operating cash inflows (see Exhibit 11.1). Differences between net income and operating cash flow are due to:
> - Depreciation and amortization expense of $1,305.9 million (similar to the addback for Java House).
> - Loss from equity method investees of $242.8 million that is included in net income. This is followed by the addition of $226.8 million from dividends received from those equity method investees. Equity income is not received in cash until the investee pays dividends to the investors (including Starbucks).

continued

continued from previous page

- Gains of $1,376.4 million on the acquisition of a joint venture and of $499.2 million on the divestiture of certain retail operations are subtracted to remove the noncash gains. The statement of cash flows shows the cash received as an investing inflow. (This is similar to the gain on sale of land for Java House.)
- Stock-based compensation expense of $250.3 million, which is noncash compensation expense paid in the form of shares of stock.

All of these noncash items are removed from reported net income to yield net cash flow from operating activities. Starbucks' operating cash flow also includes the cash generated by or used for working capital accounts as discussed above for Java House. This includes

- Decrease in accounts receivable, $131.0 million
- Increase in inventories, $41.2 million
- Increase in accounts payable, $391.6 million
- Increase in deferred revenue, $7,109.4 (from the new revenue recognition standard) representing cash received from customers but not included in net income because performance obligations had not yet been earned by year-end

Managerial Decision ■ You Are the Securities Analyst

You are analyzing a company's statement of cash flows. The company has two items relating to its accounts receivable. First, the company finances the sale of its products to some customers; the increase to notes receivable is classified as an investing activity. Second, the company sells its accounts receivable to a separate entity, such as a trust. As a result, sale of receivables is reported as an asset sale; this reduces receivables and yields a gain or loss on the sale (in this case, the company is not required to consolidate the trust). This action increases the company's operating cash flows. How should you interpret this cash flow increase? [Answer, p. 11-32]

Review 11-2 LO2

Expresso Royale's income statement and comparative balance sheets follow.

EXPRESSO ROYALE
Income Statement
For Year Ended December 31, 2020

Sales.		$385,000
Dividend income.		5,000
		390,000
Cost of goods sold	$233,000	
Wages expense	82,000	
Advertising expense.	10,000	
Depreciation expense.	11,000	
Income tax expense	17,000	
Loss on sale of investments.	2,000	355,000
Net income		$ 35,000

continued

EXPRESSO ROYALE
Balance Sheets

	Dec. 31, 2020	Dec. 31, 2019
Assets		
Cash	$ 8,000	$ 12,000
Accounts receivable	22,000	28,000
Inventory	94,000	66,000
Prepaid advertising	12,000	9,000
Available-for-sale investments	30,000	41,000
Fair value adjustment to investments	—	(1,000)
Property, plant & equipment (PPE)	178,000	130,000
Accumulated depreciation	(72,000)	(61,000)
Total assets	$272,000	$224,000
Liabilities and Equity		
Accounts payable	$ 27,000	$ 14,000
Wages payable	6,000	2,500
Income tax payable	3,000	4,500
Common stock	139,000	125,000
Retained earnings	97,000	79,000
Unrealized loss on available-for-sale investments (AOCI)	—	(1,000)
Total liabilities and equity	$272,000	$224,000

Cash dividends of $17,000 were declared and paid during 2020. PPE was purchased for cash in 2020, and, later in the year, additional common stock was issued for cash. Investments costing $11,000 and carried at $10,000 were sold for cash at a $2,000 realized loss in 2020; an unrealized loss of $1,000 on these investments had been recorded in 2019 (at December 31, 2020, the cost and fair value of unsold investments are equal).

Required
Compute Expresso Royale's operating cash flow for 2020 using the indirect method.

Solution on p. 11-56.

Computing Cash Flows from Investing Activities

Analyze Remaining Noncash Assets

Investing activities cause changes in asset accounts. Usually, the accounts affected (other than cash) are noncurrent asset accounts, such as PPE assets and long-term investments, although short-term investment accounts can also be affected. To determine the cash flows from investing activities, *we analyze changes in all noncash asset accounts not used in computing net cash flow from operating activities.* Our objective is to identify any investing cash flows related to these changes.

We can draw on our following decision rule to see how changes in assets such as investments and PPE affect cash flow.

LO3 Determine and analyze net cash flows from investing activities.

Balance Sheet Account	Increase in Account	Decrease in Account
Assets (noncash)	Cash Outflow	Cash Inflow

Java House Case Illustration
Analyze Change in Investments

Java House's comparative balance sheets (see Exhibit 11.2) show available-for-sale investments increased $15,000 during the year. The increase means investments must have been purchased, and the additional data reported indicates cash was spent to purchase investments. Purchasing investments is an investing activity. Thus, a $15,000 purchase of investments is reported as a cash outflow from investing activities in the statement of cash flows.

Cash flows from investing activities	
Purchase of investments	$(15,000)

Analyze Change in PPE

Java House's PPE decreased $20,000 during the year. PPE decreases as the result of disposals, and the additional data for Java House indicate land was sold for cash. Selling land is an investing activity. Thus, the sale of land for $28,000 is reported as a cash inflow from investing activities in the statement of cash flows. (Recall that the $8,000 gain on sale of land was deducted as a reconciling item in the operating section; see above.)

Cash flows from investing activities	
Purchase of stock investments	$(15,000)
Sale of land	28,000

Analyze Change in Accumulated Depreciation

Java House's accumulated depreciation increased $10,000 during the year. Accumulated depreciation increases when depreciation expense is recorded. Java House's depreciation expense was $10,000, so the total change in accumulated depreciation is the result of the recording of depreciation expense. As previously discussed, there is no cash flow related to the recording of depreciation expense, and we previously adjusted for this expense in our computation of net cash flows from operating activities.

Analyze Change in Patent

We see from the comparative balance sheets that Java House had an increase of $60,000 for a patent. The increase means a patent was acquired, and the additional data indicate common stock was issued to obtain a patent. This event is a noncash investing (acquiring a patent) and financing (issuing common stock) transaction that must be disclosed as supplementary information to the statement of cash flows.

Net Cash from Investing Activities

The investing activities section of the statement of cash flows appears as follows.

Cash flows from investing activities	
Purchase of stock investments	$(15,000)
Sale of land	28,000
Net cash provided by investing activities	$ 13,000

Business Insight ■ Starbucks' Investing Activities

Starbucks used $2,361.5 million cash for investing activities in 2018. Three line items on the statement of cash flows relate to investments: the buying, selling, and maturing of marketable securities throughout the year as Starbucks invests its excess cash to generate interest, dividends, and capital gains. The company used cash of $191.9 million to purchase new securities and received cash of $459.0 million and $45.3 million from security sales and maturities, respectively. Starbucks also spent $1,311.3 million cash to acquire other companies. Note that this is the cash portion of the acquisitions. The company might also have issued debt and stock to finance its acquisition, which would be excluded from the investing section of the statement of cash flows but would be specifically listed as a noncash investing activity in a footnote. The company received $608.2 million cash as proceeds from selling certain operations. This relates to the gain on sale of $499.2 million reported in the operating section of the statement of cash flows. Starbucks invested $1,976.4 million in PPE. These expenditures might have been for company-owned property or for leasehold improvements on leased property.

LO3 Review 11-3

Refer to the data in Review 11-2, to answer the requirement below.

Required

Prepare Expresso Royale's cash flows from investing activities for 2020.

Solution on p. 11-57.

Cash Flows from Financing Activities

Analyze Remaining Liabilities and Equity

LO4 Determine and analyze net cash flows from financing activities.

Financing activities cause changes in liability and stockholders' equity accounts. Usually, the accounts affected are noncurrent accounts, such as bonds payable and common stock, although a current liability such as short-term notes payable can also be affected. To determine the cash flows from financing activities, *we analyze changes in all liability and stockholders' equity accounts that were not used in computing net cash flow from operating activities*. Our objective is to identify any financing cash flows related to these changes.

We can draw on our following decision rule to see how changes in liabilities, such as short- and long-term debt, and equity accounts, such as common stock and treasury stock, affect cash flow.

Balance Sheet Account	Increase in Account	Decrease in Account
Liabilities and equity............	Cash Inflow	Cash Outflow

Java House Case Illustration

Analyze Change in Common Stock

Java House's common stock increased $70,000 during the year (see Exhibit 11.2). Common stock increases when shares of stock are issued. As noted in discussing the patent increase, common stock with a $60,000 par value was issued in exchange for a patent. This event is disclosed as a noncash investing and financing transaction. The other $10,000 increase in common stock, as noted in the additional data, resulted from an issuance of stock for cash. Issuing common stock is a financing activity, so a $10,000 cash inflow from a stock issuance appears as a financing activity in the statement of cash flows.

Cash flows from financing activities	
Issuance of common stock.................................	$10,000

Analyze Change in Retained Earnings

Retained earnings grew from $56,000 to $75,000 during the year—a $19,000 increase. This increase is the net result of Java House's $32,000 of net income (which increased retained earnings) and a $13,000 cash dividend (which decreased retained earnings). Because every item in Java House's income statement was considered in computing the net cash provided by operating activities, only the cash dividend remains to be considered. Paying a cash dividend is a financing activity. Thus, a $13,000 cash dividend appears as a cash outflow from financing activities in the statement of cash flows.

Cash flows from financing activities	
Issuance of common stock.................................	$10,000
Payment of dividends.......................................	(13,000)

Net Cash from Financing Activities

The financing activities section of the statement of cash flows appears as follows.

Cash flows from financing activities	
Issuance of common stock	$10,000
Payment of dividends	(13,000)
Net cash used by financing activities	$ (3,000)

We have now completed the analysis of all of Java House's noncash balance sheet accounts and can prepare the 2020 statement of cash flows. Exhibit 11.4 shows this statement.

If there are cash inflows and outflows from similar types of investing and financing activities, the inflows and outflows are reported separately (rather than reporting only the net difference). For example, proceeds from the sale of PPE are reported separately from outlays made to acquire PPE. Similarly, funds borrowed are reported separately from debt repayments, and proceeds from issuing stock are reported separately from outlays to acquire treasury stock.

Business Insight ■ Starbucks' Financing Activities

Highlights of **Starbucks'** 2018 financing activities include the receipt of $153.9 million cash from stock issuances. Only stock issued for cash is reflected in the statement of cash flows. Stock issued in connection with acquisitions is not reflected because it does not involve cash. Issuance of stock is often related to the exercise of employee stock options, and companies frequently repurchase stock to offset the dilutive effect of granting the options and to have stock to sell to employees who exercise their options. Starbucks reports a cash inflow of $5,584.1 million from borrowings, and no debt repayments during the year. Starbucks returned $8,876.9 million ($1,743.4 million + $7,133.5 million) to shareholders during the year in the form of dividend payments and share repurchases. The net effect is a decrease in cash of $3,242.8 million from all financing activities, including a $39.5 million reduction of cash labeled "Effect of exchange rate changes on cash and cash equivalents," which relates to the decrease in the U.S. dollar ($US) equivalent value of cash held by foreign subsidiaries as a result of a stronger $US.

Review 11-4A LO4

Solution on p. 11-57.

Refer to the data in Review 11-2, to answer the requirement below.

Required
Prepare Expresso Royale's cash flows from financing activities for 2020.

Computing Cash Flows from Balance Sheet Accounts

Drawing on the Java House illustration, we can summarize the cash flow effects of the income statement and balance sheet information and categorize them into the **operating**, **investing**, and **financing** classifications in the following table.

The current year's cash balance increases by $25,000, from $10,000 to $35,000. Formal preparation of the statement of cash flows can proceed once we have addressed one final issue: required supplemental disclosures. We discuss that topic in the next section.

Account	Change	Source or Use of Cash	Cash Flow Effect	Classification on SCF
Current assets				
Accounts receivable	+5,000	Use	−5,000	Operating
Inventories	−6,000	Source	+6,000	Operating
Prepaid insurance	+13,000	Use	−13,000	Operating
Noncurrent assets				
PPE related				Investing
Accumulated depreciation	+10,000	Neither	+10,000	Operating
Sale of land				
Proceeds	+28,000	Source	+28,000	Investing
Gain	−8,000	Neither	−8,000	Operating
Investments	+15,000	Use	−15,000	Investing
Current liabilities				
Accounts payable	−9,000	Use	−9,000	Operating
Income tax payable	+2,000	Source	+2,000	Operating
Long-term liabilities				Financing
Stockholders' equity				
Common stock	+10,000	Source	+10,000	Financing
Retained earnings				
Net income	+32,000	Source	+32,000	Operating
Dividends	+13,000	Use	−13,000	Financing
Total (net cash flow)			+25,000	

Supplemental Disclosures for the Indirect Method

When the indirect method is used in the statement of cash flows, separate disclosures are required for: (1) cash paid for interest and cash paid for income taxes, (2) a schedule or description of all noncash investing and financing transactions, and (3) the firm's policy for determining which highly liquid, short-term investments are treated as cash equivalents. Noncash investing and financing activities include the issuance of stocks, bonds, or leases in exchange for PPE assets or intangible assets; the exchange of long-term assets for other long-term assets; and the conversion of long-term debt into common stock.

Java House Case Illustration for Supplemental Disclosures

Cash Paid for Interest Java House incurred no interest cost during the year.

Cash Paid for Income Taxes Java House did pay income taxes. Our discussion of the $2,000 change in income tax payable during the year revealed that the increase meant cash tax payments were less than income tax expense by the amount of the increase. Income tax expense was $11,000, so the cash paid for income taxes was $2,000 less than $11,000, or $9,000.

Noncash Investing and Financing Activities Java House had one noncash investing and financing event: the issuance of common stock to acquire a patent. This event, as well as the cash paid for income taxes, is disclosed as supplemental information to the statement of cash flows in Exhibit 11.4.

Exhibit 11.4 ■ Statement of Cash Flows for Indirect Method with Supplemental Disclosures

JAVA HOUSE
Statement of Cash Flows
For Year Ended December 31, 2020

Net cash flow from operating activities		
Net income	$32,000	
Add (deduct) items to convert net income to cash basis:		
Depreciation	10,000	
Gain on sale of land	(8,000)	
Accounts receivable increase	(5,000)	
Inventory decrease	6,000	
Prepaid insurance increase	(13,000)	
Accounts payable decrease	(9,000)	
Income tax payable increase	2,000	
Net cash provided by operating activities		$15,000
Cash flows from investing activities		
Purchase of investments	(15,000)	
Sale of land	28,000	
Net cash provided by investing activities		13,000
Cash flows from financing activities		
Issuance of common stock	10,000	
Payment of dividends	(13,000)	
Net cash used by financing activities		(3,000)
Net increase in cash		25,000
Cash at beginning of year		10,000
Cash at end of year		$35,000
Supplemental cash flow disclosures		
Cash paid for income taxes		$ 9,000
Schedule of noncash investing and financing activities		
Issuance of common stock to acquire patent		$60,000

Review 11-4B LO4

Solution on p. 11-57.

Refer to the balance sheet for Expresso Royale, and to the solutions for Reviews 11-2, 11-3, and 11-4A, to answer the requirements below.

Required
a. Compute the change in cash by considering cash flow from operating, investing, and financing activities.
b. Use the change in cash computed in part *a* to reconcile the beginning and ending cash balances for 2020.

Analysis of Cash Flow Information

Cash Flow Components

LO5 Examine and interpret cash flow information.

Typically, established companies have positive cash flow from operating activities. This cash flow provides most (if not all) of the total cash required to grow the business while maintaining appropriate levels of net working capital. On average, net cash flow from investing activities is negative as companies grow the PPE infrastructure needed to support the business. (Any excess cash invested in marketable securities typically generates cash flow, but this is small relative to the larger cash outflow for PPE and acquisitions.) Financing activities make up the difference between cash generated by operating activities and cash used by investing activities. Companies that generate more cash from operating activities than is required to support investing activities use that excess cash to pay down indebtedness, repurchase stock, or pay additional dividends. Companies that need cash for investing activities typically generate it from financing activities.

Exhibit 11.5 presents various cash flow items as a percentage of total revenues for the S&P 500 companies in fiscal 2018. The median operating cash flow is 19.7% of total revenues, of which net income explains 11.4 percentage points, and the add-backs for depreciation and stock-based compensation explain 3.1 and 0.7 percentage points, respectively. The remaining 4.5 percentage points relate to cash inflows and outflows from net working capital accounts.

Investing activities typically represent an outflow of cash equal to 8.0% of revenues, with CAPEX comprising 45% of the total (3.6 percentage points out of 8.0). Other investing activities generally relate to investment of excess cash in marketable securities. The median S&P company generates more operating cash flow than is required for investing activities and reports negative cash flow of 8.2% of revenues for financing activities. These activities generally include the payment of dividends, the repayment of debt, and the repurchase of common stock.

Exhibit 11.5 ■ Statement of Cash Flow Items as a Percentage of Total Revenues—SP500 in 2018						
	Net Income	Depreciation and Amortization	Stock-Based Compensation	Cash from Operations	Cash from Investing	Capital Expenditure	Cash from Financing
2018 Median....	11.4%	3.1%	0.7%	19.7%	(8.0)%	(3.6)%	(8.2)%

During 2018, S&P companies were profitable (only 10 of the 500 companies report a net loss greater than 5% of revenues) and generated sizeable operating cash flows. It is common for large companies to generate more operating cash flow than is required for investing activities, thus permitting the payment of dividends, the retirement of debt, and the repurchase of common stock. We expect this profile for a healthy, mature company.

Research Insight ■ Net Income Versus Cash Flows

By definition, GAAP net income consists of two components: cash and noncash items. Accountants call the noncash items "accruals" (defined as the difference between net income and cash from operations). Finance and accounting research investigates whether, and how, net earnings, operating cash flows, and accruals each predict (1) future earnings or future cash flows (this line of research is called predictability research), and (2) stock price (this line of research is called value-relevance research).

Although the statement of cash flows is very useful in a number of analysis situations, predictability research shows it is net income and not current operating cash flow that better predicts future net income. Predictability research by Richard Sloan (*The Accounting Review*, 1996) found that the two components of net income (accruals and cash flows) have different impacts on future earnings; specifically, cash flows are more persistent, meaning they have longer-term implications for future earnings than accruals do. Later, work by Tuomo Vuolteenaho (*Journal of Finance*, 2002) found that, in addition to information about future earnings, the accruals and cash flows explain the riskiness of the firm. The interpretation is that, because accruals are less persistent and they fluctuate more, they signal additional risk. One way to use this finding in our analysis is to compute the ratio of operating cash flow to net income: the higher that number, the lower the firm's operating risk.

Early value-relevance research from the late 1960s found that when firms announced that their earnings were higher (lower) than the prior year's earnings, stock price increased (decreased). This sparked much research into the relevance of accounting earnings for stock prices. With growth in the sources and speed of information, our current understanding is that, although earnings are important for stock prices, most of the information conveyed by earnings is factored into stock price long before the company announces its official numbers. For example, Ray Ball and Lakshmanan Shivakumar (*Journal of Accounting Research*, 2008) find that earnings announcement events only account for 1% to 2% of the stock price movement each year. Later, value-relevance research investigated whether the stock market reacts differently to cash flow versus the accruals components of earnings. For example, Sloan's (1996) finding came to be known as the *accrual anomaly*—the fact that stock prices do not differentiate between accruals and cash flows—which causes mispricing because accruals fluctuate more wildly than cash flows. However, markets learn quickly from their mistakes, and evidence of the accrual anomaly has decreased steadily since 1996. In sum, both of these research streams are ongoing and active areas as academics and analysts seek to understand how the various earnings components are related to future firm profitability as well as how the income statement, balance sheet, and statement of cash flows separately and collectively inform investors about firm value and riskiness.

Cash Flow Patterns

A product life-cycle framework can be helpful in interpreting cash flow patterns. This framework proposes four stages for products or services: (1) introduction, (2) growth, (3) maturity, and (4) decline. The following figure plots the usual patterns for revenues, income, and cash flows at each of these four stages. For revenues, the top line number, we see the common pattern of growth over the first two stages, then a leveling out at maturity, then finally a decline. The length of time between introduction and decline depends on many of the factors considered by Porter's forces or a SWOT analysis. For example, products with short lives and those subject to fashion trends, technical innovation, or obsolescence will have a shorter life cycle, and revenue will be at greater risk of fluctuation. Knowledge of product life cycles can help us assess the transitory or persistent nature of revenues.

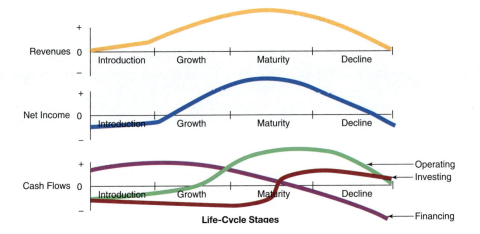

The second graph in the figure shows net income behavior over the four life-cycle stages. We commonly see losses in the introductory stage as companies struggle to recover startup costs and establish revenue streams. Net income commonly peaks during the maturity stage before a gradual decrease in the decline stage. The third graph highlights cash flows from operating, investing, and financing over the product life cycle. Although we see variations due to product success, strategic planning, and cost controls, these trends for each cash flow are fairly descriptive.

In general, during the introductory stage, revenues are limited, which results in low income and operating cash flows. The introductory stage also sees cash outflows for investing and cash inflows for financing. During the growth stage, revenues, income, and operating cash flows all increase, whereas both investing and financing cash flows increase or level out (each depending on predictions of future growth). The maturity stage sees peaks, and maybe some eventual decline, for revenues, income, and operating cash flows. This occurs as investing cash flows drop off, rendering additional financing cash inflows unnecessary. The decline stage brings large decreases in revenues, income, and operating cash flows. In decline, companies distribute cash flows for financing sources (repay debt, buy back stock, pay dividends) and realize some incoming investing cash flows as assets are gradually sold off. In summary, knowledge of product life cycles can help us understand the underlying economics, which will inform our business analysis. It can also help us interpret and possibly predict future streams of revenues, income, and cash flows.

Lowe's Companies is a solid, healthy company whose cash flow pattern (shown in Exhibit 11.6) is consistent with the pattern for mature-stage companies. Lowe's operating cash flow has grown throughout this period and provides sufficient cash to support the growth of net working capital and to partially finance the investment in PPE. Financing activities provide the remaining cash needed for investing activities. Notice how the investing and financing cash flows move in opposite directions, indicating greater financing inflows when cash outflows for investing activities increase, and vice versa. Most mature, healthy companies exhibit a similar cash flow profile.

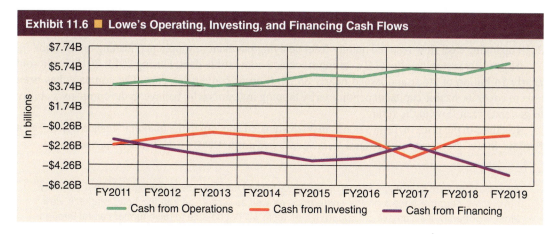

Exhibit 11.6 Lowe's Operating, Investing, and Financing Cash Flows

Southwest Airlines also provides a strong cash flow picture—shown in Exhibit 11.7. As its operating cash flows have soared, Southwest has been able to both invest in PPE and to return cash to investors via stock repurchases and dividends.

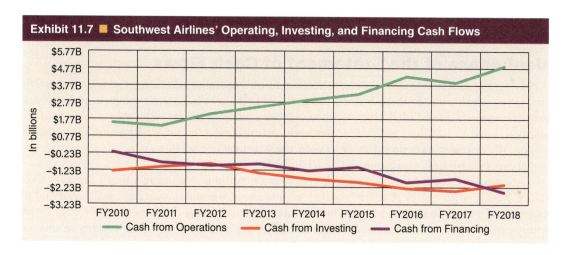

Exhibit 11.7 Southwest Airlines' Operating, Investing, and Financing Cash Flows

During 2014–2018, **Tesla Inc.** reported losses totaling nearly $5 billion and it spent nearly $10.3 billion on CAPEX—shown in Exhibit 11.8.

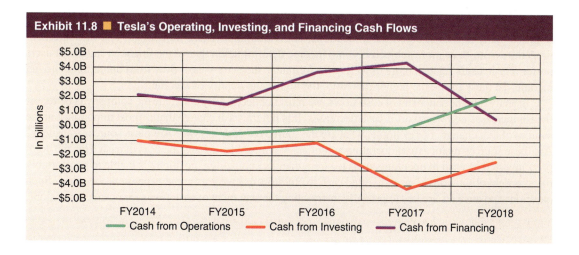

Exhibit 11.8 Tesla's Operating, Investing, and Financing Cash Flows

At first glance, in the face of significant net losses in its income statement, Tesla's positive operating cash flow in 2018 seems to indicate that the company has turned the corner. Upon closer inspection, the 2018 operating cash flow resulted mainly from delaying payment to suppliers ("leaning on the trade").

How is Tesla staying afloat? By selling stock and convertible debt. During 2014–2018, Tesla sold nearly $4 billion of stock and issued nearly $8.2 billion of convertible debt. The company has been able to cover its sizable capital expenditures by tapping investors who believe in the company's ability to generate cash flow in the future.

Declines in the price of Tesla's bonds in 2018 signaled concern to the market ("Tesla's Bonds Tell a Perilous Story," September 2018, https://seekingalpha.com/article/4205414-teslas-bonds-tell-perilous-story).

> As Tesla continues to struggle financially, it's likely to face a further credit downgrade. That will likely have some negative impact on the share price as well as further darken the bond market's view. More importantly, it's increasingly apparent that Tesla will not be able to raise further capital through the debt market without accepting far harsher terms than it has enjoyed to date. Last year, the bond market believed in Elon's promises. Now, it only believes in what he can deliver.

We can gain insight into Tesla's financial condition by analyzing its statement of cash flows as explained next.

Usefulness of the Statement of Cash Flows

A statement of cash flows shows the cash effects of a firm's operating, investing, and financing activities. Distinguishing among these different categories of cash flows helps users compare, evaluate, and predict cash flows. With cash flow information, creditors and investors are better able to assess a firm's ability to settle its liabilities and pay its dividends. A firm's need for outside financing is also better evaluated when using cash flow data. Over time, the statement of cash flows permits users to observe and access management's investing and financing policies.

A statement of cash flows also provides information useful in evaluating a firm's financial flexibility. *Financial flexibility* is a firm's ability to generate sufficient amounts of cash to respond to unanticipated needs and opportunities. Information about past cash flows, particularly cash flows from operations, helps in assessing financial flexibility. An evaluation of a firm's ability to survive an unexpected drop in demand, for example, should include a review of its past cash flows from operations. The larger these cash flows, the greater is the firm's ability to withstand adverse changes in economic conditions. Other financial statements, particularly the balance sheet and its notes, also contain information useful for judging financial flexibility.

Some investors and creditors find the statement of cash flows useful in evaluating the quality of a firm's income. As we know, determining income under accrual accounting procedures (GAAP) requires many accruals, deferrals, allocations, and valuations. These adjustment and measurement procedures introduce more subjectivity into income determination than some financial statement users prefer. These users relate a more objective performance measure—cash flow from operations—to net income. To these users, the higher this ratio, the higher the quality of income.

In analyzing the statement of cash flows, we must not necessarily conclude the company is better off if cash increases and worse off if cash decreases. It is not the cash change that is most important but the sources of that change. For example, what are the sources of cash inflows? Are these sources transitory? Are these sources mainly from operating activities? We must also review the uses of cash. Has the company invested its cash in operating areas to strengthen its competitive position? Is it able to comfortably meet its debt obligations? Has it diverted cash to creditors or investors at the expense of the other? Such questions and answers are key to properly interpreting the statement of cash flows for business decisions.

Research Insight — Cash Flow Patterns as an Indicator of Firm Life Cycle

A company can operate in several industries simultaneously and produce multiple products within each industry. This can make it difficult to identify the life-cycle stage because the company is a composite of many overlapping but distinct product life-cycle stages. Understanding a firm's life-cycle stage is important because life cycle affects the firm's production behavior, its investing activities, its market share, and many other pieces of information useful to analysis. Research shows cash flow patterns (net inflow or outflow) provide a reliable way to assess the overall life-cycle stage of the company, as follows.

	Introduction	Growth	Maturity	Decline
Operating	−	+	+	−
Investing	−	−	+/−	+
Financing	+	+	−	+/−

Using cash flow patterns to identify firm life-cycle stage, current research finds profitability ratios are consistent with expected economic behavior at each life-cycle stage. As demonstrated in the following graph, net operating profit margin (NOPM) is maximized in the growth stage when companies are able to differentiate their brands.

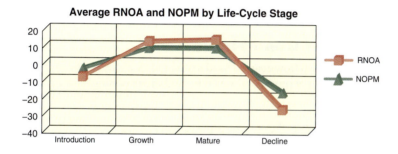

By comparison, return on net operating assets (RNOA) and net operating asset turnover (NOAT) are maximized in the maturity stage as market saturation is reached, but operating efficiencies allow the firm to maintain (or increase) profitability.

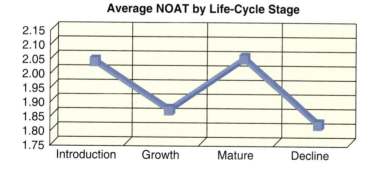

In addition, life-cycle stage as measured by cash flow patterns explains stock market valuation and stock returns. On average, mature-stage companies have abnormally high stock returns (as compared with the expected return for similar companies). One explanation is that investors underestimate the persistence of the mature company's profitability because they do not know the company's life-cycle stage and expect profits (and stock prices) to quickly revert to "normal" levels. (Source: Victoria Dickinson, "Cash Flow Patterns as a Proxy for Firm Life Cycle," *The Accounting Review*, November 2011, 86(6): 1969–1994.)

Review 11-5   LO5

The following information is taken from the Form 10-K for **Starbucks** and **Farmer Brothers**. The latter company is a small, publically traded coffee roaster.

	Revenue	Net Income	Depreciation	Stock-Based Compensation	Cash from Operations	Cash from Investing	CAPEX	Cash from Financing
Starbucks ($ millions)	$24,719.5	$4,518.3	$1,304.9	$250.3	$11,937.8	$(2,361.5)	$(1,976.4)	$(3,242.8)
Farmer Brothers ($ 000s)	$595,942	$(73,595)	$31,065	$3,674	$35,450	$(32,361)	$(34,760)	$1,456

Required

Consider the cash flow patterns for both companies in answering the following questions.

a. Compute the cash flow percentages shown in Exhibit 11.5 for both companies. How does each company's percentages compare with the medians for the S&P reported in that exhibit?

Solution on p. 11-57.   b. At what stage in its life cycle is each company? Explain.

Ratio Analyses of Cash Flows

Data from the statement of cash flows can be used to compute various financial ratios. Two such ratios are the operating cash flow to current liabilities ratio and the operating cash flow to capital expenditures ratio.

Operating Cash Flow to Current Liabilities Ratio

Two liquidity measures previously introduced—the current ratio and the quick ratio—emphasize the relation of current assets to current liabilities in an attempt to measure the ability of the firm to pay current liabilities when they become due. The **operating cash flow to current liabilities ratio** is another liquidity measure of the company's ability to liquidate current liabilities and is calculated as follows.

$$\text{Operating Cash Flow to Current Liabilities} = \frac{\text{Cash Flow from Operating Activities}}{\text{Average Current Liabilities}}$$

Net cash flow from operating activities is obtained from the statement of cash flows; it represents the excess amount of cash derived from operations during the year. The denominator is the average of the beginning and ending current liabilities for the year.

To illustrate, Starbucks reports the following amounts in its 2018 financial statements.

Cash flow from operating activities	$11,937.8 million
Current liabilities at beginning of the year	5,684.2 million
Current liabilities at end of the year	4,220.7 million

Starbucks' operating cash flow to current liabilities ratio of 2.41 is computed as follows.

$$\$11{,}937.8 \text{ million}/[(\$5{,}684.2 \text{ million} + \$4{,}220.7 \text{ million})/2] = 2.41$$

The higher this ratio, the stronger is a firm's ability to settle current liabilities as they come due. Our analysis would compare this ratio over time and against peer companies. In 2018, the average for large public companies was 0.5.

Operating Cash Flow to Capital Expenditures Ratio

To remain competitive, an entity must be able to replace and expand, when appropriate, its PPE assets. A ratio that helps assess a firm's ability to do this from internally generated cash flow is the **operating cash flow to capital expenditures ratio**, which is computed as follows.

$$\text{Operating Cash Flow to Capital Expenditures} = \frac{\text{Cash Flow from Operating Activities}}{\text{Capital Expenditures}}$$

The numerator in this ratio comes directly from the operating section of the statement of cash flows. Information for the denominator comes directly from the investing section of the statement of cash flows. Additional information about capital expenditures can be found in a number of related disclosures. Data on capital expenditures are part of the required industry segment disclosures in notes to the financial statements. Also, capital expenditures often appear in the comparative selected financial data presented as supplementary information to the financial statements. Finally, management's discussion and analysis of the statements commonly identify the annual capital expenditures.

A ratio in excess of 1.0 means the firm's current operating activities are providing cash in excess of the amount needed to provide the desired level of plant capacity and would normally be considered a sign of financial strength. This ratio is also viewed as an indicator of long-term solvency—a ratio exceeding 1.0 means there is operating cash flow in excess of capital needs that can then be used to repay outstanding long-term debt.

The interpretation of this ratio for a firm is influenced by its trend in recent years, the ratios for other firms in the same industry, and the stage of the firm's life cycle. A firm in the early stages of its life cycle, during rapid expansion, is expected to experience a lower ratio than a firm in the mature stage of its life cycle, when maintenance of plant capacity is more likely than expansion of capacity.

To illustrate the ratio's computation, **Starbucks** reported capital expenditures in 2018 of $1,976.4 million. Starbucks' operating cash flow to capital expenditures ratio for that same year is 6.04 ($11,937.8 million/$1,976.4 million). As before, our analysis would compare this ratio against Starbucks over time and against peer companies.

Free Cash Flow

Free cash flow is a common financial metric we encounter in the financial press. It is also common to see firm value estimated by discounting a company's future free cash flows (this is the DCF valuation model, which we discuss in a later module). A common definition of free cash flow (seen in finance textbooks and in use by business writers) is operating cash flows less capital expenditures (CAPEX). In this definition, "operating cash flows" is not equal to net cash flows from operating activities reported in the statement of cash flows because the latter includes items such as the effects from interest (both expense and revenue). The following table shows the definition of free cash flow commonly found in finance textbooks. The table also shows that this definition is approximately equivalent to: Free cash flow = Net operating profit after tax (NOPAT) − Increase in net operating assets (NOA). (We explain NOPAT and NOA in Module 4.)

Traditional Finance Definition	As Defined in This Text
Earnings before interest and taxes, adjusted for noncash revenues and expenses − Taxes (in the absence of interest revenue and interest expense)	Net operating profit after tax (NOPAT)
− Investments in working capital − Capital expenditures (CAPEX)	− Increase in net operating assets (NOA)
= Free cash flow	= Free cash flow

The value of a firm is related to its expected free cash flow. By expressing free cash flows in terms of NOPAT and the increase in NOA, we see two specific means to increase firm value:

- Increase NOPAT
- Control NOA growth

To increase free cash flow, companies aim to achieve both of these objectives without adversely affecting the other. For example, it is not enough to increase NOPAT by increasing revenues and operating profits if these actions increase NOA to the point that the beneficial profit effects are offset by the negative effects of higher NOA. Conversely, it is not enough to reduce NOA if doing so reduces sales and operating profit to a greater extent. The challenge to managers is to find a set of actions that optimizes net operating profit and the required level of net operating assets. This is the art of management. (We discuss this further in our valuation module.)

Review 11-6 LO6

Following is financial statement data for **McDonald's Corporation** for 2018 ($ millions).

Cash flow provided by operations	$6,966.7
Current liabilities at beginning of the year	2,890.6
Current liabilities at end of the year	2,973.5
Capital expenditures	2,741.7

Required
1. Compute the operating cash flow to current liabilities ratio.
2. Compute the operating cash flow to capital expenditures ratio.
3. From the two ratios you computed, does it appear that McDonald's is liquid and solvent? Explain.

Solution on p. 11-58.

Appendix 11A: Direct Method Reporting for Statement of Cash Flows

LO7 Explain and construct a direct method statement of cash flows.

To prepare a statement of cash flows, we need a firm's income statement, comparative balance sheets, and some additional data taken from the accounting records. Exhibit 11.2 presents this information for Java House. We use these data to prepare Java House's 2020 statement of cash flows using the direct method. Java House's statement of cash flows explains the $25,000 increase in cash (from $10,000 to $35,000) that occurred during the year by classifying the firm's cash flows into operating, investing, and financing categories. To get the information to construct the statement, we do the following.

1. **Use the direct method to determine individual cash flows from operating activities.** We use changes that occurred during the year in various current asset and current liability accounts.
2. **Determine cash flows from investing activities.** We do this by analyzing changes in noncurrent asset accounts.
3. **Determine cash flows from financing activities.** We do this by analyzing changes in liability and stockholders' equity accounts.

The net cash flows from investing and financing are identical to those prepared using the indirect method. Only the format of the net cash flows from operating activities differs between the two methods, not the total amount of cash generated from operating activities.

Cash Flows from Operating Activities

The **direct method** presents net cash flow from operating activities by showing the major categories of operating cash receipts and payments. The operating cash receipts and payments are usually determined by converting the accrual revenues and expenses to corresponding cash amounts. It is efficient to do it this way because the accrual revenues and expenses are readily available in the income statement.

Converting Revenues and Expenses to Cash Flows

Exhibit 11.9 summarizes the procedures for converting individual income statement items to corresponding cash flows from operating activities.

Java House Case Illustration

We next explain and illustrate the process of converting Java House's revenues and expenses to corresponding cash flows from operating activities under the direct method.

Exhibit 11.9 ■ Adjustments to Convert Income Statement Items to Operating Activity Cash Flows

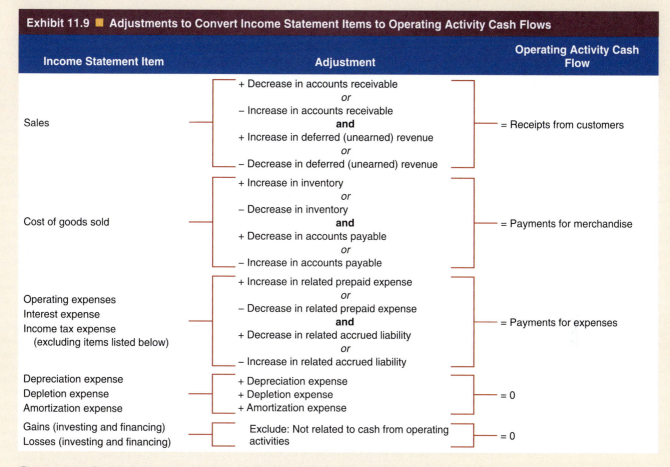

Convert Sales to Cash Received from Customers

During the year, accounts receivable increased $5,000. This increase means that cash collections on account (which decrease accounts receivable) were less than credit sales (which increase accounts receivable). We compute cash received from customers as follows:

	Sales	$250,000
−	Increase in accounts receivable	(5,000)
=	Cash received from customers	$245,000

Convert Cost of Goods Sold to Cash Paid for Merchandise Purchased

The conversion of cost of goods sold to cash paid for merchandise purchased is a two-step process. First, cost of goods sold is adjusted for the change in inventory to determine the amount of purchases during the year. Second, the purchases amount is adjusted for the change in accounts payable to derive the cash paid for merchandise purchased. Inventory decreased from $60,000 to $54,000. This $6,000 decrease indicates the cost of goods sold exceeded the cost of goods purchased during the year. The year's purchases amount is computed as follows:

	Cost of goods sold	$148,000
−	Decrease in inventory	(6,000)
=	Purchases	$142,000

During the year, accounts payable decreased $9,000. This decrease reflects the fact that cash payments for merchandise purchased on account (which decrease accounts payable) exceeded purchases on account (which increase accounts payable). The cash paid for merchandise purchased, therefore, is computed as follows:

	Purchases	$142,000
+	Decrease in accounts payable	9,000
=	Cash paid for merchandise purchased	$151,000

Convert Wages Expense to Cash Paid to Employees

No adjustment to wages expense is needed. The absence of any beginning or ending accrued liability for wages payable means wages expense and cash paid to employees as wages are the same amount: $52,000.

Convert Insurance Expense to Cash Paid for Insurance

Prepaid insurance increased $13,000. The $13,000 increase reflects the excess of cash paid for insurance during the year (which increases prepaid insurance) over the year's insurance expense (which decreases prepaid insurance). Starting with the insurance expense, the cash paid for insurance is computed as follows:

	Insurance expense	$ 5,000
+	Increase in prepaid insurance	13,000
=	Cash paid for insurance	$18,000

Eliminate Depreciation Expense and Other Noncash Operating Expenses

Depreciation expense is a noncash expense. Because it does not represent a cash payment, depreciation expense is eliminated (by adding it back) as we convert accrual expense amounts to the corresponding amounts of cash payments. If Java House had any amortization expense or depletion expense, the company would eliminate it for the same reason. The amortization of an intangible asset and the depletion of a natural resource are noncash expenses.

Convert Income Tax Expense to Cash Paid for Income Taxes

The increase in income tax payable from $3,000 at December 31, 2019, to $5,000 at December 31, 2020, means 2020's income tax expense (which increases income tax payable) was $2,000 more than 2020's tax payments (which decrease income tax payable). Starting with income tax expense, we calculate cash paid for income taxes as follows:

	Income tax expense	$11,000
−	Increase in income tax payable	(2,000)
=	Cash paid for income taxes	$ 9,000

Omit Gains and Losses Related to Investing and Financing Activities

The income statement may contain gains and losses related to investing or financing activities. Examples include gains and losses from the sale of PPE and gains and losses from the retirement of bonds payable. Because these gains and losses are not related to operating activities, we omit them as we convert income statement items to various cash flows from operating activities. The cash flows relating to these gains and losses are reported in the investing activities or financing activities sections of the statement of cash flows. Java House had an $8,000 gain from the sale of land this year. This gain is excluded; no related cash flow appears within the operating activities category.

We have now applied the adjustments to convert each accrual revenue and expense to the corresponding operating cash flow. We use these individual cash flows to prepare the operating activities section of the statement of cash flows, which we can see in Exhibit 11.10.

Exhibit 11.10 ■ Direct Method Operating Section of Statement of Cash Flows

Cash received from customers...............................		$245,000
Cash paid for merchandise purchased.....................	$151,000	
Cash paid to employees..	52,000	
Cash paid for insurance..	18,000	
Cash paid for income taxes...................................	9,000	230,000
Net cash provided by operating activities................		$ 15,000

Cash Flows from Investing and Financing

The reporting of investing and financing activities in the statement of cash flows is identical under the indirect and direct methods. Thus, we simply refer to the previous sections in this appendix for explanations.

Supplemental Disclosures

When the direct method is used for the statement of cash flows, three separate disclosures are required: (1) a reconciliation of net income to the net cash flow from operating activities, (2) a schedule or description of all noncash investing and financing transactions, and (3) the firm's policy for determining which highly liquid, short-term investments are treated as cash equivalents. The firm's policy regarding cash equivalents is placed in the financial statement notes. The other two separate disclosures are reported either in the notes or at the bottom of the statement of cash flows.

The required reconciliation is essentially the indirect method of computing cash flow from operating activities. *Thus, when the direct method is used in the statement of cash flows, the indirect method is a required separate disclosure.* We discussed the indirect method earlier in this module.

Java House did have one noncash investing and financing event during the year: the issuance of common stock to acquire a patent. This event is disclosed as supplemental information to the statement of cash flows in Exhibit 11.4.

LO7 Review 11-7

Refer to the data in Review 11-2 to answer the requirement below.

Required

Compute Expresso Royale's net cash flow from operating activities using the direct method.

Solution on p. 11-58.

Guidance Answers

You Are the Securities Analyst

Pg. 11-15 Many companies, but not all, treat customers' notes receivable as an investing activity. In 2005, the Securities and Exchange Commission (SEC) became concerned with this practice and issued letters to a number of companies objecting to this accounting classification. "Presenting cash receipts from receivables generated by the sale of inventory as investing activities in the company's consolidated statements of cash flows is not in accordance with GAAP," wrote the chief accountant for the SEC's division of corporation finance in her letter to the companies ("Little Campus Lab Shakes Big Firms—Georgia Tech Crew's Report Spurs Change in Accounting for Operating Cash Flow," March 1, 2005, *Wall Street Journal*). The SEC's position is that these notes receivable are an operating activity and analysts are certainly justified in treating them likewise. Concerning the sale of receivables, so long as the separate entity (a trust in this case) is properly structured, the transaction can be treated as a sale (rather than require consolidation) with a consequent reduction in receivables and a gain or loss on the sale recorded in the income statement. Many analysts treat this as a financing activity and argue that the cash inflow should not be regarded as an increase in operating cash flows. Bottom line: Many argue that operating cash flows do not increase as a result of these two transactions and analysts should adjust the statement of cash flows to properly classify the financing of receivables as an operating activity and the sale of receivables as a financing activity.

Questions

Superscript ^A denotes assignments based on Appendix 11A.

Q11-1. What is the definition of cash equivalents? Give three examples of cash equivalents.

Q11-2. Why are cash equivalents included with cash in a statement of cash flows?

Q11-3. What are the three major types of activities classified on a statement of cash flows? Give an example of a cash inflow and a cash outflow in each classification.

Q11-4. In which of the three activity categories of a statement of cash flows would each of the following items appear? Indicate whether each item represents a cash inflow or a cash outflow.

   a. Cash purchase of equipment.
   b. Cash collection on loans receivable.
   c. Cash dividends paid.
   d. Cash dividends received.
   e. Cash proceeds from issuing stock.
   f. Cash receipts from customers.
   g. Cash interest paid.
   h. Cash interest received.

Q11-5. Traverse Company acquired a $3,000,000 building by issuing $3,000,000 worth of bonds payable. In terms of cash flow reporting, what type of transaction is this? What special disclosure requirements apply to a transaction of this type?

Q11-6. Why are noncash investing and financing transactions disclosed as supplemental information to a statement of cash flows?

Q11-7. Why is a statement of cash flows a useful financial statement?

Q11-8.[A] What is the difference between the direct method and the indirect method of presenting net cash flow from operating activities?

Q11-9. In determining net cash flow from operating activities using the indirect method, why must we add depreciation back to net income? Give an example of another item that is added back to net income under the indirect method.

Q11-10. Vista Company sold for $98,000 cash land originally costing $70,000. The company recorded a gain on the sale of $28,000. How is this event reported in a statement of cash flows using the indirect method?

Q11-11. A firm uses the indirect method. Using the following information, what is its net cash flow from operating activities?

Net income	$99,000
Accounts receivable decrease	13,000
Inventory increase	9,000
Accounts payable decrease	3,500
Income tax payable increase	1,500
Depreciation expense	12,000

Q11-12. What separate disclosures are required for a company that reports a statement of cash flows using the indirect method?

Q11-13. If a business had a net loss for the year, under what circumstances would the statement of cash flows show a positive net cash flow from operating activities?

Q11-14.[A] A firm is converting its accrual revenues to corresponding cash amounts using the direct method. Sales on the income statement are $925,000. Beginning and ending accounts receivable on the balance sheet are $58,000 and $44,000, respectively. What is the amount of cash received from customers?

Q11-15.[A] A firm reports $86,000 wages expense in its income statement. If beginning and ending wages payable are $3,900 and $2,800, respectively, what is the amount of cash paid to employees?

Q11-16.[A] A firm reports $43,000 advertising expense in its income statement. If beginning and ending prepaid advertising are $6,000 and $7,600, respectively, what is the amount of cash paid for advertising?

Q11-17.ᴬ Rusk Company sold equipment for $5,100 cash that had cost $35,000 and had $29,000 of accumulated depreciation. How is this event reported in a statement of cash flows using the direct method?

Q11-18.ᴬ What separate disclosures are required for a company that reports a statement of cash flows using the direct method?

Q11-19. How is the operating cash flow to current liabilities ratio calculated? Explain its use.

Q11-20. How is the operating cash flow to capital expenditures ratio calculated? Explain its use.

Q11-21. For each of the following cash flow patterns, identify whether the company is in the introduction, growth, maturity, or decline stage of its life cycle.

Life-Cycle Stage	Operating Cash Flow	Investing Cash Flow	Financing Cash Flow
a.	+	–	+
b.	+	–	–
c.	–	–	+
d.	–	+	–

Assignments with the logo in the margin are available in *my*BusinessCourse.
See the Preface of the book for details.

Mini Exercises

M11-22. Classification of Cash Flows **LO1**

For each of the following items, indicate whether the cash flow relates to an operating activity, an investing activity, or a financing activity. Also indicate whether the item is a cash inflow or outflow.

a. Cash received from customers for services rendered . . . . _____ _____
b. Sale of long-term investments for cash . . . . _____ _____
c. Acquisition of PPE for cash . . . . _____ _____
d. Payment of income taxes . . . . _____ _____
e. Bonds payable issued for cash . . . . _____ _____
f. Payment of cash dividends declared in previous year . . . . _____ _____
g. Purchase of short-term investments (not cash equivalents) for cash . . . _____ _____
h. Purchases of inventory for cash . . . . _____ _____

M11-23. Classification of Cash Flows **LO1**

Fitbit Inc. reports the following items in its 2018 statement of cash flows. For each item, indicate whether it would appear in the operating, investing, or financing section of the statement of cash flows (in $ thousands).

Fitbit Inc. (FIT)

a. Change in accounts payable . . . . $ 35,207
b. Repayment of debt 747
c. Stock-based compensation 97,009
d. Proceeds from issuance of common stock 21,470
e. Change in inventories . . . . (12,860)
f. Purchase of property and equipment . . . . (52,880)
g. Acquisitions, net of cash acquired . . . . (19,253)
h. Net loss . . . . (185,829)
i. Depreciation 48,889
j. Purchase of marketable securities . . . . (353,948)

LO2 M11-24. Net Cash Flow from Operating Activities (Indirect Method)
The following information was obtained from Galena Company's comparative balance sheets. Assume Galena Company's 2020 income statement showed depreciation expense of $9,000, a gain on sale of investments of $11,000, and a net income of $40,000. Calculate the net cash flow from operating activities using the indirect method.

	May 31, 2020	May 31, 2019
Cash	$ 19,000	$ 10,000
Accounts receivable	45,000	35,000
Inventory	55,000	49,000
Prepaid rent	6,000	7,000
Long-term investments	20,000	34,000
PPE	150,000	106,000
Accumulated depreciation	42,000	33,000
Accounts payable	25,000	20,000
Income tax payable	4,000	6,000
Common stock	121,000	92,000
Retained earnings	106,000	91,000

LO2 M11-25. Interpreting Changes in Operating Assets and Liabilities
Amgen Inc. reports the following adjustments to net income in its 2018 statement of cash flows. Use the sign of each amount to indicate whether each current operating asset or liability increased or decreased during the year.

Amgen Inc. (AMGN)

Change in Current Operating Asset or Liability	
Trade receivables, net	$ (378)
Inventories	(3)
Other assets	35
Accounts payable	(143)
Accrued income taxes, net	(361)
Long-term tax liabilities	258
Other liabilities	1,214

LO7 M11-26. Operating Cash Flows (Direct Method)
Calculate the cash flow for each of the following cases.

a. Cash paid for rent:

Rent expense	$65,000
Prepaid rent, beginning year	11,000
Prepaid rent, end of year	8,000

b. Cash received as interest:

Interest income	$15,500
Interest receivable, beginning year	3,000
Interest receivable, end of year	3,800

c. Cash paid for merchandise purchased:

Cost of goods sold	$87,000
Inventory, beginning year	19,000
Inventory, end of year	23,000
Accounts payable, beginning year	11,000
Accounts payable, end of year	8,000

M11-27. Operating Cash Flows (Direct Method) LO7

Howell Company's current-year income statement reports the following.

Sales.	$785,000
Cost of goods sold	450,000
Gross profit	$335,000

Comparative balance sheets show the following (accounts payable relate to merchandise purchases).

	End of Year	Beginning of Year
Accounts receivable	$ 68,000	$60,000
Inventory	109,000	99,000
Prepaid expenses	2,000	8,000
Accounts payable	31,000	36,000

Compute current-year cash received from customers and cash paid for merchandise purchased.

M11-28. Using Statement of Cash Flow Information to Assess Company Life-Cycle Stage LO5

For each of the following cash flow amounts ($ millions), identify whether the company is in the introduction, growth, maturity, or decline stage of its life cycle.

Company	Operating Cash Flow	Investing Cash Flow	Financing Cash Flow
a	$2,281	$(3,451)	$1,907
b	6,334	3,220	(2,008)
c	(405)	(1,728)	3,518
d	3,702	(2,440)	1,330
e	70	2,005	815
f	5	(530)	876
g	(2,580)	(4,200)	7,459
h	(409)	5,581	(2,406)

M11-29. Compute and Interpret Cash Flow Ratios LO6

Use the following information to compute and interpret cash flow ratios.

Company	Operating Cash Flow	Average Current Liabilities	CAPEX
a	$2,106	$6,581	$2,425
b	5,668	2,181	1,007
c	3,702	3,365	1,220
d	2,700	5,192	1,984

Required

a. Compute the operating cash flow to current liabilities ratio for each company. Compared to the average of 0.5 for large public companies, assess each company's liquidity as low, medium, or high (i.e., its ability to settle liabilities as they come due).

b. Compute the operating cash flow to CAPEX ratio for each company. Compared to the rule of thumb of 1.0, assess the company's solvency as either low, medium, or high.

M11-30. Computing and Comparing Income and Cash Flow Measures LO1

Penno Corporation recorded service revenues of $200,000 during the current year, of which $170,000 were on credit and $30,000 were for cash. Moreover, of the $170,000 credit sales, Penno collected $20,000 cash on those receivables before year-end. The company also paid $25,000 cash for wages during the year. Its employees also earned another $15,000 in wages during the last few weeks of the year, which were not yet paid at year-end.

Required

a. Compute the company's net income for the year.

b. How much net cash inflow or outflow did the company generate during the year? Explain why Penno's net income and net cash flow differ.

Exercises

LO2 **E11-31.** **Net Cash Flow from Operating Activities (Indirect Method)**
Lincoln Company owns no PPE and reported the following income statement for the current year.

Sales.		$700,000
Cost of goods sold	$425,000	
Wages expense	110,000	
Rent expense	38,000	
Insurance expense.	15,000	588,000
Net income		$112,000

Additional balance sheet information about the company follows:

	End of Year	Beginning of Year
Accounts receivable	$56,000	$48,000
Inventory.	60,000	66,000
Prepaid insurance.	7,000	5,000
Accounts payable	22,000	18,000
Wages payable.	11,000	15,000

Use the information to calculate the net cash flow from operating activities under the indirect method.

LO2, 3, 4 **E11-32.** **Statement of Cash Flows (Indirect Method)**
Use the following information about Lund Corporation for the month of August to prepare a statement of cash flows for August under the indirect method.

Accounts payable increase.	$ 9,000
Accounts receivable increase.	4,000
Accrued liabilities decrease	3,000
Amortization expense.	6,000
Cash balance, beginning of August	22,000
Cash balance, end of August	15,000
Cash paid as dividends	29,000
Cash paid to purchase land	90,000
Cash paid to retire bonds payable at par	60,000
Cash received from issuance of common stock.	35,000
Cash received from sale of equipment.	17,000
Depreciation expense.	29,000
Gain on sale of equipment	4,000
Inventory decrease.	13,000
Net income	76,000
Prepaid expenses increase	2,000

LO2 **E11-33.** **Operating Section of Statement of Cash Flows (Indirect Method)**
Following are the income statement and balance sheet for **Nike Inc.** for the year ended May 31, 2019, and a forecasted income statement and balance sheet for 2020.

Nike Inc. (NKE)

NIKE INC.
Income Statement
For Year Ended May 31

$ millions	May 31, 2019 Actual	May 31, 2020 Est.
Revenues	$39,117	$42,246
Cost of sales	21,643	23,362
Gross profit	17,474	18,884
Demand creation expense	3,753	4,056
Operating overhead expense	8,949	9,674
Total selling and administrative expense	12,702	13,730
Interest expense (income), net	49	49
Other (income) expense, net	(78)	(78)
Income before income taxes	4,801	5,183
Income tax expense	772	1,037
Net income	$ 4,029	$ 4,146

NIKE INC.
Balance Sheet
May 31

$ millions	May 31, 2019 Actual	May 31, 2020 Est.
Current assets		
Cash and equivalents	$ 4,466	$ 6,881
Short-term investments	197	197
Accounts receivable, net	4,272	4,605
Inventories	5,622	6,083
Prepaid expenses and other current assets	1,968	2,112
Total current assets	16,525	19,878
Property, plant and equipment, net	4,744	5,259
Identifiable intangible assets, net	283	281
Goodwill	154	154
Deferred income taxes and other assets	2,011	2,155
Total assets	$23,717	$ 27,727
Current liabilities		
Current portion of long-term debt	$ 6	$ 3
Notes payable	9	0
Accounts payable	2,612	2,830
Accrued liabilities	5,010	5,407
Income taxes payable	229	253
Total current liabilities	7,866	8,493
Long-term debt	3,464	3,461
Deferred income taxes and other liabilities	3,347	3,633
Total liabilities	14,677	15,587
Shareholders' equity		
Common stock at stated value	3	3
Capital in excess of stated value	7,163	7,488
Accumulated other comprehensive income	231	231
Retained earnings	1,643	4,418
Total shareholders' equity	9,040	12,140
Total liabilities and shareholders' equity	$23,717	$27,727

Prepare the operating activities section of a forecasted statement of cash flows for 2020 using the indirect method. Treat deferred tax assets and liabilities as operating. Operating expenses (cost of sales) for 2020 include estimated depreciation expense of $751 million, amortization expense of $2 million, and stock-based compensation of $325 million. (*Hint*: Stock-based compensation is a noncash expense like depreciation and must be added back in the operating section. The amount expensed is also added to Nike's "Capital in excess of stated value" account in the balance sheet.)

LO2
Medtronic PLC
(MDT)

E11-34. Operating Section of Statement of Cash Flows (Indirect Method)
Following are the income statement and balance sheet for **Medtronic PLC** for the year ended April 29, 2019, and a forecasted income statement and balance sheet for 2020.

MEDTRONIC PLC
Income Statement
For Fiscal Year Ended

$ millions	April 2019 Actual	April 2020 Est.
Net sales..	$ 30,557	$33,002
Costs and expenses		
Cost of products sold	9,155	9,901
Research and development expense........................	2,330	2,508
Selling, general, and administrative expense...............	10,418	11,254
Amortization of intangible assets	1,764	1,914
Restructuring charges, net	198	149
Certain litigation charges, net...............................	166	150
Other operating expense, net...............................	258	258
Operating profit (loss)..	6,268	6,868
Other nonoperating income, net............................	(373)	(373)
Interest expense...	1,444	1,444
Income (loss) before income taxes..........................	5,197	5,797
Income tax provision..	547	870
Net income (loss)	4,650	4,927
Net (income) loss attributable to noncontrolling interests..	(19)	(19)
Net income (loss) attributable to Medtronic	$ 4,631	$ 4,908

MEDTRONIC PLC
Balance Sheet
At Fiscal Year-End

$ millions	Apr. 29, 2019 Actual	Apr. 30, 2020 Est.
Current assets		
Cash and cash equivalents.................................	$ 4,393	$ 7,098
Investments...	5,455	5,455
Accounts receivable, net....................................	6,222	6,732
Inventories, net...	3,753	4,059
Other current assets..	2,144	2,310
Total current assets...	21,967	25,654
Property, plant, and equipment, net	4,675	4,988
Goodwill...	39,959	39,959
Other intangible assets, net	20,560	18,646
Tax assets	1,519	1,650
Other assets..	1,014	1,089
Total assets	$ 89,694	$91,986

continued

continued from previous page

$ millions	Apr. 29, 2019 Actual	Apr. 30, 2020 Est.
Current liabilities		
Current debt obligations	$ 838	$ 2,058
Accounts payable	1,953	2,112
Accrued compensation	2,189	2,376
Accrued income taxes	567	627
Other accrued expenses	2,925	3,168
Total current liabilities	8,472	10,341
Long-term debt	24,486	22,428
Accrued compensation and retirement benefits	1,651	1,651
Accrued income taxes	2,838	3,069
Deferred tax liabilities	1,278	1,386
Other liabilities	757	825
Total liabilities	39,482	39,700
Shareholders' equity		
Ordinary shares— par value $0.0001, 2.6 billion shares authorized, 1,340,697,595 shares issued and outstanding	—	—
Additional paid-in capital	26,532	26,532
Retained earnings	26,270	28,325
Accumulated other comprehensive loss	(2,711)	(2,711)
Total shareholders' equity	50,091	52,146
Noncontrolling interests	121	140
Total equity	50,212	52,286
Total liabilities and equity	$89,694	$91,986

Begin with forecasted Net income of $4,927 million and prepare the operating activities section of a forecasted statement of cash flows for April 30, 2020, using the indirect method. Operating expenses (such as cost of sales and selling, general, and administrative expenses) for 2020 include estimated depreciation expense of $953 million. Estimated 2020 retained earnings reflects dividends of $2,853 million.

E11-35. **Operating Cash Flows (Direct Method)**
Calculate the cash flow for each of the following cases.
  a. Cash paid for advertising:

Advertising expense	$62,000
Prepaid advertising, beginning of year	11,000
Prepaid advertising, end of year	15,000

  b. Cash paid for income taxes:

Income tax expense	$29,000
Income tax payable, beginning of year	7,100
Income tax payable, end of year	4,900

  c. Cash paid for merchandise purchased:

Cost of goods sold	$180,000
Inventory, beginning of year	30,000
Inventory, end of year	25,000
Accounts payable, beginning of year	10,000
Accounts payable, end of year	12,000

E11-36. Statement of Cash Flows (Direct Method) LO3, 4, 7

Use the following information about the 2020 cash flows of Mason Corporation to prepare a statement of cash flows under the direct method.

Cash balance, end of 2020...............	$ 12,000
Cash paid to employees and suppliers......	148,000
Cash received from sale of land............	40,000
Cash paid to acquire treasury stock........	10,000
Cash balance, beginning of 2020...........	16,000
Cash received as interest.................	6,000
Cash paid as income taxes	11,000
Cash paid to purchase equipment	89,000
Cash received from customers.............	194,000
Cash received from issuing bonds payable ..	30,000
Cash paid as dividends	16,000

E11-37. Operating Cash Flows (Direct Method) LO7

Refer to the information in Exercise E11-31. Prepare the operating activities section of the statement of cash flows using the direct method.

E11-38. Investing and Financing Cash Flows LO3, 4

During the current year, Paxon Corporation's intangible assets account (at cost) increased $15,000, which was the net result of purchasing new intangible assets costing $80,000 and selling other intangible assets costing $65,000 at a $6,000 loss. Also, its bonds payable account decreased $40,000, the net result of issuing $100,000 of bonds at $103,000 and retiring bonds with a face value (and book value) of $140,000 at a $9,000 gain. What items and amounts appear in the (a) cash flows from investing activities and (b) cash flows from financing activities sections of its statement of cash flows?

E11-39. Using Graphical Statement of Cash Flow Information to Assess Company Life-Cycle Stage LO5

Facebook (FB)

Consider the following statement of cash flows information for Facebook. Does the company's cash flows conform with the typical life-cycle patterns?

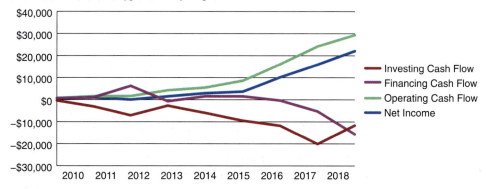

E11-40. Using Statement of Cash Flow Information to Assess Company Life-Cycle Stage LO5

Arconic Inc (ARNC)
Carmax Inc (KMX)
Flowserve Corp (FLS)
Fluor Corp (FLR)

Use the following information, taken from the 2018 statement of cash flows from each of the respective companies, to complete the requirements.

$ millions	Net Income	Cash from Operations	Cash from Investing	Cash from Financing
Arconic Inc	$642	$217	$565	$(649)
Carmax Inc	842	163	(309)	186
Flowserve Corp.......	120	191	(81)	(173)
Fluor Corp...........	225	162	1	(140)

Required
a. Identify each company's life-cycle stage (introduction, growth, maturity, or decline).
b. Rank-order each company from least to most mature. (*Hint:* All four companies have cash from operations of about $200 million. Graph the cash from investing and from financing, and then use the graphic [showing revenue, income, and cash flow by life cycle] to evaluate the relative size of the three types of cash flow.)

E11-41. **Compute Ratios from Statement of Cash Flow Information**
Use the following information, taken from each of the company's 2018 financial statements, to complete the requirements.

LO6
Arconic Inc (ARNC)
Carmax Inc (KMX)
Flowserve Corp (FLS)
Fluor Corp (FLR)

Company ($ millions)	Cash from Operations	Current Liabilities	CAPEX
Arconic Inc	$217	$3,520	$768
Carmax Inc	163	1,312	305
Flowserve Corp	191	1,081	84
Fluor Corp	162	3,553	211

Required
a. Compute the operating cash flow to current liabilities ratio for each company.
b. Rank-order each company from low to high liquidity (ability to pay liabilities as they come due). Do any of the companies have liquidity difficulties?
c. Compute the operating cash flow to CAPEX ratio for each company. Compared with the rule of thumb of 1.0, assess each company's solvency as either low, medium, or high.
d. Rank-order each company from low to high solvency. Do any of the companies have solvency difficulties?

E11-42. **Interpret Cash Flow Patterns and Ratios**
The following information is taken from the 2018 Form 10-K for each of the following technology companies.

LO5, 6
Cisco Systems Inc. (CSCO)
Oracle Corporation (ORCL)
Seagate Technology plc (STX)

Company ($ millions)	Operating Cash Flow	Investing Cash Flow	Financing Cash Flow	Average Current Liabilities	CAPEX
Cisco Systems Inc.	$13,666	$15,324	$(31,764)	$27,035	$ 834
Oracle Corporation	14,551	26,557	(42,056)	18,630	1,660
Seagate Technology plc	2,113	(1,588)	(1,211)	3,190	366

Required
a. Compute the operating cash flow to current liabilities ratio for each company. Compared to the average of 0.5, assess as low, medium, or high, each company's ability to settle liabilities as they come due.
b. Compute the operating cash flow to CAPEX ratio for each company. Compared to the rule of thumb of 1.0, assess each company's solvency as either low, medium, or high.
c. Each of the three companies is in the mature stage of its life cycle. Consider the graphic shown earlier in the module that graphs the cash flow patterns. Use the graphic to rank the companies from least mature to most mature.

Problems

LO2, 3, 4   **P11-43.**   **Statement of Cash Flows (Indirect Method)**
Wolff Company's income statement and comparative balance sheets follow.

WOLFF COMPANY
Income Statement
For Year Ended December 31, 2019

Sales..............................		$635,000
Cost of goods sold...............	$430,000	
Wages expense..................	86,000	
Insurance expense...............	8,000	
Depreciation expense............	17,000	
Interest expense.................	9,000	
Income tax expense.............	29,000	579,000
Net income......................		$ 56,000

WOLFF COMPANY
Balance Sheet

	Dec. 31, 2019	Dec. 31, 2018
Assets		
Cash.............................	$ 11,000	$ 5,000
Accounts receivable..............	41,000	32,000
Inventory.........................	90,000	60,000
Prepaid insurance................	5,000	7,000
PPE	250,000	195,000
Accumulated depreciation........	(68,000)	(51,000)
Total assets	$329,000	$248,000
Liabilities and Stockholders' Equity		
Accounts payable.................	$ 7,000	$ 10,000
Wages payable...................	9,000	6,000
Income tax payable	7,000	8,000
Bonds payable...................	130,000	75,000
Common stock...................	90,000	90,000
Retained earnings	86,000	59,000
Total liabilities and equity	$329,000	$248,000

Cash dividends of $29,000 were declared and paid during 2019. Also in 2019, PPE was purchased for cash, and bonds payable were issued for cash. Bond interest is paid semiannually on June 30 and December 31. Accounts payable relate to merchandise purchases.

Required
a. Compute the change in cash that occurred during 2019.
b. Prepare a 2019 statement of cash flows using the indirect method.

LO2, 3, 4   **P11-44.**   **Statement of Cash Flows (Indirect Method)**
Seagate Technology (STX)

Following are the income statement and balance sheet for **Seagate Technology** for the year ended June 28, 2019, and a forecasted income statement and balance sheet for 2020.

SEAGATE TECHNOLOGY PLC
Consolidated Statements of Income

For Years Ended ($ millions)	June 2019 Actual	June 2020 Est.
Revenue	$10,390	$10,910
Cost of revenue	7,458	7,833
Product development	991	1,036
Marketing and administrative	453	480
Amortization of intangibles	23	23
Restructuring and other, net	(22)	—
Total operating expenses	8,903	9,372
Income from operations	1,487	1,538
Interest income	84	84
Interest expense	(224)	(224)
Other, net	25	25
Other expense, net	(115)	(115)
Income before income taxes	1,372	1,423
(Benefit) provision for income taxes	(640)	299
Net income	$ 2,012	$ 1,124

SEAGATE TECHNOLOGY PLC
Consolidated Balance Sheet

$ millions	June 2019 Actual	June 2020 Est.
Current assets		
Cash and cash equivalents	$2,220	$2,583
Accounts receivable, net	989	1,036
Inventories	970	1,015
Other current assets	184	196
Total current assets	4,363	4,830
Property, equipment and leasehold improvements, net	1,869	1,971
Goodwill	1,237	1,237
Other intangible assets, net	111	88
Deferred income taxes	1,114	1,167
Other assets, net	191	196
Total Assets	$8,885	$9,489
Current liabilities		
Accounts payable	$1,420	$1,495
Accrued employee compensation	169	175
Accrued warranty	91	98
Accrued expenses	552	578
Total current liabilities	2,232	2,346
Long-term accrued warranty	104	109
Long-term accrued income taxes	4	4
Other noncurrent liabilities	130	142
Long-term debt, less current portion	4,253	4,253
Total Liabilities	6,723	6,854
Shareholders' equity		
Ordinary shares—par value $0.0001, 2.6 billion shares authorized	—	—
Additional paid-in capital	6,545	6,644
Accumulated other comprehensive loss	(34)	(34)
Accumulated deficit	(4,349)	(3,975)
Total shareholders' equity	2,162	2,635
Total liabilities and shareholders' equity	$8,885	$9,489

The following additional information pertains to the balance sheet and income statement for the year ended June 30, 2020 ($ millions).

Depreciation expense (included in operating expenses)	$531
Stock-based compensation	99
Amortization expense	23
Capital expenditures	633
Dividends	750

Required

Prepare a forecasted statement of cash flows for June 2020 using the indirect method. (*Hint*: Stock-based compensation is a noncash expense like depreciation and must be added back in the operating section. The amount expensed is also added to the company's "Additional paid-in capital" account in the balance sheet.)

LO2, 3, 4

P11-45. **Statement of Cash Flows (Indirect Method)**

Arctic Company's income statement and comparative balance sheets follow.

ARCTIC COMPANY
Income Statement
For Year Ended December 31, 2019

Sales		$728,000
Cost of goods sold	$534,000	
Wages expense	190,000	
Advertising expense	31,000	
Depreciation expense	22,000	
Interest expense	18,000	
Gain on sale of land	(25,000)	770,000
Net loss		$ (42,000)

ARCTIC COMPANY
Balance Sheet

	Dec. 31, 2019	Dec. 31, 2018
Assets		
Cash	$ 49,000	$ 28,000
Accounts receivable	42,000	50,000
Inventory	107,000	113,000
Prepaid advertising	10,000	13,000
PPE	360,000	222,000
Accumulated depreciation	(78,000)	(56,000)
Total assets	$490,000	$370,000
Liabilities and Stockholders' Equity		
Accounts payable	$ 17,000	$ 31,000
Interest payable	6,000	—
Bonds payable	200,000	—
Common stock	245,000	245,000
Retained earnings	52,000	94,000
Treasury stock	(30,000)	—
Total liabilities and equity	$490,000	$370,000

During 2019, Arctic sold land for $70,000 cash that had originally cost $45,000. Arctic also purchased equipment for cash, acquired treasury stock for cash, and issued bonds payable for cash in 2019. Accounts payable relate to merchandise purchases.

Required

a. Compute the change in cash that occurred during 2019.
b. Prepare a 2019 statement of cash flows using the indirect method.

P11-46. **Statement of Cash Flows (Indirect Method)** LO2, 3, 4
Dair Company's income statement and comparative balance sheets follow.

DAIR COMPANY
Income Statement
For Year Ended December 31, 2019

Sales.		$700,000
Cost of goods sold	$440,000	
Wages and other operating expenses	95,000	
Depreciation expense.	22,000	
Amortization expense.	7,000	
Interest expense.	10,000	
Income tax expense	36,000	
Loss on bond retirement.	5,000	615,000
Net income		$ 85,000

DAIR COMPANY
Balance Sheet

	Dec. 31, 2019	Dec. 31, 2018
Assets		
Cash	$ 27,000	$ 18,000
Accounts receivable	53,000	48,000
Inventory	103,000	109,000
Prepaid expenses	12,000	10,000
PPE	360,000	336,000
Accumulated depreciation	(87,000)	(84,000)
Intangible assets.	43,000	50,000
Total assets	$511,000	$487,000
Liabilities and Stockholders' Equity		
Accounts payable	$ 32,000	$ 26,000
Interest payable	4,000	7,000
Income tax payable	6,000	8,000
Bonds payable	60,000	120,000
Common stock	252,000	228,000
Retained earnings	157,000	98,000
Total liabilities and equity	$511,000	$487,000

During 2019, the company sold for $17,000 cash old equipment that had cost $36,000 and had $19,000 accumulated depreciation. Also in 2019, new equipment worth $60,000 was acquired in exchange for $60,000 of bonds payable, and bonds payable of $120,000 were retired for cash at a loss. A $26,000 cash dividend was declared and paid in 2019. Any stock issuances were for cash.

Required

a. Compute the change in cash that occurred in 2019.
b. Prepare a 2019 statement of cash flows using the indirect method.
c. Prepare separate schedules showing (1) cash paid for interest and for income taxes and (2) noncash investing and financing transactions.

LO2, 3, 4
Automatic Data Processing, Inc. (ADP)

P11-47. Statement of Cash Flows (Indirect Method)

Following are the income statement and balance sheet for **ADP Inc.**, for the year ended June 30, 2019, and a forecasted income statement and balance sheet for 2020.

AUTOMATIC DATA PROCESSING INC.
Consolidated Balance Sheets

$ millions	June 30, 2019 Actual	June 30, 2020 Est.
Current assets		
Cash and cash equivalents	$ 1,949.2	$ 2,077.6
Accounts receivable, net	2,439.3	2,755.1
Other current assets	519.6	592.7
Total current assets before funds held for clients	4,908.1	5,425.4
Funds held for clients	29,434.2	33,253.4
Total current assets	34,342.3	38,678.8
Long-term receivables, net	23.8	32.0
Property, plant and equipment, net	764.2	762.9
Capitalized contract cost, net	2,428.5	2,739.1
Other assets	934.4	1,057.2
Goodwill	2,323.0	2,323.0
Intangible assets, net	1,071.5	1,252.5
Total assets	**$41,887.7**	**$46,845.5**
Current liabilities		
Accounts payable	$ 125.5	$ 144.2
Accrued expenses and other current liabilities	1,759.0	1,986.2
Accrued payroll and payroll-related expenses	721.1	816.9
Dividends payable	340.1	365.4
Short-term deferred revenues	220.7	256.3
Obligations under reverse repurchase agreements	262.0	288.3
Income taxes payable	54.8	63.2
Total current liabilities before client funds obligations	3,483.2	3,920.5
Client funds obligations	29,144.5	32,933.0
Total current liabilities	32,627.7	36,853.5
Long-term debt	2,002.2	2,002.2
Other liabilities	798.7	897.0
Deferred income taxes	659.9	752.8
Long-term deferred revenues	399.3	448.5
Total liabilities	36,487.8	40,954.0
Shareholders' equity		
Preferred stock, $1.00 par value: Authorized, 0.3 shares; issued, none	—	—
Common stock, $0.10 par value: authorized, 1,000.0 shares; issued, 638.7 shares; outstanding 434.2 shares	63.9	63.9
Capital in excess of par value	1,183.2	1,350.5
Retained earnings	17,500.6	18,574.9
Treasury stock - at cost: 204.5 shares	(13,090.5)	(13,840.5)
Accumulated other comprehensive loss	(257.3)	(257.3)
Total stockholders' equity	5,399.9	5,891.5
Total liabilities and stockholders' equity	**$41,887.7**	**$46,845.5**

AUTOMATIC DATA PROCESSING INC.
Statements of Consolidated Earnings

For Years Ended ($ millions)	Jun. 30, 2019 Actual	June 30, 2020 Est.
Revenues, other than interest on funds held for clients and PEO revenues	$ 9,375.8	$10,594.7
Interest on funds held for clients	561.9	634.9
PEO revenues	4,237.5	4,788.4
Total revenues	14,175.2	16,018.0
Expenses		
Operating expenses	7,145.9	8,073.1
Systems development and programming costs	636.3	720.8
Depreciation and Amortization	304.4	460.5
Total cost of revenues	8,086.6	9,254.4
Selling, general, and administrative expenses	3,064.2	3,459.9
Interest expense	129.9	129.9
Total expenses	11,280.7	12,844.2
Other (income) expense, net	(111.1)	(111.1)
Earnings before income taxes	3,005.6	3,284.9
Provision for income taxes	712.8	821.2
Net earnings	$ 2,292.8	$ 2,463.7

Additional information and assumptions related to the estimated 2020 income statement and balance sheet are as follows ($ millions):

Depreciation expense	$ 184.4
Amortization expense	276.1
Stock-based compensation expense	167.3
CAPEX	183.1
Newly acquired intangibles	457.1
Stock repurchases	750.0
Dividends declared	1,389.4

Required

Prepare a forecasted statement of cash flows for 2020 using the indirect method. (*Hint*: Stock-based compensation is a noncash expense like depreciation and must be added back in the operating section. The amount expensed is also added to ADP's "Capital in excess of par value" account on the balance sheet.)

P11-48. Statement of Cash Flows (Indirect Method) LO2, 3, 4

Rainbow Company's income statement and comparative balance sheets follow.

RAINBOW COMPANY
Income Statement
For Year Ended December 31, 2019

Sales		$750,000
Dividend income		15,000
		765,000
Cost of goods sold	$440,000	
Wages and other operating expenses	130,000	
Depreciation expense	39,000	
Patent amortization expense	7,000	
Interest expense	13,000	
Income tax expense	44,000	
Loss on sale of equipment	5,000	
Gain on sale of investments	(10,000)	668,000
Net income		$ 97,000

RAINBOW COMPANY
Balance Sheet

	Dec. 31, 2019	Dec. 31, 2018
Assets		
Cash and cash equivalents	$ 19,000	$ 25,000
Accounts receivable	40,000	30,000
Inventory	103,000	77,000
Prepaid expenses	10,000	6,000
Investments—Available-for-sale	—	57,000
Land	190,000	100,000
Buildings	445,000	350,000
Accumulated depreciation—Buildings	(91,000)	(75,000)
Equipment	179,000	225,000
Accumulated depreciation—Equipment	(42,000)	(46,000)
Patents	50,000	32,000
Total assets	$903,000	$781,000
Liabilities and Stockholders' Equity		
Accounts payable	$ 20,000	$ 16,000
Interest payable	6,000	5,000
Income tax payable	8,000	10,000
Bonds payable	155,000	125,000
Preferred stock ($100 par value)	100,000	75,000
Common stock ($5 par value)	379,000	364,000
Paid-in capital in excess of par value—Common	133,000	124,000
Retained earnings	102,000	55,000
AOCI (unrealized gain on investments)	—	7,000
Total liabilities and equity	$903,000	$781,000

During 2019, the following transactions and events occurred in addition to the company's usual business activities.

1. Sold AFS investments costing $50,000 for $60,000 cash. Unrealized gains totaling $7,000 related to these investments had been recorded in earlier years.
2. Purchased land for cash.
3. Capitalized an expenditure made to improve the building.
4. Sold equipment for $14,000 cash that originally cost $46,000 and had $27,000 accumulated depreciation.
5. Issued bonds payable at face value for cash.
6. Acquired a patent with a fair value of $25,000 by issuing 250 shares of preferred stock at par value.
7. Declared and paid a $50,000 cash dividend.
8. Issued 3,000 shares of common stock for cash at $8 per share.
9. Recorded depreciation of $16,000 on buildings and $23,000 on equipment.

Required

a. Compute the change in cash and cash equivalents that occurred during 2019.
b. Prepare a 2019 statement of cash flows using the indirect method.
c. Prepare separate schedules showing (1) cash paid for interest and for income taxes and (2) noncash investing and financing transactions.

P11-49. Interpreting the Statement of Cash Flows

Following is the statement of cash flows for **Stryker Corp.**

LO1, 2, 3, 4, 5
Stryker Corp. (SYK)

STRYKER CORPORATION Consolidated Statements of Cash Flows For Year Ended December 31, 2018 ($ millions)	
Operating activities	
Net earnings (loss)	$3,553
Adjustments to reconcile net earnings to net cash provided by operating activities:	
Depreciation	306
Amortization of intangible assets	417
Share-based compensation	119
Recall charges, net of insurance proceeds	23
Sale of inventory stepped up to fair value at acquisition	16
Deferred income tax benefit (expense)	(1,582)
Changes in operating assets and liabilities	
Accounts receivable	(60)
Inventories	(385)
Accounts payable	116
Accrued expenses and other liabilities	289
Recall-related payments	(90)
Income taxes	(156)
Other, net	44
Net cash provided by operating activities	2,610
Investing activities	
Acquisitions, net of cash acquired	(2,451)
Purchases of marketable securities	(226)
Proceeds from sales of marketable securities	394
Purchases of property, plant and equipment	(572)
Other investing, net	(2)
Net cash used in investing activities	(2,857)
Financing activities	
Proceeds and payments on short-term borrowings, net	(1)
Proceeds from issuance of long-term debt	3,126
Payments on long-term debt	(669)
Dividends paid	(703)
Repurchase of common stock	(300)
Cash paid for taxes from withheld shares	(120)
Payments to purchase noncontrolling interest	(14)
Other financing, net	10
Net cash provided by (used in) financing activities	1,329
Effect of exchange rate changes on cash and cash equivalents	(8)
Change in cash and cash equivalents	1,074
Cash and cash equivalents at beginning of year	2,542
Cash and cash equivalents at end of year	$3,616

Required

a. Why does the company add back depreciation to compute net cash flows from operating activities?

b. Explain why the change in accounts receivable and inventories are reported as adjustments to net earnings. Did the accounts receivable and inventories balances increase or decrease during the year?

c. Stryker reports that it invested $572 million in property, plant and equipment. Is this an appropriate type of expenditure for the company to make? What relation should expenditures for PPE have with depreciation expense?

d. Stryker paid $300 million to repurchase its common stock in fiscal 2018 and, in addition, paid dividends of $703 million. Thus, it paid $1,003 million of cash to its stockholders during the year. How do we evaluate that use of cash relative to other possible uses for the company's cash?

e. Provide an overall assessment of the company's cash flows for fiscal 2018. In the analysis, consider the sources and uses of cash.

LO1, 2, 3, 4, 5
Verizon Communications Inc. (VZ)

P11-50. Interpreting the Statement of Cash Flows

Following is the statement of cash flows for Verizon Communications Inc.

VERIZON COMMUNICATIONS INC.
Statement of Cash Flows
For Year Ended December 31, 2018 ($ millions)

Cash Flows from Operating Activities	
Net Income	$16,039
Adjustments to reconcile net income to net cash provided by operating activities:	
Depreciation and amortization expense	17,403
Employee retirement benefits	(2,657)
Deferred income taxes	389
Provision for uncollectible accounts	980
Equity in losses of unconsolidated businesses, net of dividends received	231
Oath goodwill impairment	4,591
Changes in current assets and liabilities, net of effects from acquisition/disposition of businesses:	
Accounts receivable	(2,667)
Inventories	(324)
Prepaid expenses and other	37
Accounts payable and accrued liabilities and other current liabilities	1,777
Discretionary employee benefits contributions	(1,679)
Other, net	219
Net cash provided by operating activities	34,339
Cash Flows from Investing Activities	
Capital expenditures (including capitalized software)	(16,658)
Acquisitions of businesses, net of cash acquired	(230)
Acquisitions of wireless licenses	(1,429)
Other, net	383
Net cash used in investing activities	(17,934)
Cash Flows from Financing Activities	
Proceeds from long-term borrowings	5,967
Proceeds from asset-backed long-term borrowings	4,810
Repayments of long-term borrowings and capital lease obligations	(10,923)
Repayments of asset-backed long-term borrowings	(3,635)
Dividends paid	(9,772)
Other, net	(1,824)
Net cash used in financing activities	(15,377)
Increase (decrease) in cash, cash equivalents and restricted cash	1,028
Cash, cash equivalents and restricted cash, beginning of period	2,888
Cash, cash equivalents and restricted cash, end of period (Note 1)	$ 3,916

Required

a. Why does Verizon add back depreciation to compute net cash flows from operating activities? What does the size of the depreciation add-back indicate about the relative capital intensity of this industry?

b. Verizon reports that it invested $16,658 million in property and equipment. These expenditures are necessitated by market pressures as the company faces stiff competition from other communications companies, such as Comcast. Where in the 10-K might we find additional information about these capital expenditures to ascertain whether Verizon is addressing the company's most pressing needs? What relation might we expect between the size of these capital expenditures and the amount of depreciation expense reported?

c. Determine the net cash flow associated with debt in 2018. Verizon's balance sheet reveals that the company has $113,063 million of debt at 2018 year-end. What problem does Verizon's high debt load pose for its ability to maintain the level of capital expenditures necessary to remain competitive in its industry?

d. During the year, Verizon paid dividends of $9,772 million but did not repay a sizable portion of its debt. How do dividend payments differ from debt payments? Why would Verizon continue to pay dividends in light of cash demands for needed capital expenditures and debt repayments?

e. Provide an overall assessment of Verizon's cash flows for 2018. In the analysis, consider the sources and uses of cash.

P11-51. Reconciling and Computing Operating Cash Flows from Net Income   LO1, 2, 5

Petroni Company reports the following selected results for its current calendar year.

Net income	$130,000
Depreciation expense	28,000
Accounts receivable increase	10,000
Accounts payable increase	6,000
Prepaid expenses decrease	3,000
Wages payable decrease	4,000

Required

a. Prepare the operating section only of Petroni Company's statement of cash flows for the year.

b. Does the positive sign on depreciation expense indicate the company is generating cash by recording depreciation? Explain.

c. Explain why the increase in accounts receivable is a use of cash in the statement of cash flows.

d. Explain why the decrease in prepaid expense is a source of cash in the statement of cash flows.

P11-52. Statement of Cash Flows (Direct Method)   LO3, 4, 7

Refer to the data for Wolff Company in Problem P11-43.

Required

a. Compute the change in cash that occurred during 2019.

b. Prepare a 2019 statement of cash flows using the direct method.

P11-53. Statement of Cash Flows (Direct Method)   LO3, 4, 7

Refer to the data for Arctic Company in Problem P11-45.

Required

a. Compute the change in cash that occurred during 2019.

b. Prepare a 2019 statement of cash flows using the direct method.

P11-54. Statement of Cash Flows (Direct Method)   LO3, 4, 7

Refer to the data for Dair Company in Problem P11-46.

Required

a. Compute the change in cash that occurred in 2019.

b. Prepare a 2019 statement of cash flows using the direct method. Use one cash outflow for "cash paid for wages and other operating expenses." Accounts payable relate to inventory purchases only.

c. Prepare separate schedules showing (1) a reconciliation of net income to net cash flow from operating activities (see Exhibit 11.3) and (2) noncash investing and financing transactions.

P11-55. Statement of Cash Flows (Direct Method)   LO3, 4, 7

Refer to the data for Rainbow Company in Problem P11-48.

Required

a. Compute the change in cash that occurred in 2019.

b. Prepare a 2019 statement of cash flows using the direct method. Use one cash outflow for "cash paid for wages and other operating expenses." Accounts payable relate to inventory purchases only.

c. Prepare separate schedules showing (1) a reconciliation of net income to net cash flow from operating activities (see Exhibit 11.3) and (2) noncash investing and financing transactions.

LO1, 5, 6
Amgen Inc. (AMGN)

P11-56. Interpreting the Statement of Cash Flows
Following is the statement of cash flows of **Amgen Inc.**

AMGEN INC.
CONSOLIDATED STATEMENTS OF CASH FLOWS

For Years Ended December 31, $ millions	2018	2017	2016
Cash flows from operating activities			
Net income	$ 8,394	$ 1,979	$ 7,722
Depreciation and amortization	1,946	1,955	2,105
Stock-based compensation expense	311	329	311
Deferred income taxes	(363)	(1,330)	183
Other items, net	386	334	32
Changes in operating assets and liabilities, net of acquisitions:			
Trade receivables, net	(378)	(58)	(214)
Inventories	(3)	133	(80)
Other assets	35	(24)	(128)
Accounts payable	(143)	424	(44)
Accrued income taxes, net	(361)	523	(301)
Long-term tax liabilities	258	6,681	445
Other liabilities	1,214	231	323
Net cash provided by operating activities	11,296	11,177	10,354
Cash flows from investing activities			
Purchases of marketable securities	(18,741)	(33,607)	(28,094)
Proceeds from sales of marketable securities	28,356	24,240	17,958
Proceeds from maturities of marketable securities	5,412	6,174	2,459
Purchases of property, plant and equipment	(738)	(664)	(738)
Cash acquired in acquisition, net of cash paid	195	(19)	—
Other	(145)	(148)	(243)
Net cash used in investing activities	14,339	(4,024)	(8,658)
Cash flows from financing activities			
Net proceeds from issuance of debt	—	4,476	7,318
Repayment of debt	(1,121)	(4,405)	(3,725)
Repurchases of common stock	(17,794)	(3,160)	(2,965)
Dividends paid	(3,507)	(3,365)	(2,998)
Withholding taxes arising from shares withheld for share-based payments	(126)	(191)	(260)
Other	58	51	31
Net cash used in financing activities	(22,490)	(6,594)	(2,599)
Increase (decrease) in cash and cash equivalents	3,145	559	(903)
Cash and cash equivalents at beginning of period	3,800	3,241	4,144
Cash and cash equivalents at end of period	$ 6,945	$ 3,800	$ 3,241

Required

a. What does Amgen report as net cash from operating activities in 2018? What is net income for the year? Much of this difference is the result of depreciation. Why is Amgen adding depreciation to net income in the computation of operating cash flows?

b. In determining cash provided by operating activities, Amgen adds $311 million relating to stock-based compensation expense in 2018. What is the purpose of this addition?

c. Amgen reports $(378) million relating to trade receivables. What does the negative sign on this amount signify about the change in receivables during the year compared with the negative sign on accounts payable in 2018?

d. Calculate and compare operating cash flow with current liabilities and operating cash flow with capital expenditures for 2018 and 2017. Current liabilities were $13,488 million, $9,020 million, and $11,204 million at the end of 2018, 2017, and 2016, respectively.

e. Does the composition of Amgen's cash flow present a "healthy" picture for 2018? Explain.

P11-57. Interpreting the Statement of Cash Flows
Following is the statement of cash flows of **Thermo Fisher Scientific**.

LO1, 5, 6
Thermo Fisher Scientific (TMO)

THERMO FISHER SCIENTIFIC INC.
Consolidated Statement of Cash Flows

For Year Ended December 31, $ millions	2018
Operating Activities	
Net Income	$2,938
Adjustments to reconcile net income to net cash provided by operating activities:	
Depreciation and amortization	2,267
Change in deferred income taxes	(379)
Noncash stock-based compensation	181
Other noncash expenses, net	106
Changes in assets and liabilities, excluding the effects of acquisitions:	
Accounts receivable	(366)
Inventories	(324)
Other assets	54
Accounts payable	201
Other liabilities	(42)
Contributions to retirement plans	(93)
Net cash provided by operating activities	4,543
Investing Activities	
Acquisitions, net of cash acquired	(536)
Purchase of property, plant and equipment	(758)
Proceeds from sale of property, plant and equipment	50
Other investing activities, net	(9)
Net cash used in investing activities	(1,253)
Financing Activities	
Net proceeds from issuance of debt	690
Repayment of debt	(2,052)
Proceeds from issuance of commercial paper	5,060
Repayments of commercial paper	(5,254)
Purchases of company common stock	(500)
Dividends paid	(266)
Net proceeds from issuance of company common stock under employee stock plans	136
Other financing activities	(51)
Net cash (used in) provided by financing activities	(2,237)
Exchange Rate Effect on Cash	(297)
Increase in Cash, Cash Equivalents and Restricted Cash	756
Cash, Cash Equivalents and Restricted Cash at Beginning of Period	1,361
Cash, Cash Equivalents and Restricted Cash at End of Period	$2,117

Required

a. What amounts does the company report for net income and cash from operating activities? What one item explains most of this difference? Why does the company add these amounts in the computation of operating cash flows?

b. Thermo Fisher Scientific reports a positive amount of $181 million relating to noncash stock-based compensation. What does this positive amount signify?

c. Thermo Fisher Scientific reports a cash outflow of $758 million relating to the acquisition of PPE. Is this cash outflow a cause for concern? Explain. Did the company dispose of any PPE during 2018? How do we know?

d. Thermo Fisher Scientific's net cash flows from financing activities is $(2,237) million. For what purposes is Thermo Fisher Scientific using this cash?

e. Calculate the operating cash flow to current liabilities ratio and the operating cash flow to capital expenditures ratio. Current liabilities were $6,147 million in 2018 and $7,048 million in 2017. What do these ratios measure?

f. The cash balance increased by $756 million during the year. Does Thermo Fisher Scientific present a "healthy" cash flow picture for the year? Explain.

IFRS Applications

LO1, 5
Nutrien Ltd. (NTR)

I11-58. Interpreting Graphical Cash Flow Data

Nutrien Ltd., a Canadian agri-business company, reported the following in its 2018 annual report.

The graph below represents the significant changes in Nutrien's cash flows in 2018.

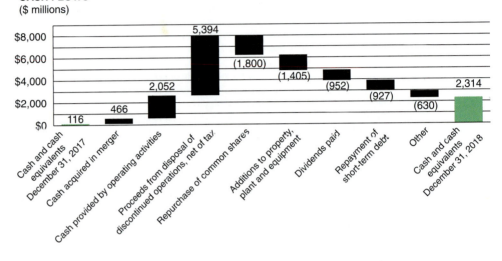

Required

a. Determine the change in cash and cash equivalents for Nutrien for 2018.
b. Classify each of the black bars in the graphic as operating, investing, or financing cash flows. Assume that "Other" relates entirely to investing cash flows.
c. Use the data to complete the following abbreviated statement of cash flows.

$ millions	2018
Cash from operating activities	
Cash from investing activities	
Cash from financing activities	
Cash flow for the year	
Cash and cash equivalents, start of year	
Cash and cash equivalents, end of year	

Solutions to Review Problems

Review 11-1—Solution

Transaction	Classification
1. Payments of dividends.	F
2. Payments to purchase PPE assets and intangible assets.	I
3. Payments to employees or suppliers.	O
4. Payments to purchase inventories.	O
5. Receipts from issuances of bonds payable, mortgage notes payable, and other notes payable.	F
6. Receipts from sales of investments in stocks, bonds, and other securities (other than cash equivalents).	I
7. Payments of interest to creditors.	O
8. Receipts from issuances of common stock and preferred stock and from sales of treasury stock.	F
9. Receipts of interest and dividends.	O
10. Payments to purchase stocks, bonds, and other securities (other than cash equivalents).	I
11. Receipts from customers for sales made or services rendered.	O
12. Payments to acquire treasury stock.	F
13. Other receipts such as lawsuit settlements and refunds received from suppliers.	O
14. Payments of taxes to government.	O
15. Payments to settle outstanding bonds payable, mortgage notes payable, and other notes payable.	F
16. Receipts from sales of PPE assets and intangible assets.	I
17. Other payments such as contributions to charity.	O
18. Receipts from repayments of loans by borrowers.	I
19. Payments made to lend money to borrowers.	I

Review 11-2—Solution

Net cash flow from operating activities	
Net income	$35,000
Add (deduct) items to convert net income to cash basis	
Depreciation	11,000
Loss on sale of investments	2,000
Accounts receivable decrease	6,000
Inventory increase	(28,000)
Prepaid advertising increase	(3,000)
Accounts payable increase	13,000
Wages payable increase	3,500
Income tax payable decrease	(1,500)
Net cash provided by operating activities	$38,000

Review 11-3—Solution

Cash Flows from Investing Activities	
Sale of investments.	$ 9,000
Purchase of PPE.	(48,000)
Net cash used by investing activities	$(39,000)

Review 11-4A—Solution

Cash Flows from Financing Activities	
Issuance of common stocks	$ 14,000
Payment of dividends	(17,000)
Net cash used by financing activities	$(3,000)

Review 11-4B—Solution

a. The change in cash = $38,000 + $(39,000) + $(3,000) = $(4,000).

b.

Net decrease in cash	$ (4,000)
Cash at beginning of year.	12,000
Cash at end of year	$ 8,000

Review 11-5—Solution

a.

	Net Income	Depreciation	Stock-Based Compensation	Cash from Operations	Cash from Investing	CAPEX	Cash from Financing
Starbucks	18.3%	5.3%	1.0%	48.3%	(9.6%)	(8.0%)	(13.1%)
Farmer Brothers	(12.3%)	5.2%	0.6%	5.9%	(5.4%)	(5.8%)	0.2%
Exhibit 11.5	11.4%	3.1%	0.7%	19.7%	(8.0%)	(3.6%)	(8.2%)

Starbucks' percentages are larger than for the median S&P 500 firm. In contrast, Farmer Brothers reports percentages that are markedly weaker. Also, Farmer Brothers' cash generated from each of its three business activities is low as compared with Starbucks and the S&P firms.

b. Both companies' cash flow patterns are roughly the same (+ – –), which reflects that both are relatively mature companies.

Review 11-6—Solution

1. $\dfrac{\$6,966.7}{(\$2,890.6 + \$2,973.5)/2} = 2.38$

2. $\dfrac{\$6,966.7}{\$2,741.7} = 2.54$

3. Yes, both ratios are strong. The operating cash flow to current liabilities ratio is much higher than the benchmark of 0.5, and the operating cash flow to capital expenditures ratio is much higher than 1.0

Review 11-7—Solution

Cash received from customers...........	$391,000	$385,000 sales + $6,000 accounts receivable decrease
Cash received as dividends..............	5,000	$5,000 dividend income
Cash paid for merchandise purchased......	(248,000)	$233,000 cost of goods sold + $28,000 inventory increase − $13,000 accounts payable increase
Cash paid to employees.................	(78,500)	$82,000 wages expense − $3,500 wages payable increase
Cash paid for advertising................	(13,000)	$10,000 advertising expense + $3,000 prepaid advertising increase
Cash paid for income taxes..............	(18,500)	$17,000 income tax expense + $1,500 income tax payable decrease
Net cash provided by operating activities....	$ 38,000	

Module 12
Financial Statement Forecasting

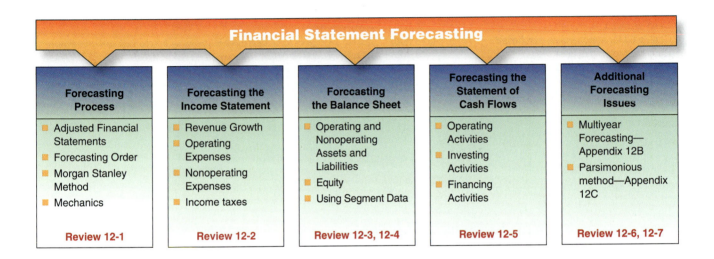

PREVIEW   PG

We describe the process for forecasting financial statements, including:

- Forecasting the income statement, including the use of company guidance.
- Forecasting the balance sheet.
- Forecasting cash as a plug figure to balance the balance sheet, and interpreting the forecasted cash balance.
- Building forecasts from the bottom up by using segment disclosures.
- Multiyear forecasting, including achieving targeted cash balances by adjusting debt levels.
- Forecasting the statement of cash flows.
- Parsimonious method of forecasting NOPAT, NOA, and RNOA.

We show excerpts from Morgan Stanley analysts' spreadsheets to illustrate the forecasting process. Appendix 12D includes excerpts of the Morgan Stanley analyst research report on Procter & Gamble, this module's focus company. The dashboard below conveys key financial information for P&G.

Consumer Discretionary Industry Asset and Revenue Growth

P&G Asset and Revenue Growth and Return on Equity

Road Map

LO	Learning Objective | Topics	Page	eLecture	Guided Example	Assignments
12-1	**Explain the process of forecasting financial statements.** Adjusted Financial Statements :: Forecasting Order :: Morgan Stanley :: Mechanics :: Consistency and Precision :: Sensitivity	12-3	e12–1	Review 12-1	1, 2, 3, 4, 9, 35
12-2	**Forecast revenues and the income statement.** Overview :: Sales Driver :: COGS :: SGA :: Income Taxes	12-8	e12–2	Review 12-2	7, 11, 12, 13, 17, 20, 21, 23, 25, 28, 32, 33, 35
12-3	**Forecast the balance sheet.** Overview :: PPE :: Intangibles :: LTD :: Retained Earnings :: Treasury Stock :: Cash Plug :: Normal Cash :: Deviation from Norm :: Capital Structure	12-12	e12–3	Review 12-3	6, 8, 10, 14, 15, 16, 18, 19, 21, 23, 25, 27, 32, 33
12-4	**Prepare forecasts using segment data.** Segment Data	12-16	e12–4	Review 12-4	28, 29, 32
12-5	**Forecast the statement of cash flows (Appendix 12A).** Operating :: Investing :: Financing	12-19	e12–5	Review 12-5	22, 24, 26, 32, 33
12-6	**Prepare multiyear forecasts of financial statements (Appendix 12B).** Motivation :: Long-Term Assumptions :: Check for Reasonableness	12-20	e12–6	Review 12-6	5, 34
12-7	**Apply a parsimonious method for forecasting net operating profit and net operating assets (Appendix 12C).**	12-22	e12–7	Review 12-7	30, 31

Forecasting Process

LO1 Explain the process of forecasting financial statements.

Forecasting financial performance is integral to a variety of business decisions. In addition to using financial forecasts to value stocks and inform investment decisions, investors and analysts might be interested in evaluating the creditworthiness of a prospective borrower. In that case, they forecast the borrower's cash flows to estimate its ability to repay its obligations, and bond ratings are influenced by those forecasts. Company managers also frequently forecast future cash flows to evaluate alternative strategic investment decisions as well as to evaluate the shareholder value that strategic investment alternatives will create. All of these decisions require accurate financial forecasts. In this module, we illustrate the most common method to forecast the income statement, balance sheet, and statement of cash flows.

Adjusted Financial Statements The forecasting process begins with a retrospective analysis. That is, we analyze current and prior years' statements to be sure that they accurately reflect the company's financial condition and performance. If we believe that they do not, we adjust those statements to reflect the company's net operating assets and liabilities and operating income that we expect to persist.

Why do we adjust historical results? The answer is that income statements can contain one-time (transitory and/or nonoperating) income or expense items that affect reported profit. Because our objective is to forecast *future* income and cash flow, we must first identify and eliminate transitory items because, by definition, they will not recur.

This adjusting process, also referred to as recasting, reformulating, or scrubbing the numbers, involves estimates. This estimation process requires judgment and varies by firm. Following are items frequently encountered.

- *Restructuring expenses* (Module 5). If the restructuring activity is unusual and management discussion indicates that it is unlikely to recur, we eliminate the expense in our forecast. If the restructuring activity is recurring, we don't eliminate but normalize the amount over the past years impacted.

- *Litigation expenses* (Module 5). Significant litigation expenses can skew results. We eliminate them from our forecast if they are transitory, or normalize the amount if litigation is a routine occurrence but the amount varies year over year.

- *Discontinued operations* (Module 5). Discontinued operations are one-time events that we eliminate because they will not affect future operations.

- *Gains and losses on asset dispositions and impairments* (Module 6). These gains and losses are one-time occurrences that we always eliminate and normalize their amounts over the periods impacted before we begin forecasting.

- *Unusual income tax expense or benefit* (Module 10). Changes in tax laws can significantly affect the effective tax rate. We need to identify unusual, one-time tax expenses and benefits to better isolate the effective tax rate that will persist.

- *Acquisitions and divestitures* (Modules 9 and 12). Acquisitions and divestitures affect the income statement from the date of the transaction. Footnote disclosures typically provide comparable historical data we can use to develop better forecast assumptions.

Forecasting Order of Financial Statements The forecasting process estimates future income statements, balance sheets, and statements of cash flows, in that order. The reason for this ordering is that each statement uses information from the preceding statement(s). For example, we update retained earnings on the balance sheet to reflect our forecast of the company's net income. And the forecasted income statement and balance sheets are used in preparing forecasts for the statement of cash flows, which follows the same process we illustrate in the module on preparing the historical statement of cash flows.

To illustrate the forecasting process, we start with the P&G financial statements for the fiscal year (FY) ended June 30, 2019 (FY2019), and use them to forecast the company's financial statements for FY2020. (See Appendix 12B for P&G financial statements for FY2019 and the FY2020 forecast.)

In Appendix 12B, we illustrate the process to extend the forecasts to FY2021 and future years. We explain interpretation of the forecasted balance for cash and the adjustments that we can make to our forecasted balance sheet and income statement to achieve a desired level of cash.

Morgan Stanley Forecasting Process Later in this module we provide excerpts from the Morgan Stanley research report on P&G and the spreadsheet Morgan Stanley analysts used in their forecasting process. Appendix 12D to this module includes excerpts from the published Morgan Stanley report. We have benefitted from conversations with Morgan Stanley analysts and are grateful for the background information that they provided us that informs the forecasting process in this module.[1]

Forecasting Mechanics The revenues (sales) forecast is, arguably, the most crucial and difficult estimate in the forecasting process. It is a crucial estimate because other income-statement and balance-sheet accounts derive, either directly or indirectly, from the revenues forecast. As a result, both the income statement and balance sheet grow with increases in revenues. The income statement reflects this growth concurrently. However, different balance sheet accounts reflect revenue growth in different ways. Some balance sheet accounts anticipate (or lead) revenue growth (inventories are one example). Some accounts reflect this growth concurrently (accounts receivable). And some accounts reflect revenue growth with a lag (for example, companies usually expand property, plant, and equipment (PPE) only after growth is deemed sustainable). Conversely, when revenues decline, so do the income statement and balance sheet, as the company shrinks to cope with adversity. Such actions include reduction of overhead costs and divestiture of excess assets. Exhibit 12.1 highlights crucial income statement and balance sheet relations that are impacted by the revenues forecast.

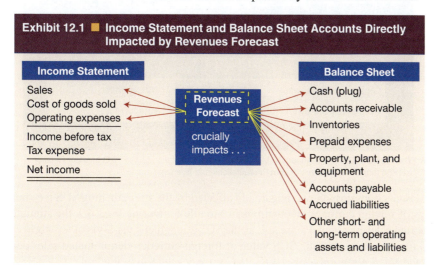

Forecasting Consistency and Precision It is important to keep two points in mind.

- **Internal consistency.** The forecasted income statement, balance sheet, and statement of cash flows are linked in the same way historical financial statements are. That is, they must articulate (link together within and across time), as we explain Module 2. Preparing a forecasted statement of cash flows, although tedious, is often a useful way to uncover forecasting assumptions that are inconsistently applied across financial statements (such as capital expenditures, depreciation, debt payments, and dividends). If the forecasted cash balance on the balance sheet agrees with that on the statement of cash flows, it is likely that our income statement and balance sheet articulate. We also must ensure that our forecast assumptions are internally consistent. For example, it is

---

[1] Please note that materials that are referenced herein comprise excerpts from Morgan Stanley research reports. MS has provided their materials here as a courtesy. Therefore, MS and Cambridge do not undertake to advise you of changes in the opinions or information set forth in these materials. These materials should not be relied on as investment advice. These materials are only as current as the publication date of the underlying Morgan Stanley research. For important disclosures, stock price charts, and equity rating histories regarding companies that are the subject of the underlying Morgan Stanley research, see www.morganstanley.com/researchdisclosures.

unadvisable to forecast an increased gross profit margin during an economic recession unless we can make compelling arguments based on known business facts about the company.

- **Level of precision.** Computing forecasts to the "nth decimal place" is easy using spreadsheets. This increased precision makes the resulting forecasts appear more precise, but they are not necessarily more accurate. As we discuss in this module, our financial statement forecasts are highly dependent on our revenues forecast. Whether revenues are expected to grow by 2% or 3% can markedly impact profitability and other forecasts. Estimating cost of goods sold (COGS) and other items to the nth decimal place is meaningless if we have imprecise revenue forecasts. Consequently, borderline decisions that depend on a high level of forecasting precision are ill-advised.

Company Guidance

Companies frequently provide guidance to analysts and other users of financial reports for forecasting purposes. P&G provided the following guidance for FY2020 when it presented its FY2019 financial results. We can use this guidance to inform our forecast assumptions.

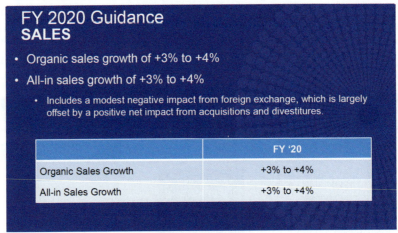

The Procter & Gamble Company Q4 2019 Earnings Presentation on the P&G Investor Relations website (http://www.pginvestor.com/Presentations-and-Events)

In FY2019, P&G's sales growth was negatively affected by the strengthening $US (see our discussion of the effects of foreign currency fluctuations in Module 5). During FY2019, the strengthening $US reduced reported sales by about 4%; recall, as the $US strengthens vis-à-vis other world currencies in which P&G transacts business, the $US value of foreign-currency-denominated sales decreases. For FY2019, in the MD&A section of its 10-K, P&G provides the following table.

Total Company	Net Sales Growth	Foreign Exchange Impact	Acquisition & Divestiture Impact/Other	Organic Sales Growth
FY2019.........	1%	4%	—%	5%

Total sales increased by 1% in FY2019, from $66,832 million to $67,684 million. Absent foreign currency effects and the effects of acquisitions and divestitures, P&G's organic sales would have increased by 5% (overall 1% net sales increase plus 4% negative foreign-currency effect). P&G does not anticipate a significant foreign currency exchange rate effect in FY2020. Consequently, P&G's All-in sales growth estimate of 3% to 4% is equal to its estimate of Organic sales growth. We use 3.5% growth, the midpoint of the range, in our forecasting process.

P&G provides guidance for its effective tax rate. For FY2020, P&G forecasts an effective tax rate of 17% to 18% (which results in the 17.5% we use in our forecasts).

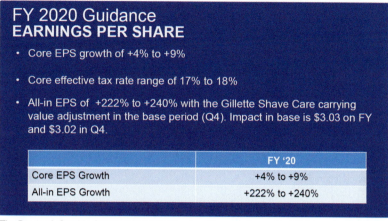

The Procter & Gamble Company Q4 2019 Earnings Presentation on the P&G Investor Relations website (http://www.pginvestor.com/Presentations-and-Events)

P&G provides guidance regarding anticipated capital spending (CAPEX), dividends, and share repurchases.

[FY 2020 Guidance — CASH GENERATION AND USAGE]
- Free Cash Flow Productivity: 90%
- Capital Spending, % Sales: 4.5% to 5.0%
- Dividends: Over $7.5B
- Direct Share Repurchase: $6 to $8B

The Procter & Gamble Company Q4 2019 Earnings Presentation on the P&G Investor Relations website (http://www.P&Ginvestor.com/Presentations-and-Events)

We use this guidance to produce the following forecasts.

- CAPEX as 4.75% of sales, the midpoint of the guidance for capital spending.
- Dividends of $7.5 billion.
- Share repurchases (treasury stock purchases) of $7 billion, the midpoint of the guidance.

LO1 Review 12-1

The FY2019 income statement and balance sheet for **General Mills**, a competitor of P&G, follow. Use them to answer the required questions.

Required
a. Which two nonrecurring items on the 2019 income statement would we consider eliminating before beginning the forecasting process?
b. In what order do we forecast the financial statements? Explain why this order is important.
c. What income statement amount do we forecast first?
d. Identify at least three forecasted expenses that are directly or indirectly related to revenue.
e. Identify at least three forecasted balance sheet accounts that are directly or indirectly related to forecasted revenue.

continued

continued from previous page

GENERAL MILLS INC.
Consolidated Statements of Earnings

12 Months Ended, $ millions	May 26, 2019
Net sales	$16,865.2
Cost of sales	11,108.4
Selling, general, and administrative expenses	2,935.8
Divestitures (loss)	30.0
Restructuring, impairment, and other exit costs	275.1
Operating profit	2,515.9
Benefit plan nonservice income	(87.9)
Interest, net	521.8
Earnings before income taxes and after-tax earnings from joint ventures	2,082.0
Income taxes	367.8
After-tax earnings from joint ventures	(72.0)
Net earnings, including earnings attributable to redeemable and noncontrolling interests	1,786.2
Net earnings attributable to redeemable and noncontrolling interests	33.5
Net earnings attributable to General Mills	$ 1,752.7

GENERAL MILLS INC.
Consolidated Balance Sheet

$ millions, except par value	May 26, 2019
Current assets	
Cash and cash equivalents	$ 450.0
Receivables	1,679.7
Inventories	1,559.3
Prepaid expenses and other current assets	497.5
Total current assets	4,186.5
Land, buildings, and equipment	3,787.2
Goodwill	13,995.8
Other intangible assets	7,166.8
Other assets	974.9
Total assets	$30,111.2
Current liabilities	
Accounts payable	$ 2,854.1
Current portion of long-term debt	1,396.5
Notes payable	1,468.7
Other current liabilities	1,367.8
Total current liabilities	7,087.1
Long-term debt	11,624.8
Deferred income taxes	2,031.0
Other liabilities	1,448.9
Total liabilities	22,191.8
Redeemable interest value	551.7
Stockholders' equity	
Common stock, 754.6 shares issued, $0.10 par value	75.5
Additional paid-in capital	1,386.7
Retained earnings	14,996.7
Common stock in treasury, at cost	(6,779.0)
Accumulated other comprehensive loss	(2,625.4)
Total stockholders' equity	7,054.5
Noncontrolling interests	313.2
Total equity	7,367.7
Total liabilities and equity	$30,111.2

Solution on p. 12-51.

Forecasting the Income Statement

Exhibit 12.2 presents the FY2019 income statement for Procter & Gamble together with our forecast of the statements for FY2020.

LO2 Forecast revenues and the income statement

Overview Here is a high-level overview—computational details follow.

- **Sales estimate.** The forecasting process begins with an estimate of the sales growth rate. For our illustration, we assume a 3.5% growth rate, informed by P&G's guidance. Given the assumed 3.5% growth in sales, forecasted 2020 sales are $70,053 million ($67,684 million × 1.035).

- **Expense estimates.** To estimate operating expenses (cost of goods sold and selling, general, and administrative [SG&A] expenses) we apply a percentage of sales ratio to forecasted sales. For nonoperating expenses (such as interest expense and interest revenue), we initially assume they will not change ("no change") unless we believe interest rates are likely to shift greatly during the forecast period. (In Appendix 12B, we relax the "no change" assumption because we add debt to achieve a desired level of cash. Additional debt causes interest expense to increase. We discuss these additional steps in Appendix 12B.)

- **One-time item estimates.** One-time items such as asset impairments and discontinued operations, are, by definition, not expected to recur. We forecast these items to be $0.

- **Tax estimate.** Income tax expense is forecasted based on PG's guidance of 17.5% of pretax income.

- **Noncontrolling interest estimate.** A common assumption is no change in the ratio of noncontrolling interest to consolidated net income. For our P&G illustration, we adopt that assumption.

For each line item in the income statement, we summarize our forecasting assumptions in the rightmost column of Exhibit 12.2, and we discuss those assumptions in depth in the following sections.

Exhibit 12.2 ■ Forecast of P&G's FY2020 Income Statement

$ millions	Actual FY2019	% of Net Sales	Computations	FY2020 Est.	% of Net Sales	Explanation
Net sales........................	$67,684	100.0%	$67,684 × 1.035	$70,053	100.0%	Use P&G's guidance that sales will increase about 3.5%. Sales forecast equals current sales × (1 + growth rate %).
Cost of products sold..............	34,768	51.4%	$70,053 × 51.4%	36,007	51.4%	Assume COGS as % of sales will remain unchanged from FY2019.
Selling, general, and administrative expense...	19,084	28.2%	$70,053 × 28.2%	19,755	28.2%	Assume SGA as % of sales will remain unchanged from FY2019.
Goodwill & indefinite lived intangibles impairment charges	8,345	12.3%	none	0		The Goodwill impairment charge is a transitory item and we eliminate that expense in FY2020.
Operating income...............	5,487	8.1%	subtotal	14,291	20.4%	
Interest expense.................	509	0.8%	computed	483	0.7%	Interest expense is discussed below.
Interest income..................	220	0.3%	no change	220	0.3%	Assume no change in interest revenue.
Other nonoperating income, net........	871	1.3%	none	0	0.0%	FY2019 nonoperating income relates to the dissolution of a partnership and early extinguishment of debt, and we assume none for FY2020 given no evidence of planned divestitures or debt retirement.
Earnings from continuing operations before income taxes.................	6,069	9.0%	subtotal	14,028	20.0%	
Income taxes on continuing operations......	2,103	3.1%	$14,028 × 17.5%	2,455	3.5%	Assume effective tax rate of 17.5% per P&G guidance.
Net earnings....................	3,966	5.9%	subtotal	11,573	16.5%	
Less: Net earnings attributable to noncontrolling interests.............	69	0.1%	$11,562 × 1.7%	197	0.3%	Assume noncontrolling interests as % of net earnings (1.7%) continues.
Net earnings attributable to P&G.........	$ 3,897	5.8%	subtotal	$11,376	16.2%	

Sales as the Income Statement Forecast Driver We forecast most income statement line items in Exhibit 12.2 as a percent of sales. (One exception is tax expense, which is commonly set as a percent of pretax profit.) Unless we are aware of transitory items that affect the current year's income statement, we use the current year percentage of sales in our forecast.

Cost of Goods Sold (COGS) Companies often discuss COGS in the Management Discussion & Analysis (MD&A) section of their 10-K report. This discussion typically provides insight into recent trends as well as anticipated effects of planned restructuring or other process improvement activities. P&G discusses its gross margin in the following excerpt from its FY2019 10-K.

> Gross margin increased 10 basis points to 48.6% of net sales in 2019. Gross margin benefited 160 basis points from total manufacturing cost savings (130 basis points net of product and packaging reinvestments), 60 basis points of positive pricing impacts and 50 basis points from lower restructuring costs. These were offset by:
> - a 100 basis-point decline from unfavorable product mix and other impacts (primarily mix within segments due to the growth of lower margin product forms and the club channel in certain categories and due to the disproportionate growth of the Fabric Care category, which is one of our largest categories and has lower than company-average gross margins),
> - an 80 basis-point negative impact due to higher commodity costs and
> - a 50 basis-point negative impact from unfavorable foreign exchange.

Gross margins did not change significantly in FY2019 as price increases and favorable manufacturing cost savings from P&G's productivity initiatives were largely offset by unfavorable product mix changes to lower gross profit products, higher commodity costs, and unfavorable foreign exchange fluctuations (exchange rate effects affect expenses in the same way they affect sales). Therefore, we use the FY2019 percent COGS to sales (51.4%).

SGA Expense To forecast SG&A for FY2020, we use the FY2019 percent SG&A to sales (28.2%) because the company does not disclose any significant operational changes to SG&A in the following excerpt from its FY2019 10-K.

> Total SG&A was relatively unchanged at $19.1 billion, as a decrease in marketing spending was offset by an increase in overhead costs and in other net operating expenses. SG&A as a percentage of net sales decreased 30 basis points to 28.2%. Reductions in marketing spending as a percentage of net sales were partially offset by an increase in overhead costs and other net operating expenses as a percentage of sales.
> - Marketing spending as a percentage of net sales decreased 80 basis points due to the positive scale impacts of the organic net sales increase, reductions in agency compensation and the impact of adopting the new standard on "Revenue from Contracts with Customers" which prospectively reclassified certain customer spending from marketing (SG&A) expense to a reduction of net sales.
> - Overhead costs as a percentage of net sales increased 30 basis points, as productivity savings and fixed cost leverage from the increased organic net sales, were more than offset by the impact of inflation, higher incentive compensation costs and other cost increases, including the ongoing and integration-related overhead costs of the Merck OTC acquisition.
> - Other net operating expenses as a percentage of net sales increased 20 basis points primarily due to an increase in foreign exchange transactional charges and the net impact of changes in indirect tax reserves, partially offset by the gain on sale of real estate in the current year.

We forecast SG&A expense as Sales × Current year SGA percentage of sales, which yields $19,755 million ($70,053 million × 28.2%).

Interest Expense We forecast interest expense as Average debt balance during the year × Estimated % interest rate. For FY2019, P&G reported $509 million of interest expense and an average debt balance of $30,689 million, yielding an average interest rate of 1.7% ($509 million/$30,689 million).

P&G begins the FY2020 year with $30,092 million ($9,697 million + $20,395 million) of short-term and long-term debt and predicts contractual payments of $3,388 for FY2020, yielding an anticipated debt balance of $26,704 for FY2020 ($30,092 − $3,388). For the initial forecast, we assume no additional borrowing during the year (we relax that assumption in Appendix 12B when we perform a multiyear forecast). Our forecast for FY2020 interest expense is $483 million calculated as 1.7% × ($30,092 + $26,704)/2.

Income Tax Expense Income tax expense (labeled "Income taxes on continuing operations" by P&G) is often a large expense item. We estimate tax expense by applying an estimated tax rate to pretax income. For FY2020, we use an effective tax rate of 17.5% as provided in PG's guidance. In the absence of company guidance, we can use disclosures in the income tax footnote to get a tax rate estimate. Following is the effective tax rate disclosure in P&G's FY2019 10-K.

Years Ended June 30 ($ millions)	2019	2018	2017
U.S. federal statutory income tax rate	21.0%	28.1%	35.0%
Country mix impacts of foreign operations	(0.5)%	(4.7)%	(6.8)%
Changes in uncertain tax positions	(0.3)%	(0.3)%	(2.0)%
Excess tax benefits from the exercise of stock options	(3.8)%	(0.4)%	(1.3)%
Goodwill impairment	22.8%	—%	—%
Net transitional impact U.S. Tax Act	—%	4.5%	—%
Other	(4.5)%	(1.2)%	(1.8)%
Effective income tax rate	34.7%	26.0%	23.1%

The aim of reviewing the tax table in the footnotes is to determine the tax rate to use for our forecasts. We look for any transitory items that affect the company's tax rate and we exclude such items in our forecast. In FY2019, for example, P&G's effective tax rate increased by 22.8 percentage points due to the Goodwill impairment that reduced pre-tax profit without a consequent reduction of income tax expense (Goodwill write-offs are generally not a tax-deductible expense). Given that the Goodwill impairment is a one-time occurrence, we would forecast a tax rate of 11.9% (34.7% effective tax rate less 22.8%). In addition, the line item labeled as "Other" increased by 2 to 3 percentage points over the previous two years. Adding that amount, then, results in an estimate of the effective tax rate that is close to the 17.5% rate in P&G's guidance.

Impact of Acquisitions When one company acquires another, the revenues and expenses of the acquired company are consolidated, but only from the date of acquisition onward (we discuss the consolidation process in an earlier module). Acquisitions can greatly impact the acquirer's income statement, especially if the acquisition occurs toward the beginning of the acquirer's fiscal year. In FY2019 P&G did not have any material acquisitions. Therefore, we use P&G's acquisition of **Gillette** in October 2005 as an example. In its June 30, 2006, fiscal year-end income statement (ending eight months following the acquisition), P&G reported the following for sales.

Years Ended June 30 ($ millions)	2006	2005	2004
Net sales	$68,222	$56,741	$51,407

These net sales amounts include Gillette product sales from October 2005 onward (for fiscal 2006), and none of Gillette's sales is reported in fiscal 2005 or fiscal 2004. P&G's 2006 sales growth of 20.2% ([$68,222 million/$56,741 million] − 1) was, therefore, not P&G's organic growth, and we would have been remiss in forecasting a 20.2% increase for fiscal 2007.

Importantly, until all three annual income statements in the 10-K include the acquired company, the acquirer is required to disclose what revenue and net income would have been had the acquired company been consolidated for all three years reported in the current annual report. This "what if" disclosure is called *pro forma* disclosure. Procter & Gamble's pro forma disclosure in the footnotes to its 2006 10-K includes the following discussion and table.

> The following table provides pro forma results of operations for the years ended June 30, 2006, 2005, and 2004, as if Gillette had been acquired as of the beginning of each fiscal year presented.
>
> | Pro Forma Results; Years Ended June 30, | 2006 | 2005 | 2004 |
> | --- | --- | --- | --- |
> | Net sales ($ millions) | $71,005 | $67,920 | $61,112 |
> | Net earnings ($ millions) | 8,871 | 8,522 | 7,504 |
> | Diluted net earnings per common share | 2.51 | 2.29 | 1.98 |

Using this disclosure, we would have been able to compute the growth rate in sales for 2006 as 4.5% ([$71,005 million/$67,920 million] − 1), and we would have used the pro forma net sales for 2006 as our forecasting base. That is, assuming a continuation of this 4.5% growth rate, we would have forecasted 2007 net sales as $74,200 million (calculated as $71,005 million × 1.045). P&G was careful to point out, however, that the pro forma earnings estimate must be viewed with caution.

> Pro forma results do not include any anticipated cost savings or other effects of the planned integration of Gillette. Accordingly, such amounts are not necessarily indicative of the results if the acquisition had occurred on the dates indicated or that may result in the future.

Impact of Divestitures When companies divest of discontinued operations, they are required to:

- Exclude sales and expenses of discontinued operations from the continuing operations portion of their income statements.
- Report net income and gain (loss) on sale of the divested entity, net of tax, below income from continuing operations.
- Segregate the assets and liabilities of discontinued operations and report them on separate line items—these are labeled "assets held for sale" or "liabilities held of sale" on the balance sheet.

In FY2019 P&G did not have any major brand divestitures. Therefore, we use FY2016 to illustrate the related forecasting issues. P&G reports assets and liabilities held for sale on its FY2016 balance sheet at $7,185 million and $2,343 million, respectively. In our FY2017 forecasts, we assume these discontinued operations will be sold in FY2017 at book value and, consequently, report both the assets and liabilities of discontinued operations at a zero balance in our FY2017 forecast.

Reassessing Financial Statement Forecasts After preparing the forecasted financial statements, it is useful to reassess whether they are reasonable in light of current economic and company conditions. This task is subjective and benefits from the forecaster's knowledge of company, industry, and economic factors. Many analysts and managers prepare "what-if" forecasted financial statements. Specifically, they change key assumptions, such as the forecasted sales growth or key cost ratios, and then recompute the forecasted financial statements. These alternative forecasting scenarios indicate the sensitivity of a set of predicted outcomes to different assumptions about future economic conditions. Such sensitivity estimates can be useful for setting contingency plans and in identifying areas of vulnerability for company performance and condition.

Review 12-2 LO2

Refer to the FY2019 income statement and balance sheet for General Mills in Review 12-1.

Required
Use the following assumptions to forecast the General Mills income statement for FY2020.
- Net sales will increase by 1.5% (150 basis points) in FY2020.
- Cost of sales: 65.9% of forecasted sales.
- SGA expenses: 17.4% of forecasted sales.
- No announced divestitures for FY2020.

continued

continued from previous page

- Restructuring, impairment, and other exit costs: 1.6% of forecasted sales.
- Tax expense as a percentage of pretax income: 17.7%
- Benefit plan nonservice income is assumed to be zero.
- The following line items remain unchanged in dollar terms:
  - Interest, net.
  - After-tax earnings from joint ventures.
  - Net earnings attributable to redeemable and noncontrolling interests.

Solution on p. 12-52.

Forecasting the Balance Sheet

Our forecast of the balance sheet in Exhibit 12.3 begins with estimates for all assets *other than cash* (which is the *plug* amount as we explain below), all liabilities, and all equity accounts.

Forecast the balance sheet.

Overview Here is a high-level overview of balance sheet forecasting—details follow.

- **Working capital accounts.** We use an assumed percentage of forecasted sales to estimated accounts receivable, inventories, accounts payable, and accrued liabilities.
- **PPE and intangible assets.** To forecast PPE, we increase the prior year's balance by estimated CAPEX and reduce the estimate by forecasted depreciation expense (we discuss the forecasting of PPE assets below). We forecast intangible assets by subtracting forecasted amortization expense.
- **Current and long-term debt.** We assume P&G will make all contractual payments of long-term debt. We reduce the prior year's long-term debt balance by the current maturities of long-term debt reported in the footnotes. We assume current and long-term debt remains unchanged. (We discuss refining this assumption later.)
- **Stockholders' equity.** We assume paid-in capital accounts remain at prior years' levels, except for planned repurchases of treasury stock, as reported by P&G in its FY2019 earnings release. Retained earnings is increased by forecasted net income and reduced by estimated dividends. (We discuss the forecasting of dividends below.)

The last step in the forecasting process is to balance the balance sheet. To do this, we determine the amount needed in the Cash account to balance the balance sheet, computed as total assets (equal to total liabilities and equity) less all other asset balances. This balancing figure is referred to as the *plug* amount.

Working Capital Accounts Working capital accounts that are operating in nature are forecasted using the historical relation of each working capital account divided by sales, then multiplied by the forecasted sales. Items that are nonoperating are usually assumed to have no change, or are predicted using company guidance such as with debt due within one year.

PPE (Property, Plant and Equipment) Assets

Capital Expenditures (CAPEX). P&G provides guidance about anticipated purchases of PPE assets (called capital expenditures or CAPEX). The company reports that FY2020 CAPEX is expected to be 4.5% to 5% of sales. We use the midpoint of 4.75% of sales and forecast FY2020 CAPEX of $3,328 million ($70,053 million of forecasted sales × 4.75%).

In the absence of company guidance (or as a check on its accuracy), we can estimate CAPEX as a percentage of forecasted sales. To compute the percentage, we use CAPEX as reported in the current period statement of cash flows along with current period sales, as follows.

$$\text{Forecasted CAPEX} = \frac{\text{Current year CAPEX}}{\text{Current year Sales}} \times \text{Forecasted Sales}$$

P&G's 2019 statement of cash flows reports CAPEX of $3,347 million, which yields an historical rate of 4.9% of sales ($3,347 million/$67,684 million). This is consistent with the 4.5% to 5% range provided in P&G's guidance.

Exhibit 12.3 Forecast of P&G's FY2020 Balance Sheet

$ millions, except per share amounts	2019 Actual	% of Sales	Computations	2020 Est.	% of Sales	Explanation
Current assets						
Cash and cash equivalents	$ 4,239	6.3%	Plug	$ (1,550)	0.1%	Plug to balance the balance sheet.*
Available-for-sale investment securities	6,048	8.9%	no change	6,048	8.6%	Assume no change.
Accounts receivable	4,951	7.3%	$70,053 × 7.3%	5,114	7.3%	Forecast working capital accounts as a % of sales using prior year's % unless information suggests otherwise.**
Inventories	5,017	7.4%	$70,053 × 7.4%	5,184	7.4%	
Prepaid expenses and other current assets	2,218	3.3%	$70,053 × 3.3%	2,312	3.3%	
Total current assets	22,473	33.2%	subtotal	17,108	26.7%	
Property, plant, and equipment, net	21,271	31.4%	$3,328 − $2,604	21,995	31.4%	CAPEX estimates are from P&G guidance, and depreciation expense is computed as a % of prior year PPE, gross.
Goodwill	40,273	59.5%	no change	40,273	57.5%	Assume no changes because goodwill is not amortized.
Trademarks and other intangible assets, net	24,215	35.8%	($359)	23,856	34.1%	Apply estimated amortization expense from footnotes of P&G.
Other noncurrent assets	6,863	10.1%	no change	6,863	9.8%	Assume no change.
Total assets	$115,095	170.0%	subtotal	$110,095	159.5%	
Current liabilities						
Accounts payable	$ 11,260	16.6%	$70,053 × 16.6%	$ 11,629	16.6%	Forecast working capital accounts as % of sales unless information suggests otherwise.
Accrued and other liabilities	9,054	13.4%	$70,053 × 13.4%	9,387	13.4%	
Debt due within one year	9,697	14.3%	($3,388) + $2,009	8,318	16.1%	Use footnotes to get current maturities of long-term debt. Assume other debt remains unchanged.
Total current liabilities	30,011	44.3%	subtotal	29,334	46.1%	
Long-term debt	20,395	30.1%	($2,009)	18,386	24.3%	Use footnotes to get current maturities of long-term debt to be repaid.
Deferred income taxes	6,899	10.2%	$70,053 × 10.2%	7,145	10.2%	Assume no change as a % of sales.
Other noncurrent liabilities	10,211	15.1%	$70,053 × 15.1%	10,578	15.1%	Assume no change as a % of sales.
Total liabilities	67,516	99.8%	subtotal	65,443	95.7%	
Shareholders' equity						
Convertible Class A preferred stock	928	1.4%	no change	928	1.3%	Assume no change in paid-in capital accounts.
Nonvoting Class B preferred stock	0	0.0%	no change	0	0.0%	
Common stock, stated value $1 per share	4,009	5.9%	no change	4,009	5.7%	
Additional paid-in capital	63,827	94.3%	no change	63,827	91.1%	
Reserve for ESOP debt retirement	(1,146)	(1.7)%	no change	(1,146)	(1.6)%	Assume no change.
Accumulated other comprehensive income (loss)	(14,936)	(22.1)%	no change	(14,936)	(21.3)%	Assume no change.
Treasury stock	(100,406)	(148.3)%	($7,000)	(107,406)	(153.3)%	Use P&G guidance.
Retained earnings	94,918	140.2%	$11,573 − $7,500	98,794	141.0%	Increased by forecasted net income less forecasted dividends.
Noncontrolling interest	385	0.6%	+ $197	582	0.8%	Increased by net income allocated to noncontrolling interests.
Total shareholders' equity	47,579	70.3%	subtotal	44,652	63.7%	
Total liabilities and shareholders' equity	$115,095	170.0%	subtotal	$110,095	159.5%	

* $(1,561) = $110,084 − $6,048 − $5,114 − $5,184 − $2,312 − $21,995 − $40,273 − $23,856 − $6,863.

** To simplify, we forecast accounts as a percent of sales, including inventories and accounts payable. Analysts sometimes use a percent of COGS for inventory and for accounts payable estimates because both are expressed in input (not output) costs. Either approach is reasonable if used consistently. One could also forecast working capital accounts using turnover rates or days as follows:

Forecasted account balance = Forecasted revenues (or COGS)/Turnover rate, or = Forecasted days outstanding × [Forecasted revenues (or COGS)/365]

Depreciation Expense. Depreciation expense is usually reported in the statement of cash flows (or in the notes). (*Note:* If depreciation expense is combined with amortization expense, we can isolate the depreciation component by subtracting amortization expense, which is frequently reported separately in footnotes—or, if not separately reported, we may use the change in accumulated amortization.) It is common to estimate depreciation as:

$$\text{Forecasted depreciation expense} = \frac{\text{Current year depreciation expense}}{\text{Prior year PPE, gross}} \times \text{Current year PPE, gross}$$

P&G's 2019 statement of cash flows reports depreciation and amortization expense of $2,824 million. Footnotes report amortization expense in 2019 of $349 million. Thus, we calculate 2019 depreciation expense as $2,475 million ($2,824 million − $349 million). The PPE footnote reports 2018 PPE, gross of $41,487 million, and 2019 PPE, gross of $43,393 million. We calculate a depreciation expense forecast assumption of 6.0% ($2,475 million expense/$41,487 million PPE, gross) and an estimated 2020 depreciation expense of $2,604 million (6.0% × $43,393 million).

PPE, net. Drawing on the forecasted CAPEX and forecasted depreciation above, the PPE, net is forecasted as:

$$\text{Forecasted PPE, net} = \text{Current PPE, net} + \text{Forecasted CAPEX} - \text{Forecasted depreciation expense}$$

Forecasted 2020 PPE, net is $21,995 million, computed as $21,271 million + $3,328 million − $2,604 million.

Intangible Assets Intangible assets, other than goodwill, are typically forecasted to decrease during the year by the amount of amortization (it is common to assume no change in amortization expense).

$$\text{Forecasted intangible assets} = \text{Current year intangible assets} - \text{Forecasted amortization expense}$$

Alternatively, the company might provide guidance. Footnotes to the P&G's FY2019 Form 10-K provide the following schedule of expected amortization expense that we use for its FY2020 forecast. We forecast that intangible assets will decrease by $359 million in FY2020.

Years Ending June 30 ($ millions)	2020	2021	2022	2023	2024
Estimated amortization expense	$359	$309	$290	$278	$267

Long-Term Debt (LTD) Companies report maturities of long-term debt for the next five years in the long-term debt footnote. We use this disclosure to forecast long-term debt:

Forecasted LTD = Current year LTD − Current maturities of LTD

Footnotes to P&G's FY2019 Form 10-K provide the following schedule of maturities of LTD that we use in our forecasts.

Years Ending June 30 ($ millions)	2020	2021	2022	2023	2024
Debt maturities	$3,388	$2,009	$2,840	$2,465	$2,461

P&G's balance sheet does not separately report current maturities of long-term debt. Instead, the current maturities amount is aggregated with other short-term debt and reported as "Debt due within one year." To forecast current maturities, we subtract $3,388 million from debt due within one year to reflect the amount that matures and will be paid in FY2020. We then add $2,009 million, the amount that comes due in FY2021. We subtract $2,009 million from long-term debt to reflect the reclassification from long-term to current.

Retained Earnings We forecast retained earnings as follows.

= Current year retained earnings + Forecasted net income − Forecasted dividends

Dividends. Companies frequently provide guidance as to expected dividends. If not, a common approach is to estimate dividends using the dividend payout ratio.

$$\text{Forecasted dividends} = \frac{\text{Current year dividends}}{\text{Current year net income}} \times \text{Forecasted net income}$$

This method will be less exact if a company reports significant one-time items. In that case, we exclude the one-time item in the payout ratio calculation. P&G's dividend payout ratio for FY2019, computed on earnings before the intangibles impairment expense, is 60.9% ($7,498 million dividends paid in FY2019 divided by $12,311 million in FY2019 net income before intangibles impairment expense). We estimate FY2020 dividends by applying the FY2019 payout ratio to forecasted net income ($11,365 million × 60.9% = $6,921 million). P&G's guidance is for dividends of "$7.5B+" (see the Company Guidance section). The forecasted dividends of $6,921 million are just slightly below that guidance. We include the guidance in our forecast because it is more precise.

Treasury Stock Many companies have multiyear stock repurchase programs, which are disclosed in footnotes or in the MD&A section of the 10-K. Often, in the year-end press release, companies provide guidance and/or disclosures about their planned treasury stock activity. Absent explicit disclosures or guidance, we can forecast future repurchases using historic data, either from the most recent year or by looking for a trend over the past two or three years. For P&G, we use the midpoint of guidance provided by managers and forecast $7B of additional repurchases in FY2020.

The forecasting process estimates the balances of all assets *other than cash*, all liabilities, and all equity accounts. The last step is to compute the amount of cash needed to balance the balance sheet (the *plug*).

Cash Plug (the *plug*) The **plug** is computed as total assets (equal to total liabilities and equity) less all other asset balances. We assess the forecasted cash balance and determine if it deviates from its historical norm. We use the current year cash-to-sales percentage as a *normal* level of cash. This assumes the amount reported in the current balance sheet represents an appropriate level of cash the company needs to conduct its operations.

Estimating the Normal Cash Level P&G's cash balance in 2019 is $4,239 million or 6.3% of 2019 sales. Applying that percentage to our forecasted sales of $70,053 million yields a normal level of cash of $4,413 million ($70,053 million × 6.3%). Our forecasted cash balance of $(1,550) million in Exhibit 12.3 is, therefore, too low.

When Cash Plug Deviates from Norm When the forecasted cash level deviates from the target cash balance, we can consider adjusting the forecasted cash balance in two ways.

- **Cash balance much HIGHER than normal** This indicates the company is generating more cash than expected, most typically from operations. Our forecasts might assume that such excess liquidity can be invested in marketable securities, used to pay down debt, repurchase stock, increase dividend payments, or any combination of these actions.

- **Cash balance much LOWER than normal** This indicates the company is not generating sufficient cash, usually as a result of net losses, significant dividend payments, stock repurchases, and/or operating assets increasing more than operating liabilities; remember, we are assuming no changes in debt and equity levels for our initial forecast. To return cash to normal levels, we might expect the company would borrow money, sell stock, and/or liquidate marketable securities. Under those assumptions, we would adjust the forecasted balance sheet by increasing cash to a normal level and adjust debt or equity to reflect the means by which additional cash was raised. Alternatively, we might expect the company would reduce dividends, cut capital expenditures, slash inventory and/or take other operating action. Raising cash in this way likely has serious costs and, for that reason, we rarely make assumptions of this sort. It is more likely the company would raise cash through investing and financing activities.

In Appendix 12B, we illustrate a method to achieve a target level of cash in our multiyear forecasts. The method involves adding debt to the balance sheet and adjusting interest expense on the income statement as needed.

Maintaining the Capital Structure When we adjust cash by forecasting an increase or decrease in debt and/or stock, we might inadvertently impact the company's capital structure—namely, the proportion of debt and equity. If we assume the company's current capital structure is appropriate, we should attempt to maintain that historic debt-to-equity ratio when we forecast additional borrowing, debt repayment, stock sales, or stock repurchases.

LO3 Review 12-3

Refer to the FY2019 income statement and balance sheet for **General Mills** along with the forecasted FY2020 income statement in Reviews 12-1 and 12-2.

Required
1. Use that information and the following assumptions to forecast General Mills balance sheet for FY2020.
   - Unless noted in other assumptions, all assets and liabilities as a percentage of FY2019 sales remain unchanged.
   - Depreciation expense for FY2020 is $580.1 million.
   - Forecast FY2020 CAPEX as 3.19% of sales.
   - Goodwill remains unchanged.
   - Form 10-K reports that amortization expense for each of the next five fiscal years will be $40 million.
   - Notes payable remain unchanged.
   - Long-term debt footnotes reveal that principal payments due on long-term debt in the next five years follow ($ millions).

Year Ending May	2020	2021	2022	2023	2024
Debt maturities	$1,396.5	$2,114.4	$1,224.1	$1,060.2	$1,750.0

   - There will be no stock repurchases in FY2020.
   - Dividends in FY2020 are forecasted as 67.4% of net income attributable to General Mills' shareholders.
   - Noncontrolling interest will increase by $33.5 million, the amount forecast as noncontrolling interest on the income statement (from Review 12-2).

2. What conclusion do we draw from the forecasted cash balance?

Solution on p. 12-52.

Building Forecasts from the Bottom Up

The sales forecast that we illustrate above relies on company guidance to form assumptions and estimates. An alternative approach that financial analysts typically use relies on information from conference calls with company management and other proprietary data sources. Analysts often prepare separate sales forecasts for the company's business segments and then sum up the segment sales to arrive at the overall sales estimate.

LO4 Prepare forecasts using segment data.

Segment Data

Companies are required to report financial data for each operating segment and to reconcile the segment totals to the reported amounts in the income statement and balance sheet for the company as a whole. Financial analysts frequently develop the sales forecasts as the sum of forecasts for the company's operating segments.[2] P&G's 10-K segment disclosure includes the following table of current and historical data for each of its five operating segments.

---

[2] GAAP defines an **operating segment** as "a component of a public entity that has all of the following characteristics. (1) It engages in business activities from which it may earn revenues and incur expenses (including revenues and expenses relating to transactions with other components of the same public entity). (2) Its operating results are regularly reviewed by the public entity's chief operating decision maker to make decisions about resources to be allocated to the segment and assess its performance. (3) Its discrete financial information is available."

Global Segment Results ($ millions)		Net Sales	Earnings (Loss) from Continuing Operations Before Income Taxes	Net Earnings (Loss) from Continuing Operations	Depreciation and Amortization	Total Assets	Capital Expenditures
Beauty	2019	$12,897	$ 3,282	$ 2,637	$ 272	$ 5,362	$ 634
	2018	12,406	3,042	2,320	236	4,709	766
	2017	11,429	2,546	1,914	220	4,184	599
Grooming	2019	6,199	1,777	1,529	429	20,882	367
	2018	6,551	1,801	1,432	447	22,609	364
	2017	6,642	1,985	1,537	433	22,759	341
Health Care	2019	8,218	1,984	1,519	294	7,708	363
	2018	7,857	1,922	1,283	230	5,254	330
	2017	7,513	1,898	1,280	209	5,194	283
Fabric & Home Care	2019	22,080	4,601	3,518	557	7,620	984
	2018	21,441	4,191	2,708	534	7,295	1,020
	2017	20,717	4,249	2,713	513	6,886	797
Baby, Feminine & Family Care	2019	17,806	3,593	2,734	861	9,271	819
	2018	18,080	3,527	2,251	899	9,682	1,016
	2017	18,252	3,868	2,503	874	9,920	1,197
Corporate	2019	484	(9,168)	(7,971)	411	64,252	180
	2018	497	(1,157)	(133)	488	68,761	221
	2017	505	(1,289)	247	571	71,463	167
Total company	2019	$67,684	$ 6,069	$ 3,966	$2,824	$115,095	$3,347
	2018	66,832	13,326	9,861	2,834	118,310	3,717
	2017	65,058	13,257	10,194	2,820	120,406	3,384

Instead of using only trends in the top line of the income statement, sales growth forecasts are more accurate when they incorporate *all* available data. In P&G's case, its product lines segment disclosures provide a wealth of information that can be used to forecast sales for each operating segment; and then summing the segment forecasts yields top line sales forecasts.

To illustrate, **Morgan Stanley** analysts use both published data (such as the segment disclosures) and proprietary databases to forecast sales growth *by product segment* and *by quarter*. Following is an excerpt from its forecasting spreadsheet for P&G's Beauty segment.

	A	B	BO	BT	BY	CD	CI	CN	CO	CP	CQ	CR	CS
1		Procter & Gamble Co. (PG)											
5		Segment Breakdown	FY2014	FY2015	FY2016	FY2017	FY2018	FY2019	Sep-19E	Dec-19E	Mar-20E	Jun-20E	FY2020E
15		Beauty Care	13,398.0	12,608.0	11,477.0	11,429.0	12,406.0	12,897.0	3,463.2	3,529.0	3,181.4	3,325.8	13,499.5
16		Organic Sales Growth	0.0 %	−1.2 %	0.2 %	3.0 %	6.5 %	8.0 %	5.0 %	4.5 %	4.0 %	4.0 %	4.4 %
17		Volume (Organic)	0.3 %	−2.9 %	−1.9 %	1.3 %	1.5 %	1.7 %	2.0 %	2.0 %	2.0 %	2.0 %	2.0 %
18		Pricing	0.2 %	2.2 %	2.0 %	0.7 %	0.0 %	2.0 %	2.0 %	1.5 %	1.0 %	1.0 %	1.4 %
19		Mix	−0.5 %	−0.5 %	0.3 %	1.3 %	5.0 %	4.3 %	1.0 %	1.0 %	1.0 %	1.0 %	1.0 %
20		FX Impact	−2.2 %	−5.1 %	−5.6 %	−1.8 %	2.2 %	−4.2 %	0.3 %	0.6 %	−0.1 %	0.3 %	0.3 %
21		Acq/Div	0.0 %	−0.3 %	−3.7 %	−2.0 %	0.0 %	0.3 %	0.0 %	0.0 %	0.0 %	0.0 %	0.0 %
22		% Sales Growth	−32.9 %	−5.9 %	−9.0 %	−0.4 %	8.5 %	4.0 %	5.3 %	5.1 %	3.9 %	4.3 %	4.7 %

We see that Morgan Stanley analysts forecast organic sales growth, including the effects of changes in *unit volume*, the effects of expected *price increases,* and the effects, if any, of expected changes in *product mix*. Their forecast includes an expected foreign-currency increase of 0.3% and no acquisition effects for that segment. In sum, Morgan Stanley analysts forecast an increase in net sales of 4.7% for the Beauty segment from $12,897 million to $13,500 million—consisting of the following components.

Organic sales growth	4.4%
Volume (organic)	2.0%
Pricing	1.4%
Mix	1.0%
Foreign exchange impact	0.3%
Acquisitions and divestitures	0.0%
Sales growth	4.7%

Similar estimates are made for the other four operating segments. Top line sales growth estimates then are the sum of sales estimates for the five operating segments along with the corporate entity.

	A	B	BO	BT	BY	CD	CI	CN	CO	CP	CQ	CR	CS
1	Procter & Gamble Co. (PG)												
3													
5	Segment Breakdown		FY2014	FY2015	FY2016	FY2017	FY2018	FY2019	Sep-19E	Dec-19E	Mar-20E	Jun-20E	FY2020E
6	Total Sales		74,401.0	70,752.0	65,299.0	65,058.0	66,832.0	67,684.0	17,718.8	18,519.8	16,987.5	17,682.9	70,909.0
7	Organic Sales Growth		2.6%	1.6%	0.8%	2.2%	1.3%	5.2%	4.0%	3.9%	3.3%	3.2%	3.6%
8	Volume (Organic)		2.4%	-1.0%	-1.2%	2.4%	1.6%	2.3%	2.0%	2.0%	2.1%	2.0%	2.0%
9	Pricing		0.7%	1.7%	1.5%	-0.3%	-1.1%	1.5%	1.6%	1.5%	0.8%	0.8%	1.2%
10	Mix		-0.5%	0.9%	0.2%	0.1%	0.7%	1.3%	0.4%	0.4%	0.3%	0.4%	0.4%
11	FX Impact		-2.5%	-5.9%	-6.2%	-1.9%	1.9%	-3.7%	0.3%	0.6%	-0.1%	0.3%	0.3%
12	Acq/Div		-0.2%	-0.2%	-1.9%	-0.7%	-0.4%	-0.1%	1.9%	1.7%	0.0%	0.0%	0.9%
13	% Sales Growth		-9.9%	-4.9%	-7.7%	-0.4%	2.7%	1.3%	6.2%	6.2%	3.2%	3.4%	4.8%

For FY2020, Morgan Stanley analysts forecast total sales growth of 4.8%. This estimate is about 1 percentage point higher than the assumption we used in our forecast, by using the midpoint of company guidance. The Morgan Stanley assumption (4.8%) includes an estimate for foreign currency effects and acquisitions that the company guidance does not include.

LO4 Review 12-4

Refer to the following information for **General Mills** to answer the requirements. The segment information footnote to General Mills' 2019 10-K reports the following sales for operating units within the company's North America retail segment.

In millions	2019	2018
U.S. Meals & Baking	$3,839.8	$ 3,865.7
U.S. Cereal	2,255.4	2,251.8
U.S. Snacks	2,060.9	2,140.5
U.S. Yogurt and other	906.7	927.4
Canada	862.4	930.0
Total	$9,925.2	$10,115.4

We assume the following estimates for growth in units for each segment.

U.S. Meals & Baking	1.5%
U.S. Cereal	2.0%
U.S. Snacks	(0.5)%
U.S. Yogurt and other	1.0%
Canada	(1.0)%

Required

a. Forecast FY2020 sales for each of the five segments. What will FY2020 sales be for the total U.S. retail segment?

b. What is the overall forecasted growth rate for the total U.S. retail segment?

Solution on p. 12-53.

Appendix 12A: Forecasting the Statement of Cash Flows

LO5 Forecast the statement of cash flows.

Forecasting the statement of cash flows is useful for a number of planning and control activities, including cash management, operating budgets, and capital budgeting decisions (CAPEX). To prepare the forecasted statement of cash flows, we use our forecasts of the income statement and balance sheet and then follow the preparation procedures explained in the statement of cash flow module. That process begins with net income, adds back or deducts any noncash expenses or revenues, and then recognizes the cash flow effect of changes in working capital followed by changes in the remaining asset, liability, and equity items. A common method is to compute changes in each of the line items on the forecasted balance sheet and then classify those changes to either the operating, investing, or financing sections of the forecasted statement of cash flows.

Exhibit 12A.1 shows the forecasted statement of cash flows for **Procter & Gamble**. It reveals operating cash flows of $15,427 million, investing cash outflows of $3,328 million, and a large financing cash outflow of $17,888 million.

Exhibit 12A.1 ■ One-Year Forecast of P&G's Statement of Cash Flows

Statement of Cash Flows
For Fiscal Year Ended 2020

$ millions	Computations	2020 Est.
Cash flow from operating activities		
Net income...............................		$11,573
Add: Depreciation........................		2,604
Add: Amortization........................		359
Change in accounts receivable...........	$4,951 – $5,114	(163)
Change in inventories....................	$5,017 – $5,184	(167)
Change in prepaid expenses and other current.....	$2,218 – $2,312	(94)
Change in accounts payable..............	$11,629 – $11,260	369
Change in accrued other liabilities........	$9,387 – $9,054	333
Change in deferred income taxes.........	$7,145 – $6,899	246
Change in other noncurrent liabilities.....	$10,578 – $10,211	367
Net cash from operating activities........		15,427
Capital expenditures......................	$70,053 × 4.75%	(3,328)
Change in available-for-sale securities....	no change	0
Net cash from investing activities.........		(3,328)
Dividends.................................		(7,500)
Increase in short-term debt...............		(1,379)
Decrease in long-term debt...............		(2,009)
Purchase of treasury shares...............		(7,000)
Net cash from financing activities.........		(17,888)
Net change in cash.......................		(5,789)
Beginning cash...........................		4,239
Ending cash..............................		$ (1,550)

The forecasted statement of cash flows highlights financing cash outflows as the main cause for the forecasted decline in cash. While operating cash flows continue to be strong, P&G's guidance includes plans to continue to repurchase common stock (approximately $7,000 million), pay dividends (approximately $7,500 million), and purchase CAPEX (approximately $3,328 million). In this first forecasting iteration, we forecast a decrease in cash of $(5,789) million, which reduces P&G's cash balance from $4,239 million to $(1,550) million. The drop in cash arises due to the planned outflows for CAPEX, the payment of dividends, and the repurchase of stock with no borrowings forecasted at this point. Such a low cash balance is not plausible. In Appendix 12B, we discuss how to modify the forecasts to derive an appropriate cash balance.

> **Business Insight** ■ Do Currency Fluctuations Affect Cash Flow?
>
> A stronger $US vis-à-vis other world currencies results in less income as foreign currency-denominated revenues are translated into fewer $US. As sales decline, so do profits. Because net income is the first line in the statement of cash flows, it is reasonable to ask whether the profit decline resulting from a strengthening $US implies P&G's cash flows will also decline. If so, we would expect such a decline to affect P&G's stock price. The short answer is that it is unlikely that P&G's cash flows will be greatly affected.
>
> Before companies can consolidate their foreign subsidiaries, the foreign-currency denominated subsidiary income statements, balance sheets, and statements of cash flows must first be translated to $US equivalents. To accomplish this, each financial statement item is multiplied by an exchange rate to yield the $US equivalent. We can think of the translation process as a spreadsheet with the foreign currency-denominated subsidiary financial statements in the first column, the exchange rate in the second, and the $US equivalent financial statements in the third, as the product of the first two columns. There are no transactions involved in this process, so it is reasonable to expect there to be no effect on cash flow from the translation process.
>
> So, why does the forecasted decline in profit not result in a decline in cash flow? P&G's balance sheet also shrinks with the strengthening $US, and the reduction in net assets (recorded as a cash *inflow* in the statement of cash flows) exactly offsets the reduction in profit (recorded as a cash *outflow*), leaving net cash unaffected, just as we would expect given there are no transactions in the translation process.

LO5 Review 12-5

Refer to the FY2019 income statement and balance sheet for **General Mills** along with its forecasted FY2020 income statement and balance sheet in Reviews 12-1, 12-2, and 12-3.

Required
Use that information to prepare the General Mills' forecasted statement of cash flows for FY2020.

Solution on p. 12-54.

Appendix 12B: Multiyear Forecasting with Target Cash and New Debt Financing

Exhibit 12B.1 shows the mechanics to forecast financial statements for more than one year ahead. Forecasting for multiple years proceeds in the same way as for one-year forecasting, illustrated above. Analysts typically need multiyear forecasts to value a firm's equity valuation, assess its ability to repay its debt, and to assign a credit rating. Managers also typically use multiyear forecasts in the planning process, including cash flow budgeting, capital expenditure plans, divestiture decisions, and mergers and acquisitions.

LO6 Prepare multiyear forecasts.

Consistent with the one-year-ahead forecasts, we balance the balance sheet with a "plug" to the cash account. We extend this example to illustrate the process to adjust the cash balance to a "normal" level, in this case by adding debt.

How much cash is "normal"? We assume that the cash-to-sales ratio in the current financial statements represents the company's "target" cash level. That is, we assume the company has made appropriate financing decisions to achieve the optimal level of cash in the current year. For FY2019, the reported cash balance of $4,239 million is 6.3% of reported sales of $67,684. If the company maintains the same level of cash as a percentage of forecasted sales, the target level of cash will be $4,413 (forecasted FY2020 sales of $70,053 × 6.3%). In Exhibit 12.3, our forecasted cash balance is $(1,550) million. Consequently, we assume additional borrowing of $6,000 million (rounded up). This additional borrowing is necessary to achieve the target cash-to-sales percentage of 6.3% because P&G will not generate sufficient cash from operating activities to cover forecasted CAPEX, debt payments, dividend payments, and anticipated repurchases of stock. With additional debt, forecasted interest expense will increase by $51 million ($6,000 million × 1.7%/2), assuming an average interest rate of 1.7% and borrowing evenly over the year. With the additional debt and after tax interest, the forecasted cash balance is $4,408 million, 6.3% of forecasted sales.

To forecast FY2021, we use the same methodology that we use for our one-year forecast. We start by forecasting sales for FY2021, assuming growth will continue to be 3.5%. We assume that expenses increase proportionately, that CAPEX will remain at the same percentage of sales, that dividends will be $7,500 million, and that the company will repurchase $7,000 million of stock. With a target cash-to-sales of 6.3%, we forecast additional borrowings of $4,150 million.

Exhibit 12B.1 ■ Forecast of P&G's FY2020 and FY2021 Income Statements and Balance Sheets

Income Statements ($ millions)	2019 Act.	% of Sales	Computations	2020 Est.	% of Sales	Computations	2021 Est.	% of Sales
Net sales	$67,684	100.0%	$67,684 × 1.035	$70,053	100.0%	$70,053 × 1.035	$72,505	100.0%
Cost of products sold	34,768	51.4%	$70,053 × 51.4%	36,007	51.4%	$72,505 × 51.4%	37,268	51.4%
Selling, general, and administrative expense	19,084	28.2%	$70,053 × 28.2%	19,755	28.2%	$72,505 × 28.2%	20,446	28.2%
Goodwill & indefinite lived intangibles impairment charges	8,345	12.3%	none	0		none	0	0.0%
Operating income	5,487	8.1%	subtotal	14,291	20.4%	subtotal	14,791	20.4%
Interest expense	509	0.8%	computed	534	0.8%	computed	574	0.8%
Interest income	220	0.3%	no change	220	0.3%	no change	220	0.3%
Other nonoperating income, net	871	1.3%	none	0	0.0%	none	0	0.0%
Earnings from continuing operations before income taxes	6,069	9.0%	subtotal	13,977	20.0%	subtotal	14,437	19.9%
Income taxes on continuing operations	2,103	3.1%	$13,977 × 17.5%	2,446	3.5%	$14,437 × 17.5%	2,526	3.5%
Net earnings	3,966	5.9%	subtotal	11,531	16.4%	subtotal	11,911	16.4%
Less: net earnings attributable to noncontrolling interests	69	0.1%	$11,531 × 1.7%	196	0.3%	$11,911 × 1.7%	202	0.3%
Net earnings attributable to Procter & Gamble	$ 3,897	5.8%	subtotal	$11,335	16.2%	subtotal	$11,709	16.1%

Balance Sheets ($ millions)	2019 Act.	% of Sales	Computations	2020 Est.	% of Sales	Computations	2021 Est.	% of Sales
Current assets								
Cash and cash equivalents	$ 4,239	6.3%	Plug	$ 4,408	6.3%	Plug	$ 4,544	6.3%
Available-for-sale investment securities	6,048	8.9%	no change	6,048	8.6%	no change	6,048	8.3%
Accounts receivable	4,951	7.3%	$70,053 × 7.3%	5,114	7.3%	$72,505 × 7.3%	5,293	7.3%
Inventories	5,017	7.4%	$70,053 × 7.4%	5,184	7.4%	$72,505 × 7.4%	5,365	7.4%
Prepaid expenses and other current assets	2,218	3.3%	$70,053 × 3.3%	2,312	3.3%	$72,505 × 3.3%	2,393	3.3%
Total current assets	22,473	33.2%		23,066	32.9%		23,643	32.6%
Property, plant, and equipment, net	21,271	31.4%	$3,328 − $2,604	21,995	31.4%	$3,444 − $2,803	22,636	31.2%
Goodwill	40,273	59.5%	no change	40,273	57.5%	no change	40,273	55.5%
Trademarks and other intangible assets, net	24,215	35.8%	($359)	23,856	34.1%	($309)	23,547	32.5%
Other noncurrent assets	6,863	10.1%	no change	6,863	9.8%	no change	6,863	9.5%
Total assets	**$115,095**	**170.0%**	total	**$116,053**	**165.7%**	total	**$116,962**	**161.3%**
Current liabilities								
Accounts payable	11,260	16.6%	$70,053 × 16.6%	$ 11,629	16.6%	$72,505 × 16.6%	$ 12,036	16.6%
Accrued and other liabilities	9,054	13.4%	$70,053 × 13.4%	9,387	13.4%	$72,505 × 13.4%	9,716	13.4%
Debt due within one year	9,697	14.3%	($3,388) + $2,009	8,318	11.9%	($2,009) + $2,840	9,149	12.6%
Total current liabilities	30,011	44.3%		29,334	41.9%		30,901	42.6%
Long-term debt	20,395	30.1%	$6,000 − $2,009	24,386	34.8%	$4,150 − $2,840	25,696	35.4%
Deferred income taxes	6,899	10.2%	$70,053 × 10.2%	7,145	10.2%	$72,505 × 10.2%	7,396	10.2%
Other noncurrent liabilities	10,211	15.1%	$70,053 × 15.1%	10,578	15.1%	$72,505 × 15.1%	10,948	15.1%
Total liabilities	67,516	99.8%	subtotal	71,443	102.0%	subtotal	74,941	103.4%
Shareholders' equity								
Convertible Class A preferred stock	928	1.4%	no change	928		no change	928	1.5%
Nonvoting Class B preferred stock								
Common stock, stated value $1 per share	4,009	5.9%	no change	4,009	5.7%	no change	4,009	5.5%
Additional paid-in capital	63,827	94.3%	no change	63,827	91.1%	no change	63,827	88.0%
Reserve for ESOP debt retirement	(1,146)	(1.7)%	no change	(1,146)	(1.6)%	no change	(1,146)	(1.6)%
Accumulated other comprehensive income (loss)	(14,936)	(22.1)%	no change	(14,936)	(21.3)%	no change	(14,936)	(20.6)%
Treasury stock, at cost	(100,406)	(148.3)%	($7,000)	(107,406)	(153.3)%	($7,000)	(114,406)	(157.8)%
Retained earnings	94,918	140.2%	$11,335 − $7,500	98,753	141.0%	$11,709 − $7,500	102,962	142.0%
Noncontrolling interest	385	0.6%	+ $196	581	0.8%	+ $202	783	1.1%
Total shareholders' equity	47,579	70.3%	subtotal	44,610	63.7%	subtotal	42,021	58.0%
Total liabilities and shareholders' equity	**$115,095**	**170.0%**	total	**$116,053**	**165.7%**	total	**$116,962**	**161.3%**

Forecasting Sensitivity Analysis Analysts commonly perform a sensitivity analysis of their forecasts. Typically, analysts prepare additional forecasts (characterized as Bull and Bear scenarios) and present these together with their "most likely" scenario forecasts. The forecasted cash flow and resulting stock price estimates are, then, recomputed under these additional assumptions to develop a possible range of stock prices that are included in the analyst's report. We provide an example of this sensitivity analysis in Appendix 12D that provides excerpts from the Morgan Stanley analysis report on P&G following its FY2019 year-end.

LO4 Review 12-6

Refer to the FY2019 income statement and balance sheet for General Mills along with the forecasted FY2020 income statement and balance sheet, in Reviews 12-1, 12-2, and 12-3.

Required

a. Adjust the 2020 forecasted financial statements to:
- Increase the current portion of long-term debt by $700 million so the ending cash balance is at the prior year cash-to-sales target of 2.7%.
- Increase interest expense due to the new debt, calculated as $700 million × (3.4%/2), which is the average new borrowing multiplied by the prior year average interest rate.

b. Forecast the 2021 balance sheet and income statement using the following assumptions:
- Sales will increase by 1.5% in FY2021.
- Operating expenses as a percentage of sales will remain unchanged from FY2020 levels.
- Restructuring, impairment, and other exit costs are expected to be 1.6% of forecasted sales.
- Add $2,100 million of additional short-term debt to achieve the targeted cash balance of approximately 2.7% of sales. Adjust interest by adding a half-year interest on the additional short-term debt using 3.4% with the same adjustment to interest expense that we used for 2020.
- Dividend payments will be 67.4% of forecasted net income attributable to General Mills' shareholders.
- CAPEX will be 3.19% of forecasted sales and depreciation expense will be $588.8 million.
- Current maturities of LTD are $1,224.1 million for 2021.

Solution on p. 12-54.

Appendix 12C: Parsimonious Method for Forecasting NOPAT and NOA

This appendix explains a parsimonious method to obtain forecasts for net operating profit after tax (NOPAT) and for net operating assets (NOA). This method requires three crucial inputs.

1. Sales growth.
2. Net operating profit margin (NOPM); defined in Module 4 as NOPAT divided by sales.
3. Net operating asset turnover (NOAT); defined in Module 4 as sales divided by average NOA. (For forecasting purposes, we define NOAT as sales divided by *year-end* NOA instead of average NOA because we want to forecast year-end values.)

LO7 Apply a parsimonious method for forecasting net operating profit and net operating assets.

Multiyear Forecasting with Parsimonious Method

We use Procter & Gamble's 2019 income statement from Exhibit 12.2, and its 2019 balance sheet from Exhibit 12.3, to determine the following measures. P&G's 2019 income statement includes a pretax goodwill impairment of $8,345 million, which is a nonrecurring item. The Form 10-K reports that the impairment is $8,000 million after-tax; we add this back to calculate a measure of persistent NOPAT. We assume that P&G's statutory tax rate is 22% on nonoperating revenues and expenses.

$ millions	2019
Sales.	$67,684
NOPAT ($5,487 + $8,000 − [$2,103 + ($509 − $220 − $871) × 22%]).	$11,512
NOA ($115,095 − $4,239 − $6,048 − $11,260 − $9,054 − $6,899 − $10,211)*.	$67,384
NOPM ($11,512/$67,384).	17%
NOAT ($67,684/$67,384)*.	1.00

*We use ending balance sheet amounts, rather than average amounts, because we forecast *ending* balance sheet amounts.

Each year's forecasted sales is the prior year sales multiplied successively by (1 + growth rate) and then rounded to whole digits. Consistent with our prior revenue growth rate assumptions for P&G, we define "1 + growth rate" as 1.035 for 2020 onward. NOPAT is computed using forecasted (and rounded) sales each year times the 2019 NOPM of 17%; and NOA is computed using forecasted (and rounded) sales divided by the 2019 NOAT of 1.00. Forecasted numbers for 2020–2023 are in Exhibit 12C.1; supporting computations are in parentheses.

This forecasting process can be continued for any desired forecast horizon. Also, the forecast assumptions such as sales growth, NOPM, and NOAT can be varied by year, if desired. This parsimonious method is simpler than the method illustrated in this module. However, its simplicity forgoes information that can improve forecast accuracy.

Exhibit 12C.1   P&G Parsimonious Method Forecasts of Sales, NOPAT, and NOA

		Horizon Period			
$ millions	Current 2019	2020 Est.	2021 Est.	2022 Est.	2023 Est.
Net sales growth.......		3.5%	3.5%	3.5%	3.5%
Sales (unrounded).....	$67,684	$70,052.94 ($67,684 × 1.035)	$72,504.79 ($70,052.94 × 1.035)	$75,042.46 ($72,504.79 ×1.035)	$77,668.95 ($75,042.46 × 1.035)
Sales (rounded).......	$67,684	$70,053	$72,505	$75,042	$77,669
NOPAT[1].............	$11,512	$11,909 ($70,053 × 17%)	$12,326 ($72,505 × 17%)	$12,757 ($75,042 × 17%)	$13,204 ($77,669 × 17%)
NOA[2]...............	$67,384	$70,053 ($70,053/1.0)	$72,505 ($72,505/1.0)	$75,042 ($75,042/1.0)	$77,669 ($77,669/1.0)

[1] Forecasted NOPAT = Forecasted net sales (rounded) × 2019 NOPM of 17%
[2] Forecasted NOA = Forecasted net sales (rounded) ÷ 2019 NOAT of 1.0

Review 12-7 LO6

Solution on p. 12-55.

Refer to Review 12-1 and the fiscal 2019 income statement and balance sheet for **General Mills** (GIS).
a. The 2019 income statement includes two nonpersistent items: Diverstiture loss and Restructuring. Assume that these are not expected to recur and that the after-tax amounts for these items are $24.4 million and $224.0 million respectively. Adjust net income (after-tax) to eliminate these two one-time items. Use the adjusted net income to calculate NOPAT and NOPM. Assume a marginal tax rate of 23%.
b. Assume a sales growth rate of 1.5% and NOAT of 0.77. Use the parsimonious forecast model to project General Mill's sales, NOPAT, and NOA for 2020 through 2023.

Appendix 12D: Morgan Stanley's Forecast Report on Procter & Gamble

Following is the **Morgan Stanley** analysts' report on Procter & Gamble that the firm issued on July 31, 2018 (pages 9–13 of the report consist of the customary disclosure information typical of analyst reports). *Please note that materials that are referenced herein comprise excerpts from Morgan Stanley research reports. MS has provided their materials here as a courtesy. Therefore, MS and Cambridge do not undertake to advise you of changes in the opinions or information set forth in these materials. These materials should not be relied on as investment advice. These materials are only as current as the publication date of the underlying Morgan Stanley research. For important disclosures, stock price charts, and equity rating histories regarding companies that are the subject of the underlying Morgan Stanley research, see www.morganstanley.com/researchdisclosures.*

Morgan Stanley | RESEARCH

July 31, 2019 10:00 AM GMT

Procter & Gamble Co. | North America

Reiterate OW; PG Results are Head and Shoulders Above Peers

UPDATE

MORGAN STANLEY & CO. LLC

Dara Mohsenian, CFA
EQUITY ANALYST
Dara.Mohsenian@morganstanley.com +1 212 761-6575

Filippo Falorni, CFA
RESEARCH ASSOCIATE
Filippo.Falorni@morganstanley.com +1 212 296-4965

Scott Rotondi
RESEARCH ASSOCIATE
Scott.Rotondi@morganstanley.com +1 212 761-9196

Sydney A Adams
RESEARCH ASSOCIATE
Sydney.Adams@morganstanley.com +1-212-761-1727

Stock Rating	Industry View	Price Target
Overweight	Cautious	$129.00

Robust 4Q topline results support our view that PG's organic sales growth trajectory has sustainably improved, which when combined with inflecting gross margins, should drive above peer EPS growth. Relative valuation vs. HPC peers remains compelling despite stock outperformance. Reiterate OW.

WHAT'S CHANGED

Procter & Gamble Co. (PG.N)	From	To
Price Target	$120.00	**$129.00**

Strong, High Quality Quarter: Following a substantial topline and EPS beat vs. fiscal Q4 consensus, PG's stock rose 4% (vs. the S&P 500 -0.3%), with very strong +7.0% (7.5% un-rounded) organic sales growth in 4Q (vs. +5% market expectations) and a gross margin inflection (+120 bps yoy and 65 bps above consensus) offset by greater than expected reinvestment on the profit line, while EPS was bolstered by below the profit line items, including a lower tax rate. Topline strength was driven by above-consensus sales in nearly every division and was PG's best organic sales growth in 13 years. PG's gross margin increase of +120 bps y-o-y was also the best result so far in US CPG this EPS season (above +110 bps at KMB and +30 bps at CL). Growth was led by Health Care (10%), Fabric and Home Care (10%), and Beauty (8%) but was broad-based with 8 of PG's 10 global categories gaining or holding share and a weighted avg market share gain of +21 bps y-o-y vs 5 bps last quarter and a 7 bp four quarter trailing average. Untracked channel growth was particularly strong with 25% organic sales growth, with e-commerce now 8% of sales mix, and strong club channel trends. Along with broad based strength across PG's portfolio and a confident tone on the growth outlook, PG was constructive on the HPC industry environment given: (a) healthy market topline growth, (b) price realization is improving, evident in PG's results and the HPC industry more broadly, and (c) promotional intensity is down on a y-o-y basis, particularly in the US, where category levels have indexed at 94 vs the prior year (and PG at 92). While pricing will likely dissipate from here as PG cycles increases and as promotion picks up with lower commodities, it sounds like the pricing environment has remained very rational so far. Net, 4Q results give us greater conviction in our call that PG organic topline growth has sustainably rebounded and GM's are inflecting, the

Procter & Gamble Co. (PG.N, PG US)
Household & Personal Care / United States of America

Stock Rating	Overweight
Industry View	Cautious
Price target	$129.00
Shr price, close (Jul 30, 2019)	$120.41
Mkt cap, curr (mm)	$319,251
52-Week Range	$121.75-78.49

Fiscal Year Ending	06/19	06/20e	06/21e	06/22e
ModelWare EPS ($)	4.52	4.86	5.07	5.33
P/E	24.3	24.8	23.7	22.6
EPS ($)§	4.47	4.74	5.05	5.51
Div yld (%)	2.5	2.4	2.5	2.6

Unless otherwise noted, all metrics are based on Morgan Stanley ModelWare framework
§ = Consensus data is provided by Thomson Reuters Estimates
e = Morgan Stanley Research estimates

QUARTERLY MODELWARE EPS ($)

Quarter	2019	2020e Prior	2020e Current	2021e Prior	2021e Current
Q1	1.12	1.21	1.26	1.29	1.32
Q2	1.25	1.34	1.37	1.42	1.43
Q3	1.06	1.09	1.11	1.16	1.16
Q4	1.10	1.08	1.12	1.15	1.17

e = Morgan Stanley Research estimates

Morgan Stanley does and seeks to do business with companies covered in Morgan Stanley Research. As a result, investors should be aware that the firm may have a conflict of interest that could affect the objectivity of Morgan Stanley Research. Investors should consider Morgan Stanley Research as only a single factor in making their investment decision.

For analyst certification and other important disclosures, refer to the Disclosure Section, located at the end of this report.

Morgan Stanley | RESEARCH

UPDATE

key drivers of our OW thesis. We see PG's stock as still compelling here, at a discounted P/E to CL and CLX despite clearly superior LT topline/EPS growth in our minds.

Raising EPS Estimates: Post initial FY20 guidance and strong Q4 results, we are raising FY20 EPS by 3% to $4.86, in the upper half of PG's $4.70-$4.92 range. Our PT increases $9 to $129 due to higher EPS and an increased multiple (26x CY20e) given greater confidence in higher PG growth than peers.

Q4 Details: PG Q4 core EPS of $1.10 was above the $1.05 consensus ($1.06 MSe) and very high quality as large topline upside, on robust +7.5% unrounded (7% rounded) organic sales growth, and a 65 bp GM beat, was mostly offset by greater than expected SG&A, driving an in-line (+0.3%) profit beat vs. consensus. EPS upside was driven by below the profit line items including a lower tax rate that flattered EPS by 3 cents vs our model. Organic sales growth of +7% (or ~7.5% un-rounded) came in far ahead of consensus of +4.3% (and 5% street expectations), while +4.25% two-year average growth also accelerated vs. +2.8% in the first three quarters of 2019. Topline growth was balanced with 3% price, 3% volume, and 2% mix. Pricing improved sequentially, up +3% vs. +2% in 3Q19, +1% in 2Q19, flat in 1Q19 and a -2% y-o-y decline in 2H18. A reported +1.4% topline beat was boosted by better than expected gross margins, which expanded a large +120 bps yoy, including -40 bps of FX, +200 bps from productivity, +160 bps from pricing, -60 bps from commodities, -120 bps of unfavorable product mix and other, and -20 bps of innovation reinvestment. Core SG&A as a % of sales decreased -20 bps yoy (worse than the -100 bps consensus, largely driven by reinvestment), including +30 bps of unfavorable FX, with -190 bps from sales leverage, -140 bps of marketing expense and overhead savings, -100 bps from the gain on Boston real estate, +170 bps from marketing reinvestment, +180 bps from capability investment in sales, R&D, and higher compensation costs, and +30 bps from Merck OTC costs. Net, operating profit beat consensus by ~0.3%, with OM's +132 bps y-o-y, as PG clearly reinvested gross profit upside.

Strong Segment Results: PG results were strong across all segments, with upside vs. consensus in each segment. Beauty was up a strong +8% (volume +1%, price +2%, mix +5%), vs. consensus of +6.8%, with Skin and Personal Care organic sales up +mid-teens driven by growth of the super-premium SK-II brand and Olay Skin Care and increased pricing, while Hair Care organic sales increased +LSD%. Health Care was +10% (volume +3%, price +3%, mix +4%), vs. consensus of +4.6%, with Personal Health Care up mid-teens due to innovation, a late season increase in cough and cold incidents and favorable mix due to higher growth in developed regions and Oral Care up +HSD% on premium innovation and positive mix. Fabric & Home Care was up +10% (volume +5%, price +4%, mix +1%), vs. consensus of +6.0%, with +DD% growth in both Fabric Care and Home Care. Baby, Feminine & Family Care organic sales were up +5% (volume +1%, price +3%, mix +1%) vs. consensus of +1.8%. Baby Care increased +LSD% due to devaluation-related price increases and positive mix from growth of premium products, partially offset by reduced volumes due to increased pricing, competitive activity and category contraction in certain markets, Feminine Care organic sales increased +HSD%, and Family Care organic sales increased +MSD%. Grooming was up +4% (volume -1%, price +3%, mix +1%), vs. consensus of +1.0%.

Initial FY20 Guidance: PG provided initial organic sales growth guidance of +3-4% for FY20, with all-in sales growth of +3-4%, including a modest negative

Morgan Stanley | RESEARCH

UPDATE

impact from FX which is largely offset by a positive impact from acquisitions and divestitures. The company expects +4-9% core EPS growth (wider than the usual range) on a base of $4.52 (implies $4.70-$4.93), which at its midpoint of ~$4.82 is ~1.7% above the prior consensus of $4.74 (MSe $4.72), or at a seemingly more realistic high-end 4% above consensus. PG's earnings guidance incorporates a modest net benefit from commodities, foreign exchange, transportation, and tariffs. PG expects the core effective tax rate for FY20 to be in the range of 17-18%. adjusted free cash flow productivity of 90% or better for FY20, $7.5 billion in dividend, repurchases of $6-8 billion of common shares, and capital spending ar 4.5-5% of sales.

Gillette Impairment: PG took an $8B after-tax non-cash impairment charge to adjust the carrying values of goodwill and trade name intangible assets in the Gillette Shave Care business primarily due to significant currency devaluations that have occurred since the 2005 deal close, as well as negative impacts from market contraction of blades and razors in developed markets due to lower shaving frequency and competitive activity. PG indicated the Shave Care business continues to be a strategic business.

Exhibit 1: PG Organic Sales Growth Accelerated in 4Q19...

Source: Company data, Morgan Stanley Research

Exhibit 2: ...Led By Improving Category Growth and More Moderate Market Share Gains

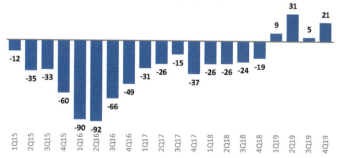

Source: Company data, Morgan Stanley Research

Morgan Stanley | RESEARCH

UPDATE

Risk-Reward: Procter & Gamble (PG)
Risk-Reward Remains Favorable

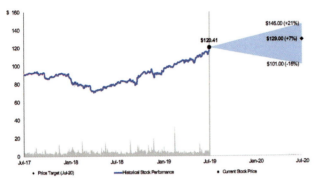

Source: Thomson Reuters, Morgan Stanley Research

Price Target $129
Derived from base case scenario

Bull $146
28x Bull Case CY20e EPS
Topline rebounds to >4.0% organic sales growth. Revenue upside (~125 bps int'l upside and ~100 bps US upside) as PG's marketing/innovation focus drives market share improvement. Cost cutting above our forecast and better than expected price realization drive margin upside, and in turn ~10% EPS growth. Valuation expands to 28x CY20e EPS.

Base $129
26x Base Case CY20e EPS
Improving sales growth + margin expansion. We forecast organic sales growth of ~3.5-4.0% going forward (above HPC peers) led by improving US results on building market share momentum. Better price realization and continued cost savings support ~70 bps of OM expansion/yr, driving HSD% EPS growth. We apply a multiple of 26x to CY20e EPS, a slight premium to PG's 3-yr avg given accelerating fundamentals.

Bear $101
21.5x Bear Case CY20e EPS
US led topline/margin downside. Our US bear case scenario plays out: -80/-50 bps pricing/volume downside along with ~20 bps of margin downside on greater reinvestment. Outside the US, ~125 bps of topline downside and ~50 bps of margin downside drive muted LSD% EPS growth. Valuation contracts to 21.5x CY20e EPS.

Investment Thesis

■ **Topline Momentum Looks Sustainable:** We believe strategy tweaks put in place in recent years are bearing fruit and can accelerate PG topline growth back to the ~3.5-4% range. In the US, improving breadth of performance and reduced promotional intensity give us confidence that market share momentum is sustainable, which, combined with an improving price outlook and greater agility as organizational changes are implemented, supports topline growth above HPC peers.

■ **Improving Margin Outlook:** Following 2 years of FY gross margin declines, we see a FY GM inflection led by improving price realization and a less onerous commodity headwind. When combined with a sizable cost savings program (worth ~15% to annual profit), we see scope for ~100 bps of annual margin expansion in FY20, and in turn HSD% EPS growth delivery over the next several years.

■ **Valuation Looks Compelling on a Relative Basis:** With PG trading at ~25x CY20e EPS, a discount to HPC peers CL and CLX, relative valuation looks compelling considering our call for PG fundamentals to positively inflect after years of underperformance vs. more expensive HPC peers.

Risks to Achieving Price Target

■ Risks include macro pressures, pricing fluctuations, cost-cutting, execution issues, market share vacillations, and currency & commodity volatility.

Exhibit 3: Bear to Bull: Topline Trends Should Be the Key Stock Driver

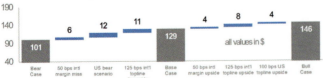

Source: Company data, Morgan Stanley Research estimates

Morgan Stanley | RESEARCH

Exhibit 4: PG Income Statement

Income Statement	FY2013	FY2014	FY2015	FY2016	FY2017	FY2018	Sep-18	Dec-18	Mar-19	Jun-19	FY2019	Sep-19 E	Dec-19 E	Mar-20 E	Jun-20 E	FY2020E	FY2021E	FY2022E
Sales	82,581.0	74,401.0	70,749.0	65,299.0	65,058.0	66,832.0	16,690.0	17,438.0	16,462.0	17,094.0	67,684.0	17,718.8	18,519.8	16,987.5	17,682.9	70,909.0	73,134.5	75,458.8
% Growth	-1.3%	-9.9%	-4.9%	-7.7%	-0.4%	2.7%	0.2%	0.2%	1.1%	3.6%	1.3%	6.2%	6.2%	3.2%	3.4%	4.8%	3.1%	3.2%
% Organic Growth	2.8%	2.6%	1.6%	0.8%	2.2%	1.3%	4.0%	4.0%	5.0%	7.0%	5.2%	4.0%	3.9%	3.3%	3.2%	3.6%	3.2%	3.2%
Cost of Sales	-39,743.0	-38,729.0	-36,537	-32,285	-32,140	-33,707	-8,438.0	-8,796.0	-8,362.0	-8,746.0	-34,342	-8,780.9	-9,156.5	-8,459.1	-8,872.7	-35,269.3	-36,193.4	-37,230.4
% of Sales	48.1%	52.1%	51.6%	49.4%	49.4%	50.4%	50.6%	50.4%	50.8%	51.2%	50.7%	49.6%	49.4%	49.8%	50.2%	49.7%	49.5%	49.3%
% of Sales Bps Change	-245	393	-41	-220	-4	103	150	86	-2	-120	30	-100	-100	-100	-99	-100	-25	-15
Gross Profit	40,373.0	35,672.0	34,212.0	33,014.0	32,918.0	33,125.0	8,252.0	8,642.0	8,100.0	8,348.0	33,342.0	8,937.9	9,363.3	8,528.5	8,810.1	35,639.8	36,941.2	38,228.4
Gross Margin %	48.9%	47.9%	48.4%	50.6%	50.6%	49.6%	49.4%	49.6%	49.2%	48.8%	49.26%	50.4%	50.6%	50.2%	49.8%	50.3%	50.5%	50.7%
Gross Margin Bps Change	-54	-94	41	220	4	-103	-150	-86	2	120	-30	100	100	100	99	100	25	15
SG&A Expense (ex Incremental Restructuring)	-25,166.0	-21,012.0	-20,348	-18,967	-18,761	-19,037	-4,625.0	-4,660.0	-4,823.0	-4,998.0	-19,106	-4,925.3	-5,004.3	-5,002.7	-5,266.9	-20,199.2	-20,550.4	-20,996.0
% of Sales	30.5%	28.2%	28.8%	29.0%	28.8%	28.5%	27.7%	26.7%	29.3%	29.2%	28.2%	27.8%	27.0%	29.4%	29.8%	28.5%	28.1%	27.8%
% Growth	-1.9%	-16.5%	-3.2%	-6.8%	-1.1%	1.5%	-2.5%	-2.6%	3.4%	3.2%	0.4%	6.5%	7.4%	3.7%	5.4%	5.7%	1.7%	2.2%
% of Sales Bps Change	-18	-223	52	29	-21	-35	-77	-78	65	-12	-28	9	30	15	55	26	-39	-27
Operating Income (ex Incremental Restructuring)	15,207.0	14,660.0	13,864.0	14,047.0	14,157.0	14,088.0	3,627.0	3,982.0	3,277.0	3,350.0	14,236.0	4,012.6	4,359.1	3,525.7	3,543.2	15,440.6	16,390.8	17,232.4
Operating Margin	18.4%	19.7%	19.6%	21.5%	21.8%	21.1%	21.7%	22.8%	19.9%	19.6%	21.0%	22.6%	23.5%	20.8%	20.0%	21.8%	22.4%	22.8%
% Growth	-3.2%	-3.6%	-5.4%	1.3%	0.8%	-0.5%	-3.0%	-0.1%	-2.0%	11.0%	1.1%	10.6%	9.5%	7.6%	5.8%	8.5%	6.2%	5.1%
Operating Margin Bps Change	-36	129	-11	192	25	-68	-73	-8	-63	132	-5	91	70	85	44	74	64	42
Interest Expense	-667.0	-710.0	-626.0	-579.0	-465.0	-506.0	-129.0	-138.0	-131.0	-111.0	-509.0	-114.2	-117.1	-116.8	-115.2	-463.3	-499.8	-495.7
Other Non-Operating Income, Net	391.9	308.0	589.0	506.0	506.0	828.0	163.0	162.0	183.5	154.9	663.4	163.0	162.0	183.5	154.9	663.4	663.4	663.4
Pretax Income	14,931.9	14,258.0	13,827.0	13,974.0	14,198.0	14,410.0	3,661.0	4,006.0	3,329.5	3,393.9	14,390.4	4,061.4	4,403.9	3,592.4	3,582.9	15,640.7	16,554.4	17,400.1
Taxes	-3,440.8	-2,949.0	-2,879	-3,437	-3,381	-3,095	-734.0	-712.0	-509.5	-488.9	-2,444	-710.8	-770.7	-628.7	-627.0	-2,737.1	-3,145.3	-3,393.0
Tax Rate	23.0%	20.7%	20.8%	24.6%	23.8%	21.5%	20.0%	17.8%	15.3%	14.4%	17.0%	17.5%	17.5%	17.5%	17.5%	17.5%	19.0%	19.5%
Minority Interests	-90.0	-141.5	-103.0	-96.0	-85.0	-111.0	-12.0	-22.0	-31.0	-4.0	-69.0	-12.0	-22.0	-31.0	-4.0	-69.0	-72.5	-76.1
Net Income	11,401.1	11,167.5	10,845.0	10,441.0	10,732	11,204.0	2,915.0	3,272.0	2,789.0	2,901.0	11,877.0	3,338.7	3,611.2	2,932.7	2,951.9	12,834.6	13,336.6	13,931.0
EPS Diluted (Core)	$3.89	$3.85	$3.76	$3.67	$3.92	$4.22	$1.12	$1.25	$1.06	$1.10	$4.52	$1.26	$1.37	$1.11	$1.12	$4.86	$5.07	$5.33
EPS % Growth	0.9%	-1.2%	-2.2%	-2.4%	6.7%	7.7%	2.5%	4.9%	5.6%	17.1%	7.1%	13.0%	9.6%	5.1%	2.1%	7.6%	4.4%	5.0%
Basic Shares	2,739.7	2,709.8	2,688.7	2,693.7	2,594.8	2,524.6	2491.4	2499.7	2508.3	2498.1	2499.4	2516.4	2510.7	2508.4	2507.3	2,510.7	2,498.3	2,494.6
Diluted Shares	2,930.6	2,904.4	2,883.6	2,844.5	2,740.4	2,656.7	2612.1	2623.0	2637.7	2645.9	2,629.7	2646.4	2640.7	2638.4	2637.3	2,640.6	2,628.3	2,614.6

Source: Company data, Morgan Stanley Research estimates

Morgan Stanley | RESEARCH — UPDATE

Exhibit 5: PG Balance Sheet

Balance Sheet	FY2013	FY2014	FY2015	FY2016	FY2017	FY2018	Sep-18	Dec-18	Mar-19	Jun-19	FY2019	Sep-19 E	Dec-19 E	Mar-20 E	Jun-20 E	FY2020E	FY2021E	FY2022E
Assets																		
Surplus Cash	0.0	0.0	0.0	0.0	0.0	0.0	0.0	0.0	0.0	0.0	0.0	0.0	0.0	0.0	0.0	0.0	0.0	0.0
Cash & Equivalents	5,947.0	8,558.0	6,836.0	7,102.0	5,569.0	2,569.0	2,545.0	3,696.0	2,738.0	4,239.0	4,239.0	4,239.0	4,239.0	4,239.0	4,239.0	4,239.0	4,239.0	4,239.0
Investment Securities		2,128.0	4,767.0	9,568.0	9,281.0	8,708.0	7,085.0	6,048.0	6,048.0	6,048.0	6,048.0	6,048.0	6,048.0	6,048.0	6,048.0	6,048.0	6,048.0
Receivables, Net	6,508.0	6,386.0	4,568.0	4,373.0	4,594.0	5,035.0	5,055.0	5,281.0	5,198.0	4,951.0	4,951.0	5,699.7	5,739.0	5,703.7	5,475.2	5,475.2	5,996.3	6,544.5
Inventories	6,909.0	6,759.0	4,979.0	4,716.0	4,624.0	4,738.0	5,182.0	5,281.0	5,358.0	5,017.0	5,017.0	5,392.6	5,497.4	5,420.2	5,089.7	5,089.7	5,391.7	5,718.0
Deferred Income Taxes	948.0	846.1	1,356.0	1,507.0	0.0	0.0	0.0	0.0	0.0	0.0	0.0	0.0	0.0	0.0	0.0	0.0	0.0	0.0
Prepaid Expenses and Other Current Assets	3,678.0	6,909.9	7,140.0	9,838.0	2,139.0	2,046.0	1,876.0	1,978.0	1,933.0	2,218.0	2,218.0	1,876.0	1,978.0	1,933.0	2,218.0	2,218.0	2,218.0	2,218.0
Total Current Assets	23,990.0	31,617.0	29,646.0	33,782.0	26,494.0	23,330.0	23,346.0	24,431.0	22,312.0	22,473.0	22,473.0	23,253.4	23,501.4	23,343.9	23,069.9	23,069.9	23,892.9	24,767.6
PP&E, Net	21,666.0	22,304.0	20,268.0	19,385.0	19,893.0	20,600.0	20,590.0	20,822.0	20,993.0	21,271.0	21,271.0	21,713.8	21,731.4	21,726.3	21,679.6	21,679.6	21,910.4	21,979.5
Goodwill, Net	55,188.0	52,832.0	42,430.0	44,350.0	44,699.0	45,175.0	45,225.0	46,932.0	46,753.0	40,273.0	40,273.0	40,273.0	40,273.0	40,273.0	40,273.0	40,273.0	40,273.0	40,273.0
Other Intangible Assets, Net	31,572.0	31,715.0	31,715.0	24,527.0	24,187.0	23,902.0	23,919.0	25,947.0	25,836.0	24,215.0	24,215.0	24,215.0	24,215.0	24,215.0	24,215.0	24,215.0	24,215.0	24,215.0
Other Assets	6,847.0	5,798.0	5,436.0	5,092.0	5,133.0	5,313.0	5,360.0	5,555.0	5,779.0	6,863.0	6,863.0	6,863.0	6,863.0	6,863.0	6,863.0	6,863.0	6,863.0	6,863.0
Total Assets	139,263.0	144,266.0	129,495.0	127,136.0	120,406.0	118,310.0	118,440.0	123,687.0	121,673.0	115,095.0	115,095.0	116,320.1	116,583.8	116,421.2	116,100.5	116,100.5	117,154.4	118,098.1
Liabilities																		
Short-Term Debt	0.0	0.0	0.0	0.0	0.0	0.0	0.0	0.0	0.0	0.0	0.0	1,853.2	1,618.3	1,722.0	743.2	743.2	586.0	203.0
Notes and Loan Payable	12,432.0	15,606.0	12,021.0	11,653.0	13,554.0	10,423.0	10,508.0	12,113.0	8,911.0	9,697.0	9,697.0	9,697.0	9,697.0	9,697.0	9,697.0	9,697.0	9,697.0	9,697.0
Current Portion of Long-Term Debt	8,777.0	8,461.0	8,257.0	9,325.0	9,632.0	10,344.0	10,243.0	10,266.0	10,207.0	11,260.0	11,260.0	10,659.3	10,686.7	10,325.5	11,423.2	11,423.2	11,693.2	11,996.8
Accounts Payable	8,828.0	9,659.0	9,512.0	9,792.0	7,024.0	7,470.0	8,469.0	8,868.0	9,252.0	9,054.0	9,054.0	8,849.3	9,270.0	9,411.5	9,224.4	9,224.4	9,343.8	9,465.1
Accrued and Other Liabilities																		
Total Current Liabilities	30,037.0	33,726.0	29,790.0	30,770.0	30,210.0	28,237.0	29,220.0	31,247.0	28,370.0	30,011.0	30,011.0	31,698.8	31,272.0	31,155.9	31,087.8	31,087.8	31,320.1	31,361.9
Long-Term Debt	19,111.0	19,811.0	18,329.0	18,945.0	18,038.0	20,863.0	20,779.0	21,514.0	21,359.0	20,395.0	20,395.0	20,395.0	20,395.0	20,395.0	20,395.0	20,395.0	20,395.0	20,395.0
Deferred Income Taxes	10,827.0	11,537.0	18,326.0	9,113.0	8,126.0	6,163.0	6,179.0	6,872.0	6,951.0	6,899.0	6,899.0	6,899.0	6,899.0	6,899.0	6,899.0	6,899.0	6,899.0	6,899.0
Other Liabilities	10,579.0	8,487.0	0.0	10,325.0	8,254.0	10,164.0	9,758.0	9,611.0	9,441.0	10,211.0	10,211.0	10,211.0	10,211.0	10,211.0	10,211.0	10,211.0	10,211.0	10,211.0
Total Liabilities	70,554.0	73,561.0	66,445.0	69,153.0	64,628.0	65,427.0	65,936.0	69,244.0	66,121.0	67,516.0	67,516.0	68,603.8	68,777.0	68,660.9	68,592.8	68,592.8	68,825.1	68,866.9
Shareholders' Equity																		
Preferred Stock	1,137.0	1,128.0	1,128.0	1,043.0	1,010.0	1,010.0	1,010.0	1,010.0	1,010.0	1,010.0	1,010.0	1,010.0	1,010.0	1,010.0	1,010.0	1,010.0	1,010.0	1,010.0
Common Stock	4,009.0	4,009.0	4,009.0	4,009.0	4,009.0	4,009.0	4,009.0	4,009.0	4,009.0	4,009.0	4,009.0	4,009.0	4,009.0	4,009.0	4,009.0	4,009.0	4,009.0	4,009.0
Additional Paid-In Capital	63,538.0	63,538.0	63,638.0	63,617.0	63,513.0	63,513.0	63,513.0	63,513.0	63,513.0	63,513.0	63,513.0	62,513.0	63,513.0	63,513.0	63,513.0	63,513.0	63,513.0	63,513.0
Retained Earnings	80,197.0	84,656.0	88,214.0	88,167.0	96,189.0	100,083.0	101,145.0	102,567.0	103,498.0	104,462.0	104,462.0	105,895.2	107,605.2	108,638.3	109,615.4	109,615.4	115,001.2	120,706.5
Accumulated Other Comprehensive Income (Loss)	-7,499.0	-4,461.0	-11,070.0	-15,330.0	-14,478.0	-14,263.0	-14,452.0	-13,184.0	-11,756.0	-18,943.0	-18,943.0	-18,239.0	-17,858.4	-17,438.0	-16,917.7	-16,917.7	-13,991.9	-11,035.4
Reserve for ESOP Debt Retirement	-1,352.0	-1,346.0	-1,289.0	-1,248.0	-1,248.0	-1,248.0	-1,248.0	-1,248.0	-1,248.0	-1,248.0	-1,248.0	-1,248.0	-1,248.0	-1,248.0	-1,248.0	-1,248.0	-1,248.0
Treasury Stock	-71,966.0	-77,648.0	-82,252.0	-82,900.0	-93,925.0	-100,929.0	-102,181.0	-102,932.0	-104,182.0	-105,932.0	-105,932.0	-107,932.0	-109,932.0	-111,432.0	-113,182.0	-113,182.0	-120,682.0	-128,432.0
Minority Interests	645.0	729.0	666.0	708.0	708.0	708.0	708.0	708.0	708.0	708.0	708.0	708.0	708.0	708.0	708.0	708.0	708.0	708.0
Total Shareholders' Equity	68,709.0	70,705.0	63,050.0	57,983.0	55,778.0	52,883.0	52,504.0	54,443.0	55,552.0	47,579.0	47,579.0	47,716.3	47,806.8	47,760.3	47,507.7	47,507.7	48,329.3	49,231.2
Total Liabilities & SE	139,263.0	144,266.0	129,495.0	127,136.0	120,406.0	118,310.0	118,440.0	123,687.0	121,673.0	115,095.0	115,095.0	116,320.1	116,583.8	116,421.2	116,100.5	116,100.5	117,154.4	118,098.1

Source: Company data, Morgan Stanley Research estimates

Morgan Stanley | RESEARCH

Exhibit 6: PG Cash Flow Statement

Cash Flow	FY2013	FY2014	FY2015	FY2016	FY2017	FY2018	Sep-18	Dec-18	Mar-19	Jun-19	FY2019	Sep-19 E	Dec-19 E	Mar-20 E	Jun-20 E	FY2020E	FY2021E	FY2022E
Net Income	11,401.1	11,167.5	10,845.0	10,441.0	10,732.0	11,204.0	2,915.0	3,272.0	2,789.0	2,901.0	11,877.0	3,338.7	3,611.2	2,932.7	2,951.9	12,834.6	13,336.6	13,931.0
Adjustments:																		
Depreciation and Amortization	2982.0	3141.0	3134.0	3078.0	2820.0	2834.0	643.0	650.0	711.0	820.0	2824.0	677.2	699.0	755.6	862.2	2994.1	3096.4	3175.7
Stock-Based Compensation Expense	346.0	360.0	337.0	335.0	351.0	395.0	102.0	79.0	118.0	216.0	515.0	104.0	90.6	120.4	220.3	525.3	535.8	546.5
Deferred Income Taxes	-307.0	-44.0	-803.0	-815.0	-601.0	-1844.0	34.0	3.0	-61.0	-387.0	-411.0	0.0	0.0	0.0	0.0	0.0	0.0	0.0
Other	-607.1	463.5	-265.0	572.0	-268.0	-1173.0	-65.0	-65.0	-13.0	-101.0	-244.0	342.0	-102.0	45.0	-285.0	0.0	0.0	0.0
Changes in A/L																		
Receivables	-415.0	87.0	349.0	35.0	-322.0	-177.0	-475.0	77.0	-151.0	273.0	-276.0	-748.7	-39.2	35.3	-524.2	-524.2	-521.1	-548.3
Inventories	-225.0	8.0	313.0	116.0	71.0	-188.0	-494.0	-37.0	-70.0	362.0	-239.0	-375.6	-104.8	77.2	228.5	-72.7	-302.0	-326.3
A/P, Accrued and Other Liabilities	1253.0	1.0	928.0	1285.0	-149.0	1385.0	933.0	208.0	300.0	415.0	1856.0	-805.4	448.1	-219.7	910.7	333.6	389.4	424.8
Other Operating Assets and Liabilities	445.0	-1226.0	-230.0	388.0	119.0	2431.0	-26.0	-180.0	-108.0	-348.0	-660.0	0.0	0.0	0.0	0.0	0.0	0.0	0.0
Cash Provided by Operations	14,873.0	13,958.0	14,608.0	15,435.0	12,753.0	14,867.0	3,567.0	4,007.0	3,517.0	4,151.0	15,242.0	2,532.2	4,592.9	3,746.5	5,219.1	16,090.7	16,535.2	17,203.5
Cash Flows from Investing Activities:																		
Capital Expenditures	-4,008.0	-3,848.0	-3,736.0	-3,314.0	-3,384.0	-3,717.0	-1090.0	-701.0	-752.0	-814.0	-3,347.0	-1,120.0	-716.7	-750.5	-815.5	-3,402.7	-3,327.2	-3,244.8
Proceeds from Asset Sales	584.0	570.0	4498.0	432.0	571.0	269.0	9.0	9.0	4.0	372.0	394.0	0.0	0.0	0.0	0.0	0.0	0.0	0.0
Payment for Acquisitions	-1145.0	-24.0	-3784.0	-166.0	-16.0	-109.0	-237.0	-3611.0	-95.0	-2.0	-3945.0	0.0	0.0	0.0	0.0	0.0	0.0	0.0
Other	-1,726.0	-805.0	132.0	-2,507.0	-2,860.0	46.0	443.0	458.0	1,416.0	1,091.0	3,408.0							
Cash Used for Investing Activities	-6,295.0	-4,107.0	-2,890.0	-5,575.0	-5,689.0	-3,511.0	-865.0	-3845.0	573.0	647.0	-3,490.0	-1120.0	-716.7	-750.5	-815.5	-3,402.7	-3,327.2	-3,244.8
Cash Flows from Financing Activities:																		
Change in Short-Term Debt	3,406.0	3304.0	-2590.0	418.0	2727.0	-3437.0	24.0	1182.0	-3038.0	-383.0	-2215.0	1893.2	-274.9	103.6	-978.7	743.2	-157.2	-383.0
Change in Long-Term Debt	-1,421.0	239.0	-1374.0	1703.0	-1328.0	2199.0	0.0	1390.0	-24.0	32.0	1398.0	0.0	0.0	0.0	0.0	0.0	0.0	0.0
Dividends Paid	-6,519.0	-6,911.0	-7287.0	-7436.0	-7,236.0	-7,310.0	-1853.0	-1850.0	-1858.0	-1937.0	-7,498.0	-1905.4	-1901.3	-1899.6	-1974.8	-7,681.2	-7,950.9	-8,225.7
Purchase of Treasury Shares	-5,966.0	-6,005.0	-4,604.0	-5,734.0	-5,204.0	-7,004.0	-1252.0	-751.0	-1250.0	-1750.0	-5,003.0	-2000.0	-2000.0	-1500.0	-1750.0	-7,250.0	-7,500.0	-7,750.0
Proceeds From Stock Options, Other	3,449.0	2,094.0	2,816.0	2,672.0	2,473.0	1,177.0	425.0	1,061.0	1,104.0	734.0	3,324.0	600.0	300.0	300.0	300.0	1,500.0	2,400.0	2,400.0
Cash Used for Financing Activities	-7,071.0	-7,279.0	-13,029.0	-9,213.0	-8,568.0	-14,375.0	-2,656.0	1,032.0	-5,066.0	-3,304.0	-9,994.0	-1,412.2	-3,876.2	-2,996.0	-4,403.6	-12,688.0	-13,208.1	-13,958.7
Cash Provided by Discontinued Operations	0.0	0.0	0.0	0.0	0.0	0.0	0.0	0.0	0.0	0.0	0.0	0.0	0.0	0.0	0.0	0.0	0.0	0.0
Exchange Rate Effect on Cash / Other	4.0	39.0	-411.0	-381.0	-29.0	19.0	-70.0	-43.0	18.0	7.0	-88.0	0.0	0.0	0.0	0.0	0.0	0.0	0.0
Net Increase (Decrease) in Cash and Cash Equivs	1511.0	2611.0	-1722.0	266.0	-1533.0	-3000.0	-24.0	1151.0	958.0	1501.0	1670.0	0.0	0.0	0.0	0.0	0.0	0.0	0.0
Cash and Cash Equivs, Beg	4,436.0	5,947.0	8,558.0	6,836.0	7,102.0	5,569.0	2,569.0	2,545.0	3,096.0	2,738.0	2,569.0	4,239.0	4,239.0	4,239.0	4,239.0	4,239.0	4,239.0	4,239.0
Cash and Cash Equivs, End	5,947.0	8,558.0	6,836.0	7,102.0	5,569.0	2,569.0	2,545.0	3,696.0	2,738.0	4,239.0	4,239.0	4,239.0	4,239.0	4,239.0	4,239.0	4,239.0	4,239.0	4,239.0

Source: Company data, Morgan Stanley Research estimates

Questions

Q12-1. Identify at least two applications that use forecasted financial statements.

Q12-2. In what order do we normally forecast the financial statements? Explain the logic of this order.

Q12-3. Why do we begin the forecasting process by adjusting the financial statements?

Q12-4. What does the concept of financial statement articulation mean in the forecasting process?

Q12-5. Analysts commonly perform a sensitivity analysis following preparation of financial forecasts. What is meant by sensitivity analysis, and why is it important?

Q12-6. Cash is forecast as the last item on the balance sheet. Why is this the case?

Q12-7. In addition to recent revenues trends, what other types and sources of information can we use to help us forecast revenues?

Q12-8. Why do we refine the forecasted cash balance? How might we deal with a cash balance that is much too low compared with the company's normal cash level?

Q12-9. Identify at least three sources of additional information we could use to refine our forecast assumptions.

Q12-10. Capital expenditures are usually an important cash outflow for a company, and they figure prominently into forecasts of net operating assets. What sources of information about capital expenditures can we draw upon?

Assignments with the logo in the margin are available in *BusinessCourse*. See the Preface of the book for details.

Mini Exercises

LO2

Automatic Data Procession (ADP)

M12-11. Forecast an Income Statement

ADP reports the following income statement.

AUTOMATIC DATA PROCESSING INC.
Statement of Consolidated Earnings
For Year Ended June 30, 2019, $ millions

Total revenues	$14,175.2
Operating expenses	7,145.9
Systems development and programming costs	636.3
Depreciation and amortization	304.4
Total cost of revenues	8,086.6
Selling, general, and administrative expenses	3,064.2
Interest expense	129.9
Total expenses	11,280.7
Other (income) expense, net	(111.1)
Earnings before income taxes	3,005.6
Provision for income taxes	712.8
Net earnings	$ 2,292.8

Forecast ADP's 2020 income statement assuming the following income statement relations. All percentages (other than total revenue growth and provision for income taxes) are based on historic percent of total revenues.

Total revenues growth	13%
Depreciation and amortization	$460.5 million
Interest expense	No change
Other (income) expense, net	No change
Income tax rate	25%

M12-12. Forecast an Income Statement

Seagate Technology reports the following income statement for fiscal 2019.

LO2
Seagate Technology PLC (STX)

SEAGATE TECHNOLOGY PLC	
Consolidated Statement of Income	
For Year Ended June 28, 2019, $ millions	
Revenue	$10,390
Cost of revenue	7,458
Product development	991
Marketing and administrative	453
Amortization of intangibles	23
Restructuring and other, net	(22)
Total operating expenses	8,903
Income from operations	1,487
Interest income	84
Interest expense	(224)
Other, net	25
Other expense, net	(115)
Income before income taxes	1,372
(Benefit) provision for income taxes	(640)
Net income	$ 2,012

Forecast Seagate's 2020 income statement assuming the following income statement relations ($ millions).

Revenue growth	5%
Cost of revenue	71.8% of revenue
Product development	9.5% of revenue
Marketing and administrative	4.4% of revenue
Amortization of intangibles	No change
Restructuring and other, net	$0
Interest income	No change
Interest expense	No change
Other, net	No change
Income tax rate	21%

M12-13. Forecast an Income Statement

Following is the income statement for Medtronic PLC.

LO2
Medtronic PLC (MDT)

Consolidated Statement of Income ($ millions) For Fiscal Year Ended	April 26, 2019
Net sales	$30,557
Costs and expenses	
Cost of products sold	9,155
Research and development expense	2,330
Selling, general, and administrative expense	10,418
Amortization of intangible assets	1,764
Restructuring charges, net	198
Certain litigation charges	166
Other operating expense, net	258
Operating profit (loss)	6,268
Other nonoperating income, net	(373)
Interest expense	1,444
Income (loss) before income taxes	5,197
Income tax provision	547
Net income (loss)	4,650
Net (income) loss attributable to noncontrolling interests	(19)
Net income (loss) attributable to Medtronic	$ 4,631

Use the following assumptions to prepare a forecast of the company's income statement for FY2020.

Net sales increase	8%
Cost of products sold	30.8% of net sales
Research and development expense	7.6% of net sales
Selling, general, and administrative expense	34.1% of net sales
Amortization of intangible assets	5.8% of net sales
Restructuring charges, net	75% of 2019 restructuring expense
Certain litigation charges	$150 million
Other operating expense, net	No change in $ amount
Interest expense	No change in $ amount
Income tax provision	15% of pretax income
Income attributable to noncontrolling interests	No change

M12-14. Adjust the Cash Balance   LO3

The forecast of the income statement and balance sheet for Next Generation yields the following.

$ millions	2019 Actual	2020 Est.
Cash and cash equivalents	$ 4,558	$ 6,127
Net sales	42,668	43,552
Marketable securities	5,980	5,980
Long-term debt	21,930	21,485
Treasury stock	(4,561)	(4,811)

Required
a. Does forecasted cash deviate from the normal level for this company?
b. Is the deviation in part *a* large enough to require adjustment? Explain.
c. Suggest three ways to adjust the forecasted cash balance.
d. If we used marketable securities to adjust the cash balance, what would be the adjusted forecast for marketable securities?
e. If we used treasury stock to adjust the cash balance, what would be the adjusted forecast for treasury stock?

M12-15. Adjust the Cash Balance   LO3

We obtain the following 2020 forecasts of selected financial statement line items for Journey Company.

$ millions	2019 Actual	2020 Est.
Net sales	$708,554	$740,439
Marketable securities	67,096	62,096
Long-term debt	346,558	308,437
Treasury stock (deducted from equity)	51,174	51,174
Cash generated by operations		57,696
Cash used for investing		(14,908)
Cash used for financing		(54,660)
Total net change in cash		(11,872)
Cash at beginning of period		51,141
Cash at end of period		$ 39,269

Required
a. Does forecasted cash deviate from the normal level for this company?
b. Is the deviation in part *a* large enough to require adjustment? Explain.
c. Identify three ways to adjust the forecasted cash balance.
d. Complete the following statement of cash flows *assuming long-term debt is used* to adjust the forecasted cash balance.

Cash generated by operations	
Cash used for investing	
Cash used for financing	_____
Total change in cash	
Cash at beginning of period	_____
Cash at end of period	======

e. Complete the following statement of cash flows *assuming marketable securities are used* to adjust the forecasted cash balance.

```
Cash generated by operations . . . . . . .
Cash used for investing . . . . . . . . . . . .
Cash used for financing . . . . . . . . . . . .
Total change in cash. . . . . . . . . . . . . . .        _____
Cash at beginning of period . . . . . . . . .
Cash at end of period . . . . . . . . . . . . .          _____
```

M12-16. Forecast the Balance Sheet

Following is the balance sheet for **Medtronic PLC** for FY2019 ended April 26, 2019.

LO3
Medtronic PLC (MDT)

Consolidated Balance Sheet ($ millions)	April 26, 2019
Current assets	
Cash and cash equivalents.	$ 4,393
Investments.	5,455
Accounts receivable, less allowances of $190	6,222
Inventories, net	3,753
Other current assets	2,144
Total current assets.	21,967
Property, plant, and equipment, net	4,675
Goodwill	39,959
Other intangible assets, net	20,560
Tax assets	1,519
Other assets.	1,014
Total assets	$89,694
Current liabilities	
Current debt obligations	$ 838
Accounts payable	1,953
Accrued compensation	2,189
Accrued income taxes.	567
Other accrued expenses.	2,925
Total current liabilities	8,472
Long-term debt	24,486
Accrued compensation and retirement benefits	1,651
Accrued income taxes	2,838
Deferred tax liabilities	1,278
Other liabilities	757
Total liabilities	39,482
Shareholders' equity	
Ordinary shares	0
Additional paid-in capital.	26,532
Retained earnings	26,270
Accumulated other comprehensive loss.	(2,711)
Total shareholders' equity.	50,091
Noncontrolling interests	121
Total equity	50,212
Total liabilities and equity	$89,694

Required

Use the following assumptions to forecast the company's balance sheet for FY2020.

Forecasted FY2020 net income including noncontrolling interest	$4,927 million
Forecasted FY2020 net sales	$33,002 million
Accounts receivable, less allowance	20.4% of net sales
Inventories, net	12.3% of net sales
Other current assets	7% of net sales
Goodwill	No change
Tax assets	5% of net sales
Other assets	3.3% of net sales
Accounts payable	6.4% of net sales
Accrued compensation (current liability)	7.2% of net sales
Accrued compensation and retirement benefits (noncurrent liability)	No change
Accrued income taxes (current liability)	1.9% of net sales
Other accrued expenses	9.6% of net sales
Accrued income taxes (noncurrent liability)	9.3% of net sales
Deferred tax liabilities	4.2% of net sales
Other liabilities	2.5% of net sales
Ordinary shares	No change
Accumulated other comprehensive loss	No change
Net income attributable to noncontrolling interest	$19 million
Dividends in FY2020	$2,853 million
CAPEX in FY2019 (to be forecast as % of net sales)	$1,134 million
Depreciation expense in FY2020	$950 million
Amortization expense in FY2020	$1,914 million
Debt due in FY2020	$838 million
Debt due in FY2021	$2,058 million

M12-17. Adjust the Income Statement

Following is information from the tax footnote from the 2018 10-K for **Honeywell International**.

Honeywell International Inc. (HON)

Years Ended December 31	2018	2017	2016
The U.S. federal statutory income tax rate is reconciled to our effective income tax rate as follows:			
U.S. federal statutory income tax rate	21.0%	35.0%	35.0%
Taxes on non-U.S. earnings	0.2	(12.8)	(8.0)
U.S. state income taxes	1.6	1.4	1.1
Reserves for tax contingencies	0.3	1.6	1.2
Employee share-based payments	(0.7)	(2.9)	(2.0)
U.S. tax reform	(5.8)	56.0	—
Reduction on taxes on unremitted earnings	(14.2)	—	—
Separation tax costs	5.5	—	—
All other items—net	0.9	(1.1)	(2.5)
	8.8%	77.2%	24.8%

The **effective tax rate for 2018** was lower than the U.S. federal statutory rate of 21% primarily attributable to internal restructuring initiatives that resulted in a reduction of accrued withholding taxes of approximately $1.1 billion related to unremitted foreign earnings. In addition, we recorded a tax benefit of approximately $440 million as a reduction to our 2017 provisional estimate of impacts from what is commonly referred to as the U.S. Tax Cuts and Jobs Act.

The effective tax rate for 2017 was higher than the U.S. federal statutory rate of 35% primarily from the estimated impacts of U.S. Tax Reform of approximately $3.8 billion, partially offset by lower tax rates on non-U.S. earnings.

a. What adjustments, if any, should we consider before forecasting Honeywell's 2020 income?
b. Adjust Honeywell's effective tax rate for each of the three years to reflect persistent factors.

M12-18. Refine Assumptions for PPE Forecast

Refer to the **Medtronic PLC** financial information in E12-25 (pertaining to 2019 fiscal year ended April 26, 2019).

Required

a. Use the financial statements along with the additional information below to forecast property, plant and equipment, net for fiscal year ended April 2020.

$ millions	April 27, 2018 Actual	April 26, 2019 Actual	April 2020 Forecast
Net sales..........................	$29,953	$30,557	$33,002
CAPEX.............................	1,068	1,134	
Depreciation expense................	821	895	
Property, plant, and equipment, gross	10,259	10,920	

b. Suppose the company discloses in a press release that accompanies its year-end SEC filing that anticipated CAPEX for fiscal year ended April 2020 is $1.5 billion. Use this guidance to refine your forecast of property, plant and equipment, net for fiscal year ended April 2020.

M12-19. Refine Assumptions for Dividend and Retained Earnings Forecast

Refer to the **Medtronic PLC** financial information in E12-25 for the fiscal year ended April 26, 2019.

Required

a. Use the financial statements along with the additional information below to forecast retained earnings for the fiscal year ended April 2020.

Forecasted net income to Medtronic shareholders for fiscal 2020.............	$4,908 million
Dividends to Medtronic shareholders in fiscal 2019.......................	2,693 million

b. Suppose the MD&A section of the Form 10-K and additional guidance from the company reveals the following additional information. "Ordinary cash dividends declared and paid totaled 50.0 cents per share for each quarter of fiscal year 2019."

At year end April 26, 2019, the company had 1,340,697,595 shares issued and outstanding. Use this information to refine your forecast of retained earnings for the fiscal year ended April 2020. Why might the two forecasted amounts differ? Which is more accurate?

M12-20. Use Segment Information to Refine Sales Forecast

To forecast sales growth for **Best Buy** for the fiscal year ended February 2, 2019, we begin with the following historical sales information.

$ millions	2015	2016	2017	2018	2019
Net sales.................	$40,339	$39,528	$39,403	$42,151	$42,879

Required

a. Determine the sales-growth rate (in percentage) for each of the years 2016 to 2019.
b. If we were to use the 2019 growth to forecast 2020 sales, what rate would we use?
c. The annual report reveals the fiscal year ended February 2018 included a 53rd week (as is common for retailers, every four years). Use this information to refine the sales-growth rates for 2018 and 2019. (*Hint:* Consider multiplying sales for a 53-week year by 52/53 to get an apples-to-apples comparison with numbers from 52-week years.)

Exercises

LO2, 3
Automatic Data Processing (ADP)

E12-21. Analyze, Forecast, and Interpret Income Statement and Balance Sheet
Following are the income statement and balance sheet of **ADP Inc.**

AUTOMATIC DATA PROCESSING INC.
Statement of Consolidated Earnings
For Year Ended June 30, 2019, $ millions

Total revenues	$14,175.2
Operating expenses	7,145.9
Systems development and programming costs	636.3
Depreciation and amortization	304.4
Total cost of revenues	8,086.6
Selling, general, and administrative expenses	3,064.2
Interest expense	129.9
Total expenses	11,280.7
Other (income) expense, net	(111.1)
Earnings before income taxes	3,005.6
Provision for income taxes	712.8
Net earnings	$ 2,292.8

AUTOMATIC DATA PROCESSING INC.
Balance Sheet

$ millions	June 30, 2019
Current assets	
Cash and cash equivalents	$ 1,949.2
Accounts receivable, net	2,439.3
Other current assets	519.6
Total current assets before funds held for clients	4,908.1
Funds held for clients	29,434.2
Total current assets	34,342.3
Long-term receivables, net	23.8
Property, plant and equipment, net	764.2
Capitalized contract cost, net	2,428.5
Other assets	934.4
Goodwill	2,323.0
Intangible assets, net	1,071.5
Total assets	$41,887.7
Current liabilities	
Accounts payable	$ 125.5
Accrued expenses and other current liabilities	1,759.0
Accrued payroll and payroll-related expenses	721.1
Dividends payable	340.1
Short-term deferred revenues	220.7
Obligations under reverse repurchase agreements	262.0
Income taxes payable	54.8
Total current liabilities before client funds obligations	3,483.2
Client funds obligations	29,144.5
Total current liabilities	32,627.7
Long-term debt	2,002.2
Other liabilities	798.7
Deferred income taxes	659.9
Long-term deferred revenues	399.3
Total liabilities	36,487.8

continued

AUTOMATIC DATA PROCESSING INC.
Balance Sheet

$ millions	June 30, 2019
Shareholders' equity	
Preferred stock, $1.00 par value: Authorized, 0.3 shares; issued, none	
Common stock, $0.10 par value: Authorized, 1,000.0 shares;	
issued, 638.7 shares; outstanding 434.2 shares	63.9
Capital in excess of par value	1,183.2
Retained earnings	17,500.6
Treasury stock, at cost: 204.5 shares	(13,090.5)
Accumulated other comprehensive loss	(257.3)
Total stockholders' equity	5,399.9
Total liabilities and stockholders' equity	$41,887.7

a. Forecast ADP's 2020 income statement and balance sheet using the following relations ($ millions). Assume total revenues grow by 13% in 2020. All other percentages (other than sales growth and provision for income taxes) are based on historic percent of total revenues.
- CAPEX for 2020 will be 1.1% of total revenue, and depreciation will be $184.4 million.
- Goodwill, long-term debt, preferred stock, common stock, and Accumulated other comprehensive loss will not change for the year.
- The company will acquire intangibles equal to 2.9% of total revenues and will record amortization expense of $276.1 million.
- Income taxes will be 25% of pretax income and income taxes payable will be 7.7% of 2020 tax expense.
- The company will award $167.3 million of stock-based compensation, which increases Capital in excess of par value by the same amount. Assume that the company routinely includes this form of compensation in operating expenses each year.
- The company will continue its stock repurchases. ADP will repurchase $750 million of treasury stock.
- Dividends will be $1,389.4 in 2020, and dividends payable will be 26.3% of dividends.

b. What does the forecasted adjustment to balance the accounting equation from part *a* reveal to us about the forecasted cash balance and related financing needs of the company? Explain.

E12-22. Forecast the Statement of Cash Flows

Refer to the **ADP Inc.** financial information in E12-21. Prepare a forecast of FY2020 statement of cash flows.

LO5
Automatic Data Processing (ADP)

E12-23. Analyze, Forecast, and Interpret Both Income Statement and Balance Sheet

Following are the income statement and balance sheet of **Seagate Technology** for fiscal 2019.

LO2, 3
Seagate Technology PLC (STX)

SEAGATE TECHNOLOGY PLC
Consolidated Statement of Income
For Year Ended June 28, 2019 ($ millions)

Revenue	$10,390
Cost of revenue	7,458
Product development	991
Marketing and administrative	453
Amortization of intangibles	23
Restructuring and other, net	(22)
Total operating expenses	8,903
Income from operations	1,487
Interest income	84
Interest expense	(224)
Other, net	25
Other expense, net	(115)
Income before income taxes	1,372
(Benefit) provision for income taxes	(640)
Net income	$ 2,012

SEAGATE TECHNOLOGY PLC
Consolidated Balance Sheet
June 28, 2019 ($ millions)

Current assets	
Cash and cash equivalents	$2,220
Accounts receivable, net	989
Inventories	970
Other current assets	184
Total current assets	4,363
Property, equipment and leasehold improvements, net	1,869
Goodwill	1,237
Other intangible assets, net	111
Deferred income taxes	1,114
Other assets, net	191
Total assets	$8,885
Current liabilities	
Accounts payable	$1,420
Accrued employee compensation	169
Accrued warranty	91
Accrued expenses	552
Total current liabilities	2,232
Long-term accrued warranty	104
Long-term accrued income taxes	4
Other noncurrent liabilities	130
Long-term debt, less current portion	4,253
Total liabilities	6,723
Shareholders' equity	
Ordinary shares— par value $0.0001, 2.6 billion shares authorized, 1,340,697,595 and 1,354,218,154 shares issued and outstanding, respectively	—
Additional paid-in capital	6,545
Accumulated other comprehensive loss	(34)
Accumulated deficit	(4,349)
Total shareholders' equity	2,162
Total liabilities and shareholders' equity	$8,885

a. Forecast Seagate Technology's 2020 income statement and balance sheet using the forecast assumptions, which are expressed as a percentage of revenue unless otherwise indicated.

Accounts receivable, net	9.5%
Inventories	9.3%
Other current assets	1.8%
Deferred income taxes	10.7%
Other assets, net	1.8%
Accounts payable	13.7%
Accrued employee compensation	1.6%
Accrued warranty	0.9%
Accrued expenses	5.3%
Long-term accrued warranty	1.0%
Other noncurrent liabilities	1.3%

- Assume that revenue will grow by 5%, and the tax rate will be 21%.
- Forecast no change in the following income statement accounts: Amortization of intangibles, Interest income, Interest expense, and Other, net.
- Forecast no change in the following balance sheet accounts: Goodwill, Long-term accrued income taxes, Long-term debt, less current portion, Ordinary shares, and Accumulated other comprehensive loss.
- Assume that in 2020, CAPEX will be 5.8% of revenue, and depreciation expense will be 5.4% of Property, equipment and leasehold improvements, gross at the start of the year, which was $9,835 million.

- Assume that in 2020, the company awards $99 million of stock-based compensation which increases Additional paid-in capital by the same amount. Assume that the company routinely includes this form of compensation in operating expenses each year.
- The company has a dividend payout ratio of 35.4% of net income.

b. What does the forecasted adjustment to balance the accounting equation from part *a* reveal to us about the forecasted cash balance and related financing needs of the company? Explain.

E12-24. Forecast the Statement of Cash Flows

Refer to the **Seagate Technology (STX)** financial information from E12-23. Prepare a forecast of its FY2020 statement of cash flows.

LO5
Seagate Technology PLC (STX)

E12-25. Forecast Income Statement and Balance Sheet

Following are the income statement and balance sheet for **Medtronic PLC**.

LO2, 3
Medtronic PLC (MDT)

Consolidated Statement of Income ($ millions) For Fiscal Year Ended	April 26, 2019
Net sales.	$30,557
Costs and expenses	
Cost of products sold	9,155
Research and development expense	2,330
Selling, general, and administrative expense	10,418
Amortization of intangible assets	1,764
Restructuring charges, net	198
Certain litigation charges	166
Other operating expense, net	258
Operating profit (loss)	6,268
Other nonoperating income, net	(373)
Interest expense	1,444
Income (loss) before income taxes	5,197
Income tax provision	547
Net income (loss)	4,650
Net (income) loss attributable to noncontrolling interests	(19)
Net income (loss) attributable to Medtronic	$ 4,631

Consolidated Balance Sheet ($ millions)	April 26, 2019
Current assets	
Cash and cash equivalents	$ 4,393
Investments	5,455
Accounts receivable, less allowances of $190	6,222
Inventories, net	3,753
Other current assets	2,144
Total current assets	21,967
Property, plant, and equipment, net	4,675
Goodwill	39,959
Other intangible assets, net	20,560
Tax assets	1,519
Other assets	1,014
Total assets	$89,694
Current liabilities	
Current debt obligations	$838
Accounts payable	1,953
Accrued compensation	2,189
Accrued income taxes	567
Other accrued expenses	2,925
Total current liabilities	8,472

continued

continued from previous page

Consolidated Balance Sheet ($ millions)—continued	April 26, 2019
Long-term debt	24,486
Accrued compensation and retirement benefits	1,651
Accrued income taxes	2,838
Deferred tax liabilities	1,278
Other liabilities	757
Total liabilities	39,482
Shareholders' equity	
Ordinary shares	0
Additional paid-in capital	26,532
Retained earnings	26,270
Accumulated other comprehensive loss	(2,711)
Total shareholders' equity	50,091
Noncontrolling interests	121
Total equity	50,212
Total liabilities and equity	$89,694

Required

a. Use the following assumptions to prepare a forecast of the company's income statement and balance sheet for fiscal year 2020, ended in April 2020.

Income Statement assumptions	
Net sales increase	8%
Cost of product sold	30.0% of net sales
Research and development expense	7.6% of net sales
Selling, general, and administrative expense	34.1% of net sales
Amortization of intangible assets	5.8% of net sales
Restructuring charges, net	75% of 2019 expense
Certain litigation charges	$150 million
Other operating expense, net	No change
Interest expense	No change
Income tax provision	15% of pre-tax income
Income to noncontrolling interests	No change
Balance sheet assumptions	
Accounts receivable, less allowances	20.4% of net sales
Inventories, net	12.3% of net sales
Other current assets	7% of net sales
Goodwill	No change
Tax assets	5% of net sales
Other assets	3.3% of net sales
Accounts payable	6.4% of net sales
Accrued compensation (current liability)	7.2% of net sales
Accrued income taxes (current liability)	1.9% of net sales
Accrued income taxes (noncurrent liability)	9.3% of net sales
Other accrued expenses	9.6% of net sales
Accrued compensation and retirement benefits (noncurrent liability)	No change
Deferred tax liabilities	4.2% of net sales
Other liabilities	2.5% of net sales
Ordinary shares	No change
Accumulated other comprehensive loss	No change
Net income attributable to noncontrolling interest	$19 million
Dividends in FY2020	$2,853 million
CAPEX in FY2019, forecast CAPEX at historic % of net sales	$1,134 million
Depreciation expense in FY2020	$950 million
Amortization expense in FY2020	$1,914 million
Debt due in FY2020	$838 million
Debt due in FY2021	$2,058 million

b. What does the forecasted adjustment to balance the accounting equation from part *a* reveal to us about the forecasted financing needs of the company? Explain.

E12-26. Forecast the Statement of Cash Flows
Refer to the **Medtronic PLC** financial information in E12-25.

Required
Use the information to forecast Medtronic's statement of cash flows for the fiscal year ended April 2020.

E12-27. Refine Cash Balance and Consider Capital Structure
Consider the following actual 2019 data along with forecasted 2020 data for selected balance sheet and income statement numbers.

$ millions	FY2019 Actual	FY2020 Est.
Net sales	$29,009	$32,102
Total assets	14,592	16,051
Total liabilities	8,755	9,923
Total equity	5,837	6,128
Cash	2,918	4,378
Marketable securities	730	730
Treasury stock	(2,189)	(2,627)

Required
a. Calculate the company's normal cash level as a percentage of net sales.
b. Determine the amount of adjustment needed to return cash to a normal level. Is an adjustment warranted? Explain.
c. Compute the liabilities-to-equity ratio for both years. What do we observe?
d. Adjust marketable securities so the forecasted cash balance is at its normal level. What affect does this have on the forecasted liabilities-to-equity ratio?
e. Adjust long-term debt so the forecasted cash balance is at its normal level. What effect does this have on the forecasted liabilities-to-equity ratio?
f. Adjust treasury stock so the forecasted cash balance is at its normal level. What effect does this have on the forecasted liabilities-to-equity ratio?
g. Adjust both long-term debt and marketable securities so as to adjust the forecasted cash balance. In so doing, make sure we preserve the company's liabilities-to-equity ratio. (*Hint:* Use "Goal Seek" under the "What-If Analysis" in Excel to determine the proportion of long-term debt versus treasury stock needed to ensure the forecasted liabilities-to-equity ratio remains at its historical level.)
h. Adjust both long-term debt and treasury stock so as to adjust the forecasted cash balance. In so doing, make sure we preserve the company's liabilities-to-equity ratio. (*Hint:* Use "Goal Seek" under the "What-If Analysis" in Excel to determine the proportion of long-term debt versus treasury stock needed to ensure the forecasted liabilities-to-equity ratio remains at its historical level.)

E12-28. Use Segment Disclosures to Forecast Income Statement
Following are revenue and cost of revenue numbers for **Thermo Fisher Scientific**.

THERMO FISHER SCIENTIFIC INC. Consolidated Statement of Income For Year Ended December 31 ($ millions)	2018	2017
Revenues		
Product revenues	$18,868	$17,374
Service revenues	5,490	3,544
Total revenues	24,358	20,918

continued

continued from previous page

THERMO FISHER SCIENTIFIC INC. Consolidated Statement of Income		
For Year Ended December 31 ($ millions)	2018	2017
Costs and operating expenses		
Product cost of revenues	9,682	8,975
Service cost of revenues	3,819	2,495
Total cost of revenues	13,501	11,470
Selling, general and administrative expenses	6,057	5,504
Research and development expenses	967	887
Restructuring and other costs, net	50	97
Total costs and operating expenses	20,575	17,958
Operating income	3,783	2,960
Other expense, net	(521)	(531)
Income from continuing operations before income taxes	3,262	2,429
Income tax expense	324	201
Income from continuing operations	2,938	2,228
Loss from discontinued operations	—	(3)
Net income	$ 2,938	$ 2,225

Required

a. Use the historic growth in total revenues (from 2017 to 2018) rounded to three decimal places, to forecast *total* revenue for 2019. Use the historic rate of total cost of revenues to total revenues to forecast *total* cost of revenues. Other forecast assumptions follow:

Selling, general and administrative expenses	24.9% of total revenues
Research and development expenses	4.0% of total revenues
Restructuring and other costs, net	$0
Other expense, net	No change
Income tax expense	23% of pretax income

b. Refine your forecast by using the separate historic growth in product revenues and service revenues (from 2017 to 2018) rounded to three decimal places, to estimate 2019 product and service revenues respectively for 2019. Also, use the historic growth in cost of revenues for each segment to forecast separate segment cost of revenues. Assume other forecast assumptions are as in part *a*.

c. Do the two forecasts differ significantly between part *a* and *b*? Which forecasted income statement do we believe is more accurate?

LO4 **E12-29. Use Segment Disclosures to Forecast Revenue**

Honeywell International Inc. (HON)

Following are 2017 and 2018 revenue data for **Honeywell International**'s four segments. Use these data to forecast its 2019 revenue.

Honeywell International Segment Sales and Business-Unit Sales by Segment		
$ millions	2018	2017
Aerospace sales		
Commercial aviation original equipment	$ 2,833	$ 2,475
Commercial aviation aftermarket	5,373	5,103
Defense and space	4,665	4,053
Transportation systems	2,622	3,148
Total aerospace sales	$15,493	$14,779
Honeywell building technologies sales		
Homes	$ 3,928	$ 4,482
Buildings	5,370	5,295
Total Honeywell building technologies sales	$ 9,298	$ 9,777

continued

continued from previous page

Honeywell International Segment Sales and Business-Unit Sales by Segment		
$ millions	2018	2017
Performance materials and technologies sales		
UOP Russell LLP	$ 2,845	$ 2,753
Process solutions	4,981	4,795
Advanced materials	2,848	2,791
Total performance materials and technologies sales	$10,674	$10,339
Safety and productivity solutions sales		
Safety	$ 2,278	$ 2,169
Productivity solutions	4,059	3,470
Total safety and productivity solutions sales	$ 6,337	$ 5,639
Total consolidated sales	$41,802	$40,534

a. Calculate historic (year-on-year) sales growth for each business unit, segment, and total consolidated sales. Calculate the rate to 4 decimal places (e.g. 2.15%).
b. Use the historic growth in Total consolidated sales (from 2017 to 2018) to estimate total consolidated sales for 2019.
c. Refine the sales forecast by using the sales growth rates for each of the four segments (from 2017 to 2018) to estimate 2019 sales for each segment. Determine a forecast for total consolidated sales for 2019.
d. Refine the sales forecast further by using the sales growth rates for each of the business units within each of the four segments. This means we use the separate historic growth for each line item in the table to estimate 2019 total consolidated sales.
e. Which approach do we believe is more accurate in forecasting total consolidated sales?

E12-30. Projecting NOPAT and NOA Using Parsimonious Forecasting Method
Following are **Target**'s sales, net operating profit after tax (NOPAT), and net operating assets (NOA) for its year ended February 2, 2019 ($ millions).

LO7
Target Corporation (TGT)

Sales	$75,356
Net operating profit after tax (NOPAT)	3,264
Net operating assets (NOA)	21,016

Use the parsimonious method to forecast Target's sales, NOPAT, and NOA for years ended February 2020 through 2023 using the following assumptions.

Sales growth per year	3.6%
Net operating profit margin (NOPM)	4.3%
Net operating asset turnover (NOAT), based on NOA at February 2, 2019	3.59

E12-31. Projecting NOPAT and NOA Using Parsimonious Forecasting Method
Following are **Logitech**'s sales, net operating profit after tax (NOPAT), and net operating assets (NOA) for its fiscal year ended March 31, 2019 ($ thousands).

LO7

Logitech Inc. (LOGI)

Net sales	$2,788,322
Net operating profit after tax (NOPAT)	211,362
Net operating assets (NOA)	571,823

Use the parsimonious method to forecast Logitech's sales, NOPAT, and NOA for fiscal years ended March 31, 2020 through 2023 using the following assumptions.

Net sales growth per year	7.00%
Net operating profit margin (NOPM)	7.58%
Net operating asset turnover (NOAT), based on NOA at fiscal year-end	4.88

Problems

LO2, 3, 4, 5
Costco Wholesale Corporation (COST)

P12-32. Forecast the Income Statement, Balance Sheet, and Statement of Cash Flows
Following are fiscal year financial statements of Costco.

COSTO WHOLESALE CORP
Consolidated Statements of Income

For Year Ended ($ millions)	Sep. 1, 2019	Sep. 2, 2018
Net sales.	$149,351	$138,434
Membership fees	3,352	3,142
Total revenue	152,703	141,576
Merchandise costs	132,886	123,152
Selling, general and administrative.	14,994	13,876
Preopening expenses.	86	68
Operating income.	4,737	4,480
Interest expense.	(150)	(159)
Interest income and other, net	178	121
Income before income taxes	4,765	4,442
Provision for income taxes	1,061	1,263
Net income including noncontrolling interests	3,704	3,179
Net income attributable to noncontrolling interests.	(45)	(45)
Net income attributable to Costco	$ 3,659	$ 3,134

COSTO WHOLESALE CORP
Consolidated Balance Sheets

In millions, except par value	Sep. 1, 2019	Sep. 2, 2018
Current Assets		
Cash and cash equivalents.	$ 8,384	$ 6,055
Short-term investments.	1,060	1,204
Receivables, net	1,535	1,669
Merchandise inventories.	11,395	11,040
Other current assets	1,111	321
Total current assets.	23,485	20,289
Property and Equipment		
Land	6,417	6,193
Buildings and improvements	17,136	16,107
Equipment and fixtures.	7,801	7,274
Construction in progress.	1,272	1,140
Gross property and equipment.	32,626	30,714
Less accumulated depreciation and amortization	(11,736)	(11,033)
Net property and equipment.	20,890	19,681
Other assets	1,025	860
Total assets	$45,400	$40,830

continued

continued from previous page

COSTO WHOLESALE CORP
Consolidated Balance Sheets

In millions, except par value	Sep. 1, 2019	Sep. 2, 2018
Current Liabilities		
Accounts payable	$11,679	$11,237
Accrued salaries and benefits	3,176	2,994
Accrued member rewards	1,180	1,057
Deferred membership fees	1,711	1,624
Current portion of long-term debt	1,699	90
Other current liabilities	3,792	2,924
Total current liabilities	23,237	19,926
Long-term debt, excluding current portion	5,124	6,487
Other liabilities	1,455	1,314
Total liabilities	29,816	27,727
Equity		
Preferred stock $.01 par value; 100,000,000 shares authorized; no shares issued and outstanding	—	—
Common stock $0.01 par value; 900,000,000 shares authorized; 439,625,000 and 438,189,000 shares issued and outstanding	4	4
Additional paid-in capital	6,417	6,107
Accumulated other comprehensive loss	(1,436)	(1,199)
Retained earnings	10,258	7,887
Total Costco stockholders' equity	15,243	12,799
Noncontrolling interests	341	304
Total equity	15,584	13,103
Total liabilities and equity	$45,400	$40,830

Required

Forecast Costco's income statement, balance sheet, and statement of cash flows for the year ended September 1, 2020. Combine all property and equipment accounts into Net property and equipment. What do the forecasts imply about Costco's financing needs in 2020?

Forecasts assumptions

Forecast Net sales *and* Membership fees using their respective historical growth rates (2018 to 2019). Forecast the following as a percentage of Net sales:

- Merchandise costs
- Merchandise inventories
- Accrued member rewards
- Receivables, net
- Accounts payable
- Forecast income tax as 23% of pretax income

Forecast Deferred membership fees as a percentage of Membership fees.

Assume no change in the balance of the following:

- Preopening expenses
- Interest expense
- Interest income
- Net income attributable to noncontrolling interest
- Short-term investments
- Preferred stock
- Common stock
- Accumulated other comprehensive loss

Debt maturing in fiscal 2020 and 2021 is $1,699 million and $1,094 million, respectively.
The company anticipates repurchasing $250 million in common stock in fiscal 2020.
The 2019 statement of cash flows reports the following:

- Depreciation expense of $1,492 million
- Dividends of $1,038 million (to forecast 2020 dividends, use the 2019 dividend payout ratio as a percentage of net income attributable to Costco shareholders)
- Stock-based compensation (a noncash expense that is included in SG&A expense and is added to Additional paid-in capital) of $595 million
- CAPEX of $2,998 million

Forecast all other items as a percentage of total revenues.
Note: Round historical rates to three decimal places. For example, round 0.04556 to 4.6%.

LO2, 3, 5 **P12-33. Forecast the Income Statement, Balance Sheet, and Statement of Cash Flows**
Following are the financial statements of Victoria Inc.

VICTORIA INC.
Consolidated Income Statements

For Year Ended December 31 ($ millions)	2019	2018
Revenues	$32,376	$30,601
Cost of sales	17,405	16,534
Gross profit	14,971	14,067
Research and development expense	3,278	3,213
Operating overhead expense	7,191	6,679
Total selling and administrative expense	10,469	9,892
Interest expense, net	19	28
Other (income) expense, net	(140)	(58)
Income before income taxes	4,623	4,205
Income tax expense	863	932
Net income	$ 3,760	$ 3,273

VICTORIA INC.
Consolidated Balance Sheets

December 31 ($ millions)	2019	2018
Current assets		
Cash and equivalents	$ 3,138	$ 3,852
Short-term investments	2,319	2,072
Accounts receivable, net	3,241	3,358
Inventories	4,838	4,337
Prepaid expenses and other current assets	1,489	1,968
Total current assets	15,025	15,587
Property, plant and equipment, net	3,520	3,011
Identifiable intangible assets, net	281	281
Goodwill	131	131
Deferred income taxes and other assets	2,439	2,587
Total assets	$21,396	$21,597
Current liabilities		
Current portion of long-term debt	$ 44	$ 107
Notes payable	1	74
Accounts payable	2,191	2,131
Accrued liabilities	3,037	3,949
Income taxes payable	85	71
Total current liabilities	5,358	6,332
Long-term debt	2,010	1,079
Deferred income taxes and other liabilities	1,770	1,479
Total liabilities	9,138	8,890
Shareholders' equity		
Class A convertible common stock	0	0
Class B common stock	3	3
Capital in excess of stated value	7,786	6,773
Accumulated other comprehensive income	318	1,246
Retained earnings	4,151	4,685
Total shareholders' equity	12,258	12,707
Total liabilities and shareholders' equity	$21,396	$21,597

Required

Forecast Victoria's 2020 income statement, balance sheet, and statement of cash flows.
- Round the revenue growth rate to the nearest whole percent.
- Round forecasts to $ millions.
- Assume no change for interest expense, net, other (income) expense, net, short-term investments, goodwill, notes payable, all classes of common stock, capital in excess of stated value, and accumulated other comprehensive income.
- For 2019, capital expenditures are $1,143 million, depreciation expense is $649 million, amortization expense is $13 million, and dividends are $1,022 million. Forecast CAPEX as a percentage of revenue. Forecast depreciation and amortization as a percentage of beginning-year PPE, net and beginning-year intangibles, respectively. Forecast dividends as a percentage of net income.
- Footnotes reveal that the current portion of long-term debt due in 2021 is $6 million.
- Estimate forecast assumptions for all other balance sheet and income statement items as a percentage of Revenues, rounded to three decimal places (for example, Inventories/Revenues is 0.14943 or 14.9%).
- Assume tax expense is 18.7% of pretax income.

What do the forecasts imply about the company's cash balance and related financing needs for the upcoming year?

P12-34. Two-Year-Ahead Forecast of Financial Statements

Following are the financial statements of **Target Corporation** from its fiscal year ended February 2, 2019.

LO6

Target Corporation (TGT)

TARGET CORPORATION
Consolidated Statements of Financial Position

For Fiscal Years Ended ($ millions)	Feb. 2, 2019	Feb. 3, 2018
Assets		
Cash and cash equivalents	$1,556	$2,643
Inventory	9,497	8,597
Other current assets	1,466	1,300
Total current assets	12,519	12,540
Property and equipment		
Land	6,064	6,095
Buildings and improvements	29,240	28,131
Fixtures and equipment	5,912	5,623
Computer hardware and software	2,544	2,645
Construction-in-progress	460	440
Accumulated depreciation	(18,687)	(18,398)
Property and equipment, net	25,533	24,536
Operating lease assets	1,965	1,884
Other noncurrent assets	1,273	1,343
Total assets	$41,290	$40,303
Liabilities and shareholders' investment		
Accounts payable	$9,761	$8,677
Accrued and other current liabilities	4,201	4,094
Current portion of long-term debt and other borrowings	1,052	281
Total current liabilities	15,014	13,052
Long-term debt and other borrowings	10,223	11,117
Noncurrent operating lease liabilities	2,004	1,924
Deferred income taxes	972	693
Other noncurrent liabilities	1,780	1,866
Total noncurrent liabilities	14,979	15,600
Shareholders' investment		
Common stock	43	45
Additional paid-in capital	6,042	5,858
Retained earnings	6,017	6,495
Accumulated other comprehensive loss	(805)	(747)
Total shareholders' investment	11,297	11,651
Total liabilities and shareholders' investment	$41,290	$40,303

TARGET CORPORATION
Consolidated Statements of Operations

12 Months Ended ($ millions)	Feb. 2, 2019	Feb. 3, 2018	Jan. 28, 2017
Total revenue	$75,356	$72,714	$70,271
Cost of sales	53,299	51,125	49,145
Selling, general and administrative expenses	15,723	15,140	14,217
Depreciation and amortization (exclusive of depreciation included in cost of sales)	2,224	2,225	2,045
Operating income	4,110	4,224	4,864
Net interest expense	461	653	991
Net other (income) expense	(27)	(59)	(88)
Earnings from continuing operations before income taxes	3,676	3,630	3,961
Provision for income taxes	746	722	1,295
Net earnings from continuing operations	2,930	2,908	2,666
Discontinued operations, net of tax	7	6	68
Net earnings	$ 2,937	$ 2,914	$ 2,734

Required
Forecast Target's income statements and balance sheets for the fiscal years ended February 2020 and 2021. Combine the forecasted property and equipment accounts into one account, titled Property and equipment, net. For cost of goods sold and for selling, general and administrative expenses, use the historic percent of revenue for forecasts. Use the following assumptions and data.

Assumptions ($ millions)	
Inventory as % Total revenue	12.6%
Other current assets as % Total revenue	1.9%
Operating lease assets as % Total revenue	2.6%
Other noncurrent assets as % Total revenue	1.7%
Accounts payable as % Total revenue	13.0%
Accrued and other current liabilities as % Total revenue	5.6%
Noncurrent operating lease liabilities	No change
Deferred income taxes as % Total revenue	1.3%
Other noncurrent liabilities as % Total revenue	2.4%
Common stock	No change
Additional paid-in capital	No change
Accumulated other comprehensive loss	No change
CAPEX/Current period total revenue	4.70%
Dividends for year ended February 2019	$1,335
Dividend payout	45.5%
Forecasted depreciation expense for year ended February 2020	$2,565
Forecasted depreciation expense for year ended February 2021	$2,778
Amortization expense	$0
Net interest expense	No change
Net other (income) expense	No change
Stock buybacks per year	$0
Tax rate (as % pretax income)	20%
Long term debt, current portion at February 2019	$1,052
Long term debt, current portion at February 2020	$1,002
Long-term debt, current portion at February 2021	$1,094

P12-35. Sensitivity Analysis of Forecasted Income Statement **LO1, 2**

Following is the income statement for **Sun Savers Inc.** for the year ended December 31, 2019.

Consolidated Statements of Operations			
For Year Ended December 31 ($ thousands)	2019	2018	2017
Net sales.	$3,578,995	$3,391,187	$3,309,616
Cost of sales.	2,659,728	2,566,246	2,444,984
Gross profit.	919,267	824,941	864,632
Operating expenses			
Research and development	130,593	143,969	134,300
Selling, general, and administrative	255,192	253,827	270,261
Production startup	16,818	5,146	2,768
Restructuring and asset impairments	—	—	86,896
Total operating expenses	402,603	402,942	494,225
Operating income	516,664	421,999	370,407
Foreign currency (loss) gain, net	(6,868)	(1,461)	893
Interest income.	22,516	18,030	16,752
Interest expense, net	(6,975)	(1,982)	(1,884)
Other expense, net.	(5,502)	(4,485)	(5,189)
Income before taxes and equity in earnings of unconsolidated affiliates	519,835	432,101	380,979
Income tax benefit (expense)	6,156	(31,188)	(30,098)
Equity in earnings (loss) of unconsolidated affiliates, net of tax	20,430	(4,949)	(163)
Net income	$ 546,421	$ 395,964	$ 350,718

Required

a. Compute the effective tax rate for Sun Savers for each of the three years presented (to four decimal places such as 0.1234 or 12.34%). What do we observe? What might explain this rate?

b. Use the following assumptions to forecast the 2020 income statement.

Net sales growth	6%
Cost of sales	74.0% of net sales
Research and development	3.6% of net sales
Selling, general, and administrative	7.1% of net sales
Production startup	0.5% of net sales
Restructuring and asset impairments	$0
Foreign currency (loss) gain, net	$0
Interest income, Interest expense, net, and Other expense, net	No change in $
Income tax benefit (expense)	Effective rate for 2019
Equity in earnings (loss) of unconsolidated affiliates, net of tax	Increase by 10% over FY2019

c. Compute the percent change in net income from actual 2019 to the 2020 forecasted net income.

d. Perform a sensitivity analysis by changing the effective tax rate and seeing the change in net income. Instead of using the 2019 effective tax rate, use the average effective tax rate that prevailed over the 2017 and 2018 period. Again, compute the tax rate to four decimal places. Compute the percent change in net income from actual 2019 to the 2020 forecasted net income. How sensitive is net income to the change in tax rate?

e. Perform a sensitivity analysis by changing the growth rate for net sales. Forecast the income statement for a range of growth rates, from 5% to 7% in 50-basis-point increments (i.e., 5%, 5.5%, 6%, 6.5%, and 7%). For this part, use an effective tax rate of 7.56%.

f. Perform a sensitivity analysis by changing the cost of sales percent to determine the effect on net income (not the entire income statement, only net income). Vary the cost of sales percent up and down by 50 basis points from 74%. For this part, use an effective tax rate of 7.56% and include the entire range of sales growth rates from 5% to 7%. That is, generate a table that shows net income for three cost-of-sales percentages and five sales-growth rates. For each cell, compute the percent change in net income from actual 2019 to the 2020 forecasted net income.

Ongoing Project

(This ongoing project began in Module 1 and continues through most of the book; even if previous segments were not completed, the requirements are still applicable to any business analysis.) This module describes methods commonly used to forecast financial statements. The module shows how to forecast a complete set of financial statements (for one or more years). The module concludes with a parsimonious forecast of select balance sheet and income statement metrics. A project can include both types of forecasts. We can use the full set of financial statements to analyze the company's near-term future performance and position. We can then use the parsimonious forecast for longer-term forecasts as inputs for valuation models that estimate the company's stock price. Importantly, use a spreadsheet for the forecasting process. The SEC website has "interactive data" for annual reports—these are spreadsheet-like arrays that can be copied into a spreadsheet. Also, many companies include on their investor relations page an Excel version of their financial statements. Define as many cells as possible with formulas, and reference income statement totals to the related balance sheet accounts. To balance the balance sheet, define the cash account to be equal to the difference between forecasted assets and liabilities plus stockholders' equity.

1. *Forecasting Preliminaries* Begin with the adjusted set of financial statements that reflect the company's net operating assets and its operating income that we expect to persist into the future. This requires that we exclude one-time items and adjust other items to reflect anticipated levels of ongoing activities.
2. *Model Assumptions and Inputs* The assumptions we use critically impact forecasted numbers. Be as thorough as possible in research and analysis in determining model inputs. The most critical assumption is sales growth. Before we begin, adjust any fiscal years to take care of the "13th week" (or 53rd week) problem. Then, use all the reported years' sales numbers to compute historical growth numbers. Observe any trends. If the company reports segment sales, compute growth of each segment and compare it with total sales growth. We should forecast each segment separately if growth differs by segment. Read the company's MD&A, the footnotes, and any guidance the company voluntarily provides. Obtain an industry report and, determine a consensus about sales expectations and the cost environment. As discussed in the module, we assume most costs (including COGS and SGA) will not deviate from their historical percentages unless there is evidence to suggest otherwise. Again, scour the footnotes. In the end, use sound judgment and remember that forecasted numbers are subjective.
3. *Forecast the Income Statement* Use the sales growth assumption to forecast sales for the next fiscal year. Use cost-level assumptions to forecast all the operating expenses. At this first stage, we typically leave nonoperating expenses and revenues unchanged from prior-year dollar levels. We return to fine-tune these after we forecast the balance sheet. Forecast a preliminary tax expense and net income. We need those numbers to complete the balance sheet.
4. *Forecast the Balance Sheet* Use the percentage of sales approach to forecast each operating asset and liability, and follow the method described in the module to forecast PPE and intangible assets. Certain operating assets and liabilities will be forecasted to remain unchanged year over year unless we learn otherwise from the financial statements. Forecast debt using the information about scheduled debt maturities. Pay careful attention to forecasting dividends and any stock repurchases or issuances.
5. *Forecast the Statement of Cash Flows* We construct a statement of cash flows from the company's current balance sheet (from the Form 10-K or annual report) and the forecasted balance sheet. The net income number forecasted will also tie in. Remember that this statement is a mechanical operation, requiring no assumptions or new calculations.

Solutions to Review Problems

Review 12-1—Solution

a. The income statement has two potential "one-time" items that we would consider eliminating:
Divestitures loss and Restructuring, impairment, and other exit costs. While restructuring has appeared on the income statement over the past three years, the amounts differ; we could also consider normalizing the adjustment to the three-year average.

b. We forecast financial statements in the following order: income statement, balance sheet, statement of cash flows. This order is important because income statement activity determines many balance sheet account balances, including retained earnings. Cash flows cannot be determined without net income (which

determines cash from operating activities) and balance sheet accounts (which affect all three types of cash flows).
c. The first, and most crucial, income statement amount forecasted is revenue.
d. The following forecasted expenses are related to forecasted revenue.
- Cost of goods sold—directly.
- Selling, general, and administrative expense—directly.
- Depreciation—indirectly to the extent that revenue drives new PPE purchases.
- Income tax—indirectly via pretax income, which increases with revenue.
e. The following forecasted balance sheet accounts are related to forecasted revenue.
- Receivables.
- Inventories.
- Prepaid expenses.
- Land, buildings, and equipment—to the extent that revenue drives new PPE purchases.
- Accounts payable—related to cost of sales, which is determined by revenue.
- Other current liabilities—those liabilities that are related to accrued operating expenses are directly determined by revenue.

Review 12-2—Solution

Income Statement ($ millions)	FY2019 Actual	% of Sales	Computations	FY2020 Est.
Net sales.	$16,865.2	100.0%	$16,865.2 × 1.015	$17,118.2
Cost of sales.	11,108.4	65.9%	$17,118.2 × 65.9%	11,280.9
Selling, general, and administrative expenses.	2,935.8	17.4%	$17,118.2 × 17.4%	2,978.6
Divestitures loss.	30.0	0.2%	Assumed $0	—
Restructuring, impairment, and other exit costs.	275.1	1.6%	$17,118.2 × 1.6%	273.9
Operating profit.	2,515.9	14.9%		2,584.8
Benefit plan nonservice income	(87.9)	0.5%	Assumed $0	—
Interest, net.	521.8	3.1%	no change	521.8
Earnings before income taxes and after-tax earnings from joint ventures	2,082.0	12.3%	subtotal	2,063.0
Income taxes	367.8	2.2%	$2,063 × 17.7%	365.2
After-tax earnings from joint ventures.	(72.0)	0.0%	no change	(72.0)
Net earnings, including earnings attributable to redeemable and noncontrolling interests	1,786.2	10.6%	subtotal	1,769.8
Net earnings attributable to redeemable and noncontrolling interests.	33.5	0.2%	no change	33.5
Net earnings attributable to General Mills	$ 1,752.7	10.4%	total	$ 1,736.3

Review 12-3—Solution

1.

Balance Sheet ($ millions)	FY2019	% of Sales	Computations	FY2020
Current assets				
Cash and cash equivalents.	$ 450.0	2.7%	Plug	$ (233.4)
Receivables	1,679.7	10.0%	$17,118.2 × 10.0%	1,711.8
Inventories	1,559.3	9.2%	$17,118.2 × 9.2%	1,574.9
Prepaid expenses and other current assets.	497.5	2.9%	$17,118.2 × 2.9%	496.4
Total current assets.	4,186.5	24.8%	subtotal	3,549.7
Land, buildings, and equipment	3,787.2	22.5%	$546.1 CAPEX − $580.1 depreciation	3,753.2
Goodwill.	13,995.8	83.0%	no change	13,995.8
Other intangible assets.	7,166.8	42.5%	Minus $40 amortization	7,126.8
Other assets.	974.9	5.8%	$17,118.2 × 5.8%	992.9
Total assets	$30,111.2	178.5%	total	$29,418.4

continued

continued from prior page

Balance Sheets ($ millions)	FY2019	% of Sales	Computations	FY2020
Current liabilities				
Accounts payable	$ 2,854.1	16.9%	$17,118.2 × 16.9%	$ 2,893.0
Current portion of long-term debt	1,396.5	8.3%	($1,396.5) + $2,114.4	2,114.4
Notes payable	1,468.7	8.7%	no change	1,468.7
Other current liabilities	1,367.8	8.1%	$17,118.2 × 8.1%	1,386.6
Total current liabilities	7,087.1	42.0%	subtotal	7,862.7
Long-term debt	11,624.8	68.9%	$11,624.8 − $2,114.4	9,510.4
Deferred income taxes	2,031.0	12.0%	$17,118.2 × 12.0%	2,054.2
Other liabilities	1,448.9	8.6%	$17,118.2 × 8.6%	1,472.2
Total liabilities	22,191.8	131.6%	subtotal	20,899.5
Redeemable interest value	551.7	3.3%	no change	551.7
Stockholders' equity				
Common stock	75.5	0.4%	no change	75.5
Additional paid-in capital	1,386.7	8.2%	no change	1,386.7
Retained earnings	14,996.7	88.9%	$1,736.3 income − $1,170.3 dividends	15,562.7
Common stock in treasury, at cost	(6,779.0)	(40.2)%	no change	(6,779.0)
Accumulated other comprehensive loss	(2,625.4)	(15.6)%	no change	(2,625.4)
Total stockholders' equity	7,054.5	41.8%	subtotal	7,620.5
Noncontrolling interests	313.2	1.9%	+ $33.5 from forecasted income statement	346.7
Total equity	7,367.7	43.7%	subtotal	7,967.2
Total liabilities and equity	$30,111.2	178.5%	total	$29,418.4

2. The negative balance for cash indicates that the company will not generate sufficient cash from operations to cover its CAPEX, debt service requirements and expected dividend payments.

Review 12-4—Solution

a.

$ millions	FY2019 Actual Sales	Estimated Growth Rate	FY2020 Est. Sales
U.S. Meals & Baking	$3,839.8	1.50%	$ 3,897.4
U.S. Cereal	2,255.4	2.00%	2,300.5
U.S. Snacks	2,060.9	(0.50)%	2,050.6
U.S. Yogurt and Other	906.7	1.00%	915.8
Canada	862.4	(1.00)%	853.8
	$9,925.2		$10,018.0

b. The overall growth rate for the total U.S. retail segment is 0.93%, which is computed as ($10,018/$9,925.2) − 1. This growth rate implies that sales are expected to increase by about 1% in FY2020.

Review 12-5—Solution

Statement of Cash Flows		
For Fiscal Year Ended 2020 ($ millions)	Computations	2020 Est.
Net earnings, including earnings attributable to redeemable and noncontrolling interests		$1,769.8
Add: depreciation		580.1
Add: amortization		40.0
Change in receivables	$1,679.7 – $1,711.8	(32.1)
Change in inventories	$1,559.3 – $1,574.9	(15.6)
Change in prepaid expenses and other current assets	$497.5 – $496.4	1.1
Change in other assets	$974.9 – $992.9	(18.0)
Change in accounts payable	$2,893.0 – $2,854.1	38.9
Change in other current liabilities	$1,386.6 – $1,367.8	18.8
Change in deferred income taxes	$2,054.2 – $2,031.0	23.2
Change in other long-term liabilities	$1,472.2 – $1,448.9	23.3
Net cash from operating activities		2,429.5
Capital expenditures	$17,118 × 3.19%	(546.1)
Net cash from investing activities		(546.1)
Dividends		(1,170.3)
Change in current maturities of long-term debt	$2,114.4 – $1,396.5	717.9
Change in long-term debt	$9,510.4 – $11,624.8	(2,114.4)
Purchase of treasury shares	none	—
Net cash from financing activities		(2,566.8)
Net change in cash		(683.4)
Beginning cash		450.0
Ending cash		$ (233.4)

Review 12-6—Solution

Income Statement ($ millions)	FY2019 Actual	% of Sales	Computations	FY2020 Forecast	% of Sales	Computations	FY2021 Forecast	% of Sales
Net sales	$16,865.2	100.0%	$16,865.2 × 1.015	$17,118.2	100.0%	$17,118.2 × 1.015	$17,375.0	100.0%
Cost of sales	11,108.4	65.9%	$17,118.2 × 65.9%	11,280.9	65.9%	$17,375.0 × 65.9%	11,450.1	65.9%
Selling, general, and administrative expenses	2,935.8	17.4%	$17,118.2 × 17.4%	2,978.6	17.4%	$17,375.0 × 17.4%	3,023.3	17.4%
Divestitures loss	30.0	0.2%	Assumed $0	—	0.0%	Assumed $0	—	0.0%
Restructuring, impairment, and other exit costs	275.1	1.6%	$17,118.2 × 1.6%	273.9	1.6%	$17,375.0 × 1.6%	278.0	1.6%
Operating profit	2,515.9	14.9%	subtotal	2,584.8	15.1%	subtotal	2,623.6	15.1%
Benefit plan nonservice income	(87.9)	(0.5)%	Assumed $0	—	—	Assumed $0	—	—
Interest, net	521.8	3.1%	$700 × (3.4%/2)	533.7	3.1%	$2,100 × (3.4%/2)	569.4	3.3%
Earnings before income taxes and after-tax earnings from joint ventures	2,082.0	12.3%	subtotal	2,051.1	12.0%	subtotal	2,054.2	11.8%
Income taxes	367.8	2.2%	$2,051.1 × 17.7%	363.0	2.1%	$2,054.2 × 17.7%	363.6	2.1%
After-tax earnings from joint ventures	72.0	0.0%	no change	72.0	0.4%	no change	72.0	0.4%
Net earnings, including earnings attributable to redeemable and noncontrolling interests	1,786.2	10.6%	subtotal	1,760.1	10.3%	subtotal	1,762.6	10.1%
Net earnings attributable to redeemable and noncontrolling interests	33.5	0.2%	Add amount from forecasted income statement	33.5	0.2%	Add amount from forecasted income statement	33.5	0.2%
Net earnings attributable to General Mills	$ 1,752.7	10.4%	total	$1,726.6	10.1%	total	$ 1,729.1	9.9%

continued

continued from prior page

Balance Sheets ($ millions)	FY2019 Actual	% of Sales	Computations	FY2020 Forecast	% of Sales	Computations	FY2021 Forecast	% of Sales
Current assets								
Cash and cash equivalents	$ 450.0	2.7%	Plug	$ 463.5	2.7%	Plug	$ 466.2	2.7%
Receivables	1,679.7	10.0%	$17,118.2 × 10.0%	1,711.8	10.0%	$17,375.0 × 10.0%	1,737.5	10.0%
Inventories	1,559.3	9.2%	$17,118.2 × 9.2%	1,574.9	9.2%	$17,375.0 × 9.2%	1,598.5	9.2%
Prepaid expenses and other current assets	497.5	2.9%	$17,118.2 × 2.9%	496.4	2.9%	$17,375.0 × 2.9%	503.9	2.9%
Total current assets	4,186.5	24.8%	subtotal	4,246.6	24.8%	subtotal	4,306.1	24.8%
Land, buildings, and equipment	3,787.2	22.5%	$546.1 − $580.1	3,753.2	21.9%	$554.3 − $588.8	3,718.7	21.4%
Goodwill	13,995.8	83.0%	no change	13,995.8	81.8%	no change	13,995.8	80.6%
Other intangible assets	7,166.8	42.5%	Minus $40 amortization	7,126.8	41.6%	Minus $40 amortization	7,086.8	40.8%
Other assets	974.9	5.8%	$17,118.2 × 5.8%	992.9	5.8%	$17,375.0 × 5.8%	1,007.8	5.8%
Total assets	$30,111.2	178.5%	total	$30,115.3	175.9%	total	$30,115.2	173.3%
Current liabilities								
Accounts payable	$ 2,854.1	16.9%	$17,118.2 × 16.9%	$ 2,893.0	16.9%	$17,375.0 × 16.9%	$ 2,936.4	16.9%
Current portion of long-term debt	1,396.5	8.3%	($1,396.5) + $2,114.4 + $700	2,814.4	16.4%	($2,814.4) + $1,224.1 + $2,100	3,324.1	19.1%
Notes payable	1,468.7	8.7%	no change	1,468.7	8.6%	no change	1,468.7	8.5%
Other current liabilities	1,367.8	8.1%	$17,118.2 × 8.1%	1,386.6	8.1%	$17,375.0 × 8.1%	1,407.4	8.1%
Total current liabilities	7,087.1	42.0%	subtotal	8,562.7	50.0%	subtotal	9,136.6	52.6%
Long-term debt	11,624.8	68.9%	$11,624.8 − $2,114.4	9,510.4	55.6%	$9,510.4 − $1,224.1	8,286.3	47.7%
Deferred income taxes	2,031.0	12.0%	$17,118.2 × 12.0%	2,054.2	12.0%	$17,375.0 × 12.0%	2,085.0	12.0%
Other liabilities	1,448.9	8.6%	$17,118.2 × 8.6%	1,472.2	0.0%	$17,375.0 × 8.6%	1,494.3	8.6%
Total liabilities	22,191.8	131.6%	subtotal	21,599.5	126.2%	subtotal	21,002.2	120.9%
Redeemable interest value	551.7	3.3%	no change	551.7	3.2%	no change	551.7	3.2%
Stockholders' equity								
Common stock, 754.6 shares issued, $0.10 par value	75.5	0.4%	no change	75.5	0.4%	no change	75.5	0.4%
Additional paid-in capital	1,386.7	8.2%	no change	1,386.7	8.1%	no change	1,386.7	8.0%
Retained earnings	14,996.7	88.9%	$1,726.6 − $1,163.7	15,559.6	90.9%	$1,729.1 − $1,165.4	16,123.3	92.8%
Common stock in treasury, at cost	(6,779.0)	(40.2)%	no change	(6,779.0)	(39.6)%	no change	(6,779.0)	(39.0)%
Accumulated other comprehensive loss	(2,625.4)	(15.6)%	no change	(2,625.4)	(15.3)%	no change	(2,625.4)	(15.1)%
Total stockholders' equity	7,054.5	41.8%	subtotal	7,617.4	44.5%	subtotal	8,181.1	47.1%
Noncontrolling interests	313.2	1.9%	$33.5 from income statement	346.7	1.8%	$33.5 from income statement	380.2	2.2%
Total equity	7,367.7	43.7%	subtotal	7,964.1	46.5%	subtotal	8,561.3	49.3%
Total liabilities and equity	$30,111.2	178.5%	total	$31,115.3	175.9%	total	$30,115.2	173.3%

Review 12-7—Solution

a. We adjust net income by adding back the effects of the two one-time items, as follows.

Net income, as reported	$1,786.2
Add back: Divestitures loss, after tax	24.4
Add back: Restructuring, impairment, and other exit costs, after tax	224.0
Net income, as restated	$2,034.6

NOPAT = Net income + NNE = $2,034.6 + [(1−23%) × ($521.8 − $87.9)] = $2,368.7

NOPM = $2,368.7/$16,865.2 = 14.0%

b.

$ millions	Current 2019	2020	2021	2022	2023
Net sales growth	1.5%	1.5%	1.5%	1.5%	1.5%
Net sales unrounded	$16,865.2	$17,118.18 ($16,865.20 × 1.015)	$17,374.95 ($17,118.18 × 1.015)	$17,635.57 ($17,374.95 × 1.015)	$17,900.11 ($17,635.57 × 1.015)
Net sales rounded		**$17,118.2**	**$17,375.0**	**$17,635.6**	**$17,900.1**
NOPM	14.0%	14.0%	14.0%	14.0%	14.0%
NOPAT	$ 2,368.7	**$2,396.5** ($17,118.2 × 14.0%)	**$2,432.5** ($17,375.0 × 14.0%)	**$2,469.0** ($17,635.6 × 14.0%)	**$2,506.0** ($17,900.1 × 14.0%)
NOAT	0.77	0.77	0.77	0.77	0.77
NOA	$21,959.4	**$22,231.4** ($17,118.2/0.77)	**$22,564.9** ($17,375.0/0.77)	**$22,903.4** ($17,635.6/0.77)	**$23,246.9** ($17,900.1/0.77)

Module 13
Using Financial Statements for Valuation

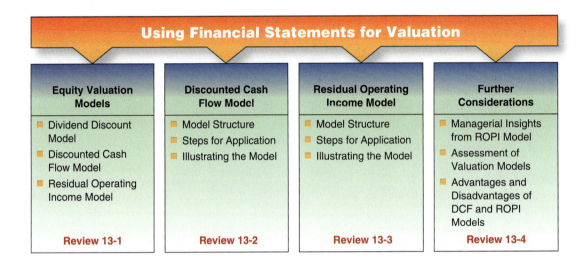

Using Financial Statements for Valuation

Equity Valuation Models
- Dividend Discount Model
- Discounted Cash Flow Model
- Residual Operating Income Model

Review 13-1

Discounted Cash Flow Model
- Model Structure
- Steps for Application
- Illustrating the Model

Review 13-2

Residual Operating Income Model
- Model Structure
- Steps for Application
- Illustrating the Model

Review 13-3

Further Considerations
- Managerial Insights from ROPI Model
- Assessment of Valuation Models
- Advantages and Disadvantages of DCF and ROPI Models

Review 13-4

PREVIEW

We explain use of financial statement information to estimate the value of a company, including use of

- Forecasts of a company's sales, profit, and cash flow.
- Discounted Cash Flow (DCF) method of valuation and illustration of its application.
- Residual operating income (ROPI) method of valuation and illustration of its application.

We also discuss managerial insights we gain from an understanding of valuation models and illustrate the types of actions managers can take to increase company value. An appendix to this module shows an example analyst report and valuation of Procter & Gamble by Deutsche Bank.

- **Procter & Gamble** is the focus company and the dashboard below conveys key financial information.

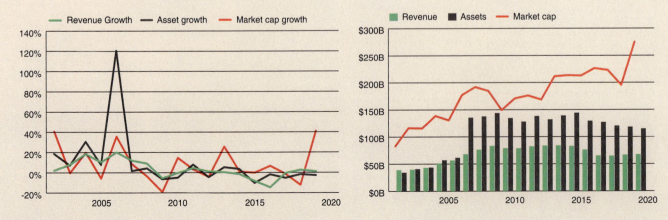

Road Map

LO	Learning Objective | Topics	Page	eLecture	Guided Example	Assignments
13-1	**Identify equity valuation models and explain the information required to value equity securities.** Dividend Discount Model :: Discounted Cash Flow Model :: Residual Operating Income Model :: Valuation Model Inputs	13-3	e13–1	Review 13-1	1, 2, 9, 20, 23, 26, 27, 30, 31
13-2	**Describe and apply the discounted free cash flow model to value equity securities.** DCF Model Structure :: Steps in Applying the DCF Model :: Illustrating the DCF Model	13-5	e13–2	Review 13-2	3, 4, 11, 13, 16, 18, 20, 21, 23, 26, 28, 30, 32
13-3	**Describe and apply the residual operating income model to value equity securities.** ROPI Model Structure :: Steps in Applying the ROPI Model :: Illustrating the ROPI Model	13-9	e13–3	Review 13-3	5, 6, 7, 10, 12, 14, 17, 19, 22, 23, 25, 27, 29, 31, 33
13-4	**Explain how equity valuation models can inform managerial decisions.** Managerial Insights :: Assessment of Valuation Models	13-11	e13–4	Review 13-4	8, 15, 24, 25, 34

Equity Valuation Models

LO1 Identify equity valuation models and explain the information required to value equity securities.

Investors, analysts, and managers use accounting information to value a company. This module describes several approaches to equity valuation. We know that the value of a debt security is the present value of the interest and principal payments that the investor *expects* to receive in the future. The valuation of equity securities is similar in that it is also based on expectations. The difference lies in the increased uncertainty surrounding the timing and amount of payments from equity securities. There are many types of equity valuation models in use today, but they share at least three common features. All equity valuation models:

- Assume that a particular fundamental variable determines equity value—we discuss three fundamental variables: dividends, free cash flows, and residual operating income.

- Forecast the fundamental variable for the remainder of the company's life. Generating an infinite stream of forecasts is not realistic; consequently, we typically estimate the fundamental variable over a horizon period, often 4 to 10 years. Then, we make simplifying assumptions about the terminal period, which encompasses the years subsequent to the horizon period. A key assumption is that the fundamental variables as forecasted for the terminal period continue into perpetuity.

- Use time value of money techniques to determine the present value of the future estimated amounts. The discount factor depends on the fundamental variable in the model. We must estimate the discount factor, which requires data from external sources and additional assumptions.

Dividend Discount Model

The basis of equity valuation is the premise that the value of an equity security is determined by the payments that the investor can expect to receive. Equity investments involve two types of payoffs: (1) dividends received while the security is owned and (2) capital gains when the security is sold. The future stock price is, itself, also assumed to be related to the expected dividends that the new investor expects to receive; as a result, the expected receipt of dividends is the sole driver of stock price under this type of valuation model. The value of an equity security is, then, based on the present value of expected dividends plus the present value of the security at the end of the forecasted holding period. The present value is determined using the firm's cost of equity capital as the discount rate. This **dividend discount model** is appealing in its simplicity and its intuitive focus on dividend distribution. As a practical matter, however, the model is not always useful because many companies that have a positive stock price have never paid a dividend, and are not expected to pay a dividend in the foreseeable future.

Discounted Cash Flow Model

The most widely used model to estimate the value of common stock is the **discounted cash flow (DCF) model**. This model focuses on the company's operating and investing activities; that is, on its ability to *generate cash*. This makes the DCF model more practical than the dividend discount model. The DCF model first estimates the value of the company (the *enterprise value*) and, then, determines the shareholders' portion, or the equity value as the enterprise value less the value of the company's debt. The DCF model takes as its fundamental input variable, the expected *free cash flows to the firm*, which are defined as operating cash flows net of the expected new investments in net operating assets (such as property, plant and equipment) that are required to support the business. The DCF model uses the weighted average cost of capital (WACC) to discount the expected future free cash flows.

Residual Operating Income Model

Another approach to equity valuation also focuses on operating and investing activities. It is known as the **residual operating income (ROPI) model**. This model uses both net operating profits after tax (NOPAT) and the net operating assets (NOA) to determine equity value (see Module 4 for complete descriptions of the NOPAT and NOA measures). This approach highlights the importance of return on net operating assets (RNOA), and the disaggregation of RNOA into net operating profit margin and NOA turnover. We discuss the implications of this insight for managers later in this module.

Valuation Model Inputs

To illustrate the valuation models, we use **Procter & Gamble** (P&G). Exhibit 13.1 provides model inputs used to estimate the models including sales, net operating profit after tax (NOPAT) and net operating assets (NOA). We obtain the model inputs for FY2019 from P&G's actual 2019 financial statements (from Exhibit 12.2). Before calculating NOPAT, we adjust for certain nonrecurring items (including a goodwill impairment of $8,000 million after-tax in 2019). The forecasted variables for FY2020 and FY2021 come from the forecasted income statements and balance sheets developed in the forecasting module and shown in Exhibits 12.2 and 12.3.[1] Forecasted financial statements (not included here) are also used to get forecasts for FY2022 and FY2023. For the terminal period, we assume a terminal growth rate of 2%. These forecasted numbers are generated using the approach we describe in our forecasting module that utilizes all of the information in the 10-K and its notes. We describe an alternate approach in our Analysis Insight Box on *Parsimonious Model Forecasts* below.

Exhibit 13.1 ■ Forecasts for Procter & Gamble

$ millions	Reported 2019	2020	2021	2022	2023	Terminal Period
Sales.	$67,684	$70,053	$72,505	$75,042	$77,669	$79,222
Sales growth.		3.5%	3.5%	3.5%	3.5%	2.0%
Net operating profit after tax (NOPAT)	$11,512	$11,776	$12,187	$12,607	$13,048	$13,309
Net operating assets (NOA)	$67,384	$66,858	$66,274	$68,846	$71,256	$72,681

To estimate the valuation models, we use a short four-year horizon period to simplify the exposition and to reduce the computational burden. In practice, investors and analysts use spreadsheets to forecast future cash flows and value the equity security, and typically have a forecast horizon of 7–10 periods. We assume a terminal period growth rate of 2% for sales, NOPAT and NOA for years 2024 and beyond.

Analysis Insight ■ Parsimonious Model Forecasts

One alternative to using detailed forecasts of the income statement and balance sheet is to use the parsimonious forecasting method that we describe in Appendix 12C. That method uses sales growth and ratios of NOPM and NOAT, computed from current (or recent) financial statements, to forecast future sales, NOPAT, and NOA. In its simple form, that method assumes that NOPM and NOAT remain unchanged during the forecast horizon and terminal period. Exhibit 13.2 shows the parsimonious forecasts for P&G (derived in Module 12) using a sales growth of 3.5% for the forecast horizon and 2% for the terminal period, along with NOPM of 17.0% (the 2019 NOPM) and NOAT of 1.00 (the 2019 NOAT). As expected, the numbers differ slightly from the full forecasted financials in Exhibit 13.1 because this parsimonious model has different assumptions.

Exhibit 13.2 ■ Valuation Model Inputs from Parsimonious Forecast Method

Procter & Gamble	Reported 2019	2020	2021	2022	2023	Terminal Period
Sales growth.		3.5%	3.5%	3.5%	3.5%	2.0%
Sales (unrounded)	$67,684	$70,052.94	$72,504.79	$75,042.46	$77,668.95	$79,222.33
		($67,684 × 1.035)	($70,052.94 × 1.035)	($72,504.79 × 1.035)	($75,042.46 × 1.035)	($77,668.95 × 1.02)
Sales (rounded).		$70,053	$72,505	$75,042	$77,669	$79,222
NOPAT (Sales rounded × 17%) . . .	11,512	$11,909	$12,326	$12,757	$13,204	$13,468
NOPM assumed to be 17.0%		($70,053 × 17.0%)	($72,505 × 17.0%)	($75,042 × 17.0%)	($77,669 × 17.0%)	($79,222 × 17.0%)
NOA	67,384	70,053	72,505	75,042	77,669	79,222
NOAT assumed to be 1.00		($70,053/1.0)	($72,505/1.0)	($75,042/1.0)	($77,669/1.0)	($79,222/1.0)

---

[1] **NOPAT** equals revenues less operating expenses such as cost of goods sold, selling, general, and administrative expenses, and taxes. NOPAT excludes any interest revenue and interest expense and any gains or losses from financial investments. NOPAT reflects the operating side of the firm as opposed to nonoperating activities such as borrowing and security investment activities. **NOA** equals operating assets less operating liabilities. (See Module 4.)

Review 13-1 LO1

We discussed three types of valuation models: dividend discount model, discounted cash flow model, and residual operating income model.

Required

For each of the following statements *a* through *j*, identify whether it is True or False for each of the three valuation models.

	Dividend Discount	Discounted Cash Flow	Residual Operating Income
a. Uses net present value concepts	_____	_____	_____
b. Operating cash flows affect value.	_____	_____	_____
c. Estimates a company's enterprise value	_____	_____	_____
d. Dividends to shareholders is a model input	_____	_____	_____
e. Free cash flow is a model input	_____	_____	_____
f. Estimates equity value of the firm.	_____	_____	_____
g. Capital expenditures affect estimated value.	_____	_____	_____
h. Requires forecasts of future amounts.	_____	_____	_____
i. Operating profit affects value	_____	_____	_____
j. Yields insight into value drivers	_____	_____	_____

Solution on p. 13-38.

Discounted Cash Flow (DCF) Model

LO2 Describe and apply the discounted free cash flow model to value equity securities.

The discounted cash flow (DCF) model defines firm value as follows.

Firm Value = Present Value of Expected Free Cash Flows to Firm

The expected free cash flows to the firm include cash flows arising from the operating side of the business; that is, cash generated from the firm's operating activities (not from nonoperating activities such as interest paid on debt or dividends received on investments). Importantly, free cash flows to the firm do not include the cash flows from financing activities.

DCF Model Structure

Free cash flows to the firm (FCFF) equal net operating profit after tax that is not used to grow net operating assets. Using the terminology of Module 4 we can define FCFF as follows (see Business Insight box below for a more traditional definition).

FCFF = NOPAT − Increase in NOA

where

NOPAT = Net operating profit after tax

NOA = Net operating assets

Net operating profit after tax is normally positive and net operating assets normally increase each year. The difference between the two (positive or negative) represents the net cash flows available to creditors and shareholders. Positive FCFF imply that there are funds available for distribution to creditors and shareholders, either in the form of debt repayments, dividends, or stock repurchases (treasury stock). Negative FCFF imply that the firm requires additional funds from creditors and/or shareholders, in the form of new loans or equity investments, to support its business activities.

Business Insight ■ Definitions of Free Cash Flow

We often see free cash flows to the firm (unlevered free cash flow) defined as follows.

$$\text{FCFF} = \text{Net cash flow from operating activities} - \text{Capital expenditures}$$

Although similar to the definition in this book, NOPAT – Increase in NOA, there are important differences.

- Net cash flow from operating activities uses net income as the starting point; net income, of course, comingles both operating and nonoperating components (such as selling expense and interest expense). Analysts sometimes correct for this by adding back items such as after-tax net interest expense. That is, the FCFF measure can be refined by beginning with earnings before interest and taxes (EBIT) and subtracting taxes.
- Income tax expense (in net income) includes the effect of the interest tax shield (see Module 4); the usual NOPAT definition includes only the tax on operating income.
- Net cash flow from operating activities also includes nonoperating items in working capital, such as changes in interest payable. NOA focuses only on operating activities.
- Capital expenditures include direct purchases of PPE assets but exclude long-term assets acquired with stock (instead of cash), say in the acquisition of a company. Changes in NOA is a more comprehensive measure of asset growth.

We must be attentive to differences in definitions for free cash flow so that we understand the analytical choices we make and their implications for equity valuation. Knowing that there is not one "universal" way to define FCFF helps us interpret analyst research reports that apply different definitions of free cash flow.

Steps in Applying the DCF Model

Application of the DCF model to equity valuation involves five steps:

1. Forecast and discount FCFF for the **horizon period**.[2]
2. Forecast and discount FCFF for the post-horizon period, called **terminal period**.[3]
3. Sum the present values of the horizon and terminal periods to yield firm (enterprise) value.
4. Subtract net nonoperating obligations (NNO), along with any noncontrolling interest (NCI), from firm value to yield equity value. If NNO is positive, the usual case, we subtract it in step 4; if NNO is negative, we add it. (For many, but not all, companies, NNO is positive because nonoperating liabilities exceed nonoperating assets.)
5. Divide firm equity value by the number of shares outstanding to yield stock value per share.

Illustrating the DCF Model

To illustrate the DCF model for Procter & Gamble, we start with the forecasted model inputs from Exhibit 13.1 and use these to compute FCFF.

---

[2] When discounting FCFF, the appropriate discount rate (r_w) is the **weighted average cost of capital (WACC)**, where the weights are the relative percentages of debt (d) and equity (e) in the capital structure applied to the expected returns on debt (r_d) and equity (r_e), respectively. P&G has two types of equity, common and preferred. Therefore, the company's weighted average cost of capital has three components: WACC = r_w = (r_d × % of debt) + (r_e × % of equity) + (r_{ps} × % of preferred stock).

[3] For an assumed growth, g, the terminal period (T) present value of FCFF in perpetuity (beyond the horizon period) is given by, $\frac{\text{FCFF}_T}{r_w - g}$, where FCFF_T is the free cash flow to the firm for the terminal period, r_w is WACC, and g is the assumed long-term growth rate of those cash flows. The resulting amount is then discounted back to the present using the horizon-end-period discount factor.

Exhibit 13.3 ■ Application of Discounted Cash Flow Model

P&G—DCF ($ millions, except per share value and discount factors)	Reported 2019	Forecast Horizon Period				Terminal Period
		2020	2021	2022	2023	
Sales.		$70,053	$72,505	$75,042	$77,669	$79,222
NOPAT		11,776	12,187	12,607	13,048	13,309
NOA		66,858	66,274	68,846	71,256	72,681
Increase in NOA.		(526)	(584)	2,572	2,410	1,425
FCFF (NOPAT − Increase in NOA).		12,302	12,771	10,035	10,638	11,884
Discount factor [$1/(1 + r_w)^t$]*		0.94491	0.89286	0.84367	0.79720	
Present value of horizon FCFF.		11,624	11,403	8,466	8,481	
Cum present value of horizon FCFF	$39,974					
Present value of terminal FCFF	247,361					
Total firm value	287,335					
Less (plus) NNO**	19,805					
Less noncontrolling interest	385					
Firm equity value	$267,145					
Shares outstanding.	2,504.7					
Stock value per share.	$106.66					

$r_w = 0.0583$
$g = 0.020$

* To simplify present value computations, the discount factors are rounded to five decimal places.
** Net nonoperating obligations (NNO) is computed as nonoperating obligations minus nonoperating assets: ($9,697 + $20,395 − $4,239 − $6,048 = $19,805). Data from 2019 financial statements, see Module 12, pages 12-8 and 12-13.

Exhibit 13.3 concludes with the estimated P&G equity value of $267,145 million, and a stock price of $106.66 per share (computed as $267,145 million/2,504.7 million shares). To determine present value, we used a weighted average cost of capital WACC(r_w) of 5.83% as the discount rate.[4] Specifically, we valued P&G's stock as follows.

1. **Compute present value of horizon period FCFF.** We compute the forecasted 2020 FCFF of $12,302 million from the forecasted 2020 NOPAT less the forecasted change in NOA in 2020. The present value of $12,302 million as of 2020 is $11,624 million, computed as $12,302 million × 0.94491 (the present value factor for one year at 5.83%). Similarly, the present value of forecasted 2021 FCFF (two years from the current date) is $11,403 million, computed as $12,771 million × 0.89286, and so on through 2023. The sum of these present values (cumulative present value) is $39,974 million.

2. **Compute present value of terminal period FCFF.** The present value of the terminal period FCFF is $247,361 million, computed as [$11,884 million/(0.0583 − 0.02)]/1.0583^4.

3. **Compute firm equity value.** We sum the present value of the horizon period FCFF and terminal period FCFF to get firm (enterprise) value of $287,335 million. We subtract the value of P&G's net nonoperating obligations of $19,805 million and the book value of its noncontrolling interest of $385 million to yield P&G's equity value of $267,145 million. We divide P&G's equity value by the 2,504.7 million shares outstanding to obtain the estimated per share value (the stock price) of $106.66.

We perform this valuation as of June 30, 2019, P&G's year-end. P&G's stock closed at $110.49 on June 30, 2019. Our valuation estimate of $106.66 indicates that the stock is slightly overvalued as of that date.

Managerial Decision ■ You Are the Chief Financial Officer

Assume that you are the CFO of a company that has a large investment in plant assets and sells its products on credit. Identify steps you can take to increase cash flow and, hence, your company's firm value. [Answer p. 13-25]

---

[4] We compute P&G's WACC as described in the text box below. To learn more about weighted average cost of capital (WACC) and how it is computed, see finance-oriented books such as *Corporate Valuation: Theory, Evidence and Practice* by Holthausen and Zmijewski, 2020, Cambridge Business Publishers.

Practice Insight — Procter & Gamble's WACC

P&G's WACC is computed as the cost of debt, common equity, and preferred stock, weighted by their proportion in the company's capital structure as follows.

	Cost	Weight
R_d (cost of debt, after tax)	1.56%	11.2%
R_e (cost of equity)	6.29%	88.5%
R_{ps} (cost of preferred stock)	28.34%	0.3%
WACC ($\sum$ cost × weight)	5.83%	

Specifically, the components of WACC are computed as follows.

- **R_d (cost of debt)**—P&G provides the effective cost of short- and long-term debt in its debt footnotes.

	%	Rate	Weighted Rate
Short-term debt	21.0%	0.5%	0.105%
Long-term debt	79.0%	2.4%	1.896%
			2.001%

To arrive at the overall cost of debt, we weight the short-term and long-term average interest rates by the relative proportion of the ST and LT debt. The result is a 2% average pretax cost of debt. We then multiply this pretax cost of debt by 1 − 22% (the federal and state combined statutory tax rate) to yield the 1.56% after-tax debt cost.

- **R_e (cost of equity)**—the cost of equity is given by the capital asset pricing model (CAPM) using the 10-year government bond rate of 2.03%, the P&G beta from Bloomberg of 0.71, both as of P&G's year-end of 6/30/19, and an assumed market premium of 6%.

$$R_e = 2.03\% + (0.71 \times 6\%) = 6.29\%$$

- **R_{ps} (cost of preferred stock)**—the cost of preferred stock is computed by dividing the dividends to preferred stockholders by the book value of the preferred stock.

$$R_{ps} = \$263 \text{ million}/\$928 \text{ million} = 28.34\%$$

LO2 Review 13-2

Following are financial data and forecast assumptions for **General Mills** (GIS) for its fiscal-year-end May 26, 2019.

General Mills ($ millions)	Reported 2019	Forecast Horizon Period 2020	2021	2022	2023	Terminal Period
Sales		$17,118.2	$17,375.0	$17,635.6	$17,900.1	$18,168.6
Sales growth		1.5%	1.5%	1.5%	1.5%	1.5%
Net operating profit after tax (NOPAT)	$ 2,368.7	$ 2,396.5	$ 2,432.5	$ 2,469.0	$ 2,506.0	$ 2,543.6
Net operating assets (NOA)	$21,959.4	$22,231.4	$22,564.9	$22,903.4	$23,246.9	$23,595.6

Equity Valuation Model Assumptions ($ and shares in millions)	
Weighted average cost of capital	5.89%
Net nonoperating obligations (NNO)	$14,591.7
Noncontrolling interest	$ 313.2
Number of common shares outstanding	601.9

Required

a. Apply the discounted cash flow (DCF) model to obtain General Mills's stock price estimate as of its fiscal-year-end May 26, 2019.

b. Compare the stock price estimate from part *a* to the actual stock price at May 28, 2019. (*Note:* May 26, 2019, was not a trading day, so use the closest prior trading day as the actual stock price.) What does our valuation estimate imply about the stock's value?

Solution on p. 13-38.

Residual Operating Income (ROPI) Model

LO3 Describe and apply the residual operating income model to value equity securities.

The residual operating income (ROPI) model focuses on net operating profit after tax (NOPAT) and net operating assets (NOA). This means it uses key measures from both the income statement and balance sheet in determining firm value.

ROPI Model Structure

The ROPI model defines firm value as the sum of two components.

$$\text{Firm Value} = \text{NOA} + \text{Present Value of Expected ROPI}$$

where

NOA = Net operating assets

ROPI = Residual operating income

Net operating assets (NOA) are the foundation of firm value under the ROPI model. The ROPI model adds an adjustment in the second term that corrects for any possible undervaluation or overvaluation of NOA. This adjustment is the present value of expected residual operating income, and is defined as follows.

$$\text{ROPI} = \underbrace{\text{NOPAT} - (\text{NOA}_{\text{Beg}} \times r_w)}_{\text{Expected NOPAT}}$$

where

NOA_{Beg} = Net operating assets at beginning (Beg) of period

r_w = Weighted average cost of capital (WACC)

Residual operating income (ROPI) is the net operating profit a firm earns over and above the return that the operating assets are expected to earn given the firm's WACC.[5] Shareholders expect the company to use NOA to generate, at least, a "hurdle" profit to cover the cost of capital (WACC). Companies that earn profits over and above that hurdle create value for shareholders. This is the concept of residual income: that is, income earned over and above the minimum amount of return required by investors.

Understanding the ROPI model helps us reap the benefits from the disaggregation of return on net operating assets (RNOA) in Module 4. In addition, the ROPI model is the foundation for many internal and external performance evaluation and compensation systems marketed by management consulting and accounting services firms.[6]

Steps in Applying the ROPI Model

Application of the ROPI model to equity valuation involves five steps.

1. Forecast and discount ROPI for the horizon period.[7]
2. Forecast and discount ROPI for the terminal period.[8]

---

[5] If the assets earn more than expected, it could be because NOA does not capture all of the firms' assets. For example, R&D and advertising are not fully and contemporaneously reflected on the balance sheet as assets though they likely produce future cash inflows. Likewise, internally generated goodwill is not fully reflected on the balance sheet as an asset. Similarly, assets are generally not written up to reflect unrealized gains. Conversely, sometimes the balance sheet overstates the true value of NOA. For example, companies can delay the write-down of impaired assets and, thus, overstate their book values. These examples, and a host of others, can yield reported values of NOA that differ from the fair value of operating assets.

[6] Examples are economic value added (EVA™) from Stern Stewart & Company, the economic profit model from McKinsey & Co., the cash flow return on investment (CFROI™) from Holt Value Associates, the economic value management from KPMG, and the value builder from PricewaterhouseCoopers (PwC).

[7] The present value of expected ROPI uses the weighted average cost of capital (WACC) as its discount rate; same as with the DCF model.

[8] For an assumed growth, g, the present value of the perpetuity of ROPI beyond the horizon period, is given by $\frac{\text{ROPI}_T}{r_w - g}$, where ROPI_T is the residual operating income for the terminal period, r_w is WACC for the firm, and g is the assumed growth rate of ROPI_T following the horizon period. The resulting amount is then discounted back to the present using the WACC, computed over the length of the horizon period.

3. Sum the present values from both the horizon and terminal periods; then add this sum to current NOA to get firm (enterprise) value.
4. Subtract net nonoperating obligations (NNO), along with any noncontrolling interest, from firm value to yield firm equity value.
5. Divide firm equity value by the number of shares outstanding to yield stock value per share.

Illustrating the ROPI Model

To illustrate the ROPI model, we return to **Procter & Gamble**. Forecasted financials for P&G (forecast horizon of FY2020 through FY2023 and terminal period of FY2024) are in Exhibit 13.4. The forecasts (in bold) are for sales, NOPAT, and NOA (the same forecasts we use to illustrate the DCF model).

Exhibit 13.4 ■ Application of Residual Operating Income Model

P&G—ROPI ($ millions, except per share value and discount factors)	Reported 2019	Forecast Horizon Period				Terminal Period
		2020	2021	2022	2023	
Sales.		$70,053	$72,505	$75,042	$77,669	$79,222
NOPAT		11,776	12,187	12,607	13,048	13,309
NOA	$ 67,384	66,858	66,274	68,846	71,256	72,681
ROPI (NOPAT – [NOA$_{Beg}$ × r_w])		7,848	8,289	8,743	9,034	9,155
Discount factor [1/(1 + r_w)^t]*		0.94491	0.89286	0.84367	0.79720	
Present value of horizon ROPI.		7,416	7,401	7,376	7,202	
Cum present value of horizon ROPI.	29,395					
Present value of terminal ROPI	190,558					
NOA	67,384					
Total firm value	287,337					
Less (plus): NNO**	19,805					
Less: NCI	345					
Firm equity value	$267,147					
Shares outstanding.	2,504.7					
Stock value per share.	$ 106.66					

$r_w = 0.0583$
$g = 0.020$

* To simplify present value computations, the discount factors are rounded to five decimal places.
** Net nonoperating obligations (NNO) is computed as nonoperating obligations minus nonoperating assets:
$9,697 + $20,395 − $4,239 − $6,048 = $19,805.

The bottom line of the ROPI valuation is the estimated P&G stock price of $106.66 per share, which is the same per share value we estimate in Exhibit 13.3 using the DCF valuation model. The present value computations use a 5.83% WACC as the discount rate. Specifically, we obtain the ROPI stock valuation as follows.

1. **Compute present value of horizon period ROPI.** The forecasted 2020 ROPI of $7,848 million is computed from the forecasted 2020 NOPAT ($11,776 million) less the product of beginning period NOA ($67,384 million) and WACC (0.0583). The present value of this ROPI as of 2020 is $7,416 million, computed as $7,848 million × 0.94491 (the present value factor for one year at 5.83%). Similarly, the present value of 2021 ROPI (two years hence) is $7,401 million, computed as $8,289 million × 0.89286, and so on through 2023. The sum of these present values (cumulative present value) is $29,395 million.

2. **Compute present value of terminal period ROPI.** The present value of the terminal period ROPI is $190,558 million, computed as [$9,155 million/(0.0583 − 0.02)]1.0583^4.

3. **Compute firm equity value.** We sum the present values from the horizon period ($29,395 million) and terminal period ($190,558 million), plus FY2019 NOA ($67,384 million), to obtain P&G's total firm (enterprise) value of $287,337 million. We then subtract the value of net nonoperating obligations of $19,805 million and noncontrolling interests of $385 million to yield firm equity value of $267,147 million. Dividing firm equity value by the 2,504.7 million shares outstanding yields the estimated per share value of $106.66.

We perform this valuation using data from the financial statements dated June 30, 2019, P&G's fiscal-year-end. P&G's stock closed at $110.49 on that date. As with the DCF model valuation, our valuation estimate of $106.66 suggests that P&G's stock is slightly overvalued as of this date.

The ROPI model and the DCF models yield identical per share estimates. This is the case so long as the firm is in a steady state, that is, when both NOPAT and NOA are growing at the same rate such that RNOA is the same each year. When this steady-state condition is not met, the two models yield different valuations. This could happen, for example, when we predict different terminal period growth rates or when profit margins are predicted to change. In practice, we often compute estimated stock values from several models and use qualitative analysis to determine an overall price estimate.

Review 13-3 LO3

Refer to the financial data and forecast assumptions for General Mills in Review 13-2.

Required
a. Apply the residual operating income (ROPI) model to obtain GIS's stock price estimate as of its fiscal-year-end May 26, 2019.
b. Compare the stock price estimate from part *a* to the actual stock price at May 28, 2019. (*Note*: May 26, 2019, was not a trading day, so use the closest prior trading day as the actual stock price.) What does our valuation estimate imply about the stock's value?

Solution on p. 13-39.

Further Considerations Involving Valuation Models

LO4 Explain how equity valuation models can inform managerial decisions.

Managerial Insights from the ROPI Model

The ROPI model defines firm value as the sum of NOA and the present value of expected residual operating income as follows.

$$\text{Firm Value} = \text{NOA} + \text{Present Value of } [\underbrace{\text{NOPAT} - (\text{NOA}_{\text{Beg}} \times r_w)}_{\text{ROPI}}]$$

Increasing ROPI, therefore, increases firm value. Managers can increase ROPI in two ways.

1. Decrease the NOA required to generate a given level of NOPAT (improve efficiency).
2. Increase NOPAT with the same level of NOA investment (improve profitability).

These are two very important observations. It means that achieving better performance requires effective management of *both* the balance sheet and the income statement. Most operating managers are accustomed to working with income statements. Further, they are often evaluated on profitability outcomes, such as achieving desired levels of sales and gross profit or efficiently managing operating expenses. The ROPI model focuses management attention on the balance sheet as well.

The two points above highlight two paths to increase ROPI and, accordingly, firm value.

Reduce NOA and maintain NOPAT First, let's consider how management can reduce the level of NOA while maintaining a given level of NOPAT. Many managers begin by implementing procedures that reduce net operating working capital, such as the following.

- Reducing receivables through
  - Better assessment of customers' credit quality
  - Better controls to identify delinquencies and automated payment notices
  - More accurate and timely invoicing
- Reducing inventories through
  - Use of less costly components (of equal quality) and production with lower wage rates
  - Elimination of product features not valued by customers

- Outsourcing to reduce product cost
- Just-in-time deliveries of raw materials
- Elimination of manufacturing bottlenecks to reduce work-in-process inventories
- Producing to order rather than to estimated demand

■ Increasing payables through
- Extending the payment of low or no-cost payables (so long as supplier relationships are unharmed)

Management would next look at its long-term operating assets for opportunities to reduce unnecessary operating assets, such as the following.

■ Sale of unnecessary property, plant or equipment
■ Acquisition of production and administrative assets in partnership with other entities for greater throughput
■ Acquisition of finished or semifinished goods from suppliers to reduce manufacturing assets

Increase NOPAT for same NOA The second path to increase ROPI and, accordingly, firm value is to increase NOPAT with the same level of NOA investment. Management would look to strategies that maximize NOPAT, such as the following.

■ Increasing gross profit dollars through
- Better pricing and mix of products sold
- Reduction of raw material and labor cost without sacrificing product quality, perhaps by outsourcing, better design, or more efficient manufacturing
- Increase of throughput to minimize overhead costs per unit (provided inventory does not build up)

■ Reducing selling, general, and administrative expenses through
- Better management of personnel
- Reduction of overhead
- Use of derivatives to hedge commodity and interest costs
- Minimization of tax expense

Before undertaking any of these actions, managers must consider both short- and long-run implications for the company. The ROPI model helps managers assess company performance (income statement) relative to the net operating assets committed (balance sheet).

> **Managerial Decision** ■ **You Are the Chief Financial Officer**
>
> The residual operating income (ROPI) model highlights the importance of increasing NOPAT and reducing net operating assets, which are the two major components of the return on net operating assets (RNOA). What specific steps can you take to improve RNOA through improvement of its components: net operating profit margin and net operating asset turnover? [Answer, p. 13-25]

Assessment of Valuation Models

Exhibit 13.5 provides a brief summary of the advantages and disadvantages of the DCF and ROPI models. Neither model dominates the other, and both are theoretically equivalent. Instead, professionals must choose the model that performs best under practical circumstances.

There are numerous other equity valuation models in practice. Many require forecasting, but several others do not. A quick review of selected models follows.

The **method of comparables model** (often called *multiples model*) predicts equity valuation or stock value using price multiples. Price multiples are defined as stock price divided by some key financial statement number. That financial number varies across investors but is usually one of the following: net income, net sales, book value of equity, total assets, or cash flow. The method then compares companies' multiples to those of their competitors to assign value.

The **net asset valuation model** draws on the financial reporting system to assign value. That is, equity is valued as reported assets less reported liabilities. Some investors adjust reported assets and liabilities for several perceived shortcomings in GAAP prior to computing net asset value. This method is commonly applied when valuing privately held companies.

There are additional models applied in practice that involve dividends, cash flows, research and development outlays, accounting rates of return, cash recovery rates, and real option models. Further, some practitioners, called *chartists* and *technicians,* chart price behavior over time and use it to predict equity value.

Exhibit 13.5 ■ Advantages and Disadvantages of DCF and ROPI Valuation Models

Model	Advantages	Disadvantages	Performs Best

DCF	• Popular and widely accepted model
	• Cash flows are unaffected by accrual accounting
	• FCFF is intuitive
		• Cash investments in PPE assets are treated as cash outflows, even though they create shareholder value
		• Value not recognized unless evidenced by cash flows
		• Computing FCFF can be difficult as operating cash flows are affected by
		  – Cutbacks on investments (receivables, inventories, plant assets); can yield short-run benefits at long-run cost
		  – Securitization, which GAAP treats as an operating cash flow when many view it as a financing activity
			• When the firm reports positive FCFF
			• When FCFF grows at a relatively constant rate

ROPI	• Focuses on value drivers such as profit margins and asset turnovers • Uses both balance sheet and income statement, including accrual accounting information • Reduces weight placed on terminal period value	• Financial statements do not reflect all company assets, especially for knowledge-based industries (for example, R&D assets and goodwill) • Requires knowledge of accrual accounting	• When financial statements reflect more of the assets and liabilities; including those items often reported off-balance-sheet

Research Insight ■ Using Models to Identify Mispriced Stocks

Implementation of the ROPI model can include parameters to capture differences in growth opportunities, persistence of ROPI, and the conservatism in accounting measures. Research finds differences in how such factors, across firms and over time, affect ROPI and changes in NOA. This research also hints that investors do not entirely understand the properties underlying these factors and, consequently, individual stocks can be mispriced for short periods of time. Other research contends that the apparent mispricing is due to an omitted valuation variable related to riskiness of the firm.

Review 13-4 LO4

Consider the following operating activities *a* through *d* that **General Mills** managers could pursue.

Required

For each action: (i) explain the likely effect on ROPI by considering how net operating profit after tax (NOPAT) and net operating assets (NOA) would be affected, and (ii) identify any potential negative consequences for such an action.

a. Delay payment on vendor invoices by two days.
b. Offer new discounts to avoid inventory spoilage by tracking shelf life more closely to identify those products for special discounts whose "sell by" date is nearing.
c. Replace certain traditional marketing media like print ads, mailers, and coupons with social media channels for in-store promotions.
d. Lease transportation equipment for peak periods instead of purchasing PPE to cover peak periods.

Solution on p. 13-39.

Global Accounting

There are no differences in the method or technique of valuing equity securities using IFRS financial statements. We can use the DCF or the ROPI method with IFRS data as inputs and determine intrinsic values. Regarding other inputs, it is important to note that WACC varies across countries. This is readily apparent when we recognize that the risk-free rate used to compute WACC is country specific; for example, the following table shows the yield on 10-year government debt for several countries as of November 2019 (www.bloomberg.com/markets/rates-bonds). In comparison to countries such as Japan and Germany, countries such as Greece and Brazil are riskier because of their debt levels and economic troubles. The higher the country risk, the higher the yield demanded on that country's debt.

Country	Yield to Maturity
Japan	(0.10)%
Germany	(0.36)%
United States	1.77%
United Kingdom	0.70%
Australia	1.10%
Brazil	6.85%
Greece	4.89%

Appendix 13A: Derivation of Free Cash Flow Formula

Derivation of the free cash flow formula follows; our thanks to Professor Jim Boatsman for this exposition.

$$\text{Assets} = \text{Liabilities} + \text{Stockholders' Equity (SE)}$$
$$\text{NOA} = \text{NNO} + \text{SE}$$
$$\Delta\text{NOA} = \Delta\text{NNO} + \Delta\text{SE} \quad \text{[in change form, where } \Delta \text{ refers to change]}$$
$$\Delta\text{NOA} = \Delta\text{NNO} + \Delta\text{Contributed Capital (CC)} + \text{Net Income} - \text{Dividends (DIV)} \quad \text{[substituting for SE]}$$
$$\Delta\text{NOA} = \Delta\text{NNO} + \Delta\text{CC} + (\text{NOPAT} - \text{NNE}) - \text{DIV} \quad \text{[substituting for NI]}$$
$$-\text{NOPAT} + \Delta\text{NOA} = \Delta\text{NNO} + \Delta\text{CC} - \text{NNE} - \text{DIV} \quad \text{[rearranging terms]}$$
$$\text{NOPAT} - \Delta\text{NOA} = \text{NNE} - \Delta\text{NNO} - \Delta\text{CC} + \text{DIV} \quad \text{[multiplying by } -1\text{]}$$

- NOPAT − ΔNOA = Free cash flows to the firm (FCFF)
- NNE − ΔNNO − ΔCC + DIV = Net payments to holders of net nonoperating obligations and of stock

Appendix 13B: Deutsche Bank Valuation of Procter & Gamble

We explain the forecasting process in Module 12 and reproduce an analyst report on forecasted financial statements for **Procter & Gamble** in Appendix 12C. In this appendix we extend that analysis and reproduce an analyst forecasted stock price for P&G. We include below an excerpt from the **Deutsche Bank** valuation report.

Qualitative and Quantitative Summary

This excerpt provides a qualitative and quantitative summary from Deutsche Bank's report as of July 30, 2019 (*reproduced with permission*).

Deutsche Bank Research

Rating
Hold

North America
United States

Consumer
Cosmetics, Household & Personal Care

Company
Procter & Gamble

Reuters	Bloomberg	Exchange	Ticker
PG.N	PG US	NYS	PG

The Profit & Growth Company

Date
30 July 2019

Forecast Change

Price at 30 Jul 2019 (USD)	120.41
Price target	124.00
52-week range	116.00 - 78.87

Valuation & Risks

Steve Powers
Research Analyst
+1-212-250 5480

Faiza Alwy
Research Analyst
+1-212-250-7611

Christopher Barnes
Research Associate
+1-212-454-0778

Katy Ansel
Research Associate
+1-212-250-1027

Key changes			
TP	116.00 to 124.00	↑	6.9%
EPS (USD)	4.87 to 4.91	↑	0.8%
Revenue (USDm)	70,216.1 to 70,647.4	↑	0.6%

Source: Deutsche Bank

Key takeaways from PG's 4Q19 results (Hint: Everything is pretty awesome)

When it's working, it's working… Earlier this morning, PG delivered well-balanced results highlighted by roughly +7.5% organic growth, broad-based across all categories/regions. Investors deservedly rewarded PG today, with the stock outperforming the market by about +4 pts. From our point of view, PG is firing on all cylinders and doing a lot of things right—from innovation, to marketing, to in-store/on-shelf execution—amidst a favorably trending macro, consumer, and retailer environment, as well as a broadly rational competitive environment. However, with interest rates near lows and a defensive market posture near highs, the market is rewarding this performance with a near-25x forward multiple (a 15-year high), implicitly discounting (to us) that the good times roll on with minimal interruption for (at least) some time longer.

Possible? Yes – the momentum is impressive. However, while we remain generally constructive/optimistic on PG's earnings power (our FY20 estimates assume the high-end of the company's guidance range: +4% organic growth, EPS $4.91), we see limited room for further multiple expansion, and see anticipated earnings growth subject to potential downside risk from heightened competition, macro deceleration, elevated retail pressure, a simple inability to cycle year-over-year comparisons as adeptly as expected, or periods/places of misexecution (even if we concur with, and have been broadly impressed by, the evolution of PG's superiority strategy). While we admire PG's current focus on expanding categories and improving overall market growth, the reality is that is likely easier done (although not to imply "easy") when consumers, retailers, and competitors appear accommodating—conditions that to us risk becoming less "awesome" over time.

We commend PG and raise our PT to $124, yet maintain our Hold rating.

Estimate changes and Valuation

We have modestly raised our FY20 EPS estimate to $4.91 (from $4.87) effectively flowing through the FY19 beat. Our EPS growth rate remains broadly unchanged at +8.5%. We have also raised our FY20 organic growth estimate to +4.0% from 3.5%, following continued strong and accelerating organic trends through FY19.

Our $124 price target is DCF-based (10-years), assuming +3.5% normalized topline growth, +5% normalized EBIT growth, implying a ~23.5x multiple on 13-24

Deutsche Bank Securities Inc.

Distributed on: 30/07/2019 22:51:08 GMT

Deutsche Bank does and seeks to do business with companies covered in its research reports. Thus, investors should be aware that the firm may have a conflict of interest that could affect the objectivity of this report. Investors should consider this report as only a single factor in making their investment decision. DISCLOSURES AND ANALYST CERTIFICATIONS ARE LOCATED IN APPENDIX 1. MCI (P) 066/04/2019.

30 July 2019
Cosmetics, Household & Personal Care
Procter & Gamble

month EPS. We assume a WACC of 6.5% and a 1.5% terminal growth rate (in-line with expected long-term category growth). Upside risks: better-than-expected top-line growth, further improvement in macro/consumer trends, higher than expected productivity savings, commodity deflation, weaker USD, and value-accretive capital deployment. Downside risks: rotation out of staples, volatility in input costs and short supplies of raw materials, stronger dollar, more challenged competitive environment, unfavorable macro and consumption environment, and greater than anticipated cost of growth.

Figure 1: Discounted Cash Flow Analysis

Terminal Value Growth Rate	1.5%										
WACC	6.5%										

Period	4Q19 TTM	4QE20 TTM	4QE21 TTM	4QE22 TTM	4QE23 TTM	4QE24 TTM	4QE25 TTM	4QE26 TTM	4QE27 TTM	4QE28 TTM	4QE28 TTM
Revenue	$67,684	$70,647	$73,200	$75,630	$78,147	$80,755	$83,457	$86,256	$89,156	$92,162	$95,276
Revenue Growth		4.4%	3.6%	3.3%	3.3%	3.3%	3.3%	3.4%	3.4%	3.4%	3.4%
Operating Margin	21.0%	21.9%	22.3%	22.6%	22.9%	23.2%	23.5%	23.8%	24.1%	24.4%	24.8%
EBIT	14,236	15,492	16,345	17,100	17,898	18,736	19,616	20,540	21,511	22,532	23,604
Tax Rate	17.5%	17.5%	17.5%	17.5%	17.5%	17.5%	17.5%	17.5%	17.5%	17.5%	17.5%
After-tax EBIT	11,745	12,781	13,484	14,108	14,766	15,457	16,183	16,945	17,747	18,589	19,474
+: D&A	2,824	3,038	3,221	3,403	3,517	3,634	3,756	3,882	4,012	4,147	4,287
+: Capital Expenditures	(3,347)	(3,364)	(3,587)	(3,706)	(3,829)	(3,957)	(4,089)	(4,227)	(4,369)	(4,516)	(4,669)
+/− : Changes in Working Capital	681	220	373	362	376	391	406	422	439	456	474
Unlevered Free Cash Flow	11,903	12,675	13,491	14,167	14,830	15,525	16,255	17,023	17,829	18,676	19,566
Terminal Value											397,192
Discounted Cash Flow		12,675	12,668	12,491	12,277	12,068	11,865	11,666	11,473	11,285	236,449

Discounted Cash Flow	344,915				EBITDA Exit	14.2x
−: Net Debt	22,254				Sales CAGR	3.4%
Implied Equity Value	322,661		13-24 mth EPS	$5.25	EBIT CAGR	4.8%
Shares Outstanding	2,611		Implied 13-24 mth P/E	23.5x	Margin growth	0.3%
Implied 12-month Target Price	$124		13-24 mth EV/EBITDA	17.6x		

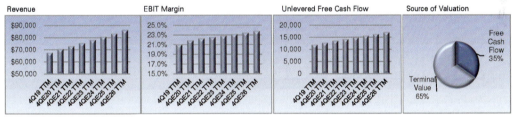

Source: Deutsche Bank estimates

30 July 2019
Cosmetics, Household & Personal Care
Procter & Gamble

Financial Model

Figure 2: PG quarterly income statement

(fy ending June, $ in millions, except per share amounts)

	FY18	2019 1Q Sep	2Q Dec	3Q Mar	4Q Jun	FY19	2020E 1QE Sep	2QE Dec	3QE Mar	4QE Jun	FY20E	2021E 1QE Sep	2QE Dec	3QE Mar	4QE Jun	FY21E
INCOME STATEMENT																
Net Sales	66,832	16,690	17,438	16,462	17,094	67,684	17,612	18,579	16,953	17,503	70,647	18,251	19,251	17,565	18,133	73,200
Cost of Goods Sold	33,707	8,438	8,796	8,362	8,746	34,342	8,728	9,195	8,544	8,798	35,265	8,990	9,470	8,799	9,060	36,319
Gross Profit	33,125	8,252	8,642	8,100	8,348	33,342	8,884	9,384	8,410	8,705	35,383	9,261	9,781	8,765	9,073	36,881
Gross margin	49.6%	49.4%	49.6%	49.2%	48.8%	49.3%	50.4%	50.5%	49.6%	49.7%	50.1%	50.7%	50.8%	49.9%	50.0%	50.4%
GM chg. in bps	-1323 bps	-150 bps	-86 bps	2 bps	120 bps	-30 bps	100 bps	95 bps	40 bps	90 bps	82 bps	30 bps	30 bps	30 bps	30 bps	30 bps
SG&A expenses	19,037	4,625	4,660	4,823	4,998	19,106	4,854	4,881	4,941	5,214	19,891	5,012	5,039	5,102	5,383	20,536
SG&A as % of sales	28.5%	27.7%	26.7%	29.3%	29.2%	28.2%	27.6%	26.3%	29.1%	29.8%	28.2%	27.5%	26.2%	29.0%	29.7%	28.1%
SG&A ratio chg. in bps	-21 bps	-77 bps	78 bps	65 bps	-12 bps	-26 bps	-15 bps	-45 bps	-15 bps	55 bps	-7 bps	-10 bps	-10 bps	-10 bps	-10 bps	-10 bps
Adjusted Operating Profit	14,088	3,627	3,982	3,277	3,350	14,236	4,030	4,503	3,468	3,491	15,492	4,249	4,743	3,663	3,690	16,345
Operating Margin	21.1%	21.7%	22.8%	19.9%	19.6%	21.0%	22.9%	24.2%	20.5%	19.9%	21.9%	23.3%	24.6%	20.9%	20.3%	22.3%
OM chg. in bps	-1302 bps	-73 bps	-8 bps	-63 bps	132 bps	-5 bps	115 bps	140 bps	55 bps	35 bps	90 bps	40 bps	40 bps	40 bps	40 bps	40 bps
Interest expense	259	76	75	79	59	289	69	69	72	72	283	69	69	72	72	283
Ann. interest rate on Total Debt	1.2%	1.3%	1.2%	1.4%	1.0%	1.2%	1.2%	1.2%	1.2%	1.2%	1.2%	1.2%	1.2%	1.2%	1.2%	1.2%
Other expense/(income)	(584)	(110)	(100)	(131)	(192)	(533)	(123)	(130)	(119)	(123)	(495)	(128)	(135)	(123)	(127)	(512)
Other expense/(income) as % of s	-0.9%	-0.7%	-0.6%	-0.8%	-1.1%	-0.8%	-0.7%	-0.7%	-0.7%	-0.7%	-0.7%	-0.7%	-0.7%	-0.7%	-0.7%	-0.7%
Adjusted Pretax Income	14,413	3,661	4,007	3,329	3,483	14,480	4,084	4,564	3,515	3,542	15,704	4,308	4,808	3,714	3,744	16,575
Adj. Pretax Margin	21.6%	21.9%	23.0%	20.2%	20.4%	21.4%	23.2%	24.6%	20.7%	20.2%	22.2%	23.6%	25.0%	21.1%	20.6%	22.6%
Adjusted taxes	3,095	734	713	509	578	2,534	715	799	615	620	2,748	754	841	650	655	2,901
Adj. effective tax rate	21.5%	20.0%	17.8%	15.3%	16.6%	17.5%	17.5%	17.5%	17.5%	17.5%	17.5%	17.5%	17.5%	17.5%	17.5%	17.5%
Noncontrolling Interest	114	12	22	31	4	69	12	22	31	4	69	12	22	31	4	69
Adjusted Net Income	11,204	2,915	3,272	2,789	2,901	11,877	3,357	3,743	2,869	2,918	12,887	3,542	3,945	3,033	3,085	13,605
Net Margin	16.8%	17.5%	18.8%	16.9%	17.0%	17.5%	19.1%	20.1%	16.9%	16.7%	18.2%	19.4%	20.5%	17.3%	17.0%	18.6%
Convert. Preferred Dividends	265	66	65	64	64	259	69	68	67	67	269	71	70	69	70	281
Net Income After Preferred	10,939	2,849	3,207	2,725	2,837	11,618	3,289	3,675	2,802	2,851	12,617	3,471	3,874	2,964	3,015	13,324
CORE EPS																
Diluted shares	2,657	2,612	2,623	2,638	2,646	2,630	2,642	2,632	2,621	2,611	2,627	2,602	2,594	2,586	2,578	2,590
CORE EPS - adjusted	$4.22	$1.12	$1.25	$1.06	$1.10	$4.52	$1.27	$1.42	$1.09	$1.12	$4.91	$1.36	$1.52	$1.17	$1.20	$5.25
Dividends	$2.79	$0.72	$0.72	$0.72	$0.75	$2.90	$0.75	$0.75	$0.75	$0.78	$3.01	$0.78	$0.78	$0.78	$0.81	$3.14
AS REPORTED																
GAAP Diluted EPS	$3.67	$1.22	$1.22	$1.04	($2.12)	$1.48	$1.27	$1.42	$1.09	$1.12	$4.91	$1.36	$1.52	$1.17	$1.20	$5.25
EBITDA																
EBIT	14,088	3,627	3,982	3,277	3,350	14,236	4,030	4,503	3,468	3,491	15,492	4,249	4,743	3,663	3,690	16,345
+: D&A	2,834	643	650	711	820	2,824	757	799	729	753	3,038	803	847	773	798	3,221
ADJUSTED EBITDA	16,922	4,270	4,632	3,988	4,170	17,060	4,787	5,302	4,197	4,244	18,530	5,052	5,590	4,436	4,487	19,565
% Growth																
Total Net Sales	2.7%	0.2%	0.2%	1.1%	3.6%	1.3%	5.5%	6.5%	3.0%	2.4%	4.4%	3.6%	3.6%	3.6%	3.6%	3.6%
Gross profit	-18.9%	-2.7%	-1.5%	1.1%	6.2%	0.7%	7.7%	8.6%	3.8%	4.3%	6.1%	4.2%	4.2%	4.2%	4.2%	4.2%
SG&A	2.0%	-2.5%	-2.6%	3.4%	3.2%	0.4%	5.0%	4.8%	2.5%	4.3%	4.1%	3.3%	3.2%	3.3%	3.3%	3.2%
Adjusted Operating profit	-36.5%	-3.0%	-0.1%	-2.0%	11.0%	1.1%	11.1%	13.1%	5.8%	4.2%	8.8%	5.4%	5.3%	5.6%	5.7%	5.5%
Adjusted Pretax income	-34.6%	-4.8%	-2.4%	-1.9%	13.5%	0.5%	11.6%	13.9%	5.6%	1.7%	8.5%	5.5%	5.4%	5.7%	5.7%	5.5%
Net income	-39.6%	-0.4%	3.1%	5.3%	18.3%	6.0%	15.2%	14.4%	2.9%	0.6%	8.5%	5.5%	5.4%	5.7%	5.7%	5.6%
Diluted EPS	-43.9%	15.5%	30.3%	9.6%	-393.8%	-59.6%	3.7%	16.8%	5.2%	-152.7%	231.1%	7.1%	6.9%	7.2%	7.1%	7.1%
Core EPS	-37.7%	2.5%	4.9%	5.6%	17.1%	7.1%	13.9%	14.0%	3.5%	1.9%	8.6%	7.1%	6.9%	7.2%	7.1%	7.1%
Dividends	3.3%	4.0%	4.0%	4.0%	4.0%	4.0%	4.0%	4.0%	4.0%	4.0%	4.0%	4.0%	4.0%	4.0%	5.0%	4.3%
Diluted EPS (GAAP)	-43.9%	15.5%	30.3%	9.6%	-393.8%	-59.6%	3.7%	16.8%	5.2%	-152.7%	231.1%	7.1%	6.9%	7.2%	7.1%	7.1%
Core EPS - 2 yr. stacked	-92.5%	-68.8%	15.0%	10.1%	27.9%	-30.6%	16.4%	18.9%	9.1%	19.1%	15.7%	21.0%	20.9%	10.7%	9.0%	15.7%

Source: Deutsche Bank estimates and analysis, Company filings

Deutsche Bank Securities Inc.

30 July 2019
Cosmetics, Household & Personal Care
Procter & Gamble

Appendix 1

Important Disclosures

*Other information available upon request

Disclosure checklist			
Company	Ticker	Recent price*	Disclosure
Procter Gamble	PG.N	116.0 (USD) 29 Jul 2019	1, 7, 8, 14, 15

*Prices are current as of the end of the previous trading session unless otherwise indicated and are sourced from local exchanges via Reuters, Bloomberg and other vendors . Other information is sourced from Deutsche Bank, subject companies, and other sources. For disclosures pertaining to recommendations or estimates made on securities other than the primary subject of this research, please see the most recently published company report or visit our global disclosure look-up page on our website at https://research.db.com/Research/Disclosures/CompanySearch. Aside from within this report, important risk and conflict disclosures can also be found at https://research.db.com/Research/Topics/Equities?topicId=RB0002. Investors are strongly encouraged to review this information before investing.

Important Disclosures Required by U.S. Regulators

Disclosures marked with an asterisk may also be required by at least one jurisdiction in addition to the United States. See Important Disclosures Required by Non-US Regulators and Explanatory Notes.

1. Within the past year, Deutsche Bank and/or its affiliate(s) has managed or co-managed a public or private offering for this company, for which it received fees.
7. Deutsche Bank and/or its affiliate(s) has received compensation from this company for the provision of investment banking or financial advisory services within the past year.
8. Deutsche Bank and/or its affiliate(s) expects to receive, or intends to seek, compensation for investment banking services from this company in the next three months.
14. Deutsche Bank and/or its affiliate(s) has received non-investment banking related compensation from this company within the past year.
15. This company has been a client of Deutsche Bank Securities Inc. within the past year, during which time it received non-investment banking securities-related services.

Important Disclosures Required by Non-U.S. Regulators

Disclosures marked with an asterisk may also be required by at least one jurisdiction in addition to the United States. See Important Disclosures Required by Non-US Regulators and Explanatory Notes.

1. Within the past year, Deutsche Bank and/or its affiliate(s) has managed or co-managed a public or private offering for this company, for which it received fees.
7. Deutsche Bank and/or its affiliate(s) has received compensation from this company for the provision of investment banking or financial advisory services within the past year.

For disclosures pertaining to recommendations or estimates made on securities other than the primary subject of this research, please see the most recently published company report or visit our global disclosure look-up page on our website at https://research.db.com/Research/Disclosures/CompanySearch

Analyst Certification

The views expressed in this report accurately reflect the personal views of the undersigned lead analyst(s) about the subject issuer and the securities of the issuer. In addition, the undersigned lead analyst(s) has not and will not receive any compensation for providing a specific recommendation or view in this report. Steve Powers.

30 July 2019
Cosmetics, Household & Personal Care
Procter & Gamble

Historical recommendations and target price: Procter Gamble (PG.N)
(as of 07/29/2019)

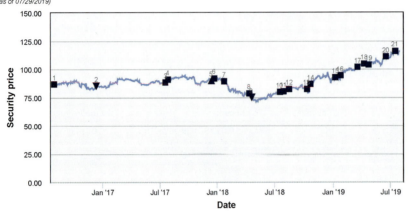

Current Recommendations
Buy
Hold
Sell
Not Rated
Suspended Rating

** Analyst is no longer at Deutsche Bank

1.	08/03/2016	Buy, Target Price Change USD 95.00 William Schmitz**	12.	08/16/2018	Hold, Target Price Change USD 85.00 Stephen Powers
2.	12/13/2016	Downgraded to Hold, Target Price Change USD 90.00 William Schmitz**	13.	10/10/2018	Hold, Target Price Change USD 82.00 Stephen Powers
3.	07/20/2017	Hold, Target Price Change USD 92.00 Faiza Alwy	14.	10/22/2018	Hold, Target Price Change USD 83.00 Stephen Powers
4.	07/28/2017	Hold, Target Price Change USD 94.00 Faiza Alwy	15.	01/08/2019	Hold, Target Price Change USD 87.00 Stephen Powers
5.	12/13/2017	Upgraded to Buy, Target Price Change USD 101.00 Stephen Powers	16.	01/24/2019	Hold, Target Price Change USD 90.00 Stephen Powers
6.	12/22/2017	Buy, Target Price Change USD 102.00 Stephen Powers	17.	03/20/2019	Hold, Target Price Change USD 99.00 Stephen Powers
7.	01/24/2018	Buy, Target Price Change USD 100.00 Stephen Powers	18.	04/10/2019	Hold, Target Price Change USD 100.00 Stephen Powers
8.	04/13/2018	Buy, Target Price Change USD 88.00 Stephen Powers	19.	04/24/2019	Hold, Target Price Change USD 106.00 Stephen Powers
9.	04/20/2018	Downgraded to Hold, Target Price Change USD 80.00 Stephen Powers	20.	06/17/2019	Hold, Target Price Change USD 109.00 Stephen Powers
10.	07/19/2018	Hold, Target Price Change USD 81.00 Stephen Powers	21.	07/16/2019	Hold, Target Price Change USD 116.00 Stephen Powers
11.	07/31/2018	Hold, Target Price Change USD 84.00 Stephen Powers			

Equity Rating Key

Buy: Based on a current 12- month view of total share-holder return (TSR = percentage change in share price from current price to projected target price plus pro-jected dividend yield) , we recommend that investors buy the stock.

Sell: Based on a current 12-month view of total share-holder return, we recommend that investors sell the stock.

Hold: We take a neutral view on the stock 12-months out and, based on this time horizon, do not recommend either a Buy or Sell.

Newly issued research recommendations and target prices supersede previously published research.

Equity rating dispersion and banking relationships

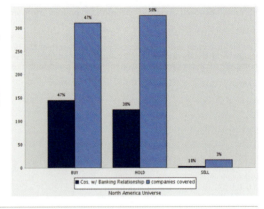

Deutsche Bank Securities Inc.

30 July 2019
Cosmetics, Household & Personal Care
Procter & Gamble

Additional Information

The information and opinions in this report were prepared by Deutsche Bank AG or one of its affiliates (collectively 'Deutsche Bank'). Though the information herein is believed to be reliable and has been obtained from public sources believed to be reliable, Deutsche Bank makes no representation as to its accuracy or completeness. Hyperlinks to third-party websites in this report are provided for reader convenience only. Deutsche Bank neither endorses the content nor is responsible for the accuracy or security controls of those websites.

If you use the services of Deutsche Bank in connection with a purchase or sale of a security that is discussed in this report, or is included or discussed in another communication (oral or written) from a Deutsche Bank analyst, Deutsche Bank may act as principal for its own account or as agent for another person.

Deutsche Bank may consider this report in deciding to trade as principal. It may also engage in transactions, for its own account or with customers, in a manner inconsistent with the views taken in this research report. Others within Deutsche Bank, including strategists, sales staff and other analysts, may take views that are inconsistent with those taken in this research report. Deutsche Bank issues a variety of research products, including fundamental analysis, equity-linked analysis, quantitative analysis and trade ideas. Recommendations contained in one type of communication may differ from recommendations contained in others, whether as a result of differing time horizons, methodologies, perspectives or otherwise. Deutsche Bank and/or its affiliates may also be holding debt or equity securities of the issuers it writes on. Analysts are paid in part based on the profitability of Deutsche Bank AG and its affiliates, which includes investment banking, trading and principal trading revenues.

Opinions, estimates and projections constitute the current judgment of the author as of the date of this report. They do not necessarily reflect the opinions of Deutsche Bank and are subject to change without notice. Deutsche Bank provides liquidity for buyers and sellers of securities issued by the companies it covers. Deutsche Bank research analysts sometimes have shorter-term trade ideas that may be inconsistent with Deutsche Bank's existing longer-term ratings. Some trade ideas for equities are listed as Catalyst Calls on the Research Website (https://research.db.com/Research/), and can be found on the general coverage list and also on the covered company's page. A Catalyst Call represents a high-conviction belief by an analyst that a stock will outperform or underperform the market and/or a specified sector over a time frame of no less than two weeks and no more than three months. In addition to Catalyst Calls, analysts may occasionally discuss with our clients, and with Deutsche Bank salespersons and traders, trading strategies or ideas that reference catalysts or events that may have a near-term or medium-term impact on the market price of the securities discussed in this report, which impact may be directionally counter to the analysts' current 12-month view of total return or investment return as described herein. Deutsche Bank has no obligation to update, modify or amend this report or to otherwise notify a recipient thereof if an opinion, forecast or estimate changes or becomes inaccurate. Coverage and the frequency of changes in market conditions and in both general and company-specific economic prospects make it difficult to update research at defined intervals. Updates are at the sole discretion of the coverage analyst or of the Research Department Management, and the majority of reports are published at irregular intervals. This report is provided for informational purposes only and does not take into account the particular investment objectives, financial situations, or needs of individual clients. It is not an offer or a solicitation of an offer to buy or sell any financial instruments or to participate in any particular trading strategy. Target prices are inherently imprecise and a product of the analyst's judgment. The financial instruments discussed in this report may not be suitable for all investors, and investors must make their own informed investment decisions. Prices and availability of financial instruments are subject to change without notice, and investment transactions can lead to losses as a result of price fluctuations and other factors. If a financial instrument is denominated in a currency other than an investor's currency, a change in exchange rates may adversely affect the investment. Past performance is not necessarily indicative of future results. Performance calculations exclude transaction costs, unless otherwise indicated. Unless otherwise indicated, prices are current as of the end of the previous trading session and are sourced from local exchanges via Reuters, Bloomberg and other vendors. Data is also sourced from Deutsche Bank, subject companies, and other parties.

The Deutsche Bank Research Department is independent of other business divisions of the Bank. Details regarding our organizational arrangements and information barriers we have to prevent and avoid conflicts of interest with respect to our research are available on our website (https://research.db.com/Research/) under Disclaimer.

Macroeconomic fluctuations often account for most of the risks associated with exposures to instruments that promise to pay fixed or variable interest rates. For an investor who is long fixed-rate instruments (thus receiving these cash flows), increases in interest rates naturally lift the discount factors applied to the expected cash flows and thus cause a loss. The longer the maturity of a certain cash flow and the higher the move in the discount factor, the higher will be the loss. Upside surprises in inflation, fiscal funding needs, and FX depreciation rates are among the most common adverse macroeconomic shocks to receivers. But counterparty exposure, issuer creditworthiness, client segmentation, regulation (including changes in assets holding limits for different types of investors), changes in tax policies, currency convertibility (which may constrain currency conversion, repatriation of profits and/or liquidation of positions), and settlement issues related to local clearing houses are also important risk factors. The sensitivity of fixed-income instruments to macroeconomic shocks may be mitigated by indexing the contracted cash flows to inflation, to FX depreciation, or to specified interest rates – these are common in emerging markets. The index fixings may – by construction – lag or mis-measure the actual move in the underlying variables they are intended to track. The choice of the proper fixing (or metric) is particularly important in swaps markets, where floating coupon rates (i.e., coupons indexed to a typically short-dated interest rate reference index) are exchanged for fixed coupons. Funding in a currency that differs from the currency in which coupons are denominated carries FX risk. Options on swaps (swaptions) the risks typical to options in addition to the risks related to rates movements.

Derivative transactions involve numerous risks including market, counterparty default and illiquidity risk. The appropriateness

30 July 2019
Cosmetics, Household & Personal Care
Procter & Gamble

of these products for use by investors depends on the investors' own circumstances, including their tax position, their regulatory environment and the nature of their other assets and liabilities; as such, investors should take expert legal and financial advice before entering into any transaction similar to or inspired by the contents of this publication. The risk of loss in futures trading and options, foreign or domestic, can be substantial. As a result of the high degree of leverage obtainable in futures and options trading, losses may be incurred that are greater than the amount of funds initially deposited – up to theoretically unlimited losses. Trading in options involves risk and is not suitable for all investors. Prior to buying or selling an option, investors must review the 'Characteristics and Risks of Standardized Options", at http://www.optionsclearing.com/about/publications/character-risks.jsp. If you are unable to access the website, please contact your Deutsche Bank representative for a copy of this important document.

Participants in foreign exchange transactions may incur risks arising from several factors, including the following: (i) exchange rates can be volatile and are subject to large fluctuations; (ii) the value of currencies may be affected by numerous market factors, including world and national economic, political and regulatory events, events in equity and debt markets and changes in interest rates; and (iii) currencies may be subject to devaluation or government-imposed exchange controls, which could affect the value of the currency. Investors in securities such as ADRs, whose values are affected by the currency of an underlying security, effectively assume currency risk.

Unless governing law provides otherwise, all transactions should be executed through the Deutsche Bank entity in the investor's home jurisdiction. Aside from within this report, important conflict disclosures can also be found at https://research.db.com/Research/ on each company's research page. Investors are strongly encouraged to review this information before investing.

Deutsche Bank (which includes Deutsche Bank AG, its branches and affiliated companies) is not acting as a financial adviser, consultant or fiduciary to you or any of your agents (collectively, "You" or "Your") with respect to any information provided in this report. Deutsche Bank does not provide investment, legal, tax or accounting advice, Deutsche Bank is not acting as your impartial adviser, and does not express any opinion or recommendation whatsoever as to any strategies, products or any other information presented in the materials. Information contained herein is being provided solely on the basis that the recipient will make an independent assessment of the merits of any investment decision, and it does not constitute a recommendation of, or express an opinion on, any product or service or any trading strategy.

The information presented is general in nature and is not directed to retirement accounts or any specific person or account type, and is therefore provided to You on the express basis that it is not advice, and You may not rely upon it in making Your decision. The information we provide is being directed only to persons we believe to be financially sophisticated, who are capable of evaluating investment risks independently, both in general and with regard to particular transactions and investment strategies, and who understand that Deutsche Bank has financial interests in the offering of its products and services. If this is not the case, or if You are an IRA or other retail investor receiving this directly from us, we ask that you inform us immediately.

In July 2018, Deutsche Bank revised its rating system for short term ideas whereby the branding has been changed to Catalyst Calls ("CC") from SOLAR ideas; the rating categories for Catalyst Calls originated in the Americas region have been made consistent with the categories used by Analysts globally; and the effective time period for CCs has been reduced from a maximum of 180 days to 90 days.

United States: Approved and/or distributed by Deutsche Bank Securities Incorporated, a member of FINRA, NFA and SIPC. Analysts located outside of the United States are employed by non-US affiliates that are not subject to FINRA regulations.

Germany: Approved and/or distributed by Deutsche Bank AG, a joint stock corporation with limited liability incorporated in the Federal Republic of Germany with its principal office in Frankfurt am Main. Deutsche Bank AG is authorized under German Banking Law and is subject to supervision by the European Central Bank and by BaFin, Germany's Federal Financial Supervisory Authority.

United Kingdom: Approved and/or distributed by Deutsche Bank AG acting through its London Branch at Winchester House, 1 Great Winchester Street, London EC2N 2DB. Deutsche Bank AG in the United Kingdom is authorised by the Prudential Regulation Authority and is subject to limited regulation by the Prudential Regulation Authority and Financial Conduct Authority. Details about the extent of our authorisation and regulation are available on request.

Hong Kong: Distributed by Deutsche Bank AG, Hong Kong Branch or Deutsche Securities Asia Limited (save that any research relating to futures contracts within the meaning of the Hong Kong Securities and Futures Ordinance Cap. 571 shall be distributed solely by Deutsche Securities Asia Limited). The provisions set out above in the 'Additional Information' section shall apply to the fullest extent permissible by local laws and regulations, including without limitation the Code of Conduct for Persons Licensed or Registered with the Securities and Futures Commission.

India: Prepared by Deutsche Equities India Private Limited (DEIPL) having CIN: U65990MH2002PTC137431 and registered office at 14th Floor, The Capital, C-70, G Block, Bandra Kurla Complex Mumbai (India) 400051. Tel: + 91 22 7180 4444. It is registered by the Securities and Exchange Board of India (SEBI) as a Stock broker bearing registration no.: INZ000252437; Merchant Banker bearing SEBI Registration no.: INM000010833 and Research Analyst bearing SEBI Registration no.: INH000001741. DEIPL may have received administrative warnings from the SEBI for breaches of Indian regulations. Deutsche Bank and/or its affiliate(s) may have debt holdings or positions in the subject company. With regard to information on associates, please refer to the "Shareholdings" section in the Annual Report at: https://www.db.com/ir/en/annual-reports.htm.

Deutsche Bank Securities Inc.

30 July 2019
Cosmetics, Household & Personal Care
Procter & Gamble

Japan: Approved and/or distributed by Deutsche Securities Inc.(DSI). Registration number - Registered as a financial instruments dealer by the Head of the Kanto Local Finance Bureau (Kinsho) No. 117. Member of associations: JSDA, Type II Financial Instruments Firms Association and The Financial Futures Association of Japan. Commissions and risks involved in stock transactions - for stock transactions, we charge stock commissions and consumption tax by multiplying the transaction amount by the commission rate agreed with each customer. Stock transactions can lead to losses as a result of share price fluctuations and other factors. Transactions in foreign stocks can lead to additional losses stemming from foreign exchange fluctuations. We may also charge commissions and fees for certain categories of investment advice, products and services. Recommended investment strategies, products and services carry the risk of losses to principal and other losses as a result of changes in market and/or economic trends, and/or fluctuations in market value. Before deciding on the purchase of financial products and/or services, customers should carefully read the relevant disclosures, prospectuses and other documentation. 'Moody's', 'Standard Poor's', and 'Fitch' mentioned in this report are not registered credit rating agencies in Japan unless Japan or 'Nippon' is specifically designated in the name of the entity. Reports on Japanese listed companies not written by analysts of DSI are written by Deutsche Bank Group's analysts with the coverage companies specified by DSI. Some of the foreign securities stated on this report are not disclosed according to the Financial Instruments and Exchange Law of Japan. Target prices set by Deutsche Bank's equity analysts are based on a 12-month forecast period.

Korea: Distributed by Deutsche Securities Korea Co.

South Africa: Deutsche Bank AG Johannesburg is incorporated in the Federal Republic of Germany (Branch Register Number in South Africa: 1998/003298/10).

Singapore: This report is issued by Deutsche Bank AG, Singapore Branch or Deutsche Securities Asia Limited, Singapore Branch (One Raffles Quay #18-00 South Tower Singapore 048583, +65 6423 8001), which may be contacted in respect of any matters arising from, or in connection with, this report. Where this report is issued or promulgated by Deutsche Bank in Singapore to a person who is not an accredited investor, expert investor or institutional investor (as defined in the applicable Singapore laws and regulations), they accept legal responsibility to such person for its contents.

Taiwan: Information on securities/investments that trade in Taiwan is for your reference only. Readers should independently evaluate investment risks and are solely responsible for their investment decisions. Deutsche Bank research may not be distributed to the Taiwan public media or quoted or used by the Taiwan public media without written consent. Information on securities/instruments that do not trade in Taiwan is for informational purposes only and is not to be construed as a recommendation to trade in such securities/instruments. Deutsche Securities Asia Limited, Taipei Branch may not execute transactions for clients in these securities/instruments.

Qatar: Deutsche Bank AG in the Qatar Financial Centre (registered no. 00032) is regulated by the Qatar Financial Centre Regulatory Authority. Deutsche Bank AG - QFC Branch may undertake only the financial services activities that fall within the scope of its existing QFCRA license. Its principal place of business in the QFC: Qatar Financial Centre, Tower, West Bay, Level 5, PO Box 14928, Doha, Qatar. This information has been distributed by Deutsche Bank AG. Related financial products or services are only available only to Business Customers, as defined by the Qatar Financial Centre Regulatory Authority.

Russia: The information, interpretation and opinions submitted herein are not in the context of, and do not constitute, any appraisal or evaluation activity requiring a license in the Russian Federation.

Kingdom of Saudi Arabia: Deutsche Securities Saudi Arabia LLC Company (registered no. 07073-37) is regulated by the Capital Market Authority. Deutsche Securities Saudi Arabia may undertake only the financial services activities that fall within the scope of its existing CMA license. Its principal place of business in Saudi Arabia: King Fahad Road, Al Olaya District, P.O. Box 301809, Faisaliah Tower - 17th Floor, 11372 Riyadh, Saudi Arabia.

United Arab Emirates: Deutsche Bank AG in the Dubai International Financial Centre (registered no. 00045) is regulated by the Dubai Financial Services Authority. Deutsche Bank AG - DIFC Branch may only undertake the financial services activities that fall within the scope of its existing DFSA license. Principal place of business in the DIFC: Dubai International Financial Centre, The Gate Village, Building 5, PO Box 504902, Dubai, U.A.E. This information has been distributed by Deutsche Bank AG. Related financial products or services are available only to Professional Clients, as defined by the Dubai Financial Services Authority.

Australia and New Zealand: This research is intended only for 'wholesale clients' within the meaning of the Australian Corporations Act and New Zealand Financial Advisors Act, respectively. Please refer to Australia-specific research disclosures and related information at https://australia.db.com/australia/content/research-information.html Where research refers to any particular financial product recipients of the research should consider any product disclosure statement, prospectus or other applicable disclosure document before making any decision about whether to acquire the product. In preparing this report, the primary analyst or an individual who assisted in the preparation of this report has likely been in contact with the company that is the subject of this research for confirmation/clarification of data, facts, statements, permission to use company-sourced material in the report, and/or site-visit attendance. Without prior approval from Research Management, analysts may not accept from current or potential Banking clients the costs of travel, accommodations, or other expenses incurred by analysts attending site visits, conferences, social events, and the like. Similarly, without prior approval from Research Management and Anti-Bribery and Corruption ("ABC") team, analysts may not accept perks or other items of value for their personal use from issuers they cover.

Additional information relative to securities, other financial products or issuers discussed in this report is available upon

30 July 2019

Cosmetics, Household & Personal Care

Procter & Gamble

request. This report may not be reproduced, distributed or published without Deutsche Bank's prior written consent. Copyright © 2019 Deutsche Bank AG

David Folkerts-Landau
Group Chief Economist and Global Head of Research

Pam Finelli Global Chief Operating Officer Research	Michael Spencer Head of APAC Research	Steve Pollard Head of Americas Research Global Head of Equity Research
Anthony Klarman Global Head of Debt Research	Kinner Lakhani Head of EMEA Equity Research	Joe Liew Head of APAC Equity Research

Jim Reid Global Head of Thematic Research	Francis Yared Global Head of Rates Research	George Saravelos Head of FX Research	Peter Hooper Global Head of Economic Research

Andreas Neubauer
Head of Germany Research

Spyros Mesomeris
Global Head of Quantitative
and QIS Research

International Production Locations

Deutsche Bank AG
Deutsche Bank Place
Level 16
Corner of Hunter & Phillip Streets
Sydney, NSW 2000
Australia
Tel: (61) 2 8258 1234

Deutsche Bank AG
Equity Research
Mainzer Landstrasse 11-17
60329 Frankfurt am Main
Germany
Tel: (49) 69 910 00

Deutsche Bank AG
Filiale Hongkong
International Commerce Centre,
1 Austin Road West, Kowloon,
Hong Kong
Tel: (852) 2203 8888

Deutsche Securities Inc.
2-11-1 Nagatacho
Sanno Park Tower
Chiyoda-ku, Tokyo 100-6171
Japan
Tel: (81) 3 5156 6770

Deutsche Bank AG London
1 Great Winchester Street
London EC2N 2EQ
United Kingdom
Tel: (44) 20 7545 8000

Deutsche Bank Securities Inc.
60 Wall Street
New York, NY 10005
United States of America
Tel: (1) 212 250 2500

Concluding Observations of Analyst Report

We make four observations on the Deutsche Bank analyst report regarding P&G's target stock price.

1. The analyst report defines free cash flow to the firm as follows:

	Earnings before interest and taxes (EBIT)
−	Taxes (EBIT × assumed tax rate)
+	Depreciation and amortization
−	Capital expenditures
−	Increase in working capital
=	Free cash flow to the firm

2. This analyst report uses the same DCF computation we describe in this module. Free cash flow estimates for the nine-year forecast horizon (4QE20-4QE28) and the terminal year (also labeled 4QE28) are discounted at the weighted average cost of capital, resulting in a total firm value of $344,915 million. The analyst, then, subtracts P&G's debt of $22,254 million, to yield the implied equity value of $322,661, or $124 per share, based on 2,611 million shares outstanding.
3. The cost of equity capital is estimated using the capital asset pricing model (CAPM) as we describe in the module. The analyst's estimated WACC of 6.5% is higher than the 5.83% WACC that we assume in the module. It is not uncommon that model assumptions differ among analysts.
4. Bottom line: We see that this analyst's $124 stock price target is higher than the $110.49 stock price estimate that we independently determined in this module. There are a number of differences between our forecast and that of the Deutsche Bank analyst, including growth rates, margins, and WACC.

Guidance Answers

You Are the Chief Financial Officer
Pg. 13-6 Cash flow can be increased by reducing assets. For example, receivables can be reduced by the following.

- Encouraging up-front payments or progress billings on long-term contracts
- Increasing credit standards to avoid slow-paying accounts before sales are made
- Monitoring account age and sending reminders to past-due customers
- Selling accounts receivable to a financial institution or special-purpose entity

As another example of asset reduction, plant assets can be reduced by the following.

- Selling unused or excess plant assets
- Forming alliances with other companies to share specialized plant assets
- Owning assets in a special-purpose entity with other companies
- Selling production facilities to a contract manufacturer and purchasing the output

You Are the Chief Financial Officer
Pg. 13-12 RNOA can be disaggregated into its two key drivers: net operating profit margin and net operating asset turnover. Net operating profit margin can be increased by improving gross profit margins (better product pricing, lower-cost manufacturing, etc.) and closely monitoring and controlling operating expenses. Net operating asset turnover can be increased by reducing net operating working capital (better monitoring of receivables, better management of inventories, carefully extending payables, etc.) and making more effective use of plant assets (disposing of unused assets, forming corporate alliances to increase plant asset capacity, selling productive assets to contract producers and purchasing the output, etc.). The ROPI model effectively focuses managers on the balance sheet *and* income statement.

Questions

Q13-1. Explain how information contained in financial statements is useful in pricing securities. Are there some components of earnings that are more useful than others in this regard? What nonfinancial information might also be useful?

Q13-2. In general, what role do expectations play in pricing equity securities? What is the relation between security prices and expected returns (the discount rate, or WACC, in this case)?

Q13-3. What are free cash flows to the firm (FCFF) and how are they used in the pricing of equity securities?

Q13-4. Define the weighted average cost of capital (WACC).

Q13-5. Define net operating profit after tax (NOPAT).

Q13-6. Define net operating assets (NOA).

Q13-7. Define the concept of residual operating income (ROPI). How is residual operating income used in pricing equity securities?

Q13-8. What insight does disaggregation of RNOA into net operating profit margin and net operating asset turnover provide for managing a company?

Assignments with the logo in the margin are available in BusinessCourse.
See the Preface of the book for details.

Mini Exercises

M13-9. Interpreting Earnings Announcement Effects on Stock Prices
On November 2, 2016, Facebook Inc. announced its 2016 third quarter results. Revenues were up nearly 50% from 2015 and earnings were up a whopping 180% ($5,944 million compared to $2,127 million.) Yet, in the ensuing days, Facebook's stock value fell 7% according to CNBC. Why do you believe that the company's stock price fell despite the good news?

LO1
Facebook Inc. (FB)

M13-10. Computing Residual Operating Income (ROPI)
Home Depot reports net operating profit after tax (NOPAT) of $12,073 million for the fiscal year ended February 3, 2019. Its net operating assets at the beginning of the fiscal year are $24,887 million. Assuming a 7.85% weighted average cost of capital (WACC), what is Home Depot's residual operating income for the fiscal year ended February 3, 2019? Show computations.

LO3
Home Depot Inc. (HD)

M13-11. Computing Free Cash Flows to the Firm (FCFF)
Home Depot reports net operating profit after tax (NOPAT) of $12,073 million for the fiscal year ended February 3, 2019. Its net operating assets at the beginning of and end of the fiscal year ended February 3, 2019, are $24,887 million and $25,546 million, respectively. What are Home Depot's free cash flows to the firm (FCFF) for the year ended February 3, 2019? Show computations.

LO2
Home Depot Inc. (HD)

M13-12. Computing, Analyzing, and Interpreting Residual Operating Income (ROPI)
In its annual report for the fiscal year ended July 27, 2019, Cisco Systems reports net operating income after tax (NOPAT) of $11,346 million. As of the beginning of the fiscal year it reports net operating assets of $22,225 million.

a. Did Cisco earn positive residual operating income (ROPI) if its weighted average cost of capital (WACC) is 7.6%? Explain.
b. At what level of WACC would Cisco not report positive residual operating income for the year? Explain.

LO3
Cisco Systems (CSCO)

M13-13. Estimating Share Value Using the DCF Model
Following are forecasts of Target Corporation's sales, net operating profit after tax (NOPAT), and net operating assets (NOA) as of February 2, 2019, which we label fiscal year 2018.

LO1, 2
Target Corporation (TGT)

$ millions	Reported 2018	Forecast Horizon Period				Terminal Period
		2019	2020	2021	2022	
Sales............	$75,356	$79,124	$83,080	$87,234	$91,596	$93,428
NOPAT..........	3,269	3,402	3,572	3,751	3,939	4,017
NOA............	23,020	24,197	25,407	26,677	28,011	28,571

Answer the following requirements assuming a terminal period growth rate of 2%, a discount rate (WACC) of 7.63%, common shares outstanding of 517.8 million, and net nonoperating obligations (NNO) of $11,723 million.

a. Estimate the value of a share of Target common stock using the discounted cash flow (DCF) model as of February 2, 2019.
b. Target Corporation (TGT) stock closed at $77.12 on March 13, 2019, the date the 10-K was filed with the SEC. How does your valuation estimate compare with this closing price? What do you believe are some reasons for the difference?

LO3
Target Corporation (TGT)

M13-14. Estimating Share Value Using the ROPI Model
Refer to the information for Target Corporation in M13-13 to answer the following requirements.

a. Estimate the value of a share of Target common stock using the residual operating income (ROPI) model as of February 2, 2019.
b. Target Corporation (TGT) stock closed at $77.12 on March 13, 2019, the date the 10-K was filed with the SEC. How does your valuation estimate compare with this closing price? What do you believe are some reasons for the difference?

LO4
Alcoa Corp. (AA)

M13-15. Assess the Effects of Managerial Actions on ROPI and Components
Alcoa's Form 10-Q for the third quarter ended September 30, 2019, included the following disclosure.

> In September 2019, Alcoa Corporation announced the implementation of a new operating model that will result in a leaner, more integrated, operator-centric organization. Effective November 1, 2019, the new operating model eliminates the business unit structure, consolidates sales, procurement and other commercial capabilities at an enterprise level, and streamlines the Executive Team from 12 to seven direct reports to the Chief Executive Officer. The new structure will reduce overhead with the intention of promoting operational and commercial excellence, and increasing connectivity between the Company's plants and leadership.

By undertaking these actions, the company hopes to improve its ROPI. Identify at least four specific ways that these actions can happen *and* the direction of the effects from each on NOPAT and NOA.

Exercises

LO2
Illinois Tool Works Inc. (ITW)

E13-16. Estimating Share Value Using the DCF Model
Following are forecasts of Illinois Tool Works Inc. sales, net operating profit after tax (NOPAT), and net operating assets (NOA) as of December 31, 2018.

$ millions	Reported 2018	Forecast Horizon Period				Terminal Period
		2019	2020	2021	2022	
Sales...........	$14,768	$15,654	$16,593	$17,589	$18,644	$19,017
NOPAT.........	2,711	2,880	3,053	3,236	3,430	3,499
NOA............	9,462	10,028	10,630	11,268	11,944	12,183

Answer the following requirements assuming a discount rate (WACC) of 7.35%, a terminal period growth rate of 2%, common shares outstanding of 328.1 million, and net nonoperating obligations (NNO) of $6,204 million.

a. Estimate the value of a share of ITW's common stock using the discounted cash flow (DCF) model as of December 31, 2018.
b. Illinois Tool Works Inc. closed at $144.21 on February 15, 2019, the date the 10-K was filed with the SEC. How does your valuation estimate compare with this closing price? What do you believe are some reasons for the difference?

E13-17. Estimating Share Value Using the ROPI Model

Refer to the information for **Illinois Tool Works Inc.** in E13-16 to answer the following requirements.

a. Estimate the value of a share of Illinois Tool Works Inc. common stock using the residual operating income (ROPI) model as of December 31, 2018.

b. Illinois Tool Works stock closed at $144.21 on February 15, 2019, the date the 10-K was filed with the SEC. How does your valuation estimate compare with this closing price? What do you believe are some reasons for the difference?

E13-18. Estimating Share Value Using the DCF Model

Following are forecasts of sales, net operating profit after tax (NOPAT), and net operating assets (NOA) as of December 31, 2018, for **Humana**.

$ millions	Reported 2018	Forecast Horizon Period				Terminal Period
		2019	2020	2021	2022	
Sales........	$56,912	$57,766	$58,632	$59,512	$60,404	$61,008
NOPAT......	2,492	2,542	2,580	2,619	2,658	2,684
NOA........	4,032	4,097	4,158	4,221	4,284	4,327

Answer the following requirements assuming a discount rate (WACC) of 7.8%, a terminal period growth rate of 1%, common shares outstanding of 135.6 million, net nonoperating obligations (NNO) of $(6,129) million, which is negative because Humana's nonoperating assets exceed its nonoperating liabilities, and no noncontrolling interest (NCI) on the balance sheet.

a. Estimate the value of a share of Humana's common stock using the discounted cash flow (DCF) model as of December 31, 2018.

b. Humana (HUM) stock closed at $307.56 on February 21, 2019, the date the 10-K was filed with the SEC. How does your valuation estimate compare with this closing price? What do you believe are some reasons for the difference?

E13-19. Estimating Share Value Using the ROPI Model

Refer to the information for **Humana** in E13-18 to answer the following requirements.

a. Estimate the value of a share of common stock using the residual operating income (ROPI) model as of December 31, 2018.

b. Humana (HUM) stock closed at $307.56 on February 21, 2019, the date the 10-K was filed with the SEC. How does your valuation estimate compare with this closing price? What do you believe are some reasons for the difference?

E13-20. Identifying and Computing Net Operating Assets (NOA) and Net Nonoperating Obligations (NNO)

Following are the balance sheets and statement of earnings for **Home Depot Inc.** for fiscal year ended February 3, 2019, which the company labels fiscal year 2018.

THE HOME DEPOT INC. Consolidated Balance Sheets		
$ millions, except par value	February 3, 2019	January 28, 2018
Assets		
Current assets		
Cash and cash equivalents......	$ 1,778	$ 3,595
Receivables, net.......	1,936	1,952
Merchandise inventories.....	13,925	12,748
Other current assets.......	890	638
Total current assets.......	18,529	18,933
Net property and equipment.....	22,375	22,075
Goodwill.......	2,252	2,275
Other assets.......	847	1,246
Total assets.......	$44,003	$44,529

continued

THE HOME DEPOT INC.
Consolidated Balance Sheets

$ millions, except par value	February 3, 2019	January 28, 2018
Liabilities and Stockholders' Equity		
Current liabilities		
Short-term debt	$ 1,339	$ 1,559
Accounts payable	7,755	7,244
Accrued salaries and related expenses	1,506	1,640
Sales taxes payable	656	520
Deferred revenue	1,782	1,805
Income taxes payable	11	54
Current installments of long-term debt	1,056	1,202
Other accrued expenses	2,611	2,170
Total current liabilities	16,716	16,194
Long-term debt, excluding current installments	26,807	24,267
Deferred income taxes	491	440
Other long-term liabilities	1,867	2,174
Total liabilities	45,881	43,075
Common stock, par value $0.05; authorized: 10,000 shares; issued: 1,782 at February 3, 2019 and 1,780 shares at January 28, 2018; outstanding: 1,105 shares at February 3, 2019 and 1,158 shares at January 28, 2018	89	89
Paid-in capital	10,578	10,192
Retained earnings	46,423	39,935
Accumulated other comprehensive loss	(772)	(566)
Treasury stock, at cost, 677 shares at February 3, 2019 and 622 shares at January 28, 2018	(58,196)	(48,196)
Total stockholders' (deficit) equity	(1,878)	1,454
Total liabilities and stockholders' equity	$44,003	$44,529

THE HOME DEPOT INC.
Consolidated Statements of Earnings

For Fiscal Year Ended ($ millions)	February 3, 2019	January 28, 2018
Net Sales	$108,203	$100,904
Cost of sales	71,043	66,548
Gross profit	37,160	34,356
Operating expenses		
Selling, general and administrative	19,513	17,864
Depreciation and amortization	1,870	1,811
Impairment loss	247	0
Total operating expenses	21,630	19,675
Operating income	15,530	14,681
Interest and other (income) expense:		
Interest and investment income	(93)	(74)
Interest expense	1,051	1,057
Other	16	0
Interest and other, net	974	983
Earnings before provision for income taxes	14,556	13,698
Provision for income taxes	3,435	5,068
Net earnings	$ 11,121	$ 8,630

a. Compute net operating assets (NOA) and net nonoperating obligations (NNO) for the fiscal year ended February 3, 2019.
b. For the fiscal year ended February 3, 2019, show that: NOA = NNO + Stockholders' equity.
c. Compute net operating profit after tax (NOPAT) for the year ended February 3, 2019. Assume a federal and state combined statutory tax rate of 22%. Also, consider the Impairment loss of $247 million before tax ($193 million after tax) to be a nonpersistent item. Exclude the after-tax amount from your NOPAT calculation.

E13-21. Estimating Share Value Using the DCF Model

LO1, 2
Home Depot Inc. (HD)

Following are forecasts of **Home Depot**'s sales, net operating profit after tax (NOPAT), and net operating assets (NOA) as of February 3, 2019, which the company labels fiscal 2018.

$ millions	Reported 2018	Forecast Horizon Period 2019	2020	2021	2022	Terminal Period
Sales	$108,203	$115,777	$123,882	$132,553	$141,832	$144,669
NOPAT	12,073	12,967	13,875	14,846	15,885	16,203
NOA	25,546	27,332	29,245	31,292	33,483	34,152

Answer the following requirements assuming a discount rate (WACC) of 7.85%, a terminal period growth rate of 2%, common shares outstanding of 1,105 million, net nonoperating obligations (NNO) of $27,424 million.

a. Estimate the value of a share of Home Depot's common stock using the discounted cash flow (DCF) model as of February 3, 2019.
b. Home Depot stock closed at $190.06 on March 28, 2019, the date the Form 10-K was filed with the SEC. How does your valuation estimate compare with this closing price? What do you believe are some reasons for the difference?

E13-22. Estimating Share Value Using the ROPI Model

LO3
Home Depot Inc. (HD)

Refer to the information for **Home Depot Inc.** in E13-21 to answer the following requirements.

a. Estimate the value of a share of Home Depot common stock using the residual operating income (ROPI) model as of February 3, 2019.
b. Home Depot stock closed at $190.06 on March 28, 2019, the date the Form 10-K was filed with the SEC. How does your valuation estimate compare with this closing price? What do you believe are some reasons for the difference?

E13-23. Explaining the Equivalence of Valuation Models and the Relevance of Earnings

LO1, 2, 3

This module focused on two different valuation models: the discounted cash flow (DCF) model and the residual operating income (ROPI) model. The models focus on free cash flows to the firm and on residual operating income, respectively. We stressed that these two models are theoretically equivalent.

a. What is the *intuition* for why these models are equivalent?
b. Some analysts focus on cash flows as they believe that companies manage earnings, which presumably makes earnings less relevant. Are earnings relevant? Explain.

E13-24. Applying and Interpreting Value Driver Components of RNOA

LO4

The net operating profit margin and the net operating asset turnover components of return on net operating assets are often termed *value drivers,* which refers to their positive influence on stock value by virtue of their role as components of return on net operating assets (RNOA).

a. How do profit margins and asset turnover ratios influence stock values?
b. Assuming that profit margins and asset turnover ratios are value drivers, what insight does this give us about managing companies if the goal is to create shareholder value?

E13-25. Quantify the Effects of Managerial Actions on ROPI and Components

LO4

Rincon Farms Inc. reports the following financial data just prior to its fiscal year ended December 31, 2019 ($ millions).

RINCON FARMS INC.
Balance Sheet

Cash.............................	$ 100	Accounts payable...............	$ 300
Accounts receivable.............	300	Long-term debt.................	600
Inventory.......................	500		
Property, plant & equipment.....	1,000	Equity........................	1,000
Total assets	$1,900	Total liabilities and equity	$1,900

	Actual Dec. 2019	Forecasted Dec. 2020
Sales.....................	$1,200	$1,310
NOPAT	$ 210	$ 216
NOA	$1,500	$1,545
WACC.....................	7%	

Required

a. Compute ROPI for 2019 and 2020. Net operating assets (NOA) at the beginning of 2019 were $1,350.
b. The company is contemplating taking the following actions before the end of 2019. (These actions are not reflected in any of the financial data reported above.) For each of the actions, determine the effect on residual operating income for the fiscal year ended December 31, 2020.
   1. Reduce inventory by 10%, which reduces accounts payable by 5%.
   2. Decrease property, plant and equipment (PPE) by 20% with no consequent impact on NOPAT.
   3. Engage in a sale leaseback of a major building. The company will sell 50% of its PPE at book value and increase rental costs by $30 after tax, per year.
   4. Increase debt $300, which increases interest expense by $15.

Problems

Cisco Systems (CSCO)

LO1, 2 P13-26. Forecasting with the Parsimonious Method and Estimating Share Value Using the DCF Model
Following are income statements and balance sheets for **Cisco Systems**.

CISCO SYSTEMS
Consolidated Statements of Operations

Year Ended ($ millions)	July 27, 2019	July 28, 2018
Revenue		
Product..	$39,005	$36,709
Service..	12,899	12,621
Total revenue.......................................	51,904	49,330
Cost of sales		
Product..	14,863	14,427
Service..	4,375	4,297
Total cost of sales	19,238	18,724
Gross margin	32,666	30,606
Operating expenses		
Research and development	6,577	6,332
Sales and marketing..................................	9,571	9,242
General and administrative...........................	1,827	2,144
Amortization of purchased intangible assets........	150	221
Restructuring and other charges.....................	322	358
Total operating expenses	18,447	18,297

continued

continued from previous page

CISCO SYSTEMS
Consolidated Statements of Operations

Year Ended ($ millions)	July 27, 2019	July 28, 2018
Operating income	14,219	12,309
Interest income	1,308	1,508
Interest expense	(859)	(943)
Other income (loss), net	(97)	165
Interest and other income (loss), net	352	730
Income before provision for income taxes	14,571	13,039
Provision for income taxes	2,950	12,929
Net income	$11,621	$ 110

CISCO SYSTEMS INC.
Consolidated Balance Sheets

$ millions, except par value	July 27, 2019	July 28, 2018
Assets		
Current assets		
Cash and cash equivalents	$11,750	$ 8,934
Investments	21,663	37,614
Accounts receivable, net of allowance for doubtful accounts of $136 at July 27, 2019 and $129 at July 28, 2018	5,491	5,554
Inventories	1,383	1,846
Financing receivables, net	5,095	4,949
Other current assets	2,373	2,940
Total current assets	47,755	61,837
Property and equipment, net	2,789	3,006
Financing receivables, net	4,958	4,882
Goodwill	33,529	31,706
Purchased intangible assets, net	2,201	2,552
Deferred tax assets	4,065	3,219
Other assets	2,496	1,582
Total assets	$97,793	$108,784
Liabilities and equity		
Current liabilities		
Short-term debt	$10,191	$ 5,238
Accounts payable	2,059	1,904
Income taxes payable	1,149	1,004
Accrued compensation	3,221	2,986
Deferred revenue	10,668	11,490
Other current liabilities	4,424	4,413
Total current liabilities	31,712	27,035
Long-term debt	14,475	20,331
Income taxes payable	8,927	8,585
Deferred revenue	7,799	8,195
Other long-term liabilities	1,309	1,434
Total liabilities	64,222	65,580

continued

continued from previous page

CISCO SYSTEMS INC.
Consolidated Balance Sheets

$ millions, except par value	July 27, 2019	July 28, 2018
Equity:		
Cisco shareholders' equity		
Preferred stock, no par value: 5 shares authorized; none issued and outstanding...	—	—
Common stock and additional paid-in capital, $0.001 par value: 20,000 shares authorized; 4,250 and 4,614 shares issued and outstanding at July 27, 2019, and July 28, 2018, respectively......	40,266	42,820
(Accumulated deficit) Retained earnings......................	(5,903)	1,233
Accumulated other comprehensive income (loss)................	(792)	(849)
Total Cisco shareholders' equity............................	33,571	43,204
Total equity..	33,571	43,204
Total liabilities and equity....................................	$97,793	$108,784

Required

a. Compute net operating assets (NOA) for 2019.
b. Compute net operating profit after tax (NOPAT) for 2019, assuming a federal and state statutory tax rate of 22%. Assume that all items on the 2019 income statement will persist.
c. Use the parsimonious forecast method, as shown in Analysis Insight box on page 13-4, to forecast Cisco's sales, NOPAT, and NOA for 2020 through 2023 *and* the terminal period using the following assumptions.

Sales growth 2020–2023......................	5%
Terminal growth.............................	1%
Net operating profit margin...................	2019 rate rounded to three decimal places
Net operating asset turnover..................	2019 rate rounded to three decimal places

d. Estimate the value of a share of Cisco common stock using the discounted cash flow (DCF) model as of July 27, 2019; assume a discount rate (WACC) of 7.6%, common shares outstanding of 5,029 million, and net nonoperating obligations (NNO) of $(8,747) million (NNO is negative, which means that Cisco has net nonoperating investments).
e. Cisco stock closed at $48.42 on September 5, 2019, the date the Form 10-K was filed with the SEC. How does your valuation estimate compare with this closing price? What do you believe are some reasons for the difference? What investment decision is suggested from your results?

LO1, 3

Cisco Systems (CSCO)

P13-27. Forecasting with Parsimonious Method and Estimating Share Value Using the ROPI Model

Refer to the information for **Cisco Systems** in P13-26 to answer the following requirements.

Required

a. Estimate the value of a share of Cisco common stock using the residual operating income (ROPI) model as of July 27, 2019.
b. Cisco stock closed at $48.42 on September 5, 2019, the date the Form 10-K was filed with the SEC. How does your valuation estimate compare with this closing price? What do you believe are some reasons for the difference? What investment decision is suggested from your results?

LO2

AT&T Inc. (T)

P13-28. Estimating Share Value Using the DCF Model

Following are forecasted sales, NOPAT, and NOA for **AT&T** for 2019 through 2022.

$ millions	Reported 2018	Forecast Horizon Period			
		2019	2020	2021	2022
Sales.......................	$170,756	$181,001	$191,861	$203,373	$215,576
NOPAT.....................	20,895	22,082	23,407	24,812	26,300
NOA.......................	369,039	390,931	414,387	439,251	465,607

Required

a. Forecast the terminal period values assuming a 2% terminal period growth rate.
b. Estimate the value of a share of AT&T common stock using the discounted cash flow (DCF) model as of December 31, 2018; assume a discount rate (WACC) of 5.7%, common shares outstanding of 7,281.6 million, net nonoperating obligations (NNO) of $175,155 million, and noncontrolling interest (NCI) from the balance sheet of $9,795 million.
c. AT&T closed at $30.85 on February 20, 2019, the date the Form 10-K was filed with the SEC. How does your valuation estimate compare with this closing price?
d. If WACC has been 6.2%, what would the valuation estimate have been? What about if WACC has been 5.2%?

P13-29. Estimating Share Value Using the ROPI Model

Refer to the information for **AT&T** in P13-28 to answer the following requirements.

Required

a. Estimate the value of a share of AT&T common stock using the residual operating income (ROPI) model as of December 31, 2018.
b. AT&T stock price was $30.85 on February 20, 2019, the date the Form 10-K was filed with the SEC. How does your valuation estimate compare with this closing price? What do you believe are some reasons for the difference? What investment decision is suggested from your results?

LO3

AT&T Inc. (T)

P13-30. Forecasting with Parsimonious Method and Estimating Share Value Using the DCF Model

Following are income statements and balance sheets for **Nike Inc.**

LO1, 2

Nike Inc. (NKE)

NIKE INC.
Consolidated Income Statements

For Year Ended ($ millions)	May 31, 2019	May 31, 2018
Revenues	$39,117	$36,397
Cost of sales	21,643	20,441
Gross profit	17,474	15,956
Demand creation expense	3,753	3,577
Operating overhead expense	8,949	7,934
Total selling and administrative expense	12,702	11,511
Interest expense (income), net	49	54
Other (income) expense, net	(78)	66
Income before income taxes	4,801	4,325
Income tax expense	772	2,392
Net income	$ 4,029	$ 1,933

NIKE INC.
Consolidated Balance Sheets

$ millions	May 31, 2019	May 31, 2018
Current assets		
Cash and equivalents	$ 4,466	$ 4,249
Short-term investments	197	996
Accounts receivable, net	4,272	3,498
Inventories	5,622	5,261
Prepaid expenses and other current assets	1,968	1,130
Total current assets	16,525	15,134
Property, plant and equipment, net	4,744	4,454
Identifiable intangible assets, net	283	285
Goodwill	154	154
Deferred income taxes and other assets	2,011	2,509
Total assets	$23,717	$22,536

continued

continued from previous page

NIKE INC.
Consolidated Balance Sheets

$ millions	May 31, 2019	May 31, 2018
Current liabilities		
Current portion of long-term debt	$ 6	$ 6
Notes payable	9	336
Accounts payable	2,612	2,279
Accrued liabilities	5,010	3,269
Income taxes payable	229	150
Total current liabilities	7,866	6,040
Long-term debt	3,464	3,468
Deferred income taxes and other liabilities	3,347	3,216
Commitments and contingencies (Note 18)		
Shareholders' equity		
Common stock at stated value:		
Class A convertible—315 and 329 shares outstanding	—	—
Class B—1,253 and 1,272 shares outstanding	3	3
Capital in excess of stated value	7,163	6,384
Accumulated other comprehensive income (loss)	231	(92)
Retained earnings	1,643	3,517
Total shareholders' equity	9,040	9,812
Total liabilities and shareholders' equity	$23,717	$22,536

Required

a. Compute net operating assets (NOA) and net nonoperating obligations (NNO) for 2019. The company's NNO is negative because cash exceeds debt.

b. Compute net operating profit after tax (NOPAT) for 2019 assuming a federal and state statutory tax rate of 22%.

c. Use the parsimonious forecast method, as shown in the Analysis Insight box on page 13-4, to forecast sales, NOPAT, and NOA for 2020 through 2023 using the following assumptions.

Sales growth	8%
Net operating profit margin (NOPM)	2019 ratios rounded to three decimal places
Net operating asset turnover (NOAT), year-end	2019 ratios rounded to three decimal places

Forecast the terminal period value assuming a 2% terminal period growth and using the NOPM and NOAT assumptions above.

d. Estimate the value of a share of Nike's common stock using the discounted cash flow (DCF) model as of May 31, 2019; assume a discount rate (WACC) of 6.8% and common shares outstanding of 1,682 million.

e. Nike's stock closed at $86.70 on July 23, 2019, the date the Form 10-K was filed with the SEC. How does your valuation estimate compare with this closing price? What do you believe are some reasons for the difference? What investment decision is suggested from your results?

LO1, 3
Nike Inc. (NKE)

P13-31. Forecasting with the Parsimonious Method and Estimating Share Value Using the ROPI Model
Refer to the information for **Nike Inc.** in P13-30 to answer the following requirements.

Required

a. Estimate the value of a share of Nike common stock using the residual operating income (ROPI) model as of May 31, 2019. For simplicity, prepare your forecasts in $ millions.

b. Nike's stock closed at $86.70 on July 23, 2019, the date the Form 10-K was filed with the SEC. How does your valuation estimate compare with this closing price? What do you believe are some reasons for the difference? What investment decision is suggested from your results?

P13-32. Estimating Share Value Using the DCF Model

Following are forecasted sales, NOPAT, and NOA for Colgate-Palmolive Company for 2019 through 2022.

LO2
Colgate-Palmolive
Company (CL)

Colgate Palmolive (CL) $ millions	Reported 2018	Forecast Horizon Period			
		2019	2020	2021	2022
Sales..........................	$15,544	$16,010	$16,491	$16,985	$17,495
NOPAT........................	2,737	2,818	2,902	2,989	3,079
NOA...........................	5,837	6,012	6,193	6,378	6,570

Required

a. Forecast the terminal period values assuming a 1% terminal period growth for all three model inputs, that is Sales, NOPAT, and NOA.
b. Estimate the value of a share of Colgate-Palmolive common stock using the discounted cash flow (DCF) model; assume a discount rate (WACC) of 5.7%, common shares outstanding of 862.9 million, net nonoperating obligations (NNO) of $5,640 million, and noncontrolling interest (NCI) from the balance sheet of $299 million.
c. Colgate-Palmolive's stock closed at $66.70 on February 21, 2019, the date the Form 10-K was filed with the SEC. How does your valuation estimate compare with this closing price? What do you believe are some reasons for the difference?
d. The forecasts you completed assumed a terminal growth rate of 1%. What if the terminal rate had been 2%. What would your estimated stock price have been?
e. What would WACC have to be to warrant the actual stock price on February 21, 2019?

P13-33. Estimating Share Value Using the ROPI Model

Refer to the information for Colgate-Palmolive in P13-32 to answer the following requirements.

LO3
Colgate-Palmolive
Company (CL)

Required

a. Estimate the value of a share of Colgate-Palmolive common stock using the residual operating income (ROPI) model.
b. Colgate-Palmolive stock closed at $66.70 on February 21, 2019, the date the Form 10-K was filed with the SEC. How does your valuation estimate compare with this closing price? What do you believe are some reasons for the difference? What investment decision is suggested from your results?

Management Applications

MA13-34. Management Application: Operating Improvement versus Financial Engineering

Assume that you are the CEO of a small publicly traded company. The operating performance of your company has fallen below market expectations, which is reflected in a depressed stock price. At your direction, your CFO provides you with the following recommendations that are designed to increase your company's return on net operating assets (RNOA) and your operating cash flows, both of which will, presumably, result in improved financial performance and an increased stock price.

LO4

1. To improve net cash flow from operating activities, the CFO recommends that your company reduce inventories (raw material, work-in-progress, and finished goods) and receivables (through selective credit granting and increased emphasis on collection of past due accounts).
2. The CFO recommends that your company lengthen the time taken to pay accounts payable (lean on the trade) to increase net cash flows from operating activities.
3. Because your company's operating performance is already depressed, the CFO recommends that you take a "big bath;" that is, write off all assets deemed to be impaired and accrue excessive liabilities for future contingencies. The higher current period expense will, then, result in higher future period income as the assets written off will not be depreciated and your company will have a liability account available to absorb future cash payments rather than recording them as expenses.

4. The CFO recommends that your company increase its estimate of expected return on pension investments. This will reduce pension expense and increase operating profit, a component of net operating profit after tax (NOPAT) and, thus, of RNOA.
5. The CFO recommends that your company share ownership of its outbound logistics (trucking division) with another company in a joint venture. This would have the effect of increasing throughput, thus spreading overhead over a larger volume base, and would remove the assets from your company's balance sheet since the joint venture would be accounted for as an equity method investment.

Evaluate each of the CFO's recommendations. In your evaluation, consider whether each recommendation will positively impact the operating performance of your company or whether it is cosmetic in nature.

Ongoing Project

(This ongoing project began in Module 1 and continues through most of the book; even if previous segments were not completed, the requirements are still applicable to any business analysis.) Two common models used to estimate the value of company's equity are the discounted cash flow (DCF) model and the residual operating income (ROPI) model. Estimate the value of equity and a stock price for the company(ies) under analysis. The aim is to determine an independent measure of value and assess whether the stock appears to be over- or under-valued. Begin with a forecast of the company's balance sheet and income statement. See Module 12 and follow the forecasting steps outlined there.

1. *Model Assumptions and Inputs.* In addition to the assumptions used for the forecasts, we require several additional inputs.
   - Weighted average cost of capital (WACC) is required to discount future amounts to derive present values. We can find estimates at a number of websites. Find the latest WACC at three or more sites and explore why they differ. One approach would be to use an average in the calculation and then perform sensitivity analysis for the high and the low in the range.
   - Net nonoperating obligations (NNO) is needed to determine the value of equity from total enterprise value.
   - Number of shares outstanding. Recall that shares outstanding is equal to shares issued less treasury shares. The balance sheet typically reports both numbers but if not, we can find the amounts in the statement of shareholders' equity or in a footnote.

2. *Model Estimation.* Use a spreadsheet and estimate the DCF and the ROPI models respectively. Here are some tips.
   - Pay close attention to the rounding conventions described in the footnotes in Exhibits 13.3 and 13.4. Use the spreadsheet rounding functions. *Note:* Setting the format of a cell to "no decimals" is not the same as rounding the number; with the former, the decimals are still there, but they are not displayed.
   - Make sure that NNO is subtracted from total enterprise value. In some cases, NNO is a negative number; this occurs when nonoperating assets such as cash and marketable securities exceed nonoperating liabilities. By subtracting this negative NNO, the value of equity will be greater than the enterprise value of the firm.
   - The stock prices obtained are point estimates derived from a specific set of assumptions. To understand the impact of each assumption, compute alternative stock prices by varying the assumptions. The point is to determine a range of stock prices that derive from a reasonable set of assumptions. One approach is to increase and decrease each of the model assumptions by a reasonable amount such as +/− 10%. Use the spreadsheet functions to perform this sensitivity analysis. Identify which assumptions are most important or impactful.
   - Determine the company's actual stock price. Compare the per share estimate to the actual stock price and form an opinion about the relative value. Is the stock over- or under-valued according to the model?

3. *Interpretation.* The final step in the project is to evaluate the companies based on all the analysis performed in the ongoing project.
   - Revisit the conclusions made about the companies' performance (profit and margin analysis), asset efficiency, solvency, liquidity, off-balance-sheet financing, and future opportunities based on analysis of

strengths, weaknesses, opportunities, and threats. Our goal is to assimilate the various components of analysis and to synthesize what we discovered and learned.

- Access one or more analyst reports for each company. How do the other professionals see the firms? How does their view differ from ours?
- Our analysis was based primarily on historical data from financial statements. What additional information would we like to have to refine our opinion? Is this missing information critical to our opinion?
- Based on our analysis, would we consider investing in the company? Explain.

Solutions to Review Problems

Review 13-1—Solution

	Dividend Discount	Discounted Cash Flow	Residual Operating Income
a. Uses net present value concepts.	True	True	True
b. Operating cash flows affect value	False	True	False
c. Estimates a company's enterprise value	False	True	True
d. Dividends to shareholders is a model input	True	False	False
e. Free cash flow is a model input	False	True	False
f. Estimates equity value of the firm	True	True	True
g. Capital expenditures affect estimated value	False	True	True*
h. Requires forecasts of future amounts	True	True	True
i. Operating profit affects value	False	False	True
j. Yields insight into value drivers	False	False	True

*Net operating assets change during the year due, in part, to CAPEX. So while CAPEX is not the only model input, expenditures for PPE do affect the ROPI model inputs.

Review 13-2—Solution

a.

GIS—DCF ($ millions, except per share value and discount factors)	Reported 2019	Forecast Horizon Period				Terminal Period
		2020	2021	2022	2023	
Sales		$17,118.2	$17,375.0	$17,635.6	$17,900.1	$18,168.6
NOPAT		2,396.5	2,432.5	2,469.0	2,506.0	2,543.6
NOA		22,231.4	22,564.9	22,903.4	23,246.9	23,595.6
Increase in NOA		272.0	333.5	338.5	343.5	348.7
FCFF (NOPAT − Increase in NOA)		2,124.5	2,099.0	2,130.5	2,162.5	2,194.9
Discount factor [1/(1 + r_w)^t]		0.94438	0.89185	0.84224	0.79539	
Present value of horizon FCFF		2,006.3	1,872.0	1,794.4	1,720.0	
Cum present value of horizon FCFF	$ 7,392.7					
Present value of terminal FCFF	39,768.0					
Total firm value	47,160.7					
Less: NNO	14,591.7					
Less: NCI	313.2					
Firm equity value	$32,255.8					
Shares outstanding	601.9					
Stock value per share	$ 53.59					

r_w = 0.0589
g = 0.015

b. The stock price on May 28, 2019 (the closest trading day prior to the fiscal-year-end) was $52.81 per share. The part *a* valuation of $53.59 per share implies that the stock is slightly undervalued on that date.

Review 13-3—Solution

a.

GIS—ROPI (In millions, except per share value and discount factors)	Reported 2019	Forecast Horizon Period				Terminal Period
		2020	2021	2022	2023	
Sales.		$17,118.2	$17,375.0	$17,635.6	$17,900.1	$18,168.6
NOPAT		2,396.5	2,432.5	2,469.0	2,506.0	2,543.6
NOA	$21,959.4	22,231.4	22,564.9	22,903.4	23,246.9	23,595.6
ROPI (NOPAT − [NOA$_{Beg}$ × r_w])		1,103.1	1,123.1	1,139.9	1,157.0	1,174.4
Discount factor [1/(1 + r_w)^t].		0.94438	0.89185	0.84224	0.79539	
Present value of horizon ROPI.		1,041.7	1,001.6	960.1	920.3	
Cum present value of horizon ROPI.	3,923.7					
Present value of terminal ROPI	21,278.0					
NOA	21,959.4					
Total firm value	47,161.1					
Less: NNO	14,591.7					
Less: NCI	313.2					
Firm equity value	$32,256.2					
Shares outstanding.	601.9					
Stock value per share.	$ 53.59					

r_w = 0.0589
g = 0.015

b. The stock price on May 28, 2019 (the closest trading day prior to the fiscal-year-end) was $52.81 per share. The part *a* valuation of $53.59 per share implies that the stock is slightly undervalued on that date.

Review 13-4—Solution

a. (i) Delaying payment would improve ROPI because accounts payable balance would increase, which would decrease NOA.
   (ii) A potential negative consequence would be if suppliers increase their prices to counter delayed payment. In that case, ROPI could be worsened because cost of goods sold would increase.
b. (i) Reducing inventory spoilage would reduce COGS, which would improve NOPAT.
   (ii) Selling at a discount may cause customers to expect the discount on other products, which could create pressure on margins.
c. (i) Using social media could cut down on advertising expenses.
   (ii) The impact of the new marketing on sales is a crucial factor. If the traditional marketing media were highly effective, moving away from them could actually harm sales. The cost savings and sales outcomes need to be determined to assess the impact on ROPI.
d. (i) If the lease costs are lower than the cash outlay needed for CAPEX, this could increase ROPI by increasing NOPAT and decreasing NOA.
   (ii) The availability of leased equipment might be questionable, which could lead to lost sales.

Appendix A—Compound Interest Tables

Table 1 ■ Present Value of Single Amount

$p = 1/(1 + i)^t$

Period	0.01	0.02	0.03	0.04	0.05	0.06	0.07	0.08	0.09	0.10	0.11	0.12
1	0.99010	0.98039	0.97087	0.96154	0.95238	0.94340	0.93458	0.92593	0.91743	0.90909	0.90090	0.89286
2	0.98030	0.96117	0.94260	0.92456	0.90703	0.89000	0.87344	0.85734	0.84168	0.82645	0.81162	0.79719
3	0.97059	0.94232	0.91514	0.88900	0.86384	0.83962	0.81630	0.79383	0.77218	0.75131	0.73119	0.71178
4	0.96098	0.92385	0.88849	0.85480	0.82270	0.79209	0.76290	0.73503	0.70843	0.68301	0.65873	0.63552
5	0.95147	0.90573	0.86261	0.82193	0.78353	0.74726	0.71299	0.68058	0.64993	0.62092	0.59345	0.56743
6	0.94205	0.88797	0.83748	0.79031	0.74622	0.70496	0.66634	0.63017	0.59627	0.56447	0.53464	0.50663
7	0.93272	0.87056	0.81309	0.75992	0.71068	0.66506	0.62275	0.58349	0.54703	0.51316	0.48166	0.45235
8	0.92348	0.85349	0.78941	0.73069	0.67684	0.62741	0.58201	0.54027	0.50187	0.46651	0.43393	0.40388
9	0.91434	0.83676	0.76642	0.70259	0.64461	0.59190	0.54393	0.50025	0.46043	0.42410	0.39092	0.36061
10	0.90529	0.82035	0.74409	0.67556	0.61391	0.55839	0.50835	0.46319	0.42241	0.38554	0.35218	0.32197
11	0.89632	0.80426	0.72242	0.64958	0.58468	0.52679	0.47509	0.42888	0.38753	0.35049	0.31728	0.28748
12	0.88745	0.78849	0.70138	0.62460	0.55684	0.49697	0.44401	0.39711	0.35553	0.31863	0.28584	0.25668
13	0.87866	0.77303	0.68095	0.60057	0.53032	0.46884	0.41496	0.36770	0.32618	0.28966	0.25751	0.22917
14	0.86996	0.75788	0.66112	0.57748	0.50507	0.44230	0.38782	0.34046	0.29925	0.26333	0.23199	0.20462
15	0.86135	0.74301	0.64186	0.55526	0.48102	0.41727	0.36245	0.31524	0.27454	0.23939	0.20900	0.18270
16	0.85282	0.72845	0.62317	0.53391	0.45811	0.39365	0.33873	0.29189	0.25187	0.21763	0.18829	0.16312
17	0.84438	0.71416	0.60502	0.51337	0.43630	0.37136	0.31657	0.27027	0.23107	0.19784	0.16963	0.14564
18	0.83602	0.70016	0.58739	0.49363	0.41552	0.35034	0.29586	0.25025	0.21199	0.17986	0.15282	0.13004
19	0.82774	0.68643	0.57029	0.47464	0.39573	0.33051	0.27651	0.23171	0.19449	0.16351	0.13768	0.11611
20	0.81954	0.67297	0.55368	0.45639	0.37689	0.31180	0.25842	0.21455	0.17843	0.14864	0.12403	0.10367
21	0.81143	0.65978	0.53755	0.43883	0.35894	0.29416	0.24151	0.19866	0.16370	0.13513	0.11174	0.09256
22	0.80340	0.64684	0.52189	0.42196	0.34185	0.27751	0.22571	0.18394	0.15018	0.12285	0.10067	0.08264
23	0.79544	0.63416	0.50669	0.40573	0.32557	0.26180	0.21095	0.17032	0.13778	0.11168	0.09069	0.07379
24	0.78757	0.62172	0.49193	0.39012	0.31007	0.24698	0.19715	0.15770	0.12640	0.10153	0.08170	0.06588
25	0.77977	0.60953	0.47761	0.37512	0.29530	0.23300	0.18425	0.14602	0.11597	0.09230	0.07361	0.05882
30	0.74192	0.55207	0.41199	0.30832	0.23138	0.17411	0.13137	0.09938	0.07537	0.05731	0.04368	0.03338
35	0.70591	0.50003	0.35538	0.25342	0.18129	0.13011	0.09366	0.06763	0.04899	0.03558	0.02592	0.01894
40	0.67165	0.45289	0.30656	0.20829	0.14205	0.09722	0.06678	0.04603	0.03184	0.02209	0.01538	0.01075

Table 2 ■ Present Value of Ordinary Annuity

$p = \{1 - [1/(1 + i)^t]\}/i$

Period	0.01	0.02	0.03	0.04	0.05	0.06	0.07	0.08	0.09	0.10	0.11	0.12
1	0.99010	0.98039	0.97087	0.96154	0.95238	0.94340	0.93458	0.92593	0.91743	0.90909	0.90090	0.89286
2	1.97040	1.94156	1.91347	1.88609	1.85941	1.83339	1.80802	1.78326	1.75911	1.73554	1.71252	1.69005
3	2.94099	2.88388	2.82861	2.77509	2.72325	2.67301	2.62432	2.57710	2.53129	2.48685	2.44371	2.40183
4	3.90197	3.80773	3.71710	3.62990	3.54595	3.46511	3.38721	3.31213	3.23972	3.16987	3.10245	3.03735
5	4.85343	4.71346	4.57971	4.45182	4.32948	4.21236	4.10020	3.99271	3.88965	3.79079	3.69590	3.60478
6	5.79548	5.60143	5.41719	5.24214	5.07569	4.91732	4.76654	4.62288	4.48592	4.35526	4.23054	4.11141
7	6.72819	6.47199	6.23028	6.00205	5.78637	5.58238	5.38929	5.20637	5.03295	4.86842	4.71220	4.56376
8	7.65168	7.32548	7.01969	6.73274	6.46321	6.20979	5.97130	5.74664	5.53482	5.33493	5.14612	4.96764
9	8.56602	8.16224	7.78611	7.43533	7.10782	6.80169	6.51523	6.24689	5.99525	5.75902	5.53705	5.32825
10	9.47130	8.98259	8.53020	8.11090	7.72173	7.36009	7.02358	6.71008	6.41766	6.14457	5.88923	5.65022
11	10.36763	9.78685	9.25262	8.76048	8.30641	7.88687	7.49867	7.13896	6.80519	6.49506	6.20652	5.93770
12	11.25508	10.57534	9.95400	9.38507	8.86325	8.38384	7.94269	7.53608	7.16073	6.81369	6.49236	6.19437
13	12.13374	11.34837	10.63496	9.98565	9.39357	8.85268	8.35765	7.90378	7.48690	7.10336	6.74987	6.42355
14	13.00370	12.10625	11.29607	10.56312	9.89864	9.29498	8.74547	8.24424	7.78615	7.36669	6.98187	6.62817
15	13.86505	12.84926	11.93794	11.11839	10.37966	9.71225	9.10791	8.55948	8.06069	7.60608	7.19087	6.81086
16	14.71787	13.57771	12.56110	11.65230	10.83777	10.10590	9.44665	8.85137	8.31256	7.82371	7.37916	6.97399
17	15.56225	14.29187	13.16612	12.16567	11.27407	10.47726	9.76322	9.12164	8.54363	8.02155	7.54879	7.11963
18	16.39827	14.99203	13.75351	12.65930	11.68959	10.82760	10.05909	9.37189	8.75563	8.20141	7.70162	7.24967
19	17.22601	15.67846	14.32380	13.13394	12.08532	11.15812	10.33560	9.60360	8.95011	8.36492	7.83929	7.36578
20	18.04555	16.35143	14.87747	13.59033	12.46221	11.46992	10.59401	9.81815	9.12855	8.51356	7.96333	7.46944
21	18.85698	17.01121	15.41502	14.02916	12.82115	11.76408	10.83553	10.01680	9.29224	8.64869	8.07507	7.56200
22	19.66038	17.65805	15.93692	14.45112	13.16300	12.04158	11.06124	10.20074	9.44243	8.77154	8.17574	7.64465
23	20.45582	18.29220	16.44361	14.85684	13.48857	12.30338	11.27219	10.37106	9.58021	8.88322	8.26643	7.71843
24	21.24339	18.91393	16.93554	15.24696	13.79864	12.55036	11.46933	10.52876	9.70661	8.98474	8.34814	7.78432
25	22.02316	19.52346	17.41315	15.62208	14.09394	12.78336	11.65358	10.67478	9.82258	9.07704	8.42174	7.84314
30	25.80771	22.39646	19.60044	17.29203	15.37245	13.76483	12.40904	11.25778	10.27365	9.42691	8.69379	8.05518
35	29.40858	24.99862	21.48722	18.66461	16.37419	14.49825	12.94767	11.65457	10.56682	9.64416	8.85524	8.17550
40	32.83469	27.35548	23.11477	19.79277	17.15909	15.04630	13.33171	11.92461	10.75736	9.77905	8.95105	8.24378

© Cambridge Business Publishers

Appendix A — Compound Interest Tables

Table 3 ■ Future Value of Single Amount

$f = (1 + i)^t$

Period	Interest Rate											
	0.01	0.02	0.03	0.04	0.05	0.06	0.07	0.08	0.09	0.10	0.11	0.12
1	1.01000	1.02000	1.03000	1.04000	1.05000	1.06000	1.07000	1.08000	1.09000	1.10000	1.11000	1.12000
2	1.02010	1.04040	1.06090	1.08160	1.10250	1.12360	1.14490	1.16640	1.18810	1.21000	1.23210	1.25440
3	1.03030	1.06121	1.09273	1.12486	1.15763	1.19102	1.22504	1.25971	1.29503	1.33100	1.36763	1.40493
4	1.04060	1.08243	1.12551	1.16986	1.21551	1.26248	1.31080	1.36049	1.41158	1.46410	1.51807	1.57352
5	1.05101	1.10408	1.15927	1.21665	1.27628	1.33823	1.40255	1.46933	1.53862	1.61051	1.68506	1.76234
6	1.06152	1.12616	1.19405	1.26532	1.34010	1.41852	1.50073	1.58687	1.67710	1.77156	1.87041	1.97382
7	1.07214	1.14869	1.22987	1.31593	1.40710	1.50363	1.60578	1.71382	1.82804	1.94872	2.07616	2.21068
8	1.08286	1.17166	1.26677	1.36857	1.47746	1.59385	1.71819	1.85093	1.99256	2.14359	2.30454	2.47596
9	1.09369	1.19509	1.30477	1.42331	1.55133	1.68948	1.83846	1.99900	2.17189	2.35795	2.55804	2.77308
10	1.10462	1.21899	1.34392	1.48024	1.62889	1.79085	1.96715	2.15892	2.36736	2.59374	2.83942	3.10585
11	1.11567	1.24337	1.38423	1.53945	1.71034	1.89830	2.10485	2.33164	2.58043	2.85312	3.15176	3.47855
12	1.12683	1.26824	1.42576	1.60103	1.79586	2.01220	2.25219	2.51817	2.81266	3.13843	3.49845	3.89598
13	1.13809	1.29361	1.46853	1.66507	1.88565	2.13293	2.40985	2.71962	3.06580	3.45227	3.88328	4.36349
14	1.14947	1.31948	1.51259	1.73168	1.97993	2.26090	2.57853	2.93719	3.34173	3.79750	4.31044	4.88711
15	1.16097	1.34587	1.55797	1.80094	2.07893	2.39656	2.75903	3.17217	3.64248	4.17725	4.78459	5.47357
16	1.17258	1.37279	1.60471	1.87298	2.18287	2.54035	2.95216	3.42594	3.97031	4.59497	5.31089	6.13039
17	1.18430	1.40024	1.65285	1.94790	2.29202	2.69277	3.15882	3.70002	4.32763	5.05447	5.89509	6.86604
18	1.19615	1.42825	1.70243	2.02582	2.40662	2.85434	3.37993	3.99602	4.71712	5.55992	6.54355	7.68997
19	1.20811	1.45681	1.75351	2.10685	2.52695	3.02560	3.61653	4.31570	5.14166	6.11591	7.26334	8.61276
20	1.22019	1.48595	1.80611	2.19112	2.65330	3.20714	3.86968	4.66096	5.60441	6.72750	8.06231	9.64629
21	1.23239	1.51567	1.86029	2.27877	2.78596	3.39956	4.14056	5.03383	6.10881	7.40025	8.94917	10.80385
22	1.24472	1.54598	1.91610	2.36992	2.92526	3.60354	4.43040	5.43654	6.65860	8.14027	9.93357	12.10031
23	1.25716	1.57690	1.97359	2.46472	3.07152	3.81975	4.74053	5.87146	7.25787	8.95430	11.02627	13.55235
24	1.26973	1.60844	2.03279	2.56330	3.22510	4.04893	5.07237	6.34118	7.91108	9.84973	12.23916	15.17863
25	1.28243	1.64061	2.09378	2.66584	3.38635	4.29187	5.42743	6.84848	8.62308	10.83471	13.58546	17.00006
30	1.34785	1.81136	2.42726	3.24340	4.32194	5.74349	7.61226	10.06266	13.26768	17.44940	22.89230	29.95992
35	1.41660	1.99989	2.81386	3.94609	5.51602	7.68609	10.67658	14.78534	20.41397	28.10244	38.57485	52.79962
40	1.48886	2.20804	3.26204	4.80102	7.03999	10.28572	14.97446	21.72452	31.40942	45.25926	65.00087	93.05097

Table 4 ■ Future Value of an Ordinary Annuity

$f = [(1 + i)^t - 1]/i$

Period	Interest Rate											
	0.01	0.02	0.03	0.04	0.05	0.06	0.07	0.08	0.09	0.10	0.11	0.12
1	1.00000	1.00000	1.00000	1.00000	1.00000	1.00000	1.00000	1.00000	1.00000	1.00000	1.00000	1.00000
2	2.01000	2.02000	2.03000	2.04000	2.05000	2.06000	2.07000	2.08000	2.09000	2.10000	2.11000	2.12000
3	3.03010	3.06040	3.09090	3.12160	3.15250	3.18360	3.21490	3.24640	3.27810	3.31000	3.34210	3.37440
4	4.06040	4.12161	4.18363	4.24646	4.31013	4.37462	4.43994	4.50611	4.57313	4.64100	4.70973	4.77933
5	5.10101	5.20404	5.30914	5.41632	5.52563	5.63709	5.75074	5.86660	5.98471	6.10510	6.22780	6.35285
6	6.15202	6.30812	6.46841	6.63298	6.80191	6.97532	7.15329	7.33593	7.52333	7.71561	7.91286	8.11519
7	7.21354	7.43428	7.66246	7.89829	8.14201	8.39384	8.65402	8.92280	9.20043	9.48717	9.78327	10.08901
8	8.28567	8.58297	8.89234	9.21423	9.54911	9.89747	10.25980	10.63663	11.02847	11.43589	11.85943	12.29969
9	9.36853	9.75463	10.15911	10.58280	11.02656	11.49132	11.97799	12.48756	13.02104	13.57948	14.16397	14.77566
10	10.46221	10.94972	11.46388	12.00611	12.57789	13.18079	13.81645	14.48656	15.19293	15.93742	16.72201	17.54874
11	11.56683	12.16872	12.80780	13.48635	14.20679	14.97164	15.78360	16.64549	17.56029	18.53117	19.56143	20.65458
12	12.68250	13.41209	14.19203	15.02581	15.91713	16.86994	17.88845	18.97713	20.14072	21.38428	22.71319	24.13313
13	13.80933	14.68033	15.61779	16.62684	17.71298	18.88214	20.14064	21.49530	22.95338	24.52271	26.21164	28.02911
14	14.94742	15.97394	17.08632	18.29191	19.59863	21.01507	22.55049	24.21492	26.01919	27.97498	30.09492	32.39260
15	16.09690	17.29342	18.59891	20.02359	21.57856	23.27597	25.12902	27.15211	29.36092	31.77248	34.40536	37.27971
16	17.25786	18.63929	20.15688	21.82453	23.65749	25.67253	27.88805	30.32428	33.00340	35.94973	39.18995	42.75328
17	18.43044	20.01207	21.76159	23.69751	25.84037	28.21288	30.84022	33.75023	36.97370	40.54470	44.50084	48.88367
18	19.61475	21.41231	23.41444	25.64541	28.13238	30.90565	33.99903	37.45024	41.30134	45.59917	50.39594	55.74971
19	20.81090	22.84056	25.11687	27.67123	30.53900	33.75999	37.37896	41.44626	46.01846	51.15909	56.93949	63.43968
20	22.01900	24.29737	26.87037	29.77808	33.06595	36.78559	40.99549	45.76196	51.16012	57.27500	64.20283	72.05244
21	23.23919	25.78332	28.67649	31.96920	35.71925	39.99273	44.86518	50.42292	56.76453	64.00250	72.26514	81.69874
22	24.47159	27.29898	30.53678	34.24797	38.50521	43.39229	49.00574	55.45676	62.87334	71.40275	81.21431	92.50258
23	25.71630	28.84496	32.45288	36.61789	41.43048	46.99583	53.43614	60.89330	69.53194	79.54302	91.14788	104.60289
24	26.97346	30.42186	34.42647	39.08260	44.50200	50.81558	58.17667	66.76476	76.78981	88.49733	102.17415	118.15524
25	28.24320	32.03030	36.45926	41.64591	47.72710	54.86451	63.24904	73.10594	84.70090	98.34706	114.41331	133.33387
30	34.78489	40.56808	47.57542	56.08494	66.43885	79.05819	94.46079	113.28321	136.30754	164.49402	199.02088	241.33268
35	41.66028	49.99448	60.46208	73.65222	90.32031	111.43478	138.23688	172.31680	215.71075	271.02437	341.58955	431.66350
40	48.88637	60.40198	75.40126	95.02552	120.79977	154.76197	199.63511	259.05652	337.88245	442.59256	581.82607	767.09142

Appendix B
Chart of Accounts with Acronyms

Assets

Cash	Cash
MS	Marketable securities
AR	Accounts receivable
AU	Allowance for uncollectible accounts
INV	Inventory (or Inventories)
SUP	Supplies
PPD	Prepaid expenses
PPDA	Prepaid advertising
PPRNT	Prepaid rent
PPI	Prepaid insurance
PPE	Property, plant and equipment (PPE)
AD	Accumulated depreciation
INT	Intangible assets
DTA	Deferred tax assets
OA	Other assets
EMI	Equity method investments
ROU	Right-of-use asset (capitalized lease)
PA	Pension assets

Liabilities

NP	Notes payable
AP	Accounts payable
ACC	Accrued expenses
WP	Wages payable
SP	Salaries payable
RNTP	Rent payable
RSL	Restructuring liability
UP	Utilities payable
TP	Taxes payable
WRP	Warranty payable
IP	Interest payable
CMLTD	Current maturities of long-term debt
UR	Unearned (or deferred) revenues
DP	Dividends payable
LTD	Long-term debt
CLO	Capital lease obligations
DTL	Deferred tax liabilities
OL	Other liabilities
PL	Pension liability

Equity

EC	Earned capital
CS	Common stock
PS	Preferred stock
APIC	Additional paid-in capital
RE	Retained earnings
DIV	Dividends
TS	Treasury stock
AOCI	Accumulated other comprehensive income
DC	Deferred compensation expense
NCI	Noncontrolling interest
EQ	Total stockholders' equity
CI	Equity attributable to controlling interest

Revenues and Expenses

Sales	Sales
REV	Revenues
COGS	Cost of goods sold (or Cost of sales)
OE	Operating expenses
AE	Advertising expense
AIE	Asset impairment expense
BDE	Bad debts expense
DE	Depreciation expense
GN (LS)	Gain (loss)–operating
INSE	Insurance expense
PE	Pension expense
RDE	Research and development expense
RNTE	Rent expense
RSE	Restructuring expense
SE	Salaries expense
SUPE	Supplies expense
TE	Tax expense
UTE	Utilities expense
WE	Wages expense
WRE	Warranty expense
ONI (E)	Other nonoperating income (expense)
IE	Interest expense
II	Interest income
UG (UL)	Unrealized gain (loss)
DI	Dividend income (or revenue)
EI	Equity income (or revenue)
GN (LS)	Gain (loss)–nonoperating

Appendix C
Comprehensive Case

Harley-Davidson

Available for free download from the book's website in the Supplements section.

Glossary

A

accelerated cost recovery system (ACRS, MACRS) A system of accelerated depreciation for tax purposes introduced in 1981 (ACRS) and modified starting in 1987 (MACRS); it prescribes depreciation rates by asset classification for assets acquired after 1980

accelerated depreciation method Any depreciation method under which the amounts of depreciation expense taken in the early years of an asset's life are larger than the amounts expensed in the later years; includes the double-declining balance method

access control matrix A computerized file that lists the type of access that each computer user is entitled to have to each file and program in the computer system

account A record of the additions, deductions, and balances of individual assets, liabilities, equity, revenues, and expenses

accounting The process of measuring the economic activity of an entity in money terms and communicating the results to interested parties; the purpose is to provide financial information that is useful in making economic decisions

accounting adjustments (adjusting entries) Entries made at the end of an accounting period under accrual accounting to ensure the proper recording of expenses incurred and revenues earned for the period

accounting cycle A series of basic steps followed to process accounting information during a fiscal year

accounting entity An economic unit that has identifiable boundaries and that is the focus for the accumulation and reporting of financial information

accounting equation An expression of the equivalency of the economic resources and the claims upon those resources of a specific entity; often stated as Assets = Liabilities + Owners' Equity

accounting period The time period, typically one year (or quarter), for which periodic accounting reports are prepared

accounting system The structured collection of policies, procedures, equipment, files, and records that a company uses to collect, record, classify, process, store, report, and interpret financial data

accounts payable turnover The ratio obtained by dividing cost of goods sold by average accounts payable

accounts receivable A current asset that is created by a sale on a credit basis; it represents the amount owed the company by the customer

accounts receivable aging method A procedure that uses an aging schedule to determine the year-end balance needed in the allowance for uncollectible accounts

accounts receivable turnover Annual net sales divided by average accounts receivable (net)

accrual accounting Accounting procedures whereby revenues are recorded when they are earned and realized and expenses are recorded in the period in which they help to generate revenues

accruals Adjustments that reflect revenues earned but not received or recorded and expenses incurred but not paid or recorded

accrued expense An expense incurred but not yet paid; recognized with an accounting adjustment

accrued revenue Revenue earned but not yet billed or received; recognized with an accounting adjustment

accumulated depreciation The sum of all depreciation expense recorded to date; it is subtracted from the cost of the asset in order to derive the asset's net book value

accumulated other comprehensive income (AOCI) Current accumulation of all prior periods' other comprehensive income; see definition for *other comprehensive income*

adjusted trial balance A list of general ledger accounts and their balances taken after accounting adjustments have been made

adjusting The process of adjusting the historical financial statements prior to the projection of future results; also called recasting and reformulating

aging schedule An analysis that shows how long customers' accounts receivable balances have remained unpaid

allowance for uncollectible accounts A contra asset account with a normal credit balance shown on the balance sheet as a deduction from accounts receivable to reflect the expected realizable amount of accounts receivable

allowance method An accounting procedure whereby the amount of uncollectible accounts expense is estimated and recorded in the period in which the related credit sales occur

Altman's Z-score A predictor of potential bankruptcy based on multiple ratios

amortization The periodic writing off of an account balance to expense; similar to depreciation and usually refers to the periodic writing off of an intangible asset

annuity A pattern of cash flows in which equal amounts are spaced equally over a number of periods

articles of incorporation A document prepared by persons organizing a corporation in the United States that sets forth the structure and purpose of the corporation and specifics regarding the stock to be issued

articulation The linkage of financial statements within and across time

asset turnover Net income divided by average total assets

asset write-downs Adjustment of carrying value of assets down to their current fair value

assets The economic resources of an entity that are owned or controlled will provide future benefits and can be reliably measured

audit An examination of a company's financial statements by a firm of independent certified public accountants

audit report A report issued by independent auditors that includes the final version of the financial statements, accompanying notes, and the auditor's opinion on the financial statements

authorized stock The maximum number of shares in a class of stock that a corporation may issue

available-for-sale securities Debt securities that do not qualify as held-to-maturity or trading

average cash conversion cycle Average collection period + average inventory days outstanding − average payable days outstanding

average collection period Determined by dividing accounts receivable by average daily sales, sometimes referred to as days sales outstanding or DSO

average inventory days outstanding (AIDO) An indication of how long, on average, inventories are on the shelves, computed as inventory divided by average daily cost of goods sold

B

balance sheet A financial statement showing an entity's assets, liabilities, and owners' equity at a specific date; sometimes called a statement of financial position

bearer One of the terms that may be used to designate the payee on a promissory note; means whoever holds the note

bond A long-term debt instrument that promises to pay interest periodically and a principal amount at maturity, usually issued by the borrower to a group of lenders; bonds may incorporate a wide variety of provisions relating to security for the debt involved, methods of paying the periodic interest, retirement provisions, and conversion options

book value The dollar amount carried in the accounts for a particular item; the book value of a depreciable asset is cost less accumulated depreciation; the book value of an entity is assets less liabilities

book value per share The dollar amount of net assets represented by one share of stock; computed by dividing the amount of stockholders' equity associated with a class of stock by the outstanding shares of that class of stock

borrows at a discount When the face amount of the note is reduced by a calculated cash discount to determine the cash proceeds

C

calendar year A fiscal year that ends on December 31

call provision A bond feature that allows the borrower to retire (call in) the bonds after a stated date

capital expenditures Expenditures that increase the book value of long-term assets; sometimes abbreviated as CAPEX

capital lease Under the pre-2019 Lease accounting standard, a capital lease is a lease that transfers to the lessee substantially all of the benefits and risks related to ownership of the property; the lessee records the leased property as an asset and establishes a liability for the lease obligation

capital markets Financing sources, which are formalized when companies issue securities that are traded on organized exchanges; they are informal when companies are funded by private sources

capitalization The recording of a cost as an asset on the balance sheet rather than as an expense on the income statement; these costs are transferred to expense as the asset is used up

capitalization of interest A process that adds interest to an asset's initial cost if a period of time is required to prepare the asset for use

cash An asset category representing the amount of a firm's available cash and funds on deposit at a bank in checking accounts and savings accounts

cash and cash equivalents The sum of cash plus short-term, highly liquid investments such as treasury bills and money market funds; includes marketable securities maturing within 90 days of the financial statement date

cash conversion cycle Measures the average time (in days) to sell inventories, collect the receivables from the sale, repay the suppliers for the inventory purchases, and return to cash. It is the amount of days to collect accounts receivable plus days sales in inventory minus days to pay account payable.

cash discount An amount that a purchaser of merchandise may deduct from the purchase price for paying within the discount period

cash-basis accounting Accounting procedures whereby revenues are recorded when cash is received and expenses are recorded when cash payments are made

cash (operating) conversion cycle The period of time (typically measured in days) from when cash is invested in inventories until inventory is sold and receivables are collected

certificate of deposit (CD) An investment security available at financial institutions generally offering a fixed rate of return for a specified period of time

change in accounting estimate Modification to a previous estimate of an uncertain future event, such as the useful life of a depreciable asset, uncollectible accounts receivable, and warranty expenses; applied currently and prospectively only

changes in accounting principles Modification of accounting methods (such as depreciation or inventory costing methods)

chart of accounts A list of all the general ledger account titles and their numerical code

clean surplus accounting Income that explains successive equity balances

closing procedures A step in the accounting cycle in which the balances of all temporary accounts are transferred to the retained earnings account, leaving the temporary accounts with zero balances

commitments A contractual arrangement by which both parties to the contract still have acts to perform

common stock The basic ownership class of corporate capital stock, carrying the rights to vote, share in earnings, participate in future stock issues, and share in any liquidation proceeds after prior claims have been settled

common-size financial statement A financial statement in which each item is presented as a percentage of a key figure such as sales or total assets

comparative financial statements A form of horizontal analysis involving comparison of two or more periods' financial statements showing dollar and/or percentage changes

comprehensive income The total change in stockholders' equity other than those arising from capital (stock) transactions; computed as net income plus other comprehensive income (OCI); typical OCI components are unrealized gains (losses) on available-for-sale securities and derivatives, minimum pension liability adjustment, and foreign currency translation adjustments

conceptual framework A cohesive set of interrelated objectives and fundamentals for external financial reporting developed by the FASB

conservatism An accounting principle stating that judgmental determinations should tend toward understatement rather than overstatement of net assets and income

consistency An accounting principle stating that, unless otherwise disclosed, accounting reports should be prepared on a basis consistent with the preceding period

consolidated financial statements Financial statements reflecting a parent company and one or more subsidiary companies and/or a variable interest entity (VIE) and its primary beneficiary

contingent liabilities A potential obligation, the eventual occurrence of which usually depends on some future event beyond the control of the firm; contingent liabilities may originate with such events as lawsuits, credit guarantees, and environmental damages

contra account An account related to, and deducted from, another account when financial statements are prepared or when book values are computed

contract rate The rate of interest stated on a bond certificate

contributed capital The net funding that a company receives from issuing and acquiring its equity shares

convertible bond A bond incorporating the holder's right to convert the bond to capital stock under prescribed terms

convertible securities Debt and equity securities that provide the holder with an option to convert those securities into other securities

copyright An exclusive right that protects an owner against the unauthorized reproduction of a specific written work or artwork

core income A company's income from its usual business activities that is expected to continue (persist) into the future

corporation A legal entity created by the granting of a charter from an appropriate governmental authority and owned by stockholders who have limited liability for corporate debt

cost of goods sold The total cost of merchandise sold to customers during the accounting period

cost of goods sold percentage The ratio of cost of goods sold divided by net sales

cost method An investment is reported at its historical cost, and any cash dividends and interest received are recognized in current income

cost principle An accounting principle stating that asset measures are based on the prices paid to acquire the assets

cost-to-cost method The extent of progress towards completion based on the ratio of costs incurred to date to the total estimated costs at completion of the contract

coupon bond A bond with coupons for interest payable to bearer attached to the bond for each interest period; whenever interest is due, the bondholder detaches a coupon and deposits it with his or her bank for collection

coupon (contract or stated) rate The coupon rate of interest is stated in the bond contract; it is used to compute the dollar amount of (semiannual) interest payments that are paid to bondholder during the life of the bond issue

covenants Contractual requirements put into loan or bond agreements by lenders

credit (entry) An entry on the right side (or in the credit column) of any account

credit card fee A fee charged retailers for credit card services provided by financial institutions; the fee is usually stated as a percentage of credit card sales

credit guarantee A guarantee of another company's debt by cosigning a note payable; a guarantor's contingent liability that is usually disclosed in a balance sheet footnote

credit memo A document prepared by a seller to inform the purchaser that the seller has reduced the amount owed by the purchaser due to a return or an allowance

credit period The maximum amount of time, usually stated in days, that the purchaser of merchandise has to pay the seller

credit rating An opinion formed by a credit-rating agency (such as Standard & Poor's, Moody's or Fitch) concerning the creditworthiness of a borrower (a corporation or a government) based on an assessment of the borrower's likelihood of default

credit terms The prescribed payment period for purchases on credit with discount specified for early payment

cumulative (preferred stock) A feature associated with preferred stock whereby any dividends in arrears must be paid before dividends may be paid on common stock

cumulative effect of a change in principle The cumulative effect on net income to the date of a change in accounting principle

cumulative translation adjustment The amount recorded in the equity section as necessary to balance the accounting equation when assets and liabilities of foreign subsidiaries are translated into $US at the rate of exchange prevailing at the statement date

current assets Cash and other assets that will be converted to cash or used up during the normal operating cycle of the business or one year, whichever is longer

current liabilities Obligations that will require within the coming year or operating cycle, whichever is longer, (1) the use of existing current assets or (2) the creation of other current liabilities

current rate method Method of translating foreign currency transactions under which balance sheet amounts are translated using exchange rates in effect at the period-end consolidation date and income statement amounts using the average exchange rate for the period

current ratio Current assets divided by current liabilities

D

days inventory outstanding Inventories divided by average cost of goods sold

days payable outstanding Ratio that reflects the average length of time that payables are deferred. Computed as 365 x average accounts payable / COGS.

days sales outstanding Ratio that reveals the number of days, on average, that accounts receivable are outstanding before they are paid. Computed as 365 x average accounts receivable / sales.

debenture bond A bond that has no specific property pledged as security for the repayment of funds borrowed

debit (entry) An entry on the left side (or in the debit column) of any account

debt-to-equity ratio A firm's total liabilities divided by its total owners' equity

declining-balance method An accelerated depreciation method that allocates depreciation expense to each year by applying a constant percentage to the declining book value of the asset

default The nonpayment of interest and principal and/or the failure to adhere to the various terms and conditions of the bond indenture

deferrals Adjustments that allocate various assets and revenues received in advance to the proper accounting periods as expenses and revenues

deferred revenue A liability representing revenues received in advance; also called unearned revenue

deferred tax liability A liability representing the estimated future income taxes payable resulting from an existing temporary difference between an asset's book value and its tax basis

deferred tax valuation allowance Reduction in a reported deferred tax asset to adjust for the amount that is not likely to be realized

defined benefit plan A type of retirement plan under which the company promises to make periodic payments to the employee after retirement

defined contribution plan A retirement plan under which the company makes cash contribution into an employee's account (usually with a third-party trustee like a bank) either solely or as a matching contribution

depletion The allocation of the cost of natural resources to the units extracted and sold or, in the case of timberland, the board feet of timber cut

depreciable asset cost Cost of assets that will be depreciated; excludes land and construction in progress

depreciation The decline in economic potential (using up) of plant assets originating from wear, deterioration, and obsolescence

depreciation accounting The process of allocating the cost of equipment, vehicles, and buildings (not land) to expense over the time period benefiting from their use

depreciation base The acquisition cost of an asset less estimated salvage value

depreciation rate An estimate of how the asset will be used up over its useful life—evenly over its useful life, more heavily in the early years, or in proportion to its actual usage

derivatives Financial instruments such as futures, options, and swaps that are commonly used to hedge (mitigate) some external risk, such as commodity price risk, interest rate risk, or risks relating to foreign currency fluctuations

diluted earnings per share The earnings per share computation taking into consideration the effects of dilutive securities

dilutive securities Securities that can be exchanged for shares of common stock and, thereby, increase the number of common shares outstanding

discontinued operations Net income or loss from business segments that are up for sale or have been sold in the current period

discount bond A bond that is sold for less than its par (face) value

discount on notes payable A contra account that is subtracted from the Notes Payable amount on the balance sheet; as the life of the note elapses, the discount is reduced and charged to interest expense

discount period The maximum amount of time, usually stated in days, that the purchaser of merchandise has to pay the seller if the purchaser wants to claim the cash discount

discounted cash flow (DCF) model The value of a security is equal to the present value of the expected free cash flows to the firm, discounted at the weighted average cost of capital (WACC)

discounting The exchanging of notes receivable for cash at a financial institution at an amount that is less than the face value of the notes

dividends account A temporary equity account used to accumulate owner dividends from the business

dividend discount model The value of a security today is equal to the present value of that security's expected dividends, discounted at the weighted average cost of capital

dividend payout ratio Annual dividends per share divided by the earnings per share or by net income

dividend yield Annual dividends per share divided by the market price per share

double-entry accounting system A method of accounting that recognizes the duality of a transaction such that the analysis results in a recording of equal amounts of debits and credits

E

earned When referring to revenue, the seller's execution of its duties under the terms of the agreement, with the resultant passing of title to the buyer with no right of return or other contingencies

earned capital The cumulative net income (losses) retained by the company (not paid out to shareholders as dividends)

earnings per share (EPS) Net income less preferred stock dividends divided by the weighted average common shares outstanding for the period

earnings quality The degree to which reported earnings represent how well the firm has performed from an economic standpoint

earnings smoothing Earnings management with a goal to provide an earnings stream with less variability

EBIT Earnings before interest and taxes

EBITDA Earnings before interest, taxes, depreciation and amortization

economic profit The number of inventory units sold multiplied by the difference between the sales price and the replacement cost of the inventories (approximated by the cost of the most recently purchased inventories)

economic value added (EVA) Net operating profits after tax less a charge for the use of capital equal to beginning capital utilized in the business multiplied by the weighted average cost of capital (EVA = NOPAT − [r_w × Net operating assets])

effective interest method A method of amortizing bond premium or discount that results in a constant rate of interest each period and varying amounts of premium or discount amortized each period

effective interest rate The rate determined by dividing the total discount amount by the cash proceeds on a note payable when the borrower borrowed at a discount

effective rate The current rate of interest in the market for a bond or other debt instrument; when issued, a bond is priced to yield the market (effective) rate of interest at the date of issuance

efficient markets hypothesis Capital markets are said to be efficient if at any given time, current equity (stock) prices reflect all relevant information that determines those equity prices

employee severance costs Accrued (estimated) costs for termination of employees as part of a restructuring program

employee stock options A form of compensation that grants employees the right to purchase a fixed number of company shares at a fixed price for a predetermined time period

equity carve out A corporate divestiture of operating units

equity method The prescribed method of accounting for investments in which the investor company has a significant influence over the investee company (usually taken to be ownership between 20-50% of the outstanding common stock of the investee company)

ethics An area of inquiry dealing with the values, rules, and justifications that governs one's way of life

executory contract A contract where a party has a material unperformed obligation that, if not performed, will result in a breach of contract

expenses Decreases in owners' equity incurred by a firm in the process of earning revenues

F

face amount The principal amount of a bond or note to be repaid at maturity

factoring Selling an account receivable to another company, typically a finance company or a financial institution, for less than its face value

fair value Value that an asset could be sold for (or an obligation discharged) in an orderly market, between willing buyers and sellers; often, but not always, is current market value

fair value method Method of accounting that records on the balance sheet, the asset or liabilities fair value, and records on the income statement, changes in the fair value

finance leases transfer **control of the lease asset** to the lessee. Finance leases are effectively like purchasing the asset and financing the purchase with a collateralized loan

financial accounting The area of accounting activities dealing with the preparation of financial statements showing an entity's results of operations, financial position, and cash flows

Financial Accounting Standards Board (FASB) The organization currently responsible for setting accounting standards for reporting financial information by U.S. entities

financial assets Normally consist of excess resources held for future expansion or unexpected needs; they are usually invested in the form of other companies' stock, corporate or government bonds, and real estate

financial leverage The proportionate use of borrowed funds in the capital structure, computed as net nonoperating obligations (NNO) divided by average equity

financial reporting objectives A component of the conceptual framework that specifies that financial statements should provide information (1) useful for investment and credit decisions, (2) helpful in assessing an entity's ability to generate future cash flows, and (3) about an entity's resources, claims to those resources, and the effects of events causing changes in these items

financial statement elements A part of the conceptual framework that identifies the significant components—such as assets, liabilities, owners' equity, revenues, and expenses—used to put financial statements together

financing activities Methods that companies use to raise the funds to pay for resources such as land, buildings, and equipment

finished goods inventory The dollar amount of inventory that has completed the production process and is awaiting sale

first-in, first-out (FIFO) method One of the prescribed methods of inventory costing; FIFO assumes that the first costs incurred for the purchase or production of inventory are the first costs relieved from inventory when goods are sold

fiscal year The annual accounting period used by a business firm

five forces of competitive intensity Industry competition, bargaining power of buyers, bargaining power of suppliers, threat of substitution, threat of entry

fixed assets An alternate label for long-term assets; may also be called property, plant, and equipment (PPE)

fixed costs Costs that do not change with changes in sales volume (over a reasonable range)

forecast The projection of financial results over the forecast horizon and terminal periods

foreign currency transaction The $US equivalent of an asset or liability denominated in a foreign currency

foreign exchange gain or loss The gain (loss) recognized in the income statement relating to the change in the $US equivalent of an asset or liability denominated in a foreign currency

forward earnings Earnings expected to be reported in the next period

franchise Generally, an exclusive right to operate or sell a specific brand of products in a given geographic area

free cash flow This excess cash flow (above that required to manage its growth and development) from which dividends can be paid; computed as NOPAT − Increase in NOA

full disclosure principle An accounting principle stipulating the disclosure of all facts necessary to make financial statements useful to readers

fully diluted earnings per share *See* diluted earnings per share

functional currency The currency representing the primary currency in which a business unit conducts its operations

fundamental analysis Uses financial information to predict future valuation and, hence, buy-sell stock strategies

funded status The difference between the pension obligation and the fair value of the pension investments

future value The amount a specified investment (or series of investments) will be worth at a future date if invested at a given rate of compound interest

G

general journal A journal with enough flexibility so that any type of business transaction can be recorded in it

general ledger A grouping of all of an entity's accounts that are used to prepare the basic financial statements

generally accepted accounting principles (GAAP) A set of standards and procedures that guide the preparation of financial statements

going concern concept An accounting principle that assumes that, in the absence of evidence to the contrary, a business entity will have an indefinite life

goodwill The value that derives from a firm's ability to earn more than a normal rate of return on the fair market value of its specific, identifiable net assets; computed as the residual of the purchase price less the fair market value of the net tangible and intangible assets acquired

gross margin The difference between net sales and cost of goods sold; also called gross profit

gross profit on sales The difference between net sales and cost of goods sold; also called gross margin

gross profit margin (GPM) (percentage) The ratio of gross profit on sales divided by net sales

H

held-to-maturity securities The designation given to a portfolio of bond investments that are expected to be held until they mature

historical cost Original acquisition or issuance costs

holding company The parent company of a subsidiary

holding gain The increase in replacement cost since the inventories were acquired, which equals the number of units sold multiplied by the difference between the current replacement cost and the original acquisition cost

horizon period The forecast period for which detailed estimates are made, typically 5-10 years

horizontal analysis Analysis of a firm's financial statements that covers two or more years; year-over-year percentage change in financial statement line items

I

IASB International Accounting Standards Board, independent, privately funded accounting standard-setter based in London, responsible for developing IFRS and promoting the use and application of these standards

IFRS International Financial Reporting Standards, a body of accounting standards developed by the International Accounting Standards Board and used for financial reports across much of the world

impairment A reduction in value from that presently recorded

impairment loss A loss recognized on an impaired asset equal to the difference between its book value and current fair value

income statement A financial statement reporting an entity's revenues and expenses for a period of time

indirect method A presentation format for the statement of cash flows that refers to the operating section only; that section begins with net income and converts it to cash flows from operations

intangible assets A term applied to a group of long-term assets, including patents, copyrights, franchises, trademarks, and goodwill, that benefit an entity but do not have physical substance

interest cost (pensions) The increase in the pension obligation due to the accrual of an additional year of interest

internal auditing A company function that provides independent appraisals of the company's financial statements, its internal controls, and its operations

internal controls The measures undertaken by a company to ensure the reliability of its accounting data, protect its assets from theft or unauthorized use, make sure that employees are following the company's policies and procedures, and evaluate the performance of employees, departments, divisions, and the company as a whole

inventory carrying costs Costs of holding inventories, including warehousing, logistics, insurance, financing, and the risk of loss due to theft, damage, or technological or fashion change

inventory shrinkage The cost associated with an inventory shortage; the amount by which the perpetual inventory exceeds the physical inventory

inventory turnover Cost of goods sold divided by average inventory

investing activities The acquiring and disposing of resources (assets) that a company uses to acquire and sell its products and services

investing creditors Those who primarily finance investing activities

investment returns The increase in pension investments resulting from interest, dividends, and capital gains on the investment portfolio

invoice A document that the seller sends to the purchaser to request payment for items that the seller shipped to the purchaser

invoice price The price that a seller charges the purchaser for merchandise

IOU A slang term for a receivable

IPO Initial public offering; the sale of shares of a private company to the public, for the first time

IRS Internal Revenue Service, the U.S. taxing authority

issued stock Shares of stock that have been sold and issued to stockholders; issued stock may be either outstanding or in the treasury

J

journal A tabular record in which business transactions are analyzed in debit and credit terms and recorded in chronological order

just-in-time (JIT) inventory Receive inventory from suppliers into the production process just at the point it is needed

L

land improvements Improvements with limited lives made to land sites, such as paved parking lots and driveways

last-in, first-out (LIFO) method One of the prescribed methods of inventory costing; LIFO assumes that the last costs incurred for the purchase or production of inventory are the first costs relieved from inventory when goods are sold

lease A contract between a lessor (owner) and lessee (tenant) for the rental of property

leasehold The rights transferred from the lessor to the lessee by a lease

leasehold improvements Expenditures made by a lessee to alter or improve leased property

lessee The party acquiring the right to the use of property by a lease

lessor The owner of property who transfers the right to use the property to another party by a lease

level 1 fair value Observable, quoted prices for identical assets or liabilities in active markets

level 2 fair value Quoted prices for similar assets or liabilities in active markets or quoted prices for identical or similar assets in markets that are not active

level 3 fair value Prices based on the best, reasonably available information

leveraging The use of borrowed funds in the capital structure of a firm; the expectation is that the funds will earn a return higher than the rate of interest on the borrowed funds

liabilities The obligations, or debts, that an entity must pay in money or services at some time in the future because of past transactions or events

LIFO conformity rule IRS requirement to cost inventories using LIFO for tax purposes if they are costed using LIFO for financial reporting purposes

LIFO liquidation The reduction in inventory quantities when LIFO costing is used; LIFO liquidation yields an increase in gross profit and income when prices are rising

LIFO reserve The difference between the cost of inventories using FIFO and the cost using LIFO

liquidation value per share The amount that would be received by a holder of a share of stock if the corporation liquidated

liquidity How much cash the company has, how much is expected, and how much can be raised on short notice

list price The suggested price or reference price of merchandise in a catalog or price list

long-term liabilities Debt obligations not due to be settled within the normal operating cycle or one year, whichever is longer

lower of cost or net realizable value (LCNRV) *also called LCM*; GAAP requirement to write down the carrying amount of inventories on the balance sheet if the reported cost (using FIFO, for example) exceeds market value (determined by current replacement cost)

M

maker The signer of a promissory note

management discussion and anaysis (MD&A) The section of the 10-K report in which a company provides a detailed discussion of its business activities

managerial accounting The accounting activities carried out by a firm's accounting staff primarily to furnish management with accounting data for decisions related to the firm's operations

manufacturers Companies that convert raw materials and components into finished products through the application of skilled labor and machine operations

manufacturing costs The costs of direct materials, direct labor, and manufacturing overhead incurred in the manufacture of a product

market cap Market capitalization of the firm, or value as perceived by investors; computed as market value per share multiplied by shares outstanding

market (yield) rate This is the interest rate that investors expect to earn on the investment in this debt security; this rate is used to price the bond issue

market value The published price (as listed on a stock exchange)

market value per share The current price at which shares of stock may be bought or sold

matching principle An accounting guideline that states that income is determined by relating expenses, to the extent feasible, with revenues that have been recorded

materiality An accounting guideline that states that transactions so insignificant that they would not affect a user's actions or perception of the company may be recorded in the most expedient manner

materials inventory The physical component of inventory; the other components of manufactured inventory are labor costs and overhead costs

maturity date The date on which a note or bond matures

measuring unit concept An accounting guideline noting that the accounting unit of measure is the basic unit of money

merchandise inventory A stock of products that a company buys from another company and makes available for sale to its customers

merchandising firm A company that buys finished products, stores the products for varying periods of time, and then resells the products

method of comparables model Equity valuation or stock values are predicted using price multiples, which are defined as stock price divided by some key financial statement number such as net income, net sales, book value of equity, total assets, or cash flow; companies are then compared with their competitors

minority interest *See* noncontrolling interest

modified accelerated cost recovery system (MACRS) *See* accelerated cost recovery system

multiple element arrangements Sales (revenue) arrangements containing multiple deliverables and, in some cases, multiple cash-flow streams

N

natural resources Assets occurring in a natural state, such as timber, petroleum, natural gas, coal, and other mineral deposits

net asset based valuation model Equity is valued as reported assets less reported liabilities

net assets The difference between an entity's assets and liabilities; net assets are equal to owners' equity

net book value (NBV) The cost of the asset less accumulated depreciation; also called carrying value

net income The excess of a firm's revenues over its expenses

net loss The excess of a firm's expenses over its revenues

net nonoperating expense (NNE) Nonoperating expenses and losses (plus any net income attributable to noncontrolling interest) less nonoperating revenues and gains, all measured after-tax

net nonoperating expense percentage (NNEP) Net nonoperating expense divided by net nonoperating obligations (NNO)

net nonoperating obligations (NNO) All nonoperating obligations (plus any noncontrolling interest) less nonoperating assets

net operating asset turnover (NOAT) Ratio obtained by dividing sales by net operating assets

net operating assets (NOA) Current and long-term operating assets less current and long-term operating liabilities; or net operating working capital plus long-term net operating assets

net operating profit after tax (NOPAT) Operating revenues less operating expenses (including taxes)

net operating profit margin (NOPM) Ratio obtained by dividing net operating profit after tax (NOPAT) by sales

net operating working capital (NOWC) Current operating assets less current operating liabilities

net realizable value The value at which an asset can be sold, net of any costs of disposition

net sales The total revenue generated by a company through merchandise sales less the revenue given up through sales returns and allowances and sales discounts

net working capital Current assets less current liabilities

nominal rate The rate of interest stated on a bond certificate or other debt instrument

noncash investing and financing activities Significant business activities during the period that do not impact cash inflows or cash outflows

noncontrolling interest The portion of equity (net assets) in a subsidiary not attributable, directly or indirectly, to a parent. A noncontrolling interest (formerly called minority interest) typically represents the ownership interest of shareholders other than those of the parent company.

noncurrent liabilities Obligations not due to be paid within one year or the operating cycle, whichever is longer

nonoperating expenses Expenses that relate to the company's financing activities and include interest income and interest expense, gains and losses on sales of securities, and income or loss on discontinued operations

no-par stock Stock that does not have a par value

NOPAT Net operating profit after tax

normal operating cycle For a particular business, the average period of time between the use of cash in its typical operating activity and the subsequent collection of cash from customers

note receivable A promissory note held by the note's payee

notes to financial statements Footnotes in which companies discuss their accounting policies and estimates used in preparing the statements

not-sufficient-funds check A check from an individual or company that had an insufficient cash balance in the bank when the holder of the check presented it to the bank for payment

O

off-balance-sheet financing The structuring of a financing arrangement so that no liability shows on the borrower's balance sheet

operating activities Using resources to research, develop, produce, purchase, market, and distribute company products and services

operating cash flow to capital expenditures ratio A firm's net cash flow from operating activities divided by its annual capital expenditures

operating cash flow to current liabilities ratio A firm's net cash flow from operating activities divided by its average current liabilities

operating creditors Those who primarily finance operating activities

operating cycle The time between paying cash for goods or employee services and receiving cash from customers

operating expense margin (OEM) The ratio obtained by dividing any operating expense category by sales

operating expenses The usual and customary costs that a company incurs to support its main business activities; these include cost of goods sold, selling expenses, depreciation expense, amortization expense, research and development expense, and taxes on operating profits

operating lease transfers control of the use of the lease asset, but not the asset itself; any lease of 12 months or more not classified as a finance lease is classified as an operating lease

operating profit margin The ratio obtained by dividing NOPAT by sales

operational audit An evaluation of activities, systems, and internal controls within a company to determine their efficiency, effectiveness, and economy

organization costs Expenditures incurred in launching a business (usually a corporation), including attorney's fees and various fees paid to the state

other comprehensive income (OCI) Current period change in stockholders' equity *other than* those arising from capital (stock) transactions and those included in net income; typical OCI components are unrealized gains (losses) on available-for-sale securities and derivatives, minimum pension liability adjustment, and foreign currency translation adjustments

outstanding checks Checks issued by a firm that have not yet been presented to its bank for payment

outstanding stock Shares of stock that are currently owned by stockholders (excludes treasury stock)

owners' equity The interest of owners in the assets of an entity; equal to the difference between the entity's assets and liabilities

P

paid-in capital The amount of capital contributed to a corporation by various transactions; the primary source of paid-in capital is from the issuance of shares of stock

par (bonds) Face value of the bond

par value (stock) An amount specified in the corporate charter for each share of stock and imprinted on the face of each stock certificate, often determines the legal capital of the corporation

parent company A company owning one or more subsidiary companies

parsimonious method to multiyear forecasting Forecasting multiple years using only sales growth, net operating profit margin (NOPM), and the turnover of net operating assets (NOAT)

partnership A voluntary association of two or more persons for the purpose of conducting a business

patent An exclusive privilege granted for 20 years to an inventor that gives the patent holder the right to exclude others from making, using, or selling the invention

payee The company or individual to whom a promissory note is made payable

payment approval form A document that authorizes the payment of an invoice

pension plan A plan to pay benefits to employees after they retire from the company; the plan may be a defined contribution plan or a defined benefit plan

percentage-of-completion method Recognition of revenue by determining the costs incurred per the contract as compared to its total expected costs

percentage of net sales method A procedure that determines the uncollectible accounts expense for the year by multiplying net credit sales by the estimated uncollectible percentage

performance obligation A promise in a contract with a customer to transfer a good or service to the customer; includes promises that are implied by business practices, published policies, or explicit statements if those promises create an expectation of the customer that the entity will perform

performance obligation The actions the seller must undertake to satisfy the customer and complete the sales contract.

period statement A financial statement accumulating information for a specific period of time; examples are the income statement, the statement of owners' equity, and the statement of cash flows

permanent account An account used to prepare the balance sheet; that is, asset, liability, and equity capital (capital stock and retained earnings) accounts; any balance in a permanent account at the end of an accounting period is carried forward to the next period

physical inventory A year-end procedure that involves counting the quantity of each inventory item, determining the unit cost of each item, multiplying the unit cost times quantity, and summing the costs of all the items to determine the total inventory at cost

plant assets Land, buildings, equipment, vehicles, furniture, and fixtures that a firm uses in its operations; sometimes referred to by the acronym PPE

pooling of interests method A method of accounting for business combinations under which the acquired company is recorded on the acquirer's balance sheet at its book value, rather than market value; this method is no longer acceptable under GAAP for acquisitions occurring after 2001

position statement A financial statement, such as the balance sheet, that presents information as of a particular date

post-closing trial balance A list of general ledger accounts and their balances after closing entries have been recorded and posted

postdated check A check from another person or company with a date that is later than the current date; a postdated check does not become cash until the date of the check

preemptive right The right of a stockholder to maintain his or her proportionate interest in a corporation by having the right to purchase an appropriate share of any new stock issue

preferred stock A class of corporate capital stock typically receiving priority over common stock in dividend payments and distribution of assets should the corporation be liquidated

premium bond A bond that is sold for more than its par (face) value

present value The current worth of amounts to be paid (or received) in the future; computed by discounting the future payments (or receipts) at a specified interest rate

price-earnings ratio Current market price per common share divided by earnings per share

pro forma income A computation of income that begins with the GAAP income from continuing operations (that excludes discontinued operations, extraordinary items and changes in accounting principle), but then excludes other transitory items (most notably, restructuring charges), and some additional items such as expenses arising from acquisitions (goodwill amortization and other acquisition costs), compensation expense in the form of stock options, and research and development expenditures; pro forma income is not GAAP

pro rata Proportionately or dollar for dollar

promissory note A written promise to pay a certain sum of money on demand or at a determinable future time

purchase method The prescribed method of accounting for business combinations; under the purchase method, assets and liabilities of the acquired company are recorded at fair market value, together with identifiable intangible assets; the balance is ascribed to goodwill

purchase order A document that formally requests a supplier to sell and deliver specific quantities of particular items of merchandise at specified prices

purchase requisition An internal document that requests that the purchasing department order particular items of merchandise

Q

qualitative characteristics of accounting information The characteristics of accounting information that contribute to decision usefulness; the primary qualities are relevance and reliability

quarterly data Selected quarterly financial information that is reported in annual reports to stockholders

quick ratio Quick assets (that is, cash and cash equivalents, short-term investments, and current receivables) divided by current liabilities

R

realized (or realizable) When referring to revenue, the receipt of an asset or satisfaction of a liability or performance obligation as a result of a transaction or event

recognition criteria The criteria that must be met before a financial statement element may be recorded in the accounts; essentially, the item must meet the definition of an element and must be measurable

registered bond A bond for which the issuer (or the trustee) maintains a record of owners and, at the appropriate times, mails out interest payments

relative selling price The price for a deliverable if the item were sold separately on a regular basis, consistent with company selling practices.

relevance A qualitative characteristic of accounting information; relevant information contributes to the predictive and evaluative decisions made by financial statement users

reliability A qualitative characteristic of accounting information; reliable information contains no bias or error and faithfully portrays what it intends to represent

remeasurement The computation of gain or loss in the translation of subsidiaries denominated in a foreign currency into $US when the temporal method is used

residual operating income Net operating profits after tax (NOPAT) less the product of net operating assets (NOA) at the beginning of the period multiplied by the weighted average cost of capital (WACC)

residual operating income (ROPI) model An equity valuation approach that equates the firm's value to the sum of its net operating assets (NOA) and the present value of its residual operating income (ROPI)

retailers Companies that buy products from wholesale distributors and sell the products to individual customers, the general public

retained earnings Earned capital, the cumulative net income and loss, of the company (from its inception) that has not been paid to shareholders as dividends

retained earnings reconciliation The reconciliation of retained earnings from the beginning to the end of the year; the change in retained earnings includes, at a minimum, the net income (loss) for the period and dividends paid, if any, but may include other components as well; also called statement of retained earnings

return The amount earned on an investment; also called yield

return on assets (ROA) A financial ratio computed as net income divided by average total assets

return on common stockholders' equity (ROCE) A financial ratio computed as net income less preferred stock dividends divided by average common stockholders' equity

return on equity (ROE) The ultimate measure of performance from the shareholders' perspective; computed as net income divided by average equity

return on investment The ratio obtained by dividing income by average investment; sometimes referred to by the acronym ROI

return on net operating assets (RNOA) The ratio obtained by dividing NOPAT by average net operating assets

return on sales (ROS) The ratio obtained by dividing net income by net sales

revenue recognition principle An accounting principle requiring that revenue be recognized when earned and realized (or realizable)

revenues Increases in owners' equity a firm earns by providing goods or services for its customers

right of use (ROU) asset A term for the lease asset once the lease is reflected on the balance sheet.

S

SAAS Software as a service: software delivery and licensing model that allows customers online access to software on a subscription basis rather than purchased and installed on individual computers

sale on account A sale of merchandise made on a credit basis

salvage value The expected net recovery when a plant asset is sold or removed from service; also called residual value

secured bond A bond that pledges specific property as security for meeting the terms of the bond agreement

Securities and Exchange Commission (SEC) The commission, created by the 1934 Securities Act, that has broad powers to regulate the issuance and trading of securities, and the financial reporting of companies issuing securities to the public

segments Subdivisions of a firm for which supplemental financial information is disclosed

serial bond A bond issue that staggers the bond maturity dates over a series of years

service cost (pensions) The increase in the pension obligation due to employees working another year for the employer

share-based payment Payment for a good or service using the entity's equity securities; an example is restricted stock used to compensate employees

significant influence The ability of the investor to affect the financing or operating policies of the investee

sinking fund provision A bond feature that requires the borrower to retire a portion of the bonds each year or, in some cases, to make payments each year to a trustee who is responsible for managing the resources needed to retire the bonds at maturity

solvency The ability to meet obligations, especially to creditors

source document Any written document or computer record evidencing an accounting transaction, such as a bank check or deposit slip, sales invoice, or cash register tape

special purpose entity *See* variable interest entity

spin-off A form of equity carve out in which divestiture is accomplished by distribution of a company's shares in a subsidiary to the company's shareholders who then own the shares in the subsidiary directly rather than through the parent company

split-off A form of equity carve out in which divestiture is accomplished by the parent company's exchange of stock in the subsidiary in return for shares in the parent owned by its shareholders

spread The difference between the return on net operating activities (RNOA) and the net nonoperating expense percentage (NNEP)

stated value A nominal amount that may be assigned to each share of no-par stock and accounted for much as if it were a par value

statement of cash flows A financial statement showing a firm's cash inflows and outflows for a specific period, classified into operating, investing, and financing categories

statement of equity *See* statement of stockholders' equity

statement of financial position A financial statement showing a firm's assets, liabilities, and owners' equity at a specific date; also called a balance sheet

statement of owners' equity A financial statement presenting information on the events causing a change in owners' equity during a period; the statement presents the beginning balance, additions to, deductions from, and the ending balance of owners' equity for the period

statement of retained earnings *See* retained earnings reconciliation

statement of stockholders' equity The financial statement that reconciles all of the components of stockholders' equity

stock dividends The payment of dividends in shares of stock

stock option The right, but not the obligation, to buy or sell a stock at an agreed upon price and date

stock split Additional shares of its own stock issued by a corporation to its current stockholders in proportion to their current ownership interests without changing the balances in the related stockholders' equity accounts; a formal stock split increases the number of shares outstanding and reduces proportionately the stock's per share par value

straight-line depreciation A depreciation procedure that allocates uniform amounts of depreciation expense to each full period of a depreciable asset's useful life

subsequent events Events occurring shortly after a fiscal year-end that will be reported as supplemental information to the financial statements of the year just ended

subsidiaries Companies that are owned by the parent company

subsidiary ledger A set of accounts or records that contains detailed information about the items included in the balance of one general ledger account

summary of significant accounting policies A financial statement disclosure, usually the initial note to the statements, which identifies the major accounting policies and procedures used by the firm

sum-of-the-years'-digits method An accelerated depreciation method that allocates depreciation expense to each year in a fractional proportion, the denominator of which is the sum of the years' digits in the useful life of the asset and the numerator of which is the remaining useful life of the asset at the beginning of the current depreciation period

T

T account An abbreviated form of the formal account in the shape of a T; use is usually limited to illustrations of accounting techniques and analysis

TCJA Tax Cuts and Jobs Act 2017 legislation that significantly affected taxes for individuals, corporations, partnerships, and other business entities

temporary account An account used to gather information for an accounting period; at the end of the period, the balance is transferred to a permanent owners' equity account; revenue, expense, and dividends accounts are temporary accounts

term loan A long-term borrowing, evidenced by a note payable, which is contracted with a single lender

terminal period The forecast period following the horizon period

times interest earned ratio Income before interest expense and income taxes divided by interest expense

total compensation cost The sum of gross pay, payroll taxes, and fringe benefits paid by the employer

trade credit Inventories purchased on credit from other companies

trade discount An amount, usually based on quantity of merchandise purchased, that the seller subtracts from the list price of merchandise to determine the invoice price

trade name An exclusive and continuing right to use a certain term or name to identify a brand or family of products

trade receivables Another name for accounts receivable from customers

trademark An exclusive and continuing right to use a certain symbol to identify a brand or family of products

trading on the equity The use of borrowed funds in the capital structure of a firm; the expectation is that the funds will earn a return higher than the rate of interest on the borrowed funds

trading securities Investments in debt securities that management intends to actively trade (buy and sell) for trading profits as market prices fluctuate

trailing earnings Earnings reported in the prior period

transitory items Transactions or events that are not likely to recur

translation adjustment The change in the value of the net assets of a subsidiary whose assets and liabilities are denominated in a foreign currency

treasury stock Shares of outstanding stock that have been acquired (and not retired) by the issuing corporation; treasury stock is recorded at cost and deducted from stockholders' equity in the balance sheet

trend percentages A comparison of the same financial item over two or more years stated as a percentage of a base-year amount

trial balance A list of the account titles in the general ledger, their respective debit or credit balances, and the totals of the debit and credit amounts

U

unadjusted trial balance A list of general ledger accounts and their balances taken before accounting adjustments have been made

uncollectible accounts expense The expense stemming from the inability of a business to collect an amount previously recorded as a receivable; sometimes called bad debts expense; normally classified as a selling or administrative expense

unearned revenue A liability representing revenues received in advance; also called deferred revenue

units-of-production method A depreciation method that allocates depreciation expense to each operating period in proportion to the amount of the asset's expected total production capacity used each period

useful life The period of time an asset is used by an entity in its operating activities, running from date of acquisition to date of disposal (or removal from service)

V

variable costs Those costs that change in proportion to changes in sales volume

variable interest entity (VIE) Any form of business organization (such as corporation, partnership, trust) that is established by a sponsoring company and provides benefits to that company in the form of asset securitization or project financing; VIEs were formerly known as special purpose entities (SPEs)

vertical analysis Analysis of a firm's financial statements that focuses on the statements of a single year; each line item expressed in percentage terms (balance sheet as % of total assets, income statement as % of total revenue)

voucher Another name for the payment approval form

W

warranties Guarantees against product defects for a designated period of time after sale

wasting assets Another name for natural resources; *see* natural resources

weighted average cost of capital (WACC) The discount rate where the weights are the relative percentages of debt and equity in the capital structure and are applied to the expected returns on debt and equity respectively

work in process inventory The cost of inventories that are in the manufacturing process and have not yet reached completion

working capital The difference between current assets and current liabilities

Z

z-score The outcome of the Altman Z-score bankruptcy prediction model

zero coupon bond A bond that offers no periodic interest payments but that is issued at a substantial discount from its face value

Index

A

AB InBev/SABMiller, 9-14–9-15
Accelerated depreciation method, 6-19
Accounting conservatism, 7-17
Accounting cycle, 3-17
    accounting adjustments
        accounting adjustments for Apple, 3-12–3-13
        accrued expenses, 3-11–3-12
        accrued revenues, 3-12
        prepaid expenses, 3-10
        types of, 3-9–3-10
        unearned revenues, 3-10–3-11
    closing books
        dividend account, 3-17
        expense and loss accounts, 3-17
        with journal entries, 3-16
        revenue and gain accounts, 3-16
        with template, 3-16
    financial statements, preparation
        balance sheet, 3-14–3-15
        income statement, 3-13–3-14
        statement of stockholders' equity, 3-15–3-16
    four-step, 3-3
    summary, 3-17–3-18
    transactions
        Apple's, 3-6
        financial statement effects template, 3-6
        journal entry and T-account, 3-6–3-9
Accounting equation, 1-10
Accounting (fiscal) year, 1-9
Accounts payable, 2-7, 11-13
Accounts payable turnover (APT), 6-15
Accounts receivable, 2-5, 11-12
    accounting for, 5-20
    aging analysis of, 5-19
    analysis of
        magnitude, 5-21–5-22
        quality, 5-22–5-24
Accounts receivable turnover, 5-21
Accruals, 3-9, 3-13, C-14
    accounting, 2-15, 3-9
    anomaly, 11-22
Accrued expenses, 3-10, 3-11–3-12
Accrued liabilities, 2-7, 11-14
    contingent liabilities, accruals for, 7-5
        warranties, 7-5–7-7
    contractual liabilities, accruals for
        deferred revenue, 7-4–7-5
        wages payable, 7-4
    defined, 7-3–7-4
Accrued revenues, 3-10, 3-12
Accumulated depreciation, 6-19
    change in, 11-17
Accumulated other comprehensive income (AOCI), 2-10, 8-4, 8-5, 9-8, 9-24
    components
        employee benefit plans, 8-20
        foreign currency translation adjustments, 8-19
        gains and losses, 8-19, 8-20

    disclosures and interpretation, 8-20–8-22
Accumulated post-employment benefit obligation (APBO), 10-23
Acquired intangible assets, accounting for, 9-22
Acquisitions, 12-3
    impact of, 12-10
    and sale, 9-4–9-5
Actuarial adjustments, 10-15–10-16
Actuarial assumption, 10-19
Additional paid-in capital, 2-10, 8-5
Adjusted financial statements, 12-3
Adjustments, accounting
    accrued expenses, 3-11–3-12
    accrued revenues, 3-12
    for Apple, 3-12–3-13
    prepaid expenses, 3-10
    types of, 3-9–3-10
    unearned revenues, 3-10–3-11
Aging analysis, 5-19
Allowance for uncollectible accounts, 5-20
Alphabet, 1-11, 1-12, 1-13, 5-18, 9-24–9-25
    equity investments with control, 9-17–9-18
    investments in debt securities, 9-8–9-10
    passive investments in equity securities, 9-4–9-8
Altria Group Inc., 9-14, 9-26
Amazon, 4-33–4-34, 5-10
American Airlines, 10-23–10-24, 10-38
Amortization, 7-14, 7-31
    of debt, 7-31
    of deferred amounts, 10-19
    of discount, 7-31
    of intangible assets, 5-25
    of premium, 7-32
Analyst reports, 2-25
Annuity, 7-10
Apple Inc., 1-1, 1-13, 1-18, 1-19, 1-25, 2-4, 2-9, 3-5, 4-10
    accounting adjustments, 3-12–3-13
    accounting equation for, 3-3–3-4
    accrued expenses, 3-11–3-12
    accrued revenues, 3-12
    articulation of financial statements, 2-21
    audit report for, 1-31
    balance sheet, 1-10–1-11, 2-4, 3-14–3-15
        liabilities and equity sections of, 2-7
    closing books, accounting
        dividend account, 3-17
        expense and loss accounts, 3-17
        with journal entries, 3-16
        revenue and gain accounts, 3-16
        with template, 3-16
    Credit Suisse on, 1-5
    description of business, 2-23
    disclosure of loan covenants, 1-6
    financial statement effects template, 3-6, 3-7
    fiscal year, 1-10
    income statement, 1-13, 2-13–2-14, 3-13–3-14
    journal entry and T-account, 3-6
    market value vs. book value, 2-11
    prepaid expenses, 3-10

    retained earnings reconciliation, 2-20
    retained earnings statement, 3-15
    statement of cash flows, 1-15–1-16, 2-19
    statement of stockholders' equity, 1-15, 2-17–2-18, 3-15–3-16
    transactions, 3-6, 3-8
    unearned revenues, 3-10–3-11
Asset turnover (AT), 1-18, 4-6
Assets, 2-4
    balance sheet, 2-4
    current, 2-5
    long-term, 2-5
    measuring, 2-5–2-6
    sales, 6-20–6-21
    utilization, 6-15
    write-downs, 6-22, 6-24
AT&T, 4-34–4-35, 7-22, 10-19–10-20
Audit Committee, 1-32, 1-34
Audit report, 1-31–1-34
Authorized shares, 8-3, 8-5, 8-7
Autozone, 8-25
Available-for-sale (AFS) debt securities, 9-8–9-10
Average cost (AC), 6-5–6-6
Average days inventory outstanding (DIO). *See* Days inventory outstanding

B

Balance sheet, 11-3, 12-4
    accounts, computing cash flows from, 11-19–11-20
    analysis with operating focus, 4-14–4-15
        net nonoperating obligations, 4-17–4-18
        net operating assets, 4-15–4-17
        return on net operating assets, 4-15
    assets, 2-4–2-6
    defined benefit pension plan on, 10-12–10-13
    effects of inventory costing, 6-7
    financing activities, 1-12
    and flow of costs, 2-3–2-4
    forecasting, 12-12–12-16
    investing activities, 1-10–1-11
    lease accounting and, 10-6–10-7
    liabilities and equity, 2-6–2-13
    long-term debt, reporting, 7-13–7-14
    operating vs. nonoperating classification, 4-30
    preparation of, 3-14–3-15
    reporting and analysis, C-9–C-10
        accounts receivable, C-10–C-11
        current liabilities, C-14
        deferred tax assets and liabilities, C-13–C-14
        derivatives, C-20
        goodwill and other intangible assets, C-13
        inventories, C-11–C-12
        long-term debt, C-15
        noncurrent employee benefits and other obligations, C-15–C-17
        operating leases, C-18–C-19
        pensions and other postretirement plans, C-19
        property, plant, and equipment, C-12–C-13

Balance sheet, *(continued)*
  reporting and analysis, *(continued)*
    stockholders' equity, C-17–C-18
    variable interest entities, C-19–C-20
  under IFRS, 2-18
Bargaining power, 1-7
  of buyers, 1-22
  of suppliers, 1-22
Barriers to entry, 1-24
Basic EPS, 8-24
BDO, 1-31
Benefits of disclosure, 1-7–1-8
Berkshire Hathaway, 8-24
Best Buy, 1-11, 1-12, 1-13
Bill-and-hold arrangements, 5-6
Bloomberg U.S. Spin-Off Index, 9-36
Board of directors, 8-4
Boeing, 5-7
Bond valuation, 7-27
Book value, 2-12, 7-15
Book value per share, 8-4
Boston Scientific Corporation, 4-3, 4-6
  common-size balance sheets, 4-39–4-40
  common-size income statements, 4-40
  current ratio, 4-36
  disaggregation of ROE, 4-7
  operating and nonoperating items
    balance sheet, 4-16
    income statement, 4-20
  return on net operating assets, 4-23
BT Group plc, 8-26
Business activities, 1-3–1-4
Business forces, 1-3
Business risk, 7-20
Business strategy, 1-3–1-4

C

Calendar-year, 1-9
Capital expenditures (CAPEX), 11-5, 12-12, 6-18
Capital IQ, 2-26
Capital leases, 10-9
Capital structure, maintaining, 12-16
Capitalization, 6-17–6-20
  lease
    using financial calculator, 10-33
    using present value tables, 10-34–10-35
Carrying value, 6-19
Cash, 2-5
Cash conversion cycle, 2-9, 4-9, 6-16–6-17
Cash dividend
  disclosures, 8-16–8-17
  financial effects, 8-17–8-18
Cash equivalents, 11-3
Cash flow
  components, 11-21–11-22
  effects of inventory costing, 6-7–6-8
  from financing activities
    balance sheet accounts, 11-19–11-20
    Java House case illustration, 11-18–11-19
    liabilities and equity, 11-18
    supplemental disclosures for indirect method, 11-20–11-21
  foreign currency and, 5-16–5-17
  free cash flow, 11-28–11-29

  hedge, 9-30
  from investing activities
    Java House case illustration, 11-16–11-18
    noncash assets, 11-16
  net income vs., 11-22
  from operating activities, 11-9–11-10
    Java House case illustration, 11-11–11-16
    steps to compute net cash flow, 11-10–11-11
  patterns, 11-23–11-25
  ratio analysis of, 11-27–11-28
  statement of. *See also* Statement of cash flows
    direct method reporting for, 11-29–11-32
    financing activities, 11-8–11-9
    investing activities, 11-8
    operating activities, 11-5–11-7
    relation among financial statements, 11-3–11-4
    structure, 11-4–11-5
    usefulness of, 11-25–11-27
Cash plug (plug), 12-15
Caterpillar Financial Services Corporation, 4-27, 4-41
Caterpillar Inc. (CAT), 1-12, 4-27, 4-41, 6-7, 6-9–6-10, 9-25–9-26
Caveat, 4-21
CBS Corporation, 9-35–9-36
Celadon Group Inc., 1-33
CFA Institute, 9-31
Charge-offs, 6-22
Chart of accounts, B-1
Chartists, 13-13
Cisco Systems Inc., 1-11, 1-13, 1-19, 2-24, 9-29
Closing books, accounting
  dividend account, 3-17
  expense and loss accounts, 3-17
  with journal entries, 3-16
  revenue and gain accounts, 3-16
  with template, 3-16
Closing process, 3-16
Coca-Cola Company, 5-24, 6-24, 8-9, 8-12, 8-16, 8-21–8-22
Colgate Palmolive, 1-11, 1-12, 1-14, 1-18, 4-21
Collateral, 7-21
Collectibility, C-10
Comcast, 1-11, 7-9, 7-13, 7-16, 7-22, 7-24
Common stock, 2-10, 8-3, 8-5, 8-7–8-8
  change in, 11-18
Common-size analysis, 2-16
Company managers, 1-3
Competitive advantage, 1-24–1-25
Competitive disadvantages, 1-8
Competitive environment, 1-22–1-23
Compound financial instruments, 8-23
Compound interest tables, A-1–A-2
Compounding, 7-25
Consignment sales, 5-6
Consolidation
  accounting, mechanics of, 9-19–9-22
  of foreign subsidiaries, 9-23–9-27
  reporting, limitations of, 9-27–9-28
Contingent liabilities, accruals for, 7-5
  warranties, 7-5–7-7
Contractual liabilities, accruals for
  deferred revenue, 7-4–7-5

  wages payable, 7-4
Contributed capital, 1-14, 2-10, 8-3
Control, equity investments with, 9-3, 9-4, 9-17–9-18
  accounting for, 9-18–9-23
  consolidation of foreign subsidiaries, 9-23–9-27
  limitations of consolidation reporting, 9-27–9-28
Controlling interest, 2-13, 4-5
Conversion option, 8-22
Conversion privileges, 8-6
Convertible securities
  disclosures and interpretation, 8-22–8-23
  financial effects, 8-23
  under IFRS, 8-23
Corning Inc., 8-6, 8-22
Corporate governance, 1-31
  structure, 1-33
Cost leader, 1-24
Cost of debt, 7-17
Cost of equity (R_e), 13-8
Cost of goods sold (COGS), 1-13, 2-3, 6-3, 12-9
Cost of preferred stock (R_{ps}), 13-8
Cost of sales, 1-13, 5-25
Costing methods, inventory, 6-3–6-4
  average cost, 6-5–6-6
  balance sheet effects, 6-7
  cash flow effects, 6-7–6-8
  financial statement effects of, 6-7–6-8
  first-in, first-out, 6-4–6-5
  income statement effects, 6-7
  last-in, first-out, 6-5
Costs of disclosure, 1-8
Cost-to-cost method, 5-7–5-8
Cost-to-cost reporting, 5-8–5-10
Cost-to-retail percentage, 6-6
Counterparty risk, 9-30
Coupon (contract or stated) rate, 7-9
Courts, 1-34
Covenants, 1-5, 4-35, 7-21
Credit analysis, 7-16–7-17
Credit facility, 1-6
Credit ratings, 1-21, 7-18–7-19
  and financial ratios, 7-19–7-21
  reasons for matter, 7-23–7-24
  Verizon, 7-21–7-23
Credit services, 2-26
Credit Suisse, 1-5
Creditors, 1-5–1-6
Cumulative translation adjustment, 9-23–9-27
Current (nonoperating) assets, 2-5, 4-36, 11-5
Current (nonoperating) liabilities, 2-7–2-9, 4-36, 11-5
Current maturities of long-term debt, 2-7, 2-9, 7-8
Current operating assets, 11-10
  accounts receivable, 11-12
  inventory, 11-12–11-13
  prepaid expenses, 11-13
Current operating liabilities, 11-10
  accounts payable, 11-13
  accrued liabilities, 11-14
Current ratio, 4-36
Customers, 1-6
CVS, 1-13, 1-18, 7-15

D

Darden Restaurants, 1-18
Data analytics
    data visualization, 1-29–1-30
    importance of, 1-29
    types of, 1-29
Data services, 2-26
Data visualization, 1-29–1-30
Date of payment, 8-5
Date of record, 8-5
Days inventory outstanding, 6-13–6-15
Days payable outstanding (DPO), 6-15–6-16
Days sales outstanding (DSO), 5-21
Dean Foods Company, 6-21
Debt, amortization of, 7-31
Debt securities
    investments in
        available-for-sale, 9-8–9-10
        financial statement disclosures, 9-10–9-11
        held-to-maturity, 9-8
Declaration date, 8-5
Deere & Company, 10-17–10-19, 10-23
Default, 7-18
Deferred tax assets
    expanded example of, 10-41
    expanded explanation of, 10-39–10-41
    reporting, 10-27–10-28
    rules for, 10-40
    timing differences create, 10-24–10-27
    valuation allowance for, 10-28
Deferred tax liabilities
    expanded explanation of, 10-39–10-41
    illustration of, 10-25
    reporting, 10-27–10-28
    rules for, 10-40
    timing differences create, 10-24–10-27
    valuation allowance for, 10-28
Defined benefit pension plan, 10-11
    on balance sheet, 10-12–10-13
    on income statement, 10-15–10-16
Defined contribution plan, 10-11
Deloitte, 1-31
Delta Airlines, 10-4
    analysis issues relating to leases, 10-10
    leasing footnote disclosure from, 10-11
    new lease accounting standard, 10-8
Demand for information
    creditors and suppliers, 1-5–1-6
    customers and strategic partners, 1-6
    investment analysts and information intermediaries, 1-5
    managers and employees, 1-4–1-5
    regulators and tax agencies, 1-6–1-7
    stockholders and directors, 1-6
    voters and representatives, 1-7
Depreciation, 2-3, 6-17–6-20
    expense, 12-13–12-14
Derivatives, 4-17, 9-29
    accounting for, 9-29–9-30
    analysis of, 9-30–9-31
Descriptive analytics, 1-29
Deutsche Bank valuation, 13-14–13-25
Diagnostic analytics, 1-29
Diluted EPS, 8-24
Direct (raw) materials, 6-3
Direct labor, 6-3

Direct method, 11-9
    reporting for statement of cash flows, 11-29–11-32
Directors, 1-6
Discontinued operations, 2-15–2-16, 5-25, 5-28–5-31, 4-17, 12-3
Discount, 7-11
    amortization of, 7-31
    rate, 10-15–10-16
Discounted cash flow (DCF) model, 13-3
    advantages and disadvantages of, 13-13
    application of, 13-7
    illustrating, 13-6–13-8
    steps in applying, 13-6
    structure, 13-5–13-6
Dissemination costs, 1-8
Divestitures, 12-3
    impact of, 12-11
Dividends, 8-5, 12-15
    in arrears, 8-18
    cash dividend disclosures, 8-16–8-17
    cash dividends financial effects, 8-17–8-18
    discount model, 13-3
    payout and yield, 8-17
    stock split in form of, 8-18–8-19
DuPont analysis
    financial leverage, 4-4–4-6
    return on assets, 4-4

E

E.I. DuPont de Nemours and Company, 4-4
Earned capital, 1-14, 2-10, 8-3, 8-4–8-5
Earnings, 1-13
    and stock prices, 1-20
Earnings per share (EPS), 8-23–8-25
EarthLink, 9-27–9-28
Effective cost of debt, 7-11–7-13
Employee benefit plans, 8-20
Employee severance or relocation costs, 6-22, 6-23
Employee share purchase plans, 8-13
Employee stock options, 8-13
Employee stock purchase plans (ESPP), 8-26
Employees, 1-4–1-5
Enron, 1-30, 1-34
Equipment, 2-3
Equity, 1-10
    analyzing, 11-18
Equity carve-outs, 9-32–9-36
    analysis of, 9-36
    IPOs, 9-32
    sell-offs, 9-32
    spin-offs, 9-32
    split-offs, 9-32
Equity method accounting, 9-12, 9-14–9-17
Equity securities, valuing, C-30–C-31
    assessment of valuation estimate, C-32–C-33
    discounted cash flow valuation, C-31–C-32
    residual operating income valuation, C-32
    summary observations, C-33
Equity valuation models
    discounted cash flow model, 13-3
    dividend discount model, 13-3
    residual operating income model, 13-3
    valuation model inputs, 13-4–13-5

Ernst & Young LLP, C-22–C-23
Expected return, 10-16
Expense recognition (matching) principle, 2-15, 8-13
Expenses and losses
    deductions from income, 5-25
    discontinued operations, 5-28–5-31
    provision (benefit) for taxes on income, 5-28
    recognizing, 2-14–2-15
    research and development
        analysis of, 5-26–5-28
        R&D spending, 5-26
Express Scripts Inc., 8-23
Expresso Royale, 11-15–11-16
Extended protection plan contracts, 5-15
EY, 1-31

F

Face amount, 7-9
Fair value, 5-5
    accounting, 10-19–10-21
    disclosures, 7-15–7-16
    hedge, 9-30
    method, 9-5
Farmer Brothers, 11-27
FedEx, 10-13–10-14, 10-20–10-21, 10-31, 10-41
Film and television revenues and costs, 5-9
Finance leases, 10-3, 10-35–10-37
Financial accounting for MBAs
    accounting principles and governance
        audit report, 1-31–1-34
        financial accounting environment, 1-30–1-31
    business activities, reporting on, 1-3–1-4
    financial statement. *See* Financial statement
Financial Accounting Standards Board (FASB), 1-8, 1-30
    financial statement presentation project, 3-19
Financial calculator, lease capitalization, 10-33
Financial flexibility, 11-25
Financial leverage (FLEV), 4-4–4-6, 4-24, 4-32, 9-16
    analysis, 4-12–4-14
Financial ratios, 1-21
Financial reporting, business environment for, C-3
Financial risk, 7-20
Financial statement
    additional information sources
        analyst reports, 2-25
        credit services, 2-26
        data services, 2-26
        Form 8-K, 2-25
        Form 10-K, 2-22–2-24
        Form 20-F and Form 40-F, 2-24
    analysis of
        components of return on assets, 1-18–1-20
        financial statements relevancy, 1-20–1-21
        return on assets, 1-18
        return on equity, 1-20
    articulation of
        financial statement linkages, 2-20–2-22
        retained earnings reconciliation, 2-20
    balance sheet. *See* Balance sheet

Financial statement, *(continued)*
  and business analysis
    competitive advantage, 1-24–1-25
    competitive environment, 1-22–1-23
    SWOT analysis of business environment, 1-23
  business environment for financial reporting, C-3
  data analytics
    data visualization, 1-29–1-30
    importance of, 1-29
    types of, 1-29
  demand for information, 1-4–1-7
  Financial Accounting Standards Board presentation project, 3-19
  forecasting, 12-3–12-5, C-27–C-30
    balance sheet, 12-12–12-16
    building forecasts from bottom up, 12-16–12-18
    company guidance, 12-5–12-7
    income statement, 12-8–12-12
    Morgan Stanley's report on Procter & Gamble, 12-23–12-30
    multiyear forecasting with target cash and new debt, 12-20–12-22
    parsimonious method for NOPAT and NOA, 12-22–12-23
    statement of cash flows, 12-19–12-20
  income statement. *See* Income statement
  independent audit opinion, C-22–C-23
  international accounting standards, 1-8–1-9
  inventory costing, effects of, 6-7–6-8
    balance sheet, 6-7
    cash flow, 6-7–6-8
    income statement, 6-7
  LIFO reserve adjustments to, 6-9–6-10
  linkages, 2-20–2-22
  preparation of
    balance sheet, 3-14–3-15
    income statement, 3-13–3-14
    statement of stockholders' equity, 3-15–3-16
  profitability and creditworthiness
    credit analysis, C-26
    RNOA disaggregation, margin and turnover, C-25
    ROE disaggregation, DuPont analysis, C-23–C-24
    ROE disaggregation, operating focus, C-24–C-25
    summarizing, C-26–C-27
  return on assets and disaggregation, 4-6–4-8
    financial leverage analysis, 4-12–4-14
    productivity analysis, 4-9–4-12
    profitability analysis, 4-8–4-9
  return on equity, 4-3
    disaggregation, DuPont analysis, 4-4–4-6
  return on net operating assets, 4-23–4-25
    disaggregation into margin and turnover, 4-25–4-29
  SEC filings, 1-26–2-28
  statement of cash flows. *See* Statement of cash flows
  statement of stockholders' equity. *See* Statement of stockholders' equity
  structure of, 1-9–1-10
    balance sheet, 1-10–1-12
    income statement, 1-13–1-14
    information beyond financial statements, 1-16
    managerial choices in financial accounting, 1-17–1-18
    statement of cash flows, 1-15–1-16
    statement of stockholders' equity, 1-14–1-15
  supply of information, 1-7–1-8
  for valuation
    assessment of valuation models, 13-12–13-13
    derivation of free cash flow formula, 13-14
    Deutsche Bank valuation of Procter & Gamble, 13-14–13-25
    discounted cash flow model, 13-5–13-8
    equity valuation models, 13-3–13-5
    further considerations involving, 13-11–13-13
    residual operating income model, 13-9–13-11
  valuing equity securities, C-30–C-31
    assessment of valuation estimate, C-32–C-33
    discounted cash flow valuation, C-31–C-32
    residual operating income valuation, C-32
    summary observations, C-33
Financial statement effects template, 3-3–3-4, 3-6–3-7
Financing activities, 1-3, 1-12, 1-16, 11-3–11-4
  cash flows from
    balance sheet accounts, 11-19–11-20
    Java House case illustration, 11-18–11-19
    liabilities and equity, 11-18
    supplemental disclosures for indirect method, 11-20–11-21
  preview, 11-8
First-in, first-out (FIFO), 6-4–6-5
Fitch Ratings, 2-26, 7-18
Flow of costs, balance sheet and, 2-3–2-4
Flow-based approach, 7-16
Footnote disclosure
  key assumptions, 10-21–10-22
  for stock-based compensation, 8-15–8-16
  valuation implications of, 10-20
Ford Credit Corporation, 4-41
Forecasting, 12-3–12-5, C-27–C-30
  adjusted financial statements, 12-3
  balance sheet, 12-12–12-16
  building forecasts from bottom up, 12-16–12-18
  company guidance, 12-5–12-7
  consistency and precision, 12-4–12-5
  income statement, 12-8–12-12
  mechanics, 12-4
  Morgan Stanley, 12-4
    report on Procter & Gamble, 12-23–12-30
  multiyear forecasting with target cash and new debt, 12-20–12-22
  order of financial statements, 12-3–12-4
  parsimonious method for NOPAT and NOA, 12-22–12-23
  segment data, 12-16–12-18
  statement of cash flows, 12-19–12-20
Foreign currency, 5-3
  and cash flows, 5-16–5-17
  and future results, 5-17–5-18
  and income, 5-17
  revenue, expenses, and cash flow, effects on, 5-15–5-16
  translation adjustments, 8-19
Foreign subsidiaries, consolidation of, 9-23–9-27
Form 8-K, 2-25
Form 10-K, 1-7, 2-22–2-24
Form 10-Q, 1-7
Form 20-F, 2-24
Form 40-F, 2-24
Forward-looking predictions, 5-27
Franchises, 5-6
Free cash flow, 11-28–11-29
  definitions of, 13-6
  formula, derivation of, 13-14
Free cash flows to the firm (FCFF), 13-5
Fundamental analysis, 1-6
Funded status, 10-12
Future value, 7-25
  of annuity, 7-30
  concepts, 7-30
  of single amount, 7-30

G

Gains and losses, 11-10
  on asset dispositions and impairments, 12-3
  on bond repurchases, 7-15
  with no cash flow effects, 11-12
  pension, unrecognized
    accounting for, 10-37
    financial statement effects from, 10-37–10-38
    PBO assumptions and, 10-38–10-39
    sources of, 10-37
General Mills, 1-12, 12-6–12-7, 12-11–12-12, 12-16, 12-18, 12-20, 12-22–12-23, 13-8, 13-11, 13-13
General Motors, 10-14
Generally Accepted Accounting Principles (GAAP), 1-8, 1-30, 5-32
  vs. International Financial Reporting Standards
    accounts receivable, 5-35
    analyzing and interpreting financial statements, 4-29–4-30
    balance sheet, 2-26
    consolidation, 9-28–9-29
    current and long-term liabilities, 7-24
    equity method investment, 9-28
    financial accounting, 1-26
    income statement, 2-26
    income taxes, 10-33
    inventory, 6-27–6-28
    leases, 10-32
    passive investments, 9-28
    pensions, 10-32
    property, plant, and equipment, 6-28
    research and development, 5-35, 6-28
    restructuring, 6-28
    revenue recognition, 5-35

Generally Accepted Accounting Principles (GAAP), *(continued)*
   vs. International Financial Reporting Standards, *(continued)*
      stock transactions, dividends, and EPS, 8-25–8-26
      transactions, adjustments, and financial statements, 3-18
      valuation, financial statements for, 13-14
Gift cards, 5-6
Gillette, 12-10
Goldman Sachs, 7-9
Goodwill, 9-21
Google, 9-13
Gross margin, 12-9
Gross profit analysis, 6-12–6-13
Gross profit, 1-13, 4-25, 6-3
Gross profit margin (GPM), 2-16, 4-8–4-9, 6-12

H

Harley-Davidson Inc., 6-15, 7-6, 7-7, 9-29, 9-30
   balance sheet reporting and analysis, C-9–C-10
      accounts receivable, C-10–C-11
      current liabilities, C-14
      deferred tax assets and liabilities, C-13–C-14
      derivatives, C-20
      goodwill and other intangible assets, C-13
      inventories, C-11–C-12
      long-term debt, C-15
      noncurrent employee benefits and other obligations, C-15–C-17
      operating leases, C-18–C-19
      pensions and other postretirement plans, C-19
      property, plant, and equipment, C-12–C-13
      stockholders' equity, C-17–C-18
      variable interest entities, C-19–C-20
   business environment for financial reporting, C-3
   forecasting, C-27–C-30
   income statement reporting and analysis
      common-size income statement, C-7–C-8
      cost of products sold and gross profit, C-5
      earnings per share, C-6–C-7
      income taxes, C-7
      management discussion and analysis, C-8–C-9
      net sales, C-3–C-5
      pension expenses, C-5–C-6
      selling, administrative, and engineering expenses, C-5
   independent audit opinion, C-22–C-23
   profitability and creditworthiness
      credit analysis, C-26
      RNOA disaggregation, margin and turnover, C-25
      ROE disaggregation, DuPont analysis, C-23–C-24
      ROE disaggregation, operating focus, C-24–C-25
      summarizing, C-26–C-27
   statement of cash flows reporting and analysis, C-21–C-22
   valuing equity securities, C-30–C-31
      assessment of valuation estimate, C-32–C-33
      discounted cash flow valuation, C-31–C-32
      residual operating income valuation, C-32
      summary observations, C-33
Heinz, 9-22
Held-to-maturity (HTM) debt securities, 9-8
Hershey Company, 9-24
Hewlett-Packard 10bII, 10-33
Hewlett-Packard Enterprise Co. (HPE), 5-30–5-31
Historical costs, 2-5, 4-41
Home Depot, 1-18, 6-6, 6-8
   analysis tools, 6-25
   cash conversion cycle, 6-16–6-17
   gross profit margin and related data for, 6-12–6-13
Honeywell, 10-20
Horizon period, 13-6
Horizontal analysis, 4-38
HP Inc., 10-27, 10-41

I

IBM, 10-20
IM Flash Technologies LLC (IMFT), 9-17
Impairment, 6-21
Income statement, 1-13–1-14, 2-13–2-14, 11-3, 12-4
   analysis with operating focus
      net nonoperating expense, 4-22–4-23
      nonoperating line items on, 4-19–4-22
      operating line items on, 4-19
   analyzing, 2-16–2-17
   defined benefit pension plan on, 10-15–10-16
   effects of inventory costing, 6-7
   forecasting, 12-8–12-12
   lease accounting and, 10-7–10-8
   long-term debt, reporting, 7-14
   operating vs. nonoperating classification, 4-30–4-31
   preparation of, 3-13–3-14
   recognizing revenues and expenses, 2-14–2-15
   reporting and analysis
      common-size income statement, C-7–C-8
      cost of products sold and gross profit, C-5
      earnings per share, C-6–C-7
      income taxes, C-7
      management discussion and analysis, C-8–C-9
      net sales, C-3–C-5
      pension expenses, C-5–C-6
      selling, administrative, and engineering expenses, C-5
   reporting of transitory items, 2-15–2-16
   under IFRS, 2-18
Income taxes
   deferred taxes, expanded explanation of, 10-39–10-41
   disclosures for, 10-29–10-30
      analysis of, 10-30–10-32
   expense, 12-10
   timing differences create deferred tax assets and liabilities, 10-24–10-27
      reporting deferred tax assets and liabilities, 10-27–10-28
      valuation allowance for deferred tax assets, 10-28
Independent audit opinion, C-22–C-23
Indirect method, 11-9
   supplemental disclosures for, 11-20–11-21
Industry competition, 1-22
Information intermediaries, 1-5
Initial public offering (IPO), 8-5
In-store and on-line sales, 5-14
Intangible assets, 2-5, 12-14
Intel, 1-12–1-13, 1-18–1-19, 9-17, 9-27–9-28
Intercorporate investments, 9-3–9-4
   debt securities
      available-for-sale, 9-8–9-10
      financial statement disclosures, 9-10–9-11
      held-to-maturity, 9-8
   derivatives
      accounting for, 9-29–9-30
      analysis of, 9-30–9-31
   equity carve-outs, 9-32–9-36
      analysis of, 9-36
   equity investments with control, 9-17–9-18
      accounting for investments with control, 9-18–9-23
      consolidation of foreign subsidiaries, 9-23–9-27
      limitations of consolidation reporting, 9-27–9-28
   equity investments with significant influence
      accounting for investments with significant influence, 9-12–9-14
      equity method accounting and ROE effects, 9-14–9-17
   passive investments in equity securities
      acquisition and sale, 9-4–9-5
      fair-value method, 9-5–9-6
      initial adoption of new accounting rules, 9-7–9-10
      marketable equity securities, 9-6
      non-marketable equity securities, 9-6–9-7
Interest cost, 10-15
Interest expense, 12-9–12-10
Internal consistency, 12-4–12-5
Internal controls, 1-33
Internal Revenue Code (IRC), 10-24
International Accounting Standards Board (IASB), 1-8
International Accounting Standards, 1-8–1-9
International Financial Reporting Standards (IFRS), 1-8
   balance sheet presentation and, 1-12
   vs. Generally Accepted Accounting Principles
      accounts receivable, 5-35
      analyzing and interpreting financial statements, 4-29–4-30
      balance sheet, 2-26
      consolidation, 9-28–9-29
      current and long-term liabilities, 7-24
      equity method investment, 9-28
      financial accounting, 1-26
      income statement, 2-26

International Financial Reporting Standards
(IFRS), *(continued)*
vs. Generally Accepted Accounting
Principles, *(continued)*
income taxes, 10-33
inventory, 6-27–6-28
leases, 10-32
passive investments, 9-28
pensions, 10-32
property, plant, and equipment, 6-28
research and development, 5-35, 6-28
restructuring, 6-28
revenue recognition, 5-35
stock transactions, dividends, and EPS, 8-25–8-26
transactions, adjustments, and financial statements, 3-18
valuation, financial statements for, 13-14
inventory measurement under, 6-11
lease accounting under, 10-10
pension funded status under, 10-15
PPE valuation under, 6-21
provisions and contingencies under, 7-7
International Paper Company, 9-32
Inventories, 2-3, 2-5, 11-12–11-13
analysis tools
cash conversion cycle, 6-16–6-17
days inventory outstanding and inventory turnover, 6-13–6-15
days payable outstanding, 6-15–6-16
gross profit analysis, 6-12–6-13
costing methods, 6-3–6-4
average cost, 6-5–6-6
balance sheet effects, 6-7
cash flow effects, 6-7–6-8
financial statement effects of, 6-7–6-8
first-in, first-out, 6-4–6-5
income statement effects, 6-7
last-in, first-out, 6-5
quality, 6-14–6-15
reporting
LIFO liquidations, 6-11
LIFO reserve adjustments to financial statements, 6-9–6-10
lower of cost or market, 6-8–6-9
turnover, 6-13–6-15
Investing activities, 1-3, 1-10–1-11, 1-15–1-16, 11-3–11-4
cash flows from
Java House case illustration, 11-16–11-18
noncash assets, 11-16
preview, 11-8
Investing equals financing, 1-10
Investment analysts, 1-5
Investment returns, 10-15–10-16
Investors and equity analysts, 1-3
Issued shares, 8-3, 8-5, 8-7

J

Java House case illustration
cash flow from financing activities
common stock, change in, 11-18
net cash from financing activities, 11-19
retained earnings, change in, 11-18
cash flow from investing activities
accumulated depreciation, change in, 11-17
long-term investments, change in, 11-16–11-17
net cash from investing activities, 11-17–11-18
patent, 11-17
PPE, change in, 11-17
cash flow from operating activities
accounts payable, 11-13
accounts receivable, 11-12
accrued liabilities, 11-14
gains and losses with no cash flow effects, 11-12
inventory, 11-12–11-13
net cash from operating activities, 11-14
prepaid expenses, 11-13
revenues and expenses with no cash flow effects, 11-11–11-12
financial data of, 11-10
for supplemental disclosures, 11-20–11-21
Johnson & Johnson, 1-11, 1-13, 1-19
accounting for stock-based compensation, 8-14–8-15
AOCI disclosures and interpretation, 8-20–8-21
common stock, 8-7–8-8
stockholders' equity
accounts, 8-3–8-4
statement of, 8-5–8-6
Journal entries, 3-5–3-6
Juniper Networks, 9-4–9-5, 9-11

K

KPMG, 1-31
Kraft Heinz Company, 9-22
Kraft, 9-22
Kroger, 6-6
Kubota, 6-10

L

Last-in, first-out (LIFO), 6-5
liquidations, 6-11
reserve adjustments to financial statements, 6-9–6-10
Lattice method, 8-15
Leases
accounting, 10-5
and balance sheet, 10-6–10-7
and income statement, 10-7–10-8
statement of cash flows, 10-8–10-9
analysis issues relating to, 10-10–10-11
capitalization
using financial calculator, 10-33
using present value tables, 10-34–10-35
finance and operating leases, 10-35–10-37
Hewlett-Packard 10bII, 10-33
imputed discount rate computation for, 10-7
lessee reporting, 10-4–10-5
liability, 10-6
Microsoft Corporation, 10-4–10-5
new lease reporting standard, 10-3–10-4
summary, 10-9–10-10
Texas Instruments BA II Plus, 10-33

Lenders, 7-16
and credit analysts, 1-3
Lessee, 10-3
reporting, 10-4–10-5
Lessor, 10-3
Level of precision, 12-5
Levi Strauss, 5-11
accounts receivable, 5-23–5-24
balance sheet, 5-12
income statement, 5-12
sales allowances
analysis of, 5-13
reporting, 5-12
Liabilities, 1-10, 2-6–2-7
analyzing, 11-18
current, 2-7–2-9
noncurrent, 2-9–2-10
-to-equity ratio, 4-37–4-38
Licenses, 5-6
Liquidity, 2-5, 7-20, 11-3
analysis, 4-36
Litigation, 1-8
expenses, 12-3
Long-term assets, 2-5
Long-term debt (LTD), 2-9, 12-14
current maturities of, 7-8
effective cost of debt, 7-11–7-13
pricing, 7-9–7-10
of bonds issued at discount, 7-10–7-11
of bonds issued at par, 7-10
of bonds issued at premium, 7-11
reporting
balance sheet, 7-13–7-14
fair value disclosures, 7-15–7-16
financial statement effects of bond repurchase, 7-14–7-15
income statement, 7-14
Long-term investments, 2-5
change in, 11-16–11-17
LookSmart, 9-17
Lowe's Companies Inc., 5-14–5-15, 6-17, 6-27, 11-23
Lower of cost or market (LCM), 6-3, 6-8–6-9
Lump-sum, 7-10, 7-26
Lyft, 5-33

M

Macy's Inc., 1-13, 1-18, 6-20
Magnitude, 5-21–5-22, C-10
Management discussion and analysis (MD&A), 2-23–2-24, C-8–C-9
Managers, 1-4–1-5
Manufacturing costs, 6-3
Manufacturing overhead, 6-3
Market (yield or effective) rate, 7-9
Market capitalization, 8-5, 8-8
Market price, 8-5
Market value, 2-12
Marketable equity securities, 9-6
Market-to-book ratio, 2-12, 8-4
McDonald's Corporation, 11-29
Measurability, 4-40
Mechanics of consolidation accounting, 9-19–9-22
Merck & Co. Inc., 4-10–4-11, 5-34–5-35

Method of comparables model, 13-12
Metropolitan Life Insurance Co., 10-21
Michael Kors Holdings LTD, 9-29, 9-30
Microsoft Corporation, 2-13, 2-26, 5-4–5-5, 5-15, 8-11–8-12, 9-11, 10-3–10-5
   assets, 10-4
   financial statements, 2-22
   imputed discount rate computation for leases, 10-7
   income statement, 2-17
   liabilities and stockholders' equity, 10-5
   statement of cash flows, 2-20
   statement of stockholders' equity, 2-18
Modified Accelerated Cost Recovery System (MACRS), 6-19, 10-25
Moody's Investors Service, 1-21, 2-26, 7-18, 7-24, C-15
Morgan Stanley, 12-17
   forecast report on Procter & Gamble, 12-23–12-30
   forecasting process, 12-4
MTV, 3-10
Multiple-element-contracts, 5-6
Multiples model. *See* Method of comparables model

N

Net asset valuation model, 13-13
Net book value (NBV), 6-19, 10-39
Net cash
   from financing activities, 11-19
   flow, 11-10–11-11
   from investing activities, 11-17–11-18
Net income vs. cash flows, 11-22
Net nonoperating expense (NNE), 4-22–4-23, 4-32
Net nonoperating expense percent (NNEP), 4-32
Net nonoperating obligations (NNO), 4-17–4-18, 4-32
Net operating asset (NOA), 4-15–4-17, 4-24, 13-4, 13-11–13-12
   parsimonious method for forecasting, 12-22–12-23
Net operating asset turnover (NOAT), 4-26–4-28, 9-16
Net operating profit after tax (NOPAT), 4-24, 13-4, 13-11–13-12
   parsimonious method for forecasting, 12-22–12-23
Net operating profit before tax (NOPBT), 4-24
Net operating profit margin (NOPM), 4-25–4-28, 9-16
Net working capital, 2-8
Netgear Inc., 9-34–9-35
New lease reporting standard, 10-3–10-4
Nissim Company, 9-18–9-21
Noncapitalized costs, 4-41
Noncash assets, 11-16
Noncontrolling interest, 4-5, 8-8, 9-19–9-20
   income attributable to, 5-25
Noncurrent liabilities, 2-9–2-10
Non-marketable equity securities, 9-6
Nonoperating assets, 4-17–4-18
Nonoperating expenses, 2-13
Nonoperating liabilities, 4-17
Nonowner financing, 1-10
Nonpension post-employment benefits, 10-23
Nonrefundable up-front fees, 5-6
Nordstrom, 1-11, 1-13, 1-19
Normal balance, 3-4
North American Consumer Packaging, 9-32

O

Operating (or cash) cycle, 2-8
Operating activities, 1-3, 1-15, 11-3, 11-4
   cash flows from, 11-9–11-10
      Java House case illustration, 11-11–11-16
      steps to compute net cash flow, 11-10–11-11
   converting net income to net cash flow from, 11-11
   preview, 11-5
Operating assets, 4-15
Operating cash flow to capital expenditures ratio, 11-27–11-28
Operating cash flow to current liabilities ratio, 11-27
Operating expenses, 2-13, 2-16
   margin, 4-9
Operating lease, 10-3, 10-35–10-37
   method, 10-9
   payments, present value of, 10-6
Operating liabilities, 4-15–4-16
Operating segment, 12-16
Options, 7-21
Ordinary annuity, 7-26
Other comprehensive income (OCI), 8-5, 8-20, 9-25
Other long-term liabilities, 2-9
Other post-employment benefits (OPEB), 10-23–10-24, C-19
Outstanding shares, 8-5, 8-8
Owner financing, 1-10

P

Pads. *See* Accruals
Paid-in capital, 8-5
Par (face) value, 7-10, 8-3, 8-5, 8-7
Parsimonious model forecasts, 13-4
Passive investments in equity securities, 9-3–9-4
   intercorporate investments
      acquisition and sale, 9-4–9-5
      fair-value method, 9-5–9-6
      initial adoption of new accounting rules, 9-7–9-10
      marketable equity securities, 9-6
      non-marketable equity securities, 9-6–9-7
Patent, 11-17
Penman Company, 9-18–9-21
Pension, 10-11–10-12
   amortization component of pension expense, 10-37–10-39
   analysis implications, 10-22–10-23
   analysis issue, 10-13–10-15
   defined benefit pension plan
      on balance sheet, 10-12–10-13
      on income statement, 10-15–10-16
   fair value accounting for, 10-19–10-21
   footnote disclosure, 10-21–10-22
   other post-employment benefits, 10-23–10-24
   pension expense smoothing, 10-16–10-19
Pension expense
   amortization component of, 10-37–10-39
   smoothing, 10-16–10-19
Pension plan assets, 10-12, 10-17, C-6
   unexpected returns on, 10-19
PepsiCo Inc., 8-8, 9-31
Performance obligation, 5-4
Periodic interest payments, 7-10
Permanent accounts, 2-3, 3-14
Pfizer, 5-3, 5-15–5-16, 5-33, 6-23
   accounts receivable, 5-19
   discontinued operations, 5-29
   expense and loss items, 5-25
   financial ratios, 5-22
   foreign currency
      and cash flows, 5-17
      and future results, 5-17–5-18
      and income, 5-17
   income statement, 5-3
   pro forma income reporting, 5-31–5-32
   R&D expense, 5-26–5-27
Plant, property and equipment (PPE), 10-39–10-40, 12-12
   analysis of, 4-11–4-12
   analysis tools
      PPE percent used up, 6-27
      PPE turnover, 6-25–6-26
      PPE useful life, 6-26
   capitalization and depreciation, 6-17–6-20
   change in, 11-17
   impairments, 6-21
   plant and equipment
      other depreciation methods, 6-19
      straight-line method, 6-18–6-19
   research and development facilities and equipment, 6-19–6-20
   restructuring costs
      analysis of, 6-23–6-24
      disclosure of, 6-22–6-23
   sales, 6-20–6-21
   turnover, 6-25–6-26
Political costs, 1-8
Posting transactions, 3-4
Potential dilution, 8-13
Predictive analytics, 1-29
Preferred stock, 2-10, 8-3, 8-4, 8-6–8-7
Premium, 7-11
   amortization of, 7-32
Prepaid advertising, 3-10
Prepaid expenses, 2-5, 3-10, 11-13
Preparation costs, 1-8
Prescriptive analytics, 1-29
Present value
   of annuity, 7-26–7-27
   concepts, 7-25
   of single amount, 7-25
   tables, lease capitalization, 10-34–10-35
Prestige Inc., 3-8–3-9, 3-13
Pricing, 7-9–7-10
   of bonds issued at discount, 7-10–7-11
   of bonds issued at par, 7-10
   of bonds issued at premium, 7-11
Prior service costs, 10-37
Pro forma disclosure, 12-10

Pro forma income reporting
  disclosures and market assessments, 5-32–5-35
  Regulation G reconciliation, 5-31–5-32
  SEC warnings about pro forma numbers, 5-32
Procter & Gamble (P&G), 1-14
  Deutsche Bank valuation of
    concluding observations of analyst report, 13-25
    qualitative and quantitative summary, 13-14–13-24
  forecasting, 13-4
    balance sheet, 12-12–12-16, 12-21
    guidance, 12-5–12-6
    income statement, 12-8–12-12, 12-21
    Morgan Stanley's report, 12-23–12-30
    parsimonious method of sales, NOPAT, and NOA, 12-23
    segment data, 12-16–12-18
    statement of cash flows, 12-19
  residual operating income model, 13-10
  weighted average cost of capital, 13-8
Product differentiation, 1-24
Productivity, 1-18
  analysis
    cash conversion cycle, 4-10–4-11
    plant, property and equipment, 4-11–4-12
    working capital, 4-9
Profit, 1-13
Profit margin (PM), 1-18, 4-6
Profitability, 1-18
  analysis
    gross profit margin, 4-8–4-9
    operating expense margin, 4-9
  and creditworthiness
    credit analysis, C-26
      RNOA disaggregation, margin and turnover, C-25
      ROE disaggregation, DuPont analysis, C-23–C-24
      ROE disaggregation, operating focus, C-24–C-25
      summarizing, C-26–C-27
Projected benefit obligation (PBO), 10-12, 10-17
Prospective adoption, 10-3
Provision (benefit) for taxes on income, 5-25, 5-28
Public Company Accounting Oversight Board (PCAOB), 1-32
PwC, 1-31, 5-9

Q

Quality of debt
  credit analysis, 7-16–7-17
  credit ratings, 7-18–7-19
    and financial ratios, 7-19–7-21
    Verizon, 7-20–7-23
    reasons for matter, 7-23–7-24
Quality, 5-22–5-24
Quick ratio, 4-36–4-37

R

R&D spending, 5-26
Ratio analysis, 11-27–11-28

Raytheon, 5-7
  cost-to-cost method, 5-7–5-8
  cost-to-cost reporting, 5-8–5-10
RBC Capital Markets, 2-25
Reasonable assurance, 1-32
Regulation, 1-7
Regulation Fair Disclosure (FD), 1-8
Regulation G reconciliation, 5-31–5-32
Regulators, 1-6–1-7
Reinvested capital, 1-14
Representatives, 1-7
Research and development (R&D)
  analysis of, 5-26–5-28
  R&D spending, 5-26
Residual claim, 8-5
Residual interest, 2-10
Residual operating income (ROPI) model, 13-3
  advantages and disadvantages of, 13-13
  illustrating, 13-10–13-11
  managerial insights from, 13-11–13-12
  steps in applying, 13-9–13-10
  structure, 13-9
Resources (assets), 1-10
Restricted stock, 8-13
Restricted stock awards, 8-27
Restricted stock units (RSU), 8-13, 8-27
Restructuring cost, 5-25, 10-41
  analysis of, 6-23–6-24
  disclosure of, 6-22–6-23
  and managerial incentives, 6-24
Restructuring expenses, 12-3
Retail inventory method (RIM), 6-6
Retained earnings, 1-14, 2-6, 2-10–2-13, 8-4, 12-14
  change in, 11-18
  reconciliation, 2-20
  statement, 3-15
Retroactive adoption, 10-3
Return on assets (ROA), 1-18, 4-4
  adjusted, 4-6
  components of, 1-18–1-20
  and disaggregation, 4-6–4-7
    financial leverage analysis, 4-12–4-14
    productivity analysis, 4-9–4-12
    profitability analysis, 4-8–4-9
Return on equity (ROE), 1-20, 4-3, 4-24, 9-14–9-17
  accounts used to compute, 4-5
  disaggregation
    DuPont analysis, C-23–C-24
    financial leverage, 4-4–4-6
    operating focus, C-24–C-25
    return on assets, 4-4. See also Return on assets
  nonoperating return, 4-31–4-32
    with noncontrolling interest, 4-34–4-35
    with substantial net nonoperating assets, 4-33–4-34
Return on invested capital (ROIC), 4-28
Return on net operating assets (RNOA), 4-15, 4-23–4-25
  disaggregation into margin and turnover, 4-25–4-29, C-25
  vs. ROA, 4-23

Revenue
  and expenses, with no cash flow effects, 11-10–11-12
  recognizing, 2-14–2-15
Revenue recognition, 5-3–5-4
  complications of, 5-5–5-6
  foreign currency effects on, 5-15–5-18
  performance obligations satisfied over time, 5-7–5-11
  principle, 2-14
  rules, 5-4–5-5
  unearned (deferred), 5-14–5-15
Right of return, 5-6
Right-of-use asset, 10-6
Risk premium, 7-17
Risk-free rate, 7-17
Rite Aid, 6-11
RSM, 1-31

S

S&P 500 Index, 4-3
Sales allowances, 5-3
  accounting for, 5-11–5-12
  analysis of, 5-13–5-14
  reporting, 5-12
Samsung Electronics, 1-18, 1-25
Sarbanes-Oxley Act (SOX), 1-17
Securities and Exchange Commission (SEC), 5-32
  enforcement actions, 1-33
  filings, 1-26–2-28
Segment data, 12-16–12-18
Self-liquidating, 4-15, 4-38
Selling, general, and administrative expenses (SG&A), 1-13, 4-9, 5-25, 12-9
Sensitivity analysis, 12-21
Service cost, 10-15
Service revenue, 5-15
Short-term debt, 2-7
  accounting for, 7-7–7-8
Short-term investments, 2-5
Significant influence, equity investments with, 9-3, 9-4
  accounting for, 9-12–9-14
  equity method accounting and ROE effects, 9-14–9-17
Single payment, 7-10
Solvency analysis, 4-37
Southwest Airlines Inc., 1-11, 9-29–9-30, 10-39, 11-24
Spitz Inc., 5-7
Spread, 4-32, 7-17
Stand-alone selling price (SSP), 5-5
Standard & Poor (S&P), 2-26, 4-3, 5-21, 7-18, 7-24, C-15
Starbucks, 11-5, 11-11–11-12, 11-18, 11-27–11-28
  adjustments for operating cash flow, 11-14–11-15
  financing activities, 11-19
  investing activities, 11-17
  statement of cash flows for, 11-6
Statement of cash flows, 1-15–1-16, 2-18–2-20, 11-3
  direct method reporting for, 11-29–11-32
  financing activities, 11-8–11-9

Statement of cash flows, *(continued)*
   forecasting, 12-19–12-20
   investing activities, 11-8
   lease accounting and, 10-8–10-9
   operating activities, 11-5–11-7
   relation among financial statements, 11-3–11-4
   reporting and analysis, C-21–C-22
   structure, 11-4–11-5
   usefulness of, 11-25–11-27
Statement of stockholders' equity, 1-14–1-15, 2-17–2-18
   preparation of, 3-15–3-16
Stock appreciation rights (SARs), 8-13, 8-28
Stock awards, 8-27
Stock issuance, 8-8–8-9
   and stock returns, 8-10
Stock options, 8-27
Stock repurchase, 8-10–8-12
Stock split, 8-5, 8-18
   in form of dividend, 8-18–8-19
Stock transactions
   stock issuance, 8-8–8-10
   stock repurchase, 8-10–8-12
Stock-based compensation, 8-12
   accounting for, 8-14–8-15
   analysis implications, 8-28–8-29
   footnote disclosures for, 8-15–8-16
   interpretation of, 8-14–8-15
   plans
      analysis of, 8-13–8-14
      characteristics of, 8-13
      types of, 8-13
   reporting and analyzing
      employee stock purchase plans, 8-26
      stock appreciation rights, 8-28
      stock awards, 8-27
      stock options, 8-27
   summary of, 8-28
Stockholders, 1-6
Stockholders' equity, 2-10–2-11
   accounts
      contributed capital, 8-3
      earned capital, 8-4–8-5
      common stock, 8-7–8-8
      preferred stock, 8-6–8-7
      statement of, 8-5–8-6. *See also* Statement of stockholders' equity
Stored-value cards, 5-15
Straight-line method, 6-18–6-19
Strategic (business) plan, 1-3–1-4
Strategic alliances, 9-12
Strategic partners, 1-6
Stryker Corporation, 4-3, 4-5–4-6, 4-14, 4-18, 4-22–4-23, 4-25, 4-29, 4-35, 4-41

Suppliers, 1-5–1-6
Supply of information
   benefits of disclosure, 1-7–1-8
   costs of disclosure, 1-8
   International Accounting Standards, 1-8–1-9
SWOT analysis of business environment, 1-23

T

T-account, 3-4, 3-6–3-9
Target Corporation, 1-13, 1-18, 10-35
Tata Consultancy Services, 5-7
Tax agencies, 1-6–1-7
Tax Cuts and Jobs Act, 10-30–10-31
Tax loss carryforwards, 10-27
Tax provision, 5-28
Technicians, 13-13
Temporary accounts, 3-16
Terminal period, 13-6
Tesla, 8-22, 11-24–11-25
Texas Instruments BA II Plus, 10-33
Thomson Reuters Corporation, 2-26
Threat of entry, 1-22
Threat of substitution, 1-22
3M Company, 1-11, 1-14, 2-9
Tiffany & Co., 5-13–5-14, 9-29, 9-30
Time value of money
   bond valuation, 7-27
   computations using calculator, 7-28
   computations using excel, 7-28–7-29
   future value
      of annuity, 7-30
      concepts, 7-30
      of single amount, 7-30
   present value
      of annuity, 7-26–7-27
      concepts, 7-25
      of single amount, 7-25
      tables, 7-25–7-26
Times interest earned, 4-38
TJX Companies Inc., 8-18
Trade credit, 2-9
Trading securities, 9-10–9-11
Transactions, accounting
   Apple's, 3-6
   financial statement effects template, 3-6
   journal entry and T-account, 3-6–3-9
Transitory items, reporting of, 2-15–2-16
Treasury shares, 8-5
Treasury stock, 2-10, 8-4, 8-7, 12-15
   companies increasingly choose retirement for, 8-11
   disclosures and interpretation, 8-11
   reissuing, 8-10–8-11
Two-step approach, 7-16

U

UBER, 5-33
Ultimate Revenues, 5-9
Unearned (deferred) revenue, 2-7, 3-10–3-11, 5-3, 5-14–5-15, 7-4–7-5
Units-of-production method, 6-19
Unusual income tax expense/benefit, 12-3
UPS, 10-20

V

Valuation and qualifying accounts, 2-24
Valuation models. *See also specific models*
   inputs, 13-4–13-5
Vanguard Group, The, 7-9
Variable interest entity (VIE), 9-18
Verizon Communications Inc., 9-29, 10-20
   accounting for short-term debt, 7-7–7-8
   accrued liabilities, 7-3–7-5
   amortization of discount, 7-31
   balance sheet reporting, 7-13–7-14
   credit ratings, 7-20–7-23
   effective cost of debt, 7-12
   loss on early extinguishment of debt, 7-14
Vertical analysis, 2-11, 4-38. *See also* Common-size analysis
Vesting period, 8-13
Voters, 1-7

W

Wage inflation, 10-15
Wages payable, 7-4
Wall Street Reform and Consumer Protection Act of 2010 (Dodd-Frank Act), 1-17
Walmart, 4-36
Walt Disney Company, 5-9
Weighted average cost of capital (WACC), 13-6
Wells Fargo (WFC), 8-18
WeWork, 5-33
Working capital, 4-9, 4-36
   accounts, 12-12
   management, 11-7
WorldCom Inc., 1-34, 5-33
Write-offs, 6-22

Y

Years of benefit payments, 10-15
Yield, 8-6

Z

Zoetis, 5-29